Woodbourne Library
Washington-Centerville Public Lib
Centerville, Ohio

D1238188

Diaries

1857–1917

Diaries

1857–1917

by Bishop Milton Wright

Wright State University

B
WRIGHT

The Wright State University Libraries
Dayton, Ohio 45435

© 1999 by Wright State University Libraries
All rights reserved.
Printed in the United States of America by Thomson-Shore, Inc.

Book design by Jane Baker

Library of Congress Card Number: 99-68525

Wright, Bishop Milton, 1829–1917
       Diaries, 1857–1917

ISBN 0-9676359-0-X

CONTENTS

ILLUSTRATIONS

Photographs

Documents

Maps

Jane Reece portraits of Bishop Milton Wright are reprinted courtesy of the Dayton Art Institute

FOREWORD

My father was named Milton Wright after his grandfather, Bishop Milton Wright, and often talked about his memories of his namesake. The Bishop kept a daily diary for almost sixty years; his Church of the United Brethren Church in Christ made an earlier transcription of those diaries, but they were never published. The original small leather-bound notebooks, now held by Special Collections and Archives at Wright State University, contain the Bishop's observations of eventful years in the history of the United States as well as those in his own family. The diaries begin with Milton's missionary days on the wild frontier of Oregon and end in the early years of the twentieth century when two of his sons, Wilbur and Orville, conceived, constructed, and flew the world's first successful flying machine and then began a fledgling aviation industry.

Bishop Milton Wright was a man with strong opinions and prodigious energy. From the time of his religious conversion at the age of fifteen, he spent his life traveling tirelessly to visit the scattered congregations—exhorting, preaching, writing, administering, formulating doctrine, and adjudicating disputes to build and strengthen his church. The Bishop traveled by whatever means were available, including train, interurban car, buggy, farm wagon, horseback, or by foot when necessary.

My father used to recall a trip he made on the circuit with his grandfather one summer. They would be met by a member of the congregation and taken to a church or perhaps a tent in the yard of a farm home. There the Bishop would preach a sermon and conduct other church business. Afterwards trestle tables would be set up on the lawn and the ladies of the flock would bring in the bounty of the countryside: fried chicken and potato salad and cole slaw and deviled eggs and pickled beets and, of course, homemade cakes and pies. Then someone would come and pick up the Bishop and his grandson and take them to another congregation where they went through the same routine the next day. My father liked particularly to recall, with some astonishment, a trip that lasted about three weeks, and in which they had a chicken dinner every day but one. On one day they managed to visit two congregations, so they had two chicken dinners that day!

My father's memories and the diaries kindled my interest in the man who was my great grandfather, and this edition of his diaries fulfills a long-time ambition of mine to have this chronicle of the Bishop's life available in a convenient, readily accessible single volume. All of this was made possible by the excellent professional assistance of the staff at Wright State University's Paul Laurence Dunbar Library where Wright family relics are carefully preserved and made available for study.

Wilkinson Wright
September 1999

PREFACE

The Special Collections and Archives Department of the Wright State University Libraries was chosen in 1975 to be the repository for an extensive collection of Wright Brothers' material. Among the thousands of photographs, books, technical journals, correspondence, financial records, and memorabilia were the diaries of Bishop Milton Wright. These diaries of the father of Wilbur and Orville Wright record the full range of experiences of his adult life from 1857 to his death in 1917. They provide a detailed chronicle of Milton Wright's dynamic, and sometimes controversial, ministry and leadership in the United Brethren Church, and his role as the father of the famed inventors of powered flight. The diaries also demonstrate the Bishop's awareness of local, national, and world events, as well as his political allegiance and support of progressive movements, such as women's suffrage. Probably the most important contribution the diaries make to present scholarship on the Wright Brothers is the greater knowledge we gain about the dynamics of the Wright family. Through his daily writings, Milton Wright allows us to know him as a husband, father, and grandfather. Taken as a whole, the diaries provide an essential resource in the study of the history of the Wright Brothers' career in aviation, the history of the United Brethren Church, and the life of a man dedicated to his family and his church.

Bishop Milton Wright recorded his life experiences daily in small, black-leather-bound volumes. While separate entries are brief, Bishop Wright provides more detailed narrative about the year's events at the end of each diary. He lists expenses and his salary for the year, family history and genealogy, and important milestones in the lives of his children and in the church he served. The diaries were originally transcribed in the 1950s by staff of the United

Brethren Church in Huntington, Indiana. In 1995, a project was undertaken at the Wright State University Libraries to compare the early transcripts with the actual diary entries. Using optical character recognition, the transcripts from the 1950s were digitized and compared to the original diaries, inaccuracies were corrected, and all previously untranscribed notes and entries were added from the originals. All spelling, punctuation, and grammar remain as written by Milton Wright, edited only where absolutely necessary for understanding. Not included are such brief entries as "At home" or "Nothing of importance today." The diaries have been indexed to make them more accessible and searchable. Individual names, places, and events are listed. As part of his ministry, the Bishop traveled extensively and visited many churches and homes. While it was impossible to list every name of every family who offered him a meal and a bed, major destinations and frequently mentioned ministers and church members are recorded in the index. This volume also includes thirty-nine photographs and seven documents from the Wright Brothers Collection, as well as four maps, which help to illustrate the life and work of Milton Wright.

The publication of the Bishop Milton Wright diaries would not have been possible without the constant support and encouragement of G. Wilkinson Wright, great-grandson of Milton Wright, who was instrumental in securing a grant from the Wright Family Fund of the Dayton Foundation to publish this book. I also wish to acknowledge Jane Baker for her exceptional contribution in the design and layout of the Diaries. Jay Gatrell, Assistant Professor of Geography in the Department of Urban Affairs and Geography at Wright State University, created the maps to illustrate the travels of Milton Wright; and Nancy Schurr, graduate student in History at Wright State University during the early stages of the project, prepared revised transcriptions of the diaries. I would also like to thank Victoria A. Montavon, University Librarian, and my colleagues in Special Collections and Archives for their assistance on this project.

Dawne Dewey
Head, Special Collections and Archives
Wright State University Libraries
October 8, 1999

INTRODUCTION

Bishop Wright and His Diaries
An Appreciation

The publication in 1818 of portions of the diary of John Evelyn, an otherwise obscure seventeenth-century English author and civil servant, marked the emergence of a new and distinct literary genre. From the incomparable *Diary of Samuel Pepys,* which first appeared in 1825, through Mary Boykin Chestnut's *Diary from Dixie,* to the *Diary of Anne Frank,* published editions of private journals have offered fascinating insight into the lives and minds of a fascinating set of individuals. They also represent an important source of historical information and provide a personal perspective that can humanize and illuminate the great events of the past in very powerful ways.

Like most diarists, Bishop Milton Wright did not intend his journal for publication. A devoted genealogist, he had spent a lifetime laboriously recovering the details of a long line of ancestral lives stretching back to sixteenth-century England. He scoured the nation for books, manuscripts, church records, personal memories, and anything else that would fill the gaps in his knowledge of the family tree. He was determined to make the process of research easier for the family historians who came after him by providing them with an accurate and detailed record of his daily activities, and those of the other members of his immediate family.

Bishop Wright's diaries are matter-of-fact records of his daily life. His entries for the spring and summer of 1899 are fairly typical. It is apparent that this was a busy time for the residents of the Wright home at 7 Hawthorne Street, in West Dayton, Ohio. Seventy-one-year-old Bishop Wright, as usual, spent a great deal of time on the road, visiting far-flung congregations, calling on relatives in Ohio and Indiana, and attending church conferences. When at home, he made periodic visits to the dentist who was fitting him with a "vulcanized" upper plate; supervised the workmen who were refurbishing the kitchen and the "east room" of the house; and handled family business, including the sale of timber on an Indiana farm.

Busy as he was, he always had time for his grandchildren, especially his son Lorin's eldest boy and girl, Milton and Ivonette, who lived just around the corner on Horace Street. At young Milton's request, the Bishop took them on walks to their grandmother's grave in lovely Woodland Cemetery. On May 10, 1899, the three of them cheered from the upper-story windows of a church office as Col. William F. "Buffalo Bill" Cody paraded his Wild West Show through the streets of Dayton. Grandfather and grandchildren enjoyed family fireworks on the Fourth of July.

It was a busy spring for Milton's twenty-four-year-old daughter, Katharine Wright, as well. Katie, as she was known to her father and friends, was the only college graduate in the family—Oberlin, Class of '98. Recently "elected" to the faculty of Central High School as a teacher of English and Latin, she spent the spring and summer preparing for and enjoying her high school reunion, and entertaining visiting college friends. She and a group of friends hosted a supper for a visiting Oberlin professor on May 20.

A college chum, Margaret "Mag" Goodwin, arrived for a visit after June 8. The two of them took a train for Oberlin, and their first college reunion, on June 16. Another friend, Harriet "Hattie" Silliman, arrived for a visit on July 20. Orville pitched in to help squire Katharine's visitors around town, and accompanied his sister and friends on a camping trip to Shoup's Mill on the nearby Stillwater River during the first week of August 1899.

Milton does not mention the fact that his sons had written to the Smithsonian for information on flying on May 30, or that, before the end of August, Wilbur and Orville would develop their critically important notion of wing warping as a means of controlling an aircraft in the roll axis, devise a practical means of incorporating that system into a structure that would be safe to fly, and build and test their first experimental flying machine, a biplane kite with a wingspan of five feet. His only entry relating to flight occurs on July 7, 1899, when he invites his grandson Milton over "to see the flying machine." In fact, there was no "flying machine" to see on that date. Wilbur and Orville must have shown their nephew pictures of aircraft in the books on flight that they had purchased the month before.

Prior to 1902, the diary offers few indications that Wilbur and Orville were deeply involved in aeronautical research, and provides little insight into the nature of their experiments. That is not too surprising. Their work in aeronautics had little impact on Bishop Wright's life during the busy and critical years 1899–1903. Despite the fact that he seems scarcely to have been aware that history was being made under his roof, however, his diary entries for this period would play a major role in the great patent battles to come.

In the spring of 1912, when the brothers were locked in a patent infringement suit with Glenn Hammond Curtiss, the precise timing of their earliest experiments became a matter of intense interest and legal importance. The Wrights had not kept any record of their earliest thinking. They were able to reconstruct precisely what had happened, and when, through the use of their father's diary, and their own memories of the other events of that spring and summer. Orville, for example, recalled that serious discussion of aeronautical issues were well underway "while Miss Goodwin . . . was visiting in our home." Their father's diary enabled them to pinpoint that date, and the date of the camping trip and other events linked in their minds to their earliest aeronautical discussions and experiments.

After the success of 1903, the activities of Wilbur, Orville and Katharine begin to take center stage in the pages of their father's diary. The Bishop treats us to an extraordinary commentary on the travels, triumphs, and struggles of his children as they turn from the process of invention to the business of dealing with the complexities of life as international figures.

The Bishop's diaries provide an invaluable window into a household where history was made. Great events do not occur in a vacuum. During the months and years when Wilbur and Orville were struggling to fly, they were also functioning as sons, brothers, uncles, neighbors, and friends. Their father's journal serves as a window into the life and times of an extraordinary family, and provides an important part of the context within which the drama of the invention of the airplane was played out. For that, biographers and historians interested in the Bishop's famous flying sons have long been grateful.

This published edition of the diaries of Milton Wright is long overdue, and very welcome indeed. It represents a significant addition to the shelf of standard reference works such as *The Papers of Wilbur and Orville Wright,* Fred Kelly's *Miracle at Kitty Hawk,* and Arthur Renstrom's invaluable *Wilbur and Orville Wright: A Biography,* and *Wilbur and Orville Wright: A Chronology.* All thanks to Dawne Dewey and the members of the Special Collections and Archives Department of the Wright State University Libraries, and to Wilkinson Wright and all of the others who have worked so hard to make this important historical document available to a wider audience.

Tom D. Crouch
Senior Curator, Aeronautics
National Air and Space Museum
Smithsonian Institution

October 8, 1999

Dedicated to the Memory of

G. Wilkinson "Wick" Wright

1922–1999

THE DIARIES

PART ONE

1857–1880

"We went out to sea, and in a few hours, many were seasick. I went forward at night, and for hours, saw the moonlight dance on the waves."
Milton Wright, July 6, 1857

Bishop Milton Wright spent the first years of his ministry miles away from the family and the home he knew in Indiana. The story of his travels to the North-west Territory by ocean steamer and his day-by-day account of his ministry by foot, horseback, and steamboat, provide us with glimpses of the life of a circuit preacher in a remote area of the country in the years just before the Civil War. Milton Wright continued to chronicle his life when he returned to Indiana, to marry Susan Koerner, begin a ministry in the Whitewater Circuit, and raise four sons—Reuchlin, Lorin, Wilbur, and Orville—and a daughter, Katharine. Bishop Wright rose in the ministry and leadership of the church during these years, becoming an elder and the editor of the Religious Telescope, *spreading the gospel, and making known his own strong beliefs on the issues of the day. In 1871 the family moved to Dayton, Ohio. When Milton Wright was elected a bishop in 1877 and assigned to the West Mississippi District, the family moved to Cedar Rapids, Iowa. Wright traveled across the West, preaching and minister-ing to members, and in 1878 brought home the Penaud helicopter, which would spark Wilbur and Orville's imaginations on the possibilities of human flight.*

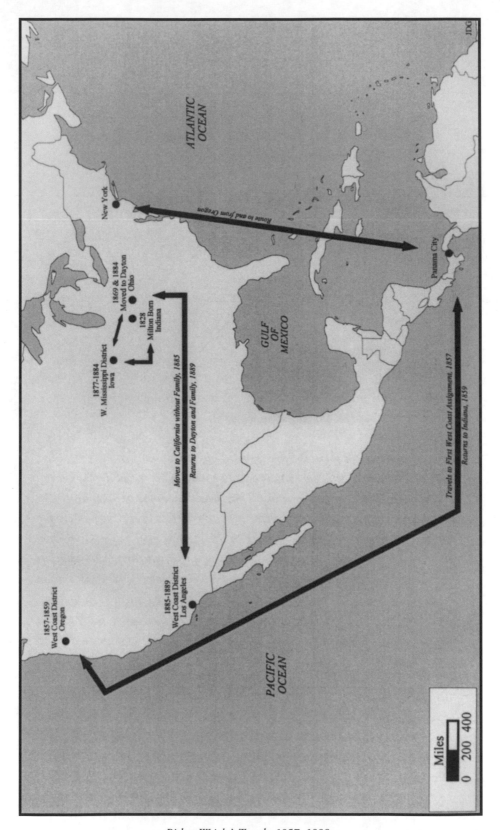

Bishop Wright's Travels, 1857–1889

1857

Thursday, January 1 I arose late. I drank water only & ate no meat. Anson Moor and his son Harvey called. I went to Hugh Wilson's and lodged there. I learn that at the M.E. meeting at Fayetteville, there have been 13 accessions. It was a revival at which I preached once.

Friday, January 2 I arose at 5:00. Home at 11:00. I went to the Crowel appointment and pr. I Cor. 10:31. Lodged at Crowel's.

Saturday, January 3 I arose at 7:30. It is cold. I dine at Epenetus Smith's. He tells of the Campbelite social meeting! We talk of Shumay's course. I learn tht Timothy Ellison has broken up. I went home and wrote a composition on the New Birth.

Sunday, January 4 I pr. at Garrison Creek at 11:00, John 3.7; at Colombia, at 3:00, Rom. 8.31. Went to Mr. Eddy's. They tell of John Null's show & of his collecting his fathers accounts!

Monday, January 5 I came home by Cramer's & Blakes & dined at Pike's. I went to Fayetteville—called at John Wagner's.

Wednesday, January 7 I staid at home. Emanuel Wagoner dined with us. I prepared two discourses. (Some notes are too dim to record).

Thursday, January 8 I stopped at Rev. Lilas Andrews, on my way to John Morgan's. It was talked that S.M. Shumway's followers included George McReady's and Charles Andrews'. I pr. Rom. 3.10.

Friday, January 9 I arose at 5:45, made fire, read 20 or 30 pages of Chemistry and talked on it. Called at Chas. Andrews', pr. Hosea 4.17. I lodged at Andrews.

Saturday, January 10 I called at S. Cramer's (M.E.C.), on the way to Qr. meeting at Andersonville. I received $1.44 subscrip to the *Rel. Telescope.* Go to Archibald Mill's to dinner, and after Qr. Conference to supper; and, after evening service go there to lodge.

Sunday, January 11 Rev. Geo. Muth, P.E., preached at 11:00, on parable of the sower, and in the evening, he preached from Isa. 5th (1–6). I dine at A. Miller's and lodged at Elihu Neff's.

Monday, January 12 Was at "lovefeast" in the forenoon. Mrs. Hulda Morgan took a shout. I visited George McReady's, Thomas Linston's & Morgan Linville's. G. Muth pr. at night, Acts 26.17. Lodged at A. Miller's.

Tuesday, January 13 I went from Miller's to John Lewis's. She is sick. Webb and sister came. Bro. Lewis returns home. He was a magnetic healer. He tells me of a woman's scull once cut & her nerves affected by it. G. Muth preached at night at Neff's Corners.

Wednesday, January 14 I lodged at John Cook's. It was my boarding place nine months, in 1854 and 1855, when teaching school at the Corners. I am about sick to-day with cold and toothache.

Thursday, January 15 I went to Peter Miller's and visited Robert Powers' school at the Corners. I preached at night, Heb. 12:28,29. I lodged at John Cook's.

Friday, January 16 I went home to my father's, by way of Wm. Nichols', Silas Andrews' and the Andersonville post-office. I got a letter from P.S. Cook. I pr. at Garrison Creek at 3, John 14:6. Returned to my father's.

Saturday, January 17 I went with Rev. Wm. Nichols to New Castle, via Wayne Smith's. I pr. at night, Mat. 16:26. I staid at Jacob Byers'.

Sunday, January 18 (My brother William filled my App'tmts at Henry Crowel's at 11:00 & Maxwell's at 3:00). I attended lovefeast and preached (New Castle) at 11:00, Rom. 8.31. I dined at Jon't Adamson's. Nichols pr. at night on conversion of Jailor. Lodge at Shopp's.

Monday, January 19 I have a controversy with Jones, Swigert's soninlaw on Campbelism. I went to the lovefeast. I dined at J. Shopp's. I then went to Jac. Byers'. I preached at night, Gal. 6.14. Mises Bell and Letty Dorr were converted & Swigert's son. I lodged at Jac. Byers'.

Tuesday, January 20 I wrote a letter to Rev. John Brown. Bro. Shouk came. I went in afternoon to Bell's Store. I pr. at night, I Chron. 28.9. There were six mourners. Miss Swigert converted. Mary Mullen struggles long. I lodge at J. Shopp's.

Wednesday, January 21 In afternoon, I went to J. Swigert's, and had a talk with Jones. At night, Rev. Aaron Worth preached, Acts 10.34,35. Three converted. I lodge at Rev. Bell's with Worth, they being American Wesleyans.

Thursday, January 22 I went to J. Shop's, and thence to Jacob Byers. I preached at night from 2 Peter 1.1–11. Rev. A. Worth came to Byers' in the afternoon. I staid at Byers' that night.

Friday, January 23 I staid at Byer's till afternoon. Afternoon, I visited Sister Sharp's, and then went to J. Shopp's and staid till meeting time. The house was crowded. I led a good lovefeast. I lodged at Johathan Adamson's.

Saturday, January 24 I called at Henry Shopp's shop, and dined at J. Shopp's, and supped at Jacob Byers'. I pr. at night, Luke 19.27. The house was crowded. J. Swigert & John Rigert joined church & E. Swigert full

member. West is a templar. I lodged at Shopp's.

Sunday, January 25 Rev. McReynolds (Lutheran) pr. at 11:00, I Cor. 12.27. I dined at Dr. Dorr's. We have a lovefeast at 2:00. McReynolds pr. at night, 2 Cor. 4.3,4. I exhorted. I lodged at Jac. Byers. (To-day was my app't. at Morgan's, which Wm. Nichols attended).

Monday, January 26 I remained at Byers' all day. I wrote to P.S. Cook, and read in Allien's Alarm, which is good. Wrote a communication to Rel. Telescope. Preached at night, Prov. 15.32. It was a high time. Two joined church. Lodged at J. Shopp's.

Tuesday, January 27 I went to Hornings about noon. Cornelius and I had quite a talk about the status of those "unsanctified" at death, i.e. those not "entirely sanctified." Justified; sanctified. The world asleep!

Wednesday, January 28 I went via John Scheildknecht's to John Richert's in New Castle, and dined. He formerly of the Otterbein Church, Baltimore. I sup at Byers', and called at J. Shopp's. Rev. Bell pr. Acts 26.28—good. I closed the meeting. Lodge at Adamson's.

Thursday, January 29 I called at J. Shopp's and Jacob Byers, and started for Dublin. I met Rev. A. Butler, saw Swartz, and went to Rev. Caleb Witt's. He reads John Sloneker's letters. W's idea of the resurrection. Edw. Beecher's Conflict of Ages! Prayer meeting at Wayne Smith's.

Friday, January 30 I went via John Huddleston's to Joshua LaMott's on Knolen's Fork. He tells me his ideas of baptism and criticises J. Ball's conduct, also Witt, Stover, Butler etc. He has 300 acres of land & huge barn. I lodged at La Mott's.

Saturday, January 31 I went to John Huddleston's and dined—saw Myers (probably Joseph); went to Wayne Smith's & saw Deitrick. My horse ran away with a post to his halter! I call at C.W. Witts. He accepted Beecher's idea of Preexistence! I went to Eli Modlin's (west) and lodged.

Sunday, February 1 I went to Salem to prayer meeting at 11:00. Dine at Wilkison Smith's. I pr. at 3:00, Eph.

5.15,16. I saw Puntney, Miller, Guire, Holly, Ward, Stiggleman & Scott. Lodged at Wm. McGeath's.

Monday, February 2 I went to John Russel's and dined. I went to New Castle & stopped at J. Shopp's. I preached at night, I Cor. 13.13. Mother Mitchell (Mrs. Byers' mother) enthusiastic over the sermon. Lodge at Jac. Byers. (Class Sunday. Bill & Dutch Henry)

Tuesday, February 3 I went to J. Shopp's. Lizzie's piano songs: "Meet me," "Way to Canada," etc. I go to J. Scheildknecht's & pr. Matt. 13.58. See Shaffer, Miles Conway, Henry Sch. & wife, I pr. at Horning's, Ps. 16.11. Lodged at Horning's.

Wednesday, February 4 I went in the afternoon to Miles Conway's, and lodged there. The next morning, I had a talk with Black Charley on religion.

Thursday, February 5 I went to Dublin, and called at Wayne Smith's, John Fohl's, and Bro. Hafer's. Was a pr. meeting. Lodged at Rev. J. Fohl's. Children: Katharine, Susan, John, George, Ottergein, Benj. Dublin men: Lippy, Gaylor, Swartz, Sis. Custer, Wood, Brown, Huddlestone.

Friday, February 6 I called at Wood's shop. I went to Wayne Smith's and dined. I went to C.W. Witt's. He has another letter from J. Sloneker on the Resurrection. W's essay on it; animal spirit resurrected! Fohl's report. Those were Witt's idiosyncracies. Probably he abandoned them.

Saturday, February 7 I went to Wayne Smith's and to Teacher's Association. Mr. Royce on the Mississip[p]i running some miles uphill by centrifugal force. I dined at Bennett Witt's. I called at A. Butler's and Wilson Scroggy's. Went to Stafford's Sch. H. Shut out in the rain at Shaffords! Lodge there, after meeting. Pr. Luke 19.27.

Sunday, February 8 I came near to being thrown into Knowlen's *Fork, by my horse. I pr. at Union, Heb. 12.1. I dined at Joshua LaMott's. I pr. at Fohlen's Chapel, Acts 2.40. I staid at Emsley Hoover's. *My wrist was lame three weeks.

Monday, February 9 I went home via Pennville, Waterloo, Connersville and Hughe's, reaching home at 10:30. (The foregoing is a three week's tour on Dublin Circuit, in exchange with Wm. Nichols.)

Tuesday, February 10 I was at home to day. I went in the evening to B.J. Gillum's and preached, Luke 19.27.

Wednesday, February 11 I went home and wrote a communication for the *Rel. Telescope.*

Thursday, February 12 I finished the communication. I went to Andersonville. Lydia Neff was married to Geroge Utter to-day. I had a talk with S.M. Shumway—the doctrine & position of his Church—Hubbardites. I lodged at Johm Lewis's.

Friday, February 13 I went to Wm. Nichols' and dined. Went to the Crowell Sch. H. and pr., Matt. 9.12. Yesterday, I married Isaac Neff to Miss Maple.

Saturday, February 14 I went to Uncle George Reeder's and heard from Charles Harris's. I lodged at Reeder's.

Sunday, February 15 I went to Neff's Corners and pr. Rom. 8.31. I dine at Archie Miller's. I pr. at 3:00, Rom. 1.16. I stay at Derbyshire's.

Monday, February 16 I went home via John Malone's. I went to Colombia, but met no congregation. I lodged at Hines'.

Tuesday, February 17 I came home.

Friday, February 20 I remain at home on account of rain and mud, and miss my appointment at Ails.

Saturday, February 21 I went to my brother Harvey's. Found only the children at home. I went to Fayetteville in the afternoon & bought some articles of wear. Went home.

Sunday, February 22 I went to Andersonville and pr., Ps. 50.2. Dined at Elihu Neff's. Went on to John Morgan's. A mistake as to the appointment. I lodge there.

Monday, February 23 I went to Fourey's and dined. The

old man's talk. I went via John Lewis's to Isaac Neff's. These Fourey's had Martha Snyder, my second cousin, living with them.

Tuesday, February 24 I went home, and went to Gillum's and pr. Ps. 16.8. I lodged at Johnson Gillum's. He was an excellent man—a brother of Rev. Raney Gillum, who was smart, but ill-balanced.

Wednesday, February 25 I went to Fayetteville and had a tooth extracted. Was assessed. (Fayetteville's original name was Danville, and later on the name was changed to Orange.)

Thursday, February 26 I went to Neff's Corners and pr. Acts 26.28. I lodged at John Cook's. (This Neff's Corners, or Cook's Corners, is a mile and one-fourth west of Andersonville).

Friday, February 27 I visited Father John Neff's, called at Squire Simmons, and went via Andersonville to Crowell's, and pr. to a good-sized congregation, Acts 2.40.

Saturday, February 28 I went to Robert Monroe's, and dined. I went to Rev. Silas Andrews' and lodged there. The title to twenty acres of his land is not good. Jesse Stubbs has sold out to Mr. Hamway; Miller to Lewis; Saml. Stubbs do.

Sunday, March 1 I put up at Jesse Stubbs'. Pr. Ps. 50.2. Dine at Isaac Umphrey's. I pr. at night, Acts 26.28, at Stubbs' Sch. House. I lodged at Jesse Stubb's.

Monday, March 2 I stay at Stubb's till afternoon, and then went to Morgan's & to James Newman's, where I preached from Ps. 16.8. I lodged at Newman's, James was a fond friend.

Tuesday, March 3 I dined at Kinion Freeman's. Called at Silas Andrews, on my way home. Kinion is my father's cousin, his father John Freeman being my grandmother Wright's younger brother.

Wednesday, March 4 I wrote off much of Rev. John Morgan's sketch of the pioneer preachers, for publication in the *Rel. Telescope*.

Thursday, March 5 I finished the transcription, and wrote a letter to my cousin Margaret Reeder in Grant Co., Indiana.

Friday, March 6 I went via John Malone's to Ails. There was a snow-storm which prevented having meeting. Ails lived not far from Buena Vista.

Saturday, March 7 I remained at Ails till afternoon when I went via A. Osborn's to Epenetus Smith's. Lodged there. He was one of the good men.

Sunday, March 8 I preached at Andersonville, Rev. 14.6. I dined at Rev. Silas Andrews'. I pr. at Neff's Corner's at 3:00, Acts 16.9, and then went home. Andrews, now aged, had once been a prominent preacher.

Monday, March 9 I remained at home, and read some.

Tuesday, March 10 I wrote a letter to Rev. John R. Brown. I went to Garrison Creek (the record does not say as to meeting). J.R. Brown was afterward of St. Joseph Conference. He married a Daily.

Saturday, March 14 I went via Malone's to Henry Crowel's, and pr. Acts 26.28. I lodged at J. Sutton's.

Sunday, March 15 I preached at Crowel's School-House, Acts 16.9. I dined at Green's. Preached afternoon at Maxwell's Sch. House from Rom. 5.

Monday, March 16 I went to Isaac Johnson's, dined and supped, and went to Columbia and pr. Acts 26.28. I went home after meeting.

Tuesday, March 17 I am not very well. I went with my Mother to my brother Harvey's. Returned home.

Wednesday, March 18 I went via John Malone's, John Lewis's and S. Cramer's to James Newman's, and pr. Rom 5.18, and lodged at Newman's. It is said that Shumway told Bluford Conner, that he had leave to join the Masons.

Thursday, March 19 James Newman and I go to John Morgan's, and stay till evening. I pr. I Thes. 5.17, at Stubb's Sch. H. (Perhaps I lodged at Jesse Stubb's.)

Friday, March 20 I returned to Morgan's in company with (Father) William Stubbs'. I went in the afternoon to Ails' and pr. Acts 26.28. Father Stubbs and wife live with their son Jesse. He has become an opium eater.

Saturday, March 21 I came home by way of John Lewis's. He was one of my parents' first neighbors and acquaintance after they moved into their half-finished cabin on the 80 which corners at the north-west of Hopewell in 1821.

Sunday, March 22 I pr. at our Andersonville Church at 11:00, Ps. 16.8. I dined at Jas. Simmond's at the Corners, and pr. at the Corners Sch. H. at 3:00, Rom 8.18. (Probably I went home, this evening).

Thursday, March 26 I was at home reading. In the evening, Rev. Wm. Nichols called and took me with him to Thomas G. Stephen's, a mile north, where he married Matilda Stephen to Alexander Mattney, a widower.

Friday, March 27 I went to Crowel's appointment and pr. I Tim 6.6. I put up at [blank] Green's. I went home by Lorenzo Springer's. I preached in the evening at Garrison Creek, Rom. 5. Lodged at Jno. Harper's.

Saturday, March 28 I went to R. Powers by the Salt Creek Baptist Church north of Andersonville, where I heard Erastus Thomas preach, a very able discourse, 2 Tim. 2.19. He had a halt in speech.

Sunday, March 29 I pr. at Gillum's App't. a missionary discourse, Mark 16.15, 1 1/2 hour long! I dined at Johnson Gillum's. I pr. at Colombia at 3:00, Rom. 5.18. Uncle Johny Malone preached at Garrison Creek (Gillum's) at night—not much!

Monday, March 30 I was at home in the forenoon. Went to Harvey's in the evening, and lodged.

Tuesday, March 31 I went to Fayetteville, and on home. In the afternoon, I plowed for William.

Friday, April 3 I harrowed for William; while he sowed oats. I went to Aile's and pr. at night 2 Cor. 5.11.

Saturday, April 4 I went to George McReady's (M.E. Ch.) and dined. I visited Sister Ramsey, and went to John Malone's and lodged.

Sunday, April 5 I went to Andersonville through the rain and preached, 2 Cor. 5.11. I dined at Archie Miller's, and had a class-meeting at the Corners. Lodged at Father Pete Miller's.

Monday, April 6 I went to John Cook's and remained till evening, when I went to A. Miller's and lodged. Mrs. Archie Miller was of the Barber family. Mrs. John Cook was Peter Miller's daughter.

Tuesday, April 7 I went home.

Wednesday, April 8 I preached at Crowels (probably at night) and lodged at Henry Crowel's.

Thursday, April 9 I went to Andersonville; wrote to cousin Samuel Wright; bought a huge bowl & Brittania ladle for B. Frank Morgan whose bowl I had broken; and went to Rob't. Monroe's, & preached. Lodged there.

Friday, April 10 No record of to-day.

Saturday, April 11 Rev. George Muth, P.E. pr. at 11:00, Ps. 103. There were few at Quarterly Conference, in the afternoon. In the evening B.F. Morgan pr. Acts 10.34,35. I lodged at J. Morgan's.

Sunday, April 12 G. Muth pr. at 11:00, I pet. 1.24,25. Afternoon, Silas Andrews pr. Isa. Evening, Rev. J.B. Ervin of Hartsville pr. Lu. 9.23.

Monday, April 13 We had a good lovefeast, in the forenoon. Muth pr. in the evening, 2 Cor. 5.10,11, and one joined as a seeker. I lodged at Samuel Stubbs.

Tuesday, April 14 I went to Charles Andrews' and dined & to John Morgans to school-meeting (?) and to Isaac Umphrey's. J.B. Ervin pr. Rev.—I lodged at John Miller's.

Wednesday, April 15 I went to John Morgan's and thence to a funeral (whose?); and went home to my father's in Fayette County, three miles south-east of Fayetteville—later named Orange.

Friday, April 17 I went to Garrison Creek, and at 3:00 pr., Ps. 50.2; to Columbia evening, Hebr. 12.28,29. John Malone was with me. I was much discouraged with my preaching. We lodged at father's.

Sunday, April 19 I preached at Andersonville, Col. 3.11. S.M. Shumway (last year's pastor who had withdrawn from the Church) was present. Dined at A. Miller's.

Wednesday, April 22 I was at home in the forenoon. Went afternoon to James Newman's, and pr. in evening, Mat. 19.27. Lodged there.

Thursday, April 23 I went ot John Morgan's, and with compasses drafted a pat[t]ern to make a quilt by. I pr. at night at Sch. H., Heb. 3.7,8. Lodged at Jno. Morgan's with John B. Ervin.

Friday, April 24 I remained at Morgan's till in afternoon; then went to Ails' and pr. in evening from 2 Cor. 4.3. Lodged at Ails'.

Saturday, April 25 I went home by Andersonville, but returned to Andersonville, and heard T.J. Connor, of Corvallis, Oregon pr. Mal. 3.18, an excellent discourse, 30 min. Lodge at A. Miller's.

Sunday, April 26 Heard Connor at 11:00, Andersonville, pr. Rev. 6.12; and at night, Rev. 15.2. We lodged at Wm. Nichols'.

Monday, April 27 I attended love-feast in forenoon. Went to John Lewis's, and to Silas Andrews'. At night Connor's text was The Christian Religion. Lodge, A. Miller's.

Tuesday, April 28 Went to lovefeast. Dined at Mother Jackman's. Went to A. Miller's. Rev. Daniel Shuck came, and preached at night Prov. 29.1.

Wednesday, April 29 I went to Peter Miller's and to William Nichols' to Kinion Freeman's and to John Morgan's, where I lodged.

Thursday, April 30 I went to Uncle George Reeder's 4 miles north of Clarksburg, where I dined and supped. Then I went to Neff's Corners, and heard P.S. Cook pr. Rom. 14.

Friday, May 1 I went to Fayetteville and purchased a hat etc. Returned and went to Garrison Creek and pr. at 3:00, Matt. 19.27; went to Colombia. Staid at Utter's.

Saturday, May 2 I came home and staid till evening. Made some sketches for sermons. Went to Neff's Corners and preached, Matt. 9.27. Lodged at John Cook's.

Sunday, May 3 I went to Crowel's and pr. Mat. 19.20. I dined at Green's. Pr. at Maxwell's, Matt. 19.27. Go to Epenetus Smith's. Pr. at Andersonville, Heb. 3.7,8. Lodge at Smith's.

Monday, May 4 I went home. Started to Morgan's, but the rain caused me to stop and stay at Kinion Freeman's.

Tuesday, May 5 I went via Morgan's to Charles Harris's, seven miles south-east of Greensburg. I looked over the farm. His wife is my sister Sarah, 4 years my senior.

Wednesday, May 6 I was about sick with a swelled face. I remained till next morning.

Thursday, May 7 I went on to Hartsville and put up at Rev. Jno. Riley's, ate a little, and went to the Missionary Board meeting. I have a talk with T.J. Connor about my going to Oregon. I lodge at Daniel Shuck's.

Friday, May 8 I went to David Shuck's. Took a walk, go to the Board meeting. Hear the reports, and discussions on sending John Fohl to Oregon. I have a walk with Connor. Sup at John Scudders. Lodge at Riley's. Literary Union—Connor lect's.

Saturday, May 9 I arose early (4:00), go via Greensburg to Neff's Corners, and dine. I went to Andersonville post-office, and to Chas. Andrews' and lodged. I had the toothache!

Sunday, May 10 I pr. at Stubbs' Sch. H. at 11:00, Mat. 19.20. Dined at Stubbs. Preached at Joliff's, I Cor. 1.23, afternoon, and at Ails', Heb. 3.7,8, evening. Lodge at Ails'.

Monday, May 11 I went home and transcribed Conner's article for the *Rel. Telescope*.

Tuesday, May 12 (To-day, the General conference is to open in Cincinnati). I worked at ploughing, and retired to bed early and slept a long time.

Wednesday, May 13 There was rain, and I wrote a letter to Rev. G.W. Keller. In the evening, I went to my brother Harvey's.

Thursday, May 14 I came home and wrote Uncle William H.H. Reeder a letter. I read some in the afternoon.

Friday, May 15 I wrote some sketches. Went to Henry Crowel's and pr. Eph. 5.15,16. I put up at Sutton's.

Saturday, May 16 I went home, and went in the afternoon to Columbia. There was a misunderstanding about the appointment there. Mother Kramer was sick. I staid at Ozro Mason's.

Sunday, May 17 I went to Gillum's and preached, Heb. 3.15. I go to Andersonville and preached from I Cof. 1.23,24. In the evening I preached at Neff's Corners, Mat. 19.20. I lodged at John Cook's.

Monday, May 18 I called at Neff's and Miller's, went by the post-office to Solomon Nichol's, and dined. I went to John Morgan's and Isaac Umphrey's, and preached at Stubb's School-house, 2 Cor. 4.3. Lodged at Umphrey's.

Tuesday, May 19 Went to John Morgan's and staid till evening. I then went to Ailes' and preached, I Cor. 1.23,24. I lodged at Ails'.

Wednesday, May 20 I went to father's in the morning, and helped Wm. cross-out, and plant corn.

Thursday, May 21 Helped plant corn, and finished at 4:30 afternoon.

Friday, May 22 I started to Peter Cook's. I went through Andersonville, Manilla, to Guynneville, to Carmare's where I supped and to Cook's. I preached at Blue River Chapel, Heb. 3.7,8.

Saturday, May 23 I preached at Blue River, Matt. 19.20. I dined at Eli Myer's. Father Silas Andrews preached at 3:00, Isa. 40.1. P.S. Cook preached at night, Amos 4.12. I lodged at William Wariton's.

Sunday, May 24 I preached at 11:00, Matt. 19.27. Silas Andrews preached at 3:00, Isa. 3.10. I preach at night, Acts 26.28. I lodged at Eli Myer's.

Monday, May 25 We had a pretty good love-feast in the forenoon. I dined at Eli Myer's. I went to Peter's brother Frue's, and preached, Luke 14.17. I staid at Eli Myer's.

Tuesday, May 26 We had a love-feast. I preached on Baptism, I pet. 3.21. I baptized Eli Myer, his wife, and her brother, Mr. Talbert, in Blue River, near Bilman's. I went home with P.S. Cook. It was my first baptizing.

Wednesday, May 27 I came to my father's by way of the Andersonville post-office, where I got a letter from D.K. Flickinger, informing me that the Mission Board had appointed me to Oregon. I gave my father the letter and walked out. I lodged at Harvey's.

Thursday, May 28 I came home, and remained all day. My mother yesterday was much affected about my going to Oregon, but was resigned. She said she had prayed that her sons might be ministers, and she ought not to complain.

Friday, May 29 I went to John Melone's and dined. I got my saddle mended, and went to Osborne's. Rev P.S. Cook preached from Ps.

Saturday, May 30 I visited a little. Bro. Cook preached. I dine at Greene's. I went afternoon to Daniel Fry's, near Franklin Church, where I saw F.J. Connor and W.H. Dougherty.

Sunday, May 31 Rev. T.J. Connor preached, Rev. 15.2. I dined at Recompense Murphey's. I preached at 3:00 from Hebrews 3.15. I supped at Samuel Fry's. Rev. T.J. Conor preached at night, Rom. 9.25. I staid at Recompense Murphy's.

Monday, June 1 I went back to Greene's. P.S. Cook preached, Ps. 117. I go to Crowell's, and preached, I Cor. 16.22. I lodged at Crowell's.

Tuesday, June 2 We had a pretty good morning meeting—I dined at Sutton's. I preached at 4:00 Isaiah [sic] 52.1.

Wednesday, June 3 I went to William Nichol's, I had my horse shod. I went by Andersonville home.

Thursday, June 4 It rained so I did not start to Grant County, Indiana.

Friday, June 5 I went to Wilkison Smith's, and lodged.

Saturday, June 6 I went on to Solomon Haynes'. I stopped at Cowing's. I preached at Washington Schoolhouse, near Haynes, Heb. 3.7,8. In Delaware County. [Perhaps the name was Cowen]

Sunday, June 7 I preached at Washington School-house, I Cor. 1.23,24. Rev. Culbertson preached, I Thes. 5.19. I preached at night I Cor. 16.22. I staid at John Buoie's.

Monday, June 8 I went to Uncle William Reeder's, and to Aunt Fanny Reeder's in the evening. I lodged there.

Tuesday, June 9 I went to Henry Richards. I called at Henry Simons and John Crawford's, and returned to Uncle William Reeder's. I preached, Matt. 19.27. I staid at Wm. Reeder's.

Wednesday, June 10 I staid at Uncle Reeder's. I visited Frank Furnish. I settled with Uncle William as my agent. Sold my double-tree etc., shovel plow, etc.

Thursday, June 11 I went to New Castle.

Friday, June 12 I called at Rev. Bells, Jont. Adams, Tom, Aman's, Luther Byer's, saw Peter Reuther. At John Shop's heard Lizzie Shop's piano songs. Saw Drs. Read and Rhea. There was hard rain. I lodged at Jacob Byers'.

Saturday, June 13 I started for home via Flat Rock Baptist Church. Reached home.

Sunday, June 14 I went to the Corners, Neffs, and preached. I dined at Peter Miller's. I preached at 4:00, *2 Cor. 4.3. I supped at Asbury Cook's. William Nichols preached Matt. 7.36,37. I lodged at Rev. Wm. Nichols. *"If our gospel be hid."

Monday, June 15 I went to Fayetteville (now Orange) to John Cook's, to Uncle George Reeder's (four miles north of Clarksburg), to John Morgan's and preached at Stubb's Sch. House. I staid at Jesse Stubbs.

Tuesday, June 16 I visited Joash Stubbs', where Rev. William Stubbs* lay unconscious, and died after I left. I dined at John Morgan's. I went to Ails'—was caught in the rain—and preached Acts 20.32. I lodged there.

Wednesday, June 17 I called at John Ails'. I saw S. M's Rome (?) and went to Crowell's. There was no congregation (rain); so I lodged there. *Wm. Stubbs was a very eloquent preacher. He fell into the opium habit, in old age.

Thursday, June 18 I went to Andersonville and purchased shoes, and to Archibald Miller's, and dined at Kinion Freeman's, my father's cousin's. They lived 2 miles south of Neff's Corners and over a quarter m. west. I went afternoon to Chas. Harris's.

Friday, June 19 Sarah Harris is my only living sister. I went to Hartsville and dined at Professor Shuck's. I supped at David's, went to Daniel's, and had my first private talk with Susan Koerner. I asked her to go to Oregon with me.

Saturday, June 20 I went to Cliffty Station and dined (I suppose at Uncle Jno. Bradens.) I went to my Uncle George Reeder's, four miles north of Clarksburg and lodged there.

Sunday, June 21 I went to Garrison Creek and preached from I John. I dined at Benj. Johnson Gilburns. I preached at Columbia at 3:00, 2 Cor. 4.3.

Monday, June 22 I came home to my father's, and in afternoon went to my brother Harvey Wright's, and lodged there. He lived on the road between Fayetteville (now Orange) and Stone's Mill.

Tuesday, June 23 I rode out to Anderson's and got $8.10, and came back and staid at Harvey's to dinner. I went home to my father's.

Wednesday, June 24 I wrote during the forenoon. Father Silas Andrew's visited me. I went to Andersonville to the post-office, and came back, calling at John Malone's.

Thursday, June 25 I staid at home to-day visiting with Harvey and Charles and all their families. Our parting affecting me not a little. I felt that the children would largely lose interest in me. They did. Though regain it in old age.

Friday, June 26 I went to Connersville with my brother William. There I got ambrotypes. I went on to Dr. Rainey Gillum's, and collected an order from Hartsville College. William took me to Caleb W. Witt's & lodged with me there. He was born Feb. 29, 1832.

Saturday, June 27 I had a kind visit with Bro. Witt. William went home. I went to Dayton, Ohio. I dined at Solomon O'Conner's. I went to the *Telescope* Office. I went to Father Adam Shuey's and lodged there.

Sunday, June 28 I went to the United Brethren Church, where T.J. Connor preached on Matt. 24 and 25 chapters. We (Connor and I) dined with Editor John Lawrence. J.C. Bright pr. afternoon Hebr. 4.9. I pr. at night Matt. 19.27. Connor and I lodged at John Dodd's.

Monday, June 29 I went about some. I dined at J.B. King's, with J.C. Bright & his wife, and Bishop Lewis Davis. Dr. Davis gives direction as to how to board us up, if buried at sea. I think I lodged at Adam Shuey's.

Tuesday, June 30 I packed my box of books. I tried to find John W. VanCleve. I had my picture taken. W.H. Daugherty packed up. I supped at Bishop David Edwards'. I went to hear Kidd's lecture on Elocution. I lodged at Adam Shuey's.

Wednesday, July 1 We started at 7:00 for New York. We went through Columbus, Crestline, Pittsburgh, and reached Altoona before daylight. We rode across the Allegheny River in an omnibus, in the dark. Our fare from Dayton to New York about $19.00.

Thursday, July 2 We went through Harrisburg to Philadelphia, and soon on to Amboy and to New York. We arrived at New York about 6:00 evening. We went by a steamboat from Amboy. Coachman [unreadable] one way; and charged another. Reached hotel at 6:00.

Friday, July 3 We put up at Lovejoy's Hotel [crossed out in original]. We visited the American Missionary Association, S.S. Union, J. Ogden Shipping Agent. Saw Jocelyn, Wm. Goodell, Hoadley, Lewis Tappan's, saw George Thompson Missionary. I saw Wall Street, Broadway. We visited R.R. Tkt. Office. I was editor of the Principle. William Goodell. We got a reduction of 25 per cent as missionaries. S.S. Jacelyn our special friend.

Saturday, July 4 Celebration. Business Houses are closed. The Military and Secret Societies make a display. There were Explosions, Balloons. There were hawkers. A great crowd. I did not see the fight between the Bowery Boys and the "Dead Rabbits." Ten killed; 50 wounded. Our room in 4th story costs 50 each.

Sunday, July 5 We spent the day in our rooms. Daugherty, wife, and child took a walk, but fell into yesterday's riot of "Bowery Boys" etc. It raged about them and they rushed into an open door. They were glad to get back to the Hotel.

Monday, July 6 Our tickets to San Francisco cost $132.00 each. Before starting aboard, I went to Tkt. Office & Post-office. The City Hall was in the Park. We started at 2:00 afternoon. We went out to sea, and, in a few hours, many were sea-sick. I went forward at night, and for hours saw the moonlight dance on the waves! I went to bed late. I slept four hours.

Tuesday, July 7 My berth was No. 102; my seat at table 63. Our Longitude was 73 degrees at noon. Latitude 38 degrees. We saw a sail ship near us. I was at one time slightly sick, but it soon passed away, and I was quite well. I slept well. Our Ship was the "Illinois."

Wednesday, July 8 I was quite well, and nothing unusual occurred. We saw no land. Wm. H. Daugherty & wife were still very sea sick. Their little boy was well. Most of the passengers were sea sick. At noon: Lat. 34 degrees, Long. 73 degrees. I slept well at night.

Thursday, July 9 We sailed as usual. There was no land in sight. All was a dreary waste of water. T.J. Connor and I attend the table almost alone.

Friday, July 10 We have the monatony of sea and sea-sickness aboard. I kept well. Nothing unusual occurred.

Saturday, July 11 Nothing occurred unusual to-day, only all were delighted in the sight of Walling Island. All looked at it as if they had never seen land before. Most passengers were getting better of sea sickness.

Sunday, July 12 Preaching at 11:00 by Rev. T.J. Brown, Episcopal minister from Jamaica. At 4:00, John Salvis, Revelation 20.11,12. Brown's texts were: Ps. 127.2 & Ps. 103. He was a great composer and reader. While he was preaching, we saw Cuba to our right hand.

Monday, July 13 In the forenoon, we came in sight of Jamaica. We rode up to the fortifications at Kingston. Diver's came about the vessel; "Give me a dime Masser." We went to the landing. Perhaps 60 colored girls carried coal in half barrels, with snatches of song & dance.

Tuesday, July 14 The city had its streets, trees and beggars—and fruit sellers. Its mansions are mostly walled in 8 or 10 feet high. Quite assailed by fruit sellers & a beggar. A poet attacks me. We sailed at 5:15, morning, for Aspinwall, now Colon. Sailed slowly.

Wednesday, July 15 I wrote part of the day. We sailed pretty well. We saw a school of porpoises. We saw flying fish daily. Some of the flying fish flew twenty rods, I think. The porpoise is nearly the length of a man.

Thursday, July 16 About 2:00, we came in sight of land. We saw Porto Bello, and before night landed at Aspinwall, now Colon. We slept at the Howard house as much as a few mosquitos would allow. Fair rooms, $2.00.

Friday, July 17 "Won't you buy of Betsy," She "liked the looks of Daugherty. Colored man: "kiss your rosy lips." Went by rail to Ranama, 20 or 25 miles an hour. Villages, huts, trees, swamps, mountains (Porto Bello) Panama Soldiers, Indians. Sailed for San Cisc.

Saturday, July 18 Qr. Meeting at Gillums to-day. God bless them. To-day we saw the spouting of whales. In the evening, we had a dance, the first I ever saw. Our steamship was the "Golden Age."

Sunday, July 19 It is a rainy day. John Salvis made a no-better effort to preach at 11:00, and F.J. Connor preached a good sermon at 4:00, on forward deck, Mal. 3:18. Salvis professed to be a Baptist Missionary—ex-perhaps.

Monday, July 20 Nothing of special interest occurred to-day, except a dance in the evening, in which not a few church members took part. A "learned" Spaniard was introduced to me by Salvis. I remarked that our country was but a child. "A very large child," he said.

Tuesday, July 21 The sea was calm, and the sun was very warm. I found a boy aboard (one of these days), who was just getting up from Panama fever. I scrutinize instrument of observation, as the Captain took observations.

Wednesday, July 22 A calm sea and warm sun, as usual. Nothing of special interest occurs. We mostly keep in sight of the mountains.

Thursday, July 23 I awoke near Acapulco. We went ashore, after seeing the fish after the refuse from our table. It is a beautiful harbor. Sorry town, fortifications. We left at 12:00 or 1:00. Ferriage at Acapulco, $1.00.

Friday, July 24 At Manzanilla about 4:00 afternoon. There we took aboard "about $400,000 of silver bars." It has fifty or sixty houses in sight. Officials. We had a Dutch visitor.

Saturday, July 25 Saturday. We sailed over the Gulf of California. The incidents were those of usual occurrence. About this time, after notifying T.J. Con[n]or of what I intended doing, and Andrew Gant, I took Daug[h]erty's purse out of his pocket in his bunk, while he washed.

Sunday, July 26 To-day we passed Cape St. Lucas. Through the request of the first cabin passengers, T.J. Connor pr. Rev. 15.2. It was a moderate effort.

Monday, July 27 We sailed on to-day as usual.

Tuesday, July 28 To-day, I had a chill, supposed to be

caused by the cold breezes on coming out of the tropics, but later it proved to be Panama Fever, probably taken from that boy in the hold of the ship.

Wednesday, July 29 I had another chill and was considerably sick.

Thursday, July 30 I had a sick day and night of it. I still supposed it a bad cold.

Friday, July 31 We reached San Francisco at 2:00, morning. We put up at Hillman's Temperance Hotel, where I lay very sick, a long forenoon. At 12:00, we sailed on the ship "Commodore." My fever raged the long day. I almost fainted on the way, walking ship.

Saturday, August 1 We sail[e]d on. I was somewhat deliri[o]us at night. We had concluded I had fever, and I had pulverized slippery elm bought for my use. We had a doctor but no medicine.

Sunday, August 2 The sea was rough, and I was very sick. At night my head, and then my feet, were highest, and I was delirious, but disturbed no one. My thoughts with painful vigor flew over the universe.

Monday, August 3 We reached Crescent City in the afternoon, where the doctor got me a little sweet spirits of nitre. We left the city at 5:00, and had a smooth sea, on to Portland, Oregon, or to Columbia Bar.

Tuesday, August 4 We had a nice sea. In the night, we passed in to Columbia River, over the Bar, and in the morning passed Astoria, which I arose to see through the port window. I did not see the ship races. They ran, however.

Wednesday, August 5 We landed at Portland, and rode to Mr. Davidson's, the first private dwelling I had been in since we left Dayton, Ohio. Very kind. We ran up the the Willamette to the shallows, laid there awhile, and ran up the shallows with Mr. Hatch to Oregon City. I was quite sick.

Thursday, August 6 We lay in the Hotel in Oregon City. We settled a small bill with our doctor. Our landlord scolded T.J. Connor for trying to find in kitchen something I could eat. Our bill was $12.50. Dr. Baily's bill was $2.50.

Friday, August 7 We left Oregon City at 11:00 on the "Hosier." We struck on a rock and pulled off by a pulley hitched to a tree. Landed at Butteville about six o'clock. We, Emeline, Dennis, and I, rode to Mother Childers' in French Prairie.

Saturday, August 8 Rev. T.J. Connor borrowed a horse and went home. Our trunks were brought from the Depot at Butteville. I was quite weak and stupid to-day. Mother Childers, Marion, and Perry were very kind. Henry stold another's "duck."

Sunday, August 9 W.H. Daugherty and the rest go to Case's School-house to meeting at 11:00. I go in afternoon to hear Bro. Daugherty preach. I am better to day.

Monday, August 10 My health is improving. I saw Mr. Randall. Sister Hall visited us.

Tuesday, August 11 I am gaining slowly. I remain at Sister Childers.

Wednesday, August 12 I am gaining in strength somewhat. I walked about a half mile to-day.

Thursday, August 13 I made a pleasant visit to Father (Rev.) J.B. Lichtenthaler's to-day. I lodged there that night. (The session of White River Conference began to-day.)

Friday, August 14 I returned to Mother Childer's, which was a very kind home for me. I had considerable fever in the evening.

Saturday, August 15 I had pretty high fever to-day, which abated in the evening. I drank Isup tea, bathed my feet, and sweat all night.

Sunday, August 16 I was pretty well in the forenoon, but had considerable fever in the afternoon and night.

Monday, August 17 I had less fever to-day, as it was not my fever day, but I lay in bed mostly.

Tuesday, August 18 I was quite weak, to-day, and lay in bed. My fever arose about dark.

Wednesday, August 19 I am a little better to-day. It had proved a relapse of Panama fever.

Thursday, August 20 I missed fever again to day.

Friday, August 21 I arose weak, but got along pretty well. Bro. W.H. Daugherty and Rev. J.B. Lichtenthaler go to Sublimity to a quarterly meeting.

Saturday, August 22 I feel tolerably well. I rode down to Henry Childer's house. Henry's wife had engaged to marry another man, but Henry got ahead of him! The Childers boys told me that cattle could not eat Oregon straw!

Sunday, August 23 I felt tolerably well. I preached my first sermon in Oregon, at Case's School-house, Acts. 26.28.

Monday, August 24 I went to Case's and lodged. The breezes had a peculiar roar in the fir trees, and the memory of the sound was lasting. Bears were often seen in the wo[o]ds, as the women told me.

Tuesday, August 25 I staid at Case's till afternoon, and I walked home, which tired me.

Wednesday, August 26 I remained at Mother Childers', and finished reading Lawrence's Church History, a now new book. I thought the history of other "United Brethren" too long. Later, I concluded it was excellent.

Thursday, August 27 I had a chill, Brother E. Cartwright staid with us at Childer's. The chill to-day was another relapse of the Panama fever, but it was more like the common chills.

Friday, August 28 We went, the family and myself, to Yam Hill Campmeeting. On the way, I sent to Young Violet, his father's gifts sent from Sanes Creek, by me. Childers saw him. I lodged at Benjamin Branson's house.

Saturday, August 29 I went to the camp-ground, and heard W.H. Daugherty preach. I had a chill and fever, and took a course of emeticks. In the afternoon, I heard Rev. Jeremiah Kenoyer preach (my first time) on "The door was shut." I slept in the tent.

Sunday, August 30 I heard Rev. W.H. Daugherty preach, at 11:00, Isa. 9.6. Rev. Doane (M.E.) preached at P. Salms, 3:00, rather dryly, though ably. Rev. J. Kenoyer preached at night. He was nearly always stirring.

Monday, August 31 I had considerable fever. Rev. J. Kenoyer spoke on baptism. Rev. W.H. Daugherty preached on Prov. Rev. —Wallace preached afternoon. I went to Benjamin Branson's, and was quite sick.

Tuesday, September 1 After the lovefeast, the meeting broke. I went with William Howe to Miller's, and lodged there. Rev. Doane was there, and said he supposed me to be a deliberate speaker, the very reverse of the fact.

Wednesday, September 2 I remained at Bro. Miller's. I missed the chills. Rev. Jer. Kenoyer and wife came.

Thursday, September 3 We start to Corvallis, but stay at night on the way.

Friday, September 4 Arrive with Kenoyer's at the Camp-meeting, in Father Hurlburt's neighborhood, on the Willamette River. I went to William Pierson's tent. This was Abraham Hurlburt's.

Saturday, September 5 I lay in Pierson's tent, my face swol[l]en, and face painted for cresipelas. Many came to see me, and I would bounce up to speak with them.

Sunday, September 6 Rev. T.J. Connor, W.H. Daugherty and P.C. Parker preached. Parker was zealous and tolerably able, but deficient in grammer and in facts. Kaugherty was a good speaker and growing. Sacrament in afternoon.

Monday, September 7 To-day, I visited Father Hurlburt's—Abraham Hurlburt's.

Tuesday, September 8 I had an other chill. We had a lovefeast and baptizing in the forenoon. I went to F.J. Connor's and lodged, two miles from Corvallis.

Walla Walla Conference, ca. 1857

Wednesday, September 9 I went with Peter Mason and wife in their covered wagon for Sublimity. We arrived at Hadley Hobson's an hour before sundown. I have a chill again.

Thursday, September 10 I remained at Hobson's, and had considerable fever.

Friday, September 11 Went to conference in the afternoon. The annual conference appropriated funds to partly pay for horses for Bro. Daugherty and myself. I had an other chill.

Saturday, September 12 I had some fever, but went to conference in the afternoon.

Sunday, September 13 Rev. W.H. Daugherty and Rev. T.J. Connor preached. I staid at Hobson's. I was appointed to Lane County Mission, but resigned by the advice of Connor, my elder, and Kenoyer, my physician.

Monday, September 14 I went to Conference and sat on the Course of Reading. I was paid $60.00 to buy a horse and $15.00 appro. on Lane Mission. I returned the $15.00, upon my resignation of the mission. Conference adjourned.

Tuesday, September 15 I went to Bro. James Campbell's four miles or more on the way to Salem. They have peaches which are rare in Oregon. Sister Campbell is sick. I went with Jesse Haritt's, who invited me to a home at their house.

Wednesday, September 16 I promise to visit Bro. Campbell's again. I go to Salem with Haritt's, and buy a watch-key, 25 cents, and an overcoat, $7.50.

Thursday, September 17 W.H. Chandler and I, arranged the minutes of the annual conference, and he wrote out part of them. I slept soundly at night. Mr. —— talked of Adams and Jefferson.

Friday, September 18 I read some to-day. Saw Pap Thompson and Mr. Barmun. Rev. A. Bennet came and brought two letters—one of them from Susan Koerner, the girl "I left behind."

Saturday, September 19 I spent the afternoon with Rev. A. Bennett. I was as well as common.

Sunday, September 20 I went to meeting and heard Bro. Harritt preach from Matthew, and Bro. Bennett from Daniel. (Probably the meeting was out west of Harritt's some three miles). Returned to Harritt's.

Monday, September 21 I spent the day at Bro. Harritt's.

Tuesday, September 22 I still remained at Rev. Jesse Harritt's, where I was shown great kindness always.

Wednesday, September 23 Rev. William H. Daugherty came in the evening.

Thursday, September 24 Rev. Daugherty left, and Rev. Jer. Kenoyer came.

Friday, September 25 I wrote too late to go to the post-office.

Saturday, September 26 It was too rainy for me to go to Salem. Mr. McCord went and brought the *Telescope*. I have symptoms of a chill, and have fever through the night.

Sunday, September 27 Rev. Harritt and Mr. McCord went over on the Ricreall to a funeral preached by Rev. T.J. Connor. Connor sent me word, that the people of Lane Mission wanted me to come to the mission.

Monday, September 28 I went to Salem, and bought a cravat, paper, etc. I returned to Harritt's.

Tuesday, September 29 Rev. Wallace Hurlburt came. He is appointed to Columbia Mission, but has never preached a sermon. I spent the day as usual.

Wednesday, September 30 As usual, I had symptoms of a chill. Rev. Wm. H. Daugherty did not come.

Thursday, October 1 Wallace Hurlburt still continued with us. I read and wrote a letter to Uncle W.H. Reeder. The folks went to prayer meeting at night.

Friday, October 2 Father J.B. Lichtenthaler and Rev. Wm. H. Daugherty came in the evening, to Harritt's.

Saturday, October 3 Bros. Lichtenthaler, Harritt and Hurlburt went to a meeting on the Santiam. Rev. W.H. Daugherty went to Corvallis. Mr. McCord got his face badly hurt.

Sunday, October 4 I was quite sick all the day, at Harritt's.

Monday, October 5 Unwell, but I had no chill till night.

Tuesday, October 6 I was quite sick to-day.

Wednesday, October 7 Sister Harritt visited Williams'. I wrote considerable "ornamental" to-day. I had a chill about dark.

Thursday, October 8 I was right sick to-day. The Chitwood girls visit us. I read the "Charmed Mother," 250 pages, through in the afternoon. Rev. W.H. Daugherty came.

Friday, October 9 Bro. Harritt went to French Prairie to meeting. I read in Newton on the Prophecies, and in Coleman's Historical Geography. I missed my chill.

Saturday, October 10 I felt rather feeble. I remained at Harritt's, reading.

Sunday, October 11 I went with Harritt's to meeting at Spring Valley. Rev. Cornwall preached, Acts 16.31; Gillamy Crawford preached, Rev. 2.20. Sister of Sam's—child condemned.

Monday, October 12 I am at Harritt's. Their children are John, 10 years old; Alice, 7; Byron Webster, 3.

Tuesday, October 13 I am at Brother Harritt's.

Wednesday, October 14 I bought a mare of Kenoyer, at $100.00. I traded my watch.

Thursday, October 15 Went to Father Emmet's to prayer meeting. I exhorted and led the meeting. Bro. Osborn came from Umqua Valley.

Friday, October 16 I had a slight chill in the evening. Rev. Wm. H. Daugherty came.

Saturday, October 17 Rev. W.H. Daugherty preached at 11:00 from Proverbs. I preached at night, 2 Pet. 1.3,4. Shaw's (from Cincinnati), Coal's, King and Walker, there. Cincinnati was 4 miles up the Willamette.

Sunday, October 18 Rev. Daugherty preached at 11:00, John 1.29. I preached at 3:00, I Pet. 3.15. Brother

Daugherty preached at night, Matt. 13.39. There was considerable feeling, but no one joined Church.

Monday, October 19 I rode a piece with Bro. Daugherty, as he went away, and I returned to Harritt's. I start at 3:30 to Campbell's, where I find Parker. I bought a satin vest at $4.00, at Salem.

Tuesday, October 20 I remained at Campbell's, reading Wesley's sermons. Irish Crontall, there. I took a walk in the afternoon, as usual. Bro. Campbell tells of his sickness and niece nurse.

Wednesday, October 21 At 9:00, I started to Lebanon. I had a map. I arrived about dark. I saw Osborn at the ferry. I saw Young Helms and his sister. Their boy was born the 16th. I staid at J.B. Helm's. Dr. Crawford and Julia Donnell, live 12 miles away, at Brownsville.

Thursday, October 22 I remained at J.B. Helm's till evening. I saw Mother Helm's. I went home with Sister Peterson who lived near Washington Butte or Peterson Butte. Mr. J.B. Helm is merchandizing and owns 160 acres of land. He is a M.E., good looking and well-behaved.

Friday, October 23 I staid at Bro. Peterson's.

Saturday, October 24 I went to Mr. Drain's, Mrs. Jackson's brother's. I dined at Hiram Jackson's, and went to Parish's. I attended a singing. I staid at Cal. Ward's. Gusta sings for me. Oliver Ward his brother was there.

Sunday, October 25 I preached at 11:00, I Pet. 3.15. I dined at Ward's. That night I lodged at Father Gallaher's. His medicine was calomel! I saw John Metzler. I took fever again.

Monday, October 26 I was quite sick with eresypelas and fever. I did not lecture on Education, as I had announced. I had also dental neuralgia. I think I was at Cal. Ward's.

Tuesday, October 27 I went to Bro. Peterson's and found my horse very sick.

Wednesday, October 28 I was quite sick in the morning.

Thursday, October 29 I was weak but better.

Friday, October 30 I was still better. I heard M.M. Crow preach on 2 Pet. 1.5–11. Preached well. I lodged at Richardson's. He is from Indiana. He has a lame child. Crow had sold his claim.

Saturday, October 31 I went to Lebanon, by way of Peterson's. I lodged at Helm. Benson and William and Young Denny had arrived from Portland at 3:00 in the morning.

Sunday, November 1 I remain at J.B. Helms. William and Elizabeth go home. I retired to bed early. I was better, but had some toothache. I studied a sermon on the Judgement Seat of Christ.

Monday, November 2 It rained considerably in the morning, and some again toward night.

Tuesday, November 3 It was still rainy. I saw Father Helms to-day.

Wednesday, November 4 I started to Rev. T.J. Connor's. I called in Corvallis at Joshua Mason's. I went through Albany Prairie on the way from Lebanon. I reached Bro. Connor's after dark, and lodged there.

Thursday, November 5 I remained at Bro. Connor's till after noon. Rev. W.H. Daugherty and William Pierson came. I went to G.W. Bether's and lodged.

Friday, November 6 I started at 9:00, for Jesse Harritt's. I saw Rev. A. Bennett. I bought a dozen steel pens for 25 cents. My mare was a slow traveler, and I was weak to whip up. I bought a bite to eat of a traveler. I found it dark in the Willamette timber, and put up at Shaw's in Cincin[n]ati.

Saturday, November 7 The morning, I went to Jesse Harritt's. I wrote some letters in the afternoon, while it was very rainy.

Sunday, November 8 I remained at Harritt's. It was a rainy day. I read Newton on the 25th Chapter of Matthew, also on Revelation. I read considerably in Clarke's commentary, on Generation of Vipers.

Monday, November 9 This was election day in Oregon. There were many pro-slavery voters. Glover and Major Walker. Vote on the State Constitution. And Slavery and no Slavery. Anti-slavery prevailed.

Tuesday, November 10 I went out to Salt Creek. I thought I had found my stray mare, but was deceived.

Wednesday, November 11 I went to Jeremia Kenoyer's. I stopped at Casper's and Branson's. Staid at Kenoyer's.

Thursday, November 12 I returned to Miller's. I hunted considerably. I passed F. Yokum's, and called at Branson's. I preached at Miller's at night, 2 Cor. 4.4. Franklin's and Dodson's.

Friday, November 13 I breakfasted at Howe's. I came to Jesse Harritt's, passed Carlisle's. I engaged a saddle at Joe Downer's. I came back by Spring Valley.

Saturday, November 14 I went via Durham's to Walling's, and talk with the old Father. I return to Harritt's by the Valley road.

Sunday, November 15 There is a meeting at Harritt's. Rev. W.H. Daugherty preached from 2 Cor. 1.21,22, and Painter exhorts. I went to Walling's and preached from 1 Cor. 1.23,24. I returned to Harritt's.

Monday, November 16 I went to James Campbell's. I saw Keen, McVary, etc.

Tuesday, November 17 I went to Sublimity, where I saw Spriggs, Kirkpatrick, Albertson, Sears, Logan, Fullbright, McDaniel, Foote, and Stayton. I lodged at Father Gabriel Brown's. Sublimity is 15 miles south-east of Salem.

Wednesday, November 18 I went to Hadley Hobson's. Rev. Jer. Kenoyer came in the afternoon, and we lodge there. We talked of Oliver the Deist, "extremes," peaches, Mormons, Clifton.

Thursday, November 19 I went to Gabriel Brown's. At a meeting of the Board of Sublimity College, I engaged to teach three months at $50 a month and they pay my board. They had a night session at G. Brown's, where I lodge.

Friday, November 20 I remained at Gabriel Brown's. I wrote a letter to Harriet Helm, my second cousin, the only relative on the coast.

Saturday, November 21 I went to Quarterly meeting at Sublimity and heard Rev. J.B. Lichtenthaler preach. I dined at James Brown's, the merchants. I preached at night 2 Pet. 1.3,4. (I heard Lichtenthaler and Harritt discuss as to whether Daugherty or I could preach best & Harritt said I was most systematic.) It was in the dark.

Sunday, November 22 I heard Rev. Jer. Kenoyer preach. I dined in the country at Read Miller's, 2 miles northeast. Rev. J.B. Lichtenthaler preached at night, and I exhorted. I lodged at Gabriel Brown's.

Monday, November 23 I began Sublimity College with 27 scholars. I board at Gabriel Brown's. They lived a mile south-west. They were old Arkansas people. Their son John, unmarried, was at home, and Robert Newel, an Indian, about 12 lived there.

Tuesday, November 24 I had 29 scholars to-day. One of them was Robert Newell, a California Indian, brought to Sublimity by James Brown, a farmer, whom he left on account of hard treatment, and lived with Brown's father.

Wednesday, November 25 I got along well with my school. My walk to Brown's was about enough for my strength.

Thursday, November 26 I carried on school as usual. I was thin and sallow, not worth fighting by enemies of the United Brethren.

Friday, November 27 We had a spelling school in the afternoon.

Saturday, November 28 I went to Allen Davies' and made a stand, which I left at Brown's when I left there the next quarter. I did not attend the debate on Slavery, where Parker was proslavery, & who angered John Greenstreet, who was antislavery.

Sunday, November 29 I went to the College building to hear a Rev. Dickens preach, who did not come. I dined at Solomon Albertson's, where I saw Mr. Rice and

Stayton. I went to James Brown's, where few attended a prayer meeting. A farmer a half-mile north of town. His wife was Miss Evans.

Monday, November 30 I continued to teach, and my school grew in numbers. I interested my scholars in manner of reading.

Wednesday, December 2 School continued, and greater interest was manifested.

Friday, December 4 I have recitations as usual in the forenoon. But I scolded at noon. We had spelling and declamations in the afternoon. Verd. Oden's family came to live at Brown's. He was their soninlaw.

Saturday, December 5 I fixed my watch to-day. John Greenstreet came in.

Sunday, December 6 I preached at the College from 2 Pet. 3.18. I dined at Hadley Hobson's. I also lodged there. My face was much swollen from my teeth.

Monday, December 7 I did not feel very well to-day.

Tuesday, December 8 My face pained me in the afternoon. Verd. Oden himself came to Gabriel Brown's.

Wednesday, December 9 Went to Hadley Hobson's in the evening. He was quite sick with a pain in his side.

Friday, December 11 We had our recitations in elocution. I lodged at Solomon Albertson's. He called forceps "pulicans," and Foote said "natur" for nature.

Saturday, December 12 I went to Gabriel Brown's and remained there.

Sunday, December 13 I preached at the College from Ps. 50.2. I went to Phillip Glover's to prayer meeting, and went home with Gabriel Brown.

Tuesday, December 15 School as usual. We had singing at night. I went to G. Brown's, my boarding place, as usual.

Friday, December 18 School as usual. I staid at Hadley Hobson's. About this time, in playing ball, Henry Wizner let his bat fly and strike Francis Hobson on the cheek, a dangerous hurt, but he recovered.

Saturday, December 19 I went to Brown's, and next to help move Jer. Kenoyer's house, near Sublimity. I took medicine to Francis Hobson's, and then went home to Gabriel Brown's, in Kenoyer's wagon.

Sunday, December 20 Rev. J.B. Lichtenthaler preached from Eph. Waller's soninlaw seems to have made a mistake sup[p]osing he had an appointment. I dined at merchant James Brown's. Mrs. Brown was an intelligent woman. Jer. Kenoyer pr. at night I cor. 13.3. I went to Gabriel Brown's, lodged.

Monday, December 21 I was at school. We had a spelling school at night.

Tuesday, December 22 I spent the day teaching school. Rev. Jer. Kenoyer staid at G. Brown's with us. My mare came home. She had got into a neighbor's field by Harritts!

Wednesday, December 23 School as usual. We had singing at night.

Thursday, December 24 I went across the Santiam River, and married Mr. D.M. Cook and E. Ann Wizner. I lodged at Dillon Hoskin's. This Cook was of Siskyou, Cal. He gave a ten dollar gold piece to me. Miss Wizner had attended school.

Friday, December 25 I rode with D.M. Cook and wife to the ferry, and found a pocket-book with about $3.00 in it, for which I found an owner later on. I went via Hobson's to Geo. W. Hunt's. Lichtenthaler preached from "Search the Scriptures." I staid there.

Saturday, December 26 Lichtenthaler and I go to Woods, over on the Willamette, via Frazer's Gap. He preached I cor. 1.18. He was the pastor of Marion Circuit.

Sunday, December 27 I preached from Matt. 19.27. I went home by way of Crump's and Force's and Delany's. I lost my way and lodged at Mr. Blenton's.

Monday, December 28 I came on to School late. My manners to C. were ill. I lodged as usual at Gabriel Brown's.

Wednesday, December 30 I had school as usual, and I staid in the evening to the singing.

Thursday, December 31 There was School, as was common. I went in the evening to Morgan Rudolph's to a watch night (M.E.) meeting. Rev. Mr. Spaulding and Rev. Mr. Wiber preached. Wilber was an early missionary. He was beloved by the imigrants.

Friday, January 1, 1858 I staid at Gabriel Brown's nearly all day.

Memoranda

A Sketch—Never Preached. Rev. 16.13 & 19.19.
I. *Spirit of Frogs*
    1. Unclean, Loud, Boastful.
II. *Emenations of Satan.*
    1. He is the Adversary.
    2. Busy & adroit.
    3. He is powerful.
III. *Proceeds out of his mouth*
    1. Dragon
    2. Beast
    3. False Prophets
IV. *Christ War[n]s against*
    1. Dragon
    2. Beast
    3. False prophets
V. *Strive against.*
    1. Not against flash only
    2. But against Principalities
    3. Powers
    4. Rulers of the Darkness
    5. Need of the Whole armor
    6. Need courage, perseverance & Divine help.
VI. *Victors Wear*
    1. Crown
    2. Obtain Eternal Glory.

The Highway Creed.
"The work of soul purification commenced in regeneration, may be perfected by an act of consecration and faith; or the carnal mind, or inbred sin, may be entirely destroyed from the soul by the power of the Holy Spirit by the virtue of the cleansing blood of Jesus."
Judge Daniel Thew Wright of Washington, D.C. formerly of Cincinnati, son of Dan, son of Nathaniel Wright, is a fourth cousin of ours. He is a great-great-grandson of Nathaniel Wright, of Hanover, New Hampshire, an older brother of Benoni Wright.

William Goodell whom we saw in New York, was of good size and a good looking elderly man of dignified deportment, very natural. He sent (to T.J. Connor) his paper a year, the "Radical Abolitionist," afterward, "The Principia." He was a very able writer. Licenses as a preacher, but not ordained. Lewis Tappan is a stout-built man of sandy complexion. He is a good-natured looking man. He is spirited, somewhat jovial in his manner, and talks freely. He is a whole-souled sort of a fellow. S.S. Jocelyn was a spare, tall, sober looking man, quite friendly and truly obliging. Tappan told an anecdote of himself and a colored man (lecturer perhaps) that some abolitionist thought ought to sleep together as they lodged at his house! I forget how they came out.

I built my house in Adair Co., Iowa, in 1880. My deed for my Dayton House & lot is dated Dec. 21, 1870.

Continued from Preceeding Page.
George Thompson, a missionary from the American Board, was a pleasant modest kind of a man. His conversation was pleasant. I learned the following anecdote of him. At Good Hope Mission, (now Bonthe), Sherbro Island, they had a refractory boy, that the natives said ought to be flogged. But Thompson said No. He would be flogged instead of the boy. So he was flogged! The boy was still stubborn. But a few days later, one evening he came to Thompson and asked him to go with him to the chapel, which he did, and there he told the Lord how mean he had been, and implored Divine forgiveness.

Children of Charles B. & Sarah (Wright) Harris.
1. Edward M. Harris married Mary Amelia (Hedrick) Harris.

2. James F. Harris m. Zena R. Harris, nee Johnson.
3. Laura (Harris) Winchell m. Austin Winchell
4. Charles Wright Harris m. May (Waite) Harris
5. Harvey B. Harris m. Hope E. (Harshbarger) Harris
6. Ella (Harris) Reese m. Napoleon Bonapart Reese.
7. Orval C. Harris m. Emma Harris
8. Kate H. Vanfleet m. Marshall H. Vanfleet
9. Estella (Harris) Petree [m] Frank Petree
10. Clara H. Gilbert [m] Leonard A. Gilbert

Charles Harris & Sarah Harris: Their two oldest died. Their first from its naval string not being properly tied. William Edgar, a large fleshy child, died at 18 months, from bowel trouble.

My days in Common School

1. James Ross	3 weeks
2. Mr. Blackburn	3 months
3. Mrs. Bowler	3 months
4. William Hogue	3 months
5. Jas. Johnson Wilder	3 weeks
6. Jeremiah Anderson	6 months
7. Jas. Wilson	8 weeks
8. Jas. K. Rhodes	6 weeks
9. Wm. Cotton	6 weeks
10. James Dickens	3 months
11. Wm. Rhodes	3 weeks
12. James Tuttle	3 weeks

Expenses in 1857

Telescope books	3.25
Inkstand	.25
Stationary	.15
Bought in Oregon	
Cholagogue	2.50
Post-office stamps	.50
3 skeins of silk	.15
Hair oil and Iodine	.50
Hymn Book	50
Quinine, iodine	1.00
Cravat	2.00
Overcoat	7.50
Sec'y Coll.	1.00
Candy	.50
watch key	.25
Lead pencil	.10
Post-office stamps	.50

Needles and thread	.25
Paper, one quire	.43
Sponge	.25
Letter envelopes	.25
Ferriage	.25
Bought mare	100.00
Bible	.75
Making shirts	1.00
Post-office stamps	1.00
Satin Vest	4.00
Ferriage	.25
Ferriage	.15
Gun coat	3.00
Mittens (mistake)	.50
Ferriage	.25
Quinine	1.00
oil cloves, tinc, iodine	.50
Ferriage	.25
Matches	.12 $^1/_2$
A coat	12.00
Silk handkerchief	.75
Writing paper	.25
Buttons and shaving soap	.25
Saddle-blanket	2.50
Ferriage	.12 $^1/_2$
Boots	5.00
Oats	5.00
Geography & Atlas	2.00
Pair Drawers	1.50
Ink	.20
To Brown	1.50
Cathartic	.25
Wrappers	.70
Black drilling	.85
Paid	5.00
Saddle blanket	2.75
Oats	5.00
Oats	5.00
Received of T.J. Connor	10.00
June 20	20
July 5th	1.50
Stamps	1.00
July cash	5.00
1858	
Bought vest	4.50
Carpet bag	1.00

Davies Bourdon	2.00
Paper for writing	1.12 $^1/_2$
Envelopes	.87 $^1/_2$
Bridle	3.00
Oil of cloves	.25
Tinct. Iodine	.50
Paid Jas. Campbell—apples	5.00
Gave to J.B. Lichtenthaler	4.00
Bought Curtains	2.00
P.O. Stamps	1.00
Hat	4.00
Ferriage	.50
Candle stick	.75
Tobacco (not to chew)	.12
pens	.10
Bills for school	2.00
Socks	1.25
Mending shoes	.50
Candles for meeting	2.10
Cholagugue	1.00
Silk thread	.15
post stamps	.50
Expenses in 1857	
Ticket to Dayton	1.70
Express box of books	.25
Express at Dayton	.25
Drayage of books	.15
Books bought	3.35

Diary of 1858 Oregon

Feb. 6 The ground is frozen. Not over two inches deep.

Feb. 7 It rains to day and carries off last nights snow.

Feb. 15 Connor came to the close of my school and the meeting of Sublimity Board. Had a good close. He brought Wm's & Harvey's letters.

May 17 My term of School closed at Sublimity. There followed a slight measles scare which soon passed away. Warm weather came about June 1st.

June 12 In my letter of June 12th, 1858, I tell of visiting

Harriet Helm on my way from Conference; her health is usual, and her children have whooping cough; a letter from her sister Martha spoke of her having typhoid pneumonia. Martha lived near Milroy, Ind.

July 12 Caswell W. Witt arrived at Sublimity, from Iowa. The forepart, at least, of this month was cool. I closed school Aug. 20th. I attended camp meeting Aug. 29, 25 miles.

Sept. 26 Commenced the fall term of School, to-day, at Sublimity.

I wrote October 5th. I attended three Camp-meetings; 35 conversions, 25 accessions. I visited Harriet Helms in the tour. She and her children in usual health. She had letters from Lavina Snyder and from her Sister Martha who talked of going to Oregon, but she moved west. Rev. Helm, her fatherinlaw, was a stiff Methodist.

Nov. 8th, I wrote of not enjoying as good health in twelve years, and tha my School was overflowing.

Feb. 1, 1859, I wrote that my health was excellent; and that the winter had been warm and rainy, the school full & prosperous.

March 2, 1859, I wrote that I was reading the *National Era,* the *New York Tribune,* the *Religious Telescope,* the *Oregonia* (Portland) the *Agnes* (Salem), the *North Western Christian Advocate,* and two or three Monthlies—as much as I liked. I added that we had a good Quarterly Meeting before the 7th of March (March 5).

May 12. At the annual conference.

May 16. Session, I had my home at S.K. Brown's. At this session, Caswell W. Witt, William Kendrickson, Wallace Hurlbert, Jas. Connor, and Levi M. Sallee joined the conference. Rev. C.B. Masters pr. at 11:00 Monday, and J. Kenoyer pr. at the School-house at night. Conference adjourned at 6:00, Monday. I was appointed to Calipooia Mission. Rev. C.W. Witt moves to Puget Sound next week. On Sunday, Rev. William H. Daugherty preached the dedicatory sermon in the new Church, May 15, (1859) from "Praise God in his sanctuary," Ps. 150.1. He tracked the course I had given him yesterday, not thinking of his using it to-day. Welcome to it.

June 6, 1859. I arrived at Corvallis this morning. We had a very interesting meeting at Cochran's yesterday, some awakened.

1860, Winter
I taught three months school at New Salem, six miles south-east of Rushville, Ind. I began Jan. 2nd. Some large scholars were insubordinate, and injured the discipline of the School. Here my wife and I were very happy. I preached frequently. In April, I removed to Andersonville, and there taught a summer school at Neff's Corners. I found the School less pleasant than the one in 1855. After the School was out, I went with my wife on a visit to Grant County, Indiana, for three weeks, and there she imbibed malaria. I came back to a meeting (Qr.) at Green's forks, and the P.E. David O'Farrell's child Eddy being sick. I preached for him, and was credited with more than I merited. I went on to Conference at Williamsburg, where we boarded at Benjamin Harris's, she Mattie, being a Hartsville student and roommate of my wife's. Her pro James. I served as assistant secretary of the annual conference. At this conference, there were almost uniform failures to preach, except Bishop David Edwards. I evaded preaching, and got Rev. D.K. Flickinger to preach for me at Greens Fork, the Washington. The conference assigned me to Marion Circuit, and the next month, I moved to my farm in Grant County, four miles east of Fairmount. To the farm, I moved by wagon, John P. Freeman being a teamster. On the way, John P. Freeman staid at the house of the uncle of his future wife, Robert Clark, on the north bank of the Kilbuck, while we staid at Mr. Joseph Cowen's on the south-side. We reached our home next day. This is introductory to some notes on my time and labors on the new Circuit, and events connected therewith. I had on Marion Circuit, Marion District, White River Conference, seven regular appointments, and others occasional. To these appointments, I devoted my time. I tried to farm a little. The next Conference elected me presiding elder and put me on Marion District. I went on a visit or errand to Franklin and Fayette Counties, and here let me begin my notes: Called to Mother Fohl's crazy daughters. I went home by Chesterfield, arriving at home through the rain. I note that Joseph and Eliza

Minton lost their babe, the day I got home, and John Richards preached its funeral from 1 Pet. 1.2. He said he had often doubted his own election. "This babe was a sinner, else it would not have died." Very comforting! At this my house in Grant Co. my oldest son Reuchlin was born March 17, 1861, just before the South began the Civil War. I wrote my brother William, near Orange, Fayette County, May 19th, that I had received his letter of April 13th. I said that Susan had had no chills for five weeks; that Reuchlin grows finely; that uncle William Reeder's had a great big girl, just two weeks old; that my Cousin Margaret is at Nottingham, and Essenior was at E. Smith's. I said: "I am but little stirred about the war. May it prove the irrepressible conflict in the fullest sense of the term, ending oppression's rule." I said nearly three companies had gone from this country, William Heal in one of them. Oct. 19, 1861, I wrote William of my Father's death. I had visited him immediately after conference, with my family. And we were to start to see him again, the 18th, but rain hindered. Yet I alone started, but a boy met me with a letter telling me of his burial. At the time of his death, we had a meeting on a circuit, with six accessions to the Church.

November 27, 1861. I wrote of John Croddy's visit— before and Nov. 27th. I stated that Reuchlin weighed, about a month before, nineteen (19) pounds, and Susan wrote *December 20th,* that he was "beginning to creep."

February 27, 1862, I tell of a good Quar. Meeting at Mt. Pleasant, ten preachers there. I also told of seeing Sereptu Wearly, a second cousin of my Mother. She was the daughter of Richard Shourd, a soldier of the war of 1812, who was the son on Amey Shourd. Sereptu was a good U.B.

April 20, 1862. I wrote I sold my gray mare about three weeks ago, for seventy-seven dollars; that I paid $60.00 on my farm and bought a colt for $25.00, which I sold a year later to John Huddleston for a nice profit. I stated that the last six quarterly meetings had been attended with mud, and generally rain—some 30 accessions. I mention our having engaged Clementine Chainey, to live with us. She was ten years old. She came, was a good natured little girl, and I took her to her mother in the fall, when we moved to my Mother's in Fayette County.

She never amounted to much. Her father had committed suicide. Her mother was much disappointed at her being brought home—would have let her move with us.

June 8, 1862. I had written Harvey, two weeks ago, that I was sick, but I had since attended two quarterly meetings. I mentioned that fruit (apples) was abundant. I speak of having seen Squire Woodbeck, a Campbelite, smarter than I expected. We had been old neighbors in Fayette County. His brother John was not prosperous. Their oldest brother, William, who built my father's barn, was now a prosperous merchant in Andrews. In later years he went to Indianapolis "to buy goods" and was seen no more. It was generally thought that he went South to a woman he had met when a soldier. I called at his soninlaw's years later, and Mr. Hutt was suspected of being William, (come home) by his daughterinlaw. William's wife was a perfect shrew.

June 18th, 1862, I had just closed a Qr. M. at Jacob Stover's. Rev. Jacob was an arbitrary man, and vain. He said to the conference, that his grandson Milton (?) Garrigns was the smartest boy in the state.

1863, December 23. I was P.E. on Indianapolis District, in time of the Civil War. On account of ill health and extreme cold, I turned back after starting to Blue River Quarterly Meeting, December 18th. I notice that Silas Koerner sold my wheat at Wabash at $1.13 a bushel—$35 worth. I went the 24th to Fairview Chruch, Palestine Circuit, to Quarterly Meeting. I wrote Dec. 23, that our county, Wayne, was cleared of a draft. Susan had rheumatism of her neck and shoulders.

Oct. 22, 1863, Thursday. I wrote of Reuchlin and Lorin being unwell for a week or two before, and Reuchlin having burned himself smartly on the stove—nearly well; and I said that Lorin was running about. I went to J.B. Ervin's Quar. Meeting the 23, near Cadiz—probably at Bennetts. I was, Oct. 19th, at Uncle Ryland T. Brown's in Indianapolis. John Braden, Eliza and aunt Mary Brown, were expected home from Grant County, that evening. And Catharine Eliza Brown was soon to go to Mt. Vernon, Ohio, to teach in the Academy. I wrote William proposing that Mother should go with me on a visit to Indianapolis, Oct. 28th; she did not go.

1864, Feb. 10. I wrote that I had been in meeting every day and night for a month, except two days spent in traveling. Irving Fox is doing swell on Honey Creek Circuit; Thomas Evans prospering on Pleasant View Circuit. I said J.B. Ervin missed appointments on Sugar Creek Circuit, last quarter, and resigned at Qr. meeting; succeeded by William Davenport. That J.S. Wall was slow at Indianapolis. I saw David O'Ferrill at Mr. Pleasant, a week ago. Jas. M. Cook had organized a class at Beach Grove—20 new members. I was at Dr. B.T. Brown's a month ago. I hoped to see William on my way to Hartsville, March 5th. I go to Olive Branch, next Friday.

1864, May 13, Friday. Next Thursday (May 19) the Parent Missionary Board met at Dublin. Bishops Glossbrenner, Edwards, Markwood were there. Dickson came advocating the abandonment of the African Mission. J. Dickson pr. one night, Ps. 123.2. David Edwards preached Wm. Barton Witt's funeral sermon, (May 22), Sunday, "Blessed are" was not a happy effort. Spiritualists rejoiced on his comment on Jesse Wilson's spiritual influence, *after his death.* The collection was almost a failure—the man Caleb Witt pressed it for Barton's sake! Afternoon, J.M. Spangler spoke well an interesting Missionary sermon. But the audience was sleepy. He said: "As sure as some of you are asleep!" and Markwood "twisted his face for Sunday," and William Davenport who sat beside me laughed so heartily, that I had hard work to keep my face saintly. At night, (May 22), Bishop Markwood was to preach. He objected, and said he would go to Germantown. I told him that if he did, it would not do for him to return to Dublin again. He took his text in Revelation, and though fluent in words, he had little sense in his discourse. I would have sunken through the floor, if possible, and wished "he had gone to Germantown!" I had heard him scrape the skies. In the debate, I advocated holding on the African Mission.

1859

Saturday, December 31, 1858 I arose at Bro. Jesse Harritt's, where I had lodged. He came from Coal's about 10:00. I left Harritt's after dinner, and went via Salem and S. Painter's to Claigett's. Rev. Jer. Kenoyer preached at Childers' Sch. H. Ps. 50:1–6, but was away Sun.

January 1, 1859 I went to Quarterly meeting at School-house in Mrs. Childers' neighborhood. I lodged at Mrs. Childers'. I saw Mr. Cone's.

Sunday, January 2 I preached at the School-house, Ps. 50,2. I dined at Goddel's and staid at William Case's.

Monday, January 3 I started home by the way of Parkersville. I passed Sappingfield's, and lodged at James Campbell's. His pronunciation of whiskey was "viskey." We talked of College matters. He told of Howel's theft.

Tuesday, January 4 I came to Sublimity, and opened school with about thirty-three scholars. I boarded with John Denny's. He was old now, and nearly blind. He was twelve years a senator in Illinois legislature, from Knox County, and was nominated for Governor in Oregon But he withdrew for reasons. I received a letter from my brother Harvey, and I read Senator Seward's speach [sic].

Wednesday, January 5 The school increased to about forty-five scholars, at Sublimity College. I visited at Rev. McMillin's, Camb. Pres. I read Senator Crittenden's speech on the Lecompton Constitution. Mr. Denny gave account of the comparative influence of slaveholders and non-slaveholders in Congress.

Thursday, January 6 We had school as usual, and prayer meeting as usual.

Saturday, January 8 I went to the Baptist meeting and heard Rev. Wilmot preach, Hebr. 1st Chapter. A Mr. Star, of Cambridge, Indiana, came after meeting. The Executive Committee of Sublimity College convened. Mr. David Hubbard staid with us, at John Denny's. (Star proved a bad egg, there, & in Indiana.)

Sunday, January 9 I went to Condit's Presbyterian Church, 5 miles south-west, and preached, Matt. 5.8. I dined at Silvanus Condit's. I came back to William Pierson's and lodged.

Monday, January 10 I met Solomon Alberson, and had a talk on Liquor Dealing. He favored it. He was a great blow. I got my mail including letters.

Tuesday, January 11 The President's Message came, and I read part of it.

Wednesday, January 12 Prayer meeting at the College. I as usual attended it.

Thursday, January 13 Dr. Adair had emgaged a Singing School, and we met for it. He uses round notes. He is a physician. He gave an introductory lecture.

Friday, January 14 We had spelling as usual in the afternoon, and essay, etc. "Sublimity," Gabriel's, Morris's, Lewis McMillin fails on address. Modest. I lecture at night, on Dress, Cleanliness, Economy.

Saturday, January 15 I hauled up from Hadley Hobson's, my oats, and trunk, to John Denny's, my present boarding place.

Sunday, January 16 Rev. Jer. Kenoyer is lame and his family sick; so I preached, Gal. 2.20. Mr. Star's family came. I preached at night, Acts 5.20.

Tuesday, January 18 I called at Father Gabriel Brown's. I lodged at Jer. Kenoyers.

Wednesday, January 19 I attended prayer meeting at College.

Thursday, January 20 In our second singing, we practice on rounds on the scale. Silas Williams got a joke on himself. (I forget it.)

Friday, January 21 Few declaimed in the afternoon. At night Rev. J.B. Lichtenthaler preached, John 1.8,9.

Saturday, January 22 I went to the Woods appointment. I saw Zink and young Woods, and Enoch Garrison. I showed James Wood how to cipher.

Sunday, January 23 I preached at Woods, Matt 5.8. I saw Ervine, Hall, Poly Jr., Helms etc. I arrived at home after seven.

Monday, January 24 The School attendance was to over fifty. David Hubbard with us.

Tuesday, January 25 Our horses are gone. I have letters from Susan, J.B. Ervin, and D.K. Flickinger. Called at Star's timeshop.

Wednesday, January 26 Rev. Thomas Small's appointment. Prayer meeting, eve. but few out.

Thursday, January 27 West came, also Rev. A. Bennett. We have singing school.

Friday, January 28 There was a candle scrape, and a fight and some swearing. Rev. Alex. Bennett lodged with me.

Saturday, January 29 I went with Bennett, to Gabriel Brown's (now in town) and to Rev. M.M. Crow's, and lodged at William Pierson's south-west of town.

Sunday, January 30 Rev. Thomas Small preached Acts 2:15, and dined with us. He is a Cumberland Presbyterian. I visited Rev. Jer. Kenoyer's; and I preached at night, Ps. 84.11. I was exceedingly happy. Fell.

Monday, January 31 I wrote a letter for Father Denny. I went to Gabriel Brown's and wrote letters. Lodged there.

Tuesday, February 1 I sent five letters: Ervin, ————, Wm. Wright, Ezra ————, Susan Koerner. [Lines appear in text]

Wednesday, February 2 There was prayer meeting at night. Revs. Berkley, Kenoyer and Crow attend. I called at Mr. Brook's, a M.E. Silas Williams lodged with me.

Thursday, February 3 We had singing, and Dr. Adair lodged with me. James Brown, the farmer, who married Miss Evans, son of Gabriel, agrees to withdraw from the Church. There were James Brown, the farmer, and James Brown, the merchant.

Friday, February 4 I miscomprehend some writing on the blackboard, and comment on it severely. "A gentleman on his feet is higher than a gentleman on his knees." Harvey Rudolph confessed writing it; and I confessed to having misunderstood it! On my way to James Campbell's, in the evening I got lost. I found the way at last. Sister Campbell is sick.

Saturday, February 5 I start to French Prairie. I saw an eagle and a deer, on the way; I also saw ducks. I reach Case's, and lodged at Mrs. Childers.

Sunday, February 6 I went to J.B. Lichtenthaler's and joined in marriage Mr. Morrow and Rebec[c]a Lichtenthaler, Rev. J.B.'s daughter. I preached at the school-house, at 11:00, Ps. 84.11. I started in the afternoon to Sublimity, rode with a Frenchman on the way. I reached James Campbell's at 10:00.

Monday, February 7 I went to Denny's. Mrs. Parker visited us. Jerome Grear and McMillin Jr. visited us, and lodged. I wrote a letter to J.C. Latimer for Father Denny.

Wednesday, February 9 Prayer meeting, and Rev. Berkley attended. I wrote till after midnight, a letter to Susan Koerner.

Thursday, February 10 Mrs. Brooks visits us. Father Denny jokes me about my return to the States.

Friday, February 11 Elder David Hubbard supped with us. There was singing-School at night.

Saturday, February 12 I attended the Baptist Monthly meeting. Rev. Berkley preached Rom. 12.1. I started on M.M. Crow's horse for Wood's appointment. Being belated, I staid at Nigh's.

Sunday, February 13 I went on to Wood's, and preached, Matt. 7.13,14. I returned and in meeting we had a warm time in prayer.

Monday, February 14 Nothing special occurred only I forgot the school-house door. I wrote till midnight.

Tuesday, February 15 Received the Salem "Argus," and read most of it. Saw Mr. Newsom's letter in the Statesman. "Conservatives." Saw a satire on free whiskey. I wrote late.

Wednesday, February 16 Nothing very especial occurs. Cornelius and Wadle came and asked me how much 5 1/2 X 5 1/2 make. I answered 30 1/4.

Friday, February 18 Afternoon, we had the usual exercises in school. Newton Parker and Amanda Parker visit us at Denny's. Dr. Adair lodged with me.

Saturday, February 19 I went across the Santiam River and called at Zevely's. I dined at James Williams: Children James, Mary Jane, Elizabeth, Martha. I preached at 2 o'clock, Ps. 84.11, spoke long and good liberty. Staid at Dillon Hoskins.

Sunday, February 20 I preached at Irvine's Sch. house, Bro. Miller, whose appointment it was, not being there, Matt. 7.13,14. I had good liberty. I dined at Irvine's.

Wallace Hurlburt and Senaca Caston came. Hurlburt preached at night, "To seek and save." It was rainy and few were out. I stay at Irvine's.

Monday, February 21 I preach, at Elias Forqua's, on Baptism, I Pet 3.21. I baptize 5 persons, some Dillon Hoskin's girls. We had a warm meeting. I dined at Wesner's, children Henry, E. Ann, etc. I got back to Sublimity, just before the School closed. I mailed a letter to Susan and one to the Telescope.

Tuesday, February 22 School as usual. The mail brings a letter from Wm. & one from Susan. There was a prayer meeting.

Wednesday, February 23 Glover and Virgil Newsome were excused for attending a ball, Morris was suspended for two days, and others were notified to give answer.

Thursday, February 24 The boys trial for attending the ball. Four are suspended for two weeks. Coons came in the evening and jawed. I went to Hadley Hobson's and talked with him. I staid at his house.

Friday, February 25 We had school. Ex. Committee met at night. They sustain my Discipline. Morgan Rudolph gave his opinion favorable to me, So Denny, Hubbard, Berkley, McMillin, Hobson and Albertson were against me. Preston Glover is called to account and is expelled. (When converted, he greatly desired my forgiveness. Freely granted.)

Saturday, February 26 I went to Albertson's Store. Peyton Glover came in and cursed me. (I did not inform on him, as he had thought). I saw Adair and Berkley. I read Susan's letters. I called at Kenoyer's. There is egg-roasting at College.

Sunday, February 27 I heard Prof. Hoyt preach, Luke 12.40. Rev. Mr. Lewis is with him. (He, Hoyt, was, years later, the editor of the *Western Christian Advocate,* when I heard him again.)

Monday, February 28 There were forty-seven in School to-day. Brooks and two or three others try to talk across the room. At night, there was a debate on Dancing. I ironically defended it.

Tuesday, March 1 I got a letter from W.H. Chandler. I called at Brown's and lodged at Wm. Pearson's.

Wednesday, March 2 Mr. Kirk came to board at Denny's. John Greenstreet calls on us. Rev. Berkley leads the prayer meeting this evening.

Thursday, March 3 The girls refuse to sweep the house at School—a trick. Ballou curses those who oppose the regulations of the College.

Saturday, March 5 Quarterly Meeting. Rev. P.C. Parker preached at 11:00, Prov. 23.23. We had a good time. Quarterly Conference in Aftern. Rev. Jer. Kenoyer preached at night, Rom. 12.1. Parker lodged with me.

Sunday, March 6 We had a love-feast—a happy time. Parker preached. Happy time, afternoon at lovefeast. Silas Williams happy. Parker pr. at night. I dine at Lowe's. Lodge at G. Brown's.

Monday, March 7 Rev. P.C. Parker leaves us.

Thursday, March 10 I ask the Scholars' leave of absence, and go to G.W. Hunts and lodge.

Friday, March 11 I borrow Hunt's young horse, but give out going to Rock Hill, south of Lebanon. Miss Condit and the Miss Pearsons, visit us.

Saturday, March 12 I change my mind and start to Rock Hill. I called an hour at Harriet Helms, in Lebanon. I fix her sewing machine. I pr. Rom. 6.14. Lodge at Gallaher's.

Sunday, March 13 I preach Gal. 2:20. Dine at Hiram Jackson's. Pr. 2 Cor. 4.3. Lodge at A.J. Richardson's.

Monday, March 14 I, with Wallace Hurlburt go to Wm. Pearson's at Sublimity. Lodge there.

Tuesday, March 15 I get a letter from Lewis Mobley, who tries to make me believe that Susan was caring for another man, but I knew he was treacherous. I went to G.W. Hunt's and lodged

Wednesday, March 16 We had school as usual. Wallace

Hurlburt preached at College at night. I lodged at Rev. M.M. Crow's, in town.

Thursday, March 17 We had Singing School at night. I lodge at Pearson's with Hurlburt.

Friday, March 18 Hurlburt starts over the Santiam. The Quarterly Meeting, M.E. Church, commences at the College. M.M. Crow preached.

Saturday, March 19 Elder [blank] Wilber pr. 11, Isa. 41.10. I exhorted. Rev. Taylor pr. at night, "Crying aloud." Rev. Ellis exhorted. I attended the meeting.

Sunday, March 20 Lovefeast in which Wilber and Crow gave striking experiences. Eld. Wilbur preached "born again," and sacrament followed. I called at Star's in the afternoon. Fletcher Denny pr. "Day of his wrath." Rev. 6.19.

Tuesday, March 22 Morgan Rudolph calls. I got a letter from Rev. T.J. Connor. Alberson, as wise as Solomon, talks on a platform & the admission of Oregon.

Wednesday, March 23 Mr. Benson called to-day at Mr. John Denny's. There is prayer meeting. I wrote a dialogue, to be acted at Sublimity, at the close of the term, by the girls.

Thursday, March 24 I lent James D. Brown, Merchant at Sublimity, Fifty Dollars. He is not a relative of Gabriel Brown.

Friday, March 25 I settled with J. Glover $1.50 for services as assistant teacher, and ($2.00) as a substitute. I went to James Campbell's and lodged.

Saturday, March 26 I went on to Salem, put up horses (M.M. Crow's and mine) at Samuel Pentar's, crossed the Willamette with Paynter in a skiff, to a quarterly meeting held by Rev. P.C. Parker at Harritt's. I preached at night, Rom. 6.14. Lodged at Harritt's.

Sunday, March 27 Rev. P.C. Parker preached at 11 o'clock, Prov. 23.23, "Buy the truth." Communion followed. I crossed the river with Penter, in Chitwood's canoe, and dined. I rode to James Campbell's. His children: Price, Finley, Virginia, and Susan. Heavy show had melted.

Monday, March 28 Finley Campbell took me to Sublimity. I lodged at Hon. John Denny's.

Tuesday, March 29 It was mail day from the States, and I received a letter from brother Harvey. In the evening, we practise [sic] on my dialogue.

Wednesday, March 30 I was at prayer-meeting at night.

Thursday, March 31 David Hubbard, M.M. Crow, and I go to Hadley Hobson's, and I had a talk with him. He was hostile and obdurate, as these brethren adjudged. David Hubbard lodged with me.

Friday, April 1 Newson's close and exhibition (?). Dr. Adair lodged with me.

Saturday, April 2 I wrote letters to Harvey and William Wright and to my father and mother. I staid at home.

Sunday, April 3 I preach at Sublimity 1 Cor. 13.13. Read Miller dines with me [and] Rector Campbell. I visit Gabriel Brown's. Read Miller leads pr. meeting.

Monday, April 4 Miss Newsom visits us. I had a practicing exhibition in the evening.

Tuesday, April 5 The Sons of Temperance had the Installation of Officers, and Rev. Thos. Small delivered a lecture. I heard one talk very largely about What a transformation the Sons of Temperance had affected at Sublimity!

Wednesday, April 6 Prayer Meeting as usual.

Friday, April 8 This day closed my teaching in Oregon. We had examinations in the day and an exhibition at night. Rev. Matoon, a Baptist, was present. Alphin, and G. Patton. My dialogue went off well. *Mary J. Williams excelled on "Sorrow for the Dead." Palmer, Virgil Newsom, and Louis McMillin had farewell addresses. Charles Jones did well. *Probably at another date.

Sunday, April 10 I walked to Condit's Church, and

preached from Ps. 84.11. I dined at the widow Condits. In afternoon, I attended the Presbyterian Prayer Meeting, and commented on the Lord's prayer. Lodged at Silvanus Condit's. The widow's husband was a Presbyterian preacher.

Monday, April 11 Silvanus and Cyrenius Conditt each gave me gold as presents. I went back to William Pierson's and saw them start back to move beyond Corvallis. I carried a box of books up to Denny's. I mailed a letter to Susan, and one to Sarah Harris. I had a talk with Alberson.

Tuesday, April 12 I call at James Brown's (the farmer's), to see Robert Newel, who is sick. I dine at Casper Rudolph's. David Hubbard comes and I go with him to Brooks' and Gabriel Brown. No mail. I lodge with Geo. W. Husitt's.

Wednesday, April 13 I came home (to John Denny's) by Jer. Kenoyer's. I am auditing my accounts. Mrs. Berkley visits us. Prayer Meeting. I lodge at home.

Thursday, April 14 The College Board meets. A committee on Rules is appointed. I sup at Gabriel Brown's. I lodge at D. Hubbard's.

Friday, April 15 The Board, having referred the rules to a special committee, takes action on its report. Solomon alberson is displeased, and resigns from the Board. The Board is instructed its Executive Committee to reemploy me as the teacher.

Saturday, April 16 I went over the Santiam to Scio. I rode with Rev. McMillin (Cumberland Presbyterian) part of the way. I dined at Miller's supped at Samuel Fleenor's. I pr. at night I Cor. 13.13. Staid with Connor, at Fleenor's.

Sunday, April 17 We had a speaking meeting in the morning. Rev. T.J. Connor pr. at 11 o'cl. Sister Griffon's funeral, 2 Samuel 14.14. Dined at Wood's. I preach at night, Phil. 3.3. Thus there were three sermons in succession with the chapter and verse the same, all unnoticed till afterward. Six joined the Church: Sisters Miller, Connor, and Flenor, Litel, and Samuel Fleenor, Jr. Staid at Wood's a merchant, in Scio.

Monday, April 18 Met T.J. Connor at Oley Hanson's. We came to Osborn's, blacksmith in Scio. Rev. w. Hurlburt pr. at night, Luke 10.42. Lodged at Osborn's.

Tuesday, April 19 I went to Samuel Fleenor's, and thence to Miller's, where I dined, we went on to Rev. McMillin's, where I lodged.

Wednesday, April 20 I went on to Sublimity. I called a few minutes at James Brown's. I hear that John Dicken's horses broke through the bridge at D.S. Stayton's. Prayer meeting. I lodged at Jer. D. Brown's.

Thursday, April 21 I spent some time recording in Qr. Conference record. I dined at M.M. Crow's, and lodged at Jer. Kenoyer's.

Friday, April 22 I went to farmer James Brown's to supper. Mrs. Evans, his motherinlaw, had a tooth drawn. I lodged at Denny's.

Saturday, April 23 I went to Mr. Hause's and dined. Then to Read Miller's, where I lodged.

Sunday, April 24 I remain at Miller's. I visit Drinkwater's. At prayer meeting, at 4:00. Lodged at [blank]

Monday, April 25 I came back to town and call at James D. Brown's. I dine at Gabriel Brown's. Lodged probably at Denny's.

Tuesday, April 26 I received a letter from Susan and one from A. Kennett. I went to Coy's and lodged.

Wednesday, April 27 I came home by where George W. Hunt worked and went on to John C. Rudolph's, where I lodged.

Thursday, April 28 I went home. Father Denny came home from Salem. I remain there.

Friday, April 29 I visit Jer. Kenoyer's and go thence home, where I drink teas, take a sweat and remain.

Saturday, April 30 Rev. McMillin's called in. I was quite unwell, and staid at home.

Sunday, May 1 Rev. Berkley preached for me, "Of whom I am chief." I exhorted from "The time is short." Hadley Hobson and family sent me a note saying they withdrew from the Church, which I read publicly.

Monday, May 2 I am at home. I lodged at Rev. Berkley's. I am quite unwell.

Tuesday, May 3 James Campbell called at the door. I stay at home, considerably unwell.

Wednesday, May 4 I went to Jer. Kenoyer's and thence to George W. Hunt's, where I lodge.

Thursday, May 5 I return to town via Jer. Kenoyer's. I help him fix his books. I borrow a horse at Henry Foster's, and stay at Gabriel Brown's.

Friday, May 6 I start to Corvallis, but meet Wm. Pierson's and Cooper's, and send my horse back, and go in a buggy to Miller's near Alphin's Ferry.

Saturday, May 7 I call at Harrington's, dine at Price Fuller's, trade at Corvallis and lodge at Pierson's.

Sunday, May 8 I started to King's Valley, but did not go on account of rain. Sisters Mason and Peter came. I lodged at Pierson's.

Monday, May 9 I went to T.J. Connor's, where P.C. Parker came. I saw C.W. Witt. I recorded in the conference journal.

Tuesday, May 10 I went to Rev. Caswell W. Witt's, after recording awhile in the journal. I went back and lodged at Connor's.

Wednesday, May 11 W.H. Daugherty came, and N.W. Allen and Canady. I went to G.W. Bethers. Oliver Brewer and Rev. C.B. Masters came.

Thursday, May 12 An. Conference convened at the New Church-house. Caswell Witt and William Hendrickson joined conference. I sup at Bales' and lodge at S.K. Brown's, my Conf. home.

Friday, May 13 The committee on Course of Reading

met. N.W. Allen and Wallace Hurlburt joined Conference. I sup at Bales'.

Saturday, May 14 The conference received James Connor and Levi M. Sallee. The committee on Finance reported. T.J. Connor and Jer. Kenoyer were elected presiding elders. Wm. Kendrickson preached at night. I lodged at S.K. Brown's, my house.

Sunday, May 15 Rev. W.H. Daugherty preached the didication sermon of the Church "Praise God in his sanctuary," Ps. 150.1. T.J. Connor at 3 o'cl., preached Conference sermon, "Contend earnestly for the faith," Jude 3, verse [blank]. I preached at night, "They that be whold need not a physician, but," Matt. 9.12.

Monday, May 16 Conference continues. Rev. C.B. Masters preached at 11:00. We adjourned about 6:00, and Jer. Kenoyer preached at School-house at night from Revelation. I was very happy. I stay at G.M. Bethers.

Tuesday, May 17 I spent the day at T.J. Connor's recording the minutes in Conf. Journal. Harritt's and Daugherty's are with us, at Connor's. I wrote to Susan. I had been appointed to Calipooia Mission.

Wednesday, May 18 I go with W.H. Daugherty to Peter Mason's and to Wm. Pearson's. I return to Mason's. I had borrowed Pearson's dun horse.

Thursday, May 19 I went to William Wyatt's and see Brother Williams' who had been much hurt. I go by A. Bennett's and T.J. Connor's to Caswell W. Witt's. I lodged at Connor's.

Friday, May 20 I went to Alex. Bennett's and dine, and return to T.J. Connor's. I met Evans. I cut stove-wood. I had a talk with James Connor, Connor's adopted son.

Saturday, May 21 I went over to Michael Crow's at Knox Bute, where Hurlburt preached at 4:00. We stay at Crow's. Seattle and his wife were there.

Sunday, May 22 I preached at the school-house, "Enoch the seventh from Adam prophecied." Jude 14 verse, my first sermon on Calipooia Mission. I dined at Young

Miller's, Rev. T.J. Connor preached at 4:00, from "They took knowledge of them" etc. Acts. 4.13. I lodge at Crow's.

Monday, May 23 I go to Sublimity. Dine at Casper Rudolph's. Get a letter from Susan. Call at Kenoyer's. I go to James Campbell's and lodge there with Wallace Hurlburt's (Allen D.)

Tuesday, May 24 Hurlburt and I go to John Hunt's. We call at George W. Hunt's, and at Jer. Kenoyer's. I go to Davies'. I lodged at Henry Foster's. I got a letter from William Wright.

Wednesday, May 25 I call at Gabriel Brown's in Sublimity. I got a letter from Cousin Sarah Wright. I fix up things. I call at John Hunt's (Senior) at Brooks', and go to Samuel Fleenor's by way of Rev. McMillin's.

Thursday, May 26 I went on to Lebanon, and stop at Cousin Harriet M. Helm's till evening. I lodge at Peterson's.

Friday, May 27 I went to Hiram Jackson's by way of Michael Ward's and the school-house. Dine at Jackson's. I go on to David Simons' and see Warren Cranston. I lodged at Simonds'.

Saturday, May 28 I am at David Simons. I call at Emmet Simon's. Smith and Lovell call.

Sunday, May 29 I preach at 11 o'cl. Ps. 84.11. I go to Rock Hill School-house, and preach, Ps. 50.2. I lodged at Hiram Jackson's, where I was invited to make my home. She was a sister to Mr. Drain, an intelligent, motherly woman, whose daughter Mary is the wife of Wallace Hurlburt. Their twin sons are Harrison and Tyler. I lodged there to-night.

Monday, May 30 I wrote in the forenoon. In the afternoon, I went to Lebanon, and heard Mr. Adams, editor of the *Statesman,* and Mr. Mack make speeches. I staid at second-cousin Harriet Helm's.

Tuesday, May 31 I called at Father Gallaher's, and dined. I go to Michael Ward's, and thence to Hiram Jackson's. There I find Wallace Hurlburt. I lodge at Jackson's.

Wednesday, June 1 I write in the forenoon. I went to Alfred Wheeldon's and dined. I went to Bogg's school-house, and thence to Fauring's, where I lodge.

Thursday, June 2 I go to H. Jackson's and write sketches of sermons, and record them. I dined, supped, and lodged there. Race after the sheep.

Friday, June 3 I go to Simons' to dinner. I preach at Bogg's School-house at 4 o'clock, Hebr. 3.7,8. I lodge at Cochran's.

Saturday, June 4 Rev. W. Hurlburt preached at 11 o'clock, I dine at Fauring's. I go and preach at Knox Butte, Rom. 6.14. I return and lodge at Fauring's.

Sunday, June 5 Rev. Mr. Miller preached 11, from Isaiah; W. Hurlburt followed Rom. 2. I dine at Cochran's, and preach at 4, Luke 19.27. Two came forward for prayers. It was a weeping and rejoicing time. I lodged at Cochran's.

Monday, June 6 I borrow a horse, and go with Hurlburt to Corvallis, where I dine at Joshua Mason's, with W.H. Daugherty. I go with him to his house. We lodge at Wm. Pearsons.

Tuesday, June 7 In the afternoon I visit Sister Mason, and L.M. Sallies, where I had supper. Return to Pearson's and lodge with C.

Wednesday and Thursday, June 8 & 9 Went with Daugherty by a bridle trail to Alsea Valley. We ascended, sometimes, steeply above tall tree top after tall tree tops till we reached the summit of the way; and then descended in like manner till we came to a small stream, on which a white fir tree, by fair measurement 31 feet in circumfrence [sic], and at least over 200 feet high. We reached Alsea Valley, about six sections of land, rich and level surrounded with mountains, a small river running through it, and the way to the ocean very difficult. There was no wagon way to it, tho one, a rough way, has since been opened. There were about six families living in this valley at that time. They packed over the pieces of wagons and other machines and set them up. The grass was tall and the river sparkling. At the salmon season, the river woudl be crowded by the salmon pushing through

from the ocean. A man could stand at a riffle with a hoe, and soon lift out a barrell [sic] of fine fish. Four of the families were professors of religion, and at Mr. Hayden's, we had meeting next day at 11 o'clock. I preached 1 Pet. 4.18, with liberty, and the man and his wife and half-grown daughter came forward for prayers. It was a melting time. We returned across the mountains in the afternoon to Rev. Daugherty's. Mother Mason, who buried her husband on the way to Oregon, was at Alsea, visiting her daughter, Mrs. McCormack, where we lodged.

Friday, June 10 I went to Connor's and thence to Father Abraham Hurlburt's, where Salee was, and we lodged there. Several preachers, at conference had agreed to hold meeting here at this time. Daugherty had promised to come, if I went to Alsea. It was at the Sch. H.

Saturday, June 11 I preached at Sch. House at 11 o'clock Ps. 84.11, with liberty. Daugherty preached at 4 o'clock, "My yoke is easy," Matt. 11.40. It was an affecting time. Two asked for prayers. I dined at Miller's and lodged at Hurlburt's.

Sunday, June 12 T.J. Connor preached, at 11:00, "Kingdon of God is preached" Luke 16.16 (Since John). I preach at 12 o'clock, Ps. 50.2. Levi M. Sallee preached at night, "The end of all things is at hand." 1 Pet. 4.7. I dined at Peter Sayers', stay there later.

Monday, June 13 Rev. T.J. Connor preached at Miller's at 11, "The sting of death is sin," 1 Cor. 15.56. I received 4 whole members and two seekers. I pr. at 4, 1 Pet. 4.18, at Sch. H., I lodge at Sayers.

Tuesday, June 14 Seekers' meeting at Sayer's. Four are converted. Hurlburt pr. at 4, Jas. 1. We organize a class of 13. I lodged at Hurlburt's.

Wednesday, June 15 I get quick breakfast at Peter Sayers, go to T.J. Connor's, and get out Cochran's mare, dine at Joshua Mason's, and go on to Deckard's, where Hurlburt preaches, Rom. 1.16. I lodge at Cochran's.

Thursday, June 16 Meeting at Cochran's. I preach Matt. 7.13,14. I go to Rock Hill and Pr. 1 Cor. 13.13. I lodge at H. Jackson's.

Friday, June 17 I go to Alfred Whealdon's. I met Hurlburt on the Prairie. I called at Smeltzer's. I dine at Leonard's. I preach at 5, Acts. I go on to Ward's.

Saturday, June 18 I go to Pollards by way of Lebanon. I see father McKinney. I dine at Mrs. Helm's. I preach at Richard Pollard's, 1 Cor. 13.13. I stay at Samuel Fleenor's with Wallace Hurlburt.

Sunday, June 19 I preach at Scio, at 11 o'clock 1 Tim. 2.6. I prcach at 4, Jude 14 verse. I lodged at Rev. James Connor's. Joseph Connor had a question in mathematics.

Monday, June 20 I go to Scio and get my horse shod by Osborn, $1.00. I call at Monkis's. Joseph Crank is badly hurt by his horses running away. His talk was like that of a saint. It vanished at the return of his health. I go on to Sublimity, and lodge at John Denny's. Mr. Clingman is teaching is Sublimity.

Tuesday, June 21 I went to David Hubbard's, Gabriel Brown's, Hadley Hobson's and Coy's. I lodged at Coy's.

Wednesday, June 22 I go to Hobsons. I get a note. I go to James Campbell's with Father Denny. Fix the needle in sewing machine. I lodge at Jesse Harritts.

Thursday, June 23 I return, afternoon to James Campbell's with Bro. Harritt's. Wallace Hurlburt there. Jer. Kenoyer comes.

Friday, June 24 Carry the mail on to Sublimity. I go to Coffeis, call at Condit's, go on to Michael Crow's, at the Butte, arriving at dark.

Saturday, June 25 I remain at Crows. We salt the cattle afternoon.

Sunday, June 26 I preach at Knox Butte at 11 o'clock. I preach at Albany at 4, 1 Tim. 2.6. I lodged at Mr. Beach's, Mr. George Mills.

Monday, June 27 I voted and went on to Bogg's Sch. house. Simons. I dine at Smeltzer's. I lodge at Emet Simon's.

Tuesday, June 28 I go to Wheaton's and dine. I see Laimebarger's. I preach Matt. 16.26. I go on to Alfred Wheeler's and lodge.

Wednesday, June 29 I went by way of H. Jackson's and Ward's to Lebanon. I attend the singing at the Academy. I lodge at my Cousin Helm's.

Thursday, June 30 My horse limps somewhat. I go to Jesse Harritt's and find Jer. Kenoyer and his wife there. I lodge there.

Friday, July 1 I go on to Campmeeting, South Yamhill. I preach at 5, 1 Thes 4.3. Rev. Levi M. Salee preached at night.

Saturday, July 2 Jer. Kenoyer preached at 11:00, "Yoke of bondage; Gal. 5.1. Rev. Flynn pr. at 4, Hurlburt at night "Worship God." Rev. 22.9.

Sunday, July 3 Jer. Kenoyer pr. at 11, "Time shall be no longer." Rev. 10.6. I pr. at 1:00, "The fool hath said in his heart," Ps. 14.1. Sacrament at sunset. Wallace Hurlburt exhorts so earnestly.

Monday, July 4 Lovefeast meeting. Wallace Hurlburt preaches, "Except your righteousness exceed." Matt. 5.20. Rev. Taylor pr. at 3. I pr. at night, "Enoch the seventh from Adam." Jude 14v.

Tuesday, July 5 We close the meeting. The news comes that Sister Huszy is dying! I go to Rev. Jesse Harritt's & lodge.

Wednesday, July 6 I go by James Campbell's to Sublimity and lodge at Denny's.

Thursday, July 7 I went to Miller's and lodged. James Williams, Sen., was there assessing.

Friday, July 8 I go to a Baptist meeting, where I see Mr. Hewit and Mrs. Wheeler baptized, after David Huffer preached. I preach at Pollard's School-house, at 4 o'clock. Lodge at Mr. Herald's. She was a cousin of William & Oscar Kendrick's.

Saturday, July 9 I go on to Quarterly Meeting, by Samuel

Fleenor's. Rev. T.J. Connor preached, "I will search Jerusalem," Zeph. 1.12. I dined at Wood's, our merchants in Scio. I preach at 4, 1 Thess. 4.3. Lodge at Fleenor's, after Quar. Conference.

Sunday, July 10 Rev. T.J. Connor preached,"The archers have shot at Joseph," Gen. 49.23. I dine at Osborn's, the blacksmith's in Scio. I preach at 4 o'clock Rev. 22.11. I go to James Connor's, and lodge. He is T.J. Connor's brother. Is much older.

Monday, July 11 I go with Bro. T.J. Connor to look at his farm in the neighborhood. I dined at Dillon Hoskin's, and lodge at James Williams'.

Tuesday, July 12 I go to Sublimity by way of School-house and Hoskins'. I receive a letter from D.K. Flickinger. I stay at Geo. W. Hunt's a mile north of Sublimity.

Wednesday, July 13 I staid at Hunt's till after dinner, and then go to Jonathan Crow's at Knox Butte's.

Thursday, July 14 I went to Nathan Newton's. He is Mrs. Alfred Wheeldon's brother. We sit up till 2:00, and talk on religion. A new convert—almost fanatical.

Friday, July 15 I go to Knox School-house, by way of Miller's. I had a talk with Young Buoy. I preach at 4, to 6 persons at S.H. and have class meeting.

Saturday, July 16 I go by Alfred Wheeldon's to Hiram Jackson's, and dine. I went on to Andrew J. Richardson's and lodge there.

Sunday, July 17 I preached at Rock Hill at 11, "Enoch the seventh from Adam," Jude 14 verse. I dined at Ward's, preach at John Metzler's at 4:30, and go to Scott's and lodge. Some one in bed differed severely with Metzler on a trouble—murder case, I believe.

Monday, July 18 I went to Metzler's, and walk to blacksmith's. I dine with John and go on to Norman Lee's, to whom I pay $1.65 for music. I lodge at Jackson's.

Tuesday, July 19 I go to Lebanon, and dine at Cousin Harriet Helm's. I go on to Samuel Fleenor's, and they

tell me of Joab Powel's backwood's talk at Baptist Meeting. I lodge at Fleenor's.

Wednesday, July 20 I go to Sublimity. I call at Wizner's on the way. I saw Griffith. The Santiam ford was very swift—my head swam. I lodged at Jer. Kenoyer's. Morgan Rudolph comes to get Kenoyer "to tie" Ben. Hutton and Catharine Donica.

Thursday, July 21 I called at John Denny's. There is a meeting of Sublimity Board. I dine at Denny's, and go on to my appointment at Ervin's School-house, where I preach at 4, Matt. 20.6. "Why stand ye here all the day idle?"

Friday, July 22 I proceeded slowly to Maxwell's ford, and thence to Froman's, and lodged at old Mr. Moore's (Lane Co.).

Saturday, July 23 I went to Fanning's and found that my horse had a nail stuck in his foot, and took it out. I helped Fanning make a horse hay-rake, and lodged at his house.

Sunday, July 24 I preached at 11, Eze. 33.11. I dine at Robert's. Preached at 4, Rev. 22.11. I lodged at Simons.

Monday, July 25 I went to H. Jackson's, my home, and thence to Jesse Harritt's, where I lodged.

Tuesday, July 26 I went to Samuel Fleenor's, and to Dillin Hoskin's where I lodged. Dillon was a Baptist, an earnest antislavery man. His son James married a Kenoyer girl and they had Bishop Hoskins.

Wednesday, July 27 I went by James Williams' and John Greenstreet's (his mother's) to Geo.W. Hunt's, and lodged there.

Thursday, July 28 I went from Hunt's to James Campbell's. Father John Denny was there, and asks our counsell about selling property to John Hunt, George's uncle.

Friday, July 29 I went to Wood's via Salem, where C. Pillow a jewler insults me for removing the wax which he said he put in to hold my watch crystal to its place!

Saturday, July 30 Wallace Hurlburt and Senaca Coston, came to Woods', and were much pleased with my sermon next day at 11, 1 John 3.2, though I had little "liberty." Senaca Coston Sunday preached at 4 (perhaps). I lodge at Wood's. Wood's was a preaching place 8 or 10 miles above Salem.

Sunday, July 31 I preached at 11, 1 John 3.2, with small freedom. Dined at Polly's. Senaca Coston preached, aftern. or night. I staid that night at Woods'.

Monday, August 1 I go to Fanning's, thence to Corvallis, thence to T.J. Connor's 3 miles from Corvallis.

Tuesday, August 2 I go from Connor's to Deckard's, where I find Mr. Guess the teacher. I lodge at Deckard's.

Wednesday, August 3 I went to Hiram Jackson's, where I find Wallace Hurlburt and wife, both unwell. They are quilting. I lodge. Mary is Mr. & Mrs. Jackson's daughter.

Thursday, August 4 I went to Drain's, and dined. He had been bitten by a hog. I go to Jonathan Crow's and lodge. Mrs. Jackson is Drain's sister.

Friday, August 5 I go to J. Crow's and remain there. It rains somewhat.

Saturday, August 6 I still remain at J. Crow's. Mr. Miller comes to see about thrashing.

Sunday, August 7 I preach at Knox Butte School-house, "Father forgive." Luke 22.34. I went to Albany and preached, Ps. 84.11. I preached at night, "As in Adam, all die." 1 Cor. 15.22. I lodged at Nathan Newton's.

Monday, August 8 I cradled oats for D. Froman's, $1.00. I saw Parish and McFadin I lodge at Nathan Newton's.

Tuesday, August 9 I went to Corvallis and dine at Joshua Mason's. I got no letter. I see Dr. Cooms & wife. He lately was arranging for a duel. Was smart Alick, now.

Wednesday, August 10 I went to Mills, where the M.E. Annual Conference convened. I see Revs. Star, Rhodes, Deal, Miller, Rutlege, Garrison and Johnson, etc. I hear Profs. Hodson and Lippincott lecture on the Bible cause. Meeting 5:00 in morn!

Thursday, August 11 I attend 5 o'clock prayer meeting. On my way to it, I found a gold coin worth over two dollars, $2.50 piece. I gave it to Bible Cause, if no owner. I was introduced to Bishop E. Baker, and by him to the Conference. The conference recommended Woodward for mission to Japan. I lodge at N. Newton's.

Friday, August 12 I breakfast at D. Froman's. I go to Sublimity, and lodge, Denny's.

Saturday, August 13 I called at Kenoyer's, and fix their clock. I dined at George W. Hunt's. I start to Mr. Herald's, and lodge there. I received a letter from Susan.

Sunday, August 14 I preached at Scio, at 11, Heb. 6.11,12. Dined at Samuel Fleenor's. Preach at Ervin's School-house, Luke 19.27. I lodged at James Williams' with Silas, his nephew.

Monday, August 15 I had my horse shod at Osborne's in Scio. I went on to Lebanon and to Jackson's, and thence to Brownsville. I lodge at Father Kirk's, after a long night-ride.

Tuesday, August 16 I went on to Michael Crow's in Scienslaw Valley, via Maxwell's Ferry and Eugene City. I thought it 46 miles from Connor's. There, I found T.J. Connor and Senaca Coston.

Wednesday, August 17 We went over Calipooia Mountain, and dined Esta's Hotel. I wrote some copies for his girls. We go on to Hendrick's and lodge.

Thursday, August 18 I go on to Rev. N.W. Allen's and lodge.

Friday, August 19 I go to Oakland and thence to Camis Swail to meeting. Rev. T.J. Connor preached at 11, and I in afternoon, Hebr. 10.35,"Cast not away." We lodge at Oliver Brewer's.

Saturday, August 20 Rev. T.J. Connor pr. at 11, Luke 18.19, Rich man & Lazarus. I preach in afternoon, Gal.

6.14. Glory in cross. We lodge at Rev. C.B. Master's.

Sunday, August 21 Rev. Connor preached 2 Pet. —[lines in original] I preached from Ps. 84.11,"The Lord." We had Sacrament at 5, o'clock. We lodge at Isaac Smith's.

Monday, August 22 I preach on Baptism, and Connor baptizes. We dined at Isaac Smith's. Connor pr. "Receive not grace in vain," 2 Cor. 6.1. We stay at William Hoskin's, a brother of Dillon Hoskins.

Tuesday, August 23 We go to the widow Brewer's and to Oliver's, where we lodge. "The Scenes Beyond the Grave" were hotly discussed, I alone condemning the book. (Connor years later came into accord with me.)

Wednesday, August 24 We went to Rev. C.B. Masters', and to brother Nathan Smith's. We did design going to a place whose name I forget.

Thursday, August 25 We go via Umqua Academy, and Winchester, to a camp-meeting about ten miles up Deer Creek of Roseburg. We found the campers preparing.

Friday, August 26 Rev. N.W. Allen preached at 11. Rev. Connor at 3, Parker at night.

Saturday, August 27 I preached at 11, T.J. Connor at 3, Senaca Coston at night. One professed conversion.

Sunday, August 28 Rev. T.J. Connor preached at 11, 2 Cor. 5.11,"Knowing the terror of the Lord." I pr. at 3, Titus 2.14, "Redeem from all iniquity." A happy time, Rev. P.C. Parker pr. at night, on value of the soul, Mark 8.37.

Monday, August 29 Morning meeting. Rev. C.B. Masters pr. at 11, 1 Cor. 15.55,"O death where is thy sting." Rev. Connor pr. at 3, Rom. 12.1, "Present your bodies a living sacrifice." I pr at night, Hosea 11.8, "How shall I give thee up, Ephraim?" We have a good meeting. T.J. Connor falls (falling-exercise), James Parker is a seeker. (I fell that evening.)

Tuesday, August 30 Morning Meeting. Sister Riggs and her son join Church. Rev. T.J. Connor pr. Acts 20.32,

"I commend you to God." Rev. N.W. Allen pr. Acts 24.25. "Go thy way," at this time.

Wednesday, August 31 We were arranging shade on the Camp-ground. At three, Father Coston, Senaca's father, preached; not much preacher.

Thursday, September 1 We had a good morning meeting. There was no preaching at 11. P.C. Parker pr. at 3, Heb. 4.11,"Give diligence to enter rest." I pr. at night, Rom. 15.13, "Now the God of peace, fill you with joy & peace."

Friday, Septmeber 2 C.B. Masters pr. at 11, "What is man?" Ps. 8.4. Rev. Cliffton pr. at 3, John 5.40, "Ye will not come to me." T.J. Connor pr. at night.

Saturday, September 3 Connor pr. at 11, "Dwell with everlasting burnings." Isai 33.14. Allen pr. at 3, Job 8.13. "Hope of the hypocrite." I pr. at night, 2 Tim. 4.1, "Who shall judge the quick and dead." Two conversions James Parker is one, son of Rev. P.C.

Sunday, September 4 Connor pr. at 11; Job 4.14,"Fear came upon me," etc. P.C. Parker pr. at 3, Matt. 22.5, "They made light of it." I pr. at night, Exodus 32.6, "Sat down to eat & rose up to play." Mr. Riggs was converted, and a number joined.

Monday, September 5 We met to close the meeting. We had read John 15, chapter and the last part of Ephesians 6, Chapt. We went on to Rev. N.W. Allen's, where we lodged.

Tuesday, September 6 We went to Esta's Hotel and dined. We crossed the Calipooia Mountains and staid at Mr. Conrad's.

Wednesday, September 7 We went to Coons' for breakfast, and I staid there till 4 o'clock. I then went on to Rev. M.M. Crow's. Rhodes was there.

Thursday, September 8 I staid at Crow's till after dinner, and went on with Senaca Coston to camp-meeting where Jer. Kenoyer pr. John 3.3, "Except a man be born again." At Hurlburts.

Friday, September 9 I preached. 2 Cor. 13.5, "Prove your ownselves." L.M. Sallee pr. Rev. 22.17. Senaca Coston pr. at night, Isa. 5.4, "What more for my vineyard!"

Saturday, September 10 Jer. Kenoyer pr. Ps. 32.10, "Many sorrows, to the wicked." N.W. Allen pr. at 3, "What shall I do to inherit eternal life?" Luke 10.25. I pr. at night, Luke 23.4. "I find no fault in thisman." There are two mourners, and one conversion. We have a rejoicing time.

Sunday, September 11 Connor pr. at 11, "If any man willeth to do his will, he shall know of the teaching," John 7.17. I pr. at 12, "Elect according to forekno[w]lege of God." W.H. Daugherty pr. at 4, Luke 24.46, "Thus it behoved Christ to suffer," a very happy discourse. He swayed the floor of the stand up and down! Jer. Kenoyer pr. at night, Rom. 6.22, "But now being made free from sin." There were six mourners and two converts.

Monday, September 12 Senaca Coston pr. at 12, Deut. 4.29, "Seek Lord with all thy heart." I spoke at 3, on Baptism, and several were baptized in the Lake by Kenoyer and two were sprinkled. In the evening two praying bands came in shouting, and shut off preaching. Several seekers.

Tuesday, September 14 [wrong date in original] After our farewell lovefeast, there were 14 accessions. Farewell march. I go to Corvallis with Jer. Kenoyer, Sallee, Kile. Jer. Kenoyer pr. at M.E. Church. I lodge at Joshua Mason's.

Wednesday, September 14 I go with Senaca Coston to my home at Hiram Jackson's by Slate's Bridge. It was a mile south of Peterson's, South of Washington's Butte, sometimes called Peterson's Butte. Lodge.

Thursday, September 15 I dined at Peterson's, and went on through Lebanon to Samuel Fleenor's, where I lodge.

Friday, September 16 Senaca Coston pr. at 11, at Malcom Millar's Schoolhouse, John 13.17, "If ye know these things, happy are ye if ye do them." It was the first sermon. We lodge at Malcom Miller's. Somewhat rainy.

Saturday, September 17 I preach at 11, Twelfth Cahp.

Isa. I dine at D. Harrold's, whose wife was a cousin of Dr. Wm. Kendrick's, Indianapolis. T.J. Connor pr. at night, Rich man & Lazarus. We stay at Joseph Crank's.

Sunday, September 18 Rev. Wm. H. Daugherty pr. at 11, Ps. 144.15. "Happy people, God the Lord." T.J. Connor pr. at 4:00. S. Coston pr. at night. "They made light of it." Matt. 22.5. I lodge with Jackson Kile at Dodridge Harold's.

Monday, September 19 I preached Matt. 13.44, "Treasure hid in a field." We all wept, even an old unbeliever, Mr. Pruett. It was an uncommon discourse, I was forced to preach with lettle preparation. I preached an hour and 30 min. Daugherty pr. at night, and I exhort with much feeling.

Tuesday, September 20 Connor pr. at 11. I baptize Susan Connor (prob. Wm's wife) and Sarah Archer. Daugherty pr. at night Jer. 8.20, "Harvest past; summer ended." Osborn and Mary Williams converted.

Wednesday, September 21 The morning meeting was most extraordinary. There were less than thirty there. It lasted all day. Much of it led itself. Everything was calm and serene. We wanted no dinner. I never saw such a meeting! I pr. at night, Luke 15.21, "I have sinned against heaven, and in thy." The night meetings were full of seekers and converts.

Thursday, September 22 We had a good morning meeting. T.J. Connor preached at night. Several joined Church. William Connor one of them.

Friday, September 23 The usual morning meeting was held. They were all extraordinary. I dined at Pruett's. I pr. at night, Col. 2.14, "Causeth us to triumph." Lodge at D. Harold's.

Saturday, September 24 Have an excellent meeting. There were ten baptized by T.J. Connor, to-day. I lodge at Samuel Fleenor's, after attending a meeting in Scio, by Rev. John Powell, a Disciple Minister. He preached and I exhorted. *Remarks:* This was one of the best meetings I ever saw. Some of the converts had been my scholars at Sublimity. I visited them some thirty years later, and found them Christians still, and very useful. Mary J.

Williams upon her conversion arose at once to the talent and knowledge of an aged Christian, and did much good. She was then receiving the addresses of Henry Follis, a Baptist, to whom she was shortly after married. Nancy Fleenor upon her conversion, from a bashful girl, became a Christian heroine. She died, years since, in the faith.

Sunday, September 25 I heard Rev. John Powell pr. a funeral discourse. I dined at Samuel Fleenor's. I start for Condit's. I have conversation with T.J. Connor on the hillside. I saw Ennis at Condit's, and he was courting Mary Condit, the widow's daughter, and afterward married her. They were students of mine at Sublimity. He was ill-contrived and unreliable. She was a choice and lovely girl.

Monday, September 26 I breakfast at Silvanus Condit's and go on by Allen Foster's to Geo. W. Hunt's and to Salem. I could not ferry the Willamette, so I lodge at Samuel Penter's.

Tuesday, September 27 I went by way of Jonathan Crow's, and Nathan Newton's and Albany to Wm. H. Daugherty's. I got there at 11, at night.

Wednesday, September 28 I go to William Pearson's. He sells my horse and saddle, while I was there, to some California traders. This saved trouble, as he had sold the horse to me, and was to take him back, and he limped somewhat. I next went to Daugherty's and to Connor's by William Wyatt's.

Thursday, September 29 I went to Hiram Jackson's through Corvallis, and Deckards. I stay that night at Alfred Wheeldon's.

Friday, September 30 Tyler Jackson goes to Brownville to get my coat. I go on by way of Lebanon to Scio and Fleenor's. I preach, "How should I give thee up, Ephraim!" Hosea 11.8. Lodge at S. Fleenor's.

Saturday, October 1 I go to James Connor's, Dillon Hoskins' and Mr. Wizner's. I pr. at Ervine's Sch. house, Gal. 6.14. I lodge at James Williams.

Sunday, October 2 I went with several to Sublimity. I preached at the College building, Matt. 6.20, "Lay up—treasures in heaven." I dined at George W. Hunt's. I call at Jeremiah Kenoyer's. After night meeting, in which the students gave me a tender farewell, I stay at Mrs. Greenstreet's.

Monday, October 3 I go to Mrs. Childer's, in French Prairie. At George W. Hunt's, we begin to sing a farewell hymn—did not sing it through! I get to Childers' at 9:30, evening.

Tuesday, October 4 I went to William Case's. They are nearly all sick. I dine at Mrs. Childer's, and visit Goodell's, and Lichtenthaler's. Lodge at Mrs. Childers'. George W. Huntt sees me there.

Wednesday, October 5 I went with William Pearson's to Judge Matlock's below Oregon City. The Judge has a brother in Wabash town, Indiana. Edwin Cartwright's Father.

Thursday, October 6 We go on to Hanson's across the river from Portland. We dine and go over the river to Portland. I saw my trunk there. Allen and Lewis [blank]. We go back to Hanson's and lodge.

Friday, October 7 We come over to Portland again. Alex. Bennett came up in a skiff to meet me. I go down the river, rowing a little awkwardly to Rev. William Hendrickson's, Bennett's fatherinlaw's, on the north side of the Columbia. I stay there till 6 o'clock, when he, Bennett takes me to the Steamer Panama, at the mouth of the Willamette. We start at 8:30 Evening. He sends gold by me.

Saturday, October 8 We reach Astoria, at 9 oclock, cross the Columbia Bar at 12, next day. Some are sea-sick. I take a nap, a little soup, & I vomited. It was my first sea-sickness. Went to bed at 7, ocl.

Sunday, October 9 I arose at 7 o'clock, morn. We are in the Strait of Fuca. Breakfast, and I pace the deck. Now, we are in sight of Victoria. Now, at Port Townsend—6, in the evening. We reach Olympia at 5:30 in the morning. Mr. Miles my room mate goes ashore.

Monday, October 10 I went ashore at 10, and spent

$7.87. On our return, we passed Steilacoom, where Mr. E.M. Meekercame aboard, and paid $50.00 fare to San Francisko [sic], while we had paid but $20.00 from Portland. Mr. Meeker and I soon became acquainted.

Tuesday, October 11 The ship Panama, goes into Esquimalt Harbor, three miles from Victoria. There are some men of ships of war lying in the Harbor. I walked to Victoria saw it and returned. I see the Indians and their huts. I describe them in a letter to the *Telescope*. We leave Esquinalt at 1:30, afternoon, and sail down the coast.

Wednesday, October 12 We sail along the coast, and about sunset, enter the Columbia River (Rough Bar), anchor in Baker's Bay, and wait till morning.

Thursday, October 13 We cross the Bar about 11 o'cl., and sail down the Coast. We hoisted sail and had a race. I spent the evening in penciling.

Friday, October 14 We sailed along the Coast, with no remarkable occurrences. The sea is as dreary as the land, as we become used to it.

Saturday, October 15 To-day, we pass Point Rayes, in the afternoon. We pass the heads. We saw the rotary light-house. We arrive at the Golden Gate at dark or dusk, and are mistaken for the "Golden Age" on which General Winfield Scott was expected, and a salute was fired as we made our way to the landing, where a dense crowd had gathered to hail the "Hero of Lundy's Lane." With the assistance of the city police at the landing, we got through to Hillman's Temperance House, on Davis St. On the way, Mr. E.M. Meeker and I had formed a very favorable acquaintance, and he changed from "What Cheer?" to Hillman's, and we ro[o]med together.

Sunday, October 16 In this morning, the "Golden Age" arrived with the very General Scott (not us) and the salutes left were given to him. Governor Weller, and all his dignitaries were out, and fine men and fine equipage graced the occasion. The General was up to overlook the San Juan Boundary Dispute. Mr. Meeker and I went that evening to hear a discourse by Dr. Scott, on the Sabbath.

Monday, October 17 I ran about town with Mr. Meeker in the forenoon, visiting wholesale stores preparatory to his purchase of goods. I wrote letters in the afternoon—one to W.H. Daugherty and one to Jer. Kenoyer. Mr. Meeker had told me that if he was not at the hotel till a certain hour in the evening I should not expect him, as a merchant had invited him to lodge with him. I waited past the hour considerably, and retired. Mr. Meeker came back, and both he and our landlord did their very best to awaken me. Said the landlord: "If this house were afire, he would burn up!" So he found another room for Mr. Meeker!

Tuesday, October 18 I spent sometime running around the city. It was then small compared with what I found in 1888. Our hotel was over the shallow water of the harbor! Plank streets with water under were quite common.

Wednesday, October 19 There was a recent opposition line of Steamers to the Isthmus, and the contention was so sharp as to publicly proclaim the "Sonora," of the regular line, "the coffin of the Pacific!" I made a careful comparison of the two steamers and preferred to drown on the Sonora rather than suffocate on the competition. I paid $54.50, to New York on the Sonora line. To-night, I went to Music Hall, with Mr. Meeker, to a lecture on the Arabs by Bayard Taylor. It was interesting, delivered with almost faultless elocution. I cannot here attempt a sum[m]ary of its parts. But he said if the Arab knew the truth of anything inquired about, he would tell it without great exaggeration; if he did not know the truth of the matter, he would give an answer any way. One with them would exaggerate fearfully. It became a habit. He said since he quit them, the habit had entirely left him!

Thursday, October 20 I bade Mr. E.M. Meeker good by. We were near one age. He was a married man, and I was going to my bride. I learned, years afterward, that the ship on which he returned to his dear family, was lost at sea. I was very much attached to him. But to-day, I went aboard the "Sonora," "the floating coffin," which bore us safely to Panama, and my choice, I approve. We started about 10:00, in the forenoon. We saw two whales sporting about two miles distant, and throwing out of the water, about one third of their bodies—fir[s]t the head and then the tail. They appeared to be from fifty to seventy feet in length. Probably seventy feet.

Friday, October 21 We sailed on with little to break the monotony. I wrote some verses on card-playing. Our reckonings said we had sailed 280 miles at noon. We had aboard a sick man by the name of Travis. He was going home to Kentucky to die. He had consumption.

Saturday, October 22 I wrote out a subscription for Travis and put my name down for $2.00. We soon had enough to hire him cared for. But about 9:00, a girl announced to her mistress in our cabin that "the boat has stopped!" I had just lain down to sleep. I arose and went to the quarter deck, where the crew were lowering a life-boat. A man had jumped overboard. The boat went out to sea, fired a sky rocket, but got no response, came back, and we sailed on. The man was a stow-away, found after we left San Francisco, being set to work heaving coal topay his passace [sic], he came on deck, talked gibberish nonsense and leaped over the bulwarks into the sea just before the left paddlebox. It was his last on earth. He was evidently insane.

Sunday, October 23 Things are as usual aboard, except no card playing. I was sitting near Mr. Dodge, an Indian Agent, and Mr. Lansing Stout a representative to Congress from Oregon, when Mr. Stout said: "We have plenty of whiskey to last this side." Mr. Dodge said he did not like whiskey, but said he had "some very good wine." Joseph H. Lane the United States Senator from Oregon was aboard, and Judge Deady, and Mr. McHibben, the second of Senator Braderick of California, in his fatal duel. The first I saw of General Lane was a man inquiring for Lansing Stout, to assist him in playing a game of cards. Besides these and others, of political notoreity, we had Bayard Taylor and his wife, among our best, and least ostentatious, passengers.

Monday, October 24 To-day, at 3:00, we passed Cape St. Lucas. We saw the fish jumping in the waters. I slept in the dining saloon, finding the air too close and hot in the cabin.

Tuesday, October 25 We saw Cape Corrientes to-day. I slept on the hurricane deck to-night.

Wednesday, October 26 We sailed on, very near land, in the morning. I slept in the dining saloon, at night. It is due that I shoud say that our passengers were very different from those of two years before going out to San Francisco. There were hardly any that did not at once show that they made no pretense to being religious. Swearing was common, and other behavior corresponding there too. I wore no clerical garb and made no pious pretensions, but was regularly marked as a minister. When I asked why, they replied, that I took no part in things irreligious. They were largely miners going home from the gold field.

Thursday, October 27 We sailed on, the whole way nearer shore than we went out in July, 1857. We reached Acapulco at 1:00 next morning, and left that place a little after 4 o'clock. There was a pleasant sea breeze in the evening, and I stayed on deck till late at night. At Acapulco the Mexicans were selling us "sugars" and nice bunches of coral, some of which I purchased.

Friday, October 28 The Gulph [sic] of Tehuantipec was rolling, and I became somewhat sea-sick. I went below, and slept till dinner. The sea was smoother in the afternoon. There was no land in sight. I slept in the dining saloon.

Sunday, October 30 Times were as usual. This voyage, we had no religious services on Sundays.

Monday, October 31 There was nothing unusual. I spoke to Senator Joseph H. Lane for the first time.

Tuesday, November 1 We reached Panama in the afternoon. While waiting aboard the "Panama," a gentleman from the east came in, and reported Ossawatomie (John) Brown's capture of Harper's Ferry, and his subsequent arrest by the Virginia authorities. General Joseph H. Lane said in a loud voice, "I would have hung him higher than Haman, without judge or jury!" He said he did not believe in unjudicial proceedings, but special cases required special treatment. It is to be remembered that Senator Lane was a zealous aspirant to the Democratic nomination for president of the United States. He was nominated for the vice-presidency, and ran on the ticket with John C. Breckenridge the next year, and received many electoral votes. His words on this occasion were measured in manner, and intended to be quoted, and no doubt were quoted, in the campaign which followed.

But "the soul of John Brown went marching on!" We after dark were carried, by rail across the Isthmus to Aspinwall, in the rain. We supped at Brook's Hotel. Our sick man Travis was deserted by a doctor hired to attend him, and had to hire himself carried by a man, a mile.

Wednesday, November 2 We left Aspinwall at 4 o'clock in the morning on the ship Atlantic and nothing of special interest occurred that day. We are all aboard.

Thursday, November 3 We have some head winds. The sea is monotonous.

Friday, November 4 We still have strong breezes, part of the day. In the evening, we pass near Cuba. We saw two sail vessels. I slept in my berth.

Monday, November 7 The sea is rough to-day. The waves rolled very high and the ship rolled fearfully.

Tuesday, November 8 The sea was fearfully rough and stormy. We "shipped sea" several times. Many were alarmed. The officers of the vessel looked anxious. On the way from Aspinwall an invalid died, but we took his body on to New York. He was profane, but of refined manners. He came aboard at Acapulco.

Wednesday, November 9 We get into the "purple sea" to-day, and it is more pleasant. We reach Sandy Hook, about 7, in the evening, and New York Harbor at 2:00 morning.

Thursday, November 10 We get ashore at New York at 4 o'clock in the morning. I put up at Lovejoy's Hotel through the rascality of the hack-driver, who said our hotel of 1857 was discontinued! I left by rail, by way of Albany. We are lodged at Syracuse, on account of a burned bridge.

Friday, November 11 Leave Syracuse, and reach Buffalo about 2:30, afternoon. I dined at the "International." I see there new gas lamps. I close a tedious waiting, at 9:00, afternoon, and reach Cleveland at night.

Saturday, November 12 I leave Cleveland at 4 o'clock, morning, and reach Dayton at 11 o'clock. I went to the

Telescope office. I lodged at Adam Shuey's, Wm. J's father's.

Sunday, November 13 I heard William J. Shuey pr. at 11 o'clock, and I dine at his house. I went to class-meeting in the afternoon, and go to Solomon Vonneida's. I preach at night, Matt. 13.44.

Monday, November 14 I went to Dublin on forenoon train. I dine at William Barton Witt's. I get his horse and sulky, and go home, arriving in the evening. I call at William's, and then at my Father's, where I lodge. We are all rejoiced. My mother almost overcome with joy. I had been away 2 yrs. 4 mo, & 19 d.

Tuesday, November 15 I visit Harvey's in the morning. I go in the afternoon to John G. Koerner's to see Susan. It is rainy and is night before I get there. Daniel's are at supper, and Silas Koerner and wife at the table with them. I sat down by the fire. At last Elmira came and said she believed "It is brother Wright." Daniel went to tell it at the other house. Rev. Franklin Morgan was there, and came back with Daniel and expressed great joy at meeting me. I go to the other house and greet the people; I talk with Susan till a late hour.

Wednesday, November 16 I remained at Father Keorner's [sic] all day.

Thursday, November 17 I went home by way of John Malone's. I went to Harvey Wright's, and lodged. My borrowed horse is sick.

Friday, November 18 I went to Dublin and took the horse home. It rained and it was dark, and it was as late as 8:00, when I got there. Bennett Witt and his wife were very kind. I lodged with them.

Saturday, November 19 I remained in Dublin. I saw Rev. J.K. Billheimer, the first time. I dine at Rev. John Fohl's. I sup at Wayne Smith's. I lodge at Wayne Smith's.

Sunday, November 20 I preached at 11, o'clock, Ps. 84.11. I dine at Wilson Scroggy's. I visit the Sunday School. They organized. I sup at Isaac Pearson's. I pr. at night, Rev. 22.11. Isaac was a brother of William Pearson.

Susan Koerner Wright,
married to Bishop Milton Wright
on November 24, 1859

Monday, November 21 I went home by Connersville. I bought a suit of Wm. H. Beck, a primitive Baptist. I rode in the rain.

Tuesday, November 22 I went to Liberty. I called at old Mr. Pierson's. I got my license, to be married. I went to Susan's father's. Saw and talked with Susan.

Wednesday, November 23 I went home by West Union, and visit Harvey Wright.

Thursday, November 24 Thanksgiving. Harvey Wright and Delila, and my brother William go with me to my wedding, which was at Daniel Koerner's, a little after 3,

o'clock. Rev. John Fohl officiated. Father Koerner pronounced a solemn blessing on us, after the marriage. Harvey, Delila, and William stay. D.K. Zeller and Caroline, and Silas Koerner and Hannah were there.

Friday, November 25 Harvey and Delila and William and Susan and myself went to my father's home, to the infair. On the way I gave Susan a gold pencil, and told her we should not go to Oregon very soon, possibly not at all. William Wright now lives at a house a half mile north-east of my Father's, but always rented the farm. William's stay with us the infair night.

Saturday, November 26 We remained together at my

Father's all day, except a I [sic] made a brief trip to Fayetteville, now Orange.

Sunday, November 27 We went to Andersonville, where Father John Morgan pr. at 11, Job 22.21, "Acquaint now thyself." We dine at Rev. Silas Andrews', joke about children. Wm. Wright pr. at 3, "How shall we escape," Hebr. 2.3. I pr. at night, Matt. 13.44, "Treas. hid." We lodge at Father Peter Miller's, at Corners.

Monday, November 28 We went to lovefeast, where John Morgan spoke so well. We dine at Elihu S. Neff's. We go to my Father's.

Tuesday, November 29 We go to Father John Gottleib Koerner's, by Columbia and West Union. We visit Daniel Koerner's and I chat with him about Oregon. We lodge a Pap Koerners.

Wednesday, November 30 I go to Liberty and William Bennett's and to George W. Hunt's. I sup at Mr. Smith's and stay at G.W. Hunt's. He has weak knees. We talk to land trade, B. Rusk's death.

Thursday, December 1 I went through rain to Samuel Goodwin's. We have quite a long talk. I dine there, and go through Liberty to Father Koerner's. I left at Liberty the Power of Attorney to be recorded, $2.50, in Bennett's hands. Mr. Bennett raised Mrs. Wm. Pearson.

Friday, December 2 We staid at Father Koerner's. He is a very interesting, full of wit and humor. I mend my harness.

Saturday, December 3 We go by Fairfield, Blooming Grove and Metamora, through Andersonville, to Archible Miller's. We lodge there. It was a cold snowy day. Stove-fires were comfortable. "Aunt Betty," an old colored lady, formerly at his Uncle Joe's, sung some songs.

Sunday, December 4 I preach at Andersonville, at 11, Ps. 84.11. We dine at Robert Ayers. Their children: Flora and Ira. We had a good time. Her Sisterinlaw, once Watkins, now Ritchey. We go home to my Father's, Dan Wright's, on Sand Creek, seven miles from Laurel, three from Orange. We see H. Muth, pastor.

Monday, December 5 We are at home to dinner. We went to William Wright's and lodged. They tell of Rev. William Nichols' having claimed to see Susan's letters from me, which Susan says is not true. Lively imagination.

Tuesday, December 6 There was a Ministerial Association at Indianapolis which I did not attend. He went to Father's in the afternoon.

Wednesday, December 7 I go to Orange (then Fayetteville) to visit Robert Gamble in the Academy. I dine at Rev. Dr. Heron's. I came home with the papers and a letter from Mr. Lefever, not the doctor, the man aboard our ships who cared for Mr. Travis, and at[t]ended him to Kentucky, where he left him. I never heard from Lefever or Travis afterward.

Thursday, December 8 We remain at my Father's. I chop wood afternoon. I write at night. It was a good day.

Friday, December 9 I went to Fayetteville, and received a letter from G.W. Hunt.

Saturday, December 10 We went to Quarterly meeting. We dined at John Allen's. David O'Farrell pr. at 11, I pr. at night, 1 Tim. 2.6, "He gave himself a ransom for." We stay at Archie Miller's.

Sunday, December 11 Rev. O'Farrell pr. "Sow in tears," Ps. 126.5. I introduce sacramental service, with much feeling. We dine at Dr. O. Martin's. I preach at night, Jude 14, "Enoch the seventh." We lodge at Dr. Martin's. Mrs. Martin was a sister of Dr. Henry Qillen. She was ever my friend.

Monday, December 12 I went to New Salem to see about getting a school, and return to Dr. Martin's. We went to Lewis's on a call. We call at Samuel Holmes, before meeting. O'Farrell pr. at night, "Ephraim is a cake" Hosea 7.8. We stay at A. Miller's.

Tuesday, December 13 We went by Kinion Freeman's, Luther Donald's, to Charles Harris's. We lodge there. Sarah is my sister. Little Charley's happy laugh—is seven years old. Much attached to me.

Wednesday, December 14 I got my horse shod, and went on to Hartsville. We stop at Lyman Chittenden's father's house. We see Prof. David Shuck. Prayer meeting at the old college Chapel. Jane Ready's cry. We call at Daniel Shuck's. We staid at Pa. Chittenden's.

Thursday, December 15 We breakfasted at Prof. Shuck's. Attended the opening of school. Girls read seventh chap. 1 Cor! We called at Father Canady's, and at Rev. Flora's, and Daniel Shuck's. Call at Rev. John Riley's, Father Joseph *Ball's, Lewis Mobley's, E. Pitman's, and sup at Rev. L.S. Chittenden's. I pr. at night, 1 John 3.2.

Friday, December 16 We go to John Braden's, my uncle's, who were from home; to W.S. Collier's, who married cousin Margaret, where we saw Aunt Eliza, and went to Quailtoron, Newburg and Greensburg to Charles Harris's, my brotherinlaw's. I went to Smyrnia and pr. Luke 19.27. I lodged at Charles Atkinson's.

Saturday, December 17 We went to Jacob Coom's. *Joseph Ball batpized me in Sands Creek June 1847. We lost our way, saw Concord Church, I preach at Stubb's School-house, Rom. 6.14. Lodge at Coom's.

Sunday, December 18 I pr. at Isaac Umphrey's at 11, on Sanctification, 1 Thes. 4.3. We dine at Umphrey's. Hulda Morgan's greeting. She picked Susan for me—but I had picked her before. We went on to Neff's Corners' and put up at Peter Miller's. Henry Muth pr. "Awake thou that sleepest." Eph. 5.14. We lodge at John Cook's.

Monday, December 19 We went to my father's, Dan Wrights, and I went to Salem, to solicit subscribers for a school. I lodged at Thomas Mitchell's.

Tuesday, December 20 I raise subscription. I go by Samuel Frazee's and Fayetteville and Harvey Wright's, to my father's. I got a letter from D.K. Zeller.

Wednesday, December 21 I write letters to T.J. Connor and James, and a foolish one to "Oscar H. Hendrick and Co," in reply to one from him. I sawed out sleigh run[n]ers.

Thursday, December 22 I worked at making a sleigh.

Saturday, December 24 William helped me finish the sleigh. Susan and I go by Neff's Corners, to Andersonville, where we hear Henry Muth preach. I preach at Neff's Corners at 3, Rom. 6.14.

Tuesday, December 27 We went to Connersville and bought furniture, and went on to Father Koerner's, seven miles south of Liberty. We found Betsy Fry and David Fry, Susan's cousins, there.

Wednesday, December 28 We load up furniture, etc., take Daniel's wagon and team, and I reach my Father's late. It was so icy that the team could hardly climb the hills.

Thursday, December 29 I hauled the load to New Salem, and put it in my rented house and returned to my Father's.

Friday, December 30 William and I, went to Connersville and hauled two loads of household stuff, bought before, to Harvey Wright's.

Saturday, December 31 We went to New Salem with the goods, unloaded in my house, and I went home with Daniels team, arriving at ten at night.

Sunday, January 1 Susan and I go [to] Bloomings grove and dine at a hotel, had a "goose 40 years old." Lodged at Father's. It is awfully cold. We warmed several times.

Monday, January 2 Susan and I went early to our home at New Salem, Rush Co., Ind., and I began school, at 8:30. It had three rooms, and it was a very happy home.

Note January 25, 1911 We lived in New Salem till sometime in April, 1860, when we removed to Andersonville. At New Salem, Rush Carly and his sister, and the Mitchell girls, all grown, were insubordinate; others were pleasant. In April, we removed to Andersonville, Franklin County, where I taught school, beginning before May, perhaps, at Neff's Corners, where I had taught none months in 1854 and 1855. This was also a very happy home. In August, we took trip to Grant County, where my farm lay, and where we had relatives, and were there about three weeks, and bought 55 acres of land, at 15 dollars and went thence to annual conference at Sugar Grove, Wayne County, where I had joined in 1853. I went first to a quarterly meeting at Washington (now Greensfork) where I preached for David O'Farrell, the Pres. elder. We also visited Benjamin Harris, whose sone James was at Hartsville and his sister Mattie. My wife imbibed malaria, in Grant County and was ailing at conference. After conference, sometime in September, I removed from Andersonville, to my farm in Grant County, five miles east of Fairmount, I having been appointed the pastor of Marion Circuit. Young John Freeman, a second cousin, hauled a load for me, and the night before we reached our new home, he staid at Robert Clark's, brother to his future fatherinlaw, Richard Clark of near Clarksburg. The rest of the movers staid on the state road, at Joseph Cown's, this side of Killbuck. That year I had about eight appointments on Marion Circuit, Rev. D. O'ferrill being my presiding elder, and a good friend. I farmed a little. Father Koerner and Mother Koerner visited us in May. Reuchlin was born March 17, 1861, in our hewed log home. (In my Diary of 1857, the rest is recorded.)

1869

[This year appears in the same book as the year 1859.]

Sunday, January 3 I made only general notes of January. I had gone to Fayette County, and to Andersonville where my Sister Sarah Harris had died, December 23, 1868. When I returned I found my protracted meeting at Hartsville greatly run down, and had to do my best for its resuscitation. I generally preached each evening, but sometimes some other minister preached. I was intent on a revival, which most of the preachers and people thought we could not have. But we had day meetings attended by a few, and the revival broke out there, especially in Mrs. Noah Elrod's wife's heart. I preached the third of January, morning and evening from texts not recorded.

Monday, January 4 We had morning and evening meetings, and in one of the day meetings, this week, the revival was manifest.

Thursday, January 7 We had morning meeting. W.J. Pruner preached in the evening, and I exhorted with great effect, and Mr. Key joined the church.

Friday, January 8 Many wanted me to close the meeting over Saturday and Sunday and attend the M.E. Quarterly meeting. Mrs. Scudder expecial[l]y insisted on it. But I persisted, that we were on the eve of a revival. If I had yielded, we should have lost all our labor.

Saturday, January 9 I attended the quarterly meeting of the M.E. Church, and heard the presiding elder, Williamson Terrell, preach from Jude. He was a great preacher in 1847, now quite old. At one annual confer-

ence he preached in the afternoon, and soared far beyond Bishop Hamline's sermon in the forenoon. He and the pastor, Rev. Mahin, dined with us, to-day.

Sunday, January 10 I heard Terrell preach at 10.30. There was nothing specially uplifting in the meeting. I preached at the College Chapel, at night, and had a very happy meeting.

Monday, January 11 I attended the M.E. love-feast. In the evening I preached at the College Chapel, and a revival broke out. A revival also broke out at the M.E. Church, and it continued at both places.

Tuesday, January 12 Our meeting continued, and three came out for prayers, in the evening.

Wednesday, January 13 We had a rich social meeting at 3:00, so many spoke, and so soon. In the evening, Sisters Graves and Ham join Church.

Thursday, January 14 We had a good speaking meeting at 1:25. Preaching in the evening and four join the Church.

Friday, January 15 In the day social meeting, one joined the Church. Rev. W.J. Pruner preached at 6:00. There were several seekers, and five join church

Saturday, January 16 Meeting at 1:15. In the evening, four join church.

Sunday, January 17 I preached at 10.30, Rev. 3.21. Morning meeting before preaching. Elizabeth Bumpas joined church. Rev. W.J. Pruner preached in the evening, at 6:00.

Monday, January 18 During last week, and this week, many came to the altar for prayers, and were converted. Preaching in the evening. Three joined church.

Tuesday, January 19 There was generally a day meeting; and preaching in the evening. I preach, 1 Cor. 15, and perhaps 58 verses, and ten joined Church.

Friday, January 22 I made no record of to-day. Previous to this, for five years, there had been no real revival in the church at Hartsville.

Saturday, January 23 There is no record for to-day. President J.W. Scribner, for the first time, since here, encouraged a revival all he could, during this meeting.

Sunday, January 24 I preached at 10.30, "Behold he prayeth." Acts 9.11. Rev. W.J. Pruner preached, in the evening.

Monday, January 25 Ten Joined the church this evening. (Rev. John Riley told me in 1902, that this was one of the most lasing revivals ever held in Hartsville.)

Tuesday, January 26 Within the past fifteen days, about fifty joined the church, and there was a larger number converted. Two joined the church to-day. A large number had profes[s]ed at the M.E. Church. Malin proved unchaste.

Wednesday, January 27 This evening, W.J. Pruner preached. Several gave their hands for prayers. The meeting was adjourned till Saturday at 10:30, when Quarterly meeting is to begin.

Thursday, January 28 We had official meeting in the evening.

Friday, January 29 The Theological Society discussed the question of Total Depravity. Rev. A.E. Evans stays at our house.

Saturday, January 30 Rev. Evans pr. at 10:30, Heb. 10.23–4. Quar. Conf. at 1:30. Wm. Fix pr. at 6:15.

Sunday, January 31 Rev. A.E. Evans preached at 10:30 Isai. 26.3,4. There were two classes at 9 o'clock. There was a very large communion at 12.00. Rev. J. W. Scribner pr. at 6:30, "Watch ye." 1 Cor. 16.13.

Monday, February 1 Good Love-feast meeting. Wagoner joined in the evening.

Wednesday, February 3 I was called to J.B. Hamilton's, as he nearly sank away. He reproved his wife for fretting about him. We had prayer-meeting and speaking meeting at 1:15, and prayer-meeting at 6:15.

Thursday, February 4 Bro. Evans leaves for Collin's via Flat Rock. He was one of the very best of my fellow-workers. I pr. at 6:15, John 21.22, good audience.

Friday, February 5 Prof. Hamilton died at 4.00 A.M. Theological Society. Addresses by eight.

Saturday, February 6 I preached N.B. Hamilton's funeral at 10:00, "Therefore there remaineth for" Hebr. 4.9. He was a very patient, good soul, a suitable companion for his wife, the fiery, gifted "Bine" Canady. I preach at 6.15, "Not another name," Acts 4:12.

Sunday, February 7 I preached at 10:30, 1 Pet. 3.21, on baptism, and baptized Woodworth, Winings, J.T. Heady, Fred. Hiner, S. Spears, Carrie Murphy, Minerva Koerner, Elvira Shellhorn. Bishop D. Shuck, preached at 6:30, "Anathema Maranatha," 1 Cor. 16.22. S. Barnet's wife came out to be prayed for.

Monday, February 8 Speaking meeting at 1.15. Rev. Hardy Wray preached at 6:30, "Choose ye this day," Josh 24.15. We adjourned the meeting, Barnet's wife still seeking.

Tuesday, February 9 I chop wood in forenoon, in a wood out east. I dine and sup at Granville Edward's. I receive letters from Rev. Monroe Gronendyke and from Rev. G. Hut Byrd. I am at home this evening for the first time in a long while.

Wednesday, February 10 We had a very good prayer and class meeting.

Friday, February 12 We visited Henry Mobley's. The Theological Society discusses the progress (retrograde) of Christianity.

Saturday, February 13 Mr. Jones, an old man, a "Texas refugee," asked leave to stay over Sunday. He remained partly with us. We visit Barnett's and Stoneypher's in the afternoon.

Sunday, February 14 I preach at 10:30, "Perfect love casteth out fear," 1 John 4:18. I preached at 6:30, "Search the Scriptures," John 5.39.

Monday, February 15 Granville Edwards and his family dine with us. They start to move to Shelby County.

Tuesday, February 16 We had a very brief Official meeting. It was followed by a donation party of about 150, who brought $40.00 of provisions, $7.30 cash, students $16.00, Wood $2.75, and a coat 25.00—total $100.00. They left wife out. Lottie and [rest is unreadable]

Wednesday, February 17 Father Apple hauled the wood. The prayer meeting was not very lively.

Thursday, February 18 I spent to-day mostly in reading and writing.

Friday, February 19 Harriet Shuck and Jane Pruner visited us. In the evening, the Theological Society debated on the rights of women.

Saturday, February 20 I spent the day in studying a text.

Sunday, February 21 I preached at 10:30, on "Grow in grace," 2 Pet. 3.18. John Huffer, one of the best of men, dines with us. In the Teachers' Class, we considered "the city." I preached in the evening, 1 John 5.3, "Commandment not grievous."

Tuesday, February 23 Rev. Aaron Davis comes and solicits me to go to Flat Rock, where Rev. Wiliam Fix "is in a revival." Rev. hardy Wray comes to our house and stays an hour or two. Some discussion.

Wednesday, February 24 Charles *Gantzkow* & Davis call for *Cynosure* subscribers. I start to Flat Rock, but find

Fix at home. I return home. The prayer-meeting is rather dull.

Thursday, February 25 I study nearly all the forenoon, in Scriptural study. I send W. Mobley's subscription toCynosure, and inquire about Wray's. I receive the Cir. *Gazette* and read till bedtime.

Friday, February 26 There are public addresses at the Theological Society, on Secret Societies: Fix, Mobley, Scribner, Wray and Thornton. I have a written address, afterward published in the Cynosure.

Sunday, February 28 I preached at 10:30, "Crown of glory & diadem of beauty." Isa. 28.5. William Smith dines with us. I preached in the evening on Ministration of the Spirit, 2 Cor. 3.7–8.

Monday, March 1 I take Minerva Koerner to the cars, at Greensburg. I saw John Cones, an old neighbor in Rush County. I als[o] saw Judge Wm. Moore, a pupil at Andersonville in 1852. I return home after dark. Mr. Brown is sick at the Pavia House, half way there.

Tuesday, March 2 Hardy Wrays visit us. I attended prayer-meeting at C.F. Gantzkow's room.

Wednesday, March 3 I had my last recitation of the Theological Class, for the term. We have a class & prayer meeting, and every professor of religion spoke.

Thursday, March 4 School examination. Concert at 6:30 afternoon. Some dissatisfaction. I did not attend.

Friday, March 5 The examination closed. Mr. Brown, Noah Elwood's soninlaw died. Pres. Scribner called to see me in the afternoon. The Theological Society discussed the Scriptural right of self-defense.

Saturday, March 6 An Irish pedlar comes along, and Susan buys two table cloths and two linen kerchiefs, for $5.00.

Sunday, March 7 Rev. Hardy Wray pr. at 10:30, the funeral discourse of Mr. Brown, "Prepare to meet thy God." Amos 4.12.

Monday, March 8 The board of trustees of College meets, and spends the day in business. I am on the committee that met at Canady's at night.

Tuesday, March 9 The Board is in session. It employs J.W. Scribner at $1000.00, Stonecypher at $600.00, Lewis Mobley at $500.00, and Miss Scribner at $400.00.

Wednesday, March 10 Rev. Jacob Scammahorn and wife visit us, and N. Miller's visit. The Board meets at 1 o'clock Prayer-meeting in the evening. Session of the Board. Rev. Jacob Scammahorn was one of the best of men.

Thursday, March 11 I write a letter to Rev. J. Dickson. I also wrote to Rev. John Morgan. I chopped wood in the forenoon, and halled [sic] it afternoon.

Friday, March 12 Chopped and hauled wood. The Thel. Society debate on Lay Representation. And we elect officers.

Saturday, March 13 I spend most of the day at home. They ask me for a Certificate of N.B. Hamilton's death, for the Life Insurance Company.

Sunday, March 14 I preached at College Chapel, at 10:30, 1 Cor. 3.15, "If any man's work he shall suffer less, yet." I preached at 7:00, Isai 55.9. "As the heavens are higher."

Wednesday, March 17 We had a good society meeting this evening.

Thursday, March 18 I taught two of Prof. Mobley's calsses in Natural Science.

Friday, March 19 Rev. W.C. Day comes to our house to board. In the Theological Class, I call Prof. Scribner to order for hypercriticism, and he gets "a tilt" over it.

Saturday, March 20 I see Leora Woodworth die. Mr. Metsker's child died last night. G.C. Mench came. Also Melisse Wilson & Minerva Koerner call.

Sunday, March 21 I preach Leora Woodworth's funeral, 2 Kings 4.26. Bishop Daniel Shuck preached at 7:10, fr.

an unrecorded text. He generally preached unconnomly well.

Wednesday, March 24 Barnett went to Greensburg, was hindered the day before. Bishop Shuck led a pretty good prayer-meeting.

Thursday, March 25 Lawrence goes to Greensburg for Barnett who chilled the day before.

Friday, March 26 I went to Greensburg, and sent postal-orders to pay my tax. I also sent to Dayton $16.00. I got Cushing's Manual, 5 copies. I sent in my resignation of the presidency of Theo. Soci.

Saturday, March 27 We had an ax-grinding. I have class on rules of order. I take M. Hacker his book, Cushing's.

Sunday, March 28 I preached a missionary discourse, Matt. 24.14, and raise over seventy-five dollars in subscription. I preached in the evening, Prov. 15.32, "He that refuseth instruction, despiseth his own soul."

Wednesday, March 31 We have an extremely good season of grace in the forenoon. We have a dull class in the evening meeting.

Friday, April 2 Philander Cranor came in the evening. He was born blind. Scribner came to solicit my attendance at Theol. Socieety. My request of leave of absence, rejected.

Saturday, April 3 I handed out 5 copies of Cushing's Manual.

Sunday, April 4 Rev. W.J. Pruner preached, "Thou God seest me," Gen. 16.13. I read Descipline. Interesting teacher's class (Sab. Sch.) on Matt. 2.1–15. I preached at night, Ps. 93.5. "Holiness becometh thine house forever."

Monday, April 5 This is a busy day of study. Philo Cranor went to his new boarding place at Key's, at noon. The class of Rules of order met at 5:00. I taught the class.

Tuesday, April 6 I visited Woodworth's. I heard of John B. Ervin's organization of an independent church at Mr.

Pleasant school-house! Is good faith a delusion?

Wednesday, April 7 We had a happy season of grace again! G.C. Mench brought me some potatoes. I heard some compositions. I went to Henry Mobley's. I visited and prayed with Mother Mobley. In the evening, we had prayer and class-meeting. Rather dull.

Thursday, April 8 We planted onions and peas.

Friday, April 9 Francis Day came, after the Theological Society meeting.

Saturday, April 10 Prof. Benj. Nyce came. He had formerly taught in the College, and Susan, my wife had recited to him. He was a fine preacher.

Sunday, April 11 Prof. Nyce preached at 10:30, "Ye are the salt of the earth," etc. I heard him on the same in 1844, at Sains Creek Church, Matt. 5.13. He preached at 7:00 on "Mary hath chosen that good part," Matt. 10.47. He lodged with us.

Monday, April 12 F.M. Day engaged boarding with us. Prof. Nyce pr. at 7:15, the rich man and Lazarus. He did good preaching.

Tuesday, April 13 Prof. Nyce went away. I hauled wood afternoon. I preached at 8:00, at Mt. Pleasant, Hebr. 12.27–8.

Wednesday, April 14 The class and prayer meeting was a little slow & dry.

Thursday, April 15 The Official meeting was short.

Friday, April 16 Rev. A.E. Evans called in the evening; also Mr. Atkinson.

Saturday, April 17 Rev. A.E. Evans preached from Heb. There were few out, only four young people. Quar. Conference at 2:00. About $90.00 were reported for me. The students visit the Falls. Rev. Aaron Davis pr. at 8:00, John 10.9. "In and out—pasture." John x.9

Sunday, April 18 Rev. A.E. Evans preached at 10:30. Bishop D. Shuck introdu. sacrament. Shuck pr. at night,

fine sermon on Ps. 145.11. "They shall talk."

Monday, April 19 We had good speaking meeting at 1:30. Bishop Shuck baptizes four by immersion. The bell was not rung at night.

Tuesday, April 20 It was a rainy day. So Rev. Evans could not go home.

Wednesday, April 21 I went to mill. The evening meeting, I lead and spoke to nearly all.

Thursday, April 22 I got grahamite flour.

Saturday, April 24 We were white-washing and we put down new carpet.

Sunday, April 25 I preached at 10:30, Ps. 137.5,6. "If I forget thee, O Jerusalem." I pr. at 7:30, Deut. 32.31. "Their Rock not as our rock."

Monday, April 26 I am troubled with dental neuralgia, and Dr. Wray extra. two of my teeth in afternoon. Prof. Scribner was absent from recitations. Dr. Everett showed himself "Lecturer on Education."

Tuesday, April 27 I went afternoon to Mother Isgrig's a mile and a half south of town, to see her son Washington. I talked to him and prayed with him. I heard Dr. Everett lecture. Impudence and tom-foolery!

Wednesday, April 28 I arose unwell, after a restless night from a sore face. I felt better after breakfast. I went in afternoon, to hear the compositions and declaimations. There was prayer-meeting at 7:00.

Thursday, April 29 We notified Dr. Everet that we considered it "cool." He lectured in the evening.

Friday, April 30 Charles Gantzko was up before breakfast to see about renting the Hall for Dr. Everet. I read an address on Providence before Theo. Soci.

Saturday, May 1 I wrote to *Cynosure*, to Charles Paddack, and to Wagner. Sent a Com. to Hart. To-night, K. Everet had a pay lecture in the College Hall.

Sunday, May 2 I preached at 10:30, Acts 17.18. John Huffer dines with us. Dr. Everet "knocks the socks off of Infidelity," and insults me. Rev. John Riley preached in the evening, and I retorted on Everet. "A stranger, he took us in."

Monday, May 3 There is some excitement over Dr. Everet, and he moves to the M.E. Church. A spoonful of Phrenology would sweeten a hogshead of error! Tuesday, May 4 I called at Emanuel Pitman's and Jac. Scammahay's. Unable to be at lecture at night.

Wednesday, May 5 I attended class-meeting in the evening. Some of the members were at the "Dr's" Phrenology lecture, which is "concentrated sweetness."

Thursday, May 6 I heard that "Dr." Everett took the Hall by the advice of Wm. Fix, which Fix positively denied.

Friday, May 7 The Theological Society discussed the question, "Sin lies in the Motive."

Sunday, May 9 I preached at 10:30. I visited and baptized Washington Isgrig in the afternoon. I supped at Louis Mobley's. Bishop Daniel Shuck preached in the evening. He preached, generally, uncommonly well.

Monday, May 10 President Scribner decides that there shall be no exhibition, and proclaims it. The students hold a meeting, and Herbaugh and Venner are seditious. I hear "Dr." Everet lecture on "Immortal."

Tuesday, May 11 There is much excitement over the exhibition. Am imperative paper is circulated. I preached Washington Isgrig's funeral. In the evening there is held a hot meting of one of the literary Societies. When the crowd started I was invited to go along. I did so, and witnessed the discussions. A student, Rimel, toward the close stormed the castle, and raised a powerful excitement. The discussion continued, and several said they would like to hear from me. At last a motion was adopted inviting me to speak. I did so, corrected some false reports and appealed to them about the labors of President Scribner which made some of them weep. Just then Professor Stonecuppher came in and his appeal was grandly eloquent. They then voted and the resolve to

have an exhibition notwithstanding some ballot-box stuffing was barely defeated. The movement at once collapsed!

Wednesday, May 12 The rebellion at once collapsed. It had not an advocate. I hear that Father John Rohrer threw himself from a window of his house, and greatly injured himself. I go with Rev. W.C. Day, to see him, and stay till morning.

Thursday, May 13 At the morning prayers, the leader's confession is read. Herbaugh's announcement. I went to see Father Rohrer, in the afternoon. F.M. Day went with me. About 8 o'clock in the evening, Father John Rohrer died.

Friday, May 14 Father Rohrer was buried at Mt. Pleasant Church. I was present. I rented my stable a month to Jerry Riley.

Saturday, May 15 I spent the day at home. I ploughed some in my garden in the evening. Simeon Rohrer engaged me to preach his his [repeated in text] father's funeral the 13th of June. For some reason, I did not preach the funeral, but Rev. Daniel Shuck did.

Sunday, May 16 I preached at 10:30, Hebr. 1.9. "Loved righteousness hated iniquity— annointed oil of gladness." Preached at 7:30, Luke 22.40. "Pray that ye enter not into temptation," to the sleeping disciples.

Monday, May 17 I start to General Conference, as a delegate. I went ot A.H.H. Beam's, near the Haw-Patch Church, and left my horse. From there, with Rev. Jacob Scammahoru, I went to Indianapolis, to Columbus, Ohio, and on toward Pittsburgh.

Tuesday, May 18 We breakfasted at Pittsburg[h] and went on toward Annville, Pa., which we reached at midnight, and went to the hotel in a company of eight, for whom I paid their rate on the cars. Probably all paid me back. I did not remember certainly.

Wednesday, May 19 We found United Brethren, and attended the meeting of the Missionary Board. I dined at C.W. Hoverton's, where I also supped, and lodged. He afterward visited me in Dayton.

Thursday, May 20 I went on to Lebanon, and found my conference home at Brother Greaf's. The General Conference opened at 2 o'clock afternoon. At 7:30 Rev. William Miller of Western Reserve Conference, preached. He was so fluent and uncertain, that he filled one with dread, but he closed up pretty well at last. At the General Conference, at 2:00, Bishop Daniel Shuck, after the reading of the 17th Chapter of the Gospel of John, and the singing of "How sweet, how heavenly is the sight," addressed a fervent prayer to a throne of divine grace, which was followed by a hymn, and Bishop David Edwards preached a short discourse from 133d Psale, 1 verse, "How good and how pleasant it is," etc. It was representative General Conference. It had not only the bishops of the church, and general officers of the church, now, but many popular preachers besides: as William Miller of Auglaize, George Plowman, R. Loggan, Isaac Kretzinger, Martin Bowman, J.N. Lemasters, J.K. Alwood, Joshua Montgomery, Z. Warner, W.B. Raber, J.K. Statton, Solomon Lindsay, J.F. Vardaman, J.A. Kenoyer, of Upper Wabash, James Griffith, and L.S. Chittenden. Bishop Glossbrenner read the address of the board of Bishops.

Friday, May 21 The committees were announced. Memorials were presented. There was a breeze over the Indianapolis memorial. I met my educational committee in the evening.

Saturday, May 22 My committee on revision met and prepared its report, nearly. I shaved and dressed at my Conference home. Rev. C. Wortman was my roommate. Report on Missions came in the afternoon. Heard Rev. A.B. Sherk preach at night.

Sunday, May 23 Bishop Weaver preached at Trinity (new) Church, but failed to raise subscription on indebtedness. Bishop D. Wdwards preached at 2:30, on Christ's prayer in Gethsamane. Rev. W.B. Raber preached at the Reformed Church, "The Golden Candlestick" Ex. 25.32.

Monday, May 24 My committee (No. 2) reported. I dined at Brother Zimmerman's with Rev. J.W. Hott. We had quite a quarrel on reading the Chapter on Secrecy in Discipline. Rev. W.B. Dick declared he would not read it. I heard Rev. H.M. Greene preach in the evening.

Tuesday, May 25 I wrote a letter home to Susan. We had a real fight on making a Sabbath School Superintendent a member of Quarterly Conference. I supped at Bro. Dill's with Rev. D. O'Farrel. Dill complemented my speech, though he favored, the policy. If I had been asked to Conference, I should have won the case. I heard John Hill preach at the evening services.

Wednesday, May 26 The debate on Secrecy was opened up. Rev. P. Hirless, D.K. Flickinger, I.L. Buchwalter, H. Garst and other spoke. I spoke in the afternoon in favor of the majority report. In the evening, Father J.G. Spayth lectured. It was a heavy one—he was too old, and was not a lecturer!

Thursday, May 27 The debate on Secrecy was continued. Many spoke. At the evening sevices, Rev. Z. Warner preached. [One day, while some of their relatives came, and we ascended Washington Monument, viewed the city, and looked many miles off. My sight proved much better than that of my conductor. This was at Baltimore another year—at the time of the Missionary Board] (This belongs elsewhere)

Friday, May 28 This was the day previously agreed upon for the vote upon the Secrecy Question. On it 71 votes were cast for the majority Report and 26 votes against it. It was about this time that an evening was given to the Mutual Aid Society, an insurance ar[r]angement. I attended it. Rev. W.B. Dick explained and W.B. Raber scolded! It turned out to be a swindling concern, after some years.

Saturday, May 29 Rev. C. Wartman and I had not been very confidential in our communications, thought, he may have known that caucuses had been talking some of me and other candidates for the editorship the the *Religious Telescope.* I had not attended any caucus. He began to show some irritation about something unexplained. To-day the chief elections occurred, and after two ballots in which my own vote for John Dickson defeated me, I was elected at 9:35, as editor of the *Religious Telescope,* by 49 to 46 votes, I having still voted for another. Following which, William J. Shuey was elected Publishing Agent by 90 votes and Hoke trustee by 89 votes, Flickinger by 86, J. Applegate by 84, D.L. Rike by 75, Sowers, by 60 votes. All, unless J. Hoke, were

Liberals. D.K. Flickinger was elected corresponding Secretary of the Missionary Society, by 84 votes, and William McKee by 60 votes, Missionary Treasurer. Afterwards the trustees, without consulting me, though I was favorable to it, elected Rev. D. Berger to assist me, as editor. During the vote for editor, Rev. J.W. Hott sat by me, saw my tickets, and testified afterward, that I did not vote for myself at any time. Some alleged that I did.

Sunday, May 30 I heard J.J. Glossbrenner preach at 10:30. I dined at Huston's. In the afternoon, Rev. W.J. Shuey's sermon was interrupted by the Decoration march. Some United Brethren ministers were in the march. I supped at Bergner's. In the evening I heard Rev. J.S. Chittenden preach.

Monday, May 31 Bishop Glossbrenner presiding. Bishop Shuck spoke warmly against abandoning the African Mission and the question as to our polity was referred back to the Board of Missions. I reported for the Committee on Education. The matter of a Theological Seminary was referred back to the committee favorably. Much business was transacted. I had supper at Kimmel's. Then, we had a night session.

Tuesday, June 1 I reported, for the Committee on Education, Submitting the establishment of a Theological Institute to the Board of Education. It was afterward named Union Biblical Seminary on my motion, and founded on my motion in the Board in Other business was transacted. The Gen. Conference adjourned with prayer by Bishop J. Dickson. I supped at my Conference home with Rev. Thomas Evans. Key lectured at night, and after it, we started for home.

Wednesday, June 2 We reached Pittsburg[h], in the morning. We went over the Pan Handle Rail-road, to Columbus, and thence to Indianapolis, where we arrived at 2:00 A.M., and lodged at Rev. Thomas Evans'.

Thursday, June 3 At Indianapolis, I saw Mr. B.F. Witt. We went on to Columbus, Ind., at 12:00. I dined at Rev. A.H.H. Beam's. I got my horse at Beam's, who charged me nothing, but I afterward paid him in presents, and went on home to Hartsville, before I was expected. I found all well except Rev. W.C. Day a boarder.

Friday, June 4 I attended College prayers. I had talks with Lewis Mobley, J.W. Scribner, Apple, Lottie Chittenden and Grandmother Chittenden.

Saturday, June 5 My brotherinlaw, Daniel Koerner and his daughters, Ellen and Elizabeth, came.

Sunday, June 6 I preached at 10:30, 1 Pet. 2.9. Jonathan Wilson came after his sister Melissa. I preached at 7:30, Matt. 6.18, "Lay not up for yourselves treasures upon earth" etc.

Monday, June 7 I visited Elias Huffer, in the country, who spoke of the editorship as the most important office in the church. I ploughed in my garden in the afternoon.

Tuesday, June 8 We had the graduating addresses at the College Chapel. We had Scribner's address. We had a dinner at College Hall. We had a brief session of the Board of Trustees.

Wednesday, June 9 We had the meeting of the Board of Trustees in the day. We had prayer meeting in the evening.

Thursday, June 10 Daniel Koerner started home. Minerva, on account of W.C. Day, wanted to stay. I know from him, that he did not wish her. She wept. The Board adjourned for a week.

Friday, June 11 W.C. Day had been sick, but he and Francis went to Columbus to-day. I saw David Fix, my landlord, and we agreed on what he would allow me for my garden.

Saturday, June 12 We visited Henry Mobley's and J.C. Mench's to-day. I adjusted with my landlord, who had rather backed out from our agreement.

Sunday, June 13 I went to Mt. Pleasant Church, three miles south-east of Hartsville, and preached, Hebr. 12.1, "Cloud of witnesses." I dined with William Smith, in the country.

Monday, June 14 Susan made ready to pack for moving to Dayton, Ohio. W.C. Day one of our boarders being sick had delayed us some.

Tuesday, June 15 Rev. W.C. Day left for home, and we went to packing up. Susan was an expert in packing dishes. We lodged at N.P. Miller's.

Wednesday, June 16 We finished packing our goods. We dined at N.P. Miller's, Supped at William Fix's, and lodged at Miller's.

Thursday, June 17 We went with goods to Greesburg and left them to be shipped by railroad to Dayton, Ohio, and went on to Rev. John Morgan's, where we lo[d]ged.

Friday, June 18 We went by way of Andersonville to Lucinda Wright's, on Sane's Creek, in Fayette County.

Saturday, June 19 We went via Connersville and Liberty, to Daniel Koerner's in Union County, arriving at 9:00, eve.

Sunday, June 20 We staid at Pap John G. Koerner's, and did not go to meeting. The girls went to the Friends' Church at Salem. Daniel went to Franklin Church.

Monday, June 21 We remained with Koerner's that day, and lodged at Daniel's.

Tuesday, June 22 We went to Richmond, arriving in the afternoon. We looked at Daniel Zellers business house.

Wednesday, June 23 I went on the early train to Dayton, arriving at 8:00 A.M. I found my goods at the Xenia Depot. I dined at P.H. Davis's. Staid at William J. Shuey's.

Thursday, June 24 I wrote an article in the morning. I rented a house (Corners of Third and Sprague) in the afternoon, and moved my goods into it. I dined at D.L. Rike's, and lodged at W.H. Lanthurn's.

Friday, June 25 I wrote a hasty article, and took the excursion train to Richmond. I went on to Elias Bowman's, arriving at 10:00, eve, in the buggy.

Saturday, June 26 I went to Millville. Went in afternoon to Hoover's Sale, to Benjamin Shaffer's and to Mr. James Taylor's. I lodged at Elias Bowman's. He was a near neighbor and warm friend.

Sunday, June 27 I preached at Bridgeport, 10:30, Ps. 145.11. We dined at Daniel McMullen's with Enos Shaffer's. I preach at 3:30. We stay at Jacob Williams. (He at last fell out on Keiter's account.)

Monday, June 28 Myself and family go, via Richmond, to Dayton, arriving before nine o'clock in the morning. We went to our house, corner of 3ed & Sprague Sts, unpacked and lived.

Tuesday, June 29 I went to the office and commenced work. I began on my salutatory address.

Thursday, July 1 Rev. William McKee dined with us. I worked in my office.

Saturday, July 3 I worked in the office. Bought some furniture.

Sunday, July 4 Attended S.S. at First Church. I had a class: Misses Logan, Rice and Crider. Rev. W.J. Shuey preached a fair sermon on the "Wall watered Garden," Jer. 31.12. I visited the Miami City Sabbath School. My essay on recapitulation was poor. I preach at night at the Colored Church on Ludlow Street.

Monday, July 5 My Salutatory was complemented.

Friday, July 9 Rev. Slater, of Western Reserve, dined with us.

Saturday, July 10 We bought Susan a hat and a sundown. Rev. D. Berger went to Springfield in the morning.

Sunday, July 11 We went to Sabbath School and to preaching at First Church. Rev. S.M. Hippard preached, "Lord, Give Prosperity," Ps. 118.25. I attended S.S. at Miami Chapel. I preached at the Fourth Presbyterian Church at at [repeated in text] 8:00. Mr. Findlay is the pastor. "Holiness becometh thine house, O Lord, forever," Ps 93.5.

Monday, July 12 I was at the office. Rev. D. Berger came back from Springfield, at 1:30. I bought some groceries at Sandemyer's grocery.

1 8 7 1

[This year appears in the same book as the year 1859.]

Sunday, July 16 I preached at Ludlow colored Church, at 11:00, "Glorious thing are spoken of thee, O city of God," Ps. 87.3. Preach in the evening, Blasphemy of the Holy Ghost, Matthew 12.31,32.

Monday, July 17 Lydia Sexton called, and John Dodds at the same time. Byers called a meeting at night. What is up? No one knew. Something hidden.

Tuesday, July 18 Rev. Aikman came. We went to prayer meeting.

Wednesday, July 19 Aikman, Julius Bronson of Oregon, C.W. Miller and John Kemp came. I had a talk with Kemp. My Bible class met in the evening.

Thursday, July 20 Julius Bronson dined with us. I go to hear Lydia Sexton at Ludlow Church in the evening. Matthews (colored) prayer was both solemn and laughable. I laughed heartily.

Saturday, July 22 Rev. Aikman calls on his way to Cambridge. I saw Telescope about put in form. Bronson lodged with us.

Sunday, July 23 We went to Miami Chapel to hear Lydia Sexton preach. "Who is the Almighty that we should serve him?" Job. 21.15. J. Bronson stays with us to-day and to-night. Boat ride defeat. J.N. Zehring says, "fogy!" Lydia Sexton preached at Summit Street at 8:00, "What more could the Lord do for his vineyard," Mark 12.9.

Monday, July 24 Lydia Sexton and Mother Rhinehart widow of Rev. William Rhinehart, dined with us. Mother Sexton described Rev. Jeremiah Kenoyer as very rude in his boyhood. There was a church council at Home St., afterward called Summit Street Church, at night.

Tuesday, July 25 Julius Bronson, who was in the east in the interest of Philomath College, dined with us to-day. In the evening I attended prayer meeting.

Wednesday, July 26 Rev. P.H. Davis called in the forenoon. I write till about 4:00. Prof. H.A. Thompson calls in the Book-store. In the evening, I was re-elected president [sic] of the teachers class, at Home St.

Friday, July 28 Bishop J.J. Glossbrenner, Rev. William McKee, Rev. D.K. Flickinger and Julius A. Bronson dine with us.

Saturday, July 29 I wrote an editorial. Mr. Christopher Shearer, the husband of Harriet (Wright) Shearer, my cousin, called in. They live a few miles north of Dayton.

Sunday, July 30 I preached at Home Street (Summit St.) Church at 10:30, on Spiritual Diligence, Hebr. 6.11,12. I attended Sunday School and had six scholars in my class. I heard Rev. J.D. Holtzinger preach in afternoon, "Let her alone." Putnam Smith asked for and had lodging with us.

Monday, July 31 Rev. P.B. Lee called at my office. There was official meeting in the evening at Home Street Church.

Tuesday, August 1 Pres's S.B. Allen and E.B. Kephart and Rev. W.C. Smith came.

Wednesday, August 2 The Educational Board was in session. Julias Bronson and Rev. William Dillon dine with us. Rev. W.S. Titus and W.J. Pruner supped with us. I proposed the name "Union Biblical Seminary," which was adopted. Pres. H.A. Thompson made an address at First Church.

Thursday, August 3 The Board of Education was in session. Revs. W.C. Smith and John Kemp dined with us. We held a committee at noon. Revs. W.J. Prener and W.C. Smith took supper with us.

Friday, August 4 Rev. W.J. Pruner dined with us. Rev. P.B. Lee supped with us. I had an talk with him on the Secrecy question. The fun in his introduction to El[l]en Koerner—She struck the wall in making her [unreadable]

Saturday, August 5 I was busy editorially all day. James Manning pays me half of the $70.00, he had borrowed of me. He payed the rest afterward. James was honest.

Saturday, August 19 Orville was born this morning.

Positively, I finished rewriting the foregoing forty-two years after the day of Orville's birth, when I am nearly eighty-five years of age.   Milton Wright

The House on Hawthorne Street into which the Wrights moved in April 1871. Photo ca. 1910.

1 8 7 7

May 5 Started with Bishops Glossbrenner & Weaver for Westfield. Staid at Next best Depot House, Indianapolis. Called at Walter S. Brown's on Ft. Wayne Avenue an hour or two, in the evening.

May 6 Went on with brethren to Vermillion, Ill., where they stop and I go go to Ashmore. Dine at the Franklin House. Go on hack to Westfield. Stop at W.C. Smith's. Call on Pres. Allen's. Alumni meeting at night.

May 7 Preached the baccalaureate, at 10 1/2. Dined at Prof. W.S. Shuey's. Heard I.G.W. Chase pr. at 8:00 Eve. Staid at Solomon Zeller's.

May 8 Spent the day partly in attending recitations. Dine at Rev. J.H. Snyder's. [Here a half month has no record.]

June 26 Reach St. Joseph, Mo. Stay at the Hote.

June 27 Get to Gairbury. Stay with Joseph Westley. Meeting there (He proved a mendacious sham.) Rev. Isaac Belknap said Westley was the ablest preacher in Nebr.

June 28 Lay *Corner Stone (What a farce!) *of a College!

June 29 I did not know. I go out to Father Marks with I.K. Belknap.

June 30 I go to Quar'y Meeting up Rose Creek. I saw Schell, D.K. Zeller's nephew. I stay at John Ackaret's.

July 1 I Preach at Fairbury Court House at 11:00 from Heb. 4:14. I preach at night from Ps. 87:3. Stay at Bowers', G.W. This Bowers was Rev. Eddy Bower's father but a weak man.

July 2 Go with Rev. E.W. Johnson to Crete.

July 3 Visit R.A. Bishop. See Mr. James Johnson. Go on via Plattsmouth to Creston, Iowa. Stay at my Uncle George Reeder's. He is my Mother's youngest brother. I boarded the summer of 1852 at his house in Rush Co., Indiana.

July 4 Left Creston for Burlington, intending to go on to Muscatine. I conclude to stop off at Fairfiled. I find no direct connection for Muscatine. Stay at Hotel. I see the fireworks. They go off in a fury! Several were reported wounded—one killed! by sky-rockets.

July 5 Go on to Columbus Junction on the early train. Breakfast at [blank] House with Prof. Fellows of Iowa City. Go on to Ely. Walk part way to Western—then get in a wagon. Go to E.B. Kephart's. Effort to keep cool with the mercury about 100 degrees! Several friends call in. Lodge at I.L. Buchwalter's.

July 6 Go to Cedar Rapids. Call at J. Bear's. Dine at Justuses. Go on to West Liberty. Stay that night.

July 7 Reach Geneseo, Ill., about 10 A.M. H—meets me. Rev. W.H. Post takes me to his house. Stay there that night.

July 8 Preach from [blank]. Raise subscription and dedicate the Church. Dine at Weiner's. Go after night meeting to John Bears. He soon after proved to be a rascal. He would allow no ventillation & we were almost suffocated. He ran off soon.

July 9 I go on to Chicago, and thence toward Jonesboro, Ind., arrive in night.

July 10 I breakfast at Hiram Simons. Go on to Fairmount. Winslow takes me over to Uncle Wm. Reeder's.

July 11 Go over to farm to-day. Stay at Uncle William's.

July 12 Robert takes me to Fairmount, and I go via Union City, and arrive home, (Dayton.) There is now a week of which I have no record.

July 20 At 8:00, M. Left on Pan-Handle train for Indianapolis. Called at Bro. D.K. Zeller's at Richmond, 5 minutes. Saw Wilde Cranor on the train to Indianapolis—daughter of Rev. J. Cranor, then of Newport, Vermill. Co. Ind. Went on via Terre Haute, Vandalia, to St. Louis, and thence (10 P.M.) to Kansas City, which I reached next day.

July 21 Reached Kansas City at about 11:00. Went on to Perryville, Kan. Called at Rev. Josiah Terrell's. Brother Beam, & Sister Frances Lippy met me and took me in a skiff down the Delaware (Grass Hopper) to Lecompton, crossing the swift current of Kansas River. Stopped at Levi Lippy's. Called at Rev. R. Loggain's. [Written as Cars were in motion, July 21] Saw Bro. Hill. Met Prof. Bartlett who accompanied me to Lippy's.

July 22 Was in morning meeting. Saw for the first Rev. A.A. Cellars, Zabriska (Sobeiska), Father Green, etc. Preached from Ps. 48:11. Dined at Mr. Hill's 3/4 mile out. At Sab. School at 3:00. Talked to Father Green's infant class, He the father of Rev. H.M. Green, on the crucifixion. Called at Lippy's. Supped at Prof. Bartlett's. I preached at 8:00—Deut 18:18,19. Lodged at Bartlett's. Talked about teachers etc. quite late.

July 23 I called at Dr. Bonebrake's And Went to Rev. J.H. Zabrisky's. I Called again at Bonebrake's, a half-hour. Bonebrake's wife was Caswell W. Witt's daughter. I went to Lippy's, and started for Perryville. Hailed boat and waited. Went on the skiff "Idle" up the Grass Hopper. Dined at J. Terrill's at Perryville. I start at 2:00 for Denver, Col. The Kaw up Kansas Valley, which is wide, level & rich. I study. I sleep about seven hours on cars.

Tuesday, July 24 We are out on plains. I saw antelopes, a Prairie-dog town & a drove of four or six thousand cattle. Stiff winds. First View of snowy mountains—Pike's and Long's peaks. Reach Denver at 3:00. At Denver I dine at Rev. St. Clair Ross', & Mary meets me & I go up to his house, 655 Larimer Street. I ride over town after "dinner." I sup at Rev. H.R. Miller's—a nice family. I call at Mr. Evans', Ross' soninlaw's, at the gate only. I go to Ross's and then to Murphy (temperance) meeting at Christian Ass. rooms. Rev. Mr. [blank] of Cincinnati, O, explains. I am called on to talk also. Others speak. Resolved to send for workers from Sedalia, Mo. Lodge at Ross's.

Wednesday, July 25 I get half-fare pass and go to Longmont, & Call at Rev. L.S. Cornell's—dine—See Montgomery's. I go in a wagon four miles. Ackerman along. Walk then to Bro. Lewis Cross's, An emigrant wagon takes my valises. Stay all night. Railroad section surveyors.

Thursday, July 26 Revs. St. Cl, Ross, Mary, Rev. Levi Debuck & wife called. Father Cross takes me to Big Thompson, Colo. Conf. met and adjourned. My home at Abraham Risto's. They not members of Church. The Conf. in afternoon. Rev. Ackaret & Miller rejected on their transfers. Examinations proceed. Rev. Harry preaches at School House at night on "Pathway of just." Prov. 4.18.

Friday, July 27 Session continues at M.E. Parsonage. Receive Jas. L. Snead into Conf. St. Ross locates. L.S. Cornell elected P.E. Ride out to Brooks. Dine at George Litell's. I preach at 8:00, Ps. 18:30.

Saturday, July 28 Finance Com. Rev. McCreary, U.P. Rev. Osborne came. Dined at Monroe's—3 miles out. Ackaret is received into Conf. Stationing Com. Cornell preaches. I read stationing Com's report. Conference finally adjourned.

Sunday, July 29 I preached Conference sermon II Tim. 4:12. Dine at George Litell's. Gen. Sab. S. meeting. Sup at D. Hershman's. His nephew of Henney, of Genesco, Ill. The people showed me great friendship. I Preach, Ps. 87:3. I stay at A. Rist's as usual. Charley very friendly.

Monday, July 30 I go with Rev. L.S. Cornell to Longmont. Lamb and DeBusk's come also. I dine at Cornell's. I go on to Denver & stop at H.R. Miller's on or near 20th Street.

Tuesday, July 31 I go to St. C. Ross' and get my trunk and clothes. I start at 11:00 for Junction City.

Wednesday, August 1 I arrive at Junction City, Kan. about 9:00. I saw Friend Mussey of New Vienna, Ohio on the way there. I find Revs. G.M. Huffman and Josiah Terrell & J. Mason who go with me on the cars to Clay Center. Rev. A.J. Clay meets us with conveyance and takes us to Jackson's near Clifton to supper, and thence 8 miles to the Conference tent. J.H. Zabriski preached that evening. Found my home at Van Campen's.

Thursday, August 2 Opened Conf. session. R. Loggan, Chairman, L.G. Cowdry secretary. Examination proceedings slow. O.A. Chapman preached in the evening.

Friday, August 3 We got along fast. A good day. Bearss preached in the evening. Crowded out of my bed that night—a hard sleep. (Spore took my bed!)

Saturday, August 4 Conf. as usual. Much business done. Stationing Com meets in the evening. Short, late night session.

Sunday, August 5 I Preached at 11:00, II Cor. 3:7-8. Much feeling in the congregation. We ordained Bros. Rose & Burkhart. Sab. Sch. Meeting in aftn. Some remarks, I made. (Coll. in forenoon about $34.00—raised to about $45 next day) Love feast and sacramental meeting in evening. It was a time of great joy in love feast and great feeling indeed all through.

Monday, August 6 We close Conf. after a two hours' session. I start with Bro. Imes and [blank] and Terrell for Clay Center. Dine at Jackson's. A threatened storm

scarcely brushes us, but it cools the air. Reach Junction City. I stay at Thompson House, a third class house. Our host is very garulous [sic].

Tuesday, August 7 I get four postal orders, two of $49 each for Susan and two for Shuey aggregating $70. Wrote letters home, etc. Wait till about 7:00 P.M.—Cars behind. Reach Kansas City at 2:00 in morning.

Wednesday, August 8 Breakfast at Coats' House. Got half-fare pass on railroad. I go on to Pleasanton. Bro. Anderson takes me, Green, and Graves to his house. Go on to Mound City. Gorsline preaches. Rev. Forbes as a singer. I Stay at Sol. Mason's.

Thursday, August 9 Conference opens and progresses. Rev. Geo. W. Keller preaches at night. Lodge at Mason's.

Friday, August 10 Conf. as usual. Dine at Alexander's. J. Riley preached at night. I stay at Conf. home and get a long night's sleep.

Saturday, August 11 We close Conference in night session. Elect Pres. Elders on first ballot. Boundary & finance Com's reports adopted without amendment.

Sunday, August 12 I preach from II Tim. 2:15. "Study," etc. Arrang[e] subject in morning. Ordain A. Mumma. Dry Sab. Sch. meeting. I preach in evening from Heb. 11:10. "City which hath foundations."

Monday, August 13 I started at 3:00 A.M. for Pleasanton, Arrive just in time for cars. Greene with me. Buy two postal orders for Susan—fifty dollars each. (perhaps at Kansas City) Take cars at 11:00 morning for Pacific Junction. Write letters on the way. Stay at Woodhurst's at Pacif. Junction.

Tuesday, August 14 I go on to Plattsmouth, Nebraska. Rev. I.N. Martin meets me and takes me to his home. I stay at Pap Horning's at night. They make much of me. Cornelius seems so pleased and overjoyed. Mrs. Adams and Shopp, their daugh. live there.

Wednesday, August 15 I Call at Cornelius Horning's. Ezra takes me to Plattsmouth. I dine at Martin's. Go to

Church in afternoon. W.S. Spooner preaches at night. Long exhorts.

Thursday, August 16 Begin Conference. Effort made to get Conference to arrange committees. It fails. Prof. R.E. Williams preaches at night.

Friday, August 17 Conference as usual. Meet Com. on Divis. I Preach at night Ps. 25:14.

Saturday, August 18 Dine at Cornelius Horning's. Night session. Several ballots on 4th P.E.

Sunday, August 19 Sunday: Preached from II Tim. 4:1,2. Dine at Mr. Jean's. Sab. Sch. Meeting. Wright, Westley, Prof. Williams, Caldwell, Johnson, & Austin speak. Van Gordon preaches at night.

Monday, August 20 We have a morning session. Rapid. A little disorderly. Agree to meet together next conference at Fairbury, and as divided conference. Start at 2:30 for Plattsmouth. Buy a draft of Nat. Bank on Chemical Nat. Bank of New York. Go on to Pacific Junction. Write to Susan and to Shuey. Baggage master treats me meanly. I reach Council Bluffs and stay at Rev. Rose's. Mapes there.

Tuesday, August 21 I go on freight wagon to North W. Depot—to Missouri Valley. Then to Sioux City. Dine at Hotel Depot. Make purchases in town. Miss train, it departing before my eyes! Confinue purchases & write to Susan. I go on to Cherokee, Starting at 6:00, p.m. Reach there at 11:00. Note from J.A. Lambert to stay at Washington House. Stay there.

Wednesday, August 22 Write to Susan and to Dr. L. Davis in morning. Bro. Lambert comes and takes me to his house, near Conference, which is at Union Ridge School House, about 4 miles from Correctionville, Woodbury County, Iowa. Bros. Bunce and Van Norman had arrived and their wives, Chase & others arrive. Chase preached.

Thursday, August 23 Began Conference. It is slow but harmonious. Dr. Bunce Preaches.

Friday, August 24 Conf. Session Continues. I preach in the grove at Lambert's from Heb. 11:27. A strong breeze—fail.

Saturday, August 25 Session of Conference closes. J.H. McNey preached.

Sunday, August 26 I preach to ministers at 11 o'clock from [blank] Tedious Sab. Sch. Convention in afternoon. Sup at [blank] Stay at Freeman's.

Monday, August 27 I go early with Rev. A.N. Kings' to Hazzard Station. Reach Sioux City about noon. Dine. Have my hair trimmed. I Go on to Sioux City. Wm Jacobs & Roberts meet me at depot. Go on hack to J. Talbot's in Des Moines.

Tuesday, August 28 Next morning go on to Creston. Stay at Uncle George Reeder's a day.

Wednesday, August 29 I go on to Lucas and thence to Norwood. Stay at Pennington's.

Thursday, August 30 Begin Conference. J.W. Baber referred for trial. Duffield contradicts Jacobs—is set down.

Friday, August 31 Examination continues.

Saturday, September 1 This is the first day of the new Discipline. Elect P.E.'s, etc. Stationing Com. sits at night.

Sunday, September 2 Preach at 11:00 from Heb. 7:27. Ordain [blank] Dine with Geo. Miller's at French's. Preach at night from Eph 2:7. While preaching I was struck with a pain in my head which passed away soon, but was felt for years.

Monday, September 3 Close Conf. at 9:00. Go on to Knoxville. Lodge at Lorimer Ardery's. Rev. Scott took me there.

Tuesday, September 4 I go on to Ainsworth via Oskaloosa. I find a number on the train. I go to Edward Stone's. Bonebrake preached.

Wednesday, September 5 Conference opens. W. Demoss is referred to a committee. Shuler preaches at night. I home at Ed. Stone's.

Friday, September 6 [somehow Thursday was lost or skipped or the numbers were mixed up in the original] Session Continued. Examination progresses. I.K. Statton preached at night.

September 7 Conference Continued. I preach at night from [blank]

September 8 Conference closes. There is quite a stampede on transfers.

Sunday, September 9 I preach at 11 from Acts 11:24. Sun. Sch. Anni. in afternoon. Sacrament at night. It is a rainy day & night.

September 10 I dine at John Stone's. I go on to Muscatine. Stay at I.K. Statton's.

Tuesday, September 11 I spend Morning in writing. Afternoon, call at Pap Hershey's; ride with Statton in Baker's rig (two shetland ponies) about Muscatine. Sup with Baker at Commerical House. I go via Junction & West Liberty to Cedar Rapids. Stay at Centennial Hotel.

Wednesday, September 12 I go to Laura & Toledo. Arrive at 10 o'clock A.M. Go to W.H. Harrison's. I have a melancholy day. I.K. Statton preaches at night.

Thursday, September 13 Conference in session. My head is ailing.

September 14 Conf. Continued. I preach—fail. Num 10:29.

Sunday, September 16 I preach from II Cor. 3:7-8. Anniv. Sab. Sch. Com. Prof. Kephart preaches at night from "Far more exceeding."

September 17 I start fr Cedar Rapids in the afternoon. Arrive abt 9:00 P.M. Wait train. Take a Sleeper for Plymouth, Iowa.

September 18 Arrive at Plymouth. Stop at Austin. At Owatona. Go on freight train to Dover. Stay at Mr. Drysdale's.

Wednesday, September 19 I go on to Rev. M.L. Tibbett's,

which is my home. S.D. Kemerer preached at night from [blank]

Friday, September 21 Conference. I preach from I Kngs 18:21.

Saturday, September 22 Conf. closes. M. Epis. minister preaches at night from Rom. 1:16.

Sunday, September 23 I preach at 11:00 from Heb. 4:14. I saw Matt. Merrick & wife . I pr. at 7 1/2 from [blank]

Monday, September 24 I go to Dover about 1:00 P.M. I go on to Wynona, Sparta, Watertwon. Stop at Wat. Junc. Hotel.

September 25 I go on to Oshkosh on 6:00 freight. Dine at M.G. Lindsay's. Stop at Spore's. Church investigation. Stay at Kaye's.

Wednesday, September 26 I go to Shore's, Buell & others Call. C.M. Clark preaches at night.

Thursday, September 27 Conf. begins. Exam nearly finished. Buell preaches on "six steps to throne."

September 28 Conf. Delap pr. in aft. 2:00. Sup at Sister Ostrum's. Gay preaches at night.

September 29 Conf. E. Collins is excused from preaching at 2:00, and I speak a few minutes on Africa & on temperance. Conf. waits on Committees. Much delayed. Stationing Com. meets at Roberts'. Bacon preached at night. Mr. Spore at home. My conf. home is at Spore's.

Sunday, September 30 I preach at 11:00, from II Cor. 3:7-8. Dine at Kay's. E. Collins & Whitney sick. I go to see Lindsay. He is rather tart. Go on to S.S. Conven. I call to see Whitney at his sister's. I preach at night from Eph. 2:4.

Monday, October 1 Leave at 9:00 for Janesville. Arrive at 3:00. G.G. Nickey awoke me on the train! Else I should have gone on! I look at town; was in Keye's large store-room. I sup at Father Nihart's—excellent old people. I go on with Bros. G.G. Nickey & G.M. Mabbott to Monroe. Dennis Whitney & others are aboard. Stop at Gillett's & lodge there.

October 2 I stay till afternoon and then go on with Charley Sargeant & others to Wiota where we sup with [blank]. It is in Lafayette Co. Go on to Pleasant Grove. Stay at our home Mr. Dryden's.

October 3 Go to Bridgman's a short time. Back to dinner. Spend afternoon in posting books, diary, etc.

October 4 Begin Conference (Wisconsin)

Sunday, October 7 Preach from Heb. 11:10. I Raise about $270 of Sub. on Pleasant Grove Church. I preach at night, from Acts 11:24, the Conf. Sermon.

October 8 Dine at Dryden's. Alderman, Bovee, etc. call. I start with Hiram Bridgman to Darlington, and go thence to Warren. Stay at [blank] with F.J. Crowder.

October 9 I go on to Polo, Ill. Dine at Rev. J.H. Grim's. Go with him to Overholser's near Coleta & lodge there.

Wednesday, October 10 The Rock River Conf. meets. Adjourn till afternoon. P. Hurless is Sec'y. Hallowell is Chariman. My home is at Father Winters. Rhinehart preached at night.

Sunday, October 14 I preach from II Tim 4:2. Aftn. S.S. Meeting. I preach at night Deut. 18:18.

Monday, October 15 Went to Sterling. Dine at Kingery's. Call at Overholser's grocery. See J. Zeller. Go on via Fulton, Rock Island, Wilton, Columbus Junction, to Burlington, Iowa. Stay at City Hotel.

Tuesday, October 16 I go on to Pulaski, Iowa & dine at Harper's with Pap Cossel. Go on with Rev. J.W. Estep to Barker's. N.E. Gardner preached: "Oh that thou hadst hearkened," etc. "Peace as a river."

October 17 Conf. opened. A.W. Geeslin preached at night.

October 19 Very rainy. No preaching, but prayer-meeting at night.

October 20 Still misty. L.D. Ambrose preached at night.

October 21 Excellent conf. love feast. I preach at 11 from Heb. 4:14. Dine on the ground. Sab. Sch. meeting, aftn. I preach at night from Eph. 3:19.

Monday, October 22 I go to Pulaski. Dine at hotel. Write letters. Take cars at 2:50 p.m. for Burlington. Ticket & check for Peoria. Stay at City Hotel.

October 23 Go on via Galesburg, Peoria, Bloomington, Crawfordsville, to Richmond. (I had held thirteen conferences in succession while gone from home.) Stay at D.K. Zellers.

October 24 I Reach home at 9:30 A.M. I go to *Convention in the afternoon. E. Ronayne works 1st degree of Masonry at Gebhart's Hall at night. Tedious. *Antisecrecy Association. I remained mostly in Dayton for about a month, and of this time I find no record till Nov. 28th. I remember we had a little snow and freezing at Thanksgiving time.

Wednesday, November 28 In afternoon, went to town & bought at Ryke's articles of wear & a large shawl. Got a watch of Reeves to carry. Called at Tizzard's (dentist) Read exchanges at Office. Hear Dr. L. Davis pr. opening sermon of protracted meeting at Summit Street Church. Preached Rom. 4.4. Powerful.

Thursday, November 29 I hear Rev. Stelling pr. a Thanksgiving sermon at First U. Brethren Church. It was able, well worded and well read, but wanting in the religious element. Susan & I dined at D.L. Davis's. Mrs Edwards, Arrilla and Miss Erb were there. Heard J.W. Hott at night on "Wilt thou not revive" Bishop Dickson Lodged with us.

Friday, November 30 I go to Christopher Shearer's at Swanders, and thence at 7:00 via Lima to Ft. Wayne arriv there at midnight. Lodge at Robinson House.

Saturday, December 1 Write to Reuchlin, Shuey, James T. Harris etc. I go to Pleasant Lake. Rev. J. Brown of N. Ohio takes me to his house for dinner. His daughter is to be married soon. I go to Levi Dondt's. Pr. from Ps. 1.6.

Lorin Wright, b. 18 November 1862

Sunday, December 2 I pr. at 11:00, Heb. 11.10. Hard to raise deficit. Brown pr. eve., & I raise the rest, and dedicate the church. Lodge at Dondt's.

Monday, December 3 I went via Auburn to Albion. There I visit Cousin Sarah E. Worth. I pr. there, Eph 2:4. Audion goes with me to the cars at midnight.
Tuesday, December 4 I reach Chicago before daylight. I breakfast at Brvoost House. A woman at R. Is. Dep. borrows 60 cts. on her way to a funeral, "Lent expecting nothing." I go via Aurora and Ottawa to Streator, Ill. Antisecrecy (that day) convention had just closed at Cumberland Pres. Church. I lodge at Dr. Wolley's.

Wednesday, December 5 Dr. Wolley is an unbeliever and claims that in six weeks of study, he made great discoveries as to the mysteries of creation in Genesis, and so forth. A chart hanging on the wall (of his own make) he explained to us for an hour. Three parts: Shem, Ham and Japheth. Flood. "Rams, i.e. Gods." Job. so explained. Three days on the cross. Resur[r]ection. Jonah in Whale's belly. Mother Eve. Mary Magdalene. Elected. Twelve baskets full. Moses smites the rock. All symbolical. He boasted much. Had astonished Dr. Swing, etc, etc! I went

to the comvention. I dined at Lawyer Buckley's. I spoke in the afternoon. I have supper at Buckley's. I lodge at Rev. Andrew Winsett's. He is a famous United Brethren revivalist, whom I had never seen before. Pres. Allen and Rev. L. Taylor speak.

Thursday, December 6 Discussion in the convention on Free Masonry. I was, in the afternoon, elected President. J. Stoddard spoke in the afternoon. H. Avery of Tonica and Prof. C.A. Blanchard spoke. I lodge at a Bro. Beaver's 3 square's south-west of the Streator House.

Friday, December 7 I go via Ottawa to Sheffield. Bro. W.H. Becker meets me and takes me to his house six miles north-east.

Saturday, December 8 Go to Rev. J.W. Lewis's, in the afternoon. I preached at night from I Cor. 16.22, "Anathema."

Sunday, December 9 I pr. at 11:00, Hebr. 11:26 & Raise $220 and dedicate the Church. It took about one-half hour to raise the amount. Dine at Sidney Barber's Pap Harrison (?) I pr. at night, Acts 16.31. I lodge at Lockard's.

Monday, December 10 I go with Bro. Lockard to Sheffield. Stop at Sheffield House for dinner. Write to family and to H.M. Greene. I ask him to send me R.R. half-fare permits. I leave at 4:20 for Muscatine, Iowa. See J.P. Stoddard and C.A. Blanchard. Reach Muscatine about 8:00. Go to Rev. I.K. Statton's.

Tuesday, December 11 I go on to Washington and stop at Mrs. Wm. Stewart's and dine. Prof. Blanchard speaks. I lodge at Mrs. Stewarts'.

Wednesday, December 12 The Convention continues. I speak at night, followed by Rev. McAyel.

Thursday, December 13 Debate on resolutions. The church exclusion party wins. Prof. McDill speaks at night. I lodge at Mrs. Stewart's.

Friday, December 14 I go on to Ainsworth. I lodge at Rev. D. Shiflet's.

Sunday, December 16 I pr. at 11, John 7:37. I pr. at night, Ps. 1:6.

Monday, December 17 Go to D. Shiflett's. Pr. at night. Lodge at E. Stone's.

Tuesday, December 18 I go to John Stone's and remain over night.

Wednesday, December 19 Pr. at night Acts 26.28. Lodge at D. S.Shiflett's.

Thursday, December 20 Dine at Wesley Nichols'. He is an old acquaintance from near Neffs Corners, Ind. I lodge at Shiflett's with Rev. R. Thrasher.

Friday, December 21 I go to Columbus City. I put up at Rev. A.S. Schwimley's.

Saturday, December 22 I call at several places. Preach at School-house 2 1/2 miles south-east in the evening. I return to Schwimley's.

Sunday, December 23 I pr. in Col. City Church, at 11, from I john 5.18,19, "We know." Dine at Shearer's. I pr. at night, I Ki. 18:21. I lodge at Schwimley's.

Monday, December 24 I go on to Lettsville (Onomwa), there John Shellabarger meets me and takes me to his house, where I lodge that night. I see Rev. E.H. Caylor, our Dayton neighbor.

December 25 I dine at Rev. E.S. Bunce's with Shellabargers and other families. Wm. Bruce and daughter. I pr. at night at Erick Church John 14.2,3.

December 26 I open the day at Bunce's. I write for Rail Road Permits.

December 27 I go on to Muscatine. I lodge at Rev. I.K. Statton's. I attend prayer-meeting.

Friday, December 28 I dine at Hershey's and sup at Bitzer's. Attend Class. Stay at Bitzer's.

Saturday, December 29 I go to Conway's to dinner. Sup at Baker's in Commercial House. I lodge at Statton's.

Sunday, December 30 I pr. at 10:30, I Cor. 15.22. Dine at H.D. Ament's. Sup at Geesler's. Pr at 7 from John 14.2,3. Lodge at J. Erb's.

Monday, December 31 I go on to Cedar Rapids, Iowa, to-day. I remember that Rev. W.I. Beatty met me at the depot & I lunched at a restaurant, and went to Bro. W.B. Smith's. *I preached at night at the rented hall west of the Cedar River. I lodged at Bro. W.B. Smith's. Rev. Beatty was in a revival. *Record said: "Preached at hall to a full house, Ps. 1.5,6. Lodged at Smiths. One forward for prayers."

1878

Tuesday, January 1 A new year. Be it to the Lord Jesus Christ. Went from Bro. W.B. Smiths, Cedar Rapids, Iowa, to Bro. Christion Bear's, two miles south of town to dinner. Preach at 7:00 from Ez. 33:11. Stay with Rev. M.S. Drury at John Bear's.

Wednesday, January 2 Go to town. Get a letter from home. Write five letters—one home—at Bro. Williams. Drury goes home. Bro. W.I. Beatty visits Bro. Williams in Derry Dale neighborhood—sick. I Preach at 7:00 Acts 16:31. I Stay at Bro. John Bear's.

Thursday, January 3 I Write at Bro. Bear's till after dinner. I go to post-office. See Rev. S. Sutton who sups with us at Bear's. I preach, 7:00, from Jer. 13:20. Stay at Jno Bear's.

Friday, January 4 Go over to Smith's. Dine at Perry's. Go to Waterloo, 52 miles north. Go out with J.D. Ferries. Cold, rough ride. Nice family, but not very well-trained religiously. Stay there.

Saturday, January 5 Remain. Spend forenoon in writing. Compose sketch on Jude 21. Revise some others. Meet trustees of Black Hawk Church. Building 32x46x16. M.M. Taylor pr 7:00 from "No other name." Stay Ferris'.

Sunday, January 6 Preach 11:00 Heb 11:26. Raise $260. Dedicate. Dine at Mr. Warren's with Taylor & wife. Call at Wilson's. Preach 6:30 from Jno. 14:2&3. Stay at Father Baldwin's.

Monday, January 7 Therm. 3 degrees below zero. Go via Ferris' to G.W. Wilson's, to dinner. Go with Andr. Baldwin to Waterloo—too late for the cars. Stop at Central House. Write a letter and article on Commercial Religion. Stay till 3:00 morning.

Tuesday, January 8 Go on to Cedar Rapids. Get letters from home, and half-fares. Remain at W.B. Smith's till meeting. Pr. I Tim. 1:1. Three seekers. Stay at John Bear's. His trial over unworthy members. Good night's rest.

Wednesday, January 9 Stay at B's till three o'clock. Go to Smith's & post-office. Call on A.D. Collin's Esq. His advice on keeping order. His stand. I preach at 7 from I Tim. 4:10. Stay at Henry Bowman's, Esq.

Thursday, January 10 Go to Bro. Smith's. A Letter from B. Beal. See Rans. Davis & Prof. J.E. Ham at Depot. Go on 11:00 freight to Stanword. Went on with Fath. Glick in bob-sled. Stopped at Easterly's till meeting. Preach Acts 26:28. Stay at Jon't. Easterly's.

Friday, January 11 Go to morning meeting at St. John's Church. Dine at Mr. Shope's. Preach from Jude 14 v. Stay at Shope's. I spend my mind on maintaining order in Church. Bad order was common there.

Saturday, January 12 Go to Samuel Easterly's in Olin to dine. Wapnesipinecon River. Kaufman, Griffith. Go back to Shope's. Preach at 7 from Luke 6.47. Stay at Hummels'.

Sunday, January 13 Preach at 11 from Rom. 7.13. Dine at Moffit's. G.W. Statton preached at 7 from Rev. 3.20. He was pastor. We stay at John Easterly's.

Monday, January 14 Go to Stamwood, Cedar Rapids, thence to Western by Ely. I get three letters from home and one from Hott. Arrive at Morgan S. Drury's—lodge there. Rev. D. Wenrich preached.

Tuesday, January 15 I attend morning prayers, and afternoon meeting at Chapel. I preach at 7 from Matt. 12:30. Stay at Bro. Drury's.

Wednesday, January 16 Attend recitation of Rhetorical Class. Dine at Rev. I.L. Bookwalter's. Meeting in afternoon. Get letter from home & from Rev. J.W. Lewis. Sup at Prof. Bookwalter's. Preach at 7, Rom 10.1. Two rise for prayers. Stay at M.M. Drury's.

Thursday, January 17 Call at G.W. Statton's. Dine at Pres. Kephart's. Aft. meeting. Tea at Pres. K's. Preach 7:00, Eph. 3:20. Stay at M.S. Drury's.

Friday, January 18 Dine at Rev. Snyder's. Aftern. M. Look at literary rooms. Tea at Father Perry's. Preach 7 from Rom. 7.13, a poor preach. Stay at Danl. Manning's.

Saturday, January 19 Call at Statton's, Bowman's, Shatto's, R. Davis'. Pres. Kephart takes me to Ely. Preach Cedar Rapids at 2:00 aftn. Get dinner at Depot. Letters. Go on to Lisbon & arrive at 9:15. Stay with Rev. D. Runkle's.

Sunday, January 20 Receive letters from home. Pr. 10 1/2 Ps. 48:11,12,13. Dine at Runkle's with Adams'. Long speaking meeting in afternoon. At Rev. T.D. Adams' for supper. I pr. at 7, Luke 15:10. Stay at D. Runkle's.

Monday, January 21 Spend afternoon visiting stores, etc. Rev. T.D.Adams pr. 7 II Chr. 15:7. I stay at Adams'.

Tuesday, January 22 Dine at Bovey's. Call at Hess's. Preach at 7 from Rom. 12:1. Rev. Bloom of Lutheran, Rev. Fouse of Ger. Ref. & Jones of M.E. present. Stay at D. Runkle's.

Wednesday, January 23 Morning meeting—good. Dine at Adam Runkle's. Call at Father Ringer's. Ride out to see town & country & Mt. Vernon. Return to Adams's. Pr at 7 Acts 16:31. Stay at Runkle's. Two forward, one converted.

Thursday, January 24 Dine at D. Runkle's. Spend after. in writing and study. Preach at night from John 1:29. One forward & professed. I stay at Runkle's. One converted.

Friday, January 25 At good morning meeting. Dine at Hess's. Stay till after prayer-meeting there begins. Pr. at 7 from Matt 13:15. Six forward for prayers—one professed. Stay at Amos Runkle's.

Saturday, January 26 Dine at D. Runkle's. Write letter home and to Dillon. Go to Rev. Adams'. Call at J. Bittering's door. Supper at Adams'. Adams pr 7 "Grieve not Holy Spirit." Stay at D. Runkle's.

Sunday, January 27 Pr. at 10 1/2 from I John 5:18. Dine at Bittering's. Pr. at 3 at Centennial Ch. I Pet. 4:18. Preach at 7 at Lisbon from I Kin. 18.21. Stay at T.D.Adams.

Monday, January 28 Went on to Cedar Rapids. Call at W.B. Smith's. Go on Burlington at 4:20; arrive there 8:40 P.M. Go on via Galesburg, Ill., to Peoria—5:00 Morning. Saw Rev. Williamson of Washington, Iowa on Burl. train.

Tuesday, January 29 Arrived at Peoria, Ill at 5:00 Morn. Breakfast at Peoria House. See McLane at Depot. Talk with Rev. Heron, Presbyterian min. of Montezuma, Iowa. Arrive at Crawfordsville. Found Darwin & George Brown (cousin) at Casket House. Supper and lodging at Darwin's. Called at Krout's & Mary Wiley's & George's my cousin.

Wednesday, January 30 After Breakfast go with Darwin to Look at Wabash College grounds & buildings. See large rock presented to Pres. Edmund G. Hovey—a second cousin of my fathers. Then to court-house. Then Krout took me to visit Public schools. Dine at George R. Brown's. Go on to Indianapolis. Stay at Walter Brown's. Call at Uncle R.T. Brown's. Snowing sharply.

Thursday, January 31 Walter helped me carry my valise to depot—the snow having delayed the street-cars. Go on to Hamilton, O. Wait there four hours. Reach home—Reuchlin meeting me at depot, at Dayton.

Friday, February 1 I remain at home. [note: Wright paraphrases his entries for Jan. 29 and 30 in this section of the diary]

Saturday, February 2 Visit offices at Telescope Building. Berger invites me to contribute to the "Bible Teacher."

Sunday, February 3 Dr. Davis preached at Summit Street to parents. Baptizes infants and convert's. Takes 10 into Church. I go in evening to hear W.G. Morehead preach at Park Street. Pres. Brilliant but not very strong.

Friday, February 8 I called at John Swaynie's to find out time of birth-day reunion of Aunty Mary Swaynie's.

Saturday, February 9 Went to Aunt Mary Swaynie's birth day party held one day before time. I saw several new friends. The day somewhat rainy.

Sunday, February 10 Preached at Summit Street I John v. 18,19. Much approved. Prof. Funkhouser commends it to his class. Called at McHenry's, Daisy Mobley's and at Hott's. Root, Pr at 7:00, "Oh that thou hadst hearkened." Several seekers. John Weaver came out.

Monday, February 11 Spent time at home. Hippard exhorts at night at S. St. Several seekers, but none converted.

Tuesday, February 12 Time spent at home. I spoke at Sum. St. at night from the theme, Reconcil[l]iation to God. One professed. Wagner converted, it is said night before.

Wednesday, February 13 Spend day in writing.

Saturday, February 16 At Hott's request, led in meeting at Summit Street. Quite good meeting.

Sunday, February 17 Heard Prof. Funkhouser in the morning. Phil. 1:9-11. I preach at the Wesleyan Ch. I Cor. 11:26. McFall present. Great excitement—house full. Heard Young Resler at night on "What shall I do with Jesus?" Exhorted and led the altar exercises. One converted at close.

Monday, February 18 Led the revival meeting at Sum. St. One professed after dismission. Meeting a little dull till toward the close when it became quite lovely.

Tuesday, February 19 Led meeting again. No new seekers. The chronic seekers (the two Smith boys) out. A lively speaking meeting near the close. Quite good.

Wednesday, February 20 I was to preach at Washington Church, but so rainy I did not go, having some neuralgia. Sent a card to the pastor next day excusing absence.

Thursday, February 21 Studied some on lesson for *Telescope*. Sheldon Arnold staid with us.

Friday, February 22 Finished the lesson for Tel. on Ahaz good reign.

Saturday, February 23 Went to office at last afternoon. Tlak with Rev. D.O. Myer, who walks frozen. Bushong's over; write some, on Miami report. Also a few words with Bushong.

Sunday, February 24 Heard Prof. Keister at Summit St at 10 1/2. Rainy in the evening. Did not hear student Powel preach in the evening. Our two boys did.

Monday, February 25 I was about sick. It was cold and neuralgia perhaps. I did little because quite feverish. Read the papers. Wrote to Bro. Dillon on the Miami report & A. Sam's letter accounts.

Tuesday, February 26 I am better. I took anti-periodics. Wrote a few letters. Staid at home.

Wednesday, February 27 I am improving. in reading, writing, etc. Went to prayer-meeting in the evening. Called at Tobey's about a half hour.

Sunday, March 3 Dr. Davis preached at 10 1/2. I was not out in evening because of cold & cough.

Saturday, March 9 Was up to town in the afternoon. Saw Lanthurn, who was just out from severe sickness. Susan with me shopping.

Sunday, March 10 Preached at Colored Church (3d U.B.) at 11:00 from Ps. 92:8. Rainy in evening.

Monday, March 11 Called at Mrs. Edwards, Cousin Sam. Wright's & also Davis & Bro. Tobey's. J.V. Pott's called the evening & staid with us.

Thursday, March 14 Bro. Hott called in the evening. Wm. Haye's story-letters. He had written Mrs. Staves, taxing her with falsehood in exposing him.

Friday, March 15 Went to town forenoon. Saw J. Weaver, D. Berger, etc.

Sunday, March 24 Went to Summit St. W.J. Shuey preaches Neh. 6:3 "Why should the work cease," etc.

Monday, March 25 Spent the day (and whole week) mostly at home.

Saturday, March 30 Bishop J. Dickson came & spent a half hour or more.

Sunday, March 31 Went in evening to hear Horace Herr: "Fight the good fight of faith."

Monday, April 1 At home footing up conf. charts, preparatory to annual report of my District.

Wednesday, April 3 Finished footing chart. Went to Dr. Davis's (eve). Discussed methods of raising funds for colleges. Also, Life Insurance question. I was opposed to Life Insur. economically.

Thursday, April 4 Finished up Annual report.
Friday, April 5 Spent the day largely in writing letters—Cornell—M.S. Drury—Wenrich—Prof. Washburn.

Sunday, April 14 Went to Summit Street. Dr. Davis preached. Rainy evening. Did not go to Browntown Cahpel in consequence. (Prob. Miami Chap.)

Friday, April 19 D.K. Flickinger and Lanthurn make a call in the evening.

Saturday, April 20 I preach Mary Ellen Molen's funeral at Beavertown—daughter of Isaac Molen. Call at Bish. H. Humler's, on return. I prayed with him at his request. His wife seemed an excellent woman.

Sunday, May 5 Bish. J. Dickson pr. Baccalaureate, Summit Street, at 10. W.C. Smith & Pres. Allen dine with us. Prof. J.W. Etter pr. 7:30.

Monday, May 6 Educa. Board meets at 9:00. Business all day & evening. Visitors from day to day. Lita. Society arrive at S.St. I not present.

Tuesday, May 7 Educa. Board forenoon.

Wednesday, May 8 Graduating Speeches at Dayton First Church.

Thursday, May 9 Day spent closely in Seminary Board. Attempt to open way for Rike, etc on Ex. Com. fails—though rule waived. Graduating addresses concluded—diploma's.

Friday, May 10 Go to Hartsville, via Greensburg. Breakfast at Cin. Depot. Ride out with Peter Wright. Stop at M. Gronendyke's. Board (Mis.) meets at 3:00. S.A. Mowers preached An. Sermon 7:30. He read it with much vigor.

Saturday, May 11 Session Board. Weaver presides. Dine at Ervin's. Sup at J. Riley's. I preside in afternoon. Night session. Addresses by Luttrell & Miss Sarah Dickey. (?) [appears in text]

Sunday, May 12 Weaver sick.* Dickson preaches. Dine at N.P. Miller's. Sab. School addresses. Sup at Pruner's after a call at Thom. Elrod's. J.K. Billheimer lectured at night. *Probably tobacco.

Monday, May 13 Came with Rev. M. Groenendyke to Greensburg. Rev. Lynch, M.E. P.E.—I find J. Kemps & come to Cin. & Dayton with him.

Wednesday, May 15 Wednesday at town. See S. Mills who is about to start to Westfiled, Ill., home.

Saturday, May 18 Went to office. I return & find Mrs. E. Culbertson on a visit over Sabbath. She is my Uncle Porter Wright's only daughter. She lives in Troy, Ohio.

Sunday, May 19 Preach Sum. St. 10:30 Ps 137:5,6. Heavy! Call to see Dr. L. Davis. Hear Student Weller at

Sum. St. "That which—saw"—in evening.

Monday, May 20 Cousin Eliza Culbertson left. I attended going to Col. J. Dickson; went on 9:35 train. Dr. Davis suffered terribly last night.

Tuesday, May 21 I go to Columbus. I obtain slight reduction on fare of family in moving. Referred to Dayton Agt. on freight, etc. Saw G.M. Rigor, I. Baltzell, Peters, Prophet. Return, 3:45=6:45. [= appears in text]

Wednesday, May 22 Harvey Wright, Delila Flora & Sarah Cath., & Laura Winchell visit us. Call with Harvey at Sam. Wrights. Call at Swaynie's and Samuel Dover's.

Thursday, May 23 Go with friends to Soldier's Home. Dine at Samuel Wright's. Harvey's go home.

Friday, May 24 Flora, Sarah Catharine & Laura, start home. Hear Joseph Cook lecture at Music Hall.

Friday, May 31 Spent the day in packing goods, etc.

Saturday, June 1 Went out to D. Koerner's arriving there about 10:00 P.M. Susan, Lorin, Orville, and Katie with me. Left Reuchlin & Wilbur at home.

Sunday, June 2 Went to Union Church with Daniel. W.C. Day preached at 10 1/2. Dine at George Beard's. I preach at 3 1/2 "Word of the Lord tried." Stay at Daniel Koerner's.

Monday, June 3 Return to Dayton alone. Packing progressing. I Stay at Saml Wrights. Boys stay at J.G. Feight's. Boys dinner at Myers—I with them there at supper.

Tuesday, June 4 Packing finished. Get goods on car. Stay at Hott's. Took supper at I. Myers—dinner at P. Lavasser's.

Wednesday, June 5 Meet Bish. J. Weaver at Telescope Office in the morning. Buy furniture. Aftn close up cars. Stay at Dr. Davis' at night.

Thursday, June 6 Start—Send Reuchlin & W. to Fairmount—I go on to Cambridge; met wife, and three children. Dine at Jay's (Huddleson house) Visit several

Wilbur Wright in 1878 (12 years old)

in Dublin. Return to Richm. Lodge at D.K. Zeller's.

Friday, June 7 Go on to Anderson. Wait till 8:35 P.M. & then go on to Fairmount. William Reeder & Reuchlin take us through rain to Uncle W.H.H. Reeder's.

Saturday, June 8 Go to my farm in afternoon. Sup at Henry Simons. Lodge at Uncle William's.

Sunday, June 9 John & Joseph Broyles & families come. We go to hear Girard preach at Brich Sch. H. I preach in aft. from Deut. 18:18. All stay at Uncle William's. (This was at Reeder's School-house.)

Monday, June 10 Rainy forenoon. Settle accts. with Uncle William. Wm. & Robert take us to Jonesboro in Aftern. through the rain. Wait at depot for 1:08 night train.

Tuesday, June 11 Reach Chicago about 8:00 morn'g.

Expressman's trick. See B. Wilson of Holden Chapel; also Bro. Kellog of Cynosure. Take family in a barough to see city. Get no reduction of fare. Go on. Dine at Dixon. Arrive at Cedar Rapids about 8:00. Stay at Grand Hotel.

Wednesday, June 12 Get removed into our new house—rented. Spend day in fixing up things. (It was the Adam's house at the border of Bohemia town, an old brick dwelling.)

Thursday, June 13 See John Drury & Summer Buchwalter.

Saturday, June 15 In aft. get a horse and take Susan out riding. Then with boys to Derry Dale. Pass Keith not knowing him.

Sunday, June 16 I.L. Buchwalter pr. 10 1/2 Rev. "Blessed the deed." Dines with us. I preach at 8:00 Isa. 12 chapt. Buchwalter stays with us.

Monday, June 17 M.S. Drury calls. See M. Bowman & Sutton.

Tuesday, June 18 Neidig's call. Sutton with them.

Thursday, June 20 A.J. Neidig & Millie J. Apt married at our house about 2:00 Aftn.

Friday, June 21 Up town, see Rock River Brethren. Griman goes home & dines with us.

Saturday, June 22 Go in afternoon to Western with Reuchlin. Sup at Buchwalter's. Hear Addresses of literary societies. Excellent. Stay at Rev. M.S. Drury's.

Sunday, June 23 Hear Pres. Kephart preach the baccalaureate. Dine at Ranson Davis'. Go in I.L. Buchwalter's buggy to Ced. Rapids. Preach 8:00.

Monday, June 24 Return to Western in afternoon. Supper at Buchwalter's. At Alumni anniversary at 8:00. Miss Hopwood & C.J. Kephart speak. Stay at Rev. M. Bowman's.

Tuesday, June 25 At Board meetings. Sup at Father Perry's. I miss transp-train by post-ponement. Hear Wood's lecutre. Much balderdash. Go with Hurliss & others home.

Wednesday, June 26 Get Telescopes of present and prece[e]ding weeks. Start after 3 hours sleep for Minnesota. Sleep in cars 3 hours.

Thursday, June 27 Reach Albert Lea at 8:00, Morning. Go on at 3:00 to Wells & Mapleton. Rev. Jas Wynn & Mr. Childs meet me. Preach at 8:00 Ps 1:6. Stay at Bro. Childs.

Friday, June 28 Bro. J.M. Tresenriter preached at 11:00. Gen. Supt of Free Meth preaches in Aftn, Hall. "Endured as seeing him—invisible." Heb. 11.27.

Monday, July 1 Come home arriving at 6:30.

Tuesday, July 2 Start for Atchison Co., Kansas. Fail of connection at Columbus Junction and return home about Midnight. C.J. Kephart called with his wife a few minutes. She was a Perry.

Thursday, July 4 Start West Iowa River bottoms low. Indian Reserve. Dine at Boone. Boyer River Valley. Stay at Rev. C.B. Davis' at Council Bluffs.

Friday, July 5 Go over to Omaha and on to Fairmount, Nebr. Elder S. Austin & Rev. Elvin F. Austen meet me. Go on to S. Austin's. Stay there in a sod house.

Saturday, July 6 Dined at Rev. E.F. Austin's. Went on to Pursel's Church. Father Pitt pr. at 3:30 from Matt 7:24,25, "House upon a rock." Supper at M. Osterhoudts. Pr. 8:30 I Cor. 1:23.24. Stay at Overhoudt's. [both spellings appear in text]

Sunday, July 7 Preach at 11 from Ps 48:11-13. Dine at Bro Purcel's. She afflicted with inflam. rheumatism. Rev. E.W. Johnson pr. afternoon. Return to S. Austin's.

Monday, July 8 Rev. E.F. Austin & family visit us at S's. Prevented going to railroad by a sudden rain & wind storm. Stay at E.F.Austin's.

Tuesday, July 9 Uncle Simeon's visit us. After dinner, I

go to Fairmount. See Rev. Curtis. Trunk checked, but not put aboard. Go on—Stay at Kearney City with David Webbert's.

Wednesday, July 10 Visit with Webbert's waiting on my trunk. View the city from Windmill platform. Cars on B&M R.R. & Union Pacific stopped by washouts.

Thursday, July 11 Train from Omaha arrives at 6:10 afternoon. I go on to Cheyenne. See some jack-rabbits hopping along.

Friday, July 12 Arrive at Cheyenne at 7:00 morn. Put up at "International Hotel." Write letters. Start at 2:00 for Ralston. Walk across & meet Bro L.S. Cornell. Sup at Bro Morrison's. Stay at Sister McChristian's. Trunk went on to Golden City.

Saturday, July 13 Conference proce[e]des. Dine at McChristian's. Preach in evening Numbers 10:29. Evening session. Stay. Stationing Com. & Finance McChristian's.

Sunday, July 14 Preach at 11 from Heb. 4:14. Dine at M. Morrison's. Pr. at 4:00 John 14:2,3. Sup & stay at Richard's. L.S. Cornell & Mary Ross stay there, also.

Monday, July 15 Call at Herod's & Morrison. Went with Rev. W.H. McCormick to Jonas Heavner's & dined. Went on to Abr. Hartzell's on the mountains height. Lodge. Bro. Morrison comes with invitation for R.R. trip. Chimney Canyon. 8000 feet high. I lodge at Rev. A. Hartzell's.

Tuesday, July 16 Went early to Golden City. Go with Bro Mc. & Prof. M. Moss to Georgetown; to Central City. Dine at Barton House. Stay at Teller House. Wind zigzag up to Central. Saw Senator H.M. Teller on the train & congressman.

Wednesday, July 17 Go to Bob Tail (Goldbearing) quartz mine. Take cars at Black-Hawk for Denver. Dine at St. Cl. Ross' 655 Larimer St. Sup at H.R. Miller's, 727 Larimer St. Pr at 8:00 S.M.E. Church Rom 3:5.

Thursday, July 18 Go about town. Dine at Aunt Ellen Mape's. Buy some stones at a store $3.25. Call on sick.

Sup at H.R. Miller's. Preach at 8:00 I King 18:21. Stay at Miller's. Mary Ross gives me geological specimens.

Friday, July 19 Go on to Boulder. Stop at Rev. L.S. Cornell's. See Judge North; editor of paper Dr. Williams & wife. There latter sup with us. Stay at Cornell's. Cora, William & other children.

Saturday, July 20 Go on to Loveland. Rev. E.J. Lamb & wife take me to Geo. Leitle's. Was at Burial of D. Hershman's wife. Attended prayer meeting at the new Church. Rains. Stay at Geo Litle's. [name spelled two different ways in text]

Sunday, July 21 Go to Archibald Litle's to see about his subscribing. Preach 11:00, II Cor 3:7. Raise $505.00 subscrip. Dine at Monroe's. Short prayer meeting there. Come back to Geo. Litle's. Preach 8:00 Deut 18:18. Stay A. Rist's.

Monday, July 22 Call at D. Hershman's & at Archibald Litle's. Go from Geo. L's to Station. Start for home at 10:00. Dine at Inter-Ocean at Cheyenne. Start at 3:00 for Omaha.

Tuesday, July 23 Breakfast at Gr. Island. $1.00 for it. Reach Omaha about 4:00 P.M. Go on to Council Bluffs. Sup on Dunlap. Got acquainted. Rcv. Mr. Jones M.E. Wisconsin, who transfers to Neb.

Wednesday, July 24 Reach home at 6:00 morning. Spend day at home. Read. A nap or two. Boys out fishing.

Thursday, July 25 Spend day at home. Wald to Post-offices & drug store in the evening. Send some postals.

Friday, July 26 Friday—at home all day. Write article for Botchafter on trip up Clear Creek Can[y]on. Boys fail in fishing.

Saturday, July 27 Go to P.O. & store. Go to Lisbon in aft. Stop at D. Runkle's. Call at several stores & at Rev. L.D. Adams'. Stay at D. Runkle's with Susan, Orville & Katie.

Sunday, July 28 Preach 10 1/2 Deut 18:18. Dine at T.D. Adams'. Class in aft. 2 1/2. Sup at Rev. Wm. Davis'. See the Davis' A.M. & Neidig's. Preach at 8:00, Luke 16:31. Stay at Rev. D. Runkle's.

Monday, July 29 Come home on 6:00 M. train. Spend day in writing.

Tuesday, July 30 Spend day in study and writing. W.B. Smith visits me. Our talk on Church. Estimate of subscription to be raised. We figured up at 1200 dollars, including Weston and Lisbon.

Wednesday, July 31 Spend day in study mostly in revising plans of sermons and getting up new ones—mostly the latter. Go in the evening to go with Smith to prayermeeting; but he gone.

Thursday, August 1 Spend forenoon in Study of Sermons.

Sunday, August 4 Preach at 11 2 Tim. 4:1-2. Preach at Dairy Dale on Ps "Great things on us," etc. Preach at May Island Ced. Rap. at 8:00 Ps 1:6.

Monday, August 5 Start at 6:00 for Col. Junc. Meet Bowman & Sutton. Reach Junction & Go on Southern Branch of Rock Is. & Pac. R.R. toward Atchison. Sleep tolerably well.

Tuesday, August 6 Pass Galatin Junction & reach Atchison about 11:00 A.M. Hired a horse at 3 (2.50) and go on to Wilkison's land. Terribly warm. See land about 7:00. Return to Brown's about 4 miles east. Lodge.

Wednesday, August 7 Start before breakfast. Rreach Atchison in time. Examine title & find two more guages & tax title of over $120.00. Go on to Topeka and Lecompton. Stop at H.D. Harris. Meredith preaches.

Thursday, August 8 Conference in session, at old college building. Room very small.

Friday, August 9 Conf. as usual. Sup at Dr. Bonebreak's, I believe.

Saturday, August 10 Sessions as usual. Dine at Brown's. Effort to divide the conference, into Kansas & West Kansas.

Sunday, August 11 Preach at 11: from 2 Tim. 4:1. Dine at Levi Lippy's. Sab. Sch. An. at 3 1/2 o'clock. J.K. Billheimer Lectures at night.

Monday, August 12 Conference in session till late at night. Divide before separation. Both Conferences to meet in joint session at Clifton, Washington Co., Kans., next year.

Tuesday, August 13 Go on to Lawrence with Willie Shuck, in the spring wagon. Just in time for train. Sup at Chanute. Reach Parsons at 11:00. Stay at A. Carey's.

Wednesday, August 14 Committees meet. H.B. Potter comes. (Accused of murder) I take some of the chart reports down. Rev. J. Riley preached at 8:00; he is of this conference. Potter brazon. [sic]

Thursday, August 15 Conf. opened at 9:00. Shockley was referred to the Com. on grievances; J.R. Evans also.

Friday, August 16 Conference continued. Prof. D. Shuck lectured on Education, or preached.

Saturday, August 17 Conference closes at 9:00. A pleasant session. J.R. Billheimer lectured at Cong. Church at 8:00.

Sunday, August 18 Preach at Cong. Church 11 from Heb. 7:26. Ordain Joel R. Chambers. Blessed occasion. Geo. W. Keller dines with me at Carey's. S.S. An. 4:00. Rev. K. Billheimer lectures at 8:00.

Monday, August 19 Go on train to Cherokee. Miss connection. Reach Ft. Scott at 10:00. Sleep at Hotel some till 3:00. Start at 3:30 on Cas. tr. for Kansas City.

Tuesday, August 20 Reach Kansas City at 8:30. Go on to St. Joseph 10:30. Reach there at 2:00. Put up at Pacif. House. Get a draft of First Nat. Bank for Fourth Nat. Bank N.Y. Spend time in writing.

Wednesday, August 21 Leave St. Jo. at 9:40. Find the Miss Dudleys & other Indiana Friends on cars. Bro. Billheimer had also staid at Bacon House St. Jo. Reach Fairbury at 7:30. Conference at work. Stop at T.R. Freeman's. Board there during the session.

Orville Wright in 1878 (8 years old on August 19)

Katharine Wright, b. August 19, 1874, 4 years old in this photograph

Thursday, August 22 Conference in session. Byron Beall preached at night from "Endued with power." It was his graduation address. It went off well.

Friday, August 23 Conference as usual. Dine at I.N. Bleknap's. J.K. Billheimer lectured at night.

Sunday, August 25 Preach at 11, from John 5:18th. Dine at I.N. Belknaps. Bro. Billheimer lectured at night.

Monday, August 26 Go on with Kenoyer & Fye to Rev. W.P. Caldwell's. Billheimer lectures at Caldwell's Sch. House. Few out. We stay at Caldwell's.

Tuesday, August 27 Go on to Crete with Dr. J.A. Kenaston. Stop at Bro. A. Shedar's. I very much wearied. B. lectures at Sch. House at night. I write a letter and go to bed.

Wednesday, August 28 Went on to Omaha and Missouri Valley Junction. Stay at Commerical House Second Class price.

Thursday, August 29 Go to Sioux City. Dine at R.R. Depot. Go on at 2:30 to Merrill 10 ms. distant. Rev. J. Brown takes us on to Bro. James Stinton's. Bro. Rust preaches at Pleasant Valley Church at 8:00.

Friday, August 30 Conference opens. Examination proceeds. Effort to arrest McVay's Char. Applicants. Weed not referred. Gallip not pronounced eligible. B. lectures on Africa at 8:00. I stay at house alone & go to bed early.

Saturday, August 31 Session Closed at 5:30 P.M. McVey tries to dissent from chair. Sta. Com. Prepare report before afternoon. D.M. Harvey P.E. Howard preaches at night. I stay at home alone to do some writing.

Sunday, September 1 Pr. at 11:00, Isa 9:6—Ordain Abram N. King. Dine at Andy Wilson's S.S. Anni. at 3 1/2 Read Stationing Com. Report. Billheimer lectures at 8:00. We go east to Wm. Stinton's & stay. Our hostess said Bro. Chase got on his 'i 'orse on a certain occasion.

Monday, September 2 Go to Merrill. On to Cedar Falls. Transfer. On to Cedar Rapids. Ar[r]ive at 4:35 morning. Find all well. W.S. Smith & wife visit us in the evening.

Wednesday, September 4 Rev. I.L. Buchwalter & D.P. Rathbun dine with us. Spend afternoon mostly in trading at stores. After a little sleep, start to Albert Lea, at 12:35.

Thursday, September 5 Reach Albert Lea about 7:00. Dine at Railroad house. Write letters. Go on to Winnebago, starting at 3:00. Arrive about 6:00. Go on to Bro. Lathrop's and to Church. Stay at Joseph H. Robinson's. Phillips preaches.

Friday, September 6 Conference opens at 9:00. Examination begins in the afternoon. Phillips & Tibbotts do not like the secrecy law. Billheimer lectures at 8:00. Does well. Stay at our house that night after the lecture.

Saturday, September 7 Business as usual. Kennerer, Tibbitts, & Phillips ask letters of dismissal. A time. Withdraw requests after evening session had progressed. Adjourn about midnight. Kennerer said I had dealt right, and they would obey the law.

Sunday, September 8 Preach at 11:00, 2 Tim 2:15. Dine at home. Sabbath afternoon, have a S.S. Anniversary & communion. Stationing Com. hold short session. B. lectures at night. Short informal session of Conf. Phillips granted a letter of dismission.

Monday, September 9 Go at day-break to Winnebago and on to Albert Lea. Talk with Tibbetts on supplying the Filmore Mission. Phillips very kind & tender. Go on at 12:00 toward Ced. Rapids. Arrive at 6:30.

Tuesday, September 10 Spend the day in writing, trading, etc. buying the boys suits & myself a hat.

Thursday, September 12 Go on Western Union R.R. via Sabula & Savanna to Milwaukee. Arrive a little before 7:00 P.M. Go on at 12:30 at night to Waldo arriving at 3:40. Stay at nearest hotel. Stay two or three hours.

Friday, September 13 Bro. Miles Akin takes us over to Cascade. Home at Wm. Akin's. Conference session progresses. Rev. C.J. Stark preaches at night.

Saturday, September 14 Conference session. Upton is elected P. Elder. In afternoon, election was reconsidered and N.G. Whitney elected presiding elder. Bro. J.K. Billheimer lectured at night. A very short session held just after. Adjourned.

Sunday, September 15 Preach at 11: from Heb. 11:26. Dine at Bro. Webb's. S.S. Anniversary in afternoon. B. Lectures at night. Stay at Akin's.

Monday, September 16 Stay at Bro. Akin's. Bro. Whitney pr. at night. Stay at Br. Aikin's. [name spelled two different ways in text]

Tuesday, September 17 Go on via Milwaukee to Lima, Wisconsin, arriving at 4:00. Sup at Rev. H. Mabbot's. Find a home at Dr. R. Henry Stetson's.

Wednesday, September 18 About town. Several ministers come in. I Preach at 8:00 John 14:2.

Thursday, September 19 Conference begins.

Sunday, September 22 I Preach at 11 from 2 Tim. 2:15. Dine at [rest is blank]

Monday, September 23 Go over to [blank] Johsnon's effort to get subscription from our host. He rough. She wife of Rev. J.J. Vaughn formerly. Sup at G.M. Mabbot's. Johnson preaches. Lent E. Bovee $25.00, which he returned some months later.

Tuesday, September 24 Went to Janesville with Father Mabbott. Dined with Rev. Jas. Johnson's at Samuel Holdridge's, his brotherinlaw. Went on to Chicago & Joliet. Stay at the Masion House in Joliet.

Wednesday, September 25 Go on to H. Kassabaum's. Considerable rain. W.H. Post preached at night.

Thursday, September 26 Conference opened. Business proceeds, Rev. Lewis pr. at 7:00.

Friday, September 27 Conference as usual. I preach at 7:00, I Tim. 3:16.

Saturday, September 28 Elections. Sister A.L. Billheimer comes. Long discussion in afternoon on the reports. Stationing Committee. Evening Session. P.E.'s Stationing Committee.

Sunday, September 29 Preach at 11 from Heb. 4:14. Ordain Dessinger, Darr, McKinley. Sabbath School anniversary in Afternoon. Mis. meeting at night. Billheimer & Wife speak. Raise a subs. of $220.00

Monday, September 30 Start early to Joliet. Go on to Chicago. Connection too close for Chi & N.W. Dine at Brevourt House. Called Cynosure. Go to Exposition. Sup at E.A. Cook's. Start home.

Tuesday, October 1 Arrive at Cedar Rapids about 7:00. At home during the day. Trains changed: so I miss starting to Missouri Conference.

Wednesday, October 2 Start at 4:20 for Missouri. Arrive at Col. Junction at 7:30. Go on to Fairfield arriving before 1:00. Dine at Legget House. Train behind time 1 1/2 hours. Reach Chariton 3:30. Put up at Railroad Hotel.

Thursday, October 3 Arose about 9:00 A.M. Breakf. at 10:00. Start at 1:00 for Leon. John Ponsh takes me to Bethel Church. Arrive about 7:30. Stay at S. Deputy's, my home.

Friday, October 4 Conference engaged in Examinations. *See Jac. Wagner & wife. E.S. Neff & wife & Isaac Neff. Dine & stay at Deputy's. J.T. Allaman preached. *Old acquaintance in Ind.

Saturday, October 5 Busy session. Several ballots for third P.E. Nice session at 7:00 of Stn. Com. Prof. C. Kephart spiaks on education. Short night session continued. Stay at Deputy's.

Sunday, October 6 Pr. 11:00 from II Tim 4:2. Dine at W.T. Haroff's. Prof. Kephart pr. tonight from Math. Raise $245.00 toward Avalon [unreadable]

Monday, October 7 Went with Bro. Moore to Leon. Went on to Chariton. Staid at Railroad House.

Tuesday, October 8 Went to Bates House. Dined. Went on with a Mr. Shaffer to Rev. H.A. Long's, six miles south. Went 1/2 mile East and staid at Thos. Vandever's.

Wednesday, October 9 Went back to Bro. Long's & dined. Went on to S. Fry's. Shiflett prea 7:00. Stay at Samuel Fry's, my home.

Thursday, October 10 Conference session. Dine & lodge at Fry's. Rained at night So we did not go to meeting. Swain was there, at Fry's.

Friday, October 11 Conference continued. I Dine at Rue's. Supper & lodge at Burton's. He was a Congregationalist.

Saturday, October 12 Stationing Com. at Goodell's. Dine at Goodell's. Session closed, 5:30. Mrs. A.L. Billheimer lectured. Stay at Fry's.

Sunday, October 13 I Preach at 11:00 from II Tim. 3:15. Dine at [blank] Sab. Sch. meeting in afternoon. Remain at church till evening meeting. I stay at Fry's.

Monday, October 14 Go via Corydon ato Allerton and start to Col. Junction at 11:00. Sup at Star House at Colum. Junction. Go on home. Arri. at Cedar Rap's at 12:20.

Tuesday, October 15 About home. Attend to a little business.

Wednesday, October 16 Go on early train to West Liberty & thence toEarlham. See several preachers on the train. Go on to Eli Cronk's. J. Surface pr. at 7:00 S.D. Snyder prays saying, "We see the friendly face of our bishop in the back part of the congregation."

Thursday, October 17 Conference begins. C.W. Miller pr. at 7:00, Eve.

Saturday, October 19 Session progresses. Long contest on the election, in the afternoon, or P.E. Night session. Stationing Committe sits till after midnight.

Sunday, October 20 I preach at 11:00 from I Tim. 4:16. Sab. Sch. anniversary in afternoon. Sister A.L. Billheimer speaks. Br. Billheimer lectured at night.

Monday, October 21 Go to Earlham & thence to West Liberty. Home on Midnight train.

Tuesday, October 22 Spend the day at home. J.K. Billheimer & Fred. calls on me. He shows me Shuey's tract.

Wednesday, October 23 Go on early train to Lisbon. I feel quite worn & unwell. Have home at D. Runkle's. Rev. G. Miller preached at 7:00.

Thursday, October 24 Conference continued. I dined at Rev. T.D. Adams'. Rev. C.W. Miller pr. 7:00, Eve.

Friday, October 25 Conference still. Dine at Bro. Hess'. Go to Bovey's for supper. Sister A.L. Billheimer lectured & organizes a Br. Society of W.M.A.

Saturday, October 26 Conference. Election of Elders on first ballot. Stationing Commit. meets at Amos Runkle's at 71/2 o'clo. Night session.

Sunday, October 27 I preach at 10 1/2 from Eph. 3:8. col of $71.00. Dined at Venerable Wm. Davis'. S. Sch. anniversary in afternoon. Rev. Billheimer lectured in the evening.

Monday, October 28 I come home at 1:00 P.M. Our pastor Rev. M.R. Drury & I hunt for houses to rent. Loan Morgan S. Drury $25.00 (which he paid.) Bro. D. stays with us.

Tuesday, October 29 Spend aftern-day in looking for houses. M.R.D. goes home on 8:10 PM train.

Wednesday, October 30 Rent House for Drury of Dudley.

Thursday, October 31 Dudley informs me that his agent Powell had previously rented that house unbeknown to Dudley.

Friday, November 1 Mrs. Epley calls to see about house-renting. Go to Epley's in the evening.

Saturday, November 2 Epley & I agree on renting his house for $270.00 for a year beginning with Nov. 1st. To draw writings & complete terms Monday.

Sunday, November 3 Went to hear Rev. Hood at 2d Pres. Church. At S. Sch. at 3:00 at Gr. Hotel. Saw Bourne. Hear Rev. Mr. Bennett pr. at M.E. Church 7:30. Orville took Diphtheria just afternoon.

Monday, November 4 Called at Epley's after being garnished by Parkhurst, Esq. Considerable trouble to find out what the law was in such contracts.

Tuesday, November 5 Saw Bowen on Contract. Opinion that nothing binding on either. Rev. M.R. Drury & family arrive at 8:00, eve. Stay at Grand Hotel.

Wednesday, November 6 Orville continues very sick. Bro. Drury rents the Lutz property at Corner of Franklin Avenue & Jackson Street. I finally abandon all idea of renting of Epley.

Thursday, November 7 Orville still sick but seems not specially dangerous till in the night. Help Drury get goods in the House. Orville has sinking spells and appears to be nearly gone. M.R. Drury stays.

Friday, November 8 Orville some better, but feeble.

Saturday, November 9 Orville much improved. Lorin gets up with fever—has diphtheria. He had nervous spells in latter part of the night.

Sunday, November 10 At home. Dr. calls at 11:00. Drury calls at 2:00. Orville very lively. Lorin seems considerably better. Day cloudy & some rain.

Monday, November 11 –Saturday, November 16 All as usual, only improving.—Reuchlin took sick with diphtheria.—All impriv. but Reuchlin.—Reuchlin is better.—R. still improving.

Sunday, November 17 Hear Dr. Buckhalter pr. at 1st Pres. Church. Sabbath School at the Grand Hotel. Hear Drury at night.

Monday, November 18 Engage in preparing an address to read at Wheaton. Called at M.R. Drury's. They starting to his fatherinlaw's.

Tuesday, November 19 Continue the preparation of address. Lent M.R. Drury $10.00. (This he afterward paid.)

Wednesday, November 20 Start early to Wheaton, Ill. Arrive about 3:00. Go to President J. Blanchard's. Convention called to order, & have addresses. Hurless, Ames, & Barlow.

Thursday, November 21 Convention continued. My address, I read, in the evening.

Friday, November 22 Convention continued. I dine at Dr. Hiatt's. I go to Naperville & take cars to Earl. I go on to Mendota & stay at Chandler's, Rev. W.H. Chandler's.

Saturday, November 23 Go to Earlville. Bro E. Thompson of Harding takes me to his house for dinner. Preach at Indian Creek at 3:00 on Golden Bells. Medler pr. at night.

Sunday, November 24 Preached, 11:00 from I John 5:18,19. Dined at Ellering's. Raised $348 & dedicated the church. E.W. Harsh preached at 7:00 from Isa. 9.6,7. Stay at Rev. S.F. Medler's.

Monday, November 25 Went on to Earlville, Le Sell Co., & thence to Mendota. F. Reibel came. Preach at 7:00 from John 1:46. Start at 11:12 for Dixon, thence to Ced. Rapids. Arrive at home about 7:00.

Tuesday, November 26 Arrive at 7:00. Stay at Home, except a little business in town.

Wednesday, November 27 Trade some at stores. Write letters to several. Attend our prayer-meeting at Post-office room.

Thursday, November 28 Attended service at Baptist Church where Rev. Mr. Hood preached at 10 1/2. Bro. M.R. Drury and family dined with us.

Friday, November 29 Look at house near Mr. West, Esq. Lorin goes after Reuchlin to Weston. I go i evening to Derry Dale with Drury to prayer-meeting.

Saturday, November 30 Call at 11 on Mr. Dore's at Bradley's to conslt on renting for church purposes. Start

at 2:35 for Moline. Met by Rev. France & wife at Depot. Stay at Parsonage.

Sunday, December 1 Preach at Moline, from Luke 15:7 in Morn. Go out at 3:00 to Coaltown Sch. house. Preach in evening at Moline from Rom. 2:5. Stay at parsonage.

Monday, December 2 A drive with P.M. France to Rock Island arsenal. Went through some of the public buildings. Drive up Mississippi & to Cemetery. Pr. at 7:00, John 14:2,3. Two forward for prayers. Called aft. Mother Jones.

Tuesday, December 3 Go to Adams Fries to dinner. Call in afternoon at Mother Heck's. Wm. Heck's & Bro. Pargonage's. Pr. at 7:00 Ps 85:6.

Wednesday, December 4 Visited Wagon factory, plow factory & called on Mother Wear. Supped at Robinson's. Preached 7:00 Ez. 33:11. Three forward & two others arose for prayer.

Thursday, December 5 Start early. Write at West Liberty. Arrive at home at 1:00. Fix up & go to town. See Epley & West on renting. Scott of Nebraska came.

Friday, December 6 Rent Epley's House & remove. Business meeting at Drury's.

Saturday, December 7 Got up stove & buy coat. Start at 2:20 to Muscatine. Sup at Nichols (town) and at Baker's. Stay at Rev. R.E. Williams'.

Sunday, December 8 Preach at 10 1/2 I John 5:18. Dine at Aments. Sabbath School afternoon. I Preach at night from I pet. 4:18. Sup & lodge at Williams'.

Monday, December 9 Dine at Father Hershey's. Ministerial meeting at 2:00. Rev. Murphy M.E. & Rev. Richards, Baptist, present. Preach at 7:00 Eph. 2:4. Lodge at Williams.

Tuesday, December 10 Call at Hetzler's. Bro Williams preaches at night. Staid at Bakers.

Wednesday, December 11 Dined at Baker's with Bro & sister Williams, Bro & Sister Isaac Neidig, Bro & Sister

Hershey. Preach at night from Ez. 33:11. Stay at Baker's. Chris. Neidig & wife & Son come.

Thursday, December 12 Dine at Baker's with Chris. Neidig's. Preach at night Acts 26:28. Stay at Parsonage.

Friday, December 13 Start at 7:00 via Wilton home. Arrive at 1:00. Quite unwell from disordered stomach & bowels.

Saturday, December 14 Still unwell. Stay at home & do little.

Sunday, December 15 Went out to Dairy Dale & pr 10 1/2 I John 5:18,19. Return for dinner.

Monday, December 16 At home. Spend part afternoon in trading at Stores. Go out to Dairy Dale. Preach 7:00 from I Ps. 6. Return home. Miss Greenlee of Toledo stays with us.

Tuesday, December 17 Br. M.S. Drury dines with us & M.R. & Miss Greenlee. Spend afternoon in writing & the evening. Letters to all the Kansas, Osage, Nebraska, & Dakota Con.

Wednesday, December 18 I Start at 2:15 for Kansas. Stop 4 hours at Col. Junction. Go on [blank] train for Leavensworth [sic] which is 2 hours behind time. Slept 5 or 6 hours on the train.

Thursday, December 19 Breakfasted at Cameron Junction. Hurried off & Leave bill partly to be settled by mail. Reach Leavenworth at 11:00 Lawrence about 1:00. Dine at Place House. Reach Lecompton at 4:00. Go to Rev. J.R. Thers'. Sup at Rsa. Lohill. Pr. Eph. 3:11th. Stay at Lippy's.

Friday, December 20 Go to Lawrence with Rev. H.D. Herr, in spring wagon. Dine at Place House. Go on to Ottawa. University students are aboard. Rev. E. Keezel meets me & takes me to his house, 1 1/2 ms. East.

Saturday, December 21 I go with Father Keezel to Jacob Fisher's at Peoria. R.Loggan comes in the afternoon. I preach at 7:00, Ps. 1:6. I lodge at Bro. Fisher's. Bro. Loggan had been holding meeting there.

Sunday, December 22 Preach at 11:00 from Heb 11.10. Congregation not very full. We raise $398.35 & dedicate Peoria Church. I dine at Fisher's. Preach at 7:00 Ez. 33:11. I stay at Fisher's.

Monday, December 23 I spent day at Fisher's. Bro. David Kerns (near Baldwin City) came. I preach at night from I Pet. 4:18. I stay at Fisher's.

Tuesday, December 24 Bro. Loggan & I go with David Kerns to Bro. K's home. Snow & snow-drifts very bad. We go to Black Jack Church & I pr. at 7:00 Ex. 28.34. Stay at Joseph Hughes', near Wellsville with Bro. Loggan.

Wednesday, December 25 I take train at 2:00, at Wellsville & reach Kan. City about sunset. I go on to Council Bluffs, starting at 10:30, at night.

Thursday, December 26 Arrive at Council Bluffs at 8:00. Breakfast & go to post-office. Am very unwell from about 10:00 a.m. Rev. L.G. Boufkin comes at night. I was at Rev. G.W. Rose's.

Friday, December 27 Start home on Chi. & N.W. Have only 7 cents after buying ticket. Arrive at 9:15. Aftn. Prof. Brookwalter comes with me from Marshaltown & stays at our house.

Saturday, December 28 Stay at home. Somewhat feverish in the afternoon. My disease proves to be diphtheria!

Sunday, December 29 Stay at home all day. Still somewhat feverish. Reuchlin & Orville attend the evening meeting at Room 13, post-office Building at 4:00. Smith preaches.

Monday, December 30 Still rather feverish & feable. M.R. Drury calls. Also Rev. I.K. Statton.

Tuesday, December 31 Some better. Write letters to J.F. Roberts, A.W. Drury and D.S. Henninger. A patent swing man calls, but sells not. This closes a year the first month of which was spent in successful protracted meetings; part of the next three in ill-health caused by severe cold. Moved to Cedar Rapids, Iowa in June. Went to Colorado in July. Severe labors on dist. for about three

Milton W. Wright in 1878, age "nearly 44"

months. Children had diphtheria. Dedications & protracted meetings follow. A good year in all, Bless the Lord.

Memoranda

Some one says that "Oldest choral melody, the book of Job, so like the summer midnight with its seas and stars." Commit "While the King sitteth at his table his spikenard sendeth forth the smell thereof." Song of Sol. 1.12v

1. Visited Browns at Crawfordsville 29 Jan. 1878.
2. Saw Wesley an[d] McFall, Feb. 17
3. Hayes lying letters, Mar. 14
4. Visit Bishop Kumler, Apr. 20
5. Weaver sick on Tobacco May 12
6. Eliza Culberlson's visit, May 18
7. Preach at Wm. Hudleston, May 2
8. Start with family, June 10
9. Neidig & Millie Apt. June 20
10. Saw Sup. Hall June 28
11. Stay in sod house July 5
12. Georgetown Central City, July 16
14. [skips 13] Land Brown Co. Kans., Aug 6
15. Billheimer, Aug. 17
16. Minnesota Fly round Sept. 8
17. Saw Neffs & Wagner, Oct. 4
18. I dine at Wm. Davis. Oct. 27
19. Garnitured Nov. 4
20. Orville nearly died Nov. 7
21. Address at Weaton, Nov. 21
22. Rent Ehley's house.

Texts Preached by Me at Dayton First Church from 1869–77.
3. What wilt thou say when he shall thee perish, Jer. 13.21
(Some not able to decipher the record) [His words]
6. Lamb of God that taketh away sin
7. Esteeming the Reproach of Christ greater riches etc. Jno. 1:29.
(Several not recorded)
Heb. 7:26 was last for many years. Hebr. For such a high-priest became us, who is holy, harmless, etc.

Texts preached Miami Chapel
From A.D. 1869-1876. "Revive thy work O Lord," Ps. 85.6 Bright & Morning star. Rev. 21.16. Reproach of Christ, Heb. 11.26. (Several undecipherable in rec) "When he shall punish," Jer. 13.21.

Miami City
1. Lamb of God, John 1.29
2. Halting between tow opin, I Ki. 18.21.
3. Righteous scarcely saved, I Pet. 4.18
4. Almost persuaded, Acts 26.22.
6. [5 was skipped] Call his name Jesus, etc. Matt. 1.21
7. Luke 15:7 "Joy in heaven."
8. Luke 23:4 "I find no fault"
(Many others) Heb 7:26, Jude 14 verse, I John v.18-19, John 16:27.

Rev. G. Fritz's sister said as she was dying: "Oh, I am so glad!" His daughter said on her death bed: "If I am not here to-morrow, I will be in heaven!"

F.A. Myers, Gen. Tkt agt. Pitt. Ft. Wayne & Chicago railroad, promises half-fare trip tickets.

1879

January 1 This is the fifty-first New Year Day that I have seen, my birth occurring Nov. 17, 1828. I was very sick with fever in the years & 1834 & 1857 (Panama fever on my way to Oregon) & 1865—typhoid. But I never suffered much pain in all those fifty years past, for which I am thankful to God. I was converted in June A.D. 1843; joined the United Brethren Church in April, 1847, preached my first sermon the evening of my 22nd birth-day anniversary Nov. 17, 1850; received into White River Conf. Aug. 1858; Appointed to Indianapolis Mission Station Aug. 1855; Ordained Aug. 1856. Went to Oregon July, 1857; Returned Nov. 1859; married Nov. 24, 1859; elected presiding elder Aug. 1861; Elected Prof. of Theology at Hartsville Aug. 1868; elected editor of the *Telescope* May 29, 1869; bishop 1877 in May. This day is quite cold. Attended quarterly conference in the afternoon at Dairy Dale.

January 2 Rev. I.K. Statton with us to dinner. Thermometer down full 20 degrees below zero. Wrote to Ch & R.I. & to C.B. & Q.R.R. for half-fare permits. Get *Telescope* & *Cynosure.*

January 3 Go down town. Get half-fare permit on B.C. & N.R. R.R. Go to Ely G.W. Statton meets me and takes me in his buggy to his house in Western, where I eat supper. He then takes me to Shueyville where I preach from Acts 26.28. Miss Ida Anderson comes out as a seeker. Mrs. Graham & other deeply affected. I stay at George Anderson's of Old Virginia. Find comfortable lodgings & thankful. Ther. morning 20 degrees-zero. At noon 1 degree below.

January 4 In afternoon hold quarterly conference.

Elected me presiding-elder *pro tem.* J.G. Bowersox, Geo. Anderson, John Kephart, Crowl, Williams, Father Henry Kephart, Geo. W. Statton etc. present. Assess $4.00 for the preacher. Preach at 6:30 from I Tim. 2:4. One forward. Stay at Anderson's. Supped at Father Kephart's. Miss Williams, sister of Prof. there.

January 5 Sabbath. Preach at 10:30 from Ex 28.34. Communion follows. Many from Western present. Dine at Father Kephart's. Pres. E.B. Kephart also there & Young Albert & Jeffries, his nephews. Preach at night from Jude 14. Many from Western there. Not a successful effort. Stay at Anderson's.

January 6 Pres. Dean calls. Dine at Bowersox's. Two of his daughters, and one son there. Prayer meeting at 1:30 at (Henry) Father Kephart's. Present: Father Frazee, Crowl & Anderson and wives, Stausfield, Mrs. Wlaters, John Kephart's wife, Statton. Good meeting. Sup at Crowl's. Rev. I.B. Betty preaches at 6:30. One rises for prayer, after I exhorted. Stay at Anderson's after a call at Prof. Williams' fathers.

January 7 Tuesday. Came home to C. Rapids with Father Kephart's. They call at Jeffries for Ida who goes along. Marion R. Drury calls at street, to leave lesson-leaves. Report a number of seekers. Said that Sutton would preach for him that evening. Write some letters.

January 8 Spend day in writing. Mrs. Knox & younger lady call to see if they would rent rooms for lodgers. They were unsuccessful.

January 10 Friday. Saw I.K. Statton about 2 o'clock &

paid him $10.25. Rev. Fusha, of West Des Moines came up from Depot & staid till 8:15 train westward. Lives 18 miles from State Centre. Told of Rose & Winebrenarians. Thanked God for Good the Churches had done. Winebrenarian said, "Thank the Devil."

January 11 Saturday. Not very well. Did but little. Wrote a few letters. Made out in the afternoon. Adams' Settels acct's—a list for Dillon.

January 12 Sunday. Go to Church in the morning. Rev. Marion R. Drury, the pastor, preaches. Sab. School. I preach at night from Ex. 28:34. Good congregation for the place (Rom. 10.13 Post-office Block.) Introduced to Richard's of Grocery on Eagle between Washington & Commercial Streets.

January 13 Monday. The night has a Sab. School present time. Reuchlin, Wilbur, & Katie go to it.

January 16 M.R. Drury came in afternoon. I went to look after houses. Saw the sch. h. thought of for a chapel. Wrote to Dessinger at some length. Was up till very late.

January 17 Started at 7:00 morn'g to Des Moines City via Ames. Arrive about 1:30. Dine at Rev. C.B. Davis's. Mother Funkhouser—Demoss—there. She tells of crowd at appointment where H. Bonebrake & John De Moss were with her. Visited Father Danl. Smith's. They of Indiana. Went to M.C. Staves'. She that detected Rev. Wm. Hayes' plagiarism in *Telescope*. His positive dinial & abusive letters to her accusing her of falsehood & tattling etc. I preach at 7:00 from Ps. 1:6. Trustees meet, Carpet. Staid at Staves'.

January 18 Trustees of 2d United Brethren Church of Des Moines City: E.Buck, M.C. Staves, S.E. Dennis, D.B. Rees, C.B. Davis. Went over to West Des Moines to get carpet. Dine at Levi Gutchel's. David Mainbeck there, of (near) Avoe. Return to Church with Rev. Geo. W. Miller & Wilson. Had seen Bro. Dennis & wife at Depot. Supped at Bro. C.B. Davis'. Father Wilson Preached at 7:00, "Royal priest." Staid at D.B. Rees.

January 19 Sunday. Went to M.C. Staves' & change clothes. Pr. at 11:00 from II Cor. 3:7,8. Raise $612.61 in Subs. & Cash. 10 mem gave $25.00 each. Dined at John H. Graham's with Bro. Geo. Miller. I Preach at 7:00 Ez 33:11. Communion followed. Bro. Wolf contended that I & Miller should come to his house; Joseph H. argues that we had promised to go there, & we did. Judge Day invites us to visit public library.

January 20 Went with Judge Day to the State Building. We saw Mr. Beams, State Treasurer, & was shown new safe with clock arrangements. State library. Through the Capitol, yet unfinished. Called at E. Buck's and Father Lawson's. M.C. Staves, Mother Funkhouser & I took Rev. Fr. to Robinson's to exposition of the trinity. Went on to Charioton arrive [blank]

January 21 Tuesday. After breakfast went to the Bates House & to the post-office—found Bro. Brun Burton, who took me via his house in a sleigh to Fry Chapel—good meeting. Several new converts. Among the brethren are S. Fry, Burton, Rev. Patterson, N. Neighbor, M. Rue, H. Goodell, Saml. Draper. Dine at Bro Parker's 1 1/2 miles east of Fry Chapel. Preach 6:30 Jer. 13:21. Stay at Saml Fry's. Mother Mason & Bennett, Bro. Kelsey & Farley, there. Fred. Burnham works there.

January 22 Morning meeting at Fry Chapel. Large attendance. H. Goodell arises and asks prayers—quite a sensation. He seems somewhat blest. Dine at Saml. Draper's. Call at H. Goodell's. Preach at the Church at 6:30 from I John 5:10. Two seekers. Excellent speaking meeting. Five rise for prayers. Saml. Draper starts afresh. Burton on the borders of shouting. I lodge at Horace Goodell's 1 1/2 miles west of New York. Father Goodell has been religious 23 years. Lamented his early neglect. Got a postal from home.

January 23 Thursday. Wrote postal to Susan. Kelsey got a note from Dr. Burton. Meeting at 11 o'clock. Dined at Mr. Neighbor's. Bro. Kelsey was called home by a messenger who brings news of the sickness of his child. I Preach from Eph. 3:19. Meeting dull. Only one seeker. Nothing goes off to good advantage. House too warm, air close, curtains hinder ventillation. Stay at Saml. Fry's. Bro. Kelsey's child is better.

January 24 Most excellent speaking meeting. Dine at Bro. Draper's with Rev. Brewer and wife. Bro Brewer (M. E. pastor) preached at 6:30. Right good meeting.

Stay with Bro. Wm. Kelsey at Bainbridge Burton's. His boys are Fred, Charley, George, Henry, etc. His daughter said "She know she was converted because The Lord makes me happy when I pray." Bro. Kelsey had returned. His Child is better.

January 25 Meeting at 11:00 Pretty good. Went to Geo. Havner's (M.E.) with Rev. Bro. Brewer & wife. After prayer go to Mr. N. Neighbor's who was unable for several days to attend Church. Pray with them. Call at Madison Rue's. Her querry about "home" dances. Bro. Kelsey preaches at 6:30. Several seekers & conversions. Stay with Kelsey at Miller's. Mother Upham an intelligent lady. Two boys—oldest 10; Sickish girl.

January 26 Sabbath. Preach after S. Sch. 2 Cor. 3:7,8. Take in 12; M.E. 4; Congr. 1. Ours: Saml. Draper, Reed & wife, Gillespie & wife (?) Jenny Fry & Fred. Burnham, Bennett boys, Rolf & boys, two Congrega. Fred Burton; M.E. Bennett boy, Neighbor girls & Miss Thomas. Dine at N. Neighbor's. Rev. Kelsey pr. at night "What shall it profit a man?" etc. I exhort. Speaking meeting. Very solemn. Stay at Saml. Fry's. Rhinehart Fry their [there] Married Son Miss Vanausdolly, Mrs. Fry & their Mother, Mrs. Mason there.

January 27 Start with [blank] Patterson, the class leader, there for Chariton. He quite talkative. Said Rev. Parker did not do much. We lunch at Chariton. Train half-hour behind time—else it would have been there. Wrote a letter on the cars to J. Riley, in Indiana & mailed it. Arrive at Burlington at 8:40. Stay at Grand Central Hotel, Burlington. No window fastening to my room. Extemporize one.

January 28 Pay bill $1.00 & start. Get home at 1 o'clock, to Cedar Rapids. Rest as much as practicable.

January 29 Rev. M. Fulcomer comes. Long talk—missed going to prayer-meeting because he did not feel able to walk there. He stays all night. I have much and entertaining conversation with him.

January 30 Long talk with M. Fulcomer. Tell him of his failings frankly & kindly. He goes on to Lisbon. Go to Prayer-meeting at Mitchell's at night. Good meeting.

January 31 Writing as usual. Attend prayer-meeting at Garlo's. Father & Mother Sweet there.

February 1 Writing etc. Prayer-meeting at John Bear's. Good.

February 2 Sabbath. Went, with John Bear to Stony Point, 4 ms. West of Cedar Rapids. Preach at 11:00 from 2 Cor. 3:7,8. I dine at Mr. Kelsey's. Bear at Mr. Howard's. I call at Dickinson's, at Howard's. Talk with the old man. John & I go to rawson's. Saw Father Sheets, Mr. & Mrs. VanDyke, the young Weatherwax, etc. Preach 6 1/2 from Jer. 3:21. Good speaking meeting. One or more asked prayers. Come home. I have Pratt, Langham, Adair, Johnson, Sutliff, Wilson, Heaton, Weed, Thompson.

February 3 Letters written & mailed. Called at M.P. Drury's & talked. Afternoon in writing. Went to prayer-meeting at Bro. Drury's. Large attendance and good meeting. Florence Drury had considerable fever.

February 4 Went to Post-office & Drury's in forenoon. Bro. J. Bear came in a little while. I Write in afternoon. None of us went to the prayer-meeting at Mr. Justice's.

February 5 Wrote most of the day and made out and sent off Conference appointments for 1879. Went to prayer-meeting at Bishop's. Three rose for prayer. Garlo, J. Bear, Corey, Sweet, Thomas, Smith, Mrs. Holecom, Ura. Justice, Two sets of Perry's, etc; there. Fair meeting.

February 6 Call at post-office. Trade at Deavendorf's. Call at Law. Gilmore's office. Away as usual. See Dean. Sec. fo State Y.M.C.A. Got Katie shoes. Her presents to Drury's children: tub & pail. Made out accts. to be sent to Dillon. I did not go to pr. m at Mitchell's.

February 7 See Drury, who failed to organize the night before at Stony-point. Mail letters; get one with ticket on Central R.R. Iowa. One from Chandler "on his ear." Get my watch from Taylor's. Go to West Union in the afternoon. Look at the Church at little. 42x55. Went on to J.K. Rosier's. Guiles spends the evening with us. Talk on prophecy science, ect. etc. Go to bed at eleven o'clock.

February 8 Went to Abraham Guiles'. Petrified wood,

partly natural wood. Mrs. Guiles' lung ailment. Went to Dennis Gray's. Mother Leo is Hinman—a granddaughter of Dan Wright's, native of Connec. & daughter of Reuben Wright's, aged 89, lives with them. Went on to the church. Much fixing of it. Arrange for subscription with little success. J.K. Rosier, Matth. Well's, Benj. Conkey, Edmund Ash, Thomas Swales. Sup at A.W. Drury's with Gray & Ash. Stay at Drury's—they away till late.

February 9 Sabbath. Preach at 10 1/2 Numbers 13.30. Raise about 4700 in cash & subscription. Dine at W.E. Drury's. Preach in the evening at 7:00, Heb. 11:26. Raise over $100 more & dedicate the church. It is of white-brick, 32x55, a bell and steeple. It was a hard struggle, but there was no damper nor sourness. Staid at Drury's.

February 10 Monday. Started home about six morning & arrived at 11:00. S. Sutton on the train from Independence. Got several letters and postals on my arrival at home. Wrote several letters. Prayer-meeting at our home in the evening. Few out on account of rain.

February 11 Tuesday. Wrote letters. Went to the post-office. Called at M.R. Durry's on my return, but find him out of town. He comes at 11:00. He had organized at Stony Point Sch. H., a class of seventeen members. I Write in the afternoon.

February 12 Wednes. Started about 5:50 M. for Polo, via Dixon, Ill. Converse with Rev. Stow, Luth Min. of Tipton, Iowa. See Rev. Wendle & Dessinger at Dixon & dine at Dessinger's Motherinlaw's. See also Bros. Marshal, Butson, Richardson & Snyder. Go on the Cars with Bro. G.W. Wendle to Polo, arriving at 2:37 P.M. Go to Rev. J.H. Grimm's. Long talk with him. Go to Dessinger's & stay all night. Called & saw Shanmaker & D. Middlekauf's, and was invited to their houses. Grimm pretty kind, but nervous. Rev. T.D. Adams came in the morning of next day, early.

February 13 Went to Church, calling awhile at Grimm's. House full & excited. P. Hurless, after devotions, conducted by myself, calls Com. on Grimm's case vs. Dessinger. No third man. Adjourn till 2:30. Grimm, Dessinger, Hurless, M.S. Drury, Chandler, Wendle & Wright meet at 1:00 at Bro.Hayes' to talk over the dif-

ferences. I conduct the services & conversations. A fine spirit and great harmonizing. Drury & Adams to draw a paper. Sup at Haye's. Preach at 7:00 Ps. 1:5,6. Parties meet awhile in basement. Drury & I stay at D. Middlekauf's. Grimm's sensitiveness.

February 14 Friday. Go to Grimm's & Dessinger's. They sign the treaty. Go to Church at 9:00. Sevices by Drury. I make remarks and read the paper twice. Sing a verse & dismiss it being near car time. We go on to Dixon. Write to Adams & Middlekauf sending a copy of the "compact" to Grimm. Names of Polo people: Hayes, Shumaker, Middlekauf, Dusing, Boone, Watson, etc. Go on at 2:30 to Cedar Rapids—arriving 8:00. Find some letters awaiting me.

February 15 Saturday. Go to Drury's and to the post-office. Spend the day largely as a day of rest. Sleep awhile in the afternoon. Go to bed early. Mrs. "Lou" Drury comes to get Reuchlin to telegraph to Toledo, Iowa, in answer to a call to preach James Harrison's funeral. Bro. D. having gone to Stony-point Sch. H. Reuchlin finds the wires out of order at the office & that the dispatch must wait till next morning.

February 16 Sabbath. Preach at Room 13 P.O. Building at 10 1/2, II Cor. 3–7,8. No special interest in the day's reading & conversation, I being rather dull. Preach again at night from I John 5–10—a short sermon. Bro. Drury worn out somewhat. Bro. Shaw, the evangelist, present, but yet unwell. A large congregation out. The meeting to be protracted. Announced that I would preach next evening.

February 17 Monday. Went to post-office & bank. Got a draft on 3d Nat. Bank of N.Y. for $267.00, to pay off note on U.B.S. endowment. Deposit $140. Loan bank $250.00 for three months, having taken up previous loan of $600 and interest $6.00. Preach at P.O. Hall at 7:30, "What shall it profit a man," etc. Good attendance.

February 18 Tuesday. At Home as usual. Eve., Rev. M.R. Drury preaches good congregation.

February 20 Write as usual. I preach at post-office Hall (No 13) from Isa. 57:21, one rises for Prayer—Mrs. Autles.

February 21 Friday. At home as usual writing, etc. Bro. M.R. Drury preaches at night at the Hall to a fair congregation.

February 22 Saturday. Went with my wife to John Bear's in the afternoon. Called on Mitchell's, who were not at home, & at Mrs. Roberts. Bro. Drury preached at night. Congregation smaller.

February 23 Sunday. M.R. Drury preaches. At S. School I teach one of the men's classes. About forty or fifty attend. I Preach at 7:30, Rom 10:1. Congregation unexpectedly large—extra seats needed. Mr. Pickering comes forward for prayers. Fine interest manifested.

February 25 Tuesday. I Spent most of the day in writing. Called at Collier's office in afternoon—talk about ganishee. Snow flies in late afternoon & evening. I preach at 7:30. About thirty out. Very pleasant meeting. Text Luke 24:46–7.

February 26 Wednesday. At home as usual. Bro. Drury preaches at 7:30 Good attendance. Fair interest.

February 27 Thursday. At Home as usual. Cooper calls to see about payment of rent. Worked on my annual report. I preach at 7:30 from I Cor. 16:22. Considerable solemnity. Rev. Mr. Duncan present.

February 28 Friday. Writing, etc, as usual. Worked on annual report. Bro. Drury preaches. Rev. S.B. Shaw present. I exhort at the close of all and call for seeker. One arose for prayers.

March 1 Saturday. Bro. Drury called; is going out to Stony Point to visit around with Bro. Heaton. I prepared Sermons. I went out to Perry's at Fair Ground, and at 7:00 Unite in marriage Edward McGown & Clara Ellen Perry. He had to marry her. His misfortune in losing $5.00! (A myth perhaps, no doubt.) Preach at 7:30 to a large congregation from I John 4:10. Mr. Reeder there. More than usual of the intelligence of the city. Very solemn meeeting.

March 2 Sabbath. Have a fair congregation. I Preach at 10 1/2 II Tim. 4:8. Short speaking meeting. After Reeder tells me his experience. Sab. School. I Preach at 7:30

from Rev. 22:11. About 175 persons in the congregation. Solemn meeting.

March 3 Monday. Start at 2:25 Aft'n for Moline. Write Some at Hise House a West Liberty. Reach Moline about 9:00. Go on to Parsonage with Rev. P.M. France. B. Frank Bash, a student from Western College there, on his way home to near Van Orin, Ill., who started on, early next morning.

March 4 Tuesday. Spend forenoon at parsonage. In the afternoon, I visit the public library, and Call at Mother Wear's, she being afflicted, her grand-daughter Gracey atten[d]ing her. I Preach at night from Matt. 13:23. Par. Sower. A good congregation. A brother of Rev. Abr. Hartzell, of Colorado, present.

March 5 Wednes. I went out to Coal-town. Dine at Wm. Giles. His grandfather was a stow-a-way on a vessel bound for South Carolina. He knew Adam Spivey's folks. Call at Wendel's. Also at Father Griffith's. I Preach at night from Mark 8:36. Congregation Small, it being muddy and rainy before & after meeting. Stay at the parsonage, in Moline. Bro. Shafer & Son. Mr. Galt the Adventist. Bro. Adam Fry's & family. Robinson Hurst.

March 6 Bro. & Sister France go to Hill part of town. I spend forenoon mostly in reading Telescope & Radical [?] I Call at post-office. Call in afternoon at Mother Jones'. Call at Prof. Smith's in South Moline. His wife is Bro. Dilling's daughter, of Western, Iowa. Call at Father Williamson's in S. Moline. Preach at 7:30, I John 4:10. One arises for prayer. I Stay at the parsonage.

March 7 Friday. I Spent the forenoon in reading, etc. Called in Afternoon at Robinson's. At Entriken's—saw Prof. Beal. He talked of going to Kansas or Colorado. Preached at 7:30, Matt. 13:44. The Prof. Smiths & wives out. Also Father and Mother Beal. Pretty fair congregation. Miss Sulivan, the last evening's seeker, not able to be present.

March 8 Saturday. Called at Duro's at A. Fries, and Mother Heck's. Rev. Philip Heck in East Desmoines Conf, is her son. Mrs. Gamble, her daughter, there working for her temporarily. I Visit Father Beal's in the afternoon. Take supper at their son's; the young lawyer's. Bro.

France preaches at night. Mrs. Beal (junior) has parents at Andalusia. Thompsons. She seems tending to consumption. They talk of going to Colorado, or Kansas.

March 9 Sabbath. Bro. France preaches at 10 1/2 on "Bear ye one another's burdens." Go with him in afternoon and preach at 3:00 at "Coal-town" school-house, from Eph 5:1. Present: Wm. Giles, Greenwood, Wendell, Miss Brown, Miss Owen, etc. Return to Moline. Preach at night (7:30) from Rev. 22:11. Mrs. Thomas & Mr. Altick join church.

March 10 Monday. Leave Moline at 6:10 Morn. Write some at Depot at W. Liberty. Go on home, arriving at 12:45, Cedar Rapids. Spend day at home. Do not go to meeting at night, being tired & sleepy.

March 11 Tuesday. Work at my report somewhat. Drury (Marion) came and staid till after dinner. Rev. M. Fulcomer came. Tells of the trouble between the faculty and students over the paper read by Rev. Buxton, said to be "smutty." Literary society deny & expel Linderman for what he said to pres. & faculty. Female Lit. Society side with the men's society. Preached at 7:30. Heb. 3:7.

March 12 At home, as usual. Feel little like mental work. M.R. Drury preaches at night. One forward for prayers.

March 13 A mild day. Take a walk with Susan and Katie up the Dabugue railroad. Begins to storm in the evening; few out. Preach Matt. 13:23.

March 14 Day cold. Worked some on annual report, etc. M.R. Drury preaches in the evening from [blank] M.S. Drury comes—is at latter part of the meeting.

March 15 M.S. Drury came & spent forenoon with me; Reeder also. Both dines with us. Go to Town in afternoon. M.R. Drury preaches at night "He that doeth the work shall know of the doctrine." One forward for prayers. Notifies me, as I start home! that he expects me to take charge of the meeting to-morrow & to-morrow night.

March 16 Sunday. Preached at P.O. Hall at 10 1/2 Zech 13:9—"I will try them as gold is tried." Preach in the evening from Rom. 1:20. "Without excuse." 150 people there. Warm meeting.

Reuchlin Wright, b. Marcxh 17, 1861

March 17 Reuchlin's eighteenth anniversary of birthday. Give him a new silver dollar. Mother & all the children give him a new silk pocket-handkerchief. Felt moderately. Did not go to Church at night. Reuchlin went; said about 100 people were out. One seeker still.

March 18 Sent off several letters. Went to West Branch to Anti-secrecy state convention. Drury elected president. 141 delegates enrolled. Found home with M.S. Drury's at John Chambers. Rev. H. Rathbun works the 1st degree of Free masonry, at 7 1/2 o'clock.

March 19 Convention continued. Rev. Joel H. Austin (P.O. Burlington, Iowa), delivered an address at 10:00. I spoke in the afternoon on Best methods of success in Antisecrecy reform. Mrs. Rathbun spoke also. Rathbun "worked" 3d degree of Masonry at night. Stayed still at John Chambers.

March 20 Call at Chambers' Bank. Start to Cedar Rapids. May, Hammond, Galloway, Kent and Altman dine with us. Galloway talks on premillenarianism [sic] before he leaves. I preach at night on Matt 13:44.

March 21 J.P. Stoddard calls in the afternoon. Drury preaches at night.

March 22 I.K. Statton preached in afternoon, at 2:30, on Duty of the people to pastor and pastor to people. Quarterly Conference followed. D.E. Middlekauf took supper with us. Statton (I.K.) preached at 7:45. "Jesus, the son of Joseph." Congregation large. Statton & Middlekauf stay with us.

March 23 Sunday. Statton preaches at 10:30 "This is he, hold him fast." Communion followed. Congregation large. John Drury & Middlekauf dine with us. Derry Dale Sabbath School met with ours. The hall have been nicely decked with evergreens the day before. Statton preaches at night House full.

March 24 D. Middlekauf left at 7:00 for Carroll, Iowa. Spend part of forenoon in shopping. Walter Burt Smith asks me to preach his wife's funeral the next day at the Church, 3 miles North-west of Shellsburg. I do not attend meeting in the evening.

March 25 Call at Smith's. Go on 1:00 train to Shellsburg & out to Church and Preach Mrs. Lurana, Adelaide Smith's funera. Bro. Arbell takes me out Bro. Greasor brings me back to the cars. I Came home on Accom. train arriving at 7:30. Go to church. Drury preaches "Blood cleanseth from all sin." I do not stay till meeting is over. Congregation large. Two seekers.

March 26 At home. I preached at 7:45 from Matt 19:29. Mrs. & Mr. Dockery profess religion. The shouting Bro. Drury absent at Stony Point where there was to be a donation to the pastor.

March 27 Start to Kansas at 2:25 afternoon. After nearly four hours waiting at Columbus Junction, I go on to Atchison—sleep about five hours on the way.

March 28 At day-light I am in Missouri. Breakfast at Cameron. Reach Atchison about 11:00. Leave for Sedgwick about noon. In company with Prentis, author of "A Kansan in Europe" A representative in Legislature, and a large profane, obscene chum, in next seat—behind me. Reach Sedgwick City about 11:00. Stay at Ithamar Lambs.

March 29 Go on to Otterbein Church, three miles South-west. Henry Shaffer & wife are present. Ithamar Lamb, Oscar Wilson, F.M. Dick, S. Fry. Black Rev. J.R. Evans; D.S. Hennonger & several others. Rev. J.R. Evans preaches a funeral—a child of less than two years old. I preach at 3:00 Ex. 28:34. Sup at Young Fry's. Br. Musty preaches at night a fair discourse. I go home with Henry Shaffer, whom I had known in Henry and Wayne counties, Ind.

March 30 Preach at 11:00 from Ps. 48:11–13. Raise $189.60. Also $300.00 to meet the Church Erection loan. Dedicate "Otterbein Church." Dine at Samuel Fry's; he a son of Joseph Henry Fry. Preach at 8:00 Ps. 16:8. Go with H. Shaffer's to I. Lamb's. Musty's there. He was raised a Catholic. She a daughter of James Allen, near Ecomony, Ind.

March 31 Start at 5:30 morning to Atchison. The greenback editor is talky. "Prof." Palmer, the long-haired tobacco-smoking phrenologist aboard, after we left Topeka, where I dined. Reached Atchison about 5:00. Put up at the Otis House.

April 1 Pay $2.50 for lodgings breakfast & dinner. Start at 2:00 for Lincoln. Arrive at 8:30. Bro. F.M. Scott meets me and takes me to Josiah Paden's. Nice family of children, but parents are unhappy.

April 2 Get a postal from home & wrote back. Start at 1:30 to depot—at 3:40 to Utica. Arrive at Utica about 7:30. Stay at Van Anken's Restaurant. Bro. Hippard to take me next morning to Conference 9 miles north-west.

April 3 Go on to conference, overtake Rev. D.D. Weimer. Conference opens pleasantly. Presiding-elders examined and passed quite favorably. My Home at Bro. Wm McCullough's, 1 mile North-west of Paol Church (Mt. Zion). Session continues. Rev. J.A. Eads preaches at night. Robert Lloyd sings and prays, at the close.

April 4 Conference continues. W.S. Spooner, Lloyds, Bishop, Bowman, etc. dine with us. Spooner's first quarterly meeting was with I.N. Martin. Reading Com's report, Bell & Elliott not referred to com. on elder's orders. I preach at 7:30 I Cor. 13:13. Stay at McCullough's.

April 5 Conference as usual. Raise over $100.00 for paying Fairbury "College" indebtedness.. Caldwell, Austin & Weimer were elected presiding-elders in afternoon. Dine at A.H. Rodger's who has brother 3 1/2 miles north-west of Cedar Rapids. After stationing committee has done its work, we go to Roger's for a bite of supper. B.C. Parker preaches. I stay at McC's.

April 6 Sunday. Call at Rogers before meeting. Some rain. Preach at 11:00 from 2 Cor. 3:7,8. Ordain S.E. & W.R. Lloyd & R.A. Bishop. Dine at Willis's. S.S. Anniversary at 3 1/2, slimly attended on account of rain. Willis' boy last winter interrupted Van Gordon, saying Satan was in him. No meeting at night on account of rain. Stay at McCullough's. Rev. S. Austin, my roommate, was absent.

April 7 Go with Rev. C.C. Kellogg of W. Neb. Conf. to C.C. Smith's to dinner. He lives on Lincoln Creek. His mother lives on Commercial St., Cedar Rapids. Boy had two little jack-rabbits whom he suckled with an old cat. Go on to Rev. S.E. Lloyd's, near the new Church with Bro. Kellogg. He lives in a large sod house, Close to his fatherinlaw's, Geo. Myers'.

April 8 Dine a G. Myer's. In afternoon, prairie fires break out, set by an Irish Catholic. Threatens the new church— injures Myers trees along his line. Revs S & E.F. Austin come. Rains in the evening. Small turn out. S. Austin preached. Stay at G. Myer's.

April 9 Stay at G. Myers'. Preach at night from Luke 16:31. A very blustery day. I took a fine walk or two in the swift wind.

April 10 Went via York to E.F. Austin's. Exchanged $53.30 of silver at York. $30.00 of it at Mr. Cobb's $23.30 for postal order. It was a Windy day, but not in our faces.

April 11 Staid at Rev. E.F. Austin's till after dinner. Go over to Rev. Simeon Austin's. Stay Rev R.A. Bishop, the pastor of West Blue Circuit, & wife come. Argument with Uncle Simeon on the Jewish Sabbath being the sixth day of creation, he affirming.

April 12 Went over to Wullbrant's with "Uncle" Simeon.

Dine. Go on to Hallock's. Sup. Go on to church, Bethel on West Blue River. Rev. R.A. Bishop preaches Luke 19:41,2. I stay at Bro. Hallock's. Rev. E.W. Johnson & wife at meeting and Rev. E.F. Austin & wife & R.B. Bishop & wife.

April 13 Sunday. Went to Bethel Church. Preached dedication sermon, John 14:23. Dedicated the house. Rev. S. Smith & wife were also present & Rev. J. Cleen. Dine at Bro. Brooke's 3 m. N. Rains about dinner-time. I Preach at 7:30 Rev. 1:10, on the Lord's day. I stay at Hallock's. I observed that in this family the children did not kneel in family prayer.

April 14 I go with Bro. Hallock to Exeter and thence to Omaha & Casey & stay at the Denning House. I was much interested in reading human nature in the conversations near me. Representa. of Malcom, Iowa, and little daughter near me from C.Blue to Casey. I got Ingersoll's "Mistakes." It is false, sensual & devilish. Dined & supped at restaurants. Casey has perhaps six or eight hundred inhabitants; is a pretty town.

April 15 Went over to see William Wright's land seven miles south of Casey. Saw Cook & David Hepler; called at Joseph Lesher's; Eben S.Roberts. Dined at David Hepler's. Mrs. Hepler told me that it was Wright's land & showed me the assessor's list—the first I knew certain, as to its being Wm's land. Met Henry A. Snyder whose office is Prussia Center. Canby is at Lesher's. Went back to Casey 4::30. Train did not come. Went on 9:32 train. Sleep 4 hours in car.

April 16 Arrive at West Liberty at 6:30, Morning. Arrive at home at 12:45 Aftn. Drury calls in.

April 17 Go with Drury to look at lots for Church building.

April 19 Went to Western with Reuchlin in buggy. Stop at M.S.Drury's. Call at Bowman's an hour, after supper. Stay at Drury's.

April 20 Preach at 10:30 Ps. 92:8. Dine at Rev. M. Bowman's. Attend class-meeting at 3:00. Go to Shatto's for supper. I.B. Beatty there M. Fulcomer comes in. Prof. Albert & wife & brother call in. Preach at 7:30 I Cor.

13:13. Stay at Rev. I.L. Bookwalter's.

April 22 Went to town. Called at Mrs. Smith's—mother of C.C. Smith of Nebraska.

April 23 Drury's call in afternoon. I go to W. Cooper's and thence to Parkhurst's and adjust garnishment, after which I pay up rent to July 1, 1879. Prayer-meeting. Reader leads. Talk over ground-plan and time of building & method of raising subscriptions.

April 25 Rev. M.S. Drury called; is going next morning to Muscatine.

April 26 Pastor Drury came in the afternoon. We inquire after lots, etc. Call & talk with Reeder.

April 27 Sabbath. Pr. at Hall, 10 1/2, Luke 22:48. Some beggar squaws in the afternoon, call at our house, & I read Greek to them. M.R. Drury pr. at 8:00—on Sacraments—Lord's Supper & baptism.

April 28 Morning as usual. Afternoon went to look after lots and then out to Mrs. Lutz. She adheres to $2,100 for her property, but seemed anxious to sell. Before this Rev. I.K. Statton & Mrs. Martin Bitzer & new wife came. Bitzers' on their way to Pennsylvania. The Congregationalists hald meeting in our Hall for consultation on Church organization.

April 29 I Walked down town. Looked some at lots & called at Drury's. Baptists (disaffected) used hall for meeting & consultation.

April 30 Wrote letters. Pastor Drury called in the afternoon. Church council after prayer meeting. Advise the trustees to buy one of three lots. Lutz, Leach, or McDaniel lots.

May 1 M.R. Drury reports in the afternoon that Mrs. Lutz deferred till Saturday to decide on sale of lot at $2000. I started at 9:20 for Dayton, Ohio on C.W.W. train.

May 2 Reach Chicago at 7:00, and take the R. Cin & St. Louis train for Logansport, Kokomo & Richmond, Ind. I dine at Logansport & reach Richmond, 6:40 p.m. I stay at

D.K. Zeller's, my brotherinlaws. Mother C. Koerner was living with them.

May 3 I remain at Zeller's till eveing & at 7:00 take the Dayton train. John Shearer is aboard. I find Hott's abed & so I go to W.O. Tobey's. Pres. S.B. Allen & W.B. Smith & H. Floyd are there.

May 4 Sunday. Bishop J. Weaver preached the baccalaureate sermon before the students of U.B.S. "We will give ourselves continually to prayer & ministry of the word." I dine at Dr. L. Davis's. Sab. School. Weaver & I make short addresses, & each also to the month's class of Church members afterward. I sup at Bro. Hotts. I stay at Dr. L. Davis's.

May 5 I call on several of the old neighbors & friends. I go to the office (*Telescope*). I return & dine at Rev. S.R. Hippard's. I visit the new Seminary building in afternoon. There is a fine view from it. There were ten at Tobey's. There was an anniversary of the literary society of the Seminary in evening. L.B. Hix, Wenrich & [blank] I stay at Cousin Sam. Wright's Cor. of 3rd and Summit Streets.

May 6 Board meeting. I dine at Philip La Vasseur's. Warm friends of our family. Bp. J.J. Glossbrenner lectured at First Church to a small congregation. I stay at J.W. Hotts.

May 7 Board Session. I dine at G.W. Funkhouser's. I sup at J.G. Feight's. Graduating address is by Crider & D.A. Mobley. I stay at Tobey's, I believe. I presented diplomas to the graduates.

May 8 Board Session of Education. Dine at Prof. Keister's. Stay at Dr. L. Davis's.
May 9 I go to Westerville. I dine at J. Dickson's. Meeting of Board of Bishops on pastoral letter. I stay at Bishop Dickson's.

May 10 Board in Session. Dine at Dickson's. Sup at Rev. N. Smith's. Stay at Bish. J. Dickson's.

May 11 S.A. Mowers preached a good sermon at Pres. Church. I attend. Dine at Pres. H.A. Thompson's. Mis Meeting at 3:00. Tea at Prof. Guitner's. Bp. Weaver preaches at night on the oft-repeated sermon on John 14:1,2. I stay at H.A. Bovey's. A very friendly family.

May 12 Early session of the Board of Bishops. Go on via Columbus, Xenia to Dayton. Dine at Hott's. Visit Cemetery—see Bishop Edwards' monument. Call at Mrs. Harriet Bond's. Simpson's family there. Mrs. Allen, Mrs. Bond's daughter called. I call at Wm. Miller's. Wm. Huffman's and Johy Swaynie's. I See Grand-Aunt Polly aged 92 years. Her grand-daughter Samantha Troup lives in Chicago. Mr. Troup superintends short-tower.

May 13 I called at Sines', Wagner's. Dine at Wm. Furgueson's, Mrs. Lehmon thee. Mrs. Whitier of St. Louis, wife of Dr. Whitier there also, & her mother, a daughter's daughter of Grand Uncle Reuben Reeder. They are Presbyterians. I call at Dr. L. Davis'. At Office a few minutes. Call at Manning's. Tea at Sines. Stay at Dr. Davis'. Cousin Paulina Langworthy lived at Dabuque & her Sister Mrs. Harris.

May 14 Went via Hamilton to Lotus. Dined at William A. Oler's, pastor of Franklin Circuit, and he takes me to Daniel Koerner's. C.F.A. Gantzscow came to Koerner's. I stay at Daniel's.

May 15 I go to Liberty & thence to Glenwood (Vienna) & go with the mail-carrier to Fayetteville. Dine at Jas. Carter's. Chester Moor takes me to Anson Moor's, where I sup and lodge.

May 16 Staid at Moor's in forenoon. Called at old farm—Greene Bird's—in afternoon, and visit Austin Winchell's and take supper there. Return to Anson Moor's.

May 17 Visit Rev. John Morgan, aged 78. Susan Bullock there. See Thomas Morgan & Sarah (Morgan) Mullen. Morgan lives in Andersonville. Came back to Austin Winchell's. Staid.

May 18 Staid at Winchell's till evening. Anson's Came. Meeting at Sanes Creek Preached Ex. 28:34. Went to Anson Moor's.

May 19 Went on cars to Rushville. Harvey Wright took me to his house. His children: Drusilla McKee, Tho-

mas, George, Francis, Dan, John, Emma, Joseph A. Rhoda, Eva. Gracie. Grand Children: Flora & Gusta McKee, etc. Spent evening & night at John McKee's, John having taken me in his buggy.

May 20 Went to Jabez Rhoads', Children: Clara (4 ys) Stella (9 mos.). Took supper at Thomas Wright's. His daughters: Effie & Cora. Went on to Harvey's. Drusilla McKee called awhile.

May 21 Went to Dunreith & took hack for New Castle. Called at Rev. M.L. Bailey's. Train at 12:20 for Anderson. Billy Wolf's excursion. At Anderson, call at Dr. G.F. Chittenden's. Supper there. Train for Fairmount—arrive there at 9:40 eve. William & Robert Reeder meet me & take me to their house.

May 22 Go to Mr. Little's to Sarah's funeral; preaching by Rev. Mr. Garrison, M.E. Ch. Saw Henry Simons & wife & Wm. Adriel, Levi & John & Joseph Pearl. Mr. Hollis, Joseph Corn & John Esom Leach & William Dealy & many others. Went home to Reeder's. Walked over & looked at the old place. A beautiful farm of 95 acres of clear land. House improved. Go back to Uncle Reeder's. James Burwick a chief-mourner on account of Miss Lyttle's death.

May 23 Stay at Uncle W.H.H. Reeder's till nearly night. John Minton comes. Same droll John! Go to Fairmount with Robert & Flora. Take train for Marion at 9:40. Sleep an hour at Depot at Marion. Train for Chicago. Sleep about three hours on train. Reach Chicago about 7:00. Call at Shot-tower but do not see Mr. Troup. Go on to Cedar Rapids. Dine at Dixon, sleep two hours. Home at 8:00.

May 24 The latter part of prece[e]ding page refers to this day. A Mr. Mitchel & wife on train for Chicago—going on the excursion to California. Lorin & Orville meet me at Depot.

May 25 Preached at Post-office Hall 10:30, I Tim. 3:16. Home in the afternoon. Sleep a nap. go to Episcopal Church in the evening. Hear Rev. Ringgold preach—or read.

May 27 Write letters. Walked out in afternoon with

our little girl & boy. Called at Drury's. L. Bookwalter called. Talk about Hartsville presidency.

May 30 Went via Vinton to Grundy, County-seat of Grundy Co., Iowa. Thence with Rev. Eben S. Bruce to Mr. Overholser's—Mother Neidig—corn & flax growing on same ground. Went on to Carvasso Bunce's. Wife sick. Went to Zion Church at Badger Hill. Origin name—a badger skin spread on Rev. E.S. Bunce's house. I preach at 8:00 from Ps. 1:6. Staid at Mr. Deloss Westcott's in Badger Hill. She a sister of E.S. Bunce.

May 31 Remained at Mr. Deloss Wescott's till after afternoon meeting. Rev. I.D. Barnard is pastor. Rev. Kearn & wife present at the meeting. I Preach at 2:00 I tim. 1:1. Go to Rev. I.D. Barnard's. Family is so amused with microscope. Rev. Keary preaches from I Tim. 1:5. Staid at Deloss Wescott's. He not church member—his wife, M.E. Church. Several brethren came up from Toledo.

June 1 Sunday. I preach dedication sermon at 10 1/2, Ps. 48.11,12,13. Raise subs. $755.00—only $550.00 called for. Also hat collection of $24.03. Dr. S.Y. Lawrence & Father Lawrence, there. I dine at Rev. G.W. Benson's. I preach at 7:30, Deut. 18:18,19. I go to Carvosso Bunce's. Mrs. B. seems better. His second daughter broke her collar bone Saturday. I gave back $4.00 of collection.

June 2 Rev. I.D. Barnard takes me to Grundy. Dine at Mother Reisinger's 3/4 mile south of depot. Start for Cedar Rapids at 1:45. Arrive at 6:30 perhaps. Saw Epley at Grundy.

June 5 Spent day in writing. I got Emphatic Diaglott—proves to be a Campbelite Affair. Went to Commencement at Presbyterian Church—Coe's Collegiate Institute—where six graduated: Miss Odell, Mr. Cooper, Murray, Marshall, Kinney, and Miss Maggie Cooper. Miss Dennis a beautiful singer. Miss Smally got the prize on Essay, Marshal second; Murray on Oration; Reuchlin Wright on Evi. Christianity; Miss Odell, Ethics; Diamond on Mathematics; etc. etc.

June 6 Went via Marshaltown and Grinnel to New Sharon [unreadable]. Met by Roos, A.L. Palmer & W.O. Smith. Went out with John Garner to Riley Case's &

lodged there. I saw Mr. Burton with Masonic lodge. Saw Mr. Carson, druggist. I took a nap at 7:00 and afterward slept well at night, arising next morning much refreshed.

June 7 Go to Jac. Grunden's, call. See Miss Hilderbrand, Bro. Smith's enamored. Bro. Palmer preached at 11 from 2Cor. 4:7, Dine at Bro. Lathrop's in Granville. Quar. Conf. in afternoon. Supper at Hood Berry's. Rev. G.W. Rose preached at night, "The great day of his wrath," etc. Rev. 6:17. Stay with Rose at Rev. Mr. Coats of the M.E. Church.

June 8 Sunday. Pr. 11 from Ps. 48.11,12,13. Raise $155 on Church & adjourn. Dine at Hugh Evans' 1 1/2 miles S.E. of Granville. Pr. at 4:00 Heb. 13:14. Raise about 60 more—the trustees assume the rest and we dedicate the church. I go to John Garner's 2 1/2 miles N.E. & stay all night. He an ex-Methodist man. Also quite a Martinite.

June 9 Go to New Sharon with Mr. Garner—Smith & Palmer along. Stop at Sharon House. Go on to Marshal about 2:00. Congregational ministers come aboard at Grinnell. Rev. Mr. Cross of Waterloo. An hour at Marshal. Reach Cedar Rapids about 10:00, at night.

June 10 Write in morning. Look at Churches in afternoon, with Drury & Reeder. Call at Orville's school room in afternoon.

June 13 Missed the 2:20 train. Much put out, as I was to lecture & preach at Avalon, Missouri, Sat. Eve. & Sabbath. I could find no way to reach Chillicothe Sat. night.

June 14 Quarterly meeting. Attended at 2:00. Bro. I.K. Statton took supper with us. He preached aft. & night. Lodged with us.

June 15 Sunday. Bro. Statton preached at 10 1/2. Sacramental service. Sabbath School. I taught women's class. Statton preached in aft. at Derry Dale. I not there. Bro. Statton preached at night, in town.

June 19 Went over to Lisbon. Stopped at T.E. Adam's to consult him on Lisbon's helping Cedar Rapids on church building. Father Haynes & Dessinger, of Polo, there. I dined at Rev. I.K. Statton's. Called at Bro. Adam's, Runkle's in store. Saw Rev. Smith, jeweler. Called at Rev. D. Runkle's with Rev. T.D. Adams. Supped at Statton's. Went home.

June 20 Went over to Western, being requested to be present at meeting of the Board of College. Dine at I. Buchwalter's. Sup at Rev. G.W. Statton's. Rev. I.L. Kephart & wife there & I.K. Statton. Kephart talks of his son. Beale lectured at night on dcision of character. I staid at Rev. M.S. Drury's. Chr. Neidig & wife & Bro. Beale there.

June 21 At the meeting of the Board of Western College. Business in forenoon. Sup at Pres. E.B. Kephert's. With Com. on Appeal of students in afternoon, and also after evening exercises, which consisted in addresses & a debate between John Drury, Miss Patten & Klinfelter & Miss [blank]. I stay at Drury's.

June 22 Lorin went after his mother. I preach Baccalaureate on "Moses, the man of God." Susan came. We dine at Bro. Drury's. Attend Gen. class in afternoon. Sup at Rev. M. Bowman's. Call at Father Perry's. Rev. J.L. Kephart preaches the "Annual sermon." Rom. 1:20, "For the invis. things," etc. W[e] stay at M.S. Drury's: I.L. Kephart was a fair preacher, not very fascinating.

June 23 Call at Pres. Kephart's & Prof. Bookwalter's & Rev. G.W. Statton's. Attend the meeting of appeal committee after about 10 o'clock. Dine with family at Bookwalter's. Wife & family go home. Committee finishes its investigation. I sup at Prof. Bookwalter's. Call at Rev. G.W. Statton's, he being sick of headache. Alumni meeting Prof. Albert lectured. A.W. Drury and A.D. Collier spoke. Miss Patterson read a poem on Samuel Johnson. I staid at Statton's.

June 24 At Western. Dine at A. Shatto's. Report of committee on appeal. Prof. Bookwalter resigns. Prof. Albert elected Prof. of Languages; Prof. Williams of Nat. science. Go to my home with Rev. G. Miller. Send $100.00 by him to pay on breaking prairie on Adair land. Stay at home. Had borrowed Drury's horse and buggy to come home with.

June 25 Went over to Western. Graduating exercises. Miss E.A. Patton & Miss E.A. Moore, & Mr. D. Miller graduate in Scientific course; Mr. W.L. Linderman & W.H. Klinefelter graduate in Classical Course. Dine at Pres. Kephart's. Call at G.W. Statton to see Howe, of Va. & Waldo Drury takes me to the train at Ely. Hurless, Reible & Chitty sup with us—Chitty stays all night.

June 26 Start at 3:00, morn. for Minnesota. Stop two hours at Cedar Falls. Dine at Al. Lea. Stop an hour at Carver. Stay at Glencoe. Draws are slpughy on the way to Carver. Run over steep Mollows west of Carver. Stay at Merchant's Hotel. Glenco[e] is a town of good size, a county seat.

June 27 Wrote letters. Start at 2:05 for Montivideo. It is a nice, rich, new country—new towns. Minnesota River. Reach there about 8:30. Learn at Dun's Hotel that Frank Fuller, livery-man, had been inquiring for me. I see him. Get room, No 25 on second floor. To go out about 6:00, to Pomme de Terre.

June 28 Alex. Berry came after me. We start at 6:30. Arrive at Camp-ground at 12:30—about 30 miles—7 miles from Appleton. Stop at Pr. David Miner's. Preach at 3:00 from Ex. 28:34. Rev. Simeon George pr. at night. "He came into world not to condemn." Supper with Rev. Berry's. Stay at Bro. Milner's. Saw Pettyjohn (blind) Dexter (deafish) Heldreth, Pickthorn, Pomeroy, Benedict, Scotts, Vandevoort, Kepner & daughters, Mother Mills.

June 29 Sabbath. Pr. at 10:30 from Ps. 18:30. Dine at Bro. John Eldredge's. Pr. in after'n. 3:00 from Matt 28:19,20, Missionary sermon. Supper at Bro. David Miner's. Bro. S.D. Kemerer preaches at night. held till 11:00. Stay at Bro. Miner's. Saw Edwards (now reclaimed backslider). Preachers: Kernerer, Tressenwriter, George, Berry, Eldredge. Mr. Underwood is M.E.

June 30 Bro. Eldridge pr. at 10:30. Dinner at Bro. Berry's. Bro. Simon Geroge preaches at 3:00. Supper at Bro. Miner's. Preach at 8:00 from Luke 24:46.

July 1 Tuesday. Rainy morning. Farewell meeting. Prayers. I make some remarks. Bro. George conducts the farewell. Dine at Bro. Miner's. Bro. King takes me to Montevideo. Put up at Dunn House.

July 2 Start at 5:00 morn. for Wisconsin. Talk with M.C. White of Minneapolis, formerly of Spiceland, Ind. Reach Hastings before dark. Reach Wynona about 2:00 night. Put up at Huff House.

July 3 Start at 7:30 for Ogdensburg. Excursion added. Note from Whitney to stop off at Amherst Junction. No one meets me—go on to Ogdensburg. Stop a short time at Bro. Rice's. Go on to Wapaca—$1.00. No one to meet me there. Put up at Lewis' Hotel. Find Glat & Morris. The latter tells me where the Camp-meeting was. Determine to go to Saxeville by stage.

July 4 Start on stage for Saxeville. Breakfast at Mr. N. Milliken's. Couple just married there—Mr. Oliolsin & Miss Milliken. Elder R. Couley (M.E. of Wautoma) officiates. Mr. Vosburg takes me on to the camp-meeting on Willow Creek $2.00. Bro. Miller preaching—"Behold I bring you glad tidings," etc. Luke. Dine, sup & lodge at Bro. Fuller's. Bro. Godde pr. 3:00 "How shall we escape?" Bro. Jas. Johnson pr. at 8:30, "Behold we have forsaken all," etc. Two came forward as seekers.

July 5 Bro. Whitney preaches at 10:30. Dine at Whitney's a layman's. I preach at 3:00 Ps. 84:12. Supper at Fuller's. Johnson preaches at 8:00. I exhort & two came out as seeker's. Names: Littleman, the Indian tenters: Bigsby's, Metcalf, Wilcox, Scott, Randall's of Oshkosh, Dr. Foster, Sister Wright. Preachers: N.G. Whitney, C.M. Clark, Miller, Goodall, Jas. Johnson, Page.

July 6 Sunday. Begin to preach at 11:00. Storm scatters us. Heavy rain is continued. Preach at Sch. House— finish forenoon text Ps 48:11,12,13. Supper at Wilcox's. A gathering storm prevents evening meeting. Stay at Fuller's.

July 7 Go on to Bigsby's—thence to Berlin. Whitney's accompany me. Start at 2:00 for Milwaukee. Arrive at 8:00. Put up at Kirby House.

July 8 Start home via Freeport, Fulton Junction, Clinton. Dine at Kraft House, Freeport. Just make close connection at Fulton. Reach home at 8:00.

July 9 Drury calls in Afternoon. Wants me to go with

him to secure subscription next day on Church.

July 10 Call with M.R. Drury at Archer's, Smith's, but get no subscription. Drury not well. Goes home & is quite sick in afternoon. G.W. Statton & J.W. Howe come about 10:00 at night. Have been to Ogden on a visit.

July 11 Go down town with Bros. Howe & Statton. Call with Howe at Drury's & Sutton's after a long search to find head-quarters of the hack driver for Western. Came home much worse for rheumatism. Howe starts for Western. Spend most of afternoon in writing.

July 12 Had considerable rheumatism. Wrote some. Drury came in the afternoon to see about to-morrow's preaching. He appeared very weak from an attack of billous Colic of a few days.

July 13 Preached at Hall at 10 1/2 Ps 84:10. Spoke most of the time sitting. Was both lame & weak. At S. Sch Discussion on predestination etc. Did not go out in evening.

July 14 Spent day in answering letters & getting ready to go to Colorado. Start on 8:00 train. Travel all night and arrive east of Dunlap, Iowa.

July 15 Breakfast at Dunlap. Transfer at Council Bluffs. Start at 12:15 for Cheyenne, Fremont, Columbus, Grand Island, etc. People harvesting with reapers and with headers. Slept in my seat five or six hours. Genial company next forenoon interested in examining flowers, etc. with my Weavers microscope.

July 16 Breakfast the company at Sidney. I buy a peach pie at bakery at 20 cts. Go on to Cheyenne. After two hours go on to Loveland arriving about 6:00. Bro. G.W. Rose meets me. I ride over with Mr. Poushnel to George Lilles. Stay there. To be my home during conference.

July 17 Rev. J.S. Cornell comes. Goes up town. Brings Rev. St. Clair Ross. I had spent fore-noon in brushing up, resting, etc. Conference begins at 2:00. Reports of fields are mostly made. Bro. McCormick preaches at 8:30 "I am the way." I get to bed late but sleep long in morning.

July 18 Conference at 8:30. Reports considered. Item in extoling Blanchard advocate of our law lost. Ross's crossness & imputation of sincerity against Rose. In afternoon, Ross & Hartzelser pouty. Transact most of the business. Rev. Rose preached at night: "Pure religion." I had a seven hours sleep.

July 19 Conference business continued. Dine at D. Hershman's. Rev. H. Ackaret's funeral in the afternoon at 3:00. Col. Robert Cowden spoke at night—on Sabbath School programme. I read Stationing Committee's report. Conference adjourned. I staid at G. Litle's.

July 20 Sunday. I preached at 11:00 from I John 5:18. Sacramental followed. Dined at Archibald Litel's. Bro. Cowden gave a black-board lesson, Sabbath. Quite interesting. Supper at Geo. Litle's. I preach at night from II Tim. 4:7. Father Ackaret's funeral. Stay at Bro. Litel's.

July 21 Spend morning in writing. Dine at Rev. M. Harry's late United Brethren now Baptist. His brother from Missouri there. Talk of the family relations, etc. Went back to Geo. Litel's. Stay there.

July 22 Morning in writing. Take my baggage to the depot. Dine at D. Hershman's. Call at Bro. Leonards. They from Oberlin. Start at 5:30 Aft. for Boulder. Arrive at Boulder. Stay at Cornell's.

July 23 Go on to Denver starting at 8:00. Reach there at 10:55. Cowden going to Lawrence Kan. & Ottawa. Get letter from Susan inclosing [sic] others. Dine at St. Cl. Ross'. Spend awhile in writing. Mail letters and call again at Mother Maples. William Evans likely to die. Had called at H.R. Millers. Visit Bro. Coustable's in West Denver. Supper at Ross's. Call at Well's. Evening at Mapes with sick man. Stay at Rev. H.R. Miller's.

July 24 Go with Miller over City north. Write. Go to P.O. See McCormick & Rose. Go back to Miller's & to depot. Start for Wilson, Kansas. Stop nearly an hour at Cheyenne Wells. The washout delay a false report. Go on. Sleep about five hours on train.

July 25 Reach Wilson at 6:00. Rev. C.U. McKee waiting to take me to Fairview Church, near Elmira Post-office in Mitchell County, to the dedication. Escape a

commencing heavy shower by arriving at Rev. E. Shepherd, the presid.-elder's. Dine there. It is in Lincoln County. Go on to Bro. McKee's. Stay there that night.

July 26 At Bro McKees that day engaged in writing in forenoon for *Telescope* and the Missionary Visitor.

July 27 Preach at 11 at church from Ps. 84:10. Raise $188.00 subscription. Rev. E. Shepherd, Brookheart, Bearss, I. W. Williams, Lewis, Bloyd, Putney etc present; also Talbot. Dine with most of preachers at C.M. McKee's. Rev. Shepherd preaches funeral of Rev. Joseph McKee in afternoon. They give me a collection of about $4.50. I go with Bro. Putney to Beloit. Lodge with Lyman Gunn's.

July 28 Rise early and breakfast at Railroad Hotel. Go on 6:00 train to Cliffton. Write some and go up to Bro. B. Berry's. Dine. Conclude to stay till next day. Go to funeral.

July 29 Go to Junction to Eagle Hotel. Get printing of formsof report at Tribune Office. Write.

July 30 Go on to Burlington, Kansas and with W. Frank Osborn to Virgil. Stay at Osborn's. I.K. Spencer preaches at night. Dined at Mr. Pepper's—She a cousin of Osborn's. A good attendance of the members of Conference.

July 31 Osage Conference convenes at 8:30, Morning. Very fine progress. S.B. McGrew preached. I staid at home to rest. Boundary Committee in room below me. Full house, I heard.

August 1 Conference continues. Dine at D. Baughman's. Col. Robert Cowden lectured on the History of the Bible. Full congregation and much interested.

August 2 Conference closes that day about 6:00. Stationing Com. meet at 7:00 at the school-house. Bro. Cowden lectures at 8:00 on History of the Books of the Bible. We got through about 10:00, stationing. Met presiding elder's committee who were unanimous.

August 3 Sabbath. Peach at 11:00 at Grove by Verdigris River from 2d Cor. 3:7,8. Dined on the ground. Col.

Robert Cowden lectured on the use of the blackboard. I preached at night from Acts 4:31. Rev. E.L. Joslin preached at the school-house. Staid at Osborns.

August 4 Left at 10:00 for Burlington. Arrived about 3:30. Took cars for Junction at 4:55. Arrive at Burlington at 9:30. Stay at Eagle Hotel.

August 5 Went on to Clifton. Put up at B. Berry's. Much crowded. Bro. Bloyd preached at tent at night. I lodge in Mr. Dobbins Dentist Office, with S.D. Stone.

August 6 Conference opened. Get along pretty well. Lodged at Mr. Dobbins' dentist office, but take meals at Bro. B. Berry's.

August 7 Conference continued. Board & lodge as usual.

August 9 A busy conference day. Dine at Jackson's, G.M. Huffman kicked by his horse at Jackson's. Stationing Com. of Kansas met at 7:30. Rev. J.I. Baber preached. Lodged as usual at Dr. Dobin's dental office.

August 10 Sabbath. Meeting at 9:00. I preach at 11:00 from Ps. 18:30. Dine at Mr. Brown's (Baber's niece) with a number of others. Read committees & stationing allotments. Bro. Cowden lectured at 3:00 teaching class of boys & girls, and then giving programmes. Supper at Bro. Berry's. O.A. Chapman preached at night. Sacrament. Rev. C.I. Aldrach's collection for pioneers. Stay at Dentist's.

August 11 Sent two fifty dollar postal orders to Susan, drawn in Reuchlin's name. Mr. Dobbins takes me to Rev. J.I. Baber's. Dine. Aldrach & wife & friend & wife & Isinan [?] dine there also. Baber & wife take us in a wagon to Bro. Livingston's twenty-five miles north. Got lost in prairie. We arrive at 9:20 evening.

August 12 Bro. Livingston took me on to Fairbury. Arrive at 1:30. Dine at Western House. Write after dinner. Go on to Hastings. Put up at Denver House. Wrote a letter home at Fairbury. Called at Dr. Freeman's. Folks away. On the way over called to see Mrs. Hungerford who is low with consumption. A daughter of Dickinson's of DeWitt, Iowa. She aiming to go home. Strong faith in God.

August 13 Spent day in writing. Go at 6:00 for Juniata. Get on wrong train. Succeed in stopping the other train. Find no one waiting. Peter Warder starts with us in carriage about dark. Arrive at Watt Davis' about 11:00. Charges $1.00. Warner, on the way preached soul-sleeping. Insisted on prophecies, but discarded plain texts.

August 14 Meeting at 10:00. Went to Benj. Davis' to dinner. Conference in the afternoon. Went to our Boarding place at Jacob Silvers. Rev. Squires preached at night. Tent by the school-house made of reaping machine canvas. P.O. here in Roseland, Adams Co., Nebraska.

August 16 Conference closed. Bro. Cowden again lectured at night. Stationing Committee met at Morgan's. Finished before night meeting.

August 17 Sunday. Preached at 10 1/2 from I Tim. 4:16. Dined at our usual place. Bro. Cowden lectured in the afternoon. I preach at night, Ps. 87:3. I stay at Silvers. He quite a friend to the church, but not a professor. Pets his little girls, Alma, Alwilde, and Mary.

August 18 Start at 5:30 for Juniata. Arrive just in time to board the cars without a ticket. Arrive at Hastings about 8:30. Go to Denver Hotel. Write. Got letter from home. The Hotel is not very well regulated. Leave Hasting next morning at 4:00. This was a weary day.

August 19 Start from Hastings at 4:00. Breakfast at [blank] arrive at St. Joseph about 5:00. Write and mail several letters. Take St. car for H & St. J. Depot. Start about 8:45 for Chillicothe, Mo., and reach Chillicothe about 12:40. Put up at Browning Hotel. Slept 2 1/2 hours on Cars and three at Hotel.

August 20 Get letter at post-office & package of books at the express office. Mr. Berry called to see me. Also Mr. Rodabaugh, father of Adam Rodabaugh, whom I knew as a student at Un. Bib. Seminary. Rev. S.H. Bagley comes after me.

August 21 Conference begins. Dine and sup at C.J. Kephert's. Nothing very extraordinary. Leander Fisher preaches at 8:00.

August 22 Bro. Kephart goes to Chillicothe to bring

Grace Jeffries, his niece Col. Cowden, arrives via Bedford. Conf. as usual. Bro. Cowden lectured at 8:00. Dined at Wm. Beauchamp's. Stay at boarding place.

August 23 Conference as usual. Dine at E.W. Carpenter's. Supper at D. Beauchamps. Stationing Committee meets at L.D. Ambrose's. Rev. A.W. Geeslin preaches at College Chapel.

August 24 I preach at College Chapel from 2 Cor. 5:20. Ordain C.J. Kephart, J.L. Zumbro, & Leander Fisher. Dine at L.D. Ambrose's. S.S. Meeting in afternoon. Supper at S.H. Bagley's. J.H. Brundige preached at night. Sacramental services. Farewell. Stay at C.J. Kepharts.

August 25 Wm. Beauchamp takes us to Chillicothe. Dine at Browning's Hotel. Prof. Bishop is along. Take cars at 4:39 for Cameron. Supper at Holland House. Start at 9:20 for Washington, Iowa, & travel all night. Sleep about six hours.

August 26 Reach Washington at 5:50 Mron. Breakfast at the Brighton House. Call on Mr. Brokaw and Rev. Mr. Johnson. Mail a letter home. Go at 10:20 to West Chester. Hire conveyance over to Joseph Smith's, two miles north. Dine there. Went on to Hiram Baker's. Staid all night. Very nice people.

August 27 Went on to T.J. Hodges. Took dinner. Neat house-keepers; nice surroundings. Stay till after supper. Went on to church. Rev. H.A. Long preached, on "What think ye of Christ?" Went to Marion. Cochran's, which was Conf. home. Bros. D. Miller & R.L. Bamford came about midnight.

August 28 Conference opened at 8:30 forenoon. Proceeded, after preliminary, to examinations. Dine & sup at Cochran's.

August 29 Conference continues. Dine at Marion Hodges. Supper at Moody's. W.S. Demoss censured. Dr. Favour dropped for nonattendance. Dessinger to be tried.

August 30 Conference continues. Dine at Cochran's. Finish business in the afternoon. Stationing committee meets at Bro. Moody's. Supper there. Bro. J.T. Allaman preaches at 7:45. Stay at Cochran's.

August 31 Sabbath. Preach at 11 from II Cor. 3:7–8. Dine at Mr. Hamilton's with Bro. Thrasher, and Rev. Boston & Melvin (M.E.) and Rev. Jameison of Ch. Union Church. Sab. Sch. meeting in the afternoon—a short sermon by M.S. Drury followed by sacrament. No night meeting. Bro. Schwimley so down-hearted. Stay at Cochran's.

September 1 Cochran brings Schwimley, Cowden & myself to Washington. Dine at Mother Grayson's, opposite to Depot. Rev. D. Miller with us. Go to Columbus Junction on freight train. Go on freight with Cowden to Ced. Rapids. Arrive at 10:15 night. Find all tolerably well. Reuchlin had been somewhat sick.

September 2 Took a drive over town with Col. Cowden. Go at 1:00 on freight to Lisbon. Dine on camp-ground, at 4:00. Sacramental service. I preach at night Rom. 7:13. Large audience. Several seekers. Dedicate the camp-grounds. Go to D. Kunkle's at town & lodge.

September 3 Go on 6:00 train next morning to Cedar Rapids. Bro. Beatty dines with us. Lorin goes with him to Western College to school.

September 5 Went down town in the morning. Spend afternoon and evening in writing, till I was quite wearied.

September 6 Went to Lisbon early. Breakfast at D. Runkles. Get some subscriptions on Church. Witness Cowden's Institute. Dine at T.D. Adams'. Supper at D. Runkle's. Go home on 7:15 train. Drury calls.

September 7 Sunday. At Church at 11. Drury preaches Missionary sermon. Subscription about $31.00. Sabbath School. Preach at 8:00, Rev. 2:17.

September 8 Col. Robert Cowden comes. Go down town with him. Call at Gilmore's. At Ham's office. Dinner. Meet M. Fulcomer. Come back after a call at Coles with Cowden and have a long talk with F. Go to bank and get a draft of $35.00 for G.F. Croddy. Consult Gilmore. Write letters. Official meeting at 7:30.

September 9 Start at Fenton, Ill., & stop off at Fulton. Walk back to East Clinton. Dinner at Clinton. Walk the R.R. bridge. Go on to Fenton, arriving about 3:00, Aft. Call at Rev. J.L. Harrison's. Go to Fred. France's. Palmer preaches at 8:00. F. France's Children: Sarah, Andrew, Orilla, Dora, Nettie.

September 10 Conference opens. P. Hurless' case occupies the day. N.E. Gardner preaches at night. Rev. C. Wendle had brought charges against Parker Hurless for immoral conduct, and Hurless had got out an injunction from the Civil Court against the trial, alledging it was a "conspiracy" against him.

September 11 Conference mostly occupied with Hurless Case. Limiting resolutions. Investigation at night. The limiting resolution resolved to allow no evidence on anything that had transpired before the last annual conference. The charges related to time previous to that time. So the case was shut out! Hurless last night had gone to the Judge and had the injunction dissolved.

September 12 Conf. Continued. Healey & Dessinger refered to a committee of investigation. Vice and tryanny were in the saddle, and partisan wrath sought vengeance.

September 13 Conference continued. Healey passed after acknowledgments. Dessinger defers. Night Session, Dessinger asks a trial. Action postponed till Monday. Bro. F. France has been sick a day or two. H.D. Healey made an abject apology to Miss Broilier, the mistress of Hurless! She was there to crack the whip over recalcitrants!

September 14 Preached at 10 1/2, 2 Pet. 1:!4. Jas. W. Robertson is ordained. Talk with Dessinger in afternoon. M.S. Drury preaches at night.

September 15 Conference continued. Stationing Com. met at noon. I start at 4:35 from Fenton to Fulton. Hackbill 75 cts each. Leave Fulton at 1:30 at night and travel all night. This was a most shameful conference. Parker Hurless, the licentious, had at least two-thirds of the conference as his partisans.

September 16 Arrive at Beloit at 5:00 Morn. Put up at Commercial House. Write and mail letters. Start at 1:40 for Madison. Rev. Eldre on train part of the way. Go on to Spring Green. Met by Young Nickey, who takes us to

Rev. G. Nickey's. Mrs. Nickey is a very small but noble woman, who has general praise.

September 17 Went to Lone Rock in wagon. Took train to Richland Centre. Dined at Hotel. Went on with Bro. Thomas Gillingham to his house. To Mt. Zion Church. Rev. J. Good preached. Rainy on our return home.

September 18 Conference opened. Several applicants in the afternoon, for an. conf. membership. Col. Cowden lectures at night. Such poor lights!

September 19 Conference continues. Basket dinner. Golden was left in Quarterly Conference. Eldred preaches. Stationing-Com. not able to get in Schoolhouse, meets at Thos. Gillingham's.

September 20 Business progresses. Basket Dinner. Much discussion of reports in the afternoon. Conference business session closes. Col. Cowden lectured.

September 21 Sunday. Preach at 11 Heb. 11:26. Dine at Conf. home. Cowden lectures at Anniversary in afternoon. I preach at night I Cor. 5:7. We had a Communion session. Stay at Thomas Gillingham's. His children are: [blank] Ellen, Nora [blank] Harley, Melvin, Victoria.

September 22 Dined at John Gillingham's. He takes us to Richland Center. Took out two postal-orders of $50 each for wife; and one for less for F.W. Wagner, New York. Wrote some letters. Arrive at Lone Rock about dark. Young Nickey meets us. Sup and lodge at Rev. G.G. Nickey's three miles N.W. of Spring Green.

September 23 Went on to Spring Green & to Madison. Dine at R.R. House. Write some letters. Go on to Portage. Put up at the Fox House. Get room 7; in Front.

September 24 Go on to Plover at 6:20. Arrive about 9:00. Dine at Empire House. Rev. Jas. Johnson comes in. Go on to Odgensburg, arriving about 4:00. Put up at Rev. C.M. Clark's, the pastor's. Col. Cowden delivers a short lecture.

September 25 Conference opens at 2:00. N.G. Whitney, C.M. Clark, E. Collins, Miller, Goode, & C.J. Stark present. J. Johnson came about 4:00. Examinations proceed. Starke preached at 7:30 & Johnson exhorted. We lodge at Clark's.

September 26 Conference proceeds. Upton's case causes a dead-lock, and I invite some one else to preside. Get it past. Some feeling over Collins' not getting more appropriation. He and Johnson are a little sharp. Jas. Johnson preaches at night, 1:13; long. Rather chaffy. He is a soft-soaping Irishman.

September 27 Business proceeded. Whitney reelected P.E. Stationing Com. met at noon at Clark's. Robt. Cowden Lectured at 2:45. Conference business is finished in the afternoon. Col. R. Cowden lectured at night on "Books of the Bible." Folks I saw here: Roberts of Oshkosh etc. Col. R. Cowden said of the shirts Mrs. Clark washed for him, that, "they looked as well after wearing them a week, as they did when first put on." Literally true!

September 28 Sabbath. Preach at 10:30 (11:00) from Ps. 25:14. Went with C.J. Stark for dinner to Mr. Gray's. We had ordained three after the sermon: C.J. Stark, Warren F. Goodell & James R. Miller. Col. Cowden lectured at 3:30 (4:00) on Use of Blackboard. I preached (33 1/2 minutes) on John 7:37, and sacrament followed.

September 29 I at Bro. Clark's. Many left for home. Dined at Clark's after calling to see staves cut at staves factory. Wrote a letter to Hillis in the morning. James Johnson preached. I exhorted. Several arose for prayer. Stay at Clark's.

September 30 Start about 10:00 for Winona. Arrive about 6:00. Stay at Huff House.

October 1 Went on to Janesville, Wis. Took Tibbetts aboard at Dover; Bacon at Eota; Hayney at Rochester, etc. Rev. E. Clow and others meet us & take us to Alma City. Make home at Daniel Bickford's. He a Mason; she an Adventist. Children: Nellie, & Frank. Rev. W.C. Bacon preached, well, in the evening.

October 2 Conference began. An experience Meeting; right good, in Conference. Thursday night, I preached, Ps. 92:8.

October 4 Conference continues. M.L. Tibbetts elected P.E. Stationing Com. met at Brickford's at 1:00. Short session at night after which Cowden lectured. We Had a short experience meeting in forenoon.

October 5 Sabbath. Preached at 10:30 from I Tim. 3:16. Ordained John M. Tresenriter, Isaac N. English & Jacob L. Berry. I Dined at Mr. Gates', a disbeliever's. Sabbath School Anniversary in the afternoon. M.S. Drury preaches at night. Sacrament followed. Stay as usual, at Daniel Bickford's.

October 6 Went on to Janesville, and take freight at 9:00 for Mankato. Delayed at the Junction waiting for the other train which was jammed and came in at 2:00. Arrive and dine at City Hotel. Cowden, Drury, & Thayer along. Go on 7:00 train for Sioux City. Arrive about 4:00 morning.

October 7 Breakfast & dine at Railroad House. Write letters. Call at Gen. Office at Dak. Southern and buy half fare tickets. Ascend the Court-House observatory and get a fine view of the City, with Bro. Drury. Start at 2:40 for Elk Point, Dakota. Arrive at 4:00 & put up at Emory Morris', my home. Get letters.

October 8 Write letters. At a funeral at M.E. Church, by D.T. Hutchison. Many conference members come during the day. Meeting at night. Dr. H.B. Bunce preaches. Preached with energy and tolerable ability, but he was a feeble brother in judgement & discretion.

October 9 Members of Church at Elk Point: Emery Morris, William Hodges, Edward Tanbert, Edith Burdick, etc. Conference opened at 2:00. Speaking meeting. Supper at Rev. Joshua V. Himes' an ex-Adventist's. Drury preached at night. This Himes was the much distinguished editor in Millerism, in 1843 & 1864, but had left the Adventists, now was Episcopal.

October 10 Conference as usual. I preach at night from John 7:37.

October 11 Conference Session. D.M. Harvey is elected P.E. Stationing Committee met at E. Morris' at 6:30. Bro. Cowden lectured at 7:30 on Books of the Bible.

October 12 I Preached at 10 1/2 Heb. 11:10. Raised subs. of $342.50 toward Church—over $100.00 more than called for—and dedicated the Church at Elk Point, Dakota. Bro. Cowden occupied at the S.S. An. in the afternoon. J.D. Rust preached at night, & I.G.W. Chase at the M.E. Church. Short 1 minute session of conference. Speaking meeting and tobacco revival. 5 renounce the use of it.

October 13 I Take train at about 10 1/2 for Sioux City. Arrive soon after noon. Dine at Railroad Hotel. Train at 2:30 for Mo. Valley & Council Bluffs. Arrive at C Bluffs about 7:00. Go to Rev. J.F. Roberts. Stay there. Bro. Cowden goes to young Talbot's & stays.

October 14 Go on to Casey. Dine at the Denning House. Called at Burns & McFarlands Store. T.J. Burns gave me as reliable men near Adair land: Lee Hoisington, North, George Lowry (north) & R.H. West. Others recommended the same. Rode out to D. Hepler's with Dutch Ludwick. Look at the broken prairie on Wm. Wright land. Call at Hepler's. Stay at George Lowry's. They not Methodists, but board M.E. preachers. He from near Cleveland, O. She from Canada.

October 15 Start about 7:00 for Casey. Ride about 3 1/2 out of the 5 1/2 miles with Henry Shelters. He recommends also Lee Hoisington, George Lowry, and Joseph Rutt, who lives 3 1/2 miles S. of Casey on Greenfield road. Go on to Van Meter. Find home at Rev. S.E. Dennis's. Statton preaches at night. Probably George.

October 16 Conference opens & progresses rapidly in examination.

October 18 Conference continues. Stationing Com. meets at noon & evening. Night session primarily on resolutions on Mis. Church Erie Education, etc.

October 19 Sunday. Preached at 10 1/2 from I John v.18–19. Dine at Bro. Jennings, a merchant's. Col. Cowden occupies the afternoon on Books of the Bible. I call at Mr. Seamen's, a M.E. man. George Statton preaches at 7:30 on "labor & heavy laden."

October 20 Started for home about 12:00. Cut across on branch-road from Iowa City to Oasis. Got home about 11:00. Found all well.

October 21 Was at home in forenoon. Went to town in afternoon. Went to Western with Rev. M.R. Drury arriving about 9:00 evening. Staid at Rev. M.S. Drury's. Orville had a chill before I left home.

October 22 Conference opened. Progressed smoothly principally on examinations. I find my home at Pres. E.B. Kephart's. W.J. Shuey & Robt. Cowden come. Shuey my room mate. Col. R. Cowden lectured at 7:30 on S. Schools. Heard by card that Orville was about right well.

October 23 Conference progresses well. I dine at Rev. I.L. Buchwalter's. Rev. Charles Wendle preaches at 7:30. "Be not weary in well-doing," etc. Heard by Drury that Orville was having another chill.

October 24 Conference continues. Dine at Prof. J.H. Albert's. Supper at Rev. Martin Bowman's. Shuey preaches at night from "Labor not for the meat," etc.

October 25 Stationing Com. meets at 7:00. Conf. continued. Dine at John Horn's. Stationing Com. at 12:30 [unreadable] on secrecy & the Cynosure. Susan & children come. Rhetorical Contest at 7:30. Night session. Adjourn at 11:00.

October 26 Sunday. Preach at 10 1/2, 2 Pet. 1:16. Ordain Theodore P. Griffith and Lemon B. Hix. Dine at Kephart's. S.S. Anniversary in Aft. Supper at I.L. Buchwalter's. D. Wenrich preached at 7:00. Harding's tripple [sic] praying. Drury's speaking-meeting. McCormack's singing. Harding's talk. Stay at Pres. Kepharts.

October 27 Went to College prayers. Harding complaining of getting missionary apportionments only according to time. I go in Kephart's buggy home. I Buy Lorin overcoat of Levi, the Jew. Spend part of aftern. in reading & arranging letters.

October 28 Went down to Church. Rev. Wm. Cunningham and wife dine with us on their way to Vinton, their home. Went down town in the afternoon. Spent some time in reading & arranging correspondence.

October 29 At home. Went down via Church to post-office. Indroduced by Mr. Collier to Rev. Mr. Bennet, the M.E. pastor. Arrange Conference appointments for 1880. I send on for publication in the Almanac. Go down to post-office and by the church. Write letters in the evening & postals.

November 2 The pastor, Bro. Drury, discoursed on duty of attendance, etc. I go to R.G. Shuey's to dinner. Preach at Dairy Dale at 3:00 from John 7:37. Had an attentive congregation. I Staid at Sabbath School. M.R. Drury preached at night from [blank] at Post-office Hall.

November 3 Called at Drury's and examine his subscription for Church & also cost of Church and present state of finances. Write in afternoon. In the evening, I go to Mr. Bever, junior, and get a subscription of $25.00 on the new Church.

November 4 Wrote letters & went to post-office, calling by the Church.

November 9 Sunday. Preached at Post-office Hall at 10 1/2 I Pet. 2:7. Taught a class in Sabbath-School. Bro. Cotton, of Dakota, came in the afternoon, he having been at work last week four miles below town. M.R. Drury preaches at night. Our boys start for Western on the 2:o'clock train in morning.

November 11 About as usual in employment. N. Fulcomer comes. I agree to forgive his debt to me on books sold, and give him $2.00 toward a buffalo overcoat. He had good talent, but lacks energy.

November 12 Spent forenoon in writing. Went afternoon with Bro. Drury to obtain subscription to Church & obtained from16–20 dollars. Went to prayer-meeting in the evening. W.B. Smith led it. Good attendance.

November 13 Went to post-office. Got the Telescope. Went by Church. Drury away. Went after subscription to S.L. Cook, Bocksmith, Averill, etc.

November 14 Start for Columbus Junction at 2:25 a.m. Breakfast at Star House. Go on to Keota. Call at Schreckengast's Store. Go with Rev. W.O. Smith & wife & Jeff. Hodge to Hodge's & dine. Go in the evening to Zion Center Church 1 m N & 3 m east of Keota, and preach, John 12.26. Stay at Rev. W.O. Smith's, lately married.

November 15 Went to Mr. ("Bro.") Robinson's. She a sister of Robt. West, who from Miami Conf. went to the Presbyterians & afterward to the Congregationalists. She as unreliable as hen's. Went to Bro. Moody's. Rev. W.O. Smith, the pastor preaches "What shall it profit a man," etc. Rather a good effort. I stay at Bro. Moody's. Ida, Nettie, Aleck.

November 16 Sunday. Preached at Zion Center Church, Wash. Co. Iowa, & raised $293.00 to—with $175.00 in notes before—pay $400.00 debt to Ch. Erection and interest. Dine at F. Marion Hodge's. Preached at 11 from Ps. 137:6; at night, John 7.37. Stay at Moody's. It rained after meeting, so I give out meeting the early train at Wellman.

November 17 Go to Keota. Dine at Isaac Schreckengast's. He a merchant at Keota, formerly of Burlington. Go on 5:00 train to Columbus Junction. Supper at the Gilbert House. Go on 9:35 train to Cedar Rapids. Arrive 12:20.

November 18 At Home. Did little as I had lost sleep and felt worn down. Slept two hours in the afternoon. Estimating Committee in Evening. Bear, Shuey & myself presant at Drury's. Estimate Dairy Dale $150.00, Stony Point $100.00.

November 19 Day much as usual, only I spent afternoon in aiding in soliciting about $30.00 toward Church.

November 20 Started at 3:10 for Burlington. Connected for Keokuk. Staid at Patterson House. Clean, hard bed & moderate breakfast, $1.25.

November 21 Went on to Quincy. Start at 3:35—lengthened to 4:35—for Brashear. Arrive at 7:30. Preach a short sermon to an expectant, but unexpected congregation, Ps. 1:6. Stay at Rev. Jas. Herbert's. Saw Rev. Mr. Caruthers of M.E. Church, etc.

November 22 Went over to Perry Garlock's. Call at Father Kelly's on the way. Stay at Perry's till after meeting.

Preach at 7:00, Acts 16:14. Stay at Perry Garlock's.

November 23 Sunday. Preach at 11 from Heb. 13:14. Raise about $220.00 & dedicate Pleasant View Chapel. Dine at A. Jackson Garlock's. He and Jacob are sons-inlaw of Father Kelly. Rev. Mr. Edmonson & his congregation there. Call at Jacob Garlock's a few minutes in the evening. Preach at 7:00 from John 7:37. Stay at Perry Garlock's.

November 24 Went early with Father Herbert to Brashear. Call at his house awhile. Start at 10:00 for Quincy. Arrive at 2:30. Start at 3:45 for Burlington. Arrive at 7:30. Connect and arrive at Cedar Rapids about 12:30 (Midnight).

November 25 Went to see new Church which is nearly all built up to within 2 ft of the square. Mother Drury comes to Marion's on a short Call. See Rev. Martin Bowman at Post-office, who has lately moved to the City—West Iowa Avenue.

November 26 At home most of the day. Got our turkey of Siniuky—rather a cheat in weight & quality. The boys came home from Western about 5:00. We went to the prayer-meeting at the hall—a sort of thanksgiving service.

November 27 Spent day at home mostly. Boys start at 2:00 for Western. Donation prayer-meeting at Drury's. We go down at 5:00, and leave $2.00.

November 28 Spent the day mostly at home. Went down in the afternoon to bank, Post-office, & new Chruch.

November 29 Spent the day mostly at home. Reuchlin came home from Western at 11:00.

November 30 Sunday. Preached at 10 1/2 at the Hall Acts 16:14. Taught the Sabbath School Class. Went to Dairy Dale. Preached Ps. 17:15. At Church at night. Bro Drury lectured on temperance.

December 1 Called in the forenoon and in the afternoon at Bever's Bank. The old man put me off with James' Subscription after all his promises.

December 2 At home in forenoon about as usual. Went in afternoon with Susan to John Bear's Dockery's, & Christian Bear's. Rented property of Epley for five months, and paid off the lease for $105.00 to W. Cooper, to whom the lease was transferred. Bought at Jackson's a casamier plants pattern at $7.50.

December 3 Spent forenoon at home in reading. Went to prayer-meeting.

December 5 At home mostly. Broke plate of Artif. teeth. Took it to Dr. Walter's. Drury called in afternoon. Went and got my (teeth) rubber plate from Walter's. Rainy day.

December 6 Went down town. Saw M.S. Drury, Kephart, etc. Did some trading. Went in afternoon to Quarterly Conference at Dairy Dale. Morgan S. Drury presided, Sutton being absent. J. Bear reported over full quota for Cedar Rapids. Came home after Drury's sermon at night. Sup at Kieths.

December 7 Went in buggy with wife to Derry Dale. Preached at 11 from Isa. 28:5,6. Sacrament followed. Came home. Preached at night from I Thess 4:3.

December 8 Morgan S. Drury came and we went to Judge Green's, who promised us $20.00 certain, and hoped to make it three or four times as much. Called at Dr. Mansfield's, who put us off, and was disinclined really. Went in afternoon with Marion Drury. Obtained promise of doing something of Dows & B.F. Mills, and $5.00 of Bradley of leatherstorc.

December 9 Spent day mostly at home & much in writing.

December 10 Spent day mostly in writing and getting ready to go away Thursday morning.

December 11 Left home at 2:00 A.M.—reached Burlington about 7:00—left for Quincy at 7:45, reached that place about 11:00. Went on a delayed train to Hannibal, arriving at 4:00 P.M. Stayed at Depot—except climbing a high hill, up the river, and a walk up town. Left for Ft. Scott at 11:00 at night. Passed Sedalia in the night, having also passed Moberly.

December 12 Awoke near Windsor. Country largely prairie, not the richest. Arrive at Ft. Scott Junction at 11:00 A.M. Mild day. Thermom. 25 degrees above zeor at noon. Wait till 3:20 for train to Cherokee—arrive about dark. Rev. J. Hogan meets me. Find Rev. E.L. Joslyn & Rev. Hinton there. There I lodge.

December 13 Stay at Bro. Hogan's till afternoon. Bor. Joslyn preaches at 2:30. Quarterly conference. Bro. Hinton preaches at 7:00, a good sermon. Rev. S.B. Graves, A.C. Easton, Rev. Foley & others come. Rev. Mr. Murray, the M.E. pastor with us. Stay with E.L. Joslyn, Hinton, at the Pastor's. Took supper at Jonathan Graves.

December 14 Sunday. Preach at 11:00 Ps 48:11, etc. Raise $361.00. Dedicate Cherokee Church. It was in quite an unfinished condition. Dine with Bro. Joslyn at Bro. Price's, M.E. people. Return to Hogan's. Mrs. Ward, Tibbett['s] sister, calls to see me. Judge E.A. Perry calls to speak about the funeral service of his brother's child at 9 1/2 next day. Preach at night from I Cor. 5:7. Sacrament. Stay at Rev. Mr. Murray's, M.E.

December 15 Jac. Brumbach comes & takes me to his house, 1 1/2 ms. N.E. of town. Dine. They were old neighbors in Henry Co., Ind. Return to Hogan's & we go to E.A. Perry's, Esq. to supper. Take the train to Parson's City. Marshal comes to my Host's, Bro. A. Carey's, to arrest me, on a discription: 5 ft 8 in., 160 lbs, slightly bald, short gray in whiskers. Marshall Hoffman is sold! He felt that he was badly beaten.

December 16 Start at 6:00 for Emporia. Reach there at 3:30. Telegraph to Oage City that I will be there on 9:00 train. Dine at European House. Write letters at post-office. Arrive at Osage City at 10:00 Revs. Cowdrey & Rosenberg wait [on] me at the train. Stay at Bro. Cowdrey's. No telegram had come. Cowdrey has seven children.

December 17 Get Card from home at post-office. Dine at Dr. J.H. Rosenberg's in S.E. outside of town. Left at 12:40 for Lecompton. Stop at Rev. Horace D. Herr's. Went to prayer-meeting at College Chapel. Called at Levi Lippy's. Stay at Bro. Herr's. Questioned the man at telegr. office at Osage for not delivering the telegram to Cowdrey. Said could not find him!

December 18 Call at Rev. R. Loggan's. Attend one of Prof. Bartlett's recitations. Dine at Lippy's. Call at Prof. Bartlett's at 2:00. Lafayette Champ came in & I go to his house a few minutes. Supper at Bartlett's. Preach at College Chapel at 6:30, I This. 4:3. Stay at Horace Herr's.

December 19 Call at Prof. Tohill's. Dine at Bro. L. Champ's. Take the train at 12:30 for Meredin via Topeka by the Court House to the State House. Got upon the rising walls & foints of the new building—walk round the old capitol building and return via the Lincoln School-building to depot. Arrive at Meredin about 3:40. Stay at Rev. G.M. Hoffman's in S.E. part of the city.

December 20 Spent morning in reading and writing. Had a financial meeting at 2:00 with good prospects. Went back to Bro. Hoffman's. Preach at 7:00, Ps. 84:11. Rev. J.H. Zabriski had come. Stay at Hoffman's. Rev. J.H. Zabriski stays there also. He Showed a card Bro Lacock had written, about Lane University and Bro. Zabriski's secrecy proclivities.

December 21 Sunday. Preach at 11:00, Matt. 13:31. Call for 500.00. Raise $670.00. Dine at Hoffman's. Preach at 6:30, Eph. 2:4. Stay at Hoffman's with Young Petty, a promising Young Baptist minister of nineteen years.

December 22 Social meeting at 10:00, led by Bro. Petty. Few present, but a pretty good meeting. Trustees give me $40.00 for my services; but I subscribe $15.00 on the Church subscription and pay it. Start at 3:25 for home. Connect at Atchison for Columbus Junction at about 6:00. Sleep about four or five hours on Cars.

December 23 Arrive at Columbus Junction about 7:00. Breakfast at Star House. Return to depot at 8:00. Start at 9:30 for home. Arrive at Cedar Rapids before one o'clock.

December 24 Lorin came home from Western. Reuchlin came on midnight train.

December 25 Spent day at home. We had a fine large turkey which weighed 18 pounds.

December 27 At home. Warm enough to work on the Church.

December 28 Sunday. At Church morning and evening. Went to Stony Point in the afternoon. Preached, John 1:29.

December 30 Went down town. Called at Church. Some hands at work on the Church-roof. Called at Gilmore's office, to see about Anson Moor's business. Called at Collier's law-office, to tell of seeing Judge Perry's. He a slow student of old. I Reported the Christmas turkey as overweighing—18 pounds instead of fifteen—no additional charge made. Bradley the contractor called on me.

December 31 Went afternoon to Bull's, Esq. and Collected some money on Church Subscription & of Olmsted on Hall dues. Went in forenoon and got tin sheets for Church. Somewhat feverish. Went to bed early and slept well. This day closed another year of ministerial and official work. It was severe but pleasant. Praise the Lord for the multitude of his mercies.

Memoranda

The Indians in Wisconsin were by name the Littleman's. His devotions were in the Indian language. Hers were in the English. She seemed to have a fine Christian spirit. At Ogdensburg Conference, they probably sleighted, and she expressed her feelings to me in a kind Christian spirit.

Incidents 1879

Mother Lois Hinman—a Wright. Mother Koerner is living at D.K. Zeller's, May 2nd, 1879. I see Uncle Reuben's relatives May 13, 1879. Relatives May 12. I see Simeon Bullock, the last time at Rev. John Morgan's, May 17, 1879, in Andersonville. Saw John Lawrence's father and Brother S.Y. Lawrence June 1. Reuchlin takes prize on Evidences of Christianity, June 5. I visited Jacob Brumbach's Dec. 15. That night I am almost arrested at Parson.

The Year 1879

Held Qr. Conference at Shueyville, Jan. 4. Project of buying a school-house in C. Rapids for a chapel, 16. Went to Des Moines the 17, saw Steve's wife whom Haye's accused of lying about his plagiarism! Jan 19, dedicate the Church. Saw State House, yet unfinished. At revival at Fry's Chapel, where we get bulk of members, the 26. Went to Stony Point Feb. 25, planned to get that class. Dedicate the church in West Union Feb. 9, Drury. Feb. 12. I start at Polo, Ill. to consider Grim's attempt to try Desinger. Much of a gathering. We get up a paper signed by both parties; home 14. March 3, I go to Moline, Ill. and hold meeting—out at Coal town to Giles'. Go home March 10. March 18, attend State anti-secrecy Convention at West Branch. Rev. Rathbun works degrees of Masonry. Mar. 22, I.K. Statton held Qr. meeting. Pr. Walter Burt Smith's wife's funeral, near Shellsburg. March 28, am in Sedgwock City, Kansas. Dine Sunday, at Samuel Fry's, Joseph Henry's son. April 1st, I go to Lincoln, Nebr. and stay with Rev. Scott at Jas. Paden's. Go to Polo Church 15 N.W. Apr. 5, we raise over $100.00 to keep good name at "Fairbury College." Next go to Myer's S.E. Loyd's fatherinlaw—sod house—prairie fire threatens [?] new Church. Awfully swift winds. Apr. 13, dedicate new church at Halbrook. Apr. 15 Saw William Wright's land for first time. Apr. 20, I am at Western preaching. Apr. 27, Sunday, Indian Squaws come in & I read Greek in an answer to their begging. I start May 1, to Dayton, Ohio. May 4, Bish. Weaver pr. baccalaureate. I stay at Samuel Wright's on Summit Street, May 5. May 7, Mobley graduates. May 9, I go to Bish. Dickson's at Westerville. I stay the 11th at H.A. Bovey's. Mowers pr. An. Mis. Sermon. Saw Harriet Bond. Aunt S[unreadable] at Dayton on my return. I dine at Wm. Ferguson's, Mrs. Lehman there. Other relatives, May 13. I go to Daniel Koerner's, May 14. Go to Glenwood 15. Visit Rev. John Morgan; saw Simeon Bullock. Saw Sarah (Morgan) Mullen, 17. Meeting at Sanes Creek, 18. Went to Harvey's, 19. Supper at Dr. G.F. Chittenden's, and to Uncle William Reeder's, 22. Sarah Little's funeral, Garrison. Start from Marion to Chicago, and home, Iowa. Went to Ebon S. Bunce's at Grundy, to Badger Hill. Pr. dedicatory sermon June 1. Dr. S.Y. Lawrence and his father there, John's relatives. Went home June 2. June 5, bought Emphatie Ciaglet; that day Reuchlin got a ten-dollar prize at Coe's Collegiate Institute, on Evidences of Christianity. Dedicate a church the 8th at Granville, Iowa. Failed to go to Avalon, Missouri, June 13th. At P.E. I.K. Statton's 2 m. at Cedar Rapids, 14th. At Western, at E.B. Kephart's settlement with Row over College fuss, June 20th. Send by Rev. Geo. Miller to settle with breakers of sod on farm June 22. Start to Minnesota, June 26. Go out to Pomme de Tere, June 27. Arrive at Camp-ground. Go via Wynona to Fox River Camp Meeting July 2. Prevented from preaching Sunday by a heavy rain, July 6. Reach home, July 8th. Preached for Drury, the pastor—he unwell. I was lame and sitting, July 13. Start to Colorado, 14th. Reach Loveland, July 16. Start to Colorado, July 15th. G.W. Rose meets me at Loveland 16. Conf. 17th. Robert Cowden with me. July 23, at Denver. Dedicate a new church at McKee's in West Kans. 22nd. July 31, at Osage Conf. Cowden with me. Preach on Verdigris River near Virgil at Conference Aug. 3. Put up at B. Berry's at Clifton. Aug 6th, Baber takes me in his wagon away north—Lost. Conf. at Juniata P.O. Roseland. Adams Co., Nebr. August 19, Chillicothe, Mo. Rodabaugh called. Ordain C.J. Kephart at Avalon, Mo. Dr. Favour dropped Aug. 29th. From East Des Moines I go to Washington and home Sept. 11. Go to Lisbon to camp-ground and dedicate it Sept. 17. Long talk with Mr. Fulcomer, Sept. 8. Our noted Rock River Conf. met.

Texts preached in Minnesota
Near Dover: "Halting between two opinions." "Pr. Christ Crucified." At Conf. in Blue Earth Co: "Take heed at thyself," etc. At Campmeeting on Colb River: "We know that he that is born of God doth not commit sin," etc. Campm. at Pomme de Terre: "Golden bells & pommegranite," "Word of Lord tried." "Go teach all nations."

Texts pr. in Fox River
2 Cor. 3:7–8. Oshkosh. Lima: John 14:2.

Received of Rev. A.L. Palmer of East Des. June 9th 1.00 on moving expenses. Received of Salary at Neb. Conference April 1879 (including present at Myers neighborhood $90.00. Church Expenses paid $2.00. Gen. S.S. (Paid Shuey) 3.50 Benefic Fund (paid) 4.40.

Sermons at Miline Ill. Ece. 1, 1878: Luke 15:7; also in evening Rom. 2:5. Dec. 2, John 14:2,3. Dec. 3, Ps. 85:6. Dec. 4 Ez. 33.11

Wm Wright's Land
South half of Section 4 Town 76 Range 32 Adair Co., Iowa. Ezra A. Cook says he can furnish 1 or 2 page tracts (20,000) at 35 cents per thousand & 4 page tracts at 65 cents per thousand.

1 8 8 0

Thursday, January 1 Another year. "His merciful kindness endureth forever." Went down town. Drury's had come home. Her sister dead. Wrote some in the morning. Got papers and read considerable.

Friday, January 2 Staid at home, my cold on my lungs continuing. I did considerable letter-writing.

Saturday, January 3 Spent the day mostly in hunting up Stationing Committee's reports, Statistics, etc. for a scrap-book of the Annual Conferences.

Sunday, January 4 Went to Hall, Drury preached. I taught the women's class in S.S. Did not go out at night.

Monday, January 5 Went to town bought a considerable amount of the groceries and some at other places.

Tuesday, January 6 Lorin went to town, to start to Western, but could not for want of room in the hack. I went to office & called at Drury's. Windows for lower part of the church came, as I left.

Wednesday, January 7 Lorin Went to Western. Drury (M.E.) in town. Pay half-term to him for Reuchlin. Called at Gilmore's Office. Gilmore is a lawyer in town.

Thursday, January 8 Reuchlin goes to Western, on 2 1/2 train to Ely.

Friday, January 9 Went to town & got papers—took out two postal-orders to John E. Hill, Greenfield, Iowa. Failed to get letter mailed on train.

Saturday, January 10 Spent forenoon at home. Dr. Reed engaged me to preach for the Congregationalists tomorrow. Everett Sutton dines with us. Go down town & buy coat & hat at Jackson's. Drury & I look after a stove. Dr. Walter donates one. Mailed letter to Hill.

Sunday, January 11 Preached at Kindergarten rooms, to Congregationalists, Heb. 7:26. Dine at home & go to Derry Dale in afternoon. Pr. at 2:30, 2 Tim. 1:7. Did not go out Sunday night.

Monday, January 12 Went down to P.O. Called at Church. Got letters from Anson Moor, card from Reuchlin & half fare permit on Bur. & Mo. Riv. R.R. Work on annual Report considerable of the day.

Tuesday, January 13 Called at the Church. Spent nearly all day and evening on my Annual report of West Mis. Dist.

Wednesday, January 14 Finished up Annual report of the District and mailed it. Called at Gilmore's in the afternoon and saw the heirs' deeds to Adair lands sent on for exchange with me. Wrote letters in the evening. Had called at Church to see how work progressed. Got letter from Bro. Joseph Hoke.

Thursday, January 15 Got form of deed from Little & Little. Go down at 10: sign and exchange. Send deeds to Greenfield for record by registered letter. Go down in evening to look up our Church building account. Lockwood (book Canvasser) there and hindered us.

Friday, January 16 Went to Drury's and looked up those

accounts. Found Total Cost so far $3,326.53 Cash received & paid out 1,441.53 Labor performed 261.00 Total indebtedness 1.664.22 Unpaid Subs. 702.20 Of this doubtful 101.20. Went with Drury to canvass in afternoon. About $25.00 promised.

Saturday, January 17 Boys came home. Wrote some in morning. Went to Western in the afternoon. Got to Kephart's about 6:15. Supper. Went to meeting. Rev. T.D. Adams was preaching. One arose for prayers. Staid at Pres. Kephart's.

Sunday, January 18 Preached at 10 1/2 from Matt. 19.27. Dined at Rev. I.L. Buchwalter's. General class at 2:30. Good. Many speak. Call at M.S. Drury's. Sup at Rev. F.O. Adam's. Preach at 6:30, Luke 23.4, "I find no fault." Stay at Adams'.

Monday, January 19 Call at A. Perry's; at Drury's; Dine at Prof. P. Wagner's. Her step-father, Samuel Denman of Circleville, Ohio. Call at Kephart's, Drury's, Churchill's & Rock's. Engaged four windows for Ced. Rapids Church. Lorin takes me to Ely. Iowa City train 2 1/2 hours behind. Call at M.R. Drury's & he comes up.

Tuesday, January 20 Went to town. Call at Drury's. He went to Lisbon at 4:00 p.m. I call at Waterhouse's, and he shows me sample chairs, and promises to put in a window in church. Go by church. Fixed up composition on an experiment on Copying letters, etc.

Thursday, January 22 Drury dines with us. Goes on the hack to Western. M.R. Drury returns from Lisbon. Had raised $39.00 subscription.

Friday, January 23 Went down and looked at the windows of Universalist Church with Bro. Drury & Mr. Fassett.

Saturday, January 24 Went down to see Mr. Fassett at Drury's. He offers to put in the 15 windows at $180.00, we paying the freight. Saw him there at 4 1/2. He at night partly promised to put them in at $170.00, Williams competing.

Sunday, January 25 Preached at P.O. Hall at 10 1/2, II Cor. 4.17, "Light afflictions." Preached at 2 1/2 at Derry Dale, Acts 11.24. M.R. Drury preaches at night, from "Labor not for the meat that perisheth," etc.

Monday, January 26 Went to town. Mifflin subscribed $10. Went to Pastor's meeting at M.E. Went in afternoon with Drury to raise subscription: Sweat, $5, Judge Wisner $5. (said "too many churches now." but Presbyterians have three!), Robine $5. W.B. Smith engaged me to address the Reform Club on temperance evening of Feb. 3d.

Tuesday, January 27 Went to town about noon. Went again in afternoon. Mr. Osgood gone. Called at the church. Plastering partly dry—nearly all beyond freezing. Mrs. Drury & Wright start out to canvass for chairs, etc. Reported back that they found many "on their last legs!"

Wednesday, January 28 Went to Western via Ely in afternoon. Call at Churchill's to see our boys also at Drury's. Sup at Pres. Kephart's. Stay at John Kephart's. Tell him of our Church-building.

Thursday, January 29 John agrees to put in a window at Ced. Rapid's Church. I Preach at College, 2 Chron. 1:10 Solomon's prayer—day of prayer for Colleges. Dine at F.D. Adams'. Call at Shatto's & at Ransom Davis' to supper. Meet Exec. Com. at College. Stay at Daniel Manning's.

Friday, January 30 Attend recitations in forenoon. Go to C.C. William's at Shueyville & he agrees to put in a window. Dine at Anderson's & he puts in 1/2 wimdow. Call at Bowersox. Brown's. Sup at Kephart's. Mother Perry gives a window. Walk to Ely. Cars delayed get home at 12:20.

Saturday, January 31 Down town, mail letters. Call at pastor Drury's. Boys come from Western, Canvass for church. Bros. Uriah Runkle & Booher come & stay till bedtime—train to Lisbon. Booher agrees to send us two cane chairs.

Sunday, February 1 At Church & Sab. Sch. Drury preached. Letter from Connor & St. J.&D. R.R. Card from I.K. Statton, saying Father Wm. Davis is dead. Died about 5:00 last evening. I Preach at church in evening.

Monday, February 2 Spent the time mostly at home. Drury called. Did not go on 4:00 train to Lisbon & before 10:00, Mr. Emerson called, to tell me the funeral was deferred till Wednesday, to await the coming of Jo from Detroit; also brought a volume of Lisbon Sun.

Tuesday, February 3 Spent forenoon mostly at home in taking notes. Went in aftern. to see Dows. Did not. Went to Lisbon on 4:00 train. Supper at I.K. Statton's. Preached at 7:00 I John 4:10. Staid at Statton's. 8 members joined that night. Called at Davis'.

Wednesday, February 4 Preached funeral of a grand man, Rev. Wm. Davis, at 10:00. Adams & Statton make remarks. Dine at Davis' with the preachers. Secured a window at Lizie S. Runkle's. Came home, arriving at 8:00.

Thursday, February 5 Went to town & got letters from Prof. C.J. Kephart & Bish. N. Castle. Called at Church. Joined in marriage Mr. H.C. Baird & Lizzie Shuey, at 3:30. Went down to town and mailed certificate of marriage to County Clerk and a complaint to Am. Book Exchange about books not coming.

Friday, February 6 Called at Church and Drury's. Paid M.S. Drury $4.25 on College tuition. Went in afternoon to see Dows at his office. He out of town. Wrote letters in the evening.

Saturday, February 7 Went to Olin. Dined at Samuel Easterly's, who was very sick. Many in to see him. Went to Jonathan Easterly's, who came after me. Preached at St. John Church at 7:00 from Haggai 1.7, "Consider your ways." Very attentive congregation. Staid at Easterly's. Good rest.

Sunday, February 8 Preached at 11 from Isa. 62.1, "lamp that owneth." Had taught a class in Sab. School. Dine at Rummel's. Preach at night from 2 Cor. 4.3,4, "Hid-lost." Bro M. Bowman exhorted. Stay at Jonathan Easterly's.

Monday, February 9 Call at Rummel's. Dine at Samuel Easterly's, in Olin. Bowman sends $100.00 by me to Henry, his son, a lawyer in Ced. Raps. Arrive at Cedar Rapids about 8:00. Examine the books received. Sit up quite late.

Tuesday, February 10 Got letter from Christopher MastersEnclosing $25.00 for upper Church windows. Called at Drury's. Drury comes up in the afternoon of next day, & shown up Church accounts. In debt deeper than he had heretofore represented.

Wednesday, February 11 Spent morning in reading. Got letter from W. Kansas & the newspapers. Read much in them, and in books. Went to prayer-meeting at Church. Rev. Mr. Gordon Bible Canvasser present. Drury come up & gives in Accts. Church.

Friday, February 13 Spent day mostly in reading, and in writing letters. Reuchlin came home on hack.

Saturday, February 14 Went to P.O. John Bear came. Had engaged a window & collected seventeen dollars for our church, at Mr. Vernon & Lisbon. Bro. D. Manning brought us 1 doz. chickens, on Ch. window account. Boys went to Western, Lorin having come on the hack, this morning.

Sunday, February 15 Went to Church, Bro. M.R. Drury preached Ex. 20.3. Ham Sexton tried to roast us. I Taught Reeder's Sab. Sc. Class, "Law of Laws." I Preach, at 7:00, Ps. 19.7. Ham renewed the coffee-roasting process. John Bear tore down the side windows & relieved me some.

Monday, February 16 At home reading some & writing a little. Andrew Ford asks me to preach at Van Buren St. Church.

Tuesday, February 17 At home mostly. Preach at 8:00 at V.B. St. Church—Acts 16.31.

Wednesday, February 18 Wrote a little. Very nervous. Went to town. Bought some articles at "10 cent" store. Morgan S. Drury came. Went to prayer-meeting.

Thursday, February 19 Wrote to Balt. & Ohio R.R. for half-fare. Went with M.S. Drury to see Judge Green. Did not find him at home.

Friday, February 20 Mostly at home. The boys come home on the midnight train.

Saturday, February 21 Went down town part of the forenoon. Missed the train to Vinton. Boys start to Western on the hack, or cars. Went on the 12:30 train to Vinton. Stay at the Really House.

Sunday, February 22 Go to Rev. J.G. Stewart's. Breakfast. They take me to Prairie Church, six miles S.E. of Vinton. Preach 11 from I John 5.18,19. Dine at John Dilling's. Preach at 7:30 I John 4.10. Stay at Dilling's. Members: Learner, Kuhn, Sinouse, Boyle, Yerkle, etc.

Monday, February 23 C.C. Garrison took us to Vinton. Dine at Rev. Wm. Cunningham's. Came home on 12:20 train. M.S. & M.R. Drury call. Upper Church window's came. Look at them. Very nice.

Tuesday, February 24 Went to Judge Green's, who subscribed $25.00. Called to see Col. May. Went in afternoon to see Dows. Did not find him in the office. Called to see Mitchell, who "went back" on the painting. Went home. Went with Susan to see the new windows.

Wednesday, February 25 Wrote letters and sent papers to E.H. Waldron, La Fayette; B. Lyman, La Fayette; John Egan, Cin. Rev. Mr. Hinman called. Pretty sharp talk over Denominationalism, on which he had criticised our church.

Thursday, February 26 Most of day in adjusting my papers in trunk & stand. Drury came in the afternoon.

Friday, February 27 Spent some time soliciting. Got subscription fron Restine firmer [lower-case]; Promise of Wear.

Saturday, February 28 Went to the church and to get carpet.

Sunday, February 29 I Preached at First Church at 10 1/2 from Matt. 18:20, "Where two or three." M.R. Drury preached at night from, "There is a way that seemeth right," etc. Prov. 14.12.

Monday, March 1 Bro. Drury came in the afternoon and we classified the names and amounts of debts & credits of the Church.

Thursday, March 4 Women met at Church & put down the carpet, scrubbed, etc. "Official" Meeting at 8:00,

after Wedding at Drury's. J. Bear & T.B. Garlow stubborn up to midnight.

Friday, March 5 Went to John & Christian Bear's prospecting on the Subscriptions for Sabbath, on Church debt.

Saturday, March 6 Rev. D. Runkle & Wife came in Morning about 10:00. Called to see P.W. Reeder twice. After dinner, get up accounts, at Drury's. Go to E.J. Keith's in evening, again prospecting. Rev. I.K. Statton pr. 7:30. Good congregation.

Sunday, March 7 Rev. T.D. Adams pr. at 10 1/2, "And the pillars of temple moved at voice," etc. I pr. at 2 1/2 Ps 48:11–13. Raise $800.00 sub. on the Church. Pres. E.B. Kephart pr. 7:30 Rev. 22.11. I then raise about $260.00 more. D. Runkle & wife, A. Runkle, Sister Adams & Sis. Stanbury stay at our house.

Monday, March 8 Went to town in the afternoon. Drury pays off Waterhouse & Tax. Lorin went to Western.

Tuesday, March 9 At home mostly. Went to Church at 8:00. Drury preached. Got home about 10:00.

Wednesday, March 10 At home in forenoon reading. Bought myself & Wilbur shoes. Went to Church at 8:00. Bro. M.R. Drury preached.

Thursday, March 11 Spent the time mostly at home. This week, one of some nervous irritation from colds & cares & labors. Went to Church at night. Drury preached.

Friday, March 12 At home. Able to do little mental work, though not at all sick, otherwise. Drury preached. Had rather an interesting speaking meeting. Rev. S. Sutton went home with me and lodged.

Saturday, March 13 Reuchlin came home at 12:20. I went with John McKey to Stony-point, he taking Bro. & Sister Loomis, Th. B. Garlow, John Bear, & Sister Mitchell, along in a wagon. S. Sutton preached II Pet. 1:8. Quarterly conf. Supper at Bro. Sutliff's a mile South. S. Sutton pr. 8:00. I came home.

Sunday, March 14 Sabbath School at 10 1/2; few. Rev. M. Bowman preached, Col. 2:9–13. Bro Bowman preached at 7:30. Both good sermons. John Drury dined with us.

Tuesday, March 16 At home writing mostly. Went down town to trade. Susan was along. M.R. Drury called.

Wednesday, March 17 I started at 7:00, morning, to Des Moines & Casey. Reached Des Moines at 1:30 P.M. Called at M.C. Staves'. No one at home. Mrs. Hugins tells me where Rev. J. Talbot lives. I call there. Wait at Depot from 3:00 till 8:00. Reach Casey at 11:00 & lodge. Denning House.

Thursday, March 18 Walk over to David Kepler's. Look at land. Stay till next morning. Kepler's boys: Alex. H.; Asa, Ed. & Dave. I authorize Mr. Kepler to rent out unrented grounds & to hire 50 acres broken on the North and of West side of farm. Saw Mr. Cook there, who lives three miles North-west.

Friday, March 19 Went over to Casey. Called at George Lowrey's. Rode in Henry Harris' wagon to town. Started right off on the accommodation to Council Bluffs. Arrive at 5:00, & transfer to Omaha. Put up at Canfield House, Cor. Ninth & Farnham Streets.

Saturday, March 20 W.H. Harrison, Jr. calls Book-keeper for W.T. Seaman 1111 Farnham St. R & Irene St., Bet. Hamilton & childs. Got half-fare on U.P. R.R. Start at 9:10 for Crete. Lunch at Lincoln. Supper at S.E. Lloyd's. S. Austin pr. at 8:00, "What good thing." Stay at A. Sheeder's.

Sunday, March 21 Preached at Crete Church from II Cor. 3.7,8. Dined at Singleton's Raise $3.80. Went after dinner to A. Sheeder's. Preach at night at the Opera House, I John 5.3 to 800 people & raise over $100.00 more. Stay at A. Sheeder's. Talk with Rev. Richards, M.E. Rev. B.C. Parker's new wife.

Monday, March 22 Called at Lloyd's & dined. Took a ride to stock yards & by the Congr. College. Mr. Bixler refused to give anything to Church. Supper at Purdy's. Preached at Church at 8:00, Heb. 11.10 & dedicated the Church. Staid at Bro. Sheeder's. Three joined

Church: Father Spores & son & wife.

Tuesday, March 23 Went to Cady's barber shop & got razor put in order; 25 cts. Went to Farlin's to dinner. Wrote in the afternoon at Sheeder's. W.R. Lloyd & wife took supper there. Rev. Eads preached at 7:30 at Church. I stayed at Purdy's.

Wednesday, March 24 Went on to Sweard with Bro. Scott. Arrive at 1:00 & put up at Abr. W. Hayeman's. Rev. J.W. Tucker calls awhile. J.W. Tucker preached at 8:00.

Thursday, March 25 Conference opened at 8:45. This day the chart examination progressed well. An excellent lofe-feast meeting at 7:30.

Friday, March 26 Conference continued. Examination nearly completed, besides considerable other business. I preach at 7:30, John 7.37. A brief speaking meeting followed. Rev. Elsea came. Staid at our home.

Saturday, March 27 Business progressed. I dine with Rev. W.P Caldwell at Barkley's, of M.E. Church. Business completed about 6:00 P.M. Stationing Committee met at M.E. Church about 7:30 P.M. J.H. Embree preached.

Sunday, March 28 Meeting at the Opera Hall at 10— love feast—and at 11, I preach from Heb. 7:26. Dine with Bro. Cone at Fletcher's, just two weeks from Dublin, Indiana. O.D. Cone pr. at 7:30 Baptist Church. Short informal conference session. I go to Alonzo Slonaker's; Tucker, Kenaston, etc. there.

Monday, March 29 I start to West Nebraska. Dine at Bro. Marshal's at York; for Bro. Simeon Austin took me in his carriage. Wind blew strongly (fiercely) from the Soth-east. We stay at R.D. Loggan's, near Fansler School-house, in a good-sized sod house. People kind. Rested well.

Tuesday, March 30 Went on to Rev. J.D. Fye's. Has nice family indeed. Dine at B.F. Fye's, and others call in the course of the evening. Preach at 7:30 from Rom. 14.17. Stay at J.D. Fye's. Raised a subscription of nearly $200.00 toward a church.

Wednesday, March 31 Went to B.F. Fye's and dined. Moore's there & Obert's. Mrs. Fye a sensible religious woman. Went with Bro. Fye to Chapman. Write at the depot. Board the train at 6:30, and arrive at Gibbon at 8:30. Get letters. Stop at J.H. Fee's.

Thursday, April 1 The Fee's are a nice family. Stay till after dinner. Bro. Fee takes me to Drury School-house. Call at Bro. George's. Conference opened & progresses. My home is at Bro. Hartman's. Intelligent, nice people. They assign me a nice room Kilpatrick preached at night.

Friday, April 2 Conference continues. Examination nearly completed. I at my home at John P. Hartman's as usual at meals & lodging. Their children are Joseph, John P, Samuel & Mary. I preach at night from I Cor. 3.6.

Saturday, April 3 C.C. Kellogg & I.N. Martin elected pres. elders. Stationing Committee meets at Hartman's at noon. Work mostly done. Session closed about 6:00. Stationing Committee finished its work. Rev. I.N. Martin preached well. Stay at Hartman's.

Sunday, April 4 I preach at 11:00, 2 Pet. 1:16. Collection $26.00. I dine at Bro. Rodger's 1 1/4 miles southeast of Sch-h, with Nichols, Knepper, Kilpatrick, S. Austin, etc. Sabbath school Anniversary at 3:30. Myself, Kellogg, Nichols, Martin, etc. speak. S. Austin preached well at night. He stays with me at Hartman's.

Monday, April 5 Samuel Hartman takes me to Kearney. Call at Rev. W.S. Spooner's on the way. Go to David Wibbert's. Rev's B.M. Allen & O.H. Bagley dine there. Send a letter & postal order for $49.27 and 50 in stamps to W.J. Shuey. Start on 9:15 train to Cheyenne. Sleep about six hours in the cars. Mailed letter to Sheuy and my dear wife on train at 2:00.

Tuesday, April 6 Lunch at Sidney. Skies cloudy. Reach Cheyenne a little after noon. My baggage mixed with that of the Southern Troup, and sent to Denver! A.D. Balcom proprietor of the International Hotel. Train waits for the east-bound train. Arrive at Loveland at 7:00. Lodge at Loveland House. Snows about 4 in. deep night & mornin[g].

Wednesday, April 7 Go to David Hershman's to breakfast. He hitches up and we go to Rev. W.H. McCormick's, Hertzing's store, Geo. Little's, Archibald Litles, Robert Leonard's, Father Leonard's, & Lorimar's. My baggage returns from Denver except an umbrella. Dine at Geo. Little's. Went on 5:30 train to Ni Wot. Wrote to Spencer & hired Stillinger to take me to Sh. House. McCormick preached. Went to Enoch Way's, my Conf. Home.

Thursday, April 8 Spent forenoon in writing. Conference opened at 2:00. Reports of fields of labor all in. Harmonious session. Rev. Patterson of Glasgow, Scotland, a Presbyterian, introduced McCormick. McCormick had not read Discip, "for lack of time." Patterson preached at 8:00. Staid at Enoch Way's. Good folks.

Friday, April 9 Session continued. Adj. at 10:00 for Committees. Dine at Danl williamson's. Afternoon session fails to elect presiding-elder. Afjourned early. I preach at 8:00 from Heb. 11:26. Stay at Way's.

Saturday, April 10 Session continued. L.S. Cornell, elected P.E. Osborn dodged election. E. said to have voted for self. Stationing Com. met at noon at Ways. L. DeBusk pr. at 2:00, "Stand fast in Liberty," etc. Finished business by 5:00. Sup—Way's. G.W. Rose preached at 8:00. "The Lord Jesus Christ." Stay at Way's. Crowded by Snede. Slept but 3 hours.

Sunday, April 11 Preached at 11:00 from II Cor. 6:3. Dined at Daniel Tracy's, 1 1/2 m E. St. C. Ross pr. at 4:00 from My "time is short." Large attendance both times. Communion after forenoon service. Went to Samuel Williamson's and staid that night. They sem to be a nice family, 5 boys, three girls.

Monday, April 12 Went to Ni Wot. Wrote at letter home. Went to Denver. Dined at Rev. G.W. Rose's. Went to Post-office, etc. & to Rev. H.R. Miller's; Supper there. Saw Bro. Van Every's—himself—wife—& three daughters. Nice family. Saw Bro. Wells. Went back to Bro. Rose's and lodged. Very nice family.

Tuesday, April 13 Went with Bros. Rose & Miller to look at lots suitable to locate a church. Dined at H.R. Miller's. Bro. Rose & I went to see Boston & Colorado smelting mills (Senator Hill's). Furnace; heating process; and tub-room, interesting. Jas. Moss called to see me. I Preached at Seventeenth Presbyterian Church, Ps 37:4. Stay at Bro. Rose's.

Wednesday, April 14 I called at the post-office & at Bro. H.R. Miller's. Start at 9:55 for Kansas. Meet the belated train. Quite windy. Nice, new car with carving instead of painting, at the sides. Get to Kansas line about 7:00 or 8:00, evening. Slept between 3 & 4 hours. Were thrown behind time somewhat in evening by a "hot box" or *journal*.

Thursday, April 15 Daylight came about the time we reached Russel, perhaps. Arrived at Junction City about 11:30. Called at Eagle Hotel. It had deteriorated. Left after dinner. Went to post-office. Sent a postal-order to Billheimer for 34.28 & 5 cents in stamp for Ch Erec. 1.00 for Benef. Fund & Gen. S.S. the rest. Put up at Bartell House which was quite good. Wrote letters. Slept 7 hours.

Friday, April 16 Arose at 4:20. Got a glass of milk & small slice of bread. Went in the "bus" to depot & aboard train for Le Roy Station. Ar[r]ive about 11.00. Go on "bus" to LeRoy town 2 1/2 miles from the station. Put up at Kent's Hotel. Rev. J.H. Spencer came and took me via Cornell to Jas. Legg's, where I stay. Very pleasant family. Hampshire the teacher there.

Saturday, April 17 Went to Bro. J.B. Tipton's and dined. Meeting of trustees at 2:00. Go to Sister Hill's. Bro. Wade comes. I preach at 8:00 from Ps. 37:4. Stay at Sister Hill's. Large family: son, daughters, daughter-in-law, visitors. Very strong wind in the night & a little rain followed. Got a letter from home. House shook much in the night. Many were alarmed.

Sunday, April 18 Preached at 11:00 Ps. 84:10. Raised $228.00 & dedicated the Church—"Cherry Mound." Took dinner at Kellerman's with Spencer & Ketcham. Called at Shaffer's. Rev. D. Baughman pr. at 8:00. "Pure Religion." Stay at James Legg's. Mr. Smith, her brother, and Charley about to start to Leadville & Walla Walla. Warm south winds changed to cool North-west winds.

Monday, April 19 Go over to Kellerman's. Go with Bro.

Spencer to Bro. Mowrey's to dinner. Go on to Greeley & to Bro. Spencer's, a little beyond. Staid there. Their Children, girls, aged about 10, 4, & 1. Passed on the way over-land beautiful, fair-looking soil, but almost unproductive. Soil as loose on the surface as ashes. Appletrees in Bloom.

Tuesday, April 20 Arose at 6:00. Wrote several letters in the day. Staid at Bro Spencer's all day. They live in a timber-land farm about 3/4 mile North of Greeley. Pleasant family. Children May 11; [blank] 9; Maud 1 year. Live in Pottawattomie bottoms.

Wednesday, April 21 Took a general brush up of clothing. Went to Greeley. Stop[p]ed at Bro. W.H. McClure's. Spent afternoon in reading, and in letter writing. Wolf & Alexander called. Preached at 8:00 from John 1.46. "Good thing?" Staid at McClure's. One son, three daughters. He owns 500 acres.

Thursday, April 22 Pr. at 11:00 Ps. 48.11,12,13. Went to Bro. D.W. Smith's for dinner. He Bro. Spencer's fatherinlaw. Bro. Bowman's there. Returned to Bro. McClure's. Preached at night from I Kings 18:21. Staid at Bro. Smith's, with Bro. Hiel Truefitt, who takes me to next appt.

Friday, April 23 Started with Bro. H. Truefitt. Stop for dinner at Bro. Jacob Ungerher's, about 18 miles on the way. Go on to Truefitts. Bro. Blake comes. We go to the new Church. I preach from Ps. 1.6. Church called Spencer Chapel. I lodge at Bro. Turefitts. Their only daughter Hattie is 14 years old.

Saturday, April 24 Staid at Bro. Truefitt's till afternoon. Went to Bro. John Hunt's. Young Speekes takes me to Br. Dennis Forester's. They make me comfortable there. Preach at 8:00 John 7:37. Spencer came. I stay at Forrester's. Remark: A nice, short shower. Considerable rain further North.

Sunday, April 25 Preached at 11:00 Heb. 11.70. Effort to raise money a failure. No trustee subscribed a cent till after we dismissed. Dined at Follis's with Rev. S.B. McGrue & Wife. Blake called. Evening friends raised the remainder of the money & we dedicated after a sermon by McGrue. Spencer & Minton there in forenoon.

Staid at Eli Turefitt's.

Monday, April 26 Call at Hiel Turefitt's. Go via Mound City to Pleasanton, with Eli Truefill. Dined at Joy House. Went on to Kansas City; and thence to Cameron, Eldon, Washington & Columbus Junction. Slept five or six hours on the cars and reach Fairfield soon after daylight.

Tuesday, April 27 Breakfast at Star House at Col. Junction. Go on at 9:30 to Cedar Rapids, arriving at 12:30. Many letters. Called at Gilmore's Office. Called at Drury's in evening.

Wednesday, April 28 Went down & made out a deed to Ellis Wright on "home" farm in Indiana. Looked all forenoon for houses to rent. Rev. I.L. Bookwalter came. Spent part of afternoon in giving him insight into Nebraska & Colorado. Thinks of a tour there. Called to see about other houses, toward evening. Rev. Nidig & Br. Shenk called with Christian Nidig, a few minutes about 1:00.

Thursday, April 29 Spent the day mostly in writing on missionary sermon.

Friday, April 30 Still looked after a houses to rent. [sic] Went down in the afternoon with Mrs. Wright to see McVan's house on Sanford Street. She liked it, but it had been rented that day.

Saturday, May 1 Still looked some after house. Lorin came. He found a house (Bradleys) in Washington St. We went in the afternoon to look at it. Spent some time in the evening writing on my missionary sermon.

Sunday, May 2 Went to church. Bro. Drury forgot to announce his text. Class meeting as usual for some weeks, followed the sermon. Mr. Coal there & had talked the Sabbath School. I went to Derry Dale & pr. at 2:30 Rom. 3:5. Did not go to church at night.

Monday, May 3 Endeavored to find a house to move to. John Bear called. Went to see Bradley's house at Cor. of Washington & Sanford; for he called to see me. Looked at Walker's house Corner of Eagle & Jackson. Met with no success as to renting.

Tuesday, May 4 Rented a room to store good[s] & moved them. Dined at Bro. Drury's with family. Supper at Drury's. Went to hotel—Grand. Bought ticket at $13.65, each, tickets to Cincinnati on M.E. Excursion train.

Wednesday, May 5 Started at 4:30 A.M. from Grand Hotel—wife, self, Orville, & Katie—via Burlington, Peoria, LaFayette. Many M.E. pastors aboard. Time made was slow. Reached LaFayette after night & Indianapolis at 1:30 A.M. Fearing losing connection at Cincinnati, I take the train for Sidney & wife & children that to Richmond. Start at 4:15.

Thursday, May 6 Reached Sidney, O. at 9:00. Stop at Valley House & dine. Write on sermon till dinner. Take train for Lima. Rev. J.W. Hott aboard. Reach Fostoria on Lake Erie & Western R.R. at 5:30. Rev. Leonard met us & conducted us to Bro. Warner's. Kindly treated. Preached Annual Miss. Sermon, Matt. 6:10. Found home at Rev. Macklin's.

Friday, May 7 Board continued at 8:30 morn. Business continued till noon. Reportson Appropriation mostly adopted in the morning. On West Miss. Dist. in afternoon. Dined at Prof. Jackson. She a sister of Robt. Shirley. Business closed in afternoon. Start with Hott & Smith for Dayton. Arrive about 3:30 & sleep till morning (later) at Hott's.

Saturday, May 8 Reaching Dayton at day-light. Breakfast at Rev. J.W. Hott's. Meet at Seminary Building about 9:00 on the Board of Education. Dine at Rev. W.O. Tobey's. Board meets in the afternoon again. Supper at Hott's. Stay at Bro. Hott's.

Sunday, May 9 Dr. Davis preached at Summit Street Church at 10:30. Dined at Rev. W.O. Tobey's. Sabbath-school at 2:00. Flickinger spoke about Wilberforce and Mambo Mission in Africa. Pres. Kephart also spoke briefly. Sup[p]er at Rev. L. Davis's, D.D. Heard Rev. Geo. Miller at Lutheran Church at 8:00. He aged 75. His wife with him. Stay at Hott's.

Monday, May 10 Write letters, etc. Keister called. Talk with him. Dined at Rev. W.J. Pruner's. Bishops' Board meet at Seminary at 1:00. My plan on Conf. Chart reports discussed; and and [repeated in text] the plan sustained in paper adopted. Supper at Prof. Funkhouser's. Literary-Society entertainment at 8:00. Stay at Bro. Hott's.

Tuesday, May 11 Seminary Board meets at 9:00. Full attendance. Dinner at Prof. Keister's. Session continued. Supper at T.J. Sines'. Weaver's address before the literary society at 8:00. Stay at J.W. Hott's.

Wednesday, May 12 Session of the Board continued. Treasurer not required to give bonds. Dine at Dr. L. Davis's. Session of the Board of bishops at 1:00. Seminary Board meets at 3:00. Business finished at 7:00. Landis added to the faculty. Graduating exercises. Hix Rodabaugh, Stiner & House. Stay at Hott's.

Thursday, May 13 Called at LaVasseur's, Billheimer's, Aunt Christina Hoffmans, Myers, Mannings, & Mrs. Edwards. Dine at Hott's. Went to Lanthurn's; Called at Aunt Polly Swaynie's. I called at the *Telescope* Office. Staid at Hott's, but at supper at J.G. Feight's. Called at LaVasseur's.

Friday, May 14 Went on 7:50 shortline train to Cincinnati. Went to M.E. General Conference at Pike's Opera. Rev. B.F. Owen with us. Dined at 11 East Fourth. Went with family to Glass-works at Covington. Called at Davidson's Fountain. Tickets re-stamped at I.C. St. L. Depot. Went via Hamilton to Geo. Beard's near Lotus, Ind.

Saturday, May 15 Went to Liberty where Daniel Koerner met us and went by Beard's and took us to his house. Staid there all day & at night. Quincy Brookbank and family came about bed time. Their boys are Charley, Freddie, & Roscoe.

Sunday, May 16 Went to Franklin to the Yearly Meeting. Preached Ps 18:30. Dined at Henry Fry's. Frank Moore preached at 4:00 from II Pet. 2:7. Communion Season introduced by me. Went to Daniel Koerner's. Saw, that day, Masters, Carters, Bassetts, etc. etc. etc.

Monday, May 17 Stay at Daniel's. Wrote many letters.

Wednesday, May 19 Went in Afternoon to Austin Winchell's & took supper there. Return to Moor's.

Thursday, May 20 Go to Glenwood & thence to Rushville. Thomas Wright meets us & takes us to Harvey's. Harvey & Delila gone to Riley Stephen's, as they had been sent for. Dan & "Rilla" came. Harvey returned. Had some rain.

Friday, May 21 Rainy day. John McKey's family came in afternoon. A very rainy day.

Saturday, May 22 Went to Thomas Wright's. Early dinner. Thomas takes us to the cars at Knightstown. I go to Dublin; Susan & children to Richmond. Go to C.W. Witt's. Then to Samuel Wright's at Cambridge. Cousin Sarah Wright there. After Supper return to Father Witt's.

Sunday, May 23 Preached at 10:30 II Cor. 4:17,18. Dined at Joseph Gray's. Called at Floyd's and "Aunt" Dru Evans. Mother Groenendyke there. Preached at 8:00, I Tim 3:16. Went to Cambridge & staid at Samuel Wright's, my cousin's.

Monday, May 24 Went on the early train to Richmond. Got letters. Wrote some. Staid at D.K. Zeller's.

Tuesday, May 25 Left at 10.20 for Anderson. Sorry lunch at New Castle. Staid at Depot at Anderson till 8:20. Start for Fairmount. Ex-Gov. Cunnback and Robeson, Esq. of Greensburg aboard. Rainy Afternoon. Stay at "Star" Hotel.

Wednesday, May 26 Went to Uncle Williams after breakfast with Robert Reeder. Go over in Afternoon to look at the place. Cousins Jo & Eliza Broyles come.

Thursday, May 27 Went to see the place & called at G.W. Dealey's—Susan & Uncle William's along. Dine & visit at Henry Simons. After return made out duplicates of our accounts.

Friday, May 28 Go to Fairmount. Start for home. Reach Indianapolis about 12:30. Saw Mr. & Mrs. Ketchum of Daleville. Go on to LaFayette & Sheldon. Put up at Taylor House. Rev. S.H. Cheadle & wife called. Invited after retiring to deliver a temperance address to a temperance meeting.

Saturday, May 29 Start at 3:55 morn. to Burlington.

Arrive there about 1:40. Dine at Bartlett House. Wait at Depot till 7:00 for Cedar Rapids train. Reach Cedar Rapids at 11:20 and put up at the Grand Hotel.

Sunday, May 30 Went to Church. Drury preached at 10:30. Baptizing at South cape of May's Island. Dined at J.D. Ham's. Meeting at night. Drury preached, or lectures on Sabbath School convention at Polo. We stay at Ham's.

Monday, May 31 Dine at the hotel. Move things into our house. Reuchlin and Clint. King. Stay at the house.

Tuesday, June 1 Fixing up. Tired & lame.

Thursday, June 3 M.S. & R.R. Drury breakfast with us. Continue to fix up things. Went to town twice to see dispatches from Chicago Nat. Republican Convention.

Friday, June 4 Lorin comes home in the morning. Considerable interest concerning the convention.

Saturday, June 5 Lorin went to Western afternoon. Convention still in session.

Sunday, June 6 Preached at First Church at 10 1/2 from Jude 20—. Drury preached at night.

Monday, June 7 Day of Considerable interest about Nominations. Spend the day at home.

Tuesday, June 8 Garfield nominated a little afternoon. Visited with Susan John Bear's. Took supper there. Called at Austin Dockery's.

Friday, June 11 At home. Drury called in afternoon & asked me to preach at Derry Dale.

Sunday, June 13 At Church morning & evening to hear Bro. Drury preach. I preach at Derry Dale at 2:30 Matt 5:8.

Tuesday, June 15 Excursion to Palisades went this morning. None of us went. Turned out to be a pretty day.

Wednesday, June 16 Did considerable writing. Went to prayer-meeting in the evening.

Thursday, June 17 Called for forms of lease. Strange forms. Called at Drury's in afternoon. Rev. L.H. Bufkin called. Rev. D. Wenrich came on 7:45 train. Staid with us. Did considerable writing to-day.

Friday, June 18 Went to town with Wenrich. Found Lichtenwalter. They dine with us & go out on Western Hack.

Saturday, June 19 Went to Ely on morning train. Bro. Lewis Kephart on the train. Lorin meets us with the Pres's buggy. I dine at Rev. T.D. Adams'. Supper at Bro. J.Y. Jones. Literary Anniversary of Philophroneans & Caliopians. Drury, Cotton, Miss Horn, & Miss Marion Bookwalter spoke. Stay at T.D. Adams.

Sunday, June 20 Pres. E.B. Kephart pr. baccalaureate at 10 1/2. I Dine at Mrs. Cath. Shuey's. Preach at 8:00, Prov. 21:2. Stay at Adams.

Monday, June 21 Board Meeting. Dine at I.L. Bookwalter's. Rev. Wm. Faucett lectures before Young Men's Institute & Altharneum Lit. Societies. Stay at Adams. Mr. Faucett also stayed there.

Tuesday, June 22 Hear grades read after M. prayer. At Board. Dine at Bro. Ransom Davis'. Sent for Susan. Lorin brought her & we supped at M.S. Drury's. Prof. Blanchard lectured before the Philophronean & Caliopean Literary societies on "The Religion of to-day." He stays at Drury's. We lodge at M.S. Drury's.

Wednesday, June 23 Commencement day at Western. J.W. Robertson, G.D. Mathewson, E. Ridenour. E.O. Kretzinger, W.I. Beatty, & Lou. Halverson graduated in the Classical course & W.O. DeMoss in scientific. Dined at Pres. E.B. Kephart's. Alumni meeting in afternoon. Supper at Prof. Wagners with Prof. Blanchard. Went in Wagon to Ely & home. Bros. D. Wenrich, L.H. Bufkins & F. Reibel stay with me.

Thursday, June 24 Went with Susan to Mt. Vernon to Cronell Ed. Commencement. Six graduated—two of them classical. We dine at the Dining Hall, at the invitation of Mrs. Henderson. Parson Colonel Granville Moody spoke at 3:00, "a fourth of July piece." We arrive home about sunset.

Friday, June 25 At home. Write some, etc.

Saturday, June 26 Went to Savanna, Illinois & Sabula, much under water. Railroad tracks largely submerged and some of it along the river washed away. Dined at Rev. B.J. Murray's. Rev. Webster, of Avalon, gave me much news about Missouri affairs. Dobson preached at 8:00 from Ps 48:1. Staid at [blank]

Sunday, June 27 Preached dedication sermon at Savanna, Ill.: Text I Cor. 1:23–4. Dined at Davis's. Went in afternoon to Rev. B.J. Murray's and Wm. Hefflebower's. Storm threatened at night. Pr. at 8:00, Ps. 87:3. Staid at Father Gunn's.

Monday, June 28 Called at Heffenbower's & dined at Murray's. Started at 3:00 for home. Arrived at 7:30.

Tuesday, June 29 At home. Wrote considerable. Sent a letter to Am. Book Exchange to send Books by Expres[s], C.O.D. M.R. Drury came. Asked me and Reuchlin to make addresses at 4th of July. Sab. Sch. Centennial. Morgan S. Drury came & staid till bed time.

Wednesday, June 30 Went to town trading at store. Sell Bro's. Show paraded. Spent most of the day writing.

Thursday, July 1 Spent the day largely in writing letters. Rev. M.S. Drury called in the afternoon & staid till Bedtime. Also Harvey McVey, student of Western, & staid till morning. Note—An impostor called in the morning wishing funds to go to Clinton. Lorin saw him drunk in hands of police aftnoon.

Friday, July 2 Wrote to A. Schwimley that I would be at Columbus Junction over Sabbath.

Saturday, July 3 Went to Columbus Junction. Celebration dispersing. Stay at Rev. A. Schwemley's.

Sunday, July 4 Preach at 10 1/2 from I John 3:2. Dined at [blank] Hard rain in afternoon. Supper at A.K. Treadway's, who was formerly at Dublin. Preach in the evening Acts 26:28. Stay at Rev. A. Schwimley's.

Monday, July 5 Came home.

Tuesday, July 6 Official meeting. Church Reports on building. Discussion on modes, etc. of prayer-meeting.

Wednesday, July 7 Went via Ames & Des Moines to Casey. Rode out to Mr. Fagan's. Arrive in a big rain. Stay with them. They very kind—are Irish Catholics.

Thursday, July 8 Went on to David Hepler's to Breakfast. Measure land with Tatman—17 acres minus 1 acre. Paid Mr. Hepler all he paid Tatman and $2.00 for trouble. A.H. took me to Greenfield. I called on Hagar & Story, Esqs. Got my deed for Adair land from recorder. Paid Hagar & Story for recording guardian's deed $1.00. Go on to Creston.

Friday, July 9 Left Creston at 5:00 morn. Reached Topeka via Hopkins, St. Joseph, & Atchison at 1:00 Aftn. Reached Lecompton at 4:00. Horse killed by Locomotive near Topeka. Go to Slade's. Preached at College Chapel at 8:00, from 2 Cor. 8.9. Staid at Bro. Horace Herr's.

Saturday, July 10 Rainy in the morning. Called at Bartletts, Bell's & Sellars. Went with Bro. Chapman & Slade & wife to [blank] for dinner; and thence to Church two miles south of Willow Springs Douglas, Co. Kan. Meeting of trustees. Supper at David Fager's. Bro. Chapman preached. Lodged at Bro. Fager's, Loggan's, Keezles, etc. there.

Sunday, July 11 Pr. at 11, Ps. 84:11. Dined with Rev. E. Shepherd's at his Bro. John's. Judge Gooden there & "tight." Called in the evening at Bro. D. Sutton's. Rev. A.G. May preached at night. We stay at Bro. Fager's. We raised $250.00, and dedicated the Church. Bro. Fager & family gave about $5.30 altogether to the church buildi[n]g.

Monday, July 12 Went on with Chapman & Slade's to M. Skaggs to dinner. Reached Lawrence just after 4:00. Kan-City train gone. Took Leavenworth train. Left Leavenworth train about 6:00—on toward Columbus Junction. Preachers at the Dedica. Loggan, Slade, Williams, Shepherd, May, Bell.

Tuesday, July 13 Arrive at the Junction at 6:00. Breakfast at Star House. Start for Cedar Rapids at 8:04. Dr.

McClallahan of the Rapids with me on the cars. Arrive at 11:00. Preached Caliphurnia Maudsley's funeral at 3:00, aged 18 mo.

Wednesday, July 14 Writing. Reuchlin went in afternoon to work in hay harvest out north-west near Raymond's. Was not at prayer meeting—tired of long meetings & two & three praying at a heat. Lorin came from it about 10:20.

Thursday, July 15 Writing considerably. M.S. Drury dined with us and went on to Marion. Bible Class at 8:00. I lead it. M.S. Drury there and came home with & staid with us.

Friday, July 16 Bro. Drury went to Toledo. I spent part of the day in writing. Saw Prof. C.J. Kephart of Avalon, Mo. at the book-store. Susan, Katie, & I took a buggy ride to Rev. M. Bowman's and Bro. Cotton's.

Saturday, July 17 Book's came from Am. Book Exchange, N.Y. Boys & Katie went to Barnum's show. I went to Lisbon. Staid at I.K. Statton's. Looked at the foundation of the new Church; about 50x70 ft.

Sunday, July 18 Went to Centennial Church. Preached at 10 1/2 Luke 22:40. Dined at Abr. Kurtz. Went with Father [blank] to Lisbon. Stopped at Statton's. Preached at M.E. Church at 8:00, Math. 9:12. Staid at Amos Runkle's.

Monday, July 19 Came home on 1:30 train. Saw M.S. Drury & Ham & Jones. Everett Sutton, Sister, & neigh[b]or girl came & stayed till after supper. Everett came back and staid all night.

Tuesday, July 20 Went to Frank Smith's & preached funeral of babe. Rev. D. Wenrich came about noon. Was looking for a telegram concerning the coming of his daughter: Waited till morning & staid with us.

Wednesday, July 21 Reuchlin & his employer dine with us. Rev. M. Bowman called. We Went out to McKee's on Boulevard. Gave us nice mess of apples.

Thursday, July 22 Sister Haynes visited us & staid till Teacher's meeting. Rev. M. Bowman & wife made us a

call. Was at teachers' meeting. Hain conducted it.

Friday, July 23 Sent off nineteen cards inquiring about crops and famine, etc., in W. Kans. & W. Nebraska. Took at buggy ride up the river on West side beyond "Time Check," the suburb. Orville had a chill.

Saturday, July 24 Spent the day mostly in writing letters. Reuchlin came home & went picnicing. We took a buggy ride in the evening to Bro Jordan's—called at John Bear's gate. Boys rode out. Thunder, but little rain in the night.

Sunday, July 25 Went to First Presbyterian Church to hear Rev. Cairn of Scotland—Text: Phil 2:9. "Above every name." Able & spiritual. John Bear dined with us. Go with Prof. P. Wagner to Stony Point S.H. His text: James 1:25. Preached at Church in town at 8:00: 2 Tim. 2:12. Sutton's daughter & little neighbor-girl staid with us.

Monday, July 26 Drury called after breakfast. Sutton's children miss train & return. I write several letters after arranging old letters. Drury dines with us.

Tuesday, July 27 Rev. Read called to see about church-building. Their lot Corner of Eagle & Medis. Went buggy-riding to John Bear's. Talked about a bill of lumber for a house on Adair land.

Wednesday, July 28 John Bear called & left a bill of lumber. Ham leads the prayer-meeting. Amos Runkle & wife lodge with us.

Thursday, July 29 Took a buggy ride to beyond Raymond's. Got to the Bible-class late.

Saturday, July 31 Reuchlin came home from Frank League's—done haying. Spent most of the day in reading in Watson, Clark, & Lee.

Sunday, August 1 Attended Church. Pastor pr. Christ Cross "foolishness to them that perish; but power of God—saved." George Cotton dines with us. Class-meeting at 4:00. Pastor pr. 8:00 on Consecration.

Tuesday, August 3 Went to post-office. Talk with P.M. Reeder at his door. Go to meeting of the trustees at Ch.

No quorum. Talk with and reprove John Bear.

Wednesday, August 4 Mostly reading & writing. I write appeal for the Kansas & Nebraska sufferers & therefore was not at prayer-meeting.

Thursday, August 5 Day spent mostly in study. I attended Bible Class at Church. Pastor leads—Drury.

Friday, August 6 Start for Nebraska at 7:00. Spend considerable of the day in study of Cushing's Manual; Some on a text also. Dine at Boone. Saw Col. Sapp, congressman, at Missouri Junction and on cars. Arrive at Omaha at 8:00. Put up at Canfield House Room No. 18. Poor place.

Saturday, August 7 Start at 9:00 for Seward via Lincoln. Get to Lincoln at 10:40. Lunch. Start on at 12:50. Reach Seward about 2:30. Preach at 3:00, Canticles 6:10. Quite a large congregation. Supper at Snyder's with Bro. Sloneker's. Bro. S.E. Lloyd preached at 8:00. I lodge at Geo. Sloniker's, four miles west of town.

Sunday, August 8 Preach dedication sermon at 11:00. Malachi 3.1 & raised $336. on church—increased in the evening to $600.00. Dined at pastor's, Rev. E.W. Johnson's. Bros. Woolbrant, Hollack, Gilmore there. Preached at 8:00 Ex. 28.34. Staid at Abraham W. Hageman's; M. Waltemire & wife & J.J. Lohr, also.

Monday, August 9 Got some items concerning I.H. Haley, an imposter, now in West Kansas, from Rev. M. Waltemire. Bro. Austin came. Went down town & to train, several brethren accompanying. Cars to Lincoln. Much interested in a *conversation between a very intelligent layman and a M.E. presiding-elder. Reach Council Bluffs & stay at Ogden House. *on sanctification.

Tuesday, August 10 Went to Chi. & R.I. Depot—too late. Go then to North-western—too late. Go to Rock Is. Dep. & take 10:00 freight train for Casey. Call on Lumber Yards & Carpenters. Go at 9:33 for Des Moines. Stay at the Aborn House.

Wednesday, August 11 See Lumber yards at Des Moines & hardware. Go across to Rev. J. Talbot's. Dine. Go at 2:20 for Ames, and home. M.S. Drury aboard from

Tama. He stays with us.

Thursday, August 12 Spent the day mostly in writing. Mail in the evening an appeal for help for the destitute in N.W. Kansas and S.W. Nebraska.

Friday, August 13 Spent the day in writing. Mailed a defense of Franklin Circuit to the *Cynosure* office. Wrote letters. Attended the official meeting at 8:00, evening.

Saturday, August 14 Went to Lisbon on 9:00 A.M. train. Hear Prof. Freerleeture on children's reading matter. Dine at Boarding Hall. I lecture at 3:00 on Silences of the Scriptures. Supper at Hall. Hott came. M.R. Drury lectured. Bro. J.W. Hott & I Stay at Bro. Bovey's.

Sunday, August 15 I teach the lecture class at S. Sch; class large. J.W. Hott pr at 10:30 "Buy the truth," etc. Quite successful. Dine at Hall. I pr. at 2 1/2 from Mal 3.1. Supper at Hall. Rev. M. Smith of Mt. Vernon preached at 7 1/2. I go to Rev. D. Runkle's and stay. A wagon upset & a young lady got her wrist injured.

Monday, August 16 I came home on early train. Day spent in visiting, etc. Getting ready to go. Sent Lumber bill to Mr. Page, where Reuchlin is at work & took one to Mr. Fay.

Tuesday, August 17 Spent forenoon in getting ready to start to Missouri. Start at 2 1/2 p.m. Tarry at Col. Junction till 9:45. Arrive at Trenton, Mo., about 5:00, next morning.

Wednesday, August 18 Hire a livery-rig for $3.00, and run out via Bancroft to Camp-ground in Harrison county. Rev. A.D. Thomas had gone to Spickardville for me. Home at Jacob Wagoner's "Holiness" furore [sic] running away with many. L.D. Ambrose preached at 8:00.

Thursday, August 19 Conference began at 8:30. It determined to examine by committee, and I was with the Committee in fornoon. Session at 1:30. Another Ex. Com. Session. "Holiness" run at 4:00. L. Fisher preached at 8:00—many exhortations follow. Flickinger came at 5:00.

Friday, August 20 Session continued. J.W. Berryman preached. Good speaker, duped with "Holiness" doctrine. Session & Memorial in afternoon of Curry. I preach, 8:00 Rom. 4:8. Anti-rant influence of it. Some out for prayers.

Saturday, August 21 Session continued. Ballot several times on second presiding elder before forenoon adjournment. Elect Geeslin in afternoon. D. Beauchamp elected on first ballot. Educational effort at 4:00. Sta. Com. meet at 7:00. Flickinger lectures on Africa at 8:00.

Sunday, August 22 Preach at 10 1/2, I John 5.18,19. Dine with Elihu Neff's on the gound; they old acqua. Lee Fisher declined to preach S.S. sermon; so Rev. D.K. Flickinger lectured on Africa. We went in Rev. D.E. Statton's rig to Elihu Neff's. He a room mate of mine at Hartsville.

Monday, August 23 Go on to Princeton with Statton & others. Cars to Allerton. Stop at Sherman House. Write letters. Write an appeal for *Telescope.* Awfully mosquitoed that night. Bro. Flickinger suffered likewise. Hard rain in afternoon & night.

Tuesday, August 24 Rainy in forenoon. Wrote some in the morning. dinner at the hotel. Hired a livery rig and went via Corydon to Samuel Fry's. Cost $2.00 for two. Bro. Fry had been sick with something like flux. Their daughter had married Burnham. Staid with them (Fry's.)

Wednesday, August 25 F.W. Burnham & Gillispia went to Allerton. Quite rainy. Brought out a number of brethren. Wrote some. I Did not go to the evening service, as it wa quite rainy. No sermon preached.

Thursday, August 26 Conference began usual progress. Rev. J. Talbot pr. at 8:00. Good sermon.

Friday, August 27 Conference continued. Dined at Rhinehart Fry's. Educational meeting in the evening. M.S. Drury lectured. Went back in the rain to Fry's.

Saturday, August 28 Session Continued. Dined at the Church & disappointed Rue's. Session closed near six o'clock. Supper at Draper's. Stationing Committee met there and finished in an hour. Flickinger lectured at 8:30.

Sunday, August 29 Preach at 10 1/2 from 2 Tim. 4:2. Dine at Fry's. Start with Bro. Shipley & Flickinger for Allerton. Flickinger pitches out of wagon & hurls himself somewhat. Call at M.E. Preacher's to speak with Schwimley. Sup & lodge at Sheridan House at Allerton. Start on train at 1:05 A.M. for Columbus Junction.

Monday, August 30 Arrive at Col. Junct. at 6:00. Breakfast at Heddrick House. Arrive at Cedar Rapids at 1:00. Write & transact business the rest of the day.

Tuesday, August 31 Start via Dixon to J.H. Middlekauf's 4 1/2 miles east of Forreston, Ill. Join in marriage Mr. Edwin H. Rushel & Miss Ella S. Middlekauf at 7:30. Lap supper. Several Kishels there & Mr. & Mrs. Dovenbarger.

Wednesday, September 1 Reached Ridott at 8:30. Home at Joseph A. Kerr's. Fair room, hard-bed. Lewis (295 lbs) my bed-fellow. Conference opened. P. Hurless referred to com. of the whole. Examination in afternoon. Education report. Mission & Ch. Erection. Palmer preached at night.

Thursday, September 2 Examination continued; much complaint. Investigation of Hurless postponed till evening at 7:00. Good order. All parties conducted well. Chandler proposed to take a rising vote as to whether there wree grounds of pardon. Lewis snores.

Friday, September 3 Report on Hurless' case adopted. Hurless passed after some confession. Still, some complaints of others. Drury lectures on education at 8:00. Many at Hayes' investigation. Lewis snores me awake!

Saturday, September 4 Conference has quite a time on Coursey & S. Healey. I lecture them. Hallowell's fling at me. I notice it after a while. Memorial service of J. Bomgardner. Father Snyder's squirming. Flickinger lectured at night.

Sunday, September 5 Preached II Cor. 3:8. Coll. $61.15. Dined at Herr's as usual. S.S. Anniversary. Called at 7:00 at Poffinbarger's. Melon & peach. Flickinger preached. Took up Miss. Subscrip. $176.00. Slept well.

Monday, September 6 Conference continued. Stationing Com. sat at 7:00. Session of Conference closed at10 1/2. Staid at Kerrs.

Tuesday, September 7 Staid at Kerr's till train in afternoon. Exchanged specie for bills. Went on to Freeport at 3:00. Bought a gold pen. Supper at E. Witters. Staid at L.B. Peck's.

Wednesday, September 8 Went on by stage via Orangeville to Thomas H. Eaton's, member of Disciple Church. Went to Bethel Church. Washburn pr. at 8:00. I Staid at Eaton's.

Thursday, September 9 Conference opened at 8:30. Snap of Crowder & Nickey. Adjourned at 11:12. Rode with Beach part way to Easton's. Examinations progressed well. Adjourned at 4:20. We rode in a single buggy to church in aftern. Flickinger lectured at 8:00 on Africa.

Friday, September 10 Conference continued. General reports mostly considered in the afternoon. Flickinger left for Willoughby, Ohio, at 4:00 p.m. Whitney preached at 8:00 p.m. Staid at Eaton's as usual.

Saturday, September 11 Conference continued. Some trouble on Elroy Seminary. Washburn takes letter of dismissal. Election of Presiding elders protracted. Stationing Committee met after supper at Hoffman's. Night session after preaching by J. Fry.

Sunday, September 12 I preached at 10 1/2 mal. 3:1. Dined at Eaton's. S.S. Anniver at 3:00. Memorial service of S.A. Potts followed. Woman's missionary meeting at night. Unofficial vote of Conference on line between Wisconsin & Fox River. Staid at Eaton's.

Monday, September 13 Bros. Talbot & Washburne called to see the *skeleton of the whale. Mr. Eaton took me to Monroe. I stopped at Rev. G.M. Mabbot's. Went to the post-off. etc. Carleton & Fritz's family there. *See page [rest is unreadable]

Tuesday, September 14 Started at 11:00 for Hanover, Madison & Elroy. Reached Elroy at 7:45. With Seminary Ex. Com. in its session. Staid at Rev. D.C. Talbot's.

Wednesday, September 15 Started at 5:30 for Necedah.

Arrived via Camp Douglas about 8:00. Put up at the Bentley House. Received letters & wrote several. Bros. Miller & DePew came for me. Home at Wm. Kent's. Clark preached at 8:00. Staid at Kent's.

Thursday, September 16 Spent forenoon in reading, getting sketches reviewed & in visiting with Miller & Clark. Conference opened at 2:00. Business proceeded. H.D. Hillis preached at 7:30 from "Sow in righteousness," etc. I Staid at Kent's.

Friday, September 17 Session as usual. D.C. Talbot & A.W. Alderman of Wisconsin present. Examination about completed & several general reports completed. Dinner & supper at Kents—& ledged there. D.C. Talbot preaches at 7:30.

Saturday, September 18 Conference as usual. Quite rainy. Whitney elected P.E. Dine, as usual, sup & lodge at Kent's. Short night sission. Adjourned at 9 1/2.

Sunday, September 19 Preached at 10 1/2 John 17.17. Dined at Mrs. Therber's with J. Fry, Whitney & Ingersolls. S.S. Anniversary at 3:30. Supper at Kent's. J. Fry preached at night.

Monday, September 20 Rev. J. Fry takes us to the train. Cars starting. They back up. Talbot and Alderman had stopped them. Rev. Harrington & Talbot dine with us at Hotel near. We go on at 7:30 toward Hastings.

Tuesday, September 21 Arrive at Hastings at 5:00. Breakfast at the Foster House. Go on to Ortonville. Dine at Glencoe. Arrive at 7:00. Stop at A. Blom's. Nice Sweedish folks.

Wednesday, September 22 Went over with Bro. Flickinger and Cook to Rev. Simon George's and Rev. Berry's. Dine at George's, in Dakota. Brethren gather in the afternoon. Prayer meeting at the School-house at 8:00.

Thursday, September 23 Conference in Ortanville began at Orton Hall at 8:30. Dine at Bloom's, as usual. Examination proceeded well. Rouse referred for trial to a committee having been suspended before. Supper at Bloom's. Rev. E. Clow pr. at Sch-h at 7:30.

Friday, September 24 Conference continued. Parley on referring Eldridge & Satterbe, Bingham declined investigation, but got it. Dinner & supper as usual, at Bloom's. I Preached at Orton Hall at 7:30 from I John 4:10. Got two letters from home & enclosed letters, etc.

Saturday, September 25 Progressed well with business. Tibbetts & Clow elected pres. elders. Stationing Com. met at 6:00 at Mr. Potter's. Clow had resigned & Kemerer was elected P.E. Supper at Potter's. Bro. Flickinger lectured at 7:30. Very short session followed. Stay at Bloom.

Sunday, September 26 Preached at Orton Hall II Pet. 1:16. Coll. for home missions $37.00. Dined at Bloom's. S.S. Anniv. at 3:00. Supper with English at Bloom's. Flickinger lectured at night.

Monday, September 27 Start at 6:10 A.M. for Shakopee & St. Paul. Dine at Glencoe at a poor place recommended by Bro. S.W. Thayer. Stop train at Carver for half-fare tickets to Shakopee. Arrive at St. Paul at 6:50. Stay at Sherman House.

Tuesday, September 28 Went over to Minneapolis. Stop at Merchant's Hotel. Run out to Minnehaha Falls. Beauty! Go to Washburn's Mills 200 ft x 100 ft. Eight stories high. Saw from it all the city. Went on at 8:20 P.M. toward Austin, Minnesota.

Wednesday, September 29 Arrive at Austin at 3:00. Take freight train to Castalia. Behind time, so we could not make connection at Postville. Stop at Castalia & Rev. J. Thornton takes us in his carriage to West Union. M. Bowman pr. My home at Mr. Hobson's.

Thursday, September 30 Conference opened at 8:00 a.m. Com to examine local preachers. Dine & Sup at Mr. Hobson's. Com. on L. pr. meets in evening. Flickinger lectured. I stay at Hobson's.

Friday, October 1 Conf. Continues. Dine at Rev. A.W. Drury's. Sup at Hobson's. I preach at 7:30. I Cor. 5:8.

Saturday, October 2 Conf. continues. Dinner at Rev. David Wenrich's. Flickinger left. Stationing Com. met at 7:00. Conf. Session closed at 10:50 p.m. Sup & stay at Mr. Hobson's.

Sunday, October 3 Preached at 10 1/2 from Acts 11:24. Sab. Sch. & Communion at 3:00. Dine & sup at Hobson's. T.D. Adams pr. at 7:30. Did not awake soon enough to go on 3:20 a.m. train.

Monday, October 4 Spend forenoon mostly in writing. Go to post-office. Go at 3:40 to Cedar Raps. Arrive at 7:40. T.D. Adams, G.W. Henson, & Klinefelter & wife stay with us.

Tuesday, October 5 Day spent in writing & fixing up for going. Rev. A.W. Drury & wife call in afternoon. John Bear called in evening.

Wednesday, October 6 Start at 7:30 for Cedar Falls. Dine. Go on 12:22 train for Aurelia, Iowa. Arrive at 11:+. Stay at Hotel. [+ appears in text]

Thursday, October 7 Bro. D.M. Harvey takes me over to C.P. Leonard's. Conference opens at 1:30. Get along well on examinations. D.T. Hutchinson pr. at 7:30. Stay at Leonard's where Bro. Harvey & wife & Dr. Darling board.

Friday, October 8 Conference as usual. Bro M.S. Drury had an educational meeting. Over $200.00 subscribed on the Western debt. (College).

Saturday, October 9 Trial of Dr. Bunce in the morning. conference as usual. Dined at Mr. Whitehead's with Chase. Session of the stationing committe at Bro. Leonard's. Chase P.E. D.T. Hutchinson & I.D. Rust elected to elder's orders. M. Fulcomer pr. 8:00.

Sunday, October 10 I preach at 10:30 Ps. 18:30. Ordain D.T. Hutchinson. Dine at Gilmore's. Falman & wife there & I.D. Rust & wife. S.S. Anniv. at 4:00. Fulcomer plays normal teacher till interrupted for organization of S.S. Normal association. Chase pr. at 7:30. Sub. for Church building. Stay at L's.

Monday, October 11 Rev. D.O. Darling M.D. takes me to Cherokee. Call at Curtis'. On to Sioux City, arrive about 11:00. Go at 2:30 for Mo. Valley & on to Council Bluffs. Stay at Metropolitan. Fire alarm at about 2:00. Wrote reply to S.Y. Miller for *Cynosure*.

Tuesday, October 12 Went on to Casey & over to Farm. Staid at Hepler's. Framework done. Plasterer was lathing. Wheat turned out over 14 bush. to acre; Oats 30; Buckwheat 13+.

Wednesday, October 13 Returned to Casey. Rode with Chas. McDonald. Did not get to see McMullin, but left $35.00 with Burns & McFarlin. Paid off Mr. Marshal, Valentine and $35.00 to Rutt & Rutt. Went on to Stuart & thence to Dale City on a 7 inch board in a lumber wagon. Home at J. Lonsdale's. D.B. Long preached.

Thursday, October 14 Conference opened. Examination progressed. Bro. Hughes preached.

Saturday, October 16 Conference continued. Stationing Com. met at 1:00. Adjourned somewhat late.

Sunday, October 17 Preached at 10 1/2 John 17:17. Dined at Kinworthy's with Robberts and Bufkin. J.W. Hott pr. at 7:30 & communion followed. Staid as usual at Lonsdales.

Monday, October 18 Went on to Stuart. Wrote some letters, at the Hotel. Went at 3:50 for Council Bluffs and Omaha. Staid at Metropolitan House. It was a very muddy time at Omaha. Rev. J.W. Hott was with me.

Tuesday, October 19 Went on at 8:40 from Omaha to Hastings & Red Cloud. Oscar Ramey met us. Hotels full; so we staid at Rev. Mr. Price's, Presbyterian, who kept a boarding house. We engaged a livery rig for four days at $10.00;—two small horses.

Wednesday, October 20 Went on to Smith Center, Kan. Dined at Hotel. Saw Dr. Albright. Bill for dinners & team 60 cts. Went on to Harlan, & to Lawrence Creek Church. Rev. J.E. French preached. Found home at John Grimes. Mother Grimes had, she told us, saved her cabbage-patch from grasshoppers by prayer! They live in a stone "half dug-out."

Thursday, October 21 Conference opened. H.C. Miller, Dierdorff, J.S. Rock, & others preached. Examination progressed. (Mother Grimes told of a cloud-burst that fills up ravine to their floor.) J.W. Hott preached at night: "Things unseen." Father Grimes laughed so much, after

he went to bed—religiously, hysterically.

Friday, October 22 Prof. Shuck came at noon. J.W. Hott left at 3:30 for Nebraska, after report on Publishing Interests was considered. Rev. H.C. Miller preached at 7:00, "Wisdom, righteousness, sanctification & redemp."

Saturday, October 23 Conference continued. Staioning Com. met at *Rev. Orlando H. Grimes. Prof. D. Shuck preached at 7:00. Conference adjourned about 9:30. *Son of mine host.

Sunday, October 24 Pr. at 11, Acts 11:24. Ordained C.U. McKee, J.H. Bloyd, & J.E. French. Dined at Father Grimes. Rev. Dierdorff preached at night. J.W. Miller exhorted with talent. Went to Rev. I.W. Williams' at Harlan. Called at Gruger's. Staid at William's.

Monday, October 25 Met Board of Gold School. Made out deed. Suggested articles of incorporation. Dined with Mr. Bailey at the hotel. Went at 2:30. Changed cars at Beloit for Topeka via Solomon. Called off at Minneapolis, Kan. & staid at Truesdale House.

Tuesday, October 26 Went out 15 miles to Harvey B. Harris's. His Sister Kate there. He is my Sister Sarah's son. Went on to Ed. M. Harris's, at Lincoln Center. Ella & Charley are there. Harvey went with me. Staid at Edward's.

Wednesday, October 27 Went to Ed's Treasurer's Office & to Charlie's Store. Went via Ed's farm, a few miles from Lincoln. Called to see Orval Harris. Went back to Harvey's. Went on via Solomon to Topeka & Grantville.

Thursday, October 28 Get conveyance after much calling. Went up to Meredin. Conference opened & progressed. Found a home at Wm. Crull's. S.D. Stone preached at night.

Friday, October 29 Business proceeded about as usual. Dined at Dr. Dawson's with Bro. J.W. Hott. Examination of local preachers, etc., on Com at 6:30. H.D. Herr preached at night.

Saturday, October 30 Educational report caused considerable discussion. Joke on Prof. D. Shuck, who curried R. Loggan. Dined at Mr. Rice's. Elected presiding elders, etc. *Shuck's warm, long speech was off the question—the election of Zabriska. Stationing Com. met at Swartz. Conf. adj. late. H.D. Healey preached.

Sunday, October 31 Preached Conf. sermon I Tim. 4:15. Ordained Edmund B. Slade, J.C. England, & Banj. A. Todd. J.W. Hott pr. at M.E. Church. Dine at Swartz S.S. meeting at 4:00. Prof. D. Shuck pr. at 7:00, H.D. Herr pr. at M.E. Ch. Rev. J.W. Hott leaves at 11:30. Both Hott and myself gave some mention of the constitutional amendments—spoke in its favor.

Monday, November 1 Dined at Swartz's. Went on via Topeka to Lecompton. Went and got a draft from Topeka State Bank on Importers & Trader's Nat. Bank, N.Y. Went in State House. Saw Hon. Bonebrake & Judge Walker. Saw Agricultural Room & Historical Room. Staid at Lecompton at Rev. W.A. Cardwell's.

Tuesday, November 2 Called at Levi Lippy's & H.D. Herr's. Dined at [blank]? Prof. Shuck's soninlaw's. Looked at Prof's farm. Supper at Rev. R. Loggan's. Preached at 7:30 Prov. 15:32. Staid with Rev. S.D. Stone's at Rev. H.D. Herr's.

Wednesday, November 3 Meeting of the Board at 10:00. I, Bell, Stone, & Meredith to meet them. Dined at Dr. J.H. Bonebrake's. Committee write out their opinion, recommending new incorporation. Debate. Report adopted. Supper at Slade's. Stay at Prof. N.B. Bartlett's.

Thursday, November 4 Start at 3:00 f or Lawrence. Dine at Place House. Zabriski along. Write in the forenoon. Went on at 11:50 to Thayer. Stop at Rev. Hugh Atkinson's. His wife was born in London, Eng.

Friday, November 5 Bro. Atkinson takes me over to David Kile's. Make home there. Conf. opens at 1:30, W.J. Shuey there. D.O'Farrell and others join on transfer. J. Riley pr. at night. Revs. Henninger, E.L. Joslyn, & R.C. Ross room with me.

Saturday, November 6 Conference progressed slowly in forenoon, & repidly in the afternoon. Dine at Rev. Stewart's, M.E. Church. Com. on Examinations met at Kile's and

reported at Night session. Zabriski pr[e]ached at 7:00.

Sunday, November 7 Preached at 11:00 Acts 11:24. Ordained R.C. Thomas. Dined at Kile's. Rev. WlJ. Shuey pr. at 6:00; and He preached in the forenoon at Erie.

Monday, November 8 Conference continued. Shuey left in afternoon. Dined at Mr. Skeel's. Stationing Com. met at Kile's in the evening. Conference adjourned at 11:00 at night. I staid at Kile's. (At this conference I last saw David O'Farrell—an old friend in White River Conf.)

Tuesday, November 9 Rev. J.W. Baughman takes Zabriski & myself to Earlville; Go on to Lawrence & Leavenworth. Arrive at St Jo. at 9:00. Stay at Sander's House. Wrote letter home. Sent $3.04 to J.W. Hott, to pay on Gen. S. School Beneficiary.

Wednesday, November 10 Went on to Hopkins & arrive at Creston, 1:10. Lunch, cost 55 cts! On to Greenfield. Stay at Kirkwood House. Paid tax, Looked after deeds, etc. There was a masquerade ball at the court-house. Boys' talk next morning..

Thursday, November 11 Went early by livery to Hepler's. Settle accounts. Wheat netted $99.75; Oats 21.78. Hepler takes me to the cars. Settle with McMullin, paying $1.00; $86 in all. Pay off balance to Rutt. Take train at 10:30 for West Liberty. Sleep four or five hours. A man aboard who swore so as to raise several protests.

Friday, November 12 Arrive at W. Liberty at 8:00. Breakfast at the Hise House. Write letters to Price, H. Wright & Mo. Pac. R.R. Got home at 12:30. All well. Found many letters waiting me.

Saturday, November 13 At Home. Lorin came at 10:00, staid till 1:30, & went to Western. I Wrote letters.

Sunday, November 14 Drury preached at 10 1/2 on holiness. S.S. followed. I preach at 7:30, Matt. 21:33.

Tuesday, November 16 At home. Writing & reading. Rev. M.R. Drury called in the afternoon. I was down in town the first time since I came home.

Wednesday, November 17 At home most of the day. Went

to post-office and cars and mailed letters. Rev. M.S. Drury called in the afternoon. Then went on home. My fifty-second Birth-day anniversary. The Lord preserves.

Thursday, Novebmer 18 Forenoon mostly spent in reading aloud in Bronson's Elocution. (Good thing to do). Lorin's birth-day anniversary, the 18th in number. Has been a real good boy, so far in life. Children got Lorin an Autograph Album. John Bear called in the evening.

Friday, November 19 Spent much of the day in writing letters. Will Baker came up with Lorin toward evening.

Saturday, November 20 Wrote in forenoon a little. Reuchlin & Baker visit Pork Estab & wagon factory. Afternoon try to buy Lorin an overcoat. He & Will Baker go back to Western Spent evening on a sermon sketch Eph. 6:11.

Sunday, November 21 Preached at 10:30 2d Pet. 1:3. Sabbath-school followed. Committee appointed on Christmas entertainment. Drury preached at night from "Whither bound?" Jonah's Case.

Monday, November 22 Engaged on a Sermon. Rev. M.R. Drury came in the afternoon and prepared a tablet for multiplying copies of any writing. I bought a copying press that day. Com. on Christmas entertainment met.

Tuesday, November 23 M.R. Drury came & argued in favor of instrumental music in Church. Spent the day largely in looking over letters and classifying them. Sketched sermon, Isa. 2.2.

Wednesday, November 24 Town in forenoon. Bought turkey. Letter from E.J. Kephart. Wrote to Cynosure & Am. Book Exchange, in afternoon.

Thursday, November 25 Went to M.E. Church to thanksgiving service. Rev. H.W. Bennett preached. *Had a fine turkey for dinner—18 pounds. Rev. M.S. Drury & wife came toward evening. At teacher's meeting. M.S. Drury's staid with us. *Turkey was cheap & the grocer refused to add to the charge.

Saturday, November 27 Lorin came home. Reuchlin went to Marion for examination to teach. (He got his certifi-

cate, and taught a term of school a few miles south of Cedar Rapids.)

Sunday, November 28 Went to the Baptist Church. Rev. H.C. Bristol preached on, "The just shall live by faith." Rev. M.R. Drury preached at 7:30 at our Church, "Orpah wept, but Ruth Clave," etc.

Tuesday, November 30 At home. Called at Rev. M.R. Drury's in the evening.

Wednesday, December 1 Started at 6:30 A.M. for Col. Junction and Princeton, Mo. Breakfasted at the Junction. Arrived at Princeton at 4:00. Campbell R. Summers & Prof. Kephart met me. Went to Bro. Summers' 2 1/2 ms. E. of Ravanna & staid.

Thursday, December 2 Talked with Bro. Summer's on giving $100 on endowment. "Shouted out" against it. Went to Mr. Cousins in the afternoon. Found Rev. A.D. Thomas had come. Lectured at 6:30 at Sch. House. Staid at Cousins'.

Friday, December 3 Bros. Thomas, Kephart, & self went on through Wyreka to St. Johns & to Rev. D.E. Statton's 2 miles N.E. Lectured at 7:00 at M.E. Chur in St. Johns. Staid at Statton's. Prof. G. Miller with us. Cloudy in the evening & almost rain.

Saturday, December 4 Gloomy morning with little rain. I stay at Statton's. Thomas, Kephart, & Miller go away for dinner. Rainy in the evening & Prof. does not go to the appt. Stay at Statton's. It turns quite cold.

Sunday, December 5 Preached at St. John Ex. 28:34. Dined at Runyon's in St. John. Nice M.E. people. Went on to Unionville. Too late for the appt. Rev. Wm. Goodison, Presbyte. preached. Stay at W.O. Underwood's not long since from Fountain Co., Ind. Goodison is brother to Mrs. M. Bowman.

Monday, December 6 Called at Bro. J.T. Miller's and Leonard Raymo's. Went via Selma by railroad to Glenwood Junction, and then walked out to Judge Wm. B. Newman's, being misdirected a mile. Lectured at Liberty Church on Education. Staid at Newman's, Saw Lucas, Mayes, etc.

Tuesday, December 7 Remained at Newman's. Old man's perpetual motion! Bros. Kephart & Thomas came about three o'clock. Prof. Kephart lectured at 7:00 on Moses. Prof. & I stay at Charles Ring's. P.O. Glenwood, Mo. His nephew is Charles Ring.

Wednesday, December 8 Went on via Savanna & Stiles to Bro. Anthony's. Took supper & went to Barke's Church & pr. John 1:29. C. Kephart talked a little about Avalon Academy. Stay with Kephart at Barker's. Mr. Grove & wife there. Mother Wheatcraft, the motherinlaw, there. Mrs. Grover, Sister to Barker.

Thursday, December 9 Went to Church. A good speaking meeting. Dine at Barker's. Talk about the school. Went to Mr. Beecraft's to see his sick son, a married man. Prof. C.J. Kephart preached in the evening. He and I stay at Barker's.

Friday, December 10 Went on to Martinstown. Dined at Lancaster. Arrived at Martinstown at 7:20. Went to antisecrecy convention at the school-house. M.N. Butler lectured. I followed at some length. Staid at Cornelius Martin's. He had preached for me at Husted's.

Saturday, December 11 Went on to Rev. Merit Husted's. Dined. Went on to Greencastle. Got a letter from home with enclosed letter's. Stopped at E.E. Prindle's. Lectured at the church on Education. His son had been to Avalon. Stay at Prindle's.

Sunday, December 12 Preached at South M.E. Church at 11:00 from John 17:17. Saw Br. Ostrum. Dine at Rev. Jas. A. Haynes', the pastor's. Bessy, Calvin, McRea, etc. there, as also Father Prindle's & Rev. M. Husted. Rev. A.D. Thomas preached at 7:00 from Prov. 9:10. Stay at Prindle's—also Husted & Thomas.

Monday, December 13 Wento on. Dined at Bro. Stahl's. Drove on through Enterprise past Henry Zumbro's (by mistake); and staid at James Fisher's. Fare free. He, a universalist. She a congregationalist. We got 6 miles South of the Church before we inquired! Missed the appointment.

Tuesday, December 14 Went on to Meadville for dinner. Thence via Bedford to Avalon. Supper at Rev. A.D.

Thomas'. Several called in. Went to Prof. C.J. Kephart's & staid.

Wednesday, December 15 Went to Father L.D. Ambrose's to dinner. At Kephart's to supper. Lectured before the students on "High Motives" at 7:00. Staid at Wm. Beauchamp's.

Thursday, December 16 Went to Kephart's. Dined there. Went to the Ex. Committee at 8:00. Supper at Kephart's. Preach at the Chapel at 6:30. Stay at Rev. L.D. Ambrose's.

Friday, December 17 Wrote for the *Telescope*. Dined with Rev. J.L. Zumbro's. Afternoon at Prof. C.J. Kephart's. Made a chromograph for him. Went to Bro. Butler's and staid all night. She the wife's sister of Rev. S.D. Spear's & formerly lived near Scipio, Indiana.

Saturday, December 18 Spent part of the day with prof. Kep. & Agt. T. in soliciting on Endowment fund. Dined at S.H. Bagley. Went to Father David Carpenter's and staid. Called at Edmund Carpenter's before starting.

Sunday, December 19 Preached at College Chapel at 10 1/2. Malachi 3:1. Dined at Father J.H. Stubbs'. Called at Ambrose's, Meek's, Thomas's, Kephart's. Preached at 6:30, Jude 14 v. Twelve came forward for prayers. I Staid at S.H. Skinner's. Several professed conversion.

Monday, December 20 Went to Kephart's & thence to Rev. Joseph L. Zumbro's with Rev. A.D. Thomas'. Dined. Had a plain talk over the situation. Called at Rev. D.A. Beauchamp's; he on his district. Led prayer-meeting at 3:00. Sup at Rev. Wm. Beauchamp's with Rev. Busby. Preach at 6 1/2 from Luke 15.7. 8 seekers. Stay Zumbro's.

Tuesday, December 21 Talk with Zumbro. Go to Kephart's. Study. Dine. Study. Attend the student's prayer meeting. Quite precious. Supper at Rev. L.D. Ambrose's. Preach at 6:30 from I Cor. 6:11. One stove in confusion. Twelve out for prayers. Staid at Saml. H. Skinner's. Slept 7 1/2 hours. Hoarseness remedied by turpentine in sugar & by bathing it in Tinecapsicum & sleeping with scarf about it.

Wednesday, December 22 Went to morning prayers at the Academy. Heard one recitation. Dine at Alfred

Miller's. Preach from John 14.2&3. Several profess conversion. Many rose for prayer. Stay at Zumbro's.

Thursday, December 23 Call at Roberts'. Dine at Rev. L.D. Ambrose's. Go up to Rev. A.D. Thomas's. Supper. Write some. Talk with Deputy. Rev. J.L. Zumbro preached at 6:30. Some seekers. Stay at Kephart's. "Sanctifying" crops out. Men mourn over sinner's return! because "Siboleth" is no sanctifiers.

Friday, December 24 Rev. A.D. Thomas took me to cars at Bedford. Start to Galatin. Lunch at 6:35; Carried to rock-quarry 3 ms. beyond; Walked back. Went on to Col. Junct. Dined at 4:00 at Eldon. Reached Cedar Rapids at 2:00 next morning. All well.

Saturday, December 25 Read letters, etc. Quarterly Conference after preaching at 2:00 by P.E., Rev. M. Bowman. Christmas entertainment at Church.

Sunday, December 26 Rev. M. Bowman preached from Matt. 12:30. Communion follows. Bowman pr. at night from John 14.2. Night grows colder.

Monday, December 27 Went to town once in the day. Spent most of the day in writing, etc. Did not go to meeting in the evening.

Tuesday, December 28 Spent much of the day in answering correspondence. Went to town, bought a cloth coat for 10:00. Called at M.R. Drury's. Got ready to start to Colorado.

Wednesday, December 29 Left home at 7:30 a.m. Annoyed till we reach Fama, by a foolkiller's nonsense with two girls. Lunch on train. Head-winds kept increasing our lateness. Arrive at Council Bluff's at 10:00; at Omaha at 11:00. Stay at Canfield House.

Thursday, December 30 See ticket office of U.R. about half-fares. Write letters. Lay in a lunch ready for possible snow-drifts. Go at 1:30 p.m. Slept three or four hours. Encounter a snow-drift west of North Platte. Hindered thereby one or two hours.

Friday, December 31 Snow lighter farther west. Reach Cheyenne at 3:00. Miss Denver Pac. train. Two Wright families aboard. Also Mr. Mason & wife & Rev. H.P. Roberts of San Juan County, Congregationalist. Arrive at Denver about 10:00, night, & go to Rev. G.W. Rose's, on 76 Glenarm St. Stay. Hear the din of bells, etc. on coming in of New Year.

Memoranda

Colorado: July 27, 1877, at Big Thompson Ps 18:30. 29, II Tim. 4:1,2 & Ps. 87:3. Ralston July 14, 78; Heb. 4:14 & John 14.2,3—13th, Numbers 10.29. At Loveland July 21 II Cor. 31:7,8 & Deut. 18:18 & July 20, 1879, I John 5:18,19 & 2 Tim 4:7.

Dakota: Heb. 11:27, Aug 24, "77." 26th 11 from I Tim. 4:2. Pleas. Valley, Sept. 1 "78." Isa. 9:6. Elk Pt. Oct 10 "79," John 7:37, Oct. 12, Heb 11:10.

Appendix—Mr. Eaton had a son in poor health who went to the Atlantic, and bought the remains of a Finback whale, 73 feet long. He removed the flesh and brought it home. Its snout was sawed off and yet the head was a cartload. Its (lower) jaw bones were fifteen feet long, following the lines. Its ribs set up had room for a horse to turn around in (perhaps an elephant). Its vertebra were at least two feet in height. Its throat, exclusive of flesh, was not over about one foot in diameter. Its strainer was such as to retain the fish it might swallow. The finback is shot by a cannon. (Skip four pages) In returning from Oregon, by ship to New York, I saw two whales sporting in the ocean, a few miles distant, apparently fifty or seventy feet long, about one third of their bodies appearing above the water (first the head and then the tail). If shot with a harpoon from a cannon, and killed at once, its body floats; otherwise it strikes for the bottom of the sea, and a few days later, if it dies, rises to the surface, when the discoverer can divest it of its oil-flesh, but he has to render a certain proportion of the oil to him that shot it.   Milton Wright

East Des Moines
Ainsworth Sept. 9, "77," Acts 11.24, Dec. 17, [blank] Dec. 19 Acts 26:28. Col. City Dec. 23, I John 5:18&19 & I Ki. 18.21, Fry Chap. Oct 13, "78" II Tim. 3:15, Jan 22, Jer. 13.21, I John 5.10, 23, Eph 3.19 26th, 2 Cor. 3:7,8. Granville June 8, Ps. 48:11. Aug. 31,79 II Cor. 3.7,8.

Items of 1880

Rev. Wm. Davis' death Jan. 31. We dedicate the Church Mch. 7. I mix my baggage April 6 at Cheyenne. I look at lots April 13 in Denver. At Junction City April 15. Dedication in Kans, 18. At W.H. McClures in Greely. Failure to raise money at Dedication. Trustees contrary. Dedicated Apr. 25 at night. May 5, Started to Cincinnati on M.E. Gen. Conf. excursion trip—Mrs. Wright and Orville & Kath. along. Ticket $13.65, each. The children mostly went free. May 6, I preach Annual Mis. sermon at Fostoria. May 9, heard Miller pr. May 13, supper at Feights. May 14, at Gen. Conf. Cinci. I pr. at Franklin, 1880. May 25, Saw Cumback on cars. Go 26, to Uncle Reeder's. May 29th, reach Cedar Rapids. Baptizing at May's Island. June 3, hear from National Republican convention. June 19, I went to Western. Lit. societies. John Drury & others. Rev. Faucett's lecture. That of Chas. Blanchard. June 23, I return home. June 27, went to Mt. Vernon, Granville Moody, June 27, dedicated Savanna Church. Shell Bros. Showparade 30. July 1 an imposter called. Went to Columbus Junction—preached July 4. Pr. dedica. church 2 m S. of Willow Springs. Judge Goodin there—"tight." Wrote for help for Kansas sufferers. George Cotton was with us. Aug. 7, Went to Seward, Nebras. to a dedication. Rev. Waltemire tells of I.H. Haley's didos. Aug. 13, controversy over Franklin's antisecrecy. Meeting Aug. 15 at Lisbon, Iowa. Aug. 19, Missouri Conf. Neff & Jac. Wagner. Conf. at Fry's. Flickinger fall out of wagon & is hurt. Rock Riv Conf. Hurless censured, Sept. 3. I shielded Coursey & Healey. Aug 8, to Wisconsin. Whale's skeleton at Eaton's. Afterward, near Ortonville, held conf. [unreadable passage] From Ortonville, we visited St. Paul & Minneapolis Sept. 28 I go to Iowa Conference at West Union. I arrive at home Oct. 4. The 6, I reach Aurelia, Iowa. The 9, the trial of Dr. Bunce. I go to Cherokee, the 11. Wrote a reply to S.Y. Miller at Council Bluffs. Went to Casey & over to my farm Oct. 12. The plastering was done. Went to Dale City to West Desmoines conf. Oct 13. I went with J.W. Hott to Red Cloud Oct. 19. We went on Livery Rig to Kansas, to Lawrence Creek Church, to John Grim's. I met Trustees of Gould School Oct. 25. Went on to Harris relatives, 26 Oct. Played a joke on Prof. Shuck Ot. 30. Both Hott and myself supported Prohibition in Constitution. Mon. Nov. 1, visited State House. Met a com. appointed to settle the college question. At Thayer held Mastro conference there. O'Farril and Shuey there. Went home. Nov. 19, Will Baker came. Nov. 27, Reuchlin gets certificate to teach School. Dec. 1, Started to Princeton. Mis. with Kephart & Thomas canvassed north Missouri. Spent a week at Avalon, Missouri at the opening of Academy. Had a fine revival. Dec. 28 I go home. Start to Colorado 29.

Bishop's Salary 1880
East Nebraska $87.14
West Nebraska 46.50

Place of the Dead

I. Where Jesus had gone. Acts 7.55. Mark 16.19. John 16.28. Heb. 1.3 & 8.1. Rom. 8.34. Eph. 1.20. col. 3.1. John 16.28

II. Where the departed go. John 17.24, Acts 7.59. John 12.26. II Cor. 5.6,8. Phil. 1.23.

III. Objections. 1. To-day in Paradise but J. not yet ascend. 2. Rich m. & Lazarus. Paradise Elysian Hesperides; Hades, Sheol, Gehenna, Tartarus. 3. II Cor. 12.3,4. 4. John 3.12,13. Rev. 2.7. "Paradise of God."

Adair Co. Land South half, Sec. 4, Town 76, Range 32. Neighbors: Lee Housington, George Lowry, R.H. West, Joseph W. Rutt 3 1/2 miles from Casey.

T.J. Burns of the firm of Burns & McFarland, at Casey Henry Shelters. Henry Harris 2 m. South.

G.W. Rose 502 New Haven St., Denver, Col.

Emory Friend, Denver, Colorado, from Beatrice Nebraska—Ch. member

McNeils' Linament
Essence Peppermint 1 oz.
Essence Cinnamon 1 oz.
Tincture of Rhubarb 1 oz.
Comp. Spirits of Lavender 1 oz.
Spirits of Camphor 2 oz.
Laudanom 3 oz.
Sulphuric Ether 4 oz.
Number Six 8 oz.

PART TWO

1881–1889

"I am thousands of miles from home. . . ."
Milton Wright, January 1, 1886

From 1881 to 1889, Milton Wright continued to be at the forefront of issues that created controversy within the United Brethren Church. His stand against secret societies caused him to fall from favor within the church leadership. Milton Wright relinquished control of the Telescope *and returned to Indiana, and eventually came back to Dayton. As a direct result of his outspoken views, he was assigned to the Pacific district and spent the next four years away from home, often six months at a time. As editor of the* Richmond Star *and later the* Christian Conservator, *he continued to be outspoken against secret societies, an issue that eventually split his church denomination. Susan Wright again managed the household and nurtured their growing family alone. Milton Wright records every letter received from the wife he left behind and writes daily to those he loved. The Bishop records the sickness that eventually claims the life of "the sweetest spirit earth ever knew." Susan Wright died on July 4, 1889.*

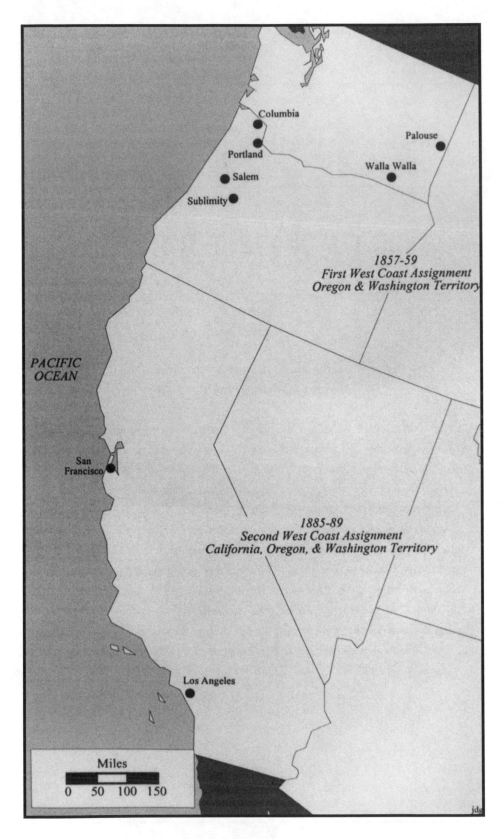

Bishop Wright's West Coast Assignments

1881

Saturday, January 1 Went to bed at Rev. G.W. Rose's, Denver Col., just after the New Year's bells, etc. rang. Awake after day-light. Mailed a card on K.P. train, home. Dinner & supper at Rose's. Rev. L.S. Cornell came afternoon. Rev. G.C. Lamb, Cong. Called in the afternoon. He married Mollie Heady of Hartsville College. Staid at Mr. J.T. Younker's.

Sunday, January 2 Preached dedicatory sermon of 1st Un. Breth. Church at 11:00, Ps. 48:11,12. Raised $331.40 for organ & pastor. Dined at J.T. Younker's. Rev. L.S.C. State Supt. Pub. Instr. preached at 7:30. Staid at Younker's. J.W. Smith & Rufus Clark, chief contributors. Gov. Evans & Crane & David Wolpert had been, before, contributors.

Monday, January 3 Went to Rose's. Wrote & studied. Dined. In the afternoon went down town. Called at Mrs. H.R. Miller's. At Chinese store at Taggy's. Went back. Preached at 7:30 John 1:29. Good congregation. Staid at Rose's.

Tuesday, January 4 Meeting at 10:00 Thurston, Baker, Kimmel, Wells, Thompson, Clark, Westlake, Rider, Mrs. Bartlett Thompson etc. present. "Potato" Clark took dinner with us at Rose's. Bro. Rose preached at 7:30 "Wilt thou be made whole." I exhorted: good attendance & interest.

Wednesday, January 5 Mailed several letters at post-office. Saw Young Sawden. Good meeting at 10:00. Went down town. Called into Krider's Drug Store. Dinner & Supper at Rose's. Pr at 7:30, Acts 26:28. Quite a good interest.

Thursday, January 6 Made a chronograph; Ink also. Inked my hands badly. Good meeting at 10:30. Talked with Thompson & others on sanctification. Dined at C.W. Wells. Meeting at 7:30.

Friday, January 7 Day as usual Meeting at 10.00 fair. Dinner & supper at Rose's. Went down town to P.O. & Krider's. Bro. Rose pr. & I exhort. Two forward for prayers—Davis & Rouches. Lodge at Rose's.

Saturday, January 8 Rev. St. Cl. Ross aired sores in Morning meeting. My indirect reply. Rose also, indirect. Dine at Rose's. Called at Krider's, [blank] and at Drugstore found Kr. and O.Fol. Clark came on message! Preach at 7:30 I Ki. 18:21. Davis & Miss Bruner professed. Wilcox & Couchey seekers.

Sunday, January 9 Preached at 11:00, II Cor 3:7,8. My best effort in the meeting. Dined at J.T. Younker's. Rose preached at 7:30, "This m receiveth sinners & eateth with them." Young Bruner came forward & professed. All other of the seekers professed; now five: Davis, Wilcox, Rouchy, Miss Polin Brunner & Mr. Henry Bruner.

Monday, January 10 Wrote in the morning. D. Wolpert called. Dined at Sister H.R. Miller's. Supper at Wilcox's. Preached at 7:30 from Acts 2:40. Ora Miller came forward and professed. Rev. Uzzell was present. Staid at Knap's, McCormick's folks.

Tuesday, January 11 Fair morning meeting Morrison of Ralston there. Dined at Rose's. Printed Circular letters. Supper at Bartletts. One conversion. Rose preached at

1 8 8 1

7:30. Staid at Knapp's. She is Mrs. McCormick's Mother.

Wednesday, January 12 Wrote in forenoon. Dined at Sister Miller's. Called in afternoon at Davis, [unreadable], & Rev. G.C. Lamb's. Supper at Rouchey's. I Preached at 7:30, Luke 23:4. No converts. Staid at Rose's. Baker Consults Rose on Holiness move.

Thursday, January 13 Supper at Mr. Philbrook's. Bartlett's there also. G.W. Rose preached. Staid Orris Knapp's.

Friday, January 14 Dined at St. Clair Evans. Went to West Denver. Supper at Smith's. Saw funeral gathering of McUne infidel. Preached at 7:30. Rom 3:5. Staid at Sister Miller's.

Saturday, January 15 Talk with Sallie on religion. Went to Rose's. Went in afternoon to town. Called at Mr. Crane's & J.W. Smith's & Krider's & Neiss's. Bought a R.R. ticket to Omaha. Saw Rev. Mr. Westwood of Cent. Pres. Ch. Supper at Bartlett's. Rose pr. Rev. 6:17. Staid at Orris Knap[p]'s. Called at St. Cl. Ross's.

Sunday, January 16 Preached at 11:00 Num. 10:29. Took 17 into the Church. Knap[p]'s, Rufus Clark, Wilcox & wife, Rouchey, Orie Miller, Westlake, Freind's daughter, Father Rose & wife, DeBusk's dutchman. Dined at Miller's. Pr. at 7:30 Acts 16:31. Stay at Rose's.

Monday, January 17 Called at Youker's & Bartlett's—he sick. Went down town & got lunch & boarded the cars. Went via Greeley. At Cheyenne wait the train. Write letter. Sleep about five hours on train. Get beyond N. Platte in night.

Tuesday, January 18 See Rev. C. Knepper at Kearney. Call at Rev. I.N. Martin's at Grand Island. Gained time somewhat. Arrived at Omaha on time. Left overshoes in the cars. Take North Western train for home. Sleep four or five hours. Lunched all the way, from Denver.

Wednesday, January 19 Arrived at home at 5:30 a.m. Spent the day at home visiting, reading, writing. Got Katie a "come-home" present, leggins; Orville, rubber overshoes. Rev. M. Bowman called in afternoon, and talked a good while. Pleasant weather.

Thursday, January 20 Spent the day at home mostly in writing. M.R. Drury came—Coniphou Tennessee Singers project—he dined with us. Got material for copying-machine & pen. Cost 50 cts for 12 oz Glycerene! 25 for 2 oz. Gelatine & 1 oz white glue; 20 cts. for pen. Preached at Church at 7:00 I Cor. 6:11. Three rose for prayers; Wilbur one of them.

Friday, January 21 Spent most of the day in writing letters. Made Copying-pad. Reuchlin came. At meeting a little while. Some arose for prayer.

Saturday, January 22 Started at 9:00 A.M. for Lisbon. Got letters before starting. Went via Father Kettering's to look at the Church. Dine at Rev. I.K. Statton's. Sup[p]er at D. Runkle's. M.S. Drury preached at Night. Stay at Adam Runkle's.

Sunday, January 23 Pr. Dedication sermon: II Cor 3:7,8, at 10:30. Raise over $2,060.00. Dedicate housing overrun the amt. Called for $467.33. Dine at Amos K. Runkle's, E.B. Kephart pr. at 7:00. Matt. 16.18. Stay at Amos K. Runkle's.

Monday, January 24 Go on early train home. Write some in forenoon. M.R. Drury called in the afternoon & invited me to preach every night in the week. Drury preached at 8:00. Prayer & speaking meeting followed.

Tuesday, January 25 Spent the day mostly in writing. Got a clergyman's permit on Ch. Mil. & St. P. R.R. Old overshoes expressed to me from Council Bluffs instead of mine! Worth nothing. Preached at 8:00 from Matt. 3:17 "My beloved Son, in whom I am well pleased."

Wednesday, January 26 Spent most of the day reading, study, & writing. Rev. M. Bowman came in the morning and staid an hour or two. Went to prayer-meeting at James Hayne's in afternoon. Preached at 8:00 Col. 1:13.

Thursday, January 27 Wrote much of the day. Preached at 8:00 from Matt. 13:58. A good congregation and considerable interest; two forward for prayers; and two others rose for prayer.

Friday, January 28 Spent all day in writing. Wrote to Rev. S. Healey admonitory. Wrote to Henry Randall

Waite on Census matters. Preached from Luke 13:24. Large congregation. Five seekers—Wilbur one. Some arose also.

Saturday, January 29 Spent day mostly in writing letters. Reuchlin went to Rhetorical at Western (but it did not occur) Preached at 8:00, Rev. 1:5,6, "Unto Him," etc. Smoke ran from one stove out at the other. Several forward for prayers.

Sunday, January 30 The Pastor pr. at 10 1/2, Isa. 52:1. About usual congregation. Sabbath-School. I preach at 7:45, I Pet. 4:18. Seven forward. Some others arose. Young Waterhouse & his mother were there. Also Rev. M.S. Drury & wife. House full.

Monday, January 31 Prepared a discourse & preached at 11:00, the funeral discourse of Enos P. Perry who was killed at the packing-house by the falling of a beam not bolted down! Overflowing house. Wrote in afternoon, to Pres. Chr. Mil. & S.P. R.R. & others. M.R. Drury preached. Six out for prayer.

Tuesday, February 1 Wrote all forenoon Epitomes of Sermons. Paid Feb. house-rent in afternoon, having written the same on sermons till 4:00. Preached at 7:45 from Matt 6:33. Several—five or six—forward—two profess conversion.

Wednesday, February 2 Wrote letter to Am. Book Exchange, etc. Got broken teeth-plate memded: $1.50. Preach at 7:45 Acts 3:10. Seven forward. Two profess. Wilbur one of them, aas he thinks. Large congregation. Meeting very spiritual. Lasted more than a half hour after discussion.

Thursday, February 3 Spent most of the day in arranging papers, writing, etc. Got half-fare Ch. R. Is. & Pac. sent for a month ago. Preached at 8:00, Isa 55:1 "Ho every one that thirsts." Six out for prayers. Miss Thuff fainted from the heat. Some sensation. Seekers: Culver, Rosa Bear, Miss Blousitt, etc.

Friday, February 4 Spent most of the day in writing (or rather in looking up facts to answer inquiries). Drury, the pastor, preached at 8:00. Eph. 2:13. Several out for

prayers. Berry professed. M.S. Drury came to the meeting.

Saturday, February 5 M.S. Drury called. Spent some time in fixing the hydrant. Preached at 8:00 Matt. 12:30. Bad night. Few out.

Sunday, February 6 Pastor Drury preached at 10:30. Congre small Mrs. Sweet joines. Rainy afternoon. I went to Dairy Dale & preached matt. 6:7 (Prayer). Preached at Cedar Rapids at 7:45, Job 31:14. Congregation small—rainy evening.

Monday, February 7 Writing. Sloppy weather. Mr. Raymond called & told his doleful story. Railed against Reuchlin. I Put a large flee in his ear. Donavin's Orig. Tennessee Concert at New Opera Hall at 8:00.

Tuesday, February 8 Went via Ely to Western. Dine at J.Y. Jones. Sup[p]er & lodging at Rev. I.L. Buchwalter's. Lorin able to be out at recitation. At Cedar Rapids, there were at our Church three seekers.

Wednesday, February 9 Called at Jones. At M.S. Drury's. John very sick. At Pres. Kephart's recitation room. At Rev. L.H. Bufkins'. Went home with I.L. Buchwalter (Rapids) in his sleigh. Letter from Ch. Mil. & St. P. R.R. giving reduced rates. Was not at meeting; but there were 2 seekers & three joiners. Slept 10 hours.

Tuesday, February 10 Spent the day in much writing. Bought apples, etc Wrong kind delivered. Prepared for going to Des Moines. Went to the Church a short time. Two seekers out. Three others arose for prayer.

Friday, February 11 Went via Ames to Des Moines— arriving at 3:00. Saw Rev. J.E. Ham at the Depot. Went with Rev. J. Talbott to his house. Dined, supped & lodged there. Went to the Church. No fire. Called at Father Lawson's. About twenty came, but returned home.

Saturday, February 12 Staid at Bro. Talbott's. Spent the day largely in writing. Dined & supped there. About 28 out to Church. Preached 2 Psalm 1 v. Staid at M.C. Staves'.

Sunday, February 13 Went to Sunday-School. In Phillip Huggin's class. Talked to the school briefly. Preached at

11:30 Deut. 18:18–19. Dined at Joseph Hague's. Went to large, good class-meeting at 3:00. Supper at Hague's. Preach at 7:30 Col. 1:13. Several rose for prayers. Stay at M.C. Stave's.

Monday, February 14 Visited Mother Funkhouser in forenoon. Wrote in afternoon, to Africa & other letters. Mailed letters at the Office. Dinner & Supper at Staves'. Preached at 7:30 Rom. 2:4. One seeker. Several arose for prayers, Dr. Rees of the number. Stay at Staves'.

Tuesday, February 15 Spent the forenoon in writing. Meeting at Staves' at 2:00. Good meeting. Remained there till ev. meeting. Preach at 7:45 Job 31:13. Rev. Wm. Jacobs there. Two out for prayers. Stay at Wilkins'—Baptist's.

Wednesday, February 16 Talk on Law—nonresistance, & Seventh day doctrine. Wrote at Stave's. Visited Rev. C.B. Davis, who has rheumatism severely. Meeting at Wilkins. Supper at Fate's. Talking-meeting at 8:00. Stay at Dr. Ree's. She lived near Dublin, Certerville, & Jonesboro, formerly.

Thursday, February 17 Called with Dr. R. at Fate's. Dined with Jacob's at Staves'. Called at J. Talbott's. Went across the river to Depot. Went on to Casey, arr. 7:00. Postal card from home. Stay at Denning House.

Friday, February 18 Wrote some. Went toward the farm. Met A.H. Hepler. Went back to Casey in a sleigh with him. Paid him $9.00. Paid Rutt & Rutt $24.91—and was credited $2.00. Dined at Denning's. Insulted. Went to Stuart, then Des Moines. Staid at Rev. J. Talbott's. His daughter, Mrs. Stivers there.

Saturday, February 19 Called after some time in writing, at Dr. Rees. His wife, disheartened religiously. Dined at Staves'. His sister Shaffer there. Took the train at 3:00 for home. Arrive at 10:00. Found all well.

Sunday, February 20 M.R. Drury preached at 10 1/2 Phil. 1:6. M.S. Drury there. Ballot for superintendent, Drury elected. Sing much in afternoon & my heart tender. Hear Rev. Reed preach at 7:30, Luke 16:10. Congre. Church.

Wednesday, February 23 Spent much of the forenoon in errands in town & much of the afternoon get[t]ing negatives for photographs for self & the children. At Prayer-meeting in the evening.

Thursday, February 24 At home most of the day. Spent afternoon in looking over Telescopes and fixing up annual Conference Book.

Friday, February 25 Went to town on business, etc. Went to cars in afternoon and to Lisbon. Called at Runkle's hardware store. Staid at Rev. I.K. Statton's.

Saturday, February 26 Went on early train to Courtland & Sycamore. Dined at an eating house. Went on to Rev. Cornelius Wendle's, three miles east, of Sycamore.

Sunday, February 27 The rain had continued over night & into the day; so that none but a cutterload of us got to the Church, which was not opened. Remained at Bro. C. Wendle's all day. Snow & wind, and drift that night.

Monday, February 28 Snow-bound. Wrote letters. Cars reported to be blockaded with snow, water, & ice. Staid that night at Wendle's.

Tuesday, March 1 Went to John Buston's. Sleigh upset. No damage. Dine at Butson's, & remain till evening meeting. Railroad blockade continued. Preach at 7:30, Hebr. xi:26. Stay at Rev. C. Wendle's.

Wednesday, March 2 Went to Sycamore, Cortland, Chicago. Visit most of the railroad general offices. Obtain reduction for delegates to Gen. Conf. from Chi. & N. Western. Dine and lodge at Brevoort House, 143 & 145 Madison St., opposite Farwell Hall, Near Corner of LaSalle & Madison Streets.

Thursday, March 3 Waded about through the snow to see Mich. Central & L. Sh. & Mich. Southern. I am snow-bound. Write letters. Stay at Brevoort House.

Friday, March 4 Look considerably after a chance to get out on the railroads. Write some. Go out at 10:10 at Night for Miline. Train arrived two hours late next morning.—No trains running west from Davenport.

Saturday, March 5 Go to Father Danl. Beall's and get a hearty lunch. Milton Beal Esq. comes home at noon. Went with him and telephoned to Davenport, but got no encouraging report for westward train. Go back and stay at Beal's.

Sunday, March 6 Attended the Congregational Church, and heard Rev. E.C. Barnard preach. Dined at Beall's. Heard Rev. A.R. Morgan & others speak on temperance. Staid at Beal's. They very kind to me.

Monday, March 7 Went at 5:30 to train & on to West Liberty and home, arr'g at 12:46. All well. Bought Problem of Human Life, of a Temp. Lecturer. Conversation with Rev. Mr. Smith, a Disciple minister of Monticello, about to remove to West Liberty.

Tuesday, March 8 At home most of the day. Went in the evening to Waterhouse's to tea. Staid at their Chapel, a quarter a way for meeting. Led the meeting.

Thursday, March 10 At home. Spent forenoon in arranging receipts and other papers. Bought a rocking-chair at W. Waterhouse's.

Friday, March 11 At home. Another snow & blockade of the railroads began.

Saturday, March 12 A[t] home. At telegram from M.R. Drury states that they were snow-bound at Marshaltown S.S. Convention.

Sunday, March 13 I preached at our Church Deut. 32:9. Drury arrived at the close of the sermon. Father Waterhouse spoke in the evening. House pretty well filled. He agreed to pay 1/10 to finish the Church.

Monday, March 14 Lorin came home a little afternoon, Several teams having come through the snow-drifts, by shoveling a good deal.

Tuesday, March 15 Got a tooth filled with cement. Wrote in the afternoon and evening.

Thursday, March 17 Spent the day largely in Writing. Children got Reuchlin a birth day present—sleve buttons, gold-washed.

Friday, March 18 Studied comments on Rom. vii. At home all day. Rev. I.K. Statton called and took dinner. Lorin went to get his photograph taken. Howard Henderson promised to stay with our boys that night.

Saturday, March 19 A snow, and the railroads blockaded again. Howard H. & a Mr. Chas. Warren staid the night with us.

Sunday, March 20 Rev. Drury, the pastor, preached at 10 1/2. S.S. review followed. George H. Cotton dined and lodged with us. I Did not go to meeting at night.

Monday, March 21 Bro. D. & McKee came in the afternoon and staid a couple of hours. At home all day.

Tuesday, March 22 At home. Got Katie's negative for a photograph at noon. Sent a number of cards on fares. Wrote many letters.

Wednesday, March 23 At home. Miss Jennie Patterson missed the train & staid with us till next morning.

Thursday, March 24 I was at home. Reuchlin went to Mt. Vernon, in the afternoon.

Saturday, March 26 Lorin came home at 11:00. Quarterly Conference in the afternoon. Lorin came at 11:00. Reuchlin came in the evening.

Sunday, March 27 Rev. M. Bowman, P.E., preached. Communion service followed & then Sabbath Sch. Walked out in the afternoon to look at the river. Eld. Bowman preached at 7:30.

Monday, March 28 Start at 7:30 for Nebraska. Dine at Boone. Reach Council Bluff's at about 8:30. Stay at Transfer Depot Hotel, there being little prospect of getting West from Omaha on account of washed out bridges.

Tuesday, March 29 Go via Pac. Junction & Plattsmouth to Lincoln, starting at 9:30 & arriving at 6:00. Man was killed in jumping off the train. Reach Aurora at 10:00 at night. Stay at the Tuthill House. The day pretty.

Wednesday, March 30 Go in afternoon with Daniel Fye,

to Rev. J.D. Fry's. Wrote in forenoon an appeal for the destitute, etc. Rev. W.S. Spooner preached at 8:00, "That wisdom that cometh from above," etc. Evening mild, but hazy.

Thursday, March 31 Rev. Current pr. at 10:30. Very strong Cold wind. Conference opens in the afternoon at 1:30. Business proceeds well. Pretty fair attendance of members. Rev. J.A. Nichols pr. at 7:30.

Friday, April 1 Conference progressed. Went to John. T. Hogue's with Bro. J.M. Walter. Considerable debate on making certain works of small membership circuits. I Preached at 8:00, I Tim. 4:10.

Saturday, April 2 Conf. Continued. Dined at B.F. Fye's. Lay delegation adopted Nichols, Kellogg, and Spooner elected presiding-elders. Stationing Com. lunch at Sch. House by B.F. Fye. H.S. Munger preaches well. Session Closed.

Sunday, April 3 Preached at 11:00, Ordained J.D. Fye & E.L. Kenoyer. Dined at my home & J.T. Squire with me. S.S. Anniversary. Pr. at 7:30 John 6:56.

Monday, April 4 From Aurora went on to Lincoln. Saw Rev. E.W. Johnon at Seward. Rev. J.I. Lohr went with me to Lincoln. Saw Caldwell & Trase at Plattsmouth. Went on to Omaha and looked after the prospect of Getting to Arizona.

Wednesday, April 6 Went on to Tekama and Arizona. Found Conf. Home at Rev. D.D. Weiner's. Rev. W.S. Field preached.

Thursday, April 7 Conference opened & progressed well. Rev. E.F. Austin preached in evening. Not much of a preacher.

Friday, April 8 Conf. continued. I preached, Rom 4:8, in the evening.

Sunday, April 10 Preached at 11:00 Heb 9:28th. Dine at Mr. Austin's. S.S. Anniversary at 3:00. Supper at Faucett's. W.P. Caldwell preached in evening.

Monday, April 11 Went on to Tekama. Dined at Astor House. N.J. Shekel, once student at Hartsville paid bill. Went with sled to Hermon & then with Rev. S.E. Lloyd to Blair. Staid at Wm. Fox's with several others.

Tuesday, April 12 Staid at Wm. Fox & Rev. M. Campbells. No trains. Preach at 8:00 at Cong. Church Heb. 11:26. Stay at Fox's.

Wednesday, April 13 Went via Freemont and Omaha & Missouri Valley home. Our company part at Valley Junction, Nebras. & Rev. L. Piper & I go on to Omaha. Go on C.W. Western for home.

Thursday, April 14 Arrive at Cedar Rapids at 7:00. At home during the day. Drury, the pastor, calls in the afternoon. Rev. I.K. Statton calls at six, on his way to see George who was hurt on cars.

Friday, April 15 Went down town. Lorin came home in the afternoon. Wrote much in the afternoon. Sent accounts and N.Y. Draft to W.J. Shuey.

Saturday, April 16 M.S. Drury came & spent an hour or two. Myself & Reuchlin wrote several letters. Went to Lisbon on 4:00 train. Staid at Rev. D. Runkle's.

Sunday, April 17 Preached at 10 1/2 from Rev. 2:17. Dined at Hess's. At class in afternoon. Pr. at 7:30, Luke 13:24. Staid at Rev. D. Runkle's

Monday, April 18 Came on 6:00 train home. Spent day in writing, etc.

Tuesday, April 19 Rev. I.K. Statton came from Ogden, where George lives, and we arrange homes for Gen. Conf. somewhat. Rev. Marion R. Drury called in the afternoon. Heard Rev. Mr. Stafford pr. at Cong. Church.

Wednesday, April 20 Wrote on Gen. Conf. Address for the Bishops. Rev. L.H. Bufkin and wife dined with us.

Saturday, April 23 Spent most of the forenoon in trading. Went to Ely in the afternoon. Walked out to Western. Supper at Jones; Pres. lectured on Astron. Staid at Drury's.

Sunday, April 24 Preached at 10 1/2 from Luke 10:31.

Dined at Pres. E.B. Kephart's. In young people's class. Supper at Prof. P. Wagner's. Preach at 7:30, Matt. 13:44. Stay at Rev. I.L. Buchwalter's.

Monday, April 25 Hack full. Lorin took me to Ely. Presbyterian preacher & I talked on Church. Arrived at home at 12:40. Worked on my usual report.

Tuesday, April 26 Worked on report. M.R. Drury called in forenoon—wanted Susan to attend the meeting to organize a Ladies Aid Society for the church. We went to town in afternoon to buy Susan & Katie hats, etc. Wrote on Annual report.

Wednesday, April 27 Finished annual report. Went town, bought hat, paid rent to June 1st. Susan went to town after I did.

Thursday, April 28 Started for Chicago & Dayton, at 10.00 at night.

Friday, April 29 Reach Chicago about 7:00. Go via Logansport & Kokomo to Richmond. Stay at D.K. Zeller's.

Saturday, April 30 Go on to Dayton. At *Telescope* office in the forenoon. Dine at Rev. W.J. Pruner's. Go to town—buy a coat, spectacles, etc. Supper & lodging at Rev. J.W. Hott's.

Sunday, May 1 Bish. J.J. Glossbrenner preached at 10 1/2. Dine at H.J. Millholland, S.S. Afternoon. Supper at H. Wagner's. I Preach at 7:30, 2 Cor. 4:2. House crowded full—(Summit St. Church.) Staid at Dr. Lewis Davis'.

Monday, May 2 Educational Board met at 9:00–10:00. Dined at Rev. W.O. Tobey's. Board in afternoon. Supper at Prof. A.W. Drury's. Philothean Society Anniversary. Stay at Rev. W.J. Pruner's.

Tuesday, May 3 Went to East Dayton. Dined at Rev. W.M. Beardshear's with W.O. Smith. Biblical Seminary Board met at 2:00. Supper at Dr. L. Davis with Bishop J.J. Glossbrenner. Call at Prof. A.W. Drury's to consider proposed changes in course of Reading. Thompson lectured at 8:00. Stay at W.J. Pruner's.

Wednesday, May 4 Board meeting. Dinner. Went to town with Hott. Supper at Hott's. Annual meeting at 8:00 Drury & McCorkle speak.

Thursday, May 5 Board meeting all day. I preside. Dined at Prof. G.A. Funkhouser's. Supper at J.W. Hott's. Start home. Call at Zeller's at Richmond. Sleep five hours on train.

Friday, May 6 Reach Chicago at 8:30 Breakfast with B.F. Booth at Brevoort House. See Assist Gen. Ticket Agt. Cent. Ill. & arrange business. Go on at 12:30 for Cedar Rapids. Hot journal impedes. Arrive at 10:00 with Booth.

Saturday, May 7 Booth started to Boone on a visit. Oregon & California delegates (D. Shuck, Jessee, Karritt, J.G. Mosher) stay with us; J.L. Field and T.J. Bauder at M.R. Drury's.

Sunday, May 8 Daniel Shuck preaches at 10 1/2. Field & Harritt dine with us. T.J. Bauder preaches at 8:00. Shuck, Mosher & Harritt stay with us.

Monday, May 9 Spend as much of the day as possible in writing. Shuck, Mosher, & Jessee Harritt stay with us. G.W. Rose came at night.

Tuesday, May 10 Delegates go on. J.W. Hott & wife came. I do some writing and more in talking & errands. Go to Lisbon at 4:00 p.m. Bishops' Board meet at 7:00. My home at A. Runkle's. C. Kellogg preached.

Wednesday, May 11 Mission Board meets at 8:00. Home at Adam Runkle's. Bishop Castle preaches the missionary sermon. Delivered it well.

Thursday, May 12 Another session of the Board of Bishops. General Conference meets at 2:00. Bishop J.J. Glosbrenner presiding. He blunderingly read the Quad. Address I wrote. Wm. Dillon preached, at night.

Friday, May 13 Session continued, progresses fairly well. Reports of Trustees, Pub. Agent, Mission Secretary, Biblical Seminary. Adjourn early in afternoon. D.K. Flickinger lectured at 8:00 on Germany.

Saturday, May 14 Session continues. Lorin came. Afternoon the conference discussed a const. amendment to a Missionary, for each annual conference, to elect a member of the Board. Dr. L. Davis lectured on Education.

Sunday, May 15 Bp. J.J. Glossbrenner preached on Isa. 32:20. Dine at Father Kettering's Love-feast at 3:00. Very precious. Bp. Weaver preached at 7:30—John 14:1–3. Same as last Gen. Conf. John 14:2

Monday, May 16 Bishop Dickson presided. Gen. Conference continued. Susan came at 10:00. Dine at Conf. Home, Adam Runkle's. Supper at Henry Booher's. J.K. Alwood preached at 8:00 on "Transfiguration."

Tuesday, May 17 Session till 10:00 Bp Castle presided. The contest of M. Bowman for M.S. Drury's seat was affirmed. Susan goes home. Woman's Missionary Meeting at night.

Wednesday, May 18 I presided at the conference. Question of examining the annual conferences was discussed on D.A. Beauchamp's motion, and Stearns amendment. Report of Com. No. 14 on Revision.

Thursday, May 19 Bp. Glosbrenner presides. The committee on Superintendency recommended a court to try a bishop. It was struck out. E. Shopherd spoke on Garst's amendment. H. Floyd preached in the evening.

Friday, May 20 Bp. Weaver presided. The conference sent greetings to Pres. Gen. Assembly (South), Stanton, Va., and Pres. Gen. Assembly North Buffalo, New York. Report on various Interests. J.W. Nye preached at night. Davis' resolution not tabled 57 to 68.

Saturday, May 21 Bp. Dickson presides. Elections at 9:00. E.B. Kephart elected by six majority as Bishop. The vote: N. Castle 104, J.J. Glossbrenner 93, J. Weaver 92, E.B. Kephart 70, J. Dickson 65, M. Wright 58, W.J. Shuey 57, George Miller 37, Wm. Dillon 30. Scattering 19.

Sunday, May 22 Bishop J. Dickson preached, at 10:30. Praise meeting in afternoon. J.W. Hott preached in the evening.

Monday, May 23 Bp. Castle presided. The Com. on Court of Appeals reported, and afternoon was indef. Postponed. The Rock River Appeal was not concurred in. Supper at Rev. Mr. Dove's, M. Episcopal.

Tuesday, May 24 I Presided. Report on Moral Reform Afternoon, debate on [unreadable]. At night it was adopted by a vote of 60 to 57, Gloss. pres. Went home on 6:00 train. E. Lorenz and E. Curtis lodged with us.

Wednesday, May 25 Bishop Weaver presided. Appeals of Bishop, Dessinger, Fohl, Bickley, were reported. Bad logic on both sides. Conf. Adjourned at 5:30. I go home at 8:00. S. Austin, J.H. Snyder, J. Kemp, David Shuck, Brenner, Nye, & Thrasher staid with us.

Saturday, May 28 Made some arrangement for cars.

Wednesday, June 1 Finished packing. Start at 9:40 p.m. in the evening for Radmould, Ind.

Thursday, June 2 Arrive in Chicago and go on to Richmond—to D.K. Zeller's; arr. at 6:30 p.m. Lorin & Wilbur at Kokomo went via Indianapolis to Glenmore to Moor's. Reuchlin at Anderson left for Fairmount & Uncle Wm. Reeder's.

Friday, June 3 Wrote in the forenoon, & up town a little Afternoon. Went to Earlham College. Called at Prof. White's. Went to Benj. Harris's. Supper there. Back to D.K. Zeller's.

Saturday, June 4 Wrote some. Went up town Looked a little for property to rent. The same in the afternoon. Went to Washington on the evening train. Staid at Evans Bailey's.

Sunday, June 5 Went through rain to Williamsburg. Few out. Dine at Madison Cranor's. Went back to Washington & preached at 4:00: "What think ye of Christ?" Staid at Wm. Hatfield's.

Monday, June 6 Went on 9:26 train to Richmond. Looked for property. Saw several pieces. Boarded at D.K. Zeller's, with family.

Tuesday, June 7 Looked further for property. Went in

afternoon with Susan to see property & we at Supper at Benj. Harris's. in Levastapol. Reuchlin came.

Wednesday, June 8 Rented property of Mrs. Joshua Haines at $20.00 per month, 211 14th St. Moved in afternoon. Lorin & Wilbur came. Supper at Zeller's. Lodge in our house.

Thursday, June 9 Breakfast at Zeller's. Engage in fixing up. Bought a load of wood & groceries. Busy all day. Emma Zeller called in the afternoon.

Friday, June 10 Went to town with Susan & bought carpets. Busy rest of the time. Mrs. Caroline Zeller & Emma come & sew carpet in afternoon.

Saturday, June 11 Wrote notes to the *Telescope* and the *Cynosure*. Busy fixing up Door-yard mowed. Mrs. Albert called in the afternoon.

Sunday, June 12 Went to United Presbyterian Church. Heard a good sermon. Older boys at Presbyterian Church. Younger children at U.P. Ch. at 2 1/2 afternoon. Went to Grace M.E. Ch. in evening. Prayer meeting, etc. there.

Monday, June 13 At home. In afternoon bought a washboiler. Called at H. Odborn's, W. Stiggleman's, and I. Huddleson's. Forgot to go to Af. M.E. Ch. to hear Editor Tanner's lecture.

Wednesday, June 15 About as usual. Benj. Harris called to see if I wanted to rent Cadwalader's property in Sevastapol.

Thursday, June 16 About as usual Called at W. Stiggleman's Photograpy Gallery. Boys look round for work in afternoon. Reuchlin engaged to a farmer over the Ohio line.

Friday, June 17 Reuchlin went to Ohio to work. Lorin looked round a little. Bought a month's bill of groceries at Coblentz. Lorin took lawn mower to Shop.

Saturday, June 18 At home. Some work and some writing. Boys mowed the door-yard with lawnmower in the evening Mrs. Isaac Huddleson & daughter called. I went

to Cambridge and stayed at Saml. Wright's.

Sunday, June 19 Went via Dublin & to Salem Ch. Preached Luke 10:37. Dined at Wilkison Smith's. David Stover Chas & Eli Holly, Jas. Tweedy, & families there. Went with Wm. Wright to Dublin. At Floyd's Pr. at 8:00 from Rev. 2:17.

Monday, June 20 Called at Har. Cook's, Savana Beatter's, W. Scroggy's, Eliz. Witt's, J. Cranor's, & dined at Mont. Groenendyke's. Went home on 1:24 train.

Tuesday, June 21 At home. Lorin went to Dayton in the afternoon. Mrs. Albert (next door) called, in the evening. Wrote to Mohler at Ced. Rapids.

Wednesday, June 22 Bought remnant of Carpet. H.O. Hutton & wife of New Paris, Ohio, visit us. Call at Peter Albert's after dinner.

Thursday, June 23 Rev. F.M. DeMumbrun visited us. Sister Yeager came after dinner. Caroline Zeller called in afternoon; then Mrs. Stiggleman called.

Friday, June 24 Read & wrote letters. Small boys went out to look after employment. They went for minnows afternoon—found none.

Saturday, June 25 At home as usual. Reuchlin came about 8:15.

Sunday, June 26 Went to U.P. Church Rev. Elihu Simpson, pastor. Text 1 Thes. 3:12,13. At that S.S. at 2 1/2. Accidentally came across David Carson, 416, S. 9th St. Heard Rev. Mr. Hughes at 8:00 Matt. 16:13.

Monday, June 27 Reuchlin went to Mr. McDonald's to work again. Called at Maj. Wm. L. Johns'. Prof. Jas. Strausburg called in the evening.

Tuesday, June 28 At home. Rev. L.N. Jones' called. Dined with him at P. Alberts. Called with Jones to see Grandmother Koerner.

Wednesday, June 29 At home. Went down to D.K. Zeller's in evening. Jacob Zeller there.

Thursday, June 30 At home as usual. Wrote to J.B. & others. Letter from Healy announcing Hurless' withdrawl, etc. Mrs. Jas. Shuey, Mrs. Jay, and Mrs. I. Huddleson called. Emma Zeller called in the evening.

Friday, July 1 At home engaged in writing & reading. Wife and self went at 7:00 eve & visited Isaac Huddleson's till bed-time.

Saturday, July 2 News of Garfield's assassination. To Dublin on 3:01 train. Lunch at Floyd's. Vardaman takes me out to Salem Ch. Stop at Bradford's J.T. Vardaman pr. at 8:00, "If any man confess me." Stay at Eli Hawley's.

Sunday, July 3 Preach Mark 16:15. Mission Coll. Dine at Chas. Hawley's with J.T. Vardaman. Go to Eli's & to Dublin with Harrison Cook. Pr. at 8:00 Ps. 25:14. Stay at H. Floyd's.

Monday, July 4 Called at H. Cook's. Went to W. Scroggy's. Talk with George Day. Dine at Seroggy's. Go on 1:26 train to Richmond. We have fire-works at night.

Tuesday, July 5 Letters from D.E. Middlekauf & others. Wrote Several letters. Caroline Zeller called in the evening.

Wednesday, July 6 Letters received. Wrote several. A very warm day & night. Rev. E.H. Caylor and son visited us and stayed all night—his son Elmore.

Thursday, July 7 Wrote letters. Very warm day. Letters and papers received. Hot, hotter, hottest!

Friday, July 8 Spent the day mostly in writing letters. Called with Susan to see her Mother, in the evening.

Saturday, July 9 Spent forenoon in writing. Went to Bloomingsport in the afternoon. Stopped off at Johnson's station. Walked over to Simeon Adamson's. Pr. at 8:30 Ex. 8:34. Staid at Otwell Hutchens'. Very, very hot.

Sunday, July 10 Pr. at 10 1/2 I John 5.18,19. Dined at Wm. Engle's, Robert Kinsey takes me on to Bethel Church, near Lynn. Pr. Ps. 25:24. Staid at John H. Moody's. Wm. Henry Johnson & wife Vienna call an hour or so. Very, very hot.

Monday, July 11 John takes me down to Johnson Stn. I go home on 9:43 train. Very, very hot. Prof. P.H. Wagner & family stay with us.

Tuesday, July 12 Spend the day principally in writing. Weather extremely hot. Nearly 100 degrees in the coolest shade.

Friday, July 15 Spent day in writing. Wrote long & severe letter to Dr. J. Blanchard who is trying to capture part of our church. Weather a little moderated.

Saturday, July 16 Day as usual. Lorin came home from Dayton. Reuchlin came at 8:30.

Sunday, July 17 Went to Friend's meeting on Main Street. Caroline Zeller and Silas called in the evening.

Tuesday, July 19 The above by mistake was assigned to Monday when it belonged to to-day. Prof. Strasburg and President C.H. Kiracofe came, Kiracofe remaining till after dinner. Then we went to Earlham and looked at collection of birds & shells & Looked at miscoscopic views at Strasburg.

Wednesday, July 20 At home. Wrote some letters Mother (Catharine) Koerner came, on a visit.

Friday, July 22 Went in the evening to Benj. Harris'. He not returned from Yellow Springs.

Saturday, July 23 Took a trip to Benj. Harris', etc. Found none at home. Mother Koerner went home. I was going to Millville on 8:10 train in Eve, but, as cars were behind, did not go.

Sunday, July 24 Went to Colored Wesleyan Camp-meeting. Elder Clemens preached at 11:00. Elder Smothers at 3:30, he went a kiting! Speaking meeting, morning & afternoon. Orville & Katie were with me.

Monday, July 25 Went to Benj. Harris's in the evening Haynes, Spence, and Coe's building, near railroad burned. Great fire truly. Very still air or the flames would have spread.

Tuesday, July 26 Went at 10:00 to Washington. Dined

at Wm. Hatfield's. Cyrus Osborn took me up to Thos. Cranor's. Came home on 6:30 train. I borrowed money of him and paid it back when due.

Wednesday, July 27 At home writing most of the day. Bought draft for $62.50, and sent in Registered letter to D. Hepler, Casey, Iowa.

Thursday, July 28 Father Peter Albert visited me this morning. Rev. W.H. Lantham & wife & daughters called in the afternoon. I start to Chicago at 10:20 P.M. via Ridgeville. Slept 5 1/2 hours on car.

Friday, July 29 Saw Rev. Shank on train. Arrived at Chicago 7:15. Start at 8:00 for Galesburg, Bushness, & Adair. Reach Adair at 9:00. Stay at Rev. A. Rigney's.

Saturday, July 30 Stay for dinner at Rigney's. Go to Solomon Walker's, 5 ms west of Adair. Preach at Union Chapel at 8:30—I Pet. 4:18. Members: Herndon & Rexroads. Stay at Walker's.

Sunday, July 31 Pr. at 10:30 from II Cor. 3:7,8: Raised $350.00 subscrip. & dedicated the Church. Dined at Herndon's. Pr. at 5:00, Luke 16:31. Stay at Solomon Walker's.

Monday, August 1 Bro. Walker takes me to McComb. Start at 9:40 for Chicago, via Galesburg, Buda, Aurora. Arrive at 7:25. Start on "Pan Handle" railroad at 7:55 for home via Ridgeville. Slept over five hours.

Tuesday, August 2 Reached Richmond at 5:00. Saw S. Moore Surface at Depot, who also called at our house an hour in the forenoon. Bought a bill of groceries.

Wednesday, August 3 Went out to the country to look for wood. Went to Dayton, O., at 2:00. Went to Henry (ex-bish) Kumler's. Found him paralyzed much but sensible. Prayed with him at his request. Visited Mrs. Polly Swaynie, aged 94.

Thursday, August 4 Had staid at Dr. Lewis Davis's. Meeting of Ex. Com. of the Board of Education. Dine at Davis'. Call at Sines & Feight's. Go to Tele. Office & return to Sines' etc. Go on 7:00 train home. Saw Rev. Tobey of Cambrid[ge].

Friday, August 5 Start at 11:10 for Marion, Ind.; Write letters while waiting at Ridgeville. Arrive at marion at 5:30. Go to Rev. W.A. Oler's & to John Y. Parlett's. Stay there. Mr. Hannah O'Farrell on the train from Richmond, from Knoxville, Ten.

Saturday, August 6 Stay at Parlett's till after dinner. Rev. W.A. Oler takes me on to Union Chapel. Call at Jeff Hamaker's. Pr. at 4:00 Ps. 1:6. Stay at Daniel Shank's.

Sunday, August 7 Preach at 10:30 in the grove. Heb. 7:26. Dine in grove with Bro. Crevinger. Rev. D.E. Myer pr. at 2:30, New Covenant. Rev. Cyrus Smith present. Go on to J.Y. Parlett's. Pr. at Ch. Church Marion at 8:00 Ps. 35:14. Stay at Rev. D.E. Myer's.

Monday, August 8 Afternoon go to John Null's, downriver. That Day Rev. A. Carroll & J.R. Brown & wife came.

Tuesday, August 9 Went to town (Maria) Called to see Dr. Chap. Nottingham Dined at Snede Thomas's. Called at D.E. Myer's. Went on 6:30 train to Conference at Salem Church near Kokomo. Day pr. Stay at David Smith's.

Wednesday, August 10 Went to place of Conference in the morning Dined at David Smith's. Conference opened at 2:00. Supper at Smith's Milton Harris pr. at 8:30 from Rom 10:1. Stay at David Smith's.

Thursday, August 11 Session as usual. Supper at Squire Farley's Met boundary Com. D.K. Flickinger preached at 8:00 "He that hath this."

Friday, August 12 Met boundary Committee at 8:00. Elected P.E. on first ballot, by 44 out of 53 votes. Floyd by 35, 2d ballot Supper at Goodwine's. Night session. Stay at Smith's as usual. Very warm.

Saturday, August 13 Stationing Com. met at 8:00 at Wm. Smith's. Also finance Com. at 9:00. A little rain. Session Closed at 10:00 at night. I was placed on Dublin Dist. W.J. Pruner preach at 8:00 Rom. 12:1. Stay at Smith's as usual. Gideon Richwind I think.

Sunday, August 14 Bp. Kephart pr. at 10:30, "While we

look at things not seen," etc. J.Y. DeMumbrion ordained. Dine on ground with Wilmore's host. Flickinger lectured on Africa at 3 1/2, after S.S. Anniversary. Supper at Squire Farley's. I preach at 8:00 I Cor. 6:11. Stay at David Smith's.

Monday, August 15 Took train at Vermont Station for Marion & thence to Fairmount. Dined at Robt. Hastings. Called at Carter hastings. Robt. took me to W.H.H. Reeder's. His daughter Flora is at Marion at Normal School. G.W. Dealey's three small children at Uncle William's.

Tuesday, August 16 Went over to see the farm. Called at Dr. George Wright's going & Coming. M. Shadrach came along. Looked at the farm & corn.

Wednesday, August 17 Went to Mr. Shadriach's; also via Fairmount to a Mr. Wright's near Gallatio. Back by dinner. Walked on settlement with Uncle Reeder. Preached at Union Church 3 1/2 ms west at 8:00: Ps. 25:1–4. Stay at Uncle William's.

Thursday, August 18 G.W. Dealey & I settle, he paying $25.00 cash for the pasture, & I agreeing to take 1/2 corn crop in the field for rent. Shadrach called again. Wm. H.H, jr, takes me to Jonesboro. Supper with him at Hotel. I stay till 1:30 & go to train. Lantern light went out.

Friday, August 19 Arrived at Ridgeville 4:30 a.m. Breakfast at Sumption House. Made inquiries of Mr. D. Kassalman & others about a rpoposed renter, Wm. Winsett. Wrote to W.H.H. Reeder & to Winsett. Call at Dr. Farquar's. Saw Rev. A. Worth & wife a moment at train. Reached home at 11:00. G.W. Beard called. Called at Zeller's.

Saturday, August 20 Emma Zeller came & helped Susan in the morning. Went to Dr. Hibbard's with Susan. Rev. Elihu Simpson of U.R. Church called to see us & invited me to preach Sab. morning.

Sunday, August 21 I pr. at 10 1/2 at U.P. Church Ps. 25:14. Afternoon Being somewhat short of sleep, I fell asleep for an hour or two. Went to hear Mr. Simpson lecture in the evening on Causes of want of Church influence.

Monday, August 22 Wrote letters in forenoon & went to the depot. Afternoon went to hear Gov. St. John at Glen Miller. Messrs. Ambrose there; also John Hetzler, & Mr. Fouts. Hear St. John at Hicksite Church at 8:00. A happy speech.

Thursday, August 25 Wrote letters. Rev. Geo. W. Beard called and left us a measure of apples, of a load he was selling in town. Susan and I call at Mr. Stiggleman's, but they not at home.

Friday, August 26 Start at 11:10 for Gr. Rapids & Caledonia. The whole land parched. Reach Gr. Rapids at 10:00 p.m. Portland, Decatur, Ft. Wayne, Kendallville, La Grange, Sturgis, Nottawa, Kalamazoo, etc, M.E. Pastor. Stay at Morton House.

Saturday, August 27 Left Gr. Rapids at 5:40 & reached Caledonia about 7:00. Stopped at Mr. A.B. Sherk's. Rev. I.H. Mourer's called. I wrote some letters. Called at Church. Bro. Shesler took me to Freeport. Quar. Conference. Supper at A.C. Clemens'. G.S. Lake preached. Stay at Cheesebro's.

Sunday, August 28 I pr at 10:30 from Heb. 7:26. Raise $780.00 on Coll for $600.00 $175 in Cash. Dedicate. Dine at J. Cheesebro's. Pr. at 7:00 Ps. 25:1–4. Stay at Job Cheesebro's.

Monday, August 29 Went in forenoon to Jac. Wing's five miles S.W. of Freeport, where Bro. Lake boards. Lodge there. Mrs. Lake's enlarged picture is real nice.

Tuesday, August 30 Rev. C.B. Sherk & wife came to dinner. We went on via Middleville (on Thorn Apple River) to Caledonia. Supper & lodging at Rev. I.H. Mourer's. J.W. Crayton pr. 7:00.

Wednesday, August 31 Spent forenoon at Mourer's. Conference opened at 2:00. Supper at Mourer's. Call at Rev. Wheeler's to see Rev. S.B. Ervin & wife. Rev. Keeny pr. 7:00, I Cor. 2:9,10. Shelley exhorts. Lodge at Shisler's. Bridenstine & others there.

Thursday, September 1 At Conference. Dine at Rev. Oudie's, (Ev. Asso.) with A. Rust & wife. Preside a little while in afternoon. Supper at Mourer's, Pr. at 7:00 Ps.

92:8. Went 10 ms. & lodged with Rev. Th. McCracken's.

Friday, September 2 Bro. McCracken takes me to Wayland for 8:30 train. Go on train. Lunch at Ft. Wayne. Lady lost ticket at end of Car seat; another gets on wrong train. Reach Richmond 6:20. All well.

Saturday, September 3 Go to Quarterly meeting via Fountain City. Ride to Winsburg with Mr. Jones. Call at Rev. H.C. Pearce's. Pr. at 2:00 Acts 16:14. Vardaman, F.M. Moore, etc. present at Qr. Conf. Sup[p]er & lodging at Washington Hutchen's. Kabrich pr. at 8:00. Good prosp. for Circuit.

Sunday, September 4 Pr. at 10L30. Ps. 92:8, Sacramental service. Dine at Herbert C. Pearce's with Kabrich. Called in afternoon at Mother Katie Johnson's, Mother Britain's, Mrs. Eliza St. Myer's, & Mrs. Hanah Blair's, with Bros. Kabrich & Pearce & Mrs. Bunwell. Pr. at 7:30 Ps 1:6. Stay at Pearce's.

Monday, September 5 Came home on the Economy hack, arriving at 9:00. Wrote a hurried letter to Rev. J.K. Alwood. Letter to Drury & Shuey & others. Called with Susan at D.K. Zeller's in evening Mother Koerner quite sick.

Tuesday, September 6 At prayer-meeting for recovery of the President, at 1st Presb. Ch; at 10:30. Susan called to see her mother.

Wednesday, September 7 Reuchlin went to Earlham, forenoon and afternoon. He was not attracted by the college. Did but little this day.

Thursday, September 8 Called at Cullaton's printing office at 9:00. Programs engaged. Wrote during the afternoon.

Friday, September 9 H. Floyd called in forenoon on his way to Qr. Meeting out north. Mailed programmes of Dist. Conference in the evening. Cost $2.50, postage 29 cts: Total: 2.79.

Saturday, September 10 Went on 11:00 (1:00) train to Cambridge. Bro. Wm. McGath took me out to Salem. Preaching over when I arrived. Qr. Conf. Went to Bro. Wilk. Smith's. Rains at night a light shower. Pr. at 8:00

Rom. 5:1. Stay at Smith's with Cranor. Rev. John Cranor.

Sunday, September 11 Pr. at 10:30 Isa. 9:6,7. Dine at Br. Chas. *Holly's. Rev. D. Stover there, sick with the flux. Bro. Cranor went to pr. at Dublin at 7:30. Speaking meeting at 7:30. I Lodge at Eli Hawley's. *Hawley.

Monday, September 12 At Micajah Modlin's funeral. F.M. DeMumbrum pr. "These are they who came" etc. I go with Rev. J. Cranor to H. Cook's. Pr. Lizzie Bever's funeral at Dublin at 3:00. Call at H. Floyd's in eve with Rev. W.C. Day. Stay at Dr. Geo. Day's. Had cholera in March. [?]

Tuesday, September 13 Went home on the early train. Felt weak all day.

Friday, September 16 Wrote some letters. Went on 8:10 train to New Castle. Staid at Bro. Harvey Root's.

Saturday, September 17 Called to see M.L. Bailey's Mother Schildknecht's & Rev. O. Jennings went with H. Root to Center Chapel, 3 ms N.W. of Cadiz. Pr. Eph 3:19. Quarterly Conf. follows. Supper at Rev. Wm. Davenport's. Rev. F.M. Moore pr. at 8:00,"Choose this day whom ye will serve." Staid at Davenport's.

Sunday, September 18 Pr. at 10:30 (11) Heb. 7.26. Dine at Bro. Reynolds'. Supper at Bro. Tully's. Rev. F.M. Moore pr. at 7:30. Job. 34.33. F.M. Moore, Williams & myself stay at Rev. Wm. Davenport's.

Monday, September 19 Went to Bro. Reynold's, & on to New Castle with Rev. Jacob Williams. Called at H. Root's meat-shop. Went on to Bro. William's—called at Mrs. Lizzie Bowman's—Dined. Took cars at 5:20 for home. Pres. Garfield died at 10:30.

Tuesday, September 20 At home reading etc. Went with Susan, Lorin, & Reuchlin to Rev. E. Simpson's, to a farewell reception.

Thursday, September 22 At home writing on revision of tract matter Caroline Zeller called in the morning. Bought a cord of wood $5.25.

Friday, September 23 Went to Anderson & Pendleton

11:00 day train. Saw Rev. J.T. Demunbrun & wife, Joseph Bradbury & lady, Jonas Hatfield & Mrs. Ed. Ogborn. Wrote letters at Anderson. Bro S.J. Ryan met me at Pendleton & took me to his house two ms. S.W. of White Chapel.

Saturday, September 24 Went to Fortville with Br. Ruan. Called at Dr. Yancey's, also at Br. Joseph Swanson's Dined at Ryan's, after going by Alfont. Simpson Jones & wife & Bro. True there. Pr. at White Chapel Luke 16:9. Quarterly confernce. Supper at Isa. Sharritt's 3 ms. S.W. F.M. Demunbrun pr. at 7:30 II Tim. 2:3. Stay at Jacob Kenerly's 2 1/2 m. S.W.

Sunday, September 25 Pr at 10:30, II Sam. 1:19. Dine at Mother George's or S.A. McCarty's, her son-in-law's. Rev. F.M. Demunbrun pr at 3:30 from "Draw nigh to God," etc. We go on to Francis M. Jackson's. Pr. at New Hope S.H. Luke 24:46 at 7:30. Stay at Jackson's Br. F.M. Denumbr. had a chill.

Monday, September 26 Br. Jackson's oldest son took me to Pendleton. President's funeral service at M.E. Church. Pastor Mr. Brewington. Biographical sketch by Mardman, Esq. I was at service at M.E. church at 2:00 in Anders[on] Rev. Joseph Franklin spoke. Revs. Hast'g P.E. M.E. McDonald pres; Virgins the pastor, etc. I spoke five minutes. Went home on 4:17 train.

Tuesday, September 27 At home arranging papers & planning my publication. I called at Zeller's in the evening.

Wednesday, September 28 I saw procession of the soldier's Reunion.

Thursday, September 29 At home in forenoon. Reuchlin & Lorin went to Glen. Miller to Soldier's reunion. Purchased suit for Reuchlin at $20, Lorin $17, Wilbur $11, etc.

Friday, September 30 Start via Indianapolis on 10:15 (11:20) train, for Whiteland. See Rev J.K. Billheimer, Rev. Wm. Hall, etc. Stay at Rev. Isaac M. Tharp's. His children are Ulyssus, Orra, Milton Wright, & Lizzie. I saw Rev. A. Worth at Richmond, as I start on the train.

Saturday, October 1 Dined at Tharp's. Go on to Quarterly meeting at Bethel. I pr. at 2:00 (3:00) Heb. 11:7.

Quar. Confer. It apportions for pastor $410.00. Quite rainy. Called at Whiteland at Nelson Scott's. I stay at Jas. Waddles, with Bro. Tharp.

Sunday, October 2 I Pr. at 10:30, Ex. 28:34. Dine at Br. Jonathan Wilson's 1 1/2 m. N.E. of Bethel. It rains so Br. Tharp and I stay there till morning. A family of movers (Campbell) stay there. The Coll. was quite small. Brethren in neighborhood: Hugh Surface, Joseph Rush, Western C. Cleary. It was a very rainy night.

Monday, October 3 I took the morning (9:14) train for Indianapolis. I saw Dr. Bebe at Whiteland. He said Henry Binkley's of Dublin lives there. Left Indianapolis at 11:00 & reached home about 2:30.

Tuesday, October 4 I took manuscript for *Reform Leaflet* to the Printer Mr. Cullaton. I worked on finishing the manuscript.

Wednesday, October 5 Finished up note on publishing *Leaflet* and *Star*. I read proof in afternoon. Joseph Boyd of Dayton called to visit the boys, & staid with us till morning.

Thursday, October 6 I got copies of *Reform Leaflet*. J. Boyd staid with us. We were folding Leaflets.

Friday, October 7 I spent day in mailing *Reform Leaflet*. Boys helped.

Saturday, October 8 Went on 10:15 (11:20) train for Indianapolis. See Rev. Z. McNew at Union Depot. Called at Benj. Groves 12 Plum St. Supper at Wm. J. Rubush's, on Park Ave. Quarterly conference at Church at 7:30. Stay at Bro. Rubush's, 409 Plum.

Sunday, October 9 Preach at 10:30. Dine at B.F. Witt's on Illinois St. Call at Haught's. Preach at 7:30 Luke 16:31. Stay at B.F. Witt's. The congregations were large morning and evening.

Monday, October 10 I went to Walter S. Brown's, and via Union Depot to Rev. Daniel Stover's. Dined. Returned to Cousin Brown's, Corner of St. Clair and Fort Wayne Avenue. Went to call on Dr. R.T. Brown 1/2 hour. Preached from Num. 10:29. I stay at F. Rubush's.

Tuesday, October 11 Went home after calling an hour on Rev. T.J. Connor, 517 N. Alabama Street. I worked with some of the boys in mailing *Ref. Leaflet.*

Wednesday, October 12 Worked hard till evening in mailing "Leaflet."

Thursday, October 13 Forenoon spent in mailing Reform Leaflets. Called at D.K. Zeller's. Finished mailing Leaflet which cost 15 days of close work.

Friday, October 14 Went on 11:10 (12:00) train to Anderson and McCordsville & to Saml. Brooks—His grand-daughter & family live with him.

Saturday, October 15 Went with Bro. Brooks to Sister Polly Ann Yaryan's & dined. Preached at Bethlehem at 2:00, I Tim. 1:7. Quart. Conf. Supper at Eliz Crook's, 1/2 mile east. Rain hindered from going to meeting. Staid at Sr. Crooks. Crook Children: Lydia & Corda.

Sunday, October 16 Pr. at Bethlehem Ch. John 14:23. Dined at "Jackey" Mitchells, with Rev. Asbury Myer & wife. Bro. Myer pr. at 7:30 on Sanctification. I stay at Wm. Mitchel's.

Monday, October 17 Called in at Bro. Myer's, who lives in Bro. Mitchel's rooms. Their boy Noitre. Talk on healing miracles of this day & on Muller's life of trust. I caution him on the subject. Dinner at Wm. Mitchell's. Went to Sister Eliz. Crook's. No meeting on account of rain.

Tuesday, October 18 Went with Rev. Asbury Myer via New Britton to Indianapolis. I call at Witt's Office. I go to Morristown on 5:50 train. Rev. Z. McNew takes me over, & I stay at Eli Myer's.

Wednesday, October 19 I stay till afternoon at Eli Myer's. Rev. L.N. Jones comes. I go to Peter Myer's & stay till evening meeting. Rev. L.N. Jones preached at 7:30 the opening sermon instead of Rev. F.M. Moore. I staid at Eli Myer's with W.C. Day.

Thursday, October 20 "Dist Conference opened W.C. Day, J.N. Jones, Z. McNew, J. Cranor & M. Wright present. Dinner at Peter Myer's. I.M. Tharp came in the evening. Cranor led the discusion of the People's duty to the Pastor. I staid at Eli Myer's."

Friday, October 21 Discussions continued. Big John Smith & Baptist Smith there. Dine at Wm. Phares', a Baptist, with Revs. McNew, Tharp & the Smith's. Supper at Eli Myer's. Profs. Kiracofe & Fix come. Temperance meeting at 7:00.

Saturday, October 22 Dist. Conference continued. Prof. Kiracofe spoke on Revised New Testament; Prof. Fix on Duty of S.S. Teachers, I dine at Peter Myer's. W.C. Day spoke on Liberalistic Tendencies. Quarterly Conf. at 2:00. I supped at Bro. Zick's. Educational meeting. Stay at Eli Myer's.

Sunday, October 23 I Preach at 10:30 Ps. 18:30. I dine at Eli Myer's. Rainy. No Sabbath School meeting at 3:00. Profs. Kiracofe and Fix had started at 8:00, Day at 3:00 & Alonzo Myer, for home. I pr at 7:00 I John 3:2. I Stay at Eli Myer's.

Monday, October 24 I go with Eli & wife to Michael Bilman's 3 1/2 miles north-east of Shelbyville. He & wife from Alsace, France, now Germany. Family: old folks grown daughter, Widow Gordon & her son and daughter. Eli's go home at four o'clock.

Tuesday, October 25 Father Billman took me to Shelbyville. Sent postal order to Susan for $30.00. Just in time for cars. Stop off at St. Louis Crossing & go on Hack to Hope. After an hour's waiting Rev. J.K. Lawrence came after me. Stop at Rev. W.C. Day's at Hartsville. Children Carl & Maggie.

Wednesday, October 26 Attend morning prayers at the College. Call at Nathaniel Miller's. Go with the pastor (Day) to secure subscr. for parsonage. Dine at John Riley's. Go with pastor to David Fix's, 3 m. west . Not at home. At prayer meeting 7 1/2. Sup & lodge with Pres. C.H. Kiracofe.

Thursday, October 27 At morning prayers. Call at Mrs. Scudder's, Coblentz & dine at G.C. Mench's. Sup & lodge at E. Pitman's. They had lost half the number of their children by scarlet fever, in April.

Friday, October 28 Called at Father Wertz and at Prof.

Mobley's. Dined at Prof. Kiracofe's. At rhetorical, and addressed the students a few minutes. Hindered by rain from going to Shiloh. Supper at Rev. W.C. Day's. Staid at Simeon Rhorer's.

Saturday, October 29 Called at Day's and Kiracofe's & dined at Josiah Lawrence's. Went with Father J.K. Lawrence to Shiloh to Qr. M. at 2:00. Pr. Titus 2:13. Qr. Conf. Supper & Lodging at Jas. eward's, 20 rds E. Rev. L.W. Crawford pr. at 7:00, John 1:29.

Sunday, October 30 Pr. at 10 1/2 I John 5:18,19. Dine at Jas. Barger's with Revs. A.C. Rice & A.H.H. Beams. A.R. Rice, pastor, pr. at 7:00. We stay at David Fix's. Their children: John, William, Elmer, & two girls.

Monday, October 31 Stay at Fix's, all day. Rice went home. I Pr. at 7:00, Isa. 55:1. I stay at Fix's that night.

Tuesday, November 1 Bro. Fix takes me to Hartsville. Dine at W.C. Day's. Canvass a little on parsonage. Supper at Day's. Lodge at Prof. Wm. Fix's.

Wednesday, November 2 At college prayers. Go to Bro. I. Tyner's. Went to Mrs. Coblentz/s, Mr Wineland's & dine. Call at J. Riley's. Supper & lodging at N.J. Miller's. Rainy evening.

Thursday, November 3 Went to J. Wertz, Pres. Kiracofe's, morning prayers, P.Office, Day's, Kir's study. Dinner at Day's. Supper and lodging at Pres. Kiracofe's. Lectured in College Chapel at 7:00 on "Our Use of Literature."

Friday, November 4 Attended morning prayers. Wrote letters to L. Davis & W.C. Smith. Dined at Jer. Dean's. He a college mate of mine, and his wife (El. Hager) a college mate of Susan's. Supper & lodging at Rev. Wm. Fix's.

Saturday, November 5 Call at Day's & Kiracofe's. Dine at Rev. A.H. Chittenden's. Pr. at 2:00, Col. Chapel, Ps. 92:8. Qr. conf. Supper and lodging at Prof. James L. Funkhouser's. Rev. John Riley pr. at 7:00. Rom. 6:22.

Sunday, November 6 Pr. at College Chapel Mal. 3:1. Large congregations, morning and evening. Dine at Alonzo Myers. S.S. 300 Supper at W.C. Day's. Pr. at 7:00 Luke 16:31. Stay at Pres. C.H. Kiracofe's.

Monday, November 7 Called at John Anderson's, Mother Fix's, Jas. Lawrence's, Susan Daley's, Dined at W.C. Day's. Rev. J.K. Lawrence took me to Hope. Went on hack to St. Louis Crossing, and on to Cambridge on cars. Staid at Saml. Wright's.

Tuesday, November 8 Went home to Richmond on 6:35 train. Took Pr. Aid Constitution to Recorder's Office for record.

Wednesday, November 9 At home forenoon. Mrs. Colvin called, being aggrieved by Rev. F.M. Demunbrun's letter. Complained of his reading the *Enquirer. Caroline Zeller called in the afternoon. *Good cause of complaint, for a minister to read the *Enquirer* before her children!

Thursday, November 10 At home all day. Called twice at the post-office. Mailed letters on the Chi. train, to Blanchard & to J.M. Habrich and to O.L. Wilson. Spent evening in looking over & classifying letters.

Friday, November 11 Spent morning in looking over old papers. Go on 3:01 train to Cambridge City. Stay at Samuel Wright's. Miss Jordan on 11th & North Sts Richmond, among their boarders. (She afterward became a newvous wreck.).

Saturday, November 12 Went on 6:00 M. train to Yellow Banks, 4 ms N.W. of Brookville. Stop at Stephen Warren's. Cross the river to Wm. P. Wilson's, where Rev. Geo. Wilson, local preacher, lives. Dine & go to Oak Forest. Pr. 20 minutes Ps. 1:5,6. Supper at Robt. White's. Pr at 7:00 Eph. 3:8. Stay at Harvey White's.

Sunday, November 13 Pr. at Oak Forest at 10 1/2 Acts 11:24. Dine at Ellis Foster's. His wife a daughter of Mr. Coffee, a Baptist friend of Bro. Harvey's. Rev. A.J. Bolen pr. at 6:30—good meeting. Stay at Saml. Foster's. a local M.E. preacher's. His nephew, Martin, teacher, boards there. His daughter teaching 7 m away.

Monday, November 14 Good morning meeting at 9:30. Dine at Robt. White's. James Coil, a local Qr. Conf. pr. Wm. Hunter there. Bro. A.J. Bolen went home. I pr. at 6:45, Mat. 16:26. Three arise for prayer. One forward for prayer. Stay at Robt. White's.

Tuesday, November 15 Went with Rev. Geo. Wilson to Harvey White's. Dined. Returned to Robt. White's. Bro. Bolen pr. A large & attentive congregation. Stay at Eilis Foster's with Geo. Wilson. Mrs. Hunter professed conversion the night before after going home.

Wednesday, November 16 Morning meeting moderately attended. Dined at Ellis Foster's with Wilson & Bolen. We fixed up the Ch. House & blacked the stove. Supper with Bolen at Robt. White's. Pr. at 7:00, I Kings 18:21. Large congregations. Stay at E. Foster's with Wilson.

Thursday, November 17 Forenoon meeting—good. Dine at E. Foster's. Call at Bro. Milburn's & Hammond's, M.E. man. Supper at William Hunter's. Pr. at 7:00 Acts 26:28. Stay at Ellis Foster's with Bro. Wilson. His two Daughters, Anna Mary & Osia.

Friday, November 18 Rev. Geo. Wilson took me to Brookville. Possibly my first sight of a town within 25 miles of where I was raised. Reach Connersville at 11:00. Call to see Thos. Little, county Clerk. Walk from Liberty to Danl. Maxwell's. Rainy. Stay at Maxwell's.

Saturday, November 19 See John Beard. Go to Alonzo Beard's. Dine. Will E. Stanton, Rev. L.N. Jones, & Rev Geo. W. Beard call. Pr. at Greenwood Church, at 2:00. John 9:4. Qr. Conf. Supper & lodging at Isaac Pearson's. I pr. at 7:00, Matt 16:26. Hard young men there. Talk during meeting.

Sunday, November 20 Pr. at 10 1/2 Heb. 13:14. Dine at John Lafuze's with Rev. L.N. Jones & wife. Mr. Lafuze and wife call, & Mr. Miller & wife. Pr. at 6:30 I Kings 18.21. Stay at Isaac Pierson's. Heard Shepherd & Gray had stopped Daniel Koerner, supposing it to be I. They mad over reproof.

Monday, November 21 Bro. Jones Called. I went with I. Pearson to Liberty Drew $26 on check from Canada at 1st nat. Bank. Went on 9:40 train via Connersville home. Staid an hour at depot at Cambridge City—over a half hour at Connersville.

Tuesday, November 22 Went on 7:25 M. train to Dayton. Called at Feight's, Sines. Went to Telescope office.

Bought fountain pen, blank-book, call at Editor's office. Dine at Dr. L. Davis'. Ex. Com. of B.Ed. at 3 1/2. Sup at Davis'. Call at Sines', Feight's, Tobey's. Stay at Davis'.

Wednesday, November 23 Call at M.R. Drury's, Mrs. Cretia Edwards, & Aunt Tena Huffman's. Go on 8:00 M. train home. Print & direct circulars on Hartsv. College.

Thursday, November 24 Print postal circulars to our itinerants of W.R. Conf. on Leaflet & Star. Hear Mr. Hughes pr. Thanksgiving sermon in Richmond. D.K. Zeller & family dine with us, this being the 22d Anniversary of mine & Susan's wedding-day. Mother Koerner of the number.

Friday, November 25 Spend the day and evening largely in writing. Inquire after Church Bells for Rev. M.R. Myer of Col. City, Iowa; and for Church seats of Haynes, Spencer & Co. for Rev. A.C. Wilmore, of Indianapolis.

Saturday, November 26 Went to Centerville on 7:15 train. Called at Daniel Aukerman's & dined. Went on to Joshua Lammott's. Pr. at Union Ch. at 2:30 II Tim. 1:7. Supper at Lammott's. Rev. O.L. Wilson pr. 6:30, Ps 92:12. I exhort. Stay with O.L. Wilson's at Lammott's.

Sunday, November 27 Pr. at 10:30 I Kings 18:21. Dine at Abr. Karch's. O.L. Wilson & Martin Coffman also there. They have a daughter, Mrs. Dennis, Cor. of N. 14 & A. Sts., Richmond. Pr at 6:30 Acts 26:28. Stay at J. Lammotts.

Monday, November 28 Dine at Mr. Dellinger's on Nat. Road, just east of "Pin Hook." Go to Wm. Leonard's. Supper. Pr. at 7:00, Luke 13:24. Call at J. Lammott's and get valise and then go on to Wm Leonard's and stay.

Tuesday, November 29 Bro. Wilson takes me on to Washington. Call at Cyrus Osborn's. Go on 9:00 train home. Willie Reeder had come after me. Allen Harris dined with us. Go on 10:20 night train to Anderson. Stay at the Doxey House.

Wednesday, November 30 Go on 7:10 (8:00) train to Fairmount. Breakffast at Winslow's Hotel. Another

Winslow (livery) takes us to W.H. Reeder's. Go to the farm & to Clark Leacher's to see G.W. Daley on a trespass in gathering corn and hauling off a Share for gathering—all unauthorized. Stay at Uncle Reeder's.

Thursday, December 1 Uncle Reeder's horse died. Found it to be from a founder or colic, as we supposed. Stay there all day. A Mr. Nick. Winslow called; also Rev. Mr. Hubert.

Friday, December 2 Went via Geo. Wright's to the farm & to Wm. Duling's. Return via cribs to Uncle's, calling to Henry Simon's. Go on to Fairmount. Stop at Mr. B. Hollingsworth's, Rev. Wm. Hall's son-in-law's. Go on 8:13 train to Anderson. Stay at the Doxey.

Saturday, December 3 Went on 7:00 train to Washington. Dine at Cyrus Osbrone's. Preach at 2:00, Eph. 2:7. Q. Conf. Supper at Nathan Brazier's. Rev. Wm. Davenport comes for Bro. Kabrich to pr. Mother Prague's funeral. I pr. at 7:00 Col. 1:13. Call at Danl. McMullin's. Stay at Wm. Hatfield's.

Sunday, December 4 Pr at 10:30, 2 Cor. 3:7,8. Dine at Wm. Hatfield's & he takes me to Dublin. Stop at Rev. J. Cranor's, Mr. Study there. Supper. Pr. at 7:00, Ps. 48:11–14. Large congregation notwithstanding Temperance meeting at M.E. Ch. Stay at Cranor's. It was Quar. Meeting.

Monday, December 5 Good speaking meeting at 10:00. Very short discourse & Qr. Conf. at 2:00. Supper at Wilson Scroggy's. Preach communion sermon at 7:00. Stay at Joseph Gray's.

Tuesday, December 6 Go home on 6:32 M. train. Engage in purchase of shoes, etc. Write a circular letter on Leaflet & the Star. Go on 4:20 aft. tr. to Anderson. On the 9:32 train to Fairmount. Stay at Winslow's Hotel, with Eli Holley (Hawley.)

Wednesday, December 7 Walk over to W.H.H. Reeder's. After Dinner go to Fairmount. Engage Foster Davis to prosecute a replevin [?] case for me. I enter suit and return to W.H.H. Reeder's, Sen.

Thursday, December 8 Go to Fairmount. See Squire Jones. Go on to Richmond, waiting in Anderson four or five hours, spending the time mostly in letter-writing.

Friday, December 9 Arise at 4:00, morning, and am busy all day, till I start to Flat Rock on 4:20 train; Aftn. supper at Jac. William's. Pr. at 6:45 Luke 13:24. Stay at Jac. Williams with Rev. F.T. Moore.

Saturday, December 10 I Pr. at 10:30, Rom. 5:1–5 Follow with Class-meeting Dine with Moore & others at Levi William's. Quarterly Conference at 2:00 after a few remarks on 122 Ps. v. 6. Supper at Mrs. Lizzie Bowman's Moore pr. at 6:45, "We are Christ's." Stay at Jac. Scheildknecht.

Sunday, December 11 Preach at 10:30 I John 5:18,19. Dine at Rev. John Austin Bailey's. Bros. Jennings, Root, Grove, & Bro. Bailey's daughters & their husbands were there. Sister Anna Bailey pr at 6:30. House very full. Stay at Nick. Milligan's, who married at Scheildtknecht.

Monday, December 12 Went to Millville, & to meeting at 10:00. Good meeting. Dine at Phillip Heddrick's. Father Miles Conway & Mother Conway live there. I Visit our old house, where Robinson's now live, & call at Hendrick's. Preach at 6:45 I Pet 4:18. Stay at Levi Williams'.

Tuesday, December 13 Meeting at 10:00 M. Good. Dine at David Bailey's 3/4 mile west of Millville. Rev. J.A. Bailey & wife & daughter, Lorinda Thornburg with us. David took me to cars. Went on 5:00 train to Anderson & thence to Fairmount.

Wednesday, December 14 Have my first lawsuit in all my life. Dine at Hotel. Remained all day at trial and till nearly 11:00 at night. Stay at Foster Davis'. Suit decided in my favor near day-light. Corn found (58 bush) awarded me.

Thursday, December 15 Leave on 10:00 train for Richmond, via Anderson. Dined at City Bakery. Wrote letters. Called at Dr. G.F. Chittenden's, Rhodes', Burtner's. Reached home at 6:30.

Friday, December 16 Forenoon in writing, and then go

to see Cullaton on publishing proposed papers. Went on 3:00 Aft. train to Knightstown. Dr. J.W. Tree met me and took me up to Warrington. Stay at Trees'.

Saturday, December 17 Write in forenoon. Pr. at 2:00 Qr. Conference. Supper at Thos. Armstrong's, an old pupil of mine. Rev. F.M. Demumbrun pr. Stay at Thos. Armstrong's. Somewhat sick that night & ate almost nothing next forenoon.

Sunday, December 18 Pr. at 10:30 2 Cor. 3:7,8. Dine at John Bridges'. His wife a school-mate of Susan's—Eliz. Cora. Saw Jas. Newkirk, also a school-mate of Susan's. Armstrong is an old acquaintance of mine. Rev. F.M. Demumbrun pr. at night. Raise $35.00 subs. for him. Stay at Bridges'.

Monday, December 19 Mr. Thorpe took me to Knightstown. Go home on 12:46 train. Home in Richmond. Write some.

Tuesday, December 20 At home, mostly writing. Start out to take names for the organization of a Church in Richmond.

Wednesday, December 21 At home till evening. Went to Albert's, Clark Yeager's, & Prof. Strausburg's.

Thursday, December 22 Very rainy day. Some small purchases in town. Went on 3:03 train to Ogden. Harvey Wright met me and took me to his house, 6miles south-by-east. Children at home. John, 25, Joseph, 21. Rhoda 16, Eva 12, Gracie 10. I Stay there.

Friday, December 23 Harvey took me to Rushville for 10:52 train, but did not board it, as it stops not till reaches Indianapolis. Go on 2:30 freight. After waiting long go on mill wagon to Freeport, and then walk to Windfall Church. Pr. Luke 13:24. Stay at John Jackson's 1 m S. by west from Church.

Saturday, December 24 Went after dinner to Windfall Church. Pr. Heb. 12:28,29. Qr. Conf. Supper at Thomas Zell's 1 m. N.W. of Church. McNew pr. 7:00 "Whatsoever thy hand," etc. Stay at Horace Patterson's 1/8 m N. of Ch. Z. McNew is the pastor.

Sunday, December 25 Pr at 11.00 Luke 2:10. Dine at Joseph Little's. Pr. at 6:30. I Kings 18:21. Take up subs. for pastor. Raise $8.00 cash & 2.50 in subscrip. Stay at John Jackson's.

Monday, December 26 Spent the day in writing letters & postals. Stay all day at Jackson's. Pr. at 6:30 Matt. 16:26. Three acces[s] sins. Stay at Jackson's.

Tuesday, December 27 Go with Rev. Z. McNew to Morristown, & thence to Indianapolis. Met Rev. Bro. Nye on cars. Met Rev. T. Evans, Dr. R.T. Brown, Walter Brown on St. Called at Rev. A.C. Wilmore's 463 N. Penn. St. Rev. J.S. Wall there. Soo Mrs. Geo. Brown & daught. on cars. Find Rev. C.C. Kellogg & Rev. H. Rupel at my house.

Wednesday, December 28 Write for the *Reform Leaflet* and engage it printed for 7:00. Spent considerable time in looking up old papers, periodicals, etc. At home all day except trip into town.

Thursday, December 29 Finish up articles for *Leaflet* and get it printed. Much time in proof reading. Get the edition about 8:00 and fold & direct many of them. Go to bed very late.

Friday, December 30 Busy directing *Ref Leaflet*. Mail them afternoon. Start at 3:03 (4:00) for Honey Creek, 4 m S.W. of Greenwood. Train misses connection. Stay at Rev. A.C. Wilmore's 463 N. Pennsylvania St. Indianapolis. Saw Rev. A. Worth on the train. Rev. C.C. Kellogg stops at Dublin.

Saturday, December 31 Start on 7:10 train for Greenwood. Walk over to Honey Creek Church. Pr at 11:00 Isa. 12th. Dine at James Jones. Quarterly Conference at 2:00. Supper at Thomas Pruner's. Pr at 7:00 Luke 15:18. Stay at James Scott's with Rev. I.M. Tharp's.

Memoranda

Presiding Elder's Salary

Williamsburg	$18.80
Dublin	18.60
New Castle	18.25

Warrington	13.75
Honey Creek	6.38
Indianapolis	3.46
Fall Creek	12.11
Blue River	18.90
Cliffty	15.06
Hartsville	11.91
White Water	11.25
Franklin	15.00
Abington	4.77
[total]	165.94

1881 Expense of Travel

Williamsburg	.40
Dublin	.85
New Castle	1.00
Warrington	2.65
Honey Creek	3.40
Indianapolis	2.90
Fall Creek	1.40
Blue River	1.00
Cliffty	.75
Home	1.35
Oak Forest	.90
Liberty	.90
Richmond	.80
Centerville	.15
Home via Washington	.20
Thence to Dublin	.24
Home	.35
Millville	.45
Knightstown & return	1.85
Morristown via Rushv.	1.10

1882

Sunday, January 1 Arose at 6:30 at James Scott's after a good night's rest. May this be a good year of grace to my soul in the Lord. Preach at Honey Creek Chapel at 10:30 I John 5:18,19. Dine at Capt. Jas. Jones. At Sab. Sch. at 3:00. Preside in the election of S.S. Officers. Return to Jones'. Preach to a good audience at 6:30 I Kings 18:21. Stay at Jas. Scott's.

Monday, January 2 Visited Mother Scott with Bro. Tharp. She long papalized. Longing to go home to heaven. Speaking meeting at 10 1/2. Few, good. Dine at Elijah Stones with Tharp & Father & Mother Sedam. Br. Tharp & I go to Whiteland. Stay at Tharp's.

Tuesday, January 3 Wrote to Burns & McFarland. Start on 9:59 train to Indianapolis. Mail letter. Dine at Walter S. Brown's. His wife's father, Mr. Shortridge there. Supper at Rev. A.C. Wilmore's. Called at Moses Hatfield's on the way to Church. Preach at 7:30 I Kings 18:21. Stay at W.G. Rubush's 409 Park Avenue.

Wednesday, January 4 Fine snow & Snowing. Write letters & stay in doors. Went and put a card & 4 letters in letter-box. Dinner & supper at Rubush's. Quar. Conf. at 7:00 & prayer-meeting at 8:00. Stay at A.C. Wilmore's. Plan of special district in connection with Indianapolis.

Thursday, January 5 Call at B.F. Witt's. His mother there. Got a card from home Busy taking down addresses for *Leaflet & Star*. Go to Witt's office and write for a clergyman's pemit on J. Mad. & Ind. R.R. Preach at 7:30 Ps 16:8. Stay at W.G. Rubush's 409 Park Ave.

Friday, January 6 Spend forenoon at T.J. Connor's, 517 Alabama St. Dine at Moses Hatfield's, on East Street. Go down town with Moses H. Call at Jon't. Elliott's Office. Go to Bro. Wilmore's. Go with Moses Hatfield to Robert Park Chapel to the revival services conducted by Harrison. Stay at Bro. Wilmore's.

Saturday, January 7 Go on 8:30 M. train from Mass. Ave. Depot to New Britton. Call at Mrs. Mary Frazier's. Pr. at 10:30 Matt. 13:31. Dined at John Crosley's. Pr. at 2:00 Ps. 16:8. Qr. Conference. Supper at Mrs. Frazier's. Rev. A. Noyer pr. at 6:30 on prayer. I stay at Sister Frazier's. Half rainy thawing day. John & Henry Frazier, her sons.

Sunday, January 8 Preach at 10:30 John 17:17. Dine at Mrs. Young's. Talk on discerning of Spirits, etc. with Myer, Brooks, etc. Pr. at 6:30 Luke 13:24. Three lifted their hands for prayer. Raised a few dollars on pastor's salary. Stay at John Crosley's.

Monday, January 9 Call at Brother Ringers. Get my valise at Sister Frazier's. Go on 10:10 train via Indianapolis home. Arrive at 2:05. Find no one at home; so call to see Mother Koerner. Return home. Read letters. Mail a few leaflets, etc.

Tuesday, January 10 Finish mailing *Leaflets*. Rev. C.C. Kellogg comes in the afternoon. He had been to Dublin West Fork Chapel, and Salem. Had collected about $30.00 for Gould College. He staid that night with us.

Wednesday, January 11 Went up town with Orville to have his teeth doctored—had two pulled to let others straight out. Consulted Judge Wm. Peele. Saw Foster Davis. Called with him after dinner at Peele's & Washburne's. Give notice at post-office about postal-order from Burns & McFarland.

Thursday, January 12 Engaged somewhat in writing & in getting ready to leave home. Go at 4:20 to Cambridge, Call at E. Wright's, and at Charley Butch's, Rev. Horace Herr's' brotherinlaw. Go that night to Whisler's but Herr's had not come. Stay at Wright's.

Friday, January 13 Went on 5:35 train to Columbus. Lunch. Call to see Spencer Esq. & Marshall Hacker, Esq., both former students and graduates of Hartsville College. Go to Rev. A.H.K. Beam's 3 ms N.E. Stay there that afternoon and night.

Saturday, January 14 Remain till afternoon at Bro. Beam's. Preach at 2:00 at Olive Branch. Rev. 2:17. Sup[p]er at Silas Anderson's. Pr. at Ps. 2:1. Stay at Anderson's. Quarterly Conference at 2:30 L.W. Crawford's license granted. Bros. Kemp. Lambert, Talley, Rothruck, [rest is blank]

Sunday, January 15 Preach at 10:30 Ps. 48:11. Sacramental service followed. Dine at Henry Lambert's Mr. Stephenson of Jennings County there. Rainy. Preach at 6:30 Rev. 22:11. Con. Generally serious. Stay at Bro. Lambert's.

Monday, January 16 A good speaking meeting at 10 1/2; about ten present. Dinner & supper at Bro. James Falley's. Their children: Charley, Adonirum, Flora, Minna, James. Pr. at 7:00 Ps. 16:11. Snowy; few out. Stay at Henry Lamberts.

Tuesday, January 17 Good meeting at 10:30. About ten out. Dine at Joshua Rothrock's. Sing after dinner. Remain to supper. Pr. at 6:30 Eph. 2:4. Congregation good, and quite serious. Stay at Silas Anderson's.

Wednesday, January 18 Good day-meeting at 10:30. Go to Simeon Bennett's. Dinner & supper there. Write full card to F. Thomas and full letter to G.W. Hunt. Preach at 6:30, I Peter 4:18. One arose for prayers—Mrs. Garitt. Stay at Bennetts.

Thursday, January 19 Rev. A.C. Rice takes me to Hartsville. Call on the way at Jas. Barger's & Jas. Seward's. Dine at Rev. Alonzo Myer's. Call at Rev. W.C. Day's & Mrs. Coblentz. Spend afternoon in Reuchlin & Lorin's rooms at Pres. Kiracofe's Supper at Kiracofe's. Bro. Day pr. at 6:30, Isa, "Let the wicked," etc. Lodge at Kiracofe's.

Friday, January 20 Attend morning prayers at College & recitation in Moral Philosophy. Attend forenoon social meeting. Dine at Rev. W.C. Day's. Attend rhetorical exercises. Supper at G.W. Lawrence's. Stay at Prof. James Funkhouser's.

Saturday, January 21 Write some in the boys' room. Dine at G. Mench's. Preach in lecture room at 1:30. 2 Cor 3:18. Quarterly Conference. Local preachers stirred on attending social worship. Supper at Isaac Tyner's. Pr. Col. Chap. Mark 8:36. Stay at Wm Fixe's.

Sunday, January 22 Pr. at 10 1/2 Ps 25:14. Dine at Rev. Hester's. Attend Sabbath School & Bible Class. Supper at Lewis Mobley's. Rev. W.C. Day pr. at 6:15. Heb. 12:29. I exhort a little & raise a collection. Stay at Nathaniel P. Miller's.

Monday, January 23 Attend morning prayers at College. Excellent warm speaking meeting at Lecture room; well-attended. Dined at Mrs. Paulina Rollins. Day called at the boy's room & talked with me some time. Supper at Day's. Preached at 6:15 Ps 16:11. Lodge at Pres. C.H. Kiracofe's.

Tuesday, January 24 Good meeting at 10:30. Dine at Emanuel Pitman's. Lorin takes me to Hope. Go on 5:00 train to Cambridge. Wreck below Cambridge. Walk on to the town. Stay at Samuel Wright's. He is a cousin of mine.

Wednesday, January 25 Went home on 6:00 train in Morning.

Thursday, January 26 At home most of the day. Mrs. Albert called. I called to see Judge Bickle.

Friday, January 27 John Y. Parlett came. Mailed letter to F. Davis. Wrote in afternoon. Called to see Judge Fox. Write to Wm Reeder, Foster Davis, etc. Go on 8:10 (8:00) train to Cambridge. Stay at Hotel.

Saturday, January 28 Start at 6:00 for Yellow Bank. Call at Stephen Warren's. Pr. at White Water at 10:30 Job 2:13 Dine at Warren's. Talk at 1:30 on I John 1 chap. Qr. Conf. Supper at James Collet's. Call in to see old folks also. Pr. at 7:00 Luke 23:4. Stay at Step[h]en Warren's.

Sunday, January 29 Preached at 10:30, Numbers 10:29. Dine at Mrs. Carrie Day's, with Rev. A.J. Bolen. Called at Stephen Warren's. Bro. Bolen pr. at 7:00, Ist Cor. 9:24. Stay at Ezekiel Collett's.

Monday, January 30 Wrote letters. Went to Wm. Wilson's & staid till evening. Preach at 7:00, Ez. 33:11. Several asked for prayers. Staid at Stephen Warren's.

Tuesday, January 31 Wrote letter[s] & mailed them. Went to Geo. W.W. Stewart's. Called at Grandfather Geo. Stewart's, aged about 93. Called at Henry Smith's Supper at G.W. Stewart's Preach at 7:00, Ps. 16:11. Stay at Joseph Nearing's.

Wednesday, February 1 Went on to Laurel. Mr. Anson Moor met me and took me to Austin Winchell's. Dine. Estella Harris there. Lucinda Moor also. Went on to Moor's. Staid there.

Thursday, February 2 Anson took me to Glenwood. Started about 12:00 for Liberty. Tarry at Connersville long. Reached Liberty after 3:00. Went with Mr. Coleman to Salem. Walked to George W. Beard's, & to Rev. L.N. Jones' to supper. Pr. at 7:00 Joel 2:13. Stay at Bro. Jones'.

Friday, February 3 Meeting at 10:00. Five or six out. Dined at Sam. B. Fry's. Go with pastor, Bro. Jones, to Mrs. Paddack's. She is aged 85 ys. Supper at Jones! Pr. at 7:00, Mark 8:36. Stay at S.B. Fry's.

Saturday, February 4 Went to Rev. L.N. Jones' Staid till after dinner. Qr. Conference at 2:00. Quiet conference. Supper at S.B. Fry's. Pr. at 7:00. Luke 13:24. Staid at Rev. G.W. Beard's. A Mr. Lee, of Mixerville, was there.

Sunday, February 5 Pr. at 11:00, Ex. 28:34. Dine at Saml B. Fry's. Martin Wyrick takes me to Abington. Supper at Wyrick's. Pr. at 6:30 from John 14:2. House over-crowded. Stay at Obadiah Holler's. At Fry's I had a plain talk with a dentist of Liberty and Sanford Fry, who denied the resur[r]ection of the body.

Monday, February 6 Called at J.H. Weaver's. Sacramental meeting followed by Quarterly Conference. Dine at John Henry Weaver's. Remain there till after supper. Preach at 6:30. Ez. 33:11. Go with George Noll's 1 1/2 m s.w. and lodge. Many lifted their hands for prayers, and four came forward for prayers. Mr. Duke joined Church.

Tuesday, February 7 Went to meeting at 10:00. Some rain but a pretty good attendance. Dine at A. Shroy's. Call at Sister Cook's, Austin Bailey's sister. Went to Obd. Holler's for supper. Pr. at 6:30 Matt. 12:30. Quite rainy but a fair congregation. Stay at Obadiah Holler's.

Wednesday, February 8 Went home with Obadiah Holler. Spent afternoon in reading letters, etc. writing, etc.

Spent forenoon at home. Went over to Dayton on 2:00 train. Call at Dr. L. Davis' & Sines. Supper & lodging at Dr. L. Davis'.

Friday, February 10 Got a note of W.L. Wright. At morning prayers at Seminary. Call at Sines', Fight's, Hotts, Tel. Office—Ed. Tel.—Ed. Gen. paper- bookroom—Dine at Aunt Polly Swaynie's. Go to Sem. Meeting at Dr. Davis Class-Room. Call at Rev. D. Miller's, Funkhouser's, Davis, Sines', Supper at Hotts. Went home on evening train.

Saturday, February 11 Went to Washington on the 11:00 train. Dine at G. Osborn's. Go to Quarterly Conference at Sugar Grove at 2:00. Full attendance. Supper at Rev. O.L. Wilson's. Pr. at 7:00, Ps. 16:11. Stay at Wm. Lamb's. 2 m N. of Church.

Sunday, February 12 Pr. at 10:30 Isa. 62:1. Communion followed. Dine at John Nicholson's. Called at John Gilmer's. Pr. at 7:00, Luke 13:3. Stay at Daniel Harris'. Milton Har[r]is there. Two young men joined church that night.

Monday, February 13 Good morning speaking meeting. Dine at Henry Franklin's. Cyrus Osborn & wife there. Call at Rev. O.L. Wilson's. Pr at 7:00 Rev. 22:11. One joined Church. Staid at John Gilmer's.

Tuesday, February 14 Went with Oscar Wilson to Washington, & on to Richmond. Washington was called Greensfork, later on.

Wednesday, February 15 Samuel Wright called & dined with us.

Friday, February 17 Went to *Telegram* & *Paladium* office to engage the printing of *Monthly*. Get prop. of *Telegram* in afternoon. Call at D.K. Zeller's in evening. Also at the Palladium office and get their bid.

Saturday, February 18 Went to Dublin on 7:15 train. Stop at Rev. J. Cranor's. Call at Mother Witt's, Rev. H. Floyd's & Wilson Scroggy's. Dine at Cranor's, & go with him to New Lisbon. Pr. at 2:0 Luke 16:9. Qr. Conf. at 3:00. Supper at David Working's. Rev. N.D. Wolfard pr. 1 Cor. 16:22. I exhort & Bro. Cranor Exh & asks for seekers to rise. Stay at George Shaffers.

Sunday, February 19 Pr. at 10 1/2 Luke 24:46. Sacramental service. Dine at John Raffensberger. Stay there till evening meeting. Pr. at 7:00 Eph. 2:4. Bro. Cranor exhorts. Stay at George Shaffer's. Day & night quite rainy.

Monday, February 20 Meeting at 10:00; fair attendance. Dine at Jacob Wiseman's & stay till meeting in the evening. Pr. at 7:00 I Kings 18:21. Rainy day & evening. Stay at George Shaffer's.

Tuesday, February 21 Go on early train to Cambridge. Arrive at home at 9:00. Go to Telegram office and see about setting up the *Star* which they had begun. Work on matter for the *Richmond Star.*

Thursday, February 23 Heading of the *Star* had not come. Continued to work on *Star*. They got too much miscellany in. Read proofs in the evening. Mrs. Samuel Wright came at 10:00 at night.

Friday, February 24 The *Star* heading had came. Make up first page and put it to press. Put up the inside of the *Star* and to press. Work at preparing for the mail. Mail some papers—5 lbs.

Saturday, February 25 Mail some more matter. Go on 11:00 train to New Castle. Dine at Father O. Jennings. Pr. on Ps. Quarterly Conference followed. Supper at Harvey Root's. Sister Anna Bailey pr. at 7:00. I follow in exhortation. Stay at Harvey Root's. Rev. F.M. Moore staid with me.

Sunday, February 26 Pr. at 10:30, II Cor. 3:8. Sacramental service. Dine at Mrs. Hilo Bailey's. Call at Harvey Root's, and stay till meeting. Pr. at 7:00, Ez. 33:11. Stay at Harvey Root's. Andrew Nicholson and wife & Mrs. Balenger dined with us at Bailey's.

Monday, February 27 Go to Mother Schildknech's and stay till morning meeting. Excellent morning meeting—about 30 present. Dine at David E. Mullen's at toll-gate at Dublin pike. Went over to Rev. O. Jennings. Supper there Mother Lydia Sexton came. Stay at Ezra Schildknecht's

Tuesday, February 28 Go on 8:04 train home. See Rev. Mr. Warbington & Bro. Poffensbarger on the train. Spend the day largely in mailing papers.

Wednesday, March 1 Receive Star subscription and wordsof cheer from Revs. W.N. Coffman & I.M. Tharp. Write postals to several requesting articles for Star.

Thursday, March 2 Samuel Horine came in the morning & staid till the next day. Went in the evening to the Depot to inquire what trains stop at Philadelphia, Ind.

Friday, March 3 Went on 7:15 train to Philadelphia, Ind. Arrived at Philadelphia at 9:20. Bro. John Parker came for me on horseback. Dined at Parker's. Went on to Union Church. Call at Wm. Wilson's. Prayer and speaking meeting at 7:00. Rev. T.J. Halsted there. Some arose for prayer. Stay at Wm. Wilson's

Saturday, March 4 Went over to A.B. Rumler's. Demumbrun, Geo Wilson, and Rev. T.J. Halsted there. Dined. Pr. at 2:00, I Thes. 5:13. Qr. Conf. Felix jar with Macedonia Brethren. Supper at Jas. H. Murphy's—an aged exhorter Rev. T.J. Halsted preached at 7:00. I stay at Rumler's. Halsted's fatherinlaw is John Apple—step fatherinlaw.

Sunday, March 5 Went to Wm. Wilson's. Pr. at 10:30, Acts 24:15, Sarah Halsted. Communion service. Dine at Wm. Wilson's Went with Sameul Brooks to Mt. Zion, 11 miles. Pr. Acts 26:28, to a good-sized congregation. Stay at Bro. S. Brook's two miles north of McCordsville. Church is Mt. Zion 3 1/2 ms N. by East from McCordsville.

Monday, March 6 Stay at Bro. Brooks till evening. Spend the day mostly in reading. Preach at 7:00 at Mt. Zion Jude 14v. Fair attendance and serious audience. Staid at Samuel Brooks.

Tuesday, March 7 Good morning meeting. On the way I lifted a sapling & its brush & put on a brush pile. Probably from strain became lame and was very lame in my side and back all day. Dined at John Heath's & staid there till morning & till next evening. He lives with his daughter, Calle.

Wednesday, March 8 Was quite lame all day. Laid on lounge awhile in the afternoon which rested me. I then walked to Church and preached Ps. 16:11. Two joined Church & 3 others arose for prayers. Rode on Bro. A. Meyer's horse to Bro. Alonzo D. Sherman's about a mile east and half mile south of Church.

Thursday, March 9 Rode over to Church for 10 1/2 meeting. Had no preaching. Talked awhile. Dined with Bro. A. Myer's at Hiram Heath's. Qr. Conf. in afternoon at 3:00. Supper at Thomas Evans Kinneman's, an exhorter's. Pr. at 7:20 I Cor. 5:7. Sacramental service. Go through rough winds on Bro. Meyer's horse to Bro Saml. Brook's. Bro. Meyer waded much.

Friday, March 10 Went with a Mr. Apple to McCordsville. Got letter from home. Wrote letter & cards to some on Fall Creek Circuit on donations. Train behind time. Reached Indianapolis. Called at Rev. A.C. Wilmore's. Saw Father Muth & daughter on train. Also Rev. S. Frazee of Fayetteville. McNew pr. at Carrolton at 7:15. I exhort. Stay at Rev. Geo Muth's—aged 83.

Saturday, March 11 Pr. at 10:30 Ps. 84:11. Few out. Go to Father Muth's for dinner. Quarterly Conference. Few out. Supper at Muth's. Conference about $26.00 behind for year so far on preacher's salary. Father Muth & Alfrey's

[unreadable] in Quarterly Conference. Father G. Muth before he embraced religion took seven degrees of Freemasonry. Says Morgan & Kernard correctly reveal it. Pr. at 7:15, Acts 26:28.

Sunday, March 12 Pr. at 10:30 Heb. 13:14. Dine at Emanuel Matilla's, it being his birth-day. Supper at Rev. A.C. Rice's with Rev. Z. McNew. Bro. McNew and Muth also dined at Matillo's. Bro. McNew preached at 7:15 Rev. 22:17 Bro McNew & myself lodge at Daniel Muth's, one mile S.E.

Monday, March 13 Went up to Carrollton and stopped at Rev. g. Muth's till toward noon. Went to A. Alfry's & dined. Remained till 4:00. Then Went up to Rev. G. Muth's & staid till meeting. Pr. at 7:15 from Ez. 33:11. Stay at Rev. G. Muth's.

Tuesday, March 14 Went in buggy with Rev. G. Muth to Greenfield, and on 11:30 train to Richmond. Susan took a hemorrage (bronchial perhaps) in the evening. Went and got medicine of Dr. Hibberd.

Wednesday, March 15 At home all day. Susan feeble.

Thursday, March 16 At home all day. Susan gaining a little. Mrs. Abert (our nearest neighbor) called in.

Friday, March 17 Susan gaining a little. Caroline Zeller came in. At home all day. Did not start to my quarterly meeting on account of Susan's sickness. Wrote to Bro. Tharp. Had written him before.

Saturday, March 18 At home all day. Caroline came in afternoon again.

Sunday, March 19 Went to hear Rev. Henry Rupe at Baptist Church. "For me to live is Christ." Go to hear Rev. Clark Skinner preach at 7 1/2. He is P.E. M.E. Church. He preached at Grace M.E. Ch. Good ability but defective scholarship.

Tuesday, March 21 At home as usual. Susan still gaining. Emma Zeller called in. John & Martha Shearer called to see us. Proofs on Star sent in.

Wednesday, March 22 Read proofs and take them to

Telegram office. Emma Zeller called in. Went to see the doctor whom I had called to see several times since Susan's sickness. Mamie Albert called in awhile.

Thursday, March 23 Finished up furnishing copy, read proofs, and got April Star to press—outside pages. Caroline Zeller came in afternoon awhile. Went at 7:45 to depot. Stay at Cambridge City, Samuel Wright's.

Friday, March 24 Went on 5:35 train to Columbus, Ind., Joseph King, who came after me, failed to find me. Called at C.N. Spencer's. Called at his house a half hour. Had dined at Eating house. Hunted a way to Salt Creek. Saw Young Sol. Vonncida, Redman, Mench, Beam. Go with Isaack [sic] King. Stay at Josh. Guffey's.

Saturday, March 25 Wrote in forenoon. Dine at Guffey's. Pr. at 2:00 Ps. 16:11. Quarterly Conf. Supper at Joseph Ohaver's with Bros. Rice & Crawford. Rev. A.H.K. Beam Pr. at 7 1/2 o'clock from Nahum 1:7. Stay at John Kings, with Rice and Crawford's.

Sunday, March 26 Pr. at 10 1/2. Heb. 13:14. Sacramental service. Dine at Joseph H. Overhaver's. Pretty day, though threatening rain. Preach at 7:30, I John 3:2. 15 or 20 out. Stay at Bro. Ohavers.

Monday, March 27 Went on to Columbus Called at Charley Spencer's. Went on 10:30 train to Indianapolis. Called at Rev. A.C. Wilmore's; also at Rev. T.J. Connor's. Went on 4:45 train home Found family well except wife, and she improving.

Tuesday, March 28 Tuesday do much writing.

Wednesday, March 29 Finish nearly the matter for April Star. Read some proof.

Thursday, March 30 Read up proofs and oversee make up of paper in afternoon. Saw Floyd & Hutchens, and Henry Franklin Star subscribers to-day.

Friday, March 31 Paper went to press. Paid F.M. Demembrun's tax $6.28—using road-receipt of 56 cts. Mailed the Star to regular subscribers. Paid Cock Co. $21.00. Went on the evening (8:10) train to Cambridge City. Staid at Central Hotel.

Saturday, April 1 Went on 5:35 train to St. Louis Crossing & Hope. Reuchlin came for me. Dine at President's. Pr. at 2:00, I John 3:2. Qr. Conf. Suppe at Funkhouser's. Pr. at 7:30 Jude 21v. Stay at Nathaniel Miller's. Mrs. Milo Bailey & daughter were on the train to Columbus to see Lawrence Bailey's wife who was very sick.

Sunday, April 2 Pr. at 10:30, Ps 137:6. About 800 people at Church. Dine at P. Rawlins. Taught S.S. class. Call at the president's & take supper at Josiah Lawrence's. Pr. at 7:30, I Cor. 5:7. Stay at Isaac Vansickle's.

Monday, April 3 Reuchlin & Lorin invited to Breakfast with me. Am at morning prayers at the College. Call at John Anderson's & Mother Fixes & Mother Coblentz & Scudders. Dine at Rev. W.C. Day's. Get horse & buggy & Pres. Kiracofe takes me to Hope. Go on via St. L. Cr. & Cambridge home. Find all well.

Friday, April 7 Write some letters. Went on 8:10 evening train to Cambridge City. Stay at Central Hotel.

Saturday, April 8 Went on to Laurel. Rev. A.J. Bolen met me and took me to Andersonville. Dine at Bolen's. Pr. at 2:00, Jude 21st. v. Supper at Rev. John Morgan's, aged 81 this month. Preach at 7:30 Ps. 1:6. Stay at Dr. F.J. Spilman's.

Sunday, April 9 Pr. at 10 1/2 Ps. 18:30. Dine at Samuel Berber's with Flora Sarah Cott & Ellis Wright & "Sonny" Bowen. Go over to Rev. A.J. Bolen's. Pr. at 7:30 I Ki. 18:21. Mrs. Wrightson joined in the morning and Isaac Cook & wife in the evening. Storm of rain just after service. Stay at Rev. A.J. Bolen's.

Monday, April 10 Spent about two hours at Father Morgan's. Go to Bro. Archi. Miller's. Dine. Call at Mrs. Eliz. Cook's an hour or more. Supper at Archi. Miller's. Call at Bolen's. Pr at 7:30 Titus 2:13. Stay at Dr. F.J. Spilman's.

Tuesday, April 11 Rev A.J. Bolen takes me to Laurel for 10:40 train to Cambridge. Go on home arriving about 2:00 P.M.

Wednesday, April 12 Emma Zeller called in the afternoon.

Thursday, April 13 Emma Zeller started with Ida Miller to Germany, on 7:00 A.M. train.

Friday, April 14 Arranged with Rev. Henry Rupe to get his horse to go to Franklin quarterly meeting. Reform Leaflet for April printed.

Saturday, April 15 Went in buggy to Daniel Koerner's. Pr. at 2:00, Luke 16:9. Quar. Conference. Sup[p]er at Henry Joseph Fry's. Pr. at 8:00, Luke 16:31. Lodge at H.J. Fry's.

Sunday, April 16 Pr. at Franklin church at 10:30, 2 Cor. 3:8. Dine at Cunnard Dorr's. Preach at 3:45, Titus 2:13. Call at Harbine's. Stay at Daniel Koerner's.

Monday, April 17 Get home about 11:30 Orville had accompanied me on the trip.

Thursday, April 20 At home. Made up first side of May Richmond Star. Went to Zellers with Susan to see Grandmother & hear from Emma.

Friday, April 21 Do some trading and some writing. Spent afternoon on editorial. Susan & Wilbur went up in the evening to Preston's to buy shoes. My pair cost $4.00; Susans $3.00; Wilbur's $3.50.

Saturday, April 22 Arose at 4:45. Start to Abbington, via Centreville at 7:15 A.M. Martin Coffman meets me and takes me to his house 2 1/2 ms. on the Ab[b]ington pike South Take dinner. Qr. Conference at Ab[b]ington at at [repeated in text] 2:00 Pr I Thes. 1:5. Supper at Obadiah Holler's. Pr. at 8:00 from Deut. 18:18. Stay at Ob. Holler's.

Sunday, April 23 Pr. at 10 1/2 Acts 11:24. Sacramental service. Dine at James Duke's. Afternoon at S. School. Rev. Steel superintendent. Went to Martin Wyrick's. Took supper there. Pr. at 8:00, Rev 22:11. Stay at John Henry Weaver's with Rev. O.L. Wilson.

Monday, April 24 Rev. O.L. Wilson takes me to Crossing of Centreville pike near Washington. Got home about 9:30. Spent the day writing for the *Star.*

Tuesday, April 25 Still at work on the *Star.* Get done

writing for *Star* that evening. Read up proofs.

Wednesday, April 26 Made up *Star.* Susan had symptom of chill.

Thursday, Arpil 27 Got quinine pills for Susan. Star delivered afternoon. Mail it in Part: that is prepare for making.

Friday, April 28 Finished directing and mailing *Star.* Went to Washington on 4:20 train. Call at Cyrus Osborn's. Kaprich & wife come. Call after supper at Evan Bailey's Stay at Wm Hatfields.

Saturday, April 29 Went on to Bethel with Wm. Hatfield's son. Pr. at 10:30 Matt. 19:27. Dine at Pleasant Adamson's. Bro. Vardaman came. Qr. Conf. at 2:00. Supper at A. Grant Mendenhall's. Rev. J. Kaprich pr at 8:00 I Pet 5:4. I exhort. Stay at Mendenhall's.

Sunday, April 30 Pr. at 10:30, I John 5:18,19. Dine at Mannings. Call after dinner at Adam Oler's with Rev. J.M. Kabrich. Bro Manning's son takes me to Hagerstown. Stay at Jessee Fox's.

Monday, May 1 Go on 4:00 a.m. train to Richmond. Breakfast & start to Dayton, O. Call at Dr. L. Davis. Board of Education convenes at Seminary building at 10:00. Dine at Dr. Davis's. Afternoon session Closes business. Supper at A.W. Drury's. Addresses by students at 8:00. Stay at Davis'.

Tuesday, May 2 Seminary Board meets. I am present, but not a member. Dine at Wm. Dillon's. Their boy quite young. Attend afternoon session of the Sem. Board. Supper at Prof. G.A. Funkhouser's with B.F. Booth & D. Speck. Prof. Jackson lectures at 8:00. Stay with Prof. S.B. Allen at Rev. W.O. Tobey.

Wednesday, May 3 Attend Board meeting But before called at Dillon's & Mrs. Fleenor's. Dined at Rev. M.R. Drury's. At afternoon session of Board. Go to Rev. J.W. Hott's to supper but find I must leave sooner to Meet the train. See Tobey & go with Allen to Richmond. Stay at home.

Thursday, May 4 Engaged in writing and looking over

business. Call at Haynes & Spencer to see about Chambersburg Church seating for Hoke. Trade some in City.

Friday, May 5 Write, etc. some after getting bathed and dressed for trip. Bishop Kephart & Rev. D. Stover Call. Go on 11:00 train to Anderson. Write some at post-office. Go on to Pendleton on 4:55 train. Ride down with Mr. Jones to Samuel A. McCarty's or Mother George's. Stay there.

Saturday, May 6 Walked down to Bro Wm. A. Gray's. Dined there. Sister Gray sick. Qr. Conference at 2:00. Pr. Salary behind. My salary short. Supper at Gray's. Pr at 8:00 Rom. 14:17. Stay at Gray's.

Sunday, May 7 Pr. at 10:30 I John 5:18,19. Dine at Isa. Sharritt's, 3 1/2 ms. S.W. Pr at 3:30, John 1:29. Supper & lodging at Gray's. His wife sick. His motherinlaw Kenner there. Children have whooping cough.

Monday, May 8 Bro. Wm. A. Gray takes me to the 5:57 morning train. Reach Fairmount about 8:00. Ride a mile & walk the rest. Dine at Uncle Wm. H.H. Reeder's. Go in afternoon to look at my farm & see rentee David Chadwick. Stay at Uncle Reeder's.

Tuesday, May 9 David Eli and John Chadwick come over. Renew the bargain as they had broken it. Spend the day in preparing two articles (duplicates).

Wednesday, May 10 Went over to see Chadwicks, Wm Leach, Owan Nottingham and Levi Simons. With Uncle Reeder look at Swamp eighty. Chadwick's come over and sign the contract. Stay at Uncle's.

Thursday, May 11 Uncle W.H.H. Reeder pays me $24.86 & I give him a receipt in full for all dues. But the Bright note remains mine. Go to Fairmount See Jones, Board the 10:00 train for home Flora Reeder with me. Stop at Doxey House at Anderson. Go on 3:54 train home.

Friday, May 12 At home. Engaged in looking over business, and in writing.

Saturday, May 13 Went on 8:50 train to Cambridge.

Went out to John Shaffers. Dined. Rev. D. Stover pr. at 2:00. Qr. Conf. followed. Rainy day. No meeting at night. Stay at John Shaffer's.

Sunday, May 14 Pr. at 10:30 Ps. 48:11–13. Dine at Noah Hieney's at S.S. in afternoon. Supper at John Shaffers. Pr. at 8:00 I Kings 18:21. Stay at Shaffers, Daniel Lawson's not having come for me. Rev. D. Stover remained till after S.S. Rev. J. Cranor did not come at all; for dental neuralgia.

Monday, May 15 Bro J. Shaffer took me to John Lawson's, who was sick, and on to Rev. John Cranor's. Dine there. Preach at 8:00 from 2 Tim. 4:5. Stay at Rev. H. Floyd's.

Tuesday, May 16 Ministerial institute Dine at Bro. Floyds. Supper at Ed. Wilson's. Went home on 6:48 train.

Thursday, May 18 At home—got the paper out—*Star*.

Friday, May 19 Went on 7:25 train to Dublin. At Min. Institute. Dine at John Robinson's. Supper at Wilson Scroggy's. Rev. A.C. Wilmore pr. at 8:00. Stay at Rev. Halleck Floyd's.

Saturday, May 20 Meeting of Teacher's at Floyd's. Institute 9:00 till 12:00. Choose Third Monday in April for next meeting. Dine at Dr. Day's. Call at Scroggy's, Cranor's, Mother Witt's, H. Floyd's, Bar. Cooks Go on 3:48 train to Indianapolis. Supper & lodging at Bro. Wilmore's.

Sunday, May 21 Pr. at 10:30 John 16:27. Communion. Dine at B.F. Witt's. Attend S. School at 2:30. Supper at W.G. Rubush's. Pr. at 8:00 Luke 24:46. Large Congr. Fletcher Rubush & wife & John & wife etc. present. Stay at Rev. A.C. Wilmore's.

Monday, May 22 Visited Rev. T.J. Connor 720–40 N. Alabama St. Dined there with Wilmore. Mrs. Hazlerig, Mrs. Connor's adopted daughter from Greensburg there. Call at post-office. Find no letter. Sup[p]er at Moses Hatfield. Qr. Conf. at 8:00. Stay at Hatfield's.

Tuesday, May 23 Call at Wilmore's, at Rev. T. Evans, at Wm. Rubash's, & Saml. Hanway's. Go home on 11:20

train. Arrive at 2:20. Wrote out an editorial.

Wednesday, May 24 Mainly finished editorials.

Friday, May 26 Made up paper in forenoon. Directed some leaflets to Virginia & Pa. preachers. Settled off square with Dr. Davis & Dr. Hibberd paying Davis $1.50 & Hibbard $3.00.

Saturday, May 27 Went on 7:25 train to Indianapolis & thence to McCordsville. Walked out to Saml Brooks'. Went with him to Qr. meeting at Bethlehem six miles n. of McCordsville. Pr. at 2:00. Prov. 6:16. Qr. Conf Supper at Jackey Mitchel's. Rev. A. Myer pr at 8:00. I stay at Joseph Becler's. 3 joined Ch.

Sunday, May 28 Call at Wm. Mitchell's & Rev. A. Myer's & Sister Crook's. Pr. at 10 1/2 Heb. 11:26. Communion. Pr at 4:00, Ps 84th. Good speaking meeting followed. Stay at Samuel Brown.

Monday, May 29 Rose early & went to McCordsville afoot. Train for Anderson would not stop. Went on 6:22 train to Indianapolis. Wrote letters at Depot. Went home on 11:20 train. Saw Profs. Mobley & Aimen at Depot at Indianapolis. Mail considerable numbers of the *Star*.

Tuesday, May 30 Mail Star in forenoon Samuel Horine and wife come on 2:00 train. He subscribes for seven Stars for others.

Wednesday, May 31 Br. Horine's go on 5:00 train home.

Thursday, June 1 At home. Write some letters. Visit Grandmother Koerner with Susan.

Friday, June 2 Write to Rice & others, Hepler, W.H.H. Reeder. Went on 2:03 train to Indianapolis. Stay at Rev. A.C. Wilmore's. His birthday. Several call in.

Saturday, June 3 Go to Greenwood on 7:40 train. Tharp meets me and takes me to his house. Dine there—Stones Crossing. Quarterly meeting at Honey Cr. Church. Qr. Conf. at 5:00. Supper at Jas. Scott's. Pr. at 8:00, I Pet 2:7. Fair congregation of younk folks out. Stay at Jas. Scott's.

Sunday, June 4 Pr. at 10:30, II Cor. 3:8. Dine at Rev. Irvin Cox's. Shelby Fullen & wife & daughter there. Also Rev. Tharp & wife, & Davis & wife. Comment on 84th Psalm. Speaking meeting followed. Went home with James Harrell. Call at B.F. Jones. Stay at Harrell's. His son Harvey, aged about 19.

Monday, June 5 Rev. I.M. Tharp takes me to Indianapolis. Go on to Richmond, on 11:15 train Arrive at 2:10.

Tuesday, June 6 Go on 5:00 M. train to Hamilton & after writing, and mailing several letters went to McGonicle's, and thence to Peter Minton's 1 1/2 m. S.E. of the station. Dine After much talk went with Bro. M. to Bro. D.D. Beal's. Supper there. Returned to Minton's. Lodged there.

Wednesday, June 7 Bro. M. takes me to Jacob Kumler's a mile N.W. of Hamilton. Take 9:00 train to Carlisle. Hack to Germantown. Call at Abr. K. Burtner. Dine at Ezra Kemp's. Call at Moyer's after calling at Rev. W.J. Pruner's. Go via Carlisle to Dayton. Call at the *Telescope* Office. Shuey's criticism. Call at Sine's & Feight's. Stay at Dr. Lewis Davis.

Thursday, June 8 Came home on 7:05 train. Daniel Koerner & Elmira there; but started home at 11:00. Went to town & wrote letters at home. Went on 8:10 A. train to Cambridge City. Stay at Stahr's Central Hotel. Rode in morn. tr. with Nick Omer of Dayton.

Friday, June 9 Went on 6:05 train to St. Louis Crossing. Rev. Martatt of Seymour, Ind, aboard. Hack to Hope Lorin meets me & takes me to Hartsville. Dine at Rev. W.C. Day's. Supper also. Call at Pres. C.H. Kiracofe's. Stay at Rev. E. Pitman's.

Saturday, June 10 Went to the Pres't. K's. At the meeting of the Board of Trustees. Dine at Pres. Kir's. Quarterly meeting at 2:00. Rev. D.B. Keller of N. Ohio pr. Quar. Conf. follows. Supper at Wm Fix's Germania Entertainment. Stay with Wm. Davenport at Prof. Wm. Fix's.

Sunday, June 11 Went to Kiracofe's. Prest. pr. bacchalaureate [sic] sermon at 10 1/2. Rainy day. Dinner at Mrs. P. Rawlins. Sab. School. Supper at Day's.

Rev. J.K. Alwood pr. at 7:00. Sacrament follows. Stay at Wm. Fix.

Monday, June 12 Dinner at W.C. Day's. Board meeting in the afternoon. Sup[p]er at Rev. J.L. Funkhouser's. Met com. on Rev. Wm. Fix's doctrines.

Tuesday, June 13 Qr. Conf. at 11:00. Fix's Case referred to An. Conf. Dinner at Mench's. Board in afternoon. Supper at C.H. Kiracofes. Sermon by Rev. D.B. Keller. Stay at Pres. Kiracofe's.

Wednesday, June 14 At morning prayers. Confer with Floyd on boundaries, etc. Closing College exercises at 1:30. Board meeting followed. Sup[p]er at Funkhouser's.

Thursday, June 15 Commencement at 10 o'clock. Addresses by J. Frank Harris and A.E. Allen. Dinner at Wesley Lawrence's. Call at S. Rhorer's. Sup[p]er at W.C. Day's. Musical concert at 8:00. Stay at Prest. Kiracofe's.

Friday, June 16 Students Leave for home. I go with Lambert's to James Seward's. Dine there. Supper also. Go with Rev. A.C. Rice to Isaac C. Bevis'. Stay all night. Storm in afternoon. Rainy night & next morning.

Saturday, June 17 After dinner went to Shiloh. Pr. Amos 6:1. Quarterly Conference. Supper at Jas. Seward's. Pr. at 8:00 Luke 23:4. Stay at Seward's with Rice.

Sunday, June 18 Rainy morning. Pr. at Shiloh 10 1/2 Isa. 9:6,7. Dine at McCaleb's. Pr. at 4:00, I Cor. 13:13. Speaking meeting followed. Stay at Jas. Barger's.

Monday, June 19 Arrived at Clifford at 6:00. Cambridge freight had started at 5:30. Go to Columbus, Indianapolis, home found Susan sick with hemorrhage of lungs.

Tuesday, June 20 Susan week [sic] and keeps her bed mostly.

Wednesday, June 21 Susan up most of the day.

Thursday, June 22 Read proof of 1 & 4 pages of July *Star*. Supervised its making up.

Friday, June 23 Went to the Dr's and got medicine for Susan.

Saturday, June 24 Went to Cleveland, Ind., McNew met me and took me to Robins'. Dine, Supper & lodge there. Pr. at 2:00 Jude 21,22. Quarterly Conf. Pr. at 8:30, Isa 57:21.

Sunday, June 25 Pr. Meeting 10:00. Pr at 10:30 I Cor. 1:23,24. Sacramental. Dine at Wagner's. Pr. at 4:00. Ps. 37:4. Stay at Wm. Myer's. 1/2 m from Gwynneville.

Monday, June 26 Take 5:35 train to Rushville, Cambridge, Richm'd. Arrive at home at 2:15. Write for Star.

Thursday, June 29 Make up July *Star* in afternoon. Paper printed Edition 2,000.

Friday, June 30 Mail *Star* to Subscribers. Start to White-Water Circuit. Miss the 8:10 Eve. pas. tr. Go on 10:00 freight. Stay at Stahr's Central Hotel.

Saturday, July 1 Go on 6:05 M. tr. Stop off at Alpine. Walk out to Wm. Perkins. Dine there. Called at Johnson's on the way. Shave there. Pr. at 2:00 Jude 20,21. Qr. Conf. Supper at Mrs. Helen Kershner's, with Rev. A.J. Bolen & family. Rev. C.S. Miller pr. at 9:00, Eve. Stay at Kershner's.

Sunday, July 2 Called at Mrs. Simeon Lewis. Preached at 10:30 Ps. 25:14. Sacramental, Dinner at John Meek's with Flora & Ellis Wright & others. Pr. at 4:00 Acts. 16:31. Supper at L. Jonas'. Go on to Anson Moor's. Stay at Moor's.

Monday, July 3 Go to early train at Glenwood—to Connersville—to Cambridge on freight tr. Dine at J. Cranor's at Dublin. Go home on 1:38 Aft. tr. Work with Lorin on lists to mail from.

Wednesday, July 5 At home. Lorin went out to hunt work.

Saturday, July 8 Went on 5:05 M. train to Hamilton. Wrote letters to Davis, Landis & others at P.O. at Hamilton. Went on 8:40 train to Oxford. Walked two miles & rode the rest of the way to Mixerville. Called at

Mrs. Mary A. Davis'. Preached at 2:00. But—greatest—is Charity I Cor. 13:13. Qr. Conf. Supper at Burch's 2 ms. S.W. Bro. L.N. Jones pr. Stay at Mrs. Davis'.

Sunday, July 9 Preach at 10:30, in grove, I Tim. 1:1. Dine at Mrs. Davis. Pr at 2:30 Numbers 10:29. Go with Bro. C. Brattons' to Rev. L.N. Jones' Benj. Huddleson's & Chas. Paddock call. Stay at Saml. B. Fry's.

Monday, July 10 Went to Jones & with him to Liberty. Saw Geo. A. Smith, Young Campbelite preacher again. Went to Connersville. Saw Wm. Cotton. Called at Saml Wright's at Cambridge. Ar[r]ived at home at 2:15.

Thursday, July 13 Gave *Leaflet* copy in hand. Spent afternoon in putting *Telescope* & other papers in Volumes to stick together.

Friday, July 14 Prepare editorial for *Leaflet*. Go in afternoon with Susan to see her mother. Prepare communications for August *Star*.

Saturday, July 15 Went on 7:10 train to Wm. Jeff. Leonard's, stopping at Jackson Hill. Took dinner there. Rev. O.L. Wilson came about 12:30. Went with him to Qr. Meeting at Union Pr. at 2:00, Ps. 119:81. Qr. Conference. Supper at Harrison Marlatt's & lodge there.

Sunday, July 16 Pr. at Union, I Tim. 1:1. Dine at Joshua LaMotte's. Pr at 3:00. Acts 16:31. Went with Rev. O.L. Wilson to Washington. Supper at Cyrus Osborn's. Lodge at Wm. Hatfield's.

Monday, July 17 Went to Richmond on 8:45 train. Lorin went out to find work. Had *Reform Leaflet* made up.

Tuesday, July 18 Lorin went out to hay-harvest at Cook's, 4 ms out on Chicago road. Boys prepared the Leaflet for mailing. Wrote art. "Reserve the Sabbath," for August *Star*.

Wednesday, July 19 Adapted an Art. from *Leaflet* for *Star*.

Thursday, July 20 Read proof and made up *Star* in the evening. Called at D.K. Zeller's He, Jerry Kimler, and Jac. Zeller had been on a visit to their old homes.

Friday, July 21 Cousin John Shearer called in the evening & staid till bedtime.

Saturday, July 22 Wrote letters in the morning Missed 11 o'clock train to Hagerstown. Failed to get a horse and buggy. Wrote letters. Went on 4:00 train to H. & Franklin. Supper & lodging at Solomon Billheimer's. W.A. Oler pr. at 8:00.

Sunday, July 23 Meeting in the grove at Hier's, 1 m. w. of Franklin. Pr. at 10:30 Mal. 3:1. Dine with Albert Thornburg's & Bailie's on the ground. Pr. at 3:00, Titus 2:13. Sup at Billheimer's. Go with Rev. W.A. Oler to Sugar Grove neighborhood & stop at Daniel Harris' & lodge.

Monday, July 24 Walked to Washington (Greensfork). Went home on 8:40 train.

Tuesday, July 25 At home till 11:00. Went to Washington. Dine at Wm. Hatfield's. Father G. Muth came before noon & Rev. L.N. Jones afternoon. Several preachers on the afternoon trains & by private conveyance. Rev. L.N. Jones pr. at 8:00, "My yoke is easy & *burden light.*" Stay at Hatfield's my Conf. home.

Wednesday, July 26 Ex. W.A. Oler in third year's reading, in forenoon. Conference opened in the afternoon at 2:00. A small attendence of members. Joseph Gomer, African Missionary lectured at night.

Thursday, July 27 Conference Continued. Wm. Dillon preached at 8:00. Father G. Muth at Sugar Grove.

Friday, July 28 Session Continued. Election of presiding elders. I got 31 votes Floyd 28—out of 34 on first ballot. W.C. Day elected on third ballot. Trial of S. Bias in afternoon. Stationing Com. at night. Prof. A.W. Drury preached at 8:00.

Saturday, July 29 Conference continued and closed about 5:00. Stationing Committee report read at 3:30, perhaps, and I assigned to Indianapolis District. Educational meeting at 8:00. Drury, Kiracofe & Kephart spoke. Tough money effort.

Sunday, July 30 Meeting of itinerants of Indianapolis

THE REFORM LEAFLET.

Entered at the P. O. at Richmond, Ind., as second class matter.   Quarterly : 10 cents a year.

MILTON WRIGHT, Publisher.]   **RICHMOND, IND., JULY, 1882.**   [VOL. I.—No. 4.

This is the last number of the first volume of the *Leaflet*. It has carried to hundreds and even thousands of homes its brief message of anti-secrecy truth. It has done something toward awakening the people on the subject of Freemasonry, and secret societies in general. For the favor shown it the publisher desires to return his sincere thanks to its patrons.

It is a strange fact that violations of the decalogue, and the precepts of Christ, under the cover of secret organization are regarded by many Christian people as a harmless thing, while the same transgressions if perpetrated outside of the cover of secretism are regarded by them as most criminal. They laud the secret systematic violators of God's law; but discipline and excommunicate those who otherwise commit the same offense. It looks like they do not so much care that the law is violated, as they care for what people will say about it.

It is not so much what is done in the lodge, bad as this is, as what its members are taught. They are taught that the most horrid oaths are tolerable; that clans to take advantage of outsiders are right and desirable; that conscience can abdicate its scepter in favor of that of another; that craftiness and guile are virtues; and that men can take upon themselves obligations, unknown to the laws of God and of their country, which are above all civil obligations, and that bind closer practically than any ecclesiastical obligations. They are thus taught that the obligations of the lodge are more sacred than those of their country, so that they would prefer one of their own to an outsider, when acting for their country, and one of the lodge to a non-lodge man, when acting for the church. There is no greater falsehood than that the lodge requires nothing inconsistent with one's duty to himself, to his country, or to his religion.

SECRETISM NOT INVINCIBLE.

Freemasonry seems to claim that the sledge-hammer of truth and the sharp blade of logic can be directed against it only for its gain and glory. It sometimes boasts that it prospers most with opposition. Some are weak enough to credit its bold vauntings.

It is true that its protean form, as seen in its varieties of lodgedoms, has a large and well-disciplined host. It has a standing army of the best moonlight drill. It has its fortifications, and is well intrenched. It rules in the churches. It prevails in Congress, the legislatures, and the courts. It controls the schools. It either muzzles or dictates the utterances of the pulpit and the press. Is not all on its side! No! not all. God, truth, the larger portion of the church of Christ, and the great body of the people are against it. The facts of the present and the records of the past are against it in all its forms and with all its shams. There is a great fund of intelligence, conscience, moral influence, and wealth in the communion of anti-secretism. It is true that anti-lodge men need to be thoroughly aroused, inspired, drilled. They slumbered while secrecy — after a feigned death — was resuscitating, growing, drilling, and intrenching.

Anti-secrecy principles have commanded the first-class minds of America, both in church and in the nation. In proof of this we need but mention such names as Samuel Adams, William Wirt,

Dist. at my room at 8:00. Bp. Kephart pr. at Grove at 10:30, "Follow me." W.A. Oler ordained. Dinner on the ground Ate with John Brooks, jr. S.S. Anniv. in Afternoon Bp E.B. Kephart pr. at 8:00 Jer. [blank] "Harvest past, etc."

Monday, July 31 Called at Lamb's. Went home on 8:45 train. Busy straightening out things. Silvanus Koerner had been at our house since Saturday, and went home after dinner.

Tuesday, August 1 Went up to town.

Wednesday, August 2 Engaged in writing most of the day. Caroline visited us in the afternoon.

Friday, August 4 Editing the *Star*. Lorin saw Pres. Kiracofe at the train on his way to Portage, O.

Saturday, August 5 Editing. Went to D.K. Zeller's, with Susan in the evening.

Sunday, August 6 Went to U.P. Church. Heard a good sermon by Rev. Gilcrest, Heb. 13:20. Attended Grace M.E. Church in the evening [blank] the pastor gave a sermon—lecture on the number, tec. of stars.

Monday, August 7 Read up proof on *Star*. Made up *Star* for press in the afternoon.

Sunday, August 13 Went to Pearl St. M.E. Church. Heard Lamport pr. on Chris. Perfection. Called in on the way home & heard Hopkins of Cin. a few minutes & Dr. [blank] of Richmond & wife called in afternoon.

Wednesday, August 16 At home till Aft'n. Start for Grant Co., on the 4:00 train, with Susan. Called at Dr. Suman's to see his mother who is paralyzed. Floyd hailed me on my way to the depot. Hailed Uncle John and Aunt Eliza Braden at Alexandria. Staid at Winslow's hotel.

Thursday, August 17 Walter & George Brown & wives, & Kath. Eliza Wiley came & we with them went to Uncle William Reeder's to the 35th anniversary of their wedding-day. Broyles' there, and many of the neighbor's there over fifty altogether. The Brown's, Braden's, & ourselves stay there.

Friday, August 18 Ourselves & relatives continue at Uncle Reeder's. John Broyles & daughters call in the afternoon. I visit the place in the afternoon with Susan.

Saturday, August 19 We go to Fairmount with Browns' and to Harrisburg & thence to Ridgeville, where Susan leaves me for home about 3:37. R.W. McCracken calls and takes me to his house where I stay. Pr at Chris. (New Light) Church at 8:00 Ps. 1:6.

Sunday, August 20 Preach Rev. Thomas McCracken's funeral at 10:30. Heb. 4:9. Dine at Mormon's. Rev. Mormon & Dr. Farquar & wife dine there. Stay at Mormon's.

Monday, August 21 Mormon's son takes me to Ridgeville. Go home on 8:50 train.

Wednesday, August 23 At home. Read up proofs on the *Star* & spent afternoon waiting, etc.

Thursday, August 24 Made up *Star* & wrote several letters.

Saturday, August 26 Rev. W.C. Day called. I went on 10:10 train to Indianapolis & to Carrollton (Reedville). Eat at lunch-room on North side, Ind. depot. Met Daniel Stover. He went with me & pr. at 8:00. We staid at G. Muth's.

Sunday, August 27 Preach dedication sermon of Welcome Chapel at 10 1/2 Mal. 3:1. Raise $133.80 to assist father Muth in its building. Dine at Squire Laraby's. S.S. Addresses at 3:30. Rev. A.C. Wilmore pr. at night. "Put on the whole armor." I stay at Mr. Bohring's.

Monday, August 28 Went on to Greenfield with Rev. G. Muth's. Called at Father Bush's. Came home arriving 2:+

Tuesday, August 29 Wrote editorials, etc. Bought Reuchlin some clothing in the afternoon—Coat vest & hat for $15.50-$1.50=$14.00. Reuchlin, Lorin, & Wilbur sup at D.K. Zeller's.

Wednesday, August 30 Wrote letters. Read *Telescope* some. Gath Rimon, (Chas. O. Wilson) dined with us. Wrote letters in evening, editorial notes in the afternoon.

Thursday, August 31 Wrote some editorials. Went with Susan to D.K. Zellers in evening. Read some proof at night.

Friday, September 1 Read up some proofs, got up the paper & to press. Directed some. Went on 8:10 (11:00) to Cambridge, arriving about midnight. Stay at Stahr Hotel.

Saturday, September 2 Go on 6:05 m. train to Columbus. Write a letter to J.W. Tucker. Go with Jas. Talley to Rev. A.H.K. Beam's. Dine there with Rev. Wm. Hall. Qr. Conf. at Olive Branch at 3:00 Pr. at 2:00, Matt. 2:23. Supper at Jas. Talley's. Pr. at 8:00. Gal. 1:4. Stay at Henry Lambert's.

Sunday, September 3 Pr. at Olive Br. at 10:30 Dinner at Silas Anderson's. Pr at 3:50 Acts 2:40. Supper and lodging at Henry Lambert's.

Monday, September 4 Bro. Lambert's Carrie takes Bro Hall & myself to Jas. Barger's 4 ms. N.E. Dine there. Walk up to Jas Leward's. Supper there. Pr. at Shiloh at 7:30.

Thursday, September 7 At home. Rev. G.W. Fast of Mich. called with us on his way to Hartsville—a few minutes— We go to Depot & see his family.

Friday, September 8 At home. Mailed Dist. Conf. Program to preachers of Indianapolis Dist.

Saturday, September 9 Went on 11:00 train to Honey Creek. Saw Rev. Frank M. Moore on the train. Pr. at Honey creek church at 2:00 Ps. 87:3. Qr. Conf. followed. Supper at Henry Fadeley's. Pr. at 7:30 Acts 16:31. Stay at Fadeley's. Father and Mother Rader of Middletown took supper with us at Fadeley's.

Sunday, September 10 Pr. at 10:30 Ex. 28:34. Dined at Asa Gossett's. S.S. Anniversary in afternoon. Staid at Asa Gosset's Bro. W.A. Oler & family there. Took supper at Bro. Strough's (Strow's) in town.

Monday, September 11 Went home arriving about 10:00.

Thursday, September 14 At home till 10:00. Stop off at Greenfield and marry Rev. G. Muth, aged 83, to Mrs. Mary Jane Hawkins, aged 62, at Reuben Riley, esq's. Dine there. Went on 5:00 train to Indianapolis & married at Geo. Kern's Rev. D. Stover and Miss Martha A. Lauries. Stay at Rev. A.C. Wilmore's.

Friday, September 15 Went over the River to Stover's— dine. Return write letters. See about permits on Railroad. Go with Moses Hatfield's home—supper. Go with them to Barn's meeting at Park Theater corner of Tenn. & Wash. Sts. Stay at Hatfield's.

Saturday, September 16 Went on 6:30 train to Fortville. Go on to Simpson Jones. Dine. To Union. Qr. Conf. at 2:00 pr. Amos 6:1. Supper at Jas. Murphy's. Rev. J.Y. Demumbrun pr. at 7:30. Stay at Wm. Wilson's.

Sunday, September 17 Pr. at 10:30, Heb. 11:26. Dine at Rumler's. Pr. at 4:00, 84th Ps., followed by speaking meeting. Go with their little boys to Jas. Frank. Reynold's, and lodge. Go to meeting at sch. house near there. A Mr. Little spoke. I talked a very little.

Monday, September 18 Bro. Reynolds takes me to Greenfield. Reach home on 2:00 train.

Friday, September 22 Made up outside pages of the *Star* for *October*. Go at 4:00 aft'n train to Anderson. Ithamer McCarty meets me and takes me to his home 2 miles down the river on the North side. Supper and lodgings there.

Saturday, September 23 Start with Bro. McCarty's to Jenkin's Sch. H. to Quarterly meeting at Fohlen's class. Arrive at 3:00 p.m. Quarterly Conference. Supper at Henry Fohlen's. His Bro. John & wife of Elwood there. Preach at 7:30, Acts 2:40. Stay at Fohlen's.

Sunday, September 24 Preach at 10:30, Ez. 33:11. Dine at Jackson Atchison's, whose wife was a sister of the Fohlens. Pr. at 4:00, Ps. 73:24. Stay at Henry Fohlen's.

Monday, September 25 Go with Shell (aged 12) stepson of Fohlen's to Frankton. Stop at John Deaton's & dine. Go on 2:48 train home. See Rev. G.B. Rogers (208 George St. Cin.) a Wesleyan preacher. Also Rev. A. Worth (cousin Sarah's husband) who comes home with me & stays till toward train time.

Tuesday, September 26 Write for the *Star.*

Wednesday, September 27 Finish another editorial & take it up just before noon.

Thursday, September 28 Get all the copy ready. Read proofs in the evening.

Friday, September 29 Take up proofs, go up and read others. Make up the forms. Get proofsheet at the depot & connect on the cars & send back. Arrive a[t] Kokomo and send several cards out. David Smith meets me and takes me to his house, 2 miles east of Salem. Stay there.

Saturday, September 30 Wrote a letter in the morning. Go to Quarterly Conf. at Salem at 2:00. Pr. Ps. 73:24. Qr. Conf. Savid Smith's Case. Some time spent on Apportionment. Supper David S. Farley's Pr at 7:30 Luke 23:4. Fair congregations. Stay at Farley's.

Sunday, October 1 Pr. at 10:30, I John 5:18,19. Dine at B.F. Learner's. Love-feast meeting at 7:30. Stay at C.P. Goodwine's.

Monday, October 2 Goodwine takes us over to Kokomo. Write letters and cards. Call at Jas. M. Reeder's. he away. Lunch at Depot. Call at Carter's on market St. Talk with Wm. Nation who lives near New Lisbon. Arrive at home at 5:15. Finish sending out the *Star.*

Tuesday, October 3 Direct a few of the *Star.* Caroline Zeller came up that afternoon.

Wednesday, October 4 Called at D.K. Zeller's to see his brother Elias & wife of Iowa, Winterset. Married at 7:30, aftern., Harry C. Lintner & Olive J. Harris at Allen B. Harris's, Corner 13th & 14 St.

Thursday, October 5 At home. Bought coal $7.50 a ton. Bought load of wood but it was not delivered. Wrote some. The man that sold me the wood acted the shote.

Saturday, October 7 Bought two loads of wood. Start on 11:00 tr. to New Castle & McKowan Station. Bro C.B.

Small meets me. Call at Bro. VanSwearingen's, Hilton Harris' soninlaw. At Harris' Moses takes me to J. Harvey Jackson's. Pr. at Mt. Pleasant Rev. 19:10, "Worship God." Stay at Jackson's.

Sunday, October 8 Pr at 10:30 Deut. 32:31. Raise $191.00. Dine at Philip Oxley's. W. Jasper Oxley & Bro. & Sister Robinson of Flatrock class there. Called at Mother Huffman's. Pr. at 7:00 I Pet. 4:18. Stay at Rev. A. Rector's.

Monday, October 9 Harvey Jackson and James Pierce come to look over accounts. Bro Rector takes me aftn. to McKowan's. Go via New Castle and Sexton to John McKee's. Supper there. Walk on to Harvey Wright's.

Tuesday, October 10 Harvey takes me to Sexton, & I go on to Rushville and Gwynnville. Walk to Wm. Myer's. Bro. I.N. Tharp pr. on Regeneration Titus 3:5. Stay at Mother Rutherford's.

Wednesday, October 11 District Conference met; good discussions. Dine at Wm. Stuart Robins'. Rev. A.C. Wilmore pr. at 7:30. "After the Resurrection." Stay at Wm. R. Wagner's 2 1/2 ms. South-west.

Thursday, October 12 Discussion's continued. Dined at Mrs. Rutherford's. Discussion's continued in Afternoon. Supper at Asbury Holmes Keaton's. Rev. Wm. Hall pr at 7:30, I Cor. 15:58. Stay at Wm. Myer's.

Friday, October 13 Go to train with Bro. Hall. Train whizzed past. Go to Indianapolis. Called at Second Presbyterian Church. Indiana Synod in session. Dine at Walter S. Brown's, my cousins. Darwin & Anna start to Crawfordsville. At Synod aftn. Saw P.S. Cook. Went to New Britton. Staid at John Frazier's.

Saturday, October 14 Called at Mr. John Crossley's, Mother Young's, and dined at Mary Frazier's. Called at Mother Ringer's. pr at 2:00, I Cor. 9:24. Quarterly conf. The pastor, M.L. Bailey, absent. Supper at Sister Frazier's. Pr. at 7:00 Matt. 1:21. Staid at John Frazier's.

Sunday, October 15 Pr. 10:30 Mal. 3:1. Communion. Dine at David Neil's, 2 ms E. Pr. 7:00 Mal. 3:16,17. Good love-feast followed. Stay at John Frazier's—Saml Brooks also staid. Saw John Callahan who lives in Knightstown, Monday Oct. 16th.

Monday, October 16 Arise at 4:00. See Comet (seen for two weeks)—good sized nucleus—train dense brilliant & broad, about 35 degrees in length. Bro John Frazier takes me to Noblesville to take Express to Indianapolis Call at Wilmore's. Start at 11:00 for home. Arrive near 2:00 See Joseph Bunger, from near Bloomington, Ind.

Tuesday, October 17 At home. A little writing, etc. Will E. Stanton dined with us. Told of B.F. Miller on N. 14th St. N. of R.R. Left my watch at Hirst's to have a new main-spring put in it.

Wednesday, October 18 Not in good plight for writing. Wrote little.

Saturday, October 21 Paid off Allen Harris. Mrs. Harris sick. Start at 3:03 for Indianapolis. Lunch at Taggart's. Stay at Rev. A.C. Wilmore's 331 Noble Street.

Sunday, October 22 Preach at 10 1/2 I Cor. 9:24. Communion. Rev. P.S. Cook present. Dine with Moses Hatfield's at Davis's. Davis' brother's wife a sister of Morgan S. Drury's. Attend Sabbath School. At B.F. Witt's in the afternoon. Pr. at 7:30 Matt. 1:21 Stay at Moses Hatfield's.

Monday, October 23 Call at W.G. Rubush's. At Rev. T.J. Connor most of the day. Call at Thos. Evan's & at Wilmore's. Qr. Conf. at Church 7:30. Moved slowly. Stay at Wm. G. Rubush's.

Tuesday, October 24 Call at Bro. Wilmore's. Go to depot. Ticket for Knightstown & Carthage. Take sick & faint. Get on train. Pres. J. Blanchard aboard. Some talk with him. So sick I went on home.

Wednesday, October 25 About town some but had fever in the afternoon. Got my watch at silversmith's—Hirst's. Paid $1.50 for new mainspring and cleaning.

Thursday, October 26 Read proofs on *Nov. Star*—outside—that evening. Saw. Dr. Hibberd & got some medicine.

Saturday, October 28 Went to see Doctor Hippard. Left on 7:20 tr. for Indianapolis & Morristown. John Jackson meets me and takes me to Windfall Church. Qr. Conf. lively over Z. McNew's salary. Apportion at $600.00. Sup[p]er & lodging at John Jackson. Did not go out to night meeting.

Sunday, October 29 Pr at 10 1/2–11—Matt. 24:3. Dine at Sim. Dennett's. See a wedding at Mr. White's. McNew pr. at 7:00 "Godliness is profitable" etc Stay at Elijah Wright's.

Monday, October 30 Go on to Wm. Myer's. Stay till noon. Take train at Gwynnesville—misinformed by conductor—go to Connersville. Return to Rushville. Put baggage in telegraph room. Find it shut at train time. Go on to Connersville & Cambridge. Stay at Stahr's Hotel.

Tuesday, October 31 Arrive home on 7:00 morn. train. Write some in forenoon. Get a letter and draft from Daniel Koerner. Pay rent in afternoon Call at Allen M. Harris'.

Wednesday, November 1 Thomas Cranor called in forenoon. I paid him interest up to Dec. 26th and $40.00 on his note. In afternoon took a note to Mother Koerner & had $200.00 credited on Daniel's note.

Thursday, November 2 At home. Able to do little mental work in consequence of biliousness & perhaps a little fever.

Friday, November 3 Went on 9:50 train to Indianapolis. Write letters. Go about 4:30 for Greenwood. Rev. I.M. Tharp meets me and takes me to his house at Stone's Crossing. Lodge there.

Saturday, November 4 Called at Cleary's. Stay till after dinner at Tharps. go on to Olive Branch with Bro. Tharp. Pr. Heb. 3:12. Qr. Conf. Supper at Jac. Sutton's Pr. at 7:00 John 7:30—fair congregation. Stay at Shelby Fullen's.

Sunday, November 5 Pr. at O. Br. 10:3[0], Matt. 13:44. Dine at Jac. Sutton's. Cox's & Tharps' there & Father Stone. Pr. at 6:30, Matt. 25:34&41. Stay at Shelby

Fullen's. Had communion in forenoon.

Monday, November 6 Go with Shelby Fullen in wagon to Indianapolis. Go on 11:00 train to Richmond.

Tuesday, November 7 Busy on *Star* Editorial.

Friday, November 10 Have last side of the Star printed. Work close at mailing.

Sunday, November 12 Heard Rev Sanders pr. at Episcopal Church.

Monday, November 13 Furnished matter to complete the Leaflet.

Wednesday, November 15 Went to Dayton Dined at Dr. Davis'. Ex. Com Board Ed. meets at 3:00. Supper at Dr. G.A. Funkhouser's. At pr. meeting at Summit St. Stay at Rev. J.W. Hott's.

Thursday, November 16 Call at Rev. W.C. Day's. Call at Mrs. Bishop Edward's. Dine at Day's. Go to Telescope Office Talk with Shuey & Lanthurn, M.R. Drury; see Rigler. Supper at J.W. Hott's. Go home on 6:30 train.

Friday, November 17 Daniel Koerner came in forenoon & staid till after dinner.

Sunday, November 19 Called at Allen Harris' in the afternoon with Susan.

Thursday, November 23 P. Albert came—a talk on Seventh Day & other theology. Make up first side of Star for December.

Friday, November 24 At Home. Katie sick in the night with measles. Just taking them.

Sunday, November 26 At Main St. Friend's Church. Spoke a few minutes. At home in the evening.

Monday, November 27 At home. Mrs. Hannah Albert came in to see if we would be at home Thanksgiving. Mrs. M.C. Zeller came to see about Thanksgiving din[n]er. We decided not to go.

Tuesday, November 28 Getting *Star* ready to print.

Wednesday, November 29 *Star* printed. Mail a considerable number. Katie's measles broke out. Reuchlin & Lorin came on evening train from Hartsville College.

Thursday, November 30 Attend Orthodox Friend's Church on Main & Fifteenth Streets. Dugan Clark & others spoke. Had our Turkey Dinner with all our children. Got the rest of the copies of the Star ready to mail.

Sunday, December 3 At Baptist Church. An old man dwelt on prophecies. Saw an Ex-United Brethren woman, Mrs. Detch. Called at Bro. B.F. Miller's in afternoon—731 N. 14th St. Little boy has measles. Go to 8th St. Presbuterian Church. Rev. Hughes pr. "Do the diligence to come before winter."

Wednesday, December 6 At home Saw Venus on her transit, a sight not to be repeated till the year A.D. 2004. The planet looked like a small black round spot.

Friday, December 8 Mrs. Hannah Albert called. Went on 4:00 train to Middletown. Rev. Mr. Lamport aboard. Had a long talk on the causes of spiritual decline, etc. Staid at Jessee Rader's.

Saturday, December 9 Stay at Father Rader's till about 11:00. Dine at Rev. Wm. A. Oler's. Went to Centre Chapel to Qr. meeting at 2:00. Light attendance. Reports pretty good. Sup[p]er with Oler at Rev. Wm. Davenport's. Preach at 6:30 Ps. 16:8. Stay at Davenport's.

Sunday, December 10 Pr. at 10:30 (11:00) Hebr. 3:12. Communion. Dine at Albert Lewis's. his older Brother & wife there. Preach at 6:30 Isa. 57:21. Stay with Oler at Lewis' of M.E. Church.

Monday, December 11 Go to Middletown with Oler's Dine on Turkey at his house. Look for a postal card from home Get none. Stay at Jessee Rader's till we start back. Supper & lodging at Davenport's. Pr. at 6:30. Luke 15:10.

Tuesday, December 12 Go to Cadiz with Oler. Call at John Baughn's and at Rev. J.M. Cook's. Go in Baughn's hack to New Castle. Call at O. Jenning's. Dine at Harvey

Root's. Rev. J.A. Bailey there. Call at Rev. Milo L. Bailey's, Mrs. Eliz. Scheildknecht's, and Mrs. Eliz. Bowman's. Went home to Richmond on 4:00 train.

Wednesday, December 13 At Home. Wrote letters, etc. Visited Mother Koerner & called to see B.F. Miller. Mrs. M.C. Zeller visited us. Susan had a spell of her ailment again.

Thursday, December 14 Spent the day at home. Rev. Crafts gave me complimentary tickets to a concert at M.E. Chrch. Mr. Thompson invited me to be at First Pres. Anniversary at 3:30 Next Sabbath—16th. Susan unwell again in the evening.

Friday, December 15 Rev. Gilcrist invited me to the U.P. Church supper. Rev. S.H. Bagley, of Avalon, Missouri, on a trip in behalf of Avalon College called & staid till next afternoon, calling also at Harris' & Alberts'. Susan having her attacks of hemorrhage of the lungs every day twice or oftener.

Saturday, December 16 At home. Susan still as for two day's past.

Sunday, December 17 None of us went from home any time in the day. Susan had hemorrhage about 7:00 in morning and 8:00 in evening.

Monday, December 18 The doctor—Hibberd—called. I called at Zeller's & wrote to D. Koerner and to *Telescope* office.

Tuesday, December 19 Mr. Albert called in the afternoon. Mrs. M.C. Zeller called and staid an hour.

Wednesday, December 20 Mrs. Albert called. Daniel McMullin lodged with us.

Thursday, December 21 At home. Susan some better.

Friday, December 22 Mrs. Lupton called in the afternoon. She was a neighbor across the street.

Saturday, December 23 Went on six o'clock train to New Castle & on 11:28 train to Kenard (Poplar Grove) Bro. Aaron Kitterman's son takes me out to their house. Pr. at Prairie School-house, at 2:00 Matt. 13:31. Qr. Con-

ference. Supper & lodge at Kitterman's. Bor. George Wilson of White water preached, "The Lord hath been mindful of us."

Sunday, December 24 Pr. Heb. 3:12,13. Communion. Small congregation. Dine at Benton Jackson's. Pr at 6:30, Matt. 13:3. Stay at Kitterman's.

Monday, December 25 Rise at 4:00. Breakfast. Reach Kenard about 6:00. Train to New Castle. Thence home 8:30 arriving at 10:00. Children had a fine Christmas. M. Caroline Zeller came in the afternoon.

Tuesday, December 26 Samuel Wright & Mr. Grimes dined with us.

Friday, December 29 Get the *Star* out. Went to Anderson on 3:20 Aft. train. Start to walk out. Met Bro. Ithamar McCarty. We called at Father John Morris' at toll-gate. Stay at McCarty's. Rev. G.W. Fast there.

Saturday, December 30 Stay till after early dinner. Went to Perkinsville. Preach at 2:00. Rev. 2:10. Qr. Conf. Supper & lodgings at Rev. Sam. Kurtz. Rev. G.W. Fast pr. at 6:30.

Sunday, December 31 Pr. at 10:30 Heb. 7:26. Dine at Henry Cole's, he being a qr. Conf. preacher. Called at M.E. Sab. Sch. At Essington's remainder of afternoon. Pr. at 6:00, Heb. 3:12. Drive McCarty's rig to his house and stay there.

Memoranda
Emma Van Cleve Geo. Reeder d. May 13, 1845.

Rev. F. Thomas South Whitley, Whitley Co., Ind. George W. Hunt, Whitaker, Marion C. Ore. Rev. G.W. Keller, Taylorsv. Christian Co., Ill. Rev. H. Elwell, Otterbein Benton C. Ind. Rev. R.L. Brengle, New Goshen, Vigo, Ind. Rev. I. Bennehoof, Harris Hill, Erie NY. Rev. J.S. Rhodes, Colfax, Wash Ter.

Paid Aug. 24, 1882 for Lorin's suit $16.20 for my pantaloons 5.40

[The final entry is a recipe for "Hair Invigorator"]

1883

Monday, January 1 Went early to Anderson. Bro. Ithamer McCarty took me there. Went home, arriving at 10:00. Arranged to get our paper—the *Star*—mailed, that is finished mailing to subscribers. D.K. Zeller called; also J.M. Strausburg & wife.

Tuesday, January 2 At Home. Mailed *Star* to exchanges and others.

Friday, January 5 Went afternoon & bought a suit each for Wilbur & Orville. Started on 3:20 train to Kokomo arriving there about 7:00 Aftn. Call at Jas. Milton Reeder's—he a cousin of my mother whose father was George Reeder. (He died 78 years old.) A son of Micaiah Reeder. Went on to Bennett's Switch. Staid at Wm. Zehring's, a cousin of Jacob & Aaron Zehring. He once a member of the legislature. His wife a daughter of Jacob Burtner of Germantown, Ohio.

Saturday, January 6 Mr. Zehring's son took me over to John Condo's two miles east of Bennet's Switch. Bro. Henry Kern came. Dine at Condo's. Squire Farley's & Bruno Miller's came. Pr. at 2:00 Rom 14:17. Qr. Conf. David Smith case reported on by a committee of investigation. Smith did not like it. Proposed to withdraw from the Church. Went home pretty sour.

Sunday, January 7 Preached at 10 1/2 Luke 24:46. Dined at John Condo's. Children there, Rev. T. Evans, Anderson's, etc. Had a speaking meeting which was quite good. Bro. Evans concluded not to protract on account of his hoarseness. David Smith and wife there & pretty offish. Went to Brown's and lodged. Live 1 m. S.E. of Bennett's Switch.

Monday, January 8 Boys took us to Station in Sled. Went to Kokomo. Stopped at Jas. Milton Reeder's He a cousin of my mothers & a son of Micaiah's. Been in Kokomo over 20 years. Once lived in Crawfordsville. Got a list of the generation of Joseph Reeder the father of Joseph Reeder, the father of George Reeder, the father of Catharin[e] Reeder the wife of Dan Wright, the father of Milton Wright Arrived at Richmond about 5:30. (This list was imperfect; Stephen Reeder youngest brother of Joseph)

Tuesday, January 9 At home. Wrote Considerable. Mrs. M. Caroline Zeller called in the afternoon.

Wednesday, January 10 At Home. Spent some hours in arranging letters that had lain loose in the stand drawer. Wrote an article in the evening. Spent some time in looking over Sermon sketches of my own production.

Thursday, January 11 At home Went & got suit refitted to Wilbur. Got Shoes at $3.50 M. Caroline Zeller called.

Friday, January 12 At home writing Got clergy permits on P. Cin. & St. L. & on Gr. Rap. Mrs Albert called in Afternoon. Wilbur went to Literary Society.

Saturday, January 13 Started at 7:20 Morn for Ind'lis. Conductor Crocker attempts to put off Mrs. Hayden's (Virginia Ave. Indianapolis) 5 year old boy! I got Clerg's permit on I.B. & Western Railroad. Applied for several others. Went on 11:10 tr. to McCordsville. Walked on to Mrs. Polly Yaryman's & then rode on to Bethlehem in Hiram Heath's buggy. Called at Samuel Brooks, but found no one at home. Preached 2:30 Gal. 6:14. Qr.

Conf. Supper & lodging at Wm. Kinneman's. Pr. at 7:00 I Cor. 16:22.

Sunday, January 14 Pr. at Bethlehem at 10:30, Luke 17:22. Sacrament. Received Jacob & Elizabeth Lemington into Church. Coll. of $11.15. Dined at Joseph Beeler's. Pr. 6:30, Jer. 13:21. Stay at Beeler's. The interest in the meeting was good, the attendance good considering the cold, and the icy roads. The congregation at night was an overflow. Beeler's from Palestine, Ind. She his second wife—were married in Southern Illinois, where she was a school-teacher. Mother Beeler, aged 88 lives part of her time at Beeler's—Was there. People about Bethlehem: Wm. Kinneman, "Jackey" Mitchel, Mrs. Crooks, Edwards.

Monday, January 15 Pr. at Bethlehem, 11:00. Ps. 16,11. Good love-feast meeting. Bro. Bailey & I dine at John Henry Wyant's. At lovefeast, C.A. Ervin, an immaterialist, screamed so in speaking. Wesley Helm spoke long & loud; once at U.B., now Baptist. Pr. at 7:00, Acts 26:28. Some ran out. Several penitent & weeping & gave hand for prayers. Staid at T.J. Mitchells 1 mile north of the Church, son of Jackey's. Rev. Clark, Meth Protestant present Sunday & Monday morning & his father & Manford's half brother & wife out Monday. Expected to join Tuesday.

Tuesday, January 16 Bro. Bailey takes me to Fortville. Go on the accom. tr. to Anderson. Lunch at 12:00 after writing some at P.O. Saw Rev. S. Kurtz and Henry Cole & wife. Knights of Pythias in uniform & with swords! Came down from Kokomo on the train I left on. Arrive at home at 5:30 aft. Saw Thronburg on the train. Damon's & Pythias' disinterested friendship taken as name to characterize bought friendship of the lodge! Why swordly knights in a peaceful Christian age? What means drill & parade of secret order of knights?

Wednesday, January 17 At home. Streets & sidewalks very icy for some days. Many boys slide till 9 o'clock or later on B Street hill, just South of us, last night. Thaws some to-day. Went to *Telegram* office & P.O. Spent the day partly, in writing.

Friday, January 19 Read up proofs. Made up First side of Feb. Went on 8:10 train to Cambridge City. Staid at

Cousin Samuel Wright's.

Saturday, January 20 Went on 6:05 morning train to St. Louis Crossing & thence by hack to Hope. Rode with Frank Beckel's to James Sweards. It rained a little. Found meeting protracting at Shiloh Church. Rev. Wm. Hall (pastor) and Rev. Irvin Cox there. Pr. at 2:00 Heb 4:9. Qr. Conf. at 3:00. Pr. at 7:00, Acts 26:28. Stay at Sweard's with Bros. Hall & Cox. It rained hard in the afternoon, and then grew quite cold in the evening.

Sunday, January 21 Quite a cold day. Pr. at 10:30, Luke 17:21. Communion. Dine at David Fix's. Reuchlin, Lorin & Jo. Kiracofe there. Miss Monta Fix face swelled from tooth-ache. Elmer & John Fix considerably stirred religiously. Walked up to Shiloh. Pr. at 7:00, Jer. 13:21. Cox exhorts. I receive David Bromfield into Church. Stay at Jas. Sweard's. Albert Seward and Hulda Jones were married at Seward's in the afternoon.

Monday, January 22 Bro Cox started home 35 miles away. I postpone going to Hartsville till to-morrow, on acct. of extreme cold weather. Love-feast meeting at 10:00. Pretty good. About 20 out to meeting. Dined at the infair at Seward's. Visited Beevis in afternoon. He had just got up from a spell of fever. His wife right sick. Supper there. Pr. at Shiloh at 7:00, Luke 15:7. Stay at Jas. Seward's.

Tuesday, January 23 Albert takes me over to near Hartsville. Cross on the ice near Mench's. Call at Pres. C.H. Kiracofe's. See Fast's a few minutes. Spend an hour with the boys. Dine with the President. Walk up to Hope. Go on Hack to St. Louis Crossing. Go on train to Cambridge City. Arrive at Richmond (& home) before 9:00 Evening. Found all in usual health.

Friday, January 26 Left home at 11:00 for Ross, Michigan. Aaron and Sarah Wroth get aboard at Briant & travel with me beyond Ft. Wayne. On account of sleet, train behind that night. Telegraphed by Rev. G.S. Lake to stop off at Moline. Went in a sleigh with Lake & Johnson's about three miles west. Snow about 2 ft deep, and drifted much in places.

Saturday, January 27 Bro. Lake takes me in sleigh to his house, 1/2 mile south of Salem Church, Allegan Co.,

Dine there and Rev. W.N. Bridenstine. Rev. H.T. Barnaby Pr. at 2:00 a good *sermon, Qr. Conf. follows. I arrange very easily with trustees to start subscription. Supper at Lake's with Barnaby. Rev. W.N. Bridenstine pr. at 7:00. Stay at Lake's. The services so far were in the school-house. Bro Lake had Married a Miss Gleason & was living in the parsonage. *First I ever heard him.

Sunday, January 28 Pr at 10:30 Matt. 13:44. Call for $650, and raise, including cash coll., $750. The Church, a frame veneered with brick, cost $2,200. It was a very pleasant occasion. I dine at Bro. Albert Twining's. Bro. Brown of Gaines there. Bro. Lowe, Bro. Bear, Stone, Waterman, Bro. Barnaby came to Twinings after dinner and spent the afternoon. Pr. at 7:00, Luke 24:46. Communion followed. Stay at Lake's. Bro Barnaby had a chill in time of meeting.

Monday, January 29 Rev. H.T. Barnaby takes me to Ross on his way home. He had a chill last night. I go on freight train to Grand Rapids. Lunch at Depot. Write letters. Go on 3:10 train to Sparta Centre. *Rev. N. Heald meets me at the Depot. Call at W.I. Ohmsted's & Israel Smith's. Supper & lodging at Rev. N. Heald's. I pr at 7:00 Ps. 1:6. Meet trustees & others. Very discouraging prospect. *Bro. Heald withdrew from the conference in 1884.

Tuesday, January 30 See Ohmsted, Smith, & others. Pr. at 10:30 2 Cor. 3:8. Good congregation; fine feeling; raise $446 easily. Called for about $330.00 Got several subs. for Star. Saw Rev. T. Brigham, J. Payne, Crips; & several ministers of other churches. Dine at W.I. Ohmsted's. Near meeting time call at Bro. N. Heald's. Pr. at 7:00, Heb. 13:14. Lodge at Ohmsted's.

Wednesday, January 31 Start on 8:40 train to Grand Rapid's, Thence on 1:00 train to Ft. Wayne. Ohmsted's Sons go with me to Gr. Rap's. Write to D.O. Darling. It Snows considerably. Snow over two feet deep at Grand Rapids. Train reaches Fort Wayne at 7:00. Next train reaches Ft. Wayne about 1:00 after midnight. I reach home aobut 6:00 Thursday morning.

Thursday, February 1 Reached home at 6:00 morn. Busy on editorial work.

Saturday, February 3 Finished reading proof and made

up the Star in the afternoon. Give out going to Indianapolis on the night train on account of continued rains & high waters The ground being frozen all the waters were precipitated into the rivers.

Sunday, February 4 Got ready & went to the train. Found it late. Went home and dined. Went back about 11:30, waited till nearly 1:00, and went on to Indianapolis arriving about 3:00. Called at Rev. A.C. Wilmore, Went in a carriage to Moses Hatfield's. After supper went to meeting & pr. 7:30, Matt. 13:30. Rev. T. Evans there. Staid at Bro. Hatfield's. Never took but one Sab. Railroad ride before—From Dublin to Ogden, about 1864, which hindered by train's not coming Sat. evening—Had a right good meeting this (Sab.) evening.

Monday, February 5 Called at Bro. Wilmore, Dined at Rev. T. Evans'. His daughter, Annetta or Jenetta whom I saw in 1855–6 as a little puny girl of about two years, dined there also, now a woman of about 150 pounds. After dinner, went down town & over to the river which is highest since 1847. Got half-fare permit on Wabash R.R. Wrote a card home. Called at Bro. Wilmore's. Supper at Bro. Davis's 35 Plum St. Prayer meeting & quarterly conference at the Church. Stay at Bro. M. Hatfield's on 411 Park Ave.

Tuesday, February 6 Staid at Bro. Hatfield's till 11:00. Dined at Wm. G. Rubush's. Rainy in the evening. Supper at Wilmore's. Prayer and speaking meeting. Quite good. Stay at Davis'. 35 Plum St.

Wednesday, February 7 Dined at Walter Brown's, on Ft. Wayne Avenue. Staid till after 2:00, Called at T.J. Connor's 840 N. Alabama St. Found no one at home. Called at A.C. Wilmore's. Supper at B.F. Witt's. Bishop Kephart pr. at 7:30, a good sermon. I stay at B.F. Witt's. On my way, half walking, half running, I draw in the cold air and bring on some irritation of the air-vessels.

Thursday, February 8 Called at Rev. A.C. Wilmore's. Called at Rev. T.J. Connor's dined, and remained till after 4:00. Supper at Wm. G. Rubush's. Rev. Z. McNew preached at 7:30. I stay at Moses Hatfield's.

Friday, February 9 Call at Rev. A.C. Wilmore's and see McNew and Wm. Myer. Stay till after dinner. Call to see Mr. Sol. Hathaway, a supposed advertising agent, but find him out of the business. Write letters at th depot. Wait for 6:30 train to Greenwood because the 4:00 train did not stop there. Arrived at Greenwood about 7:20. Walked out to L. Wash. Jone's, Levi N's father. Lodged there.

Saturday, February 10 Went over with "Capt." J. Jones to his house. Dine there. Qr. Conference at 2:00. Some revival reported at Honey Creek. Parsonage occupied, but in debt somewhat. Preaching at Ebeneezer had ceased. Salary tolerably good. Supper at Rev. Irvin Cox; Pr. at Honey Creek at 7:00, Joel 2:13. Attentive congregation. Stay at Irvin Cox's. Snow's that evening.

Sunday, February 11 Pr. at Honey Creek at 10:30, Malachi 3:1. Communion. Few communicants. Dine at Capt. J.M. Jone's. His brother from Schuyler Co., Missouri, there. Also his Uncle Harvey Jones & wife there. Call at Sab. School in afternoon. Supper at Meredith Cox's, close to the church. Pr. at 7:00, Ez. 33:11. A large congregation. There seems to be considerable interest. I lodge at Jas. M. Scott's.

Monday, February 12 Meeting at 10:00. Few out. Birthday surprise at Jas. M. Scott's. Age 44. Perhaps 75 persons there. Capt. James M. Jones; "Uncle" Harvey Jones & wife—Russell Jones, Lancaster, Mo.; Two or three families of Wadle's; Bro. Harrell's, Aquilla Jones; Meredith Cox's; Thos. Pruner; B.F. Jones; etc. Stay at Scott's till meeting time. Pr at 7:00, 2 Cor. 6:2. Bro. Cox exhorts. Mrs. Jenkins & one other join. Stay at parsonage at Stone's crossing with Rev. I.M. Tharp's.

Tuesday, February 13 Bro. Tharp takes me to Greenwood. Train arrives at Indianapolis at 10:00. Train home an hour late. Arrive at about 3:00. Found folks in about usual health.

Wednesday, February 14 At home. Considerably under the weather with cold in the air vessels.

Friday, February 16 Went on 10:30 (11:30) train to Cambridge City. Called at Samule Wright's. Found that he was at Richmond engaged on his corn planter at "Hosier Drill" shops. Went on to Connersville, and thence to Gwynville. Walked up to William Myer's about

a mile north west. Stay there. Z. McNew, nearly sick with cold on his lungs, was there, while Alonzo Myer's was carrying on meeting at Blue River Chapel, were there was a large revival. Bro. Wm. Myer lately converted, at a meeting at Otterbein. Had intended to go to Shelbyville and to Michael Bilman's, 3 miles north, but no train.

Saturday, February 17 Go with Rev. Zedekiah McNew in buggy, via Morristown to Henry Zemer's, on the banks of Blue River Chapel & 4 miles South-west of Morristown. Dine there. Go on to the Chapel & pr. at 2:00, Heb. 11:6. Qr. Conference. Supper at Rev. Peter Myer's, a Qr. Conf. preacher, father of Rev. M.R. Myer's, now in East Des Moines Conference. Rev. Asbury Myer pr at 7:00 on Christian perfection. Stay at Rev. Peter Myer's. His son Aurelius, at Hartsville College.

Sunday, February 18 Preaching at 10:30. I John 5:18.19. Communion followed; and then a missionary subscription, which with after amounts amounted to some $68.00. Dine at Alonzo Myer's (at old homestead) Eli and two daughters, and Asbury and wife there, also a Mr. Wood of Shelbyville. Eli's wife, an excellent Christian woman had died in Missouri, a few months since. He and she and her brother were the first persons I ever baptized (June 1857) in Blue River. At Sab. School. Pr at 7:00, 2 Cor. 6:2. Six joined Church—55 in the whole meeting. Stay at Peter Myer's.

Monday, February 19 Went to Henry Zemor's. Dined at 11:00. Bro. Zemer & wife had started early to Northern Ohio, his mother being very sick. Very kind family. Went with Rev. Z. McNew to Morristown & took Rushville train. Then ran north to Dunreith, that train being behind. Went home to Richmond, Ind., on 6:18 train. Found all as well as common.

Tuesday, February 20 At home. Went to town in aftern. In forenoon went to Depot and mailed letters & applied for half-fare on C.H. & D. R.R. Mr. McShay, my tenant, called in afternoon. Traded for shoes for Orville & Katie at Gilbert's.

Wednesday, February 21 Wrote cards. Read proofs on first side of . Sent them up at noon. Susan visited her mother, in afternoon.

Thursday, February 22 Made up the first enlarged outside of the *Star,* and got it ready to print. Went to Washington on 3:20 aft. train, and thence to John M. Thornburg's 1 1/2 mile south-west of Economy. Solemnized, at about 7:45, the marriage of Jabez Haley Millikan and Emma Lewis Thornburgh. It was Emma's birth-day, age 17. Mr. Millikan son on my old neighbor near Flat Rock Chapel in Henry County. Guests: Esau Fohlen & wife (Nettie) Good and wife, Oloy & John Wiles, & Dr. Clark, and Fohlen and their wifes, Wm. Thornburgh and Albert & their wives, Mr. Ogburn Mr. Jordan & sister, Mr. and Miss Millikan, etc.

Friday, February 23 Bro. John Wiles takes me to Washington. I go home on the 9:20 morn. train. Spend the day in reading and writing. It was largely a work of classifying papers which had been comming [sic] and gathering.

Saturday, February 24 Started on the 6:00 morning freight to Warrington via New Castle. Saw Rev. J.S. Walls, M.D., at the depot at New Castle. Arrived at Warrington Station 1 3/4 miles south of the Church at 12:10. Walked up to the Church & stopped at John Bridges'. Dined there. Preached on Eph 4:3 "Unity of Spirit." Qr. Conf. J.W. Trees announces purpose to withdraw from the Church. Geo. Wilson pr. on Chris. perfection "Behold the perfect man," etc. Stay at John Bridges.

Sunday, February 25 Pr at 10:30 small congregation Dine at Tharp's. Supper at J.W. Trees. Pr at 7:30. Heb 11:27, Rubbed dancing heavily. Stay at Thomas Armstrong's with Geo. Wilson.

Monday, February 26 Go to Mr. Tharp's—Mrs. Armstrong's son-in-law—Stay till after dinner. Rev. F.M. De Munbrun and Geo. Wilson take me to the station 1 3/4 ms south of Warrington. Went on to New Castle & thence home, arriving before 6:00.

Tuesday, February 27 Writing for the *Star.*

Thursday, March 1 Read proofs and gave in items, for *Star* II Vol. No. 1. Made up in afternoon and got proofs. Printed a few hundred. Paid Mrs. Haynes rent and gave notice of purpose to quit her house at end of the year.

Mailed papers till about 10:00 at night. A very pretty day.

Friday, March 2 Mailed papers till noon. Went on 2:00 train to Columbus. Arrive at 7:20. Put up at Davidson House. Paid for March *Star,* 23.25. Bought a draft of $15.00 for Reuchlin & Lorin. This was a pretty day, much like spring, though not overly warm. Read on cars some of Mr. I.O. Moody's took on secret power. Reflections there on.

Saturday, March 3 Went on 7:20 train to Rushville, Ohio via Hadley Junction. Bro. John Shaffer met me and took me to his house, near. Otterbein Church. Dined there with Householder & Rev. D.W. Lambert. Attended a business meeting of trustees & others at the Church. Supper at Mrs. Myrick's. She, W.G. Rubush's Mother-in-law. Sister Shaffer Mrs. Rubush's sister. Preach at 7:00 Luke 16:26. Stay at John Shaffer's with Rev. Lambert.

Sunday, March 4 Preached at 10:30, 2 Pet. 1:16. Raised $824.00—$174.00 more than demanded—and dedicated Otterbein Church, Perry Co., Ohio. About $252.00 paid in cash & more in evening. House a brick with a tower 46x32x16 ft., costing over $2.500, which with lot, was worth about $3,000. A very pleasant occasion. Saw Mrs. Rev. J.H. Dickson & Mrs. Rev. Price & Rev. D. Folk. Dined at Bro. Enos Middaugh's 1/4 mile east of Church. Lambert, Folk, Mrs. Price & Winegardner, and others there. Pr. at 7:00, Eph. Eph. 2:14 [repeated in text]. Stay with Lambert at John Shafer's. Trustees paid me $40.00

Monday, March 5 Bro. Shafer takes me to the train, at Rushville. Make close connection at Columbus for home. Ar[r]ive at home at 3:10. Found all as well as usual. Brought 9 1/2 Star subscribers home with me.

Tuesday, March 6 At home. Spent time in reading. In afternoon Lehman John M. Lawson—one of the best of men, aged 69 years—and Caroline Zeller called. Bro. Lawson staid till 8:10 train. Dr. Kersey had skipped to escape trial for shooting at Chas. Potts & John Zeller. Left on Sunday. Father Lawson renewed Star Subs. and for four others. He went home on 8:10 train. I went with him to the train.

Wednesday, March 7 Writing in the forenoon. Looked

some after houses to rent in Afternoon. Called at Isaac Huddleson's & at B.F. Miller's in the evening.

Thursday, March 8 Spent the day at home writing, reading, etc. In afternoon, sent off many back papers on Star, December & January & February.

Friday, March 9 Spent forenoon in writing letters, cards, etc. Went in afternoon and looked after house to rent.

Saturday, March 10 Spent forenoon in writing, etc. Went to the doctor's (Dr. Kibberd's) to get medic. for Susan. The boys (Reuchlin & Lorin) came home from Hartsville on 2:00 train from Dunreith.

Sunday, March 11 Went to 8th St. Friends' Church at 10 1/2. Heard a woman, perhaps Mrs. Chas Coffin, preach on "Selfishness & Unselfishness." Chas. F. Coffin sits at the head of the meeting. Spent part of the afternoon in recording sketches of sermons. Went to United Presbyterian Church in the evening to hear Mr. Gilcrist, who preaches on John 8:12, "I am the light of the world."

Monday, March 12 Spent forenoon in writing. Spent the afternoon about the same.

Tuesday, March 13 Went on 7:20 Morn. train to Dayton, Ohio. Dined at Dr. Davis'. Ex. Com. Meeting of Board of Education at 2:00. Sup[p]er at Davis' Called at Dillon's & at T.J. Sines'. The Dr. Davis in a hopeful mood.

Wednesday, March 14 Called at W.L. Wright's on business. Saw Albert Sheerer Called at Mrs. Edwards; but did not find her at home. Dined at Rev. W.C. Day's. We worked several hours on a Sabbath-school association Programme. Went to Stoddard's to see W.L. Wright, for money due. At A.B. Reeves, Optician, At *Telescope* Office. Left for Richmond on 6:30 train.

Friday, March 16 Went on 3:20 train to Middletown. Supper at Rev. W.A. Oler's. Pr. at 7:30 Acts 2:15, "These men are not drunken as ye suppose." Stay at Jessee Rader's He is aged 78 years. Rev. J.M. Kabrich stays with me. Congregation was quite good for week evening meeting.

Saturday, March 17 Went over to Bro. Oler's. Bro. Aaron Rinker comes after us. On the way Bro. Henry Fadely overtakes me in a buggy and I ride with him the rest of the way. Dinner at Aaron Rinker's a mile south-east of town. Preach at Church at 2:00, John 3:7. Supper at Walter Ketchum Bro. Oler pr. at 7:30 "If any man will come after me," etc. Stay at Ketchum's.

Sunday, March 18 Pr. at 10:30 John 14:2. Communion followed. Dine at Jessee Goodpasture's, with Henry Fadeley's, Oler's & Shumaker's. Went after dinner with Bro. Fadely's to Rev. J.M. Kabrich's to see his family 1/2 mile east of town, and then to Daniel Rinker's near by. Preach at 7:30 Luke 24:46. Stay at Daniel Rinker's with W.A. Oler's.

Monday, March 19 Early dinner at Daniel Rinker's. Take train for Anderson. Leave there on the 3:25 train for Richmond See Rev. F.M. Moore & wife at the depot & travel with them to Hagerstown. Arrive at home about 5:00. John Shearer & Samuel Wright called in the evening.

Tuesday, March 20 Looked some after houses. Discovered that they are rather scarce. Wrote in afternoon. Went to see Mr. Kidder and Mr. Gauze on 13th St. about property to rent.

Wednesday, March 21 Wrote in forenoon. Looked after a house in the afternoon. Wrote in the evening.

Thursday, March 22 Spent forenoon in writing. Read a little proof in the afternoon, and went to see about renting a house. Called at Haynes & saw her about renting another year. Looked at her cabinet; shells, Geological remains, etc. etc. Made up first & 4th pages on the *Star* in the evening.

Friday, March 23 Mrs. Wright and myself went in the afternoon to look at the Lowe property.

Saturday, March 24 Arranged editorial and selected matter for Second & Third pages of April Star. Went on 11:00 train to Anderson. Ithamer V. McCarty meets me & takes me to his house to dinner, just across the river from Anderson. Quarterly conference at 2:00 (3:00) pr. 126 Ps 3. Henry B. Cole, Overton E. Evans, and Ithamer

V. McCarty were licensed to preach. Supper at Joseph E. Longfellow's. Pr. at No 5 Sch. H. I Pet. 4:18. Stay at Longfellows—a farm gardner, one mile west of Anderson.

Sunday, March 25 Pr. at 10:30 (11:00) Ps. 48:11. Made some effort to get subscription on a church for the neighborhood. Dine at Geo. T. Peniston's. Preach at 7:30, Jude 14. Stay at Joseph E. Longfellow's.

Monday, March 26 Bro. Longfellow takes me to the train. Go on 7:40 train to Richmond. Look for houses in the afternoon. Reuchlin began a week with Jacobs in the grocery.

Tuesday, March 27 Looked a little about houses. Spent the day largely in writing for the Star.

Wednesday, March 28 Spent the day largely in writing for the Star.

Friday, March 30 Made some preparation to move. Made up the editorial side of the Star in the afternoon. Gave out going to Wawpecong, Miami Co. to Qr. Meeting on account of an increasing cold & hoarseness which made conversation burdensome. Also had rheumatism.

Saturday, March 31 Moved out of Mrs. Haynes property 211 N. 14th St. into Mrs. Lowe & Miss Smith's house 309 North 12th St. Susan spent most of the day at D.K. Zeller's to escape worry and excitement. She came up in afternoon. Got beds set up but much confusion in things generally.

Sunday, April 1 All staid at home all day. I was getting a little better of my cold. Nothing very unusual. The boys spent the evening singing together.

Monday, April 2 The boys mailed the April number of the Richmond Star. I spent the forenoon in sweeping out the house; the afternoon in putting up the books. Reuchlin went to Dayton on 7:20 train to work at Wight's lumber yard 1308 West Third Street.

Tuesday, April 3 Continued to work at straightening up things about the House. Mother Koerner called with Mrs. Caroline Zeller in the afternoon. Mrs. Haynes called to bring up two books that had been left at the house. Cousin Samuel Wright called in the evening.

Wednesday, April 4 Spent the day in errands and in writing.

Friday, April 6 Went on 10:50 train to Anderson and thence on 12:50 train to McCordsville. Walked out to Marion Brooks. Staid till morning. Pres. Wm. Beardshear on train from Richmond to Anderson, and Rev. F.M. Moore from Hagerstown.

Saturday, April 7 Went to Samuel Brooks and dined and thence to Mt. Zion Church at 2:00. Pr. Heb 12:1. Qr. Conference. Report from Bethel exceedingly small. Poor souls. Trustee's at Lauding's report about $1,500 raised toward a new church. John Ogle's case makes trouble in the quarterly conference. He referred for trial. Supper at Louis Wolfgang's. Pr. at Mt. Zion at 7:30. Isa. 57:21. Stay at Wolfgang's.

Sunday, April 8 Pr. at Mt. Zion at 10:30. Isa. 28:5,6. Sacramental service. Dine at Jas. Faucett's 1/2 mile N.E. Robert Faucett & wife there, he aged 68. Pr. at 7:30, Mark 16:15, a Missionary Discourse. Subscription. Stay at Louis Wolfgang's.

Monday, April 9 Called at Hiram Heath's Told Sister Shearman who is removing to Clayton, Ind., with a letter saying of Crazy Hopkins about the umpardonable sin. Hopkins was an insane preacher. Often at the towns in Indiana, he would mount a goods box, and sing a half religious & half love song till he gathered a crowd. Then he would proceed to preach. Once he said "I can tell you exactly what the unpardonable sin is. It is when a man gets religion and then goes off & joins the Campbellites." Went to Fortville & Anderson and thence to Richmond. Rev. F.M. More on train & Bail.

Tuesday, April 10 At home. Did some gardening. Considerable Reading.

Wednesday, April 11 At home. Rev. L.N. Jones came in the afternoon and staid till morning.

Sunday, April 15 Remained at home all day on account of a severe cold that has lasted for a month.

Monday, April 16 Went on 3:30 Aft. to Honey Creek Station. Supper at Rev. J.M. Kabrich's. Rev. H. Floyd pr. at 7:30 I Tim. 4:1. I stay at Kabrich's.

Tuesday, April 17 The White River Ministerial Institute begins its recitations. Dined at Kabrich's. Rev. Wm. Dillon preached on Salvation by work vs. Salvation by grace. Staid at I.M. Baker's with Rev. I.M. Tharp. Very kind but not talkative.

Wednesday, April 18 The Institute continues. Dined at Daniel Rinker's with Peter Suman & wife (Now of River Side Cal.) and several others. Supper at Walter Ketchums'. Staid at Daniel Rinker's with Rev. I.M. Tharp. Mrs. Rinker a Prussian.

Thursday, April 19 Institute continued. Dined at Gray's. A Dr. Ellis boarding there; also John Suman's son, W. Dillon also dined there. Supper at Kabrich's. Opened the discussion in the evening on the errors of Adventists. Dillon followed Stay at I.M. Baker's.

Friday, April 20 Bro. W. Dillon left for home on account of the sickness of his little boy. Institute continued. I dine at Aaron Rinker's with Rev. A.C. Wilmore. Rev. J.T. Vardaman went to Middl[e]town. Ate Supper at Rev. J.M. Kabrich's with Oler & family. Bro. Thomas & several others. Rev. Frank M. Moore pr. at 7:30, "There is no God like thee," 2 Cor. 6:18. I stay at Walter Ketchum's with W.C. Day.

Saturday, April 21 Recitations of the Institute continued, but closing before noon. Dined at Pugsley's. Met in business meeting in the afternoon. Devotional exercises of some half hour followed. Went to Kabrich's to supper. Spent the rest of the time in the evening at Walter Ketchum's. Rev. W.C. Day preached at 7:30, a real good sermon. Staid at I.M. Baker's.

Sunday, April 22 Pr. at 10:30 from Rom. 6:5. Dined at Jessee Goodpasture's with Peter Suman & wife, & Rev. F.M. Moore & wife & others. Went with Henry Fadely to Honey Creek. Supper & lodging there. Rev. F.M. Moore pr. at Honey Creek at 7:30. Rev. J.S. Wall there. Poor fellow in low circumstances. Rainy evening.

Monday, April 23 Went home on 8:07 train. Moore's

also. Saw John Bowman, Jessee Fox & others on the cars. Arrived at Richmond at 9:00. The day bleak rainy. After noon made up the first side of May Star.

Thursday, April 26 At home. Rev. C.J. Kephart of Avalon College came. We called at several places of business in town. He staid till morning with us.

Friday, April 27 We started (Susan, Kephart & I) for Dayton on 7:25 M. train. Arrived about 9:00. Went to Dr. L. Davis'. Dined there. Ex. Com. meeting of the board of Education met at 2:00. Supper at W.C. Day's. Meeting of the Board of Education at Seminary building at 7:30 I presided. Stay at Dr. Davis'.

Saturday, April 28 Board meeting continued. Dined at G.A. Funkhouser's. Board Closed its session in the afternoon. Susan took supper at Rev. J.W. Hott's. Pres. D.D. DeLong delivered an address at 7:30 at Summit St. Staid at Davis's.

Sunday, April 29 Dr. Davis preached the baccalaureate sermon at 10:30. We dined at Rev. J.W. Hott's. Attended Gospel meeting of Whittle and McGrannahan's, at the Rink. Supper at Hott's. Rev. I.K. Statton pr. at 7:30, "passed by on the other side." Staid at Davis's.

Monday, April 30 Worked with Rev. W.C. Day on Min. Inst. Program We dined at Wm. Dillon's. Programme continued. Susan went to many places. Supper at Rev. M.R. Drury's. Wrote an editorial. Did not go out to the Societies meeting said to be very good. Staid at Davis'.

Tuesday, May 1 Went to Printing Office Bought books, etc. Susan went home on 8:10 train, morn. Dined at W.C. Day's At the Meeting of the Seminary Board at Seminary building in the afternoon. S. Mills lectured on Shakespeare—idolized him. Staid at Rev. Wm. Dillon's.

Wednesday, May 2 At Board Sem. Meeting. Dined at Mullholland's below Miami Chapel Board Continues. Went to town with Rev J.W. Hott's and took supper at his house. Allumni's Meeting C.J. Kephart & F.P. Sanders speak. Stay at Dr. Davis's.

Thursday, May 3 Go home on 8:10 train.

Friday, May 4 Make up paper Get the May *Star* Spend afternoon in mailing it.

Saturday, May 5 Went on 3:03 Aft. train to Indianapolis. Stopped & staid at Rev. A.C. Wilmore's.

Sunday, May 6 Pr. at 10:30, Zech. 13:9 "Will try them as gold is tried." Dine at B.F. Witt's. At Sab. School in the afternoon. Pr. at night Rev. 22:11. Stay at Wm. G. Rubush's.

Monday, May 7 Called at Walter S. Brown's, & at Rev. A.C. Wilmore's. Dine at Wm G. Rubush's. Spend most of the afternoon at Rev. T.J. Connor's. Quarterly Conference at 7:30. Rubush & Witt rather restive about any pressure on money. Stay at Rev. A.C. Wilmore's.

Tuesday, May 8 Went home on the 5:38 train. Breakfast at home.

Friday, May 11 At home forenoon. Took five dollars to cashier of Sec. Nat. Bank that he had overpaid me by mistake, yesterday. Found it by looking at my bank book to-day. Went on 3:03 train to Indianapolis. Went on 6:30 train to Greenwood, and Rev. I.M. Tharp met me and took me to the Church—Honey Creek Chapel. Pr. Isaiah 52:1. "Awake awake. Put on thy strength, O Zion," etc. Staid at Rev. I. Cox's.

Saturday, May 12 Went to parsonage at Stone's Crossing & dined at Rev. I.M. Tharp's. Went on to qr. Meeting at Bethel. Pr. at 2:00, Ps. 137:5,6. Qr. Conf. quarterage very slim. Harrison Harrell returned to the Church Supper at Jas. Waddle's. Bro Harrell pr at 8:00. We stay at James Waddle's.

Sunday, May 13 Pr. at Bethel Church in Johnson County, 10:30, Malachi 3:1. Communion followed. Dined at Rush's. Preached at 4:00 I Tim. 1:1 "Christ our hope." Went on to Harrell's, and staid there all night.

Monday, May 14 Went over to Rev. I.M. Tharp's and he takes me to the train at Greenwood. I go on to Indianapolis & home on the train arriving at 2:00.

Saturday, May 19 Went on 7:20 train to Indianapolis, and, after an hours waiting, to Morristown. Walked to

Blue River Chapel. Rev. Asbury Myer had preached. Supper at Peter Myer's. Qr. Conference at 3:30. I pr. at 8:00. Rom. 3:5. Evening rainy. Stay at Peter Myer's.

Sunday, May 20 Pr. at 11:00. Jas. 1:12. Communion. Dine at Rev. Alonzo Myer's. At Sabbath School in the afternoon. Make a short address. Supper at Alonzo Myer's Pr. at 8:00 Rom 3:5.

Monday, May 21 Went to Michal Bilman's in the afternoon. They had taken all the stoves down except the kitchen stove. Family consists of the old folks, Mrs. Gordon and her daughter and son, and Miss Eliza Billman. Stay at Bilman's. [spelled both ways in text] The weather quite cool.

Tuesday, May 22 It snowed in large falkes in the morning, and snowed till the ground was white that day at Richmond, and till the snow was a few inches deep at Lima, Ohio. I went on 9:50 train to Indianapolis, and met Rev. Z. McNew there. Did not find Rev. A.C. Wilmore at home. Bought a piece of carpet and matting for Otterbein Church (near Morristown) Lunched on Meridian. Supper at eating-house opposite the depot. Went on to Greenwood on 6:30 train. Hired conconveyance $1.50 to Honey Creek Church. Pres. Kiracofe did not come. A.C. Wilmore preached. McNew, Wilmore & I stay at Irwin Cox's.

Wednesday, May 23 District Sabbath-School convention began at 9:00. After opening, addresses began. McNew, Wilmore, S. Moore Surface, Tharp, Cox & Myself present. Supper at Capt. Jas. Jones. Rev. Z. McNew pr. at 8:00. Staid at James Scott's.

Thursday, May 24 Convention Continues. Dinner at Cox's, Irvin's son's. Supper at G.W. Jones'. Z. McNew preached at night I appointed some to meet with the stewards of the circuit in a financial council. Went home with Rev. I.M. Tharp to the parsonage at Stone's Crossing.

Friday, May 25 Bro. Tharp took me to Whiteland. Went on to Columbus. Saw Thonton and Mrs. Elwell of Illinois, wife of H. Elwell. She is blind. Saw also at depot Lizzie M. Owen & her sister Mrs. Booth who lives east of Noblesville. Walked up to Rev. A.H.K. Beam's. Stay there till next day afternoon,—Dine, sup, & lodge & dine again there.

Saturday, May 26 Pr. at Olive Branch at 2:00. Ps. 137:6,7. Quarterly conference Supper at Talley's. Pr. at 8:00, "Reasonable service" Rom. 12:1. Stay at Henry W. Lambert's.

Sunday, May 27 Pr. at 10 1/2 Zech. 13:9. Dine at Samuel Beam's. Sabbath-school at 3:30. Pr at 4:50, Deut. 18:18,19. Stay at Henry W. Lambert's.

Monday, May 28 Stay at Bro. Lambert's till afternoon about 3:00. Go to train at Cliffton. Saw Jerry Dean there who lives a half mile S.W. Mr. Thomas, son of Peter, near Miltonville Ohio & Effie Lambert went along to Shelbyville. Arrived at Cambridge on time. Reached home about 8:00. Found all well.

Thursday, May 31 Daniel & Elmira Koerner & Mother Koerner dined with us. Went to Dublin on 3:00 train. Rev. G. Sickafoose preached the annual misionary sermon. Staid at Edmond Wilson's with Cyrus Gilbert of Germantown, Ohio.

Friday, June 1 Mis. Board in session. Dined at Wilson's Reports of Secretaries & reading of minutes of Exec. Com. in forenoon. Addressed the board on Home Missions. Mrs. Keister's & Mrs. Mair's addresses. Jacob Hoke read an address at 8:00 Staid at Dr. Robinson's. Shuey excited on Oregon.

Saturday, June 2 Dined at Floyd's Board closed & many members go home. Supper at L.N. Jones'. Flickinger lectured on Sherbro Mission at 8:00 Mrs. M. Mair spoke awhile.

Sunday, June 3 Bishop J. Dickson pr. 10:30, Acts 2:27. Rev. J.T. Demunbrun at M.E. Church. Dined at Wilson's with Bishop J. Dickson. Sab. Sch. Children's Day at 2:30. Several addresses. Witt's, mine, Cowden's black-board address on the life and character of Wm. Otterbein. Supper at Wilson Scroggy's. I pr. at 8:00, Rom. 5:3. Stay at Wilson's.

Monday, June 4 Go to Richmond on the early train Write most of the day.

Thursday, June 7 Finished up editorials, read up proofs, etc. Made up the paper.

Friday, June 8 Wrote an article for the *Cynosure* on Bishop David Edwards as an editor and bishop. Family busy mailing the *Star.* Settled for the *Star.* Went on 8:10 train to Cambridge. Staid at John Huddleston's midway to Dublin.

Saturday, June 9 Went on 6:30 train to St. Louis Crossing; and thence by hack to Hope. Walked to Hartsville—riding about a mile of the way. Dined at E. Pitman's. Qr. Conference at 2:00. Rev. J.M. Fowler pr. Qr. Conference. Prof. Armen's recommend. [He afterward proved to be the son of John Condo, and a runaway] Supper at G.W. Fast's Staid at Rev. G.W. Fast's with Rev. S.B. Ervin's.

Sunday, June 10 Pres C.H. Kiracofe Preached bacalaureate sermon on I Cor. 12:31 "Yet I show unto you a more excellent way." Dined at Bro. G. Mench's with Rev. J.M. Fowler. At Sab. Sch at 2:30 Taught a class. Supper at Pres. C.H. Kiracofe's. Rev. J.K. Alwood pr. at 8:00. Communion followed. Staid at Pres. Kiracofe's.

Monday, June 11 Dinner at J.K. Funkhouser's. Supper at Isaac Tyner's with I.M. Tharp, & Harrison Harrell, her Father. Staid at Prof. Kiracofe's with Irvin Cox.

Tuesday, June 12 Supper at Prof. S. Wertz. Staid at E. Pitman's.

Wednesday, June 13 Went over Pitman's field Board Meeting at 10 1/2 Dined at Mrs. P. Rawlins. Grades read at 2:00. board meeting in the afternoon. Reuchlin came Supper at Rev. J.D. Current, Jeffersonian Literary Society entertainment.

Thursday, June 14 Graduation day Dine at Rev. G.W. Fasts. Go on home—Dr. Davis with me. He stays at my home. Clint Galbraith graduated Wm Fix & Dr. Beck's son master oration.

Friday, June 15 Dr. Davis went home on 7:20 mor train. At home that day.

Saturday, June 16 Went on 10:55 train to Anderson & back to Middletown on local. Rev. W.A. Oler preached at 2:30 Qr. Conf. folow. I get supper at Bro. Oler's. Saw his Father-in-law & Motherinlaw—Henry Spangler, near Selma. Pr. at 8:00 92 Ps, 8 v. Stay at Jessee Rader's whose age is 78 years.

Sunday, June 17 Pr at 10:30. Zech 13:9. Rainy forenoon. Dine at Thos. Hutchens' with Rev. Wm. Davenport & wife. At Jessee Rader's for supper. Few out at Night on account of rain. Pr. I John 3:2. Stay at Rader's.

Monday, June 18 Call at Rev. W.A. Oler's. Go home on 8:00 Morn. train.

Tuesday, June 19 At home Caroline Zeller came in the afternoon.

Wednesday, June 20 Zeller's went to Presby. Picknick Susan staid at Zeller's in Aftern. with Mother Koerner I Read up Proofs.

Thursday, June 21 Made up outside of Star. Wrote in the afternoon.

Friday, June 22 Wrote in forenoon. Went on 3:03 train to Philadelphia, Ind., where John Parker meets me and takes me to his house in a buggy. Wills Parker lives about 3/4 mile east of Otterbein Church. George Parker nearer Camel W. Parker 1/4 mile south-west of Johns. Preached at Otterbein at 8:30 Ps. 92:8. Quite a congregation for such an evening. Stay at John Parker's.

Saturday, June 23 Go with John Parker to Sugar Grove Sch. House near Milner's Corners in Hancock Co. about 3 miles east of Eden & six miles east of Fortville. Dine at Wm. Collins', near Sugar Grove Sch. H. Preach at Sugar Grove Sch. House, 1/2 M West of Milner's Corners, at 2:00, Ps. 137:6,7. Qr. Conf. followed. Preached about 30 minutes. Supper at Bro. F.M. Jackson's with Rev. F.M. Dumunbrun & Bro. Wm. Wilson & wife. Pr. at S.Gr. at 8:30, Ez. 33:11. A full house. Preached 25 min. Staid at Squire Joel Manning's at Milner's Corners, with John Parker.

Sunday, June 24 Pr. at 10:30, James 1:12, at Sugar Grove Sch. House. Communion followed. Dined on the

ground with Dr. Ryan & Bro. Martin. R.N. Young came after me to take me to Bethlehem west of Fortville. Rev. F.M. Demunbrun pr. at 2:30. I went on to Young's. Pr. at Bethlehem at 8:30, Ez. 33:11. Stay at Joel Beeler's.

Monday, June 25 With R. Newton Young & Joel Beeler make an estimate of what Bethlehem members can pay on pastor's salary. Go over to Elizabeth Crook's. Dine there. Cordo talking of going to Hartsville this fall. Went to Wm. Kinneman's Found him away. Saw Wesley Helms at Cross roads. Called at Patterson's. Found all from home. Went on to John [blank] Went with Rev. M.L. Bailey to Fortville. Thence to Anderson. Stay at Joseph E. Longfellow's, 1 mile west of Anderson. He is a farm-gardner.

Tuesday, June 26 Arrived at Richmond on 9:40 train.

Thursday, June 28 Read proofs. Wrote some. Made up Star.

Friday, June 29 Made up the paper early Friday morning. Mailed papers till afternoon. Went on 3:03 train to Frankton. Staid at John Deaton's till next afternoon, but called in forenoon awhile at Richwine's.

Saturday, June 30 Called at Gideon Richwine's. Dined at Deaton's Ithamar McCarty & wife came. Went on to Montecello & pr. at 2:00 137 Ps, 5,6 v. Qr. Conf. Supper & lodging at Ben. Frazier's. Ithamar McCarty preached his first sermon at 9:00 II Kin 5:1, "He was a leper." A good effort.

Sunday, July 1 Meeting at Jas. Montgomery's grove 1/4 mile east of sch. House. Pr. at 10 1/2 Ps. 66.10. Communion followed. Dined at Mother Frazier's. People largely dined on the ground. Pr. at 3:00. Ez. 33:11. Bro. Depio a new light preacher was present both hours. Went on to Frankton with Longfellow's. Stay at Gideon Richwine's He left the Church during the war on account of politics. But is one of the best of men.

Monday, July 2 Went home on 7:12 morn. train. Called at Mr. Steffy's Drug Store. He married Bro. Richwine's youngest daughter. Spent afternoon in writing printing cards, etc. Became quite warm in the day & so continued through the night.

Tuesday, July 3 Wilbur went on the excursion to Dayton. We printed and sent off cards on Minton's list. Spent the day at home.

Wednesday, July 4 Spent the time at home. Miss Minton, of Millville, Ohio, called with Caroline Zeller. Neighbor Johnson's had considerable of fireworks in the evening. A hard rain in the afternoon caused the fireworks project at Glen Miller to be abandoned.

Thursday, July 5 Spent the day in writing. Wilbur came home from Dayton at 8:00 A party of (ice-creme supper) high school & other young folks at Johnson's—next door neighbor's.

Friday, July 6 Writing in forenoon. Shopping a little after dinner. Went on 3:03 train to Redgeville. Staid at Sumption House. Very warm day and evening.

Saturday, July 7 Called at Dr. Farquar's. His daughter, only, there. Saw Williams', a lawyer. Went on 10:06 train to McGrawsville. Observed that Xenia Station is called Converse. Bro. Geo. M. Fiser met me and took me to his house 1/2 m. South-west. Overtaken by a dashing rain. Pr. at 2:00 (2:30) Ps. 137:6. Qr. Conf. followed. Finances well up. Rain nearly all the afternoon. No meeting at night. Staid at Geo. M. Fiser's, with Rev. T. Evans. Meeting in M.E. Church House.

Sunday, July 8 Pr. at 10:30 Ps 66.10. Dined at Father Merdin's father-in-law of G.M. Fiser, with David Condo and wife. Anaker & wife, Rev. T. Evans & a Mr. Johnson & wife from near Peru, Ind. Sacramental meeting at about 4:00. No evening meeting. Stay at Henry Kern's.

Monday, July 9 Call at Henry Powel's. Go on to Geo. Fiser's & return to Powel's for dinner. Go on 11:22 train to Marion. Call at Rev. D.E. Myers'. Saw Roland Brown of Pleasant Grove class, and his wife. Go on the local freight to Fairmount arriving at 7:00. Go with Joseph Pearl to his house and stay all night.

Tuesday, July 10 Called at Henry Simons'. Look over the place. Willie McShay's take me to Uncle W.H.H. Reeder's. Shock wheat part of the afternoon. Stay at Uncle William Reeder's.

Wednesday, July 11 At Uncle Reeder's. Helped shock wheat in forenoon and afternoon awhile. Staid at Uncle's. He has a cancer on his lip beginning to advance.

Thursday, July 12 Spent a few hours in reading. Made settlement with Wm. H.H. Reeder Jr. who acts as my agent on the farm. Rained in forenoon and in afternoon. Stay at Uncle's.

Friday, July 13 Wm. Reeder, Jr. takes me to Fairmount. Collect costs advanced on the G.W. Dealey suit—of the constable, Powell. Go on 11:47 train to Indianapolis. Write many cards to Stewards, etc. of the circuits. Supper & lodging at Rev. A.C. Wilmore's, 331 N. Noble St.

Saturday, July 14 Go on 7:40 train to Greenwood. Ride out with Dr. Carnes. Quite a talk on doctors, but especially on cancers, alternatives, etc. He spoke highly of Fowler's solution of Arsenic. Walked from Honey Creek Chapel to Stone's Crossing. Dine at Rev. I.M. Tharp's. Found the qr. meeting given out for a week later. Bro. Beers takes me to Greenwood. I go on the 5:21 train to Indianapolis. Stay at Rev. A.C. Wilmore's.

Sunday, July 15 Attend Class Meeting. Pr. at 10 1/2, Ps. 92:8. Dine at Moses Hatfield Attend Sabbath School. Supper at W.G. Rubush's. Pr. at 7:45 I Cor. 5:7. Communion. Good congregation. Stay at M. Hatfield's.

Monday, July 16 Call at Walter S. Brown's. Buy umbrella, $1.85. Go over to Rev. D. Stover's on West Side. Dine there. Read old Conf. journal. Return to City. Call at W.S. Brown's again. See Miss Shortridge, Nannie Brown's Sister there. Supper at Wilmore's Qr. Conference at 7:45. Stay at Wilmore's.

Tuesday, July 17 Go home on early train. Went in afternoon and left First Page articles for the *Star*.

Wednesday, July 18 At home. Looked over Grant Co., Iowa, business letters. Writing letters and making selections in the evening.

Thursday, July 19 At home. Busy writing, etc. Read Firstside proofs on August *Star*. George Feight came on 4:59 train. Staid with us that night.

Friday, July 20 Made up First side of *Star,* in Morning. Went to Anderson. Staid at Ithamar McCarty's 3/4 m. N.W. of Depot. Went on 3:20 aft. train. Jumped off train at Anderson when in motion. Tore my new pants on gravel.

Saturday, July 21 Got Geohler to mend my pants. Little injured. Went on 9:35 train to Fortville. Walked out to Eliz. Crooks. Dined there. Pr. at Bethlehem 2:30 Ps. 87:2. Qr. Conf. Bro Bailey, pastor, was absent. Licensed Richard N. Young to preach. Supper at Joel Beeler's with Moses & Susan Hatfield's. R.N. Young Preacher His text: I Cor. 13:13. Rev. M.L. Bailey, the pastor, came. We stay at Beeler's—Bailey & Hatfield's.

Sunday, July 22 Pr. at 10:30, Jas. 1:12. Dined at Hartup's, with Bro. M.L. Bailey. Pr. at 4:00 Ps 65:4. Supper at "Jackey" Mitchels. Rev. Lowe pr. at 8:50 Does not crowd his text. "Who is the King of Glory," etc. Stay at Joel Beeler's, M.L. Bailey & Hatfield had gone away.

Monday, July 23 Wrote some cards. Went ot R. Newton Young's, Elizabeth Crooks, John (Jackey) Mitchel's & dined at Wm. Kinneman's. Wm. Helm agreed to pay $5.00 on pastor's salary, Wesley Helm some more; Sister Crook more—perhaps $4.00; had a clear talk with Kinneman; Busler promised $3.00; Both paid $3.00. Stay at Aaron Landig's. 3 1/2 S.E. Noblesville.

Tuesday, July 24 Go on to Nobleville. Just in time for cars north, 9:27, a.m. Change at Peru for Wabash. At Wabash met Prof. Hanson and Rev. F.M. Moore, of Saybrook, Ill. Called at Mrs. Henry Gillen's. Saw Albert Koerner, my wife's nephew. Went on 3:00 train to Warsaw Thence out to the Fair Ground. Pres. C.H. Kiracofe preached at 8:00. Staid in tent for the night. Supper at the Hall.

Wednesday, July 25 Breakfast at Hall. At Rev. A.M. Cummins for supper with Burtner, & wife, and Rev. Bartness. Prof. J.P. Landis spoke on the new version of New Testament. Meals, except supper at Hall.

Thursday, July 26 Bathed in the lake. 1. Elocutionary exercises by Prof. M.D. Long. 2. Evidences of Genuineness, authenticity, & inspiration of the Holy Scriptures, by Rev. F.A. Ramsey. 3. Address by Dr. J.P. Lantis, on

Origin Dinner at the hall. 1. Dr. Landis on the Authorship & languages of the books of the Bible. Good Lecture. Rev. W. Dillon lectured on Sabbath-School Teacher. Good address. Meals & lodging on the ground.

Friday, July 27 Exercises continue. I lecture at 8:00 on "The Ideal Church."

Saturday, July 28 Mrs. M.L. Wells of Indianapolis fails to Come in forenoon. So [blank] Long, [rest is blank]

Sunday, July 29 S.S. Teacher's Meeting at Sabbath Sch at 9:00. N.E. Gardner pr. at 10:30 Isa. 52:1. Flickinger, Kiracofe, and Wright talk on missions at 2:00. Lovefeast meeting at 7:30. Rev. R. Rock of Fostoria, O. pr. at 8:00, Acts 16:31. Staid on the ground.

Monday, July 30 After a meeting of the Ex. Com. & then of the Association, we went to the depot. Went on 10:10 train to Fort Wayne. After an hour and a half left for Richmond. Aaron Wroth with me from Warsaw to Bryant Stn. Several with me to Ft. Wayne Arrived at home at 5:00 p.m. Found all well.

Tuesday, July 31 Writing editorials most of the day. Orville & Katie went to the United Presbyterian S.S. picnic.

Thursday, August 2 At Home. Read up last proofs on Star and made it up.

Friday, August 3 Much of the paper mailed. Rev. L.N. Jones lodges with us.

Saturday, August 4 Went on 7:20 train to Indianapolis; and thence to Gwynne's Mills Arrived at Wm. Myers about 1:00 p.m. Dine. Go with Rev. Z. McNew to Otterbein Church pr. at 2:00 Ps 87:2. Qr. Conf. followed. Supper at Newgent's. Pr at 8:30 2 Pet. 3:9 "Not willing that any should perish," etc. Go to Wm. R. Wagner's and stay 2 miles east of Morristown. Wagners Children: Earnest, Ida, Rush, etc.

Sunday, August 5 Pr. at 10:30 I Cor. 15:12. Dine at Caton's. Rev. Z. McNew preaches at 4:00. With McNew, have supper at William Myer. Go with McNew to Blue River Chapel. Pr. at 8:45. Ps. 92:8. After election of class officers, which took a long time, we returned to Wm.

Myer's. Went to bed about 1:00 After midnight. Slept five hours.

Monday, August 6 Went on to Indianapolis & thence home arriving at 2:00 p.m. Write some letters at Indianapolis. Write at home, mail papers, etc.

Tuesday, August 7 Rev. Geo. Beard comes. We go on 11:00 train to New Castle, & thence to Monpelier. Several brethren aboard. See Rev. Smith of M.E. Church there. Go out to Balbec with B.F. Paxton, & to D.P. Smith's with his fatherinlaw, Mr. Dugdale. Supper there. Rev. H. Floyd pr. at 8:30, Job. [blank] at Gilead. Stay at Bro. Smith's Their grievance over the consolidation of two classes at Gilead.

Wednesday, August 8 Com. met on 2d year's reading at 9:00. Mattox & Wilson were examined. Dined at Smith's with Pres. C.H. Kiracofe. Conf. opened at 2:00, Bish. E.B. Kephart presiding. Wilmore & Jones secretaries. Local preachers examined. Bias' suspension referred to Com. Rev. L.N. Jones pr. at 8:30,"For he careth for you." I Pet. 5.7. Stay at Smith's, Revs. Wm. Dillon & G.H. Bonnell also staid there.

Thursday, August 9 Conference continued. Auglaize preachers (at some time) there. Z. Roberts, P.B. Williams G.H. Bonnell, C. Fields, D.F. Thomas, Ogle, Wm. Dillon, [blank] Dined as usual at D.P. Smith's Flickinger tells me he has come purposely to meet me in my own conference. Rev. Wm. Dillon of Auglaize Conf. Preaches an interesting sermon Stay at D.P. Smith's.

Friday, August 10 Conference continued. Dined at Smith's. Flickinger challenged criticism, I said I was ready as Flickinger had informed me that he was come over to meet me in my own conference of an article on the *Star* in reply to a resolution of Colorado conference, and that an article in the *Telescope* would appear on it. Stationing com. met at Gray's, in the evening Missionary meeting address by D. R. Flickinger and others. Stay at Smith's.

Saturday, August 11 Conference continued. Dine at Smith's. Stationing committee's report read about 4:30. I preach at 8:00, on resurrection, Acts 26:8. Stay at Smith's as usual.

Sunday, August 12 Go to the Grove meeting grounds soon after 9:00. Rev. J.Y. Demunbrun comes to me much hurt about what Moore had told him* I had said: That I had said he would do nothing on Marion & wanted him put on Abington mission. Bp. Kephart pr. at 11:00. John 17,3. H. Thornburg, A.J. Bolen, and C.B. Small ordained. Dine at Smith's table in the grove. Sabbath School Anniversary at 3:00. Evans, Elmore, Wright, and Kephart speak. Went on to Rev. Aaron Worth's with Cousin Sarah and Andion. Stay there. *Moore's story was false. He was perverse in this respect.

Monday, August 13 Went to Samuel W. Read's—He is Aurie's husband, & dine there. He is a Baptist man. Went home on train from Briant that reached Richmond about 5:00. Cousin Sarah E. Worth took me to Briant in the carriage.

Thursday, August 16 At home Spent at least two days in looking over old letters, classifying them and stringing them, assisted some by the children.

Saturday, August 18 Reuchlin came home on the 8:00 train from Dayton, where he has been engaged since April 1st in a lumber yard with Albert Shearer. The little ones almost wild with delight over his coming.

Sunday, August 19 Orville and Katie's birth-day. Presents, etc. A high day for them. I did not go from home that day. Had a little United Brethren prayer and speaking meeting at our house (309 N. 12th St.) at 4:00 Albert & wife & Sister Millie Roberts and Sister Huddleston there.

Wednesday, August 22 At home. Peter Albert & wife at our house in the evening. Rained that night & next morning.

Thursday, August 23 Wrote on editorials. Went at 1:00 on Hack to Liberty via Abington. Went in livery carriage thence to Daniel Koerner's arriving about sunset or dusk.

Friday, August 24 At Daniel's. Lottie Koerner, Silvanus' wife, dines with us.

Saturday, August 25 Charley and Freddie Brookbanks

came. Dine at Silvanus'. Spend the afternoon there. Supper at Silvanus's.

Sunday, August 26 Went to Franklin Church and preached for Robt. Steele. Zech. 13:9 at 10:30 o'clock. Returned to Daniel Koerner's. Quincy Brookbank's were there. They went home about five o'clock. We staid there—at Daniel's.

Monday, August 27 Daniel takes us to Liberty, and We hire a carriage at the livery stable and go home, arriving about 11:30, A.M. I finish up editorial matter for the Star, and read proofs, etc.

Tuesday, August 28 Made up *Star* in forenoon. Mail some papers and write letters in the afternoon. M.Caroline Zeller called in the afternoon.

Wednesday, August 29 Got ready and started to Auglaize Conference on 11:00 tr. Wrote cards & letter at Winchester. Met at Ansonia by a young Rohrer who took me, and C. Bodey & a Ref. Pres. Preacher Lind to Conference at Rose Hill. Found a home at Joseph Rohrer's in town. Flickinger lectured at the Church on Africa at 8:00 about one hour. Stay at Rohrer's.

Thursday, August 30 At conference. Nothing unusual. Examinations the principal thing. Dine at A.M. Keller's. Get to see (by a little strategy) a copy of the *Telescope* containing my reply to Flickinger's assault on the *Star* and on me. Got many subscribers for the *Star.* Supper at Miller's, a quarter mile north of Rose Hill. Preached at 8:00 Ps. 66:11. Stay at Joseph Rohr's.

Friday, August 31 Gathered several subscribers. Discussion on Missions. Discus[s]ion on Amendment to report of Com. on Publishing Interests. Flickinger attacks me. I reply. Dine at Wm. Rohr's. He takes Flickinger & me to Union City. Passenger tr. an hour behind. So I get a permit and go on freight. So I make connection for home.

Saturday, September 1 Went on 10:30 Morn tr. to Hamilton, Ohio. Warvel meets me at depot. Lunch there. W. takes me to Walter's. John Kemp & I.K. Morris there. Peter Minton calls and takes me to his house. I stay there till next day. Am at Temperence meeting at

Millville that evening. Make a brief address.

Sunday, September 2 Preached at 10:30 at Millville Church, Heb 7:26. Raised $392.00 on debt. Some of the principal members were not in unity with the enterprise. The debt was 8:00. Dined at Rev. G.C. Warvel's. Pr. at 7:30, Heb. 11:10. Stay at Daniel D. Beals'. Their daughter graduates next June at Otterbein College.

Monday, September 3 Bro Beal takes me to Hamilton. I go on the train to Dayton. Call at Van Ausdoll & Garman's Carpet Store where Lorin is assistant bookkeeper. Call at *Telescope* Office. See Lanthurn, Shuey, etc etc. Dine at Rev. S.A. Mowers'. Return to office and see some parties. Cross the river and See Albert Shearer & Reuchlin (my son). Visit Dr. Davis. Sup[p]er there. Called at office to see Reuchlin. Called at Rev. W.C. Day's & found them about. Staid at W. Dillon's till about 8:00. Visited the boys (Reuchlin & Lorin) at their boarding house at Recker's Cro. 3d & Euclid Sts. Staid at Rev. Wm. Dillon's.

Tuesday, September 4 Went to see Reuchlin at the lumber-yard office, & thence to Rev. W.C. Day's. Went on 8:15 train home to Richmond. Rev. C.R. Paddack dined with us. Harvey Wright (my brother) and his wife, Delilah, and daughter (Grace, 11 years of age) came to visit us. Spent the day and evening most pleasantly together.

Wednesday, September 5 Went up to the city with Harvey's. They started home on the 9:55 train, A.M. I start on 11:00 tr. to Avilla on Gr. Rap. & Ind. R.R. After waiting six hours went on to Hicksville, arriving about midnight. Was taken to Bro. J.D. Crowel's. Staid there the rest of the night. Bp. Glossbrenner and Rev. M.R. Drury there.

Thursday, September 6 At the conference. Report on Education. I spoke on it, as well as others. Pr. at 7:30 at M.E. Church Hebr. 11:10. Stay as usual at Bro. Crowl's.

Friday, September 7 At Conference. Report of Publishing Interests discussed. Complaint against the *Telescope,* Rev. M.R. Drury spoke pacifically. *Star* and *U.B.C.* approved. Dine at Bro. A. Goodin's with Rev. J.K. Alwood and wife. Missionary Report J. Dodds' long characteristic speech. Preach at 7:30, I John 5:18,19. Berger takes me to the train. Go on 11:22 train to Auburn Junction & thence to Ft. Wayne. Stay at Avaline House. They charged $1.50 for bed & breakfast.

Saturday, September 8 Wrote home. Went on 11:40 train to Montpelier. Was met by Wyant; also by Rev. M.M. Thomas. Preached at Pleasant Dale (Sch. H.) at 2:30 Ps. 137:6. Quarterly conference. M.M. Thomas pastor. Supper at James McAuley's, 2 ms. S.W. Preach at 7:30 from Ez. 33:11. Stay at G.W. Wyandt's, 1 mile North. There is a biting frost to-night.

Sunday, September 9 Preached at Pleasant Dale at 11:00, Jas. 1:12. Communion service followed. Dine at Chas. W. Bowman's 1/2 mile South. Attend S. Sch. in the afternoon, at 4:00. Supper at John H. Sipe's. Pr. at 7:30 Acts 2:40. Large congregations morning & evening. Stay at Jas. W. Pottinger's 1 mile N. West.

Monday, September 10 Stay at Bro. J.M. Pittinger's till afternoon. Bro. M.M. Thomas & wife and son come. Bro. Thomas and I visit Mr. Somerville's in the afternoon & have supper there. Call at Wiseman's. Bro. Thomas preaches on "Let your light shine," etc. I exhort. Large congregations. Go to Bro. J.G. McColly's and lodge. Thomas's also went.

Tuesday, September 11 Went with Mr. Ford's to Hartford City. Write some cards. Call at Rev. P.S. Cook's. Dine there. He once a minister of our conference. Left us on secrecy question joined the Methodist. Since, went to the Presbyterians. Now pastor at Hartford. Went on 12:50 train to Redgeville, & thence home on 3:35 aftn. tr. Found all as well as common.

Wednesday, September 12 Spent the day at home. Got *Telescope* in the morning containing Flickinger's second article against the Star. Wrote some letters.

Thursday, September 13 At home writing in reply to Flickinger. Prepared copy for the first side of the *Star* in the afternoon & evening. Caroline Zeller visited us in the afternoon. I wrote to Rev. F.M. Moore of Saybrook, Ill. (?) in the morning & to Bro Prothers of Saybrook that I could not attend their church reopening at that place Sept. 23d.

Friday, September 14 Went on 11:00 train to Ridgeville. Thence went on 2:55 train to Hartford City, where Rev. N.L. Hoopingarner met me and took me after some delay to Wm. Knox's. Pr. at Wadle Sch. H. Luke 24:46 to a fair-sized congregation. Staid at Wm. Knox's. I used to know Bro. Knox & family at Knox Chapel in Grant Co., Ind.

Saturday, September 15 Wrote in the forenoon and went immediately after an early dinner to Hartford and mailed on train my second reply to Flickinger in the *Telescope*. At 2:00 Pr. at Wadely from Psalm 87:3. Qr. Conference followed. Supper at John Russel's. They were members at Abington twenty years ago, where I knew them. Preach at 7:30, Mark 8:36 (or Luke 9:24.) Stay at Bro. Russel's with Rev. N.L. Hoopingarner.

Sunday, September 16 Pr. at Wadle Sch. House Ps. 18:30. Communion. Love-feast meeting at 9:00. Dined at David Ashbaugh's, one mile east. His wife, Eliza, a *Star* subscriber. His mother and sister live close by. It rains about night and I do not get to meeting & there was none. Bro. Hoopingarner with me.

Monday, September 17 Bro. Ashbaugh takes me to John L. Russel's and then to Bro. J.M. Pittinger's. Bro. Thomas, after dinner, takes me to Phineas Ira's at Balbec. Supper & lodging there. Call at Cyrus C. Paxton's. Preach at Gilead Chapel at 7:30, Luke 24:46,47. A good congregation. A number of old folks out.

Tuesday, September 18 Wrote some letters. Went to E.S. Cline's for dinner, after stopping about an hour at Father Dugdale's. Called at Dillon P. Smith's a few minutes. Went on to George Paxon's for supper. Rev. M.M. Thomas pr. at 7:30 Isa. 43:2. "The waters shall not overflow thee" etc. He goes home to Good Will with his wife who was at meeting. I stay at Cyrus C. Paxon's, at Balbec.

Wednesday, September 19 Spent the morning in writing letters & cards. Went John Sutton's for Dinner. Remain till perhaps four o'clock. Go to Isaac L. Walker's for supper. He is son-in-law of Bro. Sutton's. Went to Church. I pr. at 7:30, Jer. 13:21. Congregation pretty good and interest good. Stay at C.C. Paxson's. [difference in spelling in text]

Thursday, September 20 Called at Lilburn Gray's. Also at Wm. Horn's. A fair meeting at 10:00. About a dozen present. Dined at John Riley Paxson's near the Church They belong to society of Friends. Go about 4:00 to Joseph Danner's. She a member. He did, but is somewhat skeptical now. Talk on Rom. 9 chap. Preach at Gilead at 7:30. Acts 26:28. Stay with Bro. Thomas at John Sutton's 1 mile west of Balbec. Some rain in the night.

Friday, September 21 Spent forenoon at Bro. Sutton's. Bro. Thomas went home to Good Will, but continues the meeting at Gilead over the Sabbath. Went in the afternoon, via Montpelier to Mt. Zion to Silas Poling's 1 mile North of Mt. Zion. Bro. Sutton takes me in his buggy. We keep the Warren pike till we cross the river which took us two miles too far west. Had to drive east over mud road. Poling a subscriber to the *Star*.

Saturday, September 22 Bro. Sutton takes me on via Buckeye to Zion Church. Stop at Rev. W.C. Ketner's till afternoon meeting. Pr. at 2:00 Luke 16:9. Qr. Conf. followed. Pleasant session. Supper at Geroge Shafer's with Sutton & Tharp. Pr. at 7:30, Ez. 33:11 to a moderate-sized congregation. Stay at John Eubank's, Ketner's son-in-law, with Bro. Tharp.

Sunday, September 23 Pr. at Zion at 10:30 Ps 66:10 Quite a good meeting and communion. Dined at John McClure's, two miles north-west, with Chris. Wearley's & others. It rains hard in the afternoon and somewhat in the evening. A good prayer meeting in the evening at Zion. Stay at Joseph Eubank's. His son Aaron of five miles south-east of Greenville, Ohio there; also his son from close to Warren.

Monday, September 24 Bro Eubanks takes me to Warren and I go thence via Marion and Redgeville home to Richmond. See Bro. Stout of Oak Chapel there. Go to the new Courthouse to look at the building. See Foster Davis, Esq. of Fairmount. Am introduced to young Brownlee, Wright, Col. Steele and others. Arrive at home at 5:00.

Tuesday, September 25 Engaged in writing etc. Made up outside of paper.

Friday, September 28 Read up last proofs and Made up editorial side of *Star*. Start at 11:00 for Redgeville. Write letters at the depot. Go on 2:55 train to Marion. Walk up to North Marion and call to see Rev. Robt. Fryer, formerly of Union Biblical seminary (student) who keeps a grocery there. Go on 6:10 train to Van Buren. Detained 45 minutes by a freight blockade at Hanfield. Bro. Chr. Wearly meets me at Van Buren & takes me to the Appointment at his Sch. House. Pr. a few minutes— Mark 9:24 Stay at Christian Wearley's.

Saturday, September 29 Went east 1 3/4 miles to See Jacob Guard, who has a very sore toe. Dine at Wearley's. They go with me to Mt. Gilead 1 mile north & four miles west. Pt 137:4,5. Quar. Conf. followed. Supper at John Wildermuth's a half mile east with the pastor Rev. Cyrus Smith. Rev. Frank Parker pr. at 7:30 John 3:16. It was a rainy afternoon & evening. Smith and I stay at Wildermuth's.

Sunday, September 30 Pr. at Mt. Gilead at 10:30, Ps 92:8. Large comunion followed. Dine with Bro. C. Smith, Noggle, Couch, at Elias Hallowell's one mile north. Preach at 7:00, Luke 24:46. Smith exhorted. Stay at Morrow's, one half-mile West.

Monday, October 1 Went with Morrow to Bauguo 2 ms. N.W. Went on the hack to Marion. Wrote letters— first to Bishop Dickson with first 2 cent stamp. Went on 12:10 train to Ridgeville & thence home.

Wednesday, October 3 Hunted for a house to rent.

Thursday, October 4 Rented a house 38 South Thirteenth St.

Friday, October 5 Went up to town. Go on 11:00 train to Ridgeville and Marion. Stay at Rev. D.E. Myers.

Saturday, October 6 Went in buggy with Rev. D.E. Myers to Jacob Thomas' 3 miles east of La Fontaine. Dine there. Go on to Lincolnville Church. I Pr. Luke 16:9. Qr. Conf. followed. Supper at Rev. John Heavenridge's. Rev. Roland Brown pr. Heb. 4:10. Stay at John Tweedy's, with Bro. Myers.

Sunday, October 7 Pr. at Lincolnville at 10:30, Ps. 18:30.

Communion followed. Dine at John H. Martin's 2 miles north-west. Stay there till evening. Mrs. Hoch stopped there in afternoon. Jacob Thomas & wife there. Bro. D.E. Myers preached at 7:00. Stay at Jackson's with D.E. Myers.

Monday, October 8 Lovefeast meeting at 9:00. Good. Dine at Peter Brane's with Revs. Myers & Heavenridge & Carrolls & others. Went to Heavenridge's Supper there. Pr. at 7:00. Luke 9:24. Stay at Raford Copeland's with Rev. D.E. Myers.

Tuesday, October 9 Rev. David E. Myers, the pastor, went home. I call at John Tweedy's. Rev. John Heavenridge takes me to David Sailors, a grandson of Coonrod Sailors of Rush county, Ind. Dine the[re] with Raford Copeland & wife & Bro. Heavenridge. Go to Bro. A.H. Billings. Supper there with Bro. Coblentz & wife & Bro. Sailors. Pr. at Lincolnville I John 4:10. Stay at Mrs. Matthews' widow of Rev. L.W. Matthews.

Wednesday, October 10 Went on "pastoral" visits to Marshall H. Coomler's, Albert Tweedy's, Edward Owen's, C. Hummer's & dined at John Kendle's. Went after dinner to Jacob Harvey's, on the old Heavenridge farm. Went on to Jacob Thomas'. Bro. John Heavenridge went with me through the day. Staid at Thomas's.

Thursday, October 11 Staid at Bro. Thomas' till afternoon. Bor. Thomas took me to Jesse Myers'. Supper there. Pr at 7:00 at Bethlehem, Titus 2:13. Stay at Jonathan Myers', one mile South of Church.

Friday, October 12 Called at Barbary Keith's. Dine at Jont. Myers and he takes me after dinner to Marion Found that a Milton Wright had taken my postal card from the office. Went to his fathers to recover it. Found none of them at home. Went to R.W. Fryer's on North Marion. Staid there.

Saturday, October 13 Went to post-office and got that card from home. Wrote a letter to Rev. I.M. Tharp. Went on to Wysong's Dine there. Pr. at Salem at 2:00 Ps. 1:1–6. Qr. Conference. Supper at Mrs. Cath. Hillshammer's. Pr. at 7:00 Acts 2:40. Stay at Rev. J.Y. Parletts.

Sunday, October 14 Pr. at Salem, at 10:30 (11:00) Ps.

66:10. Sacrament. Dine at John Null's, two miles N.W. of Marion. Three of Mrs. Shank's sisters & a niece there. Also her brother-in-law Pratt, a brother to Emeline Daugherty, of Oregon. Pr. at 7:00 at Salem, Ps 48:12,13. Stay at John Y. Parlett's.

Monday, October 15 Called at Adam Feighner's Jr. to see Mother Fighner [different spellings] and the family. Saw John Feighner of Marion and Sisters Cox and Sanders there. Bro. J.Y. Demunbrun takes me to Marion. Pay my tax $23.39. Go on 12:10 train to Ridgeville on my way to Richmond. Arrive at home about 5:00, aft.

Tuesday, October 16 Moved from 309 N. 12th St., to 38 S. 13th St. Had two hands—four loads at 75 cts a load.

Wednesday, October 17 At home. Dr. Champs dined with us.

Friday, October 19 Made up outside of the *Star* in forenoon. At home.

Saturday, October 20 Went on accommodation train to Ridgeville and thence to Converse (Xenia). Dine at Thomas Darby's. Pr. at Xenia at 2:00, Luke 16:9. Rev. Lowry (M.E.) present. Qr. Conf. (after estimating com. had met) estimated salary with $207.00. Supper at Darby's. Pr. 7:00 Luke 24:46. Stay at Darby's.

Sunday, October 21 Pr. at Xenia at 10:30, 2 Pet. 1:16. Communion followed. Dined at Ziba Merines with Rev. I. Cox. Was at Campbellite Ch. to hear M.P. preacher. Harrison preached. Called at Thomas Darby's till evening meeting. I pr. at 7:00 Eph. 2:4. House full. Stay at Thomas Darby's.

Monday, October 22 Speaking meeting at 10:00. About 25 present. Nearly all spoke. Dine at Dennis Benbo's. Rev. Mr. White called after dinner. I called at Darby's, at Rev. Evans, M.P., and at Ziba Merine's. Rev. Mr. White, Presbyterian, preached Mark 6:6. I stay at Darby's. Saw at Xenia: Schin, Reeves.

Tuesday, October 23 Went on 11:45 train to Jonesboro. Called at Mrs. Permelia Miller's, at Hiram Simons, & at Reuben Garrison's. Went with a Mr. Wilson to

Fairmount. Went out after night with John Simons & staid at Henry Simons.

Wednesday, October 24 Went with Henry and looked at the ditch (Todd Creek) along the swamp eighty—estate of Dan Wright. Next went and looked at my farm. Walked over to W.H.H. Reeder's, Sr; and found the old folks had gone on a visit to Uncle John Braden's, at Milford, Ill. Dined there. Went over to the place with Willaim, Jr and looked after some timber for boards, lumber, etc. Returned to Uncle Reeder's.

Thursday, October 25 Stay at Reeders all day. Wm. went to town at night for his father & Mother & Robert who were returning from a visit to John Braden's at Milford, Illinois. John Minton called awhile. Wm. had me to give John some snuff-capsicum! He made an awful fuss! Uncle's came home. We went to bed about midnight.

Friday, October 26 Staid at Uncle Reeder's till after dinner, visiting, and writing. Went afternoon to Fairmount with William. Walked down to Robert Hastings. Supper there. Preached at 7:00 Ez. 33:11, at Union Church. Staid at John Smith's.

Saturday, October 27 Staid at Bro. Smith's till 10 1/2. Then went to Carter Hastings and dined there. Called at Robt. Hastings. Preached at 2:00 Ps. 137:5,6. Qr. Conf. followed. Supper at John Smith's with Rev. Wm. Hall & Rev. C.W. Rector, the pastor. Preach at 7:00, I John 4:10. Stay at John Smith's with Bro. Hall.

Sunday, October 28 Preached at Union at 10:30 (11:00) 2 Cor. 7:1. Com. followed. It was a very rainy day, and the congregation was small. Dined at Anderson's. Called at Henry Sell's. Also at Keever's on the way to Sell's. Preached at 7:00 Acts 17:31. Inclement evening. Stay at Henry Sell's with Rev. Wm. Hall.

Monday, October 29 Love-feast meeting at 9:00. Good meeting. Got a piece of pie at Robert Hasting's and go on to depot at Fairmount with [blank], the Wesleyan pastor. Go on to Anderson. Write at the depot. Get home to Richmond at 5:00. Found all as well as common. Wrote out (finished) reply to new matter in D.K. F's "closing" article.

Tuesday, October 30 Worked on editorial matter for the *Star.*

Wednesday, October 31 Grandmother & Abbie Zeller, John's wife, came awhile in forenoon.

Thursday, November 1 About home all day. Read up proofs on Star and made it up in the afternoon.

Friday, November 2 Went down town. Then went on the 10:45 train to Elwood. Went to John G. Fohler's 1 square east of depot. Rev. O.E. Evans came for me & took me to Chas. Waymire's. Supper there. Preached at Bethel sch-house at 7, Luke 24:46. Staid at Waymires, with Evans.

Saturday, November 3 Went on to Nimrod Bentleys and took dinner. Quite a smart family and well-fixed. Preached at Hopewell church at 2:00 Luke 16:9. Qr. Conference. Supper at J. Conner Elymer's 1/2 mile S. Pr at 7:00 Ez. 33:11. Hester Keller joined as a seeker. Staid at Alpheus Wiley McIntosh's 1 3/4 miles south. He is second son of Ira McIntosh at Dublin Ind., formerly.

Sunday, November 4 Preached at Hopewell I John 5:18,19. Communion. Dined at Mrs. Hannah Purtee's (widow of Rev. Samuel Purtee) with Revs. Hoffman, Evans, Neal, etc. Rev. Mr. Whit preached at 7:00. Staid at J. Conner Clymer's, with Rev. O.E. Evans.

Monday, November 5 Wrote a letter & card and sent to Elwood by Bro. Evans who went home. A few met at 10:00 for speaking meeting. Dinner & supper at Mrs. Purtee's. James aged 25 ys, and Samuel Wright, aged 22 ys, her youngest sons, steady boys, live at home with her. Preach at 7:00, Mark 8:36. One seeker. Stay at Nimrod Bentley's.

Tuesday, November 6 Remain at Bentley's till evening. Write several letters and cards. Pr. at 7:00 (at Hopewell) Matt. 19:27. Stay at Sister Purtee's.

Wednesday, November 7 Remain at Purtee's till afternoon. Write letter and cards. Go to J.C. Clymer's afternoon. Rev. O.E. Evans comes just before dusk. I pr. at 7:00, Rom. 8:7. Quite a good meeting. Stay at Joseph

Trout's 1 1/2 ms North-west.

Thursday, November 8 Speaking meeting at 10:00 (10:30). Few out, but good. Dine at Jackson Miller's with Evans. Go on to Rev. H. Huffman's (former pator's) and on to Elwood. Stop at John Fohlen's. Supper there. Saw Miss Beatty, Sister of Robt. Beatty—formerly of White River Conference. He has traveled in Warren Co., Valparaiso, near La Fayette. Is now in Knasas. Go on 7:00 train to Mill Switch (Dundee P.O.) Stay at Marion C. Carey's.

Friday, November 9 Looked after some apples. Called at Albert Chalfant's. Went on 10:00 train to Alexandria. Rode on hay wagon two miles & walked to Chas. Atkinson's. Mrs. A. Afraid, taking me for a tramp, perhaps. Dined there. Walked on to John W. Broyles'. Staid there His wife my cousin—Uncle W.H.H. Reeder's daughter, Elizabeth.

Saturday, November 10 Rainy forenoon. Pr. at 2:00 at Beech Grove Sch. house, Luke 16:9. Quarterly Conference. Supper at Henry L. Miller's Wm. Carpenter, H.L. Miller A.A. Morris, Th. J. Jackson in that neighborhood. Bro. Cook (J.M.) pr. at 7:00 "Whatsoever a man sows, that." Stay at Atwell Alonzo Morris' 1/4 mile E.

Sunday, November 11 Pr. at Beech Grove Sch. H. at 10:30, 2 Pet. 1:16. Communion. Dine at J.W. Broyles' with the Reeders and Rev. J.M. Cook. Pr at 7:00 2 Tim. 3:16. Formed a society of 6 members. Stay at Thos. J. Jacksons 1/4 m S.W.

Monday, November 12 Br. Jackson's son takes me to the train Chas. Atkinson's Atkinson takes me to Alexander Dine at Spencer House Kept by [blank] Adams a United Brethren member formerly at Galveston. Meal free and invited to call whenever I pass. Bought 24 1/4 lbs of homey of a merchant there at 15 cts a pound & a cedar bucket at 50 cts. Went on 12:10 train (1:20) to Anderson. Went thence home on 3:05 train.

Tuesday, November 13 Went on 7:25 train to Dayton. Got 1/4 Ream of pencil paper cut. Cost $1.00. Saw Mittendorf, Shuey, etc. Left deed at Recorder's office—Cemetery lot. Went over to Shearer's lumber yard. Saw Reuchlin. Had seen Lorin. Dined at Dr. Davis' with Col.

Cowden and Prest. Kiracofe. Meeting of Ex. Com. of Centr. S.S. Association at 2:00. Supper at Recher's with Reuchlin & Lorin. Meeting of Com. at 7:00. Stay at Dr. Davis'.

Wednesday, November 14 Attend prayers at Seminary. Had a meeting of Ex. Com. of Board of Education at 8:00. Visited Reuchlin at Lumber Yard. Dine at Rev. Wm. Dillon's. At funeral of Prof. Funkhouser's little girl, Catharine Staid with Reuchlin awhile. Supper at Rev. W.C. Day's. Go home on 6:30 train. Arrive about due time at home. Lived then in Richmond.

Thursday, November 15 At home all day. Went to depot before noon & called at Grand Mother's (D.K. Zeller's). In evening worked on a Conf. book compiled from minutes of An. Conferences.

Friday, November 16 Worked on Conf. book in forenoon. Addressed papers (Star) to Ontario & German Ohio ministers.

Sunday, November 18 Attended Main Street Orthodox Friends' Church at 10:30. Dr. Dugan Clark pr. Did not go out to Church in evening.

Monday, November 19 At home. Made a printing pad. Material cost about 70 cts—15 cts for 4 oz. of white glue and 55 cts for 13 oz. glycerene.

Tuesday, November 20 Silvanus & Lottie Koerner visited us. Dined with us.

Thursday, November 22 At home. Bought a dozen nice fowls one day this week—perhaps to-day.

Saturday, November 24 Caroline Zeller called. Made up the outside of the *Star* in the afternoon.

Sunday, November 25 Was at home with Katharine while the rest went to meeting. Spent a good deal of time in the evening in reading. Introduction to the Pentateuch in Critical Commentary. A grand document it is, truly.

Monday, November 26 Preparing for the last side of the *Star*. Rev. Mr. Gilchrist called either this or next day.

Wednesday, November 28 Writing for the *Star.* Reuchlin came home on the evening train which was two hours late.

Thursday, November 29 Attended thanksgiving service at the United Presbyterian Church—a union service of the Baptist and U.P. Church Rev. Mr. Allen, the Baptist, preached at good sermon: Isa. 52:16. Wrote considerably for the   Lorin returned to Dayton on the evening train.

Friday, November 30 Finished editorial on Luther's Centennial. Read up proofs. Made up the paper in the afternoon.

Saturday, December 1 Received the December number of the *Star* from the printer. Family busy mailing it. Rev. James Long, living two miles west of New Madison, Ohio called awhile in the afternoon. He was a brother of Alexander Long. I heard him preach his first sermon at Mt. Pleasant, near Hartsville, in 1853. It was good. He married a good wife who governed him.

Sunday, December 2 1 Preached at the United Presbyterian Church at 10 1/2, Ps. 92:8. In the evening attended U.P. Church. Mr. Gilchrist preached from "They sat down and watched Jesus." Mat. 27.36.

Monday, December 3 Children busy in the forenoon. Mailing Dec. Star. Reuchlin went on the afternoon train, to Dayton.

Thursday, December 6 Spent the day in writing etc. In the evening printed about 125 cards and sent out next morning.

Friday, December 7 Went on 11:00 train to Ridgeville. Wrote cards to Reuchlin, Harvey, & Anson. Waited the afternoon train to Millgrove. Stopped off at Millgrove and staid at George Ludy's.

Saturday, December 8 Dined at Ludy's. Pr. at 1:30, I John 4:4. Quarterly Conference. Supper at W.G. Stewart's, Pr. at 6:40 Ez. 11:33. Stay at Wm. G. Stewart's. Rev. W.E. Bay came in the evening. He staid at Ludy's.

Sunday, December 9 Preach at Millgrove Chapel 10:30 Ps. 92:8. Communion followed. Dined with Rev. W.S.

Bay at Wm. G. Stewart's, and remain till evening. Rev. W.E. Bay pr. at 6:00. "Never man spake like this man," Stay at Stewart's.

Monday, December 10 Went to Geo. Ludy's. Bro. M.M. Thomas called. Rev. W.E. Bay left for Fall Creek Ct. I write several letters & remain for dinner & supper at Ludy's. Pr. at 6:30 Matt. 19.27. Several seekers. Quite a good meeting. Go to W.T. Boise's 2 ms. north-west, the class-leader's.

Tuesday, December 11 At speaking meeting at 10. A well-attended good meeting. Dine at John Faqua's & stay till Meeting at 6:30. Rev. M.M. Thomas & wife there. Pr. at 6:30. Mark 8:36. Some seekers. Stay at Theodore Fuqua's, the class-steward's.

Wednesday, December 12 Good speaking meeting at 10:00. Dine at Parsonage with Thomas', Mrs. Reeves, a widow, and Miss Personett are U.B. members at Millgrove. Bro. Thomas pr. at 6:30 "The Master has come and calleth for thee." Stay at Geo. Ludy's in town.

Thursday, December 13 Good speaking meeting at 10:00. Bro. Thomas & I worked on ministerial and S. School programme before meeting & also in afternoon awhile Dinner & supper at John Everitt's. Pr. at 6:30 I John 4:10. Speaking meeting that followed very good. Good attendance for a rainy night. Stay at Lewis Reeves, the Methodist E. Class-leader's, in town.

Friday, December 14 Went over to Ludy's and staid till meeting. Good morning meeting. Dine at Harrison's White Cotton's son-in-law. Snow in the afternoon. Pr. Jer. 13.21. Stormy evening. Stay at Geo. Ludy's.

Saturday, December 15 Went on 10:40 train to Hartford City. Rev. N.L. Hoopingarner met me and took me to Westley Knox's, where I dined. Went on to Qr. Meeting at 2:00. Pr. Matt. 19:27. A very agreeable qr. Conference followed. Supper at Morris Roberts', Brother-in-law of Rev. Wm. McKee. His two daughters just home from a term in Hartsville College. Pr. at Dundee school-house at 6:30. Luke 24.46. Stay at Bro. Roberts'.

Sunday, December 16 Pr. at 10:30 (11:00) from Acts

7:59. Pretty heavy on the soul-sleepers. Communion good. Dine at Sister Robb's, a quarter west of Dundee. Go over to Roberts' in the afternoon. Bro. Bays, a Hartsville preacher student present during the meeting, the company of Alice. Pr. at 6:00, Eccl. 11:9. last clause. Stay at Roberts'.

Monday, December 17 Went on to Knox's. Warmed and dined on pies. Went on to Hartford, & took the 12:42 train for Ridgeville. Wrote some letters. Reached home about 5:00. Found all the folks well & many letters awaiting me.

Thursday, December 20 Read up proofs on *Star* and made outside in the afternoon. Elmer Caylor dined with us.

Friday, December 21 Got ready and went on the 11:00 train to Ridgeville. Wrote letters. Went on to Marion, & thence to Van Buren. Walked up to Christian Wearley's. Lodged there. Wrote a letter from Marion.

Saturday, December 22 Staid at Bro. Wearly's till after dinner. Write a letter. Pr. at Otterbein (new Church) at 1:30, Eccl. 12:12,13—on duty. Pleasant Qr. Conference. Supper with W.H.H. Myers 1/2 m West. Pr. at 6:30, Rom. 8:7, on "Carnal Mind Enmity." Stay at Chr. Wearley's.

Sunday, December 23 A snowy rainy day. Pr. at 10:30, Heb 11.10. Raised $194, and dedicated the new church, to replace the one destroyed by a cyclone. Dined at John W. Homes' 2 ms south-west. Father Ewer, his father-in-law, aged 85, lives with them. Pr. at 6:30 I Cor. 5:7. Stay at Chr. Wearly's.

Monday, December 24 Meeting at 10:30—a good speakingmeeting. Dine at Jac. Gard's. His son Cassius, of Bethlehem, and Westley there. Stay till evening meeting. Rev. I.M. Tharp preached Jer. 21.8. I followed with exhortation. One rose for prayer. Stay at Wm. Roberts' 1 3/4 miles N.W. Children: Lilly & Ora.

Tuesday, December 25 Pr. Christmas sermon at 10:30 Luke 7:10, followed by a good speaking meeting. Three rose for prayer. Dine at Jacob A. Lamones 2 m, N.E. Stay there till evening. Rev. W.C. Ketner at meeting.

Rev. I.M. Tharp pr. Acts. 8.22. I exhort. Stay with Ketner at Chr. Wearly's.

Wednesday, December 26 Chr. Wearly takes me to train to Van Buren. Go on about 10:00. See Bro. & Sister Smith on the train. Make close connection at Marion & reach Fairmount about 12.00. Mail a letter to Bp. J. Dickson & an editorial to Coe & Martin for Star. Dine at A. Anderson's. Go over to W.H.H. Reeder's. Stay there.

Thursday, December 27 Remain at Reeder's till afternoon. Go over to see the place afternoon. Go on to Fairmount and to Union Church. Pr. at Union at 6:30 Ps. 84:11. Stay at Henry Sell's, one-half mile south.

Friday, December 28 Stay at Sell's till evening. Hiatt's came. Wrote editorial on the musings of a gnat. Pr. at 6:30 at Union Ez. 33:11. Went on to Fairmount with young Wm. Lewis & on train to La Fontain. Went in sleigh to Jacob Thomas' Father Coomler sick there.

Saturday, December 29 Bro. Jacob Thomas takes me to Lincolnville. I called on Marshal Coomler's & Sister Matthews. Marshal lately *very* sick with inflamation of the stomach & bowels. Rev. J. Heavenridge took me in a sleigh to Martin Jennings'. Dine there. Pr. at 2:00, Heb. 11.6. Qr. Conf. followed. Sup[p]er at Bro. Noggles'. Rev. J. Heavenridge pr. Matt. 6:19. I exhort. Stay at Noggle's. Noggles were old neighbors at Flat Rock, near Millville.

Sunday, December 30 Pr at 10:30, Mal. 3.1. Communion followed Raised a subscription for pastor $8.40 cash & $8.00 in Subs. Dine at Jessee Hull's. His wife a daughter of William Woodbeck's. Pr. at 6:15, Mark 8.36. Stay at Jessee Hull's. The congregation at night large.

Monday, December 31 Start about 5.00 morn. to Andrews. Just in time for the train. Make close connection for Marion at Wabash. Write letters at Pan Handle Depot. See Davis of Herbst there. See Rev. A. Worth, and Reeves of Millgrove, and Hammaker (auditor) on train. Call at Dr. Farquar's at Ridgeville. Arrive at Richmond about 5:00 found all well.

Memoranda

Dedication Mt. Pleasant	$15.00
At Muth's Carrollton	10.00
Weddings Sept 14	10.00
H. Lintner's wedding	20.00
Millikan's	10.00
Mich. dedications	37.00
Otterbein Perry Co. Ohio	40.00
[total]	142.00

Expenses	
Going to Mt. Pleas	$1.25
Going to Carrollt.	3.00
Going to Weddings	.50
Going to Millikans Wed	.40
[ditto]	10.00
Otterb	7.75
[total]	22.90

Mt. Pelier Ct.
1 Qr. Pleasant Dale—Sept. 8 Ps 137:6 Ez. 4:39. Sept. 9 Jas 1:12. Acts 2:40. Gilead. Sept. 17 Luke 24:46. 19 Jer. 13:21; 20 Acts 26:28. 2 Qr. Millgrove Dec 8. I John 4.4; Ez. 33:11. Dec. 9, Ps 92:8.

Hartford Ct.
1 Qr. Sept. 14, Luke 24:46. 15 Ps 87:3 & Mark 8:36. 16, Ps. 18:30.

The two-cent postage stamp was issued in 1883. I used one Oct. 1, for the first. Nov. 14, 1883, was funeral of Catharine Funkhouser, daughter of Prof. Funkhouser.

Bell Founders
Vandusen & Tift, Cincin. McShane & Co. Troy, N.Y. Kimberly & Co. Troy, N.Y.

Rev. G.W. Fritz Torrence Road East Walnut Hills, Cincinnati, Ohio. Rev. G.W. Rose 417 S. Water St. Denver, Colorado. M.R. Harris Royerton Dela. Co., Ind. Rev. C.W. Wells, 776 Welton St. Denver Col. Rev. Z. McNew, 360 N. Pine St. Indianapolis, Ind.

1 8 8 4

Tuesday, January 1 Spent the day mostly in writing. Was at home all day except to go down to town on errands. Wrote up some editorial matter. My home was at Richmond, Indiana.

Wednesday, January 2 Sent some copy for *Star*. Read up proofs. Made up paper in afternoon. Papers all came at night, ready to mail.

Thursday, January 3 Called at Allen Harris' at D.K. Zeller's (paid Grandmother six dollars). Applied for half-fare passes at the depot. Papers (*Star*) were all mailed that day.

Friday, January 4 Started on 10:50 train via Anderson to Wabash. Make close connection and arrive at the latter place about 3:30. Bro. S.C. Sweet meets me and (after making affidavit to the marriage of T.W. & Paulina Modlin for pension prupuses & seeing Chas. Rose) I went to South Wabash with him. Supper and lodging at Samuel C. Sweet's. Rev. D.E. Myers pr. at 6:30 Prayers followed. One arose for prayers.

Saturday, January 5 Remained at Bro. Sweet's till afternoon. Pr. at old M.E. Church at 2:00. Ps. 27:14. "Wait on th Lord." Quarterly conference. Pastor's salary came nearly up except no report from Lincolnville. Pleasant session. Supper at Bro. John N. Mills. Pr. at 6:30 from xHeb. 11:6. Good speaking meeting followed. Seveal (5) asked for prayers. Stay at Bro. Sweet's. x"Without faith—impossible to please God," etc.

Sunday, January 6 Pr. at 10.30 Ex. 28:34, "Golden bell." Communion follows. Dined at John Brown's. Saw Mr. Pierson & wife (newly married) there. She Brown's daughter. Saw Mrs. Copick, also a daughter there. Called at Sweet's before meeting. Rev. D.E. Myers pr. at 6:30. I exhort. Large attendance & good attention. Stay at Sweet's.

Monday, January 7 Go after an early breadfast with Rev. D.E. Myers to depot as he goes home to Marion. Write several cards at the post-office. See Wm. L. Stone, an old school-mate of mine. His brothers Frank and Silas are dead. He lives next street west of the post-office. Return to S. Wabash and Dine at Benjamin H. Hutchins. Called toward night at Jac. Ridenour's & at Showalter's. Tea at Benj. H. Hutchens'. Pr at 6:30, Jer. 13:21. Stay at Benj. Kershner's 1 1/4 m S. West.

Tuesday, January 8 Meeting at Church at 10:00 Hutchens opened. Good meeting. Dine at Jacob Ridenour's. Long talk in afternoon. Supper at S.C. Sweets. Pr at 6:30, Acts 26.28. Several arose for prayers & four came to the altar. Stay at S.C. Sweets.

Wednesday, January 9 Wrote a few cards. Had forenoon meeting. One arose for prayer—Mrs. Florence Kershner—& joined church professing conversion today. Another backsliden one knelt & prayed for herself. Rev. J. Heavenridge and Raferd Copeland came. Dine at Jas. N. Mills. Went to Wabash—got a letter from home—wrote some cards—called at Wm. L. Stone's, an old school mate, much my senior. Supper at Br. Sweets Pr. at 6:30 Ez. 33:11. Meeting blocked by disreputable characters coming to the front and arising for prayers. Stay at Benj. Kershner's.

Thursday, January 10 Morning meeting good. Miss Mable Jenks joined church. Dine at S.C. Sweet's with Rev. D.E. Myers, who had returned, and with Rev. J. Heavenridge & Raferd Copeland. Bros. Heavenridge and Copeland go home to Lincolnville. Stay at Sweet's till after 4:00. Supper at Brown's son-in-law's. Rev. D.E. Myers preached at 6:30 Heb. 2:1. I settle some bummers who had taken fron seats for a few nights. Stay at S.C. Sweet's.

Friday, January 11 Went on 10:00 train to Marion. Silvanus C. Thomas meets me. He takes me to postoffice and thence home with him. He lives 3 miles S.W. of Marion on Liberty pike. Pr. at Liberty at 6:30, Luke 24:46. Stay at Silvanus C. Thomas's.

Saturday, January 12 Stay at Silvanus C. Thomas's till after dinner. Pr. at Liberty Church at 2:00 Ps. 27:14. Qr. Conf. followed. Supper Isaac Reynolds' 1/2 m. West. Pr. at 6:30, Matt. 13:44. Stay at Bro. Reynold's.

Sunday, January 13 Pr. at 10:30 at Liberty Ex. 28.34. Sacramental meeting. Dine at Geo. Carter's 2 m N.E. of Jonesboro with John Y. Parlett & with Wm. Carter & wife. Call in afternoon at Bro. Carter's soninlaw, Enos Bond's, and at Henry Carter's, Solomon Carter's there. Pr. at Liberty at 6:30, Mark 8:36. Stay at Henry Carter's.

Monday, January 14 Called at George Carter's. Borrow a little funds of Mrs. (Mary) Carter. George takes me to depot at Jonesboro (Harrisburg). Go via Ridgeville to Richmond. Ar[r]ive at home at half hour late. Harrisburg is called Gas City, now.

Tuesday, January 15 Go to Wm'sburg with Reuchlin. Pr. Thomas Cranor's funeral. He an old friend. A good citizen and church member. Dine at Madison Cranor's. Get home a little after dark.

Thursday, January 17 Read up proofs and in the afternoon make up the *Star,* first side.

Friday, January 18 G on 10:50 train to Kokomo. Arrive about 2:00 Go out to Vermont, Rev. I. Cox meets me & takes me to David Markland's. I Pr. at Bethany Church at 6:30, Luke 15:7, dwelling on 1 Sin 2 Repentance 3 Joy over deliverance Stay at Markland's.

Saturday, January 19 Pr. at 10:30 at Bethany, Isa. 40:31. Dine at Hugh Johnson's with James Boyer & Wm. Bowden of North Grove. Qr. Conference at 1:30 (2:00) Brief session. Supper at J. William Kester's 1 1/4 mile east. Rev. I. Cox pr at 6:30, Gen. 3:9, "Where art thou?" I exhorted. Stay at David Markland's.

Sunday, January 20 Pr. at 10:30, at Bethany, 2 Cor. 7:1, "Perfecting," etc. Communion followed. Dined at David Smith's 2 1/4 m. south-west. Attended meeting at Vermont (M.E.) and heard Rev. Mr. Knox preach. Went back to Smith's. Rev. I. Cox pr at Bethany Isa. 55:6, "Seek the Lord," etc. Four came forward for prayers. Two joined church. C. Swafford & Mrs. Johnson Stay at D. Markland's.

Monday, January 21 Love-feast Meeting at 10:30. Good meeting. Bro. Cox spoke warmly of his experience and love for the Church. Dined at Aaron Brown's Bro. Cox nearly sick. I pr. at 6:30. Jer. 13.21. Bro. Cox exhorted earnestly and for 25 minutes, his last. I stay at Jas. Wm. Kester's.

Tuesday, January 22 Went over to Chris. Swafford's. Found Bro. Cox quite unwell. He ate a little dinner and lay down again. About one o'clock he had an apoplectic attack. Easier after a while but weak. Conscious all the time till midnight & thence unconscious till he died at 4:00 next morning. I preached at 6:30 Mark 8:36. Jas. Wm. Hester & wife joined Church.

Wednesday, January 23 Went to David Smith's, and thence to Kokomo, to get Coffin, Burial suit, etc. Telegraph to friends. Dined at David Smith's. Went over to Swafford's. Short service at the Bethany Church, funeral. Go on with Mrs. Matilda Ann Cox David Smith & Sophia Smith & the corpse to Kokomo & thence to Indianapolis. Stay at the Pile House.

Thursday, January 24 Went on 7:25 train to Greenwood, & thence to Rev. Irvin Cox's late residence, 4 miles south-west. Dine at L. Washington Jones. Rev. Z. McNew & wife there. McNew is his soninlaw. Call at Mrs. Cox's. Pr. at Honey Cr. at 7:00. Rom. 4:8. Mrs. Meritbox delivered a message to me. Told of her revelations. Evidently insane. I stay at L.W. Jones.

Friday, January 25 Pr. Rev. Irvin Cox's funeral Prov. 14:32. "The righteous hath hope in his death." About two house-fulls. Rev. Z. McNew and P.B. Williams present, & Rev. Widmay & Noble of M.E. Church. Dine at Mrs. Cox's. Went in afternoon to Greenwood with Samuel Alexander. Go on 6:32 (6:40) train to Indianapolis. Stay at Rev. P.B. William's, 29 Plum Street.

Saturday, January 26 Went on 4:15 train to Anderson. Detained at Brightwood nearly an hour & thereby miss the Fairmount train. Write letters and an article at the depot. Go about 1:40 toward Fairmount. Walk down to Robt. Hastings Witt Hastings gets me a horse & buggy, and I go out to Bro. Ruboldt's 1/2 mile east of Knox Chapel. Supper there. I pr at 6:30 at Knox chapel (1 1/2 mile S.E. of Point Isabel) Rom. 4:8. Stay at Rybolt's.

Sunday, January 27 Pr. at 10:30 John 14:2. Communion follows. Dine at Aquilla Day's. They have 12 children. I Pr. at 6:30, John 15:22, by request of Wallace Titus. My throat quite sore and I become quite hoarse. I stay at Wallace titus's. Have fever and then sweat at night.

Monday, January 28 Titus takes me over to Day's, and Young Day takes me on to Connor Clymer's where we dine and then on to Elwood. Saw Daniel Clymer at Connor's. He believes the world flat and square with four corners! Saw Rev. O.E. Evans at Elwood. Came home on 2:00 train. Found all as well as common.

Tuesday, January 29 At home. Considerably unwell. Sore throat and feverish. Did a little editorial work. Found myself unable to do much with whatever of effort.

Wednesday, January 30–Tuesday, February 5 At home. Too unwell to do much of anything.—Unable to do any editorial work.—Unable to write to any advantage.—Still unwell. . . .—Wrote some for the *Star.*

Wednesday, February 6 Finished editorial writing, for the *Star.* Read up some proofs. Wrote several letters in the evening.

Thursday, February 7 Got the proofs. Made up the paper. Got the paper out just before night.

Friday, February 8 Went on the 10:17 train to New Castle & thence to Muncie. Saw John H. Smith (son of Wm.) formerly at Fayetteville. Walked from Depot to 1 m north of Muncie. Then rode in a buggy with a Mr. Acre to Joshua Null's 1 m east of Bethel. Stay there that night. Joshua had moved back from near 1/4 m Baxter Springs in Southern Kansas.

Saturday, February 9 Wrote letters to T.J. Burns of Casey, Iowa and C.S. Mosher of 719 Balt. St., Baltimore, Maryland. Joshua takes me a-horse-back to New Corner. Dine at Fred. Huber's. Pr. at 2:00 Gal. 4:18. Qr. Conf. followed. Pleasant Conference supper at J. Wesley Brock's near church. Pr. at 7:00, Ps. 16:8. Stay at David Nantz's. It is a very muddy time.

Sunday, February 10 Pr. at New Corner at 10:30, Ex. 28:34. Dine at Frederick Huber's, & stay till evening meeting. Pr. at 6:30, Rom. 12:1, "Your reasonable service." Stay at J.W. Brock's, 3/4 mile north of town. It Sleets a little that night.

Monday, February 11 Speaking meeting at 10:00. Pretty good. Dine at J. Wesley Brooks Stay till evening meeting at Brook's. Pr. at 7:00, Matt. 6:33. Fair congregation despite mud and some rain. Stay at Frederick Huber's. Was with Rev. J.M. Cook, the pastor, from the quarterly conference till I left for home.

Tuesday, February 12 Bro. Huber takes me to Muncie. Some rain in the last few miles of the way. Stay at the depot till train time. Go on to New Castle & thence home. Arrive near 5:00. My home was in Richmond, Indiana.

Thursday, February 14 At home. Did some writing of letters. Felt very nervous in the evening. Symptoms such as I never had before, for a day or two past. Whether from nervous exhaustion, spinal irritation, cold in my head, or biliousness, I cannot tell.

Sunday, February 17 Attended services at the Baptist Church and heard Rev. Allen preach a brief but good discourse on 1 Cor. 3:9. The morning was a rainy one. In the evening attended services at Grace Church. Mr. Craft pr.

Tuesday, February 19 Spent the day at home in writing. Reuchlin went on a visit to D. Koerner's and A. Moor's.

Saturday, February 23 Went to Dublin on 3:00 aft. train. Call at Rev. J. Cranor's. Stay at Wilson Scroggy's.

Sunday, February 24 Call at Rev. H. Floyd's & at Rev. Wm. Oler's & Prof. J. Cranor's. Attend class-meeting at United Brethren Church, led by [blank] a faith doctor. A humbug. Dine at Rev. J. Cranor's. Pr. at U.B. Ch. at 7:00, Ps. 16:8. Stay at Dr. G.W. Champ's.

Monday, February 25 Call at Edmond Wilson's 1/4 mile west of town. At Wm McGeath's and at Aunt Betsy Witt's. Dine at Gray's. Go home on 1:20 train. Reuchlin on same train with bad toothache which continued till following Saturday with swelling of his face. It gathered and broke on the inside of his mouth.

Tuesday, February 26 Worked on editorials.

Friday, February 29 Made up *Star* in forenoon. Began to mail papers. Samuel Wright spent the night with us.

Saturday, March 1 Continued to mail the *Star*. Finished about noon. Samuel left in the forenoon. I missed the 7:40 train to Dayton.

Sunday, March 2 Mrs. W. & Myself went to Baptist Church. Heard the pastor Mr Allen preach. Did not go to meeting in the evening.

Monday, March 3 Went to Dayton on the early train Stopped at Day's & Dr. Davis'. Dined at the latter place. Saw Dr. J.P. Landis Called at Dillon's and Day's. Meeting of Ex. Com. of Board of Education at 3:30 Supper at Rev. W.C. Day's Stay at Henry Recker's with Lorin.

Tuesday, March 4 Came home on morning train Geo. Croly (on his way to Portland, Oregon) called. Rev. C.B. Small visited us & I went with him to Allen M. Harris'. Isaac Huddleston's & Peter Albert's. Afternoon went to John Roberts' with Small.

Thursday, March 6 Went on 11:00 train to Bryant. Walk out to Samuel Read's. Stay there. Cousin Sarah E. Worth also there.

Friday, March 7 Dined at Aaron Worth's. Went in the afternoon with Cyrus Hills to Dillon P. Smith's. Rev. Wm. Hall pr. at Gilead at 7:30. I exhort. Lodge at Smith's.

Saturday, March 8 Staid at Bro. Smith's till meeting at 1:30. Pr. Matthew 11:30. Pleasant qr. conf. followed. Supper at P. Drey's Rev. M.M. Thomas pr. at 7:00. Stay at Cyrus C. Paxon's that night.

Sunday, March 9 I was at the morning meeting. Preached at 10:30 2 Cor. 3:8. Dine at Dillon P. Smith's with Saml. Read & family and Audion Worth. Rev. Wm. Hall pr at 7:00, I exhort at some length. Stay at C.C. Paxon's.

Monday, March 10 Call at Father Wm. Dugdale's. Dine at Cyrus Paxon's. Go to Camden with Cline. Stay at the store with Rev. Wm. Hall till Rev. M.M. Thomas came and took me to Lichtenfels'. East Supper there. Go on to Pleasant Dale School-House. Pr. at 7:30, Rom. 14:17. Stay at G.W. Wyandt's.

Tuesday, March 11 Rev. M.M. Thomas takes me to Hartford through the rain. Go on to Upland. Dine at Robert Wright's. Go on to Jonesboro on 3:30 train. Ride with "Buck" Ice to Uncle W.H.H. Reeder's. Muddy and dark tramp of 1/4 mile from cross-roads to the house! Lodge at Reeder's.

Wednesday, March 12 Go over to the farm. Mr. McShay is gathering corn. One third of mine ungathered! Return to W.H.H. Reeder's. Stay till morning.

Thursday, March 13 W.H.H. Reeder, Jr. takes me to the train, quite early. Just in time. Go to Jonesboro Stay there at Hiram Simons' till train time. Go to Hartford. Rev. N.L. Hoopingarner meets me & takes me to George Stallsmith's. Dinner and supper there. Pr. at Carney's Sch. H. at 7:30. Gal. 6:14. Stay at Stallsmith's.

Friday, March 14 Stay at Stallsmith's till evening. Studying mental philosophy (Joseph Haven's) Pr. at Carney's Sch. H. John 1:29. Stay at Stallsmith's Sit up with N.L. Hoopingarner till nearly 2:00. He quite sick.

Saturday, March 15 Stay at Stallsmith's till afternoon. Pr. at 1:30 (2:00) Luke 10:29. Quarterly conf. followed

Pleasant session. But reports were short. Supper at Stallsmith's. Pr at 7:30, John 3:7. Stay at Stallsmith's.

Sunday, March 16 Pr. at 10:30, Luke 16:31. Communion followed. Dine at J.W. Stallsmith's, 3/4 mile N.W. of Hartford. Pr. at 7:15, Ps. 87:3. At the close give some history of the Church. Stay at J.W. Stallsmith's.

Monday, March 17 After an early dinner, went to Hartford. Took 12:30 train for Ridgeville & thence home.

Thursday, March 20 Read up the remainder of *Star* proofs and made up the outside.

Friday, March 21 Went on 10:37 train to New CAstle and thence to Montpelier. Rev. I.M. Tharp meets me and takes me to Mt. Zion in Wells Co. Supper at Tharp's. Pr. at "Bethel" (in Mt. Zion) at 7:30 Isa. 55:1. "Ho every one that thirsts," etc. Stay at Tharp's.

Saturday, March 22 Stay at Tharp's till after dinner. Bro. Amos Alspach came about 10:30. Dine at Rev. I.M. Tharp's. Pr. at 2:00 I Pet 2:6-9 Qr. Conf. followed, pleasant & good. Supper at Thomas Clampet's. Rev. W.C. Ketner pr. at 7:30, Heb. 11:14. Large congregation. Good meeting. Stay at Thos. Clampet's, 3/4 m. North.

Sunday, March 23 Pr. at 10:30 2 Cor. 3:7-8. Communion followed. Dine at Geo. Gaizer's with Jac. Cockran, Abr. Matthias, etc. Slept an hour in the afternoon. Pr. at 7:30 I Pet. 4:18. A very large congregation. Stay at Wm. Pearce's in town.

Monday, March 24 Went with Tharp's to Elijah Morrison's. Dinner & supper there. John Beatty son of Robt. Beatty living there. Pr at 8:00, Rom. 10:1. Pretty large congregation. Stay at Rev. I.M. Tharp's.

Tuesday, March 25 It rained so that Bro. Tharp's and myself could not well go to Bro. Poling's to Dinner. Rode Bro. Tharp's horse to Buckeye and got a letter from home. Went on to David Elliot's 4 miles S.E. of Warren. It rained hard soon after I got there. Staid at Elliott's.

Wednesday, March 26 Bro. Elliott took me in a spring-wagon to James Coolman's across the Wabash River from Huntington. Very cold day. Dinner & Supper there.

Lodge there. They have a daughter, two sons & a babe.

Thursday, March 27 Bro. Jas. Coolman takes me over to Rev. Cyrus Smith's on the Etna Pike. Dinner there Sleep there an hour or two. Supper there. I Pr. at Pleasant Grove at 8:00, John 3:7. I Stay at Roland Z. Brown's.

Friday, March 28 Wrote some postal cards to Staward's on Marion Circuit. Slept nearly two hours before dinner. Dinner & Supper at Roland Z. Brown's. Conclude not to go to meeting on account of the rain. Lodge at Brown's.

Saturday, March 29 Went over to Mathias Dungan's & dined. Pr. at 2:00 at Pleasant Grove, Math 6:7. Qr. Conf. followed. Pleasant Session. Supper at Geo. Leverton's. Rev. C. Smith pr at 7:45, Eph. 2:22. Stay at Jesse Bunker's.

Sunday, March 30 I Pr. at 10:30, Jas. 1:12. Communion followed. Dine at Matt. Dungan's. Staid there till evening meeting. Pr. at 7:00, Rom. 3:5. Stay at Isaac Barker's on Etna pike, 2 1/2 miles S.W. of Huntington. He takes me to the 6:00 train next morning.

Monday, March 31 Go on early train to Ft. Wayne. Stay mostly at the depot, till 12:52 train to Richmond. Arrive at home about 5:00 Eve. Found all about in usual health.

Wednesday, April 2 Writing for paper. Read some proofs.

Thursday, April 3 Read up the remainder of proofs & made up the Editorial pages of the *Star*.

Friday, April 4 Paid my Richmond tax $7.00. Went on 10:32 train to Ridgeville and thence to Marion. Stay at Rev. D.E. Myer's.

Saturday, April 5 Went on up to Wabash on 7:03 train, with Bro. Myers. Jacob Silvius meets me & takes me to his house—Mill creek appointment. Dine there. Pr. at 2:00, John 1:16, Qr. Conference followed. Pleasant Session. Pretty well attended. Supper at Enoch Shambaugh's, the son-in-law of Kesler. Rev. D.E. Myers pr. at 7:30, "Leaving the things which are behind," etc. Stay at Wm. Dubbois.

Sunday, April 6 Preach at Mill Creek Church at 10 1/2 Zech. 13:9. Dine at Kesler's with Rev. D.E. Myers. Pr. at 7:00, Mal. 4:1 "There Shall," etc. Stay at Wm. Dubois'.

Monday, April 7 Bro. Dubois takes me to Wabash. Go thence to Fairmount. Walk & ride out to Uncle Wm. Reeder's. Stay there.

Tuesday, April 8 Wrote out a contract for myself and McShays. Go over in the afternoon and get the contract signed. Stay at Reeder's.

Wednesday, April 9 Went across the river to Mr. Park's Dined there. Returned. Sold Mr. Simons 250 bushels of corn and Joseph Pearl 25 bushels. Saw Wm. Leach & Joseph Corn. Went to Wm. Duling's Called at Geo. Simon's and at Alma Reave's. Stay at Uncle Wm. Reeder's.

Thursday, April 10 Wrote out a duplicate of lease contract. Helped raise Wm's house. Rode over in Afternoon and had duplicate signed. Called at Simons and found John had gone back on the corn contract. Staid at Reeder's.

Friday, April 11 Staid at Uncle's till after dinner. Flora took me to Fairmount afternoon. Got a letter from Susan. She having a bad cold, but better. Went on cars to Jonesboro. Walk out to G. Carter's. Supper there. Walked on to D.E. Myers at Marion. Dr. Champ there. Staid at Myers'.

Saturday, April 12 Went to post-office Got a letter from Susan. She some better. Went on to Rev. Robt. W. Fryer's in North Marion. Rev. D.E. Myers comes and takes me to Jeff. Hanimaker's to dinner. He take me on nearly to Union Chapel. Pr at 2:00, John 1:16. Pleasant Qr. Meeting. Supper at Micaga Wesner's. She was Eliz. Woohman's. R.W. Fryer pr. at 7:30, "I am the light of the world." Stay at F.A. Bradford's.

Sunday, April 13 Pr. at 10 1/2 (Union) and Easter sermon, Acts 26:8. Communion followed. Dine at Micaga Wesner's. Call in the afternoon at Harvey M. Crevaston's. Rev. W.C. Ketner pr. at 7:00, "With one consent to make excuse."

Monday, April 14 Rev. J.Y. Demumbrun takes me to

Marion. Pay my tax, borrowing $8.00. Go on 11:45 train to Ridgeville and thence home at 5:00. Read up my letters & prepared manuscript contributed for the *Star*.

Tuesday, April 15 Prepared copy for the *Star*. Went on 10:37 train to New Castle to the Ministerial Institute. Found my home at at [sic] Wm. C. Gowdy's, Father Jennings' son-in-law. Institute exercises continued. Rev. Wm. Dillon went to supper with me Rev. A. Rust pr. at 7:30. Stay at Gowdy's.

Wednesday, April 16 Institute continued. Rev. Z. McNew Dined with me. Institute continued. Rev. A.J. Bolen supped with me at Wm. C. Gowdy's. Rev. Wm. Dillon preached "In him was life, and the life was the light of men." Rev. W.C. Day staid with me at Mr. Gowdy's.

Thursday, April 17 Institute Continued Rev A.C. Wilmore dined with me. Supper at Harvey Root's Rev. Z. McNew preached at 7:30, 2 Cor. 5:17. I stay at W.C. Gowdy's.

Friday, April 18 Institute continued. Left of 11+ train for Kokomo. Stay at Kokomo narrow guage depot over two hours without fire. Caught a sharp cold in my head and throat. Went on to Vermont. Walked out to David Marklands, a mile North-east. Staid there till noon next day.

Saturday, April 19 Bro. David Markland takes me in a two horse wagon to Olive Branch 4 1/2 miles east to quarterly meeting pr. at 2:00, John 1:16. Quar. Conf. followed. Conf. aftee to retain Wm. Bowden as pastor. Supper at J.W. Phares' Rev. Mr. Spoud of Wesleyan Church pr at 7:30. An assumptions egotist, making superior profession of holiness. Lodge at J.W. Phares' who lives with his three daughters and two sons—a nice family. Emma 21, Elva 15, Anna 13, Wm. 19, Otto 10.

Sunday, April 20 Pr. at Olive Branch at 10:30, Acts 26:8. Dine at Henry Loop's, with Bros. Bowden & Fry. Call at J.W. Phares' Bro. Bowden pr. at 7:00. "Be of good courage"—with reference to Joshua. Speaking meeting followed. Stay at J.W. Phares'.

Monday, April 21 Bro. Phares takes me to the train. Go on the 9:00 local to Kokomo. Dine at Cousin James M.

Reeder's. Thence on 1:15 tr to Middletown. Daniel Rinker takes me to his house near Daleville. Call at Rev. J.M. Kabrich's & got a letter from Home. Supper at Rinker's with Rev. A.C. Wilmore & wife. Pr. Opening discourse before Woman's Branch Missionary Association Phi. 4:3. Stay at Daniel Rinker's, a half-mile east of Daleville.

Tuesday, April 22 Went after an early breakfast on 6:10 train to attend Malinda Day's funeral, wife of Rev. A.R. Day. I pr. at 10:00. Bury at Mt. Pleasant, 3 ms South of New Burlington. Short service at the Mt. Pleasant Church. Returned to Day's a half mile N.W. of Muncie. Stay there till morning. All the sons were at the funeral: Franklin, Wm. C., George, Harvey, Rufus.

Wednesday, April 23 Arose early and after an early lunch, Went to Lake Erie & Western Railroad depot. After some detention, start on local accom. train to Alexandria. Arrive there about 9:30. Mail some letters & cards. Lunch at restaurant. Go on 1:00 train to Fairmount. Cyrus Smith aboard. Walk over to Uncle W.H.H. Reeder's. Stay there.

Thursday, April 24 Stay at Uncle's till after dinner. Walked out to the fields & talked with Wm. Junior. Concluded to remain till morning. Spent most of the day outdoor, it being the first real pleasant day for some weeks.

Friday, April 25 Flora took me to Fairmount for early train. Left on 7:00 train for Marion.Called at Robt. W. Fryers in North Marion. Went on 10:02 train to Herbst. Called at Littleton Davis' & dined. An aged man by name of Wilson also dined there. Supper at Davis. Rev. C.W. Rector & wife came. Pr. at M.P. Church at 8:00 Mal. 3:18. Stay at Geo. Lane's, M.P.

Saturday, April 26 Lit. Davis & family took me in spring wagon to Geo. Conways Dine there. Pr. at 2:00, 2 Pet. 1:3 Qr. Conf. followed. Pleasant session. Supper at Father John Carpenter's, 1 mile east of Burn's Sch. House 2 1/2 miles S. of Sycamore Corners. Rev. C. Rector pr. at 8:00, Matt. 22:37. I stay at Carpenter's.

Sunday, April 27 Called at Isaac Burns'. Pr. at Burns' Sch. House at 10:30, 2 Cor. 7,8. Dine at Ervin Coston's

near Jerome 2 1/2 miles west. Bro. Rector baptizes Young Burns & wife, and Bagwell Supper at Coston's. Burns and Coston are partly African. Pr. at 7:45, Mal. 3:16,17. A good love-feast meeting followed. Many spoke and the meeting lasted till 9:00. Stay at Father john Carpenter's.

Monday, April 28 Father Carpenter takes me to Sims Station. Write some postal cards to Muncie stewards. Go on to Marion & Ridgeville. Write to some of Elwood stewards. Arrive at home about 5:00, eve.

Tuesday, April 29 Write some editorials in the forenoon. In afternoon pay rent, and pay Mother Koerner $10.00. Continue to write some. Wrote till late in the evening.

Wednesday, April 30 Rose at 4:00. Wrote for *Star*, during forenoon. Found in the afternoon that we were a colmn & a half behind. Provided this. Gathered letters & papers together such as I might need at Dayton and Germantown. Was quite worn down before I got to bed.

Thursday, May 1 Spent the forenoon in hunting up letters and reading proofs on editorials of the *Star*. Made up *Star* in afternoon. Spent evening in sending out transient copies of *Star*.

Friday, May 2 Got up matters generally. Went to Dayton in the afternoon. Saw Reuchlin & Lorin. Supper at Rev. W.C. Day's. Rev. H. Floyd there. His colloquy [sic] over Rev. H.W. Cherry's donation of $6.000 to Seminary. Meeting of the Board of Education at 8:00. Considerable business done. Stay at Rev. W.C. Day's.

Saturday, May 3 Call at Dr. L. Davis' a short time. Meet Rev. Geo. Miller in finance Committee a half hour. Board meets at 9:00. Various business and discussions of topics. Dine at Prof. G. Funkhouser's with Geo. Miller and Prof. W.R. Shuey. Com. Meeting at 1:30 Make out report. Discussion of topics on the board. Adjourned about 5:00. Supper at Prof. A.W. Drury's. She a polished lady of natural manner. He full of facts on our history of the Church. Landis lectured at 8:00. Stay at Rev. A.W. Drury's on Broadway St, near 1st. Considerable rain in the night.

Sunday, May 4 Call at Dr. L. Davis' Bp. J. Weaver pr at

10:30 baccalaureate Prov. 11:30, "He that winest souls is wise." A good discourse, well read. Dined at J.W. Hott's, with Rev. W.C. Day & family & Shupe & Freeze and Foust & Lorin (my son). Staid till after supper. Called at Recher's, to see the boys. Bp. E.B. Kephart pr. at 7:30. Zech 14:6. Topic the greater evidences to day on the truth of revelation than the past. Stay at Reeder's. Tell Lorin of Gorman's being after him wanting to see him next morning to make him chief bookkeeper.

Monday, May 5 Call to see Sines. Call at the house—at Marcus, my renter's. Called meeting of the Board of Education. Kiracofe appt. to deliver annual address at Gen. Conference. Dine at Rev. M.R. Drury's. Call at Davis'. Supper there. Called at Marcu's. He away. At entertainments of the literary societies at 7:30. J.C. Keezle's poem the best thing for the occasion. Stay at Dr. L. Davis'. He gives R. Rock a rocking. Rock said he never looked after his members, whether they were secretists or not.

Tuesday, May 6 Meeting of the U.B. Seminary Board. Dine at Mulholland's below Miami Chapel. Sister Edwards & Electa Mahan there. At board meeting in the afternoon. Supper at Recher's. Attended the lecture at Summit Street to hear Rev. Wm. G. Morehead lecture, on Students Tools. Stay at Recher's.

Wednesday, May 7 Attended board meeting at Seminary. Dine at Dillon's with Rev. J. Crayton. Attend Sem. Board meeting. It adjourned to meet next year. Supper at Rev. W.C. Day's with Bp. E.B. Kephart. Went to see Marcus my renter. He paid me one month's rent—paid up to April 4th. Attend the Alumni meeting at Summit St. Church. P.M. France, J.S. Sentman, and D.N. Howe spoke. Stay at Dr. L. Davis'.

Thursday, May 8 Called at David Huffman's to see Aunt "Tena" (Christina); also go to the pastor's study at arrange a circular for White River Ministerial Institute. Called at Wm. Dillon's—saw Jere Hoffman's widow there. Dine at S.L. Herr's. Went to Wm. Ferguson's in Dayton View. Got the names and dates relating to her father's family—Reuben Reeder's. Went to the *Telescope* office. Supper at John Gilbert's. Attend graduating exercises of Union biblical Seminary at Summit Street. M.S. Dovey, E.W. Bowers, J.S. Brown, S.D. Faust, W.O. Fries, B.F. Fritz, J.B. Hawkins, J.G. Hoffacre, J. Oliver

Fremont Spain, Jas. Turner, & L.E. Wilson spoke. Stay at Dr. Davis'.

Friday, May 9 Went over to east side. Bought a letter file. Rented pruner's property. Telephoned to Reuchlin to that effect Lunched at the Depot. Went on the C.C.C. & I. train to Miamisburg. On hack thence to Germantown, Ohio, to Meeting of Mission Board. Put up at A.K. Burtner's. Supper there, Rev. J.K. Billheimer lectured dryly that evening. I Lodge at Burtner's.

Saturday, May 10 Attend Board Meeting. Meet committee. Dine at Burtner's. Supper at A. Rodabaugh's. In afternoon, the effort to reduce *Oregon to Mission Dist. failed. Evening session before and after the annual sermon which was delivered by G.W. Funkhouser from Rom. 1:16,17. Stay at Burtner's. Burtner's children at home: Ida 18 ys.; Carrie 14; boy 10, Myrtie 7. The oldest daughter at Otterbein about to graduate in June, aged 21. *I had come to fight D.K. Flickinger's plan to reduce Oregon, but my effort was not needed.

Sunday, May 11 At Sabbath School after a call on Father Jacob Burtner's. Bishop Glossbrenner pr. at 10:30 Rev. "Behold I set before thee an open door," etc. Dine at Burtner's with Bishop J. Dickson & others. At Sabbath School address and Missions in the afternoon, at 3:00. Supper at Ezra Kenp's. Heard Mrs. Keister & Pike on Woman's missionary work, at 8:00. Stay at a Mr. Zehring's with Rev. Halleck Floyd.

Monday, May 12 Go to A.K. Burtner's before breakfast. After breakfast, take hack at Shank's for Miamisburg. Go on to Dayton. Go to 226 Zigler St. to see the corpse of David Louding, the colored boy from Africa, daughter's son of Chief Stephen Caulker. Dined at Recher's with the boys. Called at Rev. W.C. Day's. Went on 1:00 train to Richmond. H. Floyd along. Saw Jas. Martindale on cars. Says that White Water Association has about 250 members. The [unreadable] Baptist about as many or more. The churches rather diminishing within the past 25 years.

Tuesday, May 13 At home. Fixed up business in town somewhat. Sent off sample *Stars* to Parkersburg, Muskingum & Western Reserve preachers. Mr. Frindle came to look at house to rent if we got out—he and his wife.

Friday, May 16 Prepared & arranged for the first side of June *Star*. Went on 4:00 aft. train to New Castle. Stopped at Wm. C. Gowdy's, and tarried there for the night. Saw Harvey Root. Hi is rather discouraged with the propsects of the Church at New Castle. Find myself disappointed about getting a train at 6:30 in the morning.

Saturday, May 17 Called at Harvey Roots, Mrs. Eliz. Bowman's, Mrs. Betsy Schildknecht's. Went on a 9:00 freight to Muncie. Lunched at Restaurant. Rev. A.R. Day finds me a way to go out to Bethel—in Franklin Day's buggy—Call at A.R. Day's to feed the horse. Preach at Bethel at 2:00, I Cor. 13:13. A pleasant quarterly conf. followed. Supper at Joshua Null's. Pr. at 8:00, I Tim 2:6. I Stay at Null's, Rev. J.M. Cook & wife there also. Mrs. Randolph there, Mother of Horner Venneman whom Null's raised and of Lincoln Randolph, whom I stood against the door to learn him to stand 23 ys ago, now married and having two or three children.

Sunday, May 18 Pr. at 10:30, I Cor. 5:7. Communion followed. Two joined Church—Miss Huldah Iseley and Mrs. Lizzie Stephenson—I took them in the Church. Dined at John Hayden's near the Church. Call at Dr. Franklin Day's. She is a daughter of Rev. John Kiger's. At three, Rev. J.M. Cook baptizes 24 persons just below the bridge—one by trine emersion, a Mrs. Netzley. Supper at Null's. Preach at 8:00 John 7:37. Lodge at Joshua Null's.

Monday, May 19 Joshua Null takes me to Reed Station on Lake Erie & Western Railroad. Wait awhile at the store for a train. Go on 10:55 train to Muncie; then on 1:50 tr. to New Castle and on 3:20 to Richmond. Arrive at home about 5:00.

Wednesday, May 21 At home. Attempt to write some. Overhaul my files of Newspapers, etc.

Thursday, May 22 At home. Write some. Read up proofs and make up first side of June *Star*.

Friday, May 23 Wrote some in the forenoon. Got ready and went to Indianapolis on the 2:32 train. Supper at Walter S. Brown's, K. Elida Wiley and Mrs. Nannie Brown out on a visit in town. Stay at Rev. T.J. Connor's. He tells me from a letter that Walker Diffi is still raging

at Philomath, Oregon. Rev. J.E. Connor evangelizing on holiness on an undenominational basis. Bro. Jas. Edwards (Ore.) is much discouraged.

Saturday, May 24 Go on 7:15 train to Jackson Station. Stop at Geo. Rubush's. Rev. O.E. Evans, the pastor and Rev. W.C. Neal came; also Bro. N. Bentley & wife & Sister Huldah Purtee, Rev. Saml. Purtee's widow. I walked up to New Hope Sch. House. Pr. at 2:00 Rev 5:1. Seven Seals. Went up to Sharpsville and staid at Rev. D.P. Rubush's. His wife is daughter of Jacob Rubush with whom I had my home part of the time when pastor at Indianapolis in 1855-56. Her children are Clyde 12 years, Alice Ida 10, Carl 7, Ethel May 5, Leala 2.

Sunday, May 25 I rode down to New Hope to Coleman Quin's, with Rev. D.P. Rubush & boys. Pr. at 10:30, Ps 48:11,12,13. Communion followed. Dine at H. Tarkington's 1/4 S. fo Sch. H. He is nephew of M.E. P.E. Tarkington of Greensburg, Ind. pr. at 3:30 John 1:29. Walk down to Jackson Station. Supper & lodging at Geo. Rubush's. Their children are 11 in number. I had held a quarterly meeting a Jackson Station in 1861-62. I staid then at Redman's and perhaps other's houses.

Monday, May 26 Walked to Tipton Junction with Rev. E.O. Evans. Neal meets us there. Go on 9:30 train to Alexandria. Thence on 12:55 tr. to Fairmount. Prepare an article (finish) for *Star* on "Our First Frontier Mission," mail it to my publisher. Go to Anderson's & from there to Carter Hasting's. Mother Hasting had been much afflicted with eresipelas, etc. Supper there. Called at Robt. Hasting's. Then at John Smith's; he aged 76 ys. past. Rev. D.E. Myers' pr at 8:00, Rom. 8:3, an able sermon. Stay at John Smith's with I.M. Tharp. Mrs. McClure, Smith's aged widowed sister there. Her daughter was C.B. Small's first wife.

Tuesday, May 27 District Conference. Rev. William Hall on Minister's treatment of each other. Rev. M.M. Thomas on "What to do with regular appointments during revivals." N.L. Hoopingarner on Better attendance at preaching services. D.E. Myers on Missionary & other chart collections. I dine at John Smith's. Afternoon, Cyrus Smith on Increase of Biblical Knowledge among Our people. C.W. Rector on Conducting revivals. J.Y. Demumbrun on Attendance at Prayer & Class meetings. Supper at Cell's. Sermon at 8:00 M.M. Thomas I Cor. 15:50. Cook's (J.M.) unique exhortation. Stay at Ab. Anderson's with Cousin Wm. Reeder who pays me $38.50 next morning.

Wednesday, May 28 Went to town (Fairmount) with Wm. Reeder to the post-office & back with A. Anderson. Ministerial Association continues. Hall on Attendance at qr. Conferences & other business meetings. Wright on occupying our Cities. Myers reply & Wright's rejoinder Dine at Keever's. Question "box" and answers. Quite interesting. Topics continued Kethner on Christmas tree & other holiday entertainment. Wright on other churches occupying our houses with regular appoint's & organizing in—our church houses. Supper & lodging at Elwood Davis's in Fairmount. Their Children Mary Alice Harvey (Colorado Springs) 26 Clara (Cheney)22, Edwin C. 20; Willis 15, Charles 13; Albert Alfred 10; Constantine 8; Nancy 4. I.M. Tharp pr. at 8:00 Deut. 31:12.

Thursday, May 29 Session Sabbath School Convention part of the Distr. Conference. Rather hurried. Not very spirited. Called to see Mother Carter Hastings. She very much worried with eresipelas. Dinner at Robt. Hastings. Afternoon session quite good. Hall on Taking our own S.S. Literature. Milgrove chosen as the place of next year's meeting. Same time of year as now. M.M. Thomas on Home Reading Circle course of Study. Bell on Sabbath School singing Report of Com. on Resolutions. Supper at John Smith's with Wm. Hall and others. Evening experience meeting Good. I stay at Robt. Hastings with Thomas Bell & O.E. Evans.

Friday, May 30 Walked to Fairmount. Found the local train had gone to Marion. Went to Elwood Davis's. Tehy send Willis (Davis) to take me to Jonesboro. Mail article for *Star* on the noon train & go on tr. to Hartford City. Wrote considerable for the *Star*. Went over to Ft. Wayne depot to mail a communication for *Star*, but disappointed. Mailed it at Hartford. Heard Elder J. Maple speak on decoration day—short part of the speech. Saw Russel & David Stover & son Samuel. I went on 6:00 train to Red Key and thence with Frank Wonget & Rev. M.M. Thomas. Supper at Thomas's. Preach at 8:30 at Good Will Sch. H. Heb. 12:28. Lodge at Rev. M.M. Thomas' 1/4 m. west of Sch. House which is two miles

S.E. of Camden, Jay Co.

Saturday, May 31 Staid at Thomas' till about 11:00. Went to Peter McDaniel's for dinner. Pr. at 2:00, Rev. 5:1. Qr. Conference followed. Pleasant session. John Taylor Roberts recommended to annual Conference. Reports on salary short. Supper at Peter McDaniel's. Rev. Lorin H. Waldo pr. at 8:00, Luke 15:18, "I will arise" etc I exhorted. I stay at M.M. Thomas's. Their family are M.M. Aged 33; Sarah Eliz. 29; Ethelbert Lomax 10; Nancy Anna 8. She a half sister of Mrs. Elwood (Rachel) Davis—a Shugart, dau. of Henry Shugart, near Liberty Church in Grant County.

Sunday, June 1 I pr. at Good Will Grove at 10:30. Large collection of people. Communion. Dine at Bishop Addington's with Sutton's, Fuqua's & Hartup's. Rev. M.M. Thomas pr. at 3:00. Rain interferes. Supper at Rev. M.M. Thomas'. Mr. Ambrose Taylor takes me to the train at Red Key. I lodge at Mrs. Murray's boarding house till 3:00 morn. & take the fast train to Ridgeville. I had called at another "hotel" & heard the land-lord's tirade against Christians & left. Called at M.E. Church. Heard Rev. Mr. McKeg.

Monday, June 2 Awoke about 2:00. Went on 3:10 tr. to Ridgeville. Breakfast at the Sumption House, 40 cts. Wrote several cards. Went on 8:00 train to Richmond. Read some proofs on the *Star*.

Tuesday, June 3 Read up some more proofs on the *Star*. Made up the *Star* in the afternoon and got to wrapping and directing it. Also called to see Mother Koerner awhile.

Wednesday, June 4 Engaged in directing papers to subscribers, etc. all day. Finished about 4:00. Mailed a letter and card to Reuchlin on the 7:30 train. Felt quite tired. Slept perhaps 8 1/2 hours!

Thursday, June 5 Finished directing sample copies of the paper out. Spent some time in editting [sic] communications and arranging for the 1st pages of next month's *Star*. In forenoon settled for programmes $1.50 circulars $1.50, and paid for seven quires of Manilla paper $1.05, and $23.60: Total, $27.65.

Friday, June 6 I got ready and started for Fayette Co., via Dunreith, Rushville, Glenwood. Dined at Hotel at Dunreith, just south of Pan Handle depot, kept by Westerfield, an ex-Methodist, now Presbyterian. Went on 3:20 train to Rushville. There, when news came of the nomination of Jas. G. Blaine for President. i approved it, but disappointed of the nomination of Logan (afterward) for vice-president. Reached Glenwood about 6:30. Walked a mile & then rode with a Mr. McGrew to Fayetteville. Stopped awhile at Dr. Sipe's to see Estella Harris, my niece. Went on to Anson Moor's. they had gone to bed.

Saturday, June 7 Called at N.F. Bowen's. Visited the grave of my Father & Mother on the old home farm. Precious is the memory of their conspicuous integrity, affection & faithfulness. Dine at Anson Moor's. He takes me to Glenwood. I go on 3:17 train to Rushville & thence on 4:00 train to Greensburg. Found Granville Edwards and Miss Davenport on train. Go on 7:30 train to Hartsville Crossing, 3 miles N. of Hartsville. Go on Russel's hack to Hartsville. Lit. Societies hold a joint entertainment. Miss Laura Davenport, Elmer E. Fix, and Miss Fast among the speakers. I stay at Wm. Fix's—Prof. Fix's.

Sunday, June 8 Attended class-meeting at 9:30. Pres. C.H. Kiracofe pr. Phil. 4:8. Good discourse. Dine at Christian Godfrey Mensch's. At Sabbath School in the afternoon at 2:30. Few out on account of rain. Supper at Prof. C.H. Kiracofe's. Call at Roberts' and spend over a half hour. He a student from Blackford County. Rev. D.B. Keller pr. Heb. 11:6—evidences of Christianity. I stay at Rev. E. Pitman's with Rev. Halleck Floyd.

Monday, June 9 Called at John Anderson's. Attend a recitation in Language in Pres. Kiracofe's room. Dine at Rev. J.D. Current's. Board meeting at 1:30. Supper at Isaac Vansickle's. Rev. Sloss of Greensburg (Presbyterian) delivered an address before the literary societies. It was rather fragmentary, but good in ideas, clothed in good language, somewhat dramatic in portions of delivery, and earnest in manner throughout. In its tone it was manly and noble. I stay at Fix's with Halleck Floyd.

Tuesday, June 10 Board meeting at 10:00. Attended prayers at Chapel at 7:30, and had com. meetings afterward till board meeting. Dine at Jas. Funkhouser's (Prof.)

with Rev. H. Floyd. Board meeting at 1:30. A recess and Com. meetings. Resumed meeting of the board of trustees. Supper at Tyner's with Rev. A.C. Wilmore's wife & with Lizzie Billing and Miss Gordon, her niece. Board meeting at 6:30. Mr. C.N. Spencer delivered the Allumnal address at 8:00. A good address but articulation so rapid and imperfect, as to be more than half lost to the audience. Stay at Prof. Wm. Fix's.

Wednesday, June 11 Called at Rev. John Riley's. They are my old host and hostess with whom I boarded 31 years ago, now aged and feeble. Attended a meeting of the Board at 8:00. Subscription being the object. Considerable talk, but little subscription. Commencement exercises at 10:30. Music vocal & instrumental. Graduating addresses by Frank J. Bennett on Education by the State and by Alonzo Meyer on "What shall our Monument be?" Master's Oration by M.F. Daws on on [sic] "Our immortal Mission." Dine at Prof. S. Werts. Rev. A.C. Wilmore takes me to Hope. I go on hack to St. Louis Crossing & take 6:00 train to Cambridge City. At Cambridge I telegraph to J.F. Miller for leave to go home on freight train. Granted. Arrive at home about 12:30. (I then lived in Richmond.)

Thursday, June 12 At home arranging matters. I arrange for sending goods to Dayton, Saturday. Write Reuchlin & Lorin. I write to Clara & Samuel Wright to see if Clara can come & live with us. Buy ticket and mail letters on train. Engage what money we need of D.K. Zeller.

Friday, June 13 Went on 6:00 a.m. train (freight) to Ridgeville and thence by close connection to Hartford. Rev. N.L. Hoopingarner takes me to Wm. Knox's, who were from home, and thence to Samule Russell's where we dine. We go on to Bethel Church, 3 1/2 miles Southwest of Montpelier. I pr. at 2:00 I Cor. 16:2. Quarterly conference followed. Supper at John Kirk's, 1/2 m. east of the Church, with Hoopingarner. Pr. at 8:00 Matt. 19:27. Good congregation. Some went out & I rubbed them up somewhat in good humor. Stay with Rev. H. at Kirk's. Kirk's children: Retta & Ed.

Saturday, June 14 Went with Rev. N.L. Hoopingarner to dundee. I baptize Katie Robb and George Blount and George Bodine by immersion. Dine at John L. Russell's. Bro. Hoopingarner takes me on to Oak Chapel church

4 miles west of Dundee. I preach at 2:00, Rev. 5:1. Supper at Frank M. Baker's. I pr. at 8:00, I Cor. 1:23-4. Stay at John Stout's. Their boys at home are Wm. E., Geo, & John W. Our family shipped our goods today—Dayton, Ohio and Wilbur and Orville go over there.

Sunday, June 15 I pr. at Oak Chapel at 10:30, 2 Pet. 1:16. Sacramental service followed. I take up some subscription for the pastor. I dined at Jonathan Hodgson's. His mind is affected, and he is away. His sons are Benjamin, Jasper & Irvin (twin brothers), Martha, Alice, George, John, William. I go with Benj. Hodson to Bethel. Pr. at 5:00, I John 5:18,19. Communion. Go on to Wm. Knox, 4 ms. N.E. of Hartford City & stay there.

Monday, June 16 Rev. John Selig comes and after noon to Jas. W. Pittenger's in the Pleasant Dale neighborhood—perhaps 5 ms. east of Knox's. Pr. at 9:00, Matt. 5:12. "Great is your reward," and Pleas't Dale Sch. House, a brick school-house crowded. Oil out of the lamp causes considerable delay. Stay at J.W. Pittinger's with Selig. Pettinger's children: Effa 18.

Tuesday, June 17 Went over across the road to Geo. W[page torn] Rev. M.M. Thomas & wife there. They, Wyandt, & Selig, sing. Wyandt's children: Onie, 8; Ora 5, Orliepa 2. Go on over to Bro. Wm. Knox's. Stay there till 8:30, evening. Go over to Grandmother Sarah Stallsmiths & unite in marriage at 9:00 Rev. N.L. Hoopingarner and Miss Dora Emma Stallsmith the daughter of Wm. B. Stallsmith (deceased) and Mary Ann Stallsmith. John Selig along. Stay there. Quite a success as to keeping it secret about the wedding. Susan went to Dayton that day.

Wednesday, June 18 Went to Hartford City. Called at Howel's. Went to the post-office, got [unreadable] till the afternoon. Wrote cards to class-stewards. In the afternoon, got proof on the *Star*, forwarded from Richmond. Walk back to Brent Knox's. Father Joseph Runkle & wife of Forest Hill (Knox brother-in-law) [passage is unreadable] Very warm day. We move our goods into Pruner's house.

Thursday, June 19 Finished reading up the proofs on the *Star*. Very warm day. Go with Knox's to Hartford.

Send proofs to Martin & Coe. Dine at Cowel's. Found them an intelligent and pleasant family. Write some & go on 3:30 aft. tr to Marion. Mail a letter to Bish. J. Dickson. Call at Rev. Robt. W. Fryer's. Go on Narrow Guage R.R. to Buckeye. Supper at Joseph Irick's. They take me to Zion. I pr at 8:15 I Tim. 2:6. Stay at Rev. W.C. Ketner's, close by.

Friday, June 20 Called at George Shaffer's an hour. Dined at Joseph Eubanks'. Rev. W.C. Ketner takes me to Buck Eye & I go on train to Van Buren. Get letter from Susan, who had got to Dayton & found the house in miserable order. Telephoned & telegraphed to Lorin, my son, at Dayton. Walked out to Jacob Cochran's. His children at home: George Daniel Sherman, & Susan Alvira. Stay at Cochran's.

Saturday, June 21 Stop at Cochran's & write some editorials. Sleep an hour. Dine there. Go to Welcome Chapel and pr. at 2:00 I Cor 16:1. A nice Qr. Conf. followed. Supper at Cora's. Meeting at 8:30. Pr. at Welcome Rom. 7:13. A good large evening congregation. Stay at John William Hodgson's. His wife is Lucy. They are M.E. people. Amos Kapach & a Mr. Tharp stay there also.

Sunday, June 22 Pr. at Welcome 10:30, Acts 11:24. Communion. Took Wm Wesley Tharp—not a relative of Isaac M.—into the Church. Dine at Jacob Cochran Rev. W.C. Ketner pr. at 3:00, I Pet. 4:18. Bro. Jacob Cochran takes me to J.G. Parlet's and we get supper there. Bor. Parlett takes me to Rev. R.W. Fryer's in North marion. Stay there till 2:00 morning. Walk over and take the 2:12 tr. at 2:38. Go to Union City. Breakfast at Rev. W.J. Pruner's. He goes to Dayton with me.

Monday, June 23 Arriving at Dayton about 10:00, find the folks in Pruner's house, 2d lot N. of Second St., on Summit St., east side of the St. Puner goes to town and arranges for papering the House. I go to town, leave my watch, Call at book-store and at Hott's, etc. Our House is 114 N. Summit St.

Tuesday, June 24 Write for *Star*, and some letters. Pruner dined with us.

Wednesday, June 25 Write and mail editorial matter. Go over to East Side at 11:00. Fail to get my watch from

Reeves' shop. Get form of application for clergyman's ticket on C.C.C. & I. R.R. It begins a fine rain before I get back. Paper hangers begin work. Wrote an editorial and mailed on 6:10 train. At prayer-meeting at 8:00, evening.

Thursday, June 26 Call on Dr. L. Davis. Went with Susan in afternoon and bought paper to paper our house nicely on Hawthorn St. Called at Prugh & DeWies Store. Got my watch, fee $1.50, at Reeve Brothers. Went on 8:12 train to Richmond. Staid at Isaac Huddleston's, not finding D.K. Zeller's house lighted up—they being at prayer-meeting.

Friday, June 27 Read up proofs on editorial pages of the Star and made up the paper. Called at Zeller's in the morning. Went on 10:30 train to Decatur, Adams Co., Ind., and by leaving train at the corssing, and hastening, made connection with the Chicago& Atlantic & reached Huntington at about 3:00 pm. Saw Rev. John R. Brown and Rev. J.H. Simon & Young Dungan who lives there. Went on 4:13 train to Adnrews. Called at Crammer's. Went with Jesse Hall's son to Mt. Zion vicinity. Staid at Noggle's.

Saturday, June 28 Remain at Nobble's till afternoon. Went to quarterly meeting at 2:00 at Mt. Zion. Pr. at 2:00 from I Cor. 15:58. Qr. Conference followed. Pleasant session. Wm. Frank Parker and Roland Z. Brown recommended to St. Joseph Conference. Supper at Stevens' Rev. C. Smith pr at 8:30, Stay at Noggle's. 2 1/2 m. S.E. of the Church. Robt. Morrow of Marion & wife. Sister Barker of Pleasant Grove & others stay there, also.

Sunday, June 29 Pr. at Mt. Zion at 10:30 2 Cor. 3:8. Communion followed. Mrs. Vicar & Mrs. Nancy Ellen Hull joined the Church. Dined at Martin Jennings. Rev. Mr. Talbert pr at 4:00. Go on with Rev. John Heavenridge, to Lincolnville. Supper at Heavenridge's. Pr. at Lincolnville at 8:00 Matt. 5:12. A good congregation. Stay at Heavenridge's.

Monday, June 30 Dined at Raferd Copeland's with Rev. J. Heavenridge. Went on to Marshall H. Coomler's. Supper at Lewis Farrington's. They are cutting wheat. Mrs. L.W. Matthews & Kemp Matthews there. Their (F's) daughter, Mrs. Presler, sick. Bro. Heavenridge takes

me on to Jacob Thomas' three miles N.E. of La Fountain. I lodge there.

Tuesday, July 1 Went to La Fountain. Take the train to Fairmount & arrive there about 9:00. Write letters and card at the post-office. Go with Isadore McShea to the old farm. Dine there. Look over the farms. Clover nice. Timothy fair. Wheat thin. Corn small. Walked over to Uncle Wm. H.H. Reeder's. Supper & lodging there.

Wednesday, July 2 Stay at Uncle's in forenoon. Edit some Communications for the Star. Stay also in the afternoon & lodge there. Had spent some time editing Tharp's address.

Thursday, July 3 Went to Fairmount with Uncle Wm. Reeder. Write some letters and cards. Take the 1:23 train to Marion. Lunch there. Write a letter to Coe about Tharp's address. Had mailed 4 articles for first side of August *Star.* Write another card. Call at Rev. R.W. Fryer's. Walk on to the parsonage, Rev. J.Y. Demunbrun's. Call at Robinson's. Supper, at DeMunbrun's. Stay at DeMunbrun's.

Friday, July 4 After breakfast, Bro. Demunbrun takes me to train. Go on the train to La Fountaine. Saw Elias Stone; also Dr. Alex. Thomas, who used to be a boyhood associate. Got a letter from Susan. She had sent another which I got at Jacob Thomas' where I dined. Staid at Thomas's this afternoon & lodged there to-night.

Saturday, July 5 Went to Samuel Thomas'. Wm. Dubois & wife there. Dined. Went to Bethany Church. Pr. at 2:00, Rom. 11:20. Supper at Michael Myers. Henry Ketner pr. at 8:00, Ro [blank] Stay at Jonathan Myers', who lives a mile South-east of the Church, with Rev. David E. Myers.

Sunday, July 6 Pr. at 10:30, Ps. 90:17. Communion followed. Dine at Mrs. Barbary Keith's. Love-fease in the afternoon. Stay with Rev. D.E. Myers at Samuel Thomas'.

Monday, July 7 Bro Thomas' son takes me & Myers to La Fountain. See Dr. James Dickens there at Depot. Go on to Marion. Put up at D.E. Myers. Eat a lunch and go on 11:30 train to Union City. Merely call at Rev. W.J.

Pruners. Go on to Dayton, arriving about 5:00, p.m.

Friday, July 11 Get proofs on *Star* in afternoon. Go on 5:35 train to Union City Stay at Rev. W.J. Pruner's. Sleep a full night.

Saturday, July 12 Got a clergyman's pass on the C.C.C. & I. Railroad. Go on 9:16 train to North Grove. Dine at Henry Fry's. Pr. at 2 Matt. 18:20. Quarterly conference followed. Supper at Wm. H. Redman's. Pr. at 8:30, Ps. 1:6. Stay at Br. Redman's.

Sunday, July 13 Pr. at 10:30, 2 Cor. 3:8. Communion followed. Dine at Rev. Wm. Bowden's. Rev Jas. Perry preached at 4:00, Ps. 8:4. I exhort. Went to Jas. Boyer's 2 miles north-east and staid to-night. She had one son and two daughters and he one son at home. A very pleasant family to visit.

Monday, July 14 Went to Wm. Boyer's 1/2 mile south and staid till after dinner. His wife a daughter of Father Rankin that I formerly saw in the quarterly conference, 23 years ago. Jas. Boyer takes me in his buggy to town & I stop at Rev. Wm. Bowden's, the Pastor's. Call at Redman's and get my valise & at Fry's and get my thick coat. Go on 4:00 train to Xenia. Stay at Thomas Darby's.

Tuesday, July 15 Stay in forenoon at Darby's. Write letters to Revs. Tharp & Hoopingarner & Thomas. Also write a letter to Susan. Dine at Darby's. Remain at Darby's till evening. Pr. at 8:15, Ex. 28:34. Stay at Darby's.

Wednesday, July 16 Went over to Wm. Hermon's, 1 1/2 mile west of town. his mother lives with them. His wife a teacher and a well-accomplished woman. Call in at John Van Dolson's, about half way back to town. Father Merine & wife there. Go on to town & take the 4:20 train to Marion & thence to Fairmount, and to Carter Hastings! Stay there. Got a letter a Fairmount from home.

Thursday, July 17 Stay at Hasting's till after Dinner. Go to Fairmount and ride over with Dan Richards to Uncle Wm. H.H. Reeder's. Stay there.

Friday, July 18 Wm. (junior) takes me over to my farm and we look at the crops. Return to Uncle's. Stay there till morning.

Saturday, July 19 Flora takes me to 7:35 train. Go on to Marion & thence in an hour to Herbst. Stop at Littleton Davis's. Morrison's, Hastings, Cells', etc. Stop there also for dinner. Pr. at 2:00, I Cor. 16:2. Rev. Wm. Hall pr. at 8:00. "I am the true vine," etc. Supper & lodging at Enoch Babb's in town, with Rev. Wm. Hall's.

Sunday, July 20 Went down to Lit. Davis after Breakfast. Pr. at Meth. Protestant Church at Herbst at 10:30, Heb. 4:14. Communion. Raised 7.27 missionary money. Dine at Wm. Cabe's with Bro. Rector. Love-feast meeting at 4:00. Quite good. Supper at Davis'. Rev. W.C. Ketner pr. at 8:00, Rom. 6:22. A good meeting throughout. Staid at Davis' with Wm. Ketner's.

Monday, July 21 Call at John W. Rust's and at Mrs. Herbst. Go on the 9:08 train to marion, & thence on 11:40 train to Union City and on the train thence home to Dayton, arriving alittle before 5:00 p.m. Found all in common health.

Tuesday, July 22 At home. Write an editorial. Mail some editorial & communications to Richmond for the *Star.*

Wednesday, July 23 Went to Dr. Samples dentist office and he fills a tooth for me. While there an alarm of fire comes from John Dodd's rake factory on the west side of the river. With a strong west wind blowing five houses, east of the shop, and several stables are burned. The shops & lumber were partly destroyed. Damage many thousands. Writing editorials part of the afternoon. Mail some editorial matter on the 6:30 train.

Thursday, July 24 Again at the dentist shop part of the forenoon. Writing editorials. At Home. Called at Dr. Davis' about 8:00 & staid an hour.

Friday, July 25 At Home. Wrote up considerable of editorial items. Went on 1:30 train to Richmond, Ind., called at D.K. Zeller's, and then went to the office and folded & wrapped a lot of July *Stars,* and read proofs on August editorial pages. Supper & lodging at Zeller's.

Saturday, July 26 Rose early & tok a sponge bath. Prepared some July *Stars* to mail—read up proofs. Went up to *Telegram* Job office and read proofs. Mailed papers. Worked at overseeing make up of editorial side. Go on 10:15 train to Elwood. Jefferson Connor Clymer meets me & takes me home with him. Dine. Pr. at Hopewell at 3:00 Heb. 12,1. Supper at Alpheus Wiley McIntosh's, one of my old acquaintance, at Dublin, Ind. A fine rain. No meeting in consequence. Lodge at Nimrod Bentley's.

Sunday, July 27 Called at J. Connor Clymer's. Pr. in the grove 1/4 mile south at 11:00 Mal. 3:1. Communion followed. Dine on the ground with Nimrod Bentley's. Rev. Thomas Bell pr. at 3:30, Go to Mrs. Huldah Purtee's, 1/2 m. S.E. of Hopewell Church. Supper there. Rev. O.E. Evans pr. I Kings 19:31. Stay at Stretcher's 2 miles south of the Church.

Monday, July 28 Went to Ellwood. Went on train to Alexandria. Write a dozen cards. Go to Fairmount. Write a letter there. Supper at Mr. Hollingsworth's (Wm. Hall's soninlaw's). Go on 8:00 train to Jonesboro; put up at Cleeland Hotel, not succeeding in finding friends at home.

Tuesday, July 29 After breakfast, go out to J.L. Pegram's. She a second cousin of mine. Return to Jonesboro. Dine at H. Simon's. Stay at Jonesboro till evening, having given out going home this wek. Go to Fairmount on 8:00 train. Stay at Elwood Davis'. Mrs. Pegram's name is Eliza. Their son's name is Euphelius.

Wednesday, July 30 Write letters. Go to Friends meeting at 11:00. Pr. John 17.17. Dine at Elwood Davis'. Go on to Absalom Anderson's. Supper there. Go to John Smith's 1 1/2 m south of town and lodge there. They are over 70 years of age. He quite hard of hearing. They are quileless, friendly in the strongest & sincerest sense of these terms. He is an "Israelite, without quile." His sons are married; Wm., Roland, Leander. His daughter is Robert Hasting's wife.

Thursday, July 31 Went to Absalom Anderson & he takes me in a spring wagon to Fairmount. I write some & go to the depot, and find that some of my grain is hauled in. Wait at Depot for Reeders or McShay's to come in. McShay's finish sell all it brings 114. Send a draft to D.K. Zeller on Lanier & Winslow. Go on to

Uncle Reeder's with Isadore McShay, most of the way. Stay at Reeder's.

Friday, August 1 Stay at Reeder's till after supper. Then go with Uncle Wm. H.H. Reeder to Joseph A. Broyles. Stay there.

Saturday, August 2 Went to Carpenter. Met John Broyles & family on the way. They are going to Uncle Reeder's. Carpenter takes me to Olive Chapel. I pr. Supper at Rev. Arthur Rector's. He is building a new house costing him about $2,000. Rev. C.W. Rector pr. at 8:00. I go on to Rev. C.W. Rector's and lodge.

Sunday, August 3 Pr at Olive Zech. 13:9. Com. followed Dined at Edward Benbow's. Love-feast meeting & Sacramental service at 3:30. Right good. Stay at James Rector's with Rev. J.M. Cook.

Monday, August 4 Rev. J.M. Cook takes me to Muncie. Write home. Af[t]er some business, I go to the Depot & spend the time in making out my report to Annual Conference. Go on 1:50 train to New Castle & thence to Hamilton Station and to Harvey Wright's, my brother's. Stay there.

Tuesday, August 5 Called at Dan & John Wright's. Dine at Jabez Rhode's. Call again at Harvey's. See Ed. Finzer's. Take the train to Rushville & thence to Greensburg & thence to Hartsville & find my home at John Anderson's north of College Campus. Rev. J.T. Hobson my fellow-boarder.

Wednesday, August 6 The joint session of White River and Indiana Conference convened at 8:30. White River after the joint session examined the character of local preachers. Dinner at Anderson's Com. on 3d years' reading at 1:30. At night, Rev. P.B. Williams preached. Hartsville College board met at 6:30.

Thursday, August 7 Examination of White River itinerants in the forenoon. Dine at Anderson's. Com. on Boundaries in the afternoon. Supper at Rev. M.C. Dawson's. Meeting of the Board of Hartsville College at 6:30 p.m. Rev. L.S. Chittenden pr at 8:00 "The master cometh & calleth for thee." Stay at Anderson's.

Friday, August 8 Conf. proceeded. I was elected presiding-elder by 35 out of 40 votes on first ballot; McNew by 25 votes. Katerich elected on 4th ballot. Dined either to-day or to-morrow at Jery Dean's—forgot which. Stationing Committee met at Pres. Kiracofe's about 8:00 & finished its business. Rev. J.K. Billheimer & W.J. Shuey occupy the time on Missions this evening at the College Chapel

Saturday, August 9 Conference business continues. Educational meeting at night. Addresses by Rev. L.S. Chittenden, Pres. C.H. Kiracofe, and Bishop E.B. Kephart. About $2,500 subscribed toward Hartsville.

Sunday, August 10 Bishop E.B. Kephart pr. in the college chapel at 10:30 I John 5:12. C.W. Rector, G.L. Mattox, O.L. Wilson of White River & others (of Indiana Conference) ordained. Dine at Rev. D. Clark's. Memorial Services of Revs. G. Muth, J.T. Vardman & Irvin Cox. Addresses by M. Wright, Z. McNew, and F.M. Moore. Sabbath School addresses in the evening. Stay at Andersons'.

Monday, August 11 Start early to Hartsville Crossing. Go to Greensburg & thence to Rushville & Dunreith & soon to Richmond & thence to Dayton. Find all at home as well as usual.

Wednesday, August 13 At home. Dr. L. Davis & Rev. Wm. Dillon spent an hour or two in the evening with me.

Saturday, August 16 Went on 9:22 A.M. train to Akron, Ohio. Supper at Peter Shaffers west of the canal. Rev. D. Kosht pr. at 8:00 "How good & pleasant it is for brethren to dwell together in unity." A good sermon. I staid at Shaffer's.

Sunday, August 17 Preached at the new church (Corner of Hill & James St.) Deut. 32:31. Secured $4.50 subscription on the Church debt. Dined at Mrs. Wilson's. Rode over with Rev. D. Kosht to Peter Shaffer's. Rev. W.H. Miller pr. at 8:00, "Upon this Rock" etc. Preached well. Stay at Shaffer's with W.H. Millar. There was a fine & much-needed rain in the afternoon.

Monday, August 18 Start on 6:00 A.M. train to Dayton.

Saw Rev. Baldwin on the train from sterling to Ashland. Locomotive got out of order & detained us an hour at or near Richwood. Arrived at Dayton about 3:00. Spent the remainder of the afternoon in resting.

Tuesday, August 19 Anniversary of Orville & Katie's birth-day. They call in several of their playmates in the afternoon.

Thursday, August 21 At Home. Did some letter writing.

Friday, August 22 At Home. Mainly resting. Got proofs on outside of Sept. Star. Went on 6:00 train to Arcanum. Rev. Mayne pr. at 8:00, "I shall be satisfied," etc. Ps. 17:15. Staid at Mr. Oldwine's Hotel with Rev. Mayne.

Saturday, August 23 At Conference. All the forenoon. Dine at Rev. Bair's Stay to part of the memorial service. Go on home to Dayton.

Sunday, August 31 Ella Wright with us to-day. Heard Rev. Matthews pr. at 10:30. Hear Matthews at 8:00.

Saturday, September 6 Ellis & Flora Wright (My nephew & niece) come in the afternoon.

Sunday, September 7 Heard Rev. S.A. Mowers pr at 10:30, at First U.B. Church. Heard pastor of First Presbyterian Church pr. at 7:30.

Monday, September 8 Flora & Ellis go home.

Friday, September 12 Went on the evening train to Union City. Staid at Rev. W.J. Pruner's.

Saturday, September 13 Missed the early local. Wrote many letters at the depot. Went on train (about 12:30) to Selma. Found Bro. Shull at Depot. He took me to Spangler's. Spangler took me to Mt. Zion where the quarterly meeting really was. I thought it was to be at Selma. Rev. G.W. Ford pr. at 7:30 Harvest is past. etc. Rather a pleasant speaker. I took supper at David Acupon's Christian Life; also lodged there. Bros. Ford and Platt Mott & their wives also staid there. [I learned that the quarterly conference resolved to pay me only 3/4 this quarter's salary on account of my absence.]

Sunday, September 14 Pr. at 10:30, Zachariah 13:9. Dined at Life's with Rev. G.H. Byrd & others. Call in the evening at Young John Life's Pr. at 7:30. Stay at Chas. Mourmon's.

Monday, September 15 Went on to Ridgeville.

Wednesday, September 17 Went down to Marion on business and arrang with sheriff Lanfester to delay the issue on an execution on Uncle property till, at least, Oct. 15th. Called at Geroge Carter's. Went on to John Y. Parlett's & stay there. He lives 4 miles north-east of Marion. Wm. Reeder Jr. with me. The sheriff is Lenfester.

Thursday, September 18 Went on via Marion & Carter's to Fairmount and thence to Uncle Reeder's. I got a card from Susan saying she was almost sick. We also got some cancer medicine for Uncle William who has a return of cancer, this time under his jaws. Fixed out form of sale bill for Uncle's. Then went to Simons' and Curtis' to [rest is blank]

Friday, September 19 Wm. (Reeder) took me to the train at Fairmount. I go on 8:03 train to Alexander & thence to Muncie. There I get a letter from Susan saying she was better, and I felt much relieved. Went on to McKown's Station. Call at Michael Wright's—he being an old acquaintance of Henry Co., and she (his second wife) is a sister of Harvey Jackson. Supper at Robert Wright's—he a son of Chas. Wright of Grant Co., Ind. A number of women there sowing [sic] rags for a missionary carpet. Pr. at 7:30 Rom. 3:5. Darling Tuttle, an ex-U.B., now a M.E. & a Mason there. Stay at Frank Nottingham's, 2 miles South-east of McKown's. The church at McKown's provided by the will of McKown as a union church with a school-house in first story.

Saturday, September 20 Staid at Bro. Nottingham's till after Dinner. Went to Macedonia & pr. Rom. 12:13, "Given to hospitality." Supper at [blank] Pr. at 8:00 probably Ps. 1:6. Stay at [blank]

Sunday, September 21 Pr. at 10:30 Ps. 92:8. Dine at Joel Chalplast's. Rev. A.R. Day, and his new wife at meeting that day. I pr. at 4:00. Go on to Selma. At Meeting there Rev. Davenport of the "New light" Church pr. at 8:00. Stay at Henry Spangler's, Rev. W.A. Oler's Father-in-law's.

Monday, September 22 Went on to Farmland. Dine at Father Rust's Go in Afternoon on train via Union City (home) at Dayton.

Thursday, September 25 Susan went with me on afternoon train to Richmond. Stay at D.K. Zeller's. Read up proofs.

Friday, September 26 Went on train to New Castle Called at Rev. D.O. Darling's. Go on to Royerton & stay at Rev. M.R. Harris's.

Saturday, September 27 Br. Harris sends me to James Rector's. Dine there. Bro. Rector takes me on to Bethel. Have no preaching but Qr. Conf. at 3:00. Supper at Joshua Null's. Mrs. Ducket pr. at 7:30. Stay at Dr. John Haden's.

Sunday, September 28 Pr. at 10:30 It was an extraordinarily rainy day. But afternoon was pleasant. Dine at Dr. Franklin Day's. Pr. at 7:30 Rom. 3:5. Stay at Joshua Nulls. J. Madison Cook & wife also stay there.

Monday, September 29 Bro. Null takes me to Muncie. I go on the train (about 1:30 perhaps) to Union City & thence (home) to Dayton.

Tuesday, September 30 Miss Mollie Kelley came to work for us; but it appeared next day that she was seking an excuse to go to Wm. Clemmer's where she thought there was lighter work.

Wednesday, October 1 Mollie Kelley went away. [She afterward went to Clemmer's, but was dispensed with after a few months.] Dr. Davis called this evening. So I did not get to prayer meeting.

Friday, October 3 Went on the afternoon train to Richmond. Called at D.K. Zeller's. Read up proofs on Oct. Star at Coe's Office. Supper & lodging at Zeller's. Called at Hillerd & at Friend's meeting.

Saturday, October 4 Made up paper. Saw Rev. M.R. Drury at the depot Went on 10:30 train to Lynn. Dine at Thomas Moody's 1/2 mile east of Lynn. Pr. at Bethel Church at 2:00 Acts 16: [blank] about Lydia. Qr. Conf. The report that they had charges against Rev. C.B. Small.

Supper at Samuel Jennings. Rev. Ben. B. Holcomb pr. at 7:30, on Jacob's ladder. Stay at W.H.H. Johnson's.

Sunday, October 5 Pr. at 10:30, Jas. 1:12. Dine at John Roe Jennings, with Rev. O.L. Wilson, Jas. Hutchens of New Hope class, etc. Rev. A. Rust pr. at 3:30 quite a good sermon. Went to Thomas Moody's near Lynn. Bro. & Sister Rust take supper there & then go on to their home at Farmland. 16:14-16 about Lydia.

Monday, October 6 Went on 7:10 train to Arcanum & the train for Dayton having gone, I go on to Troy. Visit Cous is Eliza Culbertson (Well south on Market St.) Call at Alex. Heywood's office & see him a few minutes. Call at Mr. Kelly's book-store but do not find him in. Went on 4:00 tr. home to Dayton.

Tuesday, October 7 At home. Mail papers—Oct. *Star.*

Wednesday, October 8 At home. Spend some time arranging my books.

Friday, October 10 Went on afternoon train to Richmond Call at D.K. Zeller's. Went on to Millville and thence to Rev. Jacob William's 1/2 mile north of town. Lodged there.

Saturday, October 11 Went with Rev. Jacob Williams to New Castle. Dined at Rev. D.O. Darling's at the parsonage. Call at Mrs. Eliz. Schildtknecht's. Pr at 2:00 I Cor 15:58. Quarterly conference followed. Supper at Rev. O. Jennings'. Rev. Wm. Davenport pr. at 7:00. Ps. 3:8. Stay at Nicholas Milligan's.

Sunday, October 12 Pr. at 11:00, 2d Cor. 7:1. Dine at O. Jennings with Wm. Davenport & wife. Call at Harvey Root's. Gowdy & wife there. Supper at Rufus Day's. Rev. D.O. Darling pr. at 7:00, John 1:10. Did well. I go to Merit Bailey's, 4 miles North-west, and lodge. He a son of Henry Bailey deceased. His widow, Rev. Anna Bailey, lives together with Merit.

Monday, October 13 Return to New Castle Call at Mrs. Mary Bond's—formerly Byers. Call a few minutes at Miss Baileys and Philebraws. Dine at Rev. D.O. Darling's. Go on 1:30 train to Carlos City. Walk most of the way via Rev. C.M. Smalls to Jas. Hutchens. Sup-

per there. He takes me on to Mrs. Louisa Cranor's. Stay there.

Tuesday, October 14 Go with Martin Cranor to Williamsburg. Dine at Herbert Pierce's. Walk most of the way to Washington. Call at Cyrus Osborn's and at Charley Gray's, the latter just up from a spell of fever. Went on 4:00 train to Richmond. Saw Henry Dowell & B.F. Straton on loaning money to W.H.H. Reeder. Staid at D.K. Zeller's.

Wednesday, October 15 Called on Dowell & on Stratton again. Went on 10:30 train to Anderson & thence to Fairmount. Rode over to Uncle Wm. Reeder's with young Howard. Staid there. He afflicted with cancer under his jaws, having had one cured on his lip a year ago.

Thursday, October 16 Go with Wm. H.H. Reeder Jr. to Marion to see about borrowing money to save an execution on Uncle's property. See Norton, Mather, Wm. White, Flynn, and several real estate agents. Call at John Mull's 2 ms N.W. of town. Go on via Jonesboro to Fairmount & Uncle's.

Friday, October 17 Go to Hartford with Wm. Reeder. Call at Parks. Dine at Rev. G.L. Mattox at Hartford. Go on to Cambridge City. Call at Amos Huddleson's. Supper at Cephas Huddleson's. Go with Huddleson's to Rev. F.M. Demunbrun's. Sister Demunbrun very sick. Stay at Huddleson's.

Saturday, October 18 Go on train to Richmond & thence on 10:30 train to Washington. Dine at Cyrus Osborn's. Went on with Warren Brooks to Sugar Grove. Comment at 2:00 on I Pet. 1:1—Qr. Conf. followed. Supper at Rev. O.L. Wilson's with Rev. C.B. Small's. Pr at 7:00 Acts 16:31. Stay at Alpheus Mindenhall's with Rev. C.B. Small's.

Sunday, October 19 Pr. at 10:30 Ex. 28:34. Small communion followed. Dine at Addison Wilson's with Small, Leonard's, Jonas Hatfield etc. Love-feast meeting at 3:00 led by Martin Coffman. Supper at Louis Smith's with Small. Pr. at 7:00 Luke 16:31. Stay at Rev. O.L. Wilson's.

Monday, October 20 Went on the hack to Washington and thence to Richmond on the train. Write at the depot. Spend awhile in the Reading room. Call to see D.K. Zeller at his house to see the folks. Go home on the 2:05 train, to Dayton.

Tuesday, October 21 At home. Prepare copy for the outside of Nov. *Star.* Mail it on the evening train to Coe.

Wednesday, October 22 Write an editorial for the *Star.* At pr. meeting at Summit St.

Saturday, October 25 Went on 7:25 Morn. train to Straglton's. Eli Hawley takes me to his house 1 1/2 miles N.W. Stay there to Dinner. Rev. W.A. Oler also there. Pr at Salem Church at 2:00, Rom. 10:1—etc. Qr. Conference followed. Supper at Charles Hawley's 1/2 m. west of Elis Hawley's. Pr. at Salem at 7:00 John 21:17. Stay at Charles Hawley's.

Sunday, October 26 Go over to Eli Hawley's before meeting. Am at Sab. Sch. Pr. at 10:30 I Cor. 15:25. Communion followed. Dine at John Corbet's. Wm. McGath & wife there also. Mary Smith, Wayne's widow. Pr. at 7:00 Rom. 2:6. Stay at Corbett's.

Monday, October 27 Went to Eli Holly's. Stay till after dinner. Eli takes me to the station. Go on train to Richmond. At Zeller's in evening. Supper there. Go on the 7:15 eve. tr Home to Dayton.

Tuesday, October 28 At home. Wrote editorials. Mailed letters on the train in the evening. Heard a conversation on [blank]

Wednesday, October 29 Look up papers and write some editorial matter.

Thursday, October 30 At Home. Went over to town. Bought books for Calvin Wiles of Economy. Paid one dollar to clerk at the Book-store for John Nicholson's *Telescope* Greensfork, Ind. Bought a postal order for Rev. W.J. Pruner (Union City) to pay my rent $16.50 + .15=$16.65.

Friday, October 31 At home in forenoon. Mailed letters to many on Tel. subs. & one with Postal order to Pruner in the box at 3d & Summit. Went on Aft. tr. to Richmond. Read up proof on *Star* & made it up partly. Sup-

per at Rev. D.K. Zeller's. Went on 8:00 tr to Centreville. Staid at Daniel Aukerman's.

Saturday, November 1 Went in the forenoon with Mr. Crownover to Joshua La Mott's. Dine there. Com. at 2:00 Matt. 4:1-8. Supper at William Borough's with Rev. G.W. Fast & wife. Pr. at 7:00 Matt. 5-12. Stay at Joshua La Mott's.

Sunday, November 2 Pr at Union, Ex. 28:34. Communion. Went with Rev. G.W. Fast & wife to Gellinger's 2 ms N. on Nat. road. Dined there. Rev. G.W. Fast pr at 3 1/2 "Let him not be ashamed." Suf[f]er as a Christian, etc. I stay at Joshua Lamott's.

Monday, November 3 Rise at 4 1/2, and walk 4 miles to Centreville to take the early train 6:30 + 20. Go on to Richmond & thence to Dayton. Help mail the *Star.*

Tuesday, November 4 Sent off about 1,000 copies of the *Star.* Somewhat rainy in the forenoon. Day of presidential election. Wrote some letters.

Wednesday, November 5 At home. The news seemed to indicate Grover Cleveland's election; but the news fluctuated during the day.

Thursday, November 6 At home. Rev. Wm. Dillon called. News on the election continued fluctuating.

Friday, November 7 I at home. Wrote letters, etc. News on election still fluctuating.

Saturday, November 8 I rose at 3:00, bathed & dressed to go away. Went on 7:05 train via hamilton to Lotus. Found conveyance thence to Rev. N.L. Hoopingarner's at the parsonage. Pr at 2:00 Ps. 10:3 Pleasant Quarterly Conference. Sup[p]er at parsonage. Pr. at 7:00, I Pet. 4:18. Stay at the parsonage.

Sunday, November 9 I pr. at 10:30, I Cor. 15:4. Dine at Parsonage, with Murphy girls. Speaking meeting at 3:00 Set Atkinson back. Supper at G. Fry's with Rev. C.R. Paddack. I pr. at 7:00 Rom. 4:10 "Therefore it is of faith that it might be by grace." Lodge at parsonage.

Monday, November 10 I go via Liberty to Daniel

Koerner's. Dine there. Came back to Union. Stay at Hoopingarner's till meeting time. I pr. at 7:00 at Union Eph 5:16. Lodge at Hoopingarner's.

Tuesday, November 11 I go via Lotus to Rushville and thence to Hamilton Station. Dine at Dr. George Wright's, my Bro. Harvey's son's. He takes me to Harvey's 2 1/2 miles n-w. I Lodge there. Remarks: John Wright takes his wife and goes to Wichita Kansas. Her folks had tried to compel them to stay with them. John McKee, Harvey's son-in-law teaching school at the home school-house.

Wednesday, November 12 Stay at Harvey's all day. Drusilla McKee came in the forenoon; also in the afternoon.

Thursday, November 13 Went with Harvey to Rushville. Called a few minutes with Chas. B. Harris my deceased sister Sarah's husband, having 3rd wife. Walked about town with Harvey. Saw a good many old acquaintances. Dined with Harvey at an eating house. Hear some speaking in afternoon by Hon. Thos. A. Hendrickson, Cooper, etc. over Cleveland's ele. Walk to Fayetteville and to Austin Winchell's 1 1/2 miles s-e. Lodge there.

Friday, November 14 Went down to Anson Moor's He married my Bro. William's widow. Staid there till evening. Estelle Harris went with me. Saah Catharine Bowen, my Brother Wm's daughter was there. She is the wife of Nickolas F. Bowen. Supper and evening at Bowen's with Flora Wright, my niece. Anson also there in the evening. I stay at Anson's that night.

Saturday, November 15 Stay at Anson's till afternoon. Anson then took me via Fayetteville to Garrison Creek Church three miles west of Alpine. I pr. I Pet. 1—etc. Supper at John Meek's, 1 1/2 mile up the creek from the church. Rev. F.M. Demumbrun pr. at 7:30, Heb. 12:1. Stay at Ronan's with Demumbrun, on the old Matney place Ellen Ronan, his wife, (nee Matney) once a pupil of mine.

Sunday, November 16 Pr. at 10:30, Ps 66:10. Dine at Bro. Jonas' with Austin Winchell's and Estella Harris. Stay there till meeting time. I pr. at 7:00 Heb. 11:6. Go with Ellis Wright my nephew to Anson Moor's.

Monday, November 17 Staid at Anson Moor's till after dinner. He takes me to the train at Glenwood. Go via Hamilton to home—Dayton. Made close connections. Found all as well as common. At request, called at Dr. L. Davis' and spent the evening.

Wednesday, November 19 At home. At prayer meeting at Summit St. Church.

Friday, November 21 At home. Dr. Davis called in the afternoon. Mrs. Rebecca Davis & Mary Inglehart call in the evening.

Sunday, November 23 Went to Grace M.E. Church and heard the pastor [blank] pr. I Cor. 15:56, "The sting of death is sin," at 10:30. At home till evening. Hear Prof. G.A. Funkhouser preach at 7:00 Joshua 23:11.

Monday, November 24 At home. This is the twenty fifth anniversary of our marriage, that having occurred at the home of her parents and of her Bro. Daniel on Thanksgiving Day November 24th, 1859.

Wednesday, November 26 At home. This evening the children made a surprise on us by presention of a hanging lamp and a castor for the table.

Thursday, November 27 Thanksgiving dinner by invitation at Rev. J.W. Hott's. Guests present: Dr. L. Davis & wife; Rev. G.M. Matthews & wife, Rev. M. Wright & wife Mr. Harper & wife; Mr. John Gilbert & wife; Mrs. Edwards (widow of Bishop D. Edwards.) Mother Hott, Mrs. Shank. Had a very good day there. The weather was quite mild. Donation at Rev. G.M. Matthews in the evening. At Dillon's awhile.

Friday, November 28 Wrote some editorials. Dr. Davis called in the evening.

Sunday, November 30 Attended meeting at First Church. Funkhouser (Prof. G.A.) pr. on Communion. "Let a man examine himself," etc. Qr. Meeting occasion. Heard Rev. J.W. Hott pr. at Summit St. Church at 7:00: "I have shed innocent blood." Judas confession.

Monday, December 1 Went to town. Wrote in afternoon.

Friday, December 5 Go on to Richmond Arrange for issue of the *Star.* Call at D.K. Zeller's. Go on 10:30 train to Ridgeville. Return to Winchester, and went thence to Selma. Supper at Henry Spangler's. Pr. at Selma at 7:00 I Thess. 5:18. Stay at Rev. J.Y. Demumbrun's.

Saturday, December 6 Went to John L. Jackson's and dined, Bro. Joseph Y. Denumbrun is along. Pr. at 1:30, Ps. 119:105. Quarterly conference. Supper at Henry Spangler's. Stay that night at Spangler's.

Sunday, December 7 Pr. at 10:30, Ps. 48:12,13. Communion. Dine at Edward Shull's. Father Davis, an aged layman dined there also. Called before meeting at Rev. J.Y. Demumbrun's. Evening meeting a love feast, led by Christian Life. I went home with Platt Mott's 2 1/2 north of Selma.

Monday, December 8 Speaking meeting at 10:30 led by Rev. J.Y. Demumbrun, the pastor. Pretty good. Dined at Geo. W. Ford's, with Platt Mott & wife & Edward Shull & wife & Sister Abr. Rust. Supper at Henry Spangler's. Pr. at 7:00 John 7:37. Stay at Rev. J.Y. Demumbrun's.

Tuesday, December 9 After breakfast, get my umbrella from E. Shull's & find myself too late to get on accom. train. Go to Spangler's & write a letter home. I go to meeting an hour. I dined at Henry Spangler's He is aged 72 years. I go at 1:00 train to Winchester & after two hours to Richmond. Mail a letter and a card home, also a letter to Rev. T.D. Adams. Called & staid at Benj. Harris', an aged man in Sevastopol, formerly living in the neighborhood of Williamsburg.

Wednesday, December 10 Went to Dublin (Cambridge) & called at Susanna Huddleston's. Dined at W. Scroggy's and arranged some business. Called at Rev. W.A. Oler's and at Rev. Halleck Floyd's. Supper at Dr. Geo. W. Champ's. His son takes me to the train at Cambridge. I call at Zeller's. I go on 9:30 train to Anderson. Lodge at Doxey House.

Thursday, December 11 I go on 6:00 train to Fairmount. Breakfast at Elwood Davis' I get his horse & buggy and go to Uncle W.H. Reeder's. Dine there. I pay off my tile

bill at Fowler's. Go in the evening to Elwood Davis's at Fairmount, & lodge there.

Friday, December 12 I go to Jonesboro on tr. and walk out to Geo. Carter's. Pay off note there. Bro. Carter takes me to Marion. Pay my land tax. I go on 11:40 train to Hartford. Thence on 1:20 train to Muncie. I get a letter from Susan. Go to Selma. I take Rev. J.Y. Demumbrun's horse and go via New Burlington to Mt. Pleasant. pr. 1 Cor. 5:7. Stay at Hez. Shuttleworth's 1/4 m N.W. at old Kiger house.

Saturday, December 13 Go to Philip Oxley's for dinner. Attend meeting at Mt. Pleasant at 1:30. Talk on Revivals. Held Qr. Conference. Supper at Harvey Jackson's 1/2 mile north-west. Pr. at 7:00, John 7:37. Stay at Harvey Jackson's with Rev. F.M. Moore, the pastor, & his son Arthur.

Sunday, December 14 Pr. at Mt. Pleasant at 10:30 Ps. 66:10. Communion followed. Dine at Huffman's a half m. S.E. It is rather rainy afternoon. Pr. at 6:00, Isa. 28:56. I lodge at Hez. Shuttleworth's with Milton Harris, one of our W.R. ministers.

Monday, December 15 I go back to Selma & put up at J.Y. Demumbrun's & stay till after dinner. I go on 1:00 train to Union & thence home to Dayton, Ohio.

Thursday, December 18 At home most of the day at least. Went to "town" before noon.

Friday, December 19 Went to "town" to see about my taxes. Found they must be paid not later than January 4th. Went on 1:00 train to Union. Applied for clergymen's rates on D. & U. R.R. and C.C.C. & I. R.R. Went on to Muncie. Walk a mile, ride 5 in a Sled & wagon, walk the rest to Olive Chapel. Find Sister Vienna Johnson preaching on the Lord's prayer. I Lodge at Rev. Arthur Rector's.

Saturday, December 20 Stay at Bro. Rector's and write an article for the *Religious Telescope* in the forenoon. Dine there. Qr. Conf. at 1:30. No preaching. Bro. J.M. Cook, the pastor, not there consequence of breaking his arm Nov. 17th. Supper at Bro. A. Rector's. Pr. at 6:30 Mark 8:38. Stay at Rector's again.

Sunday, December 21 Pr. at 10:30, I John V. 18,19. Communion followed. Dine at James A. Rector's 1/2 m. east. He is to move to Oakland, Vermillion Co., Illinois soon to carry on a tile factory with his sister's husband, Johnson. Sister Vienna Johnson, wife of Reuben Johnson of Bethel Church in Randolph County, preached at 6:30.

Monday, December 22 A speaking (lovefeast) meeting at 10:00. Real good. Dine at Arthur Rector's. Borrow his horse & go through the cold to Wm. H.H. Reeder's, my Uncle's 5 ms S.E. of Fairmount. He doctoring with Mrs. Moon for the cancer under his jaw. Lodge there.

Tuesday, December 23 Take Flora to her school and come back by my farm. I find the corn all gathered. Go on to Uncle's again before dinner. Get a letter from Uncle J. Braden, etc Consult that evening with Uncle & the rest what to do about his affairs. Stay there that night.

Wednesday, December 24 Go with Wm. Jun. to Marion. On the way, dine at *John L. Pegram's. At Marion met Jonathan Myers & wife & Rev. D.E. Myers; Also Rev. A.C. Wilmore. See about business and bear a letter from Baldwin, Mrs. Burkee's attorney. Go on home via Jonesboro and Fairmount. Reach home about 9:00—that is Uncle's house. *Mrs. Pegram is James Milton Reeder's daughter, hence my second cousin.

Thursday, December 25 Went to Mr. Barritt's to see Mrs. Burke on a porposition concerning Uncle Wm's indebtedness to her. It was an eight-mile ride in the snowstorm. Returning to Uncle Wm's, find John Wilson Broyles and family there; Also Eliza Broyles and her children there. Went on to Rev. Arthur Rector's 4 ms s.e. of New Corner. Supper there. Sister Vienne Johnson pr. at 6:30 Isa. 40.31 "They that wait upon the Lord."

Friday, December 26 Went to Muncie in a sleigh with Arthur and Jas. Rector. Dined at A.R. Day's. He aged 70 married a wife of about 39—a fair woman apparently. Day takes me to the train. Go on to Winchester. There wait the train for Lynn. Went on 3:30 train to Lynn. Got a letter from home. Staid at Rev. Thomas C. Moody's 1/2 mile east of Lynn.

Saturday, December 27 Thomas Moody takes us in the spring-wagon to Mt. Pleasant, 7 miles east, 2 1/2 miles from Arba. I pr at 10:30 Matt. 13:44. Dine at Wm. Manning's, 1 1/2 miles west. Qr. Conf. at 1:30. Had a pleasant session, only reports were short. Supper at Wm. Slick's, 1/2 m east. It rained out the night meeting—rained all night.

Sunday, December 28 Very rainy still. Pr. at Mt. Pleasant at 10:30, John 1:29. Communion followed. The rain somewhat abated. Dined, Geo. W. Slick, 1 m. N.W. of the Church. John Radford & wife there also. Pr. at 6:30, Luke 23:4. Went home with Wm. Manning's & staid there.

Monday, December 29 Bro. Manning takes me part of the way to Johnson Station. It being somewhat icy on his barefoot horses, I walk the last 1 1/2 ms. Go on to Richmond. Dine at Zeller's (D.K. Z's). Go on 2:05 train home.

Tuesday, December 30 I was at home, but made no note in my diary at the time.

Memoranda
Williamsburg Thos. Cranor's Funeral: "Blessed are the dead," etc. *Honey Creek*—Jan 24, Rev. 4:8. Jan. 25, (Rev. I. Cox funeral) Prov. 14:32. *Dublin*—Feb. 24: Ps. 16:8. *Daleville,* Apr. 21 (Sermon before the Woman's Mis Association) Phil 4:3. *Near Muncie,* Apr. 22, Mrs. A.R. Day's funeral. *South Wabash*—Jan. 5, Ps. 27:14. 20, Heb. 11:6. Jan 6, Ex 28:34. Jan 7 Jer. 13:21. Jan. 8, Acts 26:28. Jan. 9, Ez. 33:11. Jan. 11: Luke 24:46. *Liberty* Qr. Conf—Jan. 12, Ps. 27:14. Matt. 13:44. Jan. 13, Ex. 28:34 Mark 8:36. *Bethany* Howard Co. Jan. 18, Luke 15:7. Jan. 19: Isa. 40:31. Jan. 20, 2 Cor. 7:1. Jan. 21, Jer. 13:21. Jan. 22, Mark 8:30. *Knox Chapel*—Jan. 26, Rom. 4:8. Jan. 27 John 14:2. John 15:22. *New Corner*—Feb. 9, Gal 4:18. Ps. 16:8. F. 10, Ex 28:34, Rom. 12:1. Feb. 11, Matt 6:33. *Gilead* (Jay Co.) March 8, Matt. 11:30. S. Feb. 9, 2 Cor. 3:8. *Pleasant Dale* (Blackford Co.) Mon. March 10, Rom. 14:17. *Carney Sch. House*—Mar. 13, Gal. 6:14. Mar. 14, John 1:29. March 15, Luke 10:29. John 3:7. March 16, Luke 16:31. Ps. 87:3. *Bethel* (Wells Co.) Mar. 21, Isa. 55:1. March 22, I Pet. 2:6-9. I Pet. 4:18. Mar. 24, Rom. 10:1. *Pleasant Grove* (Huntington Co.) Mar. 27, John 3:7. Mar.

29, Matt 6:7. March 20, Jas. 1:12, Rom. 3:5. *Mill Creek* (Wabash Co.) Apr. 5, John 1:16. Apr. 6, Zech. 13:9. *Union Chapel* (Grant Co.) Apr. 12, John 1:16. Apr. 13, Easter, Acts 26:8. *Olive Branch* (Howard Co.) Apr. 19th, John 1:16. Apr. 20. Acts 26:8. *Herbst Station* Apr. 25, Mal. 3:18. *Burns Sch House* April 26, 2 Pet. 1:3. Apr. 27, 2 Cor. 7:8. Mal. 3:16,17. *Bethel,* Del. Co. May 17, I Cor. 13:13. I Tim. 2:6. May 18, I Cor. 5:7. John 7:37. *Near Jackson Station* May 24, Rev. 5:1. May 25, Ps 48:11,12,13. John 1:29. *Good Will* (Jay Co.) May 30, Heb. 12:28. May 31, Rev. 5:1. June 1, [blank]

McNiel's Liniment
1 part Essence of peppermint
1 part Essence of Cinnamon
1 part Tincture of Rhubarb
1 part Compound Spir. Lavender
2 parts Spirits of Camphor
3 parts Laudanum
4 parts Sulphuric Ether
8 parts Number Six

Albert A. Koerner
Wabash, Ind. (Care of Charles S. Rose.)

Texts & Subjects
If any man be in Christ Jesus 2 Cor. 5:17. Graffed [*sic*] into tame olive tree. Rom. [blank]
1884

1885

Thursday, January 1 At home. Family all at home. Disappointed about getting a turkey. At home that day and feeling rather worn down with cares & labor, it was rather a dull day.

Friday, January 2 Went to court-house and paid my tax & W.J. Pruner's tax. I made application for reduced rates on railroads, but the agent, Mr. Clough, recommended me to write direct to the gen. ticket agent. Get proofs on *Richm Star* in the evening and read them.

Saturday, January 3 Went on 8:00 train to Richmond, Ind. Go to J.M. Coe's Printing Office. Hand in proofs for the first side of Jan. *Star*. Give in copy for four colums of Ed. side. Call at D.K. Zeller's. Go on 10:35 train to Hagerstown. Go up with Moses Keaver to his house close to Mt. Zion Church. Dine. Pr. at Mt. Zion Isa. 28:5, 6. Qr. Conf. followed. Supper at John Albert Locke's 1 1/2 m south with Rev. D.O.Darling, the pastor. Rev. Darling pr. at 6:30 Gal. 6:14. Stay at Aaron Locke's.

Sunday, January 4 Pr. at 10:30, 1 John 5:18, 19. Large congregation. Communion followed. Dine at Wm. Waltz's—his wife a member, but he is not, but a queer fellow. Call at Fouts' & also at John Brown's, the folks not being at home at the latter place. Call again at Aaron Locke's, till meeting. I preach at 6:30 Jer. 13:21. Speaking meeting followed. Stay at Moses Keever's.

Monday, January 5 Call at Aaron Locke's. Write for fares on "Pan Handle," and C.A. & D.R.R. Write out in part that form of deed for Mt. Zion Church. Love-feast at 10:00. Right good. Dine at John H. Thornburg's. Says that directly or indirectly he does not have any connec-

tion with the Odd Fellow's lodge. Go on with Bro. D.O. Darling, via Hagerstown & Millville to Levi Williams. Pr. at Flat Rock Chapel at 6:30 Ps. 85:6. Stay at Levi Williams.

Tuesday, January 6 Stay at Levi's and write editorials for the *Star*. Mail letter for the *Star* at 4:00 p.m. The editorials of this paper were almost all written when I was away from home. Stop at Rev. Jacob Williams' for supper. Pr. at 6:30 Matt. 5:8. Stay at Jacob Williams.

Wednesday, January 7 Spend most of the day at Jacob William's, writing editorials. Mail them to Richmond on the train as yesterday. Rev. D.O. Darling who had gone home to New Castle came toward night. Was with us at Supper. I pr. at 6:30 Luke 15:7. Stay at Jacob William's. *Remark*—Quite a good interest in the meeting. Bro. D. so hoarse as to be unfit for speaking.

Thursday, January 8 Call at Kutz to see Father Bennett, aged 96 past. Go on forenoon train to Anderson & thence to Fairmount. Ride to Uncle Wm. H.H. Reeder's in a wagon with Huston Dickinson. Stay that night at Uncle's.

Friday, January 9 Went to Marion with William Reeder Jr., pay off on the $600 contracted, and have that judgment rested & execution on Uncle's land stayed. See. Revs. J. M. Kabrich and C. Smith at the post-office. Ride in buggy with William to the Jonesboro and there take the cars to Anderson & thence to Millville. Supper at Jac. Williams. Pr. at Flat Rock at 6:30. Acts 2:40. Some ten or a dozen rose for prayers. Some came forward with the members for a season of prayer. Stay at

Levi Williams with D.O. Darling (I borrowed $100 of Mary Carter.) Paid it off since then.

Saturday, January 10 Call at Jac. Williams. Being mis-informed as to the time of the train, I miss it. Rev. D.O. Darling took me in a buggy to Taylor Nicholson's 1 1/2 miles west of Washington. Dine there. Go on with Rev. O.L. Wilson to Washington. No preach. Hold qr. Conf. About 2 1/2 o'clock. Supper at Evans Bailey's. Pr. at 6:00. Luke 15:7. Mrs. Frankie Peare follows. She for eight weeks engaged in protracted meeting at Fairfield (Friends) church near here & at town. Several seekers. Stay at Cyrus Osborn's, with Rev. C.B. Small.

Sunday, January 11 Pr. at 10:30, 48th Ps. 11,12. Communion. Dine at Daniel Nelson's with Rev. C.B. Small. Warren Brooks called in the afternoon; also Rev. Oscar L. Wilson & John Nicholson. Pr. at 6:30 John 7:37. Speaking meeting followed. Stay at Wm. Hatfield's.

Monday, January 12 Call at Nathan Brasher's, and at Cyrus Osborn's. Go on forenoon train to Richmond. Read up proofs on Jan. *Star*. Lunch. Make up *Star*. Call at D.K. Zeller's. See Daniel Koerner & David Fry & wife & Miss Fry, David's sister. Go on 2:05 train home to Dayton.

Tuesday, January 13 At home. Called at Dr. Davis' in forenoon. Went to express office in afternoon, to get this month's *Star*. Spent part of the afternoon in getting the papers ready to mail. Bro. Dillon called a few minutes.

Thursday, January 15 At home. Sent the *Star* to the express office to be forwarded to Richmond to mail.

Friday, January 16 At home till evening, except a call on Bro. Wm. Dillon. Went at 6:30 on train to Richmond, Ind. Detained at Manchester sometime by a freight locomotive off the rails. Arrive at Richmond at 10:30. Stay at Huntington House.

Saturday, January 17 Went on the 7:15 train to Dublin. Call at Wm. McGath's, Wilson Scroggy's, Rev. Halleck Floyd's, Rev. W.A. Oler's, and 1 m. N.W. at Harrison Cook's, and thence to Henry Huddleston's 2 ms from town. Dine there & he takes me to New Lisbon to qr. meeting. Pr. 15 min., Matt 5:8. Supper at J.

Raffensberger's, with the pastor.(Bro. Oler), I pr. at 1:00, Luke 15:7. Stay Benj. Perry's—he a blacksmith with Bro. Oler.

Sunday, January 18 Pr. at 10:30 Ps. 92:8. Dine at Englebert Steltzer's, an aged pious "Albright." Called at Father Wm. Hanby's. His son-in-law is Jas. Madison Mercer & [blank] Pr. at 6:30, Ex. 28:34 at the suggestion of Bro. Oler. Bro Oler & I stay at Mrs. John Adams. Her son Chester a young lawyer now teaching school. Her maiden name was Mary A. Burgoyne, with whose family I had been acquainted since about 1840.

Monday, January 19 Love-feast meeting at 10:00. Fairly attended, and of fair interest. Dined with Oler at Henry Sites 1/4 m. East. He Steltzer's son-in-law. Supper at David Werking's. Rev. Wm. Oler pr. at 7:00. Matt. 11:28. Stay at Jasper Matney's 1 1/2 miles north, on Rev. Monroe Gronendyke's old place. He a son-in-law of Mary A. Adams.

Tuesday, January 20 Stay at Jasper's till after dinner. Jesse Gilbert came to buy Jasper's hogs. Considerable conversation. His wife a Friend minister. Meeting at Wm. Hanby's at 2:30 o'clock. Real good meeting. Mrs. Frank Dare, formerly a neighbor of Daniel Koerner, was there. Supper at Hanby's. Pr. at 7:00 Acts 16:31. Two gave their hands for prayer. Stay at David Werkings in town.

Wednesday, January 21 Meeting at 10:00. Right good. Dinner at John Raffensberger's. Staid there till evening meeting. Pr at 7:00 Matt 1:21. Staid at Benj. Perry's. This was one of the coldest nights of the winter, but we slept in a stove room with fire kept up all night.

Thursday, January 22 Went to Dublin with Rev. W.A. Oler. Coldest morning of the winter. Dine at Oler's. Supper at Floyd's. Stay at Rev. Halleck Floyd's.

Friday, January 23 Call at Lanick's. Dine at Oler's. Go on 1:00 train to Centreville. Walk to Abington. Supper at Graft D. Zigler's, a Ger. Reform man from Johnsville, Ohio. Pr. at U.B. Church Acts 23:19. Stay at Alfred Schroy's in town.

Saturday, January 24 Staid at Schroy's till after dinner. Hoopingarner dined there. He pastor instead of Bro.

Fast, resigned. Pr. at 1:30 Ps 137:56. Qr. Conf. followed. Supper at Martin Wyrick's. Pr. at 7:00. Luke 23:4. Stay at Obadiah Holler's. 1 m. S.W.

Sunday, January 25 Pr. at 10:30 Ps 48:12, 13. Dined at Ed. Weaver's with Rev. N. L. Hoopingarner & wife. Called at Jas. Duke's a half hour. Pr. Rev. Robt Steel, Eph 3:14-19. I exhort. Stay at Obadiah Holler's.

Monday, January 26 Went with Holler to Philomath to protracted meeting. Dine at Henry Fricker's, 2 ms. north. Pr. at night 1 Ki. 18:21. Stay at Chas. Leistner's. Philomath is in old town where lived Kidwell, the universalist preacher, who over 40 years ago had a printing press here, and whose faith has lingered long among the people. The snow about four inches deep at this time. Very cold night.

Tuesday, January 27 At meeting at 10:30. Veal led. Noisy meeting. Dodridge there. Dine with Hoopingarner at Chas. Leistner's. Leistner & wife, both from Germany. Since from Pennsylvania. Meeting at 7:00. Veal preached John 10:11. Two seekers. I stay again at Leistner's. It snowed at night & during the night two or three inches. Still right cold.

Wednesday, January 28 Meeting at 10:30 (11:00) and quite a lively meeting we had. Four converted and all joined church. Hoopingarner & I went to Isaac Dodridge's. Mother Sutliff, her niece Miss Robinson, and Mrs. Byrme live there. They are very nice folks & Methodists. Robinson Chapel is close by. They live 3 miles from Waterloo. Meeting at night. Hoopingarner preached Gen 19:17. I exhort. Stay at Leistner's again. Weather Moderating a little.

Thursday, January 29 Meeting at 10:30. Right good. Bro. Veal led it. Two came out for prayers. One professed conversion. Dined at Jacob Shank's at Philomath. His mother-in-law, Mrs. Helmsings there. His brother-in-law, of the same name, there. Staid till evening there. Pr. at 7:00, Acts 16:31. Stay again at Leistner's. Veal miffed about not being called upon to close meeting. Two gave their hand for prayers.

Friday, January 30 Called at Henry McCashlin's 1/2 mile north of Philomath. He a M.E. member. Morning meeting at 10:30 (11:00) Pretty good. Dinner at McCashlin's with John Fender and Hoopingarner's. Meeting at 1:00. Rev. Enos Veal pr. John 3:14. Go to Obadiah Holler's & lodge.

Saturday, January 31 Start soon after 8:00. Go to Liberty. Get letters there. Mail letters to Susan, Flora Reeder, to H.D. Healey, etc. Go on to Loth's. Dine at Geo. Fry's house. Go on to Franklin Church. Pr. at 2:30, John 15:1-8. Quarterly Conference. Agreed for Hoopingarner the paster to serve Abington mission the rest of the year. Supper at Henry Fry's. Hoopingarner pr. Dan. 5:30. Stay at Henry Fry's.

Sunday, February 1 Pr. missionary Sermon, Ps. 2:8. Raise $54.75 subscription, etc. Communion. Dine at Chas. Filer's Bro. Hoopingarner returns to Philomath. Rev. John Utsler, a son-in-law of Filer's, there also. Rev C.R. Padack. Pr. at Franklin at 7:00, Titus 2:14. Go home with Daniel Koerner, my wife's brother.

Monday, February 2 Stay at Daniel's all day and write out a will to send to Uncle Wm. H.H. Reeder who is down with a cancer.

Tuesday, February 3 Daniel Koerner takes me to Liberty. I send letters to Coe at Richmond, to Wm. H.H. Reeder (Sen.) and to home, etc., etc. Stay till afternoon and go on train to Glenwood. Austin Winchell there, and I go on to his house 1 1/2 m S.E. of Fayetteville. Stay there. His wife, Laura (Harris) is my niece—Sister Sarah's daughter.

Wednesday, February 4 Went down to Anson Moor's. He is the second husband of my brother William's widow, Lucinda, or Lucy. Stay there all day and that night. Flora and Ellis, my brother's children still at home.

Thursday, February 5 Went to "Sonny" Bowen's for dinner—My niece Sarah Catharine's (Wright's) husband's. Anson and Lucy with me. Go in afternoon to Val. Conaway's to see Estella Harris, my niece. Go back to Anson Moor's. Stay there.

Friday, February 6 Anson takes me to Andersonville in the buggy. A slow, cold rough trip it was. I was chilled a good deal, and next day had much cold, perhaps from the trip, or possibly from a cold bed that night. We stopped at Rev. John Morgan's. It proved a cold, roughs afternoon and evening. At church at 7:00 p.m. Rev. Geo. Wilson preached. Stay at John Morgan's.

Saturday, February 7 Remain at Bro. Morgan's all day. He will be 84 years old next April. They think their son *Thomas has consumption. Angeline Mitchel's daughter, "Lora," who had a severe time from spinal curvature, is living with them—her grandparents. I pr. at 7:00 from Titus 2:14. In consequence of much cold got hoarse but had considerable "liberty," as preachers used to say, when commanding their own efforts. Had the large house about full. Staid at Dr. F.J. Spillman's. His mother Mrs. Righsel lives with them. (*Died a few months later.)

Sunday, February 8 Pr. at 10:30 Ps. 48:12, 13. Found myself quite hoarse. Communion service followed. Dine with Dr. Spillman's with James F. Harris, my sister's son, and his wife Zena, and his little boy. Pr. at 7:00 Luke 15:7. Stay at Samuel Barber's. His wife, Ellen Cook, a daughter of Rev. J.M. Cook's. She was raised by John Cook's where I boarded nearly thirty years ago for nine months when she was a little girl of 5 years old.

Monday, February 9 Went on the 7:00 back to Rushville via N. Salem. Mr. Jessup, the hack-driver, charged me nothing for fare. Dined at Chas. B. Harris' formerly my deceased sister's husband, now married to his third wife. Sarah was his first wife and he was divorced from his second wife. He is keeping boarders and a second-hand store. He has two little boys of about 3 & 5 years, Forest and Albert. Went on 12:10 train to Hamilton & thence to Dayton arriving about 4:00, perhaps, at home.

Tuesday, February 10 At home. Felt like doing little but rest. Sent a little copy to Coe on the evening train on yesterday evening. The day cold and growing colder. Several degrees below zero before bed time and about 12 below at 5:00 next morning. The brisk, damp wind added greatly to the coldness.

Wednesday, February 11 Weather moderated some today and at bed time it was 11 degrees above zero. At home all day. Wrote to McNew & to Lee Hossington, etc.

Thursday, February 12 At 6:00 it was about 14 degrees above zero.

Friday, February 13 At home. In the evening not getting ready to go on 6:00 Union train conclude to wait till morning at home.

Saturday, February 14 Went on 8:00 train to Richmond. Call at Coe's printing-office and left some copy for 1st page of March *Star*. Called to see my motherinlaw, Mrs. Catharine Koerner. Go on 10:50 train to Winchester. Dine at David Huston's. A Bro. B.C. Hopkin's takes me to Sparrow Creek Chapel. Comment on Matt. 3:7-17. Supper at Elisha Johnson's. Pr at 7:00, John 3:36. Stay at Johnson's with Bro. Dumunbrun Hopkins.

Sunday, February 15 Pr. at 10:30 (11:00) 2 Cor. 3:8. Cummunion followed. Dine at Leroy Starbuck's, 1 3/4 miles S.E. of Church, with David Huston & B.C. Hopkin's. Bro. Starbuck takes me to Jesse Rhinerd's, 1 1/4 m S. of the church. Call at Sarah Starbuck's, 1 m S. of Church & at George Veal's. Pr. at 7:00 Mark 8:36. Very snowy evening. Mostly young folks in the congregation. Bro. Platt Mott exhorts. Bro. Mott's, Sister Rust, and Willie stay at Elisha Johnson's 3/4 m E. of Church. I stay there too.

Monday, February 16 Bro. Elisha Johnson takes me to Winchester. Dine at David Huston's. The day is one of the coldest of the season. A little girl stops in at Johnson's with her hands almost frozen on her way to school. Mott's went home. It must have been a cold ride. I went on two o'clock train to Union City & thence to Dayton on 3:30 train. I got a clergyman's ticket on D. Union & Ind. Div of Bee Line R.R., at Union City. Arrived at home before 5:00. Found all as well as common.

Tuesday, February 17 At home all day. Read up proofs on outside of March *Star* and forwarded them in the evening. Also sent some matter for inside pages.

Wednesday, February 18 At home in forenoon. In afternoon went to "town," mailed letter to Hoopingarner & one to the treasurer of Adair Co., Iowa. Purchased various articles and paid $4.00 on Huston's, Starbucks, and Houser's *Tel's*.

Friday, February 20 Went on 12:40 train to Union City and thence on train to Muncie. Walked out to Olive Chapel, and found the people in meeting there. Staid at Rev. Arthur Rector's.

Saturday, February 21 Went with Bro. Rector to New Corner. Called at Frederick Huber's. At meeting at Meth. Prot. Church Mrs. Martha Woodworth held the meeting. A lively time. Dine at Bro. Huber's. Quarterly conference at 1:30 (2:00) at our church at New Corner. Pretty fair. Returned with Bro. A. Rector. Sup[p]er at his house. Pr. at Olive Chapel at 7:00, Titus 2:14. Stay at Cassius Marcus Rector's, 2 m N.W. of the Church. Owing to the great excitement in the meeting at M.P. Church at New Corner it was deemed inadvisable that we hald services at present.

Sunday, February 22 Pr. at Olive at 11:00 from Heb. 11:7. Geo. Benedune joined church as a seeker. Dined at Rev. C.W. Rector's 1 3/4 m. Northwest. Chas. little girl and a Downing girl take me most of the way to New Corner in a sleigh. Call at Fred. Huber's. At the M.P. Church a few minutes, but it was overcrowded. Stay at F. Hubers.

Monday, February 23 Staid at Huber's & wrote a letter home and postal-cards to Stewards of New Castel Circuit. Dine at Huber's. At the meeting awhile at M.P. Church in afternoon. Pr. at M.B. Church at 7:00 Rom 1:16 "The gospel of Christ." House full. Four at the altar. Good meeting. Quite a praise meeting.

Tuesday, February 24 At the meeting at M.P. Church in forenoon. M.E. Church gobles up most of the converts. Dine at Jas. McLaughlin's. Stay there till evening. Pr. at 7:00 Acts 16:31. Several seekers. Two joined church. Stay at Frederick Huber's. Mrs. Maria B. Woodworth closes her strange wild meetingthat day M.E. Church had meeting at their house that night.

Wednesday, February 25 I go in Huber's buggy-sleigh to Uncle W.H. Reeder's that forenoon. He thought to be better of his cancer. I go with Wm., Junior, to see Washington & John W. Fine's, and inquire of the neighbors about them as renters, etc. Return to Uncle Reeder's & stay.

Thursday, February 26 Write out a contract and rent my farm to Fines. Go in the afternoon to New Corner. Call at Jas. McLaughlin's on the way. Super and lodging at Frederick Huber's. Pr. at 7:00 John 7:37. Communion followed.

Friday, February 27 Went in a sleigh to Muncie. Wrote to Lee Housington, in Iowa. Went on the noon train to Winchester. Thence went to Lynn. Went to Jabez Osborn's near Bloomingsport. Supper there. Pr. at U.B. Church at Bloomingsport at 7:00 Hebr. 11:6. "Without Faith," etc. Stay with Hall at Jabez Osborn's.

Saturday, February 28 Dined at John Elliot's opposite to the Church. Preach at 1:30. Eph 5:15. Quarterly Conference followed. Gave a severe reproff on the slowness of the Finances. Supper at Wood. Bachelor's. Rev. Isaac Johnson of the "New Light" Church pr. at 7:00. Luke 15:2. Bro. Wm. Hall, W.J. Oxley, and I stay at Simon Adamson's one mile south of town.

Sunday, March 1 Pr. at 10:30. Mall 3:1. Communion followed. Dine with George Johnson of the Christian (or New Light) Church. I took him into the U.B. Church 19 years ago, he being converted in a meeting at Liberty Church 2 1/2 miles north of Bloomingsport, which was a fine revival with 39 accessions and perhaps 50 conversions. She a niece of David Huston's of Winchester. Call at Mother Thomas' (Anthony) and at John Henry Bales. Pr. at 7:00, Eph 2:4. A pretty large and attentive congregation. Stay at John Elliot's.

Monday, March 2 Stay at Elliot's all day. Several called in. Wrote some letters in the forenoon. No day meeting. Pr. at 7:00 (7:30) from Heb 11:16, last clause. Quite a large congregation for a week night. Stay at Elliot's.

Tuesday, March 3 Call to see the sick at Geo. Johnson's & at Mother Thomas'. Call also at Mother Engle's, widow of Wm. Engle, & at Albert's. Speaking meeting pretty fair, but a little slow. Bro. Hall led the meeting. Dine at John Hodson's 3/4 mile south. Call at Simon Adamson's. Lunch there. Pr. at 7:30, Job. 38:4. "Answer thou me."

Wednesday, March 4 Meeting at 10:30. Pretty good. Wrote home in the morning. Recast some sketches of sermons. Dine at Wood Batchelor's. Stay there till evening. Pr at 7:30 John 7:37. Stay at John Elliot's. Hall led the morning meeting.

Thursday, March 5 Meeting at 10:30. Quite good. Dine at Elliot's. 0Went to Joshua Chamness' in the afternoon. Supper there. He converted in my meeting here in 1866. Now gone to the Friends and much backslidden. Rev. Wm. Hall pr. at 7:00 Ps 103:1-5. Stay at Elliots.

Friday, March 6 Speaking meeting at 10:30. Dine at Elliots. Go to Carlos (Bloomingsport station) and thence to New Castle. Supper at Rev. D.O. Darling's. Protracted meeting going on at the Church (U.B.) and Rev D.O. Darling pr. seventy minutes "Repent and be converted." Large congregation. Stay at Harvey Roots.

Saturday, March 7 Call at Darling's. Go on 9:20 train to McCowan's station. Call at Robert Wright's. Dine with Rev. Halleck Floyd at Rinker's. He having come to attend the Qr. Meeting, that I might go to Dublin and preach a funeral, I returned on the 2:00 train & went on to Cambridge City, and walked thence to Dublin. Call at Dr. G.W. Champ's. Stay at Wilson Scroggy's.

Sunday, March 8 Pr. Wilson Scroggy's funeral, Rev. 14:13 (text Chosen by Sister Scroggy). Returned to Sister Scroggy's. Had called at Rev. W.H. Oler's in the morning; also called in the afternoon awhile. But dined at Scroggy's. Pr. at 7:00 Col. 2:6—a discourse to young converts. A revival recently. Stay at Scroggy's. Their Relatives, there, were W.E. Howry & Amelia his wife, Sarah Wilt whom they raised, as they also did Amelia; John Young Mrs. Scroggy's brother; Mrs. Stark Scroggy's half sister; Rachael Redfern his full sister, etc.

Monday, March 9 Went on 6:15 morning train to Corwin, Warren Co., Ohio, via Richmond & Xenia. Bury Wilson Scroggy, aged 79 in the cemetery there, in the family burial lot. We held a brief service at the waiting room at the depot. We had dined at Xenia. After the burial we went to the depot & remained till car time. Came home via Xenia to Dayton.

Saturday, March 14 Read up proofs on the March *Star* and partly made up the inside pages. Went on the 10:15 train to Millville 22 miles north-west. Walk up to Rev.

Jacob Williams, 1/2 m. north of town. Dine there. Walk up to Flatrock Chapel. Pr. Jas. 1:27. Qr. Conf. followed. Supper at Levi Williams Rev. D.O. Darling pr. at 7:00. Stay at Jac. William's.

Sunday, March 15 Pr. at 10:30, John 1:29. The Lutherans had meeting 1/2 mile south of ours. So our Congregation was limited—the collection small. Communion. Dine at Jac. Williams. Pr. at 7:00, 1 John 3:2. Stay at Levi Williams.

Monday, March 16 Go on 8:10 train to Richmond. Comit interest on Mother Koerner's note, make a new note & pay her $2.00 to make even numbers. Dine at Zeller's. Go on 2:05 train home. Find all well and preparing papers to mail.

Tuesday, March 17 Finish papers & mail them just afternoon.

Friday, March 20 Went on 1:00 train to Richmond & thence to Washington. Supper at Evans Bailey's. Pr. at U.B. Ch at 7:00 Rom 4:16. Stay at Daniel Nelson's.

Saturday, March 21 Go to Williamsburg with Bro. C.B. Small. Dine at Herbert Pierce's. Pr at Mt. Zion 1/2 m N.W. at 1:30 Matt. 5:8. Qr. Conf. Supper at Madison Cranor's. She paralyzed & very low. Wilson pr. 7:00. Stay at Wm. Oler's.

Sunday, March 22 Pr. at 10:30 Zech 13:9. Communion. Dine at Mrs. Martha Balenger's 2 m West. Rev. C.B. Small pr at 7:00. Stay at John Oler's 2 m N.W

Monday, March 23 Bro. Oler takes me depot at Fountain City. Go to Richmond. Dine at Zeller's. Go on 2:05 train home to Dayton. Find all as well as common.

Saturday, March 28 Went on 8:00 a.m. train to Richmond and thence to Dublin. Dine at Rev. W.A. Olers with David Werking & Wife and Bro. Riggle of Salem class. Pr at 2:00, Rev. 15:3. Qr. Conference. Supper at Halleck Floyd's. Pr. at 7:30, Rom. 4:16. Stay at Joseph Gray's.

Sunday, March 29 Prepare a discourse on Matt. 16:16. Pr. it at 10:30. Over 100 take part in the communion.

Dine at "Aunt" Amelia Scroggy's. Go to Bro. Floyd's about 4:00. Stay till meeting time. Pr. at 7:30, Acts 16:31. Stay at Dr. G.W. Champ's.

Monday, March 30 Call at Joseph Gray's. Dine at Rev. M.A. Oler's with Halleck Floyd. Spend part of the afternoon on H. Floyd's. Call at Aunt Scroggy's. Call at Wm. McGath's. Go on the 6:00 train to Richmond and thence to Dayton, having called a few minutes at D.K. Zeller's at Richmond.

Tuesday, March 31 At Home. Saw tailor in the forenoon & went over to town in the afternoon and bought a cloth coat pattern at Rike's. Austin, the tailor, said two yards would not cut me a coat. Rike and his clerk (Galloway) said it was plenty.

Wednesday, April 1 Saw my tailor and they took a day to determine. At home.

Thursday, April 2 Tailors agree that they can cut my coat. At Home.

Friday, April 3 Went on 8:00 train to Richmond. Dine at D.K. Zeller's. Walk a mile & then ride with an Irishman 4 miles and pay him a quarter. Walk on to Abington. Supper at Martin Wyrick's. Pr. at 7:30, 1 Cor. 1:23. Stay at Obadiah Holler's 3/4 m. south-west.

Saturday, April 4 Went in the Afternoon with Rev. John W. Utsler to Philomath Chapel 3/4 m west of town. Pr. at 2:00 Matt. 5:8. Supper at Chas. Leistner's in Philomath. Rev. J.W. Utsler pr at 7:30. Stay at Henry McCashlin's with Bro Utsler.

Sunday, April 5 Preached at Church 3/4 miles west of Philomath at 10:30, 8:17. Communion followed. Dine at John S. Henwood's. His mother, aged 87, is quite religious. He lives 2 ms north-west of the chapel. Preached at 7:30, at the chapel, Col. 2:6. Stay with Rev. John W. Utsler at John Leistner at (1/4 m.S.) Philomath.

Monday, April 6 We go on to Ab. Holler's. Dine early. Go on to Liberty. Visit Peter Minton in Butler Co., Ohio. Stay there.

Tuesday, April 7 Go on to Dayton on Four o'clock train

afternoon. Father Minton took me to Hamilton and gave me XX to pay on May *Star*. Reach Dayton.

Saturday, April 11 Went on 7:00 morn. train to Hamilton & thence to Oxford. Rev. Chas. H. Paddack overtakes me and takes me in his buggy to Mixersville 4 m. East. Dine at Zinks. Pr. at 2:00 at Church. Supper at Mr. Burch's. Enos Veal pr. at 7:30. Stay at Burch's.

Sunday, April 12 Pr. at Mixersville, John 7:37. Communion. Dine at Zink's. Go With Rev. N.L. Hoopingarner in the afternoon to his house 1 m. S. of Lotus. Stay there.

Monday, April 13 Called at Geo. Fry's. Went to Lotus & thence via Connersville, Cambridge, New Castle, to Muncie. Five of us (Dillon, Tharp, Oler, Wilmore, & Wright) hire a baronoke and go on to Selma. Put up at Henry Spangler's. Home during the institute there. Rev. A. G. Bolen pr. at 7:30, Job 23, 10 "When he hath tried me, I shall come forth as gold." Stay at Spangler's.

Tuesday, April 14 Institute began at 8:30. Dine at Shull's. Confer with Philip Oxley and wife who came to consult on their expulsion from the church. Supper at H. Spangler's. Rev. W. A. Oler pr. at 7:30, "Let the mind which was in Christ Jesus." Stay at Spangler's.

Wednesday, April 15 Supper at Bedwell's, with McNew, Rust's, etc. Rev. Wm. Dillon pr. at 7:30. "Have faith in God." I stay at Henry Spangler's.

Thursday, April 16 Dine at John Burchfield's. Supper at Rev. J. Y. Dumunbrun's with Rev. Z. McNew. McNew pr at 7:30 Isa. 9: "Wonderful, Counsellor," etc.

Friday, April 17 Supper at Rev. J. Y. Dumunbrun's. It rained hard and Rev. W.C. Day pr. at 7:30, "God forbid that I should glory," etc.

Saturday, April 18 Session of the institute in the forenoon. Dine at J. Martin's, 2 miles north. Love-feast at 2:30. Quite good. Supper at Platt Mott's, three miles north. Rev. Halleck Floyd pr at 7:30. A very able discourse. Stay at Spangler's.

Sunday, April 19 Pr. at 10:30, Rom. 5:2. Dine at Jas.

Simmonds. They are M.E. People and regard me with especial admiration as resembling Mr. Jas. G. Blaine, especially when speaking! Called at L.G. Saffer's, Spangler's son-in-law's. Their boy Lloyd Garrison Saffer 2 1/2 years old was a great friend, giving me his picture the evening before. Sup[p]er at Rev. J.Y. Demunbrun's. Rev. J.M. Kabrich pr. at 7:30 "Came to seek and save that which was lost." Stay at Henry Spangler's.

Monday, April 20 Went on 4:09 morning train to Muncie, & thence via Alexander to Fairmount. Walked out to Uncle Reeders, after breakfast at Elwood Davis's. Rode part of the way however with Oliver Duling. He a friend (?) to Miss Champ, of Dublin and inquired of her folks. Found Uncle Reeder as well as when I saw him last. Dined at Uncles. went over to look at the place, my farm, and returned. Lodged at Uncle's.

Tuesday, April 21 Flora took me to Fairmount. Went on the Noon train to Anderson. Went on 2:35 (late) train to New Castle. Supper at Rev. D.O. Darling's. Pr. at 7:30 before the W. Mission Asso. of W.R. Conf. from Dan. 2:44. Stay at Rev. M.L. Bailey's.

Wednesday, April 22 Went on 8:00 train to Richmond. Call to see Coe about the *Star* copy. Spent awhile in Y.M.C.A. Reading room. Went to depot. Wrote cards to A. Rector, C.B. Small, John Utsler, etc. Went on 2:05 train home. Prepared copy for the *Star* and mailed it on the 6:35 train to Richmond. After supper called at Dr. Davis'.

Thursday, April 23 At home all day. Called a few minutes to see Rev. Wm. Dillon.

Friday, April 24 Went on 8:00 tr. to Richmond. Read up proofs at Coe's, on the *Star*. Dine at D.K. Zeller's. Saw to the making up of the first side of May *Star*. Went on the 2:25 train to Cambridge City. There take the train to Matamora. Walk down the railroad to Wm. Warren's. Supper there with Rev. F.M. Demunbrun's. Demunbrun pr. at Collett's School-house at 7:30, Heb. 11:1. Stay at G.W.W. Steward's across the White Water river.

Saturday, April 25 Went in the afternoon to Oak Forest. Pr. Isa. 53 Chapter. Quarterly conference. Supper at

Robt. White's. It rains in the evening. Only seven out. Had a brief prayermeeting. Stay at Samuel B. Foster's. He a Meth. E. local preacher. Lives 1/2 mi. N. of the church. Moton also lodged there.

Sunday, April 26 Pr. at Oak Forest at 10:30, Rom. 8:17. Had a prompt love-feast meeting at 9:30. Communion at 12:00. Dine at Wm. Hunter's, 1 1/4 m. north-west, in a ravine on Indian Creek. Pr. at Oak Forest at 7:30. 1 John 3:2. A large congregation. Stay at Harvey White's 2 m. W. on Pipe Creek.

Monday, April 27 Harvey White takes me to Metamora. Go on via Connersville & Cambridge City to Richmon[d] & Dayton. See Dr. Carson of Xenia & Dr. Colinson Carr. Dine at Myers.

Tuesday, April 28 Attend John Sedgwick Manning's funeral at M.E. Church & assist Rev. Clayton.

Wednesday, April 29 At home. Write for the *Star*.

Friday, May 1 At home and writing for the paper. Finish in the afternoon. Floyd came.

Sunday, May 3 Dr. L. Davis preached the baccalaureate address from 2 Tim. 4:2. "Preach the word." Bp. Kephart & wife eat supper with us. Bp. J.J. Glossbrenner pr. at 7:30, Rom. 8:1.

Thursday, May 7 At home in the forenoon. At Woman's Missionary association in the afternoon. Mrs. Ferguson spoke for M.E. Mrs. Montgomery for Baptist, etc. Bishop N. Castle came over with me for supper. Mrs. D.D. DeLong lectured at 8:00.

Friday, May 8 At home in the forenoon. At. W.M. Association part of the afternoon.

Saturday, May 9 At home. Revs. A.J. Newgent & Bryant dine with us and take up lodging over the Sabbath etc. Came in with Floyd who lodges with us since he came.

Sunday, May 10 Attended First Church where Bp. N. Castle pr. at 10:30. Luke 9:23. At Miss Anna Edward's lecture on temperance at Summit St. Ch. at 2:30. She had charts of the human stomach, in various stages of drinking intoxicants. Bp. E.B. Kephart pr at 7:30 Summit St. "While we look not at the things which are seen."

Tuesday, May 12 Went on 10:00 train to Lima on special car. Dine with our company at Burnet house. Go on about 4:00 to Fostoria, Ohio. Put up at Rev. J.W. Rhodes, formerly in North Ohio Conference.

Wednesday, May 13 Board of Education meets in the morning at 8:30. About the Mission board in the afternoon. Missionary sermon at College Chapel at 7:30, by Rev. G.M. Matthews. Continue to board at Rhodes. Pres. C.H. Kiracofe read [rest is blank]

Thursday, May 14 Board of Education meets at 9:00. Gen. Conf. meets at 2:00. Elect secretary on second ballot. Bishop's Address. Unprecedented attempt by them to shake the Constitution! Board of Education met at 7:30.

Friday, May 15 Morning Session of Gen. Conference. Mostly reports of Pub. Agent (Shuey) and Cor. Mis. Sec. Flickinger. Board of Education met again at Chapel at Academy.

Saturday, May 16 Conference part of the forenoon and then the com's held sessions. In the afternoon the session was largely occupied with the reports on credentials.

Sunday, May 17 I attend service at the M.E. Church. Hott pr. Heb. 4:14, 15, 16. Did right well. Dine at Oversalls with Kaprich, Newgent, etc. Then went back to Rhodes'. Some delegates & others call in the afternoon. I Preach at Meth. Prot. Church at 7:30, Matt. 16:16. Stay as usual at Rhodes.

Monday, May 18 On this morning Rev. A. Bennett of Oregon was unseated because he, as alledged, was not a member of church at the time of his election. The vote was 49 to 48. The afternoon & part of the forenoon was given to committees. I was with the com. on Seminary & on Education. Heard Rev. H. Floyd of White River Conf. pr. at U.B. Church on "Not by works of righteousness which we have done."

Saturday, May 23 General Conference in session. H. Floyd read our protest. Mrs. L.R. Keister read her ad-

dress in behalf of the W.M. Association. Appeal in behalf of Rhorersville sustained. Grimm of Rockriver allowed his seat. In the election for bishops, Weaver & Kephart were elected on first ballot, Dickson & Castle on second ballot, and I for coast bishop on 6th ballot. No services this evening. Flickinger elected Foreign Missionary bishop with 69 votes. Shuey reelected agent with 80.

Sunday, May 24 Attended services at the Academy. Bishop N. Castle preached, 1 Cor. 7:31. "Fashion of this world passeth." A fine sermon. None of the bishops are in my judgment equal him as a public orator. Dined at Mr. [blank] a Methodist man. Called at Overhodes to see Wilmore & Floyd. Supper at Vaneaissoll's with Bauder. Heard Pres. W.M. Beardshear pr. "What is thy beloved more than an other beloved." Song of Songs, 5:9.

Monday, May 25 The elections were continued. Warner was elected Mission Secretary, McKee Treasurer, Light Ed. German literature, Landis of Sab. Sch. Literature, Miller Seminary Agent. Thus Billheimer, Mittendorf, Berger, etc., were slaughtered. Afternoon: Dodds, Hoke, Funkhouser, W.L. Shuey, Floyd, Hill & Luttrell elected on Missionary board. Dodds, S. Mills, Geo. Miller, Rike, McKee, Fritz, Applegate, on Pub. House Trustees. Union Bib. Sem. Trustees: L. Davis, Baldwin, Rike, Herr, Hippard, Floyd, Hott, Hoke, S.E. Kumler, Warner, K.A. Thompson, Booth, Dillon, White, McKee, etc. etc.

Tuesday, May 26 Report on Classification of the ministry. Glossbreimer, bishop Emeritus, Flickinger's resignation not accepted. Vote 42 to 42. Rev. D.W. Sprinkle lectured at Academy Chapel, on Andersonville prison. Mission Board meets at U.B. Church. They made appropriations; and agreed to pay my moving expenses.

Thursday, May 28 Reached Dayton about day-light. Slept part of the forenoon.

Friday, May 29 At home in forenoon. Dr. Davis called awhile. Went in afternoon to Union City, Farmland, and thence to Abram Hammer's. Staid there till next afternoon.

Saturday, May 30 Staid at Hammer's till afternoon. Leroy Starbrick and his older brother Walter dine there. Went Zion Chapel pr. Jude, 20, 21. Qr. Conf. followed. Supper at John Life's. Rev. G.W. Ford pr. at 8:00, "Be thou faithful unto death," etc. Stay at Martin Bartlett's, Christian Life's son-in-law's. Platt Mott & wife also staid there.

Sunday, May 31 Pr. at Zion Chapel, six miles north of Farmland, at 10:30, Matt. 16:16. Communion followed. Dine at Luther Moorman's 1 1/2 mile east. His wife scarcely able to sit up at all, but tending rapidly to consumption. Preach at 3:30, Rom. 4:16. Many of the Selma people are at Zion to-day. Go home with Father Rust and stay till after dinner next day.

Monday, June 1 Dined at Rust's. He takes me over to Farmland, a mile west. I go on 1:12 train to Union and thence to Dayton, arriving about 4:00.

Wednesday, June 3 At home. Hired Mr. McLeardie's rig and took Mrs. Wright, Estelle Harris, my niece, & Katie to Woodland cemetery, etc.

Friday, June 5 At home. Spent forenoon in work on yard fence, cutting grass, etc. Dr. Jasper Reid of Leipsic, Ohio, called to see us. He attended school formerly at Hartsville when Susan was there.

Saturday, June 6 Went on 8:00 train to Richmond, called a few minutes at D.K. Zeller's, and went to Dunreith. Dined at Shambaugh House, and wrote some letters there. Went on 3—[lines appear in text] train to Greensburg and thence to Hartsville. Revs. H. Floyd and J.M. Kabrich along from Dunreith down. Stay at Rev. A.C. Wilmore's with Br. Kabrich.

Sunday, June 7 Pres. C.H. Kiracofe pr baccalaureate sermon from Eccl. "Let us hear the conclusion," etc. A good discourse and neatly read. Dine at Pres. Kiracofe's. Children's day in the afternoon Sabbath Sch. I deliver a narration of the history of Otterbein in the absence of J. Riley, who had been appointed tospeak on that. Supper at Rev. A.C. Wilmore's. Rev. Halleck Floyd pr. at 8:00, 1 Sam. 16:18. I stay at Rev. E. Pitman's.

Monday, June 8 Board met at 8:00 A.M. Short Session. I dine at G.C. Mensch's with Kabrich. Afternoon Session. Supper at Rev. Wm. Fix's. Entertainment anniversary of the three literary societies. Stay at Prof. J.S. Funkhouser's.

Tuesday, June 9 Board met at 8:00 a.m. Dined at Rev. Isaac Van Sickle's. Afternoon session, Faculty elected. Evening session. Address of Rev. Mr. Barnard on the life and times of Wickliffe, at 8:00. Well-delivered. Stay at Van Sickles.

Wednesday, June 10 Session of the board at 8:00. Graduating addresses at 10:00 A.M. Beck, Hager Dean, Dr. Galloway, and Rev. King graduate. Addresses good and mostly well-delivered. Dine at Rev. M.F. Dawson's. Board meeting at 2:00. Supper at Wilmore's. Call at Mother Fix's, Wertz, Riley's. At concert in the evening. Stay at Rev. A.C. Wilmore's.

Thursday, June 11 Went at 5:00 A.M. to Hartsville Crossing & thence to Greensburg. Lunch there. Go on to Rushville & Hartford City, and to Jonesboro & Fairmount. Lunched at New Castle. Called at Mattox's at Hartford. Went out from Fairmount with Robt. Reeder to Uncle Reeder's. Staid there.

Friday, June 12 At Uncle's in the forenoon. His cancer is quite bad. Went over to my farm, 5 miles due east of Fairmount. Hindered by rain from seeing much. Staid at Uncle's.

Saturday, June 13 Staid at Uncle's till after dinner. Flora goes with me to Beech Grove, 5 ms. N.W. of Bethel, to Qr. meeting. Pr. James 1:27. Qr. Conference followed. Supper at John W. Broyles' one mile north. Rev. D. Miller (Qr. Conf. preacher) spoke on "the Testament." Lodge at Joseph Broyles 2 1/2 m North.

Sunday, June 14 Pr. in the grove at 10:30, Matt. 16:16. Dine at Miller's. Pr. at 3:30 sacramental sermon 1 Cor. 5:7. Went on to Rev. C.W. Rector's. Called awhile. Then to Rev. A. Rector's, 4 ms S.E. of New Corner. Staid at Rector's.

Monday, June 15 Bro. A. Rector takes me to Muncie. Go on 1:00 train to Union City and thence home, to Dayton.

Wednesday, June 17 At home. Attended prayer meeting at Summit Street Church. Rev. R.K. Little led in the services.

Thursday, June 18 At home. Had an impression taken for a new plate for upper teeth, just before noon. Attended a loyal prayer meeting at 8:00 at the Church. Led the meeting. Seven present. Dr. C. Davis, W. Dillon, Kumler, Huffman, John Nicholas, Keller, Becktel & Wright.

Friday, June 19 At home. Worked in garden most of the day.

Saturday, June 20 Went on 6:45 train to Arcanum. Write letters at the depot. Go on 1:20 train to Bloomingsport Station. John Charles, a friend, takes me part of the way & I walk the rest to New Hope Church 3 ms. N.E. of Economy. Found the Quarterly conference in session. Supper at Jas. Hutchens' 1/2 mile east. Pr. at 8:30 1 Pet. 2:4,5. Lodge at Rev. C.B. Small's, 1/4 m north.

Sunday, June 21 Pr. at 10:30, Matt. 16:15, 16. Communion followed. Dine at Charles Morrison's 1/2 mile north. Go on to Church at 4:00. Much rain and only three were there. Staid at Morrison's till morning.

Monday, June 22 Bro. Morrison took me to the train at Carlos. Go on early train to Dayton, home, via Arcanum. At home the rest of the day.

Tuesday, June 23 At home. Received a telegram from Fairmount, Indiana saying that Uncle Wm. H.H. Reeder was not expected to live till morning. The messenger brought the telegram at 1:00 in the morning.

Wednesday, June 24 Started at 7:10 via Union City & Jonesborough to Fairmount. Dined at Chrisko's, 1 mile east of Fairmount, at invitation of Friend Little. Walk on till I met John W. Broyle's coming after me. Found Uncle alive but very sick. He died a little before midnight.

Thursday, June 25 At Uncle's till funeral services by Rev. Garretson at 2:00. Bury him at Baptist Church on the state road 4 miles east. Stay at Uncle's. Uncle John Braden, & Aunt Eliza, & Joseph Broyles & family there.

Friday, June 26 Go on the 11:38 train to Anderson & to New Castle arriving at 4:00. Supper & lodging at Rev. D.O. Darling at the parsonage.

Saturday, June 27 Rainy morning. Staid at Darling's till after dinner. Preached at 2:00, Ps. 17:4. Quarterly conference followed. A very peculiar one. Little bickerings come to the surface. Conference inclined to do little. I take supper at Mother Elizabeth Schidtknecht's. Pr. at 8:00 Titus 2:14. Stay at Rev. O. Jennings' second house east of the church.

Sunday, June 28 Pr. at 10:30, Rom. 4:16, Communion followed. Dine at David Mullen's 1 1/2 ms southeast. Albert Metsker and wife dine there. Pr. at 8:00, Matt. 19:27.

Monday, June 29 Go on 8:00 train to Richmond. Susan there. Go after dinner, 2:20, to (home) Dayton.

Tuesday, June 30 Went to town in the afternoon.

Wednesday, July 1 Went to town in the afternoon at 5:00 and got my new set of upper teeth.

Saturday, July 4 Went on the 8:00 A.M. train to Richmond. Called at D.K. Zeller's. Paid grandmother Koerner $25.00. Went on to Hagerstown. Rev. P. Adamson met me and took me to his house, where I dined with Rev. C.B. Small. Pr. at 2:00 from 1 Tim. 3:15. Qr. Conf. followed. Supper at Jont. Stover's 1/4 m. north. Many traveling on the cars to-day. Preach at 8:00, Acts 2:40. Stay at A. Grant Mendenhall's, 1 1/2 miles north-east.

Sunday, July 5 Pr. at Bethel at 10:30, Matt. 5:12. Communion followed. Dine at C.C. Weyle 1 1/2 ms. west of Economy. His brother and wife, who live east of Economy there also. Lovefeast meeting at 3:30. Well-attended, and a good meeting. Supper at Adam Oler's He in quite a friendly mood. Rev. C.B. Small pr. at 8:00, Luke 14:16. Stay at George Manning's, 1/2 m. east.

Monday, July 6 Went with Bro. Small and took the Economy & Washington Hack out east & go to Washington & Richmond on railroad. Dine at D.K. Zeller's. Go on 2:20 train to Dayton.

Saturday, July 11 Went on the 8:10 train to Richmond & thence to Cambridge City. Father John H. Lawson & grandson John met me & convey me to Daniel

Lawson's, 2 ms. north-west, where I dine. Pr. at West Fork Chapel at 2:00, Heb. 12:1. Qr. Conf. followed. Resolutions on Sab. desecration & on Church Commission. Supper at Noah Heiney's 1 1/2 m. west. Pr. at 8:00 Luke 24:46. Stay at Noah Heiney's.

Sunday, July 12 Pr. at 10:30, Jas. 1. 12. Communion followed. Dinner at John Shaffer's. Lowell & wife, Jas. Tweedy, Sister Hanby, Sister Earl, Theodore Shaffer & wife, Gray & wife, Mrs. John Adams, John Stiggleman & wife, etc, etc. there. Love-feast meeting at 3:30. Quite a good meeting. Supper at Father Howard's with Bro. Oler, the pastor, His son David quite promising. David a brother to Mrs. Horace Herr. Pr. at 8:00, Acts 3:19. Stay at Daniel Lawson's.

Monday, July 13 Stay at Bro. Lawson's till after an early dinner. Father Lawson takes me to Cambridge City. Call twenty minutes at Henry Meyers. Take the 1:15/35 train to Richmond & thence to Dayton, arriving at home before 5:00. Found all well.

Friday, July 17 The *Christian Conservator* came on.

Saturday, July 18 Went on the 8:00 train to Richmond. Called at D.K. Zeller's. Went to Honey Creek Station. Br. Jones takes Bro. Moore & his wife & myself to Jacob Rinker's 4 ms north-east. Dine there. Pr. at 2:00, Exodus 15:11. Qr Conf. followed. That appeal case of P. Oxley & wife. Supper at Rinkers. Milton Harris pr. at 8:00. Rom. 10:1. Stay at Michael Groenendyke's, 1/2 m north-west.

Sunday, July 19 Pr. at 10:30, Rom. 5:1. Dine at Jac. Rinkers, 1/4 m. north-east. Bro. Moore baptized several after the forenoon meeting. Love-feast at 4:00. Real good. Supper at Michael Groenendyke's. Pr. at 8:00, Acts 2:40. Stay at Jac. Rinker's.

Monday, July 20 Bro. Rinker takes me to Honey Creek to the 8:00 train. Go on to Richmond. Stay at depot till 2:20. Write some. See Rev. A.C. Wilmore. I go on to Dayton. Reach home after 4:00.

Friday, July 24 Went on the 7:00 train to Hamilton. Saw David Beall & sons & daughter (Mrs. Bonebrake). Go on to Liberty (not noticing Lotus on account of being absorbed in reading an editorial on General U.S. Grant) and find my way back to Union a little after noon. Dine at Rev. N.L. Hoopingarner. Stay there that afternoon & night.

Saturday, July 25 Took Dinner at Mrs. Fry's. Got the two oldest copies of the United Brethren in Christ Discipline, printed in 1817 & 1819. Call at Benj. Huddleston's after dinner & go with Rev. Noah Leander Hoopingarner to Greenwood Church 3 ms north-east of Lotus. Preach at Greenwood at 2:00 p.m. Qr. Conf. followed. Text 2 Tim. 3:4. Supper at Miles La Fuse's 3 miles North-west with Daniel Koerner & Bro. Hoopingarner. Rev. John Utsler pr. at 8:30. John 14:2. Went home with Bro. Hoopingarner.

Sunday, July 26 Pr. at Greenwood Church at 10:30 Rom. 1:3, 4. Communion followed. Dine at Mother Eaton 's. Pr. at 3:30, 1 Cor. 13:13. Go home with Daniel Koerner, my wife's brother, who lives 7 ms. south of Liberty.

Monday, July 27 Stay at Daniel's all day & till morning.

Tuesday, July 28 Daniel, after an early dinner, takes me to Liberty. Go on 1:32 tr. to Hamilton & thence by close connection to Dayton. Found my folks all well.

Wednesday, July 29 At home. Prof. L. Bookwalter called in the forenoon.

Friday, July 31 Went on the 8:00 train to Richmond. Called at Bro. D.K. Zeller's. Mother Koerner now in her 89th year, is considerably worried with the hot weather. She gets about with easy movement & ascends the stairs to her room several times a day. Went on 11:00 train to Washington. Call at Evan Bailey's. Dine at Cyrus Osborne's. Meet trustees & a com. to confer on Washington Church debt. No conclusion reached. Supper at Nathan Brasier's. Go home with Sylvestor Harris' at Walnut Level. His children Clarence, Clem & Omer. His wife a Scott—John Scott's daughter.

Saturday, August 1 Sylvester takes me after an early breakfast to Hagerstown. Go on the 6:10 train to Yellow Banks five miles north-west of Brookville, Ind. Go to Ez. Collett's & dine there or at Jas. his son's, where they are threshing wheat. At 2:00, comment at the school-house on John 15:1-6. Qr. Conference. Supper at Ezekiel

Collett's. Pr. at 8:00 Ps. 16:8. Stay at Collett's. Rev. F.M. Demunbrun, the pastor, is with me supper & lodging.

Sunday, August 2 Pr. at 10:00, Rom. 3:5. Communion followed. Dined at Wilson's where lives Rev. Geo. Wilson—just across the river. Love-feast at 3:30. Fair meeting. Stay at Ez. Collett's.

Monday, August 3 Went with Rev. F.M. Demunbrun in buggy to Andersonville. Dined at John Morgan's. Went in the afternoon to Sanes Creek at the old Harris crossing, with Bro. Demunbrun. Walk up to Anson Moor's. Stay there.

Tuesday, August 4 Called at Charles Stevens at our old homestead—My father's. He was married a few months ago to my niece, Flora Wright, My brother William's oldest daughter. Also I called at N.F. Bowen's, he being married to my bro. Wm's second daughter. Dine at Moor's. He takes me to Glenwood & I go via Hamilton to my home in Dayton.

Sunday, August 9 Attended service at Summit Street Church. The pastor, Rev. G.M. Mathews preached. Rev. Wm. Dillon pr. at 8:00 at Summit Street.

Monday, August 10 Went on 7:00 A.M. train to Union City, Jonesboro, & Fairmount. Rode out with Jessee Bright's. Found Aunt Lizzie's about as usual. Went over to see my farm with Wm. H.H. Reeder, Junior. Went to see Wm. Duling about taking the agency for the heirs of the My Father's Land. Staid at Aunt Lizzie's.

Tuesday, August 11 At Aunt's. They are threshing. Staid there till next morning.

Wednesday, August 12 Just got to the early train in time to take the cars to LaFontain. Some ministers aboard. Jacob Thomas came after us and took us to his house three miles north-east and thence to Lincolnville, I riding part of the way with a Bro. Jackson. Found my home at Jas. F. Tweedy's near the Church. Conference opened at 2:00. Examination of local preachers completed. Pres. Kiracofe pr at 8:00 on "What shall I do to obtain eternal life." Stay at Tweedy's.

Thursday, August 13 Conference continues. Rev. W.C.

Day dines with me at Bro. Tweedy's. Discussion in the afternoon on Floyd's resolution on the Church Commission, in condemnation of it. Adopted by a vote of 31 to 8. Rev. Z. McNew pr. at night. Stay as usual at my home at Tweedy's.

Friday, August 14 Conference as usual. Committee on boundaries meet at 1:00 and agree on report. NcNew elected on first ballot. I.M. Tharp elected on second ballot by a majority of five. Educational meeting at night. Stationing Committee met at 7:00 at Raferd Copeland's. Stay at Tweedy's.

Saturday, August 15 Conference business continues & is concluded about 5:30, perhaps. I take supper at J. Heavenridge's with Bp. N. Castle. Castle never asked me once to preside at the conference, for an hour even. I pr. at 8:00 John 1:46. The conference gave me a farewell after the discourse. Go to Sailors two miles northwest and lodge.

Sunday, August 16 At[t]end love-feast meeting in the grove. Bp. Castle pr on Faith, an interesting sermon. I dine at my home. Sabbath School anniversary in the afternoon. Supper at Tweedy's with Rev. W.C. Day. Missionary meeting at night. Oler, Day, & myself deliver the addresses. I take up a collection of $4.28 for Chinese Walla Walla mission. Stay at Tweedy's.

Monday, August 17 Go to 8:00 m. train. Go to Fairmount & to Aunt Lizzie Reeder's. Cous. Lida Braden there, from Milford, Ill. I spend most of the day in looking over accounts on the Dan Wright estate. Go in the evening to Fairmount & thence to Marion. Go on train about Midnight toward Chicago.

Tuesday, August 18 Reached Chicago about 9:00, the train being behind time. Did some purchasing of small articles needed especially at Lehman's Fair which occupies about a half block. Went on 12:10 train westward. Reach Davenport about night. Arrive at Casey next morning about 5:00. Go out in hack which goes to Fontanello Mondays Wednesdays & Fridays.

Wednesday, August 19 Go out on hack from Casey to Lee Hoisington's. Go to see the corn on my farm a mile south, and oats. Go via Mr. Camps who is thrashing to

Lee Hoisingtons for dinner. Look over the west side of the farm. Supper at Hoisington's. Pr at 8:00 at Lowrey's school-house, Matt. 19:27. Stay at Hoisington's. Their children are Pearl a son 16, Jose 12, & Gerty 5.

Thursday, August 20 Went over to where Charles Bitner my tenant was threshing oats. He had 383 bush. I dined at Alex. H. Hepler's 1/2 m east of my corner. Went back to Hoisingtons. Saw Isaac Kerr who lives next farm south of mine. Lock a renter lives west. Raper just north of him. Brockman north of my west half, Roberts east of our school-house. Frederick a mile south.

Friday, August 21 Went to Frederick's drew up an article with Charley Bitner to whom I rented my farm. Walked back to Hoisington's. He took me in a wagon to Casey; train behind time and I did not get away till 4:00. Reached Des Moines. Stay at the Givens House near the depot.

Saturday, August 22 Start on 8:00 m. train toward St. Paul. Pass through Fort Dodge, Ogden, Humboldt, Livermore, Laverne, Albert Lea, etc. Pass up through Minnesota by Wasoca and Carver. Stop at the Pauly House, near the Manitoba Depot in Minneapolis, for lodging. Bathe quite fully & change linen.

Sunday, August 23 Went to Westminster Presbyterian Church and heard Rev. Dr. Kirkwood pr. on 1 Cor. 13:1-3. Dine as usual at the hotel. Spent afternoon mostly in my room at the hotel.

Monday, August 24 Went on early (6:30) train to St. Paul. I leave my baggage at the Union Depot. I breakfasted at a fair eating house. Went to the post-office and got a letter from Susan. I got a ticket to Palouse Junction, Washington Territory, at the Union Pacific Gen. office for $42.40. I checked my baggage and purchased articles needed on the way. I went aboard at 4:00 p.m. & started west. I mailed a card to my little daughter, Katie, at Minneapolis Depot. Ride over prairies all the afternoon. Reach Sauk Rapids on the Mississippi about dark. Did not sleep till after we passed Brainard. Slept four or five hours.

Tuesday, August 25 Awoke at Fargo. It is yet moonlight. Pass the Dalrymple farm about daylight. It is a 20,000

acre tract and is quite profitable. In on through Bismarck and Mandan. Reach the "Bad lands" before night. Wildest of scenes: Comical hills of belts of black, gray, red, and white stone. All manner of shapes and a general chaos. Night closed on us and we went through the mile tunnel in the dark.

Wednesday, August 26 Awoke at Yellow Stone Valley, near Big Horn. Yellow Stone a beautiful river. Reach Bozeman just west of Livingstone, reach Galatin valley, a fine valley truly, at Galatin see the clear stream of the upper Missouri Big Muddy's youth is as pure as can be. Reach Heron about night. Go through the mile tunnel in the night. The strange whistling of those who go in and out the door. A drip rubs the door-sill and causes it.

Thursday, August 27 Awoke on Clark River near [blank] Timbered along there for some miles with Spruce, Fir, and some Cedar. Pass Thompson Falls. Pass the Cabinet, a sort of Giants Causeway where confined waters dash between high walls of rocks. Reach Heron. Go in afternoon down Spokane valley. A nice town at Spokane Falls. The valley lies nice, but is rather gravely and stony. See a nice lake near Sprague, thought less lucid than mountain lakes.

Friday, August 28 Go on freight to Colfax. Rode out to Arrasmith's with Bro Augustus Nernitsch (to Bro. Henry Arrasmith's.) Staid there, the first home I was in since leaving Iowa.

Saturday, August 29 I go with R.I. Evans to his house five miles south of Garfield, in the afternoon. He a very decided law man on secrecy. His boys are Ernest, about 15, and George, about 7 years. His wife afflicted with dropsey, but about. One of his daughters married to an Arrasmith. Stay there till morning.

Sunday, August 30 Go to Garfield. Pr. at the Baptist church at 11:00 Heb. 11:10. Dine at Rev. W.R. Lloyd's with Bro. R.I. Evans & family. . Preach in afternoon at 4:00, Jude 14. I lodge at Bro. Lloyd's. He lives on a hill at the west end of town.

Monday, August 31 Staid at Bro. Lloyd's till nearly noon, and write up an article for the *Telescope*. Dine at J.C. Lawrence's in town. He a hardware merchant. Bro. Lloyd

& family go with me to Dr. Samuel Simpson's. He a Baptist and a great friend to the anti-secrecy cause. Supper. Go back to Bro. Lloyd's, and Rev. H.O. Kerns comes and takes me to his house after dark.

Tuesday, September 1 Stay at Bro. Kerns till after dinner. Rev. J.S. Spooneymore takes me after dinner to Rev. J.S. Rhoads. He P.E. of Walla Walla conference district. His wife a daughter of Rev. Jer. Kenoyer, and she went to school to me at Sublimity, Oregon, 27 ys ago. They have five children: Jeremiah, Chester, Precious, Adelia, & Castle.

Wednesday, September 2 Call at Rev. Jacob Antrim Kenoyer's forty rods north of Bro. Rhoads'. Go on to Henry Arrasmith's. Dine there. Go to Jac. Arrasmith's forty rods north of Bethel Church. Revs. Tressenriter, Curtis, Mitcham, and Evans come. This my conference home. People of the neighborhood: Taylor, Henry, Arrasmith, John Arrasmith, Judge Kincaid, Ells. Rev. J.C. Spoonemore pr. at 8:00.

Thursday, September 3 Conference opened. J.C. Spoonemore, secretary. Examinations. Rev. C.W. Wells pr. at 8:00.

Friday, September 4 Conference continued. Examinations. Rev. J.C. Spoonemore's resolution on "the commission" modified and adopted by a vote of 14 to 9. I pr. at 8:00—Ex. 28:34. Fair success.

Saturday, September 5 Conference continued. Rev. J.S. Rhoads elected P.E. Rev. A.K. Curtis & J.H. Vandever to assist on stationing Com. Stationing Com. met at noon at Jac. Arrasmith's. Conf. Session at night. Uncontrollable mirth over a reference on Ell's case. The report worthy of a Delphic oracle. W.C. Gallaher said: "The chair is not under obligation to furnish the conf. with understanding." Adjourned about 11:00.

Sunday, September 6 Rev. J.H. Griner called and showed me a letter from the doctor at Stockton, Cal. relating to his wife's hopeless insanity. Pr. at 11:00, Matt. 16:16. Had good liberty. A collection of $39.50 raised for me, afterward increased to $41.00. The chart collection was $26.85. Total $67.85. Read the Stationing Com. report. Several itinerants dissatisfied. Black reconciled. Sab. Sch.

Anniversary in the aftern. at 4:30. Rev. J. M. Tressenriter pr. at 8:00. Lev. 14: 5,6,7. Have some especial talk about the Ell's case etc. with Rev. J. S. Rhoads.

Monday, September 7 Rev. J.M. Tressenriter comes after me & I go with him & wife & Rev. C.W. Wells to Colfax and south. Camp on a canyon. Hills 400 ft. above us. Go on in afternoon cross Snake River on the ferry-boat and some miles below—camp at the bend of the road where we next morning leave the river. I climbed the hill four hundred ft. above the river. Sung songs till bed time. I lodge at house near by; bill 25 cts. Only cost on the way. Thos. J. Gallaher, Wm. Mitchell, Jas. Kenworthy, & A.H. Curtis with us in camp. We had dined on the Pennewana and found fine peach orchards further down on the stream.

Tuesday, September 8 Saw two steamboats going down the river in the morning. Went on over hills and came down onto the Tuchanon. Dined at the bridge with Mitchell's, Kenworthy's, Gallaher's. Went on and reach Huntsville in Columbia Co. before night. Supper at Rev. A.K. Curtis's, whom I had known in Iowa & Dakota. Rev. C.W. Wells & I lodge at Wm. Mitchell's. Bro. Mitchell is a brother of Norman Mitchell and a cousin of Rev. L.S. Chittenden. Norman became a minister of the United Brethren Church, but married, left & joined the M.E. Church—is now dead.

Wednesday, September 9 Bros. Wells & Tressenriter & wife went on home. I spend the day at Rev. A.K. Curtis'. Mend my umbrella. Write a little. Attend prayer-meeting at the chapel. Pr. a very brief discourse on Ps. 16:8. Stay at Wm. Mitchell's, and have a good night's sleep. Sister Mitchell is a daughter of Bro. Hammer who lived in the Willamet Valley on the Long Tom when I was there 26 years ago. She was the widow of Mr. Fudge.

Thursday, September 10 Went to Bro. Curtis' again. Change clothes. Write some letters & cards. Dine at Curtis & remain there till 4:00. Go to Rev. J. Black's. He going to Dayton, 8 miles east, up the Lonchett (Loosha). Go with him, excusing myself from supper engaged at James Kenworthy's. Pleasant drive. Sup. at John Bridgeman's. His wife the daughter of Rev. David Brown's, of Upper Wabash Conference, and widow of Hadley. Mother Brown there. Mrs. Hadley several years in Africa as a missionary. Prayer meeting at the Church. I speak on prayer. Stay at Bridgeman's.

Friday, September 11 Visited Calvin Ireland and family; also Kenoyer's. She a sister of Rev. G. Watrons of Iowa Conference, and he there on a visit. Dine at John Bridgman's. Her daughter is Mary Hadley. Her two small children are Maggie Bridgman, aged 7 and John, not quite 4 years. Mrs. Bridgeman a school-mate of my wife at Hartsville College. Went in the afternoon home with Bro. Black to Huntsville. Supper and lodging there.

Saturday, September 12 Went to Rev. A.K. Curtis' & spent the forenoon in writing. Rev. Parsons called. I went to Jas. Kenworthy's for dinner. I found them very friendly. I staid there that afternoon. After supper call at Bro. Curtis, Bro. J.C. Spooneymore and family being there. Pr. at Sem. Chapel at 7:30 Ps. 1:6. Stay at Bro. Kenworthy's. Jas. Kenworthy is his name.

Sunday, September 13 Pr. at Sem. Chapel at 11:00, Matt. 19:27. Rather an unsympathetic congregation, the holiness question having by division thrown a damper on the community. Bro. Wm. Mitchell sung "All Hail the Power of Jesus Name" when I had announced "Nearer My God to Thee". Dined at Rev. J.W. Black's . Bro. Black takes me to Dayton. Pr. at 4:30, Luke 24:46. Supper at John Bridgeman's. Go back to Huntsville. Hear the closing part of Rev. J.C. Spoonemore's discourse on Ps. 48:12,13. Stay at Wm. Mitchell's.

Monday, September 14 Went with Wm. Mitchell to Walla Walla, down the Tonchet (Too-sha) via Waitsburg. Cross (after 5 or 6 ms) over to Spring Valley, & then over to Dry Branch and then to Mill Creek, on which Walla Walla is situated. We had left the Blue Mountains some miles to our left out in plain sight. Saw beautiful country on our way especially on both sides of the Mill Creek. Warm clear day.
Reached Walla Walla about 12:45. Dined at Rev. C.W. Wells. Bro. Mitchell left after dinner. I staid there all day. Disappointed about a letter from home.

Tuesday, September 15 Went out with Bro. Wells. Saw Koontz, a M.E. itinerant & Strong, the M.E. pastor. Saw Egbert of the Journal, Tom Corwin's last student and Read formerly of Toledo, Ohio, brother of Reed of

Cin. Gazette. Dined at Wells. Called in afternoon at Kelso's, and Caswell Witts, son of Caswell. Supper & lodging at Witt's. She a Barker & niece to Henkle at Philomath.

Wednesday, September 16 Put letter in the office to Susan and enclosing one to Orville. Went to Bro. Wells'. Spent rest of the forenoon in writing. Went in the afternoon to call on Rev. Mr. Eslinger. Purchased Sunday School cards for Calvin Ireland of Dayton, W.T. Came home. Pr. at 7:00 Matt. 14:33. Flora Fower (Kenoyer) an old pupil at Sublimity came & staid all night. Had a very intelligent congregation. Stay at Wells'. His wife a Williamson, near NiWot, Colorado. I sent books to Orville & Katie by mail.

Thursday, September 17 Started at 11:00 for Blue Mountain Station and for Weston, Umatilla Co., Oregon. Rev. J.M. Tressenriter, meets us (Rev. C.W. Wells & wife & myself) at Blue Mountain Station, and took us to his house at Weston. Dine there. Go to post-office and get a letter of Sept. 1st from Susan (It had been forwarded from Colfax, Wash. Ter.[ ]) Also a card from Sickafoose and letter from Rev. M.M. Crow about Camp meeting at Philomath. Looked at new Church at Weston. Stay at Tressenriter's.

Friday, September 18 About town some. Dine at Tressenriter's. Stay at Tressenriter's.

Saturday, September 19 Meeting of the trustees of Weston Church. Arrange all satisfactorily. Dine at Tressenriter's. At the Church in afternoon. Supper at M.J. McDaniel's. Rev. C.W. Wells pr. at 7:30. I stay at McDaniel's. Prof. Frank A. Kumler & his sister Juan came about 9:30 & staid there.

Sunday, September 20 Pr. at 11:00 Matt. 13:44. Dedicate the First U.B. Church at Weston Umatilla Co., Oregon. Raised $407.50 of cash and subscription. Cash coll. for me, $14.10. Go to Ginn's with Bro. Wells & wife for dinner. She one of the first members here. Supper at Ginn's. Pr. at 8:00 Gen. 15:1. Prof. Frank A. Kumler spoke about thirty minutes on education. Go with Wells & wife to T.J. Gallaher.

Monday, Spetember 21 Went with T.J. Gallaher to

Pendleton in a buggy. Stop at the Golden Rule Hotel for dinner. Call at M.E. Pastor's and at J.J. Lee's. Learn of Thos. Lee and his family—he a brotherinlaw of the Mobleys. J.J. Lee calls on me with Copeland. Long talk with them. Leave Pendleton about 10:00 for Portland. Awake at Dalles City. Saw Cascades Castle Rock, Roster Rock, Multnomah Falls, etc. in the morning.

Tuesday, September 22 Reach Portland at 10:00. B.L. Haynes meets me & takes me to Rev. J.B. Leichtenthaler's 3 miles up the river. Stay there till next morning. Father L. is 83 years old and quite spry. The old lady is quite poorly. Their son Harrison is living at home.

Wednesday, September 23 Go back to Portland and Call at our Chinese Mission House. Mrs. Sickafoose at Home, only. Go on to Corvallis. Prof. G.M. Miller meets me & takes me through the rain to Philomath. Stay at Miller's.

Thursday, September 24 Called at Allen's. Attended prayers at the college chapel and called at the M.M. Crow's. Went to Camp ground. Rev. Lambert held a service on prayer. Dine with John Kitson's on the grounds. Rev. Taylor pr in afternoon on second work. Supper at Rev. E.B. Whittaker's. Rev. G. Sickafoose pr. at 7:00. Heb. 6:1. Stay at Whit[t]aker's.

Friday, September 25 Attend services at College. Call at M.M. Crow's & at Rev. E.C. Wyatt's. Go on to Camp Meeting. Rev. G. Sickafoose is Bible lesson on adoption. Dine at Rev. A. Bennett's. Stay there till evening. Sister Berry, widow of Rev. Berry, recently deceased, was there. I knew them in Minnesota. I preach at Camp meeting at 7:30, Hebr. 13:14. Stay at Prof. G.M. Miller's.

Saturday, September 26 Saturday morning I attended meeting at 10:30 Albright leads. Lambert & he shoot at each other. Dine at Whitacre's. Supper at N.W. Allen's. Sickafoose pr. at 7:00. I stay at M.M. Crow's. J.R. Crow and his son there. J.R. was one of my students at Sublimity twenty-seven years ago.

Sunday, September 27 Went to Whitacre's after my washing & thence to Prof. G.M. Miller's. Attended meeting at the Tabernacle at 11:00. Sickafoose made a polemical harangue on Second work doctrine. Dine with Rev. E. Wyatt on the ground. His wife (Mary Pierson) a stu-

dent of mine at Sublimity in 1858-9. I pr. at 3:00 Eph. 1:7. Very large audience and excellent attention. Sickafoose baptizes one man byimmersion nearby. Supper at Miller's. Sickafoose preaches at night. A real polemic, an attempted replyto me. Stay at Rev. N.W. Allen's.

Monday, September 28 Go to Prof. Miller's. Several call on me. Prof. Rankin & others. Dine there with Prof. Rankin. Go down town with Prof. Miller. I call at Hinkle's store, and talk with the younger Hinkles. Supper at Miller's. Attend Chapel at 7:00 and baptize three. Rev. Jas. R. Parker pr. at 7:00. I stay at Rev. Jas. E. Connor's. He married a daughter of Jacob Henkle. Connor, the adopted son of Rev. T.J. Connor.

Tuesday, September 29 Go to Prof. G.M. Miller's before breakfast & get ready to start. Rev. E.B. Whitacre & wife & two children & myself go via Corvallis on to Jesse Harritt's where we lodge. All seemed glad to see me. I lived with them a couple of months in 1857, while recovering from Panama fever, & they were very kind to me. We lunched at Mr. Tomlinson's on the way.

Wednesday, September 30 Staid at Bro. Harritt's. Alice, their married daughter, came. Also Emily (Stout) Luce, a student of mine at Sublimity in 1857-8. Mrs. Whitacre mends my valise. Go in afternoon to Hopewell, 3 miles north-west of Wheatland, in Yamhill county. Stay at Aaron Stephen's, a Baptist man, where my home is.

Thursday, October 1 Opened Conference at 8:30. A good attendance. Quite a discussion on the reinstatement of Rev. A. Bennett, who had been denied a seat in Gen. Conf. because not a member of a class at the time of his election as delegate, though such soon after. Dine at Stephen's. A pleasant afternoon session, five applicants. Supper at Stephen's. Rev. J.W. Pulley pr. at 7:00, John "If any man serve me" & verses preceding. A clear speaker, good language, rather graceful, not very able. Rev. S.S. Osborn exhorts. Stay at Stephens.

Friday, October 2 Session as usual. Harritt's resolution is read, & made the order for 2:00. Dine at Stephen's. Devote all aftern. on Harritt's resolution. Adopted 18 to 9. Supper at Stephen's. Rev. G. Sickafoose pr. at 7:30, "When Christ your life shall appear, then shall we appear with him in glory." Staid at Stephen's. Rev. Andrew Hunsaker staid there also.

Saturday, October 3 Mosher & Bennett elected P. Es. in aftern. Business proceeds with dispatch. Dine at Stephen's. Afternoon business progresses rapidly. Stationing Com. meets in grove near Stephen's. Supper as usual at Stephen's. Night session. Adjourn about 10:00.

Sunday, October 4 Made out credentials for licentiates & those to be ordained. Pr. at 11:00. II Sam. 22:31. Spoke about 1:45 hours. Collection $25.10 ($10.17 were added at night.) I dine with B.L. Haynes of Clackamus Mis. at his tent. Rev. J.W. Pulley pr. at 4:30. No lunch. Rev. C.N. Plowman pr. at 7:30. Ps. 8: "What is man," etc. I go with Rev. J.S. Osborn & his wife & Isaac Coy to Benj. Antrim's. Lodge there. The Philomath brethren struck tent and retired in the afternoon.

Monday, October 5 Sent to Wheatland, 1 mile distant, to see about letters, etc. Got none. Went with Rev. J.S. Osborn to Jesse Harritt's, two miles west of Salem. Dined there Isaac Coy along. Rev. Eli Whitacre & wife & Children (Frank & Johnny) along, & Rev. C.B. Masters of Rogue River. Mr. Jas. Emmit & his wife (Alice Harritt) also there. Go on after dinner to Salem. Send a letter containing a draft for $1.00 to Susan, & inclosing Oregon resolutions on the Church Commission & Allotments of labor. Go on to Bro. Osborn's on Hill Creek 6 miles below Sublimity.

Tuesday, October 6 Bro. Osborn takes me to Isaac Coy's. He an aqquaintan [sic] of mine of 1857-59 at Sublimity. She went to school to me at Sublimity. We went on to George W. Hunt's 2 1/2 miles north of Sublimity. He once a United Brethren member and a warm friend of mine. Now out of Church. His wife's name is Elizabeth, and their children: Temperance, Georgianna, Milton, Melanchthon, Jeptha, and Sara or Sally. Dine at Hunt's. Call on Melanchthon. Stay at G.W.'s.

Wednesday, October 7 Called at John Downing's. His first wife a Hunt. His second wife a Wisconsin lady. Dine at Rev. John S. Osborn's. Their children, William, Henry, Daniel, Laura. Take the cars at Turner for Portland. Arrive there at 4:20. Take a room at St Charles' Hotel Number 93. Write a little. Lunch in my room. Go to

U.B. Chinese Mission School. Rev. G. Sickafoose & wife run the school. Chinese boy of 12 ys. Moi Ling. Talk a little while to the school. Stay at Hotel.

Thursday, October 8 Breakfast at Hotel. Go to Postoffice, and thence to buy ticket on Steamer Columbia for San Francisco. Ticket at 25 per cent discount. Costs 15 dollars. It being Chinese annual festival, I visit their Joss House. Hundreds of Chinese there and along the streets. In the Joss House is on the right a horse (paddy) covered with a white cloth to the left a set of images, etc. etc. Story above was images, inscriptions, insignia, etc. Go aboard the Steamer Columbia at 7:20. My room 58, berth 3. Start at 12:00 midnight. I slept well.

Friday, October 9 Awoke. Found our Steamer running down Columbia River. Breakfast at 8:00. Reach Astoria & go ashore. Buy a little fruit; also a pair of cloth gloves. After noon go out to sea. Waters a little rough. Slightly sea-sick. Go to bed. Sleep well.

Saturday, October 10 Ate breakfast. Spend the day in writing partly. About 5:00 p.m. we pass Cape Mendocino. Write till in the night. Do not sleep as well as usual.

Sunday, October 11 Awoke. Breakfast at 7:00. Soon af[t]er we enter the Golden Gate. About 8:30 we reach the landing. I take a room at the Russ House No. 160. Attend Church at the Central Presbyterian Tabernacle. Hear a short sermon from Rev. D.E. Bushnell, D.D., on "It is finished." Rev. W.J. Smith, the retiring pastor delivers a brief address. Very affecting. Ten baptized Communion. Go to Young Men's Chr Association. Hear Dr. W.H. Pendleton on the Refuge. Hear Rev. R.L. Taber at night at 1st Congre.

Monday, October 12 Go to Oakland & thence to Stockton and Lodi, Rev. W.H. Bast being in company. Go from Lodi to Woodbridge on the stage, it being about 2 1/2 miles. Dine at Rev. Daniel Shuck's about 2:00. Stay there till morning.

Tuesday, October 13 Visited the school at Morning prayers. Wrote some at Rev. D. Shuck's. Dine at President D.A. Mobley's. Their children are Gertie, "Lota" (Mary Catharine), Blanche, and Ethel, Willie Lewis, and

Philo. Wrote some in the afternoon (Rev. Jac. L. Berry's obituary) and took supper at Shuck's, but lodged at Pres. Mobley's, with Rev. G.W. Burtner.

Wednesday, October 14 Again at prayers and heard one recitation on logic in Pres. Mobley's room. Wrote & dined at Shuck's Called in the afternoon at at [repeated in text] Rev. T.J. Bauder's. Saw there fig trees as large as large apple trees. Supper & Lodging at Rev. Daniel Shuck's. I Pr. at 7:30 Rom. 1:3,4. Not very good liberty.

Thursday, October 15 Conference opened in the morning at 8:00 (8:45) with quite spiritual devotions. Business proceeded. Dine at Rev. W.H. Klinefelter's. Rev. W.L. Demunbrun came. Business as usual. Rev. G.W. Burtner pr. Stay at Rev. Daniel Shuck's.

Friday, October 16 Business as usual. Dine at Rev. J.L. Fidl's. Business as usual. I Pr. at 7:30, Rom. 6:14. Lodge at Prof. E.H. Ridenour's, with W.H. Bast. Had only fair Liberty in speaking.

Saturday, October 17 Stationing Com. at 7:00. Business as usual. Dine at Shuck's. Stationing Com at 1:00. Conf. proceeds. Educational Meeting at 7:30. I spoke on Nature and Necessity. Klinefelter, Burtner, & Bauder spoke. Adjourned.

Sunday, October 18 Pr. at 11:00 Zech 13:9. Dine at Geo. M. Palmer's. Sab. Anniversary at 3:00. W.L. Demunbrun, W.H. Bast, F. Fisher & T.J. Bauder spok[e]. I told of Portland Chinese School. Coll. about $30 for it by Burtner. Lunch at Pres. D.A. Mobley's. Rev. W.L. Demunbrun Pr. Rom. 1:16. I introduced the Sacramental Service. Collections of the day for me amounted to $63.22.

Monday, October 19 Several called in in [repeated in text] the morning. Wrote a letter home. Dined at Shuck's. Went to Rev. T.J. Bauder's in the afternoon & staid till after supper. Rev. F. Fisher pr. at 7:30, "That we might save to the uttermost," etc. Rev. B.B. Allen made some remarks. I led a speaking meeting at the close of which four persons rose for prayer. Staid at Shuck's.

Tuesday, October 20 Attended morning prayers & one recitation in Prof. Ebersole's class in Chesar. Went back

to Shucks and spent a time in reading & writing. Dinner & supper at Shucks. I Pr. at 7:30, 1 Pet. 4:18. Three seekers came forward. Lodge at Shuck's.

Wednesday, October 21 Dined at D.J. Rush's with Daniel & Harriet Shuck, Beardsley & Fowl board there. Rush's son is John daughters, Ida & Mina. A nice family. She was a Dunning. Supper at Rush's. Demunbrun pr. at 7:00. I exhort & invite seekers. Some seven come forward. Three join church—Mrs. Walker, Zina Cowell, and Mrs. Elliot. I go to Joseph Overholser's 2 1/2 ms., N.E.

Thursday, October 22 I spend the whole day at Joseph Overholser's. His wife hard of hearing. Their children are Matthew, U.S. Grant, and Flavius Josephus. Pr. at 7:00. Rom. 5:8. Some ten are forward for prayers. A fine meeting. Stay at Shuck's.

Friday, October 23 Dined at Alfred Cowel's. The editor of the Lodi paper called in. Also Sister Shuck & Sister Lowe. Supper at Crowel's. Their children are Freddie an[d] Zina, aged 15 and 9. Rev. T.J. Bauder pr. at 7:00, "What good thing shall I do?" etc. Several seekers and 7 accessions—Bro. Elliot and two daughters & Sister Schaump and two sons. Stay at Prof. E.H. Ridenour's.

Saturday, October 24 Write and mail some letters—one home and one to Rev. J.S. Rhoads—Dine at Shucks. In the afternoon bathe and change clothes and shave. Supper at Shuck's. Rev. D.A. Mobley pr at 7:00. Several three—rose for prayer. I go home with Joseph R. Elliott. They have six children: Alice, Anna, Ida, Ernest, Warren, Milton. They live 2 miles west of town.

Sunday, October 25 Pr. at 11:00 from Ps. 48:12. One joined Church. Dined at J.A. Solinger's in town. Attend Sabbath-Sch. at three. Call at Pres. Mobley's and then go to R.W. Williams. Stay there till evening service. Rev Klinefelter pr. at 7:00. I follow—no move, but a large solemn congregation. Stay at D.A. Mobley's.

Monday, October 26 At College prayers. Call at Shuck's. Write a letter to Rev. C.W. Wells. Dine at R.W. Williams. Call at Rev. D. Shuck's. Supper at Rev. T.J. Bauder's. Rev. T.J. Bauder pr. at 7:00, II Kings 4:26. Small congregations. None arose for prayers But the prayer & speaking meeting that followed was quite good. Stay at Prof. W.H. Klinefelter's in north-west part of town.

Tuesday, October 27 Went to Rev. D. Shuck's. Stay till toward supper time. Prepare a sermon for the evening. Supper at A. Cowel's. Pr. at 7:00. 1 Tim. 2:4. Dismiss the general congregation and hold a prayer & speaking meeting. After this three arose for prayer and one came forward. Held a prayer service. Went home with Jospah Overhaltzer's and stay. Miss Shaner is a seeker who lives with them.

Wednesday, October 28 Went to town (Overhaltzer takes me) and dine at Mrs. Deal's at the boarding halls. The name however is Diehl. Dine at Mrs. H.M. Diehl's boarding-hall. Several students board there. Gillespie, Devries, Miss Maxwell, Miss Deal, Burt Diehl. Stay at Rev. T.J. Bauder's. Pr. at 7:00. Some seekers.

Thursday, October 29 Dinner at Rev. D. Shuck's. Supper and lodging at G.M. Palmer's. Pr. Acts 16:30, 31. A very solemn and deep feeling in the meeting. About seven seekers besides some who arose for prayers.

Friday, October 30 Attended morning prayers at the Chapel. Went with John Field to Rev. J.L. Field's. Spent the day there. Pr at 7:00 Acts 26:28. Seven or eight came out for prayers; others arose. Some Christian (Campbell, etc.) preachers presen[t]—Briggs, etc. An excellent meeting. Stay at Alfred Cowell's.

Saturday, October 31 Call to see Young Metcalf's. Dine at D.G. Rush's. Looked at Baptizing place. Supper at Rush's. Rev. Klinefelter pr. at 7:00. Only one or two came out for prayers, but Edith Field after dismissed, remained in much distress & John at the close came & sobbed. Aldrich also went away crying. I stay with Alfred Crowell's.

Sunday, November 1 Pres. Mobley pr at 11:00. Matt. 12:50. The house very full. I spoke on baptism about 15 minutes. We then repaired to the river a half mile north and I baptized by immersion 9 persons. Maud, Elmer & Ralph Schomp; Anna and Alice Elliott, May Keeler, Laura Shaner, Mattie Williams, & Katie Metcalf.

Dine at Burkitt's. At Sabbath School. Go to Solinger's and stay till evening meeting. Stay at Mrs. Diehl's.

Monday, November 2 Go to Schomp's and spend the day—three and a half miles north-east. He has a very fine home, nice house, door-yard, etc. Have speaking meeting at 7:00. Real good. 11 seekers, nearly all students. Four young men remain till eleven o'clock & I remain with them: two Snedigers, Van Meter, & Aldrich. Stay at Rev. Daniel Shuck's.

Tuesday, November 3 Write home and to Rev. F. Fisher. Stay at Shuck's till 4:00 p.m. Went to Pres. D.A. Mobley's. Stay till after supper. Rev. D. Shuck pr. Isa. 1:18. Quite a number of seekers and a good meeting. Stay at Cowells.

Wednesday, November 4 Dinner at D.G. Rush's. Visit Seeker in afternoon. Mrs. Rutlege, Folyers, Mother Doyle. Supper at Rush's. Pr. at 7:00 1 Chron. 28:9. Quite a number of seekers. Stay at R.W. Williams.

Thursday, November 5 Dine at Shucks. Call at Rush's to prayer-meeting of sewing circle. Call at Hastings. Supper at Rush's. Call at the two Snedigers' rooms. Pres. Mobley led the speaking meeting. Lodge at Geo. M. Palmer's.

Friday, November 6 Write Some letters. Go down town. Call at Shuck's, Rush's, post-office, and at Snediger's room. Dine at Palmer's. Write another letter. Meeting at 4:00. Real good. Supper at Mrs. Walker's. Talk with Aldrich, a student seeker. Call at Mobley's and W.L. Demunbrun, I see at Cowell's. Rev. W.L. Demunbrun opens the meeting. I follow with short exhortation. Seekers, prayer & speaking. Stay at G.M. Palmer's.

Saturday, November 7 Call at Shuck's. Attend meeting at the last of it. Several blessed, Robt. Snediger, Willis Snediger, [blank] Vanmeter, Miss Myers, Miss Hastings. The three first named seem to have been converted this morning the others blest before. Dine at Pres. D.A. Mobley's. . Go to the post-office. Stay at Shuck's till about time for evening meeting. Rev. Ebersole pr. at 7:00, 1 Tim. 1:14. I exhort. Five converted & 3 join Church: Willis Snediger, Ed. Aldrich, & Miss Myers. Stay at Ridenour's.

Sunday, November 8 Rev. Mr. Harris of the Presbyterian Church read a sermon on "Lovest thou me." Moderate attendance. Dine at G.M. Palmer's. Went to Shuck's and slept an hour. Rev. W.L. Demunbrun pr. at 7:00. I exhort & call for seekers. Two forward & one blessed. Went home with Joseph Overholtzer's & lodged.

Monday, November 9 Visit Northrup's. Dine there. A pleasant visit. Go back to Overhaltzer's. Pr. at 7:00, Mark 8:36. A large congregation, and a good meeting. There were two seekers. Stay at G.M. Palmer's.

Tuesday, November 10 Wrote to Lorin & to Lorin (my son) [repeated in text] and to Rev. F. Fisher. Dined at Alfred Cowel's. J Call at Sanlsbury, Rutlege's, D.G. Rush's, Doyle's, Blodgett's. Supper at Cowell's. Call at Hastings. Testimony Meeting. Stove-pip[e]'s threat to fall somewhat affected the meeting but it was quite good. Staid at Joseph R. Eliott's two miles S.west.

Wednesday, November 11 Came into town. Dine at Rev. A. Shuck's. Staid at Shuck's till evening.Sister Schomp called and staid an hour. Prof. D.A. Mobley led the praise meeting, which wasquite good. I staid at Alfred Cowell's.

Thursday, November 12 Called at Shuck's. Dined at D.G. Rush's. Called at Snediger's room and at the boarding Hall. Spent most of the afternoon preparing the evening discourse. Supper at D. Shucks. Pr. 7:00, Col. 1:10.— Large Con. Staid at Boarding Hall.

Friday, November 13 Went to College prayers. Spent forenoon at Rev. D. Shuck's. After an early dinner, Bro. D.G. Rush takes me to Lodi. Go on 1:10 train to Sacramento City. Put up at Rev. F.Fisher's, 1329 K St. Pr. at U.B. Church (Corner of Fourteenth & K) at 7:30, Ps. 1:6. Stay at Bro. Fisher's.

Saturday, November 14 Went down town to hotel ([blank] House) for dinner. Called at Laibein's & [blank] His talk on Judaism, etc. He bought 100 tickets for Chapman's lecture. Called on Sister Runion. She formerly lived at Camden, Ohio. Knew the Kumler's, Zellers, etc. Her daughter, Mrs. Doty there, & Zimmerman, her son. Called at Mrs. Hubbard's & at Mr. Tracy's—folks away. Pr at 7:30 Acts 2:1. Stay at Fisher's.

Sunday, November 15 Pr. at 11:00, Heb. 6:10. Dine at Theodore Tracy's. Children: Albert, Ora and Leland. Went to Y.M.C.A.'s room at 3:30. Pr. Ps. 119:9. What Hart said about secret societies. Hesswoodthe secretary. Saw Wm. T. Ross, a College chum of W.H. Lanthurn, a teacher of elocution in San Francisco, St. Ann's Building. Return to Fisher's. Pr. at 7:30, Mark 8:36. Stay at Fisher's. She sick for two days past.

Monday, November 16 Went with Bro. F. Fisher to minister's meeting at Congregational Church study. Dr. Frost (Baptist) Dr. Rice (Presbyterian) Rev. Filben of M.E., Rev. Herrick of the Baptist, and Rev. Merrill of the Congregational Ch. present. Dine at Western Hotel. Rainy afternoon. Write some. Supper as usual at Bro. Fisher's. At 8:00, hear Rev. E.S. Chapman lecture at 1st Baptist Church on the Solomons & Caesars of to-day, or Character Building. Stay at Fisher's. A windy rainy night.

Tuesday, November 17 Quite a rainy day. Dine at a restaurant on K St. Rev. Mr. Christian of the Southern M.E. Church pr. on Prayer. I stay at Rev. Fisher's.

Wednesday, November 18 It was a very rainy day. I staid indoor's nearly or quite all day, at Fisher's. Spoke in the evening on the Good Samaritan. Staid at Bro. Fisher's. The congregation was very small.

Thursday, November 19 Spent the forenoon in writing, etc. Dined at Fisher's. Went in the afternoon with Bro. Fisher. Called at Mother Hignett's, Mother Priest's— they were from Minn.—and at Mund's. Missed seeing Odells, and Rose's. Supper at a restaurant on L St. Pr. at 7:30 Matt. 1:21. Stay at Fisher's as usual.

Friday, November 20 Wrote some in the forenoon. Dined at Fisher's. Called in the afternoon at Johnston's & at Bell's. Supper at Fisher's. Rev. Hayden C. Christian of the M.E. Church South pr. at 7:30, Eph. 4:21. Quite a stirring discourse. Stay at Fisher's as usual.

Saturday, November 21 Stay at Bro. Fisher's during the forenoon. Go about 4:00 to Tracy's and have supper and stay till evening meeting. Rev. H.C. Christian and wife having come out to hear me, I contrary to expectation preached. Text Heb. 11:26. Stay at Bro. Fisher's.

Sunday, November 22 Pr. at 11:00, Matt. 16:16 to a congregation of not more than 30, a good deal of rain falling just at meeting time of assembling. -Dine at Mother Priest 's. A family by the name of Barbour boards there. Supper and lodging at Bro. Fisher 's. Pr. at 7:00, Rom. 3:23. Had a fine meeting, though the cong. was small.

Monday, November 23 Spent the day mostly in writing. Wrote to Rev. C.W. Burtner at Anderson, Shasta County, answering Disciplinary questions. Also to Susan. Dined at Rev. Francis Fisher's. Supper at Tracy's. Pr. at 7:30, Luke 24:46. A speaking meeting followed. Staid at Bro. Fishers as usual.

Tuesday, November 24 Bought an over-coat at Weinstock's & Lubins for $15.00, 2 pair socks for 80 cts. Dine at Mother Priest's. Go on Oregon Branch of Centr. Pac. R.R. to Gridley, in Butte County. It was a very rainy day, and the ground was so covered with water that we did not try to have meeting as intended, that evening. Stay at a boarding-house kept by Mr. Shirley. His wife a member of our Church.

Wednesday, November 25 Looked at Church & parsonage. Put up some notices of meeting. Dined at Boarding House. Wrote full cards to Rev. G.M. Miller & to Rev. A.K. Curtis. Called at Price's, Hill's, Dr. Todd's, Brown's, Rose's, Richardsons. Preached from Heb. 11:26. Two came forward for prayers. Stay at the boarding house.

Thursday, November 26 At the hotel. Visit Price's, Rose's, etc. Pr. at 7:30, Matt. 5:8—two raise their hands for prayer. A brief speaking meeting. Stay at boarding house.

Friday, November 27 Went to Marion Baulware's to dinner. A Mr. Bisset & wife (she a sister of Mrs. Baulware) came before dinner. Went over to Thomas Baulware's after dinner, who lives close to Biggs' Station. Went back to Gridley. Rev. P. Beck pr. at 7:00, Luke 15: "I will arise," etc. I exhort on the propriety of prayer by sinners & for sinners. Three arise for prayer. Two come forward for prayers.
Stay at Boarding house.

Saturday, November 28 Went to Sister J. Mumby's for dinner. He a ranting railer. It is a rainy day. I wrote a letter to Rev. Wm. McKee in the forenoon. Rev. P. Beck pr at 7:00 1 Tim 4:8. Only twelve or fourteen persons at meeting it being a dark rainy night. Stay at Boarding House as usual. Rainy evening, the congregation small.

Sunday, November 29 Preach at 11; Deut. 32:31. Rainy morning. Dine at Marion Baulware's. Drive from there to the Church. Pr at 7:00 from John 5:39, "Search Scrip." Large congregation. Stay at Boarding house.

Monday, November 30 Write in forenoon. Dine at boarding place. Visit several families in the afternoon. Rev. Phil. Beck pr. I exhort. Stay at boarding house.

Tuesday, December 1 Go on 7:40 train to Sacramento. Dine at Rev. Francis Fisher's, 1329 K St. Trade some in the afternoon. Supper at Theodore Tracy's, 1716 P St. Pr. at 7:30, Ps. 16:8. This meeting closed a series of about six weeks. Staid at Tracy's. She has a cousin Rev. E.H. Caylor of Miami Conference, an Uncle John Shellabarger near Letts, Iowa, and brothers near Letts. Her father was a Shellabarger.

Wednesday, December 2 Went to Fisher's. Made some change of clothing, lunched and went to the train. Start at 11:30 for Lodi. Walk over to Woodbridge. Call at Shuck's, Rush's & Bauder's. Supper at Shuck's. Call at Cowell's. Prayer meeting at 7:00, followed by official meeting. Stay at Cowell's.

Thursday, December 3 Call at Mobley's, Ridenour's, Palmer's, Klinefelter's, Solinger's, boarding hall, Salisbury's, Shucks. Dine at Rush's and he takes me to the train at Lodi. Go on train via Stockton, Lathrop, to Modesto, a town of two or three thousand inhabitants. Stay at Lorenzo Dunnings, 1 mile N.E. of depot on Burneyville Road. Their children are Charley 15, and Ellen, 3. Miss Dresser lives there.

Friday, December 4 Went down town with Bro. Dunning. Call at Howell's father, Allen's son-in-law. Call to see Mrs. Rebecca Dunning Milliner. Went to the depot and wrote some. Lunch at Restaurant. Go on 2:35 train to Selma. Arrive about 6:30. Stay at Rev. W.L. Demunbrun's. Their children are Maud, 9,Claud, 7 and Clyde 3. Get several letters: Susan, Lorin, N. Evans, Flora & Wm. Reeder, Rush's, etc.

Saturday, December 5 Stay at Demunbrun's till after dinner. Bauder came on the 1:00 train last night, having inadvertently gone on to the San Francisco train at Lathrop. Rev. Withro, late of Homer, Nebr., called in. He the M.E. Pastor here. Told me how the Rev. Griffin's conduct had troubled W.S. Spooner & J.R. Cotton, causing the latter to leave church. Cheated Father Pitt out of $200 also. Qr. Conf. at 2:30. Canvass on dedication. Supper at Jas. H. Payne's 1 1/2 ms. N.E. , T.J. Bauder pr. at 7:00, Gal. 4:1. Stay at Jas. G. Thomas; Children: Ora 14, Cora May 11, Francis O. 8, Ada Adeline 5.

Sunday, December 6 Went to Rev. Demunbrun's and changed dress. Pr. at 11:00, John 14:2,3. A very spirited meeting. Then raised $632.00 in cash and subscription & dedicated the church house. I dine at J.E. Whitson's. Her mother, Metcalf there. Her brother Staley and wife there. Rev. W.L. Demunbrun pr. at 7:00 on the Everlasting Intercessor. A fine meeting. Four joined Church. Stay at Rev. W.L. Demunbrun's. Trustees: Jas. G. Thomas, James Payne, Harrison Thomas, David S. Orr, G.J. Huffman: P.O. Selma, Fresno, Co. Cal.

Monday, December 7 Stay at De's all day. Write to Susan, N. Evans, etc. Pr. at 7:00 Heb. 11:26. Stay at J.G. Thomas' in town.

Tuesday, December 8 Saw the Telescope. Hott's gingerly notice of the results of the commission's session. Went over to Demunbrun's. Staid till after dinner. Wrote considerably. Supper at Prof. G.D. Hines, who lives in Bro. Bauder's property. Rev. T.J. Bauder pr. at 7:00. Sacramental service. Speaking meeting followed. Stay at Jas. G. Thomas' in town. They move next day 1 mile northeast.

Wednesday, December 9 Went to Bro. Demunbrun's and dine. Write before & after dinner. Walk out before night and look at Bro. Bauder's ranch. It had 1,600 fruit-trees & many vines. Supper at Rev. Nelson Young's. He formerly a Free Will Baptist—afterward a United Brethren and now out of Church, but a professor. Bro. Demunbrun pr. a very interesting sermon on Ps 126:6. Prayers followed. Stay at Jas. Payne's, 1 1/2 miles northeast.

Thursday, December 10 Went to town, calling at J.G.

Thomas'. Dined at Cyrus Van Emmons, 1 1/2 miles south-east. They were formerly of Lisbon, Iowa. She a sister of Rev. Wm. Davis' wife. Staid till evening. Pr. at 7:00, Matt. 25:46 to a large congregation. A deep solemnity distinguished the occasion. I stay at Cyrus Van Emmon's.

Friday, December 11 Went to town about noon. Dine at Demunbrun's. Supper at Whitson's. Rev. W.L. Demunbrun pr. at 7:00. Stay at Rev. W.L. Demunbrun's.

Saturday, December 12 Stay at Demunbrun's all day. Call at Whitson's. Pr. at 7:00, John 3:16. Stay at J.G. Thomas' who have moved out to their ranch a mile northeast. The congregation numbered well. I wrote several letters that day & cards.

Sunday, December 13 Walked to town. Taught a Sabbath school class. Pr. at 11: 1 Ki. 18:21. Congregation large. Dine at Jacob Emory Whitson's. Tea in the evening at Prof. G.D. Hine's. Pr. at 7:00, Acts 26:28. A very solemn meeting. Some were inclined to become seekers. While the congregation sung hymns, I went through the congregation, speaking to all the unconverted personally. Large congregation, and largely unconverted, yet mostly confessing their need of conversion. Stay at J.E. Whitson's.

Monday, December 14 Wrote letters to Susan & Lorin. Called a short time at Demunbrun's. Go to Cooper's 1 mile south & dine. Came back to Demunbrun's. He had returned from Liberty. Stayed to supper and lodged there. The congregation was small. Rev. W.L. Demunbrun pr. at 7:00, "Come thou with us, and we will do thee good," etc. Some evidently interested.

Tuesday, December 15 Stayed at Rev. W.L. Demunbrun's till about 4:00 p.m. Was rather discontent. Arranged to go to Los Angeles. Went to Rev. Nelson Young's for supper. Buy a ticket to Los Angeles, $13.50. Pr. at 7:00, Ez. 33:11. One seeker. Others deeply convicted. Sleep two hours at Demunbrun's. Go on 1:00 morn. train toward Los Angeles. Sleep perhaps two hours on the cars.

Wednesday, December 16 Morning dawn found us in the mountain pass. Many tunnels & a rough country. Reached Keene pretty early in the morning. Arrive at

Mojave after 9:00. Reach Los Angeles about 3:00 p.m. Rev. T.F. Hallowell meets me & takes me to his house (room) 341 Spring St. Attend the Meeting at the Tabernacle, where Rev. L.W. Munhall, the evangelist pr. at 7:30, "Ye will not come unto me that ye may have life." Saw Rev. P.F. Brazee, a talented preacher of the M.E. Ch. Superficial preaching & also superficial inquiry room work. Stay at Hallowell's.

Thursday, December 17 Walked to business parts. Bought rubber sandals, $1.00. Searched for Rev. D.K. Flinger's son (John perhaps) & met him on the streets. He seemed to be somewhat a doubter on religion. Dine at Bro. Hallowell's. Go on afternoon train to Downey. Got letters from Susan, Reuchlin, W.C. Day, Prest. Miller, & J.S. Rhoads, & a card from J.F. Croddy. Mr. Sin. Corum of M.E. Ch., South, takes me out to Rev. A.N. King's on New River. Mr. Thompson of Minnesota & family there. Stay at King's.

Friday, December 18 Stay at King's the forenoon. Rev. J.W. Baumgardner comes in the afternoon and takes me out riding to Norwalk, etc. Stop at Mr. Luke Charest's. Their children are Mina (11) and Clarence (18 mo.). He a Frenchman from Canada. She a niece of Emeline Day. Bro. B's wife & daughter (8) there—Katie. Pr. at New River Sch. House at 7:00, Hebr. 11:26. Stay at Charest's.

Saturday, December 19 Go over to Rev. D. McKeel's before noon & dine there. Pr. at 1:30, Matt. 5:8. Preside as P.E. protem in the Qr. Conf. M.P. Tibbett licensed to preach. Supper at Bro. McKeel's. Rev. J.W. Baumgardner pr. at 7:00 John 1:29. I stay at Rev. A.N. King's with Rev. T.F. Hallowell. King's children: Abraham 20, Edith 17, Frank, 15, Fred, Howard, Mamie, Oscar, Walter.

Sunday, December 20 Pr. at 11:00, 1 Ki. 18:21. Communion followed. I dine at Wilbur W. Curtis'. His Brothers Hubbard Curtis and Bildad M. Curtis also dine there. Call at King's. Pr. at 7:00, 1 Tim. 2:4. The congregations quite large morning and evening. Stay at Rev. A.K. King's.

Monday, December 21 Stay at King's all day, the day being quite rainy. No meeting in either afternoon or evening. Wrote some in the course of the day. Got the *Telescope* in the afternoon. Lodge at King's.

Tuesday, December 22 Staid at Bro. King's till after dinner & wrote a letter to Susan and one to Rev. Daniel Shuck. Good meeting at 2:00 at the school-house. Supper at Rev. D. McKeel's. Pr. at 7:00, Luke 18:13. Quite an interesting meeting. Stay at Rev. D. McKeel's.

Wednesday, December 23 Call at King's. Dine at Wilbur W. Curtis'. Meeting at 2:00. Supper at Charest. Pr. at 7:00, Eph. 3:19. Stay at King's. Got letters from Susan and Bp. Dickson.

Thursday, December 24 Staid at King's till meeting. Went in the afternoon to call on Dicker's & on Thompson's. Supper at Charest's. Pr. at 7:00 a Christmas sermon from Isai. 9:6. Stay at King's. Got letters from Downey, P. Beck & P. Suman.

Friday, December 25 Staid at King's all day except that I went to meeting at 2:00. Spent the day mostly in writing. Rev. J.W. Baumgardner pr. at 7:00.

Saturday, December 26 Rainy forenoon. Start after dinner for Bellona (Biona) with Rev. A. King. Go on cars via Los Angeles from Downey. Stay at Rev. Wm. P. Tibbet's.

Sunday, December 27 Went to Cold Water School-house and teach S.S. class & then pr. at 11:00, Heb. 11:10. Go on to Mr. Hurst's and took lunch. Pr. at Pass Sch. H. at 3:00 Rom. 8:32. One raised hands for prayer. Went home to Tibbet's—the whole trip over 25 miles. Supper at Tibbet's. Pr. at Bellona (Bi-o'-na) Sch. House St 7:00, John 5:39. Stay at John McLaughlin's with Rev. A.N. King. They live 1 m S. of Sch House.

Monday, December 28 Went early with Bro. A.N. King to Laubeer's and thence to Rev. W.P. Tibbet's. King starts home & I go with Tibbet to Nath. Coe's. He is sick—is Rev. J. Brown's brotherinlaw. Went via J. Brown's to Santa Monica with Bro. Tibbet's. Saw the Jones-Baker claim. Went into the Park. A central grove in it, where Campmeeting was held. Went down the "99" steps to the surf. Dined at Jacob Brown's & staid there till church-going time. Saw Eucaliptes trees two years old, 4 1/2 inches in diameter, & a beet 3 ft long weighing 42 lbs. Pr. at 7:00 John 7:37. One seeker. Stay at John McLaughlin's.

Tuesday, December 29 McL. takes me to Will Rose's for dinner. Write some letters. Go to Lowe's and call a few minutes. His wife, Coe's wife, & Brown's wife Sisters to each other. Walk over to Wm. P. Tibbet's. Supper there. Pr. at 7:00, Eccl. 12:13. Stay at Rev. Wm. R. Tibbet's.

Wednesday, December 30 Went in spring wagon (company of Revs. Tibbet & J. Brown) to Los Angeles. Dine at Rev. T.F. Hallowell's. Saw Bro. E. Luke & wife of Olive Branch Church, N. Ohio Conf., who have bought 100 acres near the Pass Sch. H. Had seen them at Matamora, Ohio, at a dedication. Got a letter from Susan & answered it. Went to New River with Rev. A.N. King. Rev. J.W. Baumgardner pr at 7:00. Eight seekers forward. Stay at Rev. A.N. King's.

Thursday, December 31 Dine at Rev. D. McKeel's. At prayer-meeting in the afternoon. Supper at McKeel's. Pr at 7:00 Ps. 40:1-3. Stay at Rev. A.N. King's.

Notes at the end of the diary

Diptheria, hoarseness, etc.

Aromatic Sulphuric Acid	3T
Tincture Sanguinarim	3T
Tincture Capsicum	3t
Spirits of Mentha	quart
Syrrup of Simplex	3T

Sip one teaspoonfull every two hours.

Fare from Marion to Chicago	3.15
Fare to Casey	11.89
Eatables	.33
Hack to Chicago	.50
Casey to Hoisingt	.50
Supper at Des Moines	.25
Lodging & breakfast	1.00
Fare from Casey	1.00
Paper at Chicago	.30
Book	1.00
Stylographic pen	1.25
Umbrella	.95

Scratchbook	.05
Copying paper	.05
Boot Blacking	.03
Fare to St. Paul (direct)	9.00
Food	.15
Church contrib.	.10
Hotel at Minneapolis	2.50
Rubber Sandals	.75
Breakfast at St. Paul	.25
McNiels Liniment & corks	.45
Postage stamps	.50
Ticket to Paluise	$42.40

St. Paul, Minn. Aug. 24

Ticket to Paluise	42.40
Com. Note paper	.50
Draft on Am. Nat. Exchange, New York	80.00
Nat. Bank Chi	25.23
[Bought at Merchants nat. Bank Chicago]	
Exchange	.25
Pant suspenders	.40
Rubber sandals	.75
McNiel's Liniment	.40
can peaches	.35
can of salmon	.35
Can of Beans	.25
Tin cup & glass	.10
Spoon	.05
Wash pan	.10
Grapes	.15
Peaches	.10
Banannas	.10
Cheese	.10
Pies (two)	.20
Buns	.15
Crackers	.05
Sweet cakes	.05
Milk	.25
Plums	.10
Lodgings & breakfast at Palouse Junction	1.00
Hotel bill at Minneapolis	2.50

Walla Walla Conf.

Public Coll. at Conf.	41.00
Chart Coll.	26.85
Dedication at Weston	14.10

Oregon Conference

Chart Collection	78.80
Coll. in forenoon	25.10
Coll. at night	10.18
Total	114. 08

Walla Walla Conf 1886

Chart Col.	29.00
Pub. Coll.	31.20

M. Wright Received at Ore. Conf.
Educational Beneficiary.

From Kitson	$2.75
From Olds	1.17

Gen. Sab. School Funds

From Kitson	1.75

Ordered my family to pay the above to treasurers'.

M. Wright Received at California Conf.

Gen Sab. Fund	7.00
Un. Bibl. Sem	3.40
Ed. Benef.	1.00
Total	11.40

Expenses of travel

From Marion, Ind to St. Paul	$16.00
To Palouse Junction	42.40
To Colfax	5.60
Colfax to Pendleton	2.50
Hotel at Pendleton	.50
Ticket to Portland	9.25
Lunch	.20
Ticket to Corvallis	3.86
Dinner on the way	.50
From Turner's to Portl.	2.25
Hotel room at Portland	.50
Food while there	.75
Ticket to San Fran.	15.00
Food while there	.80
Ticket to Lodi	3.20
Hack fare to Woodbri	.50
Ticket to Sacramento	1.45
Trip to Gridley	2.80
Back to Sacramento	2.80
To Woodbridge	1.45

To Modesto	1.70
Selma	4.30
Dinner at Modesto	.25
Trip to Los Angeles	13.50
Trip to Downey	.50
Trip to Bellona & back	1.25
To Los Angeles	.50
St. Cars at Los Ang	.20
Dinner there	.25
Ticket to Colton	2.30
Fare on hack to Riverside	.50
Hack to Colton	1.00
Ticket to Dayton	64.70
Expense on the way	.50

Trip from San Fran	
Cisco to Woodbr.	3.28
Woodbr. to Sacram.	1.45
Trip to Gridley	2.80
Trip to Sacramento	2.80
Trip to Woodbridge	1.45
Trip to Modesto	1.70
Trip to Selma	4.30
Dinner at Modesto	.25
Trip to Los Angeles	3.50
Trip to Downey	.50
to Bellona & back	1.25
To Los Angeles	.50
St Cars at Los Ang	.20
Dinner at Los Ang	.25
Fare to Colton	2.30
Stage to Riverside	.50

Received in California

Chart Coll.	86.50
Pub. Coll at Conf.	63.22
Coll after at Woodbr.	24.30
B. Wood, a ticket to Sacr.	1.00
Coll. at Sacramento	3.25
Coll at Gridley	3.45
Beck paid me	4.25
Received at New River	20.04
of Rev. A.N. King	5.00
Total	211.01

Bought of Weinstock & Lubin
4th & R St Sacramento

Overcoat	15.00
Socks 3 pr at 40 cts	1.20
Undershirts 2 at 40	.80
Drawers 1 pr	.75
Neck-tie	.25
Cuff buttons	.50
Cuffs	.40
Pantaloons	5.25

Cor J & 8th St. Sacramento
Bought of Wait Druggist

1 Bottle of Depthenalure	.25
1 " " "	.25

Bought at Woodbridge of Dr. Bentley

Cloves & hoarseness medicine	.40
Muslin 1 yd	.10
(at other store) 1 yd	.18

Rev. G.W. Burtner, Anderson, Shasta Co. Cal
Rev W.H. Bast Eureka, Humboldt Co, Cal

Post-offices of Oregon Ministers
Jessee Harrit Salem, Marion
N.W. Allen Philomath, Benton
M.M. Crow "   "
A. Bennett "   "
P.C. Parker, Oakland, Doug
J.G. Mosher, Marshfield, Coos
J.E. Connor, Philomath
A.R. Olds, Philomath, Benton
Geo. M. Stroup
M.R. Shaver, LaCentre, Clark
Jas R. Parker
Eli B. Whitacre, Philomath
C.B. Masters

Conferences, 1866
Walla Walla Confera at Weston Umatilla Co Oregon.
Oregon Conference, Abiqua Chapel, Marion Co, Oregon. Woodburn, 10 miles away is the station; Silverton the Post-office. California Com. (Bauder & others) to locate it & provide for a camp-meeting.

1886

Friday, January 1 I am thousands of miles from home. Mr. Thompson takes me to Downey (Cal.) for the 7:00 train, Bro. King having given out going with me. At Los Angeles, buy a ticket to Colton. Go up town—post office— up the hill—a way out. Call but do not see Reuben Baker. Go with Elisha Luke, wife, & Miss Jennie McComb to Colton & Riverside. Stay at Peter Suman's.

Saturday, January 2 Dine at Reuben Hall's. Luke's staid there last night & remained to-day. Go back to Peter Suman's having in forenoon called on Rev. Selah W. Brown, M.E. Pastor. Pr. at 7:00 at Y.M.C.A. Hall Eph 2:4. Stay at Halls. Their children, Samuel aged 20, William 15, Harvey 12, George 7, and two married daughters in Nebraska.

Sunday, January 3 Pr at M.E. Church at 10:45, John 6:69. Dine at Hall's with Luke's. Pr at 7:00 at Association hall, Heb. 11:26. Stay at Hall's. Luke's went to Suman's. Organized the Church after the sermon.

Monday, January 4 Went with Hall's to Peter Suman's. Hall & wife, Luke & wife, Suman & myself drive in Bro. Hall's spring-wagon over the valley & look at Orange orchards, lemons, limes, olives, vineyards, etc. Climb the butte by Shumaker's. Dinner & supper at Suman's & I lodge there. Their only child is Ida Belle Suman, about 20. Pr. at 7:00 at the hall Ps 87:3.

Tuesday, January 5–Thursday, January 7 Stay at Suman's. Pr at 7:00 at hall—pr. at 7:00 at his house, Ex. 28:34. —Pr at hall at 7:00, John 14:2. Stay at Hall's.

Friday, January 8 Naftzker came to show lot for church—one acre, too far out—and Suman went with him. Mr. Hayt came and we went out to look at the addition which he is interested in & indicated that they would give us a lot to build church on. Dine at Hall's. At 7:00 pr. at Suman's, Mark 8:36. Stay at Suman's. Rev. King & McKeel came.

Saturday, January 9 Visit the valley again with Bro. Suman, Revs. A.N. King & D. McKeel. Magnolia Ave., 150 ft wide. At Shumaker's, climb butte. Dine at Henry Cole's. Hart's cluster—oranges. Ascend Rubidoux in the afternoon (500 ft high) & see Santa Anna River, Arrowhead Mt., San Bernardino, & look on town & orange groves. Supper at Henry Bell's. King pr. at Suman's. Stay at Suman's to night.

Sunday, January 10 Pr. at 11:00 at Hall, John 5:39. Dine at Hall's with King & McKeel. King pr at 7:00, "Be ye also ready," etc. John J. Weir joined church. Stay at Hall's.

Monday, January 11 Remain at Hall's. It is a very rainy day. I help tinker at the clock. Rev. A. King leads the prayermeeting, at the hall . I stay at Bro. Hall's that night.

Tuesday, January 12 Write letters at Hall's in forenoon. In the afternoon visit Hiram A. Knapp's. Supper there. Children: Ida, 24; Eda 16 or 18, William, 11; little boy 3. A Mr. Bauter, carpenter, boards there. Pr. at the hall at 7:00, Luke 24:46. Stay at Hall's.

Wednesday, January 13–Saturday, January 16 Remain at Hall's. Pr. at the hall at 7:00, Acts 3:22, Stay at Suman's. Pr. at the hall at 7:00, Luke 15:7.

Sunday, January 17 Pr. at the hall at 10:45, Ps. 48: 12, 13. Dine at Reuben Hall's. He has a 12 1/2 acre ranch and nice brick house. Ranch cost $16,000. Hiram A. Knapp & wife joined church that day. Were Free Methodists in Minnesota.

Monday, January 18 Bro. Hall takes me to Peter Suman's 1 1/4 mile South-west of Riverside town. Rains much. Dinner & supper there. Also lodge there. Rained that day and stormed terribly at night. Caused washouts at Los Angeles & other places.

Tuesday, January 19 This the day chosen to start for Dayton. It slacks & I go to Riverside equipped for my journey. Washouts had cut off all communications. Telegraph wires down. Go to Reuben Hall's, dine & lodge there.

Wednesday, January 20 Way home closed. Bridge at San Gabriel reported to be gone and (incorrectly) at Yuma. Dine & lodge at Hall's. Slept 5 1/2 hours.

Thursday, January 21 No favorable news yet. Still stay at Hall's. Slept a full night.

Friday, January 22 Still staying at Hall's. Some mail from the east, but none for me. Talked of going to Colton, but did not. Got daily papers from Los Angeles giving account of the destruction of bridges, some houses & three lives there. Stay at Hall's. Slept 3 1/2 h.

Saturday, January 23 Went to town in the forenoon and got mail for Hall's but none for myself. Went to town after dinner & got a letter from Susan dated Jan 7th, saying that all were as well as common. Went on with Bro. Hall to Suman's & staid there.

Sunday, January 24 Pr. at Peter Suman's II Cor. 3:7, 8. Brattles of M.E. Church & wife & her friend there. Also Dr. Russell formerly of Del. Co. Ind. Go home with Reuben Hall's. Call on Judson Pulver's (in part of Halls house) in the afternoon. Stay at Hall's. No meeting that night, rainy weather.

Monday, January 25 Go to town. Telephone to Colton. Dine at Hall's. Go on hack at 2:00 to Colton. Start for Dayton at 4:15 in shabby car. Colten agent sold me via

Wab.& St. L. & told many untruths. Sleep four hours or more. Awaken at Yuma & see the river & bridge at night. From Colton had San Bernardino mts. to north & San Jacinto to the south.

Tuesday, January 26 Breakfast about Maricopa. Pass through deserts scattered over with sage-brush, greasewood, cactus, & Musquite tree: Cactus [drawing of cactus plants in diary] Ditches to guide waters from R.R. From Maricopa to Benson amid foot-hills of Mogollon Mts. Tuscon an adobe town, neat cactus. At Bowie, 250 U.S. Soldiers. 14 Apache scouts. Changed cars at Dening. Saw Rio Grande by star light, changed cars at E1 Paso. Slept 4 hours.

Wednesday, January 27 Awoke about Eagle Flats. Too much smoking & swearing aboard. But breakfast on train from lunch-box. See sky-bound plains with buttes. Midland & Germania settlements. Marionfield, 20 or 30 houses. Colorado, 800 inhab, brickish colored soil. Reached Sweet Water before dark. Slept perhaps 5 hours.

Thursday, January 28 Awoke at Ft. Worth. Dallas quite a city. Newsboy tried to swindle me on changed 30 dollars, extracting 20. Gave it back. Pine region in the afternoon. Soil at Marshall as red as a brick. Reached Texarkana after night. Passed through Little Rock in the night. Saw little. Slept three hours.

Friday, January 29 Daylight before we reach Minturn. Ground is frozen, & some snow (our first). N.E Arkansas is timbered like Indiana, and country flat. Pines begin about Piedmont. Very broken country, mostly. Reached St. Louis about 5:30. Reach Danville, Ill. at 1:00. Slept about 2 hours.

Saturday, January 30 Reached Indianapolis at 4:45 morning. Called at Rev. W.C. Day's, Corydon Heath's, and at Rev. T.J. Connor's. Start at 11:00 for Dayton via Hamilton. Reached Dayton at 4:00. At Home after nearly six month's absence. Had telegraphed home from Big Springs, Texas.

Sunday, January 31 Staid at home all day. Was somewhat worn with travel, loss of sleep, etc.

Monday, February 1 Went to town, bought a new hat &

engaged a new suit, of Church. At home the rest of the day.

Wednesday, February 3 Dr. Davis called a few minutes in the afternoon. At home all day.

Thursday, February 4 Went to town to have my new coat fitted. Called at *Telescope* Office. Paid of Chart Coll. for Califor. to Shuey 7:00, Gen. S.S. Fund, to L.O. Miller, U.B. Sem., $3.40. B. Funkhouser called in afternoon to see about note & I paid him $1.00 Edw. Benef. for California. Dillon called an hour.

Friday, February 5 Wrote for the *Telescope.* Dr. Davis called a few minutes on business.

Saturday, February 6 Went to town and got my new suit. Called at Tel. Office & read proofs of my article. Bought diary & in the afternoon copied from my unbound diary for the year.

Sunday, February 7 Attended church at Summit Street. The pastor, Rev. G.M. Matthews preached, "Choose this day whom ye will serve." Several joined church. Rev. J.W. Hott pr. at 7:00, Summit Street, Math. 25:8, "Give us of your oil," etc. About ten seekers & 4 accessions.

Monday, February 8 At home in the forenoon. Went to town in the afternoon and looked through theold *Telescope* files. Lizzie Niswonger sewing for Katie. Went to Dr. Davis's at his request & spent theevening.

Tuesday, February 9 At hime in forenoon & most of the afternoon. Wrote letters to W.E. Howry Wahpeton, Dakota, and to Mother Koerner. At home in the evening.

Wednesday, February 10 At home in the forenoon. Rev. H. Floyd called in the afternoon. Called at Rev. Wm. Dillon's in the evening. At meeting in the latter part of the evening. Incidental talk with Hott. There were two seekers. I told him Lorin had not confidence in his word.

Thursday, February 11 Was at Rev. Wm. Dillon's in the forenoon, but not at a com. meeting. Rev. Halleck Floyd dines with me. Called at J.K. Grabill's in the afternoon & then go home.

Friday, February 12 At home all day. Spent considerable time righting up my desk and papers.

Saturday, February 13 At home in the forenoon. Called in afternoon at Albert Sheerer's, to see his mother Mrs. Sam. Wright & others there. Went at 8:00 to S.L. Herr's silver wedding. About two dozen there.

Sunday, February 14 Preached at Summit Street Church at 10:30, Luke 1:32. House crowded— about 700 people. Eleven joined Church, my son Reuchlin, one of the number. At 7:00, Mott pr. "He was crucified between two thieves." Two seekers, three joiners.

Monday, February 15 Went to town in the forenoon to see the doctors about extracting Mrs. Wright's teeth. Dr. Davis & Dentist Morris came before noon & extracted 3 teeth—one a sound tooth! Used Alcohol, ether, and chloroform in equal parts as an anaesthetic. Attended 4th meeting of officers of U.B. Hist. society at 2:00. Eve. at home.

Wednesday, February 17 Mr. Samuel Horine came soon after breakfast and staid till 10:30. At home.

Thursday, February 18 Went on the 7:10 M. train to Hamilton, Ohio and thence to Peter Minton's. Dine at 2:00. At 3:00 united in marriage, Mr. William K. Hannaford and Miss Ida M. Minton, Mr. H. being from Marion, Kansas. Came home on 6:20 train.

Friday, February 19 At home. Susan had six teeth extracted. Dr. Horace Davis & Dr. Morris, the dentist, present.

Sunday, February 21 At church at Summit St. at 10:30. Qr. Meeting occasion. Rev. G.M. Matthews pr. "We love God because he first loved us." At love-feast at 3:00. Called at L. Davis', also Dillon's. The latter somewhat sick.

Tuesday, February 23 At home in the forenoon. Go to town in the afternoon and give in an article for the *Telescope,* "The constitution Valid." Spend the evening in reading.

Wednesday, February 24 At home. 7 Hawthorne St. Wrote an article for the *Christian Conservator,* on Christian Manliness & took it to Dillon in the afternoon. Called at Bro. J.K. Grabill's and at Dr. L. Davis'. Evening spent in reading.

Saturday, February 27 At home writing, considerable all day & till late in the evening.

Sunday, February 28 Attended church at Grace M.E. Rev. Mr. Dimmick preached from Heb. 12:1. At home the rest of the day. Rev. R. L. Swain & wife called an hour in the afternoon.

Monday, March 1 Spent most of the day in writing. Prepared an article for *Telescope,* "Our Work in California."

Tuesday, March 2 At home all day. Spent the day wholly in reading. Read till I was much wearied.

Friday, March 5 In the afternoon called at Rev. Wm. Dillon's. Rev. Jonathan Blanchard of Wheaton, Illinois, came in.

Saturday, March 6 Went to "town" in forenoon. Ex-President Jonathan Blanchard of Wheaton College & editor of the *Christian Cynosure,* dined with us. He recently passed into his 76th year. Spent an hour in the Evening at Lewis Davis' D.D.'s Blanchard & Pres. Thompson there.

Sunday, March 7 Heard Rev. J. Blanchard preach at Fourth Presbyterian Church at 10:30, 2 Tim. 1:10, an able, interesting sermon. Dr. Blanchard preached at 4th Pres. Ch. at 7:30, Matt. 6:10, giving a broadside on Secrecy. Congregation large.

Monday, March 8 Heard Pres. Blanchard at Seminary at 8:00 A.M. Went to "Town" in afternoon. Pres. Blanchard called an hour. Wrote letters.

Tuesday, March 9 At home in forenoon & afternoon. Went to Wesleyan Meth. Church at 8:00, evening, to hear Dr. Blanchard. His text was John 18:20, "In secret have I said nothing."

Wednesday, March 10 At home. Wrote an article for the Christian Conservator. Called at Rev. W. Dillon's in the afternoon.

Sunday, March 14 Attend meeting at Summit St. U.B. Church. Prof. A.W. Drury pr. at 10:30, 1 Cor. 3:21. At home the rest of the day.

Monday, March 15 At home. Got letters from Grant County, Ind. and from Adair Co. Iowa.

Wednesday, March 17 Anniversary of Reuchlin's birth. Gave him peesent of $50.00. Called at J.K. Grabill's, Wm. Dillon's, & L. Davis' in the afternoon & left an article on Riverside for the *Conservator.*

Thursday, March 18 At home. Reading & some study. Mrs. Bp. Edwards & Mrs. G.W. Gilbert called. Dr. Davis called in the evening.

Saturday, March 20 Went to the *Telescope* office and read proof on my annual report of the district, just before noon. The street-car drivers on 3d St. struck at noon, having run all their cars into the West End stable.

Sunday, March 21 Attended Summit St. Church at 10:30 and heard Rev. D.R. Miller deliver a discourse on Phil. 4:8. He treated of Evil literature. Rather a rainy day.

Tuesday, March 23 At home. In the afternoon, an attempt being made by the sherriff to protect the Third Street railroad company in getting cars out of their West stable, which had been detained by strikers for several days. They got two out, one clear through & one opposite the Malleable Iron Works. A mob there.

Wednesday, March 24 Reports state that a mob took that car from east stable and dashed it into a ditch. The whole thing a triumph over law and right. Gave in an article, "The Constitution of 1837," to editor of Telescope.

Thursday, March 25 At Home. Spent most of the day in arranging files of the papers— *Telescope— United Brethren— Itinerant— Christian Cynosure—* etc.

Friday, March 26 Read proofs on an article for *Conservator* in the afternoon.

Saturday, March 27 Went to market in the forenoon and read an article (in proof) for *Telescope.*

Sunday, March 28 Attended church at Summit St. U.B. Heard Rev. J.P. Landis D.D., pr. at 10 1/2, 1 Chron. 29:11. Spent the afternoon and evening on investigation of Scriptures.

Wednesday, March 31 Went to town, did some trading, and left an article, "The Constitution reasonable," at the *Telescope* Office.

Saturday, April 3 At home. Rev. Matthews called in the afternoon.

Sunday, April 4 Preached at Summit St. U.B. Church Rom. 5:4, "Endurance worketh probation." Large audience (about 500) for so sloppy a day underfoot. Remained at home the rest of the day.

Monday, April 5 Election day. Wrote up a statement of my year's work for Exec. committee. Went to town in the afternoon and gave in my written statement for the Ex. Com. of Board of Missions. Called in at the U.B. Preacher's meeting.

Tuesday, April 6 News of the election of Rep. Mayor & Waterworks trustee & all the rest Democrats elected on City ticket. At home.

Friday, April 9 At home. Rev. Wm. McKee called in the afternoon to talk about my salary. He seemed very conciliatory,

Saturday, April 10 Started at 7:30 for Union City and Marion and Fairmount. Revs. A.J. Bolen & Wm. Hall met me at the depot and took me to Bro. Bolen's for dinner. Staid at Bolen's till evening. Lectured at Union Church two miles south, on "Pacific Coast." Staid at H.C. Cell's 3/4 miles south of the Church.

Sunday, April 11 Called at Bro. McKeever's, & at John Smith's. Pr. at Union at 10:30, John 5:39. Dine at Carter Hastings. Pr. at 3:00 at Wesleyan Church at Fairmount funerals of Mary Ann and Washington R. Carter, 1 Cor. 15:22. Go to Aunt Lizzie Reeder's with Robert B. & Flora Reeder.

Monday, April 12 Went in afternoon to see the farm. Ellis Wright, my nephew, came about noon.

Tuesday, April 13 Went over in the forenoon to see the Wright heir's land. Spent afternoon at Aunt Lizzie's.

Wednesday, April 14 Went via Fairmount to Marion with Wm. & Robt. Reeder. Ellis leaves us at Fairmount. I call there on Vincent's to see Mother Parson's, aged 82 & nearly blind. Redeemed my land at Marion $51.53, paid gravel-road tax also. Went out to John Q. Thomas' & staid. He a "Friend." Quaker.

Thursday, April 15 Went to town & took 8:23 train to Vermont, Howard Co. There Rev. W.S. Fields met me and took me to his house, one mile west. Dined there. Went with Rev. W.S. Fields to John Condo's two miles east of Bennett's Switch. Pr. at Zion at 7:30, John 5.39. Rain-like evening. Stay at Condo's.

Friday, April 16 Went with Fields to Lewis C. Brown's. Dined there. He abed with a broken leg. Went after dinner to Bennett's Switch. Saw P.B. Williams & wife. Saw Rev. J.S. Cleaver. Got a letter (unexpectedly) from home. Went to Waupecong. Supper at Dr. G.C. Maughmer's. Pr. at 7:30, Heb. 11:26. Stay at Maughmer's.

Saturday, April 17 Went with Rev. W.S. Fields to Kokomo. Saw Mother Stover at M.L. Garrigner. Got a letter from home. Dined at Mother Dorman's 2 miles east of town. Went on to Church— no meeting— and to Bro. Fields'. At 7:30 had an evening meeting with addresses on missions.

Sunday, April 18 Pr. at Salem at 10:30, Mark 16:15. Took up a missionary collection of $54.00. Dine at Charles Goodwin's 1/2 m. north-west. Children's meeting at Lamp-lighting. I & Fields' made a short address each. Declamations, readings, etc. Stay at Rev. W. Shanon Fields', P.B. Williams & wife there.

Monday, April 19 Bro. Fields takes me to Kokomo. Go on to Honey Creek on afternoon train. Supper at Henry Fadeley's. Lecture at 7:00 on Pacific Coast. Stay at Rev. Wm. Gossett's. Saw Revs. Alonzo Myers and A.G. Montgomery.

Tuesday, April 20 Went on morning train to New Castle. Dine at Rev. M.M. Thomas'. Got letter from home. Supper at Rev. M.L. Bailey's. Lectured at 7:30 on Pacific Coast. Large audience. Staid at Nicholas Milligan's.

Wednesday, April 21 Wrote letters & postals. Dined at Milligan's. Went at 2:35 to Hamilton Station, now Sexton. Harvey meets me, and I go out to his house 2 1/4 miles north-west. Called at Ed. Frazier's, a half-mile north of Harvey Wright's.

Thursday, April 22 Called at Dan Thomas, and John Wright's and at Jabez Rhodes'. Dined there. McKee's, Florence Wilhelm, Erma Frazer, & Joseph A. Wright's dined there. Went to Rushville & Morristown. Supper at Peter Myers'. Lectured at Blue River Chapel at 8:00 on Pacific Coast. Staid at Myers'.

Friday, April 23 Went to the train about 8:00 & waited till 12:00. Went on to Glenwood, and home with Anson Moor, who married my brother's widow Flora Stevens & Sarah Catharine Boen, my nieces, there, & T.F. Boen. Dinner & supper there. Called at Chas. Stevens in the evening at our old homestead. Staid at Moor's.

Saturday, April 24 Went over to the graves on the old homestead. Dined at Austin Winchell's. His wife, Laura, my Sister Sarah's daughter. Went to Glenwood with Moor. Arrived at Lotus & walked out to Greenwood Church. Supper at Scott Eaton's. Rev. Z. McNew, P.E. pr. at 8:00. Let all things be done 1 Cor. 16:14. Stay at Scott Eaton's.

Sunday, April 25 Easter. Rev. Z. McNew pr. at 11:00. Sacramental meeting followed. Dined at Scott Eaton's, 2 m. N.E. Pr. at 3:30, 1 Cor. 15:22. Went with Daniel Koerner to Mrs. Sarah Fry's. Saw Hoopingarner's wife & child. Went on to Daniel's, 7 miles south of Liberty.

Monday, April 26 Just afternoon, Clarence takes me to Liberty. I go via Hamilton to Dayton, my home.

Tuesday, April 27 Reuchlin, my oldest son was married about 12:30 to Miss Lulu Billheimer, at the residence of Rev. J.K. Billheimer, her father, Wms. St. Reuchlin and Lulu go about 3:00 to their home on Second Street, fitted up afore for their occupancy.

Wednesday, April 28 Went to town. Paid $5.00 to Telescope office for Rev. N.L. Hoopingarner. Saw the doc-

tor, H.S. Davis, & paid him $20.00. Rev. H. FLoyd dined with us. Dr. L. Davis sick. Visited him.

Thursday, April 29 Called at Davis'. Called at Reuchlin's.

Saturday, May 1 At home in forenoon. Went on 12:40 train to Richmond, Indiana, to see D.K. Zeller's family, including Mother Catharine Koerner, my wife's mother. Susan was with me.

Sunday, May 2 Attended Rev. Hughe's Church. His text was 1 John 5:11. Dine at Zeller's. John G. Zeller & Abbie called. Mary, their child, not quite 2 years old. Hughes' sermon in the evening, Matt. 7:12.

Monday, May 3 Rode out in the buggy. Called at John G. Zeller's a half hour. Dined at D.K. Zeller's. Went home to Dayton on 2:20 train.

Tuesday, May 4 At home all day. Rested some; wrote some. Started to the lecture, but turned back on account of an unusual dust storm.

Wednesday, May 5 Went to town before noon. Bishop J. Dickson had called awhile before I went. In the evening, attended commencement at Summit St. Church. W.S. Blackburn, J.W. Flora, W.R. Funk, J.W. Izor, J.C. Keezel, H.D. Lehman, W.C. Niswonger, J.H. Simons, & Wm. Williamson graduated. Exercises very good.

Thursday, May 6 At home. Reuchlin & Lulu took supper with us. I gave them four books.

Friday, May 7 Wrote out a card for *Telescope*. Called at Rev. J.W. Hott's to give it to him. Bp. J. Dickson & Miss Dr. Dickson came home with me and called on us an hour or less.

Saturday, May 8 Went to "town" in the forenoon & bought several articles & a Morocco-bound Bible & Bible-Help for 7.00. Wrote at letter to Wyatt of Philomath at Philomath, Oregon. Called at Lewis Davis' D.D. Mrs. Huit & Miss Minnie Hanby called in the evening; also Rev. Wm. Dillon & Dr. L. Davis.

Sunday, May 9 Went with Emma to the First Presbyterian Church. The chaplain of the Soldier's Home preached, 2 Pet. 1:4. Rather a prosy, but scriptural preacher. Attended Summit St. Church at 7:30. Rev. West & wife talked and showed idols, sword, knives, greegrees, purrow masks, etc. from Africa.

Tuesday, May 11 At home in forenoon. Went to Reuchlin's in the afternoon. Called at Dillon's a short time.

Wednesday, May 12 Went on 9:45 a.m. train to Lima arriving at 12:30. Leave Lima at 3:15 for Ft. Wayne. Stay at Rev. J.P. Stewart's on Hammer St. a square S. of the Church. Bp. Glossbrenner also. Bp. Weaver stays at his daughter's.

Thursday, May 13 Went on 6:20 a.m. train to Roanoke. Breakfasted at Prof. D.N. Howe's. Bps. Kephart and Castle came at 9:00. All bishops here except Flickinger. Dine at Prof. Howe's. Board of bishop's meet at 1:30. Bp. J. Weaver lectures at 7:00 on Principle. Kephart offers Weaver's lecture pamphlet for sale! I sup and lodge at Ed. Olds. Flood on Wolf Creek at night.

Friday, May 14 Board meets at 8:00. Dine at Rev. F.A. Robinson's, M.E. Pastor's with all the bishops & Rev. Burton, Rev. Lynch, M.E. P.E. came. Board meets again at 4:00. Considers the address to the Church. Bout with Glossbrenner in forenoon in Bennett's case. In afternoon with Weaver over his irreverence for constitution. Hoke pr. at 8:00 Rom. 6:15. Stay at Mr. Olds'.

Saturday, May 15 Missionary Board met at 8:00. Report of the Cor. Sectetary, of the treasurer, and minutes of the Ex-Com. Flickinger & McKee's choleric tilt. Rev. J.L. Luttrell dined with me at Olds, E.C. Olds. Apropriations considered, afternoon. Session at 7:30.

Sunday, May 16 At S.S. in the morning. Rev. Z. Warner pr. at 10:30 Acts 13:2,3. Miss. Coll. about 64 dollars. Dined as usual at Ebeneezer C. Olds', Weaver & Kephart also there. Rev. D.K. Wilberforce made an address on Missions—especially Africa. Several addresses on Missions in the evening.

Monday, May 17 Met a Com. on Mis. Debt at 6:30. Board began session at 7:30. Adjourned at 11:00. Went on to Wabash. Saw Charley Rose. Went to C.W. & M.

railroad depot. Wrote several letters. Went on 6:40 train to Fairmount. Walked out to Aunt Lizzie Reeder's. Reached there about 11:00.

Tuesday, May 18 Went over to the farm. Dined early at Aunt's. Got to Fairmount just in time for the train to Anderson. Connected at Anderson for Richmond. Called at D.K. Zeller's. Saw Dr. Hibberd at his office. Supper at Zeller's with Rev. G.W. Funkhouser. Go on to Dayton, transferring to the narrow-guage R.R.

Thursday, May 20 Reuchlin & Lulu called a little before bed-time.

Friday, May 21 At home. Went with family all, to Reuchlin's for supper. Staid till 8:00.

Saturday, May 22 Went to town in the forenoon. Bought a valise, ($3.90) & Shawl straps. Went also in the afternoon to see about rates on R.R. to Portland.

Sunday, May 23 Went to High St. Church. (E.S. Lorenz, pastor) pr. Matt. 16:16. At home the rest of the day. Wm. Dillon called awhile in the evening. Also Reuchlin & wife.

Monday, May 24 Went to town & purchased a ticket to Portland, Oregon. Start on 12:10 train. Miss connection at Arcanum. Stay at Rev. J. Kilbourn's till 6:40. Go via Indianapolis on I.B.W. train to Peoria, Illinois. My delay at Arcanum cost me 24 hours' time on my journey.

Tuesday, May 25 Reached Peoria about 9:00, and Burlington, Iowa, at 12:20. I have to wait till 8:20 for a train to Council Bluffs. I spend considerable time in writing letters. I leave at 8:40 for Council Bluffs.

Wednesday, May 26 I Reach Council Bluffs at 8:30. Go aboard the cars at 9:30. We Reach North Platte after dark. It is a warm, dusty day.

Thursday, May 27 Reach Cheyenne soon after noon. Reach Laramie about 5:00. Rocky Mountain Summit at Sherman. Monument there of Oakes Ames & Oliver Ames. The Express picks up our car in the night.

Friday, May 28 Reach Green River about 9:00. Change

to Oregon Short Line R.R. Run down Bear River. Snow on the mountain sides.

Saturday, May 29 Reached Huntington, Oregon, at 9:00. We passed Baker City in the forenoon—A nice narrow valley for miles afterward. Pass through Grand Ronde Valley in the afternoon. From 12 to 15 miles wide and 2.5 long. Very level and very beautiful. Reach Pendleton at 9:00 and put up at Villard's Hotel.

Sunday, May 30 Find President Miller in the morning. I pr. at M.E. Church at 11:00, Matt. 16:16. Dine with Rev. Kirkman. We attended Congregational S.S. at 12:00 and M.E. Sab. S. at 3:00, & made addresses at both places. I pr. at 8:00 Baptist Ch. Ps. 137:5, to the union meeting of the churches of town.

Monday, May 31 Went on 7:00 hack to Adams, Centreville, and Weston. Put up at Rev. J.M. Tresenriter's. Go with Rev. Tressenriter [sic] to Caynse Station, to meet Rev. J.S. Rhodes, the round-trip being at least 20 miles, mostly through the Umatilla Reservation, a most beautiful & rich country. Stay at Tresenriter's.

Tuesday, June 1 At Tresenriter's. Rev. J.S. Rhoads pr at 8:00, an able sermon. Tresenriter's children: Maud 13; Ira 10, & Milliard, 7.

Wednesday, June 2 Walla Walla Conference convened at 8:00. Rev. J. Black pr. at 8:00, and Rev. H.O. Kern exhorts & conducts a speaking meeting. Much interest and feeling.

Thursday, June 3 Conference continued. Rev. M. Wright pr. at 8:00 from Titus 2:14. Rev. J. Kenoyer exhorts. Rather a good meeting followed.

Friday, June 4 Conference continued. Rev. J.C. Spoonemore pr. at 8:00, 40 minutes. Rev. J.J. Gallaher followed in an exhortation of perhaps over an hour in length. His is gifted, but wild.

Saturday, June 5 Conference continued. Stationing Com. met at Tresenriter's at 7:00 & again at 11:30. It was a day of much discussion. Conference adjourned about 5:30. Rev. Jeremiah Kenoyer pr. at 8:30 a very

able & eloquent discourse.

Sunday, June 6 Lovefeast at 9:30. I pr. at 11, Heb. 7:26, to a large congregation. All much elated. Dined at Ginn's, 1 mile west, with Rev. J.J. Gallaher and wife. Chinese exercises at 3:00. I raise $350.00 for Walla Ralla Chinese School. Rev . J.J. Gallaher pr. at 8:30, John 3:16, called at N.J. McDaniel's. Stay at Tresenriter's.

Monday, June 7 Go on stage to Blue Mountain & thence by train to Walla Walla, & to Rev. C.W. Wells'. Rev. Haskell, Congregationalist, calls. Also Rev. W.R. Lloyd's, Mrs. Hastings, & John Arrasmith. Stay at Wells.

Tuesday, June 8 At Rev. C.W. Wells'. Made an address on temperance at Baker Grove. Stopped by rain.

Wednesday, June 9 Went with Bro. Wells to Kelso's. Dinner and supper. Their younger children are Lilly, 10, and Mabel 7. I am dull and sleepy. Staid at Caswell Witt's, near Kelso's. They live about 2 miles east of town. His oldest son is Caleb.

Thursday, June 10 At Well's in forenoon. Dinner at Lacey's. Their children are Flora 18, Stella 13, and Fred aged 3.

Friday, June 11 At Wells. Called on Ung See Hoy. Saw ten or a dozen Chinamen, Ah Wong and Shoo Fly interpreters. Mr. Hoy has a wife and child. He is a merchant. Saw very thick cinnamon bark.

Saturday, June 12 At Wells. Call in the afternoon to see Father Wilbur in the west part of town.

Sunday, June 13 Pr. at 11:00 at U.B. Church, Ps. 87:3. Small congregation. I Dine at Wells as usual. I Pr. at M.E. Church at 8:00, Eph. 2:4. Large audience.

Monday, June 14 Went on 5:00 train to Huntsville. Dined at Rev. W.C. Gallaher's. Went in the afternoon to Rev. J. Black's. He is away. Supper at B.J. Hunt's. Called at T.Z.A. Kumler's room & staid an hour. Staid at W.E. Gallaher's.

Tuesday, June 15 Called at Jas. Kenworthy's. Board meeting at 9:00. Com. on Finance met at 11:30. I chairman.

Dine at W.C. Gallaher's. Com. on Finance met at 5:00. On Faculty met at 1:30 & at 6:00. Supper at Kenworthy's Night session. Stay at Kenworthy's.

Wednesday, June 16 Called at W.C. Gallaher's. Rev. C.W. Wells & wife came on 6:35 train. Call at Rev. J. Black's. Dine at Jas. Kenworthy's. Go in the afternoon to Hon. A.E. McCall's, nine miles beyond Dayton. Had a very lively hail storm about 5:00. Stop at Messa's. McCall the representative from Columbia Co., Democratic.

Thursday, June 17 Went on via Covello, Marengo, & Pomeroy to Patana City in Garfield County, W. Ter. Stop at Saml. Fleenor's. Rev. C.W. Wells pr. at 8:00 Mark 9:7. Congregatio[n] small. It was at the school-house. Stay at Fleenor's.

Friday, June 18 Meeting in the grove at 11:[00]. Few out. Rev. Nathan Evans pr. at 11:00 Neh. 4:6. Dine at Fleenor's. Speaking meeting at 3:00 which I led. It was right good. Supper at Fleenor's. I pr. at the night from 1 Pet. 4:18. Considerable interest in the meeting. Stay at Fleenor's.

Saturday, June 19 Meeting at 11:00. Rev. C.W. Wells pr. 1 Cor. 1:30. Dined at Fleenor's as usual. Bro. Wells led the afternoon meeting. Supper at Fleenor's. Rev. H.O. Kern & wife came. I pr. at 8:00, Eccl. 12:13. Eli Modlin & wife came about supper-time.

Sunday, June 20 I pr. at Grove at 11:00, Ps. 48:12, 13. Dine with Eli Modlin's in the grove. Saw Henry & Marion Childers & their family. I had seen those men & abode with them when sick, 29 years ago, in French Prairie, Oregon. Rev. N. Evans pr at 3:00. Job 14:20. Ah Wong read & spoke. I raised $25.00 for the Chinese Mis. School. Supper at Fleenor's. Rev. H.O. Kerns pr. at 8:00 and I exhorted. Stay at Childer's.

Monday, June 21 I start at 7:00 from Henry Childers', at Pomeroy, for Portland. Ah Wong on the train to Walla Walla. Dine at Prescott. Stay at Wallula Junction from about 5:00 till 10:30. Go on, arriving at the Dalles about 6:00 next morning.

Tuesday, June 22 Reach Portland about 10:30. Cross on a steamboat to West-side. Got a letter from Susan. Wrote letter to Susan and to Mrs. Schildtknecht & cards to G.W. Hunt & M.M. Crow. Call at Green J. Ross' in East Portland. Go on 4:00 train to Woodburn. Rev. J.W. Pulley meets me and takes me out to DeWit C. Hall's, four miles from Silverton.

Wednesday, June 23 Staid at Hall's all day, except that I called at A. Mosher's to see Rev. J.G. Mosher who was there, it being his farm. This call was in the evening. I stay at Hall's.

Thursday, June 24 Father John Whitlock called before breakfast. I stay at Hall's till after dinner. No meeting at 11:00. Call at Wm. Adair's. Was at the burial of a child at 3:00. Supper at Adair's. Pr. at 8:30, Mark 8:36. Good attention. Stay at Hall's.

Friday, June 25 Looking over diary of 1857. Stay at Bro. Hall's all the forenoon. On the grounds. Meeting at 3:00. About 20 there. Rev. J.W. Pulley pr. 116 Ps. 12. Speaking meeting. Supper at Hall's. Rev. W.H. Palmer pr. at 8:30, Prov. 18:24. About 60 persons present. Stay at Bro. Hall's.

Saturday, June 26 Spent the forenoon at Father John Whitlock's & dined there. Rev. John Osborn pr. at 3:00, 2 Cor. 5:17. Supper at Hall's. Several Campers came in the forenoon. Rev. J G. Mosher pr. at 9:00, Luke 15, 18, "I will arise and go to my father." Stay at Bro. Hall's

Sunday, June 27 I preach at 11:00 John 14:23. Formally open the Church. Though it was a rainy day, the house was very full and perhaps hundreds outside. Dine at Wm. Minear's after the marriage of their daughter M. Viletta to Grant Corby. Rev. T.H. Stinson pr. at 3:00. Supper at Hall's. Rev. J.W. Pulley pr. at 8:30. Stay at Hall's.

Monday, June 28 Meeting for prayer at 11:00. Dine at John Whitelock's. Write letter before. Rev. W.K. Palmer pr. at 3:00, John 13:17. At Whitlock's for Supper. Rev. J.G. Mosher pr. at 9:00, Acts 16:31. I stay at Hall's.

Tuesday, June 29 Meeting in the grove at 10:00, prayer. Dine at Alonzo Mosher's. She was a Chammess. Rev. T.H. Stinson pr. at 3:00, about Naanan. I have supper at Wm. Adair's. I pr. at 8:30 Matt. 19:27. One came forward for prayers & three others arose for prayer.

Wednesday, June 30 Meeting at the Church at 10:00 prayer & speaking. Father John Whitlock took very sick. Rainy. I dined at Dewit C. Hall's. Rev. N.W. Allen pr. at 3:00 I not present. Ministers come. Supper at Hall's. I preach at 8:00, Rom. 10:13. Large congregation. Stay at Hall's.

Thursday, July 1 The Oregon Conference convened at 8:30. Examination of Non-pastors. Dine as usual. Examination of non-pastors & itinerants. Adjourned at 4:30. Rev. C.C. Bell preached at 7:30. I staid at Hall's.

Friday, July 2 Conference continued. It's usual business. Geo. F. Burnett aged 48 and J.H. Bowerman, 55, referred to Com. on Applicants. Rev. J.H. Watson pr. at 7:30.

Saturday, July 3 Conf. continued. Several transfer. At 3:00 memorial services of Rev. J.B. Lichtenthaler; The "liberals" ran out to caucus. Applicants ref. back to Qr. conference. Others transfer—eight in all. Motion to not allow them to vote, Sickafoose's impudence. Supper as usual. Night session. Pulley & Ingle elected P.E.'s. Stationing Committee.

Sunday, July 4 Short meeting of Stationing Com. at 9:00. Morning meeting at Ch. at 10:00. Pr. in grove at 11:00 Heb. 4:14 to about 800 people. Very orderly & sympathetic Congregation. Coll. of 53.17 for me. Dine at John Whitelock's with Rev. J.H. Watson. Missionary anniversary at 7:30. Raise Subs. & Cash, $133.50. (Sab. Sch. Anniv. at 3:00. Read Allotments of labor) Stay at Hall's.

Monday, July 5 Conference session closed atout 9:00. I Went to see E.C. Wyatt, the conference Mission Treasurer & paid him $10.00 of minor collections on the Mis. appropriations from parent board. Dined at Abr. J. Mosher's. Rev. A. Bennett started home. I staid to supper. Rev. J.G. Mosher pr. at 7:30 from Revel. 3:20. I stay at Wm. G. Minear's. His P.O. is Butte Creek, Clockamas Co., Ore.

Tuesday, July 6 Stay at Minear's all day. Write some. Rev. J.G. Mosher came & staid till after supper. Bro. Mosher had wounded his shin by a kick of a pick. I pr. at 7:30, l Pet. 4:18. Crowd rather light. Stay at William Adair's. Wm. Adair's P.O. is Butte Creek, Clockamas Co., Oregon.

Wednesday, July 7 I go down to D.C. Hall's. Rev. Mosher came. Dined there. Mrs. Lizzie Jack and Mrs. C. Kilin start away for home. Rev. J.G. Mosher pr. at 8:00.

Thursday, July 8 Go to HllI's and stay in the forenoon. Write letters and cards. Get buggy of J. Whitlock about 5:00 and go to Silverton & mail & get letters. Supper at John Whitlock's. I pr. at 8:00, Jer. 13:21. A good-sized congregation, mostly young unconverted persons. Stay at Bro. Wm. G. Minear's. Their children are Vilette (Corby) Elmer, 17, Charley & Ella May twins, 15, & Herbert. Elmer is at his Grandfather's.

Friday, July 9 Stay at Minear's till time to go to meeting. Wrote in the forenoon and part of the afternoon. They are very nice people. Their children: Viletta 19, Elmer 17, Ella & Charley 15, Herbert 13. I Preach at 7:45 Eph. 2:4. A large and well-behaved congregation. Stay at Geo. W. Hall's. They have three nice little girls.

Saturday, July 10 I stop an hour at Abr. J. Mosher's. Had a very pleasant conversation. Go on to D.C. Hall's. Stay till after dinner. Go to Woolen's. Fix their clock. Mother Marian Eisenhart's shares in Denver Atl. Tunnel [?] Company. Pr. at 7:30 Rom. 8:1. Stay at D.C. Hall's.

Sunday, July 11 Pr. at 11:00 at Abiqna Chapel 1 John 3:2. Dine at Wm. G. Minners with Adairs and Corby's. Good cong. Prelude on infidelity. Pr. at 7:00, Acts 26:28. Prelude on Christian Sabbath. Large congregation. Stay at William R. Adair's.

Monday, July 12 Go to Dewit C. Hall's. He and wife go with me to John Whitlock's. We dine there. Sister W. asked me if I am a Mason. I read them the obligations of three degrees of Masonry. Some Masons had affirmed that I am a Mason. No! Father Whitelock took me in a buggy to Silverton & I go on cars to Aumsville. Stay at Isaac Coy's 1/3 m. west. Sister Coy's father, Mr. King, was on a visit there.

Tuesday, July 13 Went to Turner's with Ledgerwood's. I get letters— one from Susan. Go back to Rev. J.S. Osborn's. Wrote a letter to the General Convention which is to meet at Fairmount, Indiana, the 20th instant. Stay at Osborn's (after mailing the letter) till morning.

Wednesday, July 14 Borrowed a pony at Simon Morgan's and go via Sublimity to Finley Campbell's, 1 1/2 m. south-east. I dine there. Go on to Stayton; I see Wm. H. Hobson. I hunt up E.H. Geter & his wife (Martha Williams) whom I saw when she was four & five years old. Go on to West Stayton. Supper at Silvanus Condit's. Get back to Morgan's. Pr. at Turner at 8:00, John 11:27. Stayed at E.E. McKinney's.

Thursday, July 15 Went to Osborn's. Simon Morgan & wife, Mary & Bro. J.S. Osborn go with me to Wm. Pearson's, an intimate acquaintance in 1858. We dine there. Bennett & Orlando are their boys. I borrow Pierson's grey Norman & go via West Sta[y]ton to Stayton. Put up at E.H. Geter's. Pr. at 8:00, 1 John 3:2. Stay at Geter's. Henry & Mary Follis (Mrs. Geter's sister) came to the meeting.

Friday, July 16 Ride over the Santiam River to Henry Follis's. Their children are Thomas, 25, Susan, 19, William 15. Mrs. Follis went to school to me at Sublimity in 1858-9, and was converted at my meeting in 1859. I dined there. I go in the afternoon to Henry Leffler's, 3/4 mile north-east of Scio. Mrs. Eliz. Leffler was a convert of my meeting in 1859. I preach Scio. 8:30, John 15:13. Stay at Leffler's. Those converts of 27 years ago, faithful.

Saturday, July 17 Go via Lebanon to Alfred Whealdon's west of Peterson's Butte, and north of Ward's Butte. Dinner, Supper, and lodging there. Isaac & wife live there. Lambert lives S.W. Fosha comes at 9:00. Father A. Whealdon comes at dusk, having gone to Albany, 12 miles north-west for me. Josha's son, grandson of Whealdon, stays there.

Sunday, July 18 Rev. A. Bennett came. I go to Sab. Sch. at Sand-Ridge Sch-house, at 10:00. Gave short Sab. Sch. address. I pr. at 11:00, 1 John 5:18, 19. Some cheeky boys. I dine at Tyler Jackson's, near Rock Hill. Harrison, twin brother, lives with him. I pr. at Rock-Hill Church at 4:00, John 3:16. Supper at Alex. Branden's. I stay at Whealdon's. A. Bennett with me till night.

Monday, July 19 Start at 5:00, via Jefferson, to Wm. Pearson's, 2 1/2 miles north of Marion. I dine at Otto Henry Bennett Pearson's. He & Mary, his wife, are nice-looking folks, & have pretty children. He was a student of mine at Sublimity. Wm. Pearson takes me to Marion. I go to Salem & to Jesse Harritt's. I got letters at Turner & Salem.

Tuesday, July 20 I was at Bro. Harritt's. Jas. Emmit & wife (Alice Harritt) came, and they and the children stay all day. I wrote letters. Emmet's children are Eddy 15, Bertha 7, Arthur 11, and Jesse 5. John Harritt's daughter, at her grandfather's visiting, is "Dell" 10.

Wednesday, July 21 At Bro. Harritt's still. Wrote part of the forenoon. Spent the day at Harritt's. In 1857, at their invitation, I spent many weeks, with Brother Harritt's, and they were very kind to me. His name was Jesse;— hers Julia Franklin; the children, John, Alice, and Byron Webster & Elmer b. later.

Thursday, July 22 Went with Bro. Harritt's to James Emmit's, dine and return about 3:00. Go to Salem. Supper at Wm. Sargent's. Mail & get letters. Return to Harritt's.

Friday, July 23 Went to Derry Station on the stage & thence to Corvallis & to Philomath by rail. Fare 86 cts. & 24 cts. Rev. Pulley meets me and takes me to Rev. M.M. Crow's. Supper & lodging there. I pr. at 8:00, Heb. 11:26. Wm. Hartor, Rev. W.H. Best and Rev. Organ were present.

Saturday, July 24 Called at Rev. N.H. Allen's & Pres. G.M. Miller's Rev. J.W. Pulley pr. at 11:00. Qr. Conf. followed. I dined at Rev. N.W. Allen's, about 3:00 p.m. Supper at Rev. M.M. Crow's, Rev. J.W. Pulley pr. at 8:00, "I have fought a good fight," etc. I stay at N.W. Allen's.

Sunday, July 25 I Pr. at 11:00, Ps. 48:11, 12, 13. Raise $19.50 for the presideng elder, J.W. Pulley. Dine at L.N. Price's, son of Rev. Price of Umqua Valley. Call at Rev. Ezra Wyatt's. Stay till church time. Bro. Pulley pr. at 8:00, 2 Tim. 3:16. We stay at Wyatt's. Mary (Pierson) his wife was a student at 14, of mine, at Sublimity, and a nice pretty girl.

Monday, July 26 Staid at Wyatt's till 9:00. Went to Rev. N.W. Allen's and staid till after dinner. Went to Rev. Jas. R. Parker's and had a talk with him. Supper at Rev. M.M.

Crow's. I Pr. at 8:00, 2 Cor. 5:17. Stay at Crow's with Pulley.

Tuesday, July 27 Stay at Crow's sometime. Reuben Grant called. Wrote transfers and gave to J.R. Parker, J.E. Connor, and (in evening) to C.C. Bell. Went to Rev. A. Bennett 's. Dined, climbed Bennett's Butte and viewed the valley. Rev. J.W. Pulley pr., 8:00, Rev. 3:18. Stay at Rev. N.W. Allen's.

Wednesday, July 28 Go over to Rev. M.M. Crow's. Write letters. Dine there. Call at 2:00 at Prof. H. Sheak's. Stay about two hour's. Then go to Rev. N.W. Allen's & stay for supper. Call at Rev. G.M. Stropes. Pr. at 8:00, 1 John 3:2. Increased congregation. Pulley & I stay at Rev. E.C. Wyatt 's. Wyatt's wife very rheumatic.

Thursday, July 29 Call at Peter Mason's. Then call at Rev. M.M. Crow's. Mail letters to Wilbur, Rev. J.N. English, Dillon, Harvey Wright. Dine at Peter Mason's. She a cousin to Mrs. Solomon Parsons, Fairmount, Indiana. Called at Crow's. Called at John Kitson's and took supper. Bell and wife staying there. Pr. at 8:00, John 7:37. Stay at Gilbert McElroy's.

Friday, July 30 McElroy's from Illinois & acquainted with Rev. O.H. Smith & other preachers there. Children: George & William. Dine at M.M. Crows, having written several letters and cards. Called at John Aiken's drug store to see him. Called at Allen's and at S.K. Brown's. Went out with Pres. Miller to Sister Bery's. Not at home. Staid at Miller's. Jery there & wife.

Saturday, July 31 Call at Rev. Olds' recently married to Mrs. Buckingham. Rev. A. Bennett comes and takes me in a hack. Dine at Laban Case's. He once a M.E. preacher; then an unbeliever; now a reclaimed man. Go on to Joseph Gragg's & lodge there. They get news at dusk of the drowning of Arthur Buckingham, Mrs. Gragg's Nephew.

Sunday, August 1 Pr. at Simpson Chapel (M.E.) at 11:00, Heb. 11:35. Dined at Barnard's on the ground. Pr. at 2:00, Rom. 3:5. Many who were children remembered my being at a camp-meeting here 28 years ago. At the burial of Arthur Buckingham, drowned Saturday evening, in Long Tom. Staid at Jas. E. Edwards, whom I knew in 1858—a choice, good man.

Monday, August 2 Stay at Jas. E. Edwards' till 11:00. Alfred Wheeldon called. Dined at Lewis Edwards', whose wife was Margery Whealdon. Went on via Monroe to J.R. Crow's. He is a son of Rev. Malcom Crow's. He lives on the old farm 3 1/2 ms. from Junction City, in Lane County.

Tuesday, August 3 I went on to Junction City. Stop at Wm. Edwards; Son of Jas. E. Edwards. His wife an Akers, a relative of Prof. Akres of Cedar Rapids. Write and mail some letters. Go on 1:20 train to Drain. Put up at Thos. Gardner's. His fatherinlaw is Harlan, who is with them. Pr. at 8:00 John 14:3.

Wednesday, August 4 Went down to Isaac Gardner's, 4 1/2 miles below Drain, on Elk Creek. Saw our church and parsonage on the way. Stay there till next day. Children at home: Isaac & Emma.

Thursday, August 5 Stay at Isaac Gardner's till 2:00. In forenoon, I climbed the hill, 400 feet high. Went to Drain and on to Oakland. Rev. P.C. Parker met me at the train & took me to his house. Pr. at Baptist Church at 8:00, Matt. 16:16. Stay at Parker's. He is very old, but vigorous.

Friday, August 6 Staid at Bro. Parker's till nearly five o'clock p.m. I go on to Roseburg. Ride with Rev. Mr. Jones, a M.E. Evangelist, who is also a pastor at Drain. I stop at Dr. Masters, and stay there. John Newman came up to see me— talk with him.

Saturday, August 7 Write some. Go to Drug-Store and meet Prof. J.B. Horner, and call at his house an hour. Dine at John Newman's. Go out with Wm. A. Willis and lodge there. He an aged Southern M.E. preacher. He lives two miles above Pine Grove Church on Deer Creek.

Sunday, August 8 Pr. at Pine Grove U.B. Church at 11:00, Rev. 1:5, on the exalted character of Christ, as shown in the Epistle to Hebrews. Dine on the grounds with A.H. Brown's. Saw Father Dixon, Gilmore, Burt, Hunter, Clifton. Pr. at 2:30, Heb. 10:35. Speaking meeting followed. Staid at A. Hugh Brown's. Children:

Sumner (dec.) Saphone, Ellie, Etc.

Monday, August 9 Bro. Brown took me to Roseburg. Stop at Prof. J.B. Horner's. Dine there. Went down town. Got a mixture of lobelia & Glycerene for eresipelas, as a lotion. Called at Bell's office. He a M.E. South preacher, and editor of the *Register*. Supper & lodging at Horner's. Pr. at M.E. Church at 8:00, John 11:27. Large & intelligent congregation.

Tuesday, August 10 Went on the 6:30 stage to Looking-glass & to Mr. Buell's. Leave my baggage there & walk down south 1/2 mile to Edward Morgan's. Dinner & supper & lodging there. Wrote several letters. Pr. at 8:30 at Looking-glass Hall, Gal. 3:13. A good audience, but late assembling. Job Denning's wife a Wright, Luce's stepdaughter, who saw me 29 & 27 years ago.

Wednesday, August 11 Went to Buell's. Read some in their Mormon Bible, which has many Joe Smith interpolations which bear plain marks of fiction. I go on Stage to Sumner. Jas. Laird, the proprietor, was aboard. Pass the Coast Range 2,300 ft. high. Along Coquille River. Ride along the mountain side at scarey h[e]ights. Coquille falls. Lairds. Reach Sumner at about 10:20, stay at Joshua Brown's Hotel. No charge for lodging & breakfast.

Thursday, August 12 Rev. J.G. Mosher calls on his way to Rogue River. Bro. B. Frank Ross comes after me and takes me in a two-horse buggy to his house, on Ketching Slew. Ride through tallest, finest timber, down steep hills. Rev. Wm. F. Bonebrake and Josiah V. Bonebrake called. Stay at Bro. Ross's.

Friday, August 13 Go up Kitchen Slew to Unity Chapel and pr. at 11:30, Gal. 3:18. Dine at J.V. Bonebrake's. Stay at Bonebrake's. Saw Moses Stock, & Coffett, at Church. The Church is "Unity Chapel," a small, new U.B. Church.

Saturday, August 14 Call at B.F. Ross's, and walk over the hill to S. School celebration grounds. About 175 present. Make an address at the close of the exercises. Go with Mr. Yokum, in his row-boat, to the forks of Coose River. Supper with him. Go with Stephen C. Rogers to his house, two miles up Coose River. Stay there. Yocum is a blasphemous infidel.

Sunday, August 15 Walked down to Wilson's shop. Then go in a boat to Mosher Chapel. Call at J.G. Mosher's. Pr. at 11:00, Rev. 1:5. Lunch at Mosher's. Pr. at 3:00, John 20:31. Go home with Jonathan Hodson. Supper & lodging there. Coll. that day $11.85.

Monday, August 16 Went at 6:00 in Stephen C. Rodger's boat to Marsfield. Got letters from home, etc. Wrote letters home. Went back to Mosher Chapel. Supper and lodging at Abram Cutlip's, 1 1/2 miles south.

Tuesday, August 17 Go over to Nathan Smith's. Stay there till after dinner. I had visited them in 1859 in Camis Swail. Went to Marshfield on the steamboat, "Bertha". Fare 50 cts. Supper at Snyder's Hotel. Write & mail letters to Susan and Wm. Reeder. Purchase ticket and go aboard the Steamer "Coos Bay." Fare to Eureka $5.00— that is 1/2 fare. Pr. at Baptist Church at 8:00, 2 Cor. 3:8. Go aboard the steamer. Rev. Lund, Episcopal, attended me aboard. Had been in Australia.

Wednesday, August 18 Awoke at 5:00. Just going over Coos bar. Arose. "Quamish." Lay down and slept awhile. Ate a little at lunch at 12:00, and felt real well. Anchored at Crescent City. Staid till 10:30, about 4 1/2 hours. I ate a good supper. Slept about five hours.

Thursday, August 19 Awoke at 4:00 a.m., near Trinidad. Stuck in the sand, a few miles this side of Eureka, twice. Wait the rising tide. Ate a hearty breakfast. Still fast at Dinner. Loose and reach Eureka, California, about 1:00. Get a letter from Barlett of LaCentre Wash. Ter. Mail letters. Supper & lodging at Rev. E. Bast's. At Prayermeeting. Bast is W.H. Bast's father.

Friday, August 20 Mrs. Wm. Bast called in & we had quite a talk on religious topics. Went to Andrew Woolridge's, Cor. F & 9th Sts., and dined. Went down town. Sent letters & postals. Supper at Woolridge's. Called in afternoon at Charley Mentz. Talk with her on "faith healing." Call at 8:00 on Rev. F. Stearns, the pastor. Stay at Rev. E. Bast's.

Saturday, August 21 Breakfast at Woolridge's. Go at 9:00 to Sab. S. picnic across the bay, on the peninsula (or (now) island.) Fine day. Rev. F. Stearns & wife, McDonald and wife, Webster, Sisters Valier, Evans,

Woolridge, *Johnson, McCoy, Russ, Telsha, etc., there. Went on the small steamer, "Alta." Spent some hours on the beach. Stay at Woolridge's. *not a U.B. Picked up a starfish.

Sunday, August 22 Called at Rev. E. Bast's. Pr. at 11:00, Zech. 6:13, "He shall be a priest upon his throne." Dined at Woolridge's. Pr. at 7:30, Rom. 8:18, "Compar, Glor. revealed in us." Stay at the Rev. E. Bast's. Members at Eureka: Anna Wooldridge, Emma Mentz, W.B. Webster, Agnes McCoy.

Monday, August 23 Stay at Bast's till nine o'clock. Go to Rev. F. Stearns. Dine there. Go in aftern. to the red-wood forests. Supper at Mr. Maxwell's at the shingle-mill, Steam's soninlaw's. Go on back to Eureka. Stay at Wooldridge's. Saw 21 redwood stumps from 3 to 8 ft in diameter on a half (or a quarter) acre of land, at Maxwell's.

Tuesday, August 24 Went to post-office. Wrote letter to Orville & Katie. Dinner at Jas. Russ's. Call at M. McDonald's. Call at Peterson's, shop. Supper at John McLaren's. He an aged Scotchman. Call at E. Bast's. Stay at Wooldridge's. McLaren gave the lot on which our church stands, with antisecrecy provision, he being intensely antisecrecy.

Wednesday, August 25 Write letter and cards at the post-office. No mail for me. Call to see F. Peterson. I dine at Woolridge's. Go on 3:00 train to Kohnerville, F. Peterson along. I stay at Rev. Jacob Ackerson's. Sister A. quite sick. Rev. Jacob Ackerson in his 74 year.

Thursday, August 26 Go to David Eby's in town. He is helpless, but otherwise well. Dinner and supper, and lodging there. His son-in-law and daughter (Stubbs) live with them. Rev. D. Eby, 74 years of age; once a minister of Miami Conference. A strong anti-commission man.

Friday, August 27 Go to Rev. J. Ackerson's. Dine. Mother A. had a bad sinking spell yesterday, and is very weak to-day. Father Ackerson takes me to Hydesville to Fred Bernells' funeral which was preached by Rev. S.T. Sterritt. Came back and staid at Rev. Jacob Ackerson's.

Saturday, August 28 Wrote a letter home. Staid at Ackerson's all day. Dinner & supper. Wrote considerably. Staid at Rev. David Eby's.

Sunday, August 29 Pr. at 11:00, at U.B. Church, Matt. 2:10. Dined at J.R. Jordan's. Called at Frank B. Carter's. Pr. at M.E. Church at 7:30, Rom. 1:34. Stay at Rev. J. Ackerson's. Talk at Carter's with Mr. Bell on Oddfellowship. He said it is built on Scripture, and would as soon depend on its protection as on the Church.

Monday, August 30 Got several letters. Wrote all the afternoon. Dinner & Supper at Rev. J. Ackerson's. Staid at D. Eby's. Members at Rohnerville: J.F.J. Nowlan, Nancy Hauk, Jas. Smith, Frank B. Carter, J.R. Jordan, John L. Douglas.

Tuesday, August 31 Staid at Eby's till after dinner. Rev. S.T. Sterrett & wife dined with us & Gracie, their daughter, & remained till about 3:00. Supper and lodging at J. Ackerson's. Mother Ackerson had a very sick night.

Wednesday, September 1 At Ackerson's till 11:00. Dine at Rev. S.T. Sterrett's. Pleasant visit. Call at Eby's, at Carter's, and at J.R. Jordan's had my supper. Prayer meeting at 7:30, good. Saw Myrick. Stay at Rev. J. Ackerson's.

Thursday, September 2 Stay at Ackerson's till after dinner. Then get a letter at the post-office from home and from Rev. J.H. Watson, and from others, postal-cards. Went to J.F.J. Nowlan's, 1 1/2 miles toward Springville. Supper there. He brought me back to town to M.E. prayer-meeting. Stay at Rev. D. Eby's.

Friday, September 3 Write letter to Susan & some cards to P.C. Parker, Thomas Gardner, & W.H. Bast. Go to J. Ackerson's to dinner. Wrote to Rev. W.J. Campbell & some cards to Rev. A.H. Montgomery and John Newman. Go to Springsville 2 1/2 ms. north-west. Stay at Rev. J.B. Hamilton's who had just come home. Aunt Sally. They from West Desmoines, Chariton Co.

Saturday, September 4 Went before breakfast up the log-way; tramways & skids to the summit. Talk. Went to see the saw-mill. They cut a twenty-four feet board 2 ft wide in 20 seconds. Come back with Bro. (M.E.) Myrick. Dine at Ackerson's. Pr. at 2:30, 137 Ps. 5, 6. Quarterly Conf. at Rev. D. Eby's. Stay at Eby's.

Sunday, September 5 Hear at Breakfast of Mother Abigail Ackerson's death, at about 4:30. Pr. at 11:00, Zech. 13:9. Dine at Ackerson's. Stay at Ackerson's. Rest some & write an obituary to read at the funeral. Pr. at 7:30, Matt. 16:26. Stay at Ackerson's.

Monday, September 6 Pr. Mother Ackerson's funeral at 10:00, Rev. 14:13. Dinner, supper, & lodging's at Ackerson's. Spend an hour or two at Rev. D. Eby's. Got letters from Susan & Reuchlin, dated Aug. 26 & 27.

Tuesday, September 7 Went to Rev. D. Eby's. Dined there. In the morning wrote to Reuchlin enclosing a letter to Susan. Went on 1:00 train to Eureka. Rev. W.J. Bast met me. Called at Wooldridge's and went on to Bast's (Rev. E. Bast's) to supper. Gave Father Bast the Sabbath Coll. $5.00. Pr. at U.B. Church at 7:30, Mark 8:36. Stay at Andrew Wooldridge's.

Wednesday, September 8 Dinner at Wooldridge's with Mrs. Johnson and McCoy. Spent afternoon at Rev. E. Bast's. Pr. at 7:45, Deut. 18:18. Stay at E. Bast's.

Thursday, September 9 Went out to Jas. Russ's and dined. Spent the afternoon at M. McDonald's and took supper there. Talk about soul's existence between death & resurection; On Seventh-day topic also. Pr. at 8:00 Ps. 137:5, 6. Election of class-leader, Jas. Russ chosen.

Friday, September 10 Went to P.O. Got a letter from home, via Ellensburg, Ore., & Woodbridge, Cal. Write post-scripts to mine already written. Call at F. Peterson's. He measures me for pants. Go to Rev. F. Stearns & dine there. Go down town. Call at Reading Room. Supper & lodging at E. Bast's. Rev. W.H. Bast pr. 8:00, Ps.119:80.

Saturday, September 11 Call at (John) Matilda McLaren's. Went down town. Dine at E. Bast's. Afternoon went down town. Got a pair of pants of F. Peterson worth $8.00— a present. Supper at E. Bast's. Pr. at 7:30, Rom. 4:8. Preside in Qr. Conf. by election. G. W. Burris & F. Stearns licensed to preach. Stay at E. Bast's.

Sunday, September 12 Pr. at 11:00, Gen. 22:18, a missionary discourse. Raise $55.00 on the chart collections. Dine at Lois Kirk's in Pine addition. Pr. at the Hall at

3:00, 2 Thes. 2:13. Supper at Rev. E. Bast's. Administer Sacrament to him on his sick-bed. Pr. at 7:30, 1 Cor. 5:7. Sacramental service. Stay at E. Bast's.

Monday, September 13 Dined with Bro. Bast at Matilda McLaren's. Bought a ticket for the Steamer Humboldt for San Francisco, State Room 13, Berth 2. Supper & Lodging at Rev. Ephraim Bast's. Call at John McLaren's and spend 1 1/2 hours in the evening.

Tuesday, September 14 Go on the steamboat "Alta" to Arcata, and thence by car to North Fork (Mad River). There, amid a grove of large redwood trees, numbering 25 in about a radius of 200 ft., we dined heartily. We measured one round tree, 53 ft in circumference; another with three stems 56 ft. and a stump in North Fork, 19 ft across one way, and 17 the other. We measured the h[e]ight of two trees, 315 & 325 ft. I saw a board 28 ft wide sawed through in 9 sec. Return to Eureka.

Wednesday, September 15 Called at McLaren's, Stearns', and C. Metz'. Went aboard the Steamer Humboldt (Capt. John A. Howard) at 11:00. Let "sail." Bar rough. Then "trough of the sea". Many sea-sick. I mildly so. Foggy all day & all night. Wrote in the evening home. Did not see the school of whales, but was below. Slept 7 hours.

Thursday, September 16 Awoke about 5:00. Vessel stopped to take soundings. Saw a school of porpoise; also a seal. The Capt. said we went through a school of fish last night about four miles long. Foggy night & morning. Lunched at 11:00. Land at one o'clock at San Francisco. Take Room 130 at Russ House. Finish & mail letter home. View the Chinese quarters in afternoon. Stay at Russ House.

Friday, September 17 Mail home an abalonia shell, starfish, clam shells, etc. Afternoon go out on California Street by Stanwood, and Crocker buildings, to Laurel Hill Cemetery. Saw Senator Miller's and Broddrick's Monuments. Went across, via Catholic & I.O.F. Cemeteries, ran out to Golden Gate Park. To ferries via City Hall. Board "City of Stockton" to Stockton. Slept in Cabin.

Saturday, September 18 Boat Wallowed in the slew. Arrived at Stockton at 7:00 a.m. Put up at Grand Central. Visit Insane Assylum. Write letters. Go at 12:40 to Lodi. Go out on stage to Woodbridge. Stop at Rev. D. Shuck's. Dr. Jerry Riley there. Call, after supper, at Pres. D.A. Mobley's, Prof. Ridenour's, and D.G. Rush's. Stay at Rev. Daniel Shuck's.

Sunday, September 19 Pr. at 11:00, Ps. 92:8. Dine at D.G. Rush's. Supper there. Read up our papers considerably. Prof. Klinefelter pr. at 7:30, John 15:8. I stay at Rush's, which is to be my conference home. Got a letter from Wm. H.H. Reeder, my cousin.

Monday, September 20 Wrote letter and card— letter home, card to N. Evans, P.E. of Walla Walla Dist. Go to Rev. I.K. Staton's & dined. Sister Shuck brought me a letter from home. Supper & lodging at Rush's. Read up papers somewhat.

Tuesday, September 21 Wrote letters to P.E's J.W. Ingle & N. Evans. Dine at Danl. Shuck's. Staid there till evening. Bro. Shuck came home about 3:00. Staid at Rush's.

Wednesday, September 22 Dined at Alfred Cowel's with Rev. I.K. Statton, his wife & son Arthur. Got a letter from Peter Suman saying that Bro. Reuben Hall died last Friday. Supper & lodging at D.G. Rush's.

Thursday, September 23 Attended & led in the morning prayer at the college chapel. Wrote several letters & two cards. Dinner at D.G. Rush's; also supper. Sister A. Cowley dined with us and Zina and Miss Hubbard.

Friday, September 24 Went with Rev. Daniel Shuch via Stockton to Atlanta. M.E. Church. Lunch at Stockton at a restaurant. Fair week. Saw gas well, A burial at Cemetery at Atlanta, "Tea" at Rev. W.T. Mayne's, "batching" at Parsonage. Pr. at 7:30, Ps. 1:1 to a small congregation. Stay at Mrs. Harriet Foster's, with Bro. Shuck.

Saturday, September 25 Dine at Ernest Wagner's, a fun[n]y dutch-49-er. She gave me a sack of dried figs. Lunch also at Wagner's. He an Evang. Asso. man. Shuck with me. I Pr at 7:30, John 3:2, to a small congregation. Staid at Christopher Von Glahn's, five miles east of the

Church. They are M.E. folks. Their nephew quite sick & penitent.

Sunday, September 26 Pr. at Atlanta, 1 Cor. 1:23-4. Communion service followed. Dine at Atlanta, atJohn Minor's. Pr. at 7:00, 1 Ki. 18:21. Go four miles east (S.E.) and stay at Leis. He worth $100,000.

Monday, September 27 Go on toward Woodbridge. Call at Niswonger's, worth $100,000; at Hitchcock's, $100,000. Dine at John Minge's, a German M.E., who was a R. Catholic till 42 ys of age. He has a brother near Cleaves, Ohio, wants me to see him. Call at Stockton. Reach Woodbridge about 6:30. Supper at Shuck's. Got several letters. Attend Qr. Conference at 8:00. Stay at Rush's.

Tuesday, September 28 Wrote letters home, etc. Went to Rev. T.J. Bauder's to see Revs. J.R. Parker & Rev. W.H. Bast & their wives. Dine at Rush's. Spend afternoon in reading and writing. Call at Rev. D. Shuck's. Supper at my boarding place, Bro. D.G. Rush's. I Led the speaking meeting at Church. Few Conf. members there.

Wednesday, September 29 Few members were present at the opening of Conference, so it adjourned after devotional exercises and the calling of the roll. Dinner, supper & lodgings as usual. Met at 2:00 and opened the session. Preliminary business & examination. J.R. Parker pr. at 7:00. "Caleb followed Lord fully."

Thursday, September 30 Conference session proceeds fairly with business. Dine at Rev. W.H. Klinefelter's. Afternoon session. Mostly examinations. Supper at Boarding place. I pr. at 7:00, to a full house, Rom. 3:5, on Justice of God's Vengeance. Stay at Boarding place.

Friday, October 1 Business continued. Dined as usual. Conf. in forenoon determined that Bish. money above Qr. Meeting assessment, be for Qr. M. put in Church Expense column. N.W. Harrow stricken from conf. roll. Prof. Ebersole referred to Com. on Applications. Rev. I.K. Statton pr at 7:00, John 1:45.

Saturday, October 2 Business continued. Revs. J.W. Baumgardner & T.J. Bauder elected P.E.'s Stationing Com. meets at 1:00 Afternoon. Resol. on Cons. tabled.

Mis. meeting at night. I raised $109.05 in subs. & cash. Mobley moves to strike out item discouraging secred methods of temperance societies. Dinner, supper & lodging at Rush's.

Sunday, October 3 Preached at 11:00, Ps. 110:4. Dined at the Mobley's. S.S. Anniversary in the afternoon at 3:00. Supper at Rush's. Rev. Daniel Shuck pr. at 7:00, Ps. 145:11. Communion followed. Stay at D.G. Rush's.

Monday, October 4 Attend college prayers. Spend a good deal of the day in writing. Dinner supper and lodging at Rush's. Talk in the afternoon with Rollins. Rev. J.R. Parker preached at 7:00, John 1:4.

Tuesday, October 5 Attend college prayer's. At Rush's most of the forenoon. Called a few minutes at Prof. E.H. Ridenour's and at G.M. Palmer's. Dine at Rush's. Pay A. Cowell $15.05 of cash on Mission Collection, and $11.00 on Ed. Ben. & Biblical Sem. Colls. of Cal. Conf. Called at Rev. T.K. Statton's & talk with Arthur on religion. Call at Bauder's. Supper and lodging at Cowell's. I pr. at 7:00 John 21:22.

Wednesday, October 6 Went with John Fields over to Rev. J.L. Field's three miles north of Woodbridge. Spent the day there. Harry Hall, six years old, lives with them. Rev. I.K. Statton pr. at 7:00 2 Kings 3:16, 17, 18. I stay at Rush's.

Thursday, October 7 Spent the day mostly at Rush's. Wrote many letters. Rev. T.J. Bauder pr. on *Par. Prod. Son. I stay at G.M. Palmer' s. *Handed me a Careb pod while preaching, which I pocketed.

Friday, October 8 At morning prayer's. Call at Rev. Daniel Shuck's. Dine at Rush's. Call at Dr. J.J. Riley's—supper there. Children, Dessy, about 11, Ose, about 9, & [blank] about 4. I pr. at 7:00, Ex. 28:34. Good speaking meeting followed. Staid at Prof. E.H. Ridenour's.

Saturday, October 9 Went with Bro. D.G. Rush (and John & Mr. Bryant) to Stockton. Dine at Mansion House. Started to Atlanta with Jas. Carter about 3:40. From the Church, I walk up to Mrs. Harriet Foster's. Children: Anva Glenn, Early Foster, Lottie Foster; Arch, Moses.

Sunday, October 10 Pr. at Atlanta Church at 11:00, 1 Thes. 4:3. M.E. members there: Ellenwood, Hitchcock, Niswonger, Von Glohn. U.B. members: Liesy, Mrs. Wigner, Minor. Dine at Burchard Von Glahn's. Go on to Burneyville 15 miles from Atlanta. Pr. at Burneyville at 7:00, Luke 24:46. Stay at Rev. John McBride's.

Monday, October 11 At McBride's part of forenoon. Go in afternoon to Oakdale, six miles East, or north-east. Bring Ella Philips, McBride's Half-sisterinlaw to lead the music. Pr. at 7:00 Matt. 16:26. Congregation quite good. In forenoon attended the burial of Dr. Wilkinson, McBride preaching the funeral. Stay at McBride's.

Tuesday, October 12 Go about noon to Romeo E. Bangs, members, about four miles southwest of Burneyville. Dine there. He is a native of Mexico. Supper at Mrs. Nancy Livingstons, she being a member of our church. At 7:00, Rev. J. McBride preached at Burneyville, Luke 18:1. Stay at McBride's.

Wednesday, October 13 Went to B.F. Bourland's about 10:00. Stay all day and all night. Am a good deal unwell with cold and fever. Did not go out to Church But Rev. J. McBride pr. at 7:00. 2 Cor. 6:1. Bourland's children: Abbie (married), George, 21, Lemnel 19, Mamie 16, William 14.

Thursday, October 14 Staid at Bro. Bourland's till 4:00 p.m. Mr. Wm. Munsen & wife dined with us. They live 2 1/2 miles N.E. of Oakdale. Bro. Bourland takes me to Bro. McBride's. Supper there. Pr at 7:30 at Burneyville, Luke 15th and the 7th. Stay at McBride's.

Friday, October 15 Stay at Bro. McBride's in the forenoon. Go in the afternoon to Thomas Richardson's. Stay till Bro. McBride returns from Oakdale. Return to McBride's. Supper there. Pr at B.— at 7:30, Matt. 1:21. Stay at McBride's.

Saturday, October 16 Stay at McBride's all day. Took a thorough course of medicine to guard off any periodic tendencies. It sprinkled a little at different times in the day. Pr at B. at 7:30, Matt. 24:44. Stay at McBride's.

Sunday, October 17 Pr. at 11:00 Ps. 48:11-13. Dine at Thomas Richardson's, two miles east of McBride's. In evening, Richardson takes me to Oakdale. Pr. at 7:00 at Union Church Matt. 16:16. Return to Richardson's & lodge. Note—We had a time hunting up the church key at Oakland. It may have been a trick. So it seemed.

Monday, October 18 Stay at Richardson's till 4:00 Go to Thomas Snediger's. They are away. The children & Mr. Smith & Miss Capp there. Snediger's get home from Modesto after supper. I pr. at B. 7:00 Acts 2:40. Congregation about 30. Stay at McBride's.

Tuesday, October 19 Went to Mother Nancy Livingston's with Mother and Sister McBride. Dine there. Return to McBride's. McBride Pr. at 7:00, Heb. 2:3. About 55 there. Rev. J.L. Field & John there. They stay at McBride's. I stay at Robert Leighton's of M.E. Church. Mr. Yarrington & Brigden stay there.

Wednesday, October 20 Stay at Leighton's till afternoon. Come to Mother Huntley's in Burneyville, and stay a short time. Go across the Stanislaus River to Jacob Myer's. Supper there. I Pr. at 7:00, 1 Tim. 4:8. About 55 present. Three lifted their hands in token of desire to become Christians. Stay at McBride's.

Thursday, October 21 Stay at McBride's all day. McBride pr. at 7:00, John 18:40. One arose for prayer. Stay at McBride's.

Friday, October 22 Staid at McBride's all forenoon and all the afternoon. Felt weak & poorly all day. I Pr. at 7:00, 1 John 5:3. A spelling-school and a dance call away most of the young folks. Stay at McBride's.

Saturday, October 23 At McBride's in forenoon. Went to Oakdale about noon. Dinner at Mother Phillips, at Langworth. Got medicines, gloves, etc. My health some better. Supper at McBride's. I Pr. at 7:00, Luke 19:27. Three came forward for prayers. Stay at McBride's.

Sunday, October 24 Went to S. School. Heard Rev. Mr. Wolf (M.E.C.) pr at 11:00, Rom. 1:16. Dined at Wm. Wyman's, 2 1/2 ms. west of the Church. They are Baptists. Children: Elsie 14, Addle 11, Mary 5. Mother Livingston there for dinner. I lunch there. I pr. at 7:00, Rev. 22:11. Five came forward for prayer. I stay at McBride's.

Monday, October 25 Stay at McBride's that day. Wash my coat collar, etc. Supper at Salmon Blodget's. Pr at 7:00, Acts 17:31. Three forward for prayer. Stay at B.F. Bourland's. He was raised in Arkansaw [sic] on the border of the Indian Nation. Long in California & once a teamster to the mines. She is later from Georgia.

Tuesday, October 26 Staid at Bourland's all day, except that I went to Mother Brown's, at Burwood, in the afternoon. Young Mrs. Brown is Bourland's daughter, Abie. Mother Brown is a Cumberland Presbyterian. I Pr at 7:00, Heb. 3:7, 8. Stay at Salmon Blodget's. About 65 at meeting.

Wednesday, October 27 Went over about 11:00 to John McBride's. Staid till 3:30 p.m. Went to a wedding at Thompson's, three miles north. Bro. McBride unites Mr. Campbell and Maud Thompson. McBride pr. at 7:00 (7:30) at Burneyville, Mark 1:3. About 40 at meeting. The wedding and a social got up by Abbie Monroe (M.E.) took off several.

Thursday, October 28 Spend the forenoon at McBride's. Go to Salmon Blodget's in the afternoon and stay till after supper. Pr. at B. at 7:00, John 5:39. A very solemn meeting about 60 present. No move for prayers. Stay at McBride's.

Friday, October 29 Dine at McBride's. Went in afternoon to Oakdale with Ed. Blodget. Pr. at B. at 7:00. Acts 26:28. Elsie Winans deeply convicted. Go to Mother Livingston's. Grandmother Dunning is there, also.

Saturday, October 30 Rainy day. Dine at Livingston's. Spend the afternoon at Wm. Winan's. Church lit up quite late. Congregation small. We have a prayer meeting & no preaching. I stay at McBride's.

Sunday, October 31 Pr. at 11:00, Luke 16:31. Reprove some smart flirters. Poor preach. Dine at Bro. Laughlin's four miles South. Pr. at B. at 7:00. Luke 23:4. Little liberty. The house very smoky on account of a closed up stove-pipe. Stay at McBride's.

Monday, November 1 Stay at McBride's all day. Rev. J. Field and John returned from Fresno Co., having rented his ranch, six miles from Selma. Pr. at 7:00 at B. Matt. 13:44. About 40 or 50 in attendance. Stay at Robt. Leighton's.

Tuesday, November 2 Walk up to Thomas Snediger's. Thomas Richardson's to Mother Sarah Phillips's. Took the buggy and went over to McBride's where Ella had taken five letters for me. Stay there till night. Rev. J.L. Field pr. at 7:00, John 16:8. Stay at McBride's.

Wednesday, November 3 Went to Romeo E. Bangs' with Rev. John Field and Sister McBride and children. Dine. Meeting at McBride's at 2:00. I led at commenting on the 16th Ps. Coffee's & Mrs. Drake there. Supper. Rev. J.L. Field pr. at B. at 7:00, Rom. 8:1. About 55 or 60 present.

Thursday, November 4 Studied for a discourse in forenoon. Dined with J.L. Field at Blodget's. Went with them after dinner to Sister Ada Ross' to a cottage meeting at 2:00. Stay there to supper. At B., I Pr. at 7:00, Luke 13:23, 24. About 60 or 65 present. Stay at McBride's. Got a letter from home dated Oct. 23.

Friday, November 5 Visited Thomas Wallace, who is sick of typhoid fever at Copeland's, his fatherinlaw's. After dinner went to A.J. Coffey's 3 1/2 miles South of Burneyville, to meeting, at 2:00. Stay there to supper. Pr. at B. at 7:00. 1 Tim. 2:4. Stay at McBride's.

Saturday, November 6 Wrote letters in the forenoon. Walked about and rested in afternoon. Pr. at 7:00 at B. Eph. 3:19. Elsie Winans arose for prayers. Stay at McBride's. Rev. John McBride's family are Eliza (his second wife), Samuel 23, Emma Hoskins, Henry 10, Lora 8, Letta 4, Orin 2. Mother McBride, Isabel, and Jas. Wallace are living there.

Sunday, November 7 Attended S. School at B. at 10:00. Rev. Wolf (M.E.) pr. at 11:00, Jer. 8:22. Dine at Wm. Wyman's. Spend the afternoon there. Pr. at Burneyville at 7:00, Rev. 22:14. Two came out for prayer. Alice M. Keeley and Clara V. Richardson joined Church. Three had joined before: Marina Clifford & her two daughters, Alice & Lenora. Stay at McBride's.

Monday, November 8 Staid at McBride's all day. Roasted-

over my dried figs. Pr. at B. at 7:00, Ps. 16:11. One forward for prayer's. Stay at McBride's.

Tuesday, November 9 Stay at McBride's in the forenoon. Go with him in afternoon to Mrs. Drake's, four miles N.E. of Modesto, to a cottage meeting. Had a good meeting led by Bro. McBride. Supper at Mother Huntley's at Burneyville. Rev. J. McBride pr. at 7:00, Rev. 3:20. About 75 present.

Wednesday, November 10 Took Samuel McBride to Oakdale. Pr. at 7:00, Jer. 13:21. Stay at McBride's.

Thursday, November 11 Partly fix up a trunk for traveling. Call at Mr. Crow's. Dinner & supper at McBride's. Rev. J. McBride pr. at 7:00, 1 Chron. Over 50 present.

Friday, November 12 Went to Lee W. Crawford's and dined. Called at Well's and at Lowry's. Supper at McBride's. Pr. at 7:00, Prov. 3:17. Stay at McBride's. Had thought some of starting home to-morrow morning, but gave it out. Congregation over 50.

Saturday, November 13 Went to B.F. Bourland's, before noon, and staid till after dinner. Spent part of afternoon in packing my trunk and arranging my valises. Pr. at B. at 7:00, Titus 2:14. Stay at McBride's.

Sunday, November 14 Pr. at Burneyville at 11:00, Ps. 87:3, showing the glory of the Spiritual Church in all ages. Dine at Romeo E. Bangs. Bro. McBride pr. at Bell Pass Sch. H. at 3:00. Call at Thomas Hall's before Church awhile. Rev. J. McBride pr. at Bur. at 7:00 "Prepare to meet thy God." Stay at McBride's.

Monday, November 15 Went to Oakdale & take 7:20 train. Breakfast at restaurant. Go to Stockton. Dine at Mansion House. Go aboard the steamboat at 4:00 for San Francisco. Start at 5:00.

Tuesday, November 16 Arrive at San Francisco at 8:00. Lunch at a nice small restaurant on Montgomery St. Buy tickets to Chicago of an agent at 36 Montgomery St., $47.50. But two cotton comforts for $5.00. Get lunch-basket filled. Buy Shells on California St. Go to Central Pac. Depot. Start at 3:00 for Omaha. Pass Sacramento about 7:00. Wash feet on platform!

Wednesday, November 17 My birth-day anniversary. Older than wise or good! My life has been one of much enjoyment and little trouble. Bless the Lord! At Reno in the morning. Reach Humboldt about noon.

Thursday, November 18 Lorin's anniversary of birth-day. He is 24 years old to-day. Has been a steady boy all his days. Reached Ogden about 7:15. Detained at Green River for nearly 3 hours. Crowded out of a berth at Ogden. Sleep little. Nearly roasted by big fires fed by a cranky brakeman. Stay mostly afternoon and night in first-class car.

Friday, November 19 Reach Laramie about 9:00 morning. Ride in first-class car. Reach Cheyenne about noon. Get a berth on emigr. sleeper and get a tolerable night's rest. A tramp steals a ride, is put off twice, but is still along after day-light! He mashed up my hat! Wrote this on the cars.

Saturday, November 20 Reach Council Bluffs about 8:00 A.M. Run on Rock Island R.R. to Casey, Iowa. Stop over there on a "check." Go out with David Lint & "Gus" Eckert to Lee Hoisington's. Stay there.

Sunday, November 21 Stay at Hoisington's this day & night. Their children are Josie, 14, Gertie 7, and Pearl 17, the last a son. (In 1879, I had traded my share in my father's estate for a half-section of prairie land, Section 4, Town [blank] Range [blank] and this often caused me to visit Prussia Township, Adair County.

Monday, November 22 Go to Charley Bittner and rent the farm to him and Ferdinand Frederick. Dine there. Look over the farm. Supper at David Hepler's. Stay at Lee Hoisington's. He was my agent after I quit the Keplers, and always dealt honestly, and the family treated me as a friend.

Tuesday, November 23 Went with Dutch George to Casey. Buy 98 pounds of galvanized barbed wire for door and stable-yard fence. It takes 17 ounces to the rod per single stran. Posts are from 15 to 25 cts each. Dine at Denning's Hotel. Go about 2:30 on train to Chicago, Travel all night. Sleep, perhaps, 5 hours.

Wednesday, November 24 Change cars at Chicago for Dayton, Ohio, via Richmond. Reach Richmond at 5:15 p.m. Supper at D.K. Zeller's. Grandmother Koerner begins to sit up after breaking of her thigh. Reach Dayton. The children meet me at the train. I had left home six months ago to-day. Susan as usual.

Thursday, November 25 At home all day. Reuchlin and Lou dine with us & stay all day. We give Mrs. Thompson a fowl, figs, etc. for their dinner, she being our hired help.

Friday, November 26 At home all day. Reuchlin & Lou call in the evening & stay till bed time.

Saturday, November 27 At home. Did not do much. I was considerably unwell from cold contracted on my way home.

Monday, November 29 At home in forenoon. Went to town in the afternoon to make purchases, etc. Dr. Lewis Davis called a half hour. Rev. Wm. Dillon called a few minutes.

Tuesday, November 30 At home in the forenoon. Went to town in the afternoon and ordered a coat & vest, got my newly blocked hat, etc.

Wednesday, December 1 At home all day. Scoured my coat, vest, etc., in the afternoon. My cold decreasing somewhat.

Thursday, December 2 At home all day. Wrote some letters. Rev. J.W. Hott & wife called in the evening and staid till bed-time.

Friday, December 3 At home in the forenoon. Went over in the afternoon and tried new coat on. Bought kid mits at Howell's at $1.25. Bought underwear for Susan.

Saturday, December 4 At home forenoon & afternoon. Go to town in the evening for my new clothes, but they were not done.

Sunday, December 5 At home all day. A Boy came with my clothes at 1:00, and I fear the tailor worked on them that morning. I Coughed at night and I had to inhale cupsicum steam to stop it. [Charch claimed the tailor finished the clothes Saturday night.]

Monday, December 6 At home all day. Mrs. Feight called in the afternoon. Reuchlin & Lulu called in the evening.

Tuesday, December 7 Went to "town." Paid Mr. Charch $25.00 for my coat & Vest. Bought dark gray dress goods for Susan a polonaise: $2.00. Called at the mission rooms. McKee proffered me a check for $100.00, which I took.

Wednesday, December 8 Susan called at Lulu's in the afternoon & Mrs. Sines & niece & Mrs. Shaw called in, & Susan came home. Reuchlin & Lulu came in the evening.

Thursday, December 9 Afternoon, go to *Telescope* Office. See Shuey & get Oregon statistics. Call & see Hott & Drury in the editorial room.

Friday, December 10 Called at Dr. L. Davis's in the forenoon. Write some in the afternoon.

Saturday, December 11 At home in the forenoon. Went to town in afternoon.

Sunday, December 12 Heard at 10:30 Rev. G.M. Matthews pr. Acts 1:11. At home the rest of the day— most of the time in scriptural studies.

Monday, December 13 At home, working some on my annual report. Send a draft of $81.88 to Wm. H.H. Reeder to pay Fowler for tile.

Tuesday, December 14 At home. Work some on Annual report & write a long letter to Rev. T.J. Connor, at his request, on Oregon matters.

Thursday, December 16 At home. Did little. Arranged files of papers in the evening, so that I forgot that Dr. Lewis Davis lectured at Union Biblical Seminary in the evening.

Friday, December 17 Went to town. Made a variety of purchases. Dillon Called in the afternoon.

Saturday, December 18 Went to Eldorado, (having paid my tax in the forenoon) on 11:45 train. Supper at Wm. Coblentz' 1/2 m. w. of Otterbein Church. Had called at Rev. W.C. Day's, and he went with me, he being the pastor. Pr. at Otterbein at 6:30, Acts 3:19. Two forward for prayers & one arose. Stay at Wm. Coblentz.

Sunday, December 19 Pr. at Otterbein at 10:30, Matt. 19:27. Many in the congregation wept. Dine at John Coblentz (with whom his father, Goe. Coblentz lives). Pr. at 6:30, Prov. 29:1. One out for prayer. Stay at Wm. Coblentz'.

Monday, December 20 Dine at Michal Price's, 3/4 m. S. [unreadable] Meeting at 2:00. Quite good. Supper at Samuel Horine's. Pr. at 6:30, Eph. 2:4. Two forward for prayers. Stay at Wm. & Mollie Coblentz'.

Tuesday, December 21 Call at Jo. Horine's 1 1/2 ms s.-e. Dine at John Hetzler's 3/4 m. south. Got a letter from Susan. Still better meeting at 2:00 than that yesterday. Supper at John Coblentz'. Pr. at 6:30, Heb. 11:7. Four seekers. Stay at Wm. Coblentz'. Man lynched at Eaton, to-day.

Wednesday, December 22 Start early to Eldorado & go home. Spend forenoon at home. Go afternoon to town and make various purchases.

Thursday, December 23 Busy getting ready to go away. Go on 11:45 train to Eldorado & Ezra Slifer takes me to Otterbein. I get to meeting before it closes. Supper at John Hetzler's. Rev. W.C. Day pr. at 6:30, Hebr. 4:16. One seeker. One Converted Sunday, One Monday, two Wednesday. Stay at Ezra Slifer's.

Friday, December 24 Went to Michal Miller's to Dinner. His wife died a few months ago. sister Berry & Laura Baker are his house-keepers. Emeline Wilt visiting them. Supper there. Pr. at 6:30, 1 Pet. 4:18. Two conversions. Enoch Horine & Wm. H. Stover. Both join Church. Stay at Wm. Coblentz'.

Saturday, December 25 Pr. at 10:00 Isa. 9:6. Dine at Simeon Garrison's, 3/4 ms. s.w. Church. Spend the afternoon there, and write two letters. Call at W. Coblentz on the way to Church. Rev. W.C. Day pr. at 6:30, Job 21:15. Miss Roberts at the altar. Ebeneezer Wilt, aged

68, a convert of the meeting, joined Church. I stay at Wm. Coblentz'.

Sunday, December 26 Pr. at O. at 10:30, Heb. 13:14. Dine at Samuel Horine's. Their children are Enoch and Tobias. Forgot to give Coblentz the key; so they locked out of their house. Pr. at 6:30, Jer. 13:21. One converted. Charley Wertz and wife & Laura Roberts join church. I stay at Ezra Hetzler's, 1 m.s. & 1/2 m. e. Their children John 20, Clara 17, Eliza 14, Julia 9.

Monday, December 27 Ezra Hetzler took me to Eldorado. So I went to Richmond, Ind. on the morning train & staid till the 7:20, evening train. At D.K. Zellers. Mother Catherine Koerner, aged 90 years, Nov. 30th, there. Called at Allen M. Harris', Lichtenfels' Store, at Coe's, Martins, etc. Saw New Pres. Church. Reached home (Dayton) 9:00.

Tuesday, December 28 At home. Wrote to gen. R.R. officers for half-fare permits— to C.H. & D.; C.C.C. & I; Wab., St. L. & Pac.; Gr. Rap. & Ind.; N.Y.P. & O. Went to town in the afternoon.

Wednesday, December 29 At home. Forenoon on mending the rocking chair. Lulu called in afternoon. Gave her a white satin handkerchief. Broke lamp-shade, and chimney in the evening—the table of my desk breaking loose because only nailed with small nails.

Thursday, December 30 Spent forenoon mending desk & rocking chair. Keister Called to get me to preach Sab. forenoon at Summit Street Church.

Friday, December 31 At home in the forenoon. Mrs. Wm. C. Day, and Maggie, of Eldorado dined with us. I went to town in the afternoon and got medicine for Susan. Also handed to the editor of the *Telescope* the last pages of my annual report of Pacific Coast District. Got a check of McKee for $100.00 on my salary.

The past Year has been one of many blessings and mercies from the Lord. The family are all alive. Susan has stood the year full better than we could have expected. Reuchlin settled in married life, Lorin returned, after some months in Kansas City, Wilbur's health was re-stored. Orville & Katie did well morally & physically. I met my labors in good health.

Memoranda

Of the Calender year 1886, I spent seven months on the Pacific Coast. Altogether it was one of the most interesting of my life. In January, I organized our first Church in Riverside, California, which resulted in a good society there and a good church-building later on. Besides the Annual Conferences and numerous other meetings, I visited Umpqua Valley, Coos Bay, and the Humboldt Country. I had a hard-fought battle at Burneyville, California, resulting in a revival, of lasting effect and influence, and after my return to Ohio, had a prominent part in a precious revival at Otterbein Church, near Eldorado, Ohio.

When I can read my title clear. title clear, title clear. When I can read my title clear. To mansions in the skies, *Repeat*. I'll bid farewell to every fear, to every fear, to every fear, I'll bid farewell to every fear, And wipe my weeping eyes. *Chorus* O glorious kingdom, home of the blest, When shall I see thee, And be forever at rest.

I learn from Editor Phillipi, that O.F. Smith had several sons who were preachers— one a strong Congregationalist preacher. O.F. was himself a fine preacher. He died a radical.

Nov. 1881

Hotel at Stockton (Oct.)	.25
Fare fr Oakdale to Stockt.	.35
Express & St. car at Sto.	.30
Dinner at Stoc.	.25
Fare & berth to San Fran	.75
Lunch at " "	.25
St. Cars at " "	.15
Help carry trunk	.10
Fare to Chicago	47.50
Dinner at Casey	.25
Lunch-basket & contents	2.45
Tacks, screws, hoopiron (for trunk)	.60
Milk on trip	.10
Fare from Chicago	5.15
Transfer at "	.50

Sea Shells (100 & 3 for 80) 1.80
" " at San Fr 1.15
Sack-needle .05
Screw-driver .20
Shoe-mending 1.50
Hat cleaned & blacked 1.00
Cuff & collar San Fran. .75
Coat buttons & vest buttons .20
Quinine .50
Iodide of Potash .50
Tinct. Sanguinarium .25
Ayers pills 2 boxes .50
Podophylin & cinnodum .10
Oil cloves .15
Watch-spring, Marsh 2.00

1886 California Conf.
Los Angeles Dist.— J. W. Baumgardner
Los Angeles Cir.— J.W. Baungardner
Riverside M.— F. Fisher

Sacramento Dist.— T.J. Bander
Eureka Mis. Stn.— F. Stearns
Rohnerville Ct.— W.H. Bast
Petrolia M. G.W. Burris
South Eel River— J.B. Hamilton
Upper Lake Ct.— C.W. Gillett.
Shasta— G.W. Burtner
Feather River Ct.— D. Shuck.
Yolo Ct. A.W. Snepp.
Sacramento Mis. Stn. [blank]
Woodbridge Stn.— I.K. Statton.
Calaveras M. [blank]
Stanislaus Ct.— J. McBride
Semla Ct. W.L. Demumbrun
Tulare Ct. E. DeWitt
Traver M.— B.F. Kenor

1886 Bishop's Collection *Oregon Conference.*
From Pastors 68.65
Pub. Coll at Conf. 53.17
[total] $121.82
Oregon Conf. 1886
Ed. Benef. 2.81
S.S. Gen. Fund 3.56
Bib Sem. " 3.63
Total 10.00

Coll. by A.K. Olds I paid over to E.C. Wyatt. I paid over funds like the above Coll. at Cal. Conf. to Alfred Cowell.

Vote for P.E. Oregon 1886
Mosher 18
Ingle 16
Pulley 15
Wyatt 6
Bennett 5
Bartlett 1

Collection at L. Glass $22.80
" Unity Chap. 2.85
" " Mosher Chapel 11.85
" " Deer Creek 5.75
" " Sister Parson .50
[total] 23.75
Petersoon (at Eureka) 5.00
Fare to Rohnerville (Peterson donated) 1.25
Coll. at " Aug. 29 4.80
Coll. at Eureka Aug 22 7.35
" " " Sept 15 5.65
Peterson present part 7.00
Ackerson ≤ 1.25
Total 32.30

Coll. at Pataha City 3.50
C.W. Wells paid .25
[total] 3.75

Expenses to Pendleton 50.00
" at " 3.00
Hack to Weston 2.50
Cars to Walla Walla & Stay 1.30
" " Huntsville 1.85
Fare to Wallula Junc. 6.50
" " Portland 8.60
Dinner at Prescott .50
Edibles at other times .30
[total] 74.90
Fare to Aumsville 1.10
Ferriage .90
From Salem to Derry 0.00
From Derry to Corvallis 1.06
" Corvallis to Philomath .24

California

Chart. Coll.	124.75
Public Coll.	21.25
Coll at Burneyv.	16.50
" " "	10.25
Paid in Humboldt (all)	33.30

Expenses in Oregon

Portland to Woodburn	1.40
Marion " Salem	.56
Derry " Corvallis	1.06
Corwallis " Philomath	.24
Junction City " Drain	2.06
Drain to Oakland	.81
Oakland " Roseburg	.75
Hack at Oakland	.25
Hack Oakland to Sumner	5.00
Ferriage Salem & Sa[unreadable]	.90
Cars Silverton to Aumsville	1.10
[total]	14.13
Paid in Coll at Philomath	1.00
St. Boat from Coos to Marchf.	.50
Hotel at Marshfield	.25
Fare from Marsh. to Eureka	5.00
Fare to Rohnerville (Peterson pd)	1.25
" from " to Eureka	1.25
Trip to North Fork	1.00
" " San Francisco	7.50
[total]	17.75
Expense at San Fran	2.00
" " Woodbridge	1.10
Expense at Stockton	.25

Dan Wright, b. Thetford To., Orange Co., Vermont, Sept. 3, 1790; d. Fayette co., Ind., Oct. 6, 1861, aged 71 years, 1 m, 3d. Catherine Wright (Reeder) b. Hamilton Co., Ohio, March 17, 1800; d. Sept. 24th, 1866, aged 66 ys, 6m, 7d. She was born about a mile from Madisonville.

Salary for 1885 California Conference

In 1885-6. Received in California $

Chart Coll. at Conf	86.50
Pub. Coll. at Conf.	63.22
Coll. (after) Woodbr.	24.30
B. Wood (ticket)	1.00
Coll. at Sacramento	3.25

" " Gridley	3.45
Back paid me	4.25
At New River	20.04
A.N. King	5.00
Riverside	25.00
Total	$236.01

Walla Wall Conf. For 1885

Chart Coll.	26.85
Pub. Coll Conf	41.00
Dedication at Weston	14.00
total	$81.85
Oregon Conf	
Chart Collection	78.80
Pub Coll at Conf	35.28
[total]	$114.08

Annual Conferences, 1886

1. Walla Walla Conf. Weston Umatilla Co., Oregon, June 2d, 1886.
2. Oregon Conf. Abiqua Chapel, Marion Co., Oregon, Woodburn the railroad Station (10 ms); Silverton the P.O., Marion Co., July 1st.

California— at a Camp-meeting— Sept. 29th.

An Excellent Receipt
Cleaning Mixture

Sulphuric Ether	1 oz.
Castile Soap	1 oz.
Glycerene	1 oz.
Alcohol spirits	1 oz.
Aqua Ammonia 3d strength	4 oz.

Dissolve soap in two quarts of soft water; then add the other ingredients. Use with flannel rag or soft brush. Rinse in clean water until free from dirt & soap; rub with dry flannel and stretch in shape to dry.

Diphtheria Cure, and For Hoarseness

Aromatic Sulphuric Acid	2 z.
Tincture Sanguimarium	2 z.
Tincture Capsicum	1 z.
Spirits Minthea	10 drops
Surrup Simplex	2 z.

Dose for Diptheria: A teaspoonfull every two hours.

1887

Saturday, January 1 Went to town in the morning. Susan, on account of indigestion, not able to eat turkey with us. Reuchlin & Lulu called in the evening. I busy preparing a sermon I did not preach, on "O Hearer of Prayer."

Sunday, January 2 Pr. at Summit Street Church at 10:30, Heb. 3:1, it being on quarterly meeting occasion. Communion followed. Rev. S.W. Keister, P.E., pr. at 7:00, Rom. 12:11. A good sermon.

Monday, January 3 At home. Wrote some letters. Heard Bishop J. Weaver pr at 7:30, Ps. 85:5. The meeting at Summit St.

Tuesday, January 4 At home. Called at Dr. Davis & Dillon's. Halleck Floyd called an hour or more.

Wednesday, January 5 Ate no breakfast, being unwell. Rev. H. Floyd came before dinner & staid a few hours. I did little to-day.

Thursday, January 6 At home all day. Rev. H. Floyd dined with us. Printed script circular letter to preachers on my district.

Friday, January 7 At home in forenoon writing & mailing letters. Went to town in the afternoon and got my watch, etc. New mainspring cost $1.50 & guaranteed for one year. Reuchlin and Lulu called & spent the evening.

Saturday, January 8 At home all day. Got letter from Rev. J.W. Ingle giving a copy of McKee's second letter

to Rev. E.C. Wyatt, reflecting on Oregon conference.

Sunday, January 9 Attended Summit Street Church. Bp. J. Weaver pr. at 10:30, Ps. 37:3. In the evening Rev. G.M. Matthews pr. at 7:00 on Stoning of Stephen. Three mourners and all professed conversion.

Monday, January 10 Worked in forenoon on letter-writing to Coast preachers. Reuchlin & Lulu called a while in the evening.

Tuesday, January 11 Spent the day at home. Orville got his case of type pied in the evening.

Wednesday, January 12 Went to town in the forenoon. Orville printed circulars. Wrote letters in the afternoon. Called at Reuchlin's in the evening. Orville set and printed another circular—for Reuchlin.

Thursday, January 13 At home. At Summit St. Ch. at 7:00. Bp. Weaver pr. Rev. 22:17.

Saturday, January 15 Went to East Side of the river to make some purchases— bought Orville a suit of clothes for $10.00. At home in the afternoon writing. Called at Dillon's; visited Dr. Davis.

Sunday, January 16 Heard Rev. H.J. Mulholland pr. at Miami Chapel, 1 1/2 miles south of my home which is No. 7 Hawthorne St., Dayton, Ohio, which I purchased of Jas. Manning & wife in 1870, and moved into early in 1871— February, I believe. Hear Rev. A.W. Drury pr. at 7:00, John 12:32, Summit St.

Monday, January 17 At home. Reuchlin and Lulu called in the evening a little while.

Tuesday, January 18 At home. Heard Bishop J. Weaver pr. at Summit St. at 7:30, Prov. 18:24. None forward for prayers.

Wednesday, January 19 At home. Largely engaged in mending up books that had come apart. Went to Miami Chapel and preached to a large congregation, 2 Cor. 5:14. Many under conviction, deeply.

Thursday, January 20 At home during the day. Went to Miami Chapel and pr. to a large congregationMatt. 19:27. Some deeply convicted.

Friday, January 21 Went on the early train to Richmond, Ind. Called at D.K. Zeller's. Went on to Decatur, Ind. Dined at Rev. Isa. Imler's. Supper and lodging at Rev. J.W. Lower's. At Evang. Asso. Church at 7:00 and heard Rev. Oakes pr. on "One thing needful." Rev. Stoop is pastor.

Saturday, January 22 Went with Rev. J.W. Lower and family to Glenmore, 12 ms East. Dine at Elias Dull's. Meet the trustees of Bethel Church at 2:00. Supper & lodging at D.N. Hey's. Pr. at 7:00, Ps. 1:6, the first sermon in the new church.

Sunday, January 23 Pr. at 10:30 the dedication sermon of Bethel Church, one mile south of Glenmore, Ohio Math. 6:9 and raised $647.50 in subscription & cash and dedicated the church. Dine at W.G. Walters' 1 1/2 m. S.W. of Glenmore. Pr. at 7:00 Mark 8:36(?) Stay at Walters'.

Monday, January 24 Dined at Elias Dull's. Spent the afternoon at John W. Dull's & took supper there. He away. She a daughter of Rev. W.E. Bay. Bro. Lower & wife there. Pr. at 7:00, Mark 8:36(?). Congregation large. Stay at Elias Dull's, 1 1/2 m. north-west. Bro. Lower and Walters and wife there.

Tuesday, January 25 Meeting at 10:00, led by Rev. Michael Johnson. It was good. About 19 present. Dine at John Middaugh's 1/2 m. east of the church, with W.G. Walters and wife. Pr. at 7:00, Acts 3:19. Congregation large. Stay at John P. Hey's. She a strong "Radical." He

almost deaf. Lower with me.

Wednesday, January 26 Meeting at 10:00 led by Bro. Lower, 26 present. Dine at Wesley J. Walter's, 3/4 m. west of the Church, with Bros. Smith, Hurry & Lower. Supper at Franklin Dull's whose wife is a sister of W.G. Walter's wife & daughter of Smith's. Pr. at 7:00 at Bethel, Eph. 3:19. Stay at E. Dull's, with Bros. Hurry and Lower.

Thursday, January 27 Meeting at 10:00 led by Wm. G. Walters. 24 present. Dine at Solomon Kissel's 1 3/4 ms. north-west. She a member; he a confessor of the need of religion. Rev. J.W. Lower pr. at 7:00, Rom. 10:1. Stay at D.N. Hey's, close to the church.

Friday, January 28 The morning meeting at 10:00 was the best of all our day meetings. About 27 present. Dine with Lower at Jac. Smith's, 1/2 m. east. Also supper. Quite a rainy afternoon. Mrs. Smith is religious; he convicted. Pr. at 7:00 to a small congregation, Acts 16:31. Stay at John P. Hey's.

Saturday, January 29 Stay at Hey's till after dinner. Then go to D. Newton Hey's. Change clothes & bathe, as my custom for years, is. Pr. at 7:00, to a full house, Rev. 29:1. Young Fore comes as a seeker. Stay at D.N. Hey's with Bro. Lower.

Sunday, January 30 I address S.S. five min. Pr. at 10:30, Zech. 13:6. Dine at John Middaugh's with Rev. Michael Johnson, Wm. J. Walters & wife & Jac. Smith & wife & others. Rev. M. Johnson preached at 3:00, Isa. 35:8,10. Call at D.N. Hey's with Johnson, Chilcote, etc. Pr. at 7:00, Eph. 2:16. Four ask prayers. Stay at John Hey's.

Monday, January 31 Awake at 4:00. Breakfast early. Pas. train is earlier than we knew, so I go on accom. tr. to Marion, Ind. Arrived at 3:15. Mail letters to I. M. Tharp, Wilmore & D.G. Rush (Calif) there & on train home & one at Fairmount. Reach Fairmount at 9:10. Stay at Rev. A.J. Bolen's in parsonage with Littleton Davis, etc.

Tuesday, February 1 Call at Elwood Davis'. Walk on to Aunt Eliz Reeder's. Dine there. Remain in the afternoon, and till morning. Wm. Reeder comes in the evening and stays till bed-time. Robt. & Flora attend literary society at the school-house.

Wednesday, February 2 Go over via Henry Simon's and Levi's to W. Fine's, on my farm. Call at each of those places. Back to dinner at Aunt Reeder's. Write to Hoisington, Burns, and Bitner and to C.W. Wells. Supper at William's. Stay at Wm. H.H. Reeder's, Junior's. Balance Accts. He owes me $29.25.

Thursday, February 3 Have three more loads of corn sold 277 bush (about) altogether. Call at Rev. A.J. Bolen's, Fairmount. Supper & lodging there. Pr. at Union Church, 2 miles S. of Fairmount at 7:00, Acts 20:21. Three seekers came to the alter.

Friday, February 4 Went on the 7:10 train to Jonesboro, and thence on the 10:08 train to Union City, and thence on the 2:15 train to Dayton, arriving at home about 4:30. Found all about as well as common.

Saturday, February 5 At home. Called to see Dr. L. Davis, in the forenoon.

Sunday, February 6 At home in the forenoon. In the evening I heard Rev. A.W. Drury pr. at Summit St. at 7:00, on "Almost and yet not accepting Christ as a savior." Three joined Church & seven had joined in the forenoon.

Monday, January 7 At home in the forenoon, writing. In the afternoon washed my pants, with Katie's help.

Tuesday, February 8 Went to town. Saw McKee about Geo. Keller's donation. Read the proceedings of the Mis. Ex. Com. since An. Meeting of the board. Looked up Oregon matters. Ella Shell, our domestic, grew cross & Mrs. Wright sent her off in the afternoon. Bought material for pants.

Wednesday, February 9 At home. Called at Dillon's in the evening. Wrote letters in the forenoon.

Thursday, February 10 Took Susan to town to get impression for a set of lower teeth, in forenoon. Called at Davis' and Dillon's in the evening.

Sunday, February 13 Attended Church on Broadway (New Light) and heard Rev. Watson, the pastor pr. Ps. 40:1,2,3, a good sermon. Heard Rev. Marion R. Drury

pr. at 7:00 at Summit St., 1 Pet. 4:18, a good sermon.

Tuesday, February 15 At home all day, except a short trip to town in the afternoon.

Friday, February 18 Called at Bishop J. Weaver's. Called at Rev. Wm. Dillon's. Left an article: "A Misconstruction."

Saturday, February 19 Went on the noon train to Richmond and Dublin, Ind. Supper at Halleck Floyd's. Pr. at 7:00 at U.B. Church, Eph. 3:19 to a very full house. Stay at the H. Floyd's.

Sunday, February 20 Pr. at 10:30, Ps. 92:8. One seeker. Dine at Dr. G.W. Champ's. Stay till after supper. Pr. at 7:00, Luke 18:27. Five seekers and conversions. One joined. Stay at Joseph Gray's, with Rev. C.B. Small, the pastor.

Monday, February 21 Missed the early train. Breakfasted at Gray's. At meeting at 9:15. Dine at Rev. Halleck Floyd's. Go on 1:00 train home. Floyd with me. Arrive at 3:30.

Tuesday, February 22 At home. Wrote to W.H.H. Reeder. Floyd dines with us, and is with us occasionally during the week, at meals & lodging.

Wednesday, February 23 At home. Went to town in afternoon.

Thursday, February 24 At home. Declined going to the Council & Ex. Com. meeting of the radical brethren.

Saturday, February 26 At home. Went to town in the afternoon.

Sunday, February 27 Got ready too late to go to church in the morning. At home during the day. Reuchlin dined with us, as usual. In the evening at Summit Street Church heard Rev. G.M. Matthews pr. Luke 15:20, "And kissed him." Rather miscellaneous.

Monday, February 28 Went to town awhile— got some articles & saw Dr. Sample about "Mother's" teeth. Called at I.K. Gra[y]bill's in the evening & at Rev. Wm. Dillon's.

Tuesday, March 1 Changed from soft to hard coal & cleared up my room. Wrote an article for the Conservator, "A Creed on Wheels."

Wednesday, March 2 Called at W. Dillon's and at L. Davis's. Talked with G.W. Funkhouser in the evening on Oregon matters.

Thursday, March 3 At home all day. Wrote letters to L. Hoisington, C. Bitner, J.W. Ingle, J.W. Pulley, W. Fine, W.H.H. Reeder— Mrs. M.R. Drury & McHenry called in the afternoon a few minutes to see Susan.

Friday, March 4 At home all day. Wrote some letters. Called at Reuchlin's in the evening an hour.

Saturday, March 5 Rev. Halleck Floyd called an hour in the morning. Went to I.K. Graybill's & after an hour to W. Dillon's. McKee's letter for publication. H. Floyd dined with us and staid till morning. Reuchlin spent the evening till bed time with us.

Sunday, March 6 With H. Floyd heard G.M. Matthews pr. on Trial of Abraham's faith. Floyd dines with us. He went in Aftn. to W. Dillon's. Reuchlin staid to supper. Went in evening to hear Rev. P. Deveun pr. at First Pres. Church Rev. 22:17, "Spirit & bridesay," etc.

Monday, March 7 Went to town with Katie shopping. Called at Dr. L. Davis's. H. Floyd with us for dinner. Bro. Leo. Keller called an hour & more in the evening.

Tuesday, March 8 At home. Read some. Wrote to John McLaren. Sen'r at Eureka, Cal. Pretty day. Needed no fire at noon. Rev. H. Floyd called an hour or less in the evening to get paper, etc.

Thursday, March 10 Went to town & got Mrs. Wright's new teeth. Finished Article on "Flattering the People." Called at Dr. L. Davis' in the evening.

Friday, March 11 At home. Studied some on sermons in the forenoon and also in the evening. Rev. H. Floyd called in the afternoon. Also Mrs. Jas. Fleenor and Mrs. Schenck, formerly of Piqua, Ohio.

Sunday, March 13 Pr. at Summit St. Church at 10:30, 2

Pet. 1:16. Reuchlin dines with us, as he has done for some weeks. Revs. Floyd & Dillon call in the afternoon. Hear Rev. G.M. Matthews pr. at 7:30, Rev. [blank]

Monday, March 14 Went to "town" & got $100.00, the last payment of the year from McKee. Got a letter also with a draft from Wm. H.H. Reeder for 89.10.

Tuesday, March 15 At home. Spent the day on notes on my address for "Congress of Churches & Christians," at Chicago.

Wednesday, March 16–Thursday, March 17 At home. Spent the time largely in classifying the notes for my address.

Friday, March 18 Wrote on my address about the whole day— my address for the "Congress of Christians," at Chicago. Rev. H. Floyd took supper with us.

Saturday, March 19 Read in the Century Magazine much of the day. Rewrote on my address in the evening.

Sunday, March 20 Heard Rev. J.W. Hott D.D. pr. Math. 27:37. He spoke 56 minutes. Heard Rev. Thorn pr. at 7:30.

Tuesday, March 22 At home. Rel. Telescope full of bitterness comes to hand. Prof. Funkhouser comes in the afternoon.

Wednesday, March 23 Reuchlin finishes packing goods and starts afternoon for Birmingham, Alabama. He shows fine gifts in writing and planning in matters of public interest. We were sorry for him to go so far away.

Friday, March 25 Went to town in forenoon & handed in the Telescope, "Defense of Oregon Conf." Wrote a little on my Address for the Congress of Churches.

Saturday, March 26 Went over to town & read proof of article. Spent Afternoon & evening in transcribing my address.

Sunday, March 27 Heard the presiding-elder, Rev. S.W. Keister preach a good sermon, John 12:32. About 2:00 took Sacrament. At home in the afternoon and evening.

Monday, March 28 At home all forenoon. Went to town in the afternoon and got Telescope. Called at W. Dillon's & Dr. L. Davis' in the evening.

Tuesday, March 29 Worked on my address some. Started at 6:00, p.m. for Chicago. Called an hour at D.K. Zeller's with Rev. Wm. Dillon. Rev. John McFall joins us on 9:45 train & Revs. Z. McNew and O.L. Wilson at Washington (Greensfork). Revs. C.B. Small & J.M. Kabrick afterward. Slept 4 hrs.

Wednesday, March 30 Pres. C.H. Kiracofe joins our company at Crossing. Arrive at Chicago about 7:30. Breakfast. Call at Chr. Associ. Rooms, 221 W. Madison St. Take rooms at 156 Clark St. Dine at 164 Madison St. Congress of Churches & Christians meet at 9:30. C.W. Richard temp. Chm. Pres. H.H. George, D.D. perma. Chm. Addresses: 1 H. Floyd 2. E.D. Bailey 3. Rev. N. Wardner 4. Rev. John Grunirt 5. Pres. George 6. Rev. L.A. Johnston.

Thursday, March 31 Addresses: Revs. C.F. Hawley & W.H. French. Afternoon: Adds. Rev. B.F. Roberts & Pres. J. Blanchard Evening Addr's. M. Wright & Pres. E.H. Fairchild, Berea, Kentucky. The Convention was a very good one.

Friday, April 1 Start home on 7:30 train with John Fall. Waited 4 hours at Logansport. At Marion write several letters. Reach Fairmount about 9:00. Stay at the parsonage with Rev. A.J. Bolen.

Saturday, April 2 Bra. Bolen takes me to Aunt Lizzie Reeder's, 5 m. S.E. of Fairmount. Wm. & I go to the farm. Supper at William's. Stay at Aunt Lizzie's.

Sunday, April 3 Robert Reeder took me to Union Chapel 4 miles west. I Pr. 1 Cor. 13:13. Go back to Aunt Lizzie's for dinner. Oliver Glass, there. Stay at Wm. H. H. Reeder's (Jun.).

Monday, April 4 Went to Fairmount. Sold my corn. Called at Rev. A.J. Bolen's to get my valise; also at Elwood Davis's. Went on 11:30 train to Anderson & thence on 3:10 train to Richmond. Supper with Dillon at D.K. Zeller's. Went on to Dayton arriving about 9:00.

Wednesday, April 6 Went to town with Susan & got her new teeth after their being worked over. In the evening, call at Wm. Dillon's on business.

Thursday, April 7 At home all the day and sad, for our second son started away at 6:00 p.m. for Kansas City & Wichita.

Friday, April 8 At home. Read a good deal, not being well enough to write much, owing to overdoing my nerves with mental employment.

Saturday, April 9 Get Ready to go to Indiana. Start at 11:45 to Mt. Pleasant Church, Randolph Co., Ind. Called about an hour at D.K. Zeller's at Richmond. Rev. W.T. Boice met met at Johnson & took me to Sam C. Morrison's, 1 1/2 m. S. of Church. Supper & lodging there. Br. Boise pr. at 8:00, Jas. 1:27.

Sunday, April 10 I pr. at Mt. Pleasant, at 10:30, 2 Cor. 8:9, took up mission Collection $10.00. Dine at Joseph Alexander's. His daughter has scarlatina. I sat for hours in her room. Pr. at 7:30, Matt. 12:30. Stay at Alexander's. His wife is a daughter of John Coblentz, near New Paris, Ohio.

Monday, April 11 Bro. Alexander took me to Johnson. Reach Richmond about 9:30. Dine at D.K. Zeller's. Go on 1:45 train to Dayton.

Wednesday, April 13 Went to town. Whistler, the Theo. Student, called in the evening after 4:00. I called at Wm. Dillon's and Dr. L. Davis' in the evening.

Thursday, April 14 At home in the forenoon. In afternoon, I went to meet Ex. Com. (Missions) to represent my district. I Call at W. Dillon's & Dr. Davis'.

Saturday, April 16 Wrote letters in the forenoon. Went in afternoon shopping. Wrote letters in the evening.

Sunday, April 17 Attended Park Street Presbyterian Church in forenoon. It was communion day. There was baptizing of one; reception of several into Church; a short address on Christ's Glorification, etc. Rainy day & evening. Staid at home, evening.

Tuesday, April 19 At home. Made some notes for discussion. Saw Myers in the evening about Reuchlin's rent. Found Whistler had not paid it. Went to see Wh. but he away. Called a few minutes at Dr. Davis's.

Wednesday, April 20 At home. Called in the evening to see Melvin Brown about buying my lot & house. He not at house. Called to see Myers about Reuchlin's rent.

Thursday, April 21 At home writing an article for the *Telescope.*

Friday, April 22 Sent in my article in reply to McKee's last on Oregon Conference.

Sunday, April 24 Went to High St. U.B. Church. Heard Rev. J.W. Kilbourn pr. a Missionary sermon from Mark 16:19. W. Dillon called in the evening, an hour.

Monday, April 25 Went to town to see freight agent on making arrangements for Reuchlin. Wilbur ships Reuchlin's goods to Birmingham, Alabama.

Thursday, April 28 Received a letter from Lorin, who is at Cold Water, Kansas. Wrote him & mailed letter at p.o. in the afternoon.

Saturday, April 30 At Home. Orville & Katie went botanizing.

Sunday, May 1 Heard Prof. G.A. Funkhouser pr. baccalaureate sermon, Acts 20:28-35. Bishop N. Castle pr. at 7:30, 2 Cor. 5:20 "I Christ's Stead."

Monday, May 2 Board of Bishops meet at 9:00, and again at 1:30. Bishops Dickson, Castle, and Kephart at supper with us. Literary Societies exercises at 7:45.

Tuesday, May 3 Board of bishops meet at 9:00, and again at 1:30. I dine with the other bishops at Bishop Weaver's. Washington Gladden lectured on Carlisle at Sum. at 7:45. Quite interesting.

Wednesday, May 4 Graduating exercises at 9:30. L. Bookwalter, S.E. Glanden, W.B. Hartzog, Miss Ella Niswonger, R.L. Swain, C.A. Thorn, Chas. Hyer, J.H. Whistler, & W.H. Wright graduated. Go to town in the afternoon and do considerable trading.

Thursday, May 5 At home in the forenoon. Went on 3:40 train to Springfield and thence on St. Cars to Lagonda. Home at Lawrence's. Miss. Board Session at 7:30.

Friday, May 6 At Board Session. Mis. Secretary read his report, also the Missionary treasurer. Ex. Com's report read in the afternoon. Item on Oregon & N. Mich. refered to Com. Kephart, Dickson, & Castle. Mis. Meeting at night. I met Com. on Oregon at 7:00.

Saturday, May 7 Met Com. again at 7:00 AM. "Ex.Session" at 8:00. Warner's Case up. Public session about 10:00. I met Com. on Oregon at 1:00. Close the investigation. In afternoon, their *report read and adopted. Appropri. made "Ex. Session" in evening. Warner resigns. *Com. on Oregon reported in my favor.

Sunday, May 8 Rev. J. Hill pr. Annual Missionary Sermon at 10:30. Bish. Dickson dines with us. Bish. E.B. Kephart pr. at 7:30 Matt. 16:18, a labored effort. Stay as usual at Lawrence's who were very friendly and kind.

Monday, May 9 Miss St. Cars "one square," and walk to Springfield p.o. Went three squares out of the way & missed the C.C.C. & I. train one square! Buy an umbrella $2.50. Go on 11:00 train to Dayton. W.H. Whistler & Miss Rohrer on train. Wrote letters. He married her later.

Thursday, May 12 At home. Wrote letters. In morning wrote "Honor to Whom Honor," for the *Telescope.* Took a brief article "Honor to whom Honor" to the office.

Friday, May 13 Wrote out a new form of deed for Ellis Wright, in the forenoon. Went to town with Susan and acknowledged the deed and mailed it in a registered letter.

Saturday, May 14 John Dodds called a half hour, in the forenoon.

Sunday, May 15 I Pr. at High Street Ch. Rom. 5:8. Dine with the pastor, Rev. J.W. Kilbourn. Visit Rev. I.L. Buchwalter, at Prof. A.W. Drury's, on Second Street. At home in the evening.

Monday, May 16 At Home. Called a half hour at Dr. L. Davis.

Tuesday, May 17 Went to Mission Rooms & got a draft for $200.00. Saw Chas. W. Miller at the rooms. His son Dan. living at Miamisburg, Ohio.

Wednesday, May 18 Went to "town" in the afternoon. Bought a draft on Nat. Chemist's Bank, New York, No. 101493, I think & sent to Lorin Wright, Coldwater, Kansas. Bought Pantaloons at Manhattan's $5.85, thin vest, $12.25, celluloid collar .18 cts. Susan & I called at Beddell's to see Mrs. Billheimer, who had called to see us in morning.

Thursday, May 19 Went to Town Sat. for a Negative at Appleton & Hollinger's. Exchange Pantaloons at the Manhattan Clothing Store, 45 cts. less than others. Got a draft from Ellis Wright for $60.00.

Friday, May 20 Went to East Side of the City in afternoon. Got proof of negatives & attended to various items of business. Dr. L. Davis called in the forenoon.

Saturday, May 21 Went with Mrs. Wright to dentist, and attended to various items of business. Preparing to go to the Pacific Coast. Sent [blank]

Sunday, May 22 Heard A.W. Drury at Summit St. Church at 10:30, Ex. 33:18. Dr. L. Davis called in the evening. Also Rev. M.R. Drury & wife, and Chas. Keller. (Keller later in life stole a ham, was arrested, confessed—he was perhaps somewhat insane).

Monday, May 23 Started on 7:15 train for Colfax, Wash. Territory. Hard to go and leave the family so alone! Call a half hour at Richmond, Ind. at D.K. Zeller's. Went on to Chicago. John Selig & wife (First) aboard from New Castle to Anderson. Rev. Harmon Baptist from Cincinnati. Start on Chi., Mil, & St. Paul at 10:30 for St. Paul.

Tuesday, May 24 Find Rev. S.D. Badger, Baptist of Rantoul, Ill., aboard. Saw Rev.*Thomas of Lacrosse aboard; the Masonic herd. Reach St. Paul at 2:15. Get half-fare ticket at $33.75 to Palouse Junction. Start at 4:00. Interval, here, between twilight so very short. Pass Sauk Rapids about sunset. *Thomas was badly wound

up by Blanchard at Chicago "Congress."

Wednesday, May 25 Awake at Fargo. Pass Dalrymple on the great wheat farm; Jamestown, Bismarck, and Mandan on the Missouri. Dickinson, Medora in the Bad Lands. Cross the Little Missouri. Pass Mingnsville just before dark. Pass Glendive in the night.

Thursday, May 26 Awoke about Forsyth. Reached Livingston at two o'clock. Helena 7:50. A very pleasant day, it was.

Friday, May 27 Awoke on Clark's Fork of the Columbia. Passed Heron about 10:00. Passed Pendd. Oreille Lake. Reached Spokane Falls about 2:00. Got to Palouse Junction about 8:00. Stay at Warren Frank's. Had fair accomodations. A young man was there, who was going to see his affianced, who was very sick, he knew, but who died the 25th.

Saturday, May 28 Arose at 4:30. Bathe and put on fresh "linen" & socks. Go on 7:00 train to Colfax. Reach there at 2:00. Henry Arrasmith meets me and takes me to his house, near Bethel Church. Rev. J.M. Tresenriter along. Supper & lodgings there. On the whole, this is the easiest trip I have ever made to the coast.

Sunday, May 29 Pr. at 11:00 at Bethel, 1 Ki. 18:21. Dine at Jacob Arrasmith's. Pr. at 4:30, 1 Cor. 13:13. Supper & lodging at Henry Arrasmith's. I was right unwell from 2:00 morning till near meeting time. Better in the afternoon. Very hot day. Stay at Henry Arrasmith's.

Monday, May 30 At Henry Arrasmith's. Largely spend the day in reading. Feel a little the worst from yesterday's ailment and labors. Peter Arrasmith's fixing a muslin tent to go to their other ranch. Judge Kincaid brought the teacher, Miss McBride. Stay at H. Arrasmith's.

Tuesday, May 31 In the evening go to Peter Taylor's and stay till bed-time. Had staid at Arrasmith's till 4:00, and I returned there and lodged.

Wednesday, June 1 Spend forenoon in reading Revised New Testament. Read more than half of Matthew's Gospel. Read also in the life of Wm. Bramwell. Supper at John Ar[r]asmith's, 1 mile below the church. Stay at

Judge C.M. Kincaid's, 3 ms from Colfax.

Thursday, June 2 Go up to Henry Ar[r]asmith's. Spend forenoon in reading. Afternoon, Bro. Arrasmith takes me in a hack up the road, & down Clear Creek, & across the Palouse River to Rev. J.S. Rhoads'. Stay there that night. Read considerable in Finney's Lectures on Theology; on Sanctification & Election.

Friday, June 3 Went to Rev. J.A. Kenoyer's. Dined there and spent the afternoon. Went after supper, to Rev. J.S. Rhoads'.

Saturday, June 4 Rev. J.A. Kenoyer takes me to Henry Arrasmith's, and thence through the rain to Bro. Lonsh's, 1 1/2 from Elberton. After dinner to Rev. H.O. Kern's. Staid there till morning. Bro. Kenoyer also staid till morning.

Sunday, June 5 Rev. H.O. Kern took me to Rev. W.R. Lloyd's at Garfield. Went with Him to Cedar Creek, seven miles east of town. Pr. at 11:00, John 1:29. Dinner at John Horton's. Pr. at Garfield at 4:00 to a large congregation, 1 Cor. 1:23, 24. Stay at Rev. W.R. Lloyd's. Rev. S.E. Lloyd there & family: Milton 7, Rolla 4, Ray 3. Garfield is on Silver Creek.

Monday, June 6 Mailed a letter home. Went to Dr. Samuel Simpson's. He is a Baptist & strong anti-secrecy man. I dined there, and went in the afternoon back to Garfield & got a letter from home, dated May 27th. Went on to Bro. Lloyd's new house one mile out of town. Supper & lodging there. Earnest & Hattie are their children.

Tuesday, June 7 Dinner at Rev. J.M. Tressenriter's. Mother Finch and her daughter-in-law, there. Called at Wm. Carter's. They tenting there. R.I. Evans came after me, and I go to his house, five miles south-west of Garfield. Lodge there. Earnest 17, & George (9) are their children. Carter's father-in-law is Cling.

Wednesday, June 8 Stay at Bro. Evans. Write a letter home, and read some. Bro. E. lives on the east bank of the N. Palouse 300 ft above the creek (river). Pine trees, some of them 150 feet high, grow along the bluf[f]s and bottom. Bro. E. once lived near Harrisburg, Or-

egon. He was from blue-grass, in Kentucky. Was a Campbellite. Was at Walla Walla at time of the fanaticism. Rainy evening.

Thursday, June 9 At Evans. He 60, past. Went in afternoon across the bridge, 1/4 mile below, and then up the river through bushes and over loose basaltic rocks & climb the bluffs above. Fine cliffs 200 feet above the river. Rained in the evening and night. Write some. Saw Rev. S.E. Lloyd & wife & children out fishing.

Friday, June 10 Remain at Bro. Evans. Go in the afternoon a mile S.W. to look at some high basaltic bluffs on the river. Write a letter to Rev. John McBride. Stay at Bro. Evan's. His son William and daughter Clara (Mrs. Peter Arrasmith) there, that night.

Saturday, June 11 Bro. Evans goes to Colfax, and I go to Elberton afoot, about 3 1/2 ms. Dinner and lodging at Luther Kerns', a brother of Rev. H.O. Kerns. He a M.E. His wife a U.B. In afternoon, study some on a sermon on Rom. 8:21. Stay at Kern's.

Sunday, June 12 Rainy day; small congregation. Pr. at 11:00, Ps. 16:8. Dine at James Pickard's. Rev. W.R. Lloyd, R.I. Evan's & family & Mr. Erwin there. J.S. Rhoads came. Pr. at 4:00, Rom. 8:21. Few out. Go over to Rev H.O. Kern's & back to town. Stay at Luther Kern's.

Monday, June 13 Go before breakfast to Rev. H.O. Kern's. Their two younger boys have the measles. We start about 8:00 for Huntsville. I got 2 letters (Evans & H.M. Balch) and write 3 cards at Colfax. Rain ceased. Lunched between Union Flatt & the Penawawa. Cross Snake River at Penawawa ferry. Stop on the Deadmen Creek & stay. Lodge in the house. Lunch out-door. Groom's.

Tuesday, June 14 Go on via Pataha and Tucanon Creeks to Huntsville, ariving at 4:00. Home at B.J. Hunt's. He was the proprietor of the town, formerly. Called at Rev. J. Black's. Rev. A.R. Olds' pr. at 8:30. Rom. 8:28. It rained that evening & next day.

Wednesday, June 15 At Hunt's; Seminary, and Rev. W.C. Gallaher's. Rev. C.C. Bell pr. at 8:30, John 14:6; Feebly.

Thursday, June 16 Conference (Walla Walla) opened at 8:30 (9:00) Read Ps. 126. Sung "Zion Stands" & "Nearer my God." Revs. A.R. Olds and A.W. Suepp were received on transfer from Oregon. The latter not present. Afternoon. Entered onto examinations of non-pastors and pastors. Rev. T.J. Cocking pr. at 8:30. Said to be of moderate ability.

Friday, June 17 Conference opened promptly. Reports and examinations. Examinations continued. In afternoon, the proceeding on report on grievance were interrupted by chair ruling it out. Recommitted. Pres. W.S. Walker made an address on education at 8:30.

Saturday, June 18 Session continued. J.W. Tresenriter and N. Evans elected P.E.'s. Stationing Committee meets in my room at Father Hunt's at 12:45. Session afternoon. Stationing Com. retired a short time, etc. & report read. In the tabernacle, Rev. J.J. Gallaher pr. 1:45 minutes, Hebrews 12:1. I slept about 4 hours.

Sunday, June 19 Pr. at 11:00, 1 Tim. 4:16. Rubbed up all the ministers somewhat. Dine at Rev. J. Black's. At 8:00 Woman's Association organized. Pr. at 8:30, 1 Cor. 5:7. Communion. Four joined Church. Congregation lingers long; a time of rejoicing.

Monday, June 20 Remained at Father B.J. Hunt's and took a copy of the chart (Conf.) of Bro. J.C. Spoonemore. Pres. W.S. Walker & wife came and spent an hour or two, before noon. Called at Rev. J. Black's, and Rev. W.C. Gallaher's and Wm. Mitchel's. Went on the 7:20 train to Hood River. Slept about 4 hours.

Tuesday, June 21 Arrived at Hood River at 5:45 morn. Emory Eldrige met me and took me to Mrs. Hariet M. Balch's, four miles up the valley. Her children: Frederick, 25; Gertie, 17; Herbert, 13; Edna, her granddaughter, 9. Miss Bela Snyder, there. Jesse, her father lives 6 miles from Lyle, W.J. He and Mrs. Balch are my second cousins. Pr. at Sch. House at 8:30, Heb. 4:14.

Wednesday, June 22 Went at 4:30 to Hood River with Emory Eldredge. Took the train for Portland. It was 2 1/2 hours late. Dined at the Quimby House. Sent Susan (Wilbur) $29.00; Reuchlin or Lulu $20.00 present. Went

on to Albany. Staid at Russ House. Salvation singers, street.

Thursday, June 23 In Birmingham, Ala. Cath. L. Wright is born to-day. Our first grand ch. Went on 7:00 train to Corvallis. Hired a livery rig and went on to Philomath with Rev. J.W. Pulley, who had been with me from beyond Portland. Conference began before I arrived. Home at Rev. N.W. Allen's. Rev. J.W. Pulley pr. at 8:30. Jer. 17:12, 13. Supper at Jerry Hinkle's. She Father & Mother Hunt's daugh.

Friday, June 24 Conference continued. Rev. J.H. Watson pr. at 11:00 Heb. 4:9. Dine at Peter Mason's. I pr. at 8:30, Ps. 92:8.

Saturday, June 25 Conf. continued. Much business done to-day. Rev. J.W. Ingle pr. at 11:00, on Revelation. Rev. Wallace Hurlburt pr. at 8:30, Job. 14:14. Conf. Approved minutes & adjourned. I read Stn. Com. Report.

Sunday, June 26 Pr. at College Chapel at 11:00, Gal. 4:45. Coll. of $41.62 for me. Dine at John L. Aikens with Rev. T.J. Connor. Rev. T.J. Connor pr. at 3:30 Heb. 11:26. Supper at Bro. N.W. Allen's. Missionary meeting at 8:30. Revs. J.G. Mosher and P.C. Hetzler spoke. I raise $137 +, Mis. Col. & sub.

Monday, June 27 At Board meeting 8 1/2 till 12 & from 1:00 till 4:00. Dine at John Henkle's with T.J. Connor, J.G. Mosher, J.E. Edwards, M.J. Connor, etc. Supper at Rev. M.M. Crow's. Rev. J.H. Watson pr. at 8:30. Stay at Allen's with Watson. Slept 8 hours— first long sleep for a week.

Tuesday, June 28 Watson leaves for home. I stay at Allen's till 4:00 p.m. Some talk. Write a letter. Call at E.C. Wyatt's. Supper & lodging at Jer[r]y M.C. Miller's. His wife from Arbela, Mo. Would like a place in a college. A scientific graduate. Owns property here.

Wednesday, June 29 Spent forenoon at Rev. M.M. Crow's. Malcom living there. Dine there. Spend afternoon at Rev. Ezra C. Wyatt's. Supper there, also. Mrs. Wm. Pearson there. Lodge at N.W. Allen's.

Thursday, June 30 Spend most of the forenoon & afternoon in comparing charts & footing them up. Dine at

Allen's. Go in the evening to Rev. A. Bennett's across Mary's River. Stay there.

Friday, July 1 Went back to town. Dine at Jacob Henkle's. Study some at Allen's. Went to Prof. H. Sheak's. Supper there. Their little girl, Gertie, 7 years old. Stay at N.W. Allen's.

Saturday, July 2 Went on 10:00 train to Corvallis. Call at Joshua Mason's. Dine at their boarding-house. See Rev. A.W. Snepp, who is on his way to California, moving by wagon. Prof. G.M. Miller & wife & Prof. Horner come on train to Philomath. Supper & lodging at Rev. N.W. Allen's.

Sunday, July 3 Pr. at 11:00 at the College Chapel, Rom. 8:21. Dine at Rev. Ezra Wyatt's. Pr. at 4:00, John 21:17. Supper & lodgings at John Henkle's. His wife, a daughter of Reuben Gant's. Andrew Gant's son is clerking in Henkle's store. Andrew came to Oregon with our company, in 1857.

Monday, July 4 Called at Allen's. Went to Corvallis on 10:20 train. Mrs. Adie D. Miller delivered the oration. Quite good. Dined at the hotel. Returned on 2:00 tr. Called at Jac. Henkle's to see Jas. E. Connor. Called at Sister Ross', Rev. Jas. R. Parker's. Supper there. Stay at Allen's.

Tuesday, July 5 Called at Jac. Henkle's. Card to Susan. Dine at N.W. Allen's. Write letters for Bellevue and Abique. Supper at Allen's. Call at M.M. Crow's. Attend the temperance meeting at the College doorsteps. Stay at Allen's.

Wednesday, July 6 Call at M.M. Crow's. Call at J.M.C.Miller's. Call at McElroy's to see Lincoln Bennett whose eye was put out by a premature explosion of powder in a bottle. Went out with Prof. G.M. Miller & wife & Jerry's wife and their children on a picnic on Woods Creek. Supper & lodging at Allen's.Prof. G.M. Miller lectured on temperance, College.

Thursday, July 7 Called at McElroy's to see Lincoln Bennett, whose wounds were doing well. Dined at M.M. Crow's. Letter from Susan dated July 1st. Walked most of the way to Wm. W. Starr's. Rode part of the way with

the Gibbs family. Mrs. Marion Parker there— their daughter. Very friendly folks.

Friday, July 8 Rode over to John Buchanan's. Dinner and supper there. She a matron of excellent sense and piety, and is the daughter of Isaac Gardner of Elk Creek, below Drain. Children: Freddie, Alice, Earnest, etc. Bro. Jas. E. Edwards & we go to his house through "16" gates, late.

Saturday, July 9 Stay at J.E. Edwards all day, His large cherry tree has perhaps 20 bushels of Royal Ann cherries. It measures seven feet around, forty-five across, and is about thirty in height. Joseph H. Edwards there. His wife a Gardner. Their child about 8 months old is Earl.

Sunday, July 10 Pr. at Simpson's Chapel at 11:00, Matt. 12:43-45. Dine at Lewis Nelson Price's. Speaking meeting at 3:30 led by Rev. Philip Starr, an able minister of the M.E. Church. I pr. at 4:30 Eph. 2:16. Good congregations. Stay at Joseph Gragg's.

Monday, July 11 Stay at Gragg's till afternoon. Go to Father Olds'. Go on to Guilford Barnard's. Jas. E. Edwards calls in the evening. Stay at Barnard's.

Tuesday, July 12 Go to Jas. E. Edwards' (& Joseph H. Edwards) early in the morning after breakfast, and with him to Corvallis. Dine at boarding house with Edwards. Go on 2:00 train to Philomath, Prof. Condon of the State University is aboard & talks on partial inspiration. Call at Rev. M.M. Crow's. Go to A. Bennett's. Supper & lodging there.

Wednesday, July 13 Stay at Bro. Bennett's till afternoon. Bro. Pulley & Mosher there, also. Went to town & to Bro. Allen's again. Lecture at College Chapel at "8:30" on the Prohibitory Amendment to the State Constitution. Stay at Rev. N.W. Allen's. Rev. William Dickson of Prineville, Crook Co., Oregon, there.

Thursday, July 14 Stay at Allen's till afternoon. Pulley dines with us. Bro. Mosher starts to Umpqua in the morning. Dine at Allen's. Call with J.W. Pulley at G.M. Strope's. His father afflicted. Call at Underhill's a minute. We with Rev. T. Connor visit Sister Berry's family. Stay at Rev. N.W. Allen's.

Friday, July 15 Went with Rev. J.W. Pulley to Wm. Wyatt's. Stay there till next morning. Eva is their daughter. Frank, their youngest son. An older son is at home. Wrote letters & cards there and before going there. Mrs. Wyatt not at home but in very poor health at her daughter, Springer's.

Saturday, July 16 Came to Rev. N.W. Allen's. Get ready to go to Alsea. Dinner at Bro. Allen's. Go with Rev. T.P. Conner, to Alsea. Passed where Wood, Webster, Hayden, live. Stay at David Hawley's near forks of the Alsea. David Hawley's Children: Henry, Iola, Jessie, & Silvia.

Sunday, July 17 Walked to Brown's School-house. Pr. at 11:00 l Pet. 1:4. Seven arose for prayer. Dine at Chas. Malone's. He from central Georgia. Speaking meeting, at 3:00. Preaching at 3:30. My text Matt. 16:26. Supper at Mr. Hull's. Took up subs. for Conner $51.50.

Monday, July 18 Go to Hawley's & start at 7:20 for Philomath. Find a tree across a broken bridge. Hindered an hour by the burnt tree. Reached Allen's about 2:20. Dinner there with Bro. Conner's. Call at McElroy's to see Lincoln Bennett, who is improving.

Tuesday, July 19 Go on 10:00 train to Albany. Rev. Bowersox, Ev. Ass'n. P.E., on the train. Also Thomas Small, Cumb. Pres. Minister, whom I knew 29 years ago at Sublimity. Elmer Harritt meets me and takes me to Rev. Jesse Harritt's, across the new bridge & two miles west.

Wednesday, July 20 Spend forenoon in cleaning Coats & vest & writing letters. In the afternoon, Alice Emmet & children came: Eddie (here before) Bertha, Jessie. Byron Webster Harritt's wife & child (Jessie) came in the forenoon. Stay at Harritt's.

Thursday, July 21 Wrote several letters & went to Salem with a Mr. Emmett (brother of J.H.) in a cart. Walked home. Afternoon, Squire Johnson & wife came on a visit to Harritt's. They live in Salem.

Friday, July 22 Went to Jas. H. Emett's. Children Eddie (Edward) 16, Arthur 11, Bertha 8, Jessie 6. Harritt & wife along. Dine there. Also supper there. Go back and stay at Harritt's. See his peculiar fir tree in the field west of old barn. One natural limb. The rest hanging clus-

ters. A most dense shade. A regular ball.

Saturday, July 23 Went on stage at 7:00 via [blank], Zena, & Bethel, to McCoy. Wait there till 3:10 & go on train to Amity. Go with Reuben Gant to H.J. Sargeant's, 2 m's from Bellevue. Stay there. She a daughter of Gants. Dined at hotel at McCoy.

Sunday, July 24 Pr. at Bellevue U.B. Church at 11:00, Heb. 7:26. Dine at Jefferson Davis', a Disciple. Pr. at 3:30, Jer. 13:21. Rev. Hunsaker of McMinville pr. at 4:30. Stay at Sargeant's. *Remarks:* Went to Church with Reuben Gant. He not a professor, but friendly to the Church. He came to Oregon in 1845. His brother Andrew Gant went to Oregon with me in 1859, via Panama.

Monday, July 25 Went to Rev. C.C. Zumwalt's 1 1/2 miles south of Perrydale. Mr. R. Gant spends the day in hunting grouse. Killed two. *Remarks:* Bro. Zumwalt and wife (then unmarried) came to Oregon in 1845. She a sister of Gant's wife who is deceased. Zumwalt is a Qr. Conf. U.B. preacher.

Tuesday, July 26 Mr. Gant killed another Grouse & left for home. Many pass going to Dallas to preliminary trial of Abe. Blackburn, accused of being leader of the mob who hung Oscar Kelty for the murder of his wife. He is acquitted before Justice Frink. I stay at Zumwalt's, Sheriff Groves, Harry Depew, guard.

Wednesday, July 27 Bro. Zumwalt takes me to Amity (where I found no letter) and to Breidwell's where I took the cars to West Dayton a mile north of Dayton. I walked to Rev. J.W. Ingle's in Dayton. Dine there at 2:00. Go through his ware-house. Stay at Ingle's. She a daughter of Bether's. Children: Ida, etc.

Thursday, July 28 Stay at Bro. Ingle's all day. They do my washing for me. I preach at Baptist Church at 8:00 p.m. Heb. 11:26. Stay at Ingle's. Their children: Ida 16, Effa 14, Hattie 12, Fred 10, Nora 7, Calvin 2.

Friday, July 29 Stay at Ingle's till after dinner. Go on train (narrow gauge) via Dundee, Ray's landing, St. Paul, etc., to Silverton. Get a letter from home, dated 18th. Bro. W.G. Minear meets me & takes me to his house 5 miles north.

Saturday, July 30 Went with Rev. J.S. Osborn to Father Corby's. Grant Corby & his wife live with the old folks. I stay there till next morning. Read in H.B. Stowe's book on remarkable events. About Mil[l]erite excitement, J.Q. Adams fight on right of peti[ti]on, Explosion of Canon & Sec. Upshur's death, ashipboard.

Sunday, July 31 Went with Bro. Osborne to Abiqua. Called at Wm. Adair's to change clothes. Preach at 11:00, Heb. 11:26, to a house more than full. Dine at DeWitt Hall's. Speaking meeting at 3:20. I pr. at 4:00, Acts 24:25. Call a little at Hall's & at Adair's where I eat supper. Staid at W.G. Minear's, with Rev. J.S. Osborne.

Monday, August 1 Went with Bro. Osborne to Wm. Adair's. Stay there till after dinner. He troubled with eresipelas badly. Was very bad Saturday. Considerably better now. Went to Dewitt C. Hall's. Stay there till morning.

Tuesday, August 2 Call at Wm. R. Adair's. Go to John Whitlock's. Dine there. Supper at Abraham Mosher's at the cross-roads. Call at George W. Hall's. Call again at D.C. Hall's. Stay at Wm. R. Adair's.

Wednesday, August 3 Bro. D.C. Hall takes me via Fillmore (Mt. Angel) to Father Corby's, where we arrive at 2:00. Supper at Chas. Corby's. Pr. at Union Sch. H. at 7:30, Luke 24:46. After lecture on Seventh-day Adventism. Rev. Benham's (adventist) present & the Dodge folks. Stay at Father Corby's.

Thursday, August 4 Grant Corby takes me to Woodburn. Go on 8:53 train to Hubbard. Dine at Mr. Gowdy's 1 m. s. of town. Supper and lodging at Rev. W.H. Palmer's. They have four children; a daughter aged 16, and three sons.

Friday, August 5 Went on 9:00 train to Portland. Got several letters and cards. Bro. B.L. Haines takes me to his house, 9 ms. South. Their children: Albie & wife, Mary 20, Lizzie 17, Willie 16, Luther 14, Ella & Emma 11. Bro. Kenworthy & Wife called in the evening. I staid at Haines'. A fine family,

Saturday, August 6 Bro. Haines takes me to Bro. L.A. Seely's near Wilsonville. Dine there and remain there

till morning. He 67 years old. Their children all married. Seven of them are sons: Geo. B; Joseph Bem; Stephen Bishop; Franklin Flint; Judson Leach; Robert Ira; Edwin R.

Sunday, August 7 Went to Pleasant Hill Sch. H. & pr. 11:00, Rom. 1:16. More than a houseful. Lunch on the ground. Speaking meeting at 2:45. Pr. at 3:30 Acts 24:25. Supper at Geo. B. Seely's & lodging. Saw Father Voss, Mrs. Branat, Mr. Boice, Mrs. Kaufman.

Monday, August 8 George takes me to L.H. Seely's again. Dine there. Stay there till next morning. Much talk. Wrote some letters.

Tuesday, August 9 Go down to Boone's Ferry. Call at Franklin F. Seely's. Miss the steamboat by its coming 20 minutes earlier than usual. Hire mail-carrier to take me to Aurora. Dine at Grocery on canned oysters. Go on 2:00 train to Portland. Get letters & write letters. Leave teeth at C.C. Newcastle's, 167 First Street. Stay at J.B. Lichtenthaler's.

Wednesday, August 10 Went to town. Wrote letters & got letters from Susan. Saw Widdell. Called at Mission room. Saw Rev. G.W. Sickafoose there. Went on the steamboat, Lurline, to Vancouver. Stopped at Ancil Marble's. She lived near Ailey's Chapel, east of Dayton, Ohio. Her father's name was Green. Supper & lodging. Sent postal-order for $21.49 to Susan.

Thursday, August 11 Went on the Lurline to Baker's landing. Went to Oliver Hendrickson's, son of Rev. Wm. Hendrickson. His mother unable to walk—is 70 years old. Went over to see Lake VanCouver. Got into a slew. Lost my way in returning. Went back to VanCouver. Stayed at Ancil Marble's.

Friday, August 12 Stay at Schuel's store till afternoon. Go out with Wm. Cross to Rev. J.H. Alexande r's, who lives 7 Miles up country. Supper & lodging there.

Saturday, August 13 Bro. Alexander takes me up to E.J. Rickets', five miles further up. Children: James N. & Flora E., both ex-students at Philomath. Dine at Rickets. Stay there in the afternoon. Lodge there. Pr. at 8:00 at Flat Woods Sch. House, Eccl. 12:13, 14.

Sunday, August 14 Preach at 11:00, 2 Cor. 3:7,8. House over full. Dine in the school-house. Pr. at 3:00, Ps. 16:11. Goddard, Harper, Leper, Goodnight (a Disciple), Galloway, etc., I think the church Liberals. After afternoon meeting, go to Stephen Crabbe's, 3 1/2 miles S. of LaCenter. Went to Presbyterian revival at Pioneer (Union) Church. Rev. Mr. Gamble pr. Rom. 8:34. Fifteen seekers. Mr. McKinsey, Pastor.

Monday, August 15 Bro. Crabbe takes me via LaCenter to Rev. Riley Bartlett's 1 1/2 ms. N.E. of LaCenter. I stay there all day & that night.

Tuesday, August 16 Stay at Bro. Bartlett's till 4:30. Christian Olsten takes Bro. Bartlett & me to Mountain View Sch. House, 7 miles N.E., where I pr. at 8:30, Luke 24:46. See Morris, Hentsley, 2 Hazen, Granthurn, etc., & their wives. Go back to Bro. Bartlett's. Stay there. VanArsdale carried lanturn. It was a long, dark ride.

Wednesday, August 17 Having slept three hours, I rose at 4:30. Walked with Bartlett to the boat, "Lucy Walker," at LaCenter. Start at 6:00. Run down to North Fork of Lewis River, & up that & back, and on to Portland. Go to Post-office, and, on cars, to Marion. Go 3 ms. to Wm. Pearson's.

Thursday, August 18 Breakfast at Bennett Pearson's. Start at 10:00 to Marion (walk) and thence, via Albany, to Philomath. Arrive at 2:30. Many letters. Go to the campground. Speaking meeting in progress. Pulley had preached last night. Connor 10:30 this morn., Ps. 116:12. I pr. at 8:00, Luke 24:46. Supper at J. Aiken's tent. Lodge in the Preacher's tent, with Pulley, T.J. and Connor, T.J.

Friday, August 19 Breakfast at Rev. M.M. Crow's. Mail some letters. Pulley pr. at 10:30, Rev. 3:18. Dine at Allen's tent. Speaking & pr. meeting at 3:00. Right good. Supper at Allen's tent. Rev. T.J. Connor pr. at 8:00, Luke 10, Par. Samaritan. I exhort and invite seekers. Nettie Wyatt comes forward. Lodge in our tent.

Saturday, August 20 Breakfast at Rev. N.W. Allen's. Write a letter. Morning meeting at 9:30. Rev. T.J. Connor pr. at 10:30, on the Beatitudes. Dine at Allen's tent. Rev. J.W. Pulley preaches at 3:00, Jer. 2:13. Qr. Conf. follows. J.L. Garrett licensed to exhort. Supper at Jerry Henkle's tent. Pres. J.C. Keezel pr. at 8:00, John 3:18. I exhort &we had a short prayer & speaking meeting. Lodge as usual. Sanctif. hold a pr. meeting.

Sunday, August 21 Morning meeting at half past nine; runs in sanctif. line mostly. Rev. T.J. Connor pr. at 10:30, Eph. 4:11-13. Children's meeting at 2:30 addressed by Connor and Keezel. I pr. at 3:30, Isa. 52:1. At 8:00, Rev. J.C. Keezel pr. Gal. 6:7. Had meals at Allen's, all day. Lodged as usual.

Monday, August 22 Breakfast at John Henkle's. Rev. J.W. Pulley preached at 10:30, John 16:20, preceded by a prayer & speaking meeting. Dine at John Henkle's with Jacob Henkle, with whom I had a talk. Prayer & speaking meeting at 3:00 Henkle, Connor, and Mrs. Jerry Henkle, and myself talk of sanctification. Supper at Jerry Henkle's. Rev. T.J. Connor pr. at 8:00, 1 Tim 1:12,13. Lodge as usual.

Tuesday, August 23 Breakfast at Kiser's tent. Bro. Pulley left for home, on acct. of his wife's sickness. Rev. J.M. Strope pr. at 10:30 (after the brief morning meeting) from Mark 2:5. Dine at Bro. Allen's tent. Afternoon, prayer & speaking meeting well attended. Supper in town at Prof. Sheak's. Pres. Keezel pr. at 8:00, "Built house on rock"—"Sand," Mat. 7.

Wednesday, August 24 Breakfast at Allen's. Rev. J.R. Parker pr. at 10:30, after a brief prayer meeting, from Phil. 2:5. Dine at Allen's tent. Rev. T.J. Connor pr. at 3:00, John 13:1. I go to P.O. I see the paper (cons.) & get a letter. Supper at Allen's. I Pr. at 8:00, Rom. 5:8. Lodge at our preacher's tent, as every night of meeting.

Thursday, August 25 Arose early. Took a bath at the creek..We had a farewell meeting at 10:00. Mrs. Underhill joined church. Lunch at Allen's tent. Went to town. Called at John & Jerry Henkle's store; at Crow's, Wyatt's, etc. Supper at Allen's. Educational meeting at 8:00, with addresses before it by Keezel, Connor, Wright, etc. Lodge at Jerry Henkle's with Connor.

Friday, August 26 Call at Crow's, Peter Mason's, Ezra Wyatt's, Brown's, Keezel's. Start at 10:00 for Corvallis, Albany, Eugene & Roseburg. An hour at Albany; 5 hours at Eugene. Visit Luther Adair's. Start at 9:55 & arrive at Roseburg at 1:45 a.m. Lodge at McClellen House. Slept 3 1/2 hours.

Saturday, August 27 Call at John B. Newman's, Dr. Masters, etc. Dine at Newman's. Went with John S. Bonebrake's folks to his house up Deer Creek, seven miles. He is living on the South Branch, a mile from North Branch. Children: Wm. 21, George 13, Hattie, 10, Fred, 7.

Sunday, August 28 I Pr. at Pine Grove, 5 ms. east of Roseburgh at 11:00, Ex. 28:34. Dined with A.H. Brown's and Burt's on the grounds. Speaking meeting (right good) at 2:30; Preach at 3:00, Luke 16:31. Go with Casebeer to Roseburgh. Stop at Dr. S.S. Master's. Pr. at Presb. Ch. at 8:00, Luke 24:46. Rev. Mr. Smick, pastor. Rev. I. Bell. Stay at Masters'.

Monday, August 29 Call on Rev. B. Bonham. Dine at Marsters. Failed to get a gravel train to Oakland. Call at J.B. Newman's. Go out with A.H. Brown to his house. Stay there. Children: Sophionia C., Omar C., Ella M. 20, Wilbur H., Amanda *Lilian,* 17, Eliza *May,* Lizzie, *Temple,* 13, Violet 4.

Tuesday, August 30 Stay at Brown's till after dinner. Go with Wilbur to Roseburg. Call at Drug Store of S.S. Marsters. Call on errands and at Prof. J.B. Horner's. Supper and lodgings at S.S. Marsters. His son is A.C. Matsters. In climbing a butte, I broke off poison oak, forgot it, and later wiped off my forehead with my hands!

Wednesday, August 31 Dr. Marsters went with me to the depot and gave me my breakfast at the Depot Hotel. Went on freight to Ashland. Mr. Fitshugh on the train to Glendale. Gave me much information. Brakeman invited me to sit in the cupola of the caboose to see the country. Conductor gave me a watermelon. Lodge Union Hotel. Bought ticket to Coles.

Thursday, September 1 Lunched for Breakfast. Started on stage (Depot) at 9:00; from town 9:30. "His Excellency Siamese ambassador (Minister) to London, Wash., & Stockholm, in same seat. Rough trip. Start to Anderson Cal. at 2:30. A man pays 10 cts, which I had less than enough to pay my fare. I divide bread with a man who was hungry. Soda Springs on the banks of the Sacramento. Reach Anderson at 10:45. Stay at the Anderson's house. Poison oak!

Friday, September 2 Arrange my baggage somewhat. Breakfast & dinner at the hotel. Write home and to Wilmore. Get acquainted with Rev. Bateman. Also Bro. Landon & others. See Bro. Lowe, Burtner, (Rev. G.W.) comes there. Go out to Burtner's. Supper and lodging there. Children: Homer, 12; Jessie, 10; Charlie, 7; Millie & Minnie, twins, 4; Burtner went out to fight forest fires.

Saturday, September 3 Go with Rev. G.W. Burtner to Mrs. Helen G. Lowe's, 1 1/2 m. north. Children: Wm. Olin, 27; Walter F., 17; John Morris, 30; Effa Gennette, 21. Dine at Lowe's. Theirs a beautiful fruit farm, a section or two of the tract. Supper there. Pr. at Happy Valley Sch. H. at 8:00, Ps. 1:6. Stay at Lowe's. (Had to close my eyes while preaching.)

Sunday, September 4 Pr. again at the Sch. H., Heb. 12:22-24. Dine at Lowe's. Miss Clara Nutting there. Mr. Gile working there. Pr. at 8:00 at Oak Highland Sch. H., Rom. 5:8. Stay at Rev. G.W. Burtner's. He got home after meeting from a 30 miles' ride to marry a couple. Members: G.W. Landon, R.B. Landon, (Cl.Sta) Gordon E. Parker (Cl.L.)

Monday, September 5 Stay at Burtner's till about 4:00 p.m. Wrote some, read a little, and re-arranged my valise. Go to S.C. Dick's for supper. She Burtner's sister. Pr. at 8:00 at Oak Highland Sch. H., Luke 16:31. Stay at Bro. G.W. Burtner's.

Tuesday, September 6 Go to A.W. Hubbard's, 3 miles North-west. Their Son Aust. had gone to Woodbridge, and played truant, as now supposed. Came back a road to the right. Met Bro. Ed. Root. Came in sight of George Myers'. Stay at Burtner's.

Wednesday, September 7 Bro. Burtner takes me to Anderson. Go on 9:30 train to Red Bluff. Write at the depot. Lodge at National Hotel. Call, in the evening, on Rev. Wm. Leonard, a cancer doctor, and Baptist preacher. An old shed burns, in town.

Thursday, September 8 Go on 5:00 a.m. train to Biggs, Butte Co. Wm. Thos. Boulware meets me & takes me to his house 1/2 miles South. Write some. Rev. D. Shuck (ex-bishop) comes. Dinner there. Pr. at 7:30, Luke 24:46. Lodge at Boulware's. Children at home: Mary Adah 16; Belle 14. Away: Caleb Newton 30; Broderick DeKalb 27; Berthenia Moore, 25; Ellen Serviss 23; Thomas Mathew.

Friday, September 9 Go to Gridley with Rev. Daniel Shuck. Dine at his house. Return to Boulware's (Bolwer's). Supper there. Pr. at 7:30, Heb. 11:26. Called in the morning at Caleb Marion Boulware's, a few minutes. Stay at W.J. Boulware's. Mrs. Martha (Hurlbart) Boulware a cousin to Wallace Hurlbart.

Saturday, September 10 Stay at Boulware's till evening. Slept an hour in the forenoon. Had a time after my nap to subdue the itching from oak poison by bathing. In afternoon brush my clothes and use wash mixture on coat collar, etc. Supper there. Pr. at 8:00, Ex. 28:34. Good speaking meeting followed. Bro. Benj. Lambert of Bangor took me to Boulware's.

Sunday, September 11 Pr. at 11:00, Heb. 12:22-24. Dine at C. Marion Boulware's. Bro. Shuck went to an afternoon appointment. I pr. at 7:30, Jude 14v. Large congregation at night especially. Stay at W.T. Boulware's. C. Marion Boulware's children: Nelson 21, Maria 19, Berthenia 17, Albert 14; Nancy 10, babe, 2 m. Danl. Shuck's voice only a loud whisper!

Monday, September 12 Went about 11:00 to Lewis C. Smith's in Biggs. His wife, Sarah Ann, is a daughter of Rev. Aaron Farmer, of note in our church. They have three sons living. Supper there. Pr. at 8:00, Deut. 18:18 Boys' names: John A., 28; Solomon Lewis 25; Robert E. Lee 21. Stay at W. Thos. Boulware's.

Tuesday, September 13 Went to the funeral service of Mrs. Robinson. Dine at Boulware's. Mrs. Dan. Streator and daughter Mattie, called on a visit. Also Mark Kepel, the class steward at Biggs. Pr. at 7:30, Ez. 33:11. Eva Armstrong came forward for prayer. Two others arose. Stay at Boulware's.

Wednesday, September 14 Go to town on errand. Dine

at John Lewis' with Rev. D. Shuck. His wife the only religious one in the family. Daughter, Celia, going to Scissons to-night. Go home with Shuck to Gridley. Supper & lodgeing there. Pr. at U.B. Church at 7:30, Luke 16:31.

Thursday, September 15 Call at Shirley's and at Sister Bell's. She washed my clothes, but not done ironing. Dine at Shuck's. Call at W.T. Boulware's on our way to Dan Streator's. Their daughter, Mattie and the boys go to Church. Pr. at 7:45, Rev. 1:56. Berthonia Boulware converted. Stay at W.T. Boulware's.

Friday, September 16 Went to town about noon. Dined at Lewis C. Smith's. Called at Mr. Thompson's; at Wm. Armstrong's; at A.M. Pitts. Rev. Mr. Booher boards at Pitts. He is quite unwell. Pr. at 7:45, Amos 4:12. Three forward for prayers. One other arose, Mrs. Thompson and Eva Armstrong profess conversion. Mrs. Thompson probably not converted, however.

Saturday, September 17 Went to Caleb Marion Boulware's. Dine there. Nancy Hubbard, widow of Rev. Nelson Hubbard, there. She is Boulware's first wife's mother. Stay there till after supper. Turned cooler. Late to Church. Preached Luke 23:4. Cornelia Keppel, a seeker. Praise meeting. Keppel shouted. Many come forward & give their hands. Stay at Marion Boulware's.

Sunday, September 18 Go by W.J. Boulware's. Rev. Mr. Booher pr. at 11:00, 2 Cor. 8:9. Good but *lifeless. Dine at Wm. Downing's, close to the Church. Mrs. W.T. Boulware was a niece of Abraham Hurlbut, Wallace Hurlburt's father. I pr. at 7:30, Jer. 13:21. Large congregation. One forward for prayers, and two arose. Stay at W.J. Boulware's. *His health was poor.

Monday, September 19 Go to town, & thence to C. Marion Boulware's. Write letters to N. Mygrants and to A.L. Stanley. Go to L.C. Smith's for supper. Call at Wm. Armstrong's. Pr. at 7:30, Matt. 1:21. One seeker. Stay at W.J. Boulware's.

Tuesday, September 20 Stay at W.J. Boulware's till 5:00. Go to C.M. Boulware's to supper. Talk with Berthania about joining church. Talk with Albert on the way to church about becoming religious. Pr. at 7:45, Acts 26:28. M. Adah Boulware and Albert come out for prayers &

profess conversion. Stay at W.J. Boulware's.

Wednesday, September 21 Stay at Boulware's till afternoon. Go to L.C. Smith's. Not feeling well. Supper there. Pr. at 7:45, Prov. 29:1. Mary and Cornelia Keppel and Albert Boulware came out for prayers. Berthenia Boulware joined the Church. Stay at C. Marion Boulware's.

Thursday, September 22 Went to Wm. Thos. Boulware's. Stay till well in afternoon. Go to Biggs shoe-store, and Rev. Mr. R.S. Thompson's & back to Boulware's. Pr. at 7:45 on baptism, 1 Pet. 3:21. Mary Adah Boulware and Albert Boulware, her cousin, join the Church. Stay at W.J. Boulware's.

Friday, September 23 Go to A. M. Pitts & stay to Dinner & supper. Miss Kelsey, M.E.S, P.E.'s daughter from Chico there. Call at Rev. L.W. Simmons. Pr. at 7:45, Rom. 10:6-10 (about 30 minutes). Mary Cornelia, and Esther Keppel converted & join Church; daughters of Garrett Keppel, P.O. Biggs.

Saturday, September 24 Go on 7:00 a.m. train to Sacramento. Dr. Hart of Milton along. Reach Lodi at 1:30 p.m. Go out to Woodbridge. Put up at Rev. I.K. Statton's. Call at Rush's. Stay at Statton's. Could get no conveyance to Atlanta.

Sunday, September 25 Pr. at 11:00, John 21:17 "Thou knowest all things," etc. Dine at Pres. D.A. Mobley's. Go to Sabbath-School at 3:00. Short address on Sab. Sch. lesson. Stay at Statton's till church time. Sleep an hour. Pr. at Presbyterian Church at 7:30, Luke 16:31. Spoke 35 minutes. Stay at Bro. D.G. Rush's.

Monday, September 26 Led prayer at College Chapel. Wrote to Reuchlin & Mother. Go to Rev. I.K. Statton's. Saw Prof. E.P. Morey. Dine at Rev. I.K. Statton's. Wrote some letters. Call at Elliots. Supper at W.K. Klinefelter's. Stay at Statton's.

Tuesday, September 27 Wrote home. Rev. L. Stearns called. He is about to betray us at Eureka, I fear. Dine at Statton's. Write some in afternoon. Supper at B.F. Bourland's. Call at Prof. Ridenhour's. Stay at I.K. Statton's.

Wednesday, September 28 Dr. Jer. Riley took me to early train at Lodi & I go to Stockton. Stop at Grand Central Hotel for breakfast. Go to the pavilion of the fair. See squashes weighing 125, 137, 140 pounds. Go on 1:05 train to Selma. A number of ministers aboard. Reach Selma at 7:00. Get some letters. Rev. H.S. Munger pr. "He looked upon them expecting to receive something."

Thursday, September 29 Conference convened at 8:30. Exam. began. My home last night and to-day at Bro. J.G. Thomas'. Afternoon, Conf. Continued & Exam. resumed. E.L. Kenoyer received (morn) into Conf. on transfer. J.J. Smith, H.S. Munger, J.W. Ward, & A.W. Suep invited to advisory seats. Rev. J.J. Smith pr. at 7:30, Rom. 6:23. Stay at Thomas's.

Friday, September 30 Conference continued. Dine at J.E. Whitson's. Examinations continued. Supper at Thomas's. Rev. J.W. Baumgardner pr. 2 Peter 3:11. Stay at Thomas's.

Saturday, October 1 Conference continued. Progresses well. Dine at Cyrus Van Emmons'. P. Elders elected: J.W. Baumgardner, A.W. Snepp, J.W. Fisher. Supper at Renfro Hotel. Stationing Committee meets at 6:30. Educational meeting at 8:00, $203.00 subscribed for San Joaque Valley College. Conference closed at 11:00. Stay at Thomas'.

Sunday, October 2 Preach at 11:00, 1 Tim 4:15, one hour & 20 minutes. Collection $35.10. Dine at the hotel, Renfro House, at J.E. Whitson's account. Sabbath School & Memorial of E. Bast & wife, Bro. Winters, & Sister Fisher. I spoke; also A.W. Snepp & D. Shuck. Supper at Hotel. Pres. D.A. Mobley pr. II Cor. 6:19. "Ye are not your own." I took Mis. Collection & subs. $172.85. Sacramental service. Farewell. I stayed at Thomas's.

Monday, October 3 Went to town. Called at J.E. Whitson's. Dine at Thomas's. Called in afternoon at Jas. H. Payne's. Called at Rev. W.L. DeMunbrun's just before meeting. Rev. F. Fisher pr. at 7:30. He, at my suggestion takes in three members. Stay at Renfro parlor till train time 12:18 at night. Ticket to Los Angeles.

Tuesday, October 4 Pass Calientes & Keene and the Soup

Tunnel, 2 ms beyond Keene. Tehatchapie—the Salt Lake. The Cactus or palms. Mojave (mo'-ha'-ve). Arrive at Los Angeles about 1:00. Put up at New Natick House on Los Angeles St. Write some. Sleep well that night.

Wednesday, October 5 Stay at New Natick till near noon, and go with Rev. T.F. Hallowell's to his rooms on Cor. of 3d & York St. Call in the afternoon at Elisha Luke's and his soninlaw's Young's. Stay at Hallowell's. Rev. T.F. Hallowell & his wife, Margaret Hallowell.

Thursday, October 6 Go to A.N. King's office-ride out west on Cable-cars return on another cable route. Write to Robert Miller, Balbec, Ind. Shop some. Ride out on Spring Street line to Dr. Dickson's. He building. His fatherinlaw Rosecrans. Return to Hallowell's. Stay there.

Friday, October 7 Rev. I.L. Spencer of Main Street, M.E. Church called with L.H. Kingery to get me to preach for him next Sabbath, & I agreed to pr. for him Sabbath a week. Went with Bro. & Sister Hallowell on electric street-cars to the west end of it, and then to restaurant on 2d St., near Main. Buy coat for $22.00. Go to the Palms. Stay at Rev. M. Baumgardner's.

Saturday, October 8 T.F. Hallowell gave me $5.00, on coat. Went to Santa Monica with Bro. Baumgardner. Dine with Rev. W.P. Tibbet. We go with W.P. Tibbet to look at South Santa Monica and out-skirts of Santa Monica. We call on Rev. Cline of M.E. Church. Return home. Call at Rev. A.N. King's. Attend temperance meeting at Machado. Stay at Baumgardner's.

Sunday, October 9 Went to Machado Sch. H. Pr. at 11:00, Luke 16:19. Dine with Rev. A.N. King's, 11/2 m. west of "The Palms." Go in evening to Santa Monica, and pr. at 7:00, Ez. 33:11, at M.E. Church. Large Congregation for the place. Return to Bro. Baumgardner's. Met Mr. [blank] who knew me in Minnesota and Mr. Lee who knew me in Nebraska.

Monday, October 10 Went to look at the new Church at The Palms. Dine at Rev. J.W. Baumgardner's. Their daughter, Katie, is 10 years old, and their only daughter or child. Visit Henry Lowe's after dinner, and stay there till after supper. Lowe and wife go with me to Rev. A.N. King's & stay till bed-time. It rains a nice shower, the

first for months. I stay at King's.

Tuesday, October 11 Went in forenoon to Rev. Jac. Brown's, who is just from a visit to N.W. Iowa. Dine there. His daughter, Mrs. Lewis Stephens & daughterinlaw called. I look at B's Eucalyptus grove. Trees 3 years set out, last March, are some of them 10 inches through & fifty feet high. Supper & lodging at Nat. Coe's. His daughter Elsie is sick.

Wednesday, October 12 Went to Mr. Anderson Rose's in the morning with Bro. Coe's son via King's. They worth from 1/4 to 1/2 million of dollars. Dine there. Go in afternoon to Bellona Harbor. Walk and wade swails. Saw Gen. Supt. of the harbor M.L. Wicks, Esq. & Mr. Taylor Construction Supt. Rev. M.P. Tibbets comes after me & I go to his house at Santa Monica.

Thursday, October 13 Stay at Rev. W.P. Tibbet's till 3:00. I Walk on the ocean bluff in the morning and visit the old wharf in the afternoon. Go to The Palms with Rev. J.W. Baumgardner and on to "Uncle" Phineas Tibbet's. Supper & lodging there.

Friday, October 14 Go on 7:45 train to Los Angeles. Go into the Pavilion of the fair & stay till about 4:00. Pomological & Citrus exhibits. Oranges, lemons, limes, pommegranates, pears, peaches, apples, etc. Indian ornaments, quilts & fancy work, dried flowers pressed. Pumpkins 182 & 203 lbs. Beet 18 x 36. Squashes 48 x 12 inches. Sweet potato 12 inches diam. Quina 14 1/2 cir. & 1 3/4 lb. Onions 6 in. diam. Lunch at Argyle Lodge at S. H. Kingery's. Heard Bishop B.K. Hargrove on Ch. Ex.

Saturday, October 15 Called in at M. E. Ch. South annual conference. The bishop addressing the candidates for the ministry. Two received. Net increase of 107 in the laity in the year, a membership of over 1,400. Got letters—one from Katie, my daughter. Lunch at Argyle. Go to Bro. T.F. Hallowell's. Stay till 8:00. Lodge at S. H. Kingery's, 1/3 Sq. north of Main on Morris St.

Sunday, October 16 Pr. at 11:00 at Main St. M.E. Church, John 6:69. Dine at S. H. Kingery 's with Rev. J. L. Spencer. Go to Trinity (M.E. South). Hear part of a discourse by Rev. Godbey. Go to Norwalk. Rev. D.

McKeel meets me & takes me to his house for supper. Pr at 7:00 at New River Sch. H., Ez. 33:11. Two seekers. Stay at Rev. Daniel McKeel's .

Monday, October 17 Spent the day at McKeel's, mostly. Went with Bro. McKeel to Santa Fee Springs, and Whittier, a Quaker town about 6 months old. Both are largely laid out, but sparsely builded. Whittier on the Puenta foot-hills, a fine site. Pr. at New River at 7:00, Acts 26:28. Stay at Alex N. Thompson's, 1/2 mile north. Children: John, Guy, Paul, babe.

Tuesday, October 18 Stay at Thompson's in forenoon. Visit the Ostrich ranches in the afternoon. Twenty-two ostriches; 16 in one, and six in the other. Ranches 1 m. S. of Norwalk. Supper at Thompson's. Pr. at 7:00, at Sch. H., Deut. 18:18. Stay at Luke Charest's, one-third mile south. Children: Mina 13, Clarence 4, Mabel, 3 mo.

Wednesday, October 19 Stay at Charest's all day. Write up sketches. Mrs. Oscar Bloget, an invalid, comes in the afternoon. I preach at 7:00, Ps. 16:11, "At thy righteousness." Stay at Daniel McKeel's. Children: [blank]

Thursday, October 20 Stay at McK's all day. Read in Dugan Clark's "Offices of the Holy Spirit" and found many errors. Good man. Pr. at Sch. House at 7:00, Rom. 1:16. Audience smaller than heretofore. Stay at Alex. M. Thompson 's.

Friday, October 21 Stay at Thompson's till after dinner. Go via Charest's to Norwalk & back to Thompson's. Pr. at 7:00, Eph. 5:16, '"Redeem time." Stay at L. Charest's. There is a Holiness Church in Southern California— in Arizona & S. California; have about 400 or 500 members. Hardin Wallace & Ash Crafts conceived it. Wallace is their oracle.

Saturday, October 22 Stay at Luke Charest's till afternoon. Go to Norwalk, and thence with Bro. McKeel to his house. Pr. at 7:00, Rom. 8:15,16,17. I scored Quaker doctrine on special revelations, etc. A.M.T. much offended.

Sunday, October 23 Pr. at New River Sch. H. at 11:00, Ps. 87:3, treating largely of the merits of the church in all ages, and especially of the Churches in modern times. Dine at Wilbur Curtis'. Pr. at 7:00, Rom. 4:8. Close the meeting. Stay at Alex M. Thompson's.

Monday, October 24 Spent forenoon in fixing & brushing up my clothes at Bra. McKeel's. Go in afternoon to Norwalk with Bro. McK. Walk back via Charest's, W. Curtis'; and Thompson's to McKeel's. Stay there. Children: Sally 15; Elijah 14; Dan 6; Nelson 4.

Tuesday, October 25 Bro. Wilbur Curtis takes me to Downey. I go to Los Angeles. I call at King's office. Dine at Restaurant. Buy some books at Cor. Second & Main Sts. Go to Rev. T.F. Hallowell's. Stay there.

Wednesday, October 26 I attempt to go to Passadena with Bro. Hallowell. Just do miss the cars. Go to East Los Angeles. Climb a high hill and look toward Passadena. Return to Hallowell's and go to Palms with Henry Lowe. Lodge at Lowe's. Attend prayer Meeting at Rev. A.N. King's. Labeer's the Holiness folks.

Thursday, October 27 Went over to the new Church in forenoon. Ride out to Mr. Charnock's in afternoon. Return to Rev. A.N. King's. Stay there. Rev. Baumgardner & wife come to practice singing in the evening.

Friday, October 28 Go to Rev. Jacob Brown's & dine there. Call an hour at Mr. A. Stephen's. Call at Nat. Coe's & at Rev. A.N. King's. Stay at Rev. Jacob Brown's. Children: Mercy, Sarah, Caroline.

Saturday, October 29 Go to the new Church. Go to Los Angeles on 1:45 train. Call at Rev. A.N. King's office on Second St. Dine at Bakery Corner of Spring & Third St. Come back from town. Stay at Church till 9:00 pm. Stay at Rev. A.N. King's, 1 1/2 miles west.

Sunday, October 30 Pr. at 11:00, John 14:2. Raise $681.62 and dedicate the Palms Church— the 1st U.B. Church in southern California. Dine at Phineas Tibet's with Rev. M.S. Bovey. Call at Rev. J.W. Baumgardner's two hours before meeting. Rev. M.S. Bovey pr. at 7:00, Ps. 73:24. Stay at J.M. McLaughlin's.

Monday, October 31 Stay at McLaughlin's till after dinner. He takes me to Henry Lowe's. Rev. A.N. King's, and Rev. J.W. Baumgardner's. Supper at the latter place. Pr. at 7:00 at Palms, Ps. 16:11. Several asked prayers, as weak in faith. Stayed at Henry Lowe's.

Tuesday, November 1 Rev. W.P. Tibbet comes after me and takes me to his house in Santa Monica. Dine there. Take my first ocean bath in afternoon. Supper at Tibbet's. Go to meeting at Palms. Rev. M.S. Bovey pr. at 7:00, Hab. 3:2. Return with Tibbet to his house.

Wednesday, November 2 After some letter writing, another ocean bath. Letter to Simeon J. Lowe, Joslin, Illinois. Dine at Tibbet's. Ride to Santa Monica Canon & along the beach. Call at Rev. Leheigh's. His Indian adventures. Supper at Tibbet's. Sea Moss. Pr. at Palms, Acts 3:19. Praise meeting follows. Stay at Lewis Stephen's, 3 miles west.

Thursday, November 3 Went to Rev. Jac. Brown's, and thence to Palms & Machado. Take Rev. M.S. Bovey & Elizabeth, his sister, to Jac. Brown's. Stay there till 4:00. Then I go to Rev. A.N. King's. Supper there. Rev. M.S. Bovey pr. at 7:30, again from Hab. 3:2. I stay at Rev. A.N. King's. Child: Abr., Edith, Frank, Fred. Howard, Maimie, Oscar, Walter; David Bryant boards there.

Friday, November 4 Staid at King's all day. Wrote up a number of sketches. Rev. M.S. Bovey called in the afternoon on a pastoral visit. Dinner, supper, and lodging at Bro. King's. I pr. at Palm at 7:30, Ez. 33:11. Belle McLaughlin under deep conviction.

Saturday, November 5 Stay at Bro. King's till 11:00. Dine at Henry Lowe's. Pack my valises somewhat. Call at Bro. Baumgardner's— Bovey's keeping the house. Supper there. Go to Machado. Get a letter & a card. Rev. M.S. Bovey pr. at 7:30, Jas. 5:20. Cyrus Coe & preacher has a little bout over his clicking watch chain. Stay at Rev. Jac. Brown's. Four arose for prayer. Belle one.

Sunday, November 6 Preach at 11:00 at Palms from Phil. 2:9. Began dull, ended animatedly. Dine at Phineas Tibbet's. Call at Baumgardner's & find Bovey alone. Supper there. Pr. at 7:00, Rom. 7:9, 10. Bovey raised 35.00 for me. Stay at Rev. A.N. King's.

Monday, November 7 Go on cars to Los Angeles. Call at Hallowell's. Go on Santa Fee train to Pasadena, Raymond Hotel, Acme Hotel. Talk with Hayes owner of one of the first lots. Walk up the hill—fine door yards. Return to Los Angeles. Buy several books at second hand Bookstore. Go to Rev. T.F. Hollowell's. She gives me a lot of sea mosses.

Tuesday, November 8 Go to Santa Fee depot. Have to wait till 4:00. Dine at the Spencer House Restaurant. Went to A. Wood's South of Temple St. cable-road. Return to Mr. Chapin's office. Go to Depot & start for Riverside. Reach there between 8:00 & 9:00. Rev. H.S. Munger meets me & takes me to his house on Walnut betw 8th & 9th.

Wednesday, November 9 Get letters at the office. Munger takes me out to see new U.B. Church house. Call at Mrs. Martha Hall's. Dine at Bro. Munger's. Ride out to Henry Cole's on East side. Supper & lodging at Bro. Munger's. Their children: Lilly, Bessie 7, Pearly 4.

Thursday November 10 Write in forenoon till 11:00. Go to Hall's. Stay there till meeting. Prayer meeting at 7:00, followed by some calculation on the cost of the church and its indebtedness. Stay at Hall's. Children: Samuel 22; *William 17, Harvey 15; George 9. Two married daughters in Nebraska. *Wm. died.

Friday, November 11 Take Samuel Hall's rig, and with H.S. Munger, go down Magnolia Ave. Dine at Suman's. Call at Able's. See R.R. agent. Call at Church. Go home with Peter Suman. Their only living daughter is Belle, aged about 22.

Saturday, November 12 Stay at Suman's till after dinner. Go to town to the Church. Call at Martha Hall's. See Cole & Bell. Buy articles for going home. Get clothes at China town. Stay at Bro. Munger's.

Sunday, November 13 Preach at the new Church, the first Sermon preached in it, John 21:17, "Thou knowest all things, etc." Dine at Mrs. Hall's. Pr. at 3:00, dedication sermon, Rev. 21:24. Raise $505.00, & $50.00 more has been promised. Call at Munger's. Hear Connell lecture at Baptist Church at 7:00 on Temperance. I follow on Moral Aspect. Stay at Rev. H.S. Munger's.

Monday, November 14 Prepare to start home. Have to go on S. Pac. R.R. which starts from Colton at 9:10. So I stay. Dine at Munger's. Go in afternoon to see site of Reubidoux Hotel. Drive down to see Indians huts made of tule. Supper at Munger's & lodging. Attended official meeting at 7:00. Buy Comforter & tin cup.

Tuesday, November 15 Start at 6:55 to Colton. Call on Mother Suman and Mrs. Findlay & on Mrs. Kemp, of Illinois, & Miss Snyder. Buy some articles of food etc. Wait 2:20 hours on train. Start a little before 12:00. Train dines at Indio. Get to Tuxon about 8:00. Sleep five or six hours. Ticket to Dayton cost $50.50.

Wednesday, November 16 Behind time. Catch a Tarantula at Bowie & find a section of a centipede. Our car set off at last (on acct. hot box). Another halt at Deming on account of a broken rod. Reach E1paso about 6:00. Change cars for New Orleans. Travel all night.

Thursday, November 17 Awaken at Samuels. Breakfast at Langtry. Pass Del Rio, a town of 1,000 inhab. Western way is rolling winding. Cliffs on Rio Grande. Painters Cave. Reach San Antonio at 4:20 P.M. A town of about 35,000 inhabit. Nice country east of the city. Our cars wrecked at Rosenburg Junction abt. 5:00.

Friday, November 18 Arrive at Houston, about 7:00 a.m. Go on through Belmont. Cross Trinity and Sabine Rivers. In Louisiana. Ride in palace car to escape smoke. Tache Biou is a great sugar region. Connect at New Orleans for Cincinnati. Sleep about six hours. Saw Mobile by street lights.

Saturday, November 19 Awake about Evergreen. Pass Greenville. See cane-brake. Walk out on streets of Montgomery, Call at Birmingham. Pass Decatur. Reach Nashville after night. Go on through Boling Green & Louisville, toward Cincinnati. Find frost at Nashville. Slept 2 hours. Saw Dr. J.D. Barbee of Nash. *Chr. Adv.* & Col. Colier of *Nash. American.*

Sunday, November 20 Arrive at Cincinnati at 6:35. Arrive at home at 11:00, Dayton, Ohio. Being less than five days from Colton, Cal. Reuchlin & Lulu & babe came. Also Rev. H. Floyd. Also John A. Gilbert & wife & W.L. Gilbert. Slept ten hours. I had left home on May 23rd. Was away nearly six months.

Monday, November 21 At home. Feel sleepy and tired. Go over & get my trunk from Depot. Pennsylvania colored man engages to saw two cords of wood for Wilbur. Slept 8 hours.

Tuesday, November 22 At home in forenoon. Rev. Halleck Floyd came in afternoon. I called at Dr. L Davis in the evening. Slept 8 hours.

Wednesday, November 23 Spent much of the forenoon in clearing up my writing desk. Floyd called in the afternoon. In the evening, wrote an article for the *Conservator.*

Thursday, November 24 Rewrote the article on the "Millennium's Approach." Reuchlin and Lulu took dinner with us and spent the day at our house. Wrote some letters. A rainy day. Alfred Feight called in to see about Southern California.

Saturday, November 26 At home. Spent day mostly in reading and writing and in putting my clothes in order. Dr. Lewis Davis called in and spent an hour. Mrs. Glenn called a half hour in the afternoon. I went about dusk, to look after the new levy.

Sunday, November 27 Attended Summit Street Church at 10:30 about 175 or 200 present. Matthews pr. Ps. 96. 8, 9. At home the rest of the day.

Tuesday, November 29 At home in the forenoon. Went to town in the afternoon. Called at D.L. Rike's residence; at Mission Rooms; did some trading. After supper took proofs to Grabill's. Called at Rev. Wm. Dillon's a few minutes.

Wednesday, November 30 Went to Reuchlin Wright's, Grabill's, Dillon's. Got home at dinner time. Spent the afternoon mostly in brushing and sponging my clothes.

Thursday, December 1 Called at Reuchlin's in the morning. At home all the rest of the day. Called at Reuchlin's in the evening.

Friday, December 2 At home in the forenoon. Went to town in afternoon shopping with Katie.

Sunday, December 4 Attended Qr. meeting at High Street and heard the presiding-elder, Rev. S.W. Keister preach, Ex. 12:26, last clause, a good sermon. Communion service, which I conducted. At home the rest of the day.

Monday, December 5 At home. Called at Reuchlin's in the forenoon a little while. Lulu called in the afternoon.

Wednesday, December 7 At home. Went to town & did some trading in afternoon. Lost my fountain pen.

Friday, December 9 Went to town before noon. Left Katie's breast-pin at Reeve's jewelers. Could learn nothing of my lost fountain-pen. Reuchlin called in the evening. Sat up late reading.

Saturday, December 10 Arose early. Slept an hour in the forenoon. Was to attend a meeting of the Ex. Cam. Mission board. Met the committee at 2:00. Nothing of of [repeated in text] very special interest.

Sunday, December 11 Attend church at Summit Street. Rev. G.M. Matthews pr. at 10:30, Eph. 1:6 an able discourse & good so far as sound. At home the rest of the day and in the evening.

Monday, December 12 At home all day. Busy adjusting papers in my desk, etc.

Tuesday, December 13 At home all the day. Adjust the doors of the house all over. Visited Reuchlin's in the evening.

Wednesday, December 14 At home all day. Fix up things some what and write some.

Sunday, December 18 Staid at home with Mrs. Wright while Wilbur went to Church. Did not leave home all day.

Monday, December 19 Went to Richmond on 8:10 train. Go to D.K. Zeller's and stay till morning. Counted up the interest on Mother Koerner's note and paid it off in full. Got Mother Koerner pair of net slippers.

Tuesday, December 20 Went on 10:10 train to Anderson. Met Rev. Wm. Davenport & Ithamar McCarty at the depot. Called at Fairmount and then walked out to Aunt Lizzie Reeder's, 5 ms. S.E. But a Mr. White took me part of the way on a lumber wagon. Lodge at Aunt's.

Wednesday, December 21 Stay at Aunt's till afternoon. Went over to the farm and look over it, Called at Leir Simon's & Henry Simon's & went by saw-mill to see Ellis Wright's new field. Return to Aunt's & lodge there.

Thursday, December 22 Went to Wm. H.H. Reeder's and staid all day. Aunt Lizzie dined there. I wrote some letters. Stay at William's.

Friday, December 23 Remained at Wm's till after dinner made an even settlement with William and certified it with each of our names. Sold him my hay at $5.50 per ton, to be paid in fencing before summer. Wm. takes me to Fairmount. Stay at Rev. N.D. Wolfard's.

Saturday, December 24 Gave Wolfard $5.00, his wife $1.00. Went on 7:00 train to Jonesborough and Union City, arriving at home about 5:00 p.m. Cars so much crowded all the way. Talked a little with Rev. Mr. Robinson who has recently organized an independent Wesleyan church at Union City.

Sunday, December 25 This is the first Christmas, for several years, that I have been at home. Reuchlin & Luly & baby dine with us. I did not leave home through the day.

Monday, December 26 At home. Mrs. Feight called in the afternoon; Rev. H. Floyd in the evening. Suffered from dental neuralgia at night.

Tuesday, December 27 At Home. I spent much of the day in classifying my papers.

Wednesday, December 28 Col. Robt. Cowden came in forenoon & staid till after dinner.

[At the end of the diary]
Jan 1:1888.
Went to Summit St. Church. Heard Rev. G.W. Funkhouser pr. a New Year sermon, I Pet. 4:7,8. At home in afternoon. In eve. at 7:00 heard Rev Brown pr. "Set

thine house in order," Isa. "For this Year thou shalt die" Jer. One seeker.

A.D. 1887
Paid Wm. Dillon, Feb. 10th, $3.50, for all subscribers sent in up to that time by me. Paid March 18, $85.00 to Lorin on note. Paid March 10, Dr. Sample $10.00 for Mrs. W's new teeth. Paid April 9, Lorin $50 on note. Borrowed April 8th $50.00 of Rev. Wm. Dillon. Paid him Apr. 13. Got $60 on share of Father's estate. Sent $92.00 to Lorin. Rec. of Wm. Dillon $20.00. Got with it a draft for $20.00, in his name. Sent it to E.C. Wyatt. Received of McKee $200.00 of appropriation to Pac. Dist. Sent $20.00 home in June, and later in June, $29.00. Sent Reuchlin a present of $20.00. Fare to Albany .75 Salem .60 Hack & lunch at Salem .70 Total 2.05. Hack to McCoy 1.00 Hotell [sic] at McCoy .25 Fare to Amity .15.

Walla Walla Conf.
Members Received 1887. Frank J. Van Winkle, Weston. Fernin L. Hoskins. Wala Walla, Feo. W. Tenney.

McNiel's Liniment

Essence peppperment	1 Part
Essence Cinnamon	1 Part
Tinc. Rhubarb	1 Part
Comp. Spir. Lavender	1 Part
Spir. Camphor	2 Parts
Laudanum	3 Parts
Sulphuric Ether	4 Parts
Number Six	8 Parts

Anderson's Hair Invigator

Alcohol	3/4 pint
Castor Oil	1/4 pint
Oil of Clovers	20 drops
Tincture Anclusen	1 teaspoon

Shake well & let stand several hours.

For Hoarseness

Aromatic Sulphuric Acid	2 oz.
Tinc. Sanguinarim	2 oz.
Tinc. Sapsicum	1 oz.
Spirits Menatha	10 drops
Syrrup Simplex	2 oz.

Dose for dipth. a teaspoon every 2 hours.

Cleaning Mixture

Sulphuric Ether	1 oz.
Castile Soap	1 oz.
Glycerene	1 oz.
Alcohol Spirits	1 oz.
Aqua Amonia (3d Strength)	4 oz.

Dissolve the soap in two quarts of soft water; then add the other ingredients. Use with flannel rag or soft brush. Rinse in clean water until free from dirt & soap. Then rub with dry flannel and stretch in shape to dry.

Bell Founderies Vanduzen & Tift, Cin. McShane & Co., Troy, N.Y. Kimberly & Co., Troy, N.Y.

Good Mueilage
To smoothe flour paste, add oil of cloves or of peppermint, to preserve it.

Muelige
Cherrry [sic] or peach gum or gumarabic. Add carbolic acid.

Expense of trip to Washington Ter. etc.	
Ticket to Chicago	$5.15
Ticket to St. Paul	5.75
Ticket to Palouse	33.75
Lunch	1.00
Items afterward	.50
" "	.50
Ticket to Colfax	5.35
Hotel at Palouse J.	1.00
Trip to Huntsville	1.00
Fare to Portland	15.00
Philomath	4.25
Traveling in Or. & W	13.37
Through to Calif	4.45
Including all	18.35
Hotel at Anderson	1.50
Ander. to Biggs	2.55
Hotel & victuals	.65
Fare to Lodi & Woods.	3.60
Fare to Selma	4.30
Fare to Los Angeles	9.10

In Calif. cars   5.65
Fare to Dayton   50.50
Other expenses   2.50
Chas B. & Sarah Harris' Children & their Companions
Edward Harris
Mary (Heddrick) Harris
James F. Harris
Zena R. Harris
Laura Winchell
Austin Winchell
Charles W. Harris
Mary Harris
Harvey B. Harris
Hope E. Harris
Ella Reese
Napoleon B. Reese
Oral C. Harris
Emma Harris
Kate Vanfleet
Marshal H. Vanfleet
Estella (Harris) Petrie
Clara Gilbert
Leonard A. Gilbert
Frank Petrie

Walla Walla Conf. 1887. Began June 16, 1887 at 8:30
Allotments of Labor, 1887
Palouse Dist.— N. Evans, P.E.
Spokane Cir.— G.W. Tenney.
Garfield Cir.— W.H. Sherrod
South Palouse Mis.— A.E. Helm.
Moscow Cir.— M.E. Bailey
Genessee M.— J.I. Mitcham
Asotin M.— R.B. Mason
Pataha M.— A.J. Sherrod
Dayton M— W.R. Lloyd
Huntsville M. Stn.— W.S. Walker

Walla Walla Dist.— J.M. Tresenater, P.E.
Wash. Mis.— J.C. Spoonemore
Walla Walla M. Stn.— C.C. Bell
Centerville Ct.— A.R. Olds
Adams Mis.— G.W. Bailey
Umatilla Cir.— J.J. Gallaher
Lexington M.— J.T. Hoskins
Wasco M.— T.J. Cocking
Dufur M.— J.M. Pratt

Fox Valley M.— John Marquis
Grand Ronde.— C.W. Wells
Conf. Evangelist— J.S. Rhoads

Allotments of Labor
Oregon 1887

Umpqua Dist. J.G. Mosher, P.E.
Coast Mis.— C.B. Masters
Coos Mis.— J.G. Mosher
Umpqua Mis.— To be supl.

Willamette Dist.— J.W. Pulley, P.E.
Lane Mis.— A. Bennett
Linn Mis.— A. Bennett
Alsea Mis.— T.P. Connor
Philomath Cir.— J.C. Keezel
Marion Mis.— J.W. Engle
Yarnhill Mis.— Jas. R. Parker
Washington Mis.— E.C. Wyatt
Nahalem Mis.— W.H. Palmer
Columbia Mis.— J.H. Alexander
Lewis River Mis.— W.J. Campbell

Bishop's Salary, 1887
Walla Walla Conference

Chart Coll.	44.20
Pub. Coll.	35.30
Father B.J. Hunt	5.00
Other	2.00
[Total]	$86.50

Oregon Conference

Chart Coll.	82.95
Public Col. Sabbath	41.62
Joseph Gragg (after some weeks)	2.00
Bellevue Collection	6.00
Zumwalt	.75
Ingles (washing & back)	.75
Coll. at Abiqua	4.65
Given at Seely's	3.00
Mountain View	1.90
[Total]	143.62

California Conferences

Happy Valley (Shasta)	6.60
Feather River	11.00

1 8 8 8

Sunday, January 1 Heard Prof. G.A. Funkhouser pr at Summit Street Church, a New Year's sermon, 1 Pet. 4:7,8. At home all the afternoon. Heard Rev. Brown pr at 7:00 at Broadway M.E. chruch, Isa "Set thine house in order." "For this day thou shalt die," Jer. They had one seeker.

Monday, January 2 Went to town in afternoon, Bought fountain pen. Wrote letters. Paid $3.50 for pen.

Tuesday, January 3 Went to Dr. L. Davis' and paid interest on note. Gave a new note, dated Jan. 17th. Went to town & made a few purchases. Wrote some letters in afternoon and evening.

Wednesday, January 4 Went to town in forenoon and made purchases. Went in the afternoon to Rev. Wm. Dillon's to see Bro. Peter Minton. Wrote in the evening.

Thursday, January 5 At home all day. Spent much of the day in culling letters, destroying many not needing preservation. Bought watch-key and clock-cord at Henneman's. Tried my new hard coal stove.

Friday, January 6 At home all day. Spent time in lighting up my room and writing letters.

Saturday, January 7 At home all day. Wrote a card for the *Conservator* correcting the statement that I voted in 1869 for Warner's paper concerning amendment of the Constitution on Secrecy. Began to foot up charts for my an. Rep.

Sunday, January 8 Went to hear Rev. Montgomery at Third St. Presbyterian Church at 10:30, 1 Cor. 15 Chap. 46 v. Delivered in good style (not read) and with good ability. Reuchlin & family came awhile in the afternoon. Heard Rev. G.M. Matthews at 7:00, Rev. 3:20, at Summit St. U.B. Church.

Monday, January 9 Called at Davis' and Reuchlin's in the forenoon. Answered Rev. Daniel McKeel's inquiries concerning Oregon & Washington.

Tuesday, January 10 Made my annual report for the Rel. Telescope. Mrs. Sines called to see Susan.

Wednesday, January 11 At home all day. Engaged in reading & Study. Examined the Greek terms in the New Testament which are translated "servant" "served," etc.

Friday, January 13 Call at Rev. Wm. Dillon's and put in a correction for the Conservator. Call at Reuchlin's. Lulu visits us in the afternoon. Rev. J.W. Hott's calls in the evening.

Sunday, January 15 Heard Rev. W.F. McCauley, pastor at Park Pres. Ch. pr. Rom. 15.13. He a good speaker. Pr. 25 minutes. At home the rest of the day.

Monday, January 16–Friday, January 20 Went to town in forenoon. At home the rest of the day.—At home most of day. Called at Reuchlin's in the afternoon.—At home.

Saturday, January 21 Wrote letters most of the day. Called to see Dr. Davis in the afternoon.

Sunday, January 22 At home in the forenoon. Went to Raper Chapel and heard at 7:00 Rev. Royal pr. John 3:3. Katie went with me.

Monday, January 23 Went to town in the afternoon. Got a clergyman's permit on the I.B.W. R.R. Bought a crib for Catherine L. Wright as a present from her grandmother.

Tuesday, January 24 At home writing. Lulu called. Vent to Grace M.E. Church. Heard Miller, the evangelist, preach at 7:30, John 14:6. Good.

Wednesday, January 25 Gave Dillon an article on "the real authors of strife." Called at Reuchlin's. Heard Rev. J.P. Landis pr. at 7:30, Heb. 2:3.

Thursday, January 26 Went to town to see about tickets shop. Called in incidentally to hear Mr. Potter's Bible reading on Separation from world. Attended Grace meeting in the evening.

Friday, January 27 Wrote some letters in the forenoon. Went to town in the afternoon, shopping, but especially to hear the discourse at Grace Church on the Holy Ghost. Floyd called. Called at Dr. Davis' in the evening, awhile.

Saturday, January 28 Called at Dr. Davis' on financial business. Went to town in the afternoon. Got a Certif. of deposit for Dr. L. Davis in the bank & paid to Dr. Davis one hundred and fifty dollars on my note.

Sunday, January 29 Went to Miami Chapel and pr. Acts. 26.28. Thirteen joined Church. I was invited to John Rider's and other places but came home for dinner. Went in the evening to Grace M.E. Church. Heard Potter pr. Gal. 6:7. House crowded.

Monday, January 30 At home. Called in afternoon at J.K. Gra[y]bill's and Reuchlin's. Harvey Wright & his daughter Rhoda came on a visit.

Tuesday, January 31 Called in the forenoon at Reuchlin's with Harvey and his daughter. Afternoon Wilbur & Rhoda looked at the city. In the evening I went to Reuchlin's to conduct home our visitors who had supped there.

Wednesday, February 1 At Home. My Bro. Harvey and his daughter started home via Richmond & Dunreith at 12:15. Katie unwell in the evening and through the night. J.G. Feight & wife called in, an hour. Petition against change from Electr. to Gas.

Thursday, February 2 At home. Got first paper, the *Journal*. Did little except to read. Katie at home quite unwell. Coughed much at night.

Friday, February 3 Wrote an article for the Christian Cynosure, "The Situation." Mrs. Wm. Wagner called in afternoon.

Sunday, February 5 Heard Rev. Baker pr. at First Lutheran Church, 10:30, Matt. 17:5, "Hear ye him." An earnest young man of ability. At night hear Rev. H.F. Colby at 7:00, Matt. 20:34, "So Jesus had compassion on them." Preached 23 minutes. He Baptized three persons—one woman & two men—in the baptistery.

Monday, February 6 Called at Reuchlin's (Wright's) in the forenoon. In afternoon went to town, made a box and shipped Lorin's (Wright's) guitar to him at Cold Water, Kansas.

Tuesday, February 7 At home all day. Busy filing letters etc., mostly.

Wednesday, February 8 At home all day. Dr. L. Davis called in the evening to see if I would consent to go to New Orleans as a delegate to the Nat. Chr. Associa.

Thursday, February 9 Called forenoon at Reuchlin's & Dr. L. Davis'. Miller called to trade property. Mrs. Feight called in the afternoon.

Friday, February 10 At home. Wrote some letters. Mrs. McHenry called to see Susan.

Saturday, February 11 Went to "town" with Orville for purchases. At home in the afternoon writing.

Sunday, February 12 Went to High Street U.B. Church, and heard Rev. J. Kilbourn, pastor, pr., Mal. 3:10. Six joined church. I declined to preach, supposing correctly that the pastor had prepared a special discourse for the occasion. Reuchlin & fam. & Mrs. Henry Wagner called. With Katie, heard Rev. Dennis at Third St. Pres. at 7:00, Matt. 18:1-4.

Tuesday, February 14 At home. Reading. In afternoon, went to town. Got shoes, pocket compass, medicine for Susan. Called at Dr. L. Davis', in the evening & at Reuchl. Beebe's Catarrh remedy came after noon.

Friday, February 17 Wrote an article on "Variable Opinions." Dr. L. Davis called in afternoon.

Saturday, February 18 Called at L. Davis', D.D. and at Wm. Dillon's & at Reuchlin's in forenoon. Gave D. article for pub. Went to town in the afternoon. Bought a ticket for lecture, etc. Did not find Dr. Spitler at home. Katie brought Cath. Louise to see Susan.

Sunday, February 19 Hear Rector of Christ's Episcopal Church pr. at 11:00, Math. 11; 5:16. Rained as Katie & I went home. Heard Rev. F.V. Brown preach at M.E. Church, Broadway, Text Matt. 25.10.

Wednesday, February 22 Went to town with the children. Got Katie dress goods. Got Orville a coat and vest at 8.10. In afternoon took Susan out pleasure riding and on a visit to Reuchlin's.

Thursday, February 23 Start at 7:25 via Union City & Anderson to Fairmount. Arrive about 2:00. Go to Rev. N.D. Wolford's N.S. Mygrants comes. Cell & wife there. Supper & lodging there. Pr. at 7:30 Eph. 2:4. Large congregation.

Friday, February 24 Went to Jno. B. Hollingsworth's. Called at Nathan Vincent's to see Mother Parson's—Mr. Rich there. Dine at Hollingsworth's, with Rev. Wm. Hall. A rainy afternoon. Go to Rev. Jac. Hester 's. Stay there on account of rain. Robt. Carter & Frank Norton, there.

Saturday, February 25 The gas-regulator out of order and the stoves in town low. Call at Hall's and at Wolford's. Go to Aunt Lizzie Reeder's. She recovering from heart-disease. Come back to Fairmount. Supper at Wolford's. Pr. at Friend's Church, Acts 3:19. Stay at Wolford's.

Sunday, February 26 Pr. at Union 2 m. S. of Fairmount, John 21:17. Dine at Robt. Hastings. Call to see Carter Hastings & wife. He quite unwell. She blind for years. Call at Absalom Anderson. She sick for months. Call at John Smith's. She almost helpless—He very hard of hearing. Pr. at 7:00 Ps. 16.11. Stay at N.D. Wolford's.

Monday, February, 27 Get a letter from Katie inclosing one from Lorin. Call at Elwood Davis'. Dine there. Called also at Conners & see Mother Nottingham. Go on 1:16 train to Warren. Elijah Morrison took me to his house. Pr. at Bethel Ps. 16.11. Stay at Thos. Clampitt's. Kabrich there sick.

Tuesday, February 28 Meeting at 10:00. Right good. Go to Silas Poling's one mile north. Stay till evening. Pr. at 7:00 Acts 3:19. Some misbehavior. Stay at Thos. B. Clampitt's.

Wednesday, February 29 Meeting at 10:00. Few out, but a good meeting. Go to George Gaizer's. Dinner & supper there. Rains some in afternoon & evening. Pr. at 7:00, Mal. 3.1. Stay at Thos. B. Clampitt's.

Thursday, March 1 Went to David E. Elliott's, dined, & staid till after three o'clock. Returned with Bro. Clampett & wife & Bro. Kabrick to Silas Poling's. Supper there. Pr. at Bethel at 7:00, Prov. 2.9.1. It had become very muddy & we closed meeting. Staid at Elijah Morrison's, 1 1/4 mile west.

Friday, March 2 Went to George Huffmans. Got Kabrich's buggy. Mired down just N. of Mt. Zion. Dine, sup & lodge at Thos. B. Clampett's, with Rev. J.M. Kabrick. Clampitt's Children: Eldorah 14; Wm. H. 9.[Note: Spelling changes for "Clampett" exist in text of the diary]

Saturday, March 3 Start to Zion Chapel. Go to Harvey M. Trick's three miles N.W. Dine there. Go on to Zion Chapel. Supper and lodging at Joseph Eubanks. Grandchildren living there: James Eubanks, Mary Delphina.

Sunday, March 4 Pr. at Zion, 10:30, Rom. 4.8. Dine at George Shaffer's. Joseph Irick & Rev. J.M. Kabrich there. Mother Shaffer died three years ago. Pr. at 7:00, Rom.

8:35. Speaking meeting followed. Stay with Kabrich at Joseph Eubanks'.

Monday, March 5 Dine at Joseph Irick's, just north of Buck Eye Station with Bro. Kabrich. Go on 1:00 train to Marion. Call at P.O. & at Robt. W. Fryer's. Go on 5.40 train to Hartford City. Pr at U.B. Ch. at 7:00, Rom. 4:16. Stay at George Stallsmith's.

Tuesday, March 6 Rev. Robt. Miller called. Went to his house awhile. Called at Franklin Gronendyke's. Went on 10:40 train to Union City. Go on 2:15 train home to Dayton, Ohio. Arrive at 4:30.

Wednesday, March 7 At home & unwell with cold & sore throat.

Friday, March 9 Still at home. Improving a little in health. Mr. Brittain of Piqua called to see about buying our house.

Saturday, March 10 At home till afternoon when I went to "town" and got medicine for Susan.

Sunday, March 11 At home all day. The Children all went to Summit Street to meeting. Reuchlin & family came in the afternoon. Spent part of the afternoon and evening in looking up prophecies concerning the Jews.

Monday, March 12 At home in forenoon. Card from Greenfield, Io. Wilbur got a letter from Lorin. I go to town & send a draft on N.Y. to Jas. A. Hethrington of Greenfield, Iowa, for $23.67. Get a check from McKee for $100.00.

Tuesday, March 13 Went to the east side & bought material for pantaloons & in aftern took them to Austin. Went to Reuchlin's in aft'n. Called at Rev. Lewis Davis' D.D. but did not find him at home.

Wednesday, March 14 Called at Rev. L. Davis' D.D., before noon. Talk on Floyd's editorial. Reuchlin called in the afternoon awhile. Write some.

Thursday, March 15 At home. Wrote an article on "These Respects." Called at Reuchlin's in the afternoon. Mrs.

Sines & Mrs. Wm. Wagoner called to see Susan. Wrote letters in the evening.

Friday, March 16 Spent the day in looking over boxes of old magazines, newspapers, etc. Susan coughed a good deal and had a restless night.

Saturday, March 17 At home all forenoon. Spent some time preparing periodicals (Chicago pulpit, etc.) for binding. Went to town in afternoon. Bought Reuchlin a gold pen for a present, this being his birth-day. Cost $3.00—.40. Got clothes from the tailor. Susan coughed and had another restless night.

Sunday, March 18 At home all the forenoon. Not yet recovered from my cold. Susan more unwell from week to week. Katie sick with sore throat for several days past. Went in the evening and got medicine of Spitler for Susan. She rested easier.

Monday, March 19 Spent the day & evening mostly in writing letters. Susan a little better of her cough. She rested easier to-night, again.

Wednesday, March 21 Wrote letters in the forenoon. Called at Rev. Wm. Dillon's; and at Reuchlin's, in the afternoon. Gave in my article, entitled "These Respects."

Friday, March 23 At home till toward evening. Called at Reuchlin's & Dillon's.

Saturday, March 24 Called at Reuchlin's in the afternoon. Went in the evening to the drug store (Pretzinger's) to get medicine for Susan.

Sunday, March 25 At home. A rainy day. Susan about as for a week past. Reuchlin called in the afternoon. Read considerable in Blackburn's Church History. I dislike his stilted style.

Monday, March 26–Wednesday, March 28 At home. Write some letters. Read some, especially in church history.

Thursday, March 29 Called at Dr. L. Davis. Away. Dr. Davis called in the afternoon. Lulu came with Owley. Wrote some letters.

Saturday, March 31 Went to town (east-side) forenoon. Mrs. Henry Wagner, Mrs. Rebecca Davis, & Mrs. Lucretia Edwards called to see Susan.

Sunday, April 1 At home till evening. Reuchlin & family came in the afternoon & staid an hour. I heard Rev. Montgomery preach at 7:30, John 11:25, a good sermon. The father of Needham on Hawthorne St. died this morning about 5:00, suddenly.

Monday, April 2 At Home. Dr. Spitler called. Voted. Went to town. Sent tax to Grant Co., Ind. Sent for N.Y. *Tribune.*

Tuesday, April 3 Dr. H.A. Thompson called in the forenoon.

Wednesday, April 4 At home. Reuchlin called. "Aunt" Mary Inglehart called to see Susan.

Thursday, April 5 Called to see Dr. L. Davis. Write letters to my district. Clarence White, Susan's nephew, died at 10:30 a.m. they telegraphed us to that effect.

Friday, April 6 Spent the day mostly in reading. Writing some. Called at Reuchlin's.

Saturday, April 7 Went to town to Market, etc. Write a letter in afternoon. Felt little like any work. Peter Minton died this evening about 9:00.

Sunday, April 8 Hear Bp. Knickerbacker of Indianapolis pr. at 11:00, 1 John V. 11, 12., a sound revival sermon. About twenty-three persons were "confirmed." News of Peter Minton's death last evening. Reuchlin call. Hear Rev. A.B. Leonard pr. at Grace Church at 7:30, Prov. IV:23, an eloquent sermon.

Monday, April 9 Went on 8:25 train with Dr. L. Davis to Hamilton's & to Peter Minton's. His funeral at 2:00 by Dr. Davis. I made a few remarks. Burial at Hamilton Cemetery. His children: William, Harvey, Mary Kumler, Maria Clauson, Mrs. Rosencranz, Ida Hanaford, and [blank]. We came home on 6:20 train. Rainy aftern & eve.

Tuesday, April 10 At home. Rather a dull day.

Wednesday, April 11 Went to town in forenoon. Reuchlin & family dine with us, it being Lulu's birth-day. Call at Dr. L. Davis's.

Thursday, April 12 Called at Rev. Wm. Dillon's to leave dates, etc., on Peter Minton's life, death, etc. Called at Reuchlin's in the afternoon. Rev. H. Floyd supped with us. Call at Reuchlin's in the evening. Pretty, mild weather.

Friday, April 13 At home. Pretty, fair weather. Rev. Wm. B. Stoddard. Called a short time. He a son of Rev. J.P. Stoddard, and grandson of Pres. Jonathan Blanchard. He is State Agt. of Ohio Antisecrecy Association; married a few months ago. Nice weather still.

Saturday, April 14 In my study. Spent the afternoon largely in arranging a sermon & in familiarizing myself with its thought.

Sunday, April 15 Pr. for Rev. F.V. Brown at Broadway M.E. Church, 10:30, Gal 4:45. Aftn. at Rev. D.H. French's Church, U.P., heard Miss Mary Frazer of the Egyptian Mis'n and Miss Maggie McDill of Little Girl's Home, Knoxville, Tenn. Heard Rev. J.H. Graybeil, at 7:30 pr. at Fourth Pres. Church, Gal. 3:24.

Monday, April 16–Thursday, April 19 At home. Went to town. Called at Reuchlin's. Dr. L. Davis called. Write letters.

Saturday, April 21 At Home. Has been mild nice weather for weeks. Called over to town, in afternoon with Katie to get a hat for her. Called to get my vest at Rike's. Rev. B.W. Mason called an hour in the evening.

Sunday, April 22 Went to First Reformed Church & heard the Pastor, Rev. W.A. Hale pr. 1 Tim. 1:18, 19. At home the rest of the day. Rainy afternoon and evening.

Monday, April 23 At home. Rev. B.W. Mason called and staid all night.

Thursday, April 26 Went to market and shopping. After the morning, we needed no fire in the heating stoves. Called in the evening at Reuchlin's and Dr. L. Davis'.

Sunday, April 29 At Grace M.E. Church at 10:30, hear

Dr. Iliff, of Utah, 11 Pet. 1:19., pr. an eloquent discourse. Afternoon (3) at City Hall at McLean & Willit's evangelical services. At U.P. at night (7:30) hear Dr. D. McDill pr. Isa. 53.6—an able discourse Evang. Willits in aftn Pr. Isa. 40.31, at City Hall.

Monday, April 30 At home. Writing. This is the anniversary of Mrs. Wright's birthday, and we bought her a set of dishes, but they were not delivered. Called at Reuchlin's in the evening.

Tuesday, May 1 At home. Writing. Wilbur went over to see about the dishes,which they said were partly sold to some one else. He bought another set which were delivered.

Wednesday, May 2 At home. Children cleaning house. Called at Dr. Davis in forenoon for a temporary loan. Not feeling much like writing, I spent most of the day reading papers & Magazine.

Thursday, May 3 Went to town to market.

Friday, May 4 At home not feeling like doing much. Called at Reuchlin's in the evening. Winnie Billheimer there—had come the evening before.

Saturday, May 5 Went to market. Called at Reuchlin's. At home. Writing in afternoon & evening.

Sunday, May 6 Heard Rev. W. M. Beardshear pr. bacchalaureate sermon at Summit St. Heb. 12:1, 2. A rather ambitious, but not profound sermon. The sermon was at 10:30, at Summit St. Ch. At night (7:45) heard Rev. C.W. Stearn pr. at S. St., an. Sermon to students, 1 Cor. 1:21. An hour long; fair ability.

Monday, May 7 At home writing. Rev. A.H. Thompson called in the evening. Attended the entertainment of the students at Summit Street. Four orations. Brokaw, Leffler, Suter, & Coolee.

Tuesday, May 8 Meeting of the Board of Bishops. Pres. Thompson dines with us. Board of bishops still in session. Lightning struck the school-house. Rainy evening.

Wednesday, May 9 This is commencement day at U.B.

Sem. Ten graduates. Their addresses average very fine. Board of Bishops meet in after'n. Bishop Dickson & Halleck Floyd sup with us.

Thursday, May 10 Missionary Board meets at 9:00 a.m. In the afternoon some committees meet. B.F. Booth pr. Missionary sermon at 7:45, Rev. 17:14. Read quite monotonous.

Friday, May 11 Spat with McKee over an item in the An. Report. Debate in afternoon on repudiating $300 out of $416 due Oregon. Night session. I left about 10:00.

Saturday, May 12 Arose early. Wrote letters many to-day. Called at Reuchlin's in the forenoon. Lulu & Winnie called in afternoon.

Sunday, May 13 Walked to Miami Chapel with Katie. Rev. Doty pr. 10:30, John 12:32, a missionary discourse. Dealea 7 Rufus Mason dine with us. Reuchlin's call in the afternoon. Hear Rev. Baker preach at 1st Lutheran Ch. Prov. 22:29. 25 minutes.

Monday, May 14 Went to town & got a check of McKee for $200.00. Engage & buy clothes etc.

Tuesday, May 15 Went early to market. D.K. Zeller and wife came to visit us—she being Susan's sister Mary Caroline. Call with Zeller at Funkhauser's & at Reuchlin's. Reuchlin's call in the afternoon. Zellers go to Middletown, Ohio.

Wednesday, May 16 Everything tore up with house-cleaning. Call at Dillon's and Reuchlin's in the afternoon. D.K. Zeller & Caroline called an hour in the afternoon. Went to town but Dem. State Conv. had adjourned. Wrote letters.

Saturday, May 19 Called at Vleerbaums to see about R.R. fare. Wrote several letters. Called at J.H. Grabill's.

Sunday, May 20 Went to Grace M.E. Ch. Rev. J.W. Hott pr. Matt. 13.31, 32 Long discourse. Reuchlins came about 4:00 p.m. In evening at Memorial Presbyterian Church heard Rev. J.R. Hughes pr. on lectures on Sampson.

Monday, May 21 Went to town to see about R.R. fare.

Tuesday, May 22 Went to town & got of Charch my coat & pantaloons, as made to order. Had a tooth filled with "silver." Paid $1.50 for it (sample) which squares to date.

Wednesday, May 23 Went town. Charch's shorten my new pants. Pay for coat & pantaloons, $27.00. Pay Dr. Spitler $1.00 which squares up to date present. Bought 114 ft cordwood, $3.50, partly soft wood.

Saturday, May 26 At home in forenoon. Packing some for my trip. Reuchlin called. Go to town. Buy ticket, etc., for Pacif. Coast. Packing valises.

Sunday, May 27 Went toward Miami Chapel. Called in first at Warner's & then at Puterbaugh's. Hard rain & thundershower. Went back home. Katie with me. Reuchlin's call in the afternoon. Did not go anywhere in evening.

Monday, May 28 Arose about 3:00. Got ready for my trip. Leave on 6:45 C.H. & D train——Hamilton—Indianapolis—Westfield—Frankfort—Delphi—Montecello—Monon—Chicago. Left Chicago 10:30, through Milwaukee and next morning Portage City, La Crosse, and Hastings to St. Paul.

Tuesday, May 29 Reach St. Paul at 1:30 p.m. Detained by ticket agt., at Gen. Office, 3/4 of an hour and thereby miss my train, losing thereby 24 hours time. Stay at Nicollet House 3 squares N.West of depot. Slept well.

Wednesday, May 30 Good breakfast. Went to Depot and wrote letters. Bought ticket (half-fare) to Palouse Junction $33.75. Went on train which starts precisely at 4:00 p.m. Reached Bell Prairie about dusk. Slept about 5 hours & took a nap next forenoon.

Thursday, May 31 Reach Bismarck about 10:00. Detained considerably by a hot journal. Pass Glendive before night. Bad lands from Fryburg to past Glendive. Slept perhaps six hours.

Friday, June 1 Awaken about Custer. Go on to Helena & thence over the divide of the Rockies. The tunnel not yet complete. Very steep grade. Reach Horse Plains before night. Rapid running in the night. Slept four or five hours. Slept an hour next forenoon.

Saturday, June 2 Reach Spokane Falls about 4:00 a.m. Reach Palouse Junction on close time & change cars for Elberton. Reach there about 4:00 P.M. Put up at Father Jas. Pickard's. Reach the tent before meeting closed. Supper at Pickard's. Rev. J.A. Kenoyer pr. Ps. 34:6. I stay at Pickard's.

Sunday, June 3 Pr. at the tent at 11:00, 2d Cor. 3.7,8. I raise about $260.00 for new church. At 3:30 raise $95 more & formally dedicate the Church. Rev. Jer. Kenoyer pr at the church at 8:00, without a text. I stay at Jas. Pickards.

Monday, June 4 Morning meeting at 10:00. Good. Dine at Hildrith's with Kerns & wife. Rev. Brassfield comes, a M.E. South young preacher. Aftern meeting. Kerns pr. Supper at Gurnsey's. Pr at 8:00, Ez. 33.11. Stay at Pickards.

Tuesday, June 5 Stay at Pickard's all day. Rev. Brassfield pr. at 8:00, Amos [blank] "prepare to meet thy God." I stay at Pickard's.

Wednesday, June 6 Meeting at 10:00. Small attendance. Dine at [blank] Supper at Rev. H.O. Kerns'. I Pr. at 8:00, Ez. 33:11. Stay at Rev. H.O. Kern's.

Thursday, June 7 Called at Pickard's. Kerns takes me down to Rev. J.A. Kenoyer's. Dine there. Rainy day. Call at Rev. J.S Rhodes. His son, James, was drowned last week. Went back to Kerns. Stay there. He formerly at Roanoke, Indiana, and later at Western, Iowa.

Friday, June 8 Went on the 8:30 train to Colfax & thence to Pampa. Stage to Riperia on Snake River. Stay at the Hotel there. Our way from Pampa was up a gentle can[y]on 4 miles & then down the can[y]on 14 ms. Hills rose on each side of the latter from 150 to 300 feet.

Saturday, June 9 Leave on train for Huntsville at 10:00. Arrive at Bowles Junction at 12:30. Train to Huntsville comes at 4:15. Stop at B.J. Hunt's. Rev. J. Black calls and sits till bed-time. I stay at Hunt's. I had a tedious waiting at Bolles' Junction, which is a deserted depot.

Sunday, June 10 Go to M.E. Camp-meeting 1 1/2 m east. Rev. I.D. Driver pr at 11:00 Titus 2:11,13. Dine with Pollard a M.E. I Pr at 2 1/2 Mal. 3:1. Supper at Rev. Black's at Huntsville. He takes me to Dayton. Pr. at 8:00, Heb. 11:26. Stay at Rev. W.R. Lloyd's.

Monday, June 11 Go back to Huntsville. Dine at B.J. Hunt's. Call at Rev. J. Black's, at Rev. J.S. Spoonemore's and Rev. J. M. Tresenriter's . Start at 3:00 for Conference. Delay at Waitsburg. Call at Hasting's. Stay at Smith's.

Tuesday, June 12 Went on with Revs. Black and Spoonemore via Walla Walla and Milton to Weston. Dine at L.G. Bradens, 4 miles below Walla Walla. Put up at W. Helmer's in Southwest part of Weston. R. Cowden has a S.S. Lesson at 8:30.

Wednesday, June 13 Conference opened at 9:00. Secretary elected on 13th ballot. Examination in afternoon. Dinner & Supper & lodging at W. Helmer's. Rev. J.T. Hoskins pr at 8:30.

Thursday, June 14 Session continued. Spoonemore referred to Com. on Grievance. Rainy afternoon. Col. R. Cowden gives a lecture on Qualifications of Sab. School teachers. I was not present.

Friday, June 15 Conference continued. Spoonemore passed. Dine at Helmer's. Supper there. Prof. Walker's Educational Address. Small Subscriptions. Stay as usual at Helmer's.

Saturday, June 16 Quite a discussion in conference on the appointment of "Commission tellers." Afternoon N. Evans & J.N Tresenriter elected P.E.'s. Adjourn about 6:00 p.m. Stationing Com. meets at Helmer's. Rev. J.S. Rhodes pr. at 8:30. Stay at Helmer's.

Sunday, June 17 Preach Conf. Sermon at 11:00, Deut. 32:31. Ordain J.I. Mitcham. Dine at Ginn's Sab. School Anniversary at 4:30. Cowden, J.J. Gallaher, & J. Kenoyer pr. at 9:00 p.m., Matt. 28:19,20. Close at 11:00. Stay at W. Helmer's. Retire at 12:00.

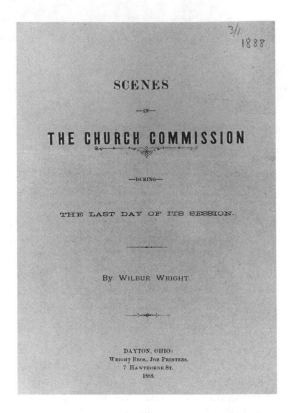

SCENES
—IN—
THE CHURCH COMMISSION
—DURING—
THE LAST DAY OF ITS SESSION.

By WILBUR WRIGHT.

DAYTON, OHIO:
WRIGHT BROS., JOB PRINTERS.
7 HAWTHORNE ST.
1888.

Monday, June 18 Rise early. Go on train to Walla Walla. Dine at restaurant. Had sat with Wells & wife and Col. Robt. Cowden at parsonage. Leave at 4:15, arrive Wallula at 6:00. Stay at depot till train at 9:35. Reach Pasco at 10:30. Lodge at hotel for 1.00. Slept four hours.

Tuesday, June 19 Arose early. Breakfast at a restaurant. Start at 5:45 for Ellensburg, Tacoma & Portland. Most of the day dark and rainy. Ran up the Yakima, across, Black and White Rivers & above the Puyallup. Ran through the Cascade tunnel in 8 minutes. Indian reserv'n. Tacoma, Tenino. Ar. Portland at 1:00 morn. Put up at Oregon H.

Wednesday, June 20 Got letters from home. Lost my umbrella. Got of O & C R.R. and Oregonian railroad half-fare permits. Did not find G.M. Miller's at home. Stay at Oregon House.

Thursday, June 21 Start on O & C (West Side) R.R. for Philomath. The banker Ladd (firm Bush & Ladd) and

Gov. S. Penoyer aboard. Get half fare permit at Corwallis on Oregon Pacific R.R. Arrive at Philomath at about 2:15. Put up at Pres. J.C. Keezel's. Attend prayer meeting at College Chapel. Stay at Keezel's.

Friday, June 22 Philomath College board meeting at 9:30. In board all day. College closing exercises at 8:00, followed by ice-cream supper. Supper & lodging at Pres. J.C. Keezel's.

Saturday, June 23 Call at J. Aiken's store. Call at Rev. M.M. Crow's. Dine at Rev. N.W. Allen's. Call at Rev. Ezra C. Wyatt's. Call at Pres. J.C. Keezel's. Supper & lodging at Mr. Jere Henkle's. Citizens at Philomath, L.F. Watkins, Peter Mason, Wm. Wyatt, John Wyatt.

Sunday, June 24 Call at Pres. J.C. Keezel's till meeting. Pr. at 11:00, Rom. 8:35. Dine at Rev. N.W. Allen 's. Attend class-meeting at 3:30. Then go to Pres. J.C. Keezel's. Pr. at 8:15, John 1:46. Large congregation. Stay at Pres. Keezel's.

Monday, June 25 Call at Rev. G.M Strope's. Also at Prof. H. Sheak's. Also at Cole's, whose wife is near death. Also at M.M. Crow's. Go on 10:00 train to Albany & thence to Woodburn & to Silverton. At Woodburn heard of Harrison's nomination for president. Go out to D.C. Hall's and stay there.

Tuesday, June 26 Called at A.J. Mosher's with Rev. J.W. Pulley. Dine at Hall's. Put some pastor's reports on the Conference Chart. Supper at Wm. Adair's. Several come in for conference. I stay at Hall's with Rev. J.W. Pulley & Mrs.Harritt.

Wednesday, June 27 Conference opened at 9:00. Few present. A. Bennett elected Sect'y. Examinations proceeded. Dine at Hall's. Examinations and chart reports continued. Supper & lodging at D.C. Hall's. Rev. A. Larkin pr at 8:30, John 14:15. Lodge at Hall's.

Thursday, June 28 Conf. continued. Adjourned at 10:30 for preaching. Rev. W.H. Palmer pr. at 10:30, Rom. 8:32. Dine at John Whitlock's. Afternoon, Boundy Com. report. Supper at Hall's. Rev. J.C. Keezel pr. 8:30, Heb. 6:1. Stay at Hall's.

Friday, June 29 Session continued. Memorial service of Rev. Jesse Harritt. Dine at John Whitlock's. Supper at D.C. Hall's. I pr at 8:30 Ps. 25:14. Lodge at Hall's.

Saturday, June 30 Session continued. Rev. J.H. Watson pr. at 11:00. Dine at Chas. Corby's cam—an old house near. Supper at D.C. Hall's. Stay at D.C. Hall's.

Sunday, July 1 I Pr. at 11:00, Ps. 68:20. It being rainy, Rev. Clark Braden lectured right after, on infidelity. He is following up Putnam an infidel lecturer. I dine at John Whitlock's with Pres. Keezel and J.R. Parker & wife. At 8:3[0] a Sacramental meeting and farewell. Stay at D.C. Hall's.

Monday, July 2 Rainy day. Watson & others call. Pulley pr at 8:30. Supper at Hall's. Stay at Hall's.

Tuesday, July 3 Dine at Mosher's. Call at Hall's. Supper at Wm. Adair's. Rev. J.W. Pulley pr at 8:30, Heb. 11:25, 26, 27. Stay at Hall's.

Wednesday, July 4 Went to Wm. G. Minear. Remain all day and night. Hall's go to take J.W. Pulley to Woodburn.

Thursday, July 5 Called at D.C. Hall's. Dine at John Whitlock's. Come back to Halls and spend the afternoon in writing. Supper at Halls. Pr. at Abiqua at 8:30, 1 Car. 15:32. Stay at W.R. Adair's.

Friday, July 6 Stay at Adair's till afternoon. Go to D.C. Hall's. Supper there. Pr. at 8:30, Job 21:15. Stay at D.C. Hall's. Wrote letters in the afternoon and prepared the evening sermon.

Saturday, July 7 Wrote letters in the forenoon. Went afternoon to Silverton. Got a letter from Rev. F. Fisher about change of California Conference time. Write letter to him, etc. Joseph Hall takes me to Warren Corby's. Stay there.

Sunday, July 8 Go to Liberty Sch. house. Pr. Jude 21st. Dine at Charley Corby's. Go to Grassy Pond Sch. house, at 6:00. Pr. Rom. 1.16, 30 min. Go back to Charles W. Corby's & lodge. Saw Geo. Vedder, Harding Baughman, Pendleton, M.E., Mrs. Van Cleve.

Monday, July 9 Went to Warren Corby's. Dine there. Write many letters—F. Stearns—A.G. Wright, H.S. Munger. Go to Woodburn and mail letters & papers. Supper at Warren Corby's. Go to Grassy Pond Sch-h. and preach, Acts 3:19 at 8:30. Stay at Charles McKee's 1/4 mile east. His wife was Luella Shank.

Tuesday, July 10 Called after dinner at Geo. Vedder's, M.E., at Wm. Gibbon's, at Abner & Belle Lenon's, and Pendleton's, M.E. Supper at Pendleton's. Pr. at 8:15, Rom. 10:1 Short speaking-meeting followed. Stay at Warren Corby's.

Wednesday, July 11 Stay at Corby's most of forenoon and part of afternoon. Dinner at Grant Corby's. Supper at W. Corby's. I went to town horse-back in afternoon and got a letter from Daughter Katie, dated July 3d. Supper at Warren Corby's. Pr. at 8:15, Rom. 14:17. Stay at Chas. W. Corby's.

Thursday, July 12 Stay at C.W. Corby's till afternoon. Go to W. Corby's and write a letter to Keezel & Stella Harris. Supper there. Stay there. Rainy day.

Friday, July 13 At W. Corby's till 5:00. Go to Woodburn. Got a letter from T.K. Gardner and answer it. Write a card to Wilbur. Stay at C.W. Corby's.

Saturday, July 14 Call at W. Corby's. Dine at Harding Baughman's. She a niece of Mrs. N.W. Allen. Go to Stn. near Pudding River and wait the Cars for McKee's station. Supper at David McKee's. Go on to George Vedder's. Stay there. He a M.E., also anti-secrecy, and a greenbacker.

Sunday, July 15 Pr. at 11:00, Gal. 4:4. Dine at Pendleton's. Pr. at 5:00 Rom. 6.21. Stay at Grant Corby's.

Monday, July 16 Grant Corby takes me to Woodburn. I get a letter from home. Go on 10:13 train to Salem. Elmer Harritt meets me and takes me to their house, two miles west of the city. Stay there. Weather hot.

Tuesday, July 17 At Harritt's all day. Byron's family come in the morning. Alice Emmit in afternoon. Wrote of trip via Tacoma to Portland, from Pasco. Went to Salem

in the evening with a pump man. Got papers. Return afoot. Warm day.

Wednesday, July 18 Dine at Byron W. Harritt's, one mile west. In afternoon go to James H. Emmit's a mile further on. Supper and lodging there. Children: Edward, Arthur, Bertha, Jessie. Warm day.

Thursday, July 19 Stay at Emmitt's till after dinner. Go with them to Mrs. Julia Franklin Harritt's. Stay there. Weather moderate.

Friday, July 20 Finish an article, "Washington Territory" in the forenoon. Write a short letter to Reuchlin. Mrs. "Melia" Harritt comes, and they all dine there: that is Byron 's. Go to Salem. Annoyancewith Chinese washers. Go on train to Cottage Grove. Stay at Cottage Grove Hotel, Jesse Thornton's. Weather moderate.

Saturday, July 21 Jackson Kile & Rev. A. Bennett come after me. I had received many letters here. Answer a few. Go out to Kile's. Dine there. Pr. at 3:00, Prov. 21:15. Supper at Jas. Lumbaugh's. Pr. at Shields Sch. H. at 11:00. Rom. 6:21. Dine on the ground. Pr. at 3:00, Acts 16.31. Stay at Samuel W. Woods'. Moderate weather.

Monday, July 23 Went to Kiles to change clothes & get writing material. Return & go with Rev. A. Bennett to John Currin's on Rowe River & dine there. Call at Simpson Lebo's on Kiser Creek, Supper at Joseph Neat's. Return to Samuel W. Wood's where I had borrowed a horse. Stay there with Bennett. Their son: Edgar Wood. Moderate weather.

Tuesday, July 24 Bennett leaves for home. By eight o'clock, I go to Jackson Kile's. Write letters. Dine there. Go in the afternoon to Cottage Grove. Supper with a Mr. Jones at Cottage Gr. Hotel by invitation. Go to Depot. Write to McKee. Go on 11:00 train to Drain's. Stay at the Hotel. Holyfield proprietor. Nice moderate weather.

Wednesday, July 25 Hotel keeper's wife is a sister to T.K. Gardner's wife. Gardner's come about 8:30. Go to Chas. Drain's house and dine there. Mother Drain one of our member's at Rock Hill, Linn Co., Oregon, thirty years ago. Supper at Hotel. Go on 11:52 train to Oakland,

Ore. Stay at hotel. Sleep nearly six hours. Nice mild weather.

Thursday, July 26 After breakfast, go to Rev. P.C. Parker's in Oakland. Stay there all day and all night. Nice weather.

Friday, July 27 Stay at Parker 's. Write some letters. Sleep till 3:30 (night) and go to depot. Train does not leave till 6:00 A.M.

Saturday, July 28 Arrive at Oakland at 7:00. Breakfast at John Newman's. Go to Dr. Marster's. We go to Rev. Elias M. Marster's near Cleaveland Post-Office. Dine there. Return. Stay at Dr. Stephen S. Marsters'. Nice mild weather.

Sunday, July 29 Pr. at Presbyterian Church at Roseburg, Ps. 92.8. Rev. Smick pastor. Dine at Smick's. Go to John Newman's. Receive Rev. E.W. Marsters into the Church from M.E. Church. Supper at Newman's. Pr. at Presby. Church at 8:00 Rom. 3:5. Stay at Newman's till 1:00. Take train at 1:40 for California. Day quite mild.

Monday, July 30 Newman with me to Gold Hill. Breakfast at Medford. Cross Siskiyon Mountain—quite grand scenery. Reach upper and lower Soda Springs sometime before night. Arrive at Biggs at almost two o'clock. Put up at Hamilton Hotel. Mild weather.

Tuesday, July 31 After Breakfast go to Lewis C. Smith 's. Write letters home and to T.K. Gardner. Get letters from home. Dine at W. Thos. Baulware's. Stay there all day and lodge there. Bro. B. very friendly and agreeable. Weather mild, but the breeze rather lively.

Wednesday, August 1 Went to Gridley. Dine at Rev. Allen G. Wright's. Come back to Biggs. Call at Caleb Marion Baulware's. Supper at W.T. Baulware's. Pr at Baptist Church in Biggs at 8:30, Rom. 6:21. Stay at W.T. Baulware's. Weather mild.

Thursday, August 2 Left Biggs at 7:15. A M.E. man Allen on the train, of Modesto. At Sacramento, put up at Western Hotel. Mr. Land proprietor. Dine there. Quinn blocks my hat. With Rev. T.J. Bauder, I visit his house, look at the church and grounds, ascend the rotunda of the Capitol, and call at Lou Winters'. Go on 5:00 train to Lodi on Woodbr. tr to Woodbridge. Stay at W.C. Day's. Very pleasant day.

Friday, August 3 Staid at Rev. W.C. Days till afternoon. Went to Post-office; got letters, called at Rev. D. Shuck's, and at Prof. E.S. Ridenour's for supper. Staid at Day's. A pleasant day.

Saturday, August 4 Went to Rev. J.L. Field's, 3 ms N.E. Stay till perhaps 4:00. Grand-nephew, Harry. Go with Day's to Lodi. Call at David Housh's. Prayer. Mrs. Housh sick. Stay at Day's. Mild fine weather.

Sunday, August 5 Pr. at Woodbridge Church at 11:00, Isa. 53.6. Dine at J.J. Riley's, M.D. Stay there till after lunch. Pr. at 8:00, 1 Pet. 4.17. Stay at Rev. W.C. Day's. Day's children: Carl, aged 14, Maggie, 10. Riley's children: Odessa 15, Ocella 10, Delphia 5. Warm but temperate day.

Monday, August 6 Went to Lodi. Called at David Housh's. His wife is low with consumption. Went on to H.D. Northrop's. Dine there. Called at Justus Schomp's. Talk on politics. I for. Benj. Harrison. Call at Northrop's & Joseph Overhaltzer's on my return. Quite a hot day. Stay at Day's.

Tuesday, August 7 Rise early. Write letters. Call at Andrew Wooldridge's awhile. Dinner and supper at Ex-bishop Daniel Shuck's. Call at Pres. Darius A. Mobley's. Stay at Rev. W.C. Day's. A very hot day. Thermometer about 110 degrees. Evening much cooler.

Wednesday, August 8 Call at B.F. Bourland's a few minutes. Dine at Prof. E.H. Ridenour's. Discussion of third party. Rev. W.C. Day & wife also there for dinner. I stay to supper. Prayer-meeting at the Church at 8:00. Stay at Day's.

Thursday, August 9 Dine at B.F. Bourland's. Supper & lodging at Prof. W.H. Klinefelter's. Wrote letters in forenoon.

Friday, August 10 Went and called at Rev. W.H. Bast's. Went to Rev. W.C. Day's. Went with Day and family to Joseph Overholtzer's, 3 ms north-east. Stay there till morning.

Saturday, August 11 Return to town to Day's. Dine there. Attend meeting at the Church and pr. at 2:30, Ps. 137:5,6. Quarterly Conf. followed. Supper at Pres. D.A. Mobley's. Rev. W.C. Day pr. at 8:00. "He must increase," etc. I stay at Mobley's.

Sunday, August 12 Pr. at 11:00, Gal. 4:4. Dine at J.A. Solinger's. Day & family also dine there. Stay till evening. Pr. at 8:00, at Presbyterian Church, Rev. D.A. Steen, pastor, Ps. 25.14. Stay at Rev. W.C. Day's.

Monday, August 13 Went to David Housh's in Lodi. His wife very low with consumption. Call at Rev. F. Fisher's. Dine at Day's. Write letters. Supper at E.H. Ridenour's. Call at A. Wooldridge's, Shuck's, G.M. Palmer's. Stay at Day's.

Tuesday, August 14 Go with Rev. W.C. Day to Stockton. Dine at the Mansion House. Review Wilbur's articles. Go on train with Rev. John McBride to Oakdale. Thence to his house. Stay there.

Wednesday, August 15 Stay at McBride's till afternoon. An agent sells McBride a Physiological chart or chartbook for the school. Dine at Mc's. Go to Salmon Blodget's. Stay there.

Thursday, August 16 Return to McBride's. Dine there. Go to Oakdale with McBride. Wrote letter to Wilbur, to Mother Koerner, Dr. L.Davis, and card to Rev. M.S. Bovey. Also wrote letter to Dr. S.S. Marsters. Return to McBride's. John Dunning stays there.

Friday, August 17 Stay at Bro. McB's till after dinner. Fix up my clothes, etc. Go via Thomas Richardson's and Thomas Snediger's Wm. Wyman's. Stay there. Children: Elsie 16, Addie 11, Mary 9.

Saturday, August 18 Go via Burneyville to McBride's. Dine there. D. Shuck came. We go to quarterly meeting at Burneyville. I pr. 2 Thes. 1:3—presided in the quarterly conference as p.e. protem. Supper at McBride's. I pr at 8:00, 1 Tim. 4:8. Stay at Salmon Blodget's with Rev. Daniel Shuck.

Sunday, August 19 Go to McBride's. Thence to Burneyville. Lovefeast meeting at 10:00. Pr. at 11:00,

John 1.29. Communion. Receive Henry Ross into the Church. Lunch with Richardson. Rev. D. Shuck speaks at 3:30 on baptism. Alice Keeler, Henry McBride, Isabelle McBride and Henry Ross were baptized by McBride. Supper at Thos. Snediger's. Pr. at 8:00, Job. 21:15. Stay at John McBride's.

Monday, August 20 Started at 9:00 for Modesto with McBride's, Shuck being along. Put up at Howell's, Rev. B.B. Allen's son-in-law. Dine there. Start for Los Angeles about 2:30. See some of the Selma folks. Get to Mojave before day-light.

Tuesday, August 21 Arrive at Los Angeles about 8:00 a.m. Go to Rev. T.F. Hallowell about 10:30. Dine there with Daniel Shuck, G.W. Burtner, & D.S. Shiflet. With Bro. H. and those brethren look at the city somewhat. Go on 5:10 train to Palms. Supper and lodging at Rev. M.S. Bovey's. Rev. H.S. Munger pr. at 8:00, 2 Cor. 4:5. A very fair effort.

Wednesday, August 22 Conference opened at 9:00, a.m. Progressed pretty well. I dine at and take up my home at Ezra Strong's. Field's and King's cases on examination excited considerable interest and remarks. Supper at Strong's. Preaching at 8:00, by A.F. Lee. Stay at Strong's.

Thursday, August 23 Conference continued. Examinations. Dine as usual. Examinations as usual. Rev. W.C. Day pr. at 8:00, I John 3:1,2.

Friday, August 24 Conference in session. Dine at Rev. J. Brown's 1 1/2 miles south-west. Session in the afternoon. Rev. W.L. Demenbrun & Rev. A.N. King elected presiding-elders. Supper at Strong's. Rev. W.L. Demunbrun pr. at 8:00 Hebr. Stay at Strong's.

Saturday, August 25 Stationing Committee met at J.W. Baumgardner's. Also at 1:00. Conf. continued. Dine at Strong's as usual. Afternoon session. Supper as usual. Pres. Mobley speaks on Christian education. Evening session of Conf. Stay at Strong's. About 9:00 read Stationing Com. Rep.

Sunday, August 26 Pr. Conf. sermon at 11:00, 2 Cor. 13.8. Dine at Strong's. Slept 1 1/2 hours in afternoon. Called near the close of Sab. Sch. anniversary, and went to Rev. A.N. King's for supper. Rev. G.W. Burtner pr at 7:30, Acts 16:31. Communion followed. Stay at Ezra Strong's. I wakeful.

Monday, August 27 More than a dozen of us went to Santa Monica and a number took an ocean bath & a plunge bath. Burtner had a nervous shock. We dine at Rev. W.P. Tibbet's. Call at Hubbard's. Go on to H. Lowe's and thence to Rev. J.W. Baumgardner's at Palms. Compare conf. charts at Strong's. Rev. A.W. Suepp pr at 8:00. Stay with Burtner's at Strong's. Sleep none after 2:20.

Tuesday, August 28 Dine at Rev. M.S. Bovey's. Slept two hours before dinner. Wrote letters in the afternoon. Sister Coe, Sister Lowe & daughter, called in. Supper at Bovey's. Rev. T.J. Bauder pr at 8:00, Ps. 33:7. I lodge at Bovey's. Slept a long nights sleep, but not very refreshing.

Wednesday, August 29 Dine at Ezra Strong's. Brush and clean up my clothes. Go to Rev. A.N. King's. Supper there. Attend prayer-meeting at Rev. Jacob Brown 's. Go back with Rev. A.N. King and stay at his house.

Thursday, August 30 Stay at Rev. A.N. King's till 11:00, and write. Dine at Enos Briant's. Children: David aged [blank] Edward [blank] Eva 17, Emma 15. Supper at King's. Go to prayer-meeting at the church. Return to Briant's & lodge there.

Friday, August 31 Go to A.N. King's. Write letters. Go to H. Lowe's. Dine there. Finish writing letter. Go to post-office and mail a letter. Call at Bovey's & Phineas Tibbetts. Return to King's and go to Rev. Jacob Brown's and stay there. Attend prayer meeting at Labier's. Give my views of Noah, Job, Daniel, John Baptist & Paul.

Saturday, September 1 Remain at Brown's till after dinner. Go to town, get my washing, brush my Sunday clothes. Supper & lodging at Phineas Tibbets.

Sunday, September 2 Rev. M.S. Bovey pr at 11:00 Acts 20.32. I dine and lunch at Ezra Ford's. Baumgardner's return from Los Angeles in aft'n. Speaking meeting at 7:30. A sort of a farewell meeting for Bros. Bovey and Baumgardner. Stay at Rev. A.N. King's 1 1/2 ms.

Monday, September 3 Staid at King's till after dinner

and wrote letters. Went to Nathan Coe's. Supper and lodging there. He in Andersonville when the fountain broke out. This seemed like a miracle.

Tuesday, September 4 Two Coe, two King, & two Bryant boys, & John Rose start for the mountains on a hunt. I go to King's. There a company of us go to Santa Monica bathing. Dinner or supper at Enos Bryant 's. Attend a temperance lecture at Palms, by Rev. J.W. Baumgardner. Stay at Enos Briant's.

Wednesday, September 5 Car ed at King's. Dined at McLaughlin's. Called at Anderson Rose's. Supper and lodging at Henry Lowe's. Prayer-meeting at Nathan Coe's.

Thursday, September 6 Went with Bro. Lowe to Los Angeles. But first called at Lorbeer's. Stop at Rev. Thomas Fairman Hallowell's and made my home there. His wife's name Margaret Eliz. Ann.

Friday, September 7 Stay at H's till afternoon. Write home and send a draft for $100.00. Call at Samuel Kingery's office. Then at Allen's. We then ride out to the S. Pac. R.R. depot. It is over 500 feet long. Go through its rooms. Return to Bro. Hallowell's. Stay there.

Saturday, September 8 Stay at Hallowell's till near night. Write a letter to Rev. J.L. Field. Study some. Go after supper to Elisha Luke's just west of the "University". Return to Hallowell's.

Sunday, September 9 Pr. at 11:00 at Main St. M.E. Church (Rev. J.L. Spencer, pastor) Job 21:15. Help raise the deficiency on salary of the pastor. Dine at Rev. Thos. F. Hallowell's. Go on 5:00 train to Palms. Lunch at Rev. H.S. Munger's. Pr. at 7:30, 1 Tim. 4.8. Stay at Rev. Jacob Brown's, 1 1/2 ms west.

Monday, September 10 Stay at Brown's till evening. Lecture on Temperance at 7:30 at the U.B. Church in the Palms. Had quite a good audience despite the tabernacle meeting held by Ellis. Ellis came to Brown's in the afternoon awhile. Once an M.E. he is not in full fellowship with holiness Ch. I stay at H. Lowes.

Tuesday, September 11 Went to Santa Monica with Bro.

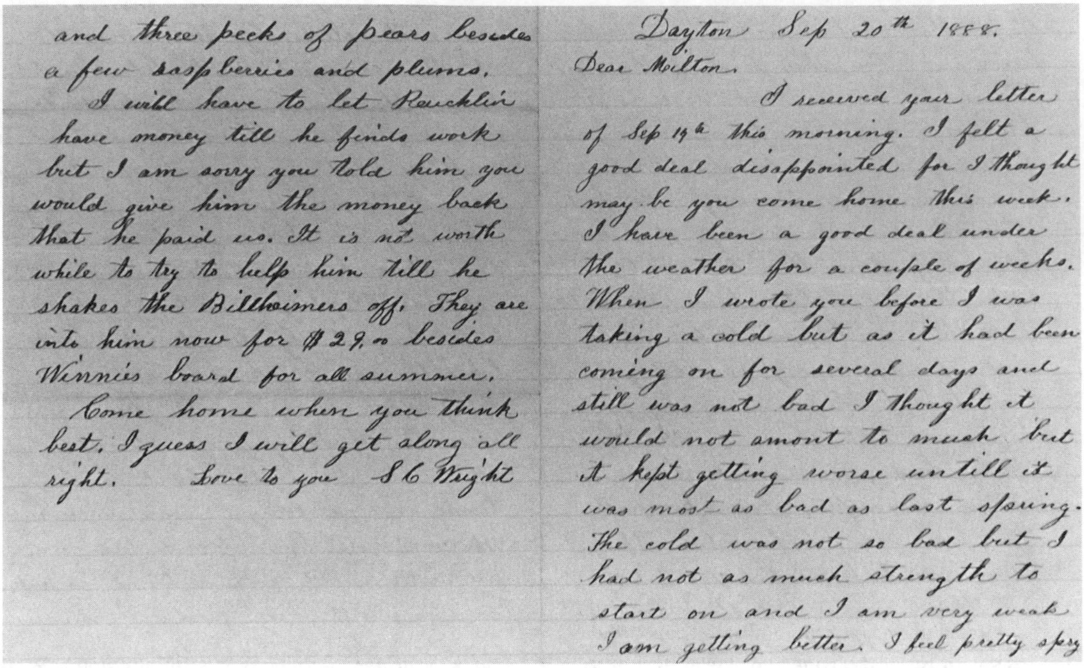

[Handwritten letter, left page]

and three pecks of pears besides a few raspberries and plums.

I will have to let Reuchlin have money till he finds work but I am sorry you told him you would give him the money back that he paid us. It is not worth while to try to help him till he shakes the Billheimers off. They are into him now for $29.00 besides Winnie's board for all summer.

Come home when you think best. I guess I will get along all right. Love to you S C Wright

[Handwritten letter, right page]

Dayton Sep 20th 1888.

Dear Milton.

I received your letter of Sep 19th this morning. I felt a good deal disappointed for I thought may be you come home this week. I have been a good deal under the weather for a couple of weeks. When I wrote you before I was taking a cold but as it had been coming on for several days and still was not bad I thought it would not amount to much but it kept getting worse untill it was most as bad as last spring. The cold was not so bad but I had not as much strength to start on and I am very weak. I am getting better. I feel pretty spry

---

H. Lowe. Stop at Rev. W.P. Tibbet's. Stay there till morning. He is about to move north—either to Fresno county or to Umpqua Valley in Oregon. Write letters.

Wednesday, September 12 Write letters. Go to the beach. See Mungers and L. Stevens. Go to Henry Lowe's. Dine there. Called at King's. Supper at Chas. Stinton's. Go to Rev. H.S. Munger's in Palms. Stay there. Stinton has two sons-in-law, both named LaForge.

Thursday, September 13 Go to Rev. Jacob Brown's with Munger's family. Dine there. Bro. Brown takes me to the train at the Palms. Go on 3:37 train to Los Angeles. Put up at Rev. T.F. Hallowell's. Supper and lodging there. Got a letter from home and one from Rev. T.D. Spyker.

Friday, September 14 Wrote letters home and to Spyker. Went down town. Inquiry on fares & about fruit. Dine at parlor Cor. Spring & 3d. Go out to Elisha Luke's about 3 squares west of "the University building." Supper & lodging there. Bro. Young's family living with them. Mrs. Luke away.

Saturday, September 15 Went to Hallowell's & thence to the depot & thence to Norwalk. Call into the town hall at a land meeting over a suit for 1/10 of certain lands. Ride out to Luke Charest's with Mr. Sackett. Dinner, supper, & lodging there. Wrote again to Spyker, card to Orville. Call in evening at Rev. A.F. Lee's.

Sunday, September 16 Arose at 6:00. Bathe thoroughly. Pr. at 11:00 at New River Sch. H. 1 Pet. 2:11. Dine at John Branscom's. Rev. A.F. Lee also there. Stay the afternoon. Rev. A.F. Lee pr at 7:30, [blank]. Stay at Luke Charest's. Lee's children are two small daughters, Gertrude 5; Mary Eliz. 1.

Monday, September 17 Call at Rev. A.F. Lee's. Dine at Alex M. Thompson's. Call in afternoon at Lee's again. Supper there. Pr. at Sch. h. at 7:30, Rom. 6:21. Stay at Thompson's. Their children are Guy, Paul, Dolly, & infant daughter.

Tuesday, September 18 Went to Charest's. Shaved. Went to Lee's & helped him to move. Dined at Lee's (or Curtis). Supper at Luke Charest's. Pr. at 7:30, Luke 15.18. Stay at Charest's. Their children are Mina 14, Clarence 4, Mabel 1.

Wednesday, September 19 Went to Mr. Woods (McLaughlin's) and dine there. Call at Rev. E.H.Curtis. Go to John Branscom's. Stay till after supper. Pr. at 7:30 Titus. 2.14. Stay at Wood's.

Thursday, September 20 Rev. A.F. Lee comes from Norwalk and takes me to the cars at Norwalk. Go to Los Angeles. Get a letter. Go to Rev. T.F. Hallowell's. Dine there. Go on st. cars to Santa Fe Depot. Cars started 100 yds before me. Write to Reuchlin. Supper at dining parlors car Spring & 3d sts. Stay at Sam, Kingery's.

Friday, September 21 Go on Sta Fee road to Riverside. Mailed a letter at Colton to Susan. Arrive at Riverside at 11:30. Din[n]er & supper at Mrs. Martha Hall's. In afternoon helped pick muscatel grapes for drying. Called with Samuel H. at Rev. M.S. Bovey's. Stay at Hall's.

Saturday, September 22 Go with Rev. M.S. Bovey to Sumans and down Magnolia Avenue as far as shade trees extend. Dine at Peter Suman's. Spend most of afternoon there. Go back to Hall's. Stay there. Was quite hoarse from cold alone.

Sunday, September 23 Pr. at U.B. Church at 11:00, Ps. 65.2. Dine at Rev. M.S. Bovey's. Lunch there. Pr. at 7:30, Heb. 9.13,14. Hoarse from cold. Stay at Bovey's.

Monday, September 24 Leave on 6:55 train for Los Angeles. Conductor had taken up my round-trip ticket but returned it this morning. Arrive at Los Angeles at 11:00. Write a letter home. Dine at Ebinger's, Cor. Spring and Third. Supper at Rev. T.F. Hallowell's. Start at 9:30 for Tulare.

Tuesday, September 25 Reach Delano and Sumner. Broad Valley. Reach Tulare at 9:20. Inquire much for exact place of Rev. E.L. Kenoyer and Rev. E. DeWitt. Go out in afternoon to Garret Hollis Hubbell's 4 ms S. of Visalia. Stay there. Children: Annie 16, Dexter 13, Archie, 3. Her bro. Spofford there.

Wednesday, September 26 Go to Vissalia. Quite a town. Good country. Spend the rest of the day at Hubbell's. Walter Spofford, brother of Rev. Spofford nee U.B. of Nebraska working there. As we sat in the evening a centipede appeared on the floor; Hubble stamped it. I put

it in alcohol and took it home with me.

Thursday, September 27 I go to Tulare. Go on 9:20 train to Selma. Dine at Rev. D.S. Shiflett's. Children: Elliot 15, Ira 10, George K., 3. Get a letter from Susan saying she had been much more unwell. I stay at Shiflett's.

Friday, September 28 I determine to start home. Pack a box & start at 10:45. Buy a ticket at Lathrop for Peoria, Ill. ($44.25) on "Burlington Route." Go on to Sacramento. Start at 8:00 for Peoria, Illinois. Pass Alta at 1:30. Reach Blue Can[y]on at 2:45. Stay till 3:30. Westbound train passes. Slept 7 hours.

Saturday, September 29 Breakfast at Reno. Saw Indians there. Women carrying papooses in a cradle on their backs. Truckee River nice. Humboldt River small and colored. Dine at Humboldt. Reach Elko about 9:00 p.m. Slept about 6 1/2 hours.

Sunday, September 30 In sight of Salt Lake. At daylight, 76 ms to Ogden. Reach Ogden at 8:00, Change cars for Denver. Stop at Salt Lake at 12:00. Attend services at Mormon Tabernacle at 2:00. Two hours long. The eccentric usher guards his seat. Angus M. Canon announces hymn. Bywater prays. J.M.S. preaches. Clear & able, Hebr. & Grant follows. I take a walk. Return to the cars. Start at 8:00. 4 hours sleep.

Monday, October 1 Awake about Sunny-Side. Breakfast at Green River. Dine at Grand Junction. Up Grand River & Gunnison. Once a lake. Much like bad lands—Heaps, crevasses, wave-marks. Pass black can[y]on. Cars stop at Gunnison till 3:30 next morning.

Tuesday, October 2 Start at 3:30 and reach Marshall Pass at 6:00. Many sweeps & curves as we descend. Pass Grand Can[y]on and Royal Gorge. Wild & grand scenery. Walk across the bridge at Royal Gorge. Reach Pueblo after 12:00. Pass Colorado Springs at 2:30. See Castle Rock. Reach Denver at 6:00. Start at 8:00 on B.M. R.R. in Nebraska. Sleep 5 or 6 hours.

Wednesday, October 3 Reach Indianola, Nebraska about day-light. Breakfast at Oxford. Change cars in afternoon at Table Rock. Arrive at Kansas City at at [repeated in text] 9:15. Put up at Adams House.

Thursday, October 4 Ride up Cable-car line a mile or two. See Post-office. New Board of Trade Building. Grand Opera House, etc. Start at 7:45 for Peoria, Ill. See O. Stott's on train for Ainsworth. See R.J. Shuey at Col. Junct. Reach Burean, Ill., after 1:00. After over 2 hours, start again for Peoria.

Friday, October 5 Arrive at Peoria, Ill., at 5:45. Breakfast at the European Hotel. Wait till 11:50 for the I.B.W. train. Start to Arcanum, Ohio. Rainy day. Reach Arcanum 12:33 a.m. Stay at Hotel. Slept 3 1/2 hours.

Saturday, October 6 Reach home at 8:00. Get my trunk from Depot. Aunt Mary calls—Mary Englehart. This is the close of four year's labor on the Pacific Coast. Providence has very greatly favored me those years. Praise His name. Reuchlin's called in the forenoon.

Sunday, October 7 Attended services at the First Reformed Church & heard Prof. Dr. Zerby preach or lecture on the Old Testament—Rom. 15:4 & II Tim. 3:16. Communion. In evening 7:30, attend installation services at First Reformed Church of Dr. Zerby and Dr. Van Horn. Dr. J.L. Swanders delivered the charge, and Dr. Van Horn read his inaugural address as Prof. in Heidleberg The. Sem. Wm. H.H. Reeder came from Troy. Reuchlin's dine with us.

Monday, October 8 Went with Wm. H.H. Reeder, who came back from Troy last evening, to see water-works, screw factory, and Barney Smith's car-shops. At home in afternoon. Reuchlin's call in the evening.

Tuesday, October 9 Wm. Reeder started home in the morning at 7:20. Mrs. A.L. Billheimer & Lulu called in the afternoon. I took articles and letter from Mrs. Day and Hallowell to Mrs. L.K. Miller. They were for Africa. She at Prof. G.A. Funkhouser's.

Wednesday, October 10 At home. Wash a quilt. Wilbur out distributing notices of registration. I attended prayer-meeting at Summit Street Church at 7:30. Near 40 present.

Thursday, October 11 Registered for November election. At home all the rest of the day. Called at Reuchlin's in the evening.

Friday, October 12 Called at Dr. L. Davis' in forenoon. Rev. Wm. Dillon called 10 minutes in the afternoon.

Saturday, October 13 Went to town in forenoon & bought over-coats for myself, Wilbur, & Orville, & carpet-stuff for druggets. Day rainy. Wilbur met with the Ten Dayton Boys at Reuchlin's in the evening.

Sunday, October 14 At Grace M.E. Church at 10:30, heard Rev. F. Iliff of Utah, John 12:24, a very able discourse. Dine at Reuchlin's with all the family. Go at 7:30 to hear Rev. F. Iliff lecture on "After Midnight in Utah." Katie with me. It is on the verge of raining. Lecture 75 minutes long.

Monday, October 15 At home all day. Spent the day mostly in writing letters. Mrs. H. Wagner called. It is An almost drizzly day, but scarcely any rain-fall.

Tuesday, October 16 At home all day engaged in writing letters. Mrs. Hott called in afternoon.

Wednesday, October 17 At home Day mostly spent in reading. Called at Dr. L. Davis' and Dr. Wm. Dillon's in the afternoon. Katie at home from School somewhat unwell. Wilbur distributing notices to register.

Thursday, October 18 A rainy day. At home clearing up medicine bottles, etc. in forenoon.

Saturday, October 20 At home most of the day. Called at Mission rooms. Got a hat.

Sunday, October 21 Attended Raper Chapel. Bishop Thoburn pr. at 10:30, Luke 9:13. Dr. Davis & Aunt Rebecca call in the afternoon. Also Reuchlin & family. I call at Reuchlin's in the evening.

Monday, October 22 Attended the Missionary convention at Raper's Chapel in forenoon. A rainy day. At home in the afternoon. In evening attend Mis. convention. Thoburn answers objections to foreign missions. Then J.E. Robinson D.D. spoke awhile, a missionary.

Tuesday, October 23 At the convention. Topic: "Home methods of raising Missionary Money." Also in the afternoon, topic: "Woman's Foreign Missionary Work."

Also in the evening. It was a "Missionary Mass Meeting."

Wednesday, October 24 At home in the forenoon. Went to town in afternoon. Lulu called in the evening. Reuchlin started to Jackson County to the coal mines as assistant pay-master and Katie staid with Lulu.

Thursday, October 25 At home all day. Wrote some letters. Wilbur is out the third time circulating, in two wards, notices to Republicans to register. I called at Dr. Davis in the evening.

Sunday, October 28 At First U.B. Church. Rev. Prentiss DeVeuve pr. Luke 8:25. Reuchlin's called in the afternoon a little while. Attend the Missionary Meeting at First Church. Mrs. L.K. Miller and Mrs. Keister told of London Mis. Conference which they attended.

Wednesday, October 31 At home. Looking over arrangement of papers, etc. Republican rally and torch-light procession and Foraker & Williams speak at the Rink.

Thursday, November 1 H. Floyd called early in the morning & staid most of the forenoon. At Ex. Com. Mis. meeting in the afternoon.

Saturday, November 3 At home all day. Bishop J. Dickson called a few minutes in the afternoon. At the funeral of Mr. Strawbridge who died at his residence on our street. Went out to cemetery. Dem. political rally in the evening. Also Ten Dayton Boy's An. Banquet.

Sunday, November 4 Attended services at the Wayne Ave. U.B. Church and heard Bishop J. Dickson preach, Luke 4:18. At home the rest of the day except a very brief call at Reuchlin's. Election of delegates to Gen. Conf. & on Commission at Summit St. Ch. Ward politicians excelled.

Monday, November 5 Republicans are circulating tickets for the election to-morrow. At home all day. Reuchlin called in the evening.

Tuesday, November 6 This is presidential election day. Voted for Benj. Harrison & L.P. Morton, about 8:40. Rain set in about 9:00. Drizzly or cloudy afternoon. Had

Dr. Spitler to come over to see Susan. Was at the place of dispatches exhibited by Garfield Club on 4th St. till a late hour.

Wednesday, November 7 News of election are some-what conflicting but indicate, Gen. Benjamin Harrison's election as dispatches did last night. Went to town in the forenoon. Also in the evening for Mother. A cloudy rainy day.

Thursday, November 8 At home all day. A rainy day. News so favorable to Harrison's election that it is generally conceded by Democratic newspapers. Wrote letters in the evening.

Friday, November 9 At home. Another very rainy day. Lulu called in the evening or afternoon awhile.

Sunday, November 11 Hear Rev. Macafee pr. at 10:30, at Grace M.E. Church, Matt. 16.24 an eloquent sermon. At home the rest of the day.

Monday, November 12 Clean house in forenoon. In afternoon, go to Library. Read in Atlantic Monthly, 17 Vol. p. 1743, Art. on Pioneer Editor G. Barley. Leave watch at Reeves. Rev. W. Dillon called in the evening.

Tuesday, November 13 At home. Cleared up my carpet in afternoon. Called at Reuchlin's in the evening.

Wednesday, November 14 Went to town, read papers, got my watch & returned. In afternoon Parade over Gen. Benj. Harrison's election. Katie & I went over to see it. Wilbur & Orville marched.

Saturday, November 17 At home all day. This is the sixtieth anniversary of my birth. I was born on the frontier settlements of Indiana, and then the whole population of the United States was about 12,000,000; and before the first railroad for public use was built in the United States, & when we reapt our grain with reap-hooks.

Sunday, November 18 At home all day. Orville took my unbrella in the morning to go to Church.

Tuesday, November 20 Went to town in forenoon. At home the rest of the day.

Wednesday, November 21 At home in the forenoon. Went to town in the afternoon. Get ready in the evening to start to Grant Co., Ind. to-morrow.

Thursday, November 22 Left home at 7:00 A.M. on D. & U. R.R. Reach Jonesbo 11:15. Cars detained about three hours. Reach Fairmount at 4:00. Call at Rev. T.E. Kinneman's. Go out with John Simons to Aunt Eliz. Reeder's. Stay there. Notes—the train from Wabash was detained by a freight-train wrecked between LaFontain & Marion. I wrote letters at Union & Jonesboro.

Friday, November 23 Stay at Aunt's till evening. Then go to Cousin Wm. H.H. Reeder's, her son's, and stay.

Saturday, November 24 Go over to my farm two miles north-east, and look over it. Call a moment at John Fine's & his father's, both being away. Dine at Henry Simon's. He aged and afflicted. Look at Ellis Wright's corn-field. Return to Aunt Eliz's. Stay there. Oliver Glass visits Flora.

Sunday, November 25 Go with cousins Wm. & Robt. to Union Church (2 ms S of Fairmount) & pr at 10:30, Job 21:15. Return to Aunt Eliz's. Pr. at Aunt's house at 6:30, John 3:16. Dan Richard's, Fowler, Glass, etc., there. Stay at Aunt's.

Monday, November 26 Write Ellis Wright a letter. Go to the farm. Mr. Fine not pleased claiming William had rented him the farm at the close of wheat cutting: not true. Supper at Aunt's. Lodge at William's.

Tuesday, November 27 Fill out a mortgage & after dinner at Aunt's, Go with Aunt & William to Fairmount & she signs & acknowledges the mortgage at Winslow's. Call at Chas. Atkinson's. Stay at the parsonage, at Rev. T.E. Kinneman's.

Wednesday, November 28 Start home on 7:00 train. Leave mortgage for record. Leave remonstrance on change of road (sent by Wm.) at Bogg's & Ratliff's. Pay Reeder's taxes for them, $32.57. Send the receipts & money left to Wm. Go on 10:50 train to Union City & thence on 2:20 train home. Found all well, as they are usually.

Thursday, November 29 Attended Thanksgiving services at the Christian (New Light) Church where Rev. L.D. Morse (Baptist) preached, Ps. 103.1. Reuchlin's dine with us. At home the rest of the day.

Saturday, December 1 At home in forenoon. Went with Katie to town shopping in the aftern.

Sunday, December 2 Went to Summit Street to Church in the forenoon. Heard Pres. elect J.W. Richards of Gettysburg Lutheran College pr. Phil. 2.12,13, a very good discourse.

Monday, December 3 At home part of forenoon. Went to town about 9:00 with Katie and got her negative for a dozen photographs. Got Susan a dress, $1.25 a yard. At home afternoon & evening. Wrote letters.

Tuesday, December 4 At home forenoon. Went to town afternoon & got salary of McKee. Deposited money in Merch. Nat. Bank. Wrote letters forenoon & evening.

Wednesday, December 5 At Dr. Davis' awhile in the forenoon. In afternoon scour my hard-coal stove. Write letters in the evening.

Thursday, December 6 Chores & reading in the forenoon, & part of the afternoon.

Friday, December 7 Called on L.L. Davis D.D. on business & on Matthews. At home the rest of the day.

Saturday, December 8 At home. Spend the day in reading and chores.

Sunday, December 9 At Third Street Presbyterian Church, Rev. Montgomery pr. at 10:30, John 20:26-29. Reuchlin's call in aft'n. I go to Trinity Reform Hall. Rev. D.W. Ebbert pr. at 7:30, 2 Chron. 20.15.

Monday, December 10 Went to town in forenoon. Library book Vol 11 Herodotus. Got 8 of Katie's photos, etc. At home in the afternoon & evening.

Thursday, December 13 Emma Zeller visited us. She dined at Reuchlin's and took supper with us. Reuchlin & Lulu also at Supper with us.

Friday, December 14 At home all day. Wrote several letters. Among them one to Hon. Benj. Harrison in behalf of Rev. G.W. Burtner of Cal. Rev. Halleck Floyd called in the evening, and staid till bedtime.

Saturday, December 15 At home in forenoon. Went to town afternoon. Spent the rest of the day and evening in reading. Look somewhat for Lorin, on a visit home from Coldwater, Kan.

Sunday, December 16 Lorin had arrived via Cincinnati & staid at Reuchlin's last night. He came in after Breakfast, this morning. In much better health than when he left home 18 months ago. None of us went from home to-day. Reuchlin came in a little while with Lorin in the morning and awhile in afternoon again.

Monday, December 17 Busy all forenoon blacking up hard-coal stove, & put it up after dinner.

Tuesday, December 18 At home as usual. Wrote some letters. The children went, in the evening to Reuchlin's to sing.

Wednesday, December 19 At home in forenoon writing cards, etc. Also at home in afternoon till evening. At 7:30 heard at Main St. Lutheran Church Dr. F.M. Conrad, First Cor. 3:21-23. He was a former pastor there. He could see his congregation only at close range.

Thursday, December 20 Got ready to go to Michigan. Hindered by the parleying of a lady over her ticket from getting a ticket. Return home. Start at 3:30 for Swanders. Stay at Christopher Shearer's, Mrs. Harriet Shearer being my cousin. Children: Albert, John, Eddy, Martha, Mary, Clara, Minnie, Charlie, Effie, Warren, Fannie.

Friday, December 21 Rev. Reichert called an hour. After early dinner, I start for Toledo. Bp. J. Weaver aboard to Columbus Grove; & Rev. D.B. Martin thence to Ottawa; & T.J. Harbaugh thence to Toledo. Wait at Toledo till 10:00 & reach Blissfield about 11:00. Stay at Simon Young's. Their only child Clarence 10.

Saturday, December 22 Dine at Wm. Rothfus', a grocer's. Daniel Palmer and wife there. Business meeting at 2:00, with devotions. Supper at Rothfus'. Rev. D. Clark pr. at 7:00, Ps. 85.6. I stay at Rev. S.H. Yeager's, the pastor's.

Church on corner of Jefferson & Depot Streets. 32 X 52 X 18 & vestibule of 13 ft. Colored glass windows. Rev. L.S. Wilmoth with us.

Sunday, December 23 I pr. at 11:00, Ps. 65.2. Then raise 1, 395.81 + 11.33 pub. Coll. at night. Dine late at Wm. Rothfus'. Call at Sime Young's & at Bailey's. Eat a little supper. Pr. at 7:00, Rom. 6:21. Stay at Simon Young's. Trustees of Church, Simon Young, Wm. Rothfus, Chas. Rothfus, E. Burk, Moses Palmer, Rev. Partee & Rev. Porter. Rev. L. Wade present.

Monday, December 24 Start home 9:30. Jam at Toledo. Weaver & Harbaugh again aboard. Reach Dayton about 5:30—an hour late. Children go to S.S. entertainment at Summit St. Church.

Tuesday, December 25 Reuchlin's come over in the morning to get Catharine's presents—two cloth dogs & a dress. Picture frame for them, etc. Reuchlin a gold pencil; Lorin's present, a white silk muffler; Wilbur's, an Alpaca umbrella; Orville's $3.50 to buy type; Katie's, new dress and handkerchief's; Mother's, red net shawl & glass tumblers. Dine at Reuchlin's.

Wednesday, December 26 Lulu has some diphtheria. Comes over. I at home reading & writing mostly. Call afternoon at Dillon's & Davis's. Dr. Davis likely to have a brush with U.B. Mutual Aid S. over a paid up promise, not fulfilled by them.

Friday, December 28 At home all forenoon. Afternoon call at Reuchlin's & go to town. Send for *Cynosure* & N.Y. *Tribune*. Buy diary for 1889 & Shakespeare for Lorin, etc. Lulu, Mrs. M.R. Drury, and Mrs. Jas. C. Manning called. Began on my annual report.

Saturday, December 29 At home. In forenoon began my report. Went to town in afternoon. Finished gathering statistics for the Annual Report of Pacific Coast District.

Sunday, December 30 Attend church at Summit Street, Rev. G.M. Matthews the pastor, preaches, Luke 24:28. Reuchlin & babe called in the afternoon. A rainy evening.

Monday, December 31 Worked on and finished my annual report of the Pacific District. Wrote letters in the evening. This closes another year of blessings, mercies, and gracious providences. Bells rang at the parting between the years. I asleep.

Memoranda at the end of the diary

Bell Foundrys.
Vandwzen & Tift. Cin. McShane & Co. Troy, N.Y. Kimberly & Co. Troy, N.Y. Meneely & Co. W. Troy, N.Y.

Expenses to Coast.	$
Half-fare Chicago	5.15
Half-fare St. Paul	5.75
Half-fare Palouse Junc.	33.75
Full fare to Elberton	6.10
Full fare to Pampa	3.20
Stage to Riparia	2.00
Fare to Huntsville	1.90
Hotel at St. Paul	1.00
Hotel at Riparia	.75
Edibles at various places	2.00
Far fr. Weston via Walla Walla to Wallula	3.00
via Pasco & Tacoma Portl	8.15
Hotel at Pasco	1.00
Hotel at Bitland	1.50
Edibles, miscellaneous, etc.	.50
Half-fare to Corvallis	1.95
Fare to Philomath	.25
Replacing a lost umbrella	1.50
Fare to Albany	.35
Fare to Woodwin	.90
Fare to Silverton	.25
Buggy (Drake) to Hall's	.35
Train fr Townsend to McKee's	.10
Train fr Woodburn to Salem	.35
To Cottage Grove	1.85
Drain	.35
Oakland	.40
Roseburg	.35
Hotel at Drain	1.00
Hotel at Oakland	1.00
Hotel at Medford	.25

Fare to Biggs	9.80
Fare to Woodbridge	3.45
Washing at Woodbridge	1.00
Fare to Oakdale	1.35
Hotel at Biggs (75 cts)	1.00
Fare fr Modesto to Palms	12.80
Expenses in Los Angeles	.30
Fare from Maitland to Palms & return	.40
Washing at Palms	.60
Celluloid Collar	.25
St Car fare	.20
Etcetaries	.15
Eye water (Thompson's)	.35
Quinine at Santa Mon.	.20
Quinine at Los Ang.	.25
St. Car fares at Los Ang.	.25
Fare & return to Norwalk	.85
Washing at Los Angeles	.50
Washing at Los Angeles	.30
Dining & St. Car fare	.35
Fare to Riverside & ret.	2.05
Street cars at Los Ang.	.25
Fare to Lodi	13.80
Fruit, ect. at L. Ang.	.15
Quinine at L. Ang.	.15
Stamps sent for L.H. pur.	.25
For fruits (Red prunes)	.50
For fruits at Selma	3.50
Nails & screws	.25
Victuals on journey	1.00
Victuals on journey	.85
Breakfast at Peoria	.20
Hotel bill Kan. City	1.00
Fare from Lathrop to Peoria	.20
Fare to Arcanum	5.75
Fare to Dayton, Ohio	.50
Hotel at Arcanum	.75
Orange	.05

Walla Walla 1887
Allotments of Labor
Palouse Dist.—N. Evans P.E.
Spokane Cir. G.W. Tenney
Garfield Cir. W.H. Sherod-Kern
South Palouse M.A. Helm
Moscow Cir.—M.E. Bailey

Genesee Mis.—J.I. Mitchum
Asotin M.—A.J. Sherrod
Dayton M.—W.R. Lloyd
Huntsville M.S.—W.S.Walker

Walla Walla Dist—J.M. Treseriter, P.E.
Wash. Mis.—J.O. Spooneman
Walla Walla M. Stn—C.C. Bell
Centerville Ct.—A.R. Olds
Adams Mis.—G.W. Bailey
Umatilla Cir—J.J. Gallaher
Lexington M.—J.T. Hoskins
Wasco Mis.—T.J. Cocking
Dufur M.—J.M. Pratt
Fox Valley M.—John Margis
Grand Ronde—C.W. Wells
Conf. Evangelist—J.S. Rhoads

Allotments of Labor
Oregon Conf.
Umpqua Dist.—J.G. Mosher
Coast Mission—J.G. Masters
Coos Mission—J.G. Mosher
Umpqua Mission—To be sup.

Willamette Dist.—J.W. Pulley.
Lane Mis.—A. Bennett
Linn Mis.—A. Bennett
Alsea Mis.—T.P. Connor
Philomath C.—J.C. Keezel
Marion M.—J.W. Ingle
Yamhill M.—J.R. Parker
Washington M.—E.C. Wyatt
Nehalem M.—W.H. Palmer
Columbia M.—J.H. Alexander
Lewis River M.—W.J. Campbell

California
Allotments of Labor
Humboldt Dist. A.W. Snepp
Rohnerville C.—A.W. Snepp
Eurek M.S.—F. Stearns
Petrolia M. G.W. Burris
Eel River
Sacramento Dist.—J.W. Fish
Upper Lake m.—
Yolo—J.J. Smith

Feather River C.—A.G. Wright
Shasta Mis.—G.W. Burtnor
Sacramento M.S.—T.J. Bauder
Woodbridge Stn—W.C. Day
Calavernus M.—
Stauislaus C.—E.S. Glandon
Liberty—W.C. DeMurbrun
Selma—D.S. Shiflet
Tulare—E.L, Kenoyer

Los Angeles Dist.—J.W. Baum
Santa Monica—J.W. Baum
Los Angeles M.—Keister
Riverside—H.S. Munger
Palms, M.S. Bovey

Walla Walla 1888
Allotments of Labor
Belouse Dist—N. Evans, P.E.
Big Bend Mis.—
Spokane Mis. Stn.—
Oakesdale Cir.—J.S. Rhoads
N. Palouse—W.H. Sherrod
S. Palouse
Julietta—H.O. Kerns
Asotin—J.A. Kenoyer
Patalia—M.E. Bailey
Dayton—J.I. Mitcham
Huntsville—J.J. Gallaher
Adams—J.C. Spoonemore
Weston—A.R. Olds
Fox Valley
Lexington—C.C. Bell
Umatilla—F.L. Hoskins
Wasco—C.B. Davis

Bish. Coll's
Salary 1886

Oregon (All Told)	$121.82
Walla Walla "	81.85
California "	144.97
Total	348.64

Coll. in 1887

Oregon	143.62
Walla Walla	86.50
California	184.00
Total	414.12

1885

Oregon 1885 (All told)	114.08
Walla Walla "	81.95
California "	211.01
[Total]	407.04

Walla Walla in 1888

Chart Collections	27.35
Public Collection	36.15
Present for B.J. Hunt	5.00
Total	68.50

Oregon in 1888

Chart Collections	92.00
Public Collections	25.80
Corby's	2.00
Blue Mountain Class	3.00
Roseburg (Newman)	1.00
[total]	123.80

California 1888

Chart Coll.	99.50
Public Col.	49.37
Presents (J.L.S.)	5.00

Index

Notes & dues	Page 2
Allotments of labor (1887)	15, 16, 17
" " " (1888)	18-20
Bish. Salary (1887) (1888)	21, 22, 23
Bell Foundries	3
Traveling Expenses	5

Members at Blissfield, Mich.

Simon Young
Wm Rothfus
Chas Rothfus
E. Burk
Moses Palmer
Dan Palmer
Pierce
Olv. Schneerer
Ezra Schnerer

1 8 8 9

Tuesday, January 1 Wea. bright. Ther. 30 degrees. The sun went down under an eclipse—partial here, total fur Ther north. Reuchlin & family dined with us—thus all the family at home, Lorin being also here. Nothing very remarkable occurred. Called at Lewis Davis', D.D., an hour in the evening.

Wednesday, January 2 Ther. 28 degrees (?). Wea. beautiful. Staid mostly at home. Went to Fergueson's in the afternoon. Mrs. Harriet Fergueson, my Mo Ther's Cousin, having died yesterday. She was the daughter of Reuben Reeder, son of Joseph, who was son of Joseph the Third.

Thursday, January 3 Ther. 23 degrees (?). Wea. fair, very fair mild day. At 10:30, attended Mrs. Fergueson's funeral at the house, Rev. J.H. Montgomery officiating. At home all afternoon and evening.

Friday, January 4 Ther. 23. Wea. fair. At home as usual, except a trip to town to get letter envelopes & apply for Clergyman's R.R. permits. Got one on Ohio, Ind, & Western—I.B.W.—of Vlierbaum. Called at Rev. Wm. Dillon's in the evening.

Saturday, January 5 Ther. 35 degrees. Wea. rainy. At home as usual. Went to town in the afternoon. Joseph Boyd & wife visited us in the evening—especially on Lorin's account.

Sunday, January 6 Ther. ab. 33 degrees. Wea. cloudy and damp. Little if any rain. I staid at home with "Mo Ther," while the children went to Church. Reuchlin called in the afternoon. I called at Dr. L. Davis' in the

evening and then at church (Baptist) on W. 3d St. Rev. L.D. Morse pr. "Is it well."

Monday, January 7 Ther. ab. 32. Cloudy Wea. At home all forenoon. Went to town in the afternoon. Got a clergyman's ticket on Cin., Ham., & Dayton R.R.

Tuesday, January 8 Ther. 34 degrees. Wea. Cloudy. Rain late in afternoon. At home all forenoon. Went to town in the afternoon. Got Clergyman's permit of Dayton Ft. W. & Chi. R.R. Nothing very unusual. Call at Reuchlin's in the evening.

Wednesday, January 9 Ther. 48 degrees. Rainy Wea. very. At home all day. Disabled by rheumatism in the joint of my head & neck, somewhat. Reuchlin left Patterson's & is again out of employment. They credit him with having succeeded well. It was to give ano Ther a place.

Friday, January 11 Ther. about 34 degrees. Fair Wea. At home all day. Reuchlin called in the evening.

Saturday, January 12 Ther. 24 degrees. Fair Wea. At home in forenoon. Did chores mostly. Went to Railroad offices. Got no answer from general offices. Mrs. Reb. Davis & Harper called.

Sunday, January 13 Ther. 36 degrees. Wea. Cloudy—sprinkles a little only. On account of rheumatism in the joint of my head & neck & the necessity of keeping my head covered, I did not go to Church. Called at Dr. Davis's in the afternoon awhile.

Monday, January 14 Ther. 32. Cloudy Wea. At home

mostly. Called at Reuchlin's in forenoon. Went to town in afternoon awhile. Got letters to-day from Gr. R. & I. R.R., Pulley, Hallowell, etc. Rutt.

Tuesday, January 15 Ther. 32 degrees. Cloudy Wea. but no rain. At home all day. Rev. Halleck Floyd came in the afternoon. Reuchlin also called.

Wednesday, January 16 Ther. 48 degrees. Rainy Wea. At home all day. Miss Lizzie Niswonger came to begin dress-making for Mrs. Wright and Katie. Boards at her boarding place, however,

Thursday, January 17 Ther. 48 degrees. Wea. fair. At home all forenoon. Go to town in the afternoon. Rev. H. Floyd dined with us. Reuchlin called in the afternoon and evening.

Friday, January 18 Ther. 26 degrees. Wea. fair. Went to Telescope Office and set Reuchlin to copying the old Journal of Indiana Conference. Called at Dr. Davis's. Mrs. Hott & Mrs. McHenry called in afternoon. Lizzie Niswonger brought Susan's new dress home.

Saturday, January 19 Ther ab 23 degrees. Fair Wea. At home in forenoon. Rev. H. Floyd called. In afternoon Mrs. Gilbert brought back Lorin's quilt, which ladies quilted. I called at Reuchlin's in the evening.

Sunday, January 20 Ther. 36 degrees. Rainy Wea. Owing to fear of catching cold in back of my neck if bared, I did not attend Church. Telegram at 1:45 from J.G. Zeller that Mo Ther Koerner died at 9:00 to-day. She was 92 y, 1 m, & 20 d of age.

Monday, January 21 Ther. 24 degrees. Fair Wea. Went to town in forenoon. Called at John Needham's after dinner, his wife being in the last stages of consumption. Reuchlin called in the afternoon awhile. Mrs. Wagner called.

Tuesday, January 22 Ther 21 degrees. Fair Wea. Went on early train to Hamilton & Liberty. Walk & ride to Roseburg. Mr. Morgan drives me in Mr. Mullen's buggy to Daniel Koerner's. Dine There. Attend Mo Ther Koerner's funeral at 2:00. Rev. J. Selig pr. the sermon, Rev. 14:13. Zeller's folks and I stay at D. Koerner's.

Wednesday, January 23 Ther. 26 degrees. fair Wea. Write up the records in Daniel's Bible. After dinner Daniel K. takes me to Union Church. Supper at the parsonage with Rev. J. Selig. I Pr. at 7:00, Acts 2:21. There is quite a stirring revival in progress. I stay at George Fry's. Geroge A. Schwab of Mixerville There, o Thers also. Chas. Filer.

Thursday, January 24 Ther. 40 degrees. Cloudy Wea. Attend morning meeting at 10:00. A wonderful meeting. Dine at Mo Ther Paddack's. John & his wife There. Bro. Selig also. Call in aftern. at Calvin Huddleston's, and at Mrs. S. Fry's. Pr. at 7:00 1 John 4:10. Stay at Logan Brockley's. Henry Fry & Selig There.

Friday, January 25 Ther. 35 degrees. Cloudy Wea. Rise at 5:00. After early breakfast, Selig takes me to Cottage Grove, but just too late to flag the train. Return to Brockley's. Go to parsonage. A glorious meeting in forenoon. Dine at parsonage & go immediately to Lotus. Go via Hamilton home arriving at 4:00 or 5:00.

Saturday, January 26 Ther. 40 degrees. Cloudy Wea. Went to town in the forenoon & engaged a coat & vest at Ryke's. At home in the afternoon. Reuchlin called. Lulu (his wife) called just before night.

Sunday, January 27 Ther. 34 degrees. Snowy Wea. There fell considerable snow, melting. Attend a sacramental meeting at First Reformed Church on N. Ludlow St. Three persons "confirmed." At Summit St. Ch. at 2:30. Rev. Chas. E. Pilgrim pr. at 2:30, 1 Cor. 16:7. A pretty good speaker. Heard at M.E. Broadway St. Pastor Brown, Jer. 13:21.

Monday, January 28 Ther. 30 degrees. Fair Wea. Went to town in forenoon. Wrote letters. Reuchlin came and we arranged for his going west. Pr. at 7:45 at Broadway M.E. Church, Rom. 10:13. Six seekers- 4 converted.

Tuesday, January 29 Ther. 17 degrees. Fair Wea. Wrote out Mo Ther Koerner's obituary for the *Rel. Telescope* in the afternoon. Attend meeting at Summit Street at 7:30. Rev. Charles E. Pilgrim pr. Acts 18:17. No seekers.

Wednesday, January 30 Ther. 26 degrees. Fair Wea. Call at J.K. Graybill's, Henry Recker's (just deceased) and Dr. L. Davis. Afternoon go to town with Katie & Catharine and get little one shoes. Attend church at Broadway. Hear Rev. Brown pr. 2 Pet. 2:21. Six seekers.

Reuchlin's came to stay.

Thursday, January 31 Ther. 38 degrees. Fair Wea. with a little snow & growing colder considerably. Went to town. Got books for G.W. Fast. Got pants and vest. At home all afternoon and evening.

Friday, February 1 Ther. 15 degrees. Fair Wea. Got up early & get ready to go to Michigan. Start at 11:45 for Richmond, Indiana. Spend the afternoon at D.K. Zeller's. Start at 11:05 for Michigan. Slept six hours on cars.

Saturday, February 2 Ther. 21 degrees. fair Wea. Arrive at Kalamazoo at 7:00 a.m. Leave on Chi. Kal. & Sag. R.R. at 7:30 for Shult's Station where I arrive at 9:00. Rev. G.W. Fast takes me to Afton Smith's 3/4 m N.E. of Rutland Church. Their Children: Mabel Maud Inez, 10, Fred 5. Pr. at Rutland at 1 1/2, Job, 21:15. Rev. W.S. Titus pr. at 7:00, Isa. 35:2. We stay at Smith's.

Sunday, February 3 Ther. 32. Cloudy Wea. Pr. 11:00 1 Tim. 3.15. Raise $204.06 & dedicate Rutland Church. Dine at Hathaway's with Titus, Fast & wife. Children, at home: Mary 19. Elmore 17, Nathan (?) 15. Pr. at 7:00, 1 John 4:10, Rev. Allen Car took me to David Bowker's in Hastings. Start at 4:25 for Gr. Rapids.

Monday, February 4 Ther 30 degrees. fair Wea. Arrive at Grand Rapids at 6:00. Start at 7:15 for Richmond. Lunched at Grand Rapids & Ft. Wayne. Saw rep. of Lagrange County. Saw Hon. Thomas Brown. Also Wm. Parry, pres. of Gr. Rap. & Ind. RR. Called at Allen Harris'. Supper at D.K. Zeller's. Go on 7:25 train to Dayton.

Tuesday, February 5 Ther. 32 degrees. Cloudy Wea. At home all forenoon. Go with Reuchlin's to get his photonegative. Settle with Dr. L. Spitler.

Wednesday, February 6 Ther. 9 degrees. Fair Wea. Reuchlin started at 7:00 for Cincinnati & perhaps for Kansas City to find employment. Wrote letters. Went to town & got proofs of negatives of Reuchlin's.

Saturday, February 9 Ther. 28 degrees. Fair Wea. At home. Bathed, and fixed up my room a little. Nettie Stokes called in the afternoon & Miss Cowell. Went to Brookville on the 6:30 train. Stay at Rev. W.J. Pruner's.

Their children: Maggie, 22; Won. May, Frank—Elizabeth, babe.

Sunday, February 10 Ther. 20 degrees. Cloudy Wea. Pr. at U.B. Church in Brookville at 10:30, Ps. 65.2. Dine at Pruner's. Supper at John Zearing's. He takes me to Arlington, where I pr. at 7:00, Eph. 2:4. Large Congregation morning & evening. Stay at Zehring's. Their children: Estolee, 18, Clara, 14, & Earnest, 6.

Monday, February 11 Ther. 28 degrees. Fair Wea. Call at Rev. W.J. Pruner's. Go home on 8:05 train. At home most of the day. Send out posters on sale of J.F. Croddy's land at Roach, Clay Co., Ill. Was at town in evening & bought Katie shoes.

Tuesday, February 12 Ther. 16 degrees. Fair Wea. At home all day. Spent most of the time arranging the files of the periodicals which I take. L.M. Brown married to Miss Landis.

Wednesday, February 13 Ther. 10 degrees Cloudy Wea. At home all day. Write some. Mail photographs to Lorin. Call at Dr. L. Davis' an hour in the evening. L.M. Brown is serenaded.

Friday, February 15 Ther. 32 degrees. Cloudy Wea. At home mostly. Called at Dillon's in forenoon. He away. Called in the afternoon & at Graybill's. Spent the evening writing.

Sunday, February 17 Ther. 42 degrees. Cloudy Wea. Attended Broadway "Christian" Church & heard Rev. J.P. Watson preach from Matt. 20:6, an excellent sermon. I pr. for Watson at 7:30, Rom. 6:21.

Monday, February 18 Ther. 34 degrees. Cloudy Wea. At home all day, writing in the forenoon and part of the afternoon. The wea Ther turned cold in the afternoon and evening.

Tuesday, February 19 Ther. 11 degrees. Fair Wea. At home all day. Daniel Lee, Lulu's old friend, called to see us and dined with us. Orville's type etc came. I read mostly to-day. When Katharine saw Lee with his long beard, she said he was Santa Claus.

Bishop Milton W. Wright in 1889

Wednesday, February 20 Ther. 8 degrees. Fair Wea. Called at Dr. L. Davis' in the forenoon. At home all the afternoon. Wrote a letter to Pres. Kiracofe. Read in Revi. Ver. several Chapters in Numbers.

Thursday, February 21 Ther. 18 degrees. fair Wea. Called at J.K. Graybill's in the forenoon. Went thence to town in the forenoon & cashed Susan's check, after a little trouble. At home in afternoon and evening.

Saturday, February 23 Ther. 6 degrees. Fair Wea Ther. Go on 12:05 train to W. Baltimore & thence to Philipsburg. Call first at Lewis W. John's (3/4 m. W. of town) then at Jas. R. Walker's. Supper There. Pr. at 7:30 1 Pet. 2:24. One seeker. Stay at Levi Goodyear's. Children: Rosie, Carrie, John Clinton.

Sunday, February 24 Ther. 10 degrees. Cloudy Wea. Pr. at 10:30, Rom. 4:16. Dine at Chas. Duckwalt's. Prayer-Meeting at 2:00. Call at Wm. Davenport's, where Rev. Ehrhart of Ev. Assocation is sick. Pr. at 7:00, Rom. 10:13, one seeker. Stay at L.W. Johns'. Members at Phillipsburg: Ullery, Hook, Binkley, Pefley, Lentz, Williamson.

Monday, February 25 Ther. 12 degrees. Fair Wea. Bro. Johns takes me to 7:40 train at Baltimore. Thence home. Go to town & buy bbl apples. At home in the afternoon.

Tuesday, February 26 Ther. 32 degrees. Clo Wea. At home in forenoon. Wrote to Reuchlin. Went to town in the afternoon.

Wednesday, February 27 Ther. 35 degrees (?). Cl. Wea. At home in the forenoon & afternoon. Dr. L. Davis called in the afternoon.

Friday, March 1 Ther. Ab. 35. Cloudy Wea. At home in forenoon. Wrote to He Therington, Toledo Blade, Reuchlin, & Hoisington. Go to town in afternoon. Lulu made an all-day visit to Charley Olinger's on Vine Street. Babe's clothes caught fire, but she was unhurt.

Saturday, March 2 Ther. ab 38 degrees. Cloudy Wea. No rain till evening, & almost none. At home all forenoon. Wrote Reuchlin, and to W.H.H. Reeder. Had intended to go to Grant Co., but unwell & concluded to wait till Lulu went to Kansas City. Went to "town" in the afternoon. Orville gets out *West Side News*.

Sunday, March 3 Ther. Ab. 40 degrees. Cloudy Wea. Attended Disciples' Church, Cor. 6th & Brown Sts. Rev. J.V. Updyke pr. Ja. 5.16. Prof. J.E. Hawes sang. At 7:30, heard Rev. John Shed lecture on Presbyterian Missions in Persia. The lecture at 3d Pres. Church. At 3:00 heard Rev. Date at Grace M.E. Church & Bro. McKoe's sing.

Monday, March 4 Ther. ab. 35 degrees. Fair Wea. News from Reuchlin, that ano Ther is promised the place he had hoped for.

Tuesday, March 5 Ther. Ab. 35 degrees. Cloudy Wea. At home all day. Daniel Koerner & Elmira came about 4:00.

Wednesday, March 6 Ther. 31 degrees. Wea. fair. At home. Afternoon bought a ticket for Lulu and checked her trunk for Kansas City. She started at 6:29 p.m. Reuchlin started just 4 weeks ago. Daniel and Elmira with us.

Thursday, March 7 Ther. 34 degrees. Wea. fair. At home all forenoon. Daniel & Elmira start at 12:29. I draw money out of the Bank.

Saturday, March 9 Ther. Ab. 24 degrees. Mixed Wea. At home most of the day. Settled with Dr. Tizzard for regulating and filling Katie's teeth. Paid the charges, $12.00.

Sunday, March 10 Ther. 30 degrees. Wea. Cloudy. As all the children went to church, I staid at home as Susan was more unwell than usual. At 7:30, heard Rev. McAfee, at Grace M.E. Church, pr. an introductory discourse to his intended Sabbath evening lectures.

Monday, March 11 Ther. 20 degrees. Wea. fair. Called to see Dr. L. Davis in the forenoon. Engaged in the afternoon and evening in writing.

Tuesday, March 12 Ther. 38 degrees. Fair Wea. At home all day. Rev. H. Floyd took supper with us. I wrote letters in afternoon & evening.

Wednesday, March 13 Ther. Ab. 39 degrees. Fair Wea. At home. Went to "town" in afternoon & got my valise mended. Called at the library.

Thursday, March 14 Day as beautiful and mild as April. At home.

Friday, March 15 Fair Wea. Went on 7:05 train to Union City & on 9:20 train to Marion. Day as mild & beautiful as spring. Paid my tax, $19.80. Went to Geo. Carter's 3 ms S. of M. Supper There. I take 8:12 eve. train to Fairmount. Stay at Rev. T.E. Kinneman's. Mrs. Carter (Mary) and Mrs. Kinneman sick.

Saturday, March 16 Go over to Aunt Elizabeth Reeder's, riding most of the way in Spring wagon with Mr. Buller, Joseph Parrill's hand. Dine at Aunt's. Go over to look at my old house to see what can be done to fix it up. Stay at Aunt's. Ellis Wright There.

Sunday, March 17 Call at Wm. H.H. Reeder's. Go with Robt. B. Reeder & Ellis to Union Church. Preach at 11:00 Matt. 5:12. Dine at Carter Hastings with Rev. Wm. Hall. Call just before meeting at Absalom Anderson's & Wm. Smith's. Pr. at 7:00 Rom. 3:5. Stay at Robt. Hastings.

Monday, March 18 Rainy Wea. Write letter to Rev. G.W. Burtner & to Susan. Abs. Anderson takes me most of the way to Aunt Reeder's. I dine There. Go in afternoon with Oliver A. Glass & wife & Wm. Reeder to look at the house again. I go by Joseph Parrill's, whom I pay in full for all past dues $5.00. Supper & lodging at Wm. Reeder's.

Tuesday, March 19 Go over to Aunt Lizzie Reeder's. Observe the work of the boys in the clearing. Joseph Broyles and wife came on an afternoon visit. I stay at Aunt's.

Wednesday, March 20 Wm., Robert, Oliver, Josh. Dickinson & I engaged in cutting & hauling logs for sills & wall, to Pearl's mill, all day. I stay at Aunt's.

Thursday, March 21 Wm. & Oliver still continue to help. Robert off the handle. We haul logs from Mill & put two logs in the wall. Stay at W.H.H. Reeder's (Jr) with Ellis Wright.

Friday, March 22 Oliver, Wm., Al. Hayden, & Ellis help me & Robt. came about 11:00. After putting in some logs, we in part pry up the house from the ground. Stay at Wm. H.H. Reeder's.

Saturday, March 23 Continue with the same hands to raise the building and put in pillars. Hayden left at 1:30 & Ellis & Robert at 3:00. Wm., Oliver, & I finish setting the pillars. Hard raising the last. Stay at Wm's.

Sunday, March 24 Brush up & go to Cumberland at Presbyterian Church. Rev. McKean pr. Matt. 22:42. Sacramental service. I return to Wm. Reeder's for dinner. Wm. takes me to Cumberland where I pr. at 7:30, Matt. 16:16 to a large congregation. Return to Wm's.

Monday, March 25 After a talk with Oliver A. Glass, I go with Wm. and make out a bill of the house as to what we want. Dine at Aunt's. Go with Oliver in afternoon & get lumber, hardware, etc. Get back after 9:00. Stay at Aunt's.

Tuesday, March 26 Wm. and I cut out logs & put in door & window checking. Oliver hauls lumber for Pearl's saw-mill & in afternoon goes to Fairmount for door & window frames. Stay at John Little's with Ellis.

Wednesday, March 27 Wm., Oliver, & I work on the house, setting in door & window frames, putting on ceiling, etc. Windy, raw day. Stay at Aunt's.

Thursday, March 28 Work on ceiling the house all day with Oliver. Wm. fixes up partition, stairs, door, etc. Stay at Wm's. And as he concludes to do o Ther work next day, I plan to go home.

Friday, March 29 Raw Wea. Flora takes me to Fairmount & thence to Jonesboro, where I take 10:00 train for Union City. Call, after noon lunch, on Rev. S.B. Ervin, pastor U.B. Church in Union. Go on home on 2:20 train arriving at 4:00. All about as usual.

Saturday, March 30 Ther. 26 degrees. Fair Wea. At home. Go to "town" afternoon & buy & express wallpaper to Fairmount for the house.

Sunday, March 31 Ther. 55 degrees. Mixed Wea. Attended Congregation Meeting at Y.M.C.A. Lecture room. Rev. Thos. Clayton pr. at 10:30, Ex. 14:15. Afterward the congregation take steps to organize a church. Called at Summit Street Church & at Dr. L. Davis'.

Monday, April 1 Ther. about 40 degrees. Cloudy Wea. At home. Wrote letters. Day of April City election. I went down and voted.

Tuesday, April 2 Ther. 43 degrees. Fair Wea. At home all day. Reading and gleaning.

Wednesday, April 3 Ther. ab 40. Hazy Wea. & fair. At home all day. Reading and collecting thoughts for my lecture to-morrow.

Thursday, April 4 Ther. 47 degrees. Wea. hazy. At home writing on lecture. President H.A. Thompson called at 2:30 and staid but a few minutes. At 3:30 I lectured before students of U. Bib. Sem. on the general principles of Church Government.

Friday, April 5 Ther. ab 40 degrees. Fair Wea. At home. Wrote an article for Conservator, The Legality question.

Saturday, April 6 Ther. 27 degrees. Fair Wea. Wrote letters etc. At home all day. Wrote letters. One to Bp. J. Dickson. Wrote one at night to Reuchlin.

Sunday, April 7 Ther. ab 30 degrees. Fair Wea. beautiful. Went to the Wesleyan Church. Rev. A.R. Bell, a colored evangelist, preached at 11:23, Ps. 51.10. W. Dillon & J.K. Graybell happened to be There also. In the evening I attended the Woman's Mis. Anniversary at Summit Street Church.

Monday, April 8 Ther. 32 degrees. Fair Wea. & beautiful. Went to town in forenoon & left measure at Charch & Wells for a new coat. Called at J.K. Graybill's.

Tuesday, April 9 Ther. 43 degrees. Hazy Wea. Called at Dr. L. Davis in the forenoon. Went to town in the afternoon. Wrote letters afterward. In the evening the Dr. Davis called with Florence. Lent me $100.00.

Wednesday, April 10 Ther. ab 45. Fair Wea. At home. Moses Hatfield called with Dillon in the evening.

Thursday, April 11 Ther. ab 45. Fair Wea. At home all day. Wrote to Reuchlin & to Lorin.

Friday, April 12 Ther. ab.50. Fair Wea. At home all day. Moved my desk and one book-case up stairs. Wrote some letters in the afternoon & evening. Wilbur began papering the front room.

Saturday, April 13 Ther. ab 35. Fair Wea. At home all forenoon. Called at Dr. L. Davis', Wm. Dillon's, & J.K. Graybill's. Went to town and got Qr. ream of Com. note paper, etc.

Sunday, April 14 Ther. 38 degrees. Fair Wea. Staid at home with Susan, the children going to church. At 7:30 at Grace M.E. Ch., heard Rev. McAfee lecture on "Which: Romanism, Protestantism, Liberalism, or Infidelity. Text John 6.68.

Monday, April 15 Ther. 42 degrees. Fair Wea. Went to town in forenoon—got my coat fitted and made a few small purchases—looked up R.R. Connections for the East. Worked most of the afternoon about house-cleaning, etc. Wrote a few cards & a letter in the evening.

Tuesday, April 16 Ther. ab 45. Fair Wea. At home all forenoon writing and most of the afternoon & evening. Called at Dillon's in afternoon a little while.

Wednesday, April 17 Ther. 58 degrees. Fair Wea. At home. Spent forenoon in clearing up papers and writing letters. Got letters from Reuchlin and Lulu. Ans'd & card to Lorin. Went to town in afternoon to see about freight rates on Reuchlin's goods.

Thursday, April 18 Ther. ab 60. Fair Wea. Look after marking loading & shipping Reuchlin's goods. Sent him bill of l[o]ading.

Friday, April 19 Ther. ab 60. Fair Wea. At home. Rev. H.H. Hinman called to see me in the afternoon.

Saturday, April 20 Ther. 60 degrees. Fair Wea. Called at the seminary. Rev. H.H. Hinman at supper and lodged with us.

Sunday, April 21 Ther. ab 40. Fair Wea. Staid at home

with Susan—all the rest at Church. Katie went on a ride to Soldier's Home with Joe Huffman's, but not admitted. At 7:30, heard Rev. Bashor pr. Matt. 5:8.

Monday, April 22 Ther. ab. 45 degrees. Fair Wea. At home. Largely a useless day. Got chilled in the morning in my bones, and could do little mental work. Sent $15.00 to Grant Co., Ind. Went to bed early. Had a good night's sleep. Oklahoma opened for settlement.

Wednesday, April 24 Ther. ab 50. Fair Wea. & Cloudy. A little rain. Doing chores and writing some. At home all day. Meeting of the Grand Army of the Republic. Their parade interfered with by showers in the afternoon.

Thursday, April 25 Ther. ab 45 degrees. A cooler day. Some fire needed all day. I remained at home all day and mostly spent the time in reading. Katie went to town to see the G.A. R. Celebration.

Saturday, April 27 Ther. ab 48 degrees. Cloudy Wea. At home all day. Studying some and doing chores. Rather cloudy day & the weather cooler, than last week.

Sunday, April 28 Ther. 50 degrees. Cloudy Wea. At Summit Street at 10:30, heard Pres. H. Garst preach the baccalaureate sermon before the students of Union Biblical Seminary. Pres. Thompson supped with us. I pr. at Miami Chapel at 7:30, Job. 21.15, Rev. Doty, the pastor.

Monday, April 29 Ther. ab 45. Fair Wea. At home writing. Went to town & bought a hat, etc. Halleck Floyd staid with us. At Literary exercises at Summit Street.

Tuesday, April 30 Ther. 48 degrees. Mixed Wea. At home looking over papers in forenoon & part of the afternoon. Called in to see U.B. Sem. Board in the afternoon and at Tea at Sem. building. Rev. Colby lectured to students Lit. society at 8:00. Floyd lodged with us.

Wednesday, May 1 Ther. ab 50. Fair Wea. At graduating exercises 9:00—12:00. W.L. Byers, Henry Doty, J.F. Lefler, and B.A. Sutton graduated. Rev. J.T. Halsted dined with us. Attended Historical Society meeting at 3:00. Bro. Floyd staid with us.

Thursday, May 2 Cloudy Wea. Chilly day. At home all day. Bro. Floyd dined with us. Dr. L. Davis called in the afternoon.

Friday, May 3 Fair Wea. Cool but moderated. Preparing to go to Pennsylvania. Went to Dr. L. Davis & Dillon's & to Town & bought a limited ticket to Harrisburg, Pa. $14.00. Sleeper $1.00 more. Start at 9:00 on fast train. Rest well, but Bro. Floyd sick.

Saturday, May 4 Lunched at Pittsburgh. Dined at Altoona. Hasty connection at Harrisburg. Reach Chambersburg about 6:00. Put up at Peter Nicklass' with Bro. Floyd and Saml. Horine.

Sunday, May 5 I pr. at King Street Church at 10:00 Micah. Dine at Rev. M.F. Keiter's. Eva his daughter is 17. At 2:00 taught the whole Sabbath School on 24th of Matthew. Lunch at Keiter's, with Bro. Floyd. Floyd pr. at 7:30. Stay at Adam Nicklass'.

Monday, May 6 Called at Bishop J. Dickson's. Board of Bishops hold a short session at 10:00. Dine at Bp. J. Dickson's. At the afternoon session, the bishops' address was read and adopted. I dissent. Supper at I. Fohl's. J. Gomer's magic Lantern Scenes at 7:00. Stay at Nic.

Tuesday, May 7 Bishops make out committees. Geo. Nicklass takes Floyd & me to Rev. J.M. Bishop's to dine. His plaster of Paris statue of Wm. Morgan. Mission Board meets at 2:30. Reports read. I do not hear Rev. J.W. Etter's Annual Mis. Sermon, as I have writing to do. Supper & lodging at A. Nicklas'.

Wednesday, May 8 At the session of Mis. Board, which adjourned at 11:30. Dine at A. Nicklass'. On 1:00 train, go to Harrisburg and thence to York on 2:30 train. Walk to Crider's store. Find my conference home at Mrs. A. Wilhelm's, 228 Market St. Spend the evening in writing.

Thursday, May 9 Remain at my boarding place till afternoon. Flickinger & Hill came. Gen. Conf. opened at 2:00. After a long time in electing secretaries, Bp. Weaver read the quadrennial address & I read my dissent. Meet the brethren at 33 Newberry St. a short time in evening, on petition.

*Photographs taken at the 20th General Conference of the Church of the United Brethren,
held at York, Pennsylvania, May 9–19, 1889*

Friday, May 10 The Commission tellers report. Report referred to a special committee of seven. Bishops try to pack the Committee. I gain some by resistance. Afternoon mostly spent on reports, as forenoon had been. Dust storm. Parret pr. at 8:00, Isa. 62:10.

Saturday, May 11 Conference as usual at 10:00, the report on regularity of, etc. of the commission, etc. Debated till after 4:00. Adopted by 110 to 20. Met the brethren at 33 Newberry St. Board as usual at Mrs. Wilhelm's, 228 Market St. Her son, Shaul; daughters, Isabelle & Sarah.

Sunday, May 12 Attended the Episcopal Church with part of the Wilhelm family. Afternoon at 3:00, go to York Opera house, and it being crowded, I go with Clay to 212 S. George St. Prayer & Counsel There. Attend no serv. evening.

Monday, May 13 Attend Council of Conservative delegates & others at 8:00 at 33 S. Newberry St. Learn at 10:30 that the "constitution" had been proclaimed. We engage the Park Opera House. At 2:00, meet at Park Opera House and open continued session of Gen. Conf. I presiding. H.J. Becker pr. at 8:00 on Battle of the giants. Wilhelms' at meeting.

Tuesday, May 14 Session continued. Report on State of Church. Aftern., action on Dillon's appeal. Rev. G.W. Story of Rock Island, fraternal delegate from Wesleyan Connection, addressed Conf. I responded. Pres. C.H. Kiracofe pr. at 8:00.

Wednesday, May 15 Session of Gen. Conference with pretty fair progress in business. I was much wearied. Rev. Jer. Kenoyer pr. at 8:00, "All scripture is given by inspiration", etc. Miss Nellie Leaf & Miss Jennings are visitors at Mrs. Wilhelm's. Emma—& Anna—waiters.

Thursday, May 16 Conference continued. In afternoon, I was elected Bishop by 28 votes (unanimously) and H.T. Barnaby by 19 votes, and H. Floyd on second ballot. H.J. Becker on 3d ballot. Becker lectured at 8:00 on Palestine & Syria.

Friday, May 17 Bishop Barnaby presided to-day. Forenoon measurably lost by reports on nominations being

poor. Referred back the nominations. In afternoon elected most of the officers. Bishop H.J. Barnaby preach[ed] at 8:00.

Saturday, May 18 Bishop Floyd presided. Business progressed well. Meeting of the Board of missions at 1:00. Meeting of the Board of Education & that of the board of missions, etc. Dillon pr. at 8:00. Closing session of Conference.

Sunday, May 19 Rev. W.O. Dinnius called. I pr. at Park Opera House, at 10:00, 1 Tim. 3:15. Temperence meeting at 3:00 addressed by Wm. Dillon & C.H. Kiracofe. Rev. H.J. Becker pr. at 7:30. Conf. delegates dispersed.

Monday, May 20 Session of the Board of bishops at Mrs. A. Wilhelm's. Start at 12:50 home. Wait an hour at Harrisburg. Reach Pittsburg[h] about 12:00. I sleep about 4 hours.

Tuesday, May 21 Lunched at Columbus, reached home between 8:00 & 9:00 morning. Called at Dr. L. Davis' in forenoon and at Rev. Wm. Dillon's. Wrote many letters in the afternoon and evening. Appointed several presiding elders.

Wednesday, May 22 Wrote part of the day. Dr. L. Davis called in the afternoon; Dillon & wife in the evening.

Thursday, May 23 Called at Drs. Davis' & Dillon's and at Graybill's. Went with Dillon & Floyd. Failed to see Dwyer and Houk but saw Hershey Esq. & paid $5.00 for the sight! Kumler Hoffman called.

Friday, May 24 Began the "Bishops' Address" to the Church & worked at it till toward evening. Bp. Floyd here part of the day. Called at Dr. L. Davis, in afternoon.

Saturday, May 25 Still wrote on the Address most of the day and evening. Called at Dr. L. Davis' to get his approval of the address. Wrote in the evening.

Sunday, May 26 Went to the Wesleyan Church & heard Dr. B.F. Porter of Franklin, Kentucky, John 7:16-18. Called at Dr. Davis' in the afternoon. Attended services at the Hall on Fitch St. at 8:00.

Monday, May 27 Go to town, mail letter, cash draft, leave watch at Reeve's. Spend forenoon & part of the afternoon in reading proofs on our (Bishops') Address.

Tuesday, May 28 Send $100.00 to H.J. Becker, Akron, Ohio. Charges $1.70. Read up proofs etc. on the Bishops' Address.

Wednesday, May 29 Saw Rev. H. Floyd about taking the publishing of the Conservator off his hands for a time. See about publishing the Bishops' Address in tract form. Write letters. Rain at night.

Thursday, May 30 Rainy Wea. Writing letters. Go to Davis', Dillon's, and Graybill's in the forenoon. Go to town at 5:00. Mail papers to Walla Walla Conference. Go to Davis and Graybill's in the evening and write letters.

Saturday, June 1 Wrote an article for the Conservator. Also opening words as Publisher.

Sunday, June 2 Rev. H.J. Mulholland called to see me in the forenoon. In the evening heard Rev. D.F. Bair pr. at the Hall on Fitch Street, Heb. 10:23.

Tuesday, June 4 Mail more tracts. Buy blank paper for subscription forms to mail to subscribers.

Wednesday, June 5 Got a letter from Rev. C.S. Miller with a check for $25.00 to pursue legal investigation.

Thursday, June 6 Mrs. M.C. Zeller visited Susan. I wrote letters and got ready to go away.

Friday, June 7 Start via Hamilton to Dublin Ind. & Hartsiille. Call to see Thomas Milligan Esq. at Hamilton. His advice. Call at Henry Huddleston's out of the rain. He takes me to town. Call at Dr. G.W. Champ's and at Rev. W.A. Oler's. Supper at Rev. A.J. Bolen's. Pr. at 8:00 Job 21:15. Stayed at Champ's.

Saturday, June 8 Wea. rainy. Call at Bp. H. Floyd's, Wray's, Gray's, Rev. John Cranor's & at Rev. W.A. Oler's and dine at Bp. Floyd's. Go after dinner to Cambridge. Oler with me to Rushville and Floyd to Hartsville Crossing. Supper at Greensburg. Lodge at Pres. C.H. Kiracofe's, Hartsville.

Sunday, June 9 Wea. drizzley. Preach baccalaureate at 10:30, 1 Cor. 13:9, 10, 11. Dine at Rev. John Riley's. Sleep a little in the afternoon, Floyd's. Supper at Rev. E. Pitman's. Bp. H. Floyd pr. at 8:00, Ps. 48:11-13. Stay at Pres. C.H. Kiracofe's.

Monday, June 10 Spent the forenoon considering plan of Bishops' visitation. Dine at Rev. N.D. Wolfard's. Call at Bro. Isaac Van Sickle's. Supper at Pres. Kiracofe's. Mr. Beck's lecture on Irish wit and oratory. Stay at Bro. Simeon Rohrer's.

Tuesday, June 11 Dine at Mrs. Bryner's (Barger's). Board of College meets at College in the afternoon. Supper at Bro. G. Mensch's. Anniversaries of the literary Societies at 8:00. Stay with F. at Mensch's.

Wednesday, June 12 Call at John Anderson's. Graduating exercises at 10:30. W.I. Alexander and Chas. Lawrence graduate. Dine at John Wesley Lawrence's. Talk with Dawson's. Supper at I.J. Tyner's. Call at Prof. O.W. Pentzer's and Mrs. P. Rawlings. Concert at 8:00. Stay at Kiracofe's.

Thursday, June 13 Wea. rain. Call at Rev. J. Riley's. Go on Hack to Crossing & thence home via Cincinnati. Arrive at home about 3:00. Called at Rev. W. Dillon's in the evening.

Friday, June 14 At Home writing. Wm. Wagner fell from his barn loft and hurt himself. Get many letters. Gave in articles: "Suggestions to our people" and Hartsville College Commencement.

Saturday, June 15 Get ready to go to Wapakonetta, but miss the train. Remain at home till 3:30. Go to Wapakonetta. Rev. R.G. Montgomery meets me and takes me to his house 8 miles south-west.

Sunday, June 16 Preach the funeral of Rev. Joseph C. Montgomery of Adah, Ohio, at Olive Branch Church at 10:30, Matt. 25.21. Dine at R.G. Montgomery's & lodge There. Supper at Fa Ther A. Montgomery's. Mrs. Hattie Montgomery & two Mr. Branham's There.

Monday, June 17 Go with R.G. M. to Bodkin, and on 10:06 train to Dayton. Arrive at home at 1:00. After dinner, go to Graybill's and Dillon's. Rev. C.S. Miller and Pres. C.H. Kiracofe stay with us.

Tuesday, June 18 Meeting of the Printing Establishment Board at our house at 9:00. Kiracofe and Floyd dine with us. Afternoon Session. Kiracofe, Rev. J.A. Brown, and Rev. C.S. Miller took supper with us. Night session of the Board at Dr. Davis'. Rev. C.S. Miller & Rev. J.A. Brown stay with us.

Wednesday, June 19 Ex. Com. on Missions meet at my house. Ex. Com. of Printing Board meet at Dr. Davis' at 11:00. Afternoon Floyd & I call on McMahon & find him retained. Telegraph Judge Wm. Lawrence. Pres. Kiracofe stays with us.

Thursday, June 20 Went on 9:20 train to Springfield and Bellefontaine. Lunch at Judge Wm. Lawrence's. Consult him on our Church case. Return to Dayton on 3:00 train. Spend evening at home. From Springfield to Bellefontaine I talked with S.L. Downey.

Friday, June 21 Called at Drs. Davis, Dillon's, Graybill's, etc. Busy all day. Dr. L. Davis delivered over the funds of *Conservator* to me in the evening. Bro. Keller called also.

Saturday, June 22 Went to town and got Katie gold-rimmed spectacles, for near-sightedness. Busy all day with business. Wrote letters in the evening.

Sunday, June 23 At 10:30 attended Congregationalist services at Y.M.C.A. Chapel. Rev. Metcalf preached. Rom. 14:1. At home in the evening.

Tuesday, June 25 Called at Davis and Dillon's and at the mailer's.

Wednesday, June 26 Went to town in the afternoon about 4:00. At home in the evening.

Thursday, June 27 At home in the forenoon. Went to town in the afternoon and took a copy of the U.B. Pub. House deed and sent to Judge Wm. Lawrence.

Friday, June 28 At home as usual and full of business. Susan has been very feeble & uncomfortable for some days past.

Susan K. Wright (n.d.)

Saturday, June 29 Looked up accounts and got orders, etc. ready to cash. Went to town cashed orders, notes, drafts, etc. Paid Graybill $50., Dillon $19.25, Mrs. Dillon $5.10, Wilbur $8.00, Myself $11.25. Dr. L. Davis quite sick with gastric trouble.

Sunday, June 30 Mrs. Henry (Rachel) Wagner called an hour or two in the forenoon. Mrs. Dillon & Mrs. Hott & Etta called in the afternoon. I called to see Dr. L. Davis who is still quite poorly. I did not get to Church to-day.

Monday, July 1 Called at Dr. Davis in the morning & the afternoon. Spent the rest of the day mostly in writing.

Tuesday, July 2 Spent the forenoon in writing. Afternoon went to town & asked for bids by Bloom and by Johnson on printing new Discipline. Went to Rev. W. Dillon's and worked an hour on editing the Discipline.

Ther.   THURS. JULY 4, 1889   Wea.

About 4:00, I found Su-
san sinking, and
about five awakened
the family. She revi-
about 7:00 somewhat, but
afterward Continued to
sink till 12:20 afternoon,
when she expired, and
thus went out the light
of my home. I went to
Woodland Cemetery in aftern
Mary Caroline Zeller came.

Ther.   FRIDAY 5   Wea.

Bought a beautiful
lot in Woodland, $135.00.
Made arrangements
as best I could for
the funeral.
*   Wilbur had me chang*
to a new lot.

Wednesday, July 3 Rev. Wm. Miller called & wished me to go to Bellefontaine to see Judge Lawrence for him. Susan said I "ought to go" and I went. Returned at 6:00. Called at Rev. Wm. Dillon's and at Dr. L. Davis'. Susan slept well to-night. Awake about 1:00 & got Susan a cool drink.

Thursday, July 4 About 4:00, I found Susan sinking, and about five awakened the family. She revived about 7:00 somewhat, but afterward continued to sink till 12:20 afternoon, when she expired, and thus went out the light of my home. I went to Woodland Cemetery in aftern. Mary Caroline Zeller came.

Friday, July 5 Bought a beautiful lot in Woodland, $135.00. Made arrangements as best I could for the funeral. Wilbur had me change to a new lot.

Saturday, July 6 D.K. Zeller and Emma came & Daniel Koerner, and our son Reuchlin. Funeral at 2:00 afternoon. Bp. Halleck Floyd pr. Ps. 116:15. "Precious in

sight." Bury Susan in Woodland Cemetery about 4:00 p.m. Daniel Koerner & Emma Zeller stay with us.

Monday, July 8 Went to town and settled funeral expenses. Ordered wrapping paper of E.B. Weston & Co. Conservator came out without a line editorial about Susan; but it was afterward inserted at my insistence!

Tuesday, July 9 Went to town afternoon and leave part of copy for new Discipline. Saw Louks. Foreman away.

Wednesday, July 10 At home writing letters etc. Left Copy for new Discipline with Bloom. Called at Dr. L. Davis in the evening.

Thursday, July 11 Worked on preparing copy for the next Discipline all forenoon & part of the afternoon with Rev. Wm. Dillon. Went to town at 1:30, cashed orders, and bought material for thin coat and vest.

Saturday, July 13 Wrote out notices for the Conservator. Went to town in the evening and got my thin coat & vest.

Sunday, July 14 Went to Oak Chapel U.B. Church and heard Rev. M.R. Bair Pr., Isa. 60.22, a good sermon. At home to dine. Dr. L. Davis sent for me to have a talk. I went. Hard rain. At home in the evening.

Monday, July 15 At home mostly. Called at Graybill's and Dillon's & saw Dr. Davis at his new building.

Tuesday, July 16 At home and writing letters. Read proof on new Discipline in the evening.

Wednesday, July 17 Rev. Wm. Miller & Rev. Wm. Dillon called in the morning. Wrote to Judge Lawrence. Read proof.

Thursday, July 18 At home in the forenoon. Went to town in the afternoon to cash orders, notes, etc. Wrote letters in the evening.

Friday, July 19 Went to Dillon's, Graybill's, & Davis' in the forenoon. Wrote an article for Conservator in the afternoon and evening, "The Legal Question".

Saturday, July 20 Called at Dillon's & Graybill's in the

morning. Went to Woodland Cemetery in the evening with Katie.

Sunday, July 21 Heard Rev. Wm. Clatworthy pr. at First Baptist Church at 10:30, 2 Tim. 4.6,7,8. It was able and good, but "aristocraticized". At home afternoon & evening. Katie rode out with Mr. & Mrs. Feight. Boys went to Summit St. Church.

Monday, July 22 Wrote up a form of notice in the evening to W.J. Shuey demanding possession of Tel. Offi. Called at Graybill's and also took proofs of Discipline to Mr. Blum. Read proofs of my article in the Conservator.

Tuesday, July 23 Wrote out Copy of notice to Shuey. Saw about printing my article in tract form. Called on Mr. Geo. W. Houk, Esq. Called at Rev. Wm. Dillon's in the evening.

Wednesday, July 24 Called again on Mr. Houk & retained him.

Friday, July 26 Wrote out & served notice to W.J. Shuey demanding possession of the Telescope Office. Went after writing articles for the paper to Richmond, Ind. Staid at D.K. Zeller's.

Saturday, July 27 Saw Rev. A.J. Bolen & Atty. Thomas Study. Went on 11:05 train to Ft. Wayne & Waterloo, Ind. Stay at Rev. A.B. Lilly's.

Sunday, July 28 Pr. at 10:30 at Corunna, Rom. 8.15. Dine at L.D. Britton's. Pr at 2:30, at Showers Corners, Ps. 92:8. Supper at Saml Husselman's. Pr. at 8:00 Waterloo Job 21.15. Stay at Rev. A.B. Lilly's.
Gave a brief address at each place on Church ques.

Monday, July 29 Go via Toledo to Dayton, arriving about 4:00 p.m. Found all well. Wrote several letters.

Wednesday, July 31 Went with Wilbur & Mr. G.W. Houk, Esq, to hold conference with Judge Wm. Lawrence. Lunch and dinner there. Spend 6 hours considering Lawrence's lengthy written opinion. Staid at the Logan House. Bill $1.50.

Thursday, August 1 Spent five hours more in consider-

ing the Opinion & o Ther matters. Bargained with Lawrence & Houk for $200.00 each as a retainer's fee, Lawrence having already worked his out & Houk to yet work his part then a bonus for success. And lawyer's rates for daily wages according to work. Came home.

Friday, August 2 Went on train to Richmond & Greens Fork. Call at D.K. Zeller's where Katie was visiting. Dine at Smith's. At Conference in afternoon. Supper at John Nicholson's. Pr. at 8:00, Rom. 8.15, 20 min. Stay at Chas. Lamb's 1 m north.

Saturday, August 3 At Conference. Dine at Joseph Lamb's near Chas. Session progressed. Memorial service for Susan. G.C. Warvel spoke. Supper at Lewis Oler's, a sonin-law [sic] of Warren Brooks'. Consecration Meeting at night. I stay at Chas. Lamb's. Stay at Mart. Kaufman's.

Sunday, August 4 Bp. H. Floyd pr at 10:30, Tim. 4 a good sermon. About $116.00 was raised to pay up salary complete. Succe[e]ded. I dine on the ground with Lamb's. Sab. School Anniversary, at 3:00. Rain. Sup[p]er at Howard's. Pr at 8, Mat. 28:19.

Monday, August 5 Went to Green's Fork. Stop awhile at Moses & Wm. Harfield's. Call at D.K. Zeller's at Richmond. Reach Dayton about 2:00 p.m. Look after proofs. At home in the evening. Got proofs & Index to Discipline from Dillon.

Tuesday, August 6 Spent from 6:00 a.m. till 5:30 p.m. revising Index to Discipline.

Friday, August 9 At home closely engaged. Read proof in the index of the *Discipline.*

Saturday, August 10 Pres. C.H. Kiracofe came. Went on 10:40 train to Sidney and thence to Marr's where I dined and then went on to Union Church. I pr. at 3:30 Rom. 8:16. Qr. Conf. followed. Supper at David Shanely's. Pr. at 8:30, Job 21:15. Stay at Shanely's.

Sunday, August 11 Preach at 11:00, Heb. 7.26. Communion. Subscrip. for Mis. & Collec. for bishop. Dine at Isaac Shanely's. Many there. Pool, Kumler, Mrs. Livingston, & families & others there. Go on to Marr's & stay there.

Monday, August 12 Take the train at Sidney to Bellefontaine & see Judge Lawrence. Come on home via Springfield, arriving about noon. Very busy. Go on 12:30 train for Union City, Pa.

Tuesday, August 13 Preach Union City at about 3:00. Put up at Rev. N.R. Luce's. Fa Ther [blank] meets me at the train. Bro. Wm. Hodge calls & stays at Bro. Luce's till bedtime.

Wednesday, August 14 Bro. Luce & I go on 8:00 train to Watt's Flatts. Mr. Rice takes us to Sugar Grove. Put up at Br. Jas. H. Coburn's. Begin Conference at 2:00 at Presbyterian Church. Rev. S. Evans pr. at 8:00, Ps. 73:25, 26.

Thursday, August 15 Conference continued. Most of us board at Bro. J.H. Coburn's. Rev. M.C. Foulk came. At night Rev. N.R. Luce preached. A very good Sermon. Stay at Bro. Coburn's.

Friday, August 16 Conference continued. Good sessions. Elected Board of trustees for incorporating the Conference & trustees of Sug. Gr. Academy & Otterbein and P. Es. I pr. at 8:00, Rom. 8:15. Speaking meeting.

Saturday, August 17 Finished up business in the forenoon mostly. Rev. T.J. Butterfield pr at 2:00. Closed business & adjourned. Rev. T.S. Bennett pr at 8:00. Howard exhorted.

Sunday, August 18 I preach at 11:00, Ps. 92:8. Dine at Coburn's. Rev. N.R. Luce preached at 2:45. I go with Rev. J.S. Amidon to his house in Corry. Emma & Fannie are his daughters. Luce stays There also.

Monday, August 19 Go to depot too late for the train. Stay at Amidon's till afternoon train at 1:40. Find Rev. S. Evans on the train after some stations. I reach home about 4:00 a.m. Slept 4 hours on cars 1 hour at home.

Tuesday, August 20 Reached home at 4:00 a.m. Busy. Rev. Wm. Armstrong of W. Meth. Ch. calls & dines with us. Cash drafts, orders, etc. Start at 4:00 via Celina to Shane's Crossing. Stay at Wm. Pontius' at Shane's Crossing with K.L. Hoffman.

Wedneday, August 21 Go with Frank Sapp to Jas. B.

Russel's near Centenary Church. Dine There, it being my Conference home. Open Conference at 2:00 with a large attendance. Rev. Jas. A. Crum sups & lodges at Russel's. Rev. G.C. Warvel pr. at 8:00. I slept 7 hours.

Thursday, August 22 Proceed with the business; the examinations. Henry Walters dined with us. Got along well with Pastor's reports. Rev. W.O. Dinnius pr. at 8:00. Good meeting.

Friday, August 23 Session Continued. Dine at Geo. Hurless', a cousin of C & P. Hurless, with Wm. Miller & o Thers. Missionary Meeting in the evening addressed by Rev. C.H. Kiracofe & Bishop Becker. I raise nearly $240.00 Mis. subs. Stationing Com. met.

Saturday, August 24 Stationing Com. at 7:00. Conf. continues. Dine with Becker at Rev. Edmiston's. Call at Br. L.F. Sapp's. Conference closed about 6:00. Supper at Solomon Shock's with Bp. Becker & o Thers. Bish. Becker pr. at 8:00, Luke 7:9. Stay at Russel's as usual.

Sunday, August 25 I pr. at 10:30 in the Grove, Ps. 93:1. Collection $87.70. Dine at Jas. B. Russel's. Sab. School Anniversary at 3:00. Bp. H.J. Becker spoke on 500 miles on Horseback in Palestine & Syria. After lunch, Bro. Russel takes us to Shane's Crossing & Bp. Becker pr. at Pres. Ch. We stay at Rev. J.H. Kiracofe's.

Monday, August 26 We start at 7:00 for home. Dine at Geo. F. Horine's at W. Manchester with Dillon's & Becker. Come home. Bp. Becker sups with us. Call at Wm. Dillon's and at Dr. L. Davis'. Bp. B. leaves at midnight for home at Akron.

Tuesday, August 27 At home in the forenoon. In afternoon go to town & cash drafts, postal orders & notes, and bank money. Pay Blum $100.00. Houk called in forenoon. Dem. Convention. Go on 1:20 night train to Crestline.

Wednesday, August 28 Arrive at Crestline abt 5:00 & go thence to Wooster arriving abt 8:20. Albert Bonewell comes abt noon & takes me and o Thers to Madisonburg, 4 miles north. Conference (East Ohio) opens at 2:00. Home at Andrew Sonnedecker. Rev. John Excell pr. at 7:30, a good discourse.

Thursday, August 29 Conference continued. Rev. H.H. Hinman came. Examinations continued. I pr. at night Eph. 2:4. Sonnedecker's Children: Allie 26; Emma 23, Clara 20. A son who graduated at Otterbein & went a year to U.B. Sem. teacher now in Pub. School at Tiffin.

Friday, August 30 Conference continued. I dine at B.A. Bonewell's. J. Noel elected pres-elder. Stationing com. met at Motte's in the evening. Bp. H.J. Becker came afternoon & pr. at night. Becker homes with us, at Sonnedecker's.

Saturday, August 31 Conference continued. I dine again at B.A. Bonewell's. Conference closed at 5:15. Bp. Becker lectured at 7:30.

Sunday, September 1 I pr. at 11:00, 2 Cor. 3:7, 8. Dine at Sonnedecker's. Mrs. Boyd, their daughter, There. Call at Mr. A. Rahl's to see Mrs. Sarah Shisler of Orrville who gave us $1,000 donation. S.S. Anniversary at 3:00. Bp. B. pr. at 7:30. I stay at Bonewell's.

Monday, September 2 Start at 3:55 a.m. for Wooster. Go on 4:20 train to Crestline. Breakfast. On 7:30 train to Delaware. Wait There till noon. Reach Dayton at 3:00 & bank money. Found Lorin had come home from Kans. Dr. L. Davis called in the evening.

Tuesday, September 3 Went to town in forenoon & again in afternoon. Saw Blum; blew up Troups; saw Houk. Called at Dillon's & Graybill's in forenoon. Went on Midnight train to Toledo, Ohio.

Wednesday, September 4 Arrive at Toledo abt 6:00. Start on Pennsylvania branch at 7:20. Stop at Helena. Find home at Rev. J. Garn's, J. French my room mate. Conf. opened at 2:00. I pr. at 7:30 Eph. 3.19. Garn's children: Helena 18, Naomia 12; Arthur 7

Thursday, September 5 Conf. contin. Rev. E.B. Maurer comes to proselyte Rev. A.J. Burkett, but fails. Bp. H.J. Becker & Rev. Wm. Dillon come. Rev. D.O. Tussing pr. at 7:30. Speaking meeting followed.

Friday, September 6 Conf. continued. Boundary Com. reported. In afternoon Rev. J. French was elected pres. elder. Stationing Com. met at 5:00 & 7:00. Bp. H.J.

Becker pr. at 7:30 on Char. & labors of Paul at Reformed Church. House full.

Saturday, September 7 Conf. continued in High School building. Rev. A.J. Burkett pr. at 2:00. Session closed at 5:00, or before, Bp. Becker Lectured at 8:00, on Palestine & Syria. House full. Supper at Wagner's.

Sunday, September 8 I pr. at 10:30, 1 Kings 18:39. Dine at Garns. Dr. Dillon pr. at 2:30, John 15:1-3. Bp. Becker lectured on Children of Palestine & Syria. I go home with Br. Wm. Shale & take supper. Pr. at Burgoon at 8:00, Rom. 8:16. Stay at Mitchell's.

Monday, September 9 Go on 7:20 train to Lima & by close connection thence to Dayton, arriving about 1:00. Bp. H. Floyd called. Felt unusually nervous. Slept only four hours & a half.

Tuesday, September 10 Went to town twice in the forenoon. Slept a little. Went on 2:45 train to Springfield and Columbus. Reach Columbus abt 6:00. Go to Rev. Jas. A. Brown's, 90 King Ave. Lodge There.

Wednesday, September 11 Went on 7:00 train to Thurston and Rushville, Ohio. N. Allebaugh meets me at Rushville and takes me to his house where I have my Conf. home. Conference opens at 2:00. Rev. Wm. Armstrong preached at 7:30. "Thou shalt love the L."

Thursday, September 12 Conference continued. Ra Ther a good session—forenoon & afternoon. Rev. G.W. Walton pr. at 7:30, 2 Cor. 5:17. Good speaking meeting. Rev. H.H. Hinman came. Noah Allebaugh's children: Frank 17; Cora 15; Oscar 13; Delpha 12.

Friday, September 13 Conference continues. Dine at Thos. L. Householder's Supper at Louis B. Lehman's. Rev. J. Hoffhines & I address on Missions. Raise $202.00 Subs. for Missions afterward increased to $223.00. Stay as usual at Allebaugh's.

Saturday, September 14 Conference continued. Stationing Com. meets at 7:00 & at 1:00. Dine at Wm. Guyton's 1 m south. Memorial service for W.K. McDaniel & Joseph McVey, at 2:30. Lecture of Rev. H.H. Hinman at 3:30. Conf. adjourned. Supper at Balser Housholder's.

Rev. Chas. McDaniel pr at 7:30, Col. 3.11. Second Granddaughter born to-night at 11:00.

Sunday, September 15 Pr. in Grove at 10:30, Heb. 4:14. Dine with the Elder Bros. Sab. Sch. Anniversary at 2:00. Supper at Allebaugh's. Rev. J. Hoffhines pr. at 7:30. Communion. Stay at Allebaugh's.

Monday, September 16 Start at 6:00 for Rushville, Col., Delaware to Dayton. Arrive at home at 1:00 p.m. Bp. H. Floyd called in the evening.

Tuesday, September 17 Called at J.K. Graybill's; also at Wm. Dillon's. Cabled at Dr. L. Davis'. Letter from Reuchlin dated 15th announcing ano Ther daughter born the 14th. Executive Mission Meeting at Kira[cofe's].

Wednesday, September 18 At home all day. Wrote some letters.

Thursday, September 19 Went to town in the forenoon. Saw Houk and printers. Went to the cemetery afternoon. Wrote some letters. Brought from Troup's 200 copies of Lawrence's Pamphlet.

Friday, September 20 Saw Mr. Houk a few minutes in the forenoon. Went to town with Pres. C.H. Kiracofe in the afternoon. Handed him a $500.00 certif. of Deposit. Sent J.A. He Therington Greenfield, Iowa $35.00.

Saturday, September 21 At home forenoon. Went to town at 4:00. Saw Houk. Got some proofs on his "Opinion." Got the remainder of the "1,500" of Lawrence Opinion.

Sunday, September 22 I Preached at the West End Mission, at 10:30, Rom. 8:14. Heard Rev. C.H. Kiracofe at Mission at 7:30.

Monday, September 23 Looking after Legal & publishing matters. Called at Rev. C.H. Kiracofe's and Dr. L. Davis' in the evening.

Tuesday, September 24 Wrote an article on East Ohio Conf. Call at Graybill's, Blum's, Houk's, etc. Look up the Gen. Conf. minutes. At home all the evening.

Wednesday, September 25 Went to town in forenoon; also in afternoon. Worked some in arranging or inspecting Gen. Conf. minutes.

Thursday, September 26 Spent considerable time running to town & back. Expressed minutes to N.R. Luce to record. Wrote several letters in the evening: E.J. Moody, C.L. Wood, B. Alter & Huffman—to Lee Hoisington.

Friday, September 27 At home. Twice go to see Mr. G.W. Houk about our Dayton answer.

Saturday, September 28 Went and was qualified to the Dayton Answer. Called at various places. Directed Legal pamphlet to several Dayton Ministers & some editors. Went on 4:00 train via Washington C.H. to Lancaster. Stay at Goetz' boarding house.

Sunday, September 29 Reached New Lexington in afternoon, afoot. Saw Butler our attorney about amending answer. Staid at Phoenix Hotel in New Lexington.

Monday, September 30 Saw Butter & Huffman about amending answer in Church case. Butter was granted by the court leave to amend. We spent the day & evening preparing answer. Dine at eating house. Evening took up regular board at Phoenix.

Tuesday, October 1 Heard Slander Case Estella [blank] vs. Emma Randolph. Lawrence, Houk, Shuey, Gunkle, & McMahon come. We spent the evening with attorneys at Mr. Huffman's Office & Butler's.

Wednesday, October 2 Our attorneys apply for a continuance. Denied it. Liberal attorney's make concessions & trial proceeds. Papers read. Afternoon Slander trial intervenes. Then our case proceeds. Evidence proceeds. Council in Eve.

Thursday, October 3 Conclude the testimony. Gunkle opens for plaintiffs. Lawrence, Furgueson, Houk, and McMahon speak in succession. Close at 10:00 at night.

Friday, October 4 My trav. Expense going & coming $5.40. Hotel at N. Lex. 5.75 on the way .85. Paid Lawr. & Houk's bill $8.00. Came via Columbus home. Arrive at 6:00. Found all well. La[w]yers at N. Lexington: Butler & Huffman; Furgueson & Johnson; Jas. D. Rebalic, L.A. Tussing.

Saturday, October 5 At Home. Went to Conserv. Office. Went late in afternoon to town with Katie & bought her a Jersey Jacket $5.00; Red Gloves .60; ribbon 28; pins 17 cents. Bp. Becker staid with us.

Sunday, October 6 Went to the Mission Church to hear Bishop Becker preach on Parable of the sower. At home the rest of the day.

Monday, October 7 Went in the evening to hear Bp. H.J. Becker lecture on Palestine.

Tuesday, October 8 Wrote out a little sketch of our trial for Conservator. Went to town in the afternoon. Got 300 more of Legal pamphlet. Saw Bp. Becker leave at 9:30 eve. for the Pacific Coast.

Wednesday, October 9 Go to town with Legal Pamphlets to mail. See Houk a few moments and also Troup Manufacturing Comp. Go to town several times to mail pamphlets, etc.

Saturday, October 12 Went to town in the forenoon. Returned via Dillon's. Afternoon spent in writing, mainly. In the evening heard Hon. Wm. McKinley speak on the tariff at the Rink on Main Street. He is a good speaker.

Sunday, October 13 I Pr. at West End Church at 10:30, II Pet. 2:15. At home till evening. Called at Rev. C.H. Kiracofe's a while before meeting. Pres. Kiracofe pr. at W. End Church at 7:00, 2 Ki. 10:15.

Monday, October 14 At home. Called at Dr. Davis' in the afternoon. He had been sick since Tuesday night.

Tuesday, October 15 At home. Write letters forenoon & afternoon. Left Dr. Davis gold watch with Henneman. Henneman was a discarded watch-tinker of mine.

Wednesday, October 16 Called at P.O., Reform Pub. House, Troup's Man'g House; at Court House.

Thursday, October 17 Called at Dillon's & Davis'. Started

at 11:50 for Richmond. Called at D.K. Zeller's and at T.J. Study's Office. Afterward saw Judge Lawrence & T.J. Study at Office. Stai at D.K. Zeller's.

Friday, October 18 After Miscellaneous business, The Court took up the Sugar Grove Church case & 1. The papers (pleadings) were read. 2. Kibley spoke till noon & then till 3:00—2 3/4 hs—Study & Witt spoke. Lawrence spoke a half hour. Board at Zeller's.

Saturday, October 19 Lawrence spoke in forenoon nearly 4 hours, very ably. Houk spoke about 3 hours with ability. Stay at D.K. Z's till after supper. Go on train to Washington. Stay at Moses Hatfield's.

Sunday, October 20 Hatfields take me to Sugar Grove Ch. I pr. 2 Pet. 2:15. Dine at Chas. Lamb's. Children Nettie 11; May 7; Nellie 5. L. takes me to Bethel. I pr. at 3:00, Ps. 92:8. Come to L's. Prayer meeting at Sug. Grove. Stay at Adam Howard's.

Monday, October 21 H. takes me to Richmond. Hear E.F. Ritter Esq. Conclude the argument on Sugar Grove Ch. case. I come home on noon train. At Dillon's, Graybill's, & Davis'

Tuesday, October 22 Read proofs on Conservator. A very rainy day. Went after 4:00 to see Mr. Houk, in vain. In the evening I go to Dr. L. Davis to see Mrs. Sarah Shisler, who come [sic] to consult about her will.

Wednesday, October 23 Went to town to see Houk etc. Call at Davis to see Mrs. Shisler. Went to town in aftern. Called at 5:00 at Dr. Davis'. After supper call at Davis' again after writing some letters.

Thursday, October 24 Went at 9:00 in buggy with C.H. Kiracofe to Germantown. Dine at Levi Zehring's. Call at Lewis Wetz & Michael Thomas'. Return to Zehring's get a 50 subscription on legal fund, and return home, arriving at 6:30.

Friday, October 25 Got up at 5:00. At home most of forenoon. Went to Dr. Davis' in afternoon a while also in the evening. All the children went to the lecture at Associational Hall.

Saturday, October 26 Called at Dr. L. Davis; at Houk's; at Troup's Man'g Co. & paid them. Mrs. Sarah Shisler dines with us. Mr. Houk called. At home in the evening. Dictated a letter to Rev. Wm. Miller.

Sunday, October 27 Went to W. End Ch. Rev. Wm. Dillon pr. at 10:30, John 15:5. Dine at home as usual. Rev. C.H. Kiracofe pr. at 7:00, Ps. 8:4.

Monday, October 28 Went to see Houk. He thought to have papers made out in afternoon, but did not. At home afternoon & evening. Much writing.

Tuesday, October 29 Called at Kiracofe's. Went to Houks. Dined at Pres. C.H. Kiracofe's. Went to town at 3:00. At 4:00, Mrs. Sarah Shisler completed her donation. Houk & Mrs. Kiracofe are the witnesses. (The donations ate it up).

Wednesday, October 30 At home in forenoon with much letter-writing. Called at Dillon's. Corrected up proofs on Richmond Answer. At home in the evening.

Thursday, October 31 Called at Rev. Wm. Dillon's and at J.K. Graybill's. Spent much of the day in arranging the pages of Dayton & Richmond answer. "Ten Annuals" have their banquet at Wilbur Landis'.

Sunday, November 3 Not very well. Staid at home all day.

Monday, November 4 Got news at 11:00 of Court decision at Richmond in Sugar Grove Case. Spent afternoon in town seeing Houk, editors of dailies, etc. & writing letters and cards. Lorin returned with decis.

Tuesday, November 5 Wrote some cards. Looked after the decision in Conservator.

Wednesday, November 6 Went to Dillon's, to Town, saw Houk, Albert Shearer, Bickham, etc. Called at Dillon's & Graybill's. Sent blank leases to Lee Hoisington.

Thursday, November 7 Went to Dillon's, Graybill's, and Davis' in forenoon. Wrote some letters. Went to town to post-office. In the evening, Bro. Dillon called with Bro. Miller & Westbarger who are in a church lawsuit at Ft. Jennings.

Friday, November 8 At home till 10:00. Get letters at Carrier's window. Go to town & send draft for $40.00 to county treasurer of Grant Co., Ind. to pay tax. Went to hear Col. Sanford's Lecture.

Sunday, November 10 Pr at West End Church at 10:30, Rom. 8:28. Dine at Jac. Swank's. Attend the funeral of Mrs. Fitch at 2:00, Cor. Williams and Fourth Sts. Pr. at 7:00, again, 2 Pet. 1:4.

Monday, November 11 Spent the day mostly at home writing notices for the paper, clearing up the accumulations of my desk, etc. Had Lorin write a half dozen letters asking for legal funds. Katie went to Young People's meeting with Flora Greenwood.

Tuesday, November 12 Read proofs morning and noon. At home afternoon. Went & spent the evening at John Weidner's.

Wednesday, November 13 Went to town in forenoon, engaged the remainder of Lawrence's pamphlet bound. Saw Houk. Bought a lamp for 75 cts. Prepared to go to Richmond, but train took off. Go at 5:20. Stay at D.K. Zeller's.

Thursday, November 14 Saw Study (T.J.) and had a talk with him. He finds me Judge Comstock's original copy of decision. Dine at D.K. Zeller's. Go on 4:50 train to Dayton. Get home at 7:30. Work on Copy till 11:00.

Friday, November 15 At home. Went to Gra[y]bill's to get decision set up. Set Lorin at it.

Saturday, November 16 At home in forenoon. Wrote letters. Went to town in afternoon. Quarterly meeting at West End Church. Rev. Wm. Miller preached at 7:00. John Forney staid with us. He is half crazy.

Sunday, November 17 Rev. Wm. Miller P.E. preached at W.E.C. at 10:30. Dine at Wm. Weidner's, with Rev. C.B. McDaniel. Supper at home, with McDaniel. McDaniel pr. at 7:00, W.E. Ch., on the temptation of Christ. McD. Stays with us.

Monday, November 18 Gave Graybill our Conservator premium list. Pres. C.H. Kiracofe & Rev. Wm. Miller calls. Meeting of the Missionary Ex. Com. at 2:00 at Dillon's. Qr. Conf. at 7:00 at W.E. Ch. W. Miller, P.E.; C.B. McDaniels, John Nicklass in dissatisfaction.

Tuesday, November 19 Mailed pamphlets, etc. Saw Houk. At home the rest of the day.

Thursday, November 21 At home most of the day. In afternoon saw the making up of the forms of Judge Comstock's tract decision. Attended and led the prayer-meeting at W.E. Ch. at 7:00.

Friday, November 22 Went to Graybill's, Dillon's, and Davis'. Went to P.O.; bought sandals, called at Houk's office and at Troup's Mfg. Co. Called at John Weidner's.

Saturday, November 23 Went to get some copies of tract form of decision and found a misprint & got type to correct it. We had orders for Judge Comstock's Decision (tract form) filled. Got Gen. Conf. record from Bro. N.R. Luce.

Sunday, November 24 Pr. at W.E. Ch. at 10:30, 1 Cor. 10:12. At home till evening. Pr. at 7:00, Ex. 28:34. A rainy evening. Much rain for several weeks past.

Monday, November 25 Corrected Publisher's notices, reducing them half. Write letters. Read & correct proofs.

Tuesday, November 26 Correct proofs & correct Premium list. Write letters.

Wednesday, November 27 Look after mailing papers. Dr. L. Davis called to see me in the afternoon.

Thursday, November 28 Attended Thanksgiving service at Ludlow St. Reformed Church & heard Prof. Scovill of Wooster University pr. a very able sermon on the Fourth Commandment. Pr. at West End Church 7:00, Acts 14:17.

Friday, November 29 Spent forenoon at home mostly writing letters, after unaccountable late rising. In afternoon went to town and purchased various articles. Read proof at night on Theologico—Legal's article.

Saturday, November 30 Went with Katie & bought her

a cloak at Meldrum & McDaniel's $10.50. At home afternoon and evening. Spidel & wife of Liberty called in.

Sunday, December 1 At W.E. Ch. Dr. Davis pr. at 10:30, without a text. At home till evening. Pr. at 7:00 W.E. Ch. Heb. 12:12-17.

Monday, December 2 At home. Wrote many of the secretaries of conferences for statistics.

Tuesday, December 3 Tizzard filled my teeth—$4.00. Consultation at Dr. Davis' at 4:00 over Kiracofe's going east and some o Ther matters.

Thursday, December 5 At home all day looking up business & writing letters. An old man called to see if I was selling Talmadge's book, as he had heard.

Friday, December 6 Got a letter from Rev. C.B. McDaniel. Went to see Davis, Dillon, and we both to see Kiracofe.

Saturday, December 7 Went up to Dillon's and Kiracofe's to see about McDaniel's moving expenses, etc. Went to town in the afternoon to take mail & trade a little. Literary meeting at Davis'.

Sunday, December 8 Dr. Lewis Davis pr. at West End Ch. at 10:30 on worship. It was much appreciated. At 7:00 Rev. Wm. Dillon pr. W.E. Ch., Acts 9:31. Speaking meeting followed.

Monday, December 9 Read some proofs on Conservator. Wrote some letters. Went to town in afternoon. Sent off affidavit. Saw Houk in forenoon. His grandchild dead.

Tuesday, December 10 Went up to mailing room and to Dillon's. Wrote letters and went to town in the afternoon.

Wednesday, December 11 Went to town before noon and saw Mr. G.W. Houk and again in the afternoon. Went to Davis', Dillon's and Kiracofe's in the afternoon & evening.

Thursday, December 12 Went to Dillon's and out to look

for a house for McDaniel, the pastor. Went in afternoon to town. Paid G.W. Houk $50.00 for McNew. Attended prayer-meeting at 7:30 at W.E. Ch.

Saturday, December 14 Arrange to meet McDaniel's family. They dine & stay at Dillon's. I go with him to rent a house. He and Wilbur move his goods into his house on Second Street.

Sunday, December 15 Rev. Chas. B. McDaniel pr. at 10:30 1 Kings 18:21. He & family dine with us. Their children are Faye 9, Winifred 7, Amey 4, & William 1 1/2. McDaniel pr. at 7:00, 2 Cor. 3:7, 8.

Monday, December 16 Went to town in forenoon and pd my tax $9.39. Saw Houk at Court room. At home in afternoon. Went to Rev. C.B. McDaniel's to donation, a bit, in the evening.

Tuesday, December 17 Called at the mailing room to see about the wrappers. Spent the rest of the day mostly in selecting distributors and sending out Judge Comstock's decision. Attended prayer-meeting at W.E. Church at 7:30. Beckner's place.

Wednesday, December 18 Called at Dr. L.Davis'. Met Judge Wm. Lawrence at G.W. Houk's office. Spent the day in consultation. Wilbur and Dr. Dillon There in afternoon. Got ready in eve. to start to Ind. Sent out many letters.

Thursday, December 19 Arose at 4:00. At 6:15 start for Fairmount, Ind. Wait at Union City till 1:00. (Reach) Marion at 2:30 & Fairmount at 4:00. Ride 2 1/2 ms. with Mr. Stresh & then walk to Aunt Lizzie Reeder's. Stay There that night.

Friday, December 20 Went to Wm. Reeder's & stay till after dinner. Call at Ellis Wright's & see his new wife Rhoda. Go to Oliver A. Glass's, where I find Aunt Lizzie & Robert. I stay There till morning.

Saturday, December 21 Oliver takes me early to Fairmount. Wait at Mation abt two hours. Arrive at Warren at 11:30. J.W. Williams takes me to his house four miles south. Go to Edward's Chapel at 7:00 & hear

Rev. A. Rust, P.E. 2 Cor. 4:7. Arrange for dedication. Stay at Geo. Lee's 1/2 m west. Very rainy.

Sunday, Decmber 22 At 10:30 pr. dedication sermon John 17:24, at Edward's Church & raise $386.00 & dedicate the Church. Dine at Saml. Elkins 1/2 m n. Rev. A. Rust pr. at 7:00, Eph. 3:19. Stay at Josiah Slusher's, 3/4 m n.e. Church is 36 X 44 X 16. Cost near $1,500.00.

Monday, December 23 Called at Mrs. H.M. Click s. Went on to Warren with Rev. A. Rust. See Rev. A. Worth & Surran. Bevington, Wesleyan, and Alexander live in Town. Go via Decatur to Richmond, Ind. See T.J. Study, Supper at D.K. Zeller's. Get home at 9:00. Trustees: C.S. Morgan, Josiah Slusher, J.W. Williams, Geo. Lee & Thomas Weeken.

Thursday, December 26 Called at Davis' Dillon's and John Nicholas'. Went in afternoon to P.O., Houk's, etc. Sent Judge Wm. Lawrence $63.25. Rev. J. Nicholas called in the evening.

Friday, December 27 At home in the forenoon. Went to Houk's in afternoon and was qualified to our recast answer in Pr. Est. Case. Children went to star course concert.

Saturday, December 28 At home all the forenoon writing, and reading proof on Lawrence' Review of Slough's decision.

Sunday, December 29 Rev. C.B. McDaniel pr. at 10:30, Prov. On Care of Child. In eve. I call at Graybill's Davis & McDaniels' on my way to church. At 7:00 McDaniel pr. Prov. "Keep the heart".

Monday, December 30 Read some proofs. Went about 11 o'clock to meet Study at Houk's office. Spent the rest of the day There. Read in the evening.

Tuesday, December 31 Called at Graybill's. At Dr. Davis. At home the rest of the day. In the evening, Bechner and afterward J. Nicholas called. I sat up and read till after midnight. The town bells rang at the incoming of 1890.

An. Conf. of 1890
Erie- Left with P.Es. Auglaize- Allentown. East Ohio-
Left to P.E. Sandusky- [blank] Scioto- Pleasant Valley,
P.O. Baltimore, Ohio. Three miles N.E. of Baltimore.

Rev. Noah Allebaugh Bremen, Ohio. Helen Wright born
Sept. 14, 1889.

Bishop's Salary.

Aug. 17 Erie Conference	29.00
Aug. 24 Auglaize Conf.	183.15
Sept. 2 East Ohio	65.01
Sept. 7 Sandusky	26.13
Sept. 14 Scioto	84.58
[total]	$387.87
Afterward Scioto	1.00
Afterward from Auglaize	5.00
March 16, Penn & Md	42.80
After	4.50
Heikes	5.00
promised	4.00
Chart Col.	51.05

Auglaize afterward (Sept 1890) on Salary of 1889, T.M.
Harvey's collection $2.50.

Bishop's Trav. Expenses

Going to Sug. Gr. Pa	[blank]
Car to Union City	9.10
Car to Watt's Flatts	.70
Hack to Sug. Grove	.25
Restaurant	.25
Return ticket	9.40
Edibles on way	.25
St Car fare	.10
Collection	[blank]
Aug. 20 Fare to Celina	1.20
Aug. 20 Fare to Shane's Cross.	.35
Return	2.25
Collections (paid on)	1.50
[total]	23.85

Traveling to E. Ohio

Delaware	1.60
Crestline	1.15
Wooster	1.60
Lunch	.15
[total]	4.50
Return Crestline	1.60
Return Delaware	1.15
Breakfast	.25
Dayton	1.50
Lunch	.10
p'd on Collections	1.00
[total]	4.60
To Springfield	.50
To Columbus	.90
To Rushville	1.10
St Car fare Dayton & Col.	.10
Return to Columbus	1.10
To Delaware	.50
Dayton	1.50
St car fare home	.05
[total]	5.75

Trip to and from N. Lexington

Wash. C.H.	.90
Lancaster	1.45
Colum	1.55
Springf.	.90
Dayton	1.50
Lodging at Lancaster O.	.50
Toll	.10
Dinner on way	.20
Hotel at N. Lexington	5.75
The foregoing was paid by breth.	11.50
Trav. Ex to Frankl'n	13.75
Hotel at Dillsburgh	.50
Restaurant	.50
Return trip	12.90
Secr'y's Coll.	.50

In 1889
Special Expenses:

Adair farm	70.00
Grant farm	120.00
Lent Reuchlin	130.00
Funeral	265.00
Total	585.00

[The diary ends with a list of attorneys.]

PART THREE

1890–1899

"This is the beginning of another year, of which I have seen sixty-six; and truly my life has been full of blessings. I think few have enjoyed life more than I have."

Milton Wright, January 1, 1895

Milton Wright's life was again marked by controversy in the United Brethren Church. He was appointed to oversee all court litigation in the church between the radicals and liberals on ownership of church property. His children had grown to adulthood, but continued to be an important part of his life and household. His sons Wilbur and Orville (or "the boys," as he called them) started a small printing business and a bicycle shop. They became interested in flight and experimented with kites. His daughter, Katharine, attended Oberlin College, graduating in 1898. Milton's Wright's two oldest sons married, and grandchildren became an important part of his daily life. He continued to write to family members and visited them often in Indiana, checking on his farm and other properties there. The Bishop records the anniversary of Susan's death each year, commenting that Independence Day was never a day of celebration after she died.

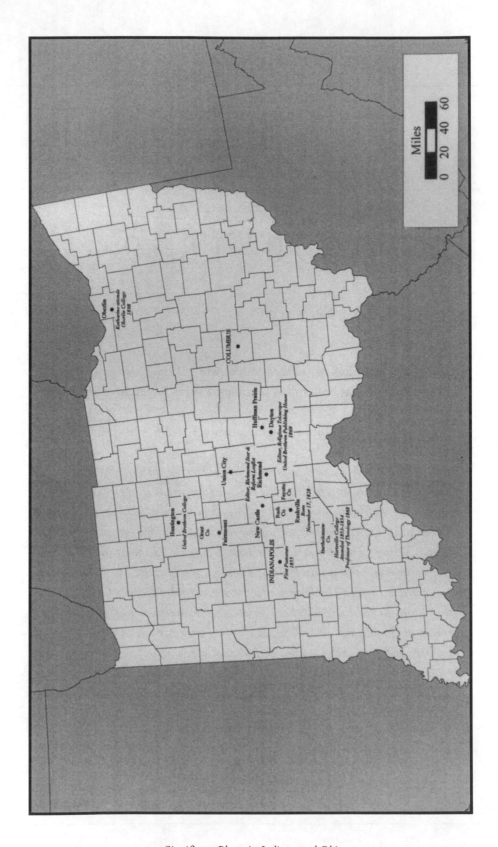

Significant Places in Indiana and Ohio

1890

Wednesday, January 1 At home all day. Have cold and do not feel very well.

Thursday, January 2 At home till evening. Katie started to school in town. Called at Dillon's in the evening. Dr. L. Davis called awhile to-day.

Friday, January 3 At home all day engaged in assorting letters and in writing letters. Lorin, Wilbur, and Katie went to the Star course concert.

Saturday, January 4 Went to Richmond on noon train. Paid off Zeller's note. Went on to Dublin. Supper at Wm. McGath's. Call at Bp. Halleck Floyd's. Pr. at 6:30, Rom. 6:21. Stay at Dr. G.W. Champ's.

Sunday, January 5 Call at Oler's. All absent. Call at Floyd's. Pr. at 10:30, Ex. 28:34. Dine at Rev. Z. McNew's. Floyd & Oler call there. Went to Floyd's awhile—supper. Pr at 6:30, 1st Psalm. Stay at Floyd's.

Monday, January 6 Went to McNew's, and then to Cambridge. Go to New Lisbon (Sexton). Dine at Robin's. Thence to Hamilton's & to John McKee's. He takes me to Harvey Wright's. Lodge there.

Tuesday, January 7 Stay at Harvey's all day, and till morning. Supper at Luther New House's.

Wednesday, January 8 Harvey takes me early to Knightstown. Go to Richmond & thence to Dayton in evening. Saw Study. Called at Zeller's. Dine at Allen Harris'.

Thursday, January 9 At home all day. Mostly writing letters, reading, etc. Katie is better.

Friday, January 10 Went to town to see Houk & Study who came from Richmond; and again in afternoon. Wrote letters in eve. Called at Davis' in forenoon.

Saturday, January 11 Went to town to see Houk. Drew money on draft. Wrote letters and cards. Called to see Drs. L. Davis & Wm. Dillon in the evening.

Sunday, January 12 Rev. C.B. McDaniel pr. at 10:30, John 15:9. I Pr. at 7:00, 2 Cor. 5.19.

Monday, January 13 Rose early & wrote several letters. Went to Graybill's and Dr. Davis' and thence to R.R. offices & make application for clergy permits. At home in afternoon.

Tuesday, January *14 At Conservator Office, Dillon's & Dr. Davis'. At home most of* the day. Settled with Lorin to Jan. 1st, 1890; allow him in all $125.00 for five months. Paid $20.00 on his trav. exp. home.

Wednesday, January 15 Went to Houk's Office in forenoon for copy of Dayton Answer. Rev. J.H. Kiracofe called in afternoon.

Thursday, January 16 At home part of day. Called at Houk's in afternoon.

Friday, January 17 At home in forenoon. Called at Dillon's & Davis' in afternoon. Telephone to Houk, twice.

Saturday, January 18 Went to Dr. L. Davis in forenoon. His deposition began on Church case. At home in the afternoon & evening, reading & writing.

Sunday, January 19 Attend Church at West End. Rev. Wm. Dillon preaches, 2 Pet. 3:9, a good sermon. Pres. C.H. Kiracofe pr. at 7:00, Ps. 1:1 4. Rainy evening.

Monday, January 20 At Dr. Lewis Davis' to see his deposition taken. At Rev. C.H. Kiracofe's in the afternoon. Com. from U.B. Sem. came! Rev. H. Floyd staid with us. Com. almost ashamed of themselves.

Tuesday, January 21 Went to town with Bishop Floyd in the Forenoon. At home in afternoon & evening.

Wednesday, January 22 Went to Dr. Davis, but Att's did not come. Call at Dillon's. Go to town in afternoon & get R.R. permits. Call at Court House, see Houk. Hear part of the pleadings in the Mc a fresh case.

Thursday, January 23 Go to town. Engage a coat & vest made. Call at the court room. Call at Dr. Davis' & Dillon's. Get ready to go to Orrville, Ohio.

Friday, January 24 Reach Crestline before day. Lunch. Reach Orrville ab. 9:00. Stay at Mrs. Sarah Shisler's. She well pleased with her donation to Church. See Mr [blank] Go on via Mt. Vernon to Centreburg. Stay at the Shaffer House.

Saturday, January 25 Go on 7:00 train to Rushville. N. Allebaugh takes me to his home. After dinner go to Zion Sch. H. & pr. at 1:30 1 Ps. 1 v. Raise $304.50 for Zion Ch. defense. Stay at N. Allebaugh's.

Sunday, January 26 Pr. at Greyton Sch. H. at 10:00. Ps. 92:8. Raise $210.00 for Pisgah & Zion's defense. Dine at Wm. Greyton's. Allebaugh takes me to Rev. A. Bateson's. His son, & his Fatherinlaw, infirm. Pr at Otterbein 6:30, Ex. 28:34. Stay at Shaffer's John Shaffer's.

Monday, January 27 Went to Rushville with John Shaffer. Thence to Columbus, Delaware, Dayton, arri. at 4:00. Gather legal documents and start at 6:00 via Greenville

at Van Wert, Ohio. Arrive at Van Wert 9:00. Put up at Hotel Marsh, Room 33. Lorin with me.

Tuesday, January 28 At Court part of the time. Telegraphed to parties to come. Our case came up about 3:00. The pleadings were read. Adjourned counsel in Houk's room.

Wednesday, January 29 Began at 8:30 examination of witnesses: Miller, John J. McKenzie & Wilson after exam. of counseller & Dr. Steman. I on the stand an hour. Kiracofe testifies. Lorin went for record. Lorin brought books after a weary night.

Thursday, January 30 Floyd & Dillon testify. Afternoon, A.W. Drury & Funkhouser testified. After Supper, We had a meeting of brethren at Mr. Houk's room. A very unprofitable time.

Friday, January 31 Trial continued. McKee, Bay, Miller and Shuey testify. We have a meeting at 7:00 in Houk's room, No. 36. Not profitable.

Saturday, February 1 Shuey closed. Floyd and I recalled in rebuttal. Adjourned to 9th instant. Pay bills of Attorneys, myself, Lorin & Floyd. Go via Lima to Dayton. Get there about 9:00.

Sunday, February 2 Pres. Elder Wm. Miller pr. at 10:30 Isa. 66:13. Communion. Dine at Rev. Wm. Dillon's. Call at Dr. L. Davis'. Supper at home. Rev. Wm. Miller pr. at 7:00, Matt. 19:27.

Monday, February 3 Dayton Circuit Qr. M. at 9:00 at Dillon's. Prepare to go to Richmond. Go at 6:00 p.m. Put up at The Huntington House. Saw Kiracofe & Floyd at the depot. See Study at home. Lodge at Huntington House.

Tuesday, February 4 Court convenes at 9:00. Judge Kibbey dismissed the suit against Sugar Grove Church. Lawrence & Houk come. Consultation. Write letters. Go to Greensfork. Stay at M. Hatfield's.

Wednesday, February 5 Pr. Philander Cranor's funeral at 11:00. Acts 24:15. Dine at Martha Ballenger's. I take the train to Greensfork & thence home. Arrive at 7:00.

Thursday, February 6 At home writing letters mostly. In the evening called at Rev. Wm. Dillon's & Dr. L. Davis'.

Friday, February 7 Went to town in the forenoon. Had Wilbur write letters in the afternoon. Took letters to the post office.

Sunday, February 9 Heard Bp. Floyd pr. at West End Church, 1 Cor. 14:8. Bp. Floyd, Pres. Kiracofe & Dr. Dillon in the afternoon. Rev. Floyd pr. at 7:00.

Monday, February 10 Went on 7:00 train to Lima & thence to Van Wert. Put up at Hotel Marsh. Col. Alexander spoke most of the afternoon & had Gunkel's brief partly read. Council in Houk's room (36).

Tuesday, February 11 Judge Wm. Lawrence spoke all forenoon & till 4:00 p.m. with great ability & power. Houk spoke two hours. Council again in Room 36. Mine & Floyd's room is 33.

Wednesday, February 12 Hon. John A. McMahon spoke till 11:30. We go via Manchester home. Arrive at Dayton about 7:00. Found all well. Judge Dennis Dwyer on the train.

Thursday, February 13 At home writing all day. Read some in the evening.

Friday, February 14 Write in forenoon. Call at Dillon's. Go to Town in the afternoon. The children go to the Star Course Concert. I wrote on an article.

Saturday, February 15 Write out article for *Christian Conservator*. Went in afternoon to see Mr. Houk who had telephoned me. He to go to N.Y. for depositions.

Sunday, February 16 Heard Dr. A.A. Willits pr. at Third St. Presb. Ch. at 10:30, 1 Cor. 12:31. Moderate preacher; witty lecturer. Call at Rev. C.H. Kiracofe's. I Pr. at West End Ch. at 7:00, Acts 17:30, 31.

Monday, February 17 Write in the forenoon. See G.W. Houk in afternoon and give him $100 to pay expenses

to & in New York. Dr. L. Davis called in the evening.

Tuesday, February 18 Spent the time in writing largely. Sent list of P.E.'s to Dr. H.K. Carroll, Supt. Religions Census, Plainfield, N.J.

Thursday, February 20 Rev. W.O. Dinnius called in forenoon & Rev. C.H. Kiracofe. Wrote in the evening.

Friday, February 21 Spent forenoon in reading. Had letters written in afternoon. In the evening, called at Revs. Wm. Dillon's and C.H. Kiracofe's.

Saturday, February 22 At home all day. Wrote some. Read some.

Sunday, February 23 At Fourth Pres. Ch. heard D.A. Sinclair comment on Ps. 103.1 5. In the evening called on Dr. Lewis Davis.

Monday, February 24 At home in the forenoon, and at Dillon's & Davis'. Went to town in the afternoon & saw Houk.

Wednesday, February 26 Went to Davis', Dillon's, & Kiracofe's in the afternoon. Wrote letters in the forenoon & in the evening.

Thursday, February 27 At home writing part of the day. Bishop Becker came at daylight. I called at Dillon's with him. Exec. Com. (Mis.) in afternoon. Bishop Becker is very sick.

Friday, February 28 At Kiracofe's in the morning. Bp. Becker is better. Call at Dillon's. At home the rest of the day. Kenan's Lecture. Telegram of Judge Day's decision in Van Wert case. We learned it by letter in afternoon.

Saturday, March 1 Wrote an article for publication. Called at Graybill's, Dillon's, & Davis'. Judge Lawrence did not come. At home till evening.

Sunday, March 2 Pr. at West End Ch., at 10:30, Heb. 12:1,2. At home the rest of the day reading much in Chalmers' Sermons & Barnes' Notes. Much interested.

Monday, March 3 Went to Bellefontaine, consult Judge

Lawrence. Dine at a restaurant. Supper at Lawrence's. Go on 6:15 train via Sidney home. Arri. at 9:00.

Tuesday, March 4 Called at Graybill's, Davis', & Dillon's. Afternoon, called on Houk, & Geo. R. Young. Employed Young on the Dayton case. Evening: Called on Rev. D.H. French with Dillon.

Wednesday, March 5 At home all day. Wrote many letters in Afternoon and evening. In morning saw Judge Day's decision in Van Wert case, as published in daily *Journal.* Thermom. 20 degrees above.

Thursday, March 6 At home in forenoon. In afternoon, went to Houk's to meet him & Judge Lawrence in counsel. Call at Davis', Kiracofe's & McDaniel's. Ther. 7 degrees above.

Friday, March 7 Went to town at 9:00. Saw Houk. Called at Dillon's and Graybill's. Saw Kiracofe & heard from Virginia. John Nicholas called in the afternoon. Wrote the rest of the day. Ther 15 degrees above.

Saturday, March 8 At home mostly. Called at Rev. W. Dillon's in the afternoon. Wrote and had written several letters in the evening.

Sunday, March 9 Heard Rev. C.B. McDaniel preach at 10:30, John 17:17. At home the rest of the day and evening.

Monday, March 10 Went to town in the forenoon & afternoon to look after question of time of Dayton trial. At the Office in afternoon. At home in evening.

Tuesday, March 11 Went to town in forenoon. Wrote a few letters. Left at 6:00 for Pennsylvania. Detained at Xenia till abt. 12:00, by freight cars off the track near Morrow. Reached Pittsburgh in the morning.

Wednesday, March 12 Reach Pittsb. about 8:00. Harrisburg at 4:00. Bought coat. Reach Dillsburg at 7:30. Put up at The Wilson House, J.H. Floyd proprietor.

Thursday, March 13 Went to Franklin town and dined at Hershey's. Conference at 2:00. Began with two preachers. Added Huber & Keiter by transfer. Home at P.D.

Baker's, with M.F. Keiter. Rev. A.K. Shank pr. at 7:30, Ps. 1:1,2.

Friday, March 14 Conf. continues. J. Fohl & J.M. Biship admitted. Bp. H.J. Becker came. Six are referred to com. on applicants. Rev. J.S. Wentz pr. at 7:00. At Baker's.

Saturday, March 15 Continue business. Afternoon, elect Keiter & Huber, P.E. Stationing Com. met at 7:00. Bishop Becker lectured at 7.30. Close Conference business. At Baker's.

Sunday, March 16 Pr. at 10:00, 1 Tim. 4:16. Dine as usual at Baker's. Sab. Sch. Anniversary at 2:00, at Lutheran Church. Supper at Baker's. Call at Hershey's. Missionary meeting at 7:30. Bp. Becker spoke. We raise $410.00 subs. for missions. Becker's.

Monday, March 17 Go to East Crossing and walk down to W. Fairview & Dine & sup at Jacob Moltz'. Go on hack to Harrisburg and leave on 7:20 train for Pittsburgh.

Tuesday, March 18 Reach Columbus about 8:00; Xenia and home at 10:30. Revs. Dillon & Kiracofe called. Look over letters, papers, etc. Call at Dr. L. Davis' in the evening. Orville came home quite sick.

Wednesday, March 19 At home in forenoon. Call at Dr. Davis' in afternoon. Go to town & see attorneys. Call at Davis' again. At home in the evening.

Thursday, March 20 Called at Dr. L. Davis'. Went on 7:30 train to Greenfield, Ind. Mr. Howard takes me out to John Parker's, 6 ms. N.W. I Preach Father Parker's funeral at 2:00. Return to Dayton. Stay at L. Davis' till 1:00. He very sick.

Friday, March 21 Call at Dr. Davis' at 11:00 & stay till 1:00. At home in afternoon. Go to Davis' at 8:30 and stay an hour. Sleep five or six hours.

Saturday, March 22 Went to Dr. Davis' at 6:30, stay till about 9:00. Go to see Houk telegraph Floyd. See Young in afternoon. Stay at Davis' till 1:00 at night.

Sunday, March 23 Rose late. At home till 3:00 afternoon. At Dr. Lewis Davis' the rest of the afternoon and part of the evening. He is near death's door. At 9:40 Dr. Davis died.

Monday, March 24 Called at Dr. Davis'. Saw Bros. Kiracofe and Dillon at their home. Return home and write some for the funeral occasion. Continue till 1:00 at night.

Tuesday, March 25 Write still on funeral papers. Funeral service at 2:00 at Summit St. Chruch. Text, 2 Cor. 4:7. Burial at Woodland Cemetery. Called at Davis'. Bp. Floyd & Rev. C.S. Miller come. Stay with us.

Wednesday, March 26 Rev. D.S. Buck comes. Go with Buck to cash draft. At home the rest of the day. Floyd, Dillon, Kiracofe, & Miller come in for counsel. Miller & Floyd stay with us.

Thursday, March 27 Went to town to see our attorneys. See them at library room. Call at Kiracofe's who are moving to Summit Street.

Friday, March 28 Judge Lawrence did not come. Called at Young's a moment & at Houk's office & did not see him. Writing some in revision of my sermon.

Saturday, March 29 Letters from Lawrence, Strawn & Norton, and Sheets & Ogan, and copy of a letter from Beeman.

Sunday, March 30 Rev. C.H. Kiracofe pr. 10:30, John 3:3. Wysong, Wood & wife join Church. I pr. at 7:00 Rom. 1:20. Three seekers at the altar.

Monday, March 31 Arose about six o'cl. Wrote some letters. Arrange to present a copy on evidence wanted, by Wilbur. Called at Graybill's, Dillon's, & Mrs. L. Davis' in afternoon. Wrote in the evening.

Tuesday, April 1 Went to town forenoon and aftern. Sent W.H. Reeder $20.00 to Treas. of Adair Co., Iowa, $40.00. Wrote Treas. of Grant Co., Ind. inquiring. Lent C.H. Kiracofe $300.00 on Mortg. notes as collateral.

Wednesday, April 2 At home. Wrote some notes on evidence, etc., etc.

Thursday, April 3 Went to town. Saw Young & Houk. Rev. C.H. Kiracofe spent afternoon with me looking up evidence, etc.

Friday, April 4 Called in Court room in forenoon. Called again in afternoon and made out affidavit in New Castle case. Attend Willett's lecture in evening.

Sunday, April 6 Hear Rev. C.B. McDaniel pr. at 10:30, West End Ch., Isa. 9:6—"the everlasting Father." Attend Gen. Class meeting at same afternoon.

Tuesday, April 8 Consultation of Lawrence, Houk & Young, and agreement between them & liberal lawyers.

Wednesday, April 9 Prof. C.H. Kiracofe goes to Cin. to see experts. I go at 4:00 p.m. to Van Wert via narrow gauge road. Stay at Marsh Hotel.

Thursday, April 10 Saw A.L. Sweet, Esq. and Richie, Esq. Went at 2:44 to Lima. Saw Borton and Schenck. At Sweet 'ssaw Mr. Conger who came to see relatives of the Stuart Child.

Friday, April 11 At home mostly. Saw Kiracofe at his house. Called at Dillon's in the evening. Kiracofe starts for Chicago 9:00 +.

Saturday, April 12 At home in forenoon. Felt exhausted. Wrote & had written a number of letters. Went to town. Saw Houk and Young.

Sunday, April 13 I pr. at W. E. Ch. at 10:30, Ps. 94:7. At home all the rest of the day & evening. Read largely in Barnes' Notes, etc.

Monday, April 14 At home in forenoon. Saw Young and Houk in the afteronoon. Planned for the week. At home in the evening.

Tuesday, April 15 Wilbur went to Bellefontaine. Lorin went to Dublin, Andersonville, etc.

Wednesday, April 16 At home. Lorin returned home from Indiana in the afternoon.

Thursday, April 17 At home mostly. Letter from Lawrence & from Wilbur.

Friday, April 18 Went to Cincinnati on the 8:10 train with Geo. R. Young, Esq. He argues the question of jurisdiction of U.S. Court of Pr. House case. Dine at Gibson house. Take Bp. Waldon's deposition. Come home on 6:00 train.

Saturday, April 19 At home in forenoon. Prof. Kiracofe called. Went afternoon with Kiracofe's to Liberty to Quar'y Meeting. Returned home at 6:00. Rev. Wm. Miller pr. at 2:30, Luke 12:32.

Sunday, April 20 Went out to Liberty with Prof. C.H. Kiracofe's, W. Miller, P.E., pr. at 10:00, Heb. 6:1 3. Communion. Dine at Hartzell's. Lovefeast meeting in aft. at 2:00. Reach home before 5:00.

Monday, April 21 At home forenoon & afternoon. Rev. Wm. Miller called in the evening & I went with him to Prof. C.H. Kiracofe's on Summit Street to consult on time & place of our Anniversaries.

Thursday, April 24 At home in forenoon, part of the time. Called at Young & Houk's in the forenoon also.

Saturday, April 26 At home all day. Pres. C.H. Kiracofe called in the afternoon. Had seen Drs. Betton & Warfield, at Princeton, N.J.

Sunday, April 27 Attended Church at West End Chapel & heard a sermon by C.B. McDaniel the pastor. At home all the rest of the day.

Wednesday, April 30 Wilbur & Orville started their daily, the *Evening Item.* Had a counsel at Rev. Kiracofe's, with him & Dillon on Board Meetings.

Thursday, May 1 Began my deposition in the Pontiac, Illinois case. Cross questioning began at about 3:30, perhaps. Meeting of the Ex. Com. of Mis. B. at 7:30.

Friday, May 2 Cross Examination continued all day. Patton grew cross & abusive in the afternoon. Dr. Alwood took supper with us.

Saturday, May 3 Cross examination closed at 12:20. Called at Graybill's, Dillon's, & Aunt Rebecca Davis'. Dictated letters to Pope, Esq., Lawrence, Esq., & to Butler, Esq.

Sunday, May 4 I pr. at W.E. Ch at 10:30, Mal. 3:1. At home then till evening. Prof. Kiracofe pr. at 7:30, 2 Pet. 3:18.

Monday, May 5 Went to town in the afternoon. Mr. Young gone to Columbus. Saw Mr. Houk.

Tuesday, May 6 Went to see Mr. Young. He at Cin. Got home 5:30. Called in forenoon & spoke a few words with Mr. Houk.

Wednesday, May 7 Petoskey depositions not arranged for to-day, somehow. Wrote many letters in the afternoon and evening.

Thursday, May 8 G.W. Houk called in the forenoon. Kiracofe called in the afternoon is going to Burbank, O, to-morrow. I wrote an article on "The Communion of Saints."

Friday, May 9 At home all day. Wrote many letters. Rev. H.H. Hinman called. He is arranging for a Church Union Convention.

Saturday, May 10 At home in forenoon. Called over in afternoon for Petoskey plaintiff depositions. Doubts about the legality. Adj. till Monday at 10:00.

Sunday, May 11 At home all day. Spent it closely in reading. Read mostly Religious anecdotes.

Monday, May 12 Called to town, but deposi. put off till 2:00. Spent about 3/4 of an hour in afternoon on W.J. Shuey's depositions.

Tuesday, May 13 —Wednesday, May 14 [Worked] on Shuey's deposition. Wilbur went to Bell[e]fontaine.

Thursday, May 15 At home most of the day writing. Wrote some items for Conservator. Called in the evening at Dillon's, Davis' and Kiracofe's.

Friday, May 16 Wrote some cards and a letter to Lawrence & mailed them in town. Felt unwell in afternoon and evening.

Saturday, May 17 Went at 11:00 to Sidney & thence to Quincy. Supper at Rev. J.H. Kiracofe's. Lodge at Rev. S.L. Livingston's 2 m. south. Children: Stanley 14, Clifford 13, Chester 9, Nellie 7, Edith 4.

Sunday, May 18 Pr. at Union at 10:30 (11:00) John 12:43. Dine at David Shanely's1/2 m. N.E. It rains & I do not go to Carysville with Kiracofe but go back to Livingston's.

Monday, May 19 Go to early train at Pemberton & thence to Sidney & Dayton. Read proofs. See Young & Houk and arrange for Young to go to Richmond. Go to Xenia & see Dr. Cardon. Come home.

Tuesday, May 20 Get ready & start to Richmond, Ind., at 11:20. Put up at Huntington House. Confer with Lawrence, Study, & Young afternoon & awhile in the evening.

Wednesday, May 21 Consult with lawyers. Dinner at D.K. Zeller's. Afternoon again at T.J. Study's office. Supper & lodging at Hotel.

Thursday, May 22 Judge Bundy did not come till 5:00 p.m. & then put off the church suit till June 23d. I dined at D.K. Zeller's & staid there at night. Lunched at a restaurant.

Friday, May 23 Start at 9:00 for Liberty & Lotus. Dine with Rev. J. Selig at Clinton Brattain's. Supper & lodging there. Children: Gertrude 13, Grace 7, Benjamin 20 months.

Saturday, May 24 Start at 10:00, for Danl Koerner's. Dine there. Pr. at 2:00 at Franklin Church, Acts 1:14. Supper at Daniel Harbine's. Children: Morris 9, Nellie 5. Pr at F. at 8:00, Heb. 2:3. "Lo great Salvation". Stay at Henry Fry's. Their daughter Anna, aged 14.

Sunday, May 25 Pr. at 10:30 (Whitsunday sermon) Joel 2:28. Dine at Jacob Wooter's 3 ms N. Rev. John Selig pr. at 4:00, Luke 7:27, 28. Rev. C.M. Paddack takes me

to Liberty. Stay with Will Stanton. Attend M.E. Church & hear Rev. Ashman Lecture. Henry Burt lives in Liberty.

Monday, May 26 Start on 6:00 A.M. train for Hamilton and Home. Arrive about 10:00. At home the rest of the day.

Tuesday, May 27 At home in forenoon. Call on Young & Houk in the afternoon. Home in the evening.

Wednesday, May 28 At home all day. Quite poorly and did not do much. Wrote a few letters in the evening.

Thursday, May 29 Lorin went at 10:25 to Cincinnati to see about printing Lawrence's Brief. He got home on a late train.

Friday, May 30 I tried to write an article for the *Conservator*, but was too unwell. Prof. Kiracofe called in the forenoon. Decoration day.

Saturday, May 31 Went to town to have my teeth plate fixed. Was unwell. Mrs. Miller helped Katie clean house.

Sunday, June 1 At home all day. Quite unwell. Spent the day in reading- mostly in Murphy on Genesis and other commentaries.

Monday, June 2 Spent all the day at home, reading the Manuscript for Judge William Lawrence's Brief.

Tuesday, June 3 Called to town. Kiracofe's deposition taken in aftern. Try to get ready to go to Hartsville.

Wednesday, June 4 Start at ab. 8:00 for Richmond, New Castle, Montpelier to Mt. Zion. Home at Elijah Morrison's. Bp. Barnaby pr. at 8:00.

Thursday, June 5 Board of Bishops meet at Rev. C.B. Small's, 1/4 m. W. Met. aftn at Morrison's. Mis. board met 7:30. Br. Becker pr. at 8:00 an Serm. "Enlarge Joph." Stay at Morrison's.

Friday, June 6 Mis. Board continues. Dine at Geo. Huffman's. Supper at E. Morrison's. Stay at Rev. C.B. Small's. Bp. Becker lectures at 8:00, on Holy Land.

Saturday, June 7 Closed the session at 9:00 & Go to Montpelier. Lunch at New Castle. Call at Rev. Hardy Robinson's. Go on home; arrive at 6:00 P.M.

Sunday, June 8 Rev. C.B. McDaniel pr. at 10:30, "Search the Scriptures." Remained at home the rest of the day. Not very well. Read, as usual on Sunday, only religious books.

Monday, June 9 Saw Houk & Young, Wilbur's deposition taken in the afternoon.

Tuesday, June 10 Wilbu[r]'s deposition continued. Conclusion of deposition in afternoon. Wrote many letters in evening.

Wednesday, June 11 At home in forenoon reading proofs, on Lawrence's brief.

Friday, June 13 Deposition still put off. Read proofs in forenoon. Called at Young's and Houk's.

Saturday, June 14 Read proofs again.

Sunday, June 15 Rev. Wm. Dillon preached at 10:30 W.E. Ch. Evidence of true discipleship. At home the rest of the day reading.

Monday, June 16 Went to town   My deposition still not taken. Called at Graybill's. Read last of the proof on Lawrence's brief.

Tuesday, June 17 Board of Trustees of Pr. Estab. met at my house. All present but Miller. Horine dines with us. Session of Boards continue in afternoon.

Wednesday, June 18 At home in forenoon. Prof. Kiracofe called in afternoon. Mrs. Bish. D. Edwards brought a copy of Discip. 1826. Went to town afternoon.

Thursday, June 19 Prof. Kiracofe's deposition being continued. Briefs came. I wrote many letters. Deposition not finished. Ex. Com. Mis. meeting at 7:00.

Saturday, June 21 At home. Recast, classified, comparison of the Old & New Creeds. Kiracofe's deposition finished in the afternoon. Hunt up documents in evening.

Sunday, June 22 Rev. C. B. McDaniel pr. on Worshipping the golden Calf. I remain at home the rest of the day.

Monday, June 23 Went over to Richmond on 7:50 a.m. train. Put up at Huntington House. The trial of the Sugar Grove Church Case began. Plaintiffs present case & defendants reply.

Tuesday, June 24–Thursday, June 26 The trial continues. Stay at Zeller's.

Friday, June 27 Trial adjourned at 4:30. I see Dugan Clark. I reach home at 9:00.

Monday, June 30 Went to the trial at Richmond. Dugan Clark testifies.

Tuesday, July 1 Trial continues. I testify.

Thursday, July 3 Trial continues. Prof. Landis examined in part.

Friday, July 4 At home. A sad day. It was the anniversary of my loss of Susan. It has been a year of the light of home gone.

Saturday, July 5 At home. Called at Young's in afternoon.

Sunday, July 6 Attend Church at West End. Rev. C.B. McDaniel preached.

Monday, July 7 Go back to trial at Richmond. Had Landis put in many quotations from Creeds of Christendom. Dine, sup & lodge at the hotel.

Tuesday, July 8 Taking testimony. Miller's & McKee's testimony. At the hotel.

Wednesday, July 9 L.B. Gunkel spoke five hours closing at 3:30. T.J. Study spoke for 2 1/2 hours, closing at 6:00. Call at Zeller's. Call at Prof. Test's.

Thursday, July 10 Geo. R. Young occupied the forenoon in an able & eloquent argument. Judge Wm. Lawrence spoke all the afternoon. I stay at D.K. Zeller's.

Friday, July 11 Lawrence concludes his argument at 12:00. McMahon closes at 5:50. I come home on train reaching Dayton at 9:00.

Sunday, July 13 Went to the Cemetery. Called at John Weidner's & C.H. Kiracofe's.

Tuesday, July 15 Went to Young's and we went to Gunckel's and presented proposition as to using Richmond evidence & as to appealing, etc.

Thursday, July 17 Went to Young's afternoon & got forms of Propositions and answers & began to copy.

Friday, July 18 Went to town and got a form of assent for attorneys to use evidence taken at Richmond. Write and print—busy.

Saturday, July 19 Mailed letters to attorneys concerning using the Richmond evidence in their cases.

Sunday, July 20 Heard Rev. C.B. McDaniel pr. at 10:30. At home the rest of the day.

Monday, July 21 Got $150 from D. Middaugh, Perry Co., to pay on New Lexington attorney's fees. Settle with Houk balance of $80.00 and send Judge Lawrence $64.35 cts as his balance.

Tuesday, July 22 At home. Wrote out report of my Dist. & shaped up Bp. Barnaby's report. Wrote letters.

Wednesday, July 23 At home in the forenoon. Go to see Young in the afternoon.

Thursday, July 24 At home. Call at Dillon's. Give in mine and Barnaby's annual reports.

Friday, July 25 Write afternoon & eve. on Invisible Church.

Saturday, July 26 Called at Dillon's & Graybill's in forenoon. I go to Zehring's 14 m W with C. Keller. Quarterly meeting at Johnsville. Rev. C.B. McDaniel pr. at 8:00. Qr. Conf. at A. Zehring's. Stay there.

Sunday, July 27 Rev. Wm. Miller pr. at 10:30 in the Grove. Dine at Zehring's. I pr at 2:20 in Grove, 11 Cor. 3:8. After this I go home. Not well evening & night. Collec. at noon. $20.00.

Monday, July 28 At home forenoon. Rev. Wm. Miller dines with us. I go to J.K. Graybill's and to C.B. McDaniel's with Miller. Unwell with indigestion or Cholera Morbus, all day.

Tuesday, July 29 Some better health. Write some letters. At home all day.

Wednesday, July 30 At home. Called at Graybill's. At Dillon's, but he is gone over to town.

Thursday, July 31 At home most of the day. Called at Dillon's in afternoon.

Friday, August 1 Called at Young's in afternoon.

Saturday, August 2 Went to town in forenoon. Saw Mr. Young & McMahon. Called at Reform Pub. House & got blank Qr. Conf. license & pastor's rep.

Sunday, August 3 At home till evening. Went & saw Prof. C.H. Kiracofe who had just returned from a trip to Ontario & Chambersburg. Very warm day. "Warmest".

Monday, August 4 Went to Young's office. Buy a coat & vest (summer) at Sol. Straus'. Go again in afternoon & we see Gunckel & McMahon. Write letters in even. Nice rain.

Tuesday, August 5 At home. Write much. Busy all day.

Wednesday, August 6 Called at Kiracofe's and at Dillon's sometime in the day.

Thursday, August 7 At home most of the day. Called at Young's in the afternoon. Left an article with Dillon on Resurrection of the body. Held the Dayton Qr. Conf. at 8:00.

Friday, August 8 Call at Young's. At home till evening. Joseph Kumler called to see me in the afternoon. I called at C.H. Kiracofe's in the evening.

Saturday, August 9 Bought a ticket on C.C.C. & I. road but train an hour & 20 late. Saw Young and Gunckel. Went on 2:50 tr. via Xenia to Col. Called at J.A. Brown's. Went to Pataskala.

Sunday, August 10 Start at 7:00 for New Albany. Pr. at 10:30, Isa. 7:14. Dine on the grounds with Noah Swickard's. Pr. again in Grove, Heb. 13:14. Sup & lodge at Father John Swickard's. Coll. $16.38.

Monday, August 11 Noah takes me to Black Lick & I go on 7:57 tr to Col. & thence via Xenia to Dayton. Call at Graybill's in aft'n. Prof. C.H. Kiracofe calls. I again call at Graybill's; also Dillon's.

Tuesday, August 12 Call at Young's. Shuey had not returned.

Wednesday, August 13 Met Mr. Mr. Gunckel at Youngs about those stipulations.

Thursday, August 14 Lorin went to D. Koerner's in Indiana. John T. McKenzie, his son & wife & daughter called. I go to Dillon's and Kiracofe's.

Friday, August 15 I call at Dillon's. McKenzies dine with us. I write article on "The Incarnation.["]

Saturday, August 16 At home forenoon. In afternoon go to town & Graybill's. Call at Young's. Write letters in the evening.

Sunday, August 17 Rev. C.B. McDaniel pr. at W. End Ch. at 10:30, Matt. 15:22 28. Dine at Long's & remain till evening. Ch. meeting at 6:45 McD. pr. at 7:30, Exodus 33:14.

Monday, August 18 At home forenoon. Called at Young's afternoon.

Tuesday, August 19 At home in forenoon. Called at Young's in afternoon. Rain at 4:00. Write letters in the evening.

Wednesday, August 20 At home in forenoon. Call at Young's & Gunckel's in aftern.

Saturday, August 23 Missed morning train & went on 11:20 train to Union City & Hartford. Supper & Lodging at Geo. Stallsmith's. Kabrich also there.

Sunday, August 24 Franklin Groenendyke takes us to grove meeting 4 miles north. I pr. at 11:00, Rom. 8:28. Dine at Wesley Knox's. A. Rust (P.E.) pr. at 3:30. I hear J. Selig pr at 7:30 at Booth's Sch. H. Stay at Selig's.

Monday, August 25 Jacob Selig takes me to Hartford & I go on 11:32 tr. to Marion & Fairmount. Mattie takes me to cousin Wm. Reeder's. Stay there. Are digging a well in the yard.

Tuesday, August 26 Made settlement with W.H.H. Reeder. Dined at Ellis Wright's with Wm. Reeder. Supper at O.A. Glass' with Reeder & Glass relatives. Stay at Aunt Elizabeth Reeder's.

Wednesday, August 27 Robert B. Reeder takes me to the 6:32 train. I go thence to Marion & Van Buren to Conference. Home at Arthur Hackney 's. Presided aftern. Rev. G.C. Warvel pr. 1 John 3:2.

Thursday, August 28 Canvass for subs. cons. Dine at Jac. Cochran's, 1 3/4 miles S.W. Pres. Payne took supper with me, at Hackney 's. Mrs. Emma Baldwin pr. at 7:30 on Consecration. Stay at Hackney 's. Crowded Church each eve.

Friday, August 29 At Conference. Meals & lodging at Hackney 's. I pr. at Welcome Chapel (Conf. room) at 8:00, 1 Tim. 3:15, on Model Church.

Saturday, August 30 At Conference. Effort to raise legal fund on White River suit. Dine at Hackney's with Rev. R.N. Young. Stay till 4:00. Lodge at Marion. Go on 2:08 tr. to Union City.

Sunday, August 31 Reach home at 9:00. Pr. at 10:30, 1 Tim. 3:15, at Swank Church, West End. At home the rest of the day.

Monday, September 1 Wrote articles for the Conservator. Went to J.K. Graybill's, Kiracofe's, & Young & Young's. Went to Young's & Gunckel's in aftern. Called at Graybill's.

Tuesday, September 2 At home writing letters and getting ready to go away.

Wednesday, September 3 Go on 9:15 train to Pennsylvania. Stay at Cambridge, Pa. at Cambridge house.

Thursday, September 4 Go on 7:20 tr. to Union City, Pa. Home at Rev. N.R. Luce's. Conf. opens at 9:00. Some business done. At 8:00 Rev. J.S. Amidon pr. Conf. held in Luce's Commercial Hall.

Friday, September 5 Business Continues. Wm. Hodge, J.A. Dieter, & Gordon Betts are licensed to preach. G.W. Bower & A.W. Potter are referred to Com. I pr. at 8:00, Rom. 8:17.

Saturday, September 6 Business Continues. Stationing Com. met at Luce's at 1:00. Business completed at 5:00. I raise 16.35 cents for Secty. Rev. S. Evans pr. at 8:00.

Sunday, September 7 I pr. at 11:00, Gal. 4:4. Dine at Luce's as usual. S.S. Anniversary at 3:00. Memorial services at 4:00- of Rev. J.L. Chapin. Missionary meeting at 8:00. Raise $51.00 of Subs. Lodge at Luce's.

Monday, September 8 Go on 7:30 train to Corry & Niagara Falls. Arrive at 4:00. See the Park, Goat Island, etc. Go to old suspension bridge. See Whirlpool Rapids. Stay at Temperance Hotel.

Tuesday, September 9 Arise early. Cross the new suspension bridge to Canada. Pass Clifton House into Queen Victoria Park. View the Falls. Take 7:46 train to Buffalo. At 2:00, go to Corry & Union City. Stay at Rev. N.R. Luce's.

Wednesday, September 10 Go to Depot at 5:00. Tr. No. 5 did not come. Went on No. 3 to Meadville, Pa. Go after night to Sterling, O. Stay at Hotel. Great rains.

Thursday, September 11 Much rain to-day. Take 8:30 tr to Canal Dover. Hindered by water. Albert Overholt takes me to his house for dinner. Home at John Overholt's. Conf. opens at 2:00. J. Excell pr. at 7:30.

Friday, September 12 Very rainy still. Conf. continues. Chas. Carter came. Rev. J.H. Shreffler there. Carter pr.

at 8:00 Titus 2:12.

Saturday, September 13 Conf. continues. M.L. Hess & Chas. Carter received into Conference. Business closed at 5:00. Rev. J.N. Lemaster pr. at 7:30, John 1:3.

Sunday, September 14 Fair Day. I pr. at 10:30, Rom. 8:30. S. School Anniversary at 3:00. Supper at Rosenbury's, 1/2 m. west. Chas. Carter pr. (John 14:17, on Mirac. healing.) I stay at John Overholt's.

Monday, September 15 Rev. J. Excel takes me to the train, to Canal Dover. Go on to New Comerstown & thence via Columbus & Xenia home arriving at 6:00, eve.

Tuesday, September 16 At home. Call in afternoon at Young's and at L.B. Gunckel's.

Wednesday, September 17 Go on 11:00 train to Lima & thence by carriage to Benedum's near Allentown. Rev. T.M. Harvey preaches at 7:30. My home at Benedum's.

Thursday, September 18 Conference opens at 9:00. Business proceeds well. Six men were referred to Com. on Applicants. Rev. J.H. Kiracofe pr. at 7:30 & we take up Mission Subs. of $214. Lodge at Benedum's.

Friday, September 19 Conf. Continues. Wm. Miller, S.L. Livingston, & S.J. Mahan elected pres. elders. Dine at S.A. Steman's in Elida. Stationing Com. met at Benedum's at 7:00. Held two or three hours.

Saturday, September 20 Brief session of the stationing com. at Church at 8:00. Business proceeds. Evening session. Raise $7.39 subscription for Legal Fund. Get to bed at 11:00.

Sunday, September 21 Pr. at Grove at 10:30, Rom. 8:17. Pub. Coll. $53.16. Dine with Benedum's & Verbryke's on the ground. S.S. Anniversary at 3:00. Conner, Dinnius, & self spoke 10 min. each. Pr. at the Church at 7:30, Eph. 2:4. Late Benedic.

Monday, September 22 Came home Monday.

Tuesday, September 23 Called at Graybill's & Dillon's.

Started at 6:00 p.m. via Winchester, to Grand Rapids, Mich.

Wednesday, September 24 Reach Howard City at 10:30 a.m. Get conveyance to Amble. Train at 4:00 to Lake View. Bp. Becker lectured on state of Church. I stay at Decker's Hotel with Bp. Barnaby.

Thursday, September 25 At the Conference. Stay at Decker's. Pr. at 7:00, Ps. 92:8.

Friday, September 26 At Conference in forenoon. Start at 11:20 for Grand Rapids with Rev. H.F. Alderton. Visit Soldier's Home. Go on 7:30 tr. to Avilla, Ind. Sleep there 3 hours.

Saturday, September 27 Go on 3:00 train to Zanesville via Chi. Junction. Go on Z & O.R. tr. to Stockport, with Rev. B.W. Mason. Wm. Hecker meets & takes us to his house, 1/2 mile from Liberty Ch. Pr at 7:00, Rom. 5:8. L. at Hecker's.

Sunday, September 28 Pr. at Liberty Ps. 95:5. Dine at Henry Zumbro's on Coal Run. Call at Abr. & Mother Zumbro's. She bed-fast, aged 81. I lecture on Church at 7:00 & raise $75.00 on Legal Fund 60 paid. Stay at Wm. Hecker's.

Monday, September 29 Benj. Zumbro takes me to Stockport & I go to Zanesville, Columbus & home ar. at 6:00 eve. Find all well.

Tuesday, September 30 At home. Found Mr. Young away. Could do nothing about stipulations.

Wednesday, October 1 Went to Rev. C.B. McDaniel's and to Graybill's. Saw Rev. Aaron Zehring & wife there. Go on 6:58 tr. to Columbus. Stay at American House. Lodging 75 c.

Thursday, October 2 Go on 7:00 train to Baltimore, O., with Rev. J.A. Brown. Thos. Warner took me up to his (Mother's) house for breakfast, 2 m. N. of B. I open Conf. at 10:00. Rev. G.W. Walton pr. at 7:00, Zech. 3:6. Noah Miller stays with me.

Friday, October 3 Conf. continued. Mason & Hofflins

are elected pres. elders. Stationing Com. meets at 6:30 at Warner's. J.A. Brown stays with me. W.O. Dinnius pr. at 7:00 & a glorius speaking meeting followed. Dined at Rev. Jas. Everhart's.

Saturday, October 4 Conf. Continues. Wm. Brown recognized. I pr. at 8:00 Matt. 1:23. Rainy evening. Stay at Warner's as usual.

Sunday, October 5 I pr. at 10.30, Rom. 8:18. Dine at John Eversole's two ms. E. S.S. Anniv. at 3:00. Dinnius and I spoke. Sacramental service followed. Supper at Eph. Blauser's 10 m. West. Pr. at 7:00, 1 Tim 3:15. Stay at Miller's, 1 m. South.

Monday, October 6 Bro. Miller takes me to Baltimore. Go on 8:28 train to Columbus. Write letters at Depot. Saw D. Bender. I go on 2:50 (one hour later) to Dayton via Xenia, arriving at 7:00. Found all well.

Tuesday, October 7 Went to see Young. Saw him again in afternoon. No wish of liberals to print Richmond evidence. Called at Rev. C.B. McDaniel's. He very sick with neuralgia. Gave him $3.15.

Wednesday, October 8 Wrote letters, packed valise, etc. Go on 11:00 train to Lima & thence to Fostoria & Rising Sun, O. Arrive at 8:30. Peter Urschel meets me and J. Park & takes us to Horace E. Smith's.

Thursday, October 9 Open Conference at 9:00. Make good progress. Rev. A.J. Burkett pr. at 7:00 Matt. 5:12 on Victory. A grand meeting. Lodge at Smith's.

Friday, October 10 Conference progresses well. J. French & D.O. Tussing elected p. elders. Stat. Com. met at Smith's at 1:00. D.O. Tussing pr. at 7:00, Eph. 5:26. I stay at Smith's.

Saturday, October 11 Rainy Day. Conf. continues. Much discussion of reports. Closed at 4:30 after Sta. Com. Rep. Supper at Peter Urschell's. A.J. Burkert pr. at 7:00, John 19:22. Lodged at Smith's.

Sunday, October 12 I pr. at 10:30, 1 John 3:2. Pub. Coll. $28.00. Dine at Wm. Bates. Funeral of Mrs. [blank] at 2:00, aged 87+. Called at A.J. Myers. "Tea" at Veach's.

Sacrament at 7:00 led by J. French. Farewell meeting & shaking hands. Stay at H.E. Smith's.

Monday, October 13 Start home at 7:30. Close connections at Fostoria & Lima. See Rev. E.B. Maurer & Family- going to York, Neb. Call at J.K. Graybill's & get home at 1:30. Write up Diary & count funds.

Tuesday, October 14 Call at Young & Young's. Looking up affairs. Write some letters.

Wednesday, October 15 Spend much of the day in arranging files of my papers & taking notes for a sketch of Dr. Davis, & writing letters.

Thursday, October 16 At home writing till 10:00. Call at Young's and Houk's. Spent the rest of the day in writing a sketch of Dr. L. Davis for the Hartsville College *Index*. Write letters in the eve.

Friday, October 17 At home all day. Write article in the afternoon for the *Conservator*. Call at Dillon's and at Mrs. R. Davis' in the evening.

Saturday, October 18 Call at J.K. Graybill's.

Sunday, October 19 Pr. at West End Church at 10:30, 1 Pet. 4:17—very dull. At home till evening. Rev. H.H. Hinman pr. at 7:00, John 17th Chap. 1. Saved from World 2. Sanctified. 3. Might be one.

Monday, October 20 Went to town. Did not see attorney. Called at Graybill's.

Tuesday, October 21 At home all day. Rev. C.R. Paddack comes at evening and lodges with us.

Wednesday, October 22 At home forenoon. Call at Graybill's in afternoon- at Young's at 5:00.

Thursday, October 23 Call at Young's at 3:30 and again at 7:30.

Friday, October 24 Call at Graybill's, Dillon's, and Kiracofe's. Dillon called in the afternoon. I write in the evening a reply to Rev. W.J. Shuey's manifesto.

Saturday, October 25 Call at Graybill's and Dillon 's. Finish my article for the Conservator. Went to East Side to see Revs. H.F. Colby & E.E. Baker. Did not see them.

Sunday, October 26 Got the children up early. Went to W.E. Church. Hear Rev. Wm. Dillon pr. 10:30, Rom. 3:24 26. Rev. C.H. Kiracofe pr at 7:00.

Monday, October 27 Read proofs on articles. Called at Wm. Dillon's. Prof. C.H. Kiracofe called at our house.

Tuesday, October 28 At home. Called at Dillon's. Took first sketch of article on "the Communion of Saints."

Wednesday, October 29 Went to town in forenoon. Wrote article for *Conservator* on "Com. of Saints". Went to town in afternoon. Saw Mr. G.R. Young. Bought cheap fountain pen, 35 cts.

Thursday, October 30 At home. Went in the evening to hear Mr. Van Bennett speak at Park Theatre Hall on Prohibition. He is called "Kansas Cyclone."

Friday, October 31 At home in the forenoon reading and writing. Wrote a card denying Bast's statement. Call at Dillon's and Graybill's. House cleaning tears up everything, and papering dining room.

Saturday, November 1 At home all day. Ten Annuals have their "banquet" in the evening at our house. I spent afternoon & evening in arranging and recording sermon sketches. Flora Greenwood stays at our house.

Sunday, November 2 Pr. at W.E. Ch. at 10:30, John 1:29. Spent rest of the day in reading commentaries. Pr. at 7:00, Acts 3:22. Pretty good congregations morning & evening. Prof. Kiracofe returned last evening.

Monday, November 3 At the Print Office (Graybill's[)] most of forenoon. Wrote in afternoon. Called at Graybill's & Kiracofe's in the evening. C.H. Kiracofe called in the evening.

Tuesday, November 4 Voted early. At home the rest of the forenoon. Spend the afternoon and evening till late in assorting and filing an accumulation of letters.

Wednesday, November 5 Rev. C.H. Kiracofe & Rev. G.W. Nelson called in the forenoon & I called at Dillon's & Graybill's. Spent afternoon and evening in writing and in examining Points to be proved.

Thursday, November 6 At Graybill's & Dillon's forenoon. Rev. J.N. Nelson took supper with us. Worked on "Points to be proved."

Friday, November 7 Worked all forenoon on "Points to be Proved." Wrote letters in afternoon. Called in the evening at Dillon's. Spoke of the fact of having many papers on trial. Called at Kiracofe's.

Saturday, November 8 Spent morning and forenoon in straightening up things about the house. So also in the afternoon.

Sunday, November 9 Rev. Wm. Dillon pr at 10:30, Matt. 3:2, at W.E. Ch. Rainy day. Called at "Aunt" Rebecca Davis'. Rev. C.H. Kiracofe was to preach at 7:00, but owing to rain did not go to Church.

Monday, November 10 At home all day except a short call at J.K. Graybill's. Wrote some letters, etc. Webster's International Dictionary came by express.

Tuesday, November 11 At home writing letters. Went in afternoon to town & called on Young's & Houk.

Wednesday, November 12 D.K. Flickinger called an hour or more. In afternoon called at Kiracofe's, Dillon's & Graybill's. Dillon called in the evening.

Thursday, November 13–Friday, November 14 At home forenoon. Saw Young in afternoon. Read proofs at Graybill's. At home in the evening.

Saturday, November 15 At home all the forenoon. Called at Graybill's in the afternoon; also at Kiracofe's & Davis' Spent the evening in reading. Rainy day.

Sunday, November 16 I pr. at West End Church at 10:30 Luke 10:27. At home the rest of the day till 7:00 when I pr. again Ps. 73:11. Rainy day, but November has had no freeze, and geraniums are out.

Monday, November 17 This is my 62nd birth-day anniversary, Praise the Lord. Rainy day. Read proofs at Graybill's. Went to town in afternoon & saw Attorney (Y.). Sent Wm. Reeder $10.00, $2.55 for boarding hand about $5.00 to pay for tile, and the rest for hauling.

Tuesday, November 18 Went to town a short time in forenoon; also in afternoon, and attended Maj. Whittle's Gospel meeting at Association Hall. Ex. Com. Miss. Meeting at office at 7:00.

Wednesday, November 19 Went to Young's and Express Office before noon. Wrote letters part of forenoon and afternoon. Read in the evening.

Thursday, November 20 Called at Young's at 2:00. Bargain on Bp. Kephart's and Dr. Carson's evidence. Katie Went to Whittle's meeting. I went to pr. meeting at West End Ch.

Friday, November 21 Writing many letters. Called at Mrs. Cretia Edwards' and at Rev. W.O. Dinnius'. Bought 1 1/2 bush. apples at $1.50.

Saturday, November 22 At home all day. Did much writing. Sent out letters to superannuated ministers & widows. Wrote to Bp. Foster & T.L. Cuyler. Katie went to Dunker meeting.

Sunday, November 23 Pr. at W.E. Ch. 10:30, Isa. 52:1. Mrs. Edwards and Davis there. C.H. Kiracofe pr. at 7:00.

Wednesday, November 26 Went to town forenoon & afternoon. Saw Young in afternoon. Calle[d] at Houk's office.

Thursday, November 27 Got my own breakfast. Wrote nine letters. Flora Greenwood ate Thanksgiving Turkey with us. I went to the post office and thence to West End Church, to Thanksgiving service.

Saturday, November 29 Went on evening train to Dublin, Ind. Stay at Bishop H. Floyd's.

Sunday, November 30 Pr. at 10:30, 2 Pet. 2:15. Dine at Dru. Wilson's. Hear [blank] Lecture at 3:00 at Friends' Church. Supper at Dr. G.W. Champs'. He rheumatic.

Pr. at 7:30, Gal. 4:4. Stay at Bp. H. Floyd's.

Monday, December 1 Took cars at Cambridge. Call at D.K. Zeller's. Bt. overcoat. Judge Bundy does not come till 7:00. Dine at D.K. Zeller's. Decision of B. averse. Go home arriving at 9:00.

Tuesday, December 2 At home forenoon after a while at Graybill's. Call at Young's afternoon. Revise "points of proof."

Wednesday, December 3 At home in forenoon. Call at Young's afternoon. Write in evening.

Thursday, December 4 Judge Elliott sat in Common Pleas Court. Printing Establishment Case opened. After form had gone through, We let the case go pro forma. Wood came.

Friday, December 5 Looked after appeals. Went to Young's in afternoon. At W.E. Church in evening. C.L. Wood pr. at 7:30 Matt. 27:21.

Saturday, December 6 Meeting of Ex. Com. of Pr. Estab. at 8:30 at my office. In afternoon at 2:00 Kiracofe & wife & Dillon, Bp. Floyd, Rev. C.L. Wood & myself went to the soldier's Home. Consult at 4:00 over D.K. Z's letters.

Sunday, December 7 I pr. at 10:30 Acts 26:8. At home till evening. Rev. Wm. Dillon pr at 7:30, Matt. 5:20.

Monday, December 8– Tuesday, December 9 Called at Graybill's print. office. At home rest of the day.

Wednesday, December 10 At home in forenoon. Went to town in the afternoon. Pr. at W. End Ch. at 7:30, Matt. 12:30.

Thursday, December 11 At Circuit Court Room in forenoon. Judge Shanck "continues" the Printing Estab. case. Go to town in afternoon, but Mr. G.R. Young not returned.

Friday, December 12 Call at Young's, but the depositions had not been opened. Wrote many letters to mail next morning.

Saturday, December 13 Called at Young's in the afternoon about 4 o'clock, and he read the depositions, to me.

Sunday, December 14 Rev. Dillon pr. at W.E. Chapel at 10:30, Heb. 12:1. I pr. at 7:00 Isa. 12:1. Large Congregation. Meeting Closes.

Monday, December 15 Called at Graybill's office and at Kiracofe's, in forenoon. Kiracofe called at my house afternoon. Take proofs to Graybill's.

Tuesday, December 16 Went to town & paid my tax. Called at Graybill's.

Wednesday, December 17 At home forenoon. Go to town at 3:00. Get draft for Lawrence $31.60; for Wolfard, $13.60; for Clay, $11.52. At library.

Thursday, December 18 Go to town, fail to see Young. See Houk about making out his bill. At home in the afternoon.

Friday, December 19 See Young a short time. Pay him $200.00. See Houk and settle with him for past services, $162.52. Write many letters.

Saturday, December 20 At home all day. Kiracofe called to see about subs. price of Homiletic Review. Was up late. [unreadable] burglars at Wagoner's. It was their hired girl.

Sunday, December 21 Went to Church at West E. Church. Kiracofe pr. a Third Party discourse. At home the rest of the day.

Monday, December 22 Called at Houk's and paid him $56.18 in full for services to date on Van Wert Lawsuit. Saw Young. Up till late 12:30 at night.

Tuesday, December 23 At home all day regulating papers, etc. Wrote on S. School address at night.

Wednesday, December 24 Got Katie a bed-room set. Spoke at West End Church Christmas entertainment.

Thursday, December 25 Spent all day at home   mostly

looking over papers, letters, etc.

Friday, December 26 Our attorneys meet at Mr. Young's office. Spent most of the day there. Settled with Wm. Lawrence in full on past services in Van Wert Case; also paid $23.20 on Richmond case.

Friday, December 27 Went on 7:08 train to Union City & Upland. Virgil Duling takes me to Wm. Duling's for supper. Rev. Lenhart & wife there. Entertainment at Salem & I lecture on Rise & progress of Sab. Schools. Stay at Wm. Reeder's.

Sunday, December 28 Pr. at 10:30, Rom. 8:17. Dine & lodge at Ellis Wright's. Wm. Reeder's, Oliver Glass's & Aunt Lizzie Reeder dine there.

Monday, December 29 Call at Henry Simons', Levi Simons, & Wm. Reeder's. Dine at Oliver Glass's. Ellis Wright, Wm. Reeder & Aunt Lizzie & families there. I stay at Aunt Lizzie's.

Tuesday, December 30 Go to Joseph Broyles' for Dinner. Kyle Secrest comes. Supper & lodging at John W. Broyles'.

Wednesday, December 31 Go to Gilman & thence to Muncie, Union City & home. Arrive at 5:00. Go to Library & p.o. At home in the evening.

Places of Annual Conf. For 1891.
1. Erie—Corry, Pa. 2. East Ohio—Chosen by P.E. 3. Auglaize—Stringtown Church—P.O. Rockford Ohio. 4. Scioto—Liberty Ch., Morgan Co. O. P.O. Stockport, Wash. Co. O. 5. Sandusky—Burgoon. 6. Penn. & Md., Chambersburg.

Paid by M. Wright
Paid March 5th for N. Lex. Case 20.00

Bishop's Salary, 1890.

Erie Chart Coll.	$50.00
East Ohio	54.63
Pub. Coll.	19.04
Auglaize (Chart)	134.61
Pub. Collec.	53.16
Scioto (Chart)	81.88
Pub. Collec.	26.78
Sandusky (Chart)	54.71
Publ. Coll.	28.60
[total]	503.41
Penn. Chart Coll.	66.52
Maryland Chart Coll.	10.31
Pub. joint Coll	42.00
Present Eliz. Hoover	5.00
Total	627.24

Traveling Expenses, 1890

To Union City	$4.70
Incidentals	.50
To Canal Dover	4.60
To Dayton	3.75
[total]	13.55
Lima & Return	2.90
Baltimore & Return	4.55
To Rising Sun & Return	6.30
[total]	27.30

Conf. Secretaries, 1889

J.C. Spoonemon	
T.P. Conner	Oregon
N.D. Wolfard	White Riv
B.A. Bonewell	E. Ohio
S.A. Myers	Sandusky
C.B. Whitaker	Mich
C.L. Wood	N. Mich
W.O. Dinnius	North Ohio
C.W. Pattee	St. Joseph
J.L. Harrison	Rock Riv
C.H. Pratt	Scioto
C.B. Sherk	Ark. Val.
F. Holm Gibbs	Adair, Mo.
W.E. Mosier	Kans.
J.P. Cotton	Elkhorn
P. Beck	Calif
O.A. Wallace	West Des.
I.C. Weidler	Penn & Maryland

Dayton Pastors

Dr. A.A. Willits	3 St. Pres.
V.F. Brown	Broadw. N.E.
D.H. French	U. Pres.

Geo. W. Belsey   Congr.
A. BowersP.E.
J.G. Vaughan   St. P. M.E.
Wm. Herr, D.D.
J.G. Neiffer   St. Johns South
E.E. Baker   Main St Lu
W.F. McCauley   Park St Pres
Herbert J. Cook   Episcopel
C.L. Work   4th Pres
W.A. Hale   Ref.
D.W. Clark   Raper M.E.
H.F. Colby   1st Baps.
Wm. Mackafee   Grace M.E.
J.R. Hughes   Memor. Pres
H.L. Lornsbury   Lain Av.
Dr. E. Herbruck   Ref.
L.D. Morse   Bap.
D.A. Sinclair
J.P. Watson   Crist.
Geo. W. Belsey   Congr.
M. Loucks

Annual Conf. Items

1. Examinations 2. Report of Com. on Reading 3. Appeals 4. Ministers died? 5. Applicants for Licensure 6. Publishing Minutes 7. Elders' Orders 8. Next Conference 9. College Trustees 10. Treasurer of Pr. Aid 11. Mis. Treasurer & Secret'y 12. Boundary Com. Rep. 13. Correct Itinerant List 14. Elect Pres. Elders 15. Stationing Committees 16. Secretary's Pay 17. Next Year's Committee 18. Are moneys paid in? 19. General Reports: 1. Missions 2. Publishing 3. Ch. Ex. 4. Education 5. Moral Reform 20. Gen. S.S. Sec. & Treas. 21. Sum up results

First Day's Session:
1. Opening Exercises. 2. Remarks. 3. Lay delegates. 4. Elect Secretary. 5. Bar of the house. 6. Meeting & Adjournm. 7. Appoint Committees 8. Any minister died? 9. Miscellaneous 10. Bishop's Examination 11. Examination of Members.

McNiel's Liniment

Dose: Adult, 1 Teaspoonful Chil. under 5 ys, 1 to 20 drops. For cholic or Cholera Morbus give a dose every 5 minutes of 1/4 teaspoonful.

Index

Cleaning Mixture

Sulphuric Ether 1, Castile Soap 1, Glycerene 1, Alcohol spirits 1, Agan Ammonia (3d Str) 4. Dissolve the soap in soft water & then add the other ingredients.

1891

Thursday, January 1 I have seen sixty two New Year Days. Mine has been a long life, yet brief span. On the whole it has been a happy one, especially from my fifteenth year till my Susan's death. In those sixty two years, how much of life, joy, & success. How much of labor & sorrow. How busy many of those years, yet how much time lost. What a multitude of of [repeated in text] Heavenly Mercies. Many trusts & honors have been accorded. Duty has been feebly done. At home mostly. Went to town & Kiracofe's. Bp. Becker came.

Friday, January 2 Pay Young & Young's (bal) Att. bill, etc., on Dayton case to date. $245.91. Bought a Waterbury Clock & expressed to Ellis Wright. At home the rest of the day. Some spinal irritation & considerably nervous of course. Wrote several letters and read proof on "Points to be Proved."

Saturday, January 3 Made out Premium Notice for Chr. Cons., price list of books, etc. At home also in the afternoon. Quarterly meeting also in evening at W.E. Church. Rev. Wm. Miller pr. Qr. Conf. followed. Wrote a number of letters to-day. Many inquire about injunctions and other legal matters. This involves much labor and care to me.

Sunday, January 4 Heard Rev. Wm. Miller pr. at W. End Ch. at 10:30 118 Ps. 25 v. He also pr. at 7:00, Acts 10:43. Sacrament in forenoon. Yost & wife joined in evening. At home the rest of the day. Bro. Miller's sermons were very good. Congregations pretty fair.

Monday, January 5 At home all day. Rev. Wm. Miller and Prof. Kiracofe called. I called at J.K. Graybill's &

Prof. Kiracofe's awhile. The weather has been very mild for some weeks, especially after Dec. 26th. In our great church struggle it is hard for me to do all that needs doing. Got a letter from Rev. I.T. Parlett, Va., saying that he is with the Radicals. Wrote several letters.

Tuesday, January 6 Called to town. Paid Houck $5.00 that I had failed by mistake but was his due. At home the rest of the day.

Wednesday, January 7 At home all day. Aaaron [sic] Eubanks of Marion, Ind., dined with us. Wrote a number of letters early and several late in the evening. In the course of the year I write a large number of letters and it often becomes wearisome.

Thursday, January 8 At home forenoon. Went to town at 2:40 and sent a N.Y. Draft of $370.00 to pay note in Con. in Richmond. Called at Young's Office 25 minutes. Got his letter of 4 lines. Applied for pass on C.C.C.& D.; D & U; and Penn. Lines. Called at W. Dillon's. Evening at home.

Friday, January 9 At home all day & at work from early to late. Letters full of difficult questions come in. Some letters showing a misapprehension of our mailing arrangements. I am overtaxed. I find it difficult to get any one who will take the burden off of me to any extent.

Saturday, January 10 Called at Graybill's Printing Office. At home the rest of the day. Kiracofe called in the afternoon. I wrote many letters. It was a very busy day.

Sunday, January 11 Preached at W. End Ch at 10:30,

Isa. 52:1. It was a rainy and snowy day. Staid at home the rest of the day.

Monday, January 12 Called at the Pr. Office of Graybill. Wrote some letters and sent out "Points to be Proved," just printed, to a few attorneys.

Tuesday, January 13 At home in forenoon. Prof. C.H. Kiracofe called in the afternoon. I went to town & got R.R. permits on C.H. & D. and D. & Ft. Wayne, and D. & U. Called five min. at Houk's & about same at Young's. Daily I write many letters.

Wednesday, January 14 Called at Hollinger's Art Gallery. Called at Mrs. Lucretia Edwards in the afternoon. In the evening wrote letters and sent Young's bill to Rev. E.J. Moody & to Rev. P. Nicklas.

Thursday, January 15 Went to Winters Nat. Bank. Called at Houk's two min. & Young's 10 m., the latter to correct Pontiac bill. Took Bp. Edwards picture to Hollinger. Got permit on C.C.C. & D R.R. In afternoon called at Hollinger's & at train depot. Went to Kiracofe's in the evening. Sent off the bill to A.B. Powel for Young.

Friday, January 16 Wrote letters. Brought back Bp. Edwards' picture from Art Gallery. In afternoon, went for S.S. Literature specimens to Reform Pub. House. Wrote letter till late in the evening. I am over taxed with work.

Saturday, January 17 Made out additions to price list of books. In afternoon, with Wilbur's help, make out Premium list for Conservator. Houk called about 5:00. Write letters in afternoon and evening. Katie & Orville go to the lake at Soldier's home to skate in the evening.

Sunday, January 18 Heard Rev. Wm. Dillon pr. (10:30) at W.E. Church, Ps. 85:6. At home till evening. Prepare a sermon. Pr. at 7:00, Luke 23:34. Pretty large congregation.

Monday, January 19 Called at Hon. G.W. Houk's Office. Got at Xenia Depot a permit on Penn. Lines West of Pittsburg. At home in afternoon, except a while at Printing Office at Graybill's. Wrote for some other R.R. Permits.

Wednesday, January 21 At home all day. Wrote out several answers to Lawrences questions for his Theological Brief. Wrote letters to several parties in the evening. Got nearly up with correspondence.

Thursday, January 22 At home in forenoon filing letters, classifying, etc. Went to town in afternoon. Saw Gunckel and gave him copy of Lawrence's second Brief. Called on Young 10 minutes. Called at Hollinger's & at Mrs. Rebecca Davis'. Pr. at 7:30 at W.E. Church Ez. 23:11.

Friday, January 23 I wrote an article for *Conservator* on Liberal Myths. Called at Dillon's & Graybill's in the afternoon. Read in Blane's Twenty Years in Congress over 100 pages in the evening.

Saturday, January 24 At home till noon. Samuel Horine called; all the forenoon spent in Reading. Afternoon Rev. W.O. Dinnius & Sam. Horine called. I went to town saw Houk, Hollinger & then went to Manchester. Staid at Geo. Horine's. His son, Wm.C. called. John C. Horine, aged 23.

Sunday, January 25 Staid at Horine's all day. In afternoon, Young Farst called. Also Overholser an [blank] Surface. I pr. at 6:00, Ps. 16:11. Large congregation. Stay at Horine's.

Monday, January 26 Went home on the 6:00 train. All well. Called at J.K. Graybill's at 10:30 and at 5:00. Called at Young's after noon 10 minutes to read Lawrence's letter. Saw Will only. Wrote letters in the evening.

Tuesday, January 27 Got cloth for coat & vest. Called at Young's and got copies of depositions, etc. Got 8 copies of Edward's picture. Read depositions all evening.

Thursday, January 29 Preparing to start to Petoskey. Take cloth to tailor's and get it cut. See Young and call at Duguerrease Gallery in the forenoon. Spend most of afternoon in getting together documents, etc., ready for trial at Petoskey, Mich. Start at 6:00 for Richmond, Ind. Call at Zeller's. Talk with T.J. Study, Esq. Go on 11:35 train toward Petoskey. Sleep abt six hours on train.

Friday, January 30 Reach Grand Rapids at 9:00. Call

on Joseph Lomax, Study's uncle, and have quite a talk with him. Go on 11:35 tr. North. Write an article on the way. Arr. at Petoskey at 7:50. Rev. G.W. Bowles & Bro. J.G. Hutchinson meet me and take me to Jacob Zollensburg's. Their children: Hattie (married to Wells), Minnie 17, Gracie 11. Katie Kitching boards there.

Saturday, January 31 Call on M.W. George, Esq., at 10:00 & in afternoon. Dine & sup at J. Van Zollenburg's. Talk with G.W. Bowles at Van Zollenburg's on his troubled domestic life. Letters to Lorin & to Judge Lawrence. Find Mr. George a sensitive sombre [sic] man. He thinks the judge will decide on the merits of the Church question; but thinks lack of incorporation important. Sore throat in night.

Sunday, February 1 I pr. at 10:30 U.B. Ch., Ps. 16:11. Dine at Van Zol's. Lecture on temperance at 4:00 in W.C.T.A. Hall. Pr. at 7:00 (U.B.C.) Rom. 8:17. Supper at Van Z's. Lodge with G.W. Bowle's at Bro. Levant Van Alstine's on [blank] St. Slept well.

Monday, February 2 Mail letter home. Call at Jacob Van Zollenburg's Grocery. See M.W. George at 10:00. D. at Van Z's. He drives me out to Bay View summer resort. Called at Robert Taylor's on Mich. St., & call at Mr. George's. Supper at Van Z's. Revs. C.L. Wood, E.J. Moody & F. Lamming come. Telegraph Judge Lawrence to come. It was a blustery day. I stay at Van Zollen's. Very good home. Slept well.

Tuesday, February 3 Went to Depot. Call at Van Alstine's for sometime. Dine at Edw. J. Moody's. Call at George's office. Trial of Church case begins in Council Chamber before Judge J.G. Ramsdell at 3:30 p.m. & continues till 6:00. I get telegrams from Lawrence and from Young. Supper & lodging at Van Z's. Slept 7 1/2 hours. Attorneys: C.J. Pailthorpe, W.B. Williams, Libs; M.W. George & O. Adams, Radicals.

Wednesday, February 4 Court opened at 9:00. Plaintiffs continued testimony till middle of afternoon & then offered Schaff, Strong & Walden's which the Defendants resisted. Question postponed. Defendants began testimony and continued till 6:00. Dine & sup at Van Zollenburg's. Lawrence came at 7:55 eve. Council at Occidental Hotel on deposition. Slept well.

Thursday, February 5 Arose at 6:00. Wrote card home. Letter from Young containing notice on depositions. Trial continued all day. Our Attys propose to use two depositions only. Dine, sup & L. at Van Zol's. Pra. meeting at U.B. C. at 7:00. Rev. C.L. Wood lodges with me. Van Zollenburg's a very agreeable family.

Friday, February 6 Attorneys stipulated the admission of D.L. Davis' and Bp. J.M. Waiden's depositions the latter liberal. All testimony finished about 4:00. Then liberal attorneys propose to abandon suit unless we *admit* the incorporation. We propose to do so if they will bind themselves to Appeal. They refuse. Case dismissed. Decree at 8:00. I go on 10:00 tr South. Saw a young man sentenced.

Saturday, February 7 Arrive at Grand Rapids abt 6:00 at Ross abt. 7:30. Leave valise & walk to Bp. H.T. Barnaby's 3 1/2 ms. east. Sleep an hour or two. Bp. was gone to Grand Rapids. Wolcott & Jones called. Barnaby's children: Alvin (at Hartsville), Horace, Milton W. (at Hartsville), Lewis, Adie, 14. All bright children.

Sunday, February 8 I pr. at Gaines Church at 10:30 (for Rev. S.E. Lane) Luke 24:46. Then taught a S.S. Class. Hanna, Mrs. Barnaby, Wolcott, Bowman & one other woman in Class. At Barnaby's dinner, supper & lodging. Pr. at 7:00, Epp. 2:4. Bechtel & wife of Caledonia called at Barnaby's before meeting. Saw several of the Bowman 's.

Monday, February 9 Bp. Barnaby's takes me to Loew's near Salem church—2 ms n. of Burnip's Corners. Dine there. Barnaby returns. Call at Austin Batdorf's whose wife L.J. Batdorf is pastor at Salem. Sup there. Daughter Estie, 15; Son [blank] 12. Pr. at 7:00 Eph. 3:19. I dedicated Salem abt. 1882. Lodge at Aaron Heasley's abt. 2 ms West to Richards, the Sch. teacher, there.

Tuesday, February 10 Bra. Heasley takes me to Allegan. Call at H.H. Pope's office. Talk with him & Charles R. Wilkes, Esq. Dine at Hotel. Interview with Pope afternoon. Go on 4:13 train to Kalamazoo, thence on 5:23 tr. to Battle Creek, & thence on 8:45 tr to Charlotte. Stay at W.S. Titus'. Children: a son at Grand Ledge, Mrs. Myers; daughter married & living in town. Daughter at home.

Wednesday, February 11 At Titus' most of day. Meyers & wife dine there. Titus & I called at Jas. A. Mouser's. Mouser takes me to the train. Go on 5:20 train via Battle Creek to Vicksburg & on 8:33 train to Richmond. Arrive at Richmond 3:40 next morning. Slept well on train.

Thursday, February 12 Called at D.K. Zeller's at 6:00. Crawford & wife there from Mansfield, Ohio. Go on 7:35 train home to Dayton, O. Found that Wilbur and Katie had been sick since I was away & were still poorly. Spent rest of day in reading letters arranging things etc.

Friday, February 13 At home writing some. Called at Dillon's. Somewhat worn down & Nervous.

Saturday, February 14 At home in the forenoon. Wrote a short article for the "Conservator". Went to Dillon's & found him nearly sick. Called at J.K. Graybill's office at Young's, Houk's, etc. Ordered a coat at Wells & Charch's. Spent evening in writing many letters. Lorin doing the penmanship.

Sunday, February 15 All got up late. Pr. at W.E. Ch. Acts 2:15. Rest somewhat in afternoon. It was a rainy evening and I did not get to Church.

Monday, February 16 Went to town. Sent $131.00 to Lawrence. Called at Blum's. At home afternoon writing letters & also in evening. Lorin helping.

Tuesday, February 17 Called at Wells & Charch's. Also at Blum's. At home the rest of the day setting papers to rights & writing letters. Lorin helps.

Wednesday, February 18 At home most of the day. Lorin helped me write letters in the evening.

Thursday, February 19 At home in the forenoon. With Wilbur read over brief & criticized it.

Friday, February 20 At home most of the day. Went to town. Called 5 min at Young's. Inquire rates East of Ag't at Xenia depot. Prepare to go East to-night, but abandon it on account of rains and high waters. Got my new coat at Wells & Charch's.

Saturday, February 21 At home in forenoon. Call in afternoon at Ref. Pub. House, to see Blum. Attend the memorial services of Gen. W.T. Sherman at Music Hall at 2:00. Hall crowded throughout. Gen. Wood presided. L.B. Gunckel, J.G. Lowe, A.A. Willits, and G.W. Houk spoke. Strange ideas of religion by Gunckel, Willitts and Houk.

Monday, February 23 Preparing to go East. Called at Graybill's. Left home at 3:00. Wait one hour in Columbus. Reached Belleair at Midnight. Pay full fare from there to Cumberland for want of a ticket.

Tuesday, February 24 Pass Oakland and other park places. Reach Cumberland about 9:00; Harper's Ferry at 11:10. Dine there; reach Weaverton at 12:00, and Rohrersville at 1:00; walked to town and thence to Robert H. Clopper's. Staid there till morning. Rev. P.O. Wagner, the pastor, boards there. Rev. S. Diller & I.C. Weidler also staid there. Went to "John Brown's Fort" at Harper's Ferry. A one story brick abt. 20 X 20 ft.

Wednesday, February 25 Called an hour at John Clopper's, father of R.H. Called at John A. Clopper's opposite to our Church. Dine at Washington McCoy's, next house south of the Church. He a Winebrenarian. His wife a Lutheran Conferences (Penn & Va.) open at 2:00. Proceed on examination of character. Rev. J. Fohl pr. at 7:30, II Kings 5:12, on Naaman. My home at McCoy's. Prof. C.H. Kiracofe with me.

Thursday, February 26 Conference progresses well. Dine, sup, & lodge at McCoy's. Nothing very unusual occurs. Rev. J.S. Wentz pr. at 7:30, Rom. 8:1. Rev. I.T. Parlett, of Virginia Conference, present & W.J. Funkhouser. Both are thorough Radicals. It appears that I.T. Parlett, Wm. Lutz, and G.W. Rexroads are Radicals & other an. Conf. Preachers express disgust with neutral position as a cheat.

Friday, February 27 Conference progresses well. Conference at 11:00 at McCoy's with I.T. Parlett, J.H. Parlett, and W.J. Funkhouser and C.H. Kiracofe. Elect pres. elder in afternoon Rev. A.H. Shank. Stationing Com. met at W. McCoy's at 6:30. Rev. A.H. Shank pr. at 7:30, Matt. 5:14. "Light of the World." Finely composed & well delivered, but his execution a little monotonous. At McCoy's as usual.

North Ohio Conference, United Brethren Church, ca. 1891

Saturday, February 28 Stationing Com. met again at 8:00, A.M. Conference began business at 9:00. Closed at 4:20. Item of S. Diller's election to elder's orders at 7:30. Missionary meeting, and Rev. C.H. Kiracofe pr. at 7:30, Mark 16:15. Raise about $250.00 subs. for Missions. Break, Dine & Sup at McCoy's. Mr. Wagoner takes photograph of the Conference at 4:30.

Sunday, March 1 I Pr. at 10:30, at Rohrersville Church, John 3:2, on future likeness to Christ. Mr. Kiracofe dines with us & after dinner C.H. Kiracofe goes home with him. Rev. J. Fohl holds a love feast at 3:00. I go to John A. Clopper's after love feast and sup there. Mother Clopper's experience. Rev. B.G. Huber pr. at 7:00, Isa. 55:2, "Delight thyself in fatness." I stay at McCoy's.

Monday, March 2 Poffenberger takes me to the station. Go on 8:10 train to Hagerstown, and thence at 12:00 to Greencastle, Pa. Dine with Rev. J.K. Nelson & wife at F.H. Barnhart's. He had given notice to Liberal trustees to return lamps to Church, as they had been out 6 weeks; search warrant, but did not find lamps. Supper & lodging at Rev. J.K. Nelson's. Their son in laws, Hicks & Freese at Fostoria, Ohio. I pr. at 7:30, Ps. 92:8 to large congregation.

Tuesday, March 3 Go on train to Chambersburg. Dine, Sup & lodge at Rev. S.J. Nicklas'. Got a copy of Find-ings of Facts, read & copied part of them. Pr. at King Street Church at 7:30, Gal. 4:4. Large congr. though evening snowy. Nicklas Children: Walter, 8; Charles 5; Anna 3. Had an interview with O.C. Bowers, Esq., at 5:00.

Wednesday, March 4 Spent forenoon in taking notes on Findings. Dine at Peter Nicklas'. Have several boys, and two daughters. The oldest, Oma Naoma, is 18. The younger about 12 is just up from typhoid fever. Call at Rev. M.F. Keiter's, Sec. Rev. B.G. Huber there. Eva Keiter 19. I study points of proof & take notes of incorrections and omissions. Call at Rev. J. Fohl's. Sup at P. Nicklas' with Keiter and Eva. Talk an hour at Store. Stay at S.J. Nicklas'. He copies notes.

Thursday, March 5 Call at Keiter's, Mrs. John Fetterhoff's, Mother Monn there, aged 88. Pray with her. Go via Nickl. store to Depot. On 9:45 train to Martinsburg, W. Va., Dine at Nicklas'. Go on 1:45 train for home. Pass Oakland. Sleep about 3:00.

Friday, March 6 Reach Newark, O., at 3:00 & Columbus at 4:00. Take 5:15 tr. to Xenia, and 7:00 tr. to Dayton, arriving at 7:35. Spent the day in adjusting matters. Went to bed at 11:00. Prof. C.H. Kiracofe called in the day. Miss Flora Greenwood called to see Katie in the evening & study lessons.

Saturday, March 7 Saturday: I adjust matters about the house. Write letters in the afternoon. At 7:00 the Ex. Com. Mis. meets at our office, Cor. Williams & Third St. Write till nearly 11:00.

Sunday, March 8 Attend Church at West End and hear Rev. W.O. Dinnius on Rom. 8:9, "If any have Spir. of Christ," etc. At home the rest of the day. It was rainy in the evening.

Monday, March 9 Called at Graybill's in the forenoon. Went to town in the afternoon, Called at Young's 15 minutes. Call then at Graybill's.

Thursday, March 12 Wrote and read in the forenoon. Afternoon Rev. W.O. Dinnius called; also Rev. C.H. Kiracofe. Also the Misses A. Osborn, F. Greenwood, Ida Graybill, and Laura Hatfield, to see Katie.

Friday, March 13 Got copy of Finding of Facts from Study. Copied changes and returned them by registered letter. Called at Young's to get them, 3 minutes. Also called again in afternoon 10 minutes.

Saturday, March 14 At home in forenoon. Afternoon made two trips to post office to see about entering Lessons Quarterly & Precious Gems. Completed it. Felt very much worn & nervous.

Sunday, March 15 Staid at home all day. Spent the time in reading and resting. Read over the S.S. Lessons for the coming quarter and comments thereon. Read till late in the evening.

Monday, March 16 Called at J.K. Graybill's office. Wrote some letters in forenoon. Spent afternoon and evening in writing.

Tuesday, March 17 In answer to a note by G.R. Young went over to his office with copies of Davis & Clark's depositions which I left there. In his office about 15 min. Wrote letters late in the evening.

Wednesday, March 18 At home till evening. Spent the day mostly in reading, not feeling much like other work. Ex. Com. Mis. met at C.H. Kiracofe's on Summit Street, 119, at 7:00. Chose Elida for the annual meeting and

Rev. I.M. Tharp to deliver the Annual Missionary discourse. Wrote till late in the evening.

Thursday, March 19 Spent the forenoon in writing and examining the letters of the past month or two. Went to Reeves' and left my watch for new main spring. Saw Mr. Houk. Saw Young 10 min. Read some in the afternoon. Wrote letters to Lawrence and on Mr. Bowers' "Exceptions to Findings" in Chambersburg case.

Friday, March 20 Called at Graybill's Office, at Dillon's and at Kiracofe's after I had gone to town where I saw Blum, and Lutzenberger the latter about a Clergyman's permit on N.Y.L.E. & W. R.R. Wrote in the afternoon and eve.

Saturday, March 21 Saw Rev. Wm. Miller at Miami City station. Wrote letters and notices. Get ready to go to Wengerlawn. Wrote till about midnight.

Sunday, March 22 At S.S. at West End. W. Dillon pr. on 139. etc. etc. on self examination. At home till evening. Hear Rev. Maurice Wilson pr at 7:30, Matt. 19:30, an able, good sermon. Katie went with me.

Monday, March 23 Went to Bellefontaine on 10:00 train. Dine, sup, & lodge at Judge Wm. Lawrence's. He reads to me a part of his argument on Differences between the Creeds. His son William was there.

Tuesday, March 24 Came home on 9:28 train after looking over the Pennsylvania paper relating to the Chambersburg case, and writing F.C. Daugherty at Kenton, Ohio. Spend afternoon in writing, going to town, etc. Write till 1:00 at night.

Wednesday, March 25 Write in the morning. Much over taxed with business. Start at 3:30 P.M. for Ontario. Go via Toledo to Detroit, reaching there at 10:50. Stay at Griswold House. On the way I had quite a talk with a Jew who is a sort of Unitarian.

Thursday, March 26 Being mistaken as to which branch of the R.R. Paris is on, I miss connection. I spend forenoon in looking up the City. Run 2 1/2 ms. out on Woodward Ave. & back on Third Ave. Call at post office, ascend elevator on the Ten story, Hammond building

& City hall tower. See Belle Island Park, Windsor Canada, Ft. Cass. Go on 12:00 train via London to Paris, arr. 5:50. Livery to Roseville. Stay D.D. Snyder's.

Friday, March 27 (Biship Barnaby absent). Conf. opened at 8:30 & progressed well. My home is at Mrs. Sarah Barton's. Children are Joseph 24; Terie 20; Lizzie 1 yr; Gracie 11; One son in Columbus. Examinations close & we elect Sherk, P.E. Stationing Com. meets at 7·00. I miss night meeting. CM.Smith pr. I did not hear him. Stay at Barton's.

Saturday, March 28 Conference continues. Reports are finished. Conference discusses theseveral reports. Afternoon Com. on Finance meets at Perrin's. Conference closes 6:00 p.m. I dined at Barton's. Sup at D.D. Snider's. They have three daughters and one son. Missionary meeting at 8:00. Backus, Clark and Plowman spoke about 15 min. each. I raise $163 missionary subscription. Stay at Barton's.

Sunday, March 29 My watch hands fall behind am late. I pr. at 10:30, 1 Tim 3:15. Collection taken for Barnaby over 29 dollars. Dine at Barton's with Bro. Sherk and others. Sabbath school anniversary at 3:00. J. Howe, Hershey, R.A. Clark & Mrs. C.M. Smith spoke & myself. Supper at Jac. Detweiler's. His son (15) takes me to Jas. Wing's in New Dundee, Lodge there. Preach at 7:30 to a full house, Gal. 4:4.

Monday, March 30 Wing's children: Effa 14; Chas. 10, Grace 4. Bra. E. Thamar takes me to Berlin (10:30) stop at Rev. D.B. Sherk's. His wife a Hershey; his son a doctor. Rev. C. W. Backus, Jac. Howe, G. Bailey & wife call & we have much talk. Supper at Prof. I.L. Bowman's. Arthur 26, Harvey 20, daughter 25. I pr. at U.B. Church at 8:00, Ps. 92:8. Thirteen of the New Menonite preachers present. House crowded. Stay at Rev. J.B. Bowman's. Son 29, daughter 26. Two Gr. Child.

Tuesday, March 31 G. Bailey, & Howe call at I.L.'s. J.B. Bowman takes me to the depot. Start at 11:+ to Fort Gratiot. Cross at Port Edwards. Stop 40 min. at Ft. Gratiot. Connect at Gratiot Ave. for L.S. & Mich.S to Toledo. Arr. at 8:20. Start at 11:40 for Dayton. Sleep perhaps four or five hours at depot & on train.

Wednesday, April 1 Reach Dayton at 5:00. Call at Graybill's, Dillon's, and Kiracofe's in forenoon. Slept two hours in afternoon. Wrote many letters in the evening. Rev. Brelsford (formerly near Jonesboro, Ind.) dines with us.

Thursday, April 2 I arose with influenza ("Grippe") and was poorly all day. Wrote considerable.

Saturday, April 4 Wrote an Article on Ontario Conference; etc. Still considerably affected with "Grippe."

Sunday, April 5 At home all day, not feeling well enough to go to Church.

Tuesday, April 7 Rev. Ephr. Eby came. He and wife dine with us. Prof. Kiracofe & Rev. Wm. Dillon call in the afternoon.

Thursday, April 9 At home all day. In evening wrote article for Conservator.

Saturday, April 11 Gloomy weather. Not able to do much. Wrote some notices of Board meetings for *Conservator*.

Sunday, April 12 Remained at home all day not feeling well, but rather weaker from the influenza.

Monday, April 13 At home. Wrote some letters. Still weak from influenza. Went to town. Saw Houk. Called at Young's. Called at Graybill's.

Wednesday, April 15 At home. Bishop Becker called with Prof. C.H. Kiracofe in the evening.

Thursday, April 16 At home. Called at Dillon's & at Prof. Kiracofe's; found noboddy [sic] at home. Bishop H.J. Becker called in the afternoon and staid to supper.

Friday, April 17 At home. Called at Wm. Dillon's in the forenoon. Saw Bp. Becker there.

Saturday, April 18 Called at C.H. Kiracofe's in the forenoon. Wrote many letters. Went to P.O., called at Young's, called at J.R. Graybill's office on my way home via St. Cars.

Sunday, April 19 I Pr. at W. End Church, Jonah 1:3, on Jonah. At home the rest of the day. Read much in Alexander's Notes, Critical Commentary, and Bunyan's Works.

Monday, April 20 Called at Kiracofe's, Dillon's & Graybill's afternoon. Called at Young's about 20 minutes. Got paper at 5:00. Wrote many letters in evening. Revised a long article in forenoon.

Tuesday, April 21 At home. Called at Mrs. L. Edwar[d]s'. Wrote letters in the evening.

Wednesday, April 22 Arose early. Wrote letters. Called at Mrs. Edwards and gave her ten of Bp. E's. photograph's. Continued to write letters.

Saturday, April 25 Went on 8:00 train to Richmond. Spent most of the day with T.J. Study, Esq., hearing his brief read. Dined at D.K. Zeller's. Called at Allen Harris'. Came home on 4:45 train.

Sunday, April 26 Heard Rev. Ephr. Eby & wife preach at W. End Church. At home rest of day till evening. I pr. at 7:30 W.E. Ch. Luke 17:21.

Monday, April 27 Called at J.K. Graybill's. After dinner went to Young's and read over my deposition in Pontiac Case, Saw Mr. Houk in his office. Spent evening in reading.

Tuesday, April 28 Went to Young's and continued my deposition, an hour. In afternoon continued 3:15 in all 3 day's of deposition! Spent the evening in letter writing.

Wednesday, April 29 Went to town to read and sign my deposition. Found *Wm. Doup, the Notary absent. Lost 1/2 day. Went in afternoon and read and signed my Pontiac deposition. (*Wm. Doup seemd a nice young man, but afterward became a forger and twice was sent to the Ohio Penitentiary).

Thursday, April 30 Spent most of the day writing an article—Liberal Victories.

Friday, May 1 At home. Spent most of the forenoon reading. Called at Dillon's & J.K. Graybill's. Afternoon, called at Rev. W.O. Dinius' and at John Collins' at Young's & Houk's, also. Evening at home writing. The children went to a concert.

Saturday, May 2 Went to town. Called at Blum's. (Ref'd Publisher) at Young's, etc.

Sunday, May 3 Rev. Wm. Dillon pr. W.E. Ch. at 10:30, Jas. 1:27 At home the rest of the day.

Monday, May 4 Went to town. Saw Houk. Saw Otto Bowman about copying depositions. Called in afternoon at Graybill's, Mrs. Rebecca Davis', and at Mrs. C. Edwards in evening.

Wednesday, May 6 Went to Marysville to Read Shuey's affidavit there.

Thursday, May 7 Learned that Study could not come to-morrow, & telegraphed him & Lawrence to come Saturday.

Friday, May 8 Went to Houk's office, Young's; saw Otto Bowman about copying depositions. In afternoon at Graybill's & Mrs. R. Davis'. In evening called at Mrs. C. Edwards. The County clerk refused to agree to certify copies any cheaper than if he made copics himself.

Saturday, May 9 Lawrence, Houk, Young and Study in consultation at Young's office. I was present. We rode out with Young in afternoon for a drive. Wrote a letter in the evening.

Sunday, May 10 I pr. at W.E. Ch. at 10:30, Ps. 25.14. At home the rest of the day. Finished reading McClelland's Canon & Interpretation of Scripture. Examined the comments on Matt. 16:18.

Monday, May 11 At home. Called at Mrs. C. Edwards in afternoon.

Tuesday, May 12 Wrote out Introductory Thoughts for Lessons Quarterly for July, etc. Bp. H. Floyd came; dined with us. I called at Mrs. Rebecca Davis', Dillon's, and J.K. Graybill's. Bp. Floyd staid with us to-night.

Wednesday, May 13 Went with Floyd & Dillon to Elida, Ohio, via Lima. Stopped at Henry Kiracofe's. Bp. Floyd & I canvass part of our work, Bps. Barnaby & Becker not arriving till 5:00 p.m. Bp. H. Floyd delivers the Annual Missionary discourse at 7:30, after a brief meeting of the Mis. Board. Dinner & Supper at Henry Kiracofe's. I stay at my home at S.A. Stemen's.

Thursday, May 14 Parent Missionary Board opens at 8:30. Coms. announced. Cor. Sec'y reports. Treasurer reports. Woman's Mis. Board meets at 2:00 & organized. After its session, Parent Board resumed session. Mrs. A.R. Kiracofe delivered an address at 7:30. I dine, sup & lodge at S.A . Steman's. Their children: Mertie 12; Mary 10; Lena Leata 9; Elva Delila 5; babe 1.

Friday, May 15 Board of Bishops meet at 8:30. Mis. Asso. of Women met at 8:30. Parent Board resumed at 10:00, Barnaby presiding. I dine at Rev. J. Freeman's 1 1/2 m north, with Bps. Floyd, Becker, & others. Session at 2:30. Adjourned at 3:15. Educational board had a session. Mis. Board resumed at 4:00. Bishop H.J. Becker lectured at 8:00, "Five Hundred miles ahorseback." I sup & stay at S.A. Stemen's.

Saturday, May 16 Womans Association met at 8:30. Parent Board met at 10:00. Aftern. met at 2:00. Retired to A.J. Stemen's to finish our session. Sup & dine at A.S. Stemen's. Barnaby pr. at 7:30 on "Blow trumpets" of Jubilee. I heard all with much interest, but sketched my sermon for the morrow. Stay at S.A. Stemen's. Slept six hours.

Sunday, May 17 Studied my sermon in bed early & walked out after breakfast & thought it over. Preach at 10:30, Rev. 6:2, "Conquests of the Rider." House very full. Dine at I.R. Spear's. His son & wife there. All the bishops there. Hear Kline pr. funeral of a boy at U.B. Church at 2:00. Called at Brenneman's. Supper at Henry Kiracofe's. Bp. Becker pr. at 7:30, Songs of Solom. 4:4. "Neck like tower of David," Stay at Stemen's.

Monday, May 18 Monday came home via Lima. Arrive at 1:00. Call at Cons. Office, Dillon's, Kiracofe's. Write letters.

Tuesday, May 19 Went to town in afternoon and called on Young 30 or 40 minutes.

Wednesday, May 20 At home. Call at Young's 15 min. Call at Dillon's & Kiracofe's.

Thursday, May 21 Went to town with Kiracofe's & they select carpets. Write letters. Wrote and sent out Circular letters to pres. elders, & to others.

Friday, May 22 Called at Graybills and Dillon's. Sent out letters and got ready to Start to Pennsylvania. Start at 9:00 p.m. for Chambersburg. Take a berth in the sleeper.

Saturday, May 23 Breakfast at Pittsburgh. Reach Harrisburg abt. 2:30 & Chambersburg abt. 5:45. Rev. P. Nicklas meets me & takes me to his house. We meet Judge Wm. Lawrence at 10:00 & take him to the McKinley Hotel. Stay at Nicklas'. Children: Christian 20; Naoma 17; Russel 15; Gracie 13; Bishop 11; Bennie 9.

Sunday, May 24 I pr. at King St. Church at 10:00. Dan. 2:34. On Conquests of Christ. Dine at Rev. M.F. Keiter's & sup there. Made an address at S. School at 2:00. Pr. at 7:30, Luke 17:21, on "Kingdom within". Stay at P. Nicklas'.

Monday, May 25 Greencastle Church case opened at 10:00 before Judge John Stewart. W. Rush Gillan spoke (mostly from manuscript and documents[)] all forenoon and a half hour afternoon. Wm. Lawrence began 20 min. after 2:00 and spoke 2 hours & 30 minutes. Sup & lodge at Rev. P. Nicklas'. I call at McKinley's Hotel to see Lawrence, at 7:30.

Tuesday, May 26 Judge Wm. Lawrence spoke all day, 6h, 15m in all 8:45. I dine & lodge at P. Nicklas'. I sup at Alson Stager's with P. Nicklas & wife & Rev. J.S. Wentz. She is Nicklas' daughter Drucilla. Call at Nicklas' store and at McKinley's; but Lawrence had retired. Talked with Peter till late.

Wednesday, May 27 Call at Hotel & see Lawrence. O.C. Bowers occupied all the forenoon. Judge Stewart gave him some posers. Judge Rowe spoke all the afternoon for plaintiffs. Consultation with attorney at O.C. Bowers' office at 7:25. Call at Lawrence room 1/2 hour. Dine, sup & lodge at P. Nicklas'.

Thursday, May 28 Call at hotel briefly. Rowe (Ro) occupied all forenoon & all afternoon closing at 5:00. I dine at P. Nicklas' sup at Adam Nicklas' and go on 6:05 train to Hagerstown, Md. Rev. Bowman on train. Call at Dunker's Tabernacle. Rainy & no meeting. Start at 11:15 for Harrisburg & at 3:10 for Pittsburgh. Sleep 4 hours.

Friday, May 29 Reach Pittsburgh abt. 12:00, & Columbus, O., at 7:15. Stay at Park Hotel. Lodging 75 cts. Write some before retiring.

Saturday, May 30 Lunch at Depot. Start on 7:25 train via Xenia to Dayton. Home about 9:00. Prof. C.H. Kiracofe called at 10:30. Put in short Article on Chambersburg trial. It is Decoration Day. Ex. Com. of the Mis. Board met at my office at 4:00. Heard Ex-pres. R.B. Hayes speak at Music Hall. Katie with me. Hayes is truly able.

Sunday, May 31 At home till evening. Took Katie to Third St. Presbyterian Church. Heard Rev. Willits pr. on "Hand writing on the wall". Dan. V.

Monday, June 1 Went of the Hill & to town in afternoon. At Young's perhaps 40 minutes. Ex. Com. Mis. met at 7:00.

Tuesday, June 2 At home all day. Wrote many letters to my district and worked on my report in the evening. Rev. Chas. S. Miller came in the afternoon and staid with us. Miller is of Rush Co., Ind.

Wednesday, June 3 Board of Trustees of Printing Establishment met at 10:00 (10:30). Z.McNew elected Chairman protem, in Floyd's absence. J.F. Horine dines with us. Seminary Board met at 2:00. Pr. Estab. Board at 3:00. Rev. Z. McNew and J.S. Miller, and Dr. G.W. Schenck sup with us. Boards both finish sessions in the evening.

Thursday, June 4 Called at Kiracofe's. S.A. Stemen & wife dine with us.

Friday, June 5 At town, Called an hour at Young's, and short time at Houk's.

Saturday, June 6 Called at Graybill's Dillon's &

Kiracofe's. Worked on Affidavit for Wooster, O., case, part of afternoon and evening.

Sunday, June 7 Pr. at West End Church on North School St. at 10:30, 1 Cor. 12.13 on "Communion of Saints." At home till evening. Hear Prof. C.H. Kiracofe pr. at 7:45, 1 Cor. 16:1, 2. on Systematic Giving.

Monday, June 8 Spent the whole day in preparing the affidavit to be used in the Wooster preliminary on the examination at Madisonburg Church case.

Tuesday, June 9 Sent off the affidavit. Wrote some letters. Saw Young. At home all afternoon.

Thursday, June 11 Called at Dillon's & Kiracofe's in forenoon. Did some writing.

Friday, June 12 Wrote on Bishop's address in the forenoon. Afternoon looked up letters received and directed answers to them, to the number of about ten.

Saturday, June 13 At home in the forenoon. Went to town (East Side) in the afternoon, 1/2 h. at Young's. Read proofs on Dr. Davis' deposition & on my articles for the Conservator.

Sunday, June 14 I Preach at W.E. Ch. at 10:30, Rev. 22:14, on "Blessedness of doing commandments." I Spent afternoon in reading Jameson's Introduction to the Pentateuch; and Anon. writer in N.Y. Tribune on "Higher Criticism;" and other writings on the same Subject. In the evening, read through the First Book of Macabees.

Monday, June 15 Made out deposition and sent it to Henry Walters, North Manchester, Ind. Saw Young & Houk.

Tuesday, June 16 Busy getting documents ready, for the trial. See Young in Aftern. Went over to learn that Lawrence had come & gone to Hon. G.W. Houk's.

Wednesday, June 17 Printing Establishment trial began. Plaintiff after reading of pleadings put in afternoon, Shuey on stand, and rested their case. We then put in documents by him. Judges: C.C. Shearer, G.H. Stewart and J.M. Smith. I was put on stand.

Thursday, June 18 I was continued on stand. Cross examination about noon. Discussion by attorneys. Cr. Examination all day. Our attorneys are Hon. Wm. Lawrence, Hon. G.W. Houk, and G.R. Young, Esq. Plaintiffs' attorneys: Hon. Lewis B. Gunckel & Hon. John McMahon.

Friday, June 19 My cross examination & re examination finished. Wilbur was examined. Shuey examined on Board of Tellers, etc. in aftern. Dr. Zach. test examined on German Discipline. He dined with us. Court adjourned till Monday.

Saturday, June 20 At home most of the day reading and writing. Called at Graybill's and Dillon's. Rev. Horace F. Alderton & wife at Dillon's.

Sunday, June 21 At W.E. Quarterly meeting. Rev. Wm. Miller P.E. preached on the "Evidence of Miracles." Alderton & wife & Rev. H.H. Hinman dined with us. Alderton pr. at 4:00 on "Grow in Grace." Rainy evening. I read & wrote.

Monday, June 22 Floyd came Dined with us. Trial resumed at 1:30.

Tuesday, June 23 Trial Continued. Kiracofe testified in the afternoon. I was put on the stand a little before adjournment.

Wednesday, June 24 My examination was continued all forenoon. Floyd dined with us. Rested our case. Weaver put on the stand. His harangue. Spoke continuously, and as an advocate. Spent a half hour or more with Lawrence at Phillips House. Call at Young's.

Thursday, June 25 Bp. Weaver cross examined. Testimony badly damaged. Drury (A.W.) used up an afternoon on his Otterbein Creed. Others likewise. Testimony closed by Liberals. Floyd dined and supped with us. I called at Dillon's & then saw Lawrence & Young at Law library room a few minutes.

Friday, June 26 Mr. L.B. Gunckel, Esq., made the opening speech for the plaintiff's. Afternoon Houk spoke 2

hr 13 m. and G.R. Young 45 min. for us. Called at Dillon's, and at Young's office. All much admired Young's speech. (Gunckel is not a pleasant speaker; Houk's was a poor argument).

Saturday, June 27 Hon. Wm. Lawrence spoke three hours. In afternoon John A. McMahon spoke for plaintiffs 3 h., 15 m. Trial Closed. Lawrence's picture taken addressing the court. His speech was a very fine one. McMahon is able and his elocution is very fine and pleasing.

Sunday, June 28 Wm. Dillon preached on Resurrection of the body at 10:30 at W.E. Ch. I dined at Jacob Swank's & staid till evening meeting. Prof. C.H. Kiracofe pr. at 8:00 on "Blessed are pure in heart," Matt. 5:8.

Monday, June 29 Busy all day preparing Lawrence's Theological Argument for printing. Called at Dillon's in forenoon.

Tuesday, June 30 Worked hard all forenoon on L's Manuscript. Went to town in afternoon. Saw Young. At my office, looked over accumulated letters.

Wednesday, July 1 Called at Graybill's & Dillon's. Went to town in afternoon. Did less than usual to-day.

Saturday, July 4 At home. Considerable proof reading on Lawrence's Dif. of the Confessions.

Sunday, July 5 Pr. at W.E. Church at 10:30, Acts 9:11. "Behold he prayeth." At home till evening. Rev. John Nicholas pr. at 7:30. Ps. 77:12, "I will medit. on thy works, and talk of thy doings."

Monday, July 6 At home. Called at Young's. Got his facts for judges to find. Wilbur read & returned. Much proof reading.

Tuesday, July 7 At home. Finish proof reading.

Wednesday, July 8 Went to Newark, Ohio. Injunction cases of Perry Co. come before Judges John W. Jenner and Chas. Follett who divide as per our request. I stay at Columbus at Leonard House till 1:30. Come home via Springfield. Hotel bill 75 cts.

Thursday, July 9 Reach home at 5:00. Call at Graybill's. At home till eve., Called at Dillon's & Printing Office.

Friday, July 10 Go to town. See Houk. Barely speak to Young as he is busy. Write short article in the evening on "Oppression's Rod Removed," for Conservator.

Saturday, July 11 Called at Kiracofe's & Graybill's.

Sunday, July 12 Pres. C.H. Kiracofe pr. at W.E. Church (School St.) at 10:30 Matt. 6:10, "Thy Kingdom Come". I pr. at Sch. St. at 7:30, on Last Six Days of Jesus previous to burial. John, XII.1.

Monday, July 13 At home. Called at Graybill's & Dillon's & Kiracofe's. Wrote letters in the evening.

Tuesday, July 14 Called at Graybill's. At home the rest of the day.

Wednesday, July 15 At home. In afternoon went to town & bought two book cases for my home office, $4.00, and I scrubbed them out in the evening.

Thursday, July 16 At home. Put book-cases in the east upper room and moved things from middle room there.

Friday, July 17 At home. Straightened out the papers in my room on book-case shelves.

Saturday, July 18 Called at Graybill's in forenoon. Called at Young's in the afternoon & telegraphed Judge Lawrence to come Monday.

Sunday, July 19 I pr. at W.E. Chapel, Matt 24:3. On the Dest. of Jerusalem Second Coming & End of the World. At home rest of the day. Pr. at W.E. Ch. 7:30, Deut. 34:3, on the Land of Palestine.

Monday, July 20 At 11:00, the Circuit Judges, C.C. Shearer & Gilbert H. Stewart gave the decision in the Printing Estab. Case against the Conservatives. Lawrence, Houk & Young read over the "finding of facts." Meet again in afternoon Houk absent at Young's office. Paper (Conservator) came out in evening.

Tuesday, July 21 Arose early. Wrote six letters & mailed

them at Union depot. C.H. Kiracofe came. Went to town in afternoon. Called at Walker's, & Chr. Asso. Reading room & at Young's with Kiracofe. Saw Young about 10 min. Wilbur had sick spell in the night.

Wednesday, July 22 Arose later than usual. Arranged Lawrence's brief for Indiana Supreme Court. Went to town in afternoon. Saw Young 15 or 20 minutes. We are promised copy of Judge's decision to-morrow morning. See. J. Collins about transl. of Weaver's Cross examination. Shuey showed himself rather short about giving us copy of the decision.

Thursday, July 23 At home. Prepare Lawrence argument for the paper. Great labor to abridge Argument.

Saturday, July 25 At home. Many proofs to read on Lawrence's Theol. Argument.

Sunday, July 26 At W.E. Church. Rev. C.H. Kiracofe pr. In the evening Rev. Wm. Dillon pr.

Monday, July 27 Wrote a Synopsis of the Decision of Ct. Ct. Read proofs on Argument of Lawrence.

Tuesday, July 28 Called at Graybill's Printing Office. Read & returned proofs. In afternoon, met Circuit Judges on Statement of facts. Judges Shearer & Stewart present. Wm. Lawrence, W.R. Young & G.W. Houk there. And McMahon & Rowe. The Judges showed no candor or fairness.

Thursday, July 30 At home. Wrote letters. Rather dull to-day. Bros. Kiracofe and Dillon called in the evening.

Saturday, August 1 Wrote some. Got ready to go to Olive Branch Dedication in Auglaize Co., O. Go on 3:45 train. Botkin meets me and takes me to his house near the Church. Supper there. Rev. S.L. Livingston pr. at 8:00 Rev. 22.14. "Blessed . . . Commandm." etc. I stay at Rev. R.G. Montgomery's. Livingston & wife there & Blakely.

Sunday, August 2 I pr. at 10:15, Ps. 122.1. Riase $350.00 in cash & subscription & dedicate Olive Branch Church. Dinner in the grove, a mile west. Preach at 2:45, 1 Cor 5:17. Sacramental Service. Stay at Shadrack S. Montgomery's.

Monday, August 3 Call at R.G. Montgomery's awhile. S.S. Montg takes me to Wapakaneta. On 10:30 train for home. Train delayed an hour on the way. Call at Graybill's. Howard Landon left Saturday.

Wednesday, August 5 Gave my deposition in the Oregon case. It took from 10:00 till about 6:00, with intermission of 1 1/2 hours.

Thursday, August 6 Called at Graybill's, Dillon's, Kiracofe's & Davis' in forenoon. In afternoon called a few minutes at Young's.

Saturday, August 8 At home. Wrote article for Conservator. Kiracofe called in forenoon.

Sunday, August 9 I pr. at W.E. Church at (30 m.) 10:30, Matt. 5:7. A very warm day. Revised several sketches of sermons. Pr. at 7:30 (30 m.) Eph. 1:7.

Monday, August 10 At Graybill's to read proof. Call at Young's & complete and read deposition.

Tuesday, August 11 Return deposition & sign it.

Wednesday, August 12 I determine on a visit to Indiana.

Thursday, August 13 Have many letters written. Start at 3:45 aftn, for Glenwood, Ind. via Hamilton, 0. Jas. C~lhertson takes me to Fayetteville and I walk to Anson Moor's 2\ms, S.E. of Fayetteville. Lucinda Moor sick with flux. I stay there. Anson Moor quite poorly.

Friday, August 14 An hour at Chas. Stevens. Flora (my niece) goes with me to Moor's. Sarah Catharine, my niece, & Laura Winchell, my niece, and Laura's daughter, Minnie and her son & Mrs. Desdemon there. After dinner, Anson takes me to Glenwood. Thence I got to Rushville & to Hamilton Station. Thence to my Bro. Harvey Wright 's.

Saturday, August 15 Spend forenoon in visiting at numerous relatives. Effa Kirkpatrick's, Drucilla McKee's, Emma Frazier's, Eva Wright's, Dan Wright's, John Wright's, Frances Rhoads. Dined at Harvey W 's. Pr. at Bapt. meeting at 2:00, Rom. 8:17, 18. Called at Thos. Wright 's. Harvey took me to Dunreith. Go to Dublin.

Supper at Edmond Wilson's. Hear Mrs. Vienna Johnson preach on Isa. 53:8. I stay at Bp. H. Floyd's.

Sunday, August 16 I pr. at 10:30 Matt. 5:14, dine at Rev. W.A. Oler's. Supper at Dr. Geo. W. Champ's. Call at Dr. Hardy Wray's. Pr. at 7:30, Matt. 5:7. Stay at H. Floyd's.

Monday, August 17 Go on hack to Cambridge City & on cars to Richmond. Call at Zeller's house & office Go on 7:40 train home. Afternoon, call at Young's. Get new pants at Dayton Tailoring Co.

Tuesday, August 18 At home. Called at Young's a few minutes. Copied for Bp. Weaver's cross examination for publ. paper.

Wednesday, August 19 Go to town. See Young two minutes. Start on 11:15 train.to Farmland. Rev. G.H. Byrd takes me out to Martin Bartlett's 1 mile S. of Zion Ch. Supper there. I pr. 8:00 1 Tim. 3:15, on Living Church. Stay at Mrs. Christian Life's. Slept abt. 5 hours.

Thursday, August 20 At Conference about an hour. G.H. Byrd takes me to Red Key. Go to Jonesboro & thence to Fairmount. Walk out to W.H.H. Reeder's on my farm. Thresher's there. Supper there. Wm. Reeder takes me to Fairmount. I go on 9:04 train to Wabash. Stay at Tremont House. Slept abt. 3 hours.

Friday, August 21 Go on 3:47 train to Huntington. Breakfast at Rev. A.G. Johnson's. Conference began at 8:30. Made good progress all day. D.T. Thomas & Rev. W.E. Street present. Rev. C.H. Kiracofe & wife came in afternoon. He pr. at 8:00 "Strive- strait gate able." I stay at Rev. A.G. Johnson's. Slept well.

Saturday, August 22 Conference continued. A.G. Johnson elected P.E. Stationing Com. met at 1:00. Session closed at 5:00. Put reports onto church chart. Rev. C.H. Kiracofe & wife spoke on missions.Slept 4 1/2 hours.

Sunday, August 23 Pr. at 10:30, Matt. 5:12. Collec. $36.04. Chart Coll. $33.00. Total $69.04. Dine at Wm. Coolman's with Rev. J. L. Powers. Hire [blank]. Go to Rev. A.G. Johnson's supper. Pr. at 8:00 at M.E. Ch. Ps. 25:14. Rev. G.H. Hill, pastor.

Monday, August 24 Start on 6:00 train for Chicago. Meet Rev. J.H. Kiracofe at Chi. Depot. I get some half fare permits. Start at 1:30 for Casey, Iowa. Travel all night. Sleep 4 hours.

Tuesday, August 25 Reach Casey 6:28 A.M. Breakfast at House. Hire a rig $1.50 & Go to L. Hoisington's & Dan R. Fagan's. Look over the farm. Dine with Fagan's. Go to Mr. Vanmeter's. Return to Fagan's and arrange for a corn crib. I go on to Casey. Stay at House. Sleep 7 1/2 hours.

Wednesday, August 26 I Go on 5:28 for Dorchester, Nebr. R.S. Austin & Rev. John Thornburg meet me and take me to Camp-ground 4 1/2 ms. S.W. I pr. at 8:00, Eph. 2:4. Stay at Bro. B.F. Duley's 2 m. north east. Slept 5 1/2 hours.

Thursday, August 27 Conf. opened at 8:30. Business proceeds. Dine at tent & supper. Rev. G.F. Albrecht pr. at 8:00. Canti 8:7. Lively testimony meeting followed. I stay again at B.F. Duleigh's. Slept 7 hours.

Friday, August 28 Conf. continued. Consecrated the tent at 3:00. Dined and supped at the tents as usual. I pr. at 7:30 1 Cor. 1:23. Stay at B.F. Duleigh with Rev. S.P. Ross. Their children are : Dwight 17 & Myrtle 11, & three married daughters.

Saturday, August 29 Conference continued. Dine & sup at the tents. Rev. L.C. Furman pr. at 3:00. Closed business at 4:30. I called at several of the tents. Rev. J.M. Sims pr. at 8:30, 1 John 3:8. I stay at B.F. Duleigh's.

Sunday, August 30 I pr. at Camp-ground at 11:00, Ps. 92:8. Dine at B.F. Mumma's. Mrs. C.H. Kyle pr. at 2:30, Col. 3:1 3. Sacrament followed. Sup at Baker's tent. I Pr. at 8:00, Rev. 22:17. Seven joined Church. I stay at Duleigh's.

Monday, August 31 Go to Camp-ground and thence to Rev. G.F. Albrecht's. Rest very much. Slept 12 hs. Two of their sons are married and two at home. The family talk German mostly.

Tuesday, September 1 Go to Dorchester with Bro. Albrecht & thence to Robt. Baker's, 3 ms. West of

Dorchester. Dine there. Revs. E.P. & O.H. Kyle call in afternoon. Write letters. Had a good night's rest. Hard rain in the night.

Wednesday, September 2 Go on 12:47 train to Lincoln. Stay at Rev. N.L. Hoopingarner's, Walker St. near Fowler Ave. Union Place. I solemnized Hoopingarner's marriage with Dora Stallsmith seven years ago, near Hartford City, Ind. He is now a M.E. evangelist. They named their oldest boy for me.

Thursday, September 3 Go on 8:10 train via Fremont to Neligh. Reach there about 3:30. Rev. E.P. Mead and N. Wilcox met me and I go with Wilcox to his house, 16 m. S.W. for supper. Rev. J.P. Cotton pr. at Free will Baptist Church, 1 mi. W. of Vim P.O. at 8:00. I stay at Ezra G. Durham's my conference home. A good single bed & room to myself.

Friday, September 4 Elkhorn Conference opened at 8:30, morn., at F Baptist Church in Antelope Co., Nebr. Examinations mostly made. I dine and sup and lodge at E.G. Durham's. Their daughter at home is Dottie. Mrs. Durham is a teacher & quite intelligent. He a preacher. Rev. L.E. Cole pr. at 8:00. I slept well.

Saturday, September 5 Conference continued. I dined at Rev. E.P. Mead's, 2 1/2 m. S.E. of Church. Stationing Com. met there. Rev. F.J. Priest pr. at 3:00. Supper at Mead's. I pr. at 8:00 Rev. 22:17. Short session after service. Conf. Adjourned. I stay at Edmund G. Durham's.

Sunday, September 6 At love feast 1/2 hour. Pr. at 11:00, 2 Cor. 4:17. Much feeling in the congregation. Dine at Rev. E.P. Mead's. S.S. Anniversary in the aftern. at 3:00. Br. Woman's Mis. Asso. meeting also. Supper at Wilson's, 2 3/4 m. S.E. She a church member. He is not. Rev. A. Brink pr. at 8:30. Stay at Durham's.

Monday, September 7 Go with C.J. Rarden, Rev. A. Brink, & Rev. F.J. Priest to Clear Water. Start at 11:05 for Ill. Arrive at Omaha about 5:30. On Motor line to Council Bluffs. Go on Chi. Mill. & St. Paul railroad to Leaf River, Ill. Reclining chair Car; slept 5 or 6 hours.

Tuesday, September 8 Reach Leaf River at 6:35. Breakfast at Rev. W.E. Mosier's. Rev. J.L. Harrison comes &

dines with us. I go to his house for supper. He is consumptive. He has sons and a daughter, Mabel, 11 years old. I stay at Mosier's. They have a niece & nephew of hers with them. Mabel Fanna & Herschell Lee Mars, aged 5 & 3.

Wednesday, September 9 Stay at Mosier's till after supper. Go with Mosier to Egan City. I pr. at 8:00, Acts 20:28, house full. I stay at Josiah Rhinehart's, 1 m. S.E.

Thursday, September 10 Conference opened at 8:30 (9:00) and business progressed well. Dinner, supper & lodging at Josiah Rhinehart's. Rev. Hetty pr. at 8:00. Fine Speaking meeting followed. I staid at Rhinehart's to read the Chambersburg decisions.

Friday, September 11 Conference continued. Home as usual. O.F. Smith elected presiding elder. Stationing Com. met at Rhinehart's at 7:00. Woman's Mis. Meeting. Miss Grace Smith read the annual address. I spoke briefly and took up subscription, 17 life members & $6.00 coll. Board as usual.

Saturday, September 12 Conference continued. A good day's session. In aft'n raised $745 subs. on Ch. House. Closed session at 5:30. Miss Grace Smith pr. at 8:00, Rom. 8:30. I exhort 5 minutes. Stay as usual at Rhinehart's.

Sunday, September 13 I Pr. in Rhinehart's grove Ps. 92:11. Dine at Rhinehart's. S.S. Anniversary at 3:00. Addressed by J. Humbert, Wm. Beers and myself. Supper at Rhinehart's. Pr. at 7:00 1 Cor. 5:7, & Sacrament. Slept 2 h at L.F. Kritzinger's. He takes me to Leaf River. Go on 4:00 train to Chi.

Monday, September 14 Arrive at Chicago about 7:30. Go on Kankakee line to Indianapolis & thence to Dayton. Call at Zeller's a few minutes. Reach home 9:00.

Tuesday, September 15 At home in forenoon. Go to town in the afternoon. Start at 6:00 for Indianapolis. Stop a few minutes at D.K. Zeller's. Arrive at Indianapolis, & stay at Circle House.

Wednesday, September 16 Go to State House and Supr. Court room. Case argued 3/4 hour on each side. J.

McBride declined to sit. Dine with Floyd at Circle House. I saw Lawrence, Young & Study at the Bates' house. I go on 5:15 train to La Fayette. Stay at Brant House.

Thursday, September 17 Go on 9:00 train to Gibson City, Ill. to visit my cousin J.F. Croddy. Call an hour in the eve. at Father Little's 1 mile out S.W. Lodge at Croddy's. Children: Edward Milton 16 years, Bertha 11. Called in afternoon at Mitchel's.

Friday, September 18 Go on 10:24 train to East Lynn. Lunch there. Ride 4 ms. N. in a wagon. Walk 2 ms. to John Judy's. Call at Jac. J. Wise's. Petichords. Stay at Judy's. Children: Chas. L., Minnie, Hattie, Tabitha, Scott.

Saturday, September 19 Conference opened at 9:00. Dine at Jacob J. Wise's. Supper at Judy's. I pr. at 8:00, John 15:13. Stay at Judy's.

Sunday, September 20 I pr. at 11:00 John 3:2. Coll. $50.00. Dine at Jac. J. Wise's. Missionary & Sacramental meeting in the afternoon about 4:00. I organized a Branch Woman's Missionary Association. No night meeting. I stay at John Judy's, 1 mile from Goodwin, 2 ms from Claytonville.

Monday, September 21 I dine at John Judy's with Rev. G.W. Alman's. Rev. C.L. Judy takes me to Milford. I go thence to Watseka. Stop at Uncle John Braden's. Children: William, Richard F. Oscar, John, Elizabeth, Eliza. Braden's wife is my mother's youngest sister, Eliza (Reeder.).

Tuesday, September 22 I stay at Braden's till next morning. J.F. Croddy, my Cousin, was also there. Uncle and Aunt started on a trip to Indiana, to visit our relatives.

Wednesday, September 23 I arise at 2:30. Go on 3:35 (4:00) train via Cassopolis, Battle Creek, to Lansing & thence to Sunfield, Eaton Co. Rough R.R. I reach Sunfield at 9:35. Stay at Valentine Myers.

Thursday, September 24 Conference opened at 8:30. Proceeded well. Rev. N. Morthland criticised [sic] the chair. Business in the afternoon proceeds well. Rev. R.W.

Keeney pr. at 7:30. Very enthusiastic meeting followed a dry discourse. I board at V. Myers. Slept 7 hours.

Friday, September 25 Conference continued. Elected B. Hamp & C.B. Whitaker presiding Elders. Stationing Com. met at 7:00 at V. Meyers'. Rev. S. Ferguson pr. at 7:30. Board at Meyers. Slept 7 hours. Very enthusiastic meeting.

Saturday, September 26 Conference proceeded well. Reports on Missions & Education. Caledonia to have next conf. Harmonious session. Close at 5:00. Rev. C.B. Whitaker pr. at 7:30. I board at V. Meyers.

Sunday, September 27 Preach in the grove near the station at 10:30, 1 John 3:2. Ordain Mrs. Sarah A. Lane, Harvey H. Halsey, Nathan F. Sheldon and Benj. D. Travis. Public Coll. $89.+. Dine at Meyers'. Sab. Sch. Anniversary at 4:00. Preach at 7:30 John 6.53, on Communion. Eucharist follows. One joined Church. I stay at V. Meyers, as usual.

Monday, September 28 Go with Mr. Morthland to George Woolett's, 3 ms. S.W. Dine there. Sleep some. Write some. Return to V. Meyers. Write some; visit some. Sleep well.

Tuesday, September 29 Write up my accounts with the office, etc., and send it home. Bro. Barnes called to bid me farewell. Dine at Meyers'. Go with M. Morthland to Portland, Ionia County. Stay at G. Marcen's. Rev. H.H. Halsey & wife called and sat an hour or more.

Wednesday, September 30 Go with M. Morthland via Pewamo, Matherton, and Hubbardston & Middleton to North Star, Gratiot Co., Mich. Dined at Philander Looke's 2 ms. N. of Hubbardston. Reached North Star at 8:00. Rev. Thos. Campbell pr. on Matt. 6:[blank] "Be ye perfect." Stay at W.S. Kleckner's 1 m. N.W. with D.H. Shelly & M. Morthland. Kleckner's children: Adah 22, Cora 18, Oliver 16, Chas. Elmer Ambrose, 24.

Thursday, October 1 Conference opened at 8:30. Business proce[e]ded well. I pr. at 7:30, Acts 20:28 on the Church. I board at W.H. Kleckner's.

Friday, October 2 Conference continued. In afternoon,

elect C.L. Wood & C.J. Moody P.Es. Stationing Committee met at thehotel at 7:00. Board at Kleckner's.

Saturday, October 3 Conference continues. Close at 4:30. Mission Meeting at 7:30, for Woman's Mis. Association, a Branch society of which was organized in afternoon. Board at Kleckner's.

Sunday, October 4 Pr. at 10:30, Heb. 13:14. Raise $60.31 & Dedicate First U.B. Church of North Star Village. Dine with Wood, Moody & Stowe at Wm. H. Kleckner's. I Pr. at 7:00 1 Cor. XI:26, On sacrament. Four join Church. Stay at Kleckner's.

Monday, October 5 Go via Owasso & Lansing & Battle Creek to Niles, Mich. Stay at Henry Evick's. Children: Gabriella; Cora Belle; Adam Winfield.

Tuesday, October 6 Write letter & cards. Start at 1:12 for Chicago. Reach the city about 4:00. Go to Union Depot. Write letters, cards, and an article for *Conservator,* the latter partly on the cars as I go toward Oxford Junction and Brush Creek, Iowa. Meet B. Deitrick & Rev. John L. Buckwalter & Chas. H. Gordon.

Wednesday, October 7 Reach Oxford Junction in the Morning at 6:00. Go on 7:05 train to Brush Creek. Meet as above. Go to Bro. Lucins Carey's in Brush Creek. Stay till morning. Rev. Swain calls to see me. I call to see J.S. Cooney, our attorney. J. Buckwalter and C.K. Gordon to meeting at Garden Prairie Church.

Thursday, October 8 Bro. Buckwalter takes me to "Deacon" W.R. Morley's, 4 ms. S.W. Dine there. He takes me to George Detrick's 6 ms. S.W. of Brush Creek, where I am to make my home. Children: Jay, 19; Nora, 14; Lora, 12; two married daughters. I pr. at Garden Prairie Church at 7:30, Rev. 23:17. Stay at Deitrick's with Rev. Chas. H. Gordon, aged 20.

Friday, October 9 Conference opened, at 9:00. Two ministers and two delegates present. Rev. J.S. Moore pr. at 2:30, Rev. 22:7. Rev. A. Smith preaches at 7:30, Luke 10:[blank] "Mary hath chosen." Board at Detrick's.

Saturday, October 10 Conference continued. Dine at Aaron Powell's. I speak at 2:30 on the State of the

Church. In forenoon, McCormack was elected Pres. Elder. Stationing Com. met at 1:30 at Church. Supper at J.W. Swales. Rev. Zabriski pr. at 7:30, Rev. 22:7.

Sunday, October 11 I pr. at 11:00 Rom. 8:18. Collect $43.75. Dine at Fred. Turner's. S.S. Anniversary at 3:00. Supper at Geo. Detrick's. Rev. R.D. McCormack pr. at 7:30, "Be of good courage," etc. Sacramental meeting. I stay at Detrick's.

Monday, October 12 Geo. Detrick takes me to Brush Creek. Dine with Lucius Carey's with Revs. John Buckwalter & Chas. H. Gordon. Write letters to Lorin, Bowles, etc. Supper & lodging at Carey's.

Tuesday, October 13 Write letters. Call at Wm. H. Benedict's. Dine at Carey 's. Call at John Mead's, to see her, as she is sick. Supper and lodging at And. J. Rosenkran's. Pr. at U. B. Church at 7:30, Gal. 4:45. Stay at Rosenkrans'.

Wednesday, October 14 Called at John Mead's and at Rev. Swain' s. Go on 10:00 train to Calmar, & on 4:10 to Boscobel, Wis. Stay at the Central House.

Thursday, October 15 Orange Scott Pound comes & takes me to his house 2 ms from Knapp Creek School house, near Excelsior. Dine, sup, & lodge there. Rev. C.M. Clark pr. 2 Cor. 8:9 at 7:30. Pound's only son: George Leroy, abt. 16. Rev. E.R. Perrin (Q. Conf.) & Rev. C.M. Clark, P.E., board there.

Friday, October 16 Conference opened at the Sch. house at 9:00. Session progressed in forenoon & afternoon. Rev. C.M. Clark pr. at 2:00, 1st John 1:[blank] . Dine & sup at O.S. Pound's & lodge there. I pr. at 7:15, John 3:16. Conference at Cedar Point or Wood Sch. House 2 1/2 ms. south of Excelsior, Richland Co., Wis.

Saturday, October 17 Conference continued. Preaching at 2:00. Rev. F.J. Crowder, Heb. 2:3. Close conf. about 4:30. I Dine, sup, & lodge at O.S. Pound's. I lecture on State of the Church at 7:30.

Sunday, October 18 Pr. at Wood Sch. House at 11:00 Heb. 11:10. Dine at Samuel Powell's with Haskins, Crowder, & Clark & their wives. Memorial services at 6:00 of Rev. L. Pound. I pr. at 7:00 Eph. 2:16. Stay at O.S. Pound's.

Monday, October 19 Stay at Bro. O.S. Pound' s. Rev. W.H. Haskins & wife (ne[e] Widow Stewart) come. Spend the day and evening in talking.

Tuesday, October 20 Bro. Pound takes me to Boscabel. Dine at the Farmer's Hotel. Take 2:00 train to Pra[i]rie DuChin. Stop with Rev. Jas. Appleby, with John Duncan, his soninlaw from Nuckols Co., Nebr., who tells me of Clem Reeves, of Grant Co., Ind., formerly. Talk with Appleby till near midnight.

Wednesday, October 21 Go on 7:20 train to Prairie DuChin and McGregor & thence via Postville & Calmar to Mason City, Iowa. Thence on Ft. Dodge and Mason City, R.R. to Ft. Dodge & thence to Dayton, Iowa. Mason City Cancer Infirmary president invites me to ride to Ft. Dodge Depot. Thence to Dayton. Stay at American Hotel.

Thursday, October 22 Call at post office and at depots. Write letters. Yound Eslick comes in for us. Dine at Amer. House. With Rev. J.E. Ham, Bros. Wallace & Ingles, I go out to McQuire's Bend on Des Moines River. Stay at W. Russell McGuire's. Rev. J.E. Ham pr. at 7:20, Acts 3:19.

Friday, October 23 Conference opened at 9:00. Short session. Resumed at 2:00. Rev. Thos. Prall pr. at 7:30. Being unwell, I did not go out to evening meeting. Board at McGuire's. Children: Lester, 5; Carrie Leota, 2.

Saturday, October 24 Conference continued. Reports discussed. Rev. J.E. Ham elected Pres. Elder almost unanimously. Stationing committee met at W.R. McGuire's after dinner. Conf. Closed at 4:30. I lecture on the state of the Church at 7:30 at the new Church. Stay at A.J. Eslick's, 1/4 mile south of Church: Children: Paul, Bertha, Ella, etc.

Sunday, October 25 Go to McGuire's. Pr. at 11:00, Acts 20:28. Dine at McGuire's with T. Day, O.A. Wallace and Thos. Prall. Call in afternoon at John Eslick's 1/4 mile west. Pr. at 7:00, John 6:54, W.K. Goodrich joined Church. Closed. Stay at W.R. McGuire's.

Monday, October 26 Arose at 5:30. Get ready to go. Go to A.J. Eslick's. At 10:00 Rev. Lewis Eslick takes Revs. J.E. Ham, S. Stoughton, Thos. Prall, and Messrs. T.D. Wallace & Geo. Engles and myself to Dayton. Dine at American House. Go on 1:35 train to Gowrie & then at 4:00 on Chi. R. Is. & Pac. to Des Moines, Eldon, to Cameron Junction.

Tuesday, October 27 Reach Kansas City at 10:10. Reuchlin meets me and takes me to his house at Ivanhoe, 3 ms. S.E. of the main City. Stay there till morning and so on.

Wednesday, October 28 Went with Reuchlin & Katie Luise to City. See town & Office. At home in rest of afternoon. Talk till bed time.

Thursday, October 29 Go to City and over to Wyandot. At home rest of the day. Came home on Grand Avenue. Walk through woods. At home the rest of the day. Lulu went to prayer meeting & Teacher's Meeting.

Friday, October 30 Went out with Reuchlin & the Children east to gather Hickory nuts, etc. Remain till 5:30. Take 7:05 tr. on H & St. J. to St. Louis. Sleep well in reclining chair.

Saturday, October 31 Reach St. Louis at 7:20. Lunch and take a short walk to see city. Go on 8:05 tr. to Indianapolis. Reach there at 2:55. See Rev. T.J. Connor & wife & Mrs. Hazwlrig, her adopted daughter of Greensburg. Send U.S. Expr. order to pay Grant Co. tax. Go on 4:00 tr. to Richmond. Call at D.K. Zeller's. Reach Dayton at 9:30. Find all well. Go to bed at 12:00. Find house remodeled.

Sunday, November 1 Arose about 8:00. Breakfast late. At home all forenoon. Called at John G. Feight's in the afternoon. Heard Rev. Chas. Weyer pr. at 7:00 at West End Church.

Tuesday, November 3 Voted my first Australian ("Kangaroo") ballot. Went to town in the afternoon. Saw G.R. Young 1/2 hour. Write Letters, to several. Prepare to go to Allegan, Michigna. Start on 9:00 train. Call at Study's, but do not see him. Call at D.K. Zeller's a few minutes. Go on Grand Rapids & Indiana train North.

Wednesday, November 4 Reach Kalamazoo at 7:05. Go on L.S. & M.S. tr to Allegan. Arrive at 8:00. See Mr. Pope. Put up at Sherman House. Salem Church case comes up at 10:00, Judge Dan Arnold. Day spent in reading bills. Counsel with Mr. C.R. Wilkes at Pope's office at 7:00.

Thursday, November 5 Documentary evidence occupies the day. Spent the evening with our attorneys. Revs. C.B. Whitaker, Stone & others come.

Friday, November 6 Bp. Weaver's testimony occupied the day. Court adjourned till December. McMahon receives a telegram announcing Indianapolis Supr. Ct. decision against us. Go on 8:30 freight to Kalamazoo. Put up at American Hotel. Slept 7 hours.

Saturday, November 7 Take 8:50 train to Richmond. Arrive at 3:55. Call at Study's. Take 7:40 train to Dayton. Reach home at 9:30. Slept well.

Sunday, November 8 Arose at 7:30. Remained at home all day, as it rained at meeting hours. Read much especially in the evening from Barnes notes on the Epistles of Peter.

Monday, November 9 Wrote an article on the Indianapolis Decision. Wrote letters. Kiracofe called in the forenoon. I called at Dillon's.

Tuesday, November 10 Engaged in writing and reading. Went nowhere till Mis. Exec. Meeting in the evening at my office at 7:00. After Ex. Com. meeting, wrote till midnight.

Wednesday, November 11 At home all day. Wrote letters. Put my office and papers to rights.

Thursday, November 12 Went to town in the afternoon. Saw Young 20 minutes. Wrote letters till midnight.

Friday, November 13 At home all day.* Got *Telescope* proofs on Indianapolis decision in the afternoon. *Went to town in the morning. Got my watch & gold pen fixed. Spend a good deal of the day arranging my files of letters, etc.

Saturday, November 14 At home all day. Did less work than usual. Prof. C.H. Kiracofe called to get me to preach next day. He is unwell.

Sunday, November 15 Pr. at West End at 10:30, Hab. 3:18, on Rejoicing in "God of my Salvation." At home the rest of the day, reading & resting.

Monday, November 16 At home Most of the day. Called at Graybill's about 5:00. Wrote a number of letters. Called at Dillon's. Had a talk with Kiracofe and Dillon over the present situation. The weather grew quite cold in the night and gave us our first taste of winter.

Tuesday, November 17 At home in the forenoon. Went to Dr. Tiz[z]ard's to have my teeth repaired. At home in the evening. Work till midnight arranging my files of papers.

Wednesday, November 18 Complete my files of papers and write some letters. Go to town in the afternoon. Call at Hollinger's Art Gallery. Get my mouth plate which Tizzard repaired.

Friday, November 20 Revise my article and take it to the office. Call at Kiracofe's. At home in the afternoon writing; also in the evening.

Sunday, November 22 Heard Rev. Chas. Weyer pr. at 10:30 Rev. 6.2. "White horse." At home then till evening. Heard Rev. [blank] the Baptist preacher, pr. at Williams St. Ch. on Publican's Prayer.

Monday, November 23 Went to town. Had measure taken for a coat. Saw Mr. Young five minutes at the Court House.

Tuesday, November 24 At home all day. Lorin helped me get up Correspondence. T.B. Arnold, of Chicago called on us relating to his S.S. Literature.

Wednesday, November 25 At home all forenoon. Getting ready to go away. In afternoon go to Merchant Tailor's, Art Gallery, and Call and see Young perhaps 15 minutes. Hear Fenton lecture on Freemasonry at West End Church at 7:30. To bed about midnight.

Thursday, November 26 Went on 9:30 train to Richmond, Logansport and South Bend to Elkhart, Ind. Stay from (11:35 p.m.) at the Standard House at Elkhart. I wrote letters at Logansport. It was rather a secular Thanksgiving Day to me as I was on a business trip for C.H. Kiracofe about a church bequest.

Friday, November 27 Went to Rev. C.E. Kidder's. Rev. J.L. Powers there and he went with me to see Dodge & Dodge, Attys. Spend the rest of the day at Kidder's. Pr. at our Church on the East Side at 7:00, 1 Cor. V.7. Stay at Kidder's.

Saturday, November 28 Start at 3:00 A.M. for Chicago & thence at abt 1:00 for Lisbon, Iowa, where I arrive at 8:30. Lodge at J. Bittinger's.

Sunday, November 29 Attend communion services at Ev. Lutheran Church at 10:30, and assist. Rev. Cresler pr. at 10:30, John 1:29. I dine at John Harris. Pr. at 2:30 at Ev. L. Ch. Zech. 13:9. Visit & sup at Rev. I.L. Buchwalter's. He is bed-fast. Pr. at 7:00 for Mr. Cresler, Matt. 25:46, on Life Eternal. Stay at J. Bittinger's.

Monday, November 30 Go on 6:10 A.M. train to Cedar Rapids and thence on 8:15 (8:35) train to Ottumwa. Call at Rev. H.D. Crawford's on [blank] Street. Go on 4:50 train to Chariton, and stay at the Bates House, 1/4 m S.E. of the Depot. Write several letters.

Tuesday, December 1 Go on 12:15 (noon) tr to Bethany, Missouri. Find the Eagleville parsonage going on, before Judge Chas. H.S. Goodman of Albany of 28th Judicial District, Radical Att'ys. Liberal att'ys: Col. D.J. Heaston, A.F. Woodruff, U.P. Wardripp. Stay at Poynter House. Met Att'ys at Wanamaker's Office opposite to the Court house & staid till 11:30.

Wednesday, December 2 Trial continued. Lib. Atty's rested at 11:00. Case closed about 4:00. I pr. at Cumberland Pres. Church at 7:00, Zech. 13:9. Many lawyers to hear me. Stay at Pointer House. W.S. Wheeler, the Showman, a rare character talks much. His employment at Little Rock as a detective to protect a liquor seller. Gets onto a Law and Order Ex. Committee! $27,000 City Bribe.

Thursday, December 3 Call at Barlow's office & at Editor's Office of Bethany *Republican*. Go on 12:15 train to Chariton, and thence via Ottumwa & Marshaltown to Jefferson where I arrive at 4:00 A.M. & Stay at the Stake House.

Friday, December 4 Arose at 8:00. Go to Court House to see the files in Mrs. Andrew Dorcas will case. See I.D. Howard, the Administrator. Employ Russel and Toliver. Talk with the latter & leave many documents. Go on 5:40 tr. via Marshaltown to Kent, Ill. Ride all night.

Saturday, December 5 Reach Kent at 6:00. Breakfast at Jacob Auman's 1/2 m. West. Stay there all day. Children: Benj. George 18; Edward 16; Lewis Wm. 10; Jac. Walter 8; Delma Eliz. 3. Rev. G.H. Wilfong pr. at 7:00. Stay at Jac. Auman's. Prospect of dedication figures very poor.

Sunday, December 6 I pr. at 10:30, Heb. 11:10, and secure $255 & dedicate the Church which is a new frame 28 X 44 X 14. I dine at Jac. Brandt's 2 ms. W. in Joe Davis County, with Wilfong & wife. I pr at 7:00, Jas. 1:29. I go back to Brandt's.

Monday, December 7 Jac. Brandt takes me in a sled to Stockton, where I go on 5:17 train to Chicago. At Chicago till 8:30 p.m. Go on to Sheldon & stay at Dunn House.

Tuesday, December 8 Write eight letters. Go on 11:15 train via Effner to Remington, Ind. Go on to Rev. G.H. Allman's, 7 miles S. Dine at Mrs. Allman's. Murphy & wife, Jas. Allman & wife & Father Goble, a street preacher, there. Pr at Shiloh at 7:00, Rom. 2:29, on a Jew inwardly. Stay at Alpheus Elmore's, 1/2 m. East.

Wednesday, December 9 Attend forenoon meeting. In the afternoon, at Alph. Elmore's we elect officers of Shiloh U.B.C. Class: Mary Allman, leader; Alpheus Elmore, steward. Mrs. Mershon pr. at Shiloh, at 7:00, 1 Thes. 4:3, on Sanctification.

Thursday, December 10 Rev. G.W. Allman takes me to the train, and I go via Logansport & Richmond to Dayton. Get home abt 7:00. Find all well.

Friday, December 11 Forenoon: Get up fire, write, etc. At home.

Saturday, December 12 At home till 2:30 p.m. Go to Johnsville and Rev. Aaron Zehring's two & a half miles north-west of the ville. Lodge there. I called at Young's in forenoon & did not find him in.

Sunday, December 13 Pr. at the school house at 10:30, Ps. 122:1. Dine at Zehring's & return to Dayton. Pr. at W.E. Church at 7:00 Rom. 2:29.

Thursday, December 17 Went to City in the afternoon. Saw Young 15 minutes.

Saturday, December 19 At home writing as usual. Read in the evening 170 pages of Irving's life of Goldsmith.

Sunday, December 20 Heard Rev Robinson pr. at Raper Chapel, M.E. Church at 10:30, Isa. 63.3. Was at home the rest of the day & in the evening, as I had a bad cold.

Tuesday, December 22 At home. Wrote for half fare permits on railroads.

Wednesday, December 23 At home. Wrote an article for Conservator "Babel in Courts." Went to town in afternoon. Called at Young's ten minutes. Made application for clergymen's rates on the Erie & Pan Hande [?] railroads.

Thursday, December 24 At home. Wrote letters. Called at Dillon's & Mrs. R. Davis'. Copied Drury's evidence on Otterbein's creed.

Friday, December 25 Arose before 6:00. Bathed all over in cold water as I have been accustomed to do almost every day since June, 1890, and have found much comfort and health in it. Christmas presents & dinner. Wrote some letters and got Shields to certify some for Applications for permits. Finished an article: "Protecting Secretis".

Saturday, December 26 At home most of the day. Called at Young's about 10 minutes in the afternoon.

Sunday, December 27 Heard Rev. Wm. Dillon preach at

West End (School Street) at 10:30, Lord's Prayer. At home the rest of the day. My knee was somewhat lame.

Tuesday, December 29 Went on 8:00 train to Union City and thence to Muncie. Dined at John Nelson's 323 Mulberry Street. Go on via Alexandria to Fairmount. Arrive abt 4:00. Ride out with Tharp two miles & walk the rest to Elis Wright's. He is my nephew, son of Wm. who died in 1868,

Wednesday, December 30 Go in morning to Aunt Elizabeth Reeder's. Dine there. Go in afternoon to Fairmount & Marion & release my share of the mortgage and receive payment, $801.68. Return to Wm. Reeder's. He lives on my farm. Get there at 10:00 at night.

Thursday, December 31 We arrange our accounts and I go to Fairmount for 12:11 train which I miss. I call at Hollingworth's and visit Wm. Hall, a minister of ours 78 years old. I go on 3:25 train to Jonesboro, walk to Harrisburg & go on 6:05 train to Union City. Stay at a hotel.

Conference Items
1. Examinations. 2. Appeals. 3. Any died. 4. Reports of Reading Coms. 5. Applicants to Preach. 6. Publishing Minutes. 7. Elders Orders. 8. Committees for next Year. 9. Next Conference. 10. College Trustees. 11. Treas. Preachers' Ac'd. 12. Mission Sec. & Treas. 13. Boundary Com. Report. 14. Correct Itinerant List. 15. Elect Pres. Elders & State Coms. 16. Secretary's Pay. 17. Conf. Sermon—Mis. Meeting—Sab. Sch. Anniversary. 18. General Reports: Missions—Chu. Erection—Publ. Interests—Education—S. Schools—Resolutions. 19. Sum up results. 20. Elders Eligible. 21. Tellers for Gen. Conf. Elec. 22. S. Sch. secr. & Treas. 23. Moneys paid in.

Bishop's Salary 1891

St. Joseph	69.00
W & W. Nebr	54.03
Elkhorn	35.89
Rock River	120.00
Up. Wabash	50.00
Michigan	190.25
N. Michigan	101.60

Wisconsin	46.00
Wisconsin	35.54
West Des Moines	39.38
[Total]	$741.72
Deduct Trav. Exp.	77.66
Nett salary	664.06

Bishops Salary, 1891

St. Joseph Pub. Col.	36.
Chart Coll's.	33.00
E. & W. Nebr. Chart Coll.	18.00
Pub. Coll.	36.03
Elkhorn Chart Coll.	24.50
Pub. Coll.	11.39
Rock River Chart Col.	69.55
Pub. Coll.	50.45
Upper Wabash Coll.	50.00
Michigan Cha. Coll.	$108.05
Pub. Coll.	82.23
[Total]	190.28
North Mich Chart	$65.60
Pub. Coll.	35.00
H.F. Alderton	1.00
[Total]	101.60
Iowa Conf.	46.00

Wisconsin Conf.	$20.00
Public Coll.	15.54
West Desmoines	39.38
Total	744.72
Trav. Exp.	77.66
[Total]	$664.06

Conference Assessments

Ontario	$125
Mich.	190
Pennsylv.	150
N. Mich	100
Maryland	40
Up. Wab	50
Erie	70
St. Joseph	100
Virginia	50
Rock River	190
East Ohio	90
Wisconsin	45

Scioto	150
Minnesota	35
Sandusky	75
Iowa	45
Auglaize	250
West Des M.	70
[Total]	1,000
Elkhorn	50
West. Nebr.	45
East Nebr.	80
[Total]	1,000
North Ohio	225
Arkan. Val.	60
Neosho	50
Kansas	100
W. Kansas	30
S. Missouri	30
Missouri	60
Illinois	30
Centr. Illin.	100
White River	225
Indiana	40
East Des Moines	50
[Total]	1,000

Bishop's Traveling Expenses, 1891

To Huntington, Ind.	$3.30
To Dorchester, Nebraska	14.39
To Neligh, Nebr	2.87
To Leaf River, Ill.	8.15
To Goodwine, Ill.	3.75
To Home & back to Ind.	4.40
To Sunfield, Mich.	7.08
To Chicago, Ill.	4.90
To Brush Creek	3.90
[Total]	52.74
To Wisconsin Conf.	3.15
Thence to Dayton, Iowa	5.07
Hotel at Dayton	.70
Kansas City	4.65
Lunch & dinner	.50
To Dayton Ohio	10.85
[Total]	77.66
Indianapolis Trial	
Trav. Expenses	7.10
Hotel Bills at Indi.	1.25

1892

Friday, January 1 Got home at 8:30 morning, from Union City, Ind. At home the rest of the day, writing.

Saturday, January 2 At home most of the day. Called at Young's in the afternoon, but found him absent. Sent for several half-fare permits.

Sunday, January 3 At School Street Church. Rev. C. Weyer pr. at 10:30 and Rev. Wm. Dillon exhorts. I pr. at 7:00, Prov. 21:2. One seeker.

Monday, January 4 Acted as pall-bearer at the funeral of Mrs. Eunice Feight, one of our nearest and best neighbors. Episcopal service at Christ's Church. I am too nervous to do much work. Called at Prof. C.H. Kiracofe's in the evening.

Tuesday, January 5 At home all day. Wrote and read some. In poor condition for mental work.

Wednesday, January 6 At home all day. Write some. Prof. Kiracofe called in the afternoon.

Saturday, January 9 At home. Wrote some. In the afternoon, I got a telegram from My son Reuchlin saying that Cath. L., his daughter, had diptheria..

Sunday, January 10 At home. Not well. Have an influenza cold. Receive telegram from Reuchlin, at Kansas City, saying Catharine Louise, was hopelessly sick (diptheria) and for me to come immediately. Cath. died that evening.

Monday, January 11 Start about 7:45 A.M. via Hamilton & Indianapolis to Danville. Take Wabash train about 6:30 for Kansas City. Talk on train with Mr. English a mail agent, who knew Westfield folks. Slept several broken hours. Cath. L. was buried this afternoon.

Tuesday, January 12 Talk with Mr. Fogleman, from vicinity of Remington, Ind. Also with a man from Greeley, Kans. who knew L. Champ, & Revs. Hinton and Forbes. Arrive at Kan. City at 9:30. Cath. L. was buried the day before. The Doctor called; also Mrs. Spohr. I staid at Mrs. Spohr's, as Reuchlin's beds were not disinfected. Lorin was Married to Nettie Stokes at 8:00, Eve. Ivonette.

Wednesday, January 13 We move somethings to Thirty-eighth Street, No. 1908. Again I stay at Mrs. Spohr's. Neighbors: Turner, Stone, Young. Reuchlin determined to remove to another house.

Thursday, January 14 Family are moved. We are busy. Jessie Reeves comes to help Lulu.

Friday, January 15 I help a little on moving. The doctor came. We Go to the cemetery in the afternoon, to see Cath. L's grave. Start at 7:20 for Union Depot. Take Wabash train for St. Louis, Decatur, Peru, to Auburn Junction.

Saturday, January 16 Reach St. Louis at 7:00. Reach Auburn about 8:00. Go on 12:08 train to Hicksville, Ohio. Stay at Schwilley House.

Sunday, January 17 Call at Mr. Shenton's. Breakfast there. M.L. Deihl came, and Lacey, & they take me out to the Wanderly School-house. Get there at close of meeting. Dine at B.F. Willets—the man who was led out of Fairview (Six Points) Church. Call at Rev. I.N. Warfield's. Pr. at Dutch Street Church at 7:00, Acts 26:28. Stay at E.R. Grier's at Six Points.

Monday, January 18 Rev. G.N. Warfield takes me in a sleigh to Bryan. I call and see Mr. Willits, Esq. Go on 11:57 train to West Manchester. Supper at G.T. Horine's. Sam'l. Horine there. Go on 8:30 train to Dayton. Found the folks in usual health.

Tuesday, January 19 At the office & home in the forenoon. Go to town in the afternoon. Get permits on C.C.C. & St. L. R'y, & on Dayton and Union. Bought underwear, etc. Called on Young, but found him away. Visit Lorin's in the evening.

Wednesday, January 20 Thermometer 12 or 15 below zero. At home all forenoon. Saw Young in afternoon a half hour. Wrote in the evening.

Thursday, January 21 At home most of the day. Wrote some. Called in the afternoon at Young's office. Did not see him. Read in the evening till a late hour.

Friday, January 22 At home in the forenoon. Went to see Young in afternoon. Interview of 20 minutes.

Saturday, January 23 At home till evening. Went on 5:40 train to Brookville. Stay at John Zehring's.

Sunday, January 24 John takes me to A. Zehring's School-h. I pr. 1 John 3:2, on Christ's Second coming. Dine at Aaron Zehring's. His wife is a daughter of Jacob Burtner's. His sons are Chas. & William & his daughter Elizabeth. Go back to John Zehring's.

Monday, January 25 Go home on 7:49 tr. Write letters. At home the rest of the day.

Friday, January 29 At home all day. Bishop H.J. Becker and Prof. Kiracofe called in the afternoon. My cold is increased.

Saturday, January 30 At home. Bishop H.J. Becker called in forenoon. Arranged my papers in the afternoon.

Sunday, January 31 At home all day, having severe cold. Lorin & Nettie called in the afternoon an hour or more. I read much in Barnes' Notes, and Newton on the Prophecies.

Monday, February 1 At home in the forenoon. Bishop Becker dined with us. I called on C. Weyer in the afternoon.

Thursday, February 4 At home; found I was too late for the cars for Bellefontaine.

Friday, February 5 Go on 8:53 tr. to Bellefontaine. Dine & sup at Judge Lawrence's. Go on 6:15 tr. to Ansonia & Sherwood. Stay at Sherwood. Saw Rev. S.L. Livingston on train from Quincy to Rockford. Robt. B. Reeder married Hattie Glass to-day.

Saturday, February 6 Go on 11:26 tr. to Hicksville. Dine at Milton L. Deihl's. Rev. W.H. Clay there. Go to Wanderly's Sch. H. Clay pr. at 2:45. Qr. Conf. followed. Supper & Lodging at B.F. Willit's. Clay pr. at 7:00.

Sunday, February 7 I pr. at 11:00. Ps. 92.8. Communion followed. Dine & sup at Willits. Pr. at 7:00 at Wm. Peeper's, in Hicksville. Stay at Pe[e]per's.

Monday, February 8 Adjourned session Qr. C. at Peeper's at 9:00. Dine at Peeper's. Cat at [blank] Crowl's where I boarded time An. Conf. years ago. Go on 11:45 tr. to Auburn Junction & thence to North Manchester. Sup at John Shaffer's in N. Manchester. On 6:38 tr. to Fairmount. Walk to W.H.H. Reeder's. Shaffer's Children: Charles, at Ogden; Minnie, invalid.

Tuesday, February 9 Dine at Ellis Wright's. Call at Oliver A. Glass'. Supper & lodging at Robt. B. Reeder's.

Wednesday, February 10 Call at Henry Simons'. His wife quite sick. Call at Wm. H.H. Reeder's. Walk to Fairmount. Dine at Elwood Davis'. Go on 12+ train to Anderson, Richmond, and Dayton. Get home at 7:00 p.m.

Thursday, February 11 Called at Dillon's & Kiracofe's. Went to town. Saw Young ten minutes. Received Young's bill & examined it.

Friday, February 12 Saw Young a half hour and paid his bill in full to date on Dayton case.

Sunday, February 14 Heard Rev. Chas. Weyer pr. at 10:30, 1 Pet. 4:3. At home the remainder of the day.

Monday, February 15 At home all day getting ready to go to Michigan. Saw Young at law library 20 or 30 minutes. Rev. C. Weyer called 1 1/2 h. in afternoon. Start, via Richmond, to Allegan at 9:40 p.m. Slept three hours.

Tuesday, February 16 Connect at Kalamazoo at 7:00 a.m. for Allegan. Put up at Sherman House. Salem Church case resumed before Judge N.P. Loveridge of Cold Water. Evidence goes in slowly. Room 34 is mine.

Wednesday, February 17 Evidence continued. McMahon, Shuey, & McKee there. Nothing remarkable occurs. Get minutes of the Commission & have Rev. C.B. Whitaker copy them in part. Meeting at Pope's at 7:00; stay till 11:00.

Thursday, February 18 Evidence continued. Wm. Lawrence came at noon. Plaintiffs close their evidence at 3:00. We began putting in depositions. Consultation at Pope's office at 7:00.

Friday, February 19 Radicals conclude their evidence at 2:30. Adjourn court till March 1st. We start on 4:13 tr. for home via Kalamazoo. Go on 8:00 train for Richmond.

Saturday, February 20 Reach Richmond at 3:30. Go on 5:00 tr. to Dayton arriving at 6:30. Find all well. At home the rest of the day, arranging & writing.

Monday, February 22 Arose at 5:50. Called in afternoon, and saw Young 5 min. Called at J. Swank's. W.O. Dinius's, C.H. Kiracofe's and at Conservator printer's. Spent evening in sorting mailing lists, to destroy copies not needed.

Tuesday, February 23 At home. Bp. H. Floyd & Prof. C.H. Kiracofe called about 8:00. Mrs. Greenwood called at 8:30. Mrs. Kiracofe called in the afternoon. I spent much of the day adjusting papers, etc., in my desk.

Wednesday, February 24 At home all day except a trip to town. Saw Young about five minutes. Boys busy with their pneumatic engine.

Thursday, February 25 Wrote "Introductory thoughts" for & revised Lesson Quarterly. . Went to town. Called on Blum; also on Young 10 minutes principally on accounts. Flora Greenwood took supper with us.

Friday, February 26 At home all forenoon. Went to town in the afternoon. Saw Young 20 or 30 minutes. Called Blum. Rev. N.D. Wolfard stayed with us.

Saturday, February 27 At home all day. Not feeling very well—the result probably of influenza. Did not get to quarterly meeting to-night.

Sunday, February 28 Heard Rev. S.L. Livingston preach at West End Ch. at 10:30, Rev. 1:7. He goes home with me & stays till evening. Revs. C. Weyer & Y. Kephart called in the evening. Rev. N.D. Wolfard pr. at 7:30, Corn. XI: 33,34.

Wednesday, March 2 At home. Went to town in the afternoon & saw Will Young. Telegrams from & to I.N. Warfield. Sent two telegrams in return.

Thursday, March 3 Received a telegram from Rev. H.H. Brundage, who was then at Toledo O, waiting for Young. Saw Young who had just returned from St. Louis, Mo., and telegraphed to Brundage to meet Young that evening at Boody House, Toledo.

Friday, March 4 Called at Dillon's and Kiracofe's. Wrote article for Conservator.

Saturday, March 5 Took to Dillon an article on the "Great Conspiracy. Went to town. Saw Young two minutes. Prof. C.H. Kiracofe called an hour. At home the rest of the day.

Sunday, March 6 Heard Rev. Mr. McAfee pr. at Grace Church, John 18:37, a good sermon on The Life worth Living.

Monday, March 7 Called at Graybill's, morning & afternoon. At home the rest of the day.

Tuesday, March 8 At home all day. Spent much time making files of the Conservator.

Wednesday, March 9 Prepared statistics for U.S. Census for H.K. Carroll, D.D. Wrote several letters.

Friday, March 11 At home. Called at Court House in afternoon.

Saturday, March 12 Went on 11:00 tr to Lima, and thence to Elida. Supper at Henry Kiracofe's. Pr. at 7:30, at U.B. Church, Luke 14:18. House overcrowded. Stay at Henry Kiracofe's. Members: Mrs. E.F. Brenneman, S.A. Stemen, G.R. Armstrong, Noah Miller.

Sunday, March 13 Pr. at 10:30, Phil. 2:12,13. Sacrament followed. About 75 communed. Dine at E.F. Brenneman's. Call in afternoon at S. Albert Stemen's & supper there. N.D. Wolfard pr. at 7:00, Matt. 13:45,46. Stay at Kiracofe's. Members: E. Sawmiller, Allen Friend, I.R. Spear, H. Kiracofe.

Monday, March 14 Start on 9:03 tr. and arrive at Dayton, 12:30. Spend afternoon mostly at Graybill's reading proofs. Sit up late.

Tuesday, March 15 Went to Graybill's early. W.O. Dinnius & C.H. Kiracofe called. I went to town. Bought 100 ft. of wood. Write letters.

Wednesday, March 16 In afternoon heard Sprigg and Patterson argue the Guenther murder case.

Friday, March 18 At town awhile in the forenoon. In the afternoon, heard Will Young argue in the Bradley will case. Wrote letters at night.

Saturday, March 19 In forenoon heard Thomas Lorne and G.K. Young argue in the Bradley case. Wrote notices in afternoon & went to J.K. Gra[y]bill's.

Sunday, March 20 Arose early. Not very well. Remained at home. Slept 1 1/2 hours. Continued at home all the evening.

Monday, March 21 Went to Graybill's in forenoon. Went to town in afternoon. Saw Young about 20 minutes.

Called at Graybill's & again in the eve[n]ing.

Tuesday, March 22 At home. Went to Graybill's & Dillon's.

Wednesday, March 23 Mis. Ex. Com. met at my house at 4:00.

Thursday, March 24 Bishop Becker called in the forenoon. I called at Graybill's. Went to town in the afternoon. Wrote many letters in the evening.

Friday, March 25 Called at Graybill's. Went to town. Saw Young five minutes. At home the rest of the day. Miss Flora Greenwood took supper with us. She is one of Katie's special friends.

Saturday, March 26 Called at Graybill's & Dillon's in the afternoon and went to town. Worked about the dooryard after my return—trimmed the grape vines.

Sunday, March 27 Heard Rev. Wm. Dillon pr at School Street Ch. at 10:30, Ps. 1:1. At home the rest of the day.

Friday, April 1 At home in forenoon, except a trip to the Post-office.

Saturday, April 2 At home in the forenoon. Went to town in afternoon or just at noon. Paid Young $11.65 in full on Bethany, Mo. case. Wrote many letters in afternoon & evening. Sat up till midnight.

Sunday, April 3 Arose at 6:00. Beeakfast at 7:15. Taught the Sab. School class at School St. Preach there at 10:30, Phil. 3:2. "Help those women." At home the rest of the day.

Monday, April 4 Municipal election. I Called at Graybill's in forenoon & evening.

Tuesday, April 5 Called at Young's in forenoon for copy of Bill of Fairview Church case. Walked out to Miller's woods in aftern. with Katie.

Wednesday, April 6 Went to town & got copy of the bill.

Friday, April 8 Bp. Floyd called in the morning an hour.

Sunday, April 10 At School St (West End) Church; heard the Pastor, Rev. Chas. Weyer preach at 10:30, 1 Tim. 6:11. At home the rest of the day.

Monday, April 11 At home. In evening, went to the Shubert Quartet entertainment at Association Hall.

Thursday, April 14 At home. Dillon called in Afternoon. Wrote in the evening, on an article (Chapt. III) on The Great Conspiracy. Up till 12:00.

Friday, April 15 Finished my article for the *Conservator*. Mrs. A.R. Kiracofe called in the afternoon.

Saturday, April 16 Arose early & get ready to go to Qr. Meeting at Zehring Sch. H., 15 ms. west. Go on 9:30 train to Brookville, Ohio. John Zehring takes me with his family to Aaron Zehring's. Quarterly conference, in which I preside. Pr. at 7:30, Luke 13:24.

Sunday, April 17 Pr. at 10:30 at Sch. H. on 2 Pet. 3:18. "Grow in Grace." Dine at Zehring's & stay till morning. Pr. at 7:30, 2 Cor. 4:3,4. A very rainy evening.

Monday, April 18 Went against the rain storm to Brookville, and on 8:40 train to Dayton. Read proofs at Graybill's. Write, and have Lorin help me.

Tuesday, April 19 Went on train via Union City, Winchester & Decatur to Hunting on. Cost $2.05 + lunch, 5. Supper & lodging at Rev. A.G. Johnson 's. Rev. E. Kidder & Bp. H.J. Becker there & Bp. Barnaby came. Bp. H.J. Becker pr. at 8:00, John 21:25, one of his best sermons.

Wednesday, April 20 The Board of Bishops met at the Church at 10:00. We all dine at Rev. A.G. Johnson's. Session in Afternoon. Supper at Bro. Coolman's. Bp. Floyd pr. at 8:00, Eph. 5:18, "Be Filled—Spir." Stay with Floyd at Coolman's.

Thursday, April 21 Board meeting at 9:00, at Church forenoon & Afternoon. Sup at Coolman's. Dine & lodge at Rev. A.G. Johnson 's. Bishops Floyd & Barnaby left at 5:00. Bp. Becker lectured at Church at 8:00. "Impersonification of John B. Gough.["] Success not the best.

Friday, April 22 I go on early train to Wabash, Fairmount, & farm, walking out to W.H.H. Reeder's, where I dine, sleep two hours, finding all away. Then walk to Aunt Eliz. Reeder's. She is very sick with indigestion. I stay at Oliver Glass'.

Saturday, April 23 Go over with Wm. Reeder's. Stake off an orchard. Look over accounts some. Walk to Aunt Elizabeth's & pr. 8:00, Eph. 3:19. "Love of Christ." Glass's, Dan Richard's, Levi Simon's, etc., at Meeting. I stay at Reeder's.

Sunday, April 24 I drive to Union Sch. House (being shut out of church) and pr. at 10:30, Matt. 2:10, "Exceed, great joy." Preach at Am. Wesleyan Ch. at 3:30, Phil. 2:12. "Work out—Salva." etc. Go to farm to look for lost document & thence to Robt. Reeder's. Aunt very sick. Stay there.

Monday, April 25 Remain & dine. Aunt very sick. Dr. Wharton of N. Cumb. came. Oliver A. Glass takes me to Fairmount. See Hall at Winslow's Shoe-shop. Go on train to Marion & thence to Delphos, 0. Stay at Wilson McKenzie's.

Tuesday, April 26 Go on 6:45 train to Monticello—slow train. Dine at Rev. J.M. Shearer's, 1 m. N.E. Rev S.T. Mahan pr. at 8:00, Matt. 19:27. Forsaken all & followed thee" etc. Stay at Chelkiah Sleutz; 20 rods west of the Church, with Rev. Wm. Miller's & others.

Wednesday, April 27 Ministerial Institute opened W. Dillon taught Bible History; I, theology, & C.H Kiracofe, Logic. Dine at Sleutz. Association exercises in the afternoon. Sup at Lewis Barnett's. I pr. at 8:00, Phil, 2:12, "Workout" etc. Stay at Chel. Sleutz.

Thursday, April 28 Institute Classes taught. Adjourn at 11:00. Dine at Rev. J.M. Sheerer's. He takes us to Spencerville. Go on 3:04 tr. to Lima & thence on tr. to Dayton, reaching home at 9:30. All tolerably well.

Friday, April 29 At home all day. Bp. H.J. Becker & Rev. C.H. Kiracofe called in the aftern. Bishop B. had bought the Davis' library.

Saturday, April 30 Went to Graybill's & Dillon's in forenoon. Arranged to pay $4.00 of Mrs. Shisler's funds to the Mis. Cause. Paid it to Kiracofe in the afternoon. Not very well to-day & yesterday.

Sunday, May 1 Attended the Williams Street Baptist Church & heard Rev. Mr. Holmes pr., John 16:7. Called at Free's funeral on Williams Street in the afternoon at 2:30. At home the rest of the day. Read up the subject of the Holy Spirit.

Monday, May 2 Attended the meeting of the Dayton pastors' association. Dr. Maurice Wilson's essay maintained the one-wine theory; that all wine is fermented. Afternoon called at Young's and found him out. Called at J.K. Graybill's printing office, Dillon's, & Kiracofe's. Telegram from Reeder's & went via Richmond to Anderson. Stay at Doxley's Hotel.

Tuesday, May 3 Reach Fairmount about 8:00. Walk to Aunt Reeder's. She very sick. Stay there all day. John Martin, who lives on Greensburg & Columbus road near Denman farm, went out from Fairmount with me. Aunt had a deep slumber about 1:00, but revived.

Wednesday, May 4 At Reeder's all day. John Broyle's family including B. Markle's came. Doctor gave over the case as hopeless. Aunt seemed stronger and more conscious in the evening and night.

Thursday, May 5 Dr. Wharton, sent for, came. I went to Ellis Wright's, & he took me to Fairmount. Went on 12:11 tr. via Anderson home. Reach home at 7:00. Slept well after losing most of three nights sleep. Found all well.

Friday, May 6 At home. Called at Young's in the afternoon, but he was at court-house. Aunt Elizabeth Reeder died at 7:00, afternoon. They telegraph me.

Saturday, May 7 Learned of telegram. Go on 8:00 tr. via Union City & Jonesboro to Fairmount. Reach Reeder's at 3:00. Stay there.

Sunday, May 8 Prepare a Memorial paper & read it at the funeral. Jacob Richards, a Baptist, preached the funeral sermon at 10:30. Burial at Baptist grave-yard, on State Road three & 1/2 miles east. Return to Aunt's, late home, and stay.

Monday, May 9 Ralph takes me to the 8:16 tr. and I go via Jonesboro & Union City home, arriving at 3:30. I saw Rev. Aaron Worth, Rev. S.L. Livingston and Rev. A.S. Whetsel, on the way.

Tuesday, May 10 At home forenoon. Called at Young's in afternoon. He not in Office, but saw him three minutes at the court-house. Called at Dillon's, Kiracofe's, & Davis's. Get ready to go to the Board meetings.

Wednesday, May 11 Go on 7:55 train to Greenville. Call at Wm. Nicholas' He takes me back to train. Go on to Bryan. Josias Swank meets us and takes us to his house 1/2 m. E. of Stryker. Board meets at 7:30. Rev. C. L. Wood preached Missionary discourse at 8:00, Mark 16:15. Stay at Swank's.

Thursday, May 12 Board meets at 8:30. Adjourns abt 10:30 for committee meetings. I dine at Swank's. Afternoon session. Supper & lodging at Swank's. Woman's Association at 3:00. Kiracofe reads an address. Rain & mud.

Friday, May 13 Rain. Session forenoon & afternoon at church. Joint Com. meets at 11:00. Close session abt 3:00. Supper at Rev. G.W. Bechtol's. Dinner & lodging at Swank 's. I Preach at 8:00, 1 Tim. 3:5, "The Church of God." Rain & Mud.

Saturday, May 14 Go on 7:21 train to Toledo & thence home arriving at Dayton abt. 4:00. Find all well. Expense of the whole trip: 5.00. Received on exp. 4.00, My own Exp. 1.00

Sunday, May 15 Rainy day. At home all day. Felt drowsy & debilitated. Spent the day in reading.

Monday, May 16 At home in the forenoon. Called at Young's 25 minutes. Called at Dr. Tizzard's. Called at J.K. Graybill's printing-office.

Tuesday, May 17 Read & wrote letters in forenoon.

Friday, May 20 Had Dr. Tizzard to fill some teeth for me. Spent from 9:30 till 11:50. At home the rest of the day.

Saturday, May 21 Got ready to go away. Got teeth-plate at Tizzard's. Go on 12:30 train to Miamisburg. Walk thence to Germantown. S.L. Livingston pr. Quarterly Conference. Supper & lodging at Michael Thomas'. I pr. at 8:00, Acts 17:18.

Sunday, May 22 Bp. H. Floyd pre'd, at 10:30. Dedication Sermon, II Cor. 6:16. Raised $262.00. I dedicate. Dine at Rev. P.Y. Gephart's. Love-feast & sacramental meeting at 3:30. Good time. Bp. Floyd & I sup at Fout's. I pr. at 8:00, Ps. 84:11. Lodge at Levi Zehring's.

Monday, May 23 Go on hack to Miamisburg & take 8:20 tr. to Dayton. At home the rest of the day. Rev. C.H. Kiracofe called in the afternoon.

Tuesday, May 24 Called at Dillon's & Kiracofe's.

Wednesday, May 25 Jac. H. Kiracofe's did not call as they had expected to do, but went home on the early train. Lorin & wife dined & supped with us.

Sunday, May 29 Heard Rev. C. Weyer preach at 10:30. At home the rest of the day. Read much in Smith's Bible Dictionary. Mr. Anson Moor, who married my Bro. Wm's widow, died at 4:00 this afternoon.

Monday, May 30 At home all day. Being decoration day, I spent the time mostly in reading. The children in forenoon working on a job in their printing office; afternoon they went to Y.M.C.A., Athletic Park exercises.

Tuesday, May 31 Made out my report as Pub. Age't. Bp. H. Floyd & Rev. C.W. Rector came in evening awhile.

Wednesday, June 1 Board of Trustees of Publishing House met—not a quorum—sent for A. Zehring. Did work on Committee. G.T. Horine dined with us. Board with Quorum met at 6:30.

Thursday, June 2 Rev. Aaron Zehring dined with us. Boys at work making our porch floor. Called at Kiracofe's & Dillon's in the evening.

Friday, June 3 Wrote letters in the forenoon. Went to dentist (Tizzard's) and Young's in the afternoon, at the last nearly a half hour.

Saturday, June 4 Wrote an article for Publisher's Column. Wrote letters. At home all day.

Sunday, June 5 Pr. at School Street Church at 10:30, 2 Chron. 1:10 on Prayer for Wisdom.

Monday, June 6 Went to Tizzard's (dentist) and Young's (about 20 minutes) and home.

Tuesday, June 7 Went to Bellefontaine to see Judge Wm. Lawrence. Came home on afternoon train.

Wednesday, June 8 Called at Dillon's. Wrote letters at home.

Thursday, June 9 At home all day. Writing. Make revision of Quarterly lessons.

Sunday, June 12 Attended Church at West End, i.e. School St. Rev. C. Weyer pr. Ex. 20:8, on the Sabbath. He dines with us.

Tuesday, June 14 Judge Wm. Lawrence came at 10:51, for a consultation. Spent the afternoon in Law Library.

Saturday, June 18 Called at Young's a few minutes. Went in afternoon to Germantown. Heavy rain on the way. Put up at Levi Zehring's. Miss Zehring of Frankfort, Ind. there & tells of Oddf., Mason's, K. P.'s, etc in Liberal Church.

Sunday, June 19 Rainy, very. Call at Michael Thomas'. Pr. at 10:30 Ps. 73:24. Dine at M. Thomas', with Jac. Slifer & wife. Much rain. At 5:30, start home. At Rev. C. Weyer's services at Sch. St. at 8:00.

Wednesday, June 22 At home. Called at Young's a few minutes. Read Watson vs. Jones Decision carefully.

Thursday, June 23 Called at Young's ten minutes.

Friday, June 24 Notes on Watson v. Jones Decision. Called at Young's 10 minutes. Wrote letters.

Saturday, June 25 Spent morning in reading mostly. Go in afternoon to Aaron Zehring's with Horace Kiracofe. Stay there.

Sunday, June 26 Pr. at 10:00 at Sch. H. John 1:29— house full. Dine at Zehring's. In afternoon, go home. Hear Dr. Work pr. at 4th Presb. Church at 8:00.

Monday, June 27 Went to Tizzard's (my dentist's). Called at Young's five minutes.

Tuesday, June28–Saturday, July 2 At home all day.

Sunday, July 3 Heard Eby pr at Conservative Dunkard Ch., Cor. Fourth & College Sreets. Good sermon. At home the rest of the day.

Monday, July 4 At home till 9:00 Aftn., when I start on train to Pontiac, via Chicago. Mr. Reynolds gives me his lower berth in Sleeper, in exchange for mine, an upper, in deference to my age.

Tuesday, July 5 Reach Chicago (Un. Depot) about 7:00. Leave on Chi. & Alton R.R. at 9:00, and reach Pontiac at 12:20. Put up at Phoenix Hotel. Hoobler Chapel Church case begins at 3:00 before Judge Thomas P. Tipton & continues with some intermission till 10:00.

Wednesday, July 6–Friday, July 8 Trial Continues.

Saturday, July 9 Evidence closed at 3:00. Half hour statement on each side. I go to Manville & thence to Rev. A.B. Powell's 3 1/2 ms north-west. Lodge there.

Sunday, July 10 Preach at Smithdale Sch. House at 11:00, Heb. 11:26, "Recompense." Dine at Powell's. Bishop H. Floyd pr. at Otterbein at 4:30, Eph. 3:15, "Whole family." I lodge at Powell 's. Called in evening at Powell's son-in-law's, Gustave Wenzlemann's.

Monday, July 11 Go to Pontiac to Phoenix Hotel again. C.C. Strawn spoke ably two hours. McMahon spoke in afternoon two hours. Patton followed in a two hour speech. Young began at 7:00 & spoke 2:20. I slept three hours.

Tuesday, July 12 Young left at 6:00. I heard the judge talk at 9:00. Adverse. Lunch at restaurant. Floyd & I start at 5:00 via Fairbury (where we wait over two hours) and Sheldon to Indianapolis.

Wednesday, July 13 Go on 5:00 train to Richmond and Dayton arriving at 9:20. Sleep some, write some.

Thursday, July 14 At home all day writing. Kiracofe called in forenoon.

Sunday, July 17 At School Street. Becker, etc. Called at Spidel's in aftn & supper there. At Sch. St. C. Weyer pr. Eph. 3:14.

Monday, July 18 Called at Graybill's in forenoon. At home the rest of the day. Write many letters.

Tuesday, July 19 At home in the forenoon. Call at Prof. C.H. Kiracofe's, 119 N. Summit St. Dillon & Weyer & wife there. Hent to dentist's (Tizzard's) and Young's five minutes.

Thursday, July 21 At home. Called at Rev. C.H. Kiracofe's about 5:00, found Bp. H.J. Becker & wife and Alta, aged 7, there.

Friday, July 22 At home. Bp. Becker & family take Supper with us

Sunday, July 24 Heard Bp. H.J. Becker pr. at School Street (West End) Church at 10:30, Matt. 10:14. Good. I dine with Bp. Becker's at Pres. C.H. Kiracofe's & stay till 5:00. Hear Dr. Work pr. at Fourth Pres. Church at 8:00, Acts 2:43. Good.

Monday, July 25 Bishop Becker & family dine with us & stay till 4:00. It rained about 4:30, a nice & much-needed shower.

Tuesday, July 26 At home. Called at Kiracofe's. Bp. Becker was packing the Davis' library.

Wednesday, July 27 At home. Went to Kiracofe's & thence with Bp. Becker and family to East side depot as they start for home.

Thursday, July 28 Got bill U.S.C. Called at Dillon's & Kiracofe's & consult with Wilbur 1 1/2 hr. At 2:00, with Kiracofe and Dillon, consult over items in U.S. bill of complaint. Write some suggestions in memoranda. Bishop H. Floyd called an hour.

Friday, July 29 Take over Bill U.S. Case to Young with suggestions. Call at Dillon's & Kiracofe's. Rev. Chas. Weyer and family called. Go to Young's & Dr. Tizzard's. In evening, compare amended bill of complaint U.S. case with copy.

Saturday, July 30 Failed to get on the 6:45 train. Go on the 11:00 train to Lima & thence on 3:30 tr. to Ft. Wayne, and thence on 6:20 tr. to New Haven, Walk 2 m & hire a man to take me to Maysville & H.H. Brundage's. Lodge there.

Sunday, July 31 Pr. at Maysville for Rev. H.C. Foote at 10:30, 73:24. Dine at Foote's. Supper & lodging at Rev. H.H. Brundage's. Saw Bros. Dresbach's, Mills, etc.

Monday, August 1 Start at 3:30 A.M. for Antwerp. See Notary & get seal. Go on 5:42 train to Toledo. Hand amended Bill in U.S. case to Doyle, Scott, & Lewis. Look around town. Take 10:15 train home—to Dayton. Call a minute at Tizzard's & Young's.

Thursday, August 4 Rise early; go on 4:50 train (1/2 h. late) to Hamilton & Glenwood. Go with Wiles to Orange (Fayetteville) & thence walk to Austin Winchell's & dine there. Supper at N.F. Bowen's. Lodge at Lucinda Moor's.

Friday, August 5 Dine at Chas. Steven's with Moor's; Mrs. Bowen, & Laura Winchell & daughter. Bertha Moor & Minnie Winchell take me to Glenwood. Supper at Harry Winchell's. Go to Indianapolis & call two hours at Walter S. Brown's. Go on Kankakee Line to Chicago.

Saturday, August 6 Reach Chicago at 7:30. Take 8:40 tr. to Mendota. Dine at Geo. F. Huck's. Go on 4:00 tr to Van Orin. Put up at Eliz. Williams'. W.H. Chandler & wife & Alice 14 & Grace 11, there. Mrs. Williams is Chandler's Motherinlaw. Confer with Rev. Wm. Beers.

Sunday, August 7 Pr. at 11:00, Ps. 73:24. Raise $902.00. Dedicate Edwards' Chapel. Dine at Mrs. Williams. Call at Henry Williams. Pr. at 8:00, Gal. 4:4. Stay at Mrs. Williams.

Monday, August 8 Call an hour at Rev. Wm. Beers. Go to Mendota. Dine at Rev. C. Bender's. Go on 3:20 tr. to Chicago. Leave Chicago on 8:20 tr. Car crowded. Slept little.

Tuesday, August 9 Reach Richmond on early tr. Got on 5:15 tr to Dayton. Found all well. D. K. Zeller called an hour in afternoon.

Wednesday, August 10 At home. Writing. Kiracofe called. D.K. Zeller of Richmond, Ind. called an hour.

Friday, August 12 At home. Get my teeth plate at Tizzard's.

Saturday, August 13 Go on the early train to Deshler, Auburn, Troy and am met by Adam Dinnius who takes me to his son Theodore's, where I meet trustees, etc. Call at Stearns: Pr at new Ch. (Zion's Chapel) at 8:00, Ps . 1: 5, 6 . Stay at Thos. Leason's .

Sunday, August 14 Pr. at 10:30, Exa. 28:34. Raise $356.00 & dedicate the Church. Revs. D. Clark, two Robinetts, Metzler, Elliott, and Phillips, Present. Dine at Adarn Dinius'. Pr. at 8: 30, Rom. 1:16. Stay at Theo. Dinius' . Supper at 11:00!

Monday, August 15 Got to 7 :13 train to Edgerton, with Theo. Dinius. Go via Toledo to Dayton. Pay my dentist. Charge $15.00. Get home about 5: 00.

Tuesday, August 16 At home; very busy. Get tired. Call at Lorin's in the evening. Pack ready to start early in the morning to White River Conference.

Wednesday, August 17 Go on 5:00 tr. (30 min. late) to Richmond: via fast tr. miss getting off at Cambridge & continue to Indianapolis. Call at Cousin Walter S. Brown's, Cor. Ft. Wayne & St. Clair & at Rev. T.J. Connor's 740 N. Alabama St. Go to Greensburg; to Hartsville by hack; 4:00, Conference; Rev. J.M. Johnson pr. at 7:30. Home at Rev. A.H.K. Beam.

Thursday, August 18 Conference continues. Dine & lodge at Beam's. Rev. I.M. Tharp pr. at 7:30 very ably. Rev. Jac. Williams, Miss Phares, etc. board at Beam's also. Called at Wertz's. At John Anderson's.

Friday, August 19 Conference continues. Dine at Nat. B. Miller's. Supper at Rev. E. Pitman's.

Saturday, August 20 Stationing Com. of Ind. Conf. met at 6:30 Library room. White River Com. met at 7:00. Call at Rev. J.Riley's.

Sunday, August 21 Pr. at 10:30, Acts 2:17,18. Collections, $52.55. Dine at Prof. 0. Pentzer's. S.S. Anniversary at 3:00. Addresses by J.T. Miller, A. Rust, S.A. Robbins & M. Wright. Supper at Beam's. Rev. Z. McNew pr. at 7:30 "Burning Bush." Ex. 3:2.

Monday, August 22 Go at 6:30 to Hartsville Crossing. Go on 7+ tr to Greensburg. Tr. to Cin. four hours slow. Go to Cin. with Littleton Davis at Herbst, Ind. See him off on Elec. St. cars. Go on 4:00 tr to Dayton. Find all well.

Tuesday, August 23 At home doing my correspondence and getting ready to go to conference. Go on midnight train to Toledo.

Wednesday, August 24 Start for Blissfield at 7:40. Go with Rev. Henry Houghtby to his house. Dine there. Begin N.O. Conference at 2:00. Progress well. Supper & Lodging at Luther Harsh 's. Children: Maud 18, Ethel 14, a little boy & girl. Rev. G.W. Dinius of Berlin, Ont. pr.

Thursday, August 25 Conference progresses well. Prof. Kiracofe arrived. Board as usual. I pr. at 7:30, Eph. 3:8. Stay at Harsh's.

Friday, August 26 Examinations completed. In afternoon elect Pres. Elds. Stationing Com. met at 6:30. Closed about 9:00. At church, a speaking meeting of much enthusiasm. Stay at Harsh's.

Saturday, August 27 Lively discussion of resolutions. Business proceeds. Sessions of stationing Com. & its report at 4:00. Close at 5:00. Woman's Missionary Association entertainment at at [repeated in text] 7:30. Great crowd. Stay at Harsh's. Educational meeting at 3:00.

Sunday, August 28 I Pr. in Stemple's grove 1 1/4 m. west. 1,000 or 1,500 people present. Text Ps. 92:8. Coll.

about $52.00. Dine with Harsh's on the ground. S.S. Anniversary in afternoon at 2:30. Go with Harsh to Blissfield Stay at Wm. Rothfress'. Rev. McMillin pr. at 7:30.

Monday, August 29 Went on 9:00 tr to Hillsdale. Dine at Restaurant. Go on 1:07 tr. to Toledo & thence on 3:05 tr to Dayton. Reach home at 9:30. My daughterinlaw Lulu, Reuchlin's wife, & daughter Helen came Friday.

Tuesday, August 30 At home in forenoon. Mrs. Billheimer & Daisy came at 10:00. Prepare to go away. Call at Dillon's in the evening. The Misses Davidson (Andrews) & Minnie Billheimer and Lorin & Nettie call in the evening.

Wednesday, August 31 Got ready and start to Appleton, Knox Co., Ill., at 11:15 via Union City, Logansport & Chicago. Reach Chi. at 8:50 & leave at 12:00 on Atch. T & Santa Fe Ry. Sleep four hours.

Thursday, September 1 Reach Appleton at 6:40. Go to E.J. Wyman's with himself. Breakfast there. Conference (joint session of Illinois and Central Illinois) convened at 9:00. My home at Frank S. Beamer's, brother of Rev. W.J. Beamer's, of Penn. Rev. E. England, of Astoria (Liberal) with us at Dinner. Aft. Session Rev. O.F. Smith pr. at 7:30, 2 Pet. 3:14. Rev. J. Stahl stays with me.

Friday, September 2 Arose at 5:25. Conference convened at 9:00. Finished the Examination in Central Illinois Conference & adopted Finance report. Rev. D.D. Fetters dined with me. Called at 5:00 at England's to see Rev. I. Kritinger. Mission meeting at 7:30. Mrs. Belle Mosier and Mrs. Kritinger spoke. Beamer's children: Harry 22; Maggie 20; Raise $21.00. Stationing Com. Cent. Ill. met at 6:30.

Saturday, September 3 Conference continued. Stationing com's short session. Dine at Charles Snell's, 1 m. N.W. Closed conf. 4:45. Party excitement. Supper at F.S. Beamer's. I Speak at 7:30 on state of the Church. Lodge as Usual at Frank S. Beamer's.

Sunday, September 4 I Preach at 11:00, Col. 3:4. Dine at England's with Rev. Isasc Kretzinger & Mrs. Belle

Mosier. S.S. Anniv. at 3:30. I lectured. Supper at Beamer's. Pr. at night, 1 Cor. 5:7. Communion. Stay at E. Wyman's with several preachers.

Monday, September 5 Go to Appleton. On 6:23 tr. to Galesburg: 10:00 tr. to Burlington; 2:00 tr. to Creston. Mistake of ticket (Greenfield, Ill. instead of Iowa). Reach Creston at 9:45. Stay at Ewing Hotel. Wrote letters & newspaper article on the way.

Tuesday, September 6 Take 7:10 tr. to Greenfield, Iowa, Leave baggage at Depot & get livery to Lee Hoisington's. Dine there. Look over the farm in afternoon. Saw Rethlefsen, S.W. neighbor. Supper at D.R. Fagan's on my farm. Their child, Julia, 6 months old. Stay at Hoisington's. Pearl H., 22; Gertie, 13.

Wednesday, September 7 Spend forenoon looking at the farm with D.R. Fagan and in settlement of accounts. Afternoon Fagan took me to Greenfield. Go thence on 4:45 tr. to Creston and on 8:35 (9:00) tr. to Ottumwa and on 1:10 train to Eldon. Sleep at Hotel 3:00.

Thursday, September 8 Go on 5:45 tr. to Drakeville. Breakfast at Hotel. Call at Ballard's (Liberal's) He starts with me for Ash Grove Ch. Rev. H.H. Williams meets us & takes me and Rev. R.L. Bauford to King's. Dine, sup & lodge there. Conference opens at 2:00. Rev. E. DeWitt pr. at 7:30.

Friday, September 9 Conference continued. Dine at Moses Phares'. Father Zigler lives there. P. Heckard stalls on reception on the tobacco question—deferred. Rev. R.L. Bamford pr. at 7:30, an interesting, rambling sermon. Stay at King's as usual. Rainy night.

Saturday, September 10 Conference proceeds. Dine as usual. Discussions in afternoon on reports. Rev. J. Lisk pr. at 7:30, or exhorts. I lecture an hour on the state of the Church. Rainy evening. Supper at John Bartlett's— Free Methodist's. Stay at King's as usual. Conf. closes about 5:00.

Sunday, September 11 Speaking meeting at 10:00. I Pr. at 11:00, 2 Cor. 4:17. Dine at Moses Phares'. J.B.L. Hendrix there & D.W. Baker, and H.H. Williams. S.S. Anniversary at 3:30. I give an address. Supper at King's.

Pr. at 8:00, 1 Cor. 11:26. Communion & farewell. I go to Frederick Zigler's & lodge—1 m. S.E. of Church.

Monday, September 12 F. Zigler takes me to Belknap, and I go at 11:25 to Centerville. Write at depots to Lorin, & to G.S. Seiple. Get a draft of $150.00 at 1st Nat. Bank to send to Lorin. Stay at Keokuk & Western Depot till 11:20. Go to Humeston. Stop at Wabash Hotel. Sleep on train and at hotel 5 hours.

Tuesday, September 13 Go on 7:25 tr. to Leon. Stay there till 1:45, and go on Pass tr. to Blythdale, Mo. Go with livery to Eagleville and stay at Rev. B.F. Miller's. Evening quite cool. No dinner to-day—hearty supper. Slept eight hours full. Miller's nephew: Milton, 6 ys; Katie McCauley, 13.

Wednesday, September 14 Awoke at 6:00. Hearty breakfast. Go to Jere Mumma for dinner. Children: Grant, White Lake, S. Dakota; Mary 21; Maggie 18; John 16; Clara 13. Returned to Bro. Miller's. Gab'l Van Sickle & W.O. Casiday sup with us. Rev. Lem. Beauchamp pr. at 7:30, 1 Cor. 16:13,14. Stay at B.F. Miller's. My Conf. home.

Thursday, September 15 Wrote many letters, in the forenoon. Conference opened at 2:00, J.F. Allaman arrived at 4:00. Col. 3:15 was Rev. A.D. Thomas' text at 7:30— an eloquent sermon. Stay at Rev. B.F. Miller's. Rev. J.T.Allaman my room-mate.

Friday, September 16 Conference continued. Dine at Miller's. Sup at B.C. Moor's. I pr. at 7:30, 1 Cor. 15:16. Stay at Miller's. Rev. L.O. Markels, M.E. Church, A.W. Allen, Disciple; Rev. Dav. McAllen, M.E. Ch. South. Rev. Wood local M.E. Mrs. Miller's nephew, Milton Haraff, 6 years, lives with them.

Saturday, September 17 Conference met at 10:00. Dine at Tal. Curry's, edge of town. Session closed at 5:00. Sup at Rev. L.O. Markel's, Stn. Com. Met at 6:30 at Rev. B.F. Miller's. Rev. J.T. Allaman pr. at 7:30, Mark 7:37. I stay at Rev. B.F. Miller's as usual. Sleep very well, as is most usual.

Sunday, September 18 Pr. at 11:00, Ps. 92:1. Dine at Charles Mumma's Supper at Henry Poush's. Pr. at 7:30,

John 6:54 Communion. Nellie Haroff joined Church. Stay at Rev. B.F. Miller's.

Monday, September 19 Start at 7:15 for Bethany with B.F. Miller, John T. Alaman, Josiah Beauchamp & Lena Beauhamp. Call at Wannamaker's and Barlow's. Dine at a nice restaurant. Go on 3:13 (3:25) train to St. Joseph & Kansas City. Went to Reuchlin's (my Son's). Katie there.

Tuesday, September 20 At Reuchlin's all day. Quite weary. Sleep an hour. Helen Margaret (grand-daughter, 3 ys) very much wrapped up in her gran[d]pa. Our walk to woods 1/2 m southeast. They live on 38 St. just west of the station of electric car line.

Wednesday, September 21 Staid at Reuchlin's in forenoon. Went down town in afternoon with Katie and Helen. Got Helen a baby-wagon & doll, $1.90. Staid at Reuchlin's. Got letters & inclosed [sic] letters from home.

Thursday, September 22 Go on 9:00 train to Lecompton, Kans, Call at Church at 11:00. My conf. home at David Kerns' 1/2 m S.E. of the new Church. Conference Continues. Rev. David Shuck pr. at 7:30, "Behold, I stand." etc. Stay at D. Kerns with D. Shuck, D.E. Walker, and W.K. Wurzbacher.

Friday, September 23 Conference continues. Dine at G.W. Brown's, 1/2 m. S. of the Church. Sup at D. Kerns' & lodge there. Stationing Com. met at D. Kerns' at 6:30. Woman's Missionary meeting at 7:30. Gleamer's exhibition; other short addresses by women & by myself.

Saturday, September 24 Conf. continues. General Reports, etc. Dine at Kerns'. Call at Rev. Lacock's. Conf. Closes a little after 5:00. Meet trustees at 5:30 to arrange for dedication to-morrow. Supper at Lacock's. Reuchlin (my son) came on 7:40 train. We lodge at K's. Rev. Erustus Atkinson Pre Matt. 5:14. Lovefeast, followed 1/2 hour.

Sunday, September 25 After sleeping five hours, arose at 6:00. Get ready for ordination & dedication meeting. Lovefeast at 10:00; ordination of John C. Hope & A.L. Hope. Pr. at 11:00, 2 Tim. 2:12. Raise $775.00 & dismiss. Dine at Rev.A.L. Hope's with Reuchlin et al. Call

at Rev. A. Lacock's, and Kerns. S.S. Anniversary, lovefeast, Communion, dedicate on $841.52. Lodge at Kerns.

Monday, September 26 Call at Hope's, Day's, Dr. Bonebrake's, etc. Go on 10:40 tr. to Topeka; call at U.S. Court room, & see Judge Wm. Lawrence; look through State-house. Call at Rev. A.A. Zeller's, aged 85. 1201 V. Buren. Go on 2:40 tr. to Strong City. Daug[h]ter Katie with me. Stay at "Bank Hotel".

Tuesday, September 27 Go on 4:00 m. train to Manchester, Minneapolis to Ada, where we breakfast & Harvey B. Harris (Sister's son) meets us & takes us to his home, 4 miles S.W. Go to Orval. Harris's Estalla Petrie & husband come. Orval takes me to Lincoln. Stay at Chas. H. Harris'. Ella Rees comes, & Nolan Rees, 9. Max Harris, 9.

Wednesday, September 28 Call at Napoleon Bonaparte Rees' & at Ed. M. Harris' & Grace E. Brunt's, Chas. W. Harris takes me to Clarks, to see Vaughan Harris, & via Beverly to Orville's, where Petrie's, Harvey's, & Katie dine. Orville takes me on to Minneapolis where at 8:00, I go to Beloit. Stay at Freeman House. & saw Ransom Davis, Min.

Thursday, September 29 Write letter and items for Conservator. Go on 11:00 tr. for Downs. Rev. J.S. Rock & M. Strayer on train. Lunch at Downs. Write letter and article for Conservator. Go on 3:00 tr. for Stockton. Write full cards on the way. Arrive at Stockton at 6:00. Rev. W.H. Davis takes us to Webster. Meeting at Baptist Church. Stay at A.D. Medley's.

Friday, September 30 Conference opened at 9:00. Only 4 members. Dine at Abner D. Medley's with Wilfong. Several Letters. Proceed with business. Supper at Medleys, Rev. J.S. Rock pr., A. Streeter exhorts. I run a speaking meeting. Quite good. Stay at Medley's.

Saturday, October 1 Write letters or cards. Elect pres. elder—W.H. Willoughby. Dine with Rev. W.H. Davis, 2 m. N. Stationing Com. met there. Closed at 5:00. Supper at Medley's. I pr. at 7:00, Ps. 1:6, 23 m. Stay at Medley's. The meeting was quite good; a large attendance. Rock exhorted well. I Slept well.

Sunday, October 2 I Pr. at Church (Baptist) at 10:00, 2 Cor. 3:8. Communion. Dine at Medley's. S.S. Anniversary at 4:00. Suppr at Medley's. Pr. on U.B. Church at 7:30, Ps. 136: [blank] Rev. W.H. Davis takes us to Stockton. Sleep 3 hours at the Hotel.

Monday, October 3 Went on 6:10 train to Concordia. Stop at Fred. Sommer's (wife, Rev. May W. Sommers). Write considerable. Sommers is Rev. A.L. Hope's father-inlaw. Dine & sup at S's. Go on 7:50 tr. to Strong City & Hutchinson, Kans. Sleep five hours.

Tuesday, October 4 Reach Hutchinson at 7:40. Lunch near Depot. Go to Dr. Lorimer Ardley's. She is my Cousin. Their children: Roy, 18; Faye, 14; Lois, 9. We ride out to see the salt works and the city in the afternoon. Stay there. I sleep 8 1/2 hours. Elisina Elizabeth Artery is Uncle George Reeder's daughter.

Wednesday, October 5 Spend most of the forenoon in writing letters. Brush & clean my clothes in the afternoon. Sina & I & Lois visit the Ice and salt works in the later afternoon. Dr. Irwin calls at 7:00. I talk on Missions at Presb. Church at 7:30. Stay at Ardery's.

Thursday, October 6 Go on 8:20 tr to Stafford. S. Fry aboard. Dine at Rev. J.K Campbell's in Stafford. Go to Zion Church 7 1/2 ms. S.W. Open conf. at 2:15. Good aft. session. Supper & home at Rev. Robt. Casselman's. Rev. S. Levick pr. at 7:30, Col. 4:6. I Slept eight hours.

Friday, October 7 Conference continued. Business progressed well. Woman's Missionary names taken. Rev. Leitner introduced [blank]. I Pr. at Church, at 7:30, Mal. 3:18. Supper & lodging at Casselman's.

Saturday, October 8 Conference continued. Dine as usual. Stationing Committee's meetings at 8:30 & 1:30. Supper at Joseph Guyer's, 1/3 m. West of Church. His wife is Ida & son Wilbur, perhaps. Rev. W.Z. Manning (aged 82) pr. at 3:40. Matt. 5.14; Mission meeting at 7:30 $146.25 subscribed. Party resolution stirs things in afternoon.

Sunday, October 9 Speaking meeting at 10:00. I pr. at 11:00, Ps. 92.8. Dine at Castlesman's. Sab. Sch. Anniversary at 3:30. Sup at Castleman's. I Pr. at 7:30, Rom.

4:8. Communion service. Go to Stafford with J.H. Campbell's and stay with them with Sam'1 Fry. Sleep 4 1/2 hours.

Monday, October 10 Go via Hutchinson to Wichita, arriving at 11:20. Write at Depot. About 3:00 go to post-office and to City Hall. Ascend the tower & look at the city. Walk south east and then north to Martin Tremain's on 615 Ohio Ave. Supper there. Call with him at Republican Meeting in Garfield Hall. Darwin speaks. Go on 9:45 tr. to Yales Center

Tuesday, October 11 Go on 3:15 train to Coffeyville & Edna. Lay at Coffeyville over two hours & reach Edna at 10:00. Wrote letters at Coffeyville. Lunched there. Rode and walked out to Mrs. McCoy's, 4 m S.W. of Edna & dined there. Miller, a Liberal U.B. there. Meeting at 2:00 & at night. B. McGrew pr. Stay at A.J. Bessey's. Miss Lucy Magie 18 there.

Wednesday, October 12 Q. Conf. at 9:30. Have a Bible Reading at 11:00, on Sin. Dine at Bessey's and sup there. I pr. at the tent at 7:30, John 1:29. Rain falls, and continues through the night. Rev. A.D. Blinn & husband an[d] Rev. G.W. Carey were in porch when we arrived at Bessey's.

Thursday, October 13 At Bessey's in forenoon. Conference opened at 2:00. Supper at Bessey's & lodging. Spring wagon breaks down on the way to Church. Rev. M.J. Wilson pr. on Change of Heart. McGrew follows. Stay at Bessey's.

Friday, October 14 Conference continued. Dine, sup & lodge as usual. Conf. elects S.B. McGrew, P.E. Sta. Com. met at Bessey's at 6:00. Rev. Mrs. A.D. Blinn pr. John 17, G.W. Carey exhorts. Stay at Bessey's. Their children: Mrs. Higginson, Elmer S. 26; Eva 16; Clifford 10; Alvan A. 24—He at Lawrence.

Saturday, October 15 Conference Continued. Mrs. S.C. Magie returned to Conf. having withdrawn, evening before. Conf. closed at 5:00. Dine, sup & lodge at Bessey's. Rev. S.B. McGrew pr. Deut. 32:9-12. I exhort. Lodge at Bessey's.

Sunday, October 16 I pr at 11:00, Acts 2:17,18. Dine

on the ground. S.S. Anniversary at 3:00. Supper at A.J. Bessey's Missionary meeting at 7:00 & love-feast. Raise $77.00 in subscription. Neighbors: Lot—McCoy—Parks.

Monday, October 17 Visit Parks and dine there. Go in afternoon with Bro. A.J. Bessey into the Nation Round Mound—etc. Go with Elmer S. Bessey to Edna and on 10:31 tr to Coffeyville & thence to Kansas City. Hard rain in the night.

Tuesday, October 18 Reach K. C'y at 7:45. Go to Reuchlin's. Katie, my daughter, there. Stay there all day. Write letters home and to Mo. conference folks. Slept a long night's sleep.

Wednesday, October 19 Went down town and to Horace D. Herr's, 12 S. Bocke St., Kan. City, Kans. Got back to Reuchlin's at 1:30. Start on 6:45 C.B. & Q tr. to Chicago. Slept well.

Thursday, October 20 Arrive at Chicago about 10:15. See most of the Columbian Exposition parade. Many thousands of people there. Start for Berlin, Ont. on C. Gr.Tr. R'y, at 3:00. Reach Port Huron at 12:35. Cross in Tunnel.

Friday, October 21 Reach Berlin at 6:00, morn. Breakfast at Rev. Jacob B. Bowman's. See Mr. Alex Miller, solicitor, at 11:00. Case postponed. Dine at Rev. D.B. Sherk's. Spend part of afternoon there. Supper at Jac. B. Bowman's. Interview with Alexander Miller, Att'y. (Q.C.) Stay at J.B. Bowman's.

Saturday, October 22 Call at Prof. I.L. Bpwman's. He afflicted in mind and body. Dine at Rev. G.W. Dinnius'. Pr. at 2:30, Heb. 1-20. Supper at Rev. D.B. Sherk's. Lodge at Rev. J.B. Bowman's. Married son, Abraham, & wife Susan, & daughters Eva 11, Marian 5. J.B. B's daughter, Nancy.

Sunday, October 23 I pr. at 11, Ex. 28:34. Communion follows. I dine at E. Eshelman's. Mother Geo. Plowman calls with Sister Woods. I sup and lodge at Rev. D.B. Sherk's. Mr. W. Becker calls for [blank] Sherk's daughter. Much talk on Law & on Theology with D.B. Sherk.

Monday, October 24 Call at Rosenberger's, at J.B. & at I.L. Bowman's. At Eshelman's. Go on 11:00 tr to Port Huron, Detroit, Toledo, Dayton. Saw Sheriff Springer, Rev. H. Dierlamm, Mr. Bingeman, etc. at Depot at Berlin. Slept several (perhaps 4) hours on the train.

Tuesday, October 25 Reach home at 5:00 A.M. Call at Kiracofe's, Davis', & Dillon's in forenoon. Slept 3 h. in afternoon. Read letters, etc., & dictated cards in the evening. Slept well.

Wednesday, October 26 News of Mrs. Benj. Harrison's death in the White House, at 1:40 this morning; the worthy wife of our ablest president in administration, and purest morally & spiritually. Settled with Lorin, on my account & with the office & paid him $15.00, for watch. Wrote letters. Called at G.R. Young's (absent) and had gold-tooth cemented.

Thursday, October 27 Got the full text of the Oregon Supr. Court Decision. Gave to printer. Wrote many letters. Busy all day.

Friday, October 28 Busy writing letters, etc. Went to town in forenoon. At home the rest of the day.

Saturday, October 29 Saw Young five minutes. Measure for suit by Charch & Wells. Call at Graybill's. Read proofs of the Oregon decision in the afternoon and evening.

Sunday, October 30 Preach at School Street Church at 10:30, Hebr. 11:1-10. Afternoon, call more than an hour at Rev. C.H. Kiracofe's. At home in the evening reading from Psalms, Song of Moses, etc. in New Version of the Bible.

Monday, October 31 Went to Graybill's Printing Office, and to town. Sent Reuchlin (my son) $250.00, in afternoon, to buy a lot in Ivanhoe (Kansas City). Read proofs further at Graybill's. Wrote letters in the evening.

Tuesday, November 1 Mailed copies of the decision to Attorneys, etc. Continued to do so. Called at Printing office, Dillon's, and Kiracofe's in the evening.

Wednesday, November 2 At home all day except I went

to Union Depot at 6:00 to meet Katie, returning from Kansas City. Wilbur is sick with Appendicitis. Sent for the doctor (Spitler) who recommended rest, diet, and care to avoid cold.

Thursday, November 3 At home all day. Wilbur easy to-day. Kiracofe called in the evening & Joe Boyd. I saw the doctor at 9:30.

Friday, November 4 At home. Wilbur improving.

Saturday, November 5 At home mostly. Went to town to try on my new coat at Charch & Wells.

Sunday, November 6 At School St. Church heard Dr. C.H. Kiracofe pr. on Parable of 5, 2 & 1 talents, a real good discourse. At home till 6:00; called at Jac. Swank's. Heard Rev. P.Y. Kephart pr. at 7:00, 1 John 4:18.

Monday, November 7 At home except to go to Pri. Office (Graybill's) twice. Wrote letters, etc.

Tuesday, November 8 This is Presidential election day. I voted for Benj. Harrison whom I regard as one of the best administrators of Government in our Country's History. Wrote etc. most of the day. Election news at night unfavorable. Lorin's Milton born this afternoon—my first grandson.

Wednesday, November 9 At home in forenoon. Called and got my new suit—$35.00. Wrote letters, etc. Election news worse and worse.

Thursday, November 10 Write letters forenoon. Ex. Com. meeting afternoon at Kiracofe's. Election news worse and worse.

Friday, November 11 Started on 9:25 train for Meadville and Shaws, Pa. Reach Shaw's at 8:30, and stay at John Counselman's. Charged no bill and sent boy to take me to McDonald's.

Saturday, November 12 Shaw's boy takes me to Harvey McDonald's 1 1/2 mile on the way. Rev. R.H. Sickler takes me to dine at his house in Custards, and then to Brook's Chapel, where at 2:00 I pr. Acts 1:11, Sup at Brook's. Pr. at 7:00, Ps. 1:5.

Sunday, November 13 Pr at 11:00, John 14:2,3. Raise $324.00 and dedicate Brooks Chapel. Dine at Brooks'. Rev. Kitchen and Wm. Loper there. Pr at 7:00, Ex. 28:34. Stay at Rev. R.H. Sickles's.

Monday, November 14 Sickler takes me to Shaw's & I go thence to Meadville, Akron, Orrville, Mansfield, home arriving next morning. Wrote many letters at Mansfield.

Tuesday, November 15 Reach home at 4:00. Sleep till 8:30. Call at my son Lorin's before noon.

Thursday, November 17 At home. Ex. Mis. Committee at 2:00. J.S. Yackey at Fayetteville, Pa. called in afternoon.

Friday, November 18 At home. Very busy all the day. Go on 8:40 train to Richmond, Ind, & thence north on Gr. R. & I. R.R. to Kendallville.

Saturday, November 19 Reach Waterbury about 7:00. Breakfast at John Bideler's. Lilly comes & we go to town. Call at Robt. Spear's. Dine at G.W. Bachtel's. Go to Husselman's and sup & lodge at G.W. Dull's. Pr. at 7:00, Rev. 1:7, first sermon in the new house.

Sunday, November 20 Pr at 10:30, Ex. 28.34. Raise $458.50—in cash $127.00. Dedicate the church (Maple Grove) worth nearly $3,000.00. Dine at Nelson Cheeney's, 1/2 m. south. Pr. at 7:00 Acts, 26.28. Stay at J.E. Amstutz, 1/4 m. W. of Dull's and 2 1/4 m. E of the Church.

Monday, November 21 Go on 9:24 tr to Ft. Wayne. Saw Bishop Barnaby at Depot. Went on 1:00 tr to Richmond & on 5:45 tr. to Dayton.

Tuesday, November 22 At Printing office. At home most of the day.

Thursday, November 24 Thanksgiving Day. Remain at home till 5:15 p.m. Go to Dublin, Ind. Stay at Bishop H. Floyd 's.

Friday, November 25 Go on train to Ogden. Train over two hours late. Harvey Wright takes me to their house 6

m. South. Stay there till morning. Gusta Scott, Emma Frazier, John & Drucilla McKee there.

Saturday, November 26 Go on noon tr to Rushville, & thence on 6:25 tr to Morristown. Balser R. Falbert takes me to Mt. Carmel Church. Stay at John Engel's, 1 m. E. Saw John Hanen at Depot at Rushville. Engel's daughter is Elmira.

Sunday, November 27 Pr. at Mt. Carmel, I Kings 18:38,39. Dedicate the church. Dine at Balser Talbert's 2 M. S.E. Pr at 7:00, Acts 20:21. Stay at Engle's.

Monday, November 28 Engle takes me to Eli Myer's. Call at Peter Myer's. Dine at Eli's. Talk on unpar. sin with Elvira. Eli takes me to Michal Billman's. Children: S. Elizabeth. Edith & Charley Gordon there. Father Billman very sick. I lodge there.

Tuesday, November 29 Go to Shelbyville. Call at S.E. Gordon's a short time. Mother Gordon there. Go on 10:00 tr. to Cambridge. Wait till 6:00. Reach home about 8:00.

Wednesday, November 30 At home. Sab. School Quarterlies engage my time.

Sunday, December 4 Pr. at School Street, Luke 17:21. At home till night. Rev. W.S. Street pr. at 7:00, Luke 18:18.

Monday, December 5 At home in forenoon. Call at Graybill's & Kiracofe's. Rev. W.S. Street & Prof. Kiracofe called in the forenoon. I do much writing and arranging of desk.

Tuesday, December 6 At home all day. Prof. Kiracofe called in the morning. Rev. N.D. Wolfard called in the afternoon.

Wednesday, December 7 Meeting of Executive meeting (Missionary) at 2:00, at Wm. Dillon's. Considered correspondence with reference to Foreign Missions. Women ratified Small's appointment to Lower Wabash.

Friday, December 9 At home. Called & saw Young three minutes as he came down stairs. Got some proofs on

Quarterlies at Reform Pub. House. Called at Lorin Wright's a half hour.

Sunday, December 11 Attend "Christ's Episcopal Church." Rev. Wm. Wilmerding Church of the Holy Communion, New York, pr. a consecration sermon, and Rt. Rev. Boyd Vincent, Bp. (Asst.) of Southern Ohio, consecrates Dwight Steel Marfield as priest. I pr. at Sch. St. at 7:00, Gal. 3:24.

Monday, December 12 Called at Ref. Pub. House. Got more proofs on Quarterly. Saw Young a minute. Monday Afternoon at 3:45. Start to Toledo. Arrive at 9:00. Put up at Boody House. G.R. Young, Wm. Lawrence, Sheley, Gunckle and McNew there.

Tuesday, December 13 Court (U.S.Ct.) met at 9:15. Our case put off till Jan. 9, and to be at Cincinnati. Judge Taft. Came home on 10:15 tr. Judge Wm. Lawrence with me to Sidney. Got home at 3:00. Write letters in the evening.

Wednesday, December 14 At home forenoon. Go to town in afternoon. Wrote letters. Prof. Kiracof came in afternoon to hear from the trial at Toledo.

Thursday, December 15 At home. Called at at [repeated in text] C.H. Kiracofe's in the afternood. [sic] Writing letters.

Friday, December 16 At home. Worked on correcting the mailing list. Went to East side of River in afternoon. Application for railroad permits.

Saturday, December 17 Went to "Town" & saw Young. Sent for periodicals—*Tribune—Independent—Homiletical review*. Rev. S.L. Livingston called an hour in the evening.

Sunday, December 18 Heard Rev. S.L. Livingston pr. at Sch. St. Ch. at 10:30, Luke 12th, a very good sermon. The spirit and discrimination of the speaker was very fine. Heard Rev. W.S. Street pr. at 7:00, same place, Mal. 3:10. Did very well.

Monday, December 19 Revs. S.L. Livingston & Rev. W.E. Streete & their wives took dinner with us. Call at Rev.

C.H. Kiracofe's in the afternoon and have a talk about his article on Law of Tithes.

Tuesday, December 20 At home mostly. Went to town before bank closed and sent $10.00 draft to Mosier out of my own fund. Busy writing letters.

Wednesday, Decmeber 21 At home forenoon busy arranging files till 3:00, when I went over with Dr. C.H. Kiracofe to hear Evangelist Mundhall at 1st Pres. Church, on separation from world. Wilbur sick in evening; Apendicitis.

Thursday, December 22 At home all day. Mrs. A.L. Billheimer called a few minutes in the morning. Prof. C.H. Kiracofe called in the afternoon. Wilbur some better.

Friday, December 23 At home all day. Wilbur improving some. Write letters. Arrang[e] files of papers at office till 10:30.

Saturday, December 24 At home. Busy looking over old conservators 1891-1892, and arranging so we can find them when wanted. Write letters, etc. At work till late. Go to bed at 12:00.

Sunday, December 25 Christmas. Lorin and family with us to dinner. Many presents. Too much to do for Sabbath.

Monday, December 26 At home and busy arranging files at the office of Conservators of 1889, 1890, 1891, so as to have more convenient access to them when wanted. Spent evening in cutting out articles from paper for use.

Tuesday, Decmeber 27 At home all forenoon. Called at Young's 10 min. in afternoon, and at Dillon's who had called at noon. Engaged the rest of the afternoon in fixing up things out of repair, & waiting on Wilbur.

Wednesday, December 28 At home all day except a short trip to "town" about 3:00. Payed my tax; saw Young two minutes. Did a vast amount of writing letters, appl. for R'y favors, etc.

Thursday, December 29 At home. Went to town in the afternoon. Wilbur still right bad off. The Doctor (Spitler) came about 3:30. Kiracofe called. Nettie & Lorin called about 7:00. Wrote letters to-day and article on Rehearing of Oregon case for the paper.

Friday, December 30 Went on 9:15 (9:45) tr. to Union City, Pa. Reach there at 9:00. Stay at N.R. Luce's.

Saturday, December 31 Go on 10:00 tr. to Riceville. Sidney Pierce took us (Luce, G.W. Davis, Sister Drury, and Sr. E.C. Scott) to his house on Briton Run. Mother Pierce robbed last August a year. Dine at Pierce's. I pr. at 2:00, Heb. 11:1-13. Supper at Welman's. Watch-night meeting. S. Evans & Nelson R. Luce pr. Stay at Pierce's.

Conference Items

1. Examinations. 2. Appeals. 3. Any died Memoirs. 4. Reports of Reading Cons. 5. Applicants to Preach. 6. Publishing Minutes. 7. Elders Orders. 8. Committees for next Year. 9. Next conference. 10. College Trustees. 11. Rep. of Treas. Preachers' Aid. 12. Rep. Pr. Aid Treasurer. 13. Boundary & Finance Com. 14. Correct Itin. List. 15. Elect Pres. Elders & Sta. Com. 16. Secretary's Pay. 17. Conference Sermon, Mis. Meeting, S. School. 18. General Reports. 19. Sum up results. 20. Elders Eligible. 21. Tellers for Gen. Conf. 22. Sabbath Sch. Treas. 23. Reports of other Collectors.

Assessments of Conf.

Ontario	125.
Pennsylvania	150.
Maryland	40.
Erie	70.
Virginia	50.
East Ohio	90.
Scioto	150.
Sandusky	75.
Auglaize	250.
North Ohio	225.
Arkansas Valley	60.
Neosho	50.
Kansas	100.
West Kansas	30.
South Missouri	30.
Missouri	60.
Illinois	30.

Centr. Illinois	100.
White River	225.
Indiana	40.
East Des Moines	10.
Michigan	190.
North Mich.	100.
Upper Wabash	50.
St. Joseph	100.
Rock River	190.
Wisconsin	45.
Minnesota	35.
Iowa	45.
West Des Moines	70.
Elkhorn	50.
West Nebraska	45.
East Nebraska	80.

Bish. Traveling Expenses

To: White River	6.25
North Ohio	3.45
Central Illinois	6.52
East Des Moines	4.51
Eagleville, Mo.	3.55
Lecompton	2.90
Webster	7.20
Stafford	5.78
Edna	3.90
Kans City	2.68
Home (Estimated)	10.00
55.84 [Total]	

Trip from Kansas City to Berlin, Ont. & Home, 20.68. Viz To Berlin 16.06. Viz to Dayton 7.50

Shuey at Richmond, Indiana trial, read an Old inscription, "This is put into my hands as the oldest Discipline." He should have read: "This is perhaps the oldest Discipline." I took his reading from the stenographer who read his notes, as I copied them.   Milton Wright

Rheumatism
Lotion: 1/2 oz. of carbonate of Potash in 9 oz of hot water & adding six fluid dr. of Battley's Liquor Opii *Sedativus.*

Internal: 1. Turpentine, Cod-liver oil, Sulphur, quaiacum, Dovers powders. 2. Muriate Ammonia. 3. Iodide of Potash in five gr. Hoses, combined with Carbonate of Ammonia, three times daily. (From Memorial Library)

Oxford Bible on "Communion of Saints." It says: "See Fellowship." "Fellowship of Saints: Acts 2:42, 2 Cor. 8:4, Gal. 2:9, Phil. 1:5, 1 John 1:3."

"Fellowship of Christ: 1 Cor. 1:9, 12:27, 2 Cor. 4:11, Phil. 3:10, 1 Cor. 10:16."

"Fellowship of Spirit: Phil. 2:1."

Temperance: Prov. 23:29-32, Isa. 5:11-22, Hosea 4:11.

From old Acct. Book.
In 1879, a trip from Cedar Rapids, Iowa to Denver Colorado, via Cheyenne, including $2.00 for sleeper & about 45 cts for lunch, etc. cost me $30.25. Thence via Wilson, Kan., via (& thence private free to Beloit) to Burlington, Iowa cost exclusive of $1.45 for food & hack $18.25

1 8 9 3

Sunday, January 1 At Britton's Run Ch. Pa. I pr. at 11:00, Ps. 48:11-13. Call for $250; raise $316. A rainy day, limiting the congregation. Dine at Barney Sturtevant's. I pr. at 7:00, 2 Tim, iv. 6-8. I go to Byron Knight's & stay till 2:30; then he takes me to Spartansburg, Pa., before day-light.

Monday, January 2 Go to Corry and thence to Dayton. Cars much crowded with holiday excursionists. Get home at 5:00. Found all well except Wilbur who is slowly improving. Expense of the trip, $14.76, received — $23.34, four days & one night. Pr. 4 times & dedication effort, $8.58.

Tuesday, January 3 Busy adjusting papers in my desk, etc., and writing, Went to town—bought tin ware, etc. Slight pleurisy. Call at Young's 5 min.

Wednesday, January 4 At home. Very busy. Write many letters. C.H. Kiracofe calls in the aftern. Up till 10:00 p.m. Still slight pleurisy.

Thursday, January 5 Wrote an article for the paper. Called at Graybill's & Dillon's. At Dillon's again in Afternoon. Went to town about 4:00.

Sunday, January 8 At Church School St. Prof. C.H. Kiracofe conducts the services. At home the rest of the day.

Monday, January 9 Went on 7:30 (Short Line) train to Cincinnati. Put up at Gibson House. Demurrer trial in Fairview Church Case begins at 10:00. After preliminaries J.A. McMahon spoke. He closed in afternoon, and Young spoke & then Judge Wm. Lawrence.

Tuesday, January 10 Lawrence spoke an hour and a quarter. Then L.B. Gunkle made the closing speech of two hours. Young & I dine hastily & we go on 1:20 Cin. Ham. & Dayton train home.

Thursday, January 12 Called at Lorin's. Went to town in Afternoon & to Prof. C.H. Kiracofe's. The doctor (Spitler) came out about 4:00 to see Wilbur who is not so well to-day.

Friday, January 13 Rev. W.E. Streete & Bro. Speidel called about noon. I went "to town" in the afternoon, and purchased book-case curtains, etc. A cold day; from 4-9 above zero.

Saturday, January 14 At home. It is snowing a little. Ella Howard, a colored girl, comes to work for Katie. It is the coldest night of the season, running many degrees below zero.

Sunday, January 15 Very cold day. At home all day. Wilbur improving considerably.

Tuesday, January 17 At home all day except a brief call at the office. Spent the day in reading and writing. Considerably warmer. At 11:00, thermometer 10 degrees above zero.

Wednesday, January 18 At home all day, reading and writing. Prof. Kiracofe called at the office. Thermometer ran 26 degrees above zero. Snow fell some.

Thursday, January 19 At home all day. Wrote an article in the afternoon on The Demurrer trial. Wrote letters

& did other literary work.

Friday, January 20 At home. I Sort out old papers containing articles I wished to cut out. Write letters. Sent Hon. Wm. Lawrence draft for $86.40.

Saturday, January 21 At home. Write letters etc. Warmer to-day. Sent Small another $12.00. He is at home (Farmland, Ind.) on account of the sickness of his little boy. Katie's sick in the evening & night.

Sunday, January 22 Katie some better. Lorin & Ivonette spend the day with us. Wm. Bartles & wife called in the afternoon; Also Cord Ruce.

Tuesday, January 24 Rev. W.E. Streete called in the morning.

Wednesday, January 25 At home. Katie made an "all day" visit to Lorin's. I Write an article in part.

Thursday, January 26 At home. Write article on Tithing.

Saturday, January 28 At home. Went to see Dr. L. Spitler, about a sore on my face. Called at Young's. Saw him about twenty or 30 minutes. In afternoon, called at Rebecca Davis' and at Kiracofe's.

Sunday, January 29 All our family dine at Lorin's. I was there three hours. At home the rest of the day.

Monday, January 30 At home all day. Still poulticing my face.

Tuesday, January 31 At home all day, except an hour at our office, and a visit to the doctor's whom I did not find at home.

Wednesday, February 1 At home all day except a visit to the office and to the city library. Prof. Kiracofe called an hour in the afternoon.

Monday, February 6 At home all day. Kiracofe came to be excused from going to Urbana to trial to-morrow. Excused. Got telegrams saying case is continued. Write much of the day.

Tuesday, February 7 At home. Called at Dillon's & Kiracofe's. Albert K. has the measles. Reuchlin's son Herbert, born this afternoon.

Wednesday, February 8 At home in the forenoon. Called at Young's ten minutes. Took Thucidides out of the public library. Wrote in the afternoon & evening.

Thursday, February 9 Took an article to Dr. Dillon for publication. At home the rest of the day.

Sunday, February 12 Attend meeting at School St. (Swank's) Church. Pres. Elder, Wm. Miller preached. Communion. Bra. Miller dines with us and stays till evening. He preaches at 7:00.

Tuesday, February 14 Call at Dillon's and at Graybill's in the afternoon.

Wednesday, February 15 Prof. C.H. Kiracofe called. Wanted an executive committee meeting.

Thursday, February 16 At home. Missionary Meeting in the Afternoon at 2:00.

Saturday, February 18 At home. Wrote many letters. Kiracofe called early in the afternoon. From 9 to 11 evening, I spent in transcribing notes of various things.

Monday, February 20 At home reading & writing. Called at Graybill's.

Tuesday, February 21 Went over to town. Saw Will Young 10 minutes. Examined Bill at law in U.S. Case and sent to Hon. Wm. Lawrence.

Wednesday, February 22 Washington's birth-day. Hence a holiday. Did some reading and a little writing of letters. I value Washington highly, but incline little to hero worship.

Thursday, February 23 At home. Write letters, read, etc. Went to Library, etc. Sent bill on U.S. Suit to Harlan. Received Flinn's supplementary brief, read it & forwarded it to Judge Lawrence.

Sunday, February 26 Heard Rev. H. Wells at Memorial

Presbyterian Church at 10:30, John 16:7, a good sermon. In the evening at Dunker Church on W. Fourth St., heard Samuel Hoover on Isa. 55.1.

Monday, February 27 At home. Wrote letters. Received Lawrence's supplementary brief.

Tuesday, February 28 Heard Rev. H. Wells at 10:00 on Holy Spirit. Nice day & mild. Katie and Flora Greenwood went in the evening to hear Dr. H. Wells on "Final Perseverance," etc. and did not relish his Calvinism.

Wednesday, March 1 At home reading & writing. Katie is sick with quinsy. A very mild, beautiful day.

Thursday, March 2 At home. Spent the time in reading and writing. Katie is sick with quinsy, still. Beautiful mild weather. Sprinkled rain a little in the evening.

Friday, March 3 Called at C.H. Kiracofe's. Saw Wm. Dillon there. Spent the rest of the day in reading & writing. Katie is up and about. Cloudy in the morning and mild. Cooler in the evening and snows a little before bed time.

Saturday, March 4 Cold day. Read & write. Kiracofe called in forenoon.

Sunday, March 5 Preached at Swank's Chapel (School Street) at 10:30, Acts 19:25. "He, himself giveth to all life & breath & all things." Heard Dr. C.H. Kiracofe at Swank's Chapel at 7:00, 2 Pet. 3:18, "But grow in grace." It was a good sermon.

Monday, March 6 Called at Graybill's & Kiracofe's in the forenoon.

Tuesday, March 7 Bishop Henry J. Becker called an hour in the evening.

Wednesday, March 8 At home. Afternoon I received proofs on Quarterlies. Bishop Becker spent part of the afternoon & evening with us.

Thursday, March 9 Got pert of the proofs on Quarterlies ready in Afternoon and took them to Mr. Blum's. Called at Kiracofe's & Dillon's in forenoon.

Friday, March 10 Worked some on Quarterlies. Wrote article on "Neutral" Virginia.

Sunday, March 12 Heard Rev. Clark pr. at Raper Chapel, Eccl. 1:1, a very interesting sermon. In the evening, heard Rev. W.E. Streete pr. at Swank's Chap., Heb. 2:1-3.

Monday, March 13 At printing office morning & afternoon awhile. Delightful weather. Wrote letters.

Tuesday, March 14 Went to town in afternoon. Saw Will Young 10 min. Wrote letters. Weather colder and blustery.

Friday, March 17 Wrote some for an article. Not being well, did not do much.

Saturday, March 18 Got ready and started to Warren, Ind., at 11:10 fore'n. Rev. Wm. Dillon on the way as far as Upland. Rev. N. D. Wolfard from Hartford to Marion. Paid tax $30.72. Reach Warren at 5:35, and walk out to Elijah Morrison's. Stay there. Rev. Cyrus Smith & wife live with them.

Sunday, March 19 Pr. at Mt. Zion, 2 Cor. 3:7,8. Dine at T.B. Clampitt's. Pr. at Mt. Z. at 7:30, Mal. 3:18. Large congregation. Stay at Elijah Morrison's.

Monday, March 20 Morrison and wife take me to Warren. I take 11:05 tr. to Marion and Fairmount. Call at Rev. Wm. Hall's an hour. Paid Chas. Atkinson $10.00 on Ch. Subscription. Wolfard there. Go with Mr. Lytler to Ellis Wright's. Stay there.

Tuesday, March 21 Go to Hm. H.H. Reeder's & thence to Oliver Glass's. Dine there. Go to Robt. B. Reeder's. Supper there. Go to Wm. Reeder's via Ellis Wright's. Stay at Wm. Reeder's.

Wednesday, March 22 Very rainy morning. Arrange accounts with Wm. Early dinner & Wm. takes me to Fairmount & I take the 11:22 train to Anderson—thence to Richmond—and arrive at Dayton (home) about 6:00.

Thursday, March 23 At home. Call at Will Young's 10 minutes. Letters from him yesterday.

Friday, March 24 At home. Wrote Article for the paper.

Saturday, March 25 Went on 11:00 tr. to Lima and Elida. Supper at S.A. Steman's. Pr. at U.B. Church at 7:30, Mal. 3:18. Stay at Hunsaker's, with R.G. Montgomery.

Sunday, March 26 Pr. at 10:30, Matt. 5:13,14. Dine at A.J. Steman's. Call at Spear's. Pr. at 7:30, Matt. 19:27. Two seekers. Stay at Henry Kiracofe's.

Monday, March 27 Start at 9:20 via Lima to Dayton. Arrive at home at 1:15. Call at Dillon's and Graybill's.

Tuesday, March 28 At home writing. Call at Lorin's in the evening.

Thursday, March 30 Tizzard filled a tooth for me. Called at Young's. Wrote an article for the Conservator in the evening. Aunt Eliza Braden died to-day.

Friday, March 31 Lorin & Nettie dined with us. At 5:45 aft., I started to Indianapolis. I stay at Circle Park hotel.

Saturday, April 1 Call at Walter S. Brown's. Go to Rev. T.J. Connor's 740 N. Alabama St. Leave at 3:00. Go on 4:00 train to Dublin. Stay at Ed. Wilson's. Their adopted daughter, Fannie Clark, gets home late from Richmond.

Sunday, April 2 I call at Wm. McGrath's a half hour. Pr. at 10:30, Dublin U.B. Church on Main St., Rev. 22:14. Dine at John Champ's, near McNews. Call in Aft. at McNew's, Rev. H.W. Robbins', & Bish. Floyd's. Pr. at 7:00, Mal. 3:18. Stay at Dr. G.W. Champ's.

Monday, April 3 Call at Dr. Hardy Wray's. Go on 9:50 tr. to Richmond. Dine at D.K. Zeller's. Go home on 2:05 aft. train. Call at Print'g Office. Bishop H.J. Becker goes home with me. Stays with us.

Tuesday, April 4 At home all forenoon. Called at Young's 5 min. in Afternoon. Geo. at home sick.

Wednesday, April 5 At home. Mailed letters at the depot to Lawrence and others. Prof. C.H. Kiracofe called in the afternoon.

Saturday, April 8 Called for by Decker and went to Napoleon, Ohio, with Wm. Dillon. We drove out in livery to John S. Blair's, 3 miles N.W. of McClure, and staid there. Employed Martin Knupp, Esq.

Sunday, April 9 We went over to Rev. S.A. Meyers, 3 ms. N. of McClure. Dine there. I pr. at 2:30, at M.E. Church, Ps. 45:5. Supper at Wm. Good's, 2 m. W. of McClure. Rev. Wm. Dillon pr. at M.E. Church near S.A. Meyers' at 7:30 on work of the Holy Spirit.

Monday, April 10 I Go with Rev. S.A. Meyers to Napoleon. Arrange matters there, and go to Toledo on 3:14 train. See Lewis' (our Att'y) & supper at a restaurant. See Gen. Stedman's monument. Go on 11:45 tr. to Dayton. Cahill & Donovan use Huffman's Attorneys.

Tuesday, April 11 Reach Dayton about 5:00 A.M. Call to see Will Young at 11:30 & again at 4:00. Rev. C.H. Kiracofe's called at 2:00. Did little in the evening being tired.

Wednesday, April 12 Called at Gunckel & Rowe's to get a form of acknowledg[e]ment of service of Notice of Petition of Slifer for sale of Frederick Thomas estate. W.O. Dinius & Dillon called in afternoon.

Thursday, April 13 At home. Dillon called in the afternoon.

Saturday, April 15 Called at Dillon's and Kiracofe's & at Graybill's.

Sunday, April 16 I pr. at School Street Church at 10:30, Eph. 1:6. At home the rest of the day. Prof. C.H. Kiracofe pr at 7:23, Matt. 6:9.

Thursday, April 20 Called an hour at Geo. R. Young's office to see him.

Friday, April 21 At home. Mis'n Exec. Meeting at 1:30.

Saturday, April 22 At home. Wrote to R'y T. Agts for half-fare permits for western de[l]egates to Gen. Conference.

Sunday, April 23 Pr at School Street at 10:30, Matt. 25:29—Parable of the talents. At home till 7:00 p.m. Heard Rev. W.E. Streete on Job. "When thou hast tried me," etc.

Monday, April 24 At home. Called at Graybill's and Dr. Kiracofe's in the forenoon.

Tuesday, April 25 At home. Called at Dillon's & Graybill's in the forenoon. Wrote several letters and went to town in the Afternoon. Paid Young two hundred and fifty dollars, and staid a half hour.

Friday, April 28 Called at Dillon's in forenoon. At Kiracofe's in afternoon. Wrote many letters.

Saturday, April 29 Called at Young's an hour and made an affidavit in the rehearing case. Wrote letters.

Sunday, April 30 Heard Rev. Mr. Haynes pr. at 10:30, Luke 8:18. "Take heed how ye hear." Called at Lorin's awhile in the evening.

Monday, May 1 Waters very high—14 ft. 6 in. Called at Dillon's and Graybill's. Wrote an article on tithing. Up till near midnight.

Sunday, May 7 Heard Rev. Nichols preach at 10:30. Was at home the rest of the day.

Monday, May 8 At home. Called at Dillon's and Graybill's.

Tuesday, May 9 Called at Dillon's. Ex. Meeting at my House. Prin. Establ. Board met at 2:00, at My Office. Finished business in the afternoon. Bishop H. Floyd & Rev. Z. McNew dined with us. Saw Prof. Kiracofe & Bp. D.H. Flickinger. Called at Dillon's.

Saturday, May 13 Called at Liberal General Conference about 10:45. Milton Matthews showed me a copy of Cin. *Tribune* giving account of Judge Taft's decision in U.S. case in our favor. Spent the day in sending out notices of it.

Sunday, May 14 Heard Rev. C.J. Kephart pr. at 10:30, Phil. 2:[blank] "Being in form of God." At home the rest of the day.

Monday, May 15 Start at 6:40 for Waterloo, Ind. via Deshler & Auburn Junction. Dine at Rev. A.B. Lilly's.

Board of bishops meet there at 2:00. Supper at Lilly's. Bishop Becker lectured at 8:00. I stay at home and write, but get to Church at Close of lecture. Stay at Hennings.

Tuesday, May 16 Bishops meeting forenoon and afternoon at Lilly's and we all dine there and sup there. Missionary Board meets at 7:00. Annual address by Rev. D.B. Sherk at 8:00. I stay at Henning's with Bps. Barnaby & Flickinger.

Wednesday, May 17 Have an hour's talk with Flickinger. Board meets at 8:00 and continues forenoon and afternoon. Bp. Becker lectures at 8:00 for Women. Subscription of over $500.00. Table and lodging at Henning's. Their only child Estelle, 17 years.

Thursday, May 18 Rev. A.B. Lilly takes the bishops to Hudson in a carriage. I was at Charlton's, G. Oberlin's, and then at Emory A. Metz's. Gen. Conference opened at 2:00. Attended to organization, etc. Rev. John Riley's pr. at 7:30, John 3:16. Supper and lodging at Metz' my conference home.

Friday, May 19 Conference continues. Wood excused and M.F. Keiter is elected secretary. I have a touch of genuine grippe. Stay at Metz in the evening. Rev. M.F. Keiter preached at 7:30. But I had an attack of "Grippe" (Soreness, pain & swelling of the bowels) and staid at Metz'.

Saturday, May 20 Conference continued. I Was weak and sore but better. E.C. Wyatt pr. at 7:30. Home at Emory A. Metz, Mrs. Camille Metz. Brotherinlaw Walter Britton. Sarah Maria Britton, the motherinlaw.

Sunday, May 21 I pr. at U.B. Church, at 10:30, Phil. 2:9: Bps. Floyd at Reformed; Barnaby at M.E. Ch.; Becker pr. some miles away. N.R. Luce pr. at 7:30, at U.B.; I.M. Tharp at 7:00 at M.E. Ch.

Monday, May 22 Conference continued. Bishop Barnaby pr. at 7:30.

Tuesday, May 23 Conference continued. Bp. Floyd pr. at 7:30.

Wednesday, May 24 Conference continued. Bishop

Becker pr. at 7:30 on "Pr. faith which he once destroyed." Collection $223.00.

Thursday, May 25 Conference continued. Dillon, Floyd, Wright, and Barnaby elected bishops in the afternoon, Kiracofe, editor; Becker, Mis. Sec'y. Dillon pr. 7:30.

Friday, May 26 Conference continued. Memorial Service of Dr. L. Davis at 7:30. Dillon, Kiracofe and Wright spoke.

Saturday, May 27 Session continued. Keiter elected Pub. Agt & Mis. Treasurer. I presided all day and in the evening. I pr. at 7:30, Matt. 16:16. Session closed *sine die.*

Sunday, May 28 9:00 Christian Experience meet'g. Bishop H.J. Becker pr. at 10:30, Col. 2:15. I go out to Stephen Ransburg 11/2 ms. west to dinner. Walk back in preference (with Bp. Barnaby) to an offer to ride. Rev. Phil. Beck pr at 7:30, 1 Cor. 13:13.

Monday, May 29 Rev. A.B. Lilly takes me and others to Summit. Go to Ft. Wayne & Richmond, and thence home to Dayton, arriving about 6:00.

Tuesday, May 30 Decoration Day, but I remain at home. Send out copies of decision of Judge Taft. Ella Howard quit working for us.

Wednesday, May 31 Called at Young's in the afternoon and paid him $55.00 in full on Oregon Case & took his receipt. Worn down, I did not do much.

Thursday, June 1 At home trying to rest and recruit. Wrote an article on Tithe-law Inconsistencies.

Friday, June 2 Still trying to recruit. Wrote some items for Conservator in the evening.

Saturday, June 3 At home. Rather in poor health. Gave out starting to Grant Co., Ind.

Sunday, June 4 Heard E.C. Simpson pr. at 11:00 at United Pres. Church Cor. of 4th & Jefferson up stairs. At home the rest of the day. Lorin & Nettie came in the afternoon.

Monday, June 5 Start at 7:00 for Fairmount, Ind. Reach there via Union City & Gas City (Jonesboro) at 1:00. Lunch at restaurant. Call with Rev. Wm. Hall. Call at Chi., Ind. & Eastern railroad office. Go with Ben. Newbarger to Ellis Wright's. Stay at W.H.H. Reeder's.

Tuesday, June 6 At Henry Simons most of the day. He makes right of way for railroad & gives place of Station. Call at Ellis Wright's. Stay at W.H.H. Reeder's on the farm.

Wednesday, June 7 Go to Oliver Glass's & Robt. B. Reeder's, and thence with Ralph Fultz to Fairmount. Lunch. Attend to business & go on 2:00 train via Anderson to Knightstown. Go 2 ms. with Mrs. Fort & thence walk & ride to Jabez Rhodes.

Thursday, June 8 My Niece, Frances, and girls (Clara 18 & Estella 14) take me to Harvey Wright's, her Father's. In afternoon, we go out to John Wright's & call at Eva Wright's, Joe's widow's. John's health poor. Stay at Harvey's.

Friday, June 9 Call at Ed. Frazier's, John McKee's, D. Kirk's, and Thos. Wright's. Go in afternoon with Harvey to Knightstown & thence to Richmond. Call at D.K. Zeller's an hour and at Allen Harris' a half hour. Reach Dayton at 6:00.

Saturday, June 10 At home. Kiracofe called in the forenoon. Wrote some, etc.

Sunday, June 11 Was at Children's service at Linden Avenue (Baptist) Church. At home the rest of the day.

Monday, June 12 At home forenoon & at Graybill's reading proofs for *Conservator.* Went to "Town" afternoon, paid taxes, etc.

Tuesday, June 13 At home. At P.O. & Called at Young's & paid a dollar I had borrowed the day before, to pay on Lorin's tax which proved more than was expected.

Thursday, June 15 At home. Bp. Wm. Dillon called in the evening.

Saturday, June 17 At home. Went to Brookville in this

county. Staid at John Zehring's.

Sunday, June 18 Went in the afternoon to Hamiel's, near Dodson, and had supper there. Stay at John Zehring's.

Monday, June 19 Came home on 6:15 train. Read proofs. See Nelson at Rev. C.H. Kiracofe's, 119 N. Summit Street. Went to town after noon. Called at Wm. Dillon's forenoon and evening.

Tuesday, June 20 At home all day. Wrote letters. Call at Lorin's an hour in the evening. Bishop William Dillon starts to the Pacific Coast at 9:00 A.M.

Friday, June 23 Call at Kiracofe's in the evening about 6:00.

Sunday, June 25 called at the Boulevard Congregational Sabbath School and at Grace M.E. Church Communion, in the forenoon.

Wednesday, June 28 Work five hours on editing the Discipline at my house, with Prof. C.H. Kiracofe.

Thursday, June 29 At home. Work on editing the Discipline three hours with C.H. Kiracofe.

Friday, June 30 At home. Work an hour on Classification of Discip. Rev. M.F. Keiter and Eva came about 4:00.

Saturday, July 1 At home. Mrs. E. Dillon's alarm, and She arranges to go away. She was alarmed lest ex-Sheriff Snyder, her lover, should try to kill Minnie.

Sunday, July 2 Hear Rev. M.F. Keiter pr. at 10:23, "Go forward." Afternoon 4:23, hear E.C. Simpson, W. Hale, Rev. Willits speak at Association Hall on Independence day. Hear W.S. Streete pr. 7:30, 1 Cor. 13:1-13.

Saturday, July 8 Go on 6:45 train via Hamilton, O., to Liberty, Ind. Stay at Hotel.

Sunday, July 9 Go to Cath. Stanton's. Call at Aaron Filer's to See Chas. Filer. Walk to Danl Koerner's. Stay there.

Monday, July 10 Call at Water's. Dine at Samuel.Harbine's. Visit Lizzie Brookbanks. Return to Koerner's. Lodge there.

Tuesday, July 11 Go via Carl (Roseburg) to Clinton Brattain's. Dine there. Go to Chas. Paddack's & thence to Liberty. Stay at Hotel. Call an hour on Chas Filer.

Wednesday, July 12 Go on 6:45 tr to Glenwood. *Laura takes me to Lucinda Moor's, my sisterinlaw's. I lodge at Chas. Steven's. *Laura Winchell is my niece.

Thursday, July 13 Go to F.N. Boen's; dine. Go thence to Glenwood. Stay at Austin Winchell's. Call at Harry Winchell's.

Friday, July 14 Go on 8:00 tr. to Indianapolis and thence to Terre Haute. Stay at Prof. Wm. H. Wiley's. Walter (27) had just brought his bride home from Mt. Pleasant, Pa. Catharine (22). Their Mother Cath Eliza my cousin is 50.

Saturday, July 15 Went on 10:00 train to Sanford. Went with Mr. Piker to Charlie Holdaway's. Dined, and they took me to New Goshen. Stay at N.F. Minnick's.

Sunday, July 16 Pr. at 10:30, Sch. house, Ps. 95:3. "Great King." Dine at Wright's & Mrs. Maria Hay's. Awhile at Noah F. Minnick's. Pr. at 8:00, Ex. 28:34. Stay at Minnick's.

Monday, July 17 Minnick takes us to Vake E. Houston's. His (H's) fatherinlaw, John Russell there. They live a mile from St. Bernice or Jonestown.

Tuesday, July 18 Went to Jas. Ammerman. Dine there. Aft. call at Wiley Jones. Supper at Mary Jones. Preach at 8:00, Gal. 4:4. Stay at Ammerman's.

Wednesday, July 19 Go to Jas K. Chapman's. Stay that day. Supper at Mrs. Margt. Jones'. Pr. Heb. 13.14. Stay at Ammerman's.

Thursday, July 20 Chapman takes Small & self to Vermillion. Dine at Jas. T. Vansickel's. Pr. at 8:00, "I Suffer & reign." Supper & lodging at Phebe Trogden's. Mrs. Marg. Stubb's there.

Friday, July 21 Call at Rev. Kershner's. Dine at Marg. Stubbs'. Go on 10:26 train to Kansas Stn. Go on Livery rig to Westfield. Call at Wm. Bussarts. Stay at Thos. W. Berkley's.

Saturday, July 22 Dine at John Sloan's. He takes us to Isaac L. Brown's, 11/2 m. north-west of town. Stay there.

Sunday, July 23 Call at Bussart's. Pr. at 10:30, Hebr. 11:26. Dine at Berkley's. Call at Geo. Reinoehl's, and lunch. Call at H. Snyder's. Pr. at 8:00, Matt. 13:44. Stay at Berkley's.

Monday, July 24 Awake at 2:00. Start at 3:00. H. Snyder takes me, with Sloan's rig, to Kansas. Take 6:15 tr. to Indianapolis. See Henry Murphy, and his sisters, Phoebe Tucker and Lizzie Orin & his brotherinlaw, Carter at depot. Arrive at home at 4:00.

Tuesday, July 25 Board Meeting for Pub. House at 10:00. Adjourn at 4:00 p.m. Bishop H. Floyd and Rev. Wm. Miller dine with us.

Thursday, July 27 See Young 5 minutes. Get ready for trip east. Go on 6:05 tr. via Xenia, Columbus, Belleair, etc. Sleep 4 hours.

Friday, July 28 Reach Harper's Ferry about 2:00 p.m. Go on freight. Sup at Winchester. Stop at hotel at Harrisonburg, Va., 3 hours.

Saturday, July 29 Go on 5:00 morn. train to Ft. Defiance. Walk to Isaac Hoover's. Breakfast there. Boy takes me to Olivet Church. "Genius" Orebaugh. Dine at Jonas Daggy's on Freemason Creek. Qr. Conference in Afternoon. J.H. Nelson pr. at 8:00, Jonah. Sup at Daggy's. Lodge J. Daggy's.

Sunday, July 30 Pr. at Olivet & dedicate church, after raising over $190.00. Text: Matt. 5:12. Dine on the ground with M. Knott's family. J.K. Nelson pr. at 3:00. Sup at Markwood Knott's. I pr. at 8:00, Matt. 1:23. Stay at Jonas F. Daggy's. Rev. J.E. Hott, pastor, talks sometime to me.

Monday, July 31 Dine at Markwood Knott's. Sup & lodge at Jonas F. Daggy's. Had much talk that day. Call

at Mother Daggy's & dine there. Go with W. H. Showalter to his house 2.00 ms. away. His wife is Abram Huffman's daughter. Son is Baldwin; daughter [rest is blank]

Wednesday, August 2 Went to the romantic Kiracofe farm. Six preachers raised there. Also to Stribbling Springs. Showalter takes me to John Baylor's. Pr. at Jerusalem Chapel at 8:00, 1 Cor. 1:23. Stay at Baylor's.

Thursday, August 3 Baylor takes me to John H. Stotamayer's, 2 ms. from Spring Hill. Dine & sup there. His son John takes me to Spring Hill. Pr. at 8:00, Mal. 3.1-4. Stay at J.T. Ewing's with Rev. A.B. Lilly of N. Chi. Conference.

Friday, August 4 Dine at J.E. Hott's. Afternoon, go to "Meyerhoeffer's Store". Out of the way. Stay at Michael J. Henkle's.

Saturday, August 5 Call at Michael Meyerhoeffer's store. At putting up tent both forenoon & afternoon. Dine, sup, & lodge at M.J. Henkle's.

Sunday, August 6 Pr in the tent 40 X 60 ft at 10:30, in Grove, Ps. 92:8. Dine at Jas. Meyerhoeffer's—hard of hearing—son-in-law of Michael Meyerhoeffer's. M.E. S.S. in afternoon. Hooks Supt. Rev. A.B. Lilly pr. at 3:00, Prov. 3:7. I pr. at 8:00, Matt. 19:27. Sup & lodge at J. Frank Hulvah's, 1 1/2 ms. north.

Monday, August 7 Go to Harrisonburg and take 8:14 tr. to Harper's Ferry. Go on via Cumberland, to Pittsburg, & Columbus. Arrive at C. at 3:55 next morning. Saw Rev. C.W. Miller on train. (Bros. Hott, Lilly & Halvay took me to Harrisonburg.)

Tuesday, August 8 Go on 7:15 tr via Springfield to Dayton. Reach home soon after 9:00, A.M. Found all well. Dine at Lorin's. Call at Keiter's Office & Store and at Bp. Dillon's and J.K. Graybill's. Arrange papers, etc.

Wednesday, August 9 At home straightening up files, writing letters, etc. Went to town in forenoon. Got my watch with new spring. Lorin & Netta Called in the eve. Wrote late.

Thursday, August 10 called at W. Dillon's and went to town. Ex. Committee meets at Kiracofe's at 7:00 eve.

Friday, August 11 At home writing. Lorin called in the evening.

Saturday, August 12 Called at Kiracofe's an hour & at Keiter's Office.

Sunday, August 13 At home. Heard Rev. W.E. Streete pr. morning and evening.

Wednesday, August 16 Went to depot; disappointed about train. See Young. No ans. in U.S. Case. Write letters. Go on 3:25 tr. to Salamanca, N.Y. Heavy rain.

Thursday, August 17 At 6:00 arrive at Salamanca, N.Y. Train at 8:00 to Carleton, 9:45 to Bradford; 11:00 to Custer City. Dine at "Hotel". Conference (Erie) at 2:00. Supper at Spencer Tibbit's & lodging. R.H. Sickler pr. at 8:00. Children: Annie Tibbits, 20.

Friday, August 18 Conference continued, and business progresses well. I pr at 8:00, Matt. 19:27, to a full house. Some rain. Board as usual.

Saturday, August 19 Conference. Luce and Butterfield elected pres. elders. Sta. Com. met at Tibbits; W.R. Hodge pr. at 8:00. Large and enthusiastic audience. Business closed. I board as usual.

Sunday, August 20 I pr. John 16:13, and ordain Hodge. Dine at Frazee Griffin's, 2 miles North-east. Rev. N.R. Luce pr. at 8:00, Ps. 23d. Sacramental service followed. Stay at Tibbit's.

Monday, August 21 Excursion to Kinzna Bridge 18 ms South. Meeting on the banks of the creek. Dine at Depot. Lecture at the Grove, on Palestine. Return at 4:00. Bridge 2,000 ft long; 202 ft. high; 40,000,000 of iron in it. Erected in 1882. I stay at Griffin's.

Tuesday, August 22 Stay at Griffins till 11:30. Dine at J.C. Young's near by. Mrs. Y. is Griffin's sister. Their children: Frazee 20; daughters 12, 14. Son 9. Y. takes me to Bradford. Fail to see Judge Ward. Go thence to W. Salamanca. Lodge at Rev. T.J. Butterfield's. Rev. Church & Jennie Rand live there.

Wednesday, August 23 Go on 9:00 tr. to Burbank, Ohio. Lunch at Meadvillw at 12:00. Arrive at Burbank at 5:15, and walk 1 1/2 m to Hiram Whitmore's. Supper there. Mrs. Eliz. A. Olmstead pr. at 8:00, "Set for tower." Stay at Hiatt's, near the Church.

Thursday, August 24 Rose early and bathed as usual. Conference at 9:00. Board at Hiatt's.

Friday, August 25 Conference continued. Dine at Showalter's. Afternoon, J. Excell was elected P.E. Mrs. E.A. Olmstead and John Gonser were received into Conference. Stationing Committee met at Hiatt's at 7:00. Sec'y H.J. Becker pr. at 8:00. I stay at Hyatt's. [the "y" in Hyatt appears in the text]

Saturday, August 26 Conference continues and Closes at 5:00, Aft'n. I pr. at 8:00 full house. Tit. 2:14. Stay at Hiatt's

Sunday, August 27 Morning meeting at the Church and at the grove. I pr. in the grove at 10:30, Heb. 11:26 last clause. Dine with Bro. Marks on the ground. Dr. H.J. Becker preached at 3:00. S.S. Anniversary at 2:00. J. Lemasters, and [blank] spoke. I sup at Judson Knapp's. Becker lectures at 8:00. Stay at Hiatt's.

Monday, August 28 Go to Creston with Rev. E.R. Kyle. Train for Dayton is 2 hs. late. Reach Dayton at 12:30. Went to dentist's after dinner. Got spectacles at A.B. Reeves. After supper, went to Ex. Com. meeting at 7:00 at M.F. Keiter's. Called at Young's a minute.

Tuesday, August 29 Went to Cottrill's and got Katie a trunk. Went to the bank to A.B. Reeves, etc. Called at Bishop Wm. Dillon's two hours. Was up till 12:30 packing, etc. for my trips.

Wednesday, August 30 Go on 7:00 tr via Union City to North Grove, Ind. Dine & sup at Anda Rank's. Conference (White River) opens at 2:00. Full attendance. Rev. W.A. Oler pr. 7:30, Ps. 37:37. I lodge at T.R. Jones', a Merchant's.

Thursday, August 31 Conf. continued. Rev. J. Selig and wife dine at Jones' with me. M.F. Keiter came. Chart examinations. I preside awhile. Board at Jones. I pr. at 7:30, Titus 2:14.

Friday, September 1 Talk with Rust at Thomas R. Jones. Go on 8:48 tr. to Marion. Write letters. Go on 2:53 tr. to Elkhart, Ind. Sup & lodge at Rev. C.E. Kidder's on State Street. Rev. Samuel Heininger pr at 8:00, Isa. 26:3. I stay at C.E. Kidder's, 404 State Street. Daughters: Maud 21, Mildred 19.

Saturday, September 2 St. Joseph Conf. continues its session—H.T. Barnaby presiding. I dine with Bp. Barnaby at Bro. H.W. Fisher's. Conf. continues till about 5:00. Sup at C.E. Kidder's. I Pr at 8:00, Titus 2:13. I stay at Geo. E. Luke's, 4 rods east. He formerly a Radical, Barnaby's home there three years ago.

Sunday, September 3 Went to Kidder's & arranged. At speaking meeting. Bishop H.T. Barnaby pr. at 11:00, Acts 26:16-18. Dine at Kidder's, as usual. Call aft'n at Luke's. Supper at H.W. Fisher's. Bp. Barnaby pr. at 7:00, 1 Pet. 5:4. Raised $57.02 in the day. Stay at Kidder's.

Monday, September 4 Call at the post-office and get card from Dillon. Stay at Kidder's all day. Bp. Barnaby, after spending the day at Albert Brubaker's on Kinsey Street, stays also at Kidder's. Rev. A.G. Johnson & wife also continue there.

Tuesday, September 5 Go on 11:10 tr. to Toledo. Write letters at depots. Go on 9:00 tr to Burgoon, Ohio. Stay at Rev. A.J. Burkett's.

Wednesday, September 6 Go to Depot & thence call at Rev. D.O. Tussing's. Dine at Mrs. E. Webster's, my conference home. Call at A. J. Burkett's. Sup & Lodge at Webster 's. I pr. at 7:30, Isa. 40.3-5. Stay at Webster's.

Thursday, September 7 Session of Sandusky began at 9:00 morn. I took dinner at Rev. A.J. Burkett's with Bros. Becker and J. Garns. Business progressed well. Sup & lodge at Webster's. Rev. H.J. Becker pr. at 7:45, Matt. 11:28. The house was crowded.

Friday, September 8 Conference continued. In afternoon,

seven are licensed to preach. Woman's Mis. As. women occupy the evening at 7:45. Miss Mary Mullen, and Mrs. Gabels and Mowry & myself occupy the evening. Mrs. Pres. Bowman raises $230.00, on Life Members & life directors. Board at Webster's.

Saturday, September 9 Conference continued. Stationing Com. finished at 8:30. Dine at Wm. Shale's, 1 m. s. Conference closed at 3:30. Supper at Daniel Garn's with a dozen other ministers. Rev. H. Akers pr. at 7:45, 1 John 1:7, on "Fellowship." P.O. Big Prairie, Ohio. I stay at Webster's.

Sunday, September 10 I pr. at 10:30, 1 Tim. 4:16. Ordain G.W. Coss. Dine at Hosford's. Call at Burkett's. Sup at Webster 's. Miss Mary Mullen pr. at 7:00, Acts 18:17, "Galio" Sacramental service. Stay at Webster's.

Monday, September 11 Call at D.O. Tussing's and A.J. Burkett's. Go on 7:30 tr to Lima and thence Dayton. Reach home at 1:00. Call at Winter's Bank; Young's 10 min.; at Tizzard's. Look over Accts. etc. Call at Bishop Wm. Dillon's in the evening.

Tuesday, September 12 At home. Call at Conservator Office, 112 S. Broadway Street & at Graybill's. Got my teeth plate at 12:00 at Dr. Wm. E. Tizzard's. Write in the afternoon. Call at Lorin's in the evening.

Wednesday, September 13 Start on the 7:05 tr. to Mackinaw Crossing at Greenville & to Rockford, Ohio, & Auglaize Conference at Pleas. Grove Church, 3 ms. from R. Dine at a restaurant at Rockford, Ohio. Go out to Pleasant Grove with Wm. Hill. Session of conference. Supped and home at J.D. Spitler's. Rev. S.L. Livingston pr. at 7:30, Ps. 10.4.

Thursday, September 14 Conference continued. Well attended. Dr. H.J. Becker came at 2:30. Dinner, supper, & lodging at Spitler's. Dr. Becker pr. at 7:30, Mark 9:8. House closely packed. He took supper at Spitler's.

Friday, September 15 Conference continued. Dined at Frederick Hill's 1 m. south of the church. Rev. Wm. Miller & Rev. Raney G. Montgomery were elected pres. elders in the afternoon. Stationing committee met at J.D. Spitler's at 6:45. Rev. W. Dillon pr. at 7:30, Rev.

11:1,2. Raised $30.00 on outfit, Scare on rain.

Saturday, September 16 Conference continued. Dine at Rev. W.H. Conner's, 2 3/4 m. south-east. Conference closed at 5:20. Supper & lodging at Spitler's. Rev. C.L. Culbertson pr. at 7:30, Phil. 4:19.

Sunday, September 17 I pr. in the grove 20 rods south at 10:30, 2d Tim. 4:2, after a lively "conference" meeting. I with Revs. Wm. Miller, Dillon, etc., dine with Rev. W.H. Conner's in the grove. S.S. Anniversary at 3:00. J. Vian, Robt. Montgomery, & W. Dillon speak. I pr. in M.E. Church at Rockford at 7:00; stay at Wm. Pontius. Rev. Carr pastor.

Monday, September 18 Go on 7:00 tr via Carlisle to Dayton in time to see Katie start to Oberlin College; Edith and Annia Pineo also go. Dine & sup at home. Bank money & see Young three minutes. At home the rest of the day. Katie has always been a good girl for her chance. The Lord bless her.

Tuesday, September 19 Dine & Sup at Lorin's. Call at M.F. Keiter's, J.K. Graybill's and C.H. Kiracofe's. Write letters. Little else of note, except letter from Knupp & answer. Proposition to Nollie Prosegni, on condition. I answer with some spirit.

Wednesday, September 20 At home. Write Letters. Board, after the breakf. at Lorin's. Call at Keiter's office & at Becker's & Rebecca Davis'.

Thursday, September 21 At home. Write letters. Bro. M.L. Oler of Labette County, Kansas called. Mary Pinneo came over so disturbed about the girls' rooms at Oberlin. They had brushed up our house in the forenoon—the Pinneo's.

Friday, September 22 At home all day. Am writing as usual. Prof. C.H. Kiracofe called. It rained nicely in the afternoon. Wrote an article in the evening for the *Conservator*.

Saturday, September 23 Finished rewriting the article for the Conservator. Called at Kiracofe's. After dinner, call at Keiter's office. Went to post-office to mail a book to Cath.

Sunday, September 24 Preached at School St. Church at 10:30, 2 Cor. 13:5. At home the rest of the day. Spent the evening at Lorin's.

Monday, September 25 Went to town in the afternoon. Called at Young's. Sent $22.26 tax to A.D. Crooks, Iowa. Call at Keiter's and at Graybill's. Wrote letters.

Tuesday, September 26 Send Cath. $30. Call at Graybill's. Call at Keiter's forenoon & in afternoon give him the Gen. Conf. Journal, etc. Wrote letters.

Wednesday, September 27 Go on 9:20 train via Xenia & Columbus to Basil. Dine at J. Everhart's. Lost purse in morn. & had 25 cts when I reached Basil. Went on 4:38 train to Junction City & thence with Geo. H. Folk to Thos. Middaugh's. H. Rev. Wm. Armstrong pr. at 7:00, Jm. 11:39. Sup at Middaugh's, & lodge there. Quite a cool night.

Thursday, September 28 Scioto An. Conference opened at 9:00. Good attendance. Business progressed well. Rev. M.F. Keiter came in afternoon & pr. Jas. 4.8 at 7:00. I board at Middaugh's. In afternoon, G.W. Walton's case excited the wisdom of the conference. Walton made effort to escape investigation.

Friday, September 29 Conference continued. Good progress. G.W. Walton bids us farewell. J. Hoffhines and B.W. Mason were elected pres. elders. I dine at "Aunt" Lydia Goble's. Stationing Com. meets at 6 1/2 at T. Middaugh's, Rev. J. Everhart pr. well, at 7:00. Keiter raises $159.00 on pub. outfit. Stay at Middaugh's.

Saturday, September 30 Conference continued. Dine at David Middaugh's. W.M.A. meet at 3:00. Adjourned about 5:00. I pr. at 7:00, Isa. 12:1. Tearing speaking meeting followed. I stay at Thos. Middaugh's.

Sunday, October 1 I pr. at 10:30, Acts 20:20. Pub. Col. $68.77. J. Guyn ordained. Dine at Gregg's (Aunt Lydia Goble's). S.S. Anniversary in aft. 3:00. I was one that spoke. Supper at Thos. Middaugh's and lodging. Pr. at 7:00, John 6:55. Spoke 45 min. Sacrament & farewell.

Monday, October 2 Many going home. I go to David Middaugh's and dine. He takes me to Junction City. Call at B.W. Mason's. Stay with several of our people at Cent. Ohio Depot an hour. Write letter. Go on 4:00 Balt. tr. to Newark. Go to Penn. Depot. Write letters, etc. Go on 9:20 tr. for Pittsb. & Harrisburg.

Tuesday, October 3 Reach Pittsburgh at 4:30. Lunch at Altoona at 8:30. Reach Harrisburg abt. 11:15. Reach Chambersburg at 3:00. Lunch & sup & lodge at Rev. John Fohl's. Attend 3:30 Meeting at Rink Opera House. Rev. G. Wilbur Chapman, the evangelist of Albany, N.Y. Text: [blank] Text at night (7:00) Eccl. 4:12. He leaves on the train at 9:00. P. P. Bilhorn singer.

Wednesday, October 4 Stay at Rev. J. Fohl's till after dinner. Arrange for conference on Committees, etc. Go to P. Nicklas' Store, then with Huber to Gen. Office Cumb. Val. R'y & get clerical permit, and apply on Penn. lines East of Pittsburgh. Sup at P. Nicklas'. Pr. at King St. Ch. at 7:30, Rom. 4:16. Stay at Rev. B.G. Huber's.

Thursday, October 5 Go via J. Fohl's to Rev. A.H. Shank's; dine there. Go in afternoon with Isaac Hoover to Salem Church, to session of Pa. Conf. Session opened at 2:00. Supper at Mrs. Emma C. Plough's. Rev. S. Diller pr. at 7:15 a good sermon, Mark 8:36. Stay at Plough's. She is Rev. J.M. Bishop's daughter.

Friday, October 6 Conference progressed finely. Afternoon A.H. Shank was re-elected pres. elder. Stationing com. met at Mrs. E.C. Plough's at 6:00. I dine, sup and lodge at Mrs. E.C. Plough's. Rev. John Fohl, aged 80, pr. a good sermon at 7:30, Luke 22.62. Rev. P. O. Wagner lodges with me.

Saturday, October 7 Rise at 5:00. Wagner and Seippel leave for early train. Conference proceeded. I dine with Rev. John Fohl at John Rotz'. Closed the session at 4:00. Supper at George Bolinger's, 1 m. east. Rev. B.G. Huber pr. Matt. 19:27, an able, eloquent sermon. I stay at Mrs. Plough's.

Sunday, October 8 Arose early. Pr. at 10:00, Acts 20:20, 1 1/2 hs; Pub. Coll. 36 dol. Ordained J.S. Solenberger, J.C. Coulson, J.A. Burkholder & W. R. Burkholder. Dine at Mrs. E.C. Plough's. Sab. Sch. Anniversary at 3:00. L.A. Wickey, B.G. Huber, etc. spoke. I sup at Mrs. J.M. Bishop's. Pr. at 7:30, Rom. 1:14—mission sermon &

$139.00 in subs. and cash. Stay at Isaac Hoover's, 2 ms from Chambersburg. His father-in-law Schlichter.

Monday, October 9 Bro. I. Hoover takes me to Chambersburg. Call at Nicklas' store, at Gen. Office of Cumb. Val. Ry. and get half-fare pass on Penn. R'y lines east of Pitts'bg. Go on 9:09 tr. to Harrisburg. Go on 3:25 tr. for Pit[t]sburg & Columbus. Reach former about 11:10; the latter at 5:10, home at 10:30, to-morrow.

Tuesday, October 10 Reach home at 10:30. Board at home. Go to bank & call at Young's two minutes & at Keiter's. Paid to Y. all claims. Call at Lorin's afternoon & evening. At home after 8:30, eve. Boys (W. & O.) at home.

Wednesday, October 11 At home. Called at Young's 20 min. in afternoon. Write letters. Paid Becker's draft to Keiter, $91.00+, for Penn. Sent drafts $8.00 to A.P. Barnaby, & $12.03 to W.H. Clay. Dinner & supper at Lorin's.

Thursday, October 12 At home. Wrote some. Arranged files of papers. Boarded at home. In afternoon, wash up three pair of pantaloons in cold water without soap & sponge my old vests. Boys at home, eve. Some rain in the night.

Friday, October 13 Call aftn. at Keiter's and Kiracofe's. Dine & sup at Lorin's. Cloudy day with some rain in the afternoon. Boys at home all evening. I finish arranging papers.

Saturday, October 14 At home. Spend the day cleaning up the wood-house, washing up things. Becker called in the afternoon. Saw Horace Stokes at Lorin's. Attend the Mission Executive Meeting at Rev. H.J. Becker's. Boys try gasoline in the stove for fuel with some success.

Sunday, October 15 Preach at School St. Church at 10:23, Matt. 7:24. Read & wrote in the afternoon. Saw Corbett & wife at Lorin's in the evening. Heard Rev. M.F. Keiter preach at 7:30, West End Church. Read in Newton on the prophecies after coming home.

Monday, October 16 Called at Keiter's office and bought, Nast's Com. of Matthew & Mark ($1.00) Parallel versions of New Testament (75 c); Finney's Sys. Theology, (75 c); Wine's commentaries (40); Wesley's Notes (40) King's Primitive Church (20); Maury's Phys. Geog. of Sea (20). Wrote letters to Reuchlin and others. Made out deed for Nicholas, on a Penn. church.

Tuesday, October 17 At home. Called at Keiter's office for postal stamps. Arrange library, etc. Arrange collection of stones, etc. Burn up old, useless rags, etc. Wrote letters.

Wednesday, October 18 At home. Writing and shaping up affairs.

Thursday, October 19 Fixing up and getting ready to go away. Afternoon, I go to town, pay Young $200.00 on U.S. Case. Go on 5:32 tr. to Bellefontiane. Put up at House.

Friday, October 20 After breakfast called at Judge Lawrence's. A short conference with him, as he had an argument in court there, that morning. At 12:45, go on to Clyde. Bought rubbers, collar, and lunch there. Wrote letters at Bellefontaine & lunched there. Go on 6:15 tr. to Oberlin. Stay at Miss Clark's, where Katharine boards.

Saturday, October 21 Go with Catharine and visit the Chapel, Halls, etc., and afterwards with her and Annie Pinneo to visit further those places. Stay at Clark's aftern till 4:00. Go on 4:37 tr to Lindsay, Ottawa Co., Chester Yeagle takes me out to his mother's and to Church at the Schoolhouse. Rev. D.O. Tussing pr. II Cor. 6:13. I stay at Yeagle's.

Sunday, October 22 Love-feast at 9:30. I pr. at 10:30, Ps. 122.1, and raise $584.00 on Bethel Church, 3 1/2 m. North of Lindsey. Dine at Jacob Overmeyer's with Tussing & Lash. I pr. at 7:20, Luke 24:46. Dunbar spoke with much ability. I stay at Mrs. Leah Yeagle's. Dunbar also staid there & Mrs. Mallet & Mrs. Best from Toledo. Trustees gave me $20.

Monday, October 23 Go to Lindsey & thence on 8:55 train to Toledo. Thence at 10:00 to Chicago. Lunch at Elkhart. Reach Chicago about 6:45. Read much on the way. A Mr. Piper (Ice Co) conducts me from 22d St. crossing to Mrs. J. Soper's, 2732 S. Park Ave., where I find lodging. I write letter to Cath. & card to Lorin.

Tuesday, October 24 At Columbian Exposition Visit the State Buildings of Iowa, New Hampshire, Mass., Connect., N.Y., Penn., Vt., Louis., Ill., Me., Mo., Cal., Minn., Col., Wash., S. Dak., & those of Germany, France, Ceylon, Norway. Also, briefly the Art Galleries; and the Electrical Department an hour, and, ou Electrical Department an hour, and outside the Exp., the Manitoba. Lodge at Soper's.

Wednesday, October 25 Visit the State Buildings. Other States: Nebraska, Kansas, Arkansas, Texas, Kentucky, W. Virginia, Utah, Montana, Ceylon, Costa Rica, Guatamala, Columbia, Government Fisheries. Got to lodgings at 7:30. Read till 10:45. Slept well.

Thursday, October 26 Visit State buildings of Ohio, Illinois, Indiana. Rode on Intermural railroad an hour. Next visited the Forestry Building. Redwood plank, 16 5/12 ft X 12 3/4 ft X 5 in., polished woods, Mammoth Generator, Sanitarium, Gorillas, busts, Cuvier, Buffon, Linnaeus, Agazziz, Darwin, Antiquities. Leather Dep Belts 1 1/2 X 10,000 ft. Belt 12 ft wide. Elephants hide, & other buildings. Art gallery. Statues, pictures, etc.

Friday, October 27 Spent the day in Arts and Government building. Saw statues, oil painting, water colors, basreliefs; Belgic, French, Italian, Holland, Great Britain, Norway, Russia, Japan, etc. Government Mint, Big Tree, Aboriginal, Animals, birds reptiles, State dep. Interior, War Dep. Spent an hour after night in art. Rev . Went to Union depot and started at 9:00.

Saturday, October 28 Reach Richmond at 6:00; home at 9:05. Stay at home and Lorin's till 5:00. Call at Young's; not in. At home after 7:00. Found the boys burning gasoline in the base-burner.

Monday, October 30 At home. Called at Keiter's office & bought two books. Went to town in the afternoon. Did not see Young. At home in the evening reading & studying.

Tuesday, October 31 Get ready & to to Elida, Ohio on the 11:05 train. Rev. W.E. Strete had called at 10:00. Spent 3 1/2 hours at Lima. Supper at Rev. C.S. Johnson's.

Rev. S.L. Livingston pr. at 7:30, Matt. 22:42. Stay at I.R. Spear's with Livingston. Read after the rest retire.

Wednesday, November 1 I teach two lessons in systematic theology. S.L. Livingston teaches two in Bible History. I preach at 7:00, Isa. 28:56. I dine at Spears', sup at Henry Kiracofe's, lodge at Isaac R. Spear's.

Thursday, November 2 I teach one lesson on Systematic Theology in forenoon. Lesson in logic and Pastoral Theology. I dine at S. Albert Stemen's. Supper at Spears' and lodging. Rev. Wm. E. Strete pr. at 7:00, Acts 20:24.

Friday, November 3 Call at Bremmeman's and at Henry Kiracofe's. Go on 9:40 tr to Delphos, & thence on 10:43 tr to Marion, Ind. See there Aaron Eubank, Revs. H.J. Ketner, and Z. McNew. Wait there 6 hours. Write some. Go on 8:04 tr to Fairmount. Stay at Hollingsworth's. Wm. Hall there.

Saturday, November 4 Staid at Hollingsworth's till 10:30. Ride to Ellis Wright's with Wm. Simons. Dine there. Ellis is away. Go to Wm. H.H. Reeder's. He at Marion. I look over the place. Wm. came at 6:00. I stay there.

Sunday, November 5 Go to Ellis Wright's. Thence to Salem to Sabbath school. Addressed the school 25 minutes on the ressurection. .Dine with Ellis Wright's, Wm. Reeder's & Robt. Reeder's at Oliver A. Glass's. Pr. at Fairmount U.B. Church at 7:00, Jude 20, 21. Stay at Rev. N.D. Wolfard's.

Monday, November 6 Go on 8:29 tr. to Jonesboro; & at Gas City, take 10:21 tr to Union City. Wait 2 1/2 hours, spent in reading & writing. Go on 2:15 tr. to Dayton. Reach home about 4:00. Spend the evening reading & writing.

Tuesday, November 7 Voted early and for all the Republican Candidates, except that I voted for Prohibition senator. Spent the day largely in adjusting the presses, sorting clothes, etc. Up till midnight. The election proved a great Republican victory.

Wednesday, November 8 At home reading and writing. Go to town in afternoon. Saw Young 20 or 40 minutes on Exceptions to Liberal answer. Wrote letters in the

eve'g. Milton Jr's. birth-day. He gets picture-book from parents & three nice glass marbles from me.

Thursday, November 9 At home. Reading and writing. Saw Prof. C.H. Kiracofe and read Young's bill of exceptions to him.

Friday, November 10 Return bill of exceptions to Young at the courthouse. Reading and writing. Boys work on gas arrangements for stove in my room.

Saturday, November 11 At home till four 45/60 o'clock. Reading, writing & getting ready. Go on 4:45 train, which was an hour late, to Brookville. Stay at John Zehring's.

Sunday, November 12 Pr. at Olivet (New) Church at 10:30, Ps. 122:1, raise $176.95 & dedicate the church. I dine with Rev. A. Zehring's & get an Old German Bible of Chris. Crider's, bought by him at Bishop Andrew Zeller's sale. I pr. at Olivet at 6:30 Gal. 3.24. I lodge at George W. Warvel's a half mile north of Olivet.

Monday, November 13 Come home on 8:15 D. & U. tr., Rev. W.E. Streete having brought me to Brookville. At home the rest of the day reading and writing.

Wednesday, November 15 At home all day. Called at Publisher's Office & got copies of Gen. Conf. Minutes 1893 and Disciplines.

Thursday, November 16 At home forenoon.Went to Town Afternoon & got bed clothes $18.00. Sent Reuchlin a draft for $40.00. Called at Kiracofe's an hour in the evening. Saw Young one minute today.

Friday, November 17 At home. Reading, writing & fixing up my room. Letter from Wilberforce. Saw Kiracofe at Union Depot. Called to see Mrs. Kiracofe about African Mission.

Saturday, November 18 Went to town. Got a certificate of deposit for Keiter of $472.11 for Missions. Bought a pair of blankets, $6.25.

Sunday, November 19 Heard Rev. W.E. Streete pr. 10:30, at School St. Matt. 14.28. At home all day after calling a half hour at Keiter's 112 S. Broadway St., and arrange for him to pr. Hear M.F. Keiter at 7:00, Isa. 52:1, a good sermon.

Tuesday, November 21 Went to town; got Letter-box, lamp-shade, etc.

Wednesday, November 22 Boys clean up my study.

Thursday, November 23 At home. Write letters, read. Fix up my books, etc. Paid my board till next Wednesday, $10.00. Mrs. Kiracofe called to see about Small's claim.

Friday, November 24 At home. Coldest morning so far; 10 degrees above at sunrise.

Saturday, November 25 At home all day except a call at the boys' office, Keiter's Office and taking meals at Lorin's as usual. I wrote letters and an article for the Conservator. Ex. Com. of Publ. Board meets at Keiter's at 7:23.

Sunday, November 26 I Pr. at Sch. St. Church at 10:30, Rom. 1:1-10. Stay at home the rest of the day. The day was mild.

Wednesday, November 29 Began to tale meals at Mrs. Greenwood's. Boarders: Mr. and Mrs. Bruner and Harry, [blank] Landis.

Thursday, November 30 Thanksgiving Day. Turkey dinner at Mrs. Greenwood's. Called at Lorin's. Ex. Misson. Comm. meeting at Prof. C.H. Kiracofe's. Rev. I.M. Tharp lodges with me. Ex. Com. determined to open a Mission in Impeth, W. Africa.

Friday, December 1 At home all day. Finish arranging files of papers, which has occupied about two days, this week. A pretty sharp day. Bp. Floyd & Tharp with me in the forenoon.

Saturday, December 2 Go on C.H. & D. tr. to Tontogany, Rev. G.W. Coss met me & took me to Bro. C.W. Thomas'. Supper there. Pr. at Union Hill Church at 7:00, 1 Cor. 15.29. Stay at Rev. G.W. Coss's. Children Edward 17, Henry 13, Bertha 11, Myrtle 7, Alta 5. Stormy eve.

Sunday, December 3 Pr. at 11:00, Ps. 48:12, 13. Raise subs. $310.00. Dine at Rev. G.H. Coss'. Pr. at 7:00, Rom. 7:13. Stay at Rev. G.H. Coss's.

Monday, December 4 Rev. Coss takes me to town. Too late for train. Wait till 4:12. Dine at Restaurant. In morn called at C.W. Thomas'. Season of prayer. Received 4.52 - 3.70 = 82 cts.

Wednesday, December 6 Wash bed clothes in forenoon.

Thursday, December 7 At home. Letter from W.H. Ely, Saying Chambersburg sisters will turn Danville mission over to us. Call at Kiracofe's after dinner. Wrote an article in the evening for Conservator, "Aggression the Watchword."

Friday, December 8 Wrote W.H. Ely and letters to our children. Also wrote cards to subscribers to Shaw's Book on Prayer, etc., etc.

Saturday, December 9 Got Wilberforce's letter to D.K.F. Called at Prof. Kiracofe's. Wrote a letter to D.F. Wilberforce. Went to "town" called at Young's 20 minutes. Went to Carlisle on 5:00 tr & thence to Germantown. Pr. at U.B. Church at 7:00 1 Cor. 15:29. Stay with Montg. at Rev. W. Stretes.

Sunday, December 10 Call at M. Thomas' a few minutes & at Levi Zehring's. Montgom. Pr at 10:30. We dine at Levi Zehring's. I pr. at 7:00, Hebr. 9:13. Stay at Zehring's. Saw Chas. Coulthard & wife, Jo. Thomas & wife, Mrs. Swartzel, & her sister Lizzie Long, etc.

Monday, December 11 Call at Shem Thomas', father of the re-building enterprise; at M. Thomas', at Rev. P.Y. Gephart's. Walked to Miamisburg. Dine at a restaurant. Reach home at 2:00.

Tuesday, December 12 Busy as usual. Ordered a suit of clothes. In the evening, only William Miller came to the Board of publication meeting. I called at Keiter's to see the absent Board.

Wednesday, December 13 Rev. Wm. Miller spent an hour with me.

Thursday, December 14 Rev. S.W. Zeller called a few minutes.

Friday, December 15 Called at Kiracofe's afternoon to see abt form of transfer of Danville Mission, West Africa. Spent day in business writing. Mailed form of transfer.

Sunday, December 17 Hear Rev. M.F. Keiter pr. at 10:30, on "Oil in the Vessel." Breakfast and supper at home. Dine at Lorin's. Pr. at School St. at 7:00, Acts. 24, 25.

Monday, December 18 Went to town. Paid Charch $35.00 for my new suit of clothes. Sent cousin Frank as present a draft of $11.00. Apply for Clergymen's permits on D & U: C.C.C. & St. L., and Erie lines. Write letters, etc. Call at Keiter's several times.

Tuesday, December 19 Went to town; bought a book for little Milton Wright, Jr. Was sick in the evening & all night, with stomach and bowel trouble.

Wednesday, December 20 At home. Ordered two mattresses and they came four inches too narrow. Board of Publication to meet at Keiter's at 7:30. No quorum. I Was better, but not well by many degrees, to-day.

Thursday, December 21 Meeting of part of the Board of Trustees of the Printing Establishment at M.F. Keiter's, but not a quorum. Advise the enlargement of the Conservator to 16 pages; price $1.50. Katharine fails of connection at Toledo & gets home from Oberlin at 8:45, evening.

Friday, December 22 Yesterday, went to town criticized the Crayon and after amendment, took (about 4:00) to picture framer. Got Telegram, Yesterday, from the Mich. Supreme Court—victory & last night labored to get out the news. Mailed 86 letters after Midnight.

Saturday, December 23 Went to town in forenoon—mail some letters & a book to Helen. Still write many letters. In evening, send Crayon of Kath. L. to Reuchlin's, about 8:00.

Sunday, December 24 Hear Rev. Mr. Clemens pr. at 11:00, Luke 2:10, Christmas Sermon.

Monday, December 25 At home. Christmas gifts. Mine a type-writer stand. Breakfast at Lorin's, dine at Greenwood's, sup at home. Write a few letters. Mail books to E.W. Ransburg & J. Kenoyer. Children go to the lecture at Chris. Associ[ati]on Hall. I am very lame in the back to night. Dine at Greenwoods'. Sup at home.

Tuesday, December 26 At home forenoon writing, etc. Went to town Aft. 3:00, bought gold-washed silver spoons holder. Board at Lorin's.

Wednesday, December 27 Get breakfast and go on 6:00 Morn. train from Union Depot. Call at Zeller's at Richmond over an hour. Get off train at Dunreith (Crossing) and go thence to Hay's Station where Thomas, Jabez Rhoads, & Ed. Frazier meet me & take me to Harvey Wright's Golden Wedding.

Thursday, December 28 Geo. Poston & wife went home yesterday. Rhoda Williams and Son Earl go this morning. Leovicy Beaver remains. His children were all there yesterday. Thomas' wife, John's wife, and Dan's widow absent. Eight children, 14 gr. chil., & 6 gr. gr. Chil. I go to May's to 5:00—reach home at 9:10.

Friday, December 29 Busy all day & till after midnight, writing, arranging documents, etc. Got a copy of Mich. decision by mail. Took it to Kiracofe's & arranged to put it in the paper for next week. Board at Greenwood's from dinner on.

Saturday, December 30 Got a copy of Decision (another) at 9:00. Arranging papers all day. Meals at Greenwood's.

Sunday, December 31 Rise at about 6:00 morn. real time—not "standard," or false time. At home till evening. Hear Rev. E.E. Baker pr. at 7:30, John 19:22, On the Year 1893—Blessings: 1. Business depression, 2. Needs & Sympathy, 3. Congress of Religions, 4. Columbian Exposition. Meals at Mrs. Greenwood's. Went to bed at 12:05. Steam whistle blew at 12:00 "Standard Time."

Bishop's Assessments

Auglaize	$220
Sandusky	110
Ontario	125
East Ohio	110
Scioto	180
Pennsylvania	180
Erie	75
$1000	
White River	225
Indiana	65
Centr. Illinois	125
Rock River	190
Missouri	50
East Des Moines	55
Kansas	100
West Kansas	40
Arkansas Valley	65
Neosho	70
Illinois	25
1,000	
St. Joseph	86
N. Ohio	236
Michigan	176
N. Michigan	116
Wisconsin	41
Upper Wabash	66
Iowa	61
West Des Moines	66
Nebraska	86
Elkhorn	66
1000	

Conferences for 1893

1. Erie:—Britton's Run, Spartan'sburg, Glynden, Pa.
2. East Ohio:—Chosen by P.E.
3. Sandusky:—Bethel Church, 3 1/2 m E. of Elmore, O., Lindsey
4. Auglaize, Kirkwood, O.
5. Scioto: Liberty Chruch Chester Hill, Morgan Co., Ohio: Stockport, & Sharpburg—6 ms away
6. Pennsylvania, Greencastle
7. Virginia,
8. Ontario, Berlin, Ontario.

Traveling Expenses

To Custer City, Pa.	6.50
Return via Creston	6.50
Lunches	.40
Home	2.45
Burgoon	1.20
Home	1.20
To Rockford & ret.	2.20
To Junction City	2.50
To Chambersburg	9.65
To Dayton (45 cents lunch)	8.93
41.53	

Other Traveling

To White River N. Grove	1.75
To Elkhart, Ind.	1.85
Lunch	.10
To Burgoon (20 cts lunch)	1.85
To Clyde & Oberlin	2.50
To Lindsey	.75
To Toledo & Chicago	5.00
Home	4.60
Expense at Chicago	7.50
To Elida & lunch	1.30
To Fairmount	1.55
Lunches	.15

Bishop's Salary

Erie Confernece	$75.00
East Ohio &1.00 add	85.17
Sandusky	109.25
Auglaize	220.00
Scioto	188.62
Pennsylvania	115.00
Virginia	59.75
Ontario	82.26
	935.05

Indiana Supr. Court

Judge Coffey, McKabe, Hackney, Howard

Penn. Supr. Judges
Sterrett, Ch. Justice, Green, Williams, Dean, McCollum,
Mitchell, Thompson. Seven in all. Taken from Pittsb.
Daily Gazette Oct. 8, 1893.

Names for Churches
Hebron, Hopewell, Hermon, Gilead, Gideon, Gilboa,
Goshen, Gainus, Gilgal, Ebel, Eden, Emmaus, Etham,
Engedi, Eshchol, Beth, Bethel, Berea, Bozrah, Bethany,
Corinth, Carmel, Antioch, Arimathea, Jordan, Joppa,
Kidron, Lebanon, Moriah, Macedonia, Nineveh, Orion.
Olivet, Patmos, Ramah, Sharon, Shiloh, Siloam, Tabor,
Tekoah, Tadmor, Troas, Farmer Chapel, Whitcom
Chapel, Newcomer Chapel, Edwards Chapel, Davis
Chapel, Hadley Chapel

Headache Cure: Phenacetine, from 5 to 10 grains. J.N.
Free (immortal) 260 Smiths in Dayton—19 Johns &
22 Williams

Grippe Medicine: Benzoate Sodium

Wash Mixture
4 oz. of White Castila soap, 1 qt. of Boiling Water, Mix
& add when cold. 4 oz. of Amonia, 2 oz. of Alcohol, 2
oz. of Ether, 2 oz. of Glycerene.

1894

Monday, January 1 Weather clear. Thermometer Abt 65 degrees. I am now sixty-five years old. I enjoy life and work as well as I ever did. God has been very good to me. This is a snowless, mild sunshiny day. I sat up till New Year. Wrote for periodicals. Went to town after dinner—got Katharine Louise's Photographs. Meals at Mrs. Greenwood's.

Tuesday, January 2 Write article, "Michigan Court." Go to town & get some railroad permits, etc. & bid Catharine good-bye. In afternoon, go to town, pay City tax, etc. Call at the Office (Keiter's) at 7:00. Read Gov. McKinley's message. Board meals at Greenwood's.

Wednesday, January 3 Sent off many papers containing Decis. Mich. Supr. Court, to Atty's etc. Read & corrected proofs on the decision.

Thursday, January 4 Kiracofe called with a copy of C.B. Grant's dissenting opinion. H.J. Becker called in the afternoon. Spent evening in reading corrected proofs of Mich. Supr. Court decision.

Friday, January 5 Bro. Becker called just before noon. In Afternoon went to town. Saw Young ten minutes. In the evening I mailed tract-copies of decisions to attorneys, etc.

Saturday, January 6 At home writing, etc., in forenoon. Went to town after dinner & sent drafts: Catharine, $15 & $25, & to Funk & Wagnall's Co., $3.00. Called at Keiter's Office. Paid for board at Greenwood's, $4.05 to close of to-day.

Sunday, January 7 Hear at 10:30 at the Fourth Presbyterian Church Rev. C.H. Morehead preach John 3.30. At home reading the rest of the day. Board at Greenwood's.

Monday, January 8 At 10:00 at Ministerial meeting, Essay on "The Church and the World" by Benj. S. Stern. Comments by nearly all. Busy at home. Called at Kiracofe's in the evening.

Tuesday, January 9 At home all day. Wrote to Wilberforce, W. Africa. Was up till about midnight.

Thursday, January 11 At home all day except meals & brief calls at Publ. Office. Editor Kiracofe called at 5:30 & asked me to write an article for the Conservator.

Friday, January 12 Busy (very) till in the night. Wrote an article, "More on the Decision." Went to R.R. Offices. Got permits on D & U & C.C.C. & St. L. Sent for Balt. & Ohio.

Saturday, January 13 Finished Article. Wrote letters. Went to "town" at 5:00. Called at Lorin's at 8:00- 9:00, eve. Read papers, etc. and went to bed at 11:00.

Sunday, January 14 Heard Rev. H.J. Becker at 10:30, Acts 8:30-1, at School Street Church. Spent the afternoon in shaping Sermon Sketches. Evening heard Dr. Fee preach Acts 3.19, an excellent sermon.

Wednesday, January 17 Went to town. Saw Young ten minutes. Made various purchases. Got drafts for J.F. Croddy ($90.00) and for McNew & Sherk $4.12 each, etc. etc. Missionary Ex. Com. met at 4:00, Keiter's. Appropriated $333 1/3 dollars to Imperek Mission, West Africa. Wrote letters in evening.

Thursday, January 18 Bp. Floyd spent most of forenoon, & dined with me at Greenwood's. Spent afternoon and evening in close work. Many letters requesting funds.

Friday, January 19 At home. Rev. W.S. Strete called an hour in afternoon. Sent out 36 letters to-day. Wrote four more.

Saturday, January 20 At home in forenoon. Went to town afternoon. See Young five minutes. Saw dentist. Made a few purchases. At home in the evening.

Sunday, January 21 Pr. at School Street at 10:30, Heb. 7.25. At home the rest of the day till meeting. M.F. Keiter pr. at 7:30, Prov. 11.19. For perhaps six weeks, the weather has been so mild that I have not used an over-coat about town, day or night.

Tuesday, January 23 At home. Rainy. Went to School Street Church. Prof. Kiracofe pr. on doing all to God's glory with a good conscience. Good attendance and in-terest.

Wednesday, January 24 At home. It began to freeze (and snow) about 7:00, and grew colder all day, & at night. Spent the day largely in reading. Wrote a few letters.

Thursday, January 25 At home after being at the den-tists at 9:00.

Friday, January 26 At home writing, etc. Sent drafts, $7.00 to Funk & Wagnall's Co.; $1.00 Cincinnati Ga-zette; $5.00 to Katie.

Saturday, January 27 At home. Wrote some letters. Ar-ranged documents to file in the Ohio Supr. Court in Printing Establishment Case. Removed legal documents from Keiter's Office. For three mornings the ther. has indicated near 6 degrees below zero.

Sunday, January 28 At Home. Read much. Pulpit sketch in the evening. Called an hour at Lorin's.

Monday, January 29 Called at Young's in forenoon and left Briefs & Decisions to file in Printing Establishment suit. Did not see George Young.

Tuesday, January 30 Called at Young's. Saw George a quarter hour.

Friday, February 2 At home engaged as usual. Took over four additional copies of bound briefs to file.

Saturday, February 3 At home till 5:00 aftn. when I went to town. Saw Will Young a few minutes & Ans'd Davis (California) & Allen's telegram for name of a Notary.

Sunday, February 4 Breakfast at home. Pr. at Broadway "Christian" Church at 10:30, Ps. 48:11,12,13. At home till evening. Hear Rev. Mr. Randolph of Louisville, Ky. at 7:30, at Colored Baptist Church, Matt. 22:28. Un-learned, ignorant, yet some striking ideas, and dramatic eloquence.

Monday, February 5 At home except to town afternoon. Saw Young two minutes. Saw Reeves.

Tuesday, February 6 Went to town. Called at Matthias Lumber office & got bill for lumber.

Friday, February 9 At home. Mrs. A.B. Kiracofe called to see whether we had second-hand clothing for West Des Moines brethren.

Saturday, February 10 Went to town afternoon. Got spectacles, (bifocal) and spent an hour in the Public Li-brary.

Sunday, February 11 Went to Union Depot, to see train with Houk's Corpse, 3:40 late. Hear Rev. M. Wilson preach at First Pres. Church Hebr. 12:27. "Things —be shaken". Attend Houk's funeral at 3:00, at "Christ's Church" —Prot. Episcopal. Call at Rev. H.J. Becker's and hear him pr. at 7:00 at Sch. St. Ch., Luke 9:37.

Monday, February 12 A very snowy-rainy night followed by a rainy, snowy day. Called at Lorin's to see the Journal. Wrote a short notice of Hon. G.W. Houk's death & char-acter. Wrote a number of letters.

Thursday, February 15 Went to town. Saw Young 15 minutes. At home, except a few minutes at Lorin's. Wrote letters.

Friday, February 16 At home till noon. Did not go on Sandusky train to Tiffin, O., as I had intended.

Saturday, February 17 At home till 11:00. Go on C.H. & D. train to Deshler & thence to Bloomdale, Ohio. Revs. John Cronenberger, H.C. DeRhodes, and Bro. Lucas on train. Stop at J.S. Blair's. Supper and lodging there. Rev. J. Cronenberger pr. at 7:30, "There is no difference," a lively discourse.

Sunday, February 18 I Pr. at 10:30, Ps. 93:5, & raise $858.00 on the church. Dine at J.F. Smith's. Pr. at 7:00, Eph. 2:16. & raise $146.00 —$1,004.00 in all. I stay at J.S. Blair's. Preachers present, J.A. Ferguson, A.J. Burkett, H.C. DeRhodes, C. Cashley, J. Ridley, Walter, J. Cronenberger.

Monday, February 19 Go on 9:30 tr. via Tiffin home. Arrive about 7:30 p.m. Supper at home.

Tuesday, February 20 At home all day except brief calls at Lorin's & at Conservator Office. Board at home.

Thursday, February 22 At home all day reading and writing. I called at Lorin's & at Cons. Office. Fire at Broadway, near Fifth, Isaac Engle's dwelling.

Saturday, February 24 At home till night. Attend quarterly meeting at School Street. Pres. Elder R.G. Montgomery pr. at 7:30, Rom. 4:7,8. Quarterly Conf. followed.

Sunday, February 25 Heard Rev. R.G. Montgomery preach at 10:30, Heb. 10:7. Eucharist followed. Dr. H.J. Becker joined the class. Rev. H.J. Becker pr. at 7:00, Gen. 50:20. Revs. R.G. Montgomery and W.S. Strete stay with me to-night.

Monday, February 26 Rev. R.G. Montgomery lunched with me in my room. Young Troxel died yesterday and was buried to-day. They live on our street a few doors south of us.

Tuesday, February 27 Called at Rev. H.J. Becker's, and at Nicholas's near there to inquire after the Flenor children. Called at Conservator Office. Went to town. Saw Young a half-hour. Rev. Becker called about 6:00.

Wednesday, February 28 At home writing, reading, etc. Our Boys again at work on the rooms.

Thursday, March 1 At home. Spent much of the day hunting up & copying documents for Moses Taggart, Esq.

Friday, March 2 At home writing letters, etc. Rev.H.J. Becker called about an hour. In the afternoon, I called at Lorin's a half hour.

Sunday, March 4 Prayer meeting at West End (School Street) Church at 10:30. Right good. I pr. at 7:00, 2 Tim. 3.15.

Monday, March 5 At 10:00, went to Ministerial meeting at Lutheran Church. Dr. Robinson gave an essay on William the Silent. Prof. C.H. Kiracofe went with me.

Tuesday, March 6 At home. Called at *Conservator* office in forenoon & spent an hour looking at books on sale. Afternoon at 3:00 met Ex. Committee of Missionary Board at Cons. Of. Chose Marion as place of Annual Missionary Meeting & 7:30 eve. as hour.

Wednesday, March 7 At home. Kiracofe called afternoon. I called at Lorin's about 4:00. Wrote some. Read some.

Thursday, March 8 Went to town afternoon. Called at P.O., Young's a half-hour. At Mrs. Hall's, dressmaker's.

Friday, March 9 Called at Keiter's Office. Saw Becker & Kiracofe. At home all the afternoon & evening.

Saturday, March 10 At home. Send to Mrs. Hall's for Katie's waists, etc. I send them to her by express. Have my valise mended and gather up things for trip East. Called at Wm. McKee's at 7:30 (morn), but he is gone to Colorado.

Sunday, March 11 Heard Rev. Mr. Dodds, the pastor of Fourth Presby. Church pr. at 10:53, Rom. 8:35, a well polished discourse but he missed the meaning of the text. Heard Rev. W.S. Street pr. at 7:30, at School Street on Naaman.

Monday, March 12 Went to East Side forenoon & afternoon. Saw Young one minute at Court House. Jacob Slifer came over forenoon. I called at Prof. Kiracofe's about noon. Called at Lorin's in the evening.

Tuesday, March 13 Arose early. Start on 9:15 train for Virginia. Miss connection at Columbus. Leave Columbus at 8:00. via Bellair & Grafton, reach the Ohio River at midnight & Cumberland at 9:20 next morning. H.J. Becker and Keiter along.

Wednesday, March 14 Reach Harper's Ferry at 12:30. Hot box —reach Harrisonburg at 7:30. Roley takes us over to Dayton, Va. 4 ms. S.E. H.J. Becker lectured an hour & 15 min. on Palestine. We stay at Father Keiter's. Two sons & a married daughter, besides Milliard Filmore, Pub. Agent, there.

Thursday, March 15 Bro. Roley takes us over to Olivet Church. Dine at Jonas Daggy's. Conference opened at 2:00. Proceeded well. I sup & home at Geo. F. Perry's. It is rainy, and there is no meeting at 7:30. Slept well, after a long talk till 11:00.

Friday, March 16 Conference continued pleasantly and well. Mr. W.J. Funkhouser dined with me at Perry's. Afternoon finished examination and discussed the reports on Sabbath Schools, Missions, and that on Education was read. I supped at Markwood Knott's. Called at Jonas Daggy's & P.O. Wagner pr. at 8:00, well. Stay at Perry's.

Saturday, March 17 Conference continued. Rev. J.E. Hott was elected presiding elder. Stationing com. met at Jonas Daggy's at 1:00. I dine there. Conference closed at 4:45. Supper at Perry's. Dr. Becker lectured at 8:00. "Five Hundred Miles in Holy Land." I stay at Geo. F. Perry's.

Sunday, March 18 Arose at 6:20. Pr. at 10:30 Matt. 16.16. Dine at Markwood Knott's. Lunch there. Call at Mrs. Daggy's. Rev. H.J. Becker pr. at 7:30, Judges 16.6. Rev. P.O. Wagner & I stay at Nelson B. Riley's, 2 ms. S.E. Slept 3 hours.

Monday, March 19 Arose at 3:00, and after breakfast, start at 4:30 to Harrisonburg. At 8:22 take cars for Hagerstown with Rev. P.O. Wagner, [blank] Hoover, R.H. Clopper & [blank] Beler. Have 1:30 at Hagerstown. Reach Chambersburg at 5:00. Sup & lodge at Rev. Peter Nicklas's. Slept 7 hours. At Weaverton Junc. saw & talked with Rev. Mease.

Tuesday, March 20 Stay at Nicklas' till afternoon & write letters. Next call at Rev. A.H. Shank's & Rev. J. Fohl's. Letter from Orville. Supper and lodging at P. Nicklas's. I preach at 7:30, John 1:29, at King Street Church. Slept 6 hours.

Wednesday, March 21 Rev. B.G. Huber calls at Nicklas's to see me. We call at Adam Nicklas' & S.J. Nicklas'. Go on 9:45 train to Harrisburg, & on 12:10 train to Elmira, N. York, connect at 5:47 for Buffalo. Lunch at Hornelaville. Reach Buffalo about 11:00. Stay at the Filmore House.

Thursday, March 22 Go on 7:30 train to Sherk's (Sherkston). Stop at Benj. Sherk's till eve. Joseph Sherk, their brother from Buffalo, is there. I pr. at 8:30, Rom. 1:16. Stay at Isaac Sherk's, 1 mile south-west of the Church, where my conf. home is.

Friday, March 23 Conference opened at 9:00. Proceeds harmoniously. Dined at I. Sherk's. Discussed Educational report in afternoon. I sup at Peter Sherk's, 2 ms. northwest. Rev. Wm. Gribble, a Moravian, pr. at 8:00, Matt. 7:9. I stay at Isaac Sherk's, 1 m. S.W. Slept 6 hours.

Saturday, March 24 Conference continued. I dine at Rev. R.A. Learn's, 1 1/2 m. East. Stationing Committee sat there. I supped at Aaron Sherk's, 1 1/2 m. north. Evening session of conference. It closed. I lodge at Isaac Sherk's as usual. Slept six hours.

Sunday, March 25 Easter morning. I pr. at 10:30, 1 John 3.2. Large congregation. I dine at M. Shupe's, same house as I. Sherk's. Pr. at 3:30, 1 Cor. 15:29. Rev. J. Howe drives with me to Stevensville. Tea at Henry Zimmerman's, opposite the church. Pr. at 7:30, Ps. 48:11-13. Stay at John Hendershot's with J. Howe. His grandfather was a tory, in U.S.

Monday, March 26 Rev. J. Howe takes me to Sherk's Station. Dine with the Sherk brothers & sisters at the store. Go on 12:32 train to Buffalo. Supper at Restaurant near L.S. & M.S. Depot. Go on 8:25 train to Elyria, Ohio. Lodge at a Hotel. Slept 4 hs.

Tuesday, March 27 Went on 6:40 train to Oberlin. Breakfast at Miss Louise Clark's, where my daughter Catharine boards, & we left at 8:48 for Home via Toledo. Dine at a fair restaurant & we ride 2 hours on the electric cars and see the city. We go on 3:30 train. Reach Dayton, at 8:40. Slept 6 hours.

Wednesday, March 28 At home all day. The boys papering the rooms. I read, and sleep some. Called at Lorin's in the forenoon. Busy the rest of the day.

Thursday, March 29 At home all day except a call at Young's office; Geo. not there. Call at McKee's at 7:00. He talked as of accommodating & pacific, on Dorcas will case. Boys at work finishing and washing windows; and Catharine also helps.

Friday, March 30 Go to town. See Young 10 or 15 minutes. Afternoon Little Milton (Lorin's Son) spent the afternoon with me. Orville & Catharine at work on carpets, etc., etc. A pretty day.

Saturday, March 31 Cloudy day, but moderate. At home. Orville & Catharine arrange the house. First time for months, we had a room to sit in, all being torn up for new cherry finish by Wilbur & Orville. Wrote some letters aft'n. Call at Keiter's office, & see Becker. Read till late in the evening.

Sunday, April 1 Hear H.J. Becker preach at 10:30, Heb. 13:5, a nice discourse. Mrs. Greenwood & Flora called an hour in after'n. Lorin & Netta also. Miss Anna Feight also. Little Milton with us all the afternoon. Heard at Broadway M.E. Church at 7:30, H.J. Becker; text Luke 18:10.

Monday, April 2 Attended an open meeting of Dayton Ministerial Association and heard E.P. Brown, editor of the Ram's Horn, on one of the Old Testament Preachers, Elijah. Spent afternoon in looking up documents. Called at Young's 10 minutes. Lorin & family called in eve.

Tuesday, April 3 Prof. C.H. Kiracofe on deposition for Tulare Co. Case, California. Direct examination about 3 hours in forenoon & 1 1/2 in Aftn. Beautiful day till 4:00 afternoon, when winds & slight rains come. Catharine started to Oberlin at 11:00, forenoon.

Wednesday, April 4 Weather cooler and considerably windy. I give my testimony (direct) for Tulare, Cal. parsonage case, full six hours. We agree to have only the forms of continuing each day till Saturday.

Thursday, April 5 Am asked a single question on deposition at Young's & answer it. I spend most of the day writing to H.C. Horsman, Tipton, Calif., and Davis & Allen, Attys, at Tulare, California.

Friday, April 6 Went to town for a question on examination, for form's sake. Did little else in the forenoon only talk with my boys, on my and their business.

Saturday, April 7 Went to town as usual, and answered one question on deposition. Sent A.P. Barnaby $8.13 of Hartsville funds col. in Ontario, and W.H. Clay $6.50 Gen. S.S. Fund from Ontario; both by bank-draft, Winter's. Came home & wrote letters, looked up papers, etc.

Sunday, April 8 I preach at 10:30, at School Street Church, Ps. 73:24. Dine at Samuel Spidel's on King Street, recently moved there. Bro. Hanely and wife dine there also; and we all remain till evening meeting. Rev. M.F. Keiter pr. at 7:23, Ps. 126:5, a lively, skillful sermon. I get home about 9:00, eve.

Monday, April 9 At home most of the day. Adjourned depositions with one question only.

Tuesday, April 10 At home mostly. Adjourned deposition as usual. Spent two hours with Young in afternoon, looking over Calif. matters & getting ready.

Wednesday, April 11 At home. Afternoon L.B. Gunckel began Kiracofe's cross-examination.

Thursday, April 12 L.B. Gunckel continued Prof. Kiracofe's cross-examination in forenoon & begged off in Afternoon.

Friday, April 13 Cross Examination of Prof. Kiracofe continued in forenoon. Met in afternoon, but Gunckel begged off. I called at W.E. Tizzard's and had gold crown renewed on upper tooth.

Saturday, April 14 Was at the completion of Prof. Kiracofe's deposition at 12:30. In the afternoon took Milton, Jr. to Town. Mailed tax money to Grant Co., Ind.; and application for favor, on Penn Lines E. of Pittsb. Bought Milton cart and cup.

Sunday, April 15 At 9:14 tr. to Brookville. Dine at John Zehring's. He and wife take me to Henry Hamiel's, Peter Rasor's, and S.A. Munbeck's. Short discourse & prayer at the two former places and prayers at the last. Reach home 9:30, S.A. Munbeck at Voorhees, Arlington.

Monday, April 16 Went to W.E. Tizzard's the dentist. Hadan impression taken for a new upper plate of teeth. Called at Young's. Received a letter announcing postponement of the deposition on account of Gunckel's being unwell.

Tuesday, April 17 Direct examination of me resumed on Deposition in Cal. case, & it continued all day. Revs. Kiracofe & Becker called a few minutes after dinner. I called at Lorin's a half hour at 7:00, eve.

Wednesday, April 18 Direct examination closed (in my case) and cross-examination was begun. Gunckel spent nearly two hours in transcribing "Outline History" into the deposition! He & Young's Affair. "Spat" with me. Adjourn till to-morrow. Call at Lorin's & at our offices.

Thursday, April 19 My cross-examination continued in the forenoon. After a late dinner, I call a few minutes at Lorin's. Write and read aftn. & eve.

Friday, April 20 Cross-examination continued forenoon. At home aftern.

Saturday, April 21 Am cross-examined most of the day, by Gunckel, who closed at 5:00, aft'n. I then go to W.E. Tizzard's and get my set of teeth (upper) just made. Paid $13.00. At home in the evening; read over my examination.

Sunday, April 22 Arose at 5:30. Attend Church at School St. Rev. W.E. Streete, the pastor, pr. at 10:30, Mark 1:24, a real good sermon. I called at Lorin's after dinner. Strete pr. at 7:30, Ps. 107.8. Not 20 present.

Monday, April 23 Call at W.E. Tizzard's, at Frizell's drug store, and at the bank, in the forenoon, and a few minutes at Lorin's. At home in afternoon.

Tuesday, April 24 At home. Prof. Kiracofe called in aft'n of yesterday, and asked me to write an article for the Conservator. I spend much of the day on the article "The Decalogue not Repealed." Hands are digging for Holly water mains on Hawthorne Street.

Wednesday, April 25 At home, the closing of my deposition being adjourned till morning. I finish my article.

Thursday, April 26 On redirect examination. Spent the forenoon. No further cross-examination. At home in after'n. The laying of the water mains is completed.

Friday, April 27 Go to town to dentist's. Call at Young's a few minutes. Buy Stetson hat and kangaroo shoes.

Saturday, April 28 Engaged Stewart to put in water pipes. Write letters. Have my stove taken down stairs. Thermometer runs about 85 degrees.

Sunday, April 29 Was at Sch. St. Church. M.F. Keiter pr. Hosea 6:3. At Home till eve. H.J. Becker pr. on (Acts 19:28) "Diana of the Ephesians." Very beautiful weather. No fire.

Monday, April 30 See Young ten minutes on the argument at Cincinnati. Write two notes for the Conservator. Beautiful day—no fire needed.

Tuesday, May 1 Went to town and pay Young & Young $211.32, on Federal Fairview case. Spend the day largely in writing a long article, The Ten Commandments Unrepealed. Sat up late.

Wednesday, May 2 Continued to write on the article for Conservator. At home all day.

Saturday, May 5 I was at Quarterly meeting this evening. Becker lectured.

Sunday, May 6 Rev. H.J. Becker pr. at 10:30. Sacrament followed. Dine at Rev. Kehring's.

Monday, May 7 Bro. Warvel takes us to the cars. Reach home about 8:00.

Saturday, May 12 Go on 11:05 train to Tontogany, O. Rev. S.C. Hilty on the car from Weston. Bro. C.W. Thomas meets me and takes me to his house to Supper, 3 ms. east. I preach at Union Hill, at 8:00, Ps. 73:24. Stay at Rev. G.W. Coss; 1 m. north-west.

Sunday, May 13 I pr. at Union Hill Church and raise $235.55. Dine at Rev. G.W. Coss'. Pr. at 8:00, Acts 1:11. Raise $40.00, & dedicate the Church. Stay at C.W. Thomas'.

Monday, May 14 Come home on 7:32 train arriving at 1:00. Arrange affairs.

Tuesday, May 15 At home. H.J. Becker called. C.H. Kiracofe called after dinner. Heavy rain.

Wednesday, May 16 Went on 6:55 train to Lima & Elida. W.M. Association is in session. Dine and lodge at Henry Kiracofe's. Miss M.M. Titus spoke.

Thursday, May 17 Session continued. I dine as usual. Afternoon session. At evening session, I spoke on Missions. Supper at S.A. Stemen's. Stay at Henry Kiracofe's.

Friday, May 18 Arose about 4:00, ate a cold lunch & start with Brenneman to Lima. Go on 5:45 train home. Go to town; call at Young's.

Saturday, May 19 At home. Quite cool. Busy as usual. Went to bed early for lack of sufficient heating apparatus.

Sunday, May 20 Preach at Sch. St. Ch., John 14:3. At home the rest of the day except a call at Lorin's about 6:00, Aft'n. Rev. W.S. Strete preached at 8:00, Gen. 5:24. "Enoch walked with God," etc. Morning rainy and cool. Evening also somewhat rainy.

Monday, May 21 Arose late—a quarter after six—and breakfast and do some clearing up. Sent a letter to Reuchlin. Called at the office and at Kiracofe's a half hour. Shipped envelopes & letter heads to Elida to pack in Imperreh box for West Africa. Slept an hour Aft'n, & bed late.

Tuesday, May 22 I get ready and start at 12:00 Aft. via Union City to Marion, Ind. Reach there abt 4:00. On street cars to North Marion. Directed to Hez. Wysongs, 2 squares S.E. of Horton Street U.B. Ch. Call at Geo. Rinker's, 1/2 m. South of the Church to see Bp. H. Floyd. Lodge at Wysong's.

Wednesday, May 23 The Board of Bishops meet at the Church at 10:30. All present: M. Wright, H.T. Barnaby, Halleck Floyd, Wm. Dillon. I dine at Rev. Cyrus Smith's. Afternoon Session. Supper & Lodging at J.Y. Parlett's, 1/4 m. East. Dr. C.H. Kiracofe delivers an address at 8:00, on Education.

Thursday, May 24 Educational Board lacked a quorum but arranged for some work anticipating a quorum, which did not come. Missionary Board convenes at 7:30, Dr. J.K. Alwood delivers the annual address at 8:00, 2 Cor. 9:7. I board at J.Y. Parlett's.

Friday, May 25 The Session of the Missionary Board continues and progresses nicely all day. I dine at John Null's, 3 ms. west, with H. Floyd, Wm. Dillon, & I.M. Tharp. Mother Shank, her mother, in quite poor health. Committees meet at J.Y. Parlett's, after dinner. Rev. Wm. Miller of Uniopolis pr. at 8:00, John 21:22. I board at Parlett's.

Saturday, May 26 Mission Board business is completed before noon. In the Afternoon, the topics concerning Missionary work are discussed for about two hours. Bp. Wm. Dillon preached at 8:00, Rom. 1:16, 17. I board at Parlett's, but sup at Mark Hillshammer's 2 ms. east. I called in morning at Calvin McRea's, who is aged & infirm.

Sunday, May 27 Bishop Horace T. Barnaby preached at 10:30, Phil. 1:27. We dine & sup at Rev. Cyrus Smith's, an aged minister of White River conference. There was a very hard shower in the Afternoon. I call at Eddie

Hillshammer's, 1 mile n.e. I pr. at 8:00, Rev. 22:20, on Christ's Second Coming. Stay at John Y. Parlett's.

Monday, May 28 I go on 7:00 train to Fairmount. Ride out 3 ms with Nat. Haden. Walk to Daren's & call there. Go with Ellis Wright to his house. Dine there. Take a nap. Ellis takes me to W.H.H. Reeder's (Jr.) & I return with him to Ellis' & lodge. Excitement over Zach Little's murder (as supposed by Young Coggle).

Tuesday, May 29 Go to W.H.H. Reeder's. Dine there. Go with William to Harmony (Baptist) cemetery. Sup at Ellis's. He & I go to Fairmount where Rev. H.J. Becker preached at 8:00. I return with Ellis & lodge there.

Wednesday, May 30 Go with Ellis to Wm. H.H. Reeder's. Look at the timber. Ellis' views on free trade and fiat money. Go after dinner with Wm. to Oliver Glass's & Robert B. Reeder's—all away. Supper at Ellis'. He and Rhoda take me to Fairmount. I pr. Isa. 21:11, at 8:00. I stay with Rev. I. M. Tharp at Rev. N.D. Wolfard's.

Thursday, May 31 I call at Rev. Wm. Hall's (at Hollingsworth's). Go on 8:50 train to Marion and on 9:22 train to Union City. Wait three hours. Reach home at 4:30. Arrange things & write some.

Friday, June 1 Went to town in the forenoon. Saw Young five minutes. At home in the afternoon & evening, except an hour's call at Lorin's—8:00-9:00.

Saturday, June 2 Call at Young's 10 min. Call at Geo. Wood's office & sign deposition in the Tulare Co. Calif. case. At home afternoon.

Sunday, June 3 Hear H.J. Becker pr. (lecture) on "Jerusalem." At home the rest of the day till evening when I hear W.S. Strete preach at 8:00, Luke 22:55: Peter's Denial. This was the first day and night for about two weeks warm enough to need no fire.

Wednesday, June 6 Board of Publication met at 10:00 at Conservator Office, 112 S. Broadway St. Floyd, McNew, Becker & Wright present. Committees appointed. I see Young 10 min. at 11:30. Session afternoon. Floyd lodges with me.

Thursday, June 7 Breakfast at Greenwood's. Board session continues. Floyd & McNew lunch with me at 5:00 P.M. & start home.

Friday, June 8 At home. Call at Lorin's about 2:00.

Saturday, June 9 At home. Call at Young's 5 min.

Sunday, June 10 Preach at School Street 10:30, Rom. 8:2. Dine at Spidel's. Attend prayer meeting at Becker's at 2:30. Pres. C.H. Kiracofe preached at 8:00 on the Journeyings of Israel.

Monday, June 11 McKee's testimony put off till to-morrow. Wilbur goes to Marion, Ind. I write some on an article.

Tuesday, June 12 McKee's testimony again deferred. I write letters.

Wednesday, June 13 Wm. McKee's testimony in California case begins at 10:30 & Continues till 5:00 with two hours' recess at noon.

Thursday, June 14 McKee's deposition resumed at 9:30 and continued till 5:30, with two hours' recess at noon. A very evasive and insolent witness, truly.

Friday, June 15 Went to town at 9:00 & had the cap on my tooth cemented on again. Various purchases. At home aftern. Engaged cement sidewalk put down at 12 cents a sq. foot.

Saturday, June 16 At home till 5:00, Aftn. Went to New Paris, Ohio. Staid at H.O. Hutton's.

Sunday, June 17 Preach at 10:30 (real time) Ps. 83:18. Dine at Jacob Surface's. Called after supper at Hutton's, and a few minutes at John Coblentz's. She is a daughter of Rev. Robinson, a pioneer minister. M.E. children's meeting at 8:00. I stay at H.O. Hutton's.

Monday, June 18 I go on 5:20 morn. train to Dayton. Fix up things some. Go to town in afternoon. Pay $40.00 on Tulare Co. Cal. suit for notary. Hands dig up sidewalk for cement pavement.

Tuesday, June 19 At home. Write an article on the Two Dispensations. Write some letters.

Thursday, June 21 Missionary Executive meeting at 2:00. Becker tries to get in Keiter's report on Hymnal, before Hymnal Committee. I was appointed on Committee also, at former meeting.

Saturday, June 23 Get a letter from Young & Young giving Judge Wm. H. Taft's decision in our favor on Exceptions to the Liberal's.Answer in Fairview U.S. case. Prof. Kiracofe called. Went to "town" and saw Young a few minutes.

Sunday, June 24 At home all day, being in less than usual vigor. Read much; and, in the evening till midnight in Bunyan's "Badman".

Monday, June 25 At home. Called at Pres. C.H. Kiracofe's at 119 Summit Street, aft'n. We made out note on our victory in U.S. Court.

Friday, June 29 In the evening, I saw the bicycle parade in "town."

Saturday, June 30 Went to "town", drew money and paid Wagner & Co. $26.88 for cement pavement.

Sunday, July 1 Heard Rev. H.J. Becker at 10:30 on Luke 2:32. At home the rest of the day. In the evening at 7:00 was at General Class at School Street. Rev. W.S. Strete pr. at 8:00, John 13:8.

Wednesday, July 4 This is the fifth anniversary of the death of my dear wife. In intellect, in sensibilities, and in disposition she was all that heart could desire. At home her shining was gentle and pure as the glory of a pearl, and she had no ambition to shine anywhere else. Her faith in Christ was unwavering. To-day I visited her grave.

Sunday, July 8 At home all day. Spent the time in reading.

Monday, July 9 At home. Called at the Printing Office 112 S. Broadway. In evening called at Lorin's a half hour. Wrote letters in the day.

Tuesday, July 10 At home. The strike blockading the railroads seems to be declining before U.S. troops.

Wednesday, July 11 Send out newspapers containing article on Judge Taft's recent decision. At 3:00, get telegram from Attorneys saying the Liberals' motion for a rehearing in Michigan Supreme Court has been refused. Wrote many letters.

Thursday, July 12 Wrote out a statement of Sarah Margaret Fowble's remarkable restoration for Rev. J.K. Alwood's book.

Friday, July 13 Wrote out a will for Henry Walters.

Saturday, July 14 Afternoon I go to Woodland Cemetery and arrange Susan's grave.

Sunday, July 15 Pr. at Sch. St. Church 2 Tim. 2:19. At home till eve. Hear Rev. W.E. Strete pr. at 7:30, John 14:2. Taught multiplicity of places in heaven & eternal progression!

Monday, July 16 Went to town. Paid Young $100.00 on Printing Estab. Case. Bought Galvanic Battery.

Tuesday, July 17 At home. Wrote for railroad favors.

Saturday, July 21 At home. Called about 5:00 at Young's to get bills—not made out.

Sunday, July 22 I preached at *10:30, at Sch. St. 2 Cor 13:4. At home the rest of the day till evening service. Dr. C.H. Kiracofe preached at *8:00, Acts 1:8. *stands for real time.

Monday, July 23 At home mostly. Called at the Office of Conservator. Called in the evening at Lorin's.

Tuesday, July 24 At home. Board of Education with other brethren assemble. Pres. W.H. Davis & Rev. N.D. Wolfard sup & lodge with me. Board meeting at 7:30.

Wednesday, July 25 Board meeting continues all day and has a session at 7:30. Bp. Barnaby dines with me. Davis and Prof. A.B. Barnaby lodge with me.

Thursday, July 26 Board members continue to leave. I at home the rest of the day.

Friday, July 27 At home. Cleanse my room.

Sunday, July 29 Rev. W.E. Strete preached at Sch. St., 2 Pet. 1:5-7. Preached well. Rev. H.J. Becker preached at 7:30.

Tuesday, July 31 Telegram from Samuel Baird, asking if I could preach Joseph Kumler's funeral to-morrow at 2:00. Went to town. Saw Peter Louding's. Saw Young & I looked over my testimony in Pr. Est. Case. Called at Becker's & at Kiracofe's.

Wednesday, August 1 C.H. Kiracofe & Myself go on 8:20 m. train to Hamilton. We visit Mrs. Joseph Gomer at Jos. Alexander's at 75 Chestnut Street. She & Mr. Gomer were African Missionaries of much success. Went on to Kumler farm. Pr. Joseph W. Kumler's funeral at 3:30 at Miltonville.

Thursday, August 2 At home. Wrote articles for the *Conservator*.

Friday, August 3 At home. Handed articles to Prof. Kiracofe for publication. Cleared up the house & woodhouse somewhat.

Saturday, August 4 At home till 5:00, afternoon. Went to Trenton, Ohio where Chas. Coulthard met me and took me to his house where I lodged. Their children, Francis & Bertha.

Sunday, August 5 Preach at Elk Creek Church at 10:30, Zach. 13:9. Dine at Meyers. Laura (Wingard), his wife, is a daughter of Catharine Hillshammer. Joe Thomas & wife also dine there. At Prayer meeting at Coulthard's at 8:00. I stay at Meyers'.

Monday, August 6 Meyers takes me to 6:00 train at Middletown & I reach home soon after seven. Went to town in the Afternoon. Saw W.H. Craighen a moment. Saw Young a few minutes.

Saturday, August 11 At home. Katie returned from Oberlin at 3:00 afternoon.

Sunday, August 12 At home all day reading. Examined Scripture questions.

Monday, August 13 At home. At Conservator office. Went to town. Rev. R.G. Montgomery called an hour in the afternoon. Lorin & family called in the evening.

Tuesday, August 14 At home, partly preparing to go away.

Thursday, August 16 Start at 9:20 for Remington, Jasper County, Indiana, via Richmond & Logansport. Arrive about 4:30 Aft. Call at C.B. McDaniel's in Remington, and then go with Alpheus Elmore to his house, my conference home. Mrs. G. Waters pr. at 8:00, 1 Cor. 13:12.

Friday, August 17 Conference opened at 8:30 in a tent. Business progressed rapidly. Dr. H.J. Becker arrived about 5:00 aft. I pr. at 8:00, Hebr. 11:25, 26. I stay at Elmore's.

Saturday, August 18 Session continued. W.H. Elliott is reelected Pres. elder on 4th ballot over Sims. Stationing Com. meets at noon at Elmore's. Session closed at 5:00. Dr. H.J. Becker pr. at 8:00, "Apples of Gold," etc. We stay at Elmore's.

Sunday, August 19 Speaking meeting, late beginning. I preach at 11:00, Luke 12:32. Dine at Jas. Foster's, Baptists. Dr. Becker pr. at 3:30, "What think ye of Christ?" I go with Mr. Noe to see Mrs. Johnson, formerly Mrs. Miner of Dublin, Ind. I stay at Alpheus Elmore's.

Monday, August 20 Bro. Elmore takes me to Remington. I dine at Rev. C.B. McDaniel's & go on the noon train to Logansport, Marion, & Fairmount. I stay at Clinton Brattain's.

Tuesday, August 21 Call at Rev. Wm. Hall's. Bro. Brattain takes me to Ellis Wright's. Dine and sup there. Ellis takes me to Wm. Reeder's & I stay there till nearly bed time.

Wednesday , August 22 Went to Oliver Glass & Robt. B. Reeder's & then to Wm. H.H. Reeder's. I stay at Reeder's till after supper, having gave over to Fowler's tile establishment. Wm. took me to Fairmount & I stay at Brattain's. Rev. N.D. Wolfard also staid there.

Thursday, August 23 Rev. N.D. Wolfard & myself go in 8:50 train to Bolivar. Rev. A.G. Johnson meets us there and takes us to Benj. Bashore's near Servia. Conference began at 1:30. J.L. Powers had been silenced. Rev. N.D. Wolfard preaches at 8:00. Sup & stay at Benj. Bashore's.

Friday, August 24 Conference continued. Examination mostly completed. J.L. Powers, was expelled for immorality. I sup at Henry Walters, 1 1/2 ms. north of Servia. He has been very sick. Rev. J. Austin (Baptist) of Goshen, preached at 8:00. A high meeting. Staid at Bashore's.

Saturday, August 25 Conference continued. Reports slow and crude. Finished business nearly in the afternoon. Stationing committee reported at 4:30. Rev. Edward White, an ex-salvationist, pr. at 8:00, Acts 16:25. I board at Benj. Bashore's.

Sunday, August 26 I preach at 10:30 (11:00) after a "second work" exercise. This second work exercise was led by A.J. Johnson who began it after preaching time and the work over Norton, which proved a shoddy job.

Monday, August 27 Went with Rev. A.A. Powels to Henry Walters, and thence in the buggy to Cromwell, Ind., where Bro. A.A. Powell lives. Supper on the way at Jacob Himes'. I stay at Powel[l]'s. I have a chill & am sick this night.

Tuesday, August 28 Write some. In afternoon, or evening call at Vina Buck's & at W.O. Roher's. Stay at Rev. A.A. Powell's. I took quinine & escaped a chill.

Wednesday, August 29 Go on 11:04 train to Auburn Junction. I send from Auburn fifty dollars to Doyle Scott & Lewis, Toledo, O. and forty dollars to Katie in Orville's name. Thomas Dowell takes me on to his house 7 miles South-east. I board there, my conf. home.

Thursday, August 30 North Ohio Conference began session at 8:30. Some time is spent in ballotings for secretary & chairman. Aftn conf. proceeded well. Rev. R.V. Gilbert pr. at 8:00, "Lord have mercy," etc. I board at Thomas Dowel's. (The meetings were in a large tent.)

Friday, August 31 Conf. Session Suspended: J.E. Bodine. Boundary com. report adopted. Reconsidered afternoon.

Examination concluded with dispatch. Board at Dowel's. Dr. H.J. Becker pr. at 8:00, Hebr. 5:12. G.S. Seipel had been appointed to preach, but yielded to Becker.

Saturday, September 1 Conference continued. A.H. Tussing, G.W. Crawford & L.S. Wilmoth elected pres. Elders. Stationing Com. met at 1:00; & again at 7:30. Conference closed (after the preaching by Rev. W.O. Dinius) with an item of business in the evening.

Sunday, September 2 I preach at 10:30, II Cor. 3:8. Dine as usual at Dowel's, & Dr. C.H. Kiracofe with me. S.S. Anniversary at 3:00. Clay, Gilbert, Becker, & myself deliver 10 min. addresses. Dr. H.J. Becker pr. at 7:30. I stay at Dowel's.

Monday, September 3 I go to Auburn. See Moody (clerk) and also get a draft for $250.00, & send home in Orville's name. Go on to Jackson, and after 3 1/2 hours to Charlotte, Mich. Stay at Phoenix Hotel. W.H. Clay and others on the train part of the way.

Tuesday, September 4 After breakfast at the Hotel, I call at Rev. J.D. Jarvis' and Rev. J. Bishop's. I go on 11:55 train to Caledonia Station. I dine with Rev. C.B. Whitaker who takes me to Simon Bowman's, 1 mile east of Gaines Church, where I stay. Children: Ward, 12; Edna, 10.

Wednesday, September 5 Write an article on the Fourth Commandment. Go in the afternoon to Bishop H.T. Barnaby's, 1/2 m. south of Gaines church. Rev. G.W. Fast pr. at 8:00, on Zaccheus. I stay at Barnaby's, my conference home.

Thursday, September 6 Conference opened at 8:30. Business progressed well. I board at Barnaby's, who is at home. Rev. B. Hamp pr. at 8:00, II Pet. 1:10, 11.

Friday, September 7 Conference progressed well & in the afternoon, J.D. Jarvis and Henry Coles were elected presiding elders. Stationing Committee met at Bp. Barnaby's at 7:00. Adjourned at 9:00. Prof. C.H. Kiracofe preached, at 8:00.

Saturday, September 8 Conference continued and made fine progress. Stationing committee met at 7:30 & at

11:30. Elders' and Sta. Com. met at 1:45. Raise $17 + for secretary and $305.00 for U.S. suit. Dined at Simon Bowman's. Adjourned at 4:40. Prof. C.H. Kiracofe preached at 7:30, "What is man?"

Sunday, September 9 I preach at 10:30, Titus 2:14, on Atonement. Coll. for me $74.07. Dine at Barnaby's. S.S. Anniversary at 3:30. R.S. Bowman, C.H. Kiracofe, A.P. Barnaby, H.J. Barnaby, & M. Wright spoke. At 7:30, I pr. 15 min. I Cor. 6:20, followed by the Communion. Stay at Barnaby's.

Monday, September 10 Went to Grand Rapids with Bp. Barnaby & I.G. Hutchinson & wife. Saw Moses Taggart, Esq. & his partners. Return with Bro. Barnaby. Rev. R.S. Bowman & wife & Myrtle (aged 3) there till bedtime. Rev. C.H. Kiracofe came at 6:00 & staid with us.

Tuesday, September 11 Went to Ross by 7:33 & Bp. Barnaby took the train south. Prof. Kiracofe & I take the 8:44 train to Grand Rapids. Write letters. We go on 3:20 train to Owassa, & on 7:30 tr. to North Star, where we arrived at 9:00, the train being a half hour late. Prof. Kiracofe & myself staid at [blank] Courtright's in North Star.

Wednesday, September 12 Rev. T. Campbell & L.B. Davis came to Cortright's. We go to Peter Hoffman's to board. Prof. Kiracofe pr. at 7:30, Ps. 1st. Stay at Hoffman's.

Thursday, September 13 Conference opened at 9:00, morn. It progressed fairly well. Woman's Mis. Association occupied the evening. Stay at Hoffman's.

Friday, September 14 Conference continued. We receive W.O. Nease, J.R. Gilbert & Sadie M. Gilbert into the conference. C.L. Wood and E.J. Moody were elected pres. elders. Stationing com. met at 7:00 at P. Huffman's. Prof. Kiracofe preached at 7:30. We stay at Hoffman's.

Saturday, September 15 Bro. Kiracofe started home. Business progressed & closed (mostly) at 4:00. Rev. B. Hamp of Mich. pr. at 7:30, Phil. 4:19. Closed the session about 9:00. I Stay at Hoffman's.

Sunday, September 16 I Pr. at 10:30 2 Cor. 4:5. Dine at Peter Hoffman's. S.S. Anniversary at 3:30, by D.H.

Shelly. Fleming, Davis, Birddal, Nease, Porterfield, etc., and I spoke. Good anniversary. Memorial services of L. Spaulding and P. Laming at 7:00. I pr. at 7:30, I Cor. 11:29. Communion followed. I stay at Peter Hoffman's.

Monday, September 17 Start at 7:39 via Durand to Chicago. Reach there at 7:30. Stay at Hotel Grace, on Jackson St. Write some cards. Saw Mr. Ring of St. Johns, Mich., on train. He a hotel keeper, and knows Rev. I. Kretzinger. Going to Mount Pulaski, Ill., on account of the expected death of his mother. We had much talk, partly on religion.

Tuesday, September 18 Went to Chi. Mill & St. P. depot & thence to Chi. and N. West'n, and start at 8:15 to Madison & Fennimore, Wis. Stop two hours at Madison. Ascend the State House Rotunda & see city. Go on to Fennimore, Wis. reaching there at 6:30, & stay at Rev. W. H. Haskins, who is in life's jeopardy.

Wednesday, September 19 Mailed cards. Rode about town with Rev. Dan'1 Smith. Rev. W.H. Haskins was thrown from his buggy the 17th and badly hurt. I Preach at 7:30, Rom. 1:16. Stay at Haskins'. He continues to sink, gradually.

Thursday, September 20 I continue at Father W.H. Haskins. He died at abt. 3:00 afternoon, aged 77 years & 9 days. Many came in to conference. I preach at 7:30 Exodus 28:34. We stay at Haskins.

Friday, September 21 Conference opened at 8:30 at the new chapel built by Bro. & Sister Haskins. Conference progresses. I preach the funeral of Nrs. Sarah Wepking at 2:00, at the M. E. Church. Session of Conf. after the funeral. Rev. D.W. Smith preached at 7:30, 2 Pet. 1:9. Speaking meeting followed. Stay at Haskins'.

Saturday, September 22 Conference continued. I preach Elder W.H. Haskins funeral at 1:00, & we bury him. Text, Rom. 8:30. Conference closed at 4:00. Called at Morden's. I preach at M.E. Church at 7:30, John 16:13. Stay at Haskins.

Sunday, September 23 I pr. at M.E. Church at 11:00, Hebr. 11:10. Dine with Rev. C. Bender at Mrs.——— [line appears in text] Dedicate "Fennimore Chapel" at

3:00. Supper at Haskins. Preach at M.E. Church at 7:30, I Cor. 5:7. Stay at McLyman's.

Monday, September 24 Start at 4:00 morn. with Daniel Smith to Boscobel. Go on 6:28 train to Prairie du Chein, McGregor, and Castalia, Iowa. Bro. A. Lambert meets me and after a drive takes me to his home 2 ms. s.e. Dine. Rev. R.H. McCormack there & we sup at Solomon Shroyer's. I preach at Castalia at 7:30, Ps. 92:8. Stay at Lambert's.

Tuesday, September 25 Bro. McCormack took me to West Union & I saw L.L. Ainsworth, Esq., and had interview with him. Went on to Fayette & sup & lodge at Rev. McCormack's. Thier children: Mabel 17, Burdette 9; Others married.

Wednesday, September 26 Went on to *Brush Creek, on 7:00 train. Put up at R. Ewings. See J.S. Cooney, atty, and "Dea." W.R. Morley Home continues at Ewing's. Rev. E. Cronk preached at 7:30, Rom. 5:3. *Later called Arlington.

Thursday, September 27 Call at Rev. J.L. Buckwalter's. John Horn dines with me at Ewing's. Conference opened at 1:30 aftn. and proceeded well. Rev. R.D. McCormack pr. at 7:30. I board at Ewing's.

Friday, September 28 Conference continued & proceeded well. Afternoon R.D. McCormack was re-elected pres. elder. Stationing Committee met at R. Ewing's at 5:00, Miss Mary Davis preached at 7:30, Genesis 7:1. I still board at Ewing's.

Saturday, September 29 Stationing Com. met again at 9:15. Conference continued. Dr. H.J. Becker came. Dine at Rev. J.L. Buckwalter's. Session closed at 5:00. Supper at Ewing's. Rev. H.J. Becker preached at 7:30, Matt. 5:8.

Sunday, September 30 I preach at 11:00, Rom. 4:16. Dine at Roberts with McCormack & Becker. Call at John Mead's. Supper at Lawrence's. Bro. H.J. Becker preached at 7:30, Matt. 5:5. He stay at Ewing's.

Monday, October 1 Stay at Ewings till 5:20. Go on 5:45 afternoon train to Cedar Rapids (Iowa) & take 12:28 tr. via Ames to Des Moines. Arrive abt. 5:30. Saw on cars Revs. Richardson, Johnson, Kenney, and Sage. Converse with Sage and Richardson on "second work."

Tuesday, October 2 I, at 6:00 morn., take electric car via Capitol to Capitol Street 1633, to Rev. Thos. Prall's. Breakfast and dine there. Go on 3:05 train to Pleasantville (Ia.) and stop & stay at Geo. M. Glenn's to see Uncle Geo. B. Reeder. Glenn's wife is Fanny & their children, Mabel 9; Georgia 6 ys.

Wednesday, October 3 Went on 1:07 tr. to Clarkson and thence with Guild (Baptist preacher) to Carlisle, to John Patterson's. Go on 5:33 tr. to Indianola & Laconia. Chas. Henderson's takes us to his house. Supper at 8:30. Lodge there with H.J. Becker and Thoedore Eslick. Saw Dr. A.H. Chase of Congo Free State Mission, on the train to Indianola.

Thursday, October 4 Go on to Norwood & to O.A. Wallace's. Conf. home there. Conf. opened at 1:30. Dr. H.J. Becker addressed the Conf. on Missions before adjournment. Supper & Lodging at Wallace's. Dr. Becker pr. at 7:30, 1 Sam'l 18:26. Got a letter from Catharine ("Katie"). Cloudy weather.

Friday, October 5 Dr. H.J. Becker left early. Conference continued. Rev. Ogier called in. I pr. at 7:30.

Saturday, October 6 Conf. continued. I dine at J.E. Ham's. Close about 4:30, after reading the allotments of labor. Rev. E. Dewitt preached at 7:30. I sup & lodge at Wallace's.

Preach at 11:00, 2 Tim. 3:15. Pub. Coll. by DeWitt, 32:00. I dine at Wallace's. Baptized Mrs. Ham at her house at 2:00. Rev. E. Dewitt preached at 3:00, and communion followed. Supper at Wallace's. I preach at 7:30, Rom. 4:8. Go on to Chas. Hendrickson's & stay there.

Monday, October 8 I go to Lacona to 7:40 train & thence via Indianola to Des Moines. Dine at Restaurant with Rev. I.W. Bennett. Go on 12:35 train to Casey. D.R. Fagan takes me to his house, 7 ms. South. Sup there. Go to L. Hoisington's & lodge there. I looked over the farm some. Mr. Thompson works for Fagan.

Tuesday, October 9 I called at D.J. Hepler's a few minutes. Went on to Fagan's and went over the farm. Dined. Afternoon, Mr. Fagan & I made settlement. I sup at Fagan's. Lodge at Lee Hoisington's. Gertie 15 years old. Pearl not at home.

Wednesday, October 10 Went to Fagan's & made out bill of lumber for a stable. Went to Casey with Fagan and family and left $50.00 with him toward lumber, etc. Go on 2:40 train to Omaha. Take 6:50 train to Lincoln. Stay at Tremont House. Bed at 9:15. Slept 8 hours.

Thursday, October 11 Go on 7:40 fr. tr. to Crete & Dorchester, where I arrived at 10:00. I go with a man named Miller to the tent near Pleasant Valley Church. I board at Edward Barnes, 1/2 mile east. Conference opened at 1:30 in church (Pleasant Valley). I read and commented on 2 Cor., 3rd Chapt. Supper at Barnes & lodging. Rev. S.P. Ross pr. at 7:30, Rev. 4:6, "Sea of Glass." Rev. J.M. Sims exhorted.

Friday, October 12 Slept late. Conference continued. Rev. W.J. Dunn dined with us. I pr at 7:30, Eph. 2:4, to a tent full of people. Board as usual. It was a pleasant day, with little of the unusual in it.

Saturday, October 13 Conference continued. S. Austin is elected pres. elder. Stationing Committee meets at 11:15 at the Church. I dine with S. Austin's, at the tent. Conference closed about 4:00. Supper at Barnes'. Rev. J.M. Sims pr. at 7:45, Rom. 14:10. He is quite a "cyclone." Stay at Barnes.

Sunday, October 14 I Preached at 11:00 at the Conference tent Zech. 4:10. Coll. $34.50. "Despise not day of small things." I dined with B.F. Duleigh's and others. I pr. at 3:30, Acts 17:24. "Dwelleth not in Temples" etc. I sup at Rev. G.F. Albrecht's. S. Austin pr. at tent at 7:30. I took one into Church. I dedicated Pleasant Valley Church about 4:30 aftern. I stay at Rev. Wm. Trace's, 3 miles S.E. of Tent.

Monday, October 15 Bro. Trace takes me to the tent. I dine at Barnes'. with Rev. Simeon Austin & wife. They (Barnes') take me to Dorchester & I put up at Robert Baker's. Mrs. Dr [blank] , Baker's daughter from Furnus County, was there.

Tuesday, October 16 I leave on 6:35 morn. train for Omaha. Go to Webster Street Depot. Go on 12:15 train to Sioux City on Western System. Meet Rev. H.J. Becker there. We lunch up town & stay at Chermey's Depot Hotel. Bro. Becker spent an hour in my room and Afterward I wrote some.

Wednesday, October 17 Wrote some cards. Went on 10:40 train via Yankton to Parkston. Rev. Asa Brink met us and took me out to his house 1 m. N.W. from Milltown, Hutchinson, Co., Dak. Rev. E.E. Bond preached, Isa. 16:10. My conference home at A. Brink's. Milltown is a store & post-office, only.

Thursday, October 18 Staid at Brink's, the forenoon. Conference opened at 1:30. I opened with report & then afterward spoke on the legal situation. Reports of P.E.'s and pastors were given. Prevails great drought. Dr. H.J. Becker pr. at 7:30, Matt. 25:25. Board at Brink 's.

Friday, October 19 Conference opened at 8:30, & progressed well. I dine at Rev. C.J. Rardin's with Davis' and Rev. Geo. Harding, all vivid Liberals except Harding. Conference progressed. Supper at Brink's. I pr. at 7:30, Rom. 4:16, "Father of us all."

Saturday, October 20 Conference continued. Dine at Wilson Shearer's. J.P. Cotton & Asa Brink elected prcs. elders. Conference closed at 4:00. Supper and lodging at Brink's. Dr. H.J. Becker lectured at 7:30, "Five Hundred miles in the Holy Land." G. Harding gave us news of the Wolverton, Oregon, opinion.

Sunday, October 21 I preach at Milltown, Psalms 16:11. Dine at J.N. Watson's, 3 miles n.e. Supper at C.J. Rardin's. At 7:00, H.J. Becker lectured on "Open Bible in Holy Land." Stay at A. Brink's.

Monday, October 22 Rev. A. Brink takes us to Parkston, and we start at 11:37, to Sioux City, where Dr. Becker goes on the Chi. & N.W. to Chicago & Dayton. I go on 7:05 train to Council Bluffs & Kansas City. I reached the latter place in the morning.

Tuesday, October 23 Arrived at Kansas City at 6:30, morn. I go on Metropolitan Cable Cars via Delaware and Vine Sts., to Reuchlin Wright's, 1908 38th St. I remain there all day. Children: Helen Margaret 5, Herbert, abt 21 months. Herbert says but few words, but climbs and runs like a monkey.

Wednesday, October 24 In the forenoon, we took a walk & hickory nut hunt with Helen 5, and Herbert 2. Nothing eventful occurred. Neighbors: Hobdey east, green house. Hobdey & Starling west; Hunt s.w. Hazard S. Turner, s.e.; Mr. Spore, s.e. Barnes n.e.

Thursday, October 25 At Reuchlin's forenoon. Dr. [blank] Merrill took dinner with us. I visited Mrs. Spore's with Lulu. Lulu went to the prayer meeting at 8:00. Reuchlin and I staid with the children. I wrote to Katie, and to John McBride, to-day. Mrs. Spore's daughter, married to Mr. Wright, lives in Connecticut.

Friday, October 26 Walk with the children in S.W. woods. Read some. Afternoon, took the children to photograph gallery cor. 18 & Campbell streets. I start at 7:00 & take 8:00 Burlington train for St. Louis. Slept five or six hours in reclining chair.

Saturday, October 27 Reached St. Louis on 8:05 "Big Four" train. Reach Indianapolis at 2:50; on 4:00 train; reach Richmond at 6:30; on 7:35 (8:00) train, reach Dayton at 10:00. At Richmond, I called at D.K. Zeller's 10 minutes.

Sunday, October 28 Attended School Street U.B. Church. Miss Hanly preached, Matt. 3:11, "Baptism of Fire." Dine at Lorin's. Called at Kiracofe's. Misses Sallie Hinter and Guitner also called there. I preach at Sch. St. at 7:30, 2 Tim. 5:15.

Monday, October 29 Write to Katie; go to town, pay Young thirty-five dollars on California suit. I order a new suit of clothes of Wells & Charch. Call twice at our publishing office.

Tuesday, October 30 At home. Writing letters on legal business etc. In the evening, I call at Lorin's an hour. Write till near midnight. Settle a bill of $21+, at Keiter's, squaring up.

Wednesday, October 31 At home writing. I read some (almost the first for a week) in the political periodicals.

Went to the post-office, and tailor's to try on the suit— or coat. Call at Lorin's and at Sines'. Wrote letters till 11:30, eve. H.J. Becker, D.D. called in the day.

Thursday, November 1 Thursday at home mostly engaged in writing. Dr. H.J. Becker called in the forenoon. Looked up files of the Conservator.

Friday, November 2 At home all day writing letters. I have had excellent health for six weeks past. The weather has been very beautiful, and to-day is so warm, as to need little if any fire, for comfort. Rained about dark.

Saturday, November 3 At home all forenoon. Go to town in the afternoon. Brought Milton, Jr. up to our house an hour. Supper at Lorin's. Spent the rest of the evening with the boys. Deposited money at Winter's National Bank and took out a bank book.

Sunday, November 4 Heard Rev. C.B. McDaniel preach at Sch. St. at 10:30, Matt. 7:21. I dine at John Weidner's on Home Ave. Her uncle Wm. Ensey being there. I go home before meeting. Rev. C.B. McDaniel preach again at 7:30, Ps. 103:2.

Monday, November 5 At home all day. Boys set up baseburner in my study. Revs. C.B. McDaniel & H.J. Becker called in forenoon. I called an hour in the evening at Kiracofe's.

Tuesday, November 6 This is the election day. I voted the Republican ticket as I do generally. I substituted the name of the Democratic candidate for Supr. Judge instead of that of Shauck. At home the rest of the day.

Wednesday, November 7 Went to town. Paid $35.00 on my suit to Charch & Wells. Saw Becker, and got L. Flinn's letter. An hour at Kiracofe's. I wrote an article in the eve for the Conservator.

Thursday, November 8 Went to town & bought Milton a little willow rocking chair, $2.00. Spent the rest of the day at home and an hour in the eve. at Lorin's.

Friday, November 9 At home. Did but little with my pen. Weather rather cold and damp.

Saturday, November 10 At home forenoon. Called at Publ. Office and went to town. Saw Young 5 minutes. Called at notion store near s.e. cor. 6th St. and at the post office. Lorin & family called an hour in the eve. Slept 9 hours. Wrote Floyd.

Sunday, November 11 Preached at Sch. St. Ch. at 10:30, Luke 2:52, on Life and character of Jesus. Dine at Lorin's. Worked till meeting time on Sketch of a sermon on Eph. 4:30. Rev. C.H. Kiracofe preached at 7:30, on Peter as a Man. Examined lines of Scrip. after meeting till 10:30.

Monday, November 12 At home. Kiracofe called to see about Dillon's article on Wolverton's decision. I spend afternoon & eve. in looking up topics, Scripture, subjects, etc.

Tuesday, November 13 In the forenoon, I got the *Conservator* and read it mostly. In the afternoon, I was copying letter, deed, etc. There was a "skiff" of snow on the ground all day.

Thursday, November 15 At home employed as usual. Went to bank in afternoon too late.

Friday, November 16 Spent the day mainly in writing. Went to town in the afternoon. Got draft and sent to Grant Co. to Ellis Wright to pay on my gas well, $100.00; also drafts, $5.00 each, for Dillon, Srrete, and copy (Canada) of decis. Bought bucket, etc. Saw Young 20 or 30 minutes. Gunckel's suggestion of pacification. Spent the evening at Pres. Kiracofe's.

Saturday, November 17 At home. Writing on the Canada decision. This is my sixty-seventh birth-day anniversary. Life to me has been crowned with blessings and blessedness. I have known but little physical suffering. Now my general health is as good as at any period in my life. I dined to-day by invitation at Lorin's. A mild clear day.

Sunday, November 18 Attended at Sch. St. Church. Dr. Kiracofe preached on Matt. 5:1-12. Dined at Lorin's. It is a mild hazy, sunshiny day. Ohio Anti-saloon league meeting at Association Hall, 3:45. Solo by Miss Cook. Russell is manager. Wheeler of Oberlin spoke. Rev. John Brandt of Clevel. I preach at School Street at 7:30, 2 Chron. 20:33, on Temperance.

Monday, November 19 At home all day. Wrote letters. Little unusual to be noted. I am in good health and have been since about Sept. 15th.

Tuesday, November 20 At home all day except calls at Publish. Office. Paid M.F. Keiter on my Mis. Subscription at Waterloo, $55.00.

Wednesday, November 21 At home all day except call at Publ. Office. Spent a half hour at Lorin's in the evening. Wrote Katie a long letter describing Smith (my oldest brother, now long deceased) and Sister Sarah, who died in 1868.

Thursday, November 22 At home. Wrote letters. Saw and talked with Dr. H.J. Becker.

Friday, November 23 Read proof on the tract Canada Decision. J.L. Whitney had a long talk with me on leasing my Grant Co., Indiana farm to a gas company. Kiracofe brought me the Evangelical Messenger, containing the Supr. Court Decision in Bay City Church case.

Saturday, November 24 Wrote letter to Wm. Lawrence and one to Katie & mailed them at the depot. Spent an hour at Young's examining the transcript of evidence. A little conversation with him. Sent out many of the traps Canada decision.

Sunday, November 25 Heard Rev. Dodd's pr. at 4th Presb. Church at 10:30, 2 Cor. 13: "Be perfect", Revs. S.L. Livingston and M.F. Keiter called; also Lorin & Nettie & Milton. At 7:30 went to School Street, hear Rev. Henley, Ed. *Firebrand*, "preached," Isa. 64:1,2. Sat up late (about 12:00) and worked on a plan of a sermon. Rev. Hanley of Shenendoah, Iowa (Page Co.)

Monday, November 26 Called at Pr. Office, and at Kiracofe's. Saw Weidner and Nicholas on the Street. Paid $2.00 to Keiter for tract Canada Decision. Kiracofe called in the evening to tell me of Prof. H.H. Thompson's talk on compromise.

Wednesday, November 28 Got the *Conservator*. Wrote much on letters. At home all day except that I called at Lorin's in the evening an hour.

Thursday, November 29 At home all day. It is the thirty-fifth anniversary (Thanksgiving anniversary) of mine & Susan's marriage. She was one of the choicest spirits earth ever knew. Our marriage was on Thanksgiving day, November 24, 1859.

Friday, November 30 Called at Pub. Office & at Prof. Kiracofe's. Mrs. Kiracofe had just returned from her brother's where her neice was very sick with typhoid fever. I spend the afternoon & night till 12:00 examining the Scriptures on immortality.

Saturday, December 1 At home in the forenoon. Dr. Kiracofe came at 2:00, going to W. Manchester at 5:15. I go to post-office, Bank, and call on Young 15 min. In the eve. 7:00, I hear a preacher, an Adventist, who lays out his ground, referred to his warning, and preached, Rev. 14:9, a good discourse on Christ, as the Creator.

Sunday, December 2 Attended S. School at School Street and taught Graybill's class, and beat the "Firebrands" Harley, Dill, & Graybill on John the Baptist's sin of unbelief & on the scribes & Pharisees "pipe." Went to Sprague St. Af Baptist Ch. & pr. for Pastor Patrick H. Williams, on Hebr. 11.10. Heard Adventist at 7:00 "Nature of the Word."

Monday, December 3 At home all day except errands to the grocery. Spent time in looking up theological views of the perpetuity of the Decalogue. Found about 22 great theologians affirming its perpetuity. At 7:00 heard at 1150 W. 3rd St., a lecture again of Rev. [blank] Subject, "Faith," somewhat mixed. Up till 12:00.

Tuesday, December 4 At home till 4:00. Took a copy Oregon Decision to Young—"Statement of the Case." Heard the Adventist preacher at 7:00 on "How to Gain the Victory."

Wednesday, December 5 At home all day except call at the Publ. Office, etc. Wrote letters. I hear the Adventist on Christ Second coming. Some strange doctrine and one contradiction of of [repeated in text] himself.

Thursday, December 6 At home. Wrote letters. Heard Adventist pr. at 7:15, on Signs of Christ's coming. He represented starts (Matt. 24) as not corresponding to the original word [a Greek word follows] which was false. "Sun-dark moon-blood, occurred May 19, 1880! "Stars fall," Nov. 1833! Webster says dark days occurred A.D. 252, 746, 775, 1716, 1732, 1762, 1785, 1780 in northern states. Falling meteors every 34 years.

Friday, December 7 At home the forenoon. Went to town in the afternoon. Called at Kumler Huffman's. Heard [blank]Adventist at 7:00. Subject the Image of Nebuchadnezzer's dream.

Saturday, December 8 At home mostly. Adventist lec. on 24th Chap. Matt.

Sunday, December 9 Attended Williams St. Baptist Church & heard Rev. Clatworthy, and Englishman, preach from John 21:7. "That disciple whom Jesus loved," an excellent discourse. In the evening at 7:00 heard the Adventist lecture on The Home of the Saved.

Monday, December 10 At home. Heard Adven. on Dan. 7th, Four Diverse Beasts.

Tuesday, December 11 At home. Very busy reading and writing. Heard text on Matt. 16:16. He said "Hell's the grave."

Wednesday, December 12 At home all day. Wrote many letters. Heard Adventist, on Dan. 8:[rest is blank]

Thursday, December 13 Not very well. Ate little till nearly noon. Make some preparation for going away to-morrow. Did not go to Adventist meeting to-night.

Friday, December 14 Left home at 7:00 via Union City & Marion, Ind. for Elkhart, Ind. Saw Charles Mundhenk of Pyrmont on the way. About two hours each at Un. City & Marion. Write Bp. Dillon & send some postal cards. Reach Elkhart at 5:29 & Go to Rev. E. Kidder's, 404 State Street & sup there. Preach at 7:30, Lu. 6:21, last half. Stay at Kidder's.

Saturday, December 15 At Kidder's in the forenoon. Call in afternoon at Rev. Evan's & Rev. Shideler's, both of Evangelical Association. I preach at 7:30, James 4:8; "Draw nigh to God," etc. Lodge at E. Kidder's. His son-in-law is Ed. Hunneryager, & daughter Maud. Mildred is the youngest daughter. The young couple live there.

Sunday, December 16 Preach at 10:30, Acts 7:59. Dine at Mother Luke's & remain till evening meeting; they away east on the street. Preach at 7:00, Rom. 2:7, "Them who by patient contin...glory, honor & immort." Warned people against expelled ministers. Stay at E. Kidder's.

Monday, December 17 Go on 8:15 train to Fairmount. Wrote letters on the train, to Rev. J.H. Greider & W.A. Weimer. Saw on the tr. a student of N. Manchester, Mr. Yoder. I reach Fairmount at 12:24. Call at the post-office and at Hollingworth's to see Rev. Wm. Hall. Go with Mr. Milspaugh to Ellis Wright's 6 miles east. Lodge there.

Tuesday, December 18 Go to Wm. H.H. Reeder's & found nobody at home; so I return to Ellis's. In the afternoon, we go to Fowler's tile factory. After supper, we return to Fowler's again to a gas meeting & arrange our by-laws. I stay that night at Elis's.

Wednesday, December 19 Ellis takes me to Fairmount. Call at Rev. N.D. Wolfard's & at Elwood Davis's. Davis's all away. Dine with Ellis at a restaurant. I go on 12:24 train to Anderson, & on 3:30 train to Richmond & on 5:15 train to Dayton. Arrive at 6:15. Miss M.M. Titus on the train from Richmond.

Thursday, December 20 At home all forenoon arranging my room, etc. Telegram from Katie. She got home about 4:40. Was unwell yesterday morning.

Friday, December 21 At home most of the day. Called at Kiracofe's in the afternoon to see about Exec. Missionary meeting the 26th. Heard Adventist at 7:15, sham [?] time.

Saturday, December 22 At home all day. Lent Lorin $200.00 to go into laundery business. Heard Adventist at 7:15 artificial time.

Sunday, December 23 Hears Rev. Maurice Wilson preach (Matt. 1:23) on Christmas; 1st Pres. Church. Called after dinner at Lorin's an hour or more. Heard the Adventist at 7:15 (lying time) on Who changed the Sabbath? He

held that it was the Catholic Church!

Monday, December 24 At home in the forenoon. In the afternoon went to town. It was a rainy afternoon. In the evening (7:15 false time) I heard the Adventist again, on the Rest in Christ. He reasons like, the "Jackpie is a Johnpie & a Johnpie is a pie-John-pigeon." Hence a jackpie is a pigeon.

Tuesday, December 25 Dined at Lorin's with Katherine and the boys. Went in evening at 7:00 to hear the Adventist on Matt. 11:28.

Wednesday, December 26 Wrote an article on Sab. school lesson for Jan. 13, 1895, on miracle of Feeding the Five Thousand Mark 6: [blank] Attend council of Ex. Com. with the W.M.A. committee; also Ex. Com. session, at Rev. M.F. Keiter's. Bishop H. Floyd supped & lodged with me. Supper at Greenwood's.

Thursday, December 27 Breakfast, Dinner & supper at Greenwood's. Go in morn. with Bp. Floyd to our printing office, Rev. S.L. Livingston dines with me at Greenwood's. See Revs. Becker, Keiter, Kiracofe & Floyd at Keiter's about our lawsuits. Supper at Greenwood's. Spend an hour (eve.) at Lorin's

Friday, December 28 Katherine started for Chicago at 8:48 R'y time; to visit Rev. E.P. Goodwin's daughter of Dr. E.P. Goodwin. I go to town.

Saturday, December 29 At home arranging my receipts of many years. Get a card from Katherine at Chicago. Rev. S.L. Livingston called also Rev. C.H. Kiracofe; the former to arrange for me not to go away, the latter to recall it. I go on 5:15 train to Germantown. Lodge at Levi Zehring's.

Sunday, December 30 Preach at 10:00, Rev. 2:7, "To him that overcometh." Dine at Shem Thomas's & supper. Preach at 7:00, Ps. 16:11. "In thy presence," Stay at Shem Thomas's. Rose E. Salisbury, Dr. L. Davis' adopted daughter, wife of Chas. A. Salisbury, died at 3:00, forenoon, at Buffalo, New York.

Monday, December 31 Call at Mr. Lane's (Michael Thomas' former residence) at Rev. P.Y. Gephart's, and at Rev.

C.B. McDaniel's. Leave on 10:15 train, via Carlisle, to Dayton. Call at Conservator Office at 1:00, at U.B. Mission rooms at 2:30 to see Weaver. *All foolishness! At home the rest of the day and evening. Rose E. Salisbury is brought a corpse, to Dayton, from Buffalo. *Dr. Becker had a communication with W.M. Bell & Bell had arranged for a meeting. Weaver had nothing to propose! He professed to expect me to make some concession!

[The following appears as notes at the end of the diary]

Sent Home, by draft August 29, to Orville 40.00, Sept. 3 to Orville 250.00, Sept. 11 to Wilbur 235.00, Sept. 15, by Kiracofe 60.00

Bishop's Salary
Upper Wabash 66.00, St. Joseph 77.91, North Ohio 236.00, Michigan 194.07, Wisconsin 27.17, Iowa 61.00, West Des Moines 56.00, Nebraska 61.50, Elkhorn 25.91 [for a total of] 921.56.

Old Saying
"If you your lips would keep from slips, Five things observe with care: Of whom you speak, to whom you speak, And how, and when, and where."

"The law does not specify how fast a person shall run after a slave while he is trying to catch him." Lincoln.

United States Court
H. S. Brown of Mich. Sup J. Wm. H. Taft, Cir. Judge, Ohio, Horace H. Lurton Cir J. Term. Augustus J. Ricks, Dist. J. Clevel. Geo. R. Sage Dist. J. Cin.

Mich. Supreme Court.
Frank A. Hooker, C. J. John W. McGrath, J, Chas. D. Young, J, C. B. Grant, J, Robt. M. Montgomery J.

Indiana Supr. Court.
Silas D. Coffey C. J. Hackney J. McCabe, J. Howard, J. Daley, J.

Pennsylvania Supr. Court.
J. P. Sterrett, C. J. H. Green J. Henry W. Williams, J. Dean J, J. B. McCollum, J. T. J. Mitchell J, Thompson J.

1895

Tuesday, January 1 This is the beginning of another year, of which I have seen sixty six; and truly my life has been full of blessings. I think few have enjoyed life more than I have. I took Milton a set of building blocks. I was at home the rest of the day.

Wednesday, January 2 A letter came from Daughter Katherine, written at Dr. E. Park Goodwin's at Chicago. I paid my tax on which there was $4.27 delinquency charges, I supposing I had paid the first half in June!

Friday, January 4 At home. Dr. H.J. Becker called an hour. Lent him a work on Spiritualism, Necromancy, etc.

Saturday, January 5 At home about all day. Rev. C.H. Kiracofe called to leave a letter relating to a mortgage on a church in North Michigan Conference.

Sunday, January 6 Preached at Sch. St. Church at 10:30, Ps. 21:6. At home the rest of the day. The day was mostly a rainy one. I spent the evening especially in examining the first Chapter of Isaiah with Joseph Addison Alexander's notes, which are excellent; expository.

Monday, January 7 At home nearly all day. Called at the Conservator office sometime in the forenoon.

Tuesday, January 8 Went to town in the forenoon. Saw Young 20 min. Went to Cash Register Manufactury, & saw R. Thurston Houk about a charge of $20.00 in Pontiac case by his father. Gave Nettie a birthday present. It proved to be her birth-day. I called two hours at Prof. Kiracofe's.

Wednesday, January 9 At home mostly. Wrote some letters. Prepared a list of Walla Walla preachers for Year Book. Sent by Lorin for Gilfillin on Sabbath, etc. Saw Dr. Becker at Keiter's office.

Thursday, January 10 Somewhat rainy & snowy, which ended in several inches of snowfall in the night. I searched for revised Old Testament & finding none, I sent Katherine my two volumes of it. Called at the Office and got a New Version Bible of Keiter's.

Friday, January 11 At home in the forenoon. Write for railroad favors on Balt. & O., and on Mich. Centr. Go to town in the afternoon; buy a return Clergyman's ticket on Penn. lines to Anderson. Rev. Wm. B. Stoddard & Rev. H. J. Becker called in the evening. Considerable snow.

Saturday, January 12 Start at 8:53 for Anderson & Marion, Indiana. Made close connection at Anderson & reached Marion at 2:00. Mark Hillshammer meets me with a sleigh and takes me to Cyrus Smith's. Supper and lodging there with Rev. I.M. Tharp, the pastor. I pr. at 7:00, Mal. 3:16, "That thought his name."

Sunday, January 13 Preach at Horton St., North Marion, at 10:30, Gal. 4:4. I dine at Hez. B. Wysong's on Bond Ave. corner of Horton. Stay till night; also lodge there. I preach at 7:00, John 14:21. Three joined the Church. Still snowy. "I will love —manifest myself to him." John 14.21.

Monday, January 14 Called at Calvin McRea's and at Alex. Keith's, and dined at Rev. W.C. Ketner's. Meeting at 2:00, led by Rev. I.M. Tharp. Supper at Ketner's. Bro. Tharp preached at 7:00, Rom. 6.23. We stay at Rev. C. Smith's. The day was clear and mild.

Tuesday, January 15 Went to Eddy Hillshammer's with Tharp. Dine at John Y. Partlett's, Jacob Wingard was there. Excellent meeting at 2:00 which I led. I go to Cyrus Smith's. I preach at 7:00, Heb. 2:3. Stay at Rev. Wm. C. Ketner's. "How shall we escape—neglect," etc.

Wednesday, January 16 Go with Rev. I.M. Tharp to Geo. Rinker's. Call at Mr. Davis's to see Barbary Keith. We dine at Aaron Eubank's, after I had gone to the post-office, and called at Lee Hall's and Robt. Fryer's, stores. Meeting at 2:00. Call at Ketner's & sup at C. Smith's with Tharp and Elijah Morrison. Pr. at 7:00 1 John 2:15. Stay at Mark Hillshammer's.

Thursday, January 17 Rev. I.M. Tharp takes me in a sleigh to C. Smith's post-office, & to Mrs. Susan Smith's on S. Bronson No. 815, where I dine. Then he takes me to "Wabash" depot. Go on noon train to Fairmount. Call at Clint Brattain's, Elwood Davis's & go on to Ellis Wright's, riding 2 ms. with Holoway Ellis's Myrl, aged 2 ys & 10 mos.

Friday, January 18 Go to Oliver Glass's. Dine there & stay till 3:00. Call an hour at Robt. B. Reeder's. Oliver's children: Marcus, 3; Mabel, 14 mo. Robert's children: Crystal, 22 mo; George abt. 7 mo. Go to Ellis Wright's. Wm. Reeder comes after me and I go to his house & stay the night. David Fultz lives there; Ralph Fultz lives at Robert's—Wm. Fultz' children.

Saturday, January 19 Wm. takes me to Fairmount & I go on 12:24 train to Anderson, & thence on 3:30 train to Richmond; thence on 5:15 tr. to Dayton, arriving at 7:25. I found the folk in about usual health.

Sunday, January 20 Heard Prof. C.H. Kiracofe preach at School Street Luke 15:23. At home the rest of the day. Lorin & Netta called in the evening an hour.

Monday, January 21 At home. Called at the Office (Keiter's). Prof. Kiracofe told me of Rev. W.E. Mosier's death, which occurred the 19th of this month.

Tuesday, January 22 Called at Keiter's office & at Kiracofe's. I go to town in the afternoon. See Young 20 min. Get some railroad permits. At home the rest of the day.

Wednesday, January 23 At home. Write letters. It was a cold day, but considerably above zero.

Thursday, January 24 At home all forenoon. Call at Lorin's a half hour in the afternoon. A right cold day. Write letters.

Sunday, January 27 Heard Rev. S.L. Livingston preach at 10:20 and at 7:20, both sermons on Col. 4:5, "Walking with wisdom," etc. I dine with Livingston at S. Spidel's. Supper at home. Quite cold.

Monday, January 28 Called at Kiracofe's a 1/2 hour in forenoon. Pretty cold day.

Tuesday, January 29 Went on 9:15 train to Xenia to Reform Convention. Dined at Rev. J.G. Carson's, D.D. Came home on the evening train—about 7:00. Cold day & night.

Wednesday, January 30 At home. Went to town in the afternoon. Cold day & night.

Thursday, January 31 At home all forenoon, writing. Called at Orville's office in the afternoon. Thermometer at 0 degrees at 8 morn. (Over 6 degrees below zero).

Friday, February 1 At home. Drs. H.J. Becker and Kiracofe called in the evening.

Saturday, February 2 Went on 12:25 train to Brookville, Ohio. Supper at John Zehring's. He takes me to Olivet. I preach at 7:00, *Matt. 19:27 Miss Mills at the altar. I stay with Rev. S.L. Livingston at G.W. Warvel's. Congregation is large. *"Les we have left all & followed thee."

Sunday, February 3 I preach at 10:30, Rom. 10:13. Dine with Livingston at Rev. Aaron Zehring's. In afternoon, call at Martha Shank's. We sup at Aaron Wysong's. I preach at 6:30. Hebr. 4:15, "Touched with a feeling— infor [?] Stay with Lew. at Warvel's. Miss Mills is converted to-day. House overcrowded in the evening.

Monday, February 4 Ephraim Warvel takes me to Brookville, & I go home on 7:48 train. Saw Kiracofe about an Ed. Note. At home the rest of the day writing letters. Dr. H. J. Becker and Moses Hull began their debate on Spiritualism, at Cor. 5th & Jeff. Sts. Wilbur & Orville there.

Tuesday, February 5 At home. Write letters. Debate continued. Becker worsted, it is said.

Wednesday, February 6 At home. Put things to rights. Mis. Ex. Committee met at 2:00. Some snow fell & the weather quite cold. Debate continued. Boys report Becker as victorious.

Thursday, February 7 A very cold day. Thermometer little if any above zero all day. I was at home all day. Did but little except try to keep warm. The boys report that Becker made a fine success and came off victorious, manifestly.

Friday, February 8 This was the coldest morning of the year so far. Thermometer away below zero. I went to town. Sent Katharine $10.00. Wrote letters.

Saturday, February 9 At home all day except on errands. Dr. C.H. Kiracofe called about 5:00, Aftn. The boys were at home after 7:00 Aftn.

Sunday, February 10 I preach at School Street Church at 10:30, *Luke 23:4. Called after dinner at Lorin's an hour. Rev. C.H. Kiracofe preached at 7:30, *Mal 3:8. *"I find no fault with this man." "Wherein have we robbed" etc.

Monday, February 11 At home all day. Wrote letters in the forenoon. Lorin came in the afternoon and assisted me in comparing my receipts and Legal Fund accounts— Book, 3 hours. Call an hour at Lorin's in the evening.

Tuesday, February 12 At home. Write some. Orville about sick with cold in his head. In the evening I go on Orville's ticket to "Association Hall to witness the sleight of hand of the Japanese Magician.

Wednesday, February 13 At home in the forenoon. Go on 4:38 train to Franklin, and thence to Christopher

Blinn's with Mr. Eyer. Stay there—about 1 1/2 miles N.E. of Red Lion & 3 miles S.E. of Springboro.

Thursday, February 14 Preach the funeral of Margaret Jane Blinn, wife of Christopher Blinn, a grandson of Rev. Joseph Henry Fry, Mother Koerner's own cousin, at 11:00, & bury her at Springborough Cemetery. Dine at C. Blinn's. Cabman takes me to Franklin. Call at Lorin's when arrived at Dayton. At home.

Friday, February 15 At home all day. Prof. Kiracofe called in the afternoon.

Saturday, February 16 At home in forenoon. Called at the Bank in the afternoon & at Young's 10 minutes. Sent $10.00 to Rev. H.J. Barnaby for Hartsv. College in behalf of C. Blinn, & $5.00 as a present to J.F. Croddy in my own behalf. The Boys spent the evening in my room.

Sunday, February 17 Heard Rev. S.L. Livingston preach at 10:30 at School Street Church, *1 Pet. 5:6. Dine with Liv. at Spidel's & stay till evening meeting. L. preached again at 7:30, 139 ps. 23, 24 verses. *"Humble yourselves therefore." "Search me, O God, & know my heart; try me and know my thoughts; and see if there be any way of sickness, etc.

Monday, February 18 Called at Wm. Bartles' (Davis's) and at Kiracofe's. Wrote many letters.

Tuesday, February 19 At home forenoon. At Mrs. Rebecca Davis's funeral at 2:00+. I prayed at the residence, and Pres. C.H. Kiracofe was left 5 minutes to speak at the church. Rev. H. Garst & Prof. G. Funkhouser were the principal speakers.

Wednesday, February 20 Called at Wm. Bartles'. Saw Mrs. Cretia Edwards, Mrs. Lesher, her daughter and Mrs. Wax. Called at C.H. Kiracofe's, 119 N. Summit Street. After dinner, went to Bank, and Mrs. Hall, the dressmaker, & at Lorin's.

Thursday, February 21 At home except a call at Keiter's office, forenoon. Prof. Kiracofe called in the afternoon.

Friday, February 22 Called at Lorin's. Went in afternoon to W.H. Craighead's office with Prof. Kiracofe about Fred. Thomas' estate suit. Mailed 24 letters to N. Mich. brethren soliciting funds for the U.S. Case.

Saturday, February 23 Went to town inforenoon. Called at Young's to get their bill. In the afternoon, called at Wm. Bartle's, he being very sick, & I went on 5:20 to Brookville, O. & staid at John Zehring's.

Sunday, February 24 John & daughter & myself go to Olivet Church, where I preach at 11:00, Gal. *4:45. Dine at Rev. A. Zehring's. Preach at 7:00, Acts 26:28. Stay at Bro. George Warvel's. *When the fullness of time had come, God sent." + "Almost thou persuadest."

Monday, February 25 Bro. Warvel takes me to 8:35 train at Brookville. I reach home in forenoon. Call at Lorin's afternoon & Milton comes home with me on a visit, and stays over a half hour.

Tuesday, February 26 Call in forenoon an hour at Wm. Bartles'. Go to town. Buy a paper file $11.00 at [blank] Got a letter from Katie saying she is sick with quinsy. Write her a letter in the evening, enclosing a draft for forty dollars to Mrs. Morrison. Wilbur staid with William Bartles.

Wednesday, February 27 At home forenoon. Call at Wm. Bartles' about 1:30 (railroad) about ten minutes after his death. Call at Kiracofe's a few minutes. Go to town. Call at Lorin's. Call an hour at Wm. Bartles. Wilbur stays there again to-night.

Friday, March 1 At home. At 1:20 was Wm. Bartles' funeral. Funkhouser, Miller & Landis officiated. Some of the brethren held counsel at Keiter's office about a place for our Church in the city. They thought of buying a lot to move School Street church onto.

Saturday, March 2 At home most of the day. Went to town and paid Young & Young in full on legal accounts; Sixty one dollars & five cents on the United States case and two hundred and twenty three and sixty seven cents, on Printing Est. Case. Rec'd a draft (own account) from Ellis, $145.

Sunday, March 3 Preached at School Street Church at 10:30, *Isa. 55.1. At home till evening. Preached again at 7:30, Hebr. 12:28, 29. It rains a very little in the night, after a fair day. In the afternoon, I was much interested in reading Nast's comments on Second chapter of Matthew. +"Wherefore receiving a kin." *"Tho everyone that thirstith."

Monday, March 4 At home. Called at Kiracofe's in evening and at Bartles'.

Tuesday, March 5 At home. Called at the bank & at Reeve's to see about spectacles. Called at Kiracofe's to see Alvin. Kiracofe, Becker, Keiter & myself met at Keiter's office to consult over Bp. Dillon's financial terms & on location of West Side Services.

Wednesday, March 6 Wednesday at home. Dr. H.J. Becker called an hour in the eve. Boys in, an hour or so.

Thursday, March 7 At home all forenoon. Begin to fill my letter file case. Go afternoon to town. Get my spectacles, which were reglued.

Friday, March 8 At home all day. Sent out many letters soliciting U.S. suit legal funds. I arranged my letters in their files.

Saturday, March 9 At home. Go on 5:00 eve. train to Brookville where George W. Warvel (laymen) meets me and takes me to Olivet Ch. where I preach at 7:45, I Kings 18.21. "If Lord". Stay at Aaron Wysong's. His fatherinlaw, Wright, a German.

Sunday, March 10 Preached at Olivet, at 10:30, *Job. 1:8, on the "Higher Life." Dine at Rev. Aaron Zehring's with John Zehring & wife. Preach at 7:00, *Jer. 13.21 to a large & very attentive congregation. Lodge at A. Zehring's. *"A perfect & upright man." "What shall thou say, when he shall punish thee."

Monday, March 11 Stay at Zehring's till after an early dinner, when Aaron takes me to Farmersville & and [both are in text] to John Reel's, he being a Radical and very aged. I call at Sharritt's in town. Go on train via Carlisle to Dayton. Saw Rev. C.B. McDaniel's & arranged for him to preach & protract at Germant.

Tuesday, March 12 Go on 8:20 morn. train to Liberty, Ind., to preach Mrs. Chas. R. Paddack's funeral. He met me at the train & took me to his house. Preached at M.E. Church at 2:30, Acts 24:15. Go with Dan'l Koerner to his house, 7 miles South.

Wednesday, March 13 Write in the forenoon on Ontario case. Go, after early dinner, to Quincy Brookbank's & stay nearly three hours. Daniel takes me to Liberty. Go on the 5:13 train to Rushville. Walk out to John McKee's. Rode two miles of the way with Dr. Greene in a ball-bearing buggy. Drucilla afflicted with cancer.

Thursday, March 14 Went on to Harvey's with Thomas Wilhelm. Staid at Harvey's all day & lodged there. Our discussion on the Trinity, etc.

Friday, March 15 Go to Luther Newhouse's & to Thomas Wright's. Dine there. Return to Harvey Wright's. Charley Gray nearly sick with cold. Thomas & wife spent the evening at Harvey's.

Saturday, March 16 Harvey takes me to Jabez Rhoads, and they to Knightstown, & I go on 11:51 (artificial time) tr. to Fairmount, where I stop at J.B. Hollingsworth's, with Rev. Wm. Hall. They have at home a son abt. 17 ys. and a daughter abt. 11 ys.

Sunday, March 17 I preached at Union Church at 11:00, *Gal. 6.15. Dine at Robt. Hastins's. Preach at our Church at 3:00, +Job 1:8. Supper at Chas. Atkinson's. Rev. I.M. Tharp pr. at 7:00, Rom. 14:12, "Give an account—ourselves to God." We stay at Clinton Brattain's. *"Neither circumcision availith anything—a new creed." +"perfect & upright man."

Monday, March 18 We stay at Clinton Brattain's till 10:00 & after an hour up town, return & dine there. With his horse & buggy, we go to Ellis Wright's, W.H.H. Reeder's & stay all night. John H. Braden had visited them, and was recently married.

Tuesday, March 19 Go back to Ellis' & thence to Fairmount. Dine at Brattain's. Go on 1:37 tr. to Marion & pay my tax. Go on 2:58 tr. to Union City, and thence on 6:15 tr. to Dayton. Found all well.

Wednesday, March 20 Called at Keiter's office. Called at Lorin's. At home sick the rest of the day & night.

Thursday, March 21 Sick at home.

Friday, March 22 Cleaned up the upper rooms, which sadly needed it, which I was far from being able to do.

Sunday, March 24 At home forenoon, till about dinner time. Go to Lorin's & dine & stay till after 6:00. Some talk about my moving into their upper front room. Return home.

Monday, March 25 At home all day abed as much as practicable. Perhaps less fever. Lorin & Nettie called in the evening, Dr. Becker in forenoon.

Tuesday, March 26 After breakfast, I went to Lorin's, 117 Hawthorn St. intending to stay till I recover health. Dr. L. Spitler called at 3:45. I sent Treasurer of Adair Co., Iowa $ draft for $35.00 on tax. Slept well.

Wednesday, March 27 Feel, as usual, better in the morning. Write to Katharine & to Reuchlin. Am very sick with Influenza. (or Eresypelas).

Thursday, March 28 Thursday, the fever continued. Quite sick.

Friday, March 29 The Dr. an[n]ounced that I had Eresepelas, and they painted my face and head with Ichthiol, and gave me a preparation of iron.

Saturday, March 30–Tuesday, April 2 I was very sick.

Wednesday, April 3 Katherine came home from Oberlin in the evening.

Thursday, April 4 Improving somewhat. Read considerably in Newspapers & in the Bible. (?) [question mark appears in text]

Sunday, April 7 Change dress after bathing. Katherine attended the 4th Pres. Church in the evening.

Monday, April 8 I was probably some better—perhaps considerably better.

Tuesday, April 9 The children greased my head & face & washed off some of the Ichthiol.

Wednesday, April 10 Katharine started on 10:53 train to Oberlin. Wrote since that she arrived on time, abt. 7:43 Eve.

Friday, April 12 Received two letters from Katharine this morning. The morning is cloudy with some rain. Rev. G.W. Allman came in the evening. Supper with Lorin's & he lodged at my house with our boys & Breakfast at Greenwood's. I slept pretty well.

Saturday, April 13 Sat up forenoon. Mostly—abed Aftn. Prof. C.H. Kiracofe called in the morn. & eve, going to & returning from Germantown. Rev. G.W. Allman called a time or two in the day. I Slept fairly well.

Sunday, April 14 A cloudy Easter. Sat up part of the forenoon below stairs. Milton is excited somewhat over his colored Easter eggs.

Monday, April 15 Wrote some letters and sat up half of the day. Feel stronger and have better action than since I began to sit up. Orville spent the evening with me.

Tuesday, April 16 Went at 10:00 to my house. Got some articles I wanted & returned at 11:30. Saw Mrs. Bessie Dillon.

Wednesday, April 17 At Lorin's till after dinner. Then went up to my house & arranged things in desk, etc. & brought some things I wanted. Rev. H.J. Becker called an hour about 5:00. Orville calle[d] about the same time. I am considerably stronger to-day.

Thursday, April 18 Wrote a difficult letter in the forenoon. Prof. C.H. Kiracofe called an hour in the afternoon. Wilbur called after dinner. I sat up all day & went to bed at 8:00 (artif. time) and slept seven & one half hours.

Friday, April 19 At Lorin's in the forenoon. I wrote letters and sent Reuchlin $75.00 and Katharine $35.00. I went up to the store (boys') and to Surface's, Bookwalter's, and to my house where I spent an hour. Wrote letters in the evening. Lorin & family spent the

evening at Hary Andrews'. I Slept about 5 hours.

Saturday, April 20 Arose at about 5:30. Wrote several letters during the day. In the afternoon Dr. Kiracofe called and showed me a report or letter, from Rev. D.F. Wilberforce, of Danville, Africa, our Superintendent of Missions there. After dark, I walked up to Nipgen's, (9 squares in all and got 50 two-cent postal stamps. Slept well.

Sunday, April 21 Arose about 6:00 Bathed, changed clothes, and dressed up for the Breakfast, about 8:00, real time. Still better in health to-day. I go up to our house and stay 2 or 3 hours. Wm. Andrews & Lottie called at Lorin's in the afternoon. I slept well full eight hours at night.

Monday, April 22 Write to Ellis, Reuchlin, W.I. Phillips, etc. Worked some on the N. Ohio responses to my appeal for U.S. Case legal fund. Went to town after 3:00. Saw Feight, Bought shoes, Saw Young, not over 10 minutes. Looked over the rest of the N. Ohio responses and noted pledges. Sat up till 10:00. Slept well till 3:00.

Tuesday, April 23 Wrote some. Went to the Boys' Store in afternoon, and to my house.

Wednesday, April 24 At home in forenoon, writing a blank will for an Illinois person. In the afternoon [rest is blank]

Thursday, April 25 Wrote Letters. Worked on points to prove in U.S. Case. Consulted Wilbur on it. Did not get it ready to take to Young.

Friday, April 26 Wrote a letter, went to town, saw Young 15 min. Paid Miss Long, Treas, Anti-Saloon League, $2.75. $3.00 in all on my subscript. Orville called & talked on business, after dinner. At Lorin's the rest of the day.

Saturday, April 27 At Lorin's. Write letters. Call at the Conservator office, in the morning and an hour about 4:30. Wrote many letters to-day . Am getting along quite well in recovery. Lorin was sick all night from the eating of a gift piece of Bologna.

Sunday, April 28 Got up at 5:00. Got breakfast for self

at 7:00. Went to School St. Church. Heard Rev. C.H. Kiracofe preach at 10:30, a good sermon. I dine at his house and remain till evening. Stay at Lorin's. Lorin was getting much better by evening.

Monday, April 29 At home. Prepared to go away to Indiana. Wrote a set of notes on Mr. L.B. Gunckel's proposed agreement of Attorneys, in U.S. case. Saw Mr. Young 10 min. Sent my observations to Young by Orville.

Tuesday, April 30 Self home about 7:00 morn. and via Union City & Gas City & Jonesboro, arrive at Fairmount, Ind., at 12:24 Aftn. I saw Mr. Paddock, the real estate & railroad man. A Mr. Foster watched for me for Kibbey with whom I rode out to Ellis Wright's where I supped & lodged.

Wednesday, May 1 With Ellis I called on Frank Kirkwood & on Henry Simons. Looked at our town site and agreed on terms on which we would option. Stay at Ellis's.

Thursday, May 2 Went to Fairmount with Kibbey again. I stay at Clinton Bratain's.

Friday, May 3 Pliny Wolfard takes me to Ellis Wright's. Visit Robert Reeder's. Attend an oil meeting. Stay at Oliver K. Glass'.

Saturday, May 4 Return to Ellis W's. Call on Simons who is away in Afternoon. Look at railroad & its workers. The track is within 3/4 mile of the depot. Sup & lodge with Wm. H.H. Reeder.

Sunday, May 5 Wm. Reider [Reeder?] takes me to Fairmount. We call at Brattain's and I return there for dinner. We attend Quaker meeting at 11:00. Prof. Ellis spoke & I followed. I preach at 3:30, *Zach. 9:12. I stay at Chas. Atkinson's. I called at Asa Driggs' whose wife is Rhoda Wright's mother's sister. Ellis there.

Monday, May 6 Dine at Wm. Heath's, west of Quaker Church. Stay 2 hours at I.A. Anderson's. Robt. Hastings there. Tea & lodging at Clinton Bratain's. Mr. Hobbs & wife spend the evening with us, he a school teacher; she Wm. DuLing's daughter.

Tuesday, May 7 Went on 8:50 tr. to Marion & thence at 12:07 to Chicago, via Logansport. Waiting train. I called on Wysong's, Keith's & Smith's in North Marion. I reach Chicago at 5:00. Call at Carpenter Building a few minutes, 221 W. Madison St. Stay at Galt House.

Wednesday, May 8 Met with the Board of managers first; then with the Corporate members of Nat. Chris. Ass'n., both in Carpenter Building. Dine at a neighboring restaurant & sup there. Go on 6:30 tr. to Ravenswood, to Bennett's Hall. Heard Rev. Wm. B. Stoddard & Pres. Chas. A. Blanchard speak. I Stay at Robt. Bennett's. He in the Orient.

Thursday, May 9 Mrs. McCune & daughter, a son of Mr. Bennett's, & a cousin Bennett are our company at Breakfast. I attend the Convention & hear Bp. W. Dillon & Mr. Fenton. Dine at Rev. E.P. Goodwin's, D.D., at 354 Washington Bolavard. Call at Carpenter B'ldg. Go on 8:30 train with Wm. Dillon home.

Friday, May 10 Arrive about 6:30. Fix up. Write some. Sleep some. At home about all day except to see my house & to see the boys about painting it. Went to bed early & slept long.

Saturday, May 11 At home mostly, at Lorin's. Wrote several letters. Went to the house in the afternoon and to see my boys at their store and office. Went to bed early & slept long. Sleight frost, to-night.

Sunday, May 12 Read Solomon's song at 6:00 & then took another nap. Went to Sch. Street & pr. 10:30, *Col. 1:13,14. Call at Bp. Dillon's, go to Lorin's. After dinner, I spend an hour with Wilbur at old home. Went nearly to School Street and found Keiter had sent word I was not coming! Call an hour at old home, cold-like day. *"Delivered us from darkness," etc.

Monday, May 13 At Lorin's all day except a trip to East side. Saw Will Young, George being out of town & to be absent all the week, and I called at the Boys' Store and at our house. Wrote letters. The day is rainy and cold.

Tuesday, May 14 Called at Conservator Office. Saw Rev. Covert of Anderson, Ind. Paid M.F. Keiter $168.98 of

Mis. money, being residue of Mrs. Andrew Dorcas Will (of $300.00) after litigation. Was at Dr. Becker's Exposure of Spiritualism at 8:00, eve. Covert exhibited his "live" ghosts.

Wednesday, May 15 Spent part of the day at my old study (room) on Hawthorn Street. Wrote several letters.

Thursday, May 16 Spent most of the day at my old study. Wrote some letters. Studied and wrote some on the book of Ecclesiastes & worked some about the door-yard.

Friday, May 17 Spent nearly all day at my old home writing to Katharine & Reuchlin. Wrote K. at length on the authorship of the book of Ecclesiastes, which I proved to be Solomon's. The weather has been cold for a week past. Lorin went to inspect Hull's Seance.

Saturday, May 18 Went early to my own house. The painters came to put on the finishing coat on our house. Wrote letters. Sent $1.00 for type-writer ribbon; $4.50 for Hom. Review & Faucett's Cyclopedia. Sent Kath. $20.00. Pd J.G. Feight $10.10 for finishing carpenter work on our house, 7 Hawthorne Street.

Sunday, May 19 Heard Rev. C.B. McDaniel pr. at Sch. St. Church at 10:30, real time, Ps. 91:2, on "Trust in God." Dined with him at Sam'l Spidel's & remained till eve. I pr. at the same Church at 8:00 real time, *Rev. 6:9-11, on Persecution of those who are for Experiemntal Religion & Heroes for nonpopular truths. Lodge at Lorin's. *"Opened the 5th seal."

Monday, May 20 At home. Write letters or cards. Called at Keiter's office in afternoon. Beacham's painters nearly finish the second coat on our house. Rev. C.H. Kiracofe & Alvin called at my study in the evening about 8:00.

Tuesday, May 21 At home get ready to go away & busy writing. Had a consultation with the ministers at 7:00 eve. Little results.

Wednesday, May 22 Went on 8:52 tr. to Richmond. Stopped at D.K. Zeller's till after dinner. Saw Mrs. Susan Zartman & Mrs. Joseph V. Zartman of Marion, Ind. Went on 1:10 tr. to Dublin to W.M. Assoc. Put up at Lewis Cranor's. Children: One (oldest) near

Williamsburg; Ottie 19; Mable 16. Rev. R.S. Bowman's Annual address at 8:00. Good. I stay at Cranor's with N.D. Wolfard.

Thursday, May 23 Called at Dr. G.W. Champ's with N.D. Wolfard. Talk on Prohibition party. At Committees & Association. Dine at Bp. H. Floyd's. Called at Gray's. Rev. John Cranor's, & Mary Smith's. At the Association Supper at Lewis Cranor's & went on 5:52 tr. to Richmond & thence on 7·00 excursion tr to Dayton, arriving about 8:30.

Friday, May 24 At home writing. In afternoon called at Best's & got my watch, $3.00 charges; at Young's 15 minutes; and at Wilbur's bicycle store, 23 W. Second Street.

Saturday, May 25 At home writing. Called at the office and at Prof. C.H. Kiracofe's about 5:00 afternoon. In eve., spent half-hour with Young at residence.

Sunday, May 26 I pr. at Sch. St. Church at 10:30 (true time) Col. 4:5. Rains on the way home. Call at M.F. Keiter's at 4:00; see Mrs. W.H. Conner there. Do some writing in Aftern. & evening. *"Walk in wisdom—without redeeming the time."

Monday, May 27 Start at 5:00 to Richmond. Call at D.K. Zeller's office & negotiate loan. Call at T. Study's office. Call at Zeller's house. Go to Elwood on 10:35. Stop for dinner at Bro. Shatterly's, C.W. Rector, A.L. Stanley, & others there. Go on to Gibson City & stay at J.F. Croddy's, my cousins.

Tuesday, May 28 Walk about town with Bertha, calling at Mary James', & at other of her Aunts & Uncles. Dine at Frank's. Call at 5:20 at Little's. Supper at James Mitchell's. Mrs. Ellen [blank] called at Franklin's in the evening.

Wednesday, May 29 Leave Gibson at 7:16; reach Bloomington about 9:00. Go to Court House & ascend and have bird'seye view of he city. Call in the Courtroom & hear statement of the Hinshaw Murder case by Att'y of the defense. Leave on 11:23 train.

Thursday, May 30 Board of Bishops meet at 9:00 at

Mrs. Elizab. Williams & continued all day. Dine at Same & sup there. Missionary Board meets at 7:30. Dr. C.H. Kiracofe delivers the annual address at 8:00.

Friday, May 31 Board in Session. We continue business forenoon & afternoon. Dine & lodge at Mrs. Williams' as usual. In evening, have a discussion of Missionary topics. Charlotte, Mich. chosen as place of next annual meeting; Third Thurs. May.

Saturday, June 1 Morning session. At 10:30, Rev. W. Edwin Mosier's Memorial. Dine at Mrs. Arabelle Mosier's. Closed business in the afternoon. I took supper at Lewis Long's. Bp. William Dillon pr. at 8:00, "In him light," John 1:4. Rev. J.K. Alwood pr. at 3:15 Phil. 4:6. Stay at Elizabeth Williams'.

Sunday, June 2 Heard Bp. H.T. Barnaby ,*Ez. 36:25. Dine at Mrs. Williams. Call at Mrs. A. Mosier's with Robt. Montgomery and at Lewis Long's, 20 rods north. Supper at Long's on ice cream. Dr. H.J. Becker pr. on "Walls of Jerico" at 8:00. We go at 11:15 to Mendota. Stay at Hotel there. *"I will sprinkle clean water,["] etc.

Monday, June 3 Go on 7:00 tr. to Chicago. On 10:20 to Logansport. Lunched & staid till 3:30. Call at D.K. Zeller's two hours at Richmond. Go on 8:43 tr. to Dayton. Stay at home—No. 7 Hawthorne St.

Tuesday, June 4 Spent the day in necessary work & some preparation for the visit to Columbus.

Wednesday, June 5 Board (Publishing) did not convene tin 1:30. Bp. Floyd and Rev. R.G. Montgomery dine with me at Mrs. Greenwood's. Rev. Wm. Miller took supper with me at Lorin's & also staid with me & breakfasted at Mrs. Greenwood's, next morning.

Thursday, June 6 Board adjourned at 12:00 & I dine at Dr. H.J. Becker's. Then we organize the Publishing Ex. Committee at 2:00. I go on 5:37 tr to Columbus. Put up at Neil House. Young was there; Lawrence came later.

Friday, June 7 Rose at 5:00. Young very unwell. Argument began at 8:45, by Mr. G.R. Young. After 15 min., the Court postponed the case till Thurs. the 13th. We came home on Big Four train arriving about 1:00.

Spend afternoon at my old home.

Saturday, June 8 Go on 7:00 train via Union City and Gas City to Fairmount, Ind. Lunch at Jonesboro. Call at Wm. Hall's. Went with Ellis Wright to his house. Supper & lodging there.

Sunday, June 9 Go to Fairmount & pr. at U.B. Church,*Gal. v.14. Dine at Clinton Bratain's. Peter Wright & wife there. Go home with Ellis' folks & lodge there. *"God forbid that I should glory."

Monday, June 10 Go with Ellis up to the New Depot. Dine at Ellis'. Plan town ( ) [appears in text] and go to Depot again. Supper and eve. at W.H.H. Reeder's. He takes me to Ellis'. I stay there.

Tuesday, June 11 Go to Fairmount with Ellis. Dine at Wm. Heath's 1/4 m. west of Friends' Church. Go on 1:37 tr to Marion. I pay my R'y tax—$93.81. Go on 3:03 tr. to Union City. Go on 8:40 tr. to Dayton. Lodge at Lorin's.

Wednesday, June 12 At House forenoon. Go to town afternoon. Go on 5:31 tr. to Columbus. Stay at Neil House. Prof. Kiracofe with me. W. Lawrence also there. Young & Young arrive at 10:00, night.

Thursday, June 13 Our case is argued in Supreme Court beginning at 9:30 and closing at 5:00. Dine at Neil house. We go on Big 4 train, 5:45, to Dayton.

Friday, June 14 Went to town forenoon & afternoon. Paid R.T. Houk $20.00 in behalf of Pontiac case. Sent Katharine $35.00 in drafts. Wrote to Rev. A.3. Powel

Saturday, June 15 At my study at 8:00. Got letters from Wm. Lawrence & from Katharine. Write to P.E.'s of East Des Moines, W. Kansas & Ark. Valley. Send a draft of $19.00 to Katharine. Saw Young a half hour or more.

Sunday, June 16 Preach at School Street at 10:30 true time, *Mark 12:31. Dine at Lorin's. Call in Afternoon at old home. In the evening, hear Wilbur Craft at Engl. (Main St.) Lutheran Church on Observance of the Sabbath. Wilbur Wright was with me. *"Thou shalt love— neighbor."

Monday, June 17 Went over to see Young. Learn that arrangements are made to take evidence in U.B. case tomorrow at 10:00. Get Wilbur to assist in the afternoon and evening in preparing documentary evidence. Call at Keiter's office & at Kiracofe's, & Dillon's.

Tuesday, June 18 Continue preparation. Go over to Young's & learn of a hitch in the agreement. Return home. Car at Kiracofe's in the afternoon. Katharine came home about 9:00 from Oberlin, we not expecting her till Thursday.

Wednesday, June 19 At home. In afternoon was called over to Young's to see about an agreement on taking evidence in United States case. Effected it. We to file Gen. Conf. minutes of 1885 & 1889 marked & the Disciplines of 1885 & 1889.

Saturday, June 22 Meals at the old home, where I stay this summer with Katharine and the boys. Went over to see Young about 10:00. Showed me the Gen. Conf. minutes of 1885, 1889 marked by the Liberals. Worked on marking the rest of the day, in our behalf.

Sunday, June 23 Meals at home. Went to Grace M.E. Church. Heard Rev. Robinson on Eccle. XI.1, a good sermon—a poor financial effort after it. I preach at 8:00, Sch. St., *Rom. 2:29. *"He is not a Jew which is one outwardly, and cir."

Monday, June 24 At home. Call at Lorin's in forenoon.

Tuesday, June 25–Friday, June 28 At home all day. Did considerable reading.

Saturday, June 29 At home. Got new coat & vest at Charch & Wells. Paid by check $31.00 for them.

Sunday, June 30 Heard Rev. C.B. McDaniel, at Sch. St., *John 19:28. Dine at home. A little rain. I Pr. at Sch. St. at 8:00, John VI:67, "Will ye also go away?" * "I thirst."

Monday, July 1 Went in forenoon to see Mr. Young, about 15 min. Sees no opening to ask a rehearing under rulings of the Supreme Court.

Thursday, July 4 At home in the forenoon. I go in the afternoon to Woodland Cemetery with Katharine & Nellie Barry.

Friday, July 5 At home mainly reading. Wrote letters. Lorin's called in the evening.

Saturday, July 6 Went to town in the afternoon. Wrote six letters to Railroad Offices for permits. Lorin's called awhile in the evening.

Sunday, July 7 Heard Rev. Work, pastor of the Third St. Presb. Church pr. at 11:00, l Sam. 4:1. Kath. with me. At home the rest of the day. Lorin's called in the evening.

Monday, July 8 At home. The girls cleaned up my room. I called at Lorin's in the evening & Milton came up with me & went to candy store!

Tuesday, July 9–Saturday, July 13 At home.

Sunday, July 14 Heard Dr. H.J. Becker preach, at S. St. at 10:30, Eph. 2:5. At home the rest of the day.

Monday, July 15 At home all day, reading most of the time, except a call at Kiracofe's in the forenoon.

Tuesday, July 16 At home all day except a brief call at the *Conservator* Office. Day spent closely in reading. Milton (Junior) supped with us & Lorin and Nettie came up awhile & got a dish of iced pineapple.

Wednesday, July 17 Read papers mostly in the forenoon. Wrote a letter & went to town. Read in Hermon on Estopel (& Res. adjudicata) at office. Nettie called.

Thursday, July 18 At home mostly till afternoon. Went on 6:00 train to Union City & thence to Gas City. Staid at the Hotel.

Friday, July 19 Went on 7:20 train to Fairmount and walked out to the Farm. Dine, sup, & lodge with Wm. H. Reeder on the farm.

Saturday, July 20 Dine, sup & lodge at Ellis Wright's. In afternoon, go up to Matthew's. Ellis is very sick in the night with cholera Morbus.

Sunday, July 21 Go to Robert B. Reeder's. Stay till after supper. Mr. Slanker & Katie Broyles there. I call at Oliver Glass' and find no one at home, so I walk on to Ellis Wright's and lodge.

Monday, July 22 Go to Gas City & just miss the 9:17 east bound train. Go on with Ellis to Fairmount. Go on 1:40 train to Anderson & thence on 3:30 train to Richmond & home, arr. at 6:50. Lorin's call in the evening.

Thursday, July 25 At home. Took out Origen's *De Principias.*

Friday, July 26 At home. Returned Origen. Went to Public Library and got out Plato's *Day in Athens with Socrates.*

Saturday, July 27 At home. Returned Plato. Took out Vol. 1 of Iraenaus on Hereises.

Sunday, July 28 Preached at School St. at 10:30, *Deut. 6:4,5. Called a few minutes at Kiracofe's; also an hour in afternoon, to see Mrs. Shisler who came last evening. Preached at 8:00, John 12.25. *"Thou shalt love the Lord, +"He that loveth his life shall lose it."

Tuesday, July 30 At home. Harvey Wright, my brother, and his wife and his granddaughter, Stella Rhoads came, about 7:00, aftn.

Wednesday, July 31 Mrs. S. Shisler came in the forenoon and staid till towards evening. The women rode out in a rig to the Soldiers Home and about the city. Harvey rode out to the East End on the St. cars; came back & called to see Lorin; looked at the Prospective Van Cleve Park; returned home.

Thursday, August l Harvey &folks went on 5:00 m. train. Mrs. S. Shisler called again & staid till about 3:00. She has given largely of her income to our Church.

Sunday, August 4 I pr. at School St. at 10:30, 1 Tim 1.11, "Accor. to the glory of the blessed gospel.["] At home after service till evening. We had a speaking meeting at 8:00, at Sch. St.

Monday, August 5 Getting Ready to go to conferences.

Tuesday, August 6 Called at Young's but George was away. We failed to have a meeting of the Missionary Ex. Com. Spent an hour in the evening at Keiter's office. Lorin's called a few minutes.

Wednesday, August 7 At home in forenoon. Go on 12:30 via Union City to Indianapolis. Stay at Spencer House, near the Depot.

Thursday, August 8 Go on 3:55 morn. train to Louisville, Ken. Lunch there. Go on 8:07 train to Winslow. John Henniger met us and took us to his house. My home at Wheeler's. John Riley homes with me. He pr. at 8:00. We stay at Wheeler's.

Friday, August 9 Conference opened at 9:00 in the New Church. It rained in the evening, so I did not preach.

Saturday, August 10 Conference continued. In the evening, J.M. Johnson preached at 8:00. Very short session followed.

Sunday, August 11 I pr. dedication sermon at 11:00 & raised $75.00 in subscription. Dine at Wm. T. Roe's. I pr. at 8:00 John 1:46, "Can any good thing come out of Nazareth?" Stay at Wheeler's.

Monday, August 12 Young Roe takes me to Oakland City. Call at O.A. Kelsey's store. Go on 10:18 tr. via Worthington to Terre Haute, & on to Vermilion. Call at Jas. Vansickel's & then have supper & lodging at Mrs. Phebe Trogdon's with Rev. C.B. Small.

Tuesday, August 13 Dine at Margaret Stubbs with C.B. Small. Supper & lodging at Mrs. Phebe Trogdon's.

Wednesday, August 14 At Trogden's till after dinner, and till evening except a call at James Vansickle, who was sick yesterday and to-day. I preach at 8:00, John 1:46. Stay at Trogdon's.

Thursday, August 15 We hired Mr. Dusthammer to take us to New Goshen, seven miles, have a soldiers' picnic. Stop at Rev. Noah Minnick's. Dinner and supper there.

Friday, August 16 The session of the conference of the Lower Wabash Mission District began at 9:00 & continued till about noon. I continue at Noah Minnick's. I preach at 8:00, Ex. 28:34. Stay at George S. Minnich's in the edge of town.

Saturday, August 17 Conference continued. I dined at Rev. J.M. Whitesel's 1 1/2 m. S.W. of town. Conference closed. I stay at Geo. S. Minnich's.

Sunday, August 18 I Pr. at Edwards Chapel at 10:30, John 14.2. Dine at Charles Beam's & Supper. Kershner & others there also. Pr. at 7:30, Acts 26.28. Stay at Geo. S. Minnich's. This Rev. Kershner is a son of a blacksmith that lived on the ridge beyond Sanes Creek Church, near my old home in Indiana.

Monday, August 19 Spend the day at Rev. N.J. Minnick's. At 4:30, we go to James M. Whitesel's. They called away on account of Sickness at his Mother's.

Tuesday, August 20 I go early to Rev. N.J. Minnick's. Geo. S. Minnich takes me to Vermillion. Dine and sup at Mrs. Phebe Trogdon's. I call in afternoon at Jas. Vansickle's & at Mrs. Margaret Stubb's. Go on 5:50 train to Mattson. Stay at Dole House.

Wednesday, August 21 Go on 5:00 morn. tr. to Delavan. Bro. Moses Shade meets me & takes me to the Church (Bethel) and thence to his house. My Conf. home. Rev. W.H.. Knupple pr. at 8:00. With A.B. Powell, I stay at our conf. home.

Thursday, August 22 Conference began at 9:00 morn. Business proceeded well. I Dine & Sup at Shade's. I preach at 8:00, Deut. 18:17-19. Stay at Shade's. "I will raise up a prophet.["]

Friday, August 23 Conference continued. I dine at Mother Curtis'. I again preach (at 8:00) Hebr. 11:10. Stay at Shade's. Dr. C.H. Kiracofe came this morning.

Saturday, August 24 Conference Continued. I dine at C.C. Burton's. Conference Closed about 5:00. Supper at "home" (Shade's).

Sunday, August 25 I preach at 11:00, Ps. 48:11-13, "Go round about Zion." Dine at John Donaldson's, 2 m. N.W. Addresses S.S. Anniversary—mine of Palestine.

Ordain D.D. Fetters. Supper at Shade's, & lodging. Dr. C.H. Kiracofe pr at 8:00, "Seek first." Communion followed.

Monday, August 26 Go to Hopeville and go on via Bloomington & Indianapolis to Dayton, Ohio. Found all well at home.

Tuesday, August 27 At home. Went to town in the afternoon; saw Young. Call at C.H. Kiracofe's. Call at Lorin's in the evening.

Wednesday, August 28 Went on 7:00 train via Union City & Anderson back to Daleville, Ind. Stop at Silas Guerien's, my conference home. Conference opened at 2:00 and proceeded well. C.B. Small preached at 8:00 a good sermon. I stay at Guerin's.

Thursday, August 29 Conference Continued & progressed well. M.F. Keiter came about 11:00. I sup at Clinton Goodpasture's. Report on Missions discussed & adopted. H.J. Becker pr. at 8:00, "Launch out," etc.

Friday, August 30 Conference Continued. I dine at J.M. Kabrich's. N.D. Wolfard & C.W. Rector were elected presiding elders. Stationing Committee met at 7:00 at Guerin's. M.F. Keiter pr. at 8:00.

Saturday, August 31 Conference progressed and closed at 5:00. I dine with N.D. Wolfard at Dale's. Raise $201.00 subscription at 3:00 for Legal purposes. Educational Meeting at 8:00.

Sunday, September 1 I pr. in tent at 11:00, 2 Tim. 4:2. Dine at Jesse Goodpasture's. Pr. at tent at 3:00, Ps. 84:11, raise $78.50 and dedicate the tent. Rev. Z. NcNew pr. at 8:00, John 1:14. I sup & lodge at Guerin's.

Monday, September 2 Call at Walter Ketchum's. Go on 10:50 train to Union City, & on to Dayton on 2:30 train. Called at Lorin's a few minutes, and Lorin's Called in the evening.

Tuesday, September 3 At home. Go to town. Get ready to go away. Called at Kiracofe's in the afternoon.

Wednesday, September 4 Go on 8:40 train to Richmond

& Logans Port. Train leaves me & I go on 4:30 train to Chicago & thence on 10:35 tr. to Leaf River. Lodge at Rev. W.J. Byer's, having arrived on 1:40 night train.

Thursday, September 5 Home at Henry J. Schrauder's. Conference began at 9:00 & progressed well. Rev. W.H. Davis pr. at 7:45, "She did what she could." Very lively exhortation by J.J. Margileth & lively speaking meeting followed.

Friday, September 6 Conference continued & progressed well. Rev. C. Bender was elected pres. elder. Board as usual. Rev. A.J. Bolen pr. at 8:00. Neh. 4:9. He is agent for Hartsville College.

Saturday, September 7 Conference continued & closed at 5:00. Rev. O.F. Smith pr. at 7:45. I boarded as usual. Bro. Smith is an old time, eloquent preacher.

Sunday, September 8 I pr. at 11:00, Gen. 49:10. Dine at Mrs. W.H. Harrison's. S.S. Anniv. at 3:00. I spoke of Joseph. Supper at H.J. Schrader's. I pr. at 7:45, 2 Pet. 2:15. Stay at Schrader's.

Monday, September 9 Weather fair. Stay at Schrader's till 4:40, and go via Forreston to Mendota. Stay at George F. Huck's. He is a member of the church, a very confident and talkative Dutchman.

Tuesday, September 10 Weather fair. Stay at Huck's all day except a ride to the post-office.

Wednesday, September 11 Weather fair. Go on 11:23 train to Galesburg. Go on local freight to Applcton. Supper at Earnest Steffen's. Stay at E.J. Wysman's, 1 1/2 m. northwest. Mrs. Steffen is Wyman's daughter.

Thursday, September 12 Weather fair. Stay at Wyman's. Rev. J. Stahl and Amos Worman come. Rev. W.M. Davis also came. He is a young preacher, formerly of North Ohio Conference, who launched out with his horse and buggy to Central Illinois Conference.

Friday, September 13 Weather fair. Conference opened at 9:00. Few present. Committees meet on afternoon. P.J. Wintz & wife come. She is a distant relative of my wife. Austin Platt also at Conference. I board at Wyman's.

No conf. in the afternoon. Rev. W.M. Davis pr. at 7:30, 1 John v.3. Did well.

Saturday, September 14 Conf. continued. At 2:00, Rev. A. Worman pr. Rev. 2:8-10. Close Conf. at 5:00. Supper at Chas. Snell's. I preach at 7:45, Phil, 2.12-13. Stay at E.J. Wyman's.

Sunday, September 15 Weather hazy. Preach at Mound Chapel at 11:00, Isa. 21:11-12. Dine at Nelson Iker's, 4 ms. N.E. Call at Henry England's, 1/4 m. n. of Church. It Rains & no meeting. Stay at England's.

Monday, September 16 Go via Wyman's to Appleton, Galesburg, via Colona to Rock Island. Ride on electric car to Davenport. Stay at depot & write letters till night. Lodge at the Hotel Downs, 2 squares S. of the depot.

Tuesday, September 17 Go on 3:20 morn'g train to Casey, Iowa. Arrive at 10:18 tr. Dan. R. Fagan takes me to his house on Adair Co. farm. Dine & sup there. Look at the corn crop. Lodge at Lee Hoisington's, 1 mile North.

Wednesday, September 18 Weather clear. Thermometer warm. Measure the pasture fields. There are 85 acres in the main pastures, and 6 4/10 in the other. Agreed on $115.00 this year on pasture and hay lands; $80 on pasture, and $35 on slough & 2 acres of timothy. Fagan takes me to Casey. Go on 4:38 train to Des Moines & Oskaloosa. Stay at Birdsall House.

Thursday, September 19 Go on 10:15 train to Delta. F.L. Donahoo meets me and takes me to Union Chapel & to L. Pierson's to dine. Conf. continues. Find boarding at Mrs. Susan Wharton 's. Rev. P. Haynes pr at 7:30, Acts 19:2. "Have ye rec'd the Ghost?" Stay at Wharton's, Matthew Wharton's late residence.

Friday, September 20 Conf. in forenoon. Rev. H.H. Williams dines with us. Also Conf. in the afternoon. I pr. at 7:30, 1 Ki. 18:38.

Saturday, September 21 Weather warm. Conference continued & closed at 4:00, aftn. I dine at Henderson's 1 1/4 m. north, with J.D. Jessop. Rev. F.L. Donahoo pr. at 7:30, Luke v:31,32. I sup & lodge at Susan Wharton's as usual.

Sunday, September 22 Weather Fair. Thermometer Warm. I pr. at 11:00, Ps. 145:11. Dine at Wharton's It rained after meeting. Rainy afternoon. Rev. J.E. Runion pr. at 7:30, 1 Cor. 15:21. Speaking and halleluia meeting followed. I stay at Wharton's. Cool in the afternoon & evening.

Monday, September 23 Weather fair. Thermometer Cool. Stay at Wharton's after calling at Wm. Wharton's to see Rev. I.F. Beach, who has a sore foot, laming him. Wrote some on Young People's constitution. Rather cool without fire.

Tuesday, September 24 Weather fair. Go with Wm. Wharton to Tioga & thence to Atwood & thence to Sigourney. Arthur Williams takes me to Rev. H.H. William's. I send a draft to A.D. Crooks, Treas., Greenfield, Iowa, $35.00 to pay tax. Can ed to see Father Thompson, a M.E. Minister.

Wednesday, September 25 Went on 10:29 train to Chillicothe, Missouri, which I reached at 4:15 & B.W. Miller & Bro. Price met me & took me to Avalon, 15 miles away. I sup, lodge & board at Sam'l Skinner's. Rain comes up about 6:00.

Thursday, September 26 Conf. opened at 9:00. Few present. But business progressed well. Joseph L. Beauchamp dined & supped with me at Skinner's. I pr. at 7:30, Zech. 13:9. Stay as usual at Skinner's.

Friday, September 27 I conduct the College services at 7:45. Dine at Prof. Gehrell's. Conference progressed well. Supper at Skinner's. Rev. H.A. Cunningham pr. at 7:30, "Guide you into all truth," Acts, 16:13.

Saturday, September 28 Session in the forenoon. Dine at Rev. Mendenhall's, M.E. Minister's. S.S. Convention at College Chapel afternoon. Rev. Anderson (M.E.) of Chillicothe spoke 40 m; I 10 m.; Gehrett, 20 m. Rev. B.F. Miller pr. at 7:30, "Endure hardness," etc., 2 Tim 2.3.

Sunday, September 29 Weather beautiful. Preach at College Chapel at 11:00, Matt. 16:16. Dine at Carpenter's. Supper at Rev. A.D. Thomas's. Preach at 7:30, Rev. 22. Stay at Jas. M. Price's.

Monday, September 30 Weather fair. Breakfast at 3:30. Brother Price takes me to Chillicothe, & I go on 7:00 tr. to Kansas City. Get to my Son Reuchlin's in "Ivanhoe" before noon. I visit there the rest of the day.

Tuesday, October 1 Weather fair. At Reuchlin's except afternoon at the Flower Parade. Helen, aged 6, is a pretty and nice girl. Herbert, about 2 2/3 years, is a nice-looking fine boy.

Wednesday, October 2 Weather fair. I Remain at Reuchlin's till evening, except at the Bicycle Parade in afternoon. I go on 8:40 train to Formosa, Kans. Breakfast at Hotel. Dine at Mrs. J.M. Adams, 4 1/2 m Northwest. Children: Marinda & Arthur—the latter of whom came after me. Go with Rev. J.S. Rock to Mankato. Stay at Rock's.

Thursday, October 3 The last part of the record of the above is of to-day.

Friday, October 4 Weather cloudy. Conference opened at 9:00. Progressed fairly. Rev. John H. Mapes pr. at 7:30, Matt. 16:18 Rev. S.J. Foster exhorted, with much ability. He is aged.

Saturday, October 5 Weather cloudy. Conference continued. Rev. J.S. Rock was elected presiding elder. Stationing committee met at Rock's at 1:00. Finish business. Conference adjourned at 5:00. I pr. at 7:30, 1 K. 18:21. I stay at Rock's. Rev. J. McMillin was present, of Liberal U.B. Church.

Sunday, October 6 Weather fair. Moderate thermometer. I preach at 11:00, Ps. 145:11. Dine as usual. Several call in the afternoon. I preach at 7:30, Zech. 4:10, "Who hath despised the day of small things." Stay at Rock's. It was a beautiful day.

Monday, October 7 Weather fair. Cool thermometer. Staid at Bro. Rock's and made out the minutes of the conference for the *Conservator,* and recorded them. It took all day. In evening, wrote a letter.

Tuesday, October 8 Start on Mo. Pac. R'y to Abilene, at 8:22; arrive at 10:30; dine at Exchange. Write letters and cards. Go on 8:10 train to Abilene. Arrive at 10:30. Find my conference home at Fred. Volkman's, second house west of the church, a good home. Rev. H. D.Tatman & family board there also.

Wednesday, October 9 Conference opened at 9:00. Progressed fairly well. Dine, sup, and lodge at my "home." Rev. A.L. Hope pr. at 7:30, Mark 16:16, "Go ye," etc. I exhorted.

Thursday, October 10 Conf. continued. Good forenoon & afternoon sessions. Rev. E. Atkinson pr. at 7:30 Prov. 11:30, "He that winneth souls," etc. I board at Volkman's. Rev. H.M. Branham followed. A fine speaking meeting closed the services.

Friday, October 11 Conference continued. In the afternoon, Revs. W.H. Willoughby and A.L. Hope were elected presiding elders. Stationing committee met at F. Volkman's at 6:30. Rev. F.W. Bertschinger pr. at 7:30. I did not hear him. H.D. Tatman was referred to a committee of investigation.

Saturday, October 12 Conference continued. Adjourned from 11:00 to 3:00, for the Tatman committee. He refused to be investigated, and a prosecutor was appointed. A.L. Hope. Tatman preached at night, 2 Tim. 4:2, "Preach the word." Stalling was licensed. May Sommers, not present, was received on transfer. I exhort after Tatman.

Sunday, October 13 I pr at 11:00, 2 Cor. 3:8. I spoke at S.S. Anniversary at 2:30. I pr. at 7:30, 2 Pet. 2:15. I dine, sup & lodge at Fred Volkman's. They are of Evang. Association.

Monday, October 14 Several called at Bro. Volkman's. I went to Minner's to dinner. Went back to Volkman's. W.H. Spidel came and took me to his house to supper. He takes me back to Volkman's.

Tuesday, October 15 Go on 10:43 tr. to Herrington. Wait ther 4 1/2 hours. I then go on to Hutchinson, and lodge at Lorimer Ardery's, a druggist's. Elsina, his wife, is my cousin. Uncle Geo. C. Reeder, her father, is with them. Son: Roy, 21; Daughters: Faye 17, Lois 12.

Wednesday, October 16 At 4:00 p.m. I go on Mo. Pac. tr. to Haven. George R. Manning meets me & takes me

to his house, 6 ms S.W. near Sumner Church. Rev. C.B. Sherk preaches at 7:30, Col. 1:9-11 . We stay at Manning's. His father, Rev. Z. Manning, and his mother live with George.

Thursday, October 17 Conference opened at 9:00. Proceeded well. Rev. S.F. Fite pr. at 7:30, Rev. 11:14—quite woeful. Boarded at G.R. Manning's. His wife showed great energy in caring for many of the people.

Friday, October 18 Conference continued. J.H. McNew was, in the afternoon, elected presiding elder. Stationing com. met at 7:00 at Manning's. Rev. A.W. Cummings pr. at 7:30, Matt. 5.8—"Holiness." Stay at Manning's.

Saturday, October 19 Conference continued. Mrs. M.R. Williams pr. at 3:00. Close conf. about 5:00. I pr. at 7:30, Ps. 48:12,13.

Sunday, October 20 I pr. at 11:00, Dan. 12:3. Dine at Manning's. S.S. Anniversary at 3:00. Rollins, McNew & Wright spoke. I pr. at 7:30, 1 Cor. 11:28. Communion followed. Board at Manning's as usual. The attendance throughout was large & conf. harmonious.

Monday, October 21 The preachers and people mostly left in the morning. I staid at Manning's, eve. Wrote many letters & full cards in the afternoon and evening.

Tuesday, October 22 Bro. G.R. Manning takes me to Mt. Hope and to [blank] Wright's, 2 ms. South of the village. He a son of Charles Wright, our Grant Co., Ind. neighborhood & grandson of the Reynold's. Saw at his house Milton Brewer, son of John Brewer of Fairmount, Grant Co., Ind. Went on 4:40 train to Wichita. Lodge at Wichita.

Wednesday, October 23 Go on 5:00 p.m. train to Winfield & thence to Longton. Spent the day partly in writing. I thought to go on the Mo. Pac. R'y but found its connections bad. I went on 5:00 train to Winfield & thence at 9:00 to Longton & staid at Gordon House.

Thursday, October 24 Go by livery at 8:00 for the conference at Belleville Sch. H. Arrive there at 10:00. After devotions and a Bible Reading (Hebr. 11:1-10) we dismissed till aftn. conference opened at 2:00. Few present.

Dine & sup & lodge at Mon. Miller's. Rev. G.W. Carey pr. at 7:30, Acts 3.19. Rev. D.S. Buck exhorted. A good congregation.

Friday, October 25 Conference continued. Nothing unusual occurred. Board at Monica Miller's. A. Carey, of Parson's, Kans., came in the evening. I pr. at 7:30, Matt. 5:12. Speaking meeting followed. Rev. D.S. Buck staid with me at Miller's.

Saturday, October 26 Conference continued. Stationing committee met at Mon. Miller's at 1:00—at Robt. Burk's at 6:00—Conference adjourned about 4:30. Mrs. A.D. Blinn pr. at 3:00. Suppr at Burks. Rev. D.S. Buck pr. at 7:30, Isa. 30.7. We stay at Mon. Miller's.

Sunday, October 27 I Preach at 11:00, Gen. 49.10. I dine at Monica Miller's. Rev. S.B. McGrew preached at 7:00, 2 Chron. 6:18. I stay at Miller's as usual.

Monday, October 28 Go with Rev. J.B. Croms to Buxton. Got several letters there. Go on with A. Carey & C.B. Burg to Fredonia, and with S.B. McGrew to Benedict, and then alone to Chanute, arriving 12:00. Thence on 12:30 train to Kansas City. Arrive at 5:20 & go on to Reuchlin's. Found all well.

Tuesday, October 29 At Reuchlin's till 7:15, Eve. I then go on 8:45 train to St. Louis. Sleep near six hours. Best reclining chairs I have found.

Wednesday, October 30 See Vandalia Agent at St. Louis & get rates to Indianapolis on fast train. I get to Dayton soon after 6:00. Supper at Mrs. Greenwood's. I found all well at home. Found many letters awaiting me.

Thursday, October 31 Called at Lorin's & went to town; Saw Young 20 minutes or less. Supper at Lorin's. Wrote in aftn. & read eve.

Friday, November 1 At home all day reading, & called at Kiracofe's in the evening.

Saturday, November 2 At home all day except a call at Young's office of 5 minutes. Call at Lorin's in eve. but found no one at home.

Sunday, November 3 Heard Rev. W.H. Conner, the pastor, pr. at School Street Church, at 10:30, Acts 7:58, an interesting sermon. Dined at Dr. H.J. Becker's. At home then till evening. Heard Conner again at 7:30, John 12:26.

Monday, November 4 Went to Young's office at 3:00 (about 10 minutes of conference).

Tuesday, November 5 Vote at 8:40 & Go to Young's office. Spend 10 minutes, also return in Afternoon & spend two hours with him in considering points of evidence. Call at Keiter's office and at Kiracofe's. Spend the evening in reading Weaver's evidence, in the Dayton Case.

Wednesday, November 6 Spent forenoon in writing for witnesses on "Notice" etc. Went to Young's & thence to Kiracofe's. Spend the evening in reading McKee's deposition on Califor. case, to be filed by agreement in this case, U.S. Cir. Court.

Thursday, November 7 Weather rainy. To-day I was about four hours on the stand as a witness in U.S. case, to append to Calif. deposition of mine & use in this case by agreement. Spent the evening at home with Wilbur in talking.

Friday, November 8 Weather rainy. At home mostly. At town about noon. Bought Milton a hobby-horse, with which he was much pleased. Attended Ex. Com. Meeting (Missionary) at 7:00 at Keiter's office.

Saturday, November 9 Weather rainy. Went to town and got Kiracofe's deposition & read much of it. Was called at 12:00 to telephone with Quincy, Ohio about Livingston's appointments at Germantown. Wrote some on type-writer. Went after my new coat & pantaloons to Charch & Wells, but did not get them.

Sunday, November 10 Weather fair like. At home in the forenoon. Go to M.M. Chr. Association Hall. B. Frank Butts, is the singer, and John H. Elliott, the preacher, whose text was, Zech. 4:6. "Not by might, but by Spir."

Monday, November 11 Weather fair. Went to Young's & to Charch & Wells. Bought a new Stetson hat for $3.50. Wrote for U.S. Case, copies of certain parts of old disciplines—between 1819 & 1885. Wrote letters in eve'g. Klracofe called at 6:00 eve.

Tuesday, November 12 Weather fair. Finished copies of extracts from old Disciplines, to be filed as evidence in U.S. case.

Wednesday, November 13 Weather fair. Began at 9:00 the taking of Bishop J.W. Hott's deposition in U.S. case. Adjourned from 11:30 till 2:00, & afterward continued till 5:00. Latitudinous. Lorin's called in the evening. Milton as usual much interested in playing on the Keys of my type-writer.

Thursday, November 14 Rainy eve. Hott's cross examination lasted till 4:00, aftn. Evasive, not responsive, etc., but put in valuable testimony on our side. Rev. R.G. Montgomery called, at 2:00.

Friday, November 15 Bishop E.P. Kephart's deposition taken by L.B. Gunckel; Cross-examination by G.R. Young. It took all day.

Saturday, November 16 C.H. Kiracofe's former testimony continued. I went on 11:15 train to Sidney, O. & there wrote Wm. Lawrence. Called at Ed. Shearer's & saw his mother, Harriet, and sister, Effa. Went on to Quincy & home with Rev. W.E. Strete—sup there. Pr. at Bethel at 7:00, Ps. 73.24. Stay at David Shanley's, who married a Wright of Henry Co., Ind. not my relatives.

Sunday, November 17 I Pr. at 10:30 (Text Ps. 93.5) & dedicate the new Church. Raise $54.00, the debt being before provided for. I dine at Rev. Samuel L. Livingston's. I pr. at 7:00, Ps. 145.11. I stay at Isaac Shaneley's 3/4 of a mile west.

Monday, November 18 Isaac Shaneley takes me to Sidney, & I get home at 12:00. Senseny testifies for the Liberals in the afternoon. Did not know well anything. Spent the evening in planning a logical index to testimony.

Tuesday, November 19 Go to Prof. Kiracofe's to see Bp. Barnaby, just arrived, and there to Young's Office. Barnaby under examination from 10:30 till 2:45 without dinner, and went on 2:55 train to Findlay, O. A dutchman on the witness stand. Wesley Adcock & Griggs

(witnesses) stay with us. Closed testimony without examining them.

Wednesday, November 20 Called at Young's ten or 15 min. Spent the day in writing, etc. Wilbur prepares an index to some of the evidence, to file with the judge.

Thursday, November 21 Get ready to go away. Work hard to-day and in the evening to get case ready for trial to-morrow. I type-write Wilbur's Index to some evidences in our U.S. Case. Met Judge Wm. Lawrence at the depot at 12:05, who goes on to Cincinnati.

Friday, November 22 Go to Cincinnati & hear U.S. Case argued before Judge Taft. Our attorneys spoke three hours and thirty minutes; theirs 3 hours. Kiracofe and I return home on 6:30 train. Young's was his very best. Lawrence below his usual.

Saturday, November 23 Go on 7:30 train via Union City, Indianapolis & Terre Haute to Shelbyville, Illinois. Oscar Weakley meets me at the depot & takes me on to his father's, where I sup & go on to Obed. Council at the Church on dedication. It is a rainy afternoon & evening. Stay at Obed Brinker's, at Obed.

Sunday, November 24 I Preach at 11:00, Ps. 93:5, & raise about $680.00 nicely. Dine at Rev. D.W. Hamilton's, 1 1/4 mile North, with Rev. A.B. Powell, W.H. Davis, G.W. Loving. Very rainy afternoon & evening. I call at John Neakley's. Pr. at 7:00, John 1:29. Communion. Stay at O. Brinker's with Rev. A.B. Powell.

Monday, November 25 Go with Bro. D. Moll to Moewequa, and call an hour & thence at 10:30 tr. to Pana. Leave Pana on 2:18 train and reach Anderson at 8:00. Stay at Hotel Madison. Rainy day & violently stormy night. Doxy House.

Tuesday, November 26 Weather snowy. Reach Fairmount at 9:50. Ride to East Branch & walk thence via railroad to Wm. H.H. Reeder's on my farm. Dine & lodge there. Called in forenoon at James Tuttle's to see Esther Freeman, daughter of my Father's cousin Kinion Freeman & Flavia Freeman.

Wednesday, November 27 Go with Wm. Reeder to Ellis

Wright's & I dine there. We go up & look at our new "town", Leach in Afternoon. Wm. takes me to Fairmount. I preach at 7:00 (U. B. Church), John 3.16. Supper at Clinton Brattain's. Return to Reeder's & lodge there. Night quite cold.

Thursday, November 28 Weather cold. Go to Henry Simons', & thence to Oliver Glass's. The families of Robert Reeder, Wm. Reeder, & Joseph Broyles, Eliza Catharine's (Reader's) husband there, including Mr. Slanker & Katie (nee Broyles). Oliver takes me to Fairmount & I pr. at 7:00, Acts 10:43. I lodge at Bratain's. Large congregation.

Friday, November 29 Weather rainy. Go to 2:00 meeting & thence to Latham's & thence to J.C. Valentine's, the pastor's (his age 26) & get supper there. His wife is Rev. Job Kersner's daughter. I pr. at 7:00. The congregation small, as it was rainy. I lodge at C. Brattain's.

Saturday, November 30 Weather rainy. I go to see Rev. Wm. Hall (aged) at Hollingsworth's, & dine there. I call at Henry Cooper's & get a note (on hay sold him nearly two years ago), of $14.72. Call at James Tuttle's, & then at Charles Atkinson's. His son Elmer & daughter Cora there, only. Supper at Brattain's. Preach at 7:00, Ps. 73:24. Lodge at Brattain's. Good congregation.

Sunday, December 1 I pr. at 11:00, Gen. 49.10. It is a rainy day. I dine at Wm. Heath's. Call at 5:00 at Chas. Atkinson's. Very rainy evening. I pr. at 7:00, 1 Tim 1.11. I lodge at C. Atkinson's. Oliver Glass & family were at meeting at 11:00. She is a member at Union Society, 2 miles south of Fairmount.

Monday, December 2 Call at Rev. J.C. Valentine's & at C. Brattain's, & go by buggy to Summitville with Peter Wright & dine with them. Go on 12:57 train to Anderson & on 3:45 tr to Dayton, arriving at about 7:00. Found all well.

Tuesday, December 3 Went to town before noon. Wrote letters before and after going. Called at Lorin's a few minutes, on my way to town.

Wednesday, December 4 At home all day. Write some letters. Wilbur & Orville spent the evening in my room.

Thursday, December 5 At home all forenoon except a call at Lorin's of a half hour; also at home afternoon.

Friday, December 6 At home all day, arranging files of periodicals, cutting articles of value in some daily's, concerning Court decisions, Liberal Gen. Conference, etc. Boys came home tolerably early; for we three occupy the house.

Saturday, December 7 At home all day. Young McNeil of Kirkwood called to see about their suit on the church there. Busy fixing up things nearly all day. It is the finest day for a good while, sunshiny, and thawing considerably.

Sunday, December 8 Heard the pastor, Rev. W.H. Conner pr. at 11:00 on John 20, at Sch. Street. Called at Lorin's. Maud (Francisco) Snyder & husband & child Margaret were there.

Monday, December 9 At home all day. Arranging manuscripts, letters, etc. in order. Mrs. Kiracofe and Mabel called in the afternoon to see about Oklahoma affairs. W.O. Dinnins to go there three months—to where Mrs. McKay is etc.

Tuesday, December 10 Went to town in forenoon. Paid Young &Young $100.00 on U.S. suit by check on Winter's Nat. Bank. Bought socks & underwear. Called at Lorin's. A letter this morn from Katherine.

Wednesday, December 11 At home. Meeting of a committee of Ex. Com. of Mis. Board and trustees of W.M. Association at M.F. Keiters. Heard Bishop Floyd pr. at 7:00 at School Street Church, Hebr. 11:4.

Thursday, December 12 Ex. Com. Mis. Meeting at M.F. Keiters at 7:00 morn. Determined terms. Bp. H. Floyd visited me in forenoon. Write letters in afternoon & evening.

Friday, December 13 Went to town just before noon & got eyeglasses (repaired) from Reeve's. This morning my illuminum spectacles were returned by mail from E.J. Wyman's near Appleton, Ill. Dr. D.K. Flickinger came at 1:00 & we met at 4:00 at Keiter's house in counsel & employed him at Kiracofe's at 7:00. Called at Young's 10 minutes.

Saturday, December 14 Flickinger's employment yesterday was by counsel & then ratified by Ex. Com. as Gen'l Supt. of Foreign missions, $600.00 a year. Woman's M.A. trustees in part met with us. To-day I explained some misunderstandings between the Boards. Got ready at 6:00 aftern to go to Messick, Ind., but train is too late. Wrote letters.

Sunday, December 15 Arose early. Heard at 10:30, Rev. W.H. Conner preach, Acts 26.14. Go at 3:30 to Association Hall to hear Howard H. Russell on A. Lawyer's Reasons for the Christian Faith—a fine address. Heard him in the eve, 7:30, explain the success of the Anti-Saloon League & the nature of the Haskell Bill.

Tuesday, December 17 At home. Went to town. Made application for clergyman's permits on Big Four & Penn. Lines, and D. & Union.

Wednesday, December 18 Went to town & sent a $35.00 draft to Katherine. At home the rest of the day. Sister Kiracofe called to get a certificate for Rev. W.O. Dinnins, so he can get half fare on the General Traffic R'ys.

Thursday, December 19 Weather mild. At home most of the day. Wrote letters. Wilbur came home sick—perhaps indigestion. I get a ton of coal of Huffman & King.

Friday, December 20 Weather rainy eve. Wilbur better, and going about. Arose at 6:00, and work as usual. Heard Rev. Wm. G. Morehead, D.D. lecture at Assocation Hall at 8:00, eve. on Studies in the Book of Job. Katherine expected home on the evening train. She came 8:10 train via Clyde & Springfield. All sat up till 12:00.

Saturday, December 21 Weather mild. At home all day. Wrote letters. Set up cookstove, sat up till 11:30 examining scriptures. Got a telegram about 6:00 eve., telling of death of Rev. A.B. Powell, one of our best and most useful itinerants. So loved, trusted & missed! So judicious; so happy a balance; humble, yet confident.

Sunday, December 22 Weather mild, fair. Appointment to preach at Christian Church at 10:30. Pr. Gen. 49.10—somewhat embarrassed. We began vacation Housekeeping this morning & ate, all of us together, the first time for nearly four months. Called at "Davis's" & Prof.

Kiracofe's in the afternoon. At home in the evening.

Monday, December 23 Weather rainy. Thermometer high. At home all day, and I overhalled, arranged, and put away my letters and periodicals; a long & tiresome job.

Tuesday, December 24 At home till about 4:00 p.m. when I called at Keiter's office & at Kiracofe's. Went to town after supper. Wrote letters & prefaced and transcribed an 1884 letter of Joseph Gomer's for the Conservator.

Wednesday, December 25 Weather mild. Katherine got a present of gold-framed nose glasses, etc. Orville, a rug for his bed room, Wilbur, of a fountain pen & pen knife, I of a silk, and three linen handkerchiefs, & a leather box of blocking brushes, etc. Lorin & Nettie various presents, and Milton of Christmas tree & it's fruits. Rev. A.J. Bolen called. Turkey dinner at home. Wrote till midnight.

Thursday, December 26 Weather rainy. Sent in article for the Conservator, which I rewrote with type-writer this morning. Rainy day.

Friday, December 27 Weather fair. Thermometer high. At home all day, busily engaged in setting things to rights, and in writing. Write to various persons.

Saturday, Decmeber 28 Went to Town, mailed some letters, drew some money ($25.00) and called on Young a minute. Made application for C.H. & D. permit. Wrote to L.S.M. S. & to Grand Rapids & I for permits; & to Western Pass. Association also. Wrote to W.O. Dinnins and to M.N. McNeil. Paid King $6.50 for our last ton of coal.

Sunday, December 29 Attended Baptist Church on Williams Street, and heard [blank], the pastor, pr. Acts 4:13, a good discourse. Call at Lorin's with Katherine about 3:00. Horace Stokes & Mrs. Corbett there. Clare's little alligator! Heard Rev. W.H. Conner preach at School Street at 7:00, Heb. 11.24,25.

Monday, December 30 Go to town. Send N.Y. draft for $2.70 cents to Arthur Hinds & Co., New York, for Interlinear N. Testament (Greek-English), & $1.50 (Chicago) for Chr. Cynosure. Nettie & Milton came aftern. & Lorin in eve. Wrote to Rev. T.J. Connor.

Tuesday, December 31 I was at home all day. I looked up clothing for the destitute of Oklahoma, some of my own. In the evening, I wrote a long letter to Judge Wm. Lawrence of Bellefontaine. The boys are preparing for a cycle show at Y.M. Chris. Asso. building. I sat up till the New Year.

1896

Wednesday, January 1 Weather Beautiful. Ther. 16-40 degrees. This is Bicycle Exhibit day at Y.M.C.A. Building & our boys are very busy preparing for it. I attend Reception dinner at Rev. W.H. Conner's at 1517 W. Second St. At home the rest of the day.

Thursday, January 2 Weather fair. Thermometer 16 degrees. At home all day. Wrote many letters and some articles. Sat up till 1:30 ("to-morrow") reading proofs, & revising them, on Year Book for 1896.

Friday, January 3 Finished reading proofs on Year Book. Went to town. Merely saw Young. Sent regular application to Western Passenger Association for clergyman's rates on their many lines. Wrote many letters in Afternoon & evening. Slept 7 1/2 hours.

Saturday, January 4 Weather clear & Cold. At home. Wrote long letters to Bp. Dillon & H. Durfee. Wrote several Railroads for clergymen's rates: L.E. & W., B.O. & S. Western; D.D.E. Up till midnight.

Sunday, January 5 Heard Rev. W.H. Conner's sermon at 11:00, Ps. 1:2. Called an hour at Lorin's in the afternoon. At home in the evening.

Monday, January 6 At home all day. Spent most of the day in classifying and arranging letters, documents, etc., for greater convenience. Katherine, at 4:00 Aft. started on her return to Oberlin.

Tuesday, January 7 At home most of the day continuing in the forenoon my classification of letters, etc. Wonderfully tired. Go to town and draw some spending money.

Wednesday, January 8 At home nearly all day writing. Called over in town a short time. Gave Nettie a fine fruit dish. Wilbur started to Chicago about 9:00 morn.

Thursday, January 9 At home all day engaged in writing letters. Rev. W.B. Stoddard called in the afternoon.

Friday, January 10 Arose very late for me; drank only a cup of coffee; so my dinner was a hearty one. Read proofs on the last section of the Ministerial Register for the Year Book of 1896, a close two hours task.

Saturday, January 11 Went to town about 3:00. Call at Keiter's about 5:00. Dr. Becker called in the forenoon. Wrote letters.

Sunday, January 12 Heard W.H. Conner preach at 11:00, Gen. 32.28. In the afternoon heard Prof. Wilbur W. White lecture at Association Hall, on The Failure of Success, of the Success of Failure— Which?" At home the rest of the day except an hour at Lorin's in the evening.

Wednesday, January 15 Call at Youngs 5 min. Get half-fare on D & U R'y. Write communications.

Thursday, January 16 Started on 7:05 train to Fairmount via Union and Gas Cities. Go out to Jefferson Township line on hand car. Go to Ellis Wright's & stay. Dr. H.J. Becker called in the afternoon & read me his argument in the Walla Walla case. Washington Academy, Huntsville, Wash.

Friday, January 17 Go to W.H.H. Reeder's & thence to

Henry Simons & to Oliver Glass's. Dine there. Call at Robt. B. Reeder's, Frank Kirkwood's, & Fowler's, to Ellis Wright's. Sup there & go to Wm. Reeder's & stay all night.

Saturday, January 18 At Wm's. till after 3:00 p.m. Robt. Reeder & Donaldson called. Robt. dines at William's. Go in afternoon to Fairmount. Call to see Wm. Hall who had a severe chill yesterday. Supper at Rev. J.C. Valentine's. Pr. at Union at 7:30, Acts 2.40. Stay at Clinton Brittain's.

Sunday, January 19 Weather thaws. Was at the U.B. Sab. Sch. at 10:00. Attended Friends' Church at 11:00 & heard Wm. S. Wooton, 1 Cor. 3.23, "Ye are Christ's." It was an able & good sermon. Dine at Chas. Atkinson's. Wilbur Kester & wife there. Call at Rev. J. Valentine's, then at Burges Hollingsworth. Supper at Valentine's. Pr. at Union at 7:00, Matt. 25:46. Lodge at Valentine's.

Monday, January 20 Weather thaws. Call at C. Brattain's & get my valise, & I go on 8:50 tr. to Jonesboro, and thence on 9:17 train to Union City. Saw Alonzo Meyer, who stopped off at Upland. He has a son there at school. Wait 3 1/2 hours at Union, during which I write letters to Harvey Wright & to Jas. K. Harris. Arrive at home before 5:00. Talk business with the boys at night.

Tuesday, January 21 Weather warm. At home all day. Busy writing. Called at Conservator Office, in afternoon, perhaps.

Wednesday, January 22 Weather misty. At home. Call 5 m at Young's, mail letters, etc. Rain in the night.

Friday, January 24 At home. Kiracofe called in the afternoon. I called at Lorin's in the evening a half hour.

Saturday, January 25 At home. Fix up my gas lamp, etc. Kiracofe called a minute to see if I could fill the appointments at Germantown to-morrow, if needed. Rev. S.L. Livingston went to Germantown.

Sunday, January 26 Heard Rev. W.H. Conner preach at 11:00, Ps. 17.15. At home till evening, except a few minutes call at Lorin's. Preach at Clemmer St. at 7:00, Luke 4.32.

Tuesday, January 28 Called at Young's Office a few minutes. At home the rest of the day, mostly writing. Call [rest is blank]

Wednesday, January 29 At home all day writing. Bp. H. Floyd called in the afternoon a half hour, being on his way home from the State Anti-secrecy Convention at Columbus, Ohio. Call at Lorin's a half hour in the evening.

Thursday, January 30 Weather mild, fair. I got Mr. J.G. Feight, my next door neighbor, north, to make out a bill for lumber for a stable in Grant Co., Ind., bill to be sawed there. I began at breakfast to board at Mrs. Greenwood's boarding house on 3rd St., me still rooming at home. Called at Lorin's in the evening for an hour, or more.

Friday, January 31 At home. Engaged in writing & in figuring on a plan for double cribs.

Saturday, February 1 At home. Dr. C.H. Kiracofe called in the afternoon. Sent in morning a lumber bill to Wm. Reeder for double cribs.

Sunday, February 2 Some rain. Thermometer high. Heard Rev. S.L. Livingston pr. at Clemmer St. Church—formerly called School St., or West End church— at 11:00, Ps. 34.1-6. Livingstone dines with me. In the evening, I heard L. again, Ps. 91.1. He preached both sermons in good spirits & with his usual gifts of speech.

Tuesday, February 4 At home writing. Called at Conservator office just before noon & left a subscriber sent by D.S. Buck & an order for Disciplines, $2.00. Called at Lorin's 15 min. in the morning. The boys went to the concert at Association Hall in the evening.

Thursday, February 6 Called at Lorin's. Milton put out because I did not stay till he had finished his "plan for house." Engaged mostly in writing. Went to Town in afternoon. Young had not looked up corrections on bill of costs. (Record of Wednesday. Mistake)

Friday, February 7 At home all day except that I made a swift trip to town. Young was not in his office, 4:00 aft. Mrs. A.R. Kiracofe called in the afternoon to see about temporary pastor for Richmond, etc. Oklahoma. (This is record of Thursday)

Saturday, February 8 Weather mild. Left Dayton at 8:38; called at D.K. Zeller's at Richmond, Ind., about 10 minutes, went on to Ft. Wayne. At Ft. Wayne, got a cup of coffee. Reach Ross at 8:50, eve. Bp. H.T. Barnaby met me and took me to his house, 4 m. away. Lewis 22, Milton over 20, Addie about 17.

Sunday, February 9 Weather fair. Pr. at Gaines at 10:30, 1 John 5:18,19. Lunch with Rev. C.B. Whitaker in Caledonia. Pr. there at 2:00, Gen. 18:25. Supper at W's. Preach at Gaines at 7:00, Luke 24:46. Large congregation. Stay at Bp. Barnaby's.

Monday, February 10 Weather fair. Thermometer low. Remain at Barnaby's till 12:20. Go with him to Ross & Grand Rapids. Call at Moses Taggart's. Put up at Eagle Hotel. Supper, lodging & breakfast $1.00. Rev. E.J. Moody also there.

Tuesday, February 11 Weather windy. Thermometer low. Saw Taggart awhile. Staid preparing for trial till 2:00. Trial began at 2:00. Arnold, Congregationalist, and other local Liberal witnesses examined. Then others of their witness the rest of the day. We went to Rodney C. Sessions & supped and lodged.

Wednesday, February 12 Snow. Called at Taggart's Office. Goshert & Shisler on the stand. Then W.J. Shuey the rest of the day. I dine & sup at Dixon's restaurant, an excellent eating house. Call an hour at the office. Lodged at Sessions again. Theodore Sessions there. Sleighs running.

Thursday, February 13 Weather cold. McKee on the stand till 3:00. Then Shelly & Wood, for Radicals. Dine & sup at Dixon's. Lodge at Eagle's Hotel. Barnaby & Wood there.

Friday, February 14 Bishops H.T. Barnaby & M. Wright on the stand, & Wood recalled. Close at 12:00. Lunch at Dixon's. Go on 2:00 train to Ft. Wayne. On 11:45 tr. to Richmond & on 5:10 to Dayton.

Saturday, February 15 Arrive at Dayton at 6:30. Read letters. Go to Town in the afternoon. Pay personal tax. Called forenoon at Keiter's Office & pd. for a Discipline to Barnaby and one to Rev. F.A. Smith. Began again to Board at Mrs. Greenwood's, at Breakfast.

Sunday, February 16 Called at Lorin's a short time in forenoon. At home the rest of the day.

Monday, February 17 Received letters from Rev. J.H. Williams enclosing a letter to [blank] from Rev. W.O. Dinins & a card from Rev. C.B. Sherk. I copied much of them for Mrs. A.R. Kiracofe. Rev. C.H. Kiracofe called in afternoon & I went with him to consult his wife on Oklahoma matters.

Tuesday, February 18 Weather Fair. Thermometer low. Went to town aftern. Got Registered letter from Mrs. Buck containing $10.00 on salary. Called at Young's. Called at Lorin's a few minutes on my return.

Wednesday, February 19 At home all forenoon, assorting legal papers, etc. Coleman, the insurance Agent called.

Friday, February 21 At home till afternoon. Go to town. Rev. R.G. Montgomery called a few minutes just before I started to the depot. Go on train to Dublin. Put up at Bishop H. Floyd' s. Rev. C.B. Small is there.

Saturday, February 22 Dine at Gray's. Return to H. Floyd's— Rev. J. Cranor there. I call at Mrs. Mary Snith's, and at Wm. McGath's. After a call at Floyd's, make a call at Ed. Wilson's & sup at Lewis Cranor's. I preach at 7:00, at U.B. Church, 1 Pet 4.18. I stay with C.B. Small at Floyd 's. Edgar W. Nye (Bill Nye died this day.)

Sunday, February 23 I preach at 10:30, 1 Pet. 1.23. Being born again. Dine at Joseph Gray's. Rev. Peter S. Cook called there. I sup at Dr. G.W. Champ's. I pr. at 7:00, Ps. 73.24. Bro. Small then closed the protracted meeting. Stay at Beecher Johnson's. His wife J. Gray's daughter. His daughter is Estella aged 16.

Monday, February 24 Missed the early train; walked to Cambridge; went on 7:03 train to Richmond, & reached Dayton about 9:15. At home, except a half hour's call at M.F. Keiter's office, in the evening.

Tuesday, February 25 Meet at 8:30 the Ex. Com. of the Educational Board, at Dr. H.J. Becker's. Dine at Becker's. Revs. N.D. Wolfard & A.G. Johnson called. Rev. R.G. Montgomery also called & supped with me at Greenwood's.

Wednesday, February 26 I was at home in the forenoon. Afternoon, went to town, & sent a $50.00 draft to pay my tax in Iowa. I sent a draft of $517.75 to S.L. Livingston. At home the rest of the day.

Thursday, February 27 Called at C.H. Kiracofe's; at H.J. Becker's, & at Conservator Office. Kiracofe called on me a minute before noon.

Friday, February 28 Went to town in the afternoon. Saw Young & paid him for costs on Rike vs. Floyd $172.52, he having given his check to the Clerk for it.

Saturday, February 29 At home all day. Arranged my own business letters in files. Wrote Wm. Reeder and D.R. Fagan. Studied the text Ps. 19.8.

Sunday, March 1 Arose early. Tired waiting for breakfast. Pr. at Clemmer St. Church at 11:00, Ps. 19.8. "Thy come," etc. At 3:30, hear H.L. Hastings of Boston on "Nuts for Infidels to crack." He is large, aged, bald, vigorous at 80 or more. Not an orator, but is able, original, humorous & peculiar. Also heard him at 8:00 on "Atheism & anarchy."

Monday, March 2 Weather mild. At home. Spent the day largely in revising & recording plans of sermons.

Tuesday, March 3 Weather mild. At home. Rev. C.B. McDaniel called an hour in the afternoon.

Thursday, March 5 Largely engaged in examining & verifying my day-books. Spent some time at Keiter's office. The boys brought up their gas-engine that Wilbur made, & try it somewhat in the evening.

Friday, March 6 Went to Marion via Union City. Paid my tax. Saw Stover. Went on evening train to Fairmount. Staid at Rev. John C. Valentine's. Call an hour at C. Brattain's.

Saturday, March 7 Go on train to Fowlerton. At the saw mill (Price's) an hour. Dine at W.H.H. Reeder's. Go to Ellis Wright's. Go back to Fairmount, and stay at Chas. Atkinson's. That day, I looked over the place and planned for ditching the north field.

Sunday, March 8 Rev. J.C. Valentine pr. at 11:00. I dine at Brattain's. I visit Wm. Halls' (Hollingworth's) in Afternoon. Sup at Valentine's. Preach at Union, 1 1/2 miles South at 7:00, Ex. 28:34. I stay at Robt. Hasting's.

Monday, March 9 Go on 9:15 tr. to Fowlerton. Dine at Wm. Reeder's. Afternoon went to Ellis Wright's-eve rather. I redrove stakes in my town plat, that the frost had raised. Sup & lodge at Ellis's. Went in eve. to Henry Simons's, awhile.

Tuesday, March 10 Went on 7:00 train to Fairmount & thence to Wabash & Huntington. Dine, sup & lodge at Rev. A.G. Johnson's. Board of Education met at 4:00 & in Eve. Some of us went out at 3:00 to view the College Grounds north of the City.

Wednesday, March 11 Snow. Board of Education met again & arranged with Mr. Kintz to bring our Educational institution to this city. After dinner, I went on 12:25 tr to Ft. Wayne & thence via Richmond home, arriving at 6:30. Supper at home.

Thursday, March 12 Weather thaws. At home. Got letter from Rev. D.B. Sherk, saying the Ontario Court of Appeals had decided the Port Elgin case against us. Dr. H.J. Becker called in the forenoon. Mr. Fitch called in the afternoon to get sketch of my life for Dayton History by Frank Conover.

Friday, March 13 Weather moderate. At home. Boys trying to adjust business. Bicycle frame came. Dr. C.H. Kiracofe called twice in Afternoon to see about Ontario decision & Oklahoma affairs.

Sunday, March 15 Heard Rev. Prichard pr. at Williams Street Baptist Church at 11:00, Mat[t]. 13.9, a good sermon, on Parable of the Sower. Called at Lorin's after dinner, a half hour.

Wednesday, March 18 Went to town in the morning,

saw the dentist; saw Young a minute. Mrs. Kiracofe called in the afternoon to get my signature to her application for rates of travel on Gen. Pas. Ass'n. Lines. Very busy, mostly writing.

Thursday, March 19 Wrote letters to Titus and others. C. Hiram Kiracofe called in afternoon to get signature to his application for favors on W. Pas. A'n. lines.

Saturday, March 21 Went to Tizzard's & called Young's. At home rest of the day.

Sunday, March 22 I pr. at Clemmer St. at 11:00, Rev. 20.3- 18.23.Dine at Greenwood's, but other meals at home. Pres. Kiracofe pr. at 7:00, Acts 16.30. I called at Lorin's a few minutes in forenoon.

Monday, March 23 At home all day. Spend a good while looking over old volumes of the Telescope for a date, also in running over copies of the Itinerant. Dined at Greenwood's. Dr. Becker calle[d] a few minutes— wanted a meeting of Mis. Ex. Com.

Tuesday, March 24 Went to Bank & got a draft of $40.00 & sent it to Katie. Sent $1.00 draft to Harper & Bros. Called at Kiracofe's in forenoon. After session of Mis. Ex. Com. at 7:00 at Keiter's residence.

Friday, March 27 Weather beautiful. At home and engaged mostly as usual. Make a facsimile of an old flyleaf containing the records of my Great-Great-Grandfather & Grandmother's Joseph Reeder (Senior) and Susana Reeder's family— the document written about A.D. 1757-8. Kiracofe called in the afternoon.

Saturday, March 28 Weather cloudy. At home reading & writing. Went to City library, etc. in Afternoon. Weather warm and promising rain.

Sunday, March 29 Weather warm. Heard W.H. Conner pr. at 11:00, Matt. 4:17, Clemmer St. Church. Heard at 3:30, at Association Hall, Dr. Carlos Martyn, Editor of the Christian Citizen, Chicago, on "The Young Man's Scepter," a very able and eloquent address. I was at home in the evening. Rainy.

Monday, March 30 At Home most of the day. Went to the Conservator office, and to C.H. Kiracofe's. Saw S.L. Livingston and Jacob Slifer there. Called at Craighead's and at Young's. Wrote letters.

Tuesday, March 31 At home most all the day. Called at Conservator office a minute. Katharine came home from Oberlin at 9:00 aft. via Clyde, so Orville missed her. Margaret Goodwin along. At midnight, the great noise begins about the first settlement of Dayton, one hundred years ago.

Wednesday, April 1 Weather cloudy. Having gone to the old court house, I witness the great centennial noise. It was steam whistles, bells, mortars, musquetry,etc. I staid about an hour. Slept over three hours and in the day an hour. At home all day. Called at Lorin's an hour in the evening.

Thursday, April 2 Weather fair. At home all forenoon. Went to town afternoon, saw Young a minute. Call at Joseph Zenas Reeder's and at the Herald office to see him. Write letters till a very late hour.

Friday, April 3 At home all forenoon. Go to the post-office in the afternoon. Wrote much to-day. Editor Kiracofe called in the afternoon.

Saturday, April 4 At home in the forenoon, & afternoon except a trip to town. Drew the balance in my favor out of the Winters National Bank, $46.25 cents, it all being Church fund. Katie, and Margaret Goodwin, go to town to shop.

Sunday, April 5 Katherine sick to day. I was at home all day except a walk or two.

Monday, April 6 At home all day. The girls went to town and visited Lorin's in the evening. I looked up Legal Fund subscriptions and over Conservator list to find post-offices of subscribers and wrote some letters. Telegram concerning California decision in our favor. Wrote the rest of the night.

Tuesday, April 7 Wrote letters forenoon. Katherine and Miss Goodwin start to Oberlin on 11:15 train. Kiracofe called in afternoon.

Wednesday, April 8 Wrote Katie. Lorins have a little girl Ivonette, born near 4:00 this morning. Went to town, got a draft for $29.28, and sent to William to pay Fultz for ditching in north field & woods.

Thursday, April 9 Rain. At home all forenoon. Wrote J.Z. Reeder, R.V. Gilbert & John Ebersole. Called to see Mrs. Edwards at Kiracofes. Eat supper there.

Saturday, April 11 Wrote a multitude of letters— largely to subscribers to legal fund. At home all day. Letter from Katie about getting her $25.00 prize for an Essay on the Monroe Doctrine. Letter from Reuchlin.

Sunday, April 12 Wrote none. Went to hear Dr. H.F. Colby preach at the 1st Baptist Church. Text: Luke 11.13. On Holy Spirit. Spent the remainder of the day at home. Rev. H.J. Becker called at 4:00 & staid 2 hours, a part of the time in a walk on the streets.

Monday, April 13 Received the California Decision in Tulare Parsonage case, & arranged for it to go in this week's Conservator.

Tuesday, April 14 Write an article on Dayton's Centennial. Write letters.

Wednesday, April 15 Write letters. Left copies of California decision at the daily paper offices.

Friday, April 17 Called at Lorin's.

Saturday, April 18 Went on 7:00 train to Union & Gas Cities to Fairmount. Call at Rev. Wm. Hall's. Go with Oliver Buller's to Elis Wright's. Supper there. E. takes me to Wm. H.H. Reeder's. I lodge there.

Sunday, April 19 I go with Ralph Fultz to Oliver Glass's. Dine there with The Reeder families. Go at 3:00 to Hickory Sch. H. & thence to Leach S. Sch. H. I address S.S. 15 min. Supper at Grass's. Pr. at 8:00, Jas. 1:12. Lodge at Glass's.

Monday, April 20 Call at Robt. Reeder's & thence with 1st Oliver Glass & then with Ellis Wright via Parina to Ellis Wright's & dine there. Write letters & stay to supper & lodging. It rained considerably.

Tuesday, April 21 Was at Wm. Reeder's. Looked at the place. Stay at [rest is blank]

Wednesday, April 22 Went to Wm. Reeder's and helped David Fults plow out the fence corners. Began a fence on Indiana Street. Worked till late. Was very tired. Staid at William's.

Thursday, April 23 Remain at Wm. Reeder's & began to work on the straight rail-fence. It rained very much. Went to Ellis Wright's toward night. Lodge there.

Friday, April 24 Went to Fairmount on the 7:00 tr. Call at Post-office, Brattain's, etc. Come back on 9:15 train. Go to Wm. Reeder's. Stay till after supper. We looked over the place. I began a sermon for the Missionary Anniversary. Stay at Ellis Wright's. Sat up late.

Saturday, April 25 Stay at Ellis's till afternoon. He takes me after dinner to F. Kirkwood's & to Henry Simons & to Parina. I get supper at Wm. Reeder's & then go on the train to Fairmount. Stay at Clinton Brattain's.

Sunday, April 26 Went to Union, 1 1/2 m south. Pr. Luke 19.31. Dine at Keever's. Go about 4:30 to Knox Chapel with Rev. J.C. Valentine. Call at Day's; then at Jo Miller's. Pr. at 8:00 at Knox's. Acts 2:39, a Missionary sermon. Stay at Miller 's. Children: Gertrude & Willie.

Monday, April 27 Go with V. to Fairmount, & thence with Ellis Wright. Talk with Simmons on Furniture factory site. Dine at Ellis Wright's. Ellis & I look over town site etc. Stay at Ellis's.

Tuesday, April 28 Went to Leach & mail letters. Dine at W.H.H. Reeder's. We meet at Ellis' in railroad council & factory. I remain at Ellis'.

Wednesday, April 29 Go to town for Ellis. Got Myrl a little piana. Dine at Ellis's. Meet at Frank Kirkwood's at 4:00. Simmons does not appear. Sup & lodge at Ellis's. Pr. at Henry Simons at 8:00, 1 John 4.16. Madams Kimes & Noes of Fairmount there.

Thursday, April 30 Go on 7:00 tr. to Fairmount. Thence

intending train to Jonesboro home. But Frank Kirkwood met me at depot & I returned to Ellis's with him. Stay there except a walk with Little Myrl to the farm. Factory meeting at Simons at 8:00. Concluded to contract with Simmons. Stay at Simons.

Friday, May 1 Go on 7:00 train to Fairmount & thence on 8:50 to Jonesboro, Union City.

Saturday, May 2 At home in foren. busy. Called at Kiracofe's. Went to town about 5:00, got Kangaroo shoes & some sandals. Met brethren in counsel at Keiter's office. Slept 8 hours.

Sunday, May 3 Heard Rev. W.H. Conner pr. at 11:00, John 8:37. Dined at H.J. Becker's. At home the rest of the day and evening, except a call at 3:00, at Lorin's.

Monday, May 4 Went on 7:00 morn. train to Union City, Gas City, & Fairmount, Indiana. Stop at C.D. Brattain's. Go on 7:40 train to Fowlerton. Stay at Wm. H.H. Reeder's.

Tuesday, May 5 Go to Ellis Wright's. See Oliver Buller & talk with him. Stay at Ellis' till next morning.

Wednesday, May 6 Go on 7:00 train to Fairmount. Called at Rev. J.C. Valentine's, R.W. Hasting's, Chas. Atkinson's. Dine at Valentine's. Call at Hasting's, Atkinson's, Hall's, Cain's, Bartholomew's, M.M. Hain's, Henry Cell's. Stay at Atkinson's.

Thursday, May 7 Call at Wm. Heath 's. Call on various persons and get subscriptions. Dine at Wm. Heath's. Gather other subscriptions in the afternoon. Supper at Charles Atkinson's. Go on 7:40 tr. to Fowlerton. Go to Henry Simons. Mr. Simmond's does not come to meet us. I stay at Simons.

Friday, May 8 Go to Ellis Wright's. Dine there. Spend the day there, largely in writing on the annual missionary address. Lodge at Ellis's.

Saturday, May 9 Remain at Ellis's till after supper. Write on the Missionary address. Help a little in forenoon on mowing the door yard. Go at 7:00 eve. to Leach P.O. & to Willis P. Parker's and settle on the wire fence paying

him $13.93 cents additional to $7.00 heretofore sent him.

Sunday, May 10 Attend Qr. Meeting at Salem M.P. Church, & hear Rev. M.F. Iliff pr. at 11:00. Sacramental service. Dine at Levi Simons. Pr. at Salem at 8:00, Gen. 49.10. Stay at Ellis Wright's.

Monday, May 11 Go with Oliver Buller to see F. Kirkwood. Talk on Advertising & on name of our town, about changing it. Ellis & family go to Fairmount & I with them to the 12:38 train. Go via Anderson & Richmond home. Found all well. I arrived about 6:00.

Tuesday, May 12 Called at Lorin's, at the Office, and at Prof. Kiracofe's. Wrote some letters, etc.

Wednesday, May 13 Called at Lorin's. Milton went home with me & staid to dinner & till 3 or 4 oclock. Slept an hour & ate no supper. Spent an hour thinking on the subject of an article for Conservator. I spent much of the day in fixing up the neglected door-yard.

Thursday, May 14 At home. Mrs. Kiracofe called in the afternoon to see about editorial work.

Saturday, May 16 Went to town in the forenoon. Saw Young 10 minutes. Revise my An. Mis. address awhile. At home the rest of the day. The boys got the first "Wright Special" bicycle ready for sale & a ladies' wheel about so— both their own manufacture.

Sunday, May 17 Attended church & heard W.H. Conner pr. at Clemmer Street. At home the rest of the day.

Monday, May 18 At home. Did some work on articles contributed to the Conservator. Bp. D.K. Flickinger come[s] at 5:00, aftn. Went with him to Young's residence. For six weeks or more, we have had the longest continued uniform spring, that I ever knew.

Tuesday, May 19 Mr. F.H. Short of Cincinnati & Mrs. Semele Short, my Mother's cousin, came to the City on Railroad business; also Mrs. Caroline Donahue, daughter of Mt. Auburn, Cincinnati, 2117. We go to the Soldier's Home & spend the day. Supper at M.F. Keiter's. Go again to Young's with D.K.F.

Wednesday, May 20 Left on 8:43 train to Charlotte, Mich., via Richmond & Vicksburg. Lunch at Richmond, supper at Vicksburg. Rev. D.K. Flickinger with me. We took Prof. C.H. Kiracofe aboard at LaOtto & Bp. H. Floyd at Battle Creek. We arrived at 9:26, eve. I staid at Rev. R.S. Bowman's with Prof. K. & Bp. H.T. Barnaby.

Thursday, May 21 Board of Bishops met at R.S. Bowman's at 8:30 & continued in session there all day. I dine & sup at Rev. S.S. Pennington's & I also lodged there with Rev. C. Bender my fellow boarder. I delivered the Annual Missionary address at 8:00. Mission Board organized at 7:30. Pennington's children Lulu 10; Floyd 16 mo.

Friday, May 22 Session at 8:00. I preside all day. Bout over Indiana appropriation $300 or 200.00. I write an article for the Conservator which had required me spare time till bed time, so I missed hearing Dr. D.K. Flickinger's address on Africa.

Saturday, May 23 Board session continued. Bp. H.T. Barnaby presided in the forenoon. Rev. I.M. Tharp dined with me. Bishop Floyd presided. Adjourned at 5:00. Rev. J.K. Alwood supped with me. Rev. I.M. Tharp pr. at 8:00, Matt. 16:24. Stay at Pennington's as usual.

Sunday, May 24 Attended Love-feast meeting in the U.B. Church. Rev. J.K. Alwood pr. at 10:30, 1 Cor. 15.35. I dine at Pennington's. I call a few minutes at Rev. R.S. Bowman's, and two hours at Rev. W.S. Titus'. Rev. D.K. Flickinger talked to children at 6:30. I pr at 7:30, Gen. 49.10. Stay at Pennington's.

Monday, May 25 Left on 7:26 tr. for Richmond. Reach Vicksburg, Ft. Wayne, & Richmond. Rev. C. Bender continued on Gr. Trunk R'y. Pres. I.M. Tharp continue to Ft. Wayne, & Floyd to Richmond. Kiracofe continues to Dayton. I stay at D.K. Zeller's.

Tuesday, May 26 Miss 7:50 train. Call at Allen Harris. Dine at Zeller's. Call an hour at Otto Williams to see Mrs. Sarah Williams, who has been very sick. I take 7:30 tr. to Dayton. After supper, call at Lorin's a few minutes.

Wednesday, May 27 At home. Have less vigor than usual. Overworked for two weeks past.

Thursday, May 28 At home. I have not usual vigor. It is not dullness. I feel well, only an inertness of body and mind.

Friday, May 29 At home. About as yesterday only growing more vigorous .

Sunday, May 31 Heard Rev. W.H. Conner preach at Clemmer St. Church at 11:00, 1 Cor. 15.58. I dine at Samuel Spidel's far east on King St. Heard Conner pr. again at 7:30, Matt. 10.34.

Monday, June 1 At home all day writing, and cleaning up my windows. Called at Lorin's in the evening. The weather has been very fine, and almost without frost for over two months— the finest earliest spring that I ever saw.

Tuesday, June 2 At home in forenoon writing & in making out my report on Legal Affairs. Publishing Board met at Rev. M.F. Keiter's. Some controversy.

Wednesday, June 3 Business of publishing Board in forenoon. More "scrapping." Meeting of Ex. Commit[t]ees in afternoon. Dr. Flickinger present. He called at my house at 1:30 aftn. Women conclude to make a loan to Wilberforce.

Saturday, June 6 Finished up editorials & read proofs.

Sunday, June 7 Heard Rev. Wm. Miller pr. at 11:00, John 14.2. Dine with Miller & Keiter at Rev. W.H. Conner's. Stay till Experience meeting at 6:00. Rev. Miller pr. at 7:00, 1 Thes. 5.19.

Tuesday, June 9 Did work on the paper—wrote an anonymous article on The Christian's Anchor. Revised some communications.

Wednesday, June 10 Work on a Sabbath school Lesson, and other editorial work.

Thursday, June 11 Thursday, write editorials, Ed. Notes, read proofs. Did 16 hours of close work.

Friday, June 12 Busy forenoon on editorial work. Go on 12:30 Short-line train to Cincinnati, & thence on

2:30 train to Greensburg, Ind. Supper at Rev. T.J. Conner's with her daughter, Mrs. Hazelrigg. Lodge at John H. Braden's. His first wife, Eliza Reeder, was my Mother's sister. His motherinlaw Mrs. Dobbins lives with them.

Saturday, June 13 Call at Hamilton's a half hour, and on Dr. Johnson a few minutes. Go on to Rugby and to Hartsville with Young Plumley. Dine at Rev. H.W. Robbins' with Floyd. Call at Mrs. Kershner's and at Simion Rohrer's and then at Rev. A.J. Bolen's. I pr. at 8.00, Ps. 119.9 before Y. P. Chris. A. of H. Col. Stay at Bolen's.

Sunday, June 14 Call at Rev. John Riley's and at Rominer's to see Mother Noah Elrod. Bish. H. Floyd pr. baccalaureate sermon at 10:30. I dine & Sup at Prof. A.P. Barnaby's. Hamilton of Grisb. & wife dine with us. Call at Lawrence's. I pr. at 8:00 before Trustees Ps. 92.8. Stay at N.P. Miller's.

Monday, June 15 Start at 7:00 & via Greensburg & Cin. Reach home at 2:00. "Scrap" with Keiter, as is his wont.

Wednesday, June 17 At work. Go to town in Afternoon. Saw Young.

Sunday, June 21 At Baptist Church on Williams St., heard pastor pr. John 15.5. Dine at Lorin's. Stay till 4:00. At home in the evening.

Tuesday, June 23 At home. Meeting of Council on Building at Huntington, Indiana at M.F. Keiter's at 7:00, Eve. Busy writing.

Wednesday, June 24 Meeting of the Exec. Com. of Publishing Board met at 7:00. Busy writing.

Saturday, June 27 At home except a trip to town afternoon. Busy on the Conservator. Not very well in the night.

Sunday, June 28 Not very well to-day, so I slept late, which is not usual on Sundays, and went no where, only I made a call at Lorin's.

Monday, June 29 At work on the Conservator, which is somewhat behind, Mr. Graybill being off last week a day in the job room and all work in News room being without a head.

Wednesday, July 1 At home busy on editing the paper.

Thursday, July 2 Busy editing the paper. Dr. Flickinger called forenoon and afternoon.

Friday, July 3 Went to town before noon. Got a draft for $30.00 and sent to Katie.

Saturday, July 4 Seven Years ago to-day went out the spirit of my dear Susan. Ever since this National holiday has been a sad anniversary to me. Spent the forenoon partly in resting. Went to the Cemetery at 4:00, and arranged the grass on our grave lot. Perennial flowers grow over Susan's grave.

Sunday, July 5 Attended Park Presbyterian Church and hear the Pastor, Rev. F.L. Bullard, Jr., preach Matt. 16.16-17, spoke of the Pope's encyclitical.

Monday, July 6 Finished up reading proofs and writing for the paper, and wrote a few letters.

Friday, July 10 Dr. C.H. Kiracofe, the editor, came home.

Saturday, July 11 Worked on the paper. Meeting of the Building Committee at 3:00.

Sunday, July 12 Heard W.H. Conner pr. 2 Kings 20.1-3.

Monday, July 13 At noon, I closed my five weeks work on the Conservator.

Thursday, July 16 Bp. W. Dillon & B.F. Fleenor, of California, called a half hour in the forenoon. Dr. C.H. Kiracofe called in afternoon.

Friday, July 17 Called at Kiracofe's in forenoon, and thence went to town and paid my tax and paid Young & Young $200.00 on the U.S. case.

Saturday, July 18 At home, mostly writing. Call at C.H. Kiracofe's in the evening.

Sunday, July 19 Pr. at Baptist Church on Sprague St., Gal. 5:18. The pastor's name is Grant.

Monday, July 20 At home till evening. Prof. Kiracofe called in the afternoon. I attend a building committee meeting at Dr. H.J. Becker's, at 7:00. Call at Kiracofe's.

Tuesday, July 21 Went to town in forenoon. Busy all day in getting ready to go away to-morrow.

Wednesday, July 22 Go on 8:58 tr. to Richmond. Dine at D.K. Zeller's. Harvey Wright meets me at Dunreith and takes me via Mays, to his house. Delilah has some rheumatism.

Thursday, July 23 Call an hour at Sam'l. Kirkpatrick's. Dine at John McKee's. Thos. Wilhelm & Florence and Cora 12, and [blank] there also. Aftn, we went to Preston Scott's. Children Alma & [blank] Eve'n, called an hour at Luther Milhouse's. Lodge at Harvey's. Dr. Geo. Wright comes at 8:00, from his home at Indianapolis.

Friday, July 24 Chas. Gray takes myself & Geo. Wright to Knightstown. On the way, we stop abt 40 min. at Thos. Wright's and 30 min. at Jabez Rhoads. Go on 11:35 train to Anderson & to Fairmount. Go out to Ellis Wright's with Oliver Buller. Clifford & Bertha Long there on a visit.

Saturday, July 25 Go to Wm. H.H. Reeder's. I look over the place some. Go to Oliver A. Glass's. Dine there. Call at Robert B. Reeder's. Go back to Wm's. Look at corn & clover. Fix up accounts. Sup there. Go to Ellis Wright's and stay there.

Sunday, July 26 Ellis takes me to Fairmount. I pr. at U.B. Church at 11:00, Prov. 3.5,6. Dine at B. Hollingsworth's. Sup at Rev. J.C. Valentine's, south of town. Pr. at Union, Gal. V:18. Stay at Valentine's. Called at Brattain's and Robt. Hastings. It was Berge Hollingsworth above.

Monday, July 27 At Brattain's till after dinner. Go on 1:33 tr. to Jonesboro. See all the feed stores in Jonesboro and Gas City. Go out to the Carter neighborhood. Return to Jonesboro & stay at Whittier House.

Tuesday, July 28 Sold my corn to John W. Roush at 22 cents a bushel, at the crib. I go on the 9:01 train to Wabash. See Rose, cousin of Albert A. Koerner & Mr. Cora, Uncle of Albert. Toledo tr. over an hour late— two hours at Toledo; so connection for Oberlin was close. Reach Oberlin at 7:35. Katie and Katie Siliman met me.

Wednesday, July 29 Stay at Mrs. A.W. Brooke, 40 S. Professor Street. Very warm day. Took a walk in eve. Miss Clark & others call. Mrs. Johnson called. Down on bonneted speakers, she was.

Thursday, July 30 Go on 11:47 tr to Toledo. On 3:00, L.S. & M.S., to Detroit. Put up at Franklin House. Lodging 50 c., Breakf. 35 c.

Friday, July 31 Go about the city. Then on 10:15 train to Port Huron & thence to Berlin, Ont., arriving at 5:10. D.B. Sherk meets me & I go to his house. Meet Bro. Eshelman at Rev. J.B. Bowman's at 8:00. Lodge at Sherk's. Slept four hours.

Saturday, August 1 Go on 9:30 train to Port Elgin. R.A. Clark meets me and we go to his house. Children: John D.; Alberta, Viola, Anna Mary, Robt. Fry. Slept 8 hours.

Sunday, August 2 Preach at Pt. Elgin U.B. Church (the church under litigation) at 10:30, Gen. 49.10. Dine at W. Nicholson's, who is in second marriage, aged, well to do. Pr. at "the elbow" North of Bruce at 2:30, Ps. 92.8. Supper at J.H. Wismer's. Pr at Pt. Elgin, 7:00, Hebr. 11.10. Stay at R.A. Clark 's. Write in Albums. Saw J. Bechtel, trustee, at Elbow.

Monday, August 3 Start on 5:30 tr. for Berlin. Meet at depot, and on train Mr. [blank] of Toronto, solicitor for the Liquor Traffic aboard. Our conversation on parties in Canada. Dine & sup at J.B. Bowman's. I pr. at Freeport, at 8:00, Ps. 73.24.

Tuesday, August 4 Visit Chr. D. Rosenberger's & dine there. Rev. Angus R. Springer came & took me to Montrose. Supper at Samuel Bowman's. Pr. at Montrose at 8:00, Isa. 9:7. Stay at Frank Snyder's. Slept 6 hours. It rained considerably in the night.

Wednesday, August 5 Talk till 10:00 at Frank Snyder 's.

We go on to Berlin; dine at Rev. J.B. Bowman's, with Rev. Angus Springer. Go to William Becker's (Sherk's soninlaw's) for supper. Pr. at U.B. Church at 8:00, Gen. 49.10. Stay at Jacob B. Bowman's.

Thursday, August 6 Arose late. Breakfast about 8 o'clock. Wrote some letters. Called at Rev. D.B. Sherk's in the afternoon. Went at 6:30 to Manheim Church. Stay at John Ware's 1 m. west. I pr. at 8:00, 2 Tim. 2:15.

Friday, August 7 Ministerial Association convened at 8:30. I elected critic. Dine at Nathan Woods. Afternoon session. Supper at Henry Becker's. Rev. D.B. Sherk pr. at 8:00, written sermon. We stay at Henry Ware's.

Saturday, August 8 I go with Bro. Ware & his son (Horace?) 17, to Berlin. Stop an hour at Rev. J.B. Bowman's. Go to E. Eshelman's & thence to Miller & Simm's (atty's office). Henry Becker took me to his house 6 ms S. Quar. Conference after Sermon by D.B. Sherk. Pres. elder, Rom. 8.32. Sup at Becker's. Rev. J. Howe pr. at 8:00 at Church, Prov. 3. I stay at H. Becker['s].

Sunday, August 9 Pr. at Becker's Grove, at 10:30, Jas. 1.12. Dine at Becker's. Pr. at 2:30, Matt. 5.12. Sup at Jac. C. Hallman's. Pr. at New Dundee at 7:30, Gal. 4.4,5. Stay at Elias Hallman's.

Monday, August 10 Bro. Hallman takes Rev. J. Howe & Myself to Drambro, & we go on to Sherkston. Dine at Isaac Sherk's. In afternoon, go to Benj. Stroup's. Supper there. Pr. at Sherkton U.B. Church at 8:00, Ps. 73.24. Stay at Merner B. Shupe's.

Tuesday, August 11 Bro. Shupe takes me to Sherks & I go on 8:00 train to Black Rock & thence on St. cars to Buffalo. Get Canada money changed into U.S. money. Go on 9:20 train to Erie. At E., I write letter to S.H. Blake, etc. Have a time to exchange Ont. money for American. Reach Union City at 5:00. Stay at Rev. N.R. Luce's.

Wednesday, August 12 Spend forenoon in writing letters. Send Katharine $25.00. Go on 1:36 train to Geneva & Shaw's. David Loper takes us to Washington Loper's to Supper. I then go to David Loper's and lodge. Rev. S. Evans pr. at the Brooks Chapel at 8:00. I did not attend.

Thursday, August 13 Conference opened at Brooks Chapel at 8:30. Bro. Luce & I board at Abram R. Williams. Conference progressed well. Rev. J.A. Higley pr. at 8:00, Ps. 26:11. Stay at Williams.

Friday, August 14 Conference continued. Dine, sup & lodge at Williams'. Stationing committee met at Williams at 5:00. I pr. at 8:00, 1 John 1.9.

Saturday, August 15 Conference Continued. Dine, sup & lodge as usual. Read the Stationing Com. report about 3:00. Adjourn at 4:00. Rev. N.R. Luce pr. at 8:00, Rev. 21:4.

Sunday, August 16 Pr at 11:00, Isa. 9:7. Dine at Wm. Loper's near West Fairfield Church. Bro. Loper takes W.R. Luce, Saml. Evans & myself to Meadville. I stay at [blank] House.

Monday, August 17 Went on 4:00 train to Cleveland, O., & on 10:45 to Toledo, & on 4:25 to Huntington. Walk to Rev. A.G. Johnson's & stay. Rev. C.H. Kiracofe there also.

Tuesday, August 18 Go to depot & meet Bishop Barnaby, Dr. H.J. Becker, et al. I go out to College Grounds. Dine at A.G. Johnson's, lay corner stone of the College Building at 2:00. Supper and lodging at Sarah Jane Custard's with Dr. D.K. Flickinger.

Wednesday, August 19 Awake at 3:00, and go at 3:30 to the depot. Train 40 m. late. Start at 4:45 via Ft. Wayne to Massilon & Strasburg, Ohio. Augustus Slemmer meets us & takes us to his house where my home is to be during conference. Rev. D.K. Flickinger pr. at 8:00, 2 Chron. 15.7.

Thursday, August 20 East Ohio Conference meets at 8:30. Business progresses well. Dine & lodge at Slemmer's. Rev. H.J. Becker pr. at 7:30, "Take ye away the stone." Supper at Kohr's.

Friday, August 21 Conference continues. Dine at Whitaker's, whom I knew in Oregon. H.H. Young elected presiding-elder, after many ballots. Stationing Com. met at Slemmer's at 7:00. Rev. D.K. Flickinger lectured on Africa at 7:30, Coll. $20.00. Stay at Slemmer's.

Saturday, August 22 Conference Continued. I dine at Solomon Sease's 1 1/2 m. east. Conference closes at 4:30. Rev. A.H. Roach pr. at 7:30 Gen. 4.7, "Sin lieth at door." I stay at Slemmer's.

Sunday, August 23 I pr. at 11:00, Acts 26.17,18. Collection is $48.38. I dine at Slemmer's. Pr. at 7:30, Rev. 1.5, "Unto Him that loved." Stay at Gust. Slemmer's.

Monday, August 24 Go to Strasburg with A. Slemmer. Hence at 9:20, go to Cleveland. Call at Fox Lake Coal Company, 520 Western Reserve Building to see certificates of 1893, 1894. Go on 3.20 tr. to Toledo. Put up at St. James Hotel, Cor. Summit & La Grange Sts. Mailed a card to Katherine.

Tuesday, August 25 Go on 7:30 train to Rising Sun. Stop at Rev. Peter Urschell's. Dine there. Thence go to Horace Smith's, where I boarded at Conference six years ago, where I am to board during conference. At prayer meeting at 8:00. Few present.

Wednesday, August 26 At Smith's to day. Rev. C.H. Kiracofe came in the afternoon. Rev. Edward L. Day pr. at 8:00, Heb. 6:1. I stay at Smith 's. Diarrhea in the night.

Thursday, August 27 Conference opened at 8:30. I spoke at greater lenghth than usual on lesson of scripture. Conference well attended. There seemed a good interest.

Friday, August 28 Conference Continued. Dr. C.H. Kiracofe present. Dr. D.K. Flickinger and Sister A.R. Kiracofe came. Dr. Flickinger lectured at Ch. of God at 8:00, on Africa.

Saturday, August 29 Conference continued. Very busy day. Rev. H.D. Yant pr. at 8:00. Session closed before 10:00. Stationing committee meets at H. Smith's at 7:00.

Sunday, August 30 Preach at 10:30, John 3.30. Ordain Mary B. Mullen and Geo. C. Lashley. Dine at Zimmerman's. Sup at Horace Smith's. Sacramental meeting at 7:30; D.K. Flickinger lectures at 8:15. Sandusky W. M. Asso. raises 90$ a year for five years. Stay at H. Smith's.

Monday, August 31 Dine at Misses M.B. Mullen & Cora Yeagle's with Mrs. Kiracofe. Return to Smith's but go back to Mullen's to supper. Lodge at Smith's.

Tuesday, September 1 Go on 8:13 train to Carey. Mrs. Kiracofe stops off at Fostoria. Flickinger & I dine at hotel. Go on to Kenton & thence to John Burris's. I preach at Otterbein Church Acts 11:24. Stay at Burris's.

Wednesday, September 2 Open Conference at Otterbein Church at 8:30. Board at Burris's. Bishop D.K. Flickinger lectured at 8:00 on Africa.

Thursday, September 3 Conference Continued. Elected F.M. Harvey & Wm. Miller elder. Stationing committee met at 6:45 at Burris's & adjourned about 9:00. M.F. Keiter pr. at 8:00, "He saved others."

Friday, September 4 Conference Continued. Dine at Burris & Rev. C. Weyer takes Keiter & Myself to Kenton. Reach Dayton at 4:30. Found Orville very sick with typhoid fever. The temperature at one time, days ago, ran to 105.5 degrees. Temperature is now about 102 or 103 degrees.

Saturday, September 5 Arrange matters a little. Dr. Spitler came at 11:30. Go to town; found the banks closed. Go on 4:27 train to Kenton. Scott meets me & takes me to John L. Burris's. I lodge there.

Sunday, September 6 I pr. at 11:00 in the Conf. tent in Burris's grove, Dan. 2:44. Dine, sup, & lodge at Burris's. Rev. S.T. Mahan pr. at 8:00 at the church. The house was crowded & suffocated for lack of ventilation. S.S. Anniversary at 3:00, Mahan, Wright, and R.G. Montgomery spoke.

Monday, September 7 Bro. Burris takes me to Kenton, and I go on 8:50 tr. to Dayton. Orville had been better since Saturday. At home the rest of the day, and to remain till about Sept. 23.

Tuesday, September 8 At home in forenoon, except a call at Keiter's office. Go in afternoon to town & send a draft of $100.00 to Reuchlin as a loan. Call at Lorin's in the evening. Orville seems to be getting along fairly well.

Wednesday, September 9 At home. Orville is about the same.

Thursday, September 10 At home. Orville's fever is possibly decreasing a little.

Friday, September 11 At home. This 24 hours proved Orville's best since his sickness. Called at Keiter's office in the afternoon.

Saturday, September 12 Orville seemed some better this morning. Called at Kiracofe's about 10:00 forenoon.

Sunday, September 13 At home all day, except a little while at Lorin's. Orville is still doing well.

Monday, September 14 At home except a half hour at Keiter's office, and an hour in town in forenoon. Orville was better in the morning than any day since his sickness. Got a draft of $89.50 from Fagan on my oats. Sat up late reading the Scriptures.

Tuesday, September 15 At home all day. Orville is still improving.

Wednesday, September 16 This is Dayton Centennial parade day in the forenoon. I did not go to see it. No mail delivery in forenoon. I called at Lorin's at 7:00. Milton showed how the drum major keeps time and how the soldiers drill. Sat up till about 2:00 morn.

Thursday, September 17 At home all forenoon. Orville is still better. Nothing very new.

Friday, September 18 At home. Orville is still doing well.

Saturday, September 19 Go to town at 10:30, to have new coat fitted. Buy Orville a nice boquet. At home the rest of the day.

Sunday, September 20 At home all day except a half hour's call at Lorin's & dinner at the boarding- house, Mrs. Greenwood 's. Rev. Klinefelter called in teh aftern. & saw Orville a moment. Orville had little if any fever, but has some delirium, part of the time.

Monday, September 21 Orville seems better. At home all day, Mostly writing letters. Orville's fever seems to have left him.

Tuesday, September 22 Orville is still improving. Went to town afternoon & got an umbrella, $2.25, Cohen's. Went again at 6:00 and got a new suit. I paid by bank check for it, $35.00. Sat up till midnight & wrote letters. Orville slept finely.

Wednesday, September 23 Start on 9:24 morn. train to Junction City. Train being behind time, I miss connection at Columbus 20 minutes and have to wait till 5:00. Go on to Junction City, reaching there at 6:47. Ride out to Mt. Zion Ch. with Wm. Gregg's. C.H. Kiracofe preached "Harvest great." Home at Joshua Folks.

Thursday, September 24 Conference opened at 9:00, real time. Proceded. Fair progress. Board at Joshua Folk's 1/2 mile south. D.K. Flickinger lectured on Dark Africa.

Friday, September 25 Conference opened at 9:00. Proceded well. Dine at W.S. Tuttle's. C.N. Smith & N. Alleborough are elected presi. elders. Stationing com. met at Joshua Folks at 6:00, & we get through so as to hear Rev. C.H. Kiracofe pr. on John 3:3.

Saturday, September 26 Conference proceded. I dine at David Middaugh's. I take up subscription on legal fund. Memorial of W.R. Burnsworth. Adjourn at 5:00. I pr. at 7:30, 1 John 1.9. Stay at Folk's as usual.

Sunday, September 27 I preach at 10:30, Ps. 145.11. Enjoyed it. Dine at Mr. Greggs', "Aunt" Lydia Gables'. Address S.S. Anniversary at 3:30. Supper at Folk's. Rain in afternoon & evening. Love feast at 7:30. Congregation not so large on account of rain. Fine meeting.

Monday, September 28 Peter Folk takes me to Junction City abt 3:00. Go on 4:50 tr to Newark. Go on 9:00 train to Pittsburgh, etc.

Tuesday, September 29 Lunch at Altoona, reach Harrisburg abt 10:00. Lunch on fruit. Go on 11:30 tr. to Shippensburg. Stop at Rev. J.M. Smiley's, which is afterward determined to be our conf. home by com. on homes, which met at Smiley's that evening. Long Wingard & Smiley.

Wednesday, September 30 At Smiley's. Walk in town. Dine; & this to be our boarding place. Remain in afternoon. Several preachers came in the evening. Dr. D.K. Flickinger pr. at our Church at 7:30, Ez. 18.4, a good discourse. Stay at Smiley's.

Thursday, October 1 Conference opened at 8:30. Session thinly attended first hours. Full afterward. Rev. A.H. Shank pr. at 7:30, Matt. 5:6, an able sermon.

Friday, October 2 Conference Continued. Dr. M.F. Keiter came. Rev. D.K. Flickinger lectured on Africa at 7:30. Stationing committee met at 6:00 at Smiley's; B.G. Huber, Smiley & myself. We got to hear the lecture.

Saturday, October 3 Conference progressed well. Closed Saturday, at 4:30. Rev. J. Fahl pr. at 7:30 a good sermon, on Naaman the leper.

Sunday, October 4 I pr. at 10:30, at Orange Street U.B. Church, Ps. 103.19. Raise about $500 and dedicate the Church. Attend Y.M.C.A. at Presb. Church and speak on Prov. 11.28, after Pres. pastor, Rev. McCarroll, and sup at Wingart's. Pr. at 7:30 at Reformed Church, Genesis 49.10. Stay at Smiley's.

Monday, October 5 Start on 7:32 train home. Leave Harrisburg at 11:30 & Pittsburgh at 9:30. Revs. Hench and Pease aboard, and Hench continues 25 miles West of Harrisburg. Slept abt. 4:00.

Tuesday, October 6 Reach Dayton at 5:00. Find Orville improving nicely but not yet sitting up. All the rest well. In forenoon, put money in the bank. Slept two hours in afternoon. Slept abt 8 hours at night.

Wednesday, October 7 At home all forenoon. Nothing of especial interest to day.

Thursday, October 8 At home all day except a call in the forenoon at Keiter's office. Orville had tapioca to-day for the first time. He has lived for six weeks on milk, with a little beef broth for a couple of weeks past. He also sat up in bed for the first time in six weeks.

Friday, October 9 Katherine started for Oberlin at 10:30 forenoon.

Sunday, October 11 At home all day. W.H. Wagner called an hour in the evening.

Monday, October 12 Rev. C.H. Kiracofe called.

Wednesday, October 14 At home. Went with Lorin & Netta to Winnie (Bilheimer) Shupe's funeral in Riverdale (suburb) at 7:00.

Thursday, October 15 At home. Wrote letters. Called at Lorin's in the evening. Corbetts & Andrews there also. Mrs. Booth of Selma, O., and Mrs. Lewis, Netta's Uncle Walter Stokes' daughters.

Sunday, October 18 At home all day. Prof. Kiracofe & wife called in the afternoon. Lorin & the Children called in. [rest is blank]

Monday, October 19 At home forenoon. Went to bank at 3:00 and to Fairground. Barely saw W.J. Bryan, the Candidate for president.

Tuesday, October 20 Arranged to go on the 7:00 train to Marion and Fairmount; but concluded to wait a day. Went to town. Sent $30.32 to Iowa (J.S. Hulburt, Treas.) to pay the second installment of my Iowa tax.

Wednesday, October 21 Went on 7:00 tr to Union City & to Marion. Pay fall tax $21.17. Go with Jont. Winslow to Fairmount in buggy. At Bryan meeting at Fairground. Go to Wm. Reeder's with Hust. Dickinson. Lodge at Wm's. A man jumped onto my head off Fairground fence, but did not kill me.

Thursday, October 22 Go over to Robt's. I burn logs, brush, grass. Go in eve to Fowlerton and hear Mr. Saunders, Ed. of Marion Chronicle, speak on politics. Stay at Wm. Reeder's.

Friday, October 23 Go afternoon to Ellis Wright's. Lodge there.

Saturday, October 24 Go to Oliver A. Glass's, & dine at Robt. B. Reeder's, & stay there.

Sunday, October 25 Stay at Robert's till even'g. Go home with Oliver's & lodge there. Flora & children had been sick but were about again.

Monday, October 26 Go to Robert's & employ Wm. Fultz to build my horse-barn & double cribs for $80.00. Dine at Ellis Wright's. Go to Fairmount. Call at Atkinson's livery stable. Go on 6:20 tr. to Anderson. Hear Lafe Johnson speak. Wait at Doxie House till 2:50, & go on to Richmond.

Tuesday, October 27 Go on 5:20 train to Dayton. Found all as well as usual. Remained at home all day— made up some lost sleep. To-day hands began to dig for our natural gas pipes.

Wednesday, October 28 At home, and little out of the ordinary occurred.

Thursday, October 29 Rev. J.W. Chambers of Scioto Conference called on me & a Bro. Fox with him. Young Chambers is a minister of much promise.

Friday, October 30 At home all forenoon. Afternoon I visited Cousin Sarah Wright at the Deaconess Hospital, paid Young & Young $100.00 on U.S. Suit, and $19.00 to Misses Rhoads & Frazier, dress makers for Katherine. Wrote letters in the evening.

Saturday, October 31 Wrote letters to Wm. Reeder, Rev. E. Atkinson, etc.

Tuesday, November 3 At home. Voted about 8:30. In the evening went to Association Hall to hear the dispatches read concerning the election of president.

Wednesday, November 4 Largely engaged in reading. Lorin down with malarial fever. Democrats claimed the election of Bryan and made a rally.

Thursday, November 5 Election of McKinley reassured. Got book out of library. Lorin still sick.

Friday, November 6 Lorin is better. Sarah Worth and Miss McFadden call in the Afternoon.

Sunday, November 8 Heard Rev. Maurice Wilson pr. at 11:00, "He would fair [?] have been filled." Heard Rev. J.W. Hott at Association Hall at 3:30.

Monday, November 9 At home. Prof. Wahl called in the afternoon.

Tuesday, November 10 Went to town in afternoon to mail many letters, and to get type-writer ribbon. $1 paid. Attended a meeting of Mis. Ex. Com. at Conservator Office at 7:30.

Wednesday, November 11 At home writing letters all day. Called at Dillon's an hour in the evening.

Saturday, November 14 At home all day. Wrote letters. Lorin Called in the evening with with [repeated in text] little Ivonette, who felt strange to the house and cried.

Monday, November 16 At home in the forenoon. In the afternoon go to the Public Library, return Adam Smith's "Wealth of Nations" & take out Dr. Peter's "Gen'l History of Connecticut," and Palfrey's "Hist. of New England," and I examine Genealogical Hist of New England a little. I read till after midnight.

Tuesday, November 17 At home all day. This is my birthday anniversary, I being to-day 68 years old. Read till eleven o'clock at night. Did not notice that it was my birth-day.

Wednesday, November 18 At home all day, busy in my study. Read till 10:30.

Thursday, November 19 At home. Read till late at night.

Friday, November 20 At home in forenoon. In the afternoon, I read in Public Library reading room. Found Register of N.J. Revolutionary Soldiers— John Van Cleve included, also Ships' registers of Immigrants to America in the year, 1735. Meeting at Keiter's Office to counsel over Huntington College.

Saturday, November 21 At home most of the day. Quite busy. Kiracofe Called.

Sunday, November 22 At Main Street Lutheran Church, hear Rev. Miller, Supt. of the Deaconess Hospital, preach on the Ministrations of Christ. He has a German Accent, but is earnest and able. At home the rest of the day. Read till after 11:00 at night.

Wednesday, November 25 At home. Called again at Reading room of Books of Public Library.

Thursday, November 26 Attend Thanksgiving services at Broadway M.E. Church (Cor. Fourth and Broadway Streets) and heard Rev. Prichard of Williams St. Baptist Church pr. an excellent sermon, Neh. 8:10. Prof. Kiracofe called.

Friday, November 27 Start at 8:20 Morn. via Xenia, Washington ,Chillicothe to Vigo & thence N. to Pike Run or "Jimtown," 8 miles, with Rev. J.A. Conaway, of Christian Union Church, to Byron Conaway's, where I lodge. Went 7:00 to Pike Run Church to prayer meeting. Rev. Chas. N. Smith, P.E. there.

Saturday, November 28 Smith called and we went to Bro. J.J. Speakman's & dine & lodge. I pr at 1:30, Q. Conf. My text Ps. 16.8. Smith preach at 7:00, well, "Prepare to meet thy God."

Sunday, November 29 I preach at 11:00, Matt. 13:44, "Treasure hid in a field." Raise $70.00 and dismiss. Dine at B. Conaway's with Smith. In evening pr. at 6:30, Col. 3.4, "Appeal with him in glory." Raise $67.00 more (the rest vouched for) and dedicate Pike Run Church. Methodists counting on it, and people had no concert. Rev. Laton Ervin & others there.

Monday, November 30 Start home at 7:30; Rev. J.A. Bethel, of Bible Christian Church, takes me to Vigo; I wait 4 hours at Chillicothe & reach home at 6:30. Attend a missionary council at Dr. Kiracofe's. We resolve to begin Publication of Missionary Instructor. Slept eight hours.

Tuesday, December 1 At home. Went to town in the afternoon.

Wednesday, December 2 At home. I write an editorial "The Christmas" in the evening.

Thursday, December 3 At home, working on the ed. work of the *Conservator*. Mrs. Mary Gomer's funeral at Summit Street. Burtner, Flickinger & Mc Spoke. Flickinger dined with us to day. I called at Dillon's after the funeral. Revise copy eve.

Friday, December 4 I am busy writing for the Conservator, editorial. Called at Lorin's. H.J. Becker called in the afternoon.

Saturday, December 5 Working on the Conservator. Read proofs in the afternoon. Lorin called in the evening.

Sunday, December 6 Heard Rev. Robinson at Grace M.E. Church pr. Matt. 3.17. At 3:30 heard Rev. E.E. Baker speak at Y.M.C.A. Hall, "The new social law." Savage, Cannibal, Liquor. 2. Civilized Live & Let Live. 3. Christianized, Live & help live.

Monday, December 7 At home, editing & reading proofs. Mrs. Kiracofe called in the forenoon, to see about arrangements for the annual meeting of the Boards of Missions.

Wednesday, December 9 At home working at editing the Conservator. Lorin and family call in the evening.

Thursday, December 10 Working on the paper. Lorins called in the evening.

Saturday, December 12 Read proofs after dinner. Wrote editorial.

Sunday, December 13 Remained at home till evening. Called at Lorin's a half hour in the afternoon. Preached at Broadway M.E. Church at 7:00, Ps. 16.8. Milton was much interested to hear me preach.

Monday, December 14 At the office and read proof much of the day.

Tuesday, December 15 Went to town in the afternoon and refuted a statement that I had not returned Palfrey's History. Spent an hour in the reading room.

Thursday, December 17 Reading proofs a large part of the day.

Friday, December 18 Working on Editorial. Received a letter from Levi B. Ward of Mt. Vernon, Ohio, whose wife now 81 years of age is a daughter of Luther Freeman, a half-brother to my Grandmother Wright. Ward is aged 88. The letter gives some history of the Freeman's.

Saturday, December 19 Busy at work all day on editorial matters. Conner came to bring a dictatorial message from Keiter.

Sunday, December 20 At home except attendance at Association Hall at 3:30, where I heard Dr. John Pierson speak on concentration of one's powers.

Monday, December 21 At home editing. Prof. Kiracofe called a half hour in the morning.

Wednesday, December 23 Wednesday, Katherine came home at 7:15 eve. from Oberlin College for vacation.

Friday, December 25 Spent Christmas at home with the children, but mostly at work on the paper. I called with Katie at Lorin's an hour in the evening. Milton is having so fine a Christmas.

Saturday, December 26 At work on proof reading, etc.

Sunday, December 27 Heard Rev. Prichard preach at Williamstreet Baptist Church.

Thursday, December 31 Still on editorial duties. Worked on an editorial at night.

Memoranda

1. Judge John Cleaves Symmes first landed at the Miami [?] September 22, 1788, prospecting for settlement.
2. About the 24th of December, 1787, Colonel Robert Patterson, Major Israel Ludlow & others surveyed the town of Losantiville, now the city of Cincinnati. The proprietors were Matthias Denman, Robert Patterson, and John Filson. The last named gave it the name Losantiville: L for licking, os for mouth, anti for opposite, and ville for city. About January 2, 1790, Gov. St. Clair changed the name to Cincinnati. There was no record of the original plat of Losantiville, perhaps the plat lost by the death of John Filson, who was killed by an Indian. The first recorded plats were by Israel Ludlow and Joel Williamson, April 29, 1802, under the name of Cincinnati, one of the plats certifying that the town had formerly been called Losantiville. Judge Symmes states November 4th, 1790, that there were built, or building, forty framed or hewed-log two story houses in the town. My Grandmother— then Margaret Van Cleve— stated that at their coming January 1890, [1790] Major Ludlows hewed-log house was the best in the town. M. Wright.

1897

Friday, January 1 I am at home at work on the "Conservator" editorial, mostly to-day. Since Nov.17th, I am in my sixty-ninth year. My health is good and I can do much more mental work than I could thirty years ago. The mercy and goodness of the Lord are unspeakable.

Saturday, January 2 Left home, after some editorial work, about 9:00 Morn. Prof. J.E. Guetner on cars with me with whom I had some conversation; also a half hour's talk with Horace Stokes. Saw Rev. D.K. Flickinger, at Depot at Columbus. Reached Adelphia about 4:00, Jas. F. Martin meets me. Supper at F. Polings. Pr. Ps. 16.11. Stay at Martin's.

Sunday, January 3 Weather fair. High Ther. Martin's are two miles from Church. I pr at 10:30, Ps. 48:13,14. Raise abt $26.00 on Dry Ridge Church and dine at Beugher's, 1/2 m away with Rev. Blauser. Pr. at 6:30, Ps. 73.24, "Receive me to glory." Raise abt. $43.00 & dedicate the church. Stay at Fielding Poling's, a cousin to W.H. and E.O. Wright, Liberal preachers in Scioto.

Monday, January 4 Weather colder. I start at 5:00 for Adelphia and go via Kingston & Columbus & Xenia home arriving at 12:00. Spent the rest of the day reading, etc.

Tuesday, January 5 Weather cold. I spent most of the day writing very busily. Was at a counsel of officials & meeting of Mis. Ex. Com. Remained till almost midnight. The question mostly discussed was who should be publisher of the Mis. Magazine, Dr. Becker insisting that it should be Keiter, which was not agreed to.

Wednesday, January 6 Weather cold. At home writing most of the day. I call at C.H. Kiracofe's an hour in Aftn. & then go to town & pay Artif. Gas bill, $2.00! I read in the evening.

Thursday, January 7 Weather moderate. Engaged mostly in reading & writing. I send Application for Clergy Certificate to B.D. Caldwell, 721 Rookery Bldg., Chicago. I receive Clergy Certificate from F.C. Donald,Commissioner,Central Passenger Committee, Monadnock Building, Chicago. Go to town & buy several articles. Write letters.

Friday, January 8 Weather thawing. At home reading and writing. I call at 10:30 at Lorin's & give a china dish to Netta for a birthday present, and toys to Milton and Ivonette.

Sunday, January 10 Weather mild & bright. At home in forenoon. Preached at the Soldier's Home Church at 3:00, for Chaplain E. Light, to 300 or 350 soldiers. Text, Gen. 15.1. "Fear not Abram," etc. Lorin's called an hour in the evening.

Monday, January 11 At home writing in the forenoon. Called at the Pub. Office at 11:30 and again at 2:00 to Mis. Ex. Com.

Tuesday, January 12 Tuesday, at home forenoon, writing an article for the "Independent." Went to "town" in the afternoon, to attend errands & read a little in the City Library.

Wednesday, January 13 of them. Spent the evening in

looking up the documents relating to Oregon Mission. Called at Bp. Dillon's and Dr. Kiracofe's in the afternoon.

Thursday, January 14 Spent the forenoon in writing and afternoon & evening in writing and reading and mailing Gray's decision. Called at Lorin's a half hour in the evening.

Friday, January 15 At home reading & writing. In the afternoon Wilbur put a new radiator in my study. Getting ready to go away to-morrow. Dr. Becker called in the afternoon. Go to Lorin's in evening.

Saturday, January 16 Started at 7:05 Morn. via Union City & Gas City to Fairmount, and went thence with Wm. Corn to Ellis Wright's, and thence with Abner G. Conch to Wm. Reeder's. Pr. at Leach Sch- house, near Robert Reeder's at 7:00, Deut. 32.31. Stay at Wm. Reeder's.

Sunday, January 17 Preach at 11:00 Luke 6:23, "Reward in heaven." Dine at Oliver Glass's with Robt. Reeder and wife, and stay there till eve. I preach at 7:00, Ps. 16:8, "Set O Lord always before me." I stay at Robt. Reeder's.

Monday, January 18 I went to Wm. H.H. Reeder's and stay till after dinner. I go with Wm. Reeder and look at my farm and buildings. I then go to Ellis Wright's, supper & lodging.

Tuesday, January 19 I go to Fowlerton & call at the planing & shingle factory and at the saw mill, and at Wm. Fultz's, and go thence to the farm, and thence to Wm. Reeder's and dine there. Go to Oliver A. Glass's and lodge there.

Wednesday, January 20 Go to Wm. Reeder's & dine & lodge there. We fix up our accounts.

Thursday, January 21 I go over to Fowlerton to the mills and to Fultz. Paid Wm. Fultz ten dollars more on the buildings. I called at Ellis Wright's and got my umbrella, they being away at Fairmount. I then rode out with a Mr. Wood (Near Summitville) to Fairmount. I took tea at Burges Hollingsworth's. I lodged at Clinton Brattain's.

Friday, January 22 I staid at Brattain's till after dinner. I then go to Robert Hasting's and after an hour or two go to Jo. D. Cain's. I call at James Tuttle's and thence went to C. Brattain's & lodged.

Saturday, January 23 Dine at Wm. Heath 's. Go to Chas. Atkinson's and stay till morning. Rev. J.E. Rector stays with me.

Sunday, January 24 I preached at Fairmount U.B. Church at 11:00, Luke 6:23, "Great reward." Dine at Burges Hollingsworth's with Rev. J.E. Rector, Rev. [blank].Mr. Iliff pr. at U.B. Church at 3:00, Num. 13, 30. "Able to overcome it." I had supper at W. Heath's. I preach at the Church at 7:00, Rev. 3:20. I stay at Atkinson's.

Monday, January 25 I dine at C. Brattain's. Told her her name was marked "withdrawn" and she was much troubled at it. I go on aftn tr. to Wabash & thence to Huntington. Stay at Rev. A.G. Johnson's. Walter and Floyd much interested in the stories I told them. Jack & the Bean Stalk, etc. Pig & wagon with five wheels.

Tuesday, January 26 I go out with Bro. Johnson to look after the new College Building. It is now mostly under roof. We decide to approve the work. We agree to have the lower story in Oak finish; the second story in ash, the third, Georgian pine. I go on Aftn tr. to Wabash and Fairmount & stay at B. Hollingsworth's.

Wednesday, January 27 I wrote out terms of renting and rent my farm to Robt. Wilson White, whom Rev. J.E. Rector had brought over. We dine at C. Atkinson's. I go out to Fowlerton with Hayden, call at shingle Mill & via barn & sup & lodge at Oliver Buller's. I go to Fowlerton to meeting. Rector preached.

Thursday, January 28 Pay Rector seven dollars on quarterage. Go on to Fairmount, with M. Harrison. Dine at Hollingsworth's. Go on 12:44 tr. to Anderson & thence to Richmond & Dayton. Ar[r]iving at the last named place about 7:00.

Friday, January 29 At home in the forenoon. Go to town in the afternoon, after calling at Lorin's, and buy underwear, etc.

Saturday, January 30 Call at Keiter's office & pay him (Eva) $6.25; $5.25 for D.B. Sherk and $1.00 for Rev. Wm. Hall. Write letters.

Sunday, January 31 Spent the day at home. Lorin & Milton called in the afternoon.

Tuesday, February 2 At home. Called at Kiracofe's in the evening. Rev. Hyatt called to get me to take Oakland, Cal., Adventist paper. Talk with him on Seventh day.

Wednesday, February 3 At home in the forenoon writing letters. Went to the Public Library in the afternoon. Spent the evening reading. Got a letter from (I.F.D.), Sandwich, Mass., relating to Fred-erick Freeman's book, "Genealogy of the Freeman Family." The letter was from Isabella Freeman Dillingham, a second cousin of my Father.

Friday, February 5 Wrote in the forenoon. Went to town in afternoon and to Deaconess Hospital to see Cousin Sarah Wright. She is comfortable, content and resigned, but her eyes will not bear reading. I read for her the 4th Psalm and the 103 Psalm.

Sunday, February 7 Heard Rev. C.W. Choate pr. a good sermon, at 11:00, Matt. 20.27, at Congre. Church. I was at home the rest of the day. Lorin and Milton called in the evening a half hour. (Herbert Wright, my Grandson, born in Kansas City, Missouri, Feb. 7, 1893, in Ivanhoe Suburb.)

Monday, February 8 Received a letter from Otis Freeman, second cousin of my Father, 99 May St., Lawrence, Mass. and from him a book, the "Genealogy of the Freeman family" by his father, Rev. Frederick Freeman, published in 1876.

Tuesday, February 9 Wrote all day, nearly. Went to town before noon. Called at Young's. Geo. not in. Replied to Otis Freeman's letter & sent $2.65 to pay for book & postage.

Wednesday, February 10 At home. Called at Prof. Kiracofe's just before noon. Prof. Kiracofe called in the evening. Read late, after an hour's consultation and conversation with the boys, Wilbur and Orville.

Thursday, February 11 At home mostly. Went to town. Called at Public Library.

Friday, February 12 Wrote all forenoon. In afternoon H.J. Becker called an hour.

Saturday, February 13 Wrote all the forenoon and part of the afternoon. C.H. Kiracofe called in the afternoon a half hour. I went to Leibold's and got my mended slippers. Bought three laundered shirts. Called at Lorin's. Sat up late.

Sunday, February 14 At 11:00 heard Rev. Pritchard preach at Williams St. Baptist Church from Revelation 1.10, a good sermon on the subject of the Sabbath & Sabbath Observance. At home the rest of the day. Called at Lorin's in the evening. Harry, and Will Andrews and their wives there. Will Andrew's house burglarized while he was at Lorin's.

Monday, February 15 At home mostly. Prof. Kiracofe called in the afternoon. Rearranged shelves and wrote some letters.

Wednesday, February 17 At home. C.H. Kiracofe called. Rev. C.B. McDaniel called an hour.

Thursday, February 18 At home. H.J. Becker called. Am very busy.

Saturday, February, 20 Called at the office and gave Bro. Graybill $5.00 for the preacher and $1.00 for the presiding elder. Kiracofe came to get me to go to Germantown to supply in the P.E.'s absence. Went on traction line to Miamisburg & thence with Swartzell on to Germantown. Held Q. Conf. supper at McDaniel's. Pr. at 7:30. Stay at Shem Thomas's.

Sunday, February 21 Pr. after love-feast at 11:00, Matt. 22:36-40. Dine at Shem Thomas's. Pr. at 7:30, Rev. 3:20. Stay at Thomas's.

Monday, February 22 Had a talk with Levi Zehring. Dine and sup with him. Go on 5:51 train to Carlisle and thence at 6:35 to Dayton.

Tuesday, February 23 Wrote a dozen letters to-day and

mostly important ones. Called at Lorin's in the evening.

Wednesday, February 24 Went to the Library. Got Captain James Smith's Captivity among the Indians, a book I had read in childhood.

Thursday, February 25 Called at Kiracofe's in the forenoon. Prof. Kiracofe called in the afternoon. Meeting of the building Committee of the College of Huntington at 7:00, about Smead's not putting in the furnaces right.

Friday, February 26 The day is quite cold. Some snow flying. Write letters.

Saturday, February 27 Went to Library in afternoon. Returned Col. Jame's Smith's Captivity and took out Neander's Church History and "Miami Woods,["] Gallaher. Read till 11:00 eve.

Sunday, February 28 Awaken at about 6:00. I attend Church at West End, the last for our people at that place, as the Progressive Dunkers have rented it. Bp. Dillon, led a speaking meeting. I called at Lorin's about 5:00. (Our twin children, Otis and Ida, were born twenty-seven years ago to-day, on Second Street about 100-150 ft. east D&W R'y.)

Tuesday, March 2 Bishop H.T. Barnaby, with H.J. Becker, called in the forenoon; and the Bishop also called an hour in the afternoon. He had been to Perry County to dedicate a church. I wrote an article for the Missionary paper on the Origin of Oregon Mission.

Wednesday, March 3 Bishop William Dillon called two hours in the forenoon. He is to start to Oregon, Friday evening. I called an hour in the eve. at Lorin's.

Thursday, March 4 At home writing. Called at Bp. Dillon's in the forenoon. Lorin called in the evening.

Saturday, March 6 At home in forenoon. Go in afternoon to Grant Co., Ind., via Union City & Anderson. Stay at John Burges Hollingsworth's.

Sunday, March 7 Call five minutes at James Tuttle's. He is sick. David Glass and wife there; he Tuttle's soninlaw. Rev. N.D. Wolfard preached at 11:00. I dine with

Wolfard at Chas. Atkinson's & stay till morning. Wolfard went on to Summitville.

Mondays, March 8 Call at Brattain's & at Wm. Heath's. They to move Friday to Muncie. Go out to Fowlerton & the farm. Supper at Robert Wilson White's who moved onto my farm the 3rd inst. Meet church building committee at Henry Simond's. I lodge there.

Tuesday, March 9 Call at Ellis's. He takes me over to Oliver Glass's. I dine at Wm. Reeder's. (My son Otis died 27 years ago to-day, aged 13 days.)

Wednesday, March 10 Stay at Reeder's till after dinner. He takes me over to the place & to Fairmount. I stay at C.D. Brattain's.

Thursday, March 11 I go to Atkinson's. Call at hardware & at Bryan's to see about bill's. Go on 8:50 train to Jonesboro & Gas City & thence to Union City & home, reaching home at 4:00.

Friday, March 12 At home writing some and resting some.

Saturday, March 13 Went to town in the forenoon. Paid the natural gas bill $4.50, returned Neander's Ch. Hist. to the Library etc. Rested some in Aft'n & swept the house.

Sunday, March 14 Felt not very well to-day and did not go from home, only a short call at Lorin's in the afternoon. (Our daughter Ida, died 27 years ago to-day, aged 18 days.)

Monday, March 15 Went to town in forenoon. Saw Young five minutes. Called on Penn. tkt. Agt. Dr. H.J. Becker called an hour in the Aft'n.

Tuesday, March 16 Getting ready to start to Rohrersville, Md., to Virginia Conference. Dr. Keiter called about 5:00, afternoon. I start on 10:00 train to Pittsburgh, reach there at 6:00, morn. Take Balt. & Ohio tr. at 8:00 for Cumberland, etc.

Wednesday, March 17 Go on to Cumberland, Harpers Ferry, to Weverton. Wait there till 7:40, and then go on to Rohrersville, where Rev. G.S. Seiple meets me and takes me in a carriage to his house. I reach the Church just as meeting was dismissed. (This is anniversary of birth of Mother (1800) and Reuchlin, 1861).

Thursday, March 18 Home to Bro. Seiple's. Children, Lura and Earl Dillon, aged 5 & 3 ys. Conference opened at 9:45. In Aft'n nearly finished examination. Eve. at 7:30, J.E. Hott pr. Judg. 7.19,20, on Gideon.

Saturday, March 20 Conference Continued. Memorial Service in Aft'n, of Rev. J.K. Nelson. Closed about 4:00.

Sunday, March 21 I Pr. at 11:00, Isa. 12.2, "The Lord J. in strength." Dine at Mr. Gouff's with Rev. W.J. Funkhouser. Called at Bro. Beeler's. His son Sam sick. Pr. at 7:30, Ps. 145.15. Called before services at Mrs. McCoy's with whom I boarded at Conf. here six years ago.

Monday, March 22 Call at R.H. Clopper's awhile. Go on 11:03 tr. to Weverton, Cumberland to Pittsburgh. Go on to Orrville, Ohio; stay at Hurd House, a third class Hotel, 80 cts.

Tuesday, March 23 After Breakfast, go to Mrs. Sarah Shisler's and stay over an hour. Go on 10:00 tr. to Crestline, & thence to Dayton, arriving at 4:30. Found all well. Called at Lorin's in the eve.

Wednesday, March 24 At home in the forenoon. Slept an hour. Wrote a letter aft'n & went to town & bought various articles. Katharine came home on 6:30 train. She has suffered from boils frequently & concluded to come home earlier than vacation, wh. is a week later.

Thursday, March 25 At home. Mrs. Bessie Dillon called in the forenoon. Katie & I took supper at Lorin's.

Saturday, March 27 Katharine went to town in the After'n. to see the doctor, who prescribes richer diet and the lancing of boils.

Sunday, March 28 Slept late. Lay abed most of the day resting. Lorin and Milton called an hour in the forenoon.

Monday, March 29 Went to town in the afternoon and got double-lens glasses —$1.25, at Reeve's. Feel better than for some weeks.

Tuesday, March 30 At home except a walk to the post-office. I do not feel so well to-day. Lorin & family called in the evening a half hour or more.

Wednesday, March 31 At home forenoon, setting things to rights. Kath. went to town.

Friday, April 2 At home. Kiracofe called in the afternoon.

Saturday, April 3 At home. Katie & Mrs. Milton cleaned up the house in the afternoon.

Sunday, April 4 At home all day, not feeling very well. Read many pages in Eusebin's Church History.

Monday, April 5 This is election day. I voted about 9:00. The Phillips House had a great fire in it, this forenoon. I went to town in the after'n. Sent a draft to Katie for $20.00.

Wednesday, April 7 At home all day. Look over my accounts, and then write 8 letters & 1 card to Rock Riv. subs. to legal fund; also wrote to C.M. Cochran, at Leach, Ind.

Thursday, April 8 Went to town. Take back Eusebius's Church History which I read through the past two weeks. Its account of Cruelties inflicted on the heroic martyrs is too horrible for print. Called at Kiracofe's. (Ivonette Wright, my grand-daughter, was born, Apr. 8, 1896, 117 S. Horace St., Dayton, Ohio.)

Saturday, April 10 Go on 12:25 tr. via Union City & Anderson to Fairmount. Stay at Charles Atkinson's.

Sunday, April 11 Go to Union Church & pr. at 10:30, Rom. 1:16, taking up Paul's doctrine in the epistle. Dine at Robt. Hasting's. Pr. at 7:00, "Psalms of David and Asaph the seer." Stay at Hasting's. Bro. Alexander of Upland was with us. (Lulu (Billheimer) Wright, daughter of J.K. & A.L. Billheimer, born at Westerville, Oh, Apr. 11, 1865.)

Monday, April 12 Walked over to the farm. Dine at R.W. White's. Look at farm some. I go to Ellis Wright's. Supper there. Go to William Reeder's & lodge.

Wednesday, April 14 Paid my tax $32.71. Left Marion on 9:13 tr. via Wabash, Toledo, Detroit to St. Thomas, Ontario, arriving at 9:00 Western time—10:00 eastern time. I put up at Hotel Wilcox.

Thursday, April 15 Leave on 7:10 tr. for Galt; thence 4 miles to Blair. Dine at A.H. McNally's, a woolen mill man, & a Mennonite, they being very kind. Went on at 4:00 to Bro. John Perrin's, a half-mile east of Roseville. Hear Rev. R.A. Clark pr. at 8:00, John 3:16. Stay at Mrs. Jane Barton's with Sherk.

Friday, April 16 Good Friday. Ontario Conference at 8:00, Morn. continued. I pr. at 3:00, "It is finished & gave up the ghost." Rev. Wm. H. Nash pr. at 8:00. Board at Mrs. Jane Barton's. Sherk lodged with me. (This is the anniversary of my son Wilbur's birth-day, 1867, Henry Co., Ind.)

Saturday, April 17 Conference Continued. Rev. A.F. Stoltz pr. at 8:00. Closed a short Conf. Session after the preaching. Stay at Mrs. Barton's.

Sunday, April 18 Easter. I pr. at Roseville, at 10:00, Rom. 1:1, "Separated, etc." Dine at D.D. Snyder's, 3/4 m s.w. I spoke at 3:00 at S.S. Anniversary. Supper at D.D. Snyder's. He took me to Rev. C.W. Backus's, near New Dundee. Pr. at German Baptist Church at 7:30, 1 Cor. 15:29. Stay at Bro. Backus's.

Monday, April 19 Very cold day. Rev. A.R. Springer takes me to Henry Becker's, where we dine. We go on to Berlin and stop at Rev. J.B. Bowman's. I pr. at U.B. Hall at 8:00, Gen. 15.1. Lodge at Rev. D.B. Sherk's.

Tuesday, April 20 Dine at Rev. J.B. Bowman's. In afternoon, call two hours at Moses Eshelman's. Henry Becker takes me to his house. Supper & lodging there. I pr. at N. Mennonite Church at 8:00, 1 Pet. 2.1.

Wednesday, April 21 H. Becker takes me to J.B. Bowman's. I stay there till afternoon. Go to Freeport with Bro. Bowman. Call at Pogson's & Meriam's. Re-

turn toward Centerville and have supper at Sam'l. Deltwiler's. Mrs. Geo. Plowman lives there aged 88 years. I pr. at the Town Hall at Centerville at 8:00, Acts 26:28. Return to J.B. Bowman's, Berlin.

Thursday, April 22 Went to Robt. Bricknell's & dined. He wounded by a fodder cutter. Call at Sherman's. Supper at Geo. Latsh's. Return with Bowman to Berlin. Stay at Rev. D.B. Sherk's.

Friday, April 23 Call at Rosenberg's, Rev. A.F. Stoltz & Rev. W. Greible's. Dine at Rosenburg's. He is quite aged. Go on 3:10 tr to Sherkston, arriving there at 8:00. Go to new Church. Then to Merner Shupe's, 1/3 mile from Sherk's station. Rev. D.B. Sherk was with me.

Saturday, April 24 Bro. Sherk & I dine at Aaron Sherk's. Call at Allen Sherk's; supper at Samuel Sherk's, lodge at Isaac Sherk's. Aaron's daughters are Grace & Stella, the former attending high school at Welland.

Sunday, April 25 Conference meeting at 10:00, pr at 10:30, 1 Chr. 29:9. Raise $258.00 & dedicate Grace Church at Sherkston. Dine at Walter Sherk's with D.B. Sherk. Supper at Learn's. Rev. Learn takes me to Stevensville. I pr. at 8:00, 2 Cor. 3.8. I lodge at John Henderhott's.

Monday, April 26 Go on 10:50 train to Buffalo, and thence at 11:50 to Oberlin, arriving at 8:20. Call at my daughter's room at Mrs. Ruth A. Miller's till about 10:00, and then go to Park Hotel & lodge.

Tuesday, April 27 After breakfast, go to my daughter Katharine's room, and thence with her to Astronomy Class. (Prof. Churchill); to French Class and to Ethics Class. Dine at Munson's eating house. Spend some time in Library. Then go to Forensic Class & to Chapel service. Evening at Katherine's after supper with girls. Stay at Park H. Munson's. Reuchlin & Lulu m. by Dr. Davis, Apr. 27, 1886, on Wms. St.

Wednesday, April 28 Arise at 5:00. Breakfast at Restaurant on Main St., north side of it. Katharine and Miss Goodwin, her room mate, go with me to depot. I go via Berea, Delaware, Columbus, Springfield, home, arr. at 3:25. All well. Call at Lorin's at 7:30. Ivonette running about the room like a partridge.

Thursday, April 29 At home. Called at Keiter's & paid him $21.00 on Conservator subscriber. Called at Kiracofe's & paid $2.50 on Mis. Monthly subs. Spent the rest of the day in resting, reading, writing, etc.

Friday, April 30 Dr. H.J. Becker called in the forenoon an hour. Wrote many letters. Meeting of the Mis. Ex. Com. at 7:00, eve. (My wife, Susan Catharine, daughter of John Gotleib & Catharine Koerner, was born in Hillsboro Londoun Co., Virginia, April 30, 1831. Her Grandfather Philip Fry's house in Va, was a U.B. Preacher's place. Her grandmother Dorothy (Boher) Fry.

Sunday, May 2 At home. Supper at Lorin's.

Monday, May 3 Bishop H. Floyd called in the forenoon. At 2:00, the Publishing Board met at the Conservator Office. The Committee on Finance met at my house at 4:30, & again after Supper, Floyd and Miller. Rev. Wm. Miller lodged with me.

Tuesday, May 4 I take Miller & breakfast at Greenwood's. Board meeting continues. Keiter in answer to Miller's inquiry explains the "trust fund" which is a loan (?) [question mark appears in text] of Mrs. Bealer of Rohrersville, Md. of $1,000.00. After dinner, Rev. R.G. Montgomery and Bishop Floyd each called awhile. I sat up late.

Wednesday, May 5 At home most of the day. Dined at Lorin's.

Saturday, May 8 At home in the forenoon. In the afternoon call at Kiracofe's to leave some matter for publication. Spend an hour at Bp. Dillon's.

Sunday, May 9 Heard Rev. F.H. Colby at First Baptist Church preach a good sermon on Christ, at 11:00, but I was too far back to hear fully. In the aftn at 3:30, heard Hon. S.E. Nicholas, author of the Nicholson Temperance Bill in Indiana, lecture on Good Citizenship. It was fine in spirits and trend. He is comparatively a young man.

Monday, May 10 At home in forenoon. In afternoon, went to town, paid Natural Gas bill, mailed letter and cards, and rode home with Mr. Morehouse.

Tuesday, May 11 At home in the forenoon. Wrote letter. In afternoon with Milton, Jr., went to Huffman's Hill

Thursday, May 13 At home all day. C.H. Kiracofe called at 7:00 eve'g. I worked on my Annual report of the (Eastern) District in the afternoon and evening.

Friday, May 14 Continued to work on my Annual report till 2:00, & then took it up to the editor—Kiracofe.

Sunday, May 16 Heard Dr. Lyman S. Sperry's Address at 3:30 in Association Hall, on "Deadly Enemies." At home the rest of teh day. Sperry's lecture was good but he failed on his eagle story in the round up.

Monday, May 17 At home. Called at Lorin's at 7:00 even'g & Milton came up with me and spent the evening amusing himself with pocket compass, prism, syringe, & books.

Tuesday, May 18 Weather beautiful and mild. Bought a hat at Williams' $5.00. Met Mr. F.H. Short, and Semele Short, his wife, Mrs. Caroline Donohue, Miss Donohue, Flora Maloy, kinsfolks from Cincinnati, and after the An. railroad meeting at Third St. Depot, went with them to the Soldiers' Home & spent the day.

Wednesday, May 19 At home. Afternoon, Mr. Metz, from Paine, Ohio, formerly resident 6 ms. s.w. of Ohio City called with Prof. Kiracofe, he being on applicant for teacher of Music at our coming College at Huntington, Indiana.

Thursday, May 20 At home. Spent afternoon in looking over my book of Accounts, the evening in writing.

Saturday, May 22 At home. Call at Kiracofe's in the forenoon. His Uncle Harvey Showalter is there, from Virginia.

Monday, May 24 See Showalter & others start from Miama City Station to Messick. Busy getting ready. Start at 6:05, via Arcanum to Messick. Arrive at 9:00. Find home at A. Messick's. I had known and visited them over thirty years ago.

Tuesday, May 25 Board of Bishops meet at 8:00, in Messick's house. Have a full and close day's work. In the evening at 8:00, the Board of Missions convene. Bishop Barnaby pr. at 8:20, Acts 4:12, "Neither is there salvation in any other," etc. I lodge at Albert Messick's, by my home with Barnaby.

Wednesday, May 26 Board of Missions meet at 8:00, session two & a half hours. Board again at 2:00, recess at 4:10 half hour, finish at 5:00. Sup at Messick's. Snyder takes us to New Castle. Go on 7:30 tr. to Cambridge & by hack to Dublin. D.O. Tussinger pr. I find conference home, S. Crull's.

Thursday, May 27 Gen. Conference meets at 2:00. I preside in the first. I board at Solomon F. Crull's on Main Street pretty well east of the Church. Their children at home are George Boyd, her son 12 ys, & Elsie 5 years old. Rev. J. Kenoyer pr. at 8:00. Gal. 6:7. "Be not decieved God is not mocked." Stay at Crull's. A great sermon.

Friday, May 28 Morn. rain, rather cool. Conference at 9:00, Bishop H.T. Barnaby presiding. Adjourn at 11:00. Dine as usual. I had read the plan of Young People's Society. Floyd had read Bishop's Address. Aftern Pub. Quad. Report. Even'g Barkley at Cambridge & H.C. Foote called & I did not get to hear Rev. D.B. Shuck preach. Aftn., beautiful.

Saturday, May 29 Weather beautiful. Thermometer moderate. Conference Continued. Report of Pub. Trustee's. Treas. Report. Com. on Relocation Reported. Floyd presided. Aftern, Missionary Reports considered. I met Y.P. Society Committee at Olers at 7:00, Huber pr. very finely at 8:00, Hebr. 12:2, "Looking to Jesus." Meals & lodging at Crull's as usual.

Sunday, May 30 Bp. H.T. Barnaby pr. at 10:30 Heb. 12.2, "Who for the joy," etc. Lovefeast at 3:00. Soldiers' meeting at 3:30. Bishop Dillon pr. at 8:00, Hebr. 12:6. Gave his own Greek etymologies & expositions! Board as usual at S.F. Crull's. Bp. D. taught that Christ bore all our sins away, and that we first learn it in Conversion.

Monday, May 31 Weather fine. Thermometer mod. Conference continues. Some reports considered, espe-

cially in Aftn. I go on 6:59 tr. to Richmond, to see about a note, due, but found all fixed up. Stay at my brotherinlaw's, D.K. Zeller's, cor. Main & Fourteenth Sts. Bp. Dillon presided to-day. P.B. Williams pr. in the evening. Text: "Religion" of course I did not hear it.

Tuesday, June 1 Return on 6:25 train to Dublin. Board as usual. I presided to-day. Missionary meeting at night. Addresses by Miss Mary B. Mullen, and Dr. D.K Flickinger.

Wednesday, June 2 Conference continues. I Board as usual. A.G. Johnson of St. Joseph pr. at 8:00. Rom. 1:16. As usual, we Board at Crull's, an excellent home. Bishop H.T. Barnaby presided to-day.

Thursday, June 3 Bishop Floyd presided to-day. W.H. Clay pr. at 8:00 Rom. 12:11. Bishop Floyd presided.

Friday, June 4 Bishop Dillon presided. Election of Gen. Officers. I was elected on first ballot by 45 votes out of 52; Barnaby by 43; Floyd by 41, H.B. Barkley on 1st ballot by 33 votes, Wm. Dillon as Editor of Chris. Conservator by 50 votes out of 57. On 1st ballot, Keiter was elected as Publisher by 30 out of 57 votes, & Flickinger Mis. Sec'y by 30 out of 58. S.A. Stemem was elected Mis. Treas. on 4th ballot by 31 out of 55. Bp. Dillon lectured on Pacif. Coast & Becker, "A man's a man, at 5:00. Coll. taken to help [rest is unreadable]

Saturday, June 5 I presided. Business moved deliberately but rapidly. Evening Session after an address by L.B. Baldwin, H.J. Becker, and C.H. Kiracofe, on Education. Evening Session followed, Bp. Barnaby presiding. We had a Board of Ed. Meeting & elected on my motion president of Central College and resolved on my motion to open school in September. Gen. Conf. Adj. Sine die at 10:30.Talk with A.K. Shank.

Sunday, June 6 I pr. at U.B. Church at 10:30, Rom. 1:9, "The Gospel of His Son." Dine at S. Crull's as usual. Communion in Afternoon at 3:00. Many communicants. Call at Rev. John Cranor's. Supper at Dr. G.W. Champ's. Call at "Aunt" "Dru" (Evans) Wilson's, she being paralyzed. Bishop H.L. Barkley pr. at 8:00, John vii.46. "Never man spake like this man." Spoke an hour & 10 min. One was converted at the close.

Monday, June 7 Meeting of Printing Est. Board at Church at 6:30. A.G. Johnson, I.M. Tharp, & myself, elected as Ex. Com. Board of Education meets at Solomon F. Crull's, at 7:00, and elected T.H. Gragg, Miss Lena Barnes, & A.P. Barnaby for Central College professors, and elected an Ex. Com. etc., etc. I go on 10:10 morn tr. via Richmond home, arriving on accom. tr. about 1:50 aftn. Found all well. Called at Lorin's in evening. Ivonette romps with me.

Tuesday, June 8 At home. I call at Lorin's an hour in the evening.

Wednesday, June 9 I call at Young & Young's an hour or more.

Thursday, June 10 Exec. Mis. Committee met at my house at 10:00. Drs. Flickinger & Becker dine with me at Greenwood's and Flickinger remains till morning.

Friday, June 11 At home. Prof. Kiracofe called about 11:00, an hour. I go with Flickinger to visit Peter Louding's at 7:30. He is always interested in D.F. Wilberforce & the African Mission.

Saturday, June 12 Called at Young's 10 minutes at the utmost. After dinner (12:25) I start via Union City & Anderson to Fairmount. Go out with Perry Simons to Henry Simon's (or Oliver Buller's) and lodge there.

Sunday, June 13 Go to Ellis Wright's & remain there till about 4:00 Aftn. Ed. Frazier & family came about 10:00 to Ellis's, and I went with them at 4:00 via Wm. Reeder's to Robert's. Return to Wm. Reeder's & have supper there. Lodge at Oliver Glass's. Left a Bible at Ellis's before I went in afternoon.

Monday, June 14 Go to Leach early, and to Robt. W. White's later in the forenoon, and dine there. I stay there till evening & lodge at Levi Simon's. In the day look over the farm of which White is tenant. Went to Leach in afternoon to see about selling my corn.

Tuesday, June 15 Went to Leach again at 7:00. Sold my corn at 19 cts a bushel. Look over accounts of White's work, which amounted to just $17.00. In Afternoon, went to Fairmount with Rev. John E. Rector. Sup at

Chas. Atkinson's with Rev. E. Atkinson, of Kansas, who preached a good sermon at U.B. Church at 8:00. I lodge at Wilbur Kester's. Text Matt. 18.19.

Wednesday, June 16 I go on 8:50 train via Wabash to Andrews. Dine at Jesse Hull's, old acquaintances. He takes me across the river to see [blank] Bittinger's farm. Look at the place. Very hard rains. I go on 6:13 train to Huntington. Stay at Rev. A.G. Johnson's. Ex. Com. meeting of Board Ed. McMurray & Metz chosen as teachers.

Thursday, June 17 Ride out with Kiracofe and Johnson to look after my lot & especially to see the College Building. Return & K. & I take the 11:07 tr. to Ft. Wayne. Get home via Richmond at 6:00. Found all well. Mose Cohen's Carnival in the evening. I did not attend it, but saw a little of it.

Friday, June 18 Dr. Flickinger called in the forenoon an hour. I rested mostly to-day. Dr. [blank] Bittinger and Geo. Bittinger called about 8:00 to look at my house. I called at Lorin's a half hour at 5:00 afternoon. I was at the boy's store at 8:30; saw Lorin.

Saturday, June 19 Wrote to Reuchlin & Katherine— sent her draft for $20.00.

Sunday, June 20 Pr. at Zion Baptist Church at 11:00 2 Cor. 8.9. In afternoon at the same Church to Children's Exercises. Lorin & family called in the evening, awhile.

Monday, June 21 At home. Called at Pres. Kiracofe's and at Editor Dillon's. Rev. W.P. Tibbets of Cal. came in the afternoon to Dillon's.

Wednesday, June 23 At home all day. Knights of Pythias had a march in the evening along Third Street on West Side. (My granddaughter, Catharine Louise Wright, born Birmingham, Alabama, June 23, 1887, d. in Kansas City, Jan. 10, 1892, aged four years, seven months, and eighteen days.)

Thursday, June 24 I was home nearly all day to-day, except 15 minutes at Mr. Young's office.

Sunday, June 27 Pr. at American Wesleyan Church at

11:00, 28:34. At home the rest of the day.

Monday, June 28 Wrote letters. Revs. W.P. Tibbet, & John McBride came & also Bro. D.K. Zeller. They dine with us. Wrote letters in the evening.

Tuesday, June 29 At home. The meeting of the Mis. Executive Committee was held at my house at 8:30. Made apportionments to the conferences. D.K. Flickinger called again at 3:30, and we went to Keiter's and Dillon's to consult on editing the Discipline & Gen. Conf. Procedings.

Wednesday, June 30 At home. I spent some time looking after letters, etc.

Thursday, July 1 At home. Sarah Wright, an inmate of the Deaconess Hospital in this city, about 10:00 at night, fell from the roof of the third floor, and died a few moments afterward. It was not adjudged to be an intentional act.

Friday, July 2 At home working on the General Conference short-hand reports. Albert Shearer informed me after dinner of his Aunt Sarah's death and of the funeral to-morrow morning at 8:30. Neither Katharinenor I went to the great bicycle parade.

Saturday, July 3 Went out to Rev. [blank] Richard's and took his wife to the funeral at the hospital, and him to the cemetery & home. Called at Lorin's a few minutes.

Sunday, July 4 Went to Woodland Cemetery as usual on the Fourth. Heard M.R. Drury preach at 11:00 at the Congregational Church. At home the rest of the day. My wife, Susan Catharine (Koerner) Wright died eight years ago to-day, at 7 Hawthorne St., Dayton, Ohio, aged 58 years, 2 mo. & 5 days; was born in Hillsboro, Loudoun Co., Virginia.

Monday, July 5–Tuesday, July 13 At home.

Wednesday, July 14 At home. Went to the bank. Saw Young at the Recorder's office not over three minutes.

Thursday, July 15 Started at 7:00 morn. for Union City & Marion & Wabash & Huntington, Ind. Reach there

at 6:15 aftn. Call at Rev. A.G. Johnson's. An Executive Com. Meeting of the Board of Education at Pres. C.H. Kiracofe's. I stay there.

Friday, July 16 I go with Flickinger and Steman to look at Johnson's building on Jefferson Street, talked of for a publishing house. I dine & sup at Johnson's. Ex. Com. meets again at Kiracofe's with Messrs. Kintz and Cobb. I stay with Flickinger at Kiracofe's. We held an Ex. Com. of Board of Education at A.G. Johnson's. I.M. Tharp there.

Saturday, July 17 I go on wagon with Fli. & Steman to Johnson building & thence to Johnson's and Prof. A.P. Barnaby's. Start at 8:40 train to Fairmount. Reach there at 12:43. Go out to Hopewell with Ol. A. Glass. Supper at White's. Pr. at Hopewell 8:00, Matt. 5:12. "Your reward in heaven." Stay at O.A. Glass's.

Sunday, July 18 I preach at 11:00, Ps. 93.5. Raise $209.50 & dedicate Hopewell Church. Dine in the grove with the Reeder's and Broyle's & Glass's. I pr. at 4:00 Gal. 4:4, and a sacramental service followed. I stay at Oliver Buller's. (My oldest brother, Samuel Smith Wr. died fifty-five years ago to-day.)

Monday, July 19 Weather temperate. Call at R.W. White's and go with Ol. Buller to Fairmount. Go on 8:00 tr. via Gas City, Union City home, arri. at 4:10.

Tuesday, July 20–Monday, July 26 At home . . . and spent the day mainly in reading.

Tuesday, July 27 At home and spent the day in reading and writing. Lorin's called an hour in the evening.

Wednesday, July 28 At home and spent the day in writing. Called at W. Dillon's after supper.

Thursday, July 29 The eclipse of Sun 9:54 morn. we saw. I wrote many letters. In Afternoon, I worked on editing the Discipline a little perhaps.

Friday, July 30 At home. Worked at the editing of the Disciple in the afternoon. Called at Albert Shearer's an hour in the evening.

Saturday, July 31 Worked on editing the Discipline. Went to town afternoon. [Note: Bishop Wright uses the word "Discipline" on July 29 and 31, and the word "Disciple" on July 30]

Sunday, August 1 Attended the African Methodist Church on Hawthorne St. & heard Rev. Turner, the pastor, preach quite a good sermon from Acts 18:9,10. At home rest of the day.

Monday, August 2 At home. Keiter called to see about Genl. Conf. Proceedings. Busy writing letters.

Tuesday, August 3 Too warm to do much but read; and I read much and till a very late hour. But I spent part of the afternoon in the City library. Paid my Dayton tax.

Wednesday, August 4 Very warm. Worked on editing the Discipline in the afternoon. Read all the evening and till 11:30. It turned a little cooler in the evening and night.

Friday, August 6 At home working on editing the Discipline. Took the revision up to Dillon in the afternoon, having finished it.

Saturday, August 7 At home. Saw Rev. M.F. Keiter in the evening, and we arranged to have Bp. Barnaby call the Publ. Board together August 17th.

Sunday, August 8 At home. Lorin & the children came & staid an hour in the forenoon.

Tuesday, August 10 At home in the forenoon, reading & writing. Dr. Flickinger called just after dinner. I went to the bank & the library in the afternoon. Came by Lorin's & brought Ivonette home with me. Wrote in the evening.

Wednesday, August 11 At home. Had a counsel of Com. to edit Proceedings of Gen'l. Conference, and it advise against its publication.

Thursday, August 12 At home. Read proof all forenoon on the Discipline of 1897. Read some, & sent out bills to collect over $200.00 on Legal Fund. Sat up late.

Saturday, August 14 I went on 11:00 tr. to Columbus &

thence to Logan. Rev. D. Folk met me & took me to Geo. Helber's 4 miles N.W. I pr. at 7:30, at Pleasant Valley Church. I supped & lodged at Helbers.

Sunday, August 15 I pr. at 10:30, Ps. 93.6 & dedicate the church. I dine at Squire Frasure's. I pr. at 7:00 on ["]Love of God," 1 John 4.8. I stay at Father Gotleib Helber's.

Monday, August 16 D. Folk takes me to Enterprise. Go on via Marion to Huntington. I stay at Pres. C.H. Kiracofe's.

Tuesday, August 17 The Printing Estab. Board of Trustees met at the Johnson Building at 8:30 & 2:00. I dine at Johnson's. The Board contracted with A.G. Johnson for his brick business house at $10,000, $2,000 payable in two years, he donating $2,000 of it; interest six per cent. I stay at A.J. Steman's.

Wednesday, August 18 Go on 11:00 tr. to Toledo & thence to Lindsey, Ohio. I find my Conf. home at Jacob Overmeyer's. Rev. G.W. Coss pr. at $ [this is in text] 8:00, on holiness.

Thursday, August 19 Conference opened at $ [this is in text] 8:30. Business proce[e]ded well. W. Dillon comes at 5:00 & Mrs. A.R. Kiracofe. (This is the anniversary of the birth of my son Orville, in 1871, and of my daughter Catharine, in 1874 —both born at our home, 7 Hawthorn St., Dayton, Ohio.)

Friday, August 20 Conference continues. Missionary meeting at 8:00. Mrs. Kiracofe, Miss Mary B. Mullen, and Rev. W. Dillon spoke. Stationing Committee met after supper.

Saturday, August 21 Conference continued. We adjourn at 4:00. W. Dillon pr. at 8:00.

Sunday, August 22 I pr. at 10:30, Rom. 2:16, on the "Gospel." S.S. Anniversary at 3:00. W. Dillon pr. at 7:30.

Monday, August 23 I go to Limestone & thence direct to Orrville, Ohio. Call at Mrs. Shisler's. Stay at John Lefever's, where I boarded till I left town.

Tuesday, August 24 A am still at Lefever's. Call awhile in eve. at Mrs. Shisler's. I did not get to see David Walmer, one of our brethren in Orrville, as he was from home.

Wednesday, August 25 I go on 11:00 train to Dalton, and Frank Swisher takes me to his Father's. Rev. J.N. Lemasters pr. at 7:30, a good sermon.

Thursday, August 26 Conference opened at 8:30 & progressed well. Mrs. E.O. Olmsted pr. at 7:30, on holiness. W. Dillon came. My home at Swisher's.

Friday, August 27 Conference continued. I dine at Keiter's. Missionary meeting at 7:30. Miss Mullen & Dr. Dillon spoke. I raise about $82.00 in Missionary subscription, & $6.00 cash. Stationing Com. met at Swisher's, at 6:00.

Saturday, August 28 Conference continued as usual. Dillon pr. at 7:30 on immortality. The sermon was admired.

Sunday, August 29 I pr at 10:30, Gal 1:8 on gospel. Sab. Sch. Anniversary at 3:00. Dr. Dillon pr. at 7:30. Dillon did well on the collection in the forenoon.

Monday, August 30 Frank Swisher took us to Massilon, and I go thence to Cleveland, Erie, & Union City & stay at N.R. Luce's. He is full of chores. He has enough chores outside of school or church to load a man down.

Tuesday, August 31 Go on to Corry at 3:00. Sup at J.S. Amidon's. I lodge at Rev. S. Evans' with Father T.S. Bennett. He talks well but is helpless. How well he thinks, and quotes scripture.

Wednesday, September 1 Dine at J.S. Amidon's. He is paralyzed, but very pious. Go after dinner to Glynden, with Bennett & Evans. Walk out to Pickard's. Sup there. Rev. S. Evans pr. at 8:00. We stay at M.E. Pickard's, where was our conference home.

Thursday, September 2 Erie conference opens at 8:30. Rev. S.J. Cummins pr. at 8:00, eve. Supper at Mrs. [blank] Fralick's. Lodge at Pickard's. He is an Oddfellow & drinks some. She is a member of our church.

Friday, September 3 Conference continued. I dine at Platt's. Conference somewhat excited over election of presiding elder. Stationing com. at 6:00 at Pickard's. (Anniversary of my Father's birth in 1790—Dan Wright, b. Thetford To., Orange County, Vermont; son of Dan and Sarah Wright.)

Saturday, September 4 I dine & sup at Platt's. They are M.E. people. Conf. closes in Afternoon. Stay at M.E. Pickard's, pr at 8:00.

Sunday, September 5 I pr. at 11:00, 2 Cor. 3:[blank]. Dine at Platt's. Funeral of a child of McRay's at 3:00, by *Higley. I pr. at 8:00. Pickard much affected, but really groggy. *He proved to be a worthless fellow.

Monday, September 6 Melvin E. Pickard takes Rev. S. Evans & myself to Spartansburg. Saw Wallings & Wright, editors, and others. Go on to Corry, U. City, Eric, Toledo & Delphos, Ohio. Stay at Wilson McKenzie's.

Tuesday, September 7 Go on 9:00 tr. to Wilshire. O. Sheets meets us & takes us out to Sarah Sheets, at Wren, where I have our Conf. home. Rev. W.E. Strete pr. at 8:00, a good sermon.

Wednesday, September 8 Auglaize Conference opened at 8:30. Business moves well. D.K. Flickinger pr. at 8:00 on Missions.

Thursday, September 9 Conference continued. I held a missionary meeting at 8:00. Raised a subscription of $163.00. Dr. Dillon, Mrs. T.M. Harvey & Dr. Kiracofe spoke. (My brother Harvey Wright, born in Centreville, Ohio, Sept. 9, 1820.)

Friday, September 10 Conference continues. Stationing Com. met at 6:30 at Mrs. Sheet's. Dr. C.H. Kiracofe pr. at 8:00, John 3:16, for 35 min.

Saturday, September 11 Conference closed at 4:30; communion at 10:30. Rev. P.B. Williams pr. at 8:00, in a tent in 0. Sheets' grove. Receive W.H. Kindel into the conference at a called session. I boarded at the session at Mrs. S. Sheets'.

Sunday, September 12 I pr. in O. tent at 10:30. Rom. 6:17. Pub. Coll. $49.00. I spoke in S.S. Anniversary at 2:30. I then went with J.W. Harris in Mr. Matthew's conveyance to Convoy. Stay at Mullen's Hotel, they being Harris' relatives. I pr. at M.E. Church for Rev. Martin at 8:00, Rom. 4:1-8.

Monday, September 13 Go on 6:31 tr. to Lima. See Rev. C. Whitney, Liberal on the train. See Rev. P.B. Williams, Lay & Mullen hour at C.H. & D. Depot. Go on home arriving at Dayton about 12:00 noon. Found all well. Went to Winter's Bank.

Tuesday, September 14 At home. Called at Conservator Office. Rev. W. Dillon called aftn. Busy writing etc. Weather very hot. (Helen Margaret Wright, my granddaughter, was born in Kansas City, Missouri, Sept. 14, 1889.)

Wednesday, September 15 At home. Read & write. Weather still very hot.

Thursday, September 16 At home. evening. Called at Lorin's a half hour in the evening. It rained some in the night & turned cooler.

Friday, September 17 Milton came home with me and staid till after dinner. It grows cooler all day.

Saturday, September 18 At home. Was measured for a suit at Perry Meredith's. Called at Rev. W.H. Klinefelter's a half hour in the evening.

Sunday, September 19 At home. Called at Lorin's in afternoon & Lorin, Netta, and the children called later on.

Monday, September 20 Left home at 6:50 Morn., via Lima and Ft. Wayne to Huntington, Ind., and arrive at 1:13 aftn. Go to Central College Building. Attend the Ed. Board meeting at 3:00 in College Auditorium. Stay at Rev. A.G. Johnson's.

Tuesday, September 21 The Ed. Board meets at 8:00, in our new Publishing House on Jefferson Street. I dine at Pres. C.H. Kiracofe's. Rev. P.S. Henson preaches at 2:00, the dedication sermon from 2 Tim. 2:16. "All scripture," etc. Pres. Kiracofe raises $1,000—afterward increased

to $1,400. I go on 6:25 tr. to Bucyrus, Ohio. Stay at hotel.

Wednesday, September 22 Go on 5:15 tr. to Centersburg and thence to Mt. Vernon. Call on Levi B. Ward & Mary Spencer Ward, & dine there. She is a half-cousin of my Father. Go on 1:00 train to Centerburg, & thence on 4:30 to Bremen. Bro. D.F. Housholder takes me out to the Church and thence to Adam B. Lecrone's. Children: Anna, Emma, Verne, Gurley; & Ida Red is there.

Thursday, September 23 Conference opened at 8:30. Wm. Dillon dined with us. He preached at 7:30, Matt. 19:25. "Who then can be saved?"

Friday, September 24 Conference continued. I dine at J.A. Lecrone's, he having been quite sick. J.A. Hoffhines and N. Allebaugh were elected pres. elders. Stationing committee met at 6:30. D.K. Flickinger pr. at 7:30. I raise a Mis. Subs. of $133.00 afterward. Mrs. Josh. Folk spoke & so did I. (My mother, Catharine Wright, died 31 years ago, at her home in Fayette Co., Indiana.)

Saturday, September 25 Conference continued and closed at 4:00. I pr. at 7:30, Rom. 3:19.

Sunday, September 26 I pr. at 10:30, 2 Cor. 3:6. S.S. Anniversary at 2:30, consisting of children's singing & recitations. I pr. at 7:30, Titus, 2:14, & sacramental service followed.

Monday, September 27 Bro. A.B. Lecrone takes us to Logan. Go on to Athens. Get drafts. Send one to pay Iowa tax. Write letters. Go on 3:10 train to Parkersburg, and on 6:40 train to Martinsburg, W. Va., arriving at 4:35 morn. A man & his wife going to Winchester, Va., to see a cancer doctor.

Tuesday, September 28 Go on 8:20 train to Greencastle, Pa. Write a few letters. Stop at F.W. Barnhart's east side of town. Renovate myself thoroughly! I sleep well this night.

Wednesday, September 29 Go on 9:35 train to Chambersburg. I dine at Rev. John Fohl's. I call at Rev. B.G. Huber's, 644 Phil. Ave., at Nicklas' carpet store, and at Rev. A.H. Shank's, 333 Catherine Street. Return on 5:39 train to Greencastle. I attend prayer-meeting at 7:30, and at the church. I sup & lodge at Barnhart's.

Thursday, September 30 Few Came on the early train; so conference opened about 10:00. Business progressed well. Rev. J.A. Burkholder preached well at 7:30, Rom. 8:23. I board at F.W. Barnhart's. Also A.H. Shank, D.K. Flickinger, J.M. Smiley, G.S. Seiple, etc.

Friday, October 1 Conference continued. In the afternoon, B.G. Huber was elected on 1st ballot by a small majority. The stationing committee met at 6:30, at Barnhart's. Rev. G.S. Seiple preached at 7:30, a fine sermon, on [blank] and went to Middleburg after meeting.

Saturday, October 2 Conference continued. Memorial services on I.C. Weidler, Paper by S. Diller, and remarks by LA. Wickey, J.S. Wentz and B.G. Huber, all unusually good. We raise 29 subs. for the Conservator. Adjourn at 4:30. Dr. Flickinger pr. at 7:30, Eph. 3:8, and I raise $240.00 Missionary subscription.

Sunday, October 3 I preached at 10:30, 2 Cor. 8:9, and raised $800.00 on the debt of the Church. Before preaching, we ordain W.O. Weidler and Dyson M. Hench. Dine and sup at [blank] Staley's. I pr. at 7:30, Rom. 4:8, and raise $77.00 more on the Church debt; and the brethren take a cash coll. of $27.82 for me. A well begged people! I stay at Barnhart's as usual.

Monday, October 4 After settlement with D.K. Flinkinger on Cons. Subs. I go on 9:35 train to Harrisburg, Pittsburgh train 50 min. late. Start at 12:15 for Pittsburgh. Write letters at Pittsburgh & mail them in train box. Start at 8:20 (Western time) for Dayton on a through car. The trip home cost me $12.33. I slept four or five hours.

Tuesday, October 5 Arrive at home at 5:00 morn. Breakfast at Mrs. Greenwood's. Dine and sup at home. I am busy fixing up things. Make settlement with M.T. Keiter on subs. to Cons. & saw Becker. Slept two hours. Called at Lorin's a half hour in the evening, Corbetts & Mrs. ————————there. [Line appears in text]

Wednesday, October 6 Went to town and deposited a draft for $150.00 in Winter's Nat. Bank. Called at Dr.

Tizzard's office, and arranged for a new Upper teeth plate. Lorin's called an hour in the evening. (My father, Dan (not Daniel) died 36 years ago, to-day, at his home abt 1 1/2 m. from the West line & 2 m. from the s. line of Fayette Co., Indiana.)

Thursday, October 7 Took supper at Lorin's. Went to Music Hall after supper and heard Hon. Joseph B. Foraker, Gov. Asa Bushnell and Hon. Mark Hanna speak. The speeches all good, but Hanna excelled.

Friday, October 8 Called at Lorin's in the morning & at home the rest of the day.

Saturday, October 9 Went to town and got a draft of $100.00 and sent it to Kiracofe to pay $75 on Mrs. Hisler's [?]sub. to Central College and $25 on Mine, making payment full in both cases. I market some. Go at 4:00 aftn & get my new teeth plate. Call a half hour at the public Library.

Sunday, October 10 Slept surprisingly late for me. Hear at W. Baptist, Rev. Prichard preach on Ex. 14:15, "Speak—go forward." After dinner call at Lorin's and give the children cups. Go to Samuel Spidel's and stay two hours. It rained in the night.

Monday, October 11 Rains early, and then a nice shower later in the day.

Tuesday, October 12 Go on 8:10 train via Lebanon Junction to Centerville. Call at Joseph Nutt's & dine. See the places where my Grandfather Reeder and Grandfather Wright lived abt. 1814-1822, also where Aaron Nutt, Robins, and Archer's lived adjoining town (& Nutt in town) and where the old Potter Shop of Grandfather's was.

Wednesday, October 13 Went to town and bought typewriter ribbon etc. Was rather dull in the afternoon.

Thursday, October 14 Went to town in the forenoon & had a tooth fixed. Was dull & inactive in the afternoon. Milton came home with me and he had a good time with Wilbur at the office. I lay down most of the afternoon being inane.

Friday, October 15 About as usual. I lie down much of the day, the nervous force seeming dormant or deficient.

Saturday, October 16 At home mostly. I feel very trifling, though I am not sick. Went to Dr. Tizzard's in the afternoon, who kept me waiting about an hour to renew the cotton in my tooth! Read considerably. Began taking quinine in the evening.

Sunday, October 17 Kept my bed most of the day, not sick but having little appetite or energy. Restrict myself mostly to a milk diet.

Tuesday, October 19 Worked on accounts. Called at the dentists and at the bank.

Wednesday, October 20 Fail to get onto the 8:15 train. After an early dinner, I take the C.H. & D. train for Indianapolis and two miles below Dayton, our locomotive collides with a freight train, demolishing each and destroying six or eight cars. Several were bruised, and the engineer was thrown under the locomotive & died some days later. Mrs. Betty Frederick of Kingston, Ross Co., Ohio was badly hurt.

Thursday, October 21 I reached Chicago early via Hamilton & Indianapolis. Staid there till 10:10 at night & took R.Is. & Pac. tr. to Casey, Iowa. In the afternoon, I visited Dr. Dowey's Healing establishment and his tabernacle, & attended a children's service at 2:30 or 3:00. Saw and heard Dowey's father and Dowey's wife. Am impressed that he is a humbug.

Friday, October 22 Reached Casey abt. 10:30, but fell asleep & got off at Adair & hired a livery ($1.50) & go to Lee Hoisington's. Take a ride with D.R. Fagan over the place. Settle with Fagan as to terms of pasture, etc. and stay at Hoisington's.

Saturday, October 23 Fagan takes me to town after I had rented the farm to Thos. Lovell. I go on to Des Moines, but miss the 1:00 train to Kansas City and wait till 8:15 tr. at night. Slept about five hours. I misunderstood the agent, who, I suppose, said train went in five minutes. I understood to say 25 minutes; so went to lunch.

Sunday, October 24 Reach Kansas City at 7:00 & go out to Reuchlin's, where I breakfast and spend the day. We took a walk over east in the afternoon—all the family.

Monday, October 25 Still at Reuchlin's.

Tuesday, October 26 In the afternoon, I go down town & get some presents for the children.

Wednesday, October 27 I start home at 9:00 even'g on Wabash train.

Thursday, October 28 We reach St. Louis at 7:00. I go on Vandalia Lines to Indianapolis, arriving about 2:30. I stop with Geo. W. Snyder whose business is 125 S. Meridian, and his residence on N. Penn. Street. Their son's name is Albert.

Friday, October 29 I go on 9:30 tr. via Union City home, arriving at abt. 4:00. Found all well.

Saturday, October 30 Went to town before noon. Go on 2:05 tr. via Springfield to Columbus. Go on 5:00 tr. to Baltimore, O. and go out with John Reef to Maple Grove Church. I pr. at 7:30, John 14:3. I stay at John Eversole's, 2 m. east. Dr. Flickinger stays with me.

Sunday, October 31 Meet the trustees of the Church at 10:00 & name the Church & arrange for their subscriptions. I pr. at 10:30 (11:00) Ps. 122:9, "Because of the house," etc. Raise $420.00 subs. & dedicate. I dine at Jas. Huston's near Eversole's. D.K. Flickinger pr at 7:00, 2 Chr. 15:2, a fine sermon. We stay at John Eversole's. It rains at night & next day.

Monday, November 1 J. Eversole takes us to Thurston. We go on C.S. H. R'y to Columbus. I dine at Rev. D.K. Flickinger's, 201 Front St. On 3:15 tr., I go via Xenia home. The boys had resumed self-boarding, and henceforth I board with them.

Tuesday, November 2 At home. It is election day. I voted mostly for the Republicans.

Wednesday, November 3 Election news: Ohio Republican; they defeated in Cin.; Tammany triumphs in Greater

New York; Md. repub.; also N.J.; Ky. dem. S. Dak. repub.; also Kans. Sat up very late.

Thursday, November 4 Called at Lorin's. Milton called to get his little wagon.

Friday, November 5 At home. Went to Library & took out Tudor's Life of James Otis, and read much of it.

Saturday, November 6 At home. Went to town in the evening to the dentists and to the library. Took out Croly's Life & Times of George IV, which I had read over fifty years ago.

Monday, November 8 Wrote letters. I went to see Graybill's, whom I found at Jacob Swank's. They expect to ship their goods to-morrow to Harvey, Ill., & go to-morrow eve. to New Rumley to visit Graybill's father. (Milton Wright, my grandson, was born Nov. 8, 1892, at 117 S. Horace St., Dayton, Ohio.)

Wednesday, November 10 Wrote letters. J.K. Graybill called and borrowed $25.00 (which he paid some months later.)

Saturday, November 13 At home. Wrote letters. Went to the dentists, & called at the Library afterward.

Sunday, November 14 At home. Read much. Afternoon, called at John Weidner's on Kilmer St., & "First" St.

Monday, November 15 At home. Wrote letters. Read in the evening with much pleasure, 1 Cor. Chaps. 13, 14, 15, in the interlinear New Testament, published by Arthur Hinds, N.Y.

Tuesday, November 16 Went to dentists in the afternoon.

Wednesday, November 17 At home. This is the anniversary of my birth, Nov. 17, 1828 in John Quincy Adams' administration—six presidents before my birth; nineteen since. I was born in Rush County (3/4 m. north of the south line and 1 1/2 m. from the east line), Ind; Samuel Smith, Harvey, and Sarah being older, & William younger than I; & George older than Sarah; & Kate,

younger than William d. young.) George died at 6 mo, & Kate at birth.

Thursday, November 18 At home. Spent some time in letter writing. (This is the anniversary of the birth of my son Lorin, at my father's house in Fayette County, Ind., Nov. 18, 1862.)

Friday, November 19 Went to Tizzard's at 9:00, had a gold crown put on a tooth, & paid him $10.00 for that and some other dentistry. Wrote letters.

Sunday, November 21 Attended Park Presbyterian Church at 10:30 & heard Rev. W.P. Miller, the new pastor, John 4:35, who seemed to be evangelical, and preached a good sermon. Heard in afternoon part of an address by Mr. Wilder of India. Wrote an article on Self Denial Week (Anniversary of birth of Samuel Smith Wright, 1818, Sarah Wright, 1894.)

Monday, November 22 Went on 9:25 train via Richmond & Anderson to Huntington, Ind. Supper with Flickinger at restaurant. Was at meeting at U.B. Church; R.S. Bowman conducted the meeting. I stay at A.G. Johnson's.

Tuesday, November 23 Missionary Ex. Com. meeting at 7:30 & at 1:30. Go to Kiracofe's in afternoon. Supper at W. Dillon's with R.S. Bowman. I pr. at 7:30, Rev. 3:20. Stay at A.G. Johnson's.

Wednesday, November 24 Saw Judge Sayler & his son Samuel. Learn how we are to incorporate. Dine, sup & lodge at Johnson 's. We spent the Afternoon in making out a form incorporation—a busy half-day's work. (I married Susan C. Koerner, Nov. 24, 1859 at her home in Union Co., Ind., about six miles from East line and two from S. line.)

Thursday, November 25 Wrote out a clean draft of incorporation and with Johnson sign & acknowledge it, and go on the forenoon train to Wabash & Fairmount. Call at Chas. Atkinson, and then go in the mail-carriage to Leach, and to White's on our farm. Preach at Leach (Hopewell) U.B. Church. Stay at Oliver A. Glass's.

Friday, November 26 Oliver takes me to Ellis Wright's.

They have a son about five weeks old. O. takes me to R.W. White's. They have a little son. I fix up accounts with him & pay him $8.00. We look over the place and go to Chas. Leach's elevator. Collect $21.49 on last spring's corn. Called in to talk & pray with Mr. Culbert who is very sick. Stay at Henry Simons.

Saturday, November 27 Weather cool. His hand takes me to Fairmount, & I go on 8:50 tr. to Wabash, Toledo, and Wallbridge. Pr at U.B. Church at 7:30, Rev. 3:20. Supper and Lodging with Adam Kusian's, with Rev. H.D. Yant, the pastor.

Sunday, November 28 Weather cold. Pr. at 12:00, Ps. 48:11,12. Dine at Wicks 1 1/2 m. north. I pr. at 7:30, *1 Pet. 4:18. One arose for prayers. We stay again at A. Kusian's. They had been up to a Presbyterian dedication in the forenoon. *"If the righteous scarcely be saved, where" etc.

Monday, November 29 Weather cold. Go on 8:50 tr to Union Depot, Toledo, & on 10:10 (late) train to Dayton, arriving at 3:20—behind time some. Found all well at home.

Tuesday, November 30 Weather moderate. Spent the time at home. Rev. D.K. Flickinger came, dined with us, & stayed till about 3:30. Read much & till 11:00 at night.

Wednesday, December 1 At home. Called at Young's in the afternoon to see about appealing the U.S. case to U.S. Court of Appeals.

Thursday, December 2 Called at Young & Youngs & at Library. Went over at 4:00 to learn what Doyle & Lewis had to say about appealing our case. Also went over to Young's at 9:00 to see about appeal matters.

Friday, December 3 Went to Cin. with Will H. Young & had our Appeal allowed by Judge Taft in U.S. case. Called at F.H. Short's car. Mound & Kenyan Streets— 609 Mound St. Dined with Young at Gibson House.

Saturday, December 4 At home all day. Read much; wrote some. Called at Lorin's an hour in the evening. He put up his second gas radiator. Ivonette wanted to go with me.

Sunday, December 5 At home all day. Read in the forenoon. An unusual thing in my life, I wrote to-day an article for publication, "A Secular Miracle." Myself & the boys spent an hour in the evening at Lorin's.

Monday, December 6 Went to town , engaged a Publishing Establishment seal, called at Young's.

Tuesday, December 7 Went to post-office, Stencil Shop & Library. Read nearly all day & evening.

Wednesday, December 8 Wrote letters to Floyd, & R.G. Montgomery. Called at Lorin's.

Thursday, December 9 Called at Lorin's. Wrote and read all day.

Friday, December 10 Busily employed in reading and taking notes.

Saturday, December 11 At home reading. Went to the Library in afternoon.

Sunday, December 12 Heard Rev. Chas. W. Kurtz talk at Summit St. Church on Communion, at 11:00. Wrote an Article on "Pulpit Mistakes." Present, at 3:30, at Steroptican Views of Joseph's life—Y.M.C.A. Hall. Called a few minutes at Lorin's.

Monday, December 13–Saturday, December 18 At home. Reading and writing. Sent an article for the *Conservator* on Miraculous Illusions. Wrote an other article.

Sunday, December 19 At home in the forenoon. In the Afternoon, Samuel Spidel sent for me to come to his house on King St., his wife having took sick Fri. night, and being now unconscious. At 3:30, heard Maj. D.W. Whittle the evangelist a few minutes at Y.M.C.A. Hall, who stated that 400,000 are in state prisons, and 750,000 altogether in prisons in this Country. Went to Spidel's. She is very sick.

Monday, December 20 At home till in the Afternoon. Went to Spidel's, she being deceased, & made some notes for a Memorial notice. I wrote an obituary for publication also that evening.

Tuesday, December 21 At home all day, except that I went to Spidel's an hour that evening or Afternoon rather.

Wednesday, December 22 Went to Spidel's at 9:20 & to Home Ave. (Liberal) church at 10:00 and preached Mrs. Mary Ann Spidel's funeral, Acts. 24:14, "Hope toward God." Dr. H.J. Becker & F.G. Grigsby assisted. Burial at Mem. Chapel Cemetery. I dine at Spidel's & stay till about 3:00. Katharineand her room mate, Margaret Goodwin came from Oberlin at 8:30.

Friday, December 24 At home most of the day. Went afternoon to Library, and bought some Christmas presents at Pruden's.

Saturday, December 25 This is the birthday anniversary of my niece, Flora (Wright) Stevens, (1858), and of my grand-daughter, Bertha E. Wright (1896). To-day I went down to Lorin's & took presents to the children. At home the rest of the day till I called at Lorin's in the eve. Wm. Andrews & Lottie there.

Sunday, December 26 Gas was turned off in the night by the bursting of a pipe in the gas main, leaving Dayton in darkness and cold, as to natural gas. (It was off about 24 hours.)

Monday, December 27 Go on 9:25 tr. via Richmond and Anderson to Huntington, Ind. Arrive at H. at 5:40 and go to Rev. Wm. Dillon's and thence via Rev. A.G. Johnson's to church. Dr. Dillon pr. at 7:30, on Christian perfection, Matt. 7:48. I lodge at A.G. Johnson's.

Tuesday, December 28 The Publishing Establishment Board met at Publishing Establishment at 10:00. We all dine at Keiter's Restaurant. Session afternoon. Dine at same Restaurant with Flickinger. Confer with Flickinger at Publ. Building. Rev. W.H. Clay pr. at 7:30, John 3:7,8, on new birth, a good sermon. I lodge at Johnson's.

Wednesday, December 29 I go out with Bp. Barnaby to Kiracofe's in College addition. Return & take 11:07 tr. via Ft. Wayne to Richmond and Dayton, reaching home about 6:00 eve. Found all well. Talk with a monarchist on the train from Richmond.

Thursday, December 30 At home. Reading and taking notes thereon. Milton comes to go to the boy's shop to see about things to be made for his Magic Lantern show. Eats supper with us. Has a private show, with me as sole spectator by his invitation!

Friday, December 31 At home, reading and writing. Milton Has a show with the girls (Katie & Miss M. Goodwin) and Mrs. Wagner and her girls for auditors, and Lorin & family.

Marriage Formula

Do each and both of you mutually and solemnly promise and covenant that you will live together in the relation of husband and wife, and that you will be faithful to each other in all the obligations of the marriage covenant as long as you both shall live? Do you? Do you? Having witnessed your plighted faith and solem[n] vows, I pronounce you husband and wife according to the ordinance of God and the laws of our country. Let us pray.

A Few of Many Namesakes

James Milton Cook, Rev. J.M. Cook, John Milton Bell, Rev. James Bell, Milton Morton Tharp, Rev. A. Tharp, Milton Wright Tharp, I.M. Tharp, Wright Barnaby Becker Small, C.B. Small, Samuel Wright Purtee, S. Purtee, Milton Gronendyke, Monro Gronendyke, Milton Wright Reed, [blank] Reed, Milton Wright Barnaby, Bp. Barnaby, Milton ——Lake, G.S. Lake, Karl Wright Harritt, B.W. Harritt, Leo Wright McBride, J. McBride, Milton W. Lloyd, S.E. Lloyd, Milton W. Kelly, Wm. Kelley, Wade Wright Tuttle, W.S. Tuttle, Milton F. Cole, L.E. Cole, Melanchthon Wright Hunt, G.W. Hunt.

1898

Saturday, January 1 Spent the day at home, reading & writing.

Sunday, January 2 Went to the Episcopal Church, for once in a long time and heard Rev. E. Peyton Morgan pr. Luke 2:21, "His name was called Jesus," and he talked about the naming of babies, and about the advantages of baptizing them. His profanity. At home the rest of the day, reading and writing.

Monday, January 3 At home. Took notes on reading. Writing an article for the paper. Wrote in the morning and sent to the Conservator an Article on New Testament Miracles.

Tuesday, January 4 Tuesday—Katharine & Miss Margaret Goodwin start at 7:20 for Oberlin, having been here about two weeks.

Wednesday, January 5 At home. A letter from K. this afternoon says they arrived at Oberlin, safe, but tired.

Thursday, January 6 At home. Got up a clearer summing up of the Reeder Ancestry from fullest and latest investigations. Went to town; made some purchases.

Friday, January 7 At home all the forenoon. Write letters to Robt. White, Grant Co., and to Wheeler & Griffith at Casey, Iowa. Go to town, mail letters, attend to small purch[as]es including this diary. Read most of the evening.

Saturday, January 8 Spent the day largely in writing, some in reading. At home all day. Read over my Diary of last year in the evening.

Sunday, January 9 Heard in forenoon Rev. Robinson at Grace M.E. Ch., Acts 17:30, on Repentenance, a good sermon. At home the rest of the day. It rained last night and most of the day, but very moderately. Spent the evening largely in examining some scriptural questions.

Monday, January 10 Spent forenoon in Reading on Scripture points, in writing, & hunting up documents to be used by U.B. Cir. Ct. Clerk in making out a transcript of our case. In the afternoon again saw Mr. Young & gave him more documents for the same purpose. Called at Lorin's. Wrote letters in the evening.

Tuesday, January 11 Examined old papers in the forenoon. Wrote some letters. Got Central Pas. Aso. Clerical Certificate. At home all day. Wrote a letter to Katharine in the evening.

Wednesday, January 12 At home all forenoon, except a call on Lorin's, arranging and examining business letters—a hard day's work. Went to town about 3:30; learned that M. Hannah was elected Senator on 1st ballot: Hannah 73, McKisson 70, Lentz 1. Same also on long term.

Thursday, January 13 At home reading and writing except a trip to town. Lorin came in the evening to see about our business.

Friday, January 14 Wrote an article,—"Miracles of the Apostles." Took books to the Library about 5:00, Aft.

Saturday, January 15 At home. Reading and writing. In the evening, wrote letters to Kath. as I had one to Reuchlin earlier.

Sunday, January 16 Heard Rev. Maurice Wilson pr. at 11:00, Rev. 2:7, an excellent and able sermon, "To him that overcometh," etc. In the afternoon visited Samuel Spidel, and remained till after supper.

Monday, January 17 At home all day closely. Spent the day in writing. Also a little time in looking over the accumulated letters of the past months, saving those that I might need and destroying those I will not need. Spent the evening talking with the boys.

Wednesday, January 19 At home all day. Wrote an article on the purpose of Miracles.

Thursday, January 20 Finished my article of yesterday, in the forenoon. Went to town in the afternoon- Library—Young's—Post-office— made some purchases at Wider 's. Rev. Thos. Weyer & wife called in the afternoon.

Friday, January 21 Go on 7:00 train via Union City & Jonesboro to Leach, Ind., or rather to O.R. Glass's, 1 1/4 miles south of Leach. I called at Chas. Atkinson's in Fairmount, whose son, J.T. Atkinson, from Sioux City, Iowa, was there on a visit. Then I went with Oliver Glass & wife out to W.H.H. Reeder's, where I staid that night.

Saturday, January 22 I borrowed of Robt. B. Reeder a horse and of O.R. Glass a saddle and went to Leach & to R.W. White's. It proved a rainy day. I went to Ellis Wright's that evening & lodged. They were all about sick, and the babe had pneumonia, but was getting much better.

Sunday, January 23 I staid at Ellis's till after dinner & then went to S.S. at Hopewell Church in Leach. Then I went to Oliver Buller's (at Henry Simon's) for supper. I preached at Hopewell at 6:30, Jude 14 & 15 verses, "Enoch the 7th from Adam prophecied of these," etc. Lodge at Buller's.

Monday, January 24 Went to Wm. Reeder's & got him to go with me to Leach to see Ailes & Smith about our

accounts on timber sold, & sawing done, & we found I owed them $9.22. We dined at R.W. White's, and looked over the place, and then I went to O.R. Glass's, and there I had supper & lodging.

Tuesday, January 25 I exchanged horses with Oliver & went to Buller's to get my umbrella, and got rained on as I went. Dined at Buller's. Called at Ellis's. Went to Leach and to White's. Hired him to gather my corn, giving him hay-stack and $4.00 for the same. Went to Glass's and staid. It was rainy.

Wednesday, January 26 Went to White's & to Fairmount with him and sold my clover seed at $2.60 per bushel. I then took the train to Dayton, via Anderson and Richmond. Reached home at 6:20. Found all well.

Thursday, January 27 At home till afternoon when I went to City Library and got out two books; called at Young's but George was not in. Read Townsend's "Faith Work" etc. through. It is an excellent work.

Friday, January 28 At home in the forenoon, reading the papers mostly. In the afternoon see Young & get a list of duplicates needed of papers etc. in U.S. Case.

Saturday, January 29 At home. Spent the afternoon looking up Telescopes & Conservators for the U.S. Dist. Clerk to use in a transcript of evidence to be printed in the Fairview case. Took them to Young. Went thence to Rev. H.J. Becker's and got out of his loose papers duplicates of about half of them. Sat up till 1:00, arranging paper, etc.

Sunday, January 30 Breakfasted at 8:30. Wrote Katie a letter. Attend services at Park Pres. Church. The paste pr. at 11:00, Mark 10:38, a very good sermon. At home the rest of the day. The text was Burtimeas's cry: "Have mercy on me."

Monday, January 31 Spent the whole day and evening in preparing an article, "Utility of miracles," for our paper. Mailed it at 10:00 eve.

Tuesday, February 1 Went to Dr. H.J. Becker's and got two more papers, needed in my files. Spent the afternoon and eve. in looking over old papers & letters, destroying some that could not be of future use.

Wednesday, February 2 Spent most of the day in examining and refiling letters & papers stowed away in my closet.

Friday, February 4 Went to City Library and got out "Ohio Valley Historical Miscellanies," containing "The story of the "Leatherwood God."

Saturday, February 5 Spent the day largely in assorting old letters & papers.

Sunday, February 6 Hear Rev. J.P. Miller pr. at Park St. Church on 2 Cor. 9:12, an interesting discourse on "Earnest Endeavor." In afternoon called at Lorin's. Harry Andrews & Wilbur Landis & families came in there. Spent the evening in reading.

Wednesday, February 9 Reading and writing much of the day. Went to town to library, saw Young but a minute, bought shoes, etc. Sat up till midnight.

Sunday, February 13 Heard the Evangelist Peters pr. at the Broadway Christian Church Phil. 2:5, "Mind— Christ Jesus." He is a nice speaker & spoke well, but missed his text as many do. Wrote an article for the Conservator on various Readings of Scripture.

Monday, February 14 Went to town & called on Lorin's on my return. At home the rest of the day.

Tuesday, February 15 At home all day except a call at Lorin's & at the office. Wrote a good deal.

Wednesday, February 16 At home all day, except the usual calls. News came of the blowing up of the warship Maine in Havana Harbor. Is is accidental, or is it Spanish Treachery?

Thursday, February 17 Milton came and spent most of the day with me. He enjoyed it very much. Lorin and Netta called in the evening.

Friday, February 18 At home till afternoon. Wrote letters. Called at H.J. Becker's & at Mrs. Bartles to see "Aunt" Mary Englehart.

Saturday, February 19 At home most of the day. Wrote to T.J. Burns & Co, to sell my corn in Iowa & mailed the letter at the Post-office. Got out old boxes of periodicals, letters & spent some time on them.

Sunday, February 20 Heard Rev. Prichard pr. at Williams St. Baptist Church, 1 Sam. 13:13, a good sermon. Called at John Weidner's and Jacob Swank's. And in the evening at Lorin's. Wm Ensy so desirous to die.

Wednesday, February 23 Engaged in Writing. Went to the Library and returned books & took out Cyprian's works, & "Watchman what of the Night?" by Dr. Cummings. I found Cyprian very interesting.

Friday, February 25 Went to Library and copied from Genealogical Dictionary of New England, the Wright family.

Saturday, February 26 At home forenoon mostly reading, and getting ready to go to the Quarterly meeting. Go on 5:30 train to Germantown via Carlisle. Preach at 7:15, Ps. 73:24. Three seekers & one conversion—Mrs. Vergna. Stay with W. Miller at Rev. Thos. Weyer's.

Sunday, February 27 Attend Sabbath school. Speaking meeting. Rev. Wm. Miller preached. I introduce the sacramental service. Dine at Shem Thomas's. Mrs. Selby, his niece, there and W. Miller, who has neuralgia considerably. I pr. at 7:00 Rom. 8:2, Law of Spirit of Life, etc. Two seekers. Miller & I go home with Isaac Swartzell's 2 1/2 ms. out east of town.

Monday, February 28 I. Swartzel, Arthur, Eva, Earl, Nellie, Marguerite. Mrs. Ella Swartzel. Bro. Swartzel takes us to Miamisburg & we go on the traction line to Dayton. Miller stops with D.R. Miller. I Read and wrote.

Tuesday, March 1 Went to town and sent drafts: $1.44 to Eaton & Mains for books and $1.25 to Tribune for Weekly & Almanack. Called at Lorin's. Studied & prepared sketches of sermons.

Wednesday, March 2 Arranged unfired Copies of the *Richmond Star*, a paper I edited and published from 1881 to 1885.

Thursday, March 3 Went to town. Paid Young $35.00 for U.S. Clerk's docket fee. Spent the rest of the day at home.

Saturday, March 5 Write letters. Milton (my grandson) comes, dines with us & stays till 3:30.

Sunday, March 6 Attended the Hawthorne African M.E Church & heard a young preacher on "Abide in the vine." In the Afternoon at 3:30, heard Ex-pres. John W. Simpson lecture on Words, "An Uncured Tongue."

Wednesday, March 9 Called at Young's and learned of the arrangements on printing the transcript in U.S. case.

Thursday, March 10 Took over some books to Young to use in the record of evidence in U.S. Appeal case. Attended prayer-meeting at Jac. Swank's, in the evening.

Saturday, March 12 Took over copies of Volume containing Disciplines from 1815 to 1841.

Sunday, March 13 At home all day, busy looking up Scriptures on some points of Doctrine. Sat up late in the evening.

Monday, March 14 Start at 10:15 to Delphos, Ohio. Arrive at Delphos. Call at Jesse McKenzie's, Wilson H. Mc Kenzie's and at Chas. McKenzie's grocery. Supper at W.H. Mc's. Pr. at the Church at Marbletown at 7:30, Ez. 33:11. I stay at W.H. McKenzie's with Rev. J.M. Sherer, who is quite unwell.

Tuesday, March 15 Go on 10:20 train to Ft. Wayne & Huntington, arriving at the latter at 1:13. Meet Prudential Com. of Publish. Establishment at Rev. J.G. Johnson's 36 Bingham St. Supper at Johnson's. Com. met at our Publ. Building at 7:00 & stay till late. I stay at Rev. Wm. Dillon's.

Wednesday, March 16 I met Ex. Com. of the Mis. Board at 7:00 & remain to help make out a programme for the Annual Board meeting. Dine with Flickinger. Saw Alfred S. Goodin, who lives near Roanoke, and who agrees to give for the bringing of Joseph Wilberforce to America for his education $175.00. Supper at Prof. Kiracofe's. Lodge at Dillon's.

Thursday, March 17 Start at 6:19 via Ft. Wayne & Lima and reach home 12:30.

Friday, March 18 At home in the forenoon. In the morning get a draft from T.J. Burns & Co., Casey, Iowa, for $440.68 for corn sold to A. Rutt. See Young in Afternoon five minutes. Call at Lorin's on my way home.

Saturday, March 19 Went to town. Left some Mich. briefs with Mr. Young.

Sunday, March 20 Called at S. Spidel's & H.J. Becker's in the afternoon. Supper at Spidel's. Hear Rev. T. Weyer pr. at Midway mission at 7:00, Luke 24:32. It was a rainy afternoon & evening. The meeting is to be protracted.

Monday, March 21 Getting ready to go away. Called at Young's twice to see George, but he was in Court. In the Afternoon, deposited in Winter's Nat'l Bank $440.68 Chi. draft, $95.00, boys' check, and $12.00 in currency. Handed Will Young a check for $675.00. Lorin called in the evening & left $7.00.

Tuesday, March 22 Arose at 5:00. Start about 9:00 for Orrville, Ohio, on my way to Pennsylvania. I was hindered five hours at Brink Haven by a washout at Millersburg. Had just one hour at Orrville. Called at Mrs. S. Shisler's, who had fallen & hurt her right arm. Start 8:30 for Pittsburgh. Water very high. Reach P. at 2:00.

Wednesday, March 23 Leave Pittsburgh at 6:00 and reach Harrisburg at 2:00. Go on eve. train & at 6:00 stop at Mason & Dixon. Supper at Huet's, 1/2 m. east. D.L. Perry preached at Middleburg at 7:00. D.M. Hench, the evangelist, conducted revival services. I stay at J.S. Lesher's at State Line post-office, right by the church.

Thursday, March 24 Opened Conference at about 9:00. Examinations. Rev. G.W. Allmun was received on a belated transfer. He preached a fair sermon at 7:00.

Friday, March 25 Conference continued. J.E. Hott made a peculiar speech on finance. Huber preached a fine sermon at 7:00.

Saturday, March 26 Session Continued. Hott does the discussions. His illogical speech on party prohibition. W. Lutz memorial at 3:00, addresses by J.E. Hott & W.J. Funkhouser. J.E. Hott pr. a fine sermon at 7:00, Rev. 3:20.

Sunday, March 27 I preached at 10:30, Matt. 7:24. "House on a rock." Hott collects $42.68 for me. I dine at Crunkelton's in the north part of the town. S.S. Anniversary at 3:00. I summed up the quarter's lessons, pr. at 7:00, Matt. 12:30. I had supper at Mr. Bovey's with W.J. Funkhouser.

Monday, March 28 I go to Greeneastle on 9:15 train. The Liberal, Brubaker sat by me. Dine & sup with F.W. Barnhart's, & lodge there. Pr. at 7:30, Col. 1.8. "Love in the Spirit."

Tuesday, March 29 Go on 9:00 train to Chambersburg. Dine and sup at Rev. John Fohl's. He had fallen Friday the 25th and hurt his left leg. I lodged at Adam Nicklass's. He has one son in Philadelphia, another in Martinsburg and one is a lawyer in town. His daughters are Rebecca, Mary 18, and Rachel 12.

Wednesday, March 30 Dine at Peter Nicklass's. Go to Rev. J.A. Hamilton's. I preach at 7:30, Ps. 25.14. I lodge at A. Nicklas's.

Thursday, March 31 I go to Shippensburg on 9:45 train. Put up at Rev. J.M. Smiley's. I call at 6:00 at Rev. J. Dohner's. A nice family. He has his second wife. I preach at 7:00. Lodge at Smiley's.

Friday, April 1 I returned at 9:00 train to Chambersburg. I dined at John Fohl's. His son Benj. an optician, is at home for a time. I sup and lodge at A. Nicklas's.

Saturday, April 2 I dined at Rev. B.G. Huber's. With Rev. J.A. Hamilton, I call at Levi Oyler's in the edge of the country, and at Mrs. J.M. Bishop's, and at Rev. S.J. Nicklas's. I have supper and lodgings at Adam Nicklass'.

Sunday, April 3 I Preached at 10:30, Isa. 9.7. Mis. Coll. small. Dined at P. Nicklass'. At 3:00, I addressed the S.S on the Syro-phenician woman's faith. S.S. Collection for missions was about $11.00. Preach at 8:00, Rom.

8:2. Supper & lodging at A. Nicklass'.

Monday, April 4 With P. Nicklass, I went to C.V. R'y office and got a permit on that road, for half-fare. I then go on 9:45 train to Carlisle, and dine at P.O. Wagner's—the pastor's. Their little girl is Edith. I go with Bro. Wagner to look at the church and call on W.O. Weidler & sup there. Preach at 7:45, Rom. 4:8. Stay at Spangler's, Eve.

Tuesday, April 5 There is a driving snow. Start on 10:38 train to Buffalo & make close connection at Harrisburg. Go up W. Branch of the Susquehana, via Williamsport, Elmira, Watkins (Senaca Lake) Canandaqua. Reach Starkey at sunset, Penyan at twilight, and Rochester. Reach Buffalo at 11:20. Stay at the hotel across the street.

Wednesday, April 6 Go on 7:20 train of Grand Trunk R'y to Sherkston. Stop & dine at Andrew Sherk's, at the upper Store. Supper at the same. Meeting in the evening at Church, to fix homes for Conference. I stay at Isaac Sherk's.

Thursday, April 7 I dine with D.B. Sherk at Geo. Zavits' (Father House's home) and also sup there. I preach at the Church at 8:15, John 1:29. Sherk & I stay at Benj. Troup's, 1 m. west of the Church. This is our conference home. He has a grist mill.

Friday, April 8 The Ontario Conference opened at 8:30, at Grace Church, and progressed well. I dine, sup & lodge at Troup's. Rev. August F. Stoltz of Berlin pr at 3:00, Heb. 8:8–12. Rev. C.W. Backus pr at 8:00, but as I felt tired, I staid at home and got a good night's rest. A.F. Stoltz received into conf. from New Menonites.

Saturday, April 9 Conference progressed. Sherk re-elected presiding elder. Stationing Com. met at Isaac Sherk's at noon. Wm. Gribble was elected to elders orders. He preached at 8:00. I board as usual, except dinner at Merner Shoup's.

Sunday, April 10 I preach at 10:30, Acts 20.28. I dine with Gribble at Aaron Sherk's two miles north. S.S. Anniversary at 3:00. I sup at Werner Shoup's. I preach at 8:00. Go to bed at 11:40 & awake at 3:00.

Monday, April 11 Breakfast at 5:00. Troup takes me to Andrew Nelson Sherk's, and we start early to Buffalo. I go on 9:15 train and reach Cleveland at 1:10. At 3:10, I go on to Oberlin. Call at Mrs. Miller's, and lunch there. Go to Katharine's Society & hear her debate. Stay at the Hotel.

Tuesday, April 12 We go to Cleveland, where Katie shop's. Dine at Park Restaurant. Go on 1:10 train to Toledo, and on 4:25 train to Huntington. Stay at A.G. Johnson's.

Wednesday, April 13 Settle with Keiter. Meeting of Mis. Ex. Com. Go on 10:10 train to Wabash & thence to Fairmount. Go with Holliway & then with Lewis through rain & then walk to Robt. W. White's, on the farm. Stay there.

Thursday, April 14 Look over the farm. Go to Fowlerton & thence via White's to Ellis Wright's to Fairmount & take 12:43 train to Anderson & Richmond, and home to Dayton. Find all well.

Friday, April 15 I arose about 5:30. Go to town. Arrange Bank-Book. Am rather dull to-day. David Middaugh sends me a hundred dollars from his father's estate, to be used for church purposes when I think it will do the most good. I put it into bank for the present. Decedent is Thomas Middaugh.

Saturday, April 16 I arose about 5:30. At home in forenoon. Milton called, & also in afternoon. Rev. Thomas Weyer called afternoon. John Weidner called. I went to town and bought a book for Wilbur's birth-day. (Senate passed Cuban resolutions.)

Sunday, April 17 At home all day. Felt very dull & trifling.

Monday, April 18 At home. Felt rather dull. House refused to concur in Senate Cuban resolution without amendment. Conference committee. Finally the houses agreed and the Senate adopted the resolutions which render war inevitable. The form of resolution was needlessly, provoking.

Thursday, April 21 To-day Mr. Woodford, our Ambassador to Spain received his passports without asking for it. Hence war exists with Spain. Out Atlantic Squadron is ordered to Cuban waters.

Friday, April 22 The Fourth Atlantic Squadron, Captain Sampson's, starts early for the blockade in Havana, etc. U.S. Cruiser Nashville captured the Spanish Ship Buena Vera of 1,000 tons, having a cargo of lumber from the Texas Coast.

Saturday, April 23 Spent the day at home. Wrote letters. It is a rainy day.

Sunday, April 24 Attended the Congregational Church on the Boulevard and heard Rev. Jas. W. Rain preach an interesting anti-saloon sermon at 11:00.

Thursday, April 28 At home except a trip to town in the forenoon; paid Young $100.00 on services U.S. case. In afternoon went to John Weidner's on Kilmer & 1st Sts. Wm. Ensey is very low.

Saturday, April 30 Go at 5:30, Aft., on Traction to Miamisburg where Isaac Swartzel meets me and takes me to his house half way & more to Germantown. Lodge there. Children, two boys and Eva, Nellie, and Margaret.

Sunday, May 1 I preach at Germantown at 10:30, Rev. 2:17, "To him that overcometh," etc. Dine at L. Weitz. Call at C.B. McDaniel's for supper. Call at Shem Thomas' and pray with him. I preach at 7:30, Ex. 28:34. Lodge at McDaniel's.

Monday, May 2 I call on Shem Thomas'. McDaniel takes me to Miamisburg & I reach home about 11:00. John Weidner came after me to tell me of the death of Wm. P. Ensey Sunday at his house on Kilmer St.

Tuesday, May 3 At home most of the day. In the afternoon, I went to Weidner's to write a memorial paper on Mr. Ensey.

Wednesday, May 4 Attended Wm. P. Ensey's funeral at 9:30, Text, "I would not have you ignorant," etc. 1 Thes. 4.13. I spent the evening in adding up the footings of the chart of my District.

Thursday, May 5 At home mostly. Went to town in the afternoon on business. Called at Young's office, but did not see him.

Friday, May 6 Wrote several letters. Called at Young's one minute to see about extra copies of the printed record in the U.S. Case.

Sunday, May 8 Heard Rev. W.P. Miller preach at Park Presbyterian Church, Gen. 2.18, on Home and companionship.

Wednesday, May 11 At home. Correspondence.

Friday, May 13 At home. News that Admiral Sampson began yesterday morning to bombard the Spanish fortifications at San Juan, Porto Rico. Called at Weidner's in the Afternoon.

Sunday, May 15 Not well in the forenoon. Spent the day at home.

Tuesday, May 17 Mr. F.H. Short and Mrs. Semele Short come to the railroad meeting (C. H.& D.) and I dine with them at the Atlas Hotel. Before dinner we visited the High School —Saw Prof. Woerthner & Prof. Wm. Reeder. After dinner we visit Woodland Cemetery, Library Building, & Herald Office to see J.Z. Reeder.

Wednesday, May 18 Katharine(my daughter) came home from Oberlin on 6:10 eve. train.

Saturday, May 21 Go on 8:20 train via Chillicothe to Athens, 0. and thence to Garden for a dedication tomorrow. Reach Athens at 3:16. J.M. Beam takes me out to his house near Garden. I lodge there.

Sunday, May 22 I pr. at 10:30 Ps. 84.10, and raise subscription & dedicate Zion Church. Dine at Erastus Curtis's in Garden. I pr. at 8:00, Job 23:10. Communion followed. I stay at J.M. Beam's. Children at home - daughter 18 or 20 & Floyd who is about 5 1/2.

Monday, May 23 Bro. Beam takes me to Athens. Take dinner with him at Palmer House. I go on 12:25 train to Chillicothe & thence on 3:20 train to Dayton, arriving at Dayton at 6:15.

Saturday, May 28 Rev. Wm. Miller called at 10:00; D.K. Flickinger at 11:00. We all dine at eating house on N. Williams St. Bro. Miller goes on to Brookville, and I to Dr. H.J. Becker's with Dr. Flickinger. I go on 6:05 tr. to Brookville & stay at John Zehring's.

Sunday, May 29 Go with Aaron Zehring's to Olivet.S. School, love feast. Rev. Wm. Miller pr. at 10:30, Isa. 66:13. Have sacrament. I dine with Miller at A. Wyandt's. I preach at 8:00, Eccl. 12:1, to the Young people. Return to Brookville with Aaron Zehring's & stay.

Monday, May 30 Came home on 8:51 train. Go to town. See Peter Louding's about reports on African Massacre.

Tuesday, May 31 Saw Dr. Spitler & got some medicine.

Wednesday, June 1 Wrote many letters.

Friday, June 3 Went to town in afternoon. Saw Louding's, Rev. Wm. McKee & Mrs. Miller & Witt abt. African masacres.

Sunday, June 5 At home. Called at P. Louding's & at Lorin's. Wrote on a sermon some.

Monday, June 6 At home. Wrote on a sermon part of the day.

Tuesday, June 7 Went via Richmond and Anderson to Fairmont & the farm. Supper at R.W. White's on the farm. Lodge at Ellis Wright's.

Wednesday, June 8 Call at Oliver Glass's. Dine at Wm. Reeder's. Great rain. Wm. takes me to Fairmount & I lodge at Hollingworth's. (Wm. Hall's home).

Thursday June 9 Sold small ash and small linn timber to Joseph Hinkle for $1.00 for linn and $1.75 per cord for ash. Go on to Huntington via Wabash. Put up at Lou. Bailey's next door of Etna Ave. Church. Mission Ex. Com. have a consultation at Mission Room at 2:00. Board meeting at 7:30. Coll. $170.00 after sermon.

Friday, June 10 Board's session at 8:00 at Etna Ave. Ch. Afternoon session W. Mis. Association had meeting at

8:00, eve. Miss Titus & Barnes & Mullen spoke. Stay at Bailey's, Flickinger's home. This meeting was at College Chapel.

Saturday, June 11 Session continued & closed at 11:00. Attend W.M. Association at 3:00—Memorial service. Hard rain. I sup at Kiracofe's. Did not stay to Floyd's sermon at 8:00, but rested what I could at Bailey's.

Sunday, June 12 I preached in the College Auditorium at 10:30, 2 Cor. 1:7 -"of a sound mind." Dined at Rev. Rufus A. Morrison's. Heard Dr. H.J. Becker at 3:00, and Miss Mary B. Mullen at 8:00, & Bishop H. Floyd. Sup & lodge at Bailey's.

Monday, June 13 Educational Board met at 2:00 at College Chapel. I sup at S. Albert Stemen's. Musical entertainment at 8:00. I stay one hour there and then walk home to Bailey's.

Tuesday, June 14 Publishing Establishment board met at 9:00. Dine at M.F. Keiter's. At 2:00 Edu. Board had another session. I sup at Prof. Jas. H. McMurray's. Literary Societies' entertainment at 8:00. I go back to Bailie's [Bailey's]. At 6:30, we had a Publ. Board Ses. at the College.

Wednesday, June 15 Publ. Board Session at 8:00. Hear Dr. H.J. Becker at 10:00 & others. Dine at Prof. T.H. Gragg's. Publ. board met at 1:30 (2:00) and again at 8:00. I sup at Wm. Dillon's. Lodge at Bailey's .

Thursday, June 16 Consultation with sisters at 8:00 on differences in treasuries' accounts. I go on 11:07 train via Ft. Wayne & Richmond home. Called a few minutes at D.K. Zeller's in Richmond. Called at Lorin's at 7:30.

Friday, June 17 In forenoon, went to town mailed postal cards on C.H. & D. train north. Bought some clothes at Mose's. Saw Young two minutes. At home Afternoon. Wrote letters.

Saturday, June 18 Went to Union Depot to go via Toledo to Lindsey; but had left my Clergy Certificate at home. In afternoon at 4:10, go via Bellefontaine to Clyde, and thence to Fremont. Stay at Croghan Hotel.

Sunday, June 19 Hire livery to take me to Jac. Overmeyer's, near Bethel Ch. before breakfast. Attend S.S. and pr. at Bethel, 10:30, Matt. 24:3. Dine at Boyer's in Lindsey. He takes me to Ballville, near Freemont. where I have supper at [blank] Reynold's. I pr. at Church at 8:00, 1 Cor. 12:31. Stay at Rev. Silvanus Stevens.

Monday, June 20 Remain at Stevens' all day, except I call an hour in the eve at S.L. Spayd's.

Tuesday, June 21 Remain at Stevens' till afternoon. He takes me to 4:28 train at Fremont. Go to Oberlin. Supper at the bakery. Walked with Daughter Katharine. I lodged at room at a hall.

Wednesday, June 22 This is Oberlin Commencement day. At 10:00, hear an address by Rev. Edward Everet Hale. The class of 1898—about 98 in number—receive their diplomas, including C.H. Kiracofe, Jr., Margaret Goodwin, Harriet Sillaman & my Katharine. Attend Alumni dinner. Go via Cleveland home.

Thursday, June 23 Arrive at Dayton about 5:30, and home. Largely spend the day in rest.

Friday, June 24 Spent the day largely in resting. Katharine got home from Oberlin about 7:00. All up late. Election of teachers occurred at High School building to-night.

Saturday, June 25 At home all day. The day is very warm. A hard rain in the afternoon. The children were up till about midnight.

Saturday, June 26 Breakfast too late to get to church to-day. Heard Rev. Mr. Robinson, pastor of Grace M.E. Church preach at 8:00, Heb. 6:18,19. It was a very warm evening.

Monday, June 27 Telegraph or cablegram from Africa: "Sierre Leone, D.K. Flickinger, Huntington, Ind. Wilberforce and family safe."

Tuesday, June 28 Received a letter from Flickinger, telling of the cablegram announcing safety of Wilberforce and family. In the evening I called at Louding's and Dr. Webster's to talk of Wilberforce's salty.

Katharine Wright, 1898 Oberlin College graduate

Wednesday, June 29 Called at Jac. Swank's. Dr. Becker's & at "Aunt" Mary Englehart's. No one at home at Becker's.

Friday, July 1 House-cleaning to-day. Dr. H.J. Becker called at an hour in the forenoon. I called at Albert Shearer's in the evening. His sisters Effie and Fanney there, and Charlie's little girl.

Saturday, July 2 Milton dined with us. Rev. S.L. Livingston called a half hour—had come to the city to see about a trade with young Chadwick. Lorin ran bicycle into a wagon. Went with Katharine to look at chairs and dishes, but bought little.

Sunday, July 3 Heard Rev. Maurice Wilson preach at First Presbyterian Church at 11:00 on Christian nations. At 3:30, I heard Rev. Wilbur T. Crafts of Wash., D.C. speak on Dead and Living Nations at Association Hall. Y.M.C.A. Orchestra and Double Male Quartett, rendered music. Called at Samuel Spidel's.

Monday, July 4 I realized vividly in memory the scene of nine years ago—Susan's death. In the afternoon, with Katharine, I visited her grave as I usually do every Fourth. A little rain in the morning. Lorin's, Andrew's, Olinger's etc. picniced near New Lebanon.

Tuesday, July 5 The news of the destruction of Cervera's

fleet, Sunday Morning, is confirmed. I went to town and paid my water meter ($1.00) and water tax ($1.20); also my Nat. Gas meter tax ($3.00) and gas bill ($1.00).

Wednesday, July 6 Called at Doctor Spitler's in the forenoon and got medicine for a slight inflamation of the stomach which has affected me for several months, and much weakened my nervous force. My Second-Cousin G.W. Snyder died at 1:20 this morning at Battle Creek, Mich.

Friday, July 8 Spent much of the day lying down. I took a walk however. Lorin and "Sister" called an hour in the evening.

Saturday, July 9 I did nothing today but read. I took a walk of eight squares in the evening.

Sunday, July 10 Attended Memorial Presb. Ch. & heard the new pastor, Rev. F.N. MacMillin preach, Phil. 1:27. He is a solemn looking young man, of small stature, of fair delivery, and of promising talent. Geo. Feight brought a letter saying Mrs. Shisler was seriously ill.

Monday, July 11 Went via Columbus and Mt. Vernon to Orrville, Ohio, and find Mrs. Shisler very low. Saw Mrs. Cane, Mrs. Case, Mrs. Stender, Miss Susie Hurst, and Mrs. Arick there. Saw Dr. Gwenamyer in the evening at his office. I had called at Mrs. Lefever's on arriving. Called at David Walmers, but no one in. Staid at Mrs. Shislers.

Tuesday, July 12 Called an hour at David Walmer's in the morning. Dined at Mrs. John Lefever's. Spent the day largely at Mrs. Shisler's. Mrs. John Noel came in the evening. Miss Mary Rufer mostly caring for Mrs. Shisler by day, Miss [blank] came at nights. Mrs. Stender had some care of her. I lodged at Walmer's.

Wednesday, July 13 Mrs. Noel and I consulted Mrs. Shisler somewhat as to her affairs & as to her means on hand for present use & as to where her will was deposited, & she said of the latter that it was with the judge at Wooster. She told us where to find her pocket-book which contained some sixteen dollars and some Coal Co. Checks. Said she had $80.00 at Arick's. I lodge at Walmer's.

Thursday, July 14 Engage boarding at Walmer's. Go in Afternoon to Canton and pay her tax, $90.49. Steamwhistle's noise over the surrender of Santiago de Cuba, at Canton. I call an hour at John Noel's, on Woodland Ave. Railroad expense 70 cts. Prayer & singing with Mrs. Shisler. Very warm day. Rains hard at night. Stay at Walmer's.

Friday, July 15 Went to Mrs. Shisler's & go on 11:20 train to Wooster to pay tax. Expense of trip 40 cts. A very warm day. Tax accounts having been sent to Orrville. Pay Mrs. Shisler's Wayne Co. tax, which was just $15.00. Prayer and singing with Mrs. Shisler in the evening. Cooler at night. I stay at Walmer's where I had engaged regular board.

Saturday, July 16 Pretty warm. Mrs. S. seemed stronger in the morning, but grew weaker. Expressed less suffering. I called in the eve. 5 minutes at Mrs. Lefever's. Staid at Mrs. Shisler's till 9:20 eve.. Saw Miss Linburger, Mrs. Ida Heller and others. As Mrs. Shisler died at 10:15, I staid till near 2:00 morn. Stay at Walmer's.

Sunday, July 17 Went with David Walmer and arranged with Herbst, trustee and agent of the board, for a grave in Newman's Creek graveyard. There was a hard rain on our return. Board and lodge at Walmer's.

Monday, July 18 I write out a memorial paper in the forenoon and prepare notes for a brief discourse. Rev. J. Noel came. Funeral at the house at 1:00. I spoke about 15 minutes on l Cor. 15:26. I had invited John Noel to preach the funeral discourse. Buried Mrs. Shisler at Newman's Creek Cemetery. Staid at her former residence with Noel's & Kiracofe.

Tuesday, July 19 Arranged to put all her papers in a trunk and leave at Mr. Arick's. Mary Rufer & Mrs. Noel are busy clearing up and washing up things. Kiracofe and I go to Wooster & find the will & take measures to have it probated. I return to Orrville and see Mrs. Lefever & Mrs. Heller about her next of kin. Stay at the Shisler residence.

Wednesday, July 20 I arrange under the instruction of the Judge to have the keys of the house left at Mr. Arick's, and start home at 11:03, via Mt. Vernon & Columbus. I arrived at home at 5:00.

Friday, July 22 At home in enfebled health caused by my care, loss of sleep, etc. at Orrville.

Saturday, July 23 Called at the Bank. Paid the Collin's sisters for Katie's hats, $7.00.

Sunday, July 24 Felt quite unwell and staid at home all day.

Wednesday, July 27 Miss Minnie Swank called about 9:00 to ask me to preach James Cook's funeral. Went to Cook's about 5:00 and wrote out a memorial paper.

Thursday, July 28 Funeral of James Cook at the residence on W. First St. near Western Ave. at 9:00. Text 1 Cor. 15:29. Burial at Miami Chapel.

Friday, July 29 At home. Rev. Thomas Weyer and wife called at 3:00. Rev. D.K. Flickinger came at 4:00 and staid till morning. We consulted over the situation in Africa.

Saturday, July 30 At home. (Prince Bismarck died this evening. The great German Chancellor.)

Sunday, July 31 At home reading. Mr. Potts died suddenly to-day.

Monday, August 1 At home. Called at Lorin's in the evening.

Wednesday, August 3 Go to Young's at 9:00 & remain till noon to hear him read the manuscript of his brief in the United States case appealed. The rest of the day was at Home. Mr. Potts on Wms. St. was buried in the forenoon.

Thursday, August 4 Spent most of the day in writing letters. Write Kiracofe and to Judge McClarran.

Friday, August 5 William A. Broyles came at 5:00 aftn on his bicycle, having rode ninety miles to-day. He is a son of my cousin Eliza K (Reeder) Broyles.

Saturday, August 6 I stay at home mostly. Katie went with Wm. in forenoon to look at town, and Wilbur went with him in afternoon to the Soldiers' Home.

Sunday, August 7 I remained at home, being as usual, not very well. Katie and Orville attended Broadway M.E. Church in the evening and heard Harrison, a local preacher.

Monday, August 8 Rainy forenoon. I see Dr. Spitler and get some Medicine, in the afternoon; for since last spring I have had stomach ailment, originating in a cold caught at State Line, Pa., by sitting in a room without fire after meeting at night—inducing a mild form of influenza.

Tuesday, August 9 Wm. Broyles starts to Cincinnati, about 8:00, on his bicycle.

Wednesday, August 10 I was at home in the forenoon. In the Afternoon, I went to town and paid Gas bill $1.00 & Assessment on insurance on my house "Richland Mutual" $2.00.

Thursday, August 11 At home. In the evening I called at Lorin's.

Friday, August 12 Milton and Ivonette came and took dinner with us. Milton staid till night.

Saturday, August 13 At home writing letters in the forenoon. In the Afternoon got a registered letter from Judge John C. McClarran, Wooster, Ohio.

Sunday, August 14 At 10:40 heard Rev. King preach in the basement of First Baptist Chruch.

Monday, August 15 Went on 6:05 train to Lima, & thence with Dr. Kiracofe to Wooster. Saw Judge J.C. McClarran & Mahlon Rouch. Dine & sup at the Musser House. Go on 8:03 tr. to Orrville. Stay at Mrs. Lefever's.

Tuesday, August 16 Called at D. Walmer's, Sue Hurst's, Mrs. Kane's, Mr. Arick's. Come home on 11:00 train via Columbus. Saw Rev. C. Whitney on the train from Columbus. Reached home about 6:00.

Wednesday, August 17 At home. Wrote some letters. Went to town in the afternoon. Quite a hot day.

Thursday, August 18–Wednesday, August 24 At home. . . . Margaret Goodwin came in the eve [23rd].

Thursday, August 25 Go on 9:20 train via Richmond & Anderson to Fairmount. Go with Ben. Leach to the farm. Look over accounts with White. Lodge at Ellis Wright's.

Friday, August 26 Ellis takes me to White's. I send my oats to Fairmount & get 19 cts per bush—175 b. Meet Wm. Reeder & go to his house & dine & visit with him and Robert. Sup & lodge at O.A. Glass's.

Saturday, August 27 Went to Fairmount & thence to Wabash & Huntington. Sup & lodge at W. Dillon's. Rev. C.B. Small pr. at 8:00 at Conf. Room. Oliver Glass takes me to White's. Look over the farm, arrange on crops, and rent to him for another year. Go to Fairmount after an early dinner. Got $44.00 for 44 cords of small linn timber. Go on via Wabash to Huntington. Small pr. at Aetna Ave. Stay at Dillon's.

Sunday, August 28 At St. Joseph Annual Conf., Bishop Barnaby pr. at 10:30. I dine at Bailey's. Aftn. shouting meeting: Perry and Jealison! Dillon pr. at 8:00, on Resurrection & commended shouting.

Monday, August 29 A meeting of the Ex. Com. Mis. at 8:00. I dine at Keiter's with Barnaby. Supper at A.G. Johnson's. Stay at Dillon's with Barnaby.

Tuesday, August 30 Went with Kiracofe, Flickinger & Dillon via Ft. Wayne & Van Wert to Tama. Called at Sister Forney's and Miss ———[lines appear in text] a neighbor, took us down to Wm. Morrow's near Union Church. Rev. T.M. Harvey pr. at 8:00.

Wednesday, August 31 Tent raised in the forenoon. Auglaize Conference opened in Afternoon at 2:00 & progressed well. D.K. Flickinger spoke in the eve. at 8:00 in the tent, and raised some on Memorial fund. Our home at Wm. Morrow's.

Thursday, September 1 Conference continued. Kiracofe spoke on Education at 10:00. He and Flickinger left at 11:00. Dillon pr. at 8:00 on the atonement, 1 Cor. 15:3. His bad theology & he repeats his demagoguery on

shouting. There was a very large crowd. Mrs. Kiracofe came in evening.

Friday, September 2 Conference Continued. Keiter & Miss Mullen came. Had Mis. report at 3:00. Miss Mullen, Mrs. Kiracofe & Dillon spoke. Montgomery & Harvey were elected presiding elders. Stationing Com. met at 6:00. M.F. Keiter pr. at 8:00 & Mary Mullen spoke on Af. war. About $10.00 collec. for Miss Mullen.

Saturday, September 3 Nearly Completed Conf. business in the forenoon. Sacramental meeting at 2:30, 175 or 200 communicants. Precious season. Adjourned at about 4:30. I preach at the tent at 8:00, Malachi 1:14, "Great King." J.M. Shearer exhorts.

Sunday, September 4 Rains in the night & morning. I pr. at 11:00, Matt. 10:16. "Wise as serpents," etc. S.S. Anniversary at 3:00 & Conner, T. Weyer & I spoke. Conner pr. at 8:00, Rom. 3:23, a good sermon in the Church. Stay as usual at Wm. Morrow's, who took excellent care of me.

Monday, September 5 I go on 7:04 train from Oregon to Dayton. Excursionists from the north to Gr. Army Encampment at Cincinnati. At home in the afternoon.

Tuesday, September 6 At home writing letters, etc. Go to bank in afternoon. Called 5 minutes at Young's.

Wednesday, September 7 Start on 9:30 tr. to Sandusky Conference, via Tiffin, at Burgoon. David Harley meets me and takes me to his home for supper. John French pr. at 7:30. I find my home at Samuel Harley's.

Thursday, September 8 Conference opened at 9:00, at Olive Branch Church. John Cronenberger pr. at 7:30.

Friday, September 9 Conference continued. Flickinger and Mary B. Mullen held a missionary meeting in the eve. and raise about $100.00 African Memorial Fund.

Saturday, September 10 Conference continued. M.F. Keiter preached in the eve., "He saved others," etc. Conference closed with a sacramental meeting.

Sunday, September 11 I pr. at 11:00, Matt. 24:3, on

prophecy. Collection asked for carelessly, and consequent small Coll. D.O. Tussing, who took up the Collection, did not like my sermon because I preached the post-millenarian doctrine.

Monday, September 12 I staid at Samuel's and called at David Harley 's.

Tuesday, September 13 Stay at Harley's till eve. and go to Rev. Hilty's & lodge.

Wednesday, September 14 Went on 8:26 train to Wooster via Mansfield. J.D. Zook meets me and takes me to Mrs. Guyer's, near Guyer's Chapel. G.F. Hall pr. at 7:30, a fair sermon. Board at Guyer's.

Thursday, September 15 Conference opened at 9:00 (East Ohio) and progressed well.

Friday, September 16 Conference continued. H.J. Becker pr. at 7:30, "It is good to be here," He was in fine mood. J.N. Lemasters was elected Pres. elder. But Bonewell withdrew. Stationing Com. met at Guyer's at six o'clock.

Saturday, September 17 Conference continued and closed at 4:00. I sup at J.D. Zook's, 1 1/4 m. north-west. Becker lectured at 8:00, "Cuba Libra" & Four Cities of Palestine. Collection is over $9.00.

Sunday, September 18 I pr. at 11:00, Mark 16:15,16. Large S.S. Anniversary at 3:00. Becker pr. at 7:00, "Made man in his own image."

Monday, September 19 Henry Guyer takes me to Smithville Summit. I go on 7:26 train to Lawrence, and walk out to the Shisler farm & to Clover Hill Coal mine. I see Frank Brown & he takes me to Daniel Levers', 2 m. N.E. of Lawrence. I dine there and go to Orrville on even. train and stay at Mrs. John Lefever's.

Tuesday, September 20 I call at Squire Niswonger's & see the contract with Daniel Bartman. I call on Arick's, Strous's, & Mrs. Kane's. I then go on 9:40 tr. to Cleveland, and on 1:00 tr. to Erie, and on 5:20 tr. to Corry. Stay at Rev. J.S. Amidon's. He has been paralyzed for over one year, but his faith in Christ is strong.

Wednesday, September 21 I call at Samuel Evans. I then go on 9:00 tr. to Centerville. Mr. Laughlin meets me and takes me to W.H. Bevins. Painton & wife are there. They are evangelists. Rev. I. Borum pr. at Hemlock Church, at 7:30, fairly well. I stay at R.A. Dey's. Borinn & his boy board there.

Thursday, September 22 Conference opened at 9:00. It is a rainy day & evening. Jas. A. Perkins pr. at 7:30. I was not at eve. meeting. N.R. Luce was with me at Dey's.

Friday, September 23 Conference continued. Luce pr. grandly at 7:30. Rainy day.

Saturday, September 24 Conference Continued. S.J. Cunnings withdrew from conference. N.R. Luce was elected P.E. Stationing Com. met at 12:30. Conf. closed at 4:00. Sta. Com. met again at 6:00. R.W. Mercer pr. 7:30, John 2:[blank] "Corn of wheat."

Sunday, September 25 I pr. at 11:00, 2 Tim 2:15. Mercer pr. at 7:00, T.S. Bennett at 6:30, I at 7:30, 1 Cor. 13:13. Stay at Dey's.

Monday, September 26 R.A. Dey takes me to Centerville, and thence I go on Pem. Lines to Ridgeway, where I stop two hours & dine & then go on to Harrisburg via Williamsport, arriving at 10:15. I stay at the Hershey House. Fare from Centerville $9.63; Hotel 80 cts.

Tuesday, September 27 Go on 7:55 tr. to Chambersburg. Stop at Adam Nicklas's. In the afternoon I visit Rev. John Fohl's, and Rev. B.G. Huber's. Sup & lodge at A. Nicklas's.

Wednesday, September 28 Call at A.H. Hamilton's in the morning. Go on 9:55 tr. to Marion. Go to Rev. J.S. Wentz' and dine. J.A. Burkholder, L. Ditzler and Leininger come. Burkholder takes me to D.M. Rumler's. I pr. at St. James Church at 7:30, 1 Cor. 13:13. I lodge at Deikl's, who are Lutherans, with B.G. Huber.

Thursday, September 29 Pennsylvania Conference opened at 9:00. Rev. M.F. Keiter came at 11:00. Rev. P.O. Wagner pr. at 7:30.

Friday, September 30 Conference Continued. We held a

mis. meeting at 7:30 & raised $101.00 on Memorial Fund. In the aftn J.S. Solenberger and S. Diller were elected presiding elders. The Stationing Com. met at Deihl's at 6:30.

Saturday, October 1 Conference Continued. Memorial of J.N. Smiley at 3:00, followed by Sacramental meeting. Conference closed at 5:00. M.F. Keiter pr. at 7:15 "He saved others."

Sunday, October 2 I pr at 10:00, Rev. 6:2, "Went forth conquering," and raise $303.00 & dedicate St. James Church. Dine at Deihl's. Pr. at 7:00, Rom. 4:8. Stay at John Scleichter's two miles north. Mrs. Dornbush of Mechanicsburg had her home there.

Monday, October 3 Schlichter takes me to Chambersburg. I call at Nicklas' Carpet Store & dine at Stager's with Keiter & P. Nicklas. Supper & lodging at Adam Nicklas'. Pr. at King St. Church at 7:30, Matt. 24:3.

Tuesday, October 4 Call at "Aunt Susie" Fetterhoff's. Go to Nicklas' Store. Dine at A. Nicklas's. Sleep two hours in chair and start at 5:00 for Columbus, Ohio, & arrive at 7:00 morn.

Wednesday, October 5 Arrive at Columbus at 7:00. Go to Flickinger's, 201 Front St. Dine there and go with Flickinger to Baltimore, Ohio. Call at Wm. Geil's and Rev. W.S. Tuttle takes me to John Eversole's, our home. Rev. J.C. Beery pr. at 7:30.

Thursday, October 6 Conference opened at 9:00. Business proceeds well. H.J. Becker comes about 4:00, and pr. at 7:30, Job, "What is man."

Friday, October 7 Conference progresses well. Hoffhines & G.W. Tuttle are elected presiding elders. Stationing Com. meets at Eversole's at 6:30. Becker & Flickinger spoke at 7:30 on Missions and raised African Memorial fund. Ex. Com. of Mis. Board met at Bidler's at 8:00 morning. Eversole is very sick to-night.

Saturday, October 8 Conference proceeds and closes at 4:00 afternoon. H.J. Becker speaks to the preachers 25 min. at 10:45. He pr. at 7:30, "whose hearts the Lord touched." I board as usual.

Sunday, October 9 Love-feast at 9:30. Preach at 10:30, Rev. 6:2. "He went forth." Ordain Jas. W. Burton. Dine at John Eversole's as usual. Sab. School entertainment at 3:00. Was reproved by Burton. Supper at Amos Miller's. Pr. at 7:30, Zeck. 9:10. Stay at Thomas Warner's, with Hoffhines & wife.

Monday, October 10 Go on 9:00 train to Columbus. Dine at D.K. Flickinger's at 201 Front St. Go on 1:00 tr. to Dayton. Arrive at 3:25. Found all the family and Lorin's well. Call at Lorin's in the evening.

Tuesday, October 11 At home in the forenoon. Rev. Wm. B. Stoddard calls at 10:00. I go to town at 2:30. Deposit $496.46 in Winters' Bank.

Wednesday, October 12 I was at home all day. Rev. H.J. Becker called in the Afternoon an hour or more. Kath. went to the Woman's League in the evening.

Sunday, October 16 At home till evening and then heard Rev. C.W. Gullette pr. Matt. 9:9. "He saw a man." Quite an orator, but trifled with the purport of the text, emphasizing man.

Tuesday, October 18 Got word that Daniel Koerner's were coming. Met Koerners on the 2:40 train. Lorin & Ivonette called in the evening.

Thursday, October 20 Rev. Wm. B. Stoddard and H.J. Becker called at 9:00. Daniel and I go to see High School building and other places; also Elmira and Katie took a like trip. In afternoon, Koerner's visit Lorin's, but return after supper.

Friday, October 21 Daniel Koerner's start home on the electric cars at 10:00.

Sunday, October 23 At 11:00 heard Bishop J. Weaver preach at Main St. Lutheran Church, John 7:46. "Never man spake," etc., a good sermon. Wrote on my address for the Convention.

Monday, October 24 Wrote all forenoon on my address. Go in afternoon to the convention. At 2:05 address the convention for 42 minutes. W.B. Stoddard spoke about 20 minutes. Prof. David McDill spoke an hour and a third on what we know of the Lodges. D. McDill staid with us.

Tuesday, October 25 The Com. on Resolutions met at H. J. Becker's at 8:30. Convention at 9:30. Pres. S.P. Long of Lima College spoke on the Lodge & Family. Rev. Krehbeil and H.O. Hutton and Rev. T. Weyer & wife dine with us. It is open parliament in the afternoon. W.R. Sterrill at supper and lodging. Pres. C.A. Blanchard spoke about 80 min in eve. on Contract of Church & Lodge.

Wednesday, October 26 Went to town in the forenoon. Called at Young's 5 min. and bought bi-focal spectacles at New Salts—$2.00. Wrote letters in Aftern.

Thursday, October 27 At home all day writing up Van Cleve genealogy, at request.

Saturday, October 29 Spent the day in writing up the Van Cleve Ancestry for C. Herbert Allen.

Sunday, October 30 At 10:30 railroad or show [?] time, I heard Rev. McCabe pr. at Raper Chapel Gal. 6.18, a good sermon. In the afternoon, at 3:30, I heard Rev. Elijah P. Brown tell the story of his conversion from infidelity at Association Hall. Called a half-hour at Lorin's on my return. Brown an editor of "Ram's Horn."

Monday, October 31 Wrote up Reeder ancestry for Richard Braden of Watseka, Illinois.

Wednesday, November 2 At home reading. Mr. Young sent me a copy of Mr. McMahon's Brief in the U.S. Ap[p]eal case.

Friday, November 4 At home in the forenoon. Sent $40.00 in Afternoon to pay my Grant Co. land tax. Called at Mrs. Sarah Swayne's my Mother's cousin, now 82 years old. She lives on Bainbridge St., near Fifth St.

Sunday, November 6 Heard Rev. Ross F. Wicks at his church on Conover St,. at 10:30, on the Good Samaritan. At home the rest of the day reading.

Tuesday, November 8 Voted about 9:00. Rev. D.H. Flickinger came at 10:00 & went on the 11:30 train to

Union City. I went to town in afternoon and bought a chair for Milton and a plate each for him and Ivonette. Called at Young's and found him busy.

Wednesday, November 9 Election news indicate a pretty large Republican victory & later returns increase it.

Saturday, November 12 At home till evening. Go on 4:30 tr. to Richmond and stay at D.K. Zeller's.

Sunday, November 13 Attended 19th St. Presbyterian Church & heard Rev. Stanley Hughes pr. at 10:30 on "The Heavenly vision," Acts 26:19. Dine at John G. Zeller's. Call at Allen Harris's an hour in afternoon. Supper & lodgings at D.K. Zeller's. Called on Peter Albert about an hour in the evening.

Monday, November 14 Came home on 8:05 train.

Wednesday, November 16 At home. Called at Young's five minutes.

Thursday, November 17 At home. Wrote out some ideas of our U.S. Argument.

Friday, November 18 Took my type-writer to the agent to cleanse and repair. Called at Young's and left him a statement of our argument. Lorin and Netta called in the evening.

Saturday, November 19 Called at Rev. H.J. Becker's in the forenoon. I was at home the rest of the day. Flora Greenwood and Eva Keiter called in the evening.

Sunday, November 20 Laboring under quite a cold, I thought best to remain indoors to-day; and I spent the day in reading.

Tuesday, November 22 At home. Called in afternoon at Young's but he was attending a trial in Court. Spent an hour in the Library in afternoon.

Wednesday, November 23 Spent the day largely in reading in "Historical Recollections of Massachusetts." Visited the Library in the afternoon. It is a pleasant day, tho' rather cold.

Thursday, November 24 To-day Lorin and family dined with us.

Friday, November 25 Went to Young's (5m) and to the Library in the afternoon. Spent several hours in the evening in rearranging my books and pamphlets, they having been disarranged by the woman who cleaned up my room.

Saturday, November 26 Spent some hours in assorting pamphlets. Went to Young's in the forenoon—spent about 15 minutes. Sat up till about 11 o'clock putting to rights scattered pamphlets and tracts.

Sunday, November 27 Heard in the forenoon, Rev. Mr. Wones at Broadway M.E. Church on Temperance. Heard Dr. H.J. Becker at 1:30 address the children in the annex of the Broadway Church on Jerusalem. Heard at 3:30 the Yale students at Association Hall. Heard Becker on Temperance at Broadway, 7:30.

Monday, November 28 Went to Young's at 11:00. Dr. Becker called about 7:00. Wrote letters to H.C. Horsman, Lee Hoisington and R.W. White.

Tuesday, November 29 Called at Young's. Went to post-office. Got business ready to go to Cincinnati tomorrow. Dr. Becker called in the evening.

Wednesday, November 30 Went on 8:00 train to Cincinnati with G.R. Young and H.J. Becker to argue the Fairview Church case in U.S. Court of Appeals. Mr. Young spoke 40 min on it. Dine at restaurant. I call at F.H. Short 's. We put up at the Gibson House. Becker went home.

Thursday, December 1 Mr. Young resumed and spoke an hour and 10 m. L.B. Gunckel followed & spoke over an hour. John A. McMahon followed and spoke till adjournment. We remain at the Gibson House. Called in eve. at Robt. Clark's and bought a revised Bible with revised references.

Friday, December 2 Mr. McMahon spoke another hour. Mr. Young spoke an hour and a half and closed at 12:00. All spoke ably. Mr. Young outdid himself to-day. We dined at the Gibson, went on to Hamilton. Called at

Thos. Milligan's, and went on to Dayton, reaching home by 6:00.

Saturday, December 3 At home. Wrote letter to J. Noel and to R.W. White. Went to town at 4:00, called on Young three minutes & at Library. Read till late, in Bancroft's Hist. U.B. Wilbur & Kath. went to the Ten Dayton Boys' Anniversary.

Sunday, December 4 Attended 4th Presbyterian Church & heard Rev. [blank] Dodds pr. Hebr. 2.1–4. An inclement day. I preached at 7:30, Gen. 49.10. "Unto Him xx gathering xx people be." [xx appears in text] Rainy evening.

Friday, December 9 At home. Went to town in the afternoon. Saw Young one minute, called at the Library, and at Gas office. Katie's class in Literature met at our house. Wrote letters to-day.

Saturday, December 10 At home all day except a walk out and call at Lorin's in the eve.

Sunday, December 11 I was at home all day—not very well. I read much and slept some, as my sleep had been short the past two nights when I sat up very late reading.

Saturday, December 17 Went to Library and Bank and Post-office before noon, to Becker's & Cook's in the aftern.

Sunday, December 18 Heard Rev. C.W. Gullett pr. at Grace M.E. Church at 10:30, Ex. 33:14, a fine discourse. He is the finest orator in Dayton. At 3:30, Heard Prof. Henderson of Chicago University lecture at Association Hall on "The Young Man in Social Service." A poor speaker & poor lecture, it was.

Monday, December 19 I have quite a cold. I write up the Van Cleve ancestry for Richard Braden.

Tuesday, December 20 My cold is somewhat troublesome. Rev. S.L.Livingston dines with us. He has just completed the sale of most of his town land, here.

Wednesday, December 21 Katharine got word to come

over to High School and teach as a substitute and went. I sent sketches of the Reeder and Van Cleve ancestry to Gabriella Evick, Niles, Mich.

Thursday, December 22 Called at Lorin's. I have a troublesome influenza cold.

Friday, December 23 My cold perhaps abates a little.

Saturday, December 24 Margaret Goodwin came in the afternoon. I spent the day closely taking Notes on the old Journal of Indiana Conference.

Sunday, December 25 Attended the First Pres. Church and at 10:30 heard Rev. Maurice Wilson pr. Gal. 4:4, a Christmas Sermon. Not much of a sermon.

Monday, December 26 Sent an application for Joint Clergy Certificate. Read up and thought up the question whether the washing of the disciples' feet was at Bethany of Jerusalem and conclude that it was at Bethany.

Tuesday, December 27 Wrote to Harvey, my brother. Went to Library & bank & post office in the afternoon.

Wednesday, December 28 Nothing of special interest. I am very busy writing.

Saturday, December 31 At home. Margaret Goodwin left about 10:00 for her school at Canal Dover. The year just closing has been eventful. A great but brief war with decisive victories on Sea and land. Liberation of Cuba, cession of Puerto Rico, Philipines, and Guam. Treaty of Paris signed. Hawaii annexed. Unprecedented imports, great crops and great prosperity. In its course Prince Bismark and (the greater) Gladstone passed away. The Queen of Holland is assassinated. Crete secures independence of Turkish tyranny.

Connecticut *Register of Soldiers in the Revolution, Dayton Public Library.* On page 509, the name of Dan Wright ocurs, as of Captain Skinner's Company, Col. Jonathan Lattimer's Regiment; which fought in the Campaign, 1777, against Burgoyne, in Gen. Schuyler's (afterward Gates') army. The Connecticut regiments suffered more severely than any others, at Bemis H[e]ights, Sept. 19, 1777, and this was the decisive battle of the campaign. Mr. Wright was in the Army from August 25, 1777 till November 8th. He was 20 years old the preceeding Apr. 7th. I have heard my father say that his father (Dan Wright, Senior) was in this battle, Bemis Height. In the Connecticut Soldier's Register, page 167, Daniel Wright is registered as having enlisted Sept. 29, 1779, and having been discharged Jan. 15th; but this was not my grandfather, whose name was Dan, not Daniel. Milton Wright, Dec. 26, 1898.

Van Cleve; Revolution "Men in Revolution from New Jersey." Dayton Pub. Library, Genealogical Department. *Page 795* Record of John Van Cleve of Monmouth, as a soldier. Page 415, registered as a captain, John Van Cleve of Monmouth. Page 57 & p. 64: Col. David Forman; as Col. of "Forman's Regiment" in Continental Army; also Brig. General of Militia. See Irivng on gen. battle. Feb. 28, 1720, Benjamin Van Cleve was grandjuryman of Quarter sessions, held at Freehold, N.J. He was not our ancestor Banjamin, who was born in 1712. It may have been an uncle or cousin (Since) It was an uncle.

Edmund Freeman as a Soldier My Great-grandfather, Edmund Freeman, was a Revolutionary Soldier from New Hampshire, and commanded a company in the Saratoga Campaign, and was present at the Surrender of Burgoyne. (See Rev. Frederick Freeman's Genealogy of the Freeman family, page 119, and eulogy on 120 page. Edmund was Frederick's uncle, and my father's estimate of Edmund was very high.

Milton Wright, Dec. 22, 1989.

1899

Sunday, January 1 It is a moderately cold day. I am in my 71st year. To-day I was at Dunkard Church on Amity or Fourth and College St., at Sabbath School & at Preaching. Rev. Hoover pr. at 10:30, a New Year discourse, on the Supreme Need of the Present. To-day the American Flag is raised in Havana.

Tuesday, January 3 I spent the day closely, writing an article on the perpetuity of the Decalogue, especially in citing quotations from eminent men maintaining this view. The weather is very mild.

Wednesday, January 4 I awakened early, read some in Science Primer on Physics, while in bed. Got up at 5:45. Drank a pint of hot water for health. In the night, there had been a little rain, and the morning is cloudy with a considerable breeze. I receive and answer important letters.

Thursday, January 5 Mild day. I am busy writing letters. Lorin, wife, and children call in the evening. Katharine is at the G.H. Club. Wilbur attends the meeting of the School Board. After many ballots, Miss Hall and Mr. [blank] are elected High School Teachers.

Friday, January 6 About three inches of snow fell in the night. The weather is cold but milder. Katharine went to see Mr. Werthner about the position of Librarian at High School, but he had already recommended one. In the evening, Katie attends her literary class at Women's League.

Saturday, January 7 In the night there was an inch of snow fell, and in the morning the window panes were beautifully frescoed by the frost. I wrote letters. I got my Clergy Certificate to day from Central Pas.Association. Wrote an article in the evening on Self Denial Week.

Sunday, January 8 Weather moderate. I called an hour in the forenoon at Samuel Spidel's on King Street. He is to move to his son John Frederick's near Home Ave., Puterbaugh Cluster. In the evening, I attend Grace M.E. Church and hear the P.E. Rev. J.F. Harley on John 4:4 a good sermon.

Monday, January 9 Wrote letters in the forenoon. Went over the river in the afternoon, and bought presents for Lorin's family etc. etc. Lorin's & children spent an hour with us in the evening; Milton has fun with his jumping lion & Ivonette with her wooly dog.

Tuesday, January 10 Went over the river and paid my tax and got the number for our house. Rev. T. Weyer took dinner with us. He tells me of Shem Thomas' death this morning, in Germantown, aged 90 years & 9 months.

Wednesday, January 11 Weather moderate. Wrote letters and read some. In the evening I walked over to town and back, mainly for the walk.

Thursday, January 12 Weather thawing. Went on 9:00 traction to Franklin, missed connection & walked to Germantown, and dined at S. Thomas'. At 1:30, I preached Shem Thomas' funeral, Ps. 90:12. Rev. Thos. Weyer assists. Present: C.B. McDaniel, Huber, Burket & other preachers. Supper at Mother Thomas'. I stay at

Rev. T. Weyer's. S. Thomas was just 90 yrs. & 9 mo.

Friday, January 13 After a rainy night, I stay at Weyer's till 11:00, Write Thomas' obituary. It quit raining. I dine at L. Wett's, and at 1:30 preach his wife's funeral at the U.B. Ch. assisted by T. Weyer. Matt. 5:12. Burial, as yesterday, 3/4 m. W. of Church. Supper at Lewis Wett's. Lodge at T. Weyer's. Called at C.B. McDaniel's in fore-noon.

Saturday, January 14 Stay at Weyer's till 10:30. Dine at Chas. Colthard's & remain till 5:00. Call a half hour at Mother Thomas' and Stay at Chas. B. McDaniel 's. She is in very bad health.

Sunday, January 15 Preached at the Church at 10:30, Ps. 73.24. Dine at Lewis Wett's. Sophia Zehring & Lizzie Long are there. Supper there. Rev. T. Weyer pr. at 7:00, 85 Ps. 6v. I go to Swartzel's & lodge.

Monday, January 16 Bro. Swartzel takes me to Miamisburg & I get home on Traction line about noon. Write letters.

Tuesday, Janaury 17 At home in forenoon writing let-ters and reading. Go to H.J. Becker's, Jacob Swank's, and Joseph Richley's, in the afternoon. Write letters in the evening.

Wednesday, January 18 Write Ronch twice to-day. Dr. D.K. Flickinger came at 10:00 to consult over question of Wilberforce being ordered to America for a vacation and consultation. He goes at 1:00 to Miamisburg. Lorin & the children came in the evening and had a good time singing and playing.

Thursday, January 19 Wrote letters and read in the fore-noon. Went to town in the afternoon. Wrote out a record of the Minutes of the Board of Bishops for the Quadreninium for the years 1889 1893.

Friday, January 20 Weather fair. At home. Wrote many letters. Went in Afternoon to see the doctor, and paid Young a check for $300.00 for services in U.S. Case. Wrote again in the evening. Lorin and children called.

Saturday, January 21 Went on 9:25 tr. to Richmond

and thence by Anderson to Fairmount. Meet R.W. White & Jas. Rector & go with them to Quar. Conf. at Union; Payne's Child's funeral, instead. Kinneman rants & roars. Go to White's on our farm for supper. Pr. at 7:00, at Hopewell, Ps. 73:21,22. Lodge at Oliver Buller's.

Sunday, January 22 Call at Ellis Wright 's. Preach at Hopewell Church at 10:30, Zech. 13:9. Dine with [blank] Fear, 2 m. s.e. Preach at 7:00, John 1.17. House is overcrowded. I lodge at John Corn's, 1 mile west.

Monday, January 23 I went to R.W. White's. Wrote out contract on renting the farm. Went on 1:01 tr. to Fairmount, and made Hasty connection for Wabash & Huntington. Saw Mrs. George H. Dunn of Shelbyville, Ind., who told me of Tom. Adams, Esq. & Benj. Love, Esq. & of Bilman's. Lodge at A.G. Johnson's.

Tuesday, January 24 Called at Bailey's next house to Etna Ave. Ch. Went to Publ. Estab. Dine with Flickinger at Coolman's. Go to A.G. Johnson 's. I.M. Tharp came & we had an Ex. Com. Meeting at the Publ. Est. at 3:00. I sup & lodge with Tharp at C.H. Kiracofe's.

Wednesday, January 25 Attended prayers at the College at 8:15. Went to town at 9:00. Tharp went home. Dine at Wm. Dillon's and remain till morning. See Kiracofe at the College at 9:00. Next morning, go on 11:07 train to Ft. Wayne & thence to Wooster. See Mahlon Rouch, Esq. at his home. Lodge at the Hotel.

Friday, January 27 Go on 7:00 train to Canton. Call at John Noel's. Call with Noel's son at Allen Cook's. Go on 10:15 train to Orrville & thence via Columbus & Xenia home to Dayton arriving about 5:00. Read many letters.

Saturday, January 28 At home reading many letters and answering a few; also other reading. Lizzie Long called in the afternoon, to get some Oregon letters she had sent by mail relating to May Ling's Chinese School. Lorin callld.

Sunday, January 29 Arose at six o'clock. Got ready for meeting. Heard Rev. Carl Summerbell preach on Eph. 5.19. He is a pleasant, but not able or earnest speaker.

Thursday, February 2 At home. Rev. T. Weyer & wife called before noon. Katharine was sent for by Prof. Werthner to teach the succeeding weeks in High School for Prof. Eastman.

Friday, February 3 Kath. attended Eastman's recitations preparatory to taking his Classes while he is away. Rev. H.J. Becker called an hour. Thinks of a trip around the world. Is sanguine of making his arbitration scheme a means of leveling the Liberals.

Saturday, February 4 At home. Wrote letters. Aguinaldo attacks the Americans at Manilla, and begins the Phillipine War.

Sunday, February 5 At Memorial Reform Church, I heard Rev. D. Burghalter on Matt. 16.18, a good sermon. At 3:30, heard Pres. W.O. Thompson's address on "International Relations," and at 8:00 John P. Quinn give an *exposé* of gambling, both at Asln. Hall. In the forenoon the battle of Manilla continues. Insurgents defeated.

Monday, February 6 News of the battle of Manilla comes. It was Sat. eve. & Sunday. In the afternoon, news comes that the U.S. Senate has ratified the American Spanish treaty by a vote of 57 to 27. Republicans in the negative: Hale, Hoar; and Pettigrew, Populist. Kath. began to teach Prof. Eastman's classes in Latin to-day.

Tuesday, February 7 At home. In the afternoon, returned Hist. Huguenot Emigr. & took out Vol. VI, of Annals of Amer. Pulpit. Sketch of John and Stephen Gano, descendants of Francis Gerneaux, a Huguenot from Rochelle, France. (John Gano is found to be a younger brother of Susan Gano.)

Sunday, February 12 Thermometer ran to 23 below. Heard Pres. W.O. Thompson preach at 4th Presb. Church, Ps. 51.11,12, On Joy of Salvation. A good preacher he is, but not a good orator. In the afternoon at 3:30, I heard Dr. W.O. Thompson on "Your Relations", at Y.M.C.A. Hall. After meeting, Questions: Allows his little boys to play checkers Sunday afternoon. Discards progressive end.

Wednesday, February 15 Thermometer rises a little. At home. Col. Robt. Cowden called in the evening.

Thursday, February 16 Weather fair. Thermometer, 38. At home. The weather has changed to thawing. Rev. J.V. Potts, of North Robinson, Ohio, called and spent the day with me. Went to the library & got out Ossian's Poems.

Saturday, February 18 Weather, cloudy. Thermometer 36 degrees. I received a check (draft) from Lee Hoisington for $287.70 cents on corn, wheat and grass, on Adair farm. Went to town in the afternoon and paid gas bill and deposited $280 in Com. Nat. Bank. Wrote letters.

Sunday, February 19 Heard Rev. C.W. Gullette pr. Matt. 6:28. He did not preach the text, but made good points illustrated by the lilly. Heard at 3:30 Pres. W.O. Thompson on Inspiration on our Relations. Lorin's children came up awhile in the evening.

Monday, February 20 Arose 5:45. Go on 8:00 trac. car to Franklin, and thence to Germantown. Dined at Rev. C.W. McDaniel's (at Levi Zehring's); and, at 2:00, preached Mrs. McDaniel's fureral, Gen. 24:67, at our Church & Huber & T. Weyer made some remarks. After supper at McDaniel's, went home on the R.R. & Traction lines. Read carefully the Book of Habakkuk.

Tuesday, February 21 At home. Feel rather dull. Spent some time in examining my Diary of 1879, & retracing parts written with pencil, or with dim ink.

Wednesday, February 22 Washington's birth-day, & there is no High School to-day.

Friday, February 24 Katharine gets through teaching as a substitute for Prof. Eastman, in the High Sc[h]ool.

Saturday, February 25 Went on 8:00 Traction to Franklin & thence to Germantown. Dine at Rev. T. Weyer's— Rev. W.E. Strete there; also supper at Weyer's. Strete preached at 3:00, Ps. 16.8. Qr. Conf. followed. Strete pr. at 7:00, Isa. 36.5. I stay at Rev. C.B. McDaniel's.

Sunday, February 26 Talk with Levi Zehring. Strete pr. a good sermon at 10:30, Isa. 40.11. I dine at Lewis Wett's.

Sarah Iseley is keeping house for him. Praise Meeting at 2:30. Quite good. Strete & I sup at Mother Long's. I pr. at 7:00, Matt. 26.25. I stay at T. Weyer's. My sermon is rather tame.

Monday, February 27 I call at Mother Thomas's, Sophia Zehring's, & C.B. McDaniels'. Go on 10:07 train via Franklin, home arriving at 12:30. At home the rest of the day.

Tuesday, February 28 At home reading, writing and resting. Katharine is still teaching at Miss Thomas's School four lessons a week.

Wednesday, March 1 Robert Sutton, Agent of the Indianapolis Gas Co., calls to lease our Grant Co. farm for gas & oil. I did not lease.

Saturday, March 4 At home. Lorin & Milton called in the evening. Congress LIV, Adjourned about noon, after the opposition had defeated or modified several valuable measures.

Sunday, March 5 Attended Memorial Pres. Ch. Communion. Dr. W.O. Thompson preached. In Afternoon, I heard at 3:30, Pres. W.O. Thompson lecture on Our Institutional Relations.

Monday, March 6 At home. Lorin & Nettie called in the evening.

Tuesday, March 7 At home. Heard, by a letter from Young, that the decision of United States Court of Appeals, Cincinnati, is against us. Decision rendered today. Wrote letters.

Thursday, March 9 Walked down to Miami Chapel to see the graves of Otis & Ida, a walk of three miles; also Rev. Wm. R. Rhinehart's grave. His monument is a plain stone slab about 4 ft 4 in. high, 22 inches wide, and 1 1/2 inches thick with only these words: "William R. Rhinehart, died May 9, 1861, aged 60 years, 6 mo & 11 days."

Friday, March 10 Sent for Tribune Almanac, etc. Called at Lorin's.

Saturday, March 11 Go at 3:00 on Dayton & Western Traction cars to Johnsville and thence to Olivet. George W. Warvel's married son meets me at cross roads (Crawford's) 1 mile west of Johnsville. I sup & lodge at Warvel's. I teach Bible Class at Church; 24th & 25th Chapters Matt.

Sunday, March 12 Rev. Thomas Weyer preaches at 10:30, Ps. 66.18. We dine at Warvel's. At 3:00, I teach a Bible Class at Olivet, John 13th Chap. Supper at Aaron Wysong's. At 7:00 I preach, Heb. 12:1,2. We stay at G. Warvel's.

Monday, March 13 Rev. T. Weyer takes me to Brookvill[e], and I go on 9:10 traction car to Dayton. Went to Town & to the Library. Called at Young's and he not in.

Tuesday, March 14 Spend considerable part of the day in looking over my accounts. Lorin's children spent the evening with us.

Wednesday, March 15 Dr. H.J. Becker called an hour or two in the forenoon.

Thursday, March 16 Rev. T. Weyer & wife took dinner with us.

Friday, March 17 Went to town. Saw Young a few minutes. Called at Lorin's in the evening.

Saturday, March 18 Went on 7:00 M. tr. via Arcanum & New Castle to May's Station, where Harvey Wright met me and took me to his house. I pr. at Baptist Monthly meeting at 3:00, John XIII.27, on The Betheny Supper. Stay at Harvey 's.

Sunday, March 19 I pr. at 10:30, Rev. 1.5,6. Dine at Luther Newhouse's. His Father called. Return to Harvey 's. Drucilla & Gusta called, & Effie. I stay at Harvey 's.

Monday, March 20 Go to John McKee's with Harvey, Delilah, and Eva. Stay till 4:00. Then Harvey & I call at Eva Wright's. John's and Thomas's. Stay at Harvey 's.

Tuesday, March 21 Go with Thomas to Rushville. See James F. Harris, my nephew at the Court-house. Write

& mail letters. Go on 12:02 tr. to Glenwood. Lucinda Moor meets me and takes me to her house. I stay there.

Wednesday, March 22 Go with Lucinda to Harry Winchell's, and to Charles Steven's. We stay there till about 5:00. Go to Moor's, examine old papers. Stay there. Nicholas Francis Bowen & Sarah Catharine live with Lucinda.

Thursday, March 23 Ralph Bowen takes me to Glenwood. We call at Alex. Matney's, Glenwood. I go on 12:02 tr. via Hamilton home, arriving at 3:00. In eve. attend the Am. Sabbath Union Convention at Park Pres. Ch. at 7:30. I spoke on the "Civil Sabbath."

Friday, March 24 Sabbath Observance Convention at 9:30, 2:00, & 7:30. I sup at Col. Robt. Cowden's. The addresses at the convention were generally very good. A Mr. Veasley of "Zion" and Rev. J.G. Wood, Seventh Day Adventist, were present & spoke.

Saturday, March 25 I spent the day at home. Milton came up in the afternoon, and staid till after supper. I took Nell, (bird dog) home in evening. Battle in Philippines, toward Rolo.

Sunday, March 26 Heard Rev. C.W. Gullette, pastor of Grace M.E. Church, preach from John 13.34, an able and very eloquent sermon. At home the rest of the day, except a short call at Lorin's.

Monday, March 27 At home in the forenoon. In the Afternoon, called on Young, at the Carpet Store, a few minutes, and bought four shirts at Elder and Johnson's at $2.07. This was Tuesday's record.

Wednesday, March 29 Go to town in the forenoon. Leave Young a check of $300 on U.S. Case. Get ready to start to Ontario, and start at 2:35 via Toledo & Port Huron. Mrs. Henry Simons died to-night, I afterward learned.

Thursday, March 30 Reach Berlin, Ont., about 5:00, Morn. D.B. Sherk meets us and takes Dr. Flickinger and me to his house to breakfast. Went in a sleigh. I call on Rosenberger, where F's home is & get "Americus Vespucius," Conference opened at 2:00. Dr. F. Pr. at

8:00, "Because I live ye shall live also." My home at Sherk's.

Friday, March 31 Conference Continued. Henry A. Brubaker and Simon H. Swartz joined Conference. Flickinger Spoke on Africa, and the Women's Aid took up a collection: $13.00+. I stay at Sherk's.

Saturday, April 1 Conference Continued. Flick. & I dine at Rev. J.B. Bowman's. Stationing Com. met there. We took Supper at Mrs. I.L. Bowman's. W.M. As. held a meeting at night. I stay at Sherk's.

Sunday, April 2 I pr. at 10:45, Rev. 1.5,6. Coll. amounted to over $45.00. ($45.21). We dine at Rev. A.F. Stoltz's, at Orphan's Home. S.S. Anniv. at 3:00. Supper at W.H. Becker's. I pr. at 7:00, Rev. 1.18. Stay at Sherk's.

Monday, April 3 Start at 11:00, via Pt. Huron & Detroit & Toledo, and reach home at 5:00 next morning.

Tuesday, April 4 Reach home about 5:00, and remain at home all day, sleeping a couple of hours.

Wednesday, April 5 A home. Called at Lorin's in the evening. He is having sore throat and sore eyes.

Thursday, April 6 Telegram from Katherine that she would not be at home till Sat. at 5: I call at Lorin's. He is better.

Friday, April 7 Feel rather weak to day. It is a day of slight rain.

Saturday, April 8 Moses Nigh, converted Jew of Newark, Ohio, came in forenoon, saying "The Lord has sent me here." Katharine came home from Canal Dover about 5 o'clock. Got a letter from Mrs. Semele Short, saying Susana Guno, our ancestress was an older sister of Rev. John Gano.

Sunday, April 9 At 10:30 I attended Rev. Jas. Monroe Gilmore's, a M.E. Church on Eaker St., and heard Moses Nigh, the "converted Jew". Residence, 214 Maple St. At 3:30, heard Rev. Maurice E. Wilson on Athletic sports at Asso'n Hall. At 6:15, heard Paul M.C.Liu, Christian Chinaman, educated at DePauw University.

Monday, April 10 Went to town. Walked over with J.V. Potts and H.A. Thompson. Did not see Geo. Young.

Tuesday, April 11 Went to town afternoon. Saw Young five minutes about taking case up to Supr. Ct. U.S. Walk with Thompson. Start at 6:20, via Cincinnati and Huntington, W.Va., to Long Glade, Va. I Walked from town with H.A. Thomspon, in the Afternoon, car fare & St. cars, $7.00.

Wednesday, April 12 Reach Staunton, Va. at 11:06. H.W. Lindamood & Mrs.[blank], M. Knott's daughter, meet me and take me to Palmer House. John J. Stotamyer meets me there and takes me to Spring Hill (Long Glade) and I find my home at Rev. J.E. Hott's, with G.S. Seiple. W.J. Funkhouser pr. at 8:00.

Thursday, April 13 Conference opened at 9:00 (10:00) and proceeded. H.W. Lindamood preached at 8:00. Hott's family are J.E. Hott, aged 52; Nettie, his wife; children: Guy DeWitt 24, Mary Estelle, 12, Blair Hulvey, 9; Alpha Hazel 8; Charley Hughes, 7; Ion Von Kert, 18 m.

Friday, April 14 Conference continued. Hott was elected P.E. & A.H. Shanholtz on the stationing com. Stationing Committee met at Hott's at 5:00. Shanholtz & I walked to the Middle River Bridge, and called at Mr. Connell's.

Saturday, April 15 Conference continued. G.S. Seiple preached at 8:00, Isa. 52.1. Conference closed after preaching.

Sunday, April 16 Testimony meeting continued till 11:00. I Preach, Titus 3.4,5,6. Dine at J.T. Ewing's. Rev. G.S. Seiple preached at 3:00, [blank] at the Pres. Church. I preach in the eve. 8:00, Matt. 16.18, last clause. Stay at Hott's.

Monday, April 17 Met W.J. Funkhouser at Mr——'s. [line appears in text] Bro. Thomas Burton, takes me and Seiple to Staunton, & we sup at Palmer House. I go on 7:05 train (eastern time) to Cincinnati. Slept 4 or 5 hours. Awaked at Kanova; saw the way to Cin. along the Ohio River. Reached Dayton at 10:00 next morn.

Tuesday, April 18 Reached Dayton at 10:00. At home the rest of the day.

Wednesday, April 19 At home. Called at Lorin's a few minutes in the evening.

Thursday, April 20 At home. Went to town in the forenoon, Paid gas bill, $8.25. Got a draft to pay Iowa tax, $65.00. Saw Tizzard. Am to see him Monday at 2:00 on a tooth cap.

Friday, April 21 Went to town. In Afternoon, walked into North Dayton and Geo. R. Young & Mother brought me home, from near the old Wm. Ferguson place. Mrs. Ferguson was my Mother's cousin. Reuben Reeder's daughter.

Saturday, April 22 Went to town in forenoon; also to Jac. Swanks in the evening.

Sunday, April 23 Heard Rev. Grant, of Sprague St. Baptist Church on Rom. Eth. Ch. on death to sin and on Baptism (Colored Baptist). In the afternoon, called at John Weidner's & Silvester Spidel's. Weidner lives on Kilmer St.north of 2nd, S. Spidel lives at Mathison & first Sts.

Monday, April 24 Went to dentists at 2:00, & got gold cap renewed on my teeth, but it was unsuccessful. Went after Supper to John Frederick Spidel's on Putterbaugh Avenue, 7th house north of Home Ave. Afternoon, sent $65.00 to Greenfield, Iowa, to pay taxes.

Tuesday, April 25 At home. Called at Henrietta Sophia Simpson's, 227 W. McPherson St. She is a second cousin. Went in the eve to see Samuel Spidel at J.F. Spidel's, Putterbaugh Ave.

Thursday, April 27 Went on 10:45 train to Tadmor, and thence by Phoneton to Catherine McFadden's. She is nearly 84 years of age. I saw in Bethel Church Cemetery the tombstones of Grandfather Dan Wright & of his wife, of Asahel Wright & his wife, etc. Returned. Called at Mary Inglehart's. Dr. H.J. Becker calls.

Friday, April 28 At home. Called a minute at Lorin's. Wrote to Ex. Com.

Saturday, April 29 Started at 7:00, Morning, for Fairmount, via Union and Gas Cities. Ride out with Shoemaker's children to Shoemaker's, and then with Mrs. Harris to Robt. W. White's on my farm. After supper, White takes me to Wm. H.H. Reeder's. Stayed there.

Sunday, April 30 Called at Robt. B. Reeder's. O.A. Glass takes me to Hopewell. I pr. at 11:00, Matt. 24.3. Dine at Oliver Glass'. At 8:00, pr. at Hopewell, Rom. 5:8. I stay at Oliver Buller's.

Monday, May 1 I spent the forenoon at Ellis Wright's. Go to R.W. White's. He takes me to Oliver Glass' & I go after supper to R.B. Reeder's. I lodge there.

Tuesday, May 2 Call at Wm. Reeder's and at Ellis Wright's. I dine at R.W. White's; Oliver A. Glass concludes to tend the north field. White takes me to Edmund Duling's and thence to Fairmount. Supper at Vergil Hollingsworth's Wm. Hall's. I stay at Clinton Brattain's. I felt rather unwelcome.

Wednesday, May 3 Call at Mrs. Charles Atkinson's. Go on 8:50 train to Wabash and thence to Huntington. I dine at Rev. Wm. Dillon's, who has bought one square N.E. of the M.E. Church. Meet Ex. Com. at 3:00, at Publ. Establ. Supper at Keiter's. Go to prayer meeting at College. Stay at Dr. C.H. Kiracofe's.

Thursday, May 4 Call at Rev. A.B. Lilly's. Attend & led college prayers. Have a meeting of the Ex. Com. Publ. at A.G. Johnson' s. Go on 11:12 train to Ft. Wayne & thence to Lima. Saw Rev. A.J. Steman there. Got home before 7:00, to Dayton.

Sunday, May 7 Heard Rev. J. Wilbur Chapman at 3:30, at Association Hall.

Monday, May 8 A[t] 2:00 at Dr. Tizzard's and he took an impression for a new upper plate in my mouth.

Wednesday, May 10 Took Milton & Ivonette to Young's Office, from the window of which they saw Col. Cody's Wild West show; "Buffalo Bill" headed the procession. Went to town again about 4:00 Depot, Gas Office, Young's, Tizzard's.

Thursday, May 11 Got my revulcanized plate. Went on 9:53 tr. to Bellefontaine to Judge Wm. Lawrence's funeral with G.R. Young from Springfield. Dined at Hotel. Masonic Knights officiate. Haviland meets us. Patterson takes us out to the cemetery. Arrive at Dayton at 8:00. Supper at Springfield.

Friday, May 12 At home forenoon. Go to town afternoon. Saw Young. Bought garbage box.

Saturday, May 13 Went to town, mailed letters, paid Tizzard in full for dentistry $2.50. Looked into law library. In the afternoon, about 4:00 went to Young's and examined books. Got Desty's Federal Proceedings (Eighth Edition), & read some in it at home.

Sunday, May 14 At 3:30, heard Moses Nigh at Association Hall. Lorin & Milton & Ivonett[e] came up and stayed a half hour.

Tuesday, May 16 Mr. & Mrs. Short came on Director's car and I met them & visited them on the car & with Katharine lunched with them on the car. They came at 9:50 & returned on 12:50 train.

Wednesday, May 17 Went on the 1:00 Traction train to Miamisburg. Rev. T. Weyer takes me to Germantown to Lewis Wetz. I call at Rev. Coulthard's & McDaniel's in the evening. Supper and lodging at Wetz.

Thursday, May 18 L. Wetz gives me $1000.00 to be used as follows: $400 for Parent Board of missions, $300 for Central College, $200 to pay on Publishing House; $100 for U.S. Legal Fund. I immediately mailed a draft for $900 to S.A. Steman, to be put in the respective treasuries. Came home on 10:40 train.

Saturday, May 20 At home. Prof. John F. Peck of Oberlin came back from Hamilton (Cincinnati) in the afternoon. Maud Spitler, Dr. [blank] Steward, Agnes Osborn, & Katharine, had a supper for Prof. Peck at the Hotel Atlas.

Sunday, May 21 Heard Rev. C.W. Gullette, M.E., at 10:30, 2 Cor. 8.9. At home the rest of the day.

Monday, May 22 Carpenters have the house all torn up.

I went to town to Baughman's Bakery in the Afternoon.

Tuesday, May 23 Went to town. Called at Albert Shearer's Hardware Store.

Thursday, May 25 Went in the afternoon to Post office and bought postal-cards, & sent one to Pres. C.H. Kiracof[e]. Fixed on the type-writer a decoration address for Milton.

Friday, May 26 Wrote many letters. Went to town; saw Young. Called at Lorin's in the evening.

Saturday, May 27 Went to town at 11:00; cashed a check; bought a trunk ($4.25) & saw at Depot abt. times of trains. Went on 3:00 D&W Traction for Germantown, via W. Alexandria. Reach G. at 5:07, sup at C.B. McDaniel's, stay at Lewis Wetz. Sarah Esele, his house keeper.

Sunday, May 28 Call at Sarah Thomas' and at Sunday's. Pr at "10:30", Phil 2.5. Dine at Chas. Coulthard's & sup there. Pr. at "7:30", Mal. 3:1. Stay at Lewis Wetz.

Monday, May 29 Call at Levi Zehring's & at Mother Long's. Go on 11:07 tr. via W. Alexandria, arriving at home at "12:20."

Tuesday, May 30 Go out with Katharine and Milton to Woodland Cemetery to Susan's grave, and plant flowers. Milton had suggested to his mother that we should decorate his grandmother's grave.

Wednesday, May 31 Go to town twice—forenoon & evening.

Thursday, June 1 Called at Louding's to see if Wilberforce's family has come from Africa. No word from them. Wrote many letters. Katharine went at night to High School Commencement.

Friday, June 2 Went to town in forenoon. Made out my tax list in the afternoon. Katharine attended and served at Miss Thomas' reception of Patrons of her school.

Saturday, June 3 Carpenters are about to finish our kitchen. I paid gas bill etc. The Wilberforce's came about

10:00 from Africa. Sent a draft for $10.00 to Samuel Evans for Erie Mis. money.

Sunday, June 4 Peter Louding came about 7:30 A.M. informing me of the arrival of Mrs. Lizzie Wilberforce and her family from Africa. I telegraph to Rev. Wm. Dillon, Huntington, of their arrival yesterday morning. Heard Rev. Mr. Brown, agent Tract Society, pr. at Main St Lutheran Ch., Matt. 14.19,20.

Tuesday, June 6 Called to loan Mrs. Wilberforce $30.00. Afternoon called at Becker's, saw Jac. Swank, called at Mrs. Cook's.

Wednesday, June 7 At home writing on sermons most of the day. Called at P. Loudings to see if any of the Wilberforce's were going to the Board meeting.

Thursday, June 8 Went on 7:00 tr. via Greenville to Rockford. Call at W.E. Strete's. Went on to Allen W. Koeppel's. The Board meets at 8:00, W.H. Clay pr. the annual sermon 1 Cor. 13.6.

Friday, June 9 Meet a com. at 7:00, at A.A. Sutton's, Board met at 8:00, Becker pr at 8:00 (eve) on his mission round the world. I continue to Board at Koeppel's.

Saturday, June 10 The session of the Board closed at 11:00. I dine at A.C. Byce's. Rev. U. Miller takes us to Rockford. We go on 12:54 tr. to Van Wert & thence on 3:21 tr. to Fort Wayne. Lunch. Thence to Huntington, & I to Kiracofe's. Lodge there. Rev. L.B. Baldwin delivers the Annual address before the Literary Societies at 8:00.

Sunday, June 11 I preach at 10:30, Phil. 2.5. Spoke 48 minutes in Davis Memorial Hall. Dine at Joseph William Sell's. Pres. Chas. Hiram Kiracofe pr. the baccalaureate sermon at 3:00, 1 Cor. 12:31. Supper at J.A. Wildman's, C.L. Wood with me. Rev. H.J. Becker, at 8:00 pr. the Annual sermon, Sol. Songs, 4.4. I Lodge at Kiracofe's.

Monday, June 12 Council of Ex. Com. and Women of W.M.A. at 9:00. I dine at Prof. T.H. Gragg's. Board of Education meets at 2:00. Supper at S.A. Steman's. Glee Club Chorus at 8:00. I lodge at C.H. Kiracofe's, Rev.

Aaron Zehring being my bedfellow during all my stay at Huntington.

Tuesday, June 13 Publishing Establishment Board meets at 8:00, at Publ. House. I dine with D.K. Flickinger (at Coolmans) The Educational Board meets at 2:00 at the College. Floyd's financial plans carried, but on reconsideration were ejected. I sup at Rev. R.S. Bowman's Bish. Barnaby, too, Lit. entertainment 8:00. Lodge at Kirac[ofe's].

Wednesday, June 14 First College Commencement of C. College at 10:00, Joseph William Sell (Sci); Rufus A. Morrison & Elizabeth C. Zehring (clas course) graduating. All did well in Addresses. Allumnal dinner at Prof. James Henry McMurray's. After dinner speeches by myself, Bish. Barnaby, Flickinger. Supper at Kiracofe's. Musical concert at 8:00. Lodge at Kiracofe's.

Thursday, June 15 Bishops' Board meets at Prof. A.P. Barnaby's at 8:00. I and others go on 11:12 tr. to Ft. Wayne. Lunch. On 12:+ tr. to Richmond. Call at D.K. Zeller's. Reach Dayton about 6:30. Find all well.

Friday, June 16 Katharine and Miss M. Goodwin go at 9:45 for Toldeo & Oberlin. I get valises mended & buy Milton a knife. At home all the Afternoon.

Saturday, June 17 I was at home all day writing letters. Carpet for east room was brought and laid.

Sunday, June 18 Heard Dr. J.W. Simpson preach at Fourth Presbyterian Church. "Be of good courage." Called at Lorin's in the Afternoon. Called at P. Louding's & with him walked to the depot.

Monday, June 19 D.K. Flickinger came about noon, and I went with him to see Louding, and went with him to the depot. Wrote some letters.

Tuesday, June 20 Dr. H.J. Becker came and we called at P. Louding's to see the Wilberforce family. It rained in the evening.

Wednesday, June 21 Miss Mary Mullen came by with Peter Louding, going to Dr. H.J. Becker's.

Thursday, June 22 Becker and Miss Mullen came by. She much incensed at W. M. A . I go with her to Louding's and to the depot. I call at Dr. Beckers in the afternoon.

Friday, June 23 Called in the forenoon and engaged the pat[t]ern of carpet for to-morrow Van Ansdal's. In the evening I walked out to Allen H. Reeder's, 707 Superior Ave.

Saturday, June 24 Went to Louding's and the bank in the forenoon. Carpet for the sitting room came and was laid in the afternoon. Dr. Becker called after supper.

Sunday, June 25 In afternoon went to Junior League of Trinity Church (M.E.) and came by Woodland Cemetery home.

Tuesday, June 27 Rev. J.V. Potts supped with us. Paid Mr. J.G. Feight 168.52 for our kitchen.

Wednesday, June 28 Wrote & received letters. Went to town in the Afternoon & bought envelopes & postage. Rev. J.V. Potts called in the forenoon & dined with us.

Thursday, June 29 Rev. J.V. Potts called & staid most of the forenoon. He proposes to take work with us. In the evening, I called at Dr. H.J. Becker's.

Friday, June 30 At home writing. In the evening, I went to the post office and called to talk with Mr. & Mrs. Louding about rates of boarding for Wilberforce's famly. Nothing definite was proposed.

Saturday, July 1 Wrote letters. Went to the bank, Deposited $400.00 received of the boys, and saved out $100.00. Paid $13.20 to Van Ansdall on carpets & $20.90 to Beacham for painting & papering. Go on 2:35 tr. to Wapakoneta. Robt. Montgomery meets me & I go to stay at his house 8 ms south-west.

Sunday, July 2 Weather, fair. Thermometer, 95 degrees. I delivered an address on Education, Acts 7:14, and took up more than $20.00 collection & subscription at Olive Branch Church. Dined at Shadrack Montgomery's. Shadrack takes me and Rev. C.S. Johnson to Moulton Ed. Att. Gen. 1:27. Raised over $41.00. Stay at Mr.

Tester's. In eve., hear Rev. Berry McCoy at M.E. Ch.

Monday, July 3 Weather, fair. Thermometer 100 degrees. Cora Tester & sister Mattie takes me to Wapakoneta. I stop off at Christopher Shearer 's. Go on 2:00 train home. Katie gets home about 6:00.

Tuesday, July 4 At home in the forenoon. In the afternoon, I go to Susan's grave. Lorin's have fireworks in the evening.

Wednesday, July 5 At home in the forenoon. Go to town in the afternoon. Call at Lorin's in the evening.

Friday, July 7 Went to Town in the afternoon. Give Young a check for Doyle & Lewis on Costs of U.S. Suit: $132.95. Milton came up in the eve. to see the flying machine.

Saturday, July 8 To-day I settled with Young &Young for services in the United States case, he rebating $37.39 and giving receipts in full for services in this case, and in the Printing Establishment case.

Sunday, July 9 Attended Colored M.E. Church on Hawthorne St., and Rev. D.K. Flickinger pr. at 11:00, Ps. 15. He dined with me. We spend part of the afternoon with Louding's. He lodges with me.

Tuesday, July 11 At home—mostly reading & arranging. Spent most of the day, closely in arranging and putting away legal documents. Lost a half day by a press shelf breaking down and disarranging all previously done.

Wednesday, July 12 At home a very hot day. Pelt rather feeble. Called at Rev. H.J. Becker's and he and I visit Father Jacob Swank's folks an hour. By bathing thoroughly, I get a good night's rest.

Thursday, July 13 At home all day. In the Afternoon, we had one of the finest rains of the summer.

Friday, July 14 At home. Went to town in the afternoon. Rev. C.H. Kiracofe came about 7:30, eve. We call at Louding's to see the Wilberforce's. Joe Caulker was there. Kiracofe lodged with us.

Saturday, July 15 At home all day till I start at 5:30 eve. for Union City. Rev. C.H. Kiracofe dines with us. He leaves on 3:00 car for W. Alexandria & Germantown. I stay at John F. Judy's at Union City.

Sunday, July 16 I attend S. School at Liberal U.B. Church and pr. at 10:30, Rom. 4.8, "Blessed is he whose sins are covered," etc. Dine at Judy's. Pr at Free Meth. Church at 3:30, 1 John 4.10, "Herein is love." Supper at Mr. Lefever's, Bennett's soninlaw. Pr. at 8:00, at Mission Hall, Ps. 1.6. Stay at Judy's.

Monday, July 17 Start at 10+ for Gas City & Fairmount. Call at Wm. Hall's, who is sick. Go with Mr. Nottingham to Fowlerton. Supper at Robt. Wilson White's. Stay at Ellis Wright's.

Tuesday, July 18 I go to White's and thence to see Wm. Duling. Dine at Levi Simon's. Sup at E. Wright's. Stay there.

Wednesday, July 19 Go to White's. Dine and sup there. Stay at Ellis Wright's.

Thursday, July 20 Go to Oliver Glass's. Dinner & supper there. Stay at Wm. Reeder's.

Friday, July 21 Call at Robert Reeder's. He takes me to the farm. I go to Ellis Wright's. Stay there.

Saturday, July 22 I call at L. Hayden's and Henry Simons'. Go on 9:00 train to Fairmount. Call at Clinton Brattain's. Go on electric car to Alexandria. Dine at Ed. Frazier 's. Go via Anderson & Richmond to Dayton. Hattie Sillaman our visitor since Thursday.

Sunday, July 23 At home not well yesterday, last night and to-day. Am better toward evening.

Monday, July 24 In better health. I am at home all day. Some visitors called on Katharine. Hattie is sick to-day. Get proofs in the eve. of Timber sale circular.

Sunday, July 30 Not being well, I staid at home.

Monday, July 31 I feel some better but stay at home

closely. Katharine came in the forenoon awhile. Milton called in the afternoon.

Thursday, August 3 Went out with the Osborne's to the camp N.E. of Fairview Park.

Sunday, August 6 Attended First Baptist Church & heard Rev. D.D. Odell, Gal. 6.2, preach a very good sermon, on the true ideal of Doing good to others. Called an hour in the afternoon at Peter Louding's. The Wilberforce's there.

Monday, August 7 At home. Mrs. Martha Hott died at 8:00.

Tuesday, August 8 Katharine and Orville and others return from camping near Shoup's Mill on Stillwater. I call at Louding's & at Post office. Saw D.K. Flickinger a few minutes. My niece, Rhoda Newhouse died to-day.

Wednesday, August 9 Attended the funeral of Mrs. (J.W.) Hott at 12:00. W.J. Shuey and J. Weaver officiated.

Saturday, August 12 Considerably unwell in the forenoon. Went in the afternoon to Germantown, via West Alexandria. Supper & lodging at Rev. T. Weyer's. Rev. T.M. Harvey pr. at 8:00, Phil. 2:8,9. Very sultry evening.

Sunday, August 13 Rev. T.M. Harvey, P.E. pr. at 10:30, Phil. 3.8. I dine at Isaac Swartzel's, 3 m S.E. Go to town and to C.B. McDaniel 's. I gave Mc. $5.00 in all $15.00, within a few months. Harvey pr. at 8:00, 2 Cor. 4.7. All three sermons were fine. Stay at Lewis Wettz's.

Monday, August 14 Came home on 11:07 train. Had to wait an hour at West Alexandria. Slept some in the afternoon. Read till midnight.

Thursday, August 17 Went on 7:00 train to Union City & thence to Hartford City. Went to Fairview Church to Conference 4 ms right north. Home at Fuller 's. Rev. M.F. Keiter pr. at 8:00, Gen. 45:26 28, in the tent. Rev. Pliny Wolfard my "coachman."

Friday, August 18 Conference continued. In the afternoon, N.D. Wolfard and Z. McNew are elected presiding elders, Mc. on the 8th ballot. Bro. Pierce takes me

to Hartford, and I go home arriving after 10:00, p.m.

Saturday, August 19 At home. Went to town in forenoon.

Sunday, August 20 At home all day. Lorin & family dine with us.

Tuesday, August 22 Went on 7:00 tr. to Union City, Anderson, & Fairmount. Stay at the Hotel. Terribly warm bed-room!

Wednesday, August 23 Call at Wm. Hall's, Asa Drigg's, C. Bratain's. Go on 11:11 tr. to Fowlerton. Dine and sup at R.W. White's. Stay at Ellis Wright's. In the forenoon, I accepted Wm. H. Lindsey's proposal of $917.25 for my timber & received a draft for the same.

Thursday, August 24 Go to town with Ellis Wright. Look at houses for Ellis. Call at Hall's. Lunch at Depot. Go on 12:44 tr. to Anderson & Richmond. Call at D.K. Zeller's office. Come home on 5:20 train.

Friday, August 25 Went to town. Banked draft. Sent $508.75 in check, for payment of a note & interest.

Monday, August 28 Went to town in afternoon. Made some small purchases.

Tuesday, August 29 Start on 9:40 train via C.H. & D. R'y to Cridersville, Ohio, to Auglaize Conference at Victory Church. Bro. Core meets me at Cridersville and takes me to Henry Sellers 1 m E. of Victory Church. I pr. at 8:00, Phil. 3.8. "The excellency of the Knowledge," I board at H. Seller's.

Wednesday, August 30 Conference opened at 9:00. Examinations. R.G. Montgomery came. D.K. Flickinger pr. at 8:00. He and Montgomery among the Boarders at H. Seller's.

Thursday, August 31 Conference continued. I dine at Wm. Seller's. Wm. Dillon pr. at 8:00, Matt. 5:20. The room was so hot, I remained outdoors, but heard the sermon.

Friday, September 1 Conference proceeds. I dine at Elmer

Sellers, 2 ms South. Election of Montgomery & Harvey as pres. elders in Afternoon. Stationing com. meets in eve. at Henry Sellers'. S.T. Mahan pr. at 8:00 at tent.

Saturday, September 2 Conference Continues and Closes about 4:00. Stationing Committee met at the tent at 7:30 morn. Vian memorial service at 3:00. Rev. C.H. Kiracofe lectured on Education at 8:00.

Sunday, September 3 I pr. at the tent at 10:30, Isa. 21.11, "What of the night." Dine at Henry Sellers', Wm. Dillon delivers S.S. address at 3:00. R.G. Montgomery takes me to Eugene McCullough's in Wapakoneta—1 str. S. & several Sts west of the Courthouse.

Monday, September 4 McCullough takes me to Depot, and I go on 6:10 train home.

Tuesday, September 5 Go to High School with Wilberforce's, to the bank, Doctor, etc. Pres. C.H. Kiracofe comes before noon. He also lodged with us.

Wednesday, September 6 I go on 9:40 train via Deshler to Bloomdale, Ohio, C.H. Kiracofe with me. Put up at R.A. Emmerson's, my conference home. H.D. Yant pr. at 8:00.

Thursday, September 7 Sandusky Conference session opened at 9:00. Examinations proceeded. Prosecutor appointed for S.A. Myer's. B.F. Flenor's whole report not being accorded a place in the minutes, he is much offended. C.H. Kiracofe pr. at 8:00, quite well.

Friday, September 8 Conference continued. J.A. Ferguson is elected P.E. in afternoon. B.F. Fleenor is dismissed. Stationing com. meets at Emmerson's, at 7:00. D.K. Flickinger pr. at 8:00, and M.F. Keiter exhorts. S.H. Baldwin is referred to a com. of investigation.

Saturday, September 9 Conference continues. E.L. Day makes a "holiness" report on publishing interests. Adjourned at 4:00. Mary B. Mullen pr. at 8:00. I read Stationing com. report after.

Sunday, September 10 I pr. at 10:30, 1 Tim. 3:16, and ordained F.D. Coss and O. Leyons. Sabbath School in the afternoon. E.L. Day pr. at 7:30, Ps. 119:11. Fleenor

came to the altar, and after made much public confession. Communion service followed.

Monday, September 11 J. Riddle and others called. Mary B. Mullen called; and she consented to be appointed conf. evangelist in Erie. I get a bank draft, and call an hour at J.S. Blair 's. I stay at Emmerson's. He and his son Jay go to Chicago on the night train.

Tuesday, September 12 I stay at R.A. Emmerson's till 2:09, and go to Chicago Junction & thence to Lodi. Rev. John Gonser meets me and takes me to his house, near Cherry Corners Church, where Conference is to meet. I lodge there.

Wednesday, September 13 I stay at J. Gonser's till after noon, and go at 3:00 to Samuel Kimes', my conference home. Hall, Strayer, and some others arrive. John Excell pr. at 7:00, John 13:35. I lodge at Kime's.

Thursday, September 14 East Ohio conference session opens at 9:00 and proceeds well. Publishing report discusses in the afternoon. D. Traver pr. at 7:30, Job 14:14, "If a man die."

Friday, September 15 Conference contunues well. John Excel is elected P.E. Stationing com. met at Kimes at 6:00. A.H. Roach pr. at 7:30, an able sermon.

Saturday, September 16 Conference continued. There were discussions of reports, especially on moral reform. Rev. H.H. Young pr. at 7:30, in Evan. As. Church close by. Some of our women were dissatisfied about having our meetings there.

Sunday, September 17 I pr. at Ev. As. Church at 10:30, Gal. 2:20. Lemasters & Excel dine with me at Kimes', S.S. Anniv. at 3:00. H.H. Young, B.O. Hazzard, and G.F. Hall and wife sup with us. J.N. Lemasters pr. a very able sermon at 7:00, Luke 8:35. His delivery was very powerful.

Monday, September 18 I go to Rev. J. Gonser's in afternoon and stay to Supper. I stay to-night at Hagan's. Went to town (Lodi) with S. Kimes & got a bank draft and we came back through the muckland-onions and celery in the forenoon.

Tuesday, September 19 Go to S. Kimes write some letters. He takes me via Burbank to Lodi. I go on the 7:02 tr. to Akron, and lodge at Windsor Hotel.

Wednesday, September 20 I go on the 6:25 morn. train to Cleveland, and on the 8:20 tr. to "North East," Pa. I get letters & express package there. Mrs. Whitney takes me to Orson Whitney's, her fatherinlaw's, my conference home. No appointment for preaching, at night.

Thursday, September 21 Erie Conference opens at 9:00, at Wilkison's Church. Mrs. Jennie Ranglink is chosen as Secretary. Conference proceeds. The attendance is light. Isaac Boorman pr. at 7:30, "Harvest is great."

Friday, September 22 Conference continues. R.W. Mercer pr. at 7:30, an interesting sermon. He joins the conference this session from Gr. Conf., but formerly from the Free Methodists.

Saturday, September 23 Conference continued and closed at 4:30, aftn. I dine at Wilkinson's. Rev. N.R. Luce pr. an able sermon at 7:30.

Sunday, September 24 I pr. at 11:00, Phil. 2:9, not very well. We ordain Isaac Boorum, and then have communion. I pr. at 7:00, Rev. 1.5,6, and have fair freedom.

Monday, September 25 Wilkinson takes us to North East, and I go at 8:38 to Erie, where I write many letters at the depot. Start on 4:20 tr on Penn. R'y to Harrisburg.

Tuesday, September 26 I arrive at Harrisburg about 5:00 morning, and make close connection for Chambersburg, which I reach at 7:00.

Wednesday, September 27 Get many letters. J. Couldon pr at 7:30. Good sermon.

Thursday, September 28 Pennsylvania Conference opened in King Street Church at 9:00 A.M. and made good progress. Rev. J. Doner pr. at 7:30, John 9:25, and followed it with a speaking meeting.

Friday, September 29 Conference progresses well. Solenberger and Diller were elected P.E.'s. Sta. Com. met at Solenberger's at 6:00. Rev. G.S. Seiple pr. at 7:30, Isa.

52:1, "Awake [unreadable], put on", etc.

Saturday, September 30 Sta. Com. met at Huber's at 8:00. Conference progresses well and closes at 4:30. At Mis. meeting at 7:30, addresses by Miss Rilla Huber, B.G. Huber, and J.S. Solenberger. I raise Subscrip. & Cash, $329.22.

Sunday, October 1 I pr. at King Street Church at 10:30, Gal. 2:20. Dine at Solenberger's & sup there, as usual. Attend the usual afternoon testimony meeting. Pr. at 7:30, Rev. 1:5,6. Church, including gallery, full. Stay as usual, at Solenberger's.

Monday, October 2 Many callers in the morning. I dine at Father John Fohl's, with a Bro. Slaybaugh. I sup at Fred Seiple's. Call in eve. at Peter & Adam Nicklas' with J.S. Solenberger. Stay at Solenberger's.

Tuesday, October 3 Write to D.F. Wilberforce and others. Call on Mother Jas. Bishop and Mother John Fetterhoff. Dine at P. Nicklas'. His son takes me to 1:05 tr. and I go on to Harrisburg & on 3:25 tr. to Pittsburgh & on 2:10 train to Trinway, O.

Wednesday, October 4 Arrive at Trinway at 5:35; at Zanesville at 7:10; at Stockport at 9:20, where Wm. Zumbro takes me to his house near Liberty Church, his wife being Lydia Hecker. Rev. G.W. Tuttle supped with us. C.W. Smith declined to preach, so we had testimony meeting. I slept 9 hours.

Thursday, October 5 Scioto Conference opened its session at 9:00. We had a good day's session. Burton, Adcock & wives supped with us. J.C. Beery pr. at 7:30, Dan. 3:17, a good sermon. I slept 8 hours.

Friday, October 6 Conference progressed well. In aftern. J. Hoffhines & G.W. Tuttle were elected P.E.'s. Sta. Com. met at Church at 5:00. Mrs. A.R. Kiracofe came. Rev. J.Wesley Chambers pr. at 7:30, "I am resolved what I will do." Park stays with me.

Saturday, October 7 Sta. Com. met at Wm. Zumbro's at 8:00. Conf. continued & closed at 5:00. I dined at Wm. Hecker's. Garibrant talks very wildly. Missionary meeting at 7:00, addressed by J. Hoffbines and Mrs. Kiracofe.

We raise $163.00. I Stay as usual at William Zumbro's.

Sunday, October 8 It was a rainy day. House about full. I pr. at 10:30, Gal. 1:4. Dine at Rev. C.B. Tuttle's. J.W. Burton holds S.S. An. at 3:00. Chambers, Mrs. Kiracofe, and I spoke. I pr. at 7:00, John 1:29. Communion followed. Stay at Wm. Zumbro's.

Monday, October 9 Wm. Zumbro takes me to Sharpsburg. Go on 9:30 tr. to Palos, and thence on 11:48 tr to Columbus; and on 3:25 tr. home to Dayton. Arrive at 5:15. Called after supper at Lorin's.

Tuesday, October 10 At home. Went to the bank in the afternoon. In morning looked over letters; also wrote several. Becomes quite warm by evening. Look over periodicals in the evening.

Thursday, October 12 At home. Wrote many letters. Went to the post office and called to see the Wilberforce family, in the evening.

Friday, October 13 Went on 9:35 morn. tr. via Xenia (where I missed connection) reached Columbus abt. 12:30; Go on 4:20 tr. to Mt. Vernon & call at L.B. Ward's; he very sick. See Dr. Freeman Ward & wife; also Wm. Hathaway & wife. Staid at Hotel Smith till 2:00 morn. Go on to Akron.

Saturday, October 14 Arrive at Akron abt 6:00. Miss Curtis, at a milk stand tells me how to reach Paxton and the new church. Go on 8:00 tr. to Paxton, and go out with Horace Young to Rev. H.H. Young's and thence to John B. Jones' to meeting of trustees. Rev. E.R. Kile pr. at 7:30, I stay at J.B. Jones.

Sunday, October 15 I pr at 10:30, Ps. 122:1, 1/2 hr & raise $395.00. I dine at Jones'. Rev. J. Excell pr. at 7:00, and I raise $160.00 more & dedicate the Coddingville Church. I lodge at John B. Jones'.

Monday, October 16 I stay all day at Jones'. Pr. at 7:30, 1 Pet. 1:24,25. I lodge at Rev. H.H. Young's.

Tuesday, October 17 We remain at Young's. Owing to rain, there was no meeting that nght.

Wednesday, October 18 Go with Rev. B.O. Hazzard to Dalbert Kimes'. We dine and sup there. I pr. at 7:30, 1 Pet. 4:18. There were fully fifty persons there. I staid at Jones's.

Thursday, October 19 Hazzard & I go to Montrose, and dine and sup at Nick. Hanson's. He has a small grocery; is 74 years of age. Rev. D. Traver & wife dine with us. Hazzard pr. at 7:30, Isa. 53:6, a good sermon. Rain is threatened, and abt. 25 or 30 are present. I stay at Young's.

Friday, October 20 Remain at Young's all day, it being a bright day. I pr. at 7:30, Rev. 22:14. Young exhorts well. Abt. 55 present. I stay at Young's.

Saturday, October 21 I went to J.B. Jones' and dined. H.H.Young goes to his circuit, at Honey Creek. It is a beautiful day. Hazzard pr. at 7:30. I overheard Jones talking strongly Democratically. I stay at Young's.

Sunday, October 22 I pr. at 11:00, 2 Pet. 1:16. Hazzard & I dine at P.S. Stonebrake's. I pr. at 7:00, Rev. 1:5,6. House well filled & congregation very solemn. I stay at H.H. Young's.

Monday, October 23 Rev. B.O. Hazzard takes me to Paxton. On 8:30 tr. to Medina; on 10:30 tr. to Lorain; on 12:08 tr. to Fort Wayne, on 5:42 to Huntington. Stay at Rev. Wm. Dillon's.

Tuesday, October 24 Publishing Exec. Com. met at 9:00. Keiter's report was too brief for satisfaction. I discuss editor & Agent's work, & sub. editor. Dine at M.F. Keiter's with Tharp & Clay. Supper at Morrison's. Lodge at C.H. Kiracofe's with Clay.

Wednesday, October 25 Missionary Ex. Com. meets at 8:00, at Mis. Room. Mrs. A.R. Kiracofe and Eva Keiter, meet with us. I dine with Flickinger at Bailey's. I sup with Johnson at his brother's. I reach prayer meeting before it closes, at College Chapel. I stay at Prof. A.P. Barnaby's.

Thursday, October 26 Attended and led Chapel prayers, and addressed the School 10 min. Go on 10:42 tr. to Wabash and thence on tr. to Fairmount. Lunch at

Wabash. Called at Burges Hollingworth's and sup & lodge at Ellis Wright 's. In the eve heard Mrs. Ellen Lease lecture at Cong. Church on Topics of the Day.

Friday, October 27 Write letters at Driggs, Miller & Wright's hardware store. Go on 11:11 tr. to Fowlerton. Dine at Caines'. Call an hour at Robt. Wilson White's. His children are having typhoid fever. Walk to Oliver A. Glass's, and lodge there. It is quite a rainy day & night.

Saturday, October 28 I call at Wm. Reeder's. Dine at Glass'. Go in Aftn. to Hopewell in Leach. Rev. Z. McNew pr. at 2:00. Qr. Conf. followed. I sup at Reeve's. I pr. at 8:00, 2 Pet. 4.18. Lodge at John Corn's.

Sunday, October 29 Z. McNew pr. at 11:00, 2 Cor. 3:3, and put a little blood purification of the heart into the sermon; sacrament. I dine at Robert B. Reeder's with Joseph Broyles & wife and boys. I pr. at 7:00 to large audience, 1 John 1:70. I lodge at Oliver Buller's.

Monday, October 30 I dine at Ellis Wrights, having after a call at R.W. White's gone to Fairmount on the train. I lease my gas at $200.50 a year to Mr. Walla. Go on the electric car to Gas City, and on 6:00 train to Union City. Reach home about 11:00 p.m.

Tuesday, October 31 At home. Write some letters. Sent $64.82 cents to pay my Grant Co. tax. Called at Lorin's, and at Louding's.

Wednesday, November 1 Wrote a letter to C.V. Read daily paper, and recorded diary of my recent trip from blotter. Attended Democratic meeting at Victoria Hall, & heard John R. McLean, Chas. W. Baker, James E. Campbell &   [lines in actual text] Newman. Also heard Mayor S. Jones at court house Steps.

Thursday, November 2 At home, reading and writing. Mr. Kellogg called in the afternoon. I call at Lorin's in eve.

Friday, November 3 Katherine went to Richmond, Ind. I deposited gas-check in bank. Bought "Review of Reviews." Read most of the day. Wrote Rev. B.O. Hazzard. Day somewhat drizzly.

Saturday, November 4 *Wrote letters in the forenoon. I went on 1:00 Elec. Car to 1* m. w. of Johnsville, and walk to Olivet, 2 1/4 ms. Montgomery presided in Quar. Conference. Sup & lodge at Geo. Warvell's. Montgomery pr. at 7:00. I close meeting. Congregation good.

Sunday, November 5 I attend S.S. & teach Bro. Wysong's class. Rev. R.G. Montgomery preached at 10:30, I Cor. 1:30. I introduce the sacrament. Dine at [blank] Miller's with Weyer's & Montgomery. I pr. at 7:00, John 3:7. Large attentive & solemn congregation. Stay at Geo. Warvel's.

Monday, November 6 Warvels take us to the car. Reach home at 9:00 a.m. Montgomery also. I Rest, read & write.

Tuesday, November 7 This is Election Day. I voted about 9:00 for Judge Nash for Governor. In the evening, I went to town and staid till late (mostly at Association Hall) hearing the election dispatches read. They were quite confusing.

Wednesday, November 8 News that Fusionists in Nebraska had carried the election, the Democrats in Maryland, and the Republicans in Kansas, Iowa, Kentucky, Ohio, New York, New Jersey, and Massachusetts, and South Dakota. Wrote letters. Went to town. Got presents for grandchil[dren].

Thursday, November 9 At home. H.J.B. called at 9:00 A.M. I call at Lorin's in the evening.

Friday, November 10 Called at Lorin's in the evening to give him a book. I found him sick. Sent for Dr. Spitler.

Saturday, November 11 Engaged as usual in forenoon. Rev. Rufas A. Morrison came at 1:00, on his way to Africa. We called at Telescope Office. Saw McKee & Mrs. Witt & Miller. Went to the Soldiers' Home. Called at Dr. H.J. Becker's in the evening. We also called at Loudings, to see Wilberforce family.

Sunday, November 12 Morrison & Myself heard Rev. Maurice Wilson preach an excellent sermon on 1 Cor. 3.9 16. We dined at Dr. H.J. Becker's. Becker supped with us. We hear Rev. [blank] McCabe pr. at 7:00, Prov.

14:9, a good sermon. We both spoke in Epworth league (i.e. Morrison & I.)

Monday, November 13 Rev. R.A. Morrison, after a call at Mrs. Wilberforce's (P. Louding's) went on 9:20 train via Cincin. to New York, and thence to Liverpool to Bonth and Danville, Imperreh. After calling at Book store & music store went home. Wrote letters.

Tuesday, November 14 At home mostly. Called at Young's to look after the Porter genealogy. Wrote letters.

Thursday, November 16 At home. Writing letters & recording sketches of sermons.

Friday, November 17 At home largely recording sketches of sermons. Lorin called in the evening.

Saturday, November 18 Dr. Becker called in the forenoon with a letter from R.A. Morrison, on board the Oceanic. In Afternoon at 5:35, Katharine and I go to Brookville, O. and stay at John Zehring's. Their daughters are Estelle and Clare; their son Earnest.

Sunday, November 19 I went with Rev. Aaron Zehring's to Olivet Church at New Richmond. I teach the little class in Sabbath School. I pr. at 11:00, 1 Tim. 3:16, "Mystery of Godliness." I dine at Geo. Warvel's and sup there. I preach at 7:00, Rom. 5:11. "Rejoicing in Christ." Large and attentive congregation. Go home with A. Zehring's to Brookv[ille].

Monday, November 20 Come on the 8:35 train home. Rest in the forenoon. Read some in the afternoon. See about change of time on R'y's. Write letters in the evening.

Tuesday, November 21 I go via Richmond to Portland, Ind. to the meeting of the Board of Bishops. Meet at Ev. Associaiton Church at 3:30. Sup & lodge at Dr. John Morehouse's. Bp. H.L. Barkley preached at the Evang. As. Church at 7:30, Heb. 4:6. Bp. Barnaby pr. at *1st Chris. Ch. & Bp. Floyd at M.E. Church. *Fred Slovenour, pastor.

Wednesday, November 22 Bp. Floyd & I attend, by invitation of Prof. Griffith, the High School devotions, and

I led in devotions & each spoke a few minutes. Board met at 9:15. The bishops and Morehouse, and Rev. Stoops dine together at Rev. W.H. Conner's. Barkley left at 2:30. I pr. at 7:30 at Ev. As. Ch. & Barnaby at M.E. Ch. We supped at the Hotel with Rev. Harlan. Discussion of questions kept us up late. All stay at Morehouse's.

Thursday, November 23 Last night I called at D.V. Baker's, before & after meeting he called at Morehouse. I go this morning to Briant & to Rev. A. Worth's, 2 1/2 ms N.W. of town. Call at at [repeated in text] Audion's in the evening and lodge there. Mrs. Worth is my cousin and Andion her son. Ruby Reed, her daughter Aurie's child lives with them. She is 10 years old.

Friday, November 24 Audion married Miss Oler. His children are Mabel, 14; Irven 11 [blank] 8, [blank] 6. Irven takes me to Briant, and I go via Richmond home. Called at Geo. Lanes', 135 N. 7th St. a few minutes. Reach home at about 7:00.

Saturday, November 25 Spend part of the day in copying a Benham genealogy. Learn in the afternoon that Samuel Spidel is sick at the Deaconess' Hospital.

Sunday, November 26 Went to the Wesleyan Church, and heard Rev. Bass pr. from 35th Chap. of Isaiah. Went in the afternoon to see S. Spidel at the Hospital. Called in the Wesleyan S. School, at Louding's, and at Lorin's. Ivonette & Leontine sick with tonsilitis. Milton came home with me. At home in the evening.

Wednesday, November 29 At home, reading and writing. I visit the Library in the afternoon.

Thursday, November 30 Thanksgiving. Of Lorin's family, only Milton could be with us to dine; so we sent them their dinner. Nettie has tonsilitis, and Ivonette & Leontine are just recovering from it. I write letters & mail them and call on Peter Louding & wife. Wilberforces away.

Friday, December 1 At home writing. Called at Dr. H.J. Becker's about five o'clock.

Sunday, December 3 Attended M.E. Colored Church,

Hawthorne St., and preached for pastor Turner, 30 min. Revela. 1:5,6, "Unto home loved us," etc. At home the rest of the day.

Tuesday, December 5 Spent much of the afternoon in setting my books and documents in order.

Wednesday, December 6 Took much pains to give D.K. Freeman of Muncie, Ind., a genealogy of the Freeman Family. He is a son of John Porter Freeman which was also his great grandfather's name

Thursday, December 7 At home writing. Katie went to Ivonette's candy pulling in the evening.

Saturday, December 9 Went to Library and bought many small articles, in the forenoon. Went on 4:00 car to Crawford's Road. Walk up to New Richmond. Supper at William Eubank's. Pr. at 7:00, Luke 19:27, "Those mine enemies   bring Slay before." I stay at Aaron Wysong's. House quite full to-night.

Sunday, December 10 I preach again at Olivet, Rom. 10.1. Dine at Wm. Eubank's. Call at [blank] Miller's. Sup at Geo. Warvel's. Pr. at 6:30, Jere. 13:21. I stay at Daniel Wagoman's. She was a Sipes. Their child Miriam is 17 mo. old. Church moderately filled at 10 1/2; packed at 6:30.

Monday, December 11 Bro. Wagoman takes me to Crawford's crossing. I wait 40 min. at house and get home about 9:00.

Tuesday, December 12 At home reading and writing. Visited the Public Library in the afternoon. Got medicine for Lorin, of Spitler.

Wednesday, December 13 At home. Spent most of the afternoon in the public library.

Thursday, December 14 At home writing. Sent receipt for clerical rates. Spent the whole evening in examining old sketches of sermons and sketchbooks, destroying some sketch leaves not valuable.

Friday, December 15 At home busy on Indexing Sermon Sketch books.

Saturday, December 16 At home till 3:00 p.m. Went to Crawford's road 1 mile west of Johnsville, and walked up to Prizor's to supper. I preached at Olivet at 7:00, Isa. 1:18. I stay at George Warvel's with Weyer's. The congregation was large.

Sunday, December 17 I attend Sabbath school and then preach at 10:30, 2 Tim. 1:5, to a small congregation. Dine at G. Warvel's. His son Ephriam lives in the house near by. His son John lives at home, aged 14. His daughter is Wm. Eubank's wife. I pr. at 6:30, Luke 11:32. The house crowded. Weyer & I stay at Aaron Wysong's.

Monday, December 18 Wysong's children are Lottie Warvel, [blank] Wogaman, [blank] Hanshu, John 16, Elsie 14, Orville, Harrison & [blank]. Spent the afternoon and evening in writing. Milton lost his mother's spy glass out of his pocket.

Tuesday, December 19 Wrote in the forenoon, and went to P. Louding's, the post -office, and Young's, and the Library.

Thursday, December 21 At home till 3:00, writing. Go to Crawford's Road and to Wm. Eubank's to supper. John, his brother there, and is to be married the 24th in Dark[e] County. I preach at Olivet, at 7:00, 2 Pet. 1:3,4, "Exceed great and precious promises."

Friday, December 22 Bro. Weyer goes to Germantown. I wrote a letter to Rev. R.A. Morrison. I preach at 7:00, Matt. 3.44 "Treas hid—field." Stay at G. Warvel's.

Saturday, December 23 Stay at Warvel's. Rainy day & evening. No meeting. Send Morrison's letter to Bro. Dill [?]

Sunday, December 24 I teach infant class in Sabbath School. Rev. T. Weyer pr. at 10:30. We dine at Samuel Pontins' 2 1/2 ms N.W. I preach a Christmas sermon at 6:30, *Luke 2:34. I stay at Geo. Warvel's. *"This child shall be set for the fall & rising of many."

Monday, December 25 Ephraim Warvel takes me to Crawford's Crossing. I get home at 9:00. Call at Lorin's morning and evening. At home the rest of the day, examining my manuscripts, etc.

Tuesday , December 26 At home writing. Call at Lorin's in the evening.

Wednesday, December 27 Wrote in the forenoon and in the afternoon and evening.

Thursday, December 28 D.K. Flickinger calls an hour just before noon. Oberlin Glee Club appeared to-night. Our children attended.

Friday, December 29 Prof. [blank] Peck called an hour in the afternoon. Rev. S.L. Livingston and his wife Candace (Gilbert) called for supper. Flora Greenwood called. I wrote a letter to N. Allebaugh of Avlon, O. Looked over and retraced part of my diary of 1887, of which the ink had been poor.

Saturday, December 30 Sent for Tribune Almanack; and for Apocraphy, and "Cincinnati Present & Past." Called at Public Library. Called at Lorin's in eve. Slept full seven hours. It was a pretty cold night.

Sunday, December 31 At home till evening reading and writing all day. Heard Creighton Wones preach at Broadway, at 7:30, Heb. 10.32. Go to bed about 10:00, and slept nearly 7 hours. Thus ends a year of God's great goodness and mercy.

Facts, Etc.
Anson Moor died May 29, 1892.

Fact from Old Letters.
1. Nathaniel Heywood died Dec. 15, 1840, when his son Alexander was about 2 months old. He and Eliza and child Thomas visited us in Sept. 1839.

Alexander and Sarah Haywood's daughter was Aurie Eliza, who married [blank] Reed, died l[e]aving dau. Ruby Alexander d. in Spr8ing, 1856. John Whitten Van Cleve, d. Sept. 1858.

Henry Richards moved to Kansas, Apr. 1858? L.G. Richards m. Feb., 1858.

Olivet Class. 1899.
at New Richmond, O.

George Warvel, Lydia Warvel, Ephraim Warvel, Lottie Warvel, Aaron Wysong, Sarah Wysong, Daisy Hanshu, Daniel Woggoman, Rachel Woggoman, William Eubank, Lizie Eubank, Julia King, Isaac King, Perry Mills, Elizabeth Mills, Jessie Mills, dau. Wm. Prisor, Martha Shank, Gertrude Davis McDuff, Isaac Miller, C.L. (Ezra Zigler, Ronnie Zigler, Sarah Woggoman) Isaac Martin, Amelia Martin, Mandy Martin, dau. E.A Kiger, lives W. Alexandria, Frank Gerhart

John Reel died Sept. 16, 1899

PART FOUR

1900–1905

"The past year was full of stirring events. I was serene and happy through it all, though grieved at the folly of many and the wickedness of not a few. I believed that God would at last vindicate the right."

Milton Wright, December 31, 1903

During the early years of the new century, Milton became embroiled in a bitter lawsuit over the misuse of United Brethren Publishing House funds by another churchman, Millard Keiter. These years would see many changes at home. Katharine Wright was teaching in the Dayton Public Schools and becoming active in the Young Women's League. Her friends from Oberlin visited often. Wilbur and Orville Wright had embarked on their adventure to build a practical airplane. Milton Wright's diaries record their trips to Kitty Hawk, North Carolina—their failures and successes. He begins to call his sons "the Wright Brothers." The Bishop travels by train to Indiana frequently to see family and friends. His diaries record local, national, and world events. He continues to preach when needed and writes articles for United Brethren Publications. Expelled from the White River Conference, and growing weary of the fight, he retired from the ministry in 1905.

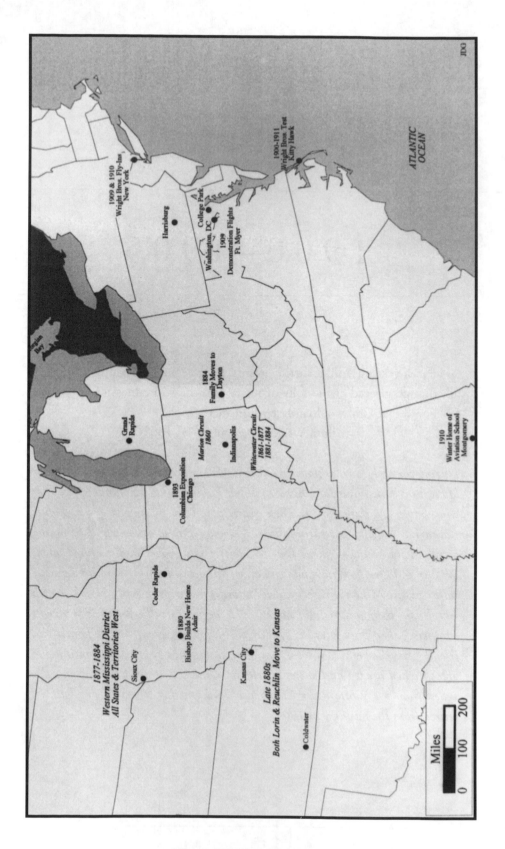

ATLANTIC
OCEAN

1900-1911
Wright Bros. Test
Kitty Hawk

1909 & 1910
Wright Bros. Fly-Ins
New York

Harrisburg

College Park

Washington, DC

1909
Demonstration Flights
Ft. Myer

1884
Family Moves to
Dayton

Grand
Rapids

Marion Circuit
1860

Indianapolis

Whitewater Circuit
1861-1877
1881-1884

1893
Columbian Exposition
Chicago

1910
Winter Home of
Aviation School
Montgomery

Cedar Rapids

1880
Bishop Builds New Home
Adair

1877-1884
Western Mississippi District
All States & Territories West

Sioux City

Kansas City

Late 1880s
Both Lorin & Reuchlin Move to Kansas

Coldwater

Miles

0   100   200

Historic Aviation and Other Sites

1900

Monday, January 1 Since Nov. 17th, I have been in my seventy second year. I have spent most of this day at home. I went about 4:00 p.m. to John Weidner's; and thence to Jesse Spidel's to see Samuel Spidel—had prayers with him. He is somewhat paralyzed, and his mind much affected.

Tuesday, January 2 I arose at 5:00. Called at Lorin's in foren. I wrote many letters. It is cold, pleasant winter weather. I arrange to go to Grant County, Ind., Friday, and to Huntington Tuesday.

Wednesday, January 3 Paid my Dayton tax. Called at Lorin's. Wrote many letters. Sat up very late.

Thursday, January 4 Spent the forenoon in writing; went to the store & bought two blankets and gave them to Wilbur and Orville —and a bed comfort for Lorin's. Milton spent the day with us.

Friday, January 5 I went on 9:00 train to Richmond, Ind., and called at Zeller's house and Office; a few minutes; and on 11:00 tr., go via Anderson to Fairmount; call at Ellis Wright's house and hardware store, and at Hollingsworth's. Go on 3:39 tr. to Fowlerton (Leach) and go home with O.A. Glass.

Saturday, January 6 I went to Wm. H.H. Reeder's and remained till after dinner, and Mattie takes me to Fowlerton. I write to M.F. Keiter. Go to Robt. W. White's, look over the Woods & fields, and over Leach and Fowlerton. Supper & lodging at White's.

Sunday, January 7 I Preach in Hopewell Ch. in Leach,

10:30, Acts 26.8, on the Resurrection. Dine at Oliver Buller's, and he takes me to Fairmount. I see Laura Winchell, my niece, and Rhoda Wright, at Asa Drigg's, 40 minutes. Go on the electric car to Marion, and thence to Delphos, Ohio. See Henry J. Dalrymple of Bluffton. Lodge at Jesse McKenzie's.

Monday, January 8 Go on 5:50 tr. to Canton, Ohio; Call at the Office of Allen Cook, Esq. Go to Rev. J. Noel's. Get a deed to Central College for 2 Harvey lots. Rollin A. Noel takes me to the train. Go on to Ft. Wayne, arriving at 4:00 morn. Write letters at the depot. Lost pocket knife by a sneak thief, at depot at Ft. Wayne!

Tuesday, January 9 I go on 10:00 tr. to Huntington, Ind.; dine at Bailey's with Flickinger. Prudential Com. of the Publishing board meets at 2:00, and continues till supper; at M.F. Keiter's. Meet again at 7:00, Adjourn at 8:00. Stay at Wm. Dillon's with I.M. Tharp & W.H. Clay.

Wednesday, January 10 Meeting of the Executive Com. of the Missionary society in forenoon. I go on 10:42 tr. via Wabash, Anderson, & Richmond home, arriving at 6:00.

Thursday, January 11 Went to town in forenoon and afternoon. Got a new suit of clothes, $24.50. Left Porter Memorial at Telescope Bindery, to cost $1.00, each volume. Spent part of Afternoon & eve in assorting & putting away pamphlets & other documents.

Friday, January 12 At home in the forenoon. Went in the afternoon to the Public Library; walked home; called at Lorin's.

Sunday, January 14 At First Baptist Church heard Dr. H.C. Mabie the Home Secretary of the Am. Baptist Mis. Union, John 12.30, "Voice—your sake." Intelligent but not a very good speaker.

Monday, January 15 Spent full half the day in retracing my diary of 1857, which was written with a lead pencil. Went to town in the afternoon, got a draft of $5.00 and sent to pay A.P. Wiggins, Saratoga, N.Y. for Porter Memorial; bought hat etc.

Tuesday, January 16 At home all forenoon. Went in the afternoon, and expressed "Cin. Present & past," back to Calrke, and went to the post office. Came back by Lorin's.

Wednesday, January 17 I call on Young, one minute. Buy a hat, and get large envelopes at the post office. Read and wrote the rest of the day. Called at Lorin's.

Thursday, January 18 Went to the bank, and to the bindery and got the volumes of the Memorial of the Porter Family $1.00 each. Read and wrote the most of the day. Katharine goes to the Helen Hunt Club. About midnight, Oscar Needham and Dr. Long call to tell Katharine that she is elected teacher in High School. They, her friends.

Friday, January 19 At home reading and writing. It is a semi rainy day, and rainy night. I call at Lorin's in the evening .

Saturday, January 20 It rained all night. But this is a pleasant day. I was a home all day. Lorin and Milton came in the evening and staid an hour or more. Agnes Osborn spent tne evening with us. H.J. Becker called in the afternoon, also on his return from town.

Sunday, January 21 Weather fair. Arose early. Got ready for meeting. Heard Rev. C.W. Gullette preach at Gr. M.E. Church 11:00, Lev. 19.18. "Thou shalt love—neighbor—self." Severely condemned the Maysville mob. Heard Rev. I.L. Kephart at Association Hall on, "What shall we do?" Lorin's took supper with us. I called at Louding's, on my return from Association Hall.

Monday, January 22 Nettie (Lorin's Wife) and the little girls called. I was home. Katharine visited Woerthner to see about her duties as teacher, etc., in the High School. I spent the day in reading & writing.

Tuesday, January 23 At home in the forenoon. Visit in the Afternoon, Jacob Swank's, on North-western Ave., Dr. H.J. Becker's and Aunt Mary Inglehart's. Call at Faeler's to see about the facts of Father John Reel's obituary. Katharine goes to the Gymnasium in the evening. Dr. Becker had gone to Rome, Ind.

Wednesday, January 24 Received letters from Rev. John Jackson, C.H. Kiracofe, Mrs. Eliza H. Wolcott, Robt. Clarke Company, and Rev. D.P. Boyd, Newberry, S.C. Wrote letters. Lorin's called in the evening. Orv. & Kath. call at Dr. Mitchell's, who move[s] to Miamisburg tomorrow.

Thursday, January 25 At home engaged as usual. Wrote to the folks at Brookville, Ind., that I expect to be there Feb. 1st. There was a change to right cold weather in the afternoon.

Friday, January 26 A home, and engaged as usual. Went to J. Spidel's in afternoon, to see his father, Samuel Spidel, who is partially paralyzed, and mentally affected. Katharine visited High School. Lorin's called in the evening.

Saturday, January 27 To town —trains all behind. Trade at Cohen's home—Go at 10:00, again; met Flickinger & in counsel 45 minutes at Hoffman House. Went on 12:00 traction car to Miamisburg, where Rev. T. Weyer meets me and takes me to his house. Pr at 2:00 1 Pet. 1:2. I preside—Qr. Conf. Sup Weyer's. Pr at 7:30, Matt. 13.31,32. Lodge at L. Wett's.

Sunday, January 28 Attend speaking-meeting at 9:15. Pr. at 10:30, 2 Cor 13.5. Sacrament. Dine at L. Long's, & sup there. Call at T. Weyer's. Pr. at 7:00, Isa. 5.4. I stay again at Lewis Wetz.[Written as Wett's above]

Monday, January 29 Call at Charles Coulthard's. Go on 10:07 tr. to Franklin, and thence home on traction. Today Katharine began as regular teacher in High School;

and Miss Hariet Osborn began to keep house for us. Went to town; got pantaloon, cloth brush, underwear, etc, etc.

Tuesday, January 30 At home in the forenoon reading and writing. Went to town in the afternoon, a short time, and made small purchase.

Wednesday, January 31 At home in the forenoon. Go on 3:17 train to Richmond & after a call at D.K. Zeller's & supper, to Cambridge & lodge at Henry Myer's.

Thursday, February 1 Go on 6:27 train to Brookville and Bro. Geo. Moulton takes me to his house. We go and look at the German Methodist Church, which the brethren propose to buy; and we visit Miss Sally Lewis, daut. of Clark Lewis. Bro. G.W. Stewart comes. I go after dinner to Daniel Koerner's. Pr. at Bath at 7:00, Rom. 5.8.

Friday, February 2 I remain at my wife's brother's, Daniel Koerner's, 12 miles north of Brookville, till after dinner. Go in Moulton's buggy to Brookville. Sup and lodge at Moulton's. Pr. at Ger. Methodist Church at 7:30, Matt. 5.12.

Saturday, February 3 I went on 11:45 train to Laurel. Lunch at the restaurant. Hire livery rig and go to Andersonville and call at Samuel Barber's. Mr. Shriner and Smith Scott—old acquaintances—come in; call at James More's house. Go on to Philam, Le Forge's, & Vern Young's. Lewis takes me to James F. Harris's. I pr. at Clarkburg. Eph. 2:4.

Sunday, February 4 My nephew, James Harris, takes me to Mt. Zion, 2 1/4 ms. south-west of Andersonville, where I preach at 10:30, Rom. 4.9. I dine at Rev. Chas. S. Miller's. Jesse LeForge and wife (Miller's daut.) dine there. Sister (Ann) Miller was James Simmond's daughter, of Neff's Corners. I pr. at 7:00, 2 Pet. 1.4. Dr. George Wright, my Nephew, goes with me to James Harris's; lodge there.

Monday, February 5 I take James' conveyance and go to old Hopewell Cemetery & get the dates of the Freeman's buried there etc. I call at Otis Porter Freeman's, 1/2 m. east of Cone's Corners. I dine at Morgan Linville's, 1/4

m. north of the Worth farm, where I was born. James Franklin Linville goes with me over the Worth farm. I return to Harris's. Pr. at Clarksburg, Rom. 8.1.

Tuesday, February 6 My nephew, James F. Harris, after dinner, takes me to Milroy. On the way, we call at the Richland Church Cemetery, and look at Grandfather & Grandmother Reeder's graves—immediately west of the nice granite monument of John & James McCorkle & Sally McCorkle & Eliz. Butler & A.P. Butler. At Rushville, call at Artemas Moor's.

Wednesday, February 7 I had gone last eve. on train to Sexton & walked out to Samuel David Kirkpatrick's & lodged. Effie takes me to Harvey Wright's. John & Flora Kirkpatrick and Mrs. Lizzie Wright visit there. Jabez Rhoads & Frances, my niece,and Stella call a half hour in afternoon. I lodge at my brother Harvey's. He is 79 years old, but walks nimbly & Preaches frequently.

Thursday, February 8 I call at Thomas Wright's, my nephew's & he takes me back to Harvey's. Charley Gray takes me to Rushville, & I go on 11:48 train to Glenwood. Nicholas Frank Bowen met me and took me to his house. Dine there. He takes me via Lucinda Moor's to Charles Steven's, on our old home place. I Sup & lodge there.

Friday, February 9 Charley & Flora, my niece, and Ray, their son, go with me to Lucinda Moor's, she having been my brother William's wife. Cliff Long & wife live with her. After supper, I went to N.F. Bowen's, and he takes me to Fayetteville, where I preach at 7:00, at Disciple's Church, Gal. 2.20. I return to Bowen's & lodge. His wife is my niece.

Saturday, February 10 After very early dinner, N.F. Bowen takes me to Glenwood, and I go on 12:02 train to Hamilton & thence to Dayton, home. Found all well, and that Carrie Kayler was doing work for us. Many letters to read.Went to bed at 9:00. Slept about 8 hours.

Sunday, February 11 Attended the Episcopal Church. Rev. John Dows Hills preached on the Parable of the Sower. Saw Albert and Edith Shearer, his dau., on the way home. Agnes Osborn called in the afternoon. I was at home the rest of the day.

Tuesday, February 13 At home all day, except to town to bank, gas office, P.O., etc. Called at P. Louding's, Joseph Wilberforce came in the evening to get a problem in Arithmetic solved, and Orville solved it and explained it to him.

Wednesday, February 14 At home all day writing letters. Lorin, Milton and Ivonette came and staid an hour, in the evening.

Thursday, February 15 At home writing most of the day. Went to Depot & Bate's store and got several paper boxes. Katharine went to the meeting of the Helen Hunt Club in the evening.

Friday, February 16 At home, mostly reading. Went in the afternoon about 5:00 to call on Jacob Swank. Called also at Rev. H.J. Becker's five minutes.

Saturday, February 17 Called just before noon at Jesse Spidel's to see his father, Samuel Spidel, who is much afflicted, and prayed with them. Read the papers and wrote a letter, and went on the electric to Crawford's and Sulphur Springs Road, & walked up to Aaron Wysong's. Lost my muffler, but recovered it next morning .

Sunday, February 18 I preached at Olivet, at 10:30, 1 John v:3, "This is the love of John."etc. Dined, supped & lodged at Geo. Warvel's. I preached at 7:00, "consider your ways" Haggai 1.5. The congregations were small. In the evening, some boys misbehaved, and I thought the brethren were inclined to tolerate their conduct.

Monday, February 19 I went home on 8:00 traction. Carrie K. was unwell, yesterday, and did not come to work to-day.

Tuesday, February 20 At home writing and reading. Carrie K. back, but went home at 3:00. Katharine came from school complaining of her throat and ear. Saw Dr. Becker at the boys' store, and had much talk with him. Dr. L. Spitler called and left medicine for Katharine.

Wednesday, February 21 Banked to day from Hoisington $63.62; from Grant on produce, clover seed, $41.48;

wheat, $21.00. Katharine teaches as usual.

Thursday, February 22 Washington's Birth Day holiday to-day. Katharine is quite unwell. I spent the day reading and writing. Nothing extraordinary occurs.

Friday, February 23 I was at home all day, busy, as I usually am; but nothing of special interest occurs. Katharine taught as usual, but had fever in the afternoon & evening.

Saturday, February 24 At home all day, reading and writing. In afternoon, Katharine has fever and sends for the doctor again. Lorin and Milton called in the evening.

Sunday, February 25 At 10:30, at Broadway "Christian" Church, I heard Dr. J.J. Summerbell, Ed. of the "Herald of Gospel Liberty," pr. from Rev. 19.13, "Clothed in vesture dipped in blood," an able and interesting sermon. At 3:30, at Association Hall, I heard Rev. Albert Read, Del. Ohio pr. on Gal. 2.20. Loved* *me* and gave himself for *me,* good sermon. Called at Lorin's. At home in the evening. * Emphasized me improp.

Monday, February 26 At home, mostly reading. Went to town in afternoon; called five minutes at Young's; went to the Library. Joseph Goodin Wilberforce came at 5:30, remained till after supper. Lorin called a while in the evening.

Tuesday, February 27 I arose quite early; was at home all day, except a trip to post office, Newsalt's, and store; bought a clock, $4.50.

Wednesday, February 28 I am at home to-day. It is quite rainy, after sleet in the morning. I spent the forenoon in copying letters on the type-writer. I attended Rev. E. Lorenz' funeral at Ger. U.B. Church at 2:00; four Germans, including G. Fritz, spoke, and Shuey, Weaver & Hott. He died Saturday eve. the 24th, aged 72.

Thursday, March 1 At home reading and writing. Nothing of special interest occurred, but in the past day or so, we get news of Gen. Cronie's surrender in South Africa, and of the relief of the British garrison at Ladysmith.

Friday, March 2 At home reading and writing—have considerable cold, and lumbar rheumatism. Lorin & wife & children called a few minutes in the evening. Orville & Catharine went to hear Paul Lawrence Dunbar, at the High School Building. He was a school-mate of Orville's, in High School.

Saturday, March 3 This is a very fair day & the temperature mild. In the afternoon, many women were on the streets. Nothing of especial interest occurs. I hear of the death of Mrs. Mary Clemmer, who died last night, at Bellefontaine. Lorin and "Tugers" (Milton) called. Mrs. Clemmer had lived here much of her life and was a sister of Mrs. Rev. John Huffman.

Sunday, March 4 Started for Baptist First Chruch, but car far out of time. My nose bled till I had to abandon the idea of going to meeting at all. Staid at home the rest of the day. It did not seem a very good Sabbath. I had a cold in my head.

Monday, March 5 At home all day. It is a damp, rather rainy day. My cold still affects me, somewhat. Mrs. Mary Clemmer's funeral occurred this afternoon.

Tuesday, March 6 This was a beautiful but windy day. I went to town in the afternoon, bank, post office, Young's. Katharine went to Miamisburg to see Mrs. Dr. Mitchell. I called at Lorin's a few minutes. Katharine returned at 9:00.

Wednesday, March 7 This is a fair, mild day. At home. Went to "town" in the afternoon, paid gas bill ($8.00), bought various articles.

Thursday, March 8 At home. Reading and writing. Mr. A. Burton Jowett, with Joseph Wilberforce called about 5:00. He offers to go to Africa as our missionary. He has been in America nearly 20—years   knew Wilberforce in Africa—graduated in Fisk University—attended Chicago Theo. Seminary awhile—is 39 years old—is lecturing on Africa.

Friday, March 9 At home. Reading and writing. Called at Sines' in the evening.

Saturday, March 10 Weather nice. Thermometer about 60 degrees. At home all the forenoon. In the afternoon, I called on Rev. Mr. Reichard, who is low with consump[t]ion. He is intelligent, thoughtful, modest, & pious. Kath. and Agnes go to Miamisburg. Lorin's went to "town" and left the children at our house. I am nearly well of my cold.

Sunday, March 11 Weather mild. Thermometer abt. 60 degrees. Lorin & the children called about an hour. In the afternoon, I heard Rev. Mr. Bigelow of Vine Street Congregational Church, at Cin. speak at Assoc. Hall, text, Luke 9:60, "Let the dead bury," etc. He is quite a good speaker, but a freak in his theories. I called at Louding's an hour or less.

Monday, March 12 Wrote some letters, and made out a program of the Missionary Board Meeting in June. To-day, Rev. C.M. Sheldon began to edit the "Topeka Capital," for which I have subscribed one week. He orders it to be non partisan, to not circulate scandals, to make only brief mention of crimes, and to give their cause. Right!

Tuesday, March 13 Weather fine. Thermometer high. I arose very early. At home. In the evening was the elections primaries. I called at Lorin's in the evening. Nothing remarkable occurred here to-day. The war cloud in Kentucky seems less threatening.

Wednesday, March 14 I arose about 5:00. Went to town to bank and Library, and post office.

Friday, March 16 I called in the forenoon at H.J. Becker's and at Jacob Swank's. Becker not at home. Swank feeble. This is a pretty cold afternoon & *night*.

Saturday, March 17 I was at home till in the afternoon, I called at Dr. Becker's and at "Aunt" Mary Inglehart's. Wrote a good many letters. This is quite cold March weather.

Sunday, March 18 Weather fair. Lorin and the children called in the forenoon. I heard Dr. H.F. Colby preach at 10:30, Luke 12:21, "Rich toward God." At 3:30 I heard W.O. Thompson, Pres. of the Ohio State University, speak on the needed young man, a very fine discourse, at Y.M.C.A. Hall. Called at Lorin's.

Tuesday, March 20 Weather changeable. Went to see two buildings. Called to see Mrs. Sarah Swayney, my Mother's cousin. Got a draft for $60.07, and enclosed 30 cts. with it as fee to S.H. Moffitt, Greenfield, Iowa for tax; and draft $2.70 for Arthur Hinds for Interlinear Greek English New Testament. Bought a few articles. Walked out to see some properties in Dayton View, toward evening.

Wednesday, March 21 I was at home, except a walk in the afternoon, to visit Samuel Spidel, at his son Jesse's, in the Putterbaugh Addition. They are to move to Liberty next Monday. He is partially paralyzed, and cannot walk without assistance.

Thursday, March 22 Went to town in forenoon; got various articles, especially envelopes, postage, etc. In afternoon, bought a postal guide, $2.00.

Friday, March 23 At home, except a trip to Bolton and Brown Streets to look at property. I received a letter from D.K. Flickinger, and one from R.A. Morrison, Danville, Imperrah. Answered them. Wrote other letters, among these, to Montgomery, Ferguson, and Hoffhines about a place for next General Conference.

Saturday, March 24 I was at home all day. Carrie, on account of a sore foot, did not come to work, to-day. This was a very fine day—scarcely cool enough for any fire. I wrote an article for the Missionary Monthly, for May. To-day—Wharton Golden testified in the preliminary trial of Secretary of State Caleb Powers, at Frankfort, Kentucky.

Sunday, March 25 Heard Rev. Maurice Wilson preach on "I was wounded in the house of my friends," Zech. 13.6, a good sermon. Bible Agent Pierson presented the Bible Society Cause.

Wednesday, March 28 At home. Men tore off the old paper in room and stairway hall.

Friday, March 30 At home. The paper hanger was at work on the sitting room and hall of stairway.

Saturday, March 31 Spent most of the day in making out deeds for 80 acres apiece, to each of my four boys,

for Adair Co. farms, and of the Dayton house and lot to Katharine and the cancel[l]ing of a $300 note of Reuchlin's $136 note & four years interest to Lorin's and $500 note and one year's interest of Wilbur and Orville's note.

Sunday, April 1 Heard President Holden, of Wooster University preach at Third St. Presbyterian Church, at 10:30, 1 Tim. 3:15, "Church of the living God," etc. Lorin's children with us much of the day. Milton and I walked to Dayton View, and on cars went to Woodland Cemetery; was at Philena Slentz; at Mother's Grave, at summer house observatory.

Monday, April 2 Got ready for trip, and went to Columbus on 2:30 Big 4 train, and go to D.K. Flickinger's at 201 S. Front St. We consult on the African situation. I lodge with him.

Tuesday, April 3 We call in forenoon at Mr. Timmerman's office and talk with him. His mother is a Flickinger. Dine at a restaurant at the corner of High & Town Streets with Flickinger. I go on 12:55 (noon) train (Pennsylvania Lines) to Pittsburgh and thence on B&O tr. to Cumberland & Harpers Ferry to Weaverton.

Wednesday, April 4 Went on to Rohrersville, and to J.W. Chambers, at the parsonage, my conference home. Rev. J.E. Hott pr. at 7:30, 1 Ki. 19:13, "What doest thou here?" Kiracofe came.

Thursday, April 5 Conference opened at 9:00. Business proceded well. Rev. G.S. Seiple pr. at 7:30.

Friday, April 6 Conference proceded well. Dr. C.H. Kiracofe pr. at 7:30, Luke 9.23, "Let him deny himself & take up his cross,"etc.

Saturday, April 7 Conference continued. Memorial service, at 3:00, for Rev. I.T. Parlett. I pr. at 7:30, John 17.17. Sanctify them through thy truth.

Sunday, April 8 I preach at 10:30, 1 Tim 3.15. I dine at Bro. Potter's, a butcher's, just out of town. I pr. at 7:30, Rom. 6.14. Sup and lodge at Rev. J.W. Chambers.

Monday, April 9 Go early with Revs. J.W. Chambers,

G.W. Allman and H.W. Lindamood to visit Antietam Battle Ground. Lunch at the Monument of Massachuset[ts] Soldiers. Feed down at the Potomac River. Lindamood takes me on to Hagerstown. I go thence by rail to Greencastle. I sup & stay at F.W. Barnes'. Had called an hour at Rev. C.B. McDaniel's.

Tuesday, April 10 Call an hour at Rev. W.R. Burkholder's. I dine at Rev. C.B. McDaniel's. I go on 12:42 tr. to Chambersburg. Call at Rev. G.S. Seiples, J.S. Solenberger's, A. Nicklas's, and Rev. P. Nicklas's, & at their carpet store & Huber's. I go on 5:00 tr. to Harrisburg. Stay at the Hershey House, and slept 6 hours.

Wednesday, April 11 I arose at 3:00, and lunched at the depot. Leave at 3:35 (3:50) for Buffalo Go via Williamsport, Elmira, Canadaigna, and Rochester, to Buffalo, and thence on 5:00 train to Sherkston, Ont. Sup and lodge at Merner Shupe's. I pr. at Sherkton Church at 8:00, Eph. 5.1, "Be ye followers of God, as dear Children."

Thursday, April 12 Go on 7:50 tr. to Drumbro, with Rev. J.W. Howe, Shupe, and others. Reach there at 11:00. Part of us go with Elias Hallman, to his house, 7 miles away, where we dine. Hallman then took us to New Dundee to Conference, which began at 2:00, and much business was dispatched. I board at Mrs. M.J. Cassel's. Rev. J.G. Connor pr. at 6:00, Rom. 8:37.

Friday, April 13 Conference continued. Examinations mostly closed in forenoon. Woman's Branch Mis. Association held from one to three & a half, after which Conference took up reports on Missions, Sabbath schools, and Moral Reform. I pr. at 8:00, Titus 2:14, In Christ's sacrifice. Board as usual at Mrs. Cassel's.

Saturday, April 14 Conference continues. General reports were discussed. I dined at Shipley's. I sup at Current's. Missionary meeting at 8:00, Rev. Deitweiler, of Alberti spoke. Raise many life memberships.

Sunday, April 15 I pr. at 10:30. Ordained J.G. Connor and A.R. Springer. Sacrament followed. I dine at Rev. C.W. Backus. Deitweiler takes me to Berlin. Sup at E. Eshelman's. Pr. at 7:00, 1 Tim. 3.15, "The house of God." I stay at W.H. Becker's.

Monday, April 16 I dine at Rev. A.B. Sherk's. In afternoon I call on Rosenberger's & Rev. J.B. Bowman's. Sup at Mrs. Isaac Bowman's. Her son Hervey is there. I pr. at 8:00, 1 Tim. 3.15, "Pillar and ground of the truth," I lodge at W.H. Becker's, Sherk's soninlaw's.

Tuesday, April 17 I breakfast at Rev. D.B. Sherk's. I visit Rev. A.F. Stoltz, and dine at Rev. J.B. Bowman's. I go on 3:05 tr. via Galt to Brantford, and to Buffalo. Stay at the Arlington Hotel.

Wednesday, April 18 Leave Buffalo at 8:10, on N.Y. Central R'y, and via Rochester, Utica and Troy; reach N. York at 7:00, Go to Flathush and lunch, and stay at St. George's Hotel, Brooklyn. Read to-day of Sheldon's "In His Steps."

Thursday, April 19 Went to Newtown, and returned to Brooklyn. Spent the afternoon and evening in the library of Brooklyn Historical Society. Found considerable on the Genealogy of the Reeders, Van Cleves, and Vanderbilts, my mother's ancestors of Newtown and Flatbush, and Staten Island, & New Ulrecht. Lodged at Clarenden Hotel.

Friday, April 20 Spent forenoon in libraries. Went afternoon to Carnegie Hall, in N.Y., and got Delegate's ticket, etc. Go to Grand Union Hotel, corner of 42nd St. and Park Avenue, to board. Flickinger called in the evening. No meeting to-night.

Saturday, April 21 Rev. D.K. Flickinger changed to our hotel, and we occupy a double bed room No. 79. We visited Mrs. A.R. Kiracofe at Grand Hotel (on Sunday). First meeting at Carnegie Hall at 2:30, ex Pres. Benj. Harrison presided. He and Dr. Judson Smith, R. Wardlow Thompson, Drs. J. King, and J. Chamberlain spoke.

Sunday, April 22 I, with Flickinger, attended the 2nd Reform Pres. Church. Met Dr. H.H. George; heard Rev. J.G. Paton, "apostle to New Hebrides" pr. at 11:00. At 3:30, I (alone) heard Rev.———[line in text of diary] of Syria. At night, we attended "The Heavenly Rest" Episcopal Church. Easter service, and address by a missionary, perhaps Bishop of British Colombia.

Monday, April 23 9:30, at Carnegie Hall, heard Augustus H. Strong of Union Theol. Seminary, J. Hudson Taylor, and Robt. E. Speer, Sec'y of B. of For. Missions. Pres. Church. In aftn, at Union M.E. Church, heard discussions on Africa, & found Prof. Scribner. Eve. at Carnegie, heard E. Stock, J.S. Dennis, and A.T. Pierson's.

Tuesday, April 24 Not getting good seat, I went to Astor Library in forenoon; went to Fifth Ave. Pres. Church at 2:30; passes on polygamy; that is, discussion. Eve. at Carnegie, heard Canon W.J. Edmonds, Dennis and Ashmore.

Wednesday, April 25 Heard (morning) R. Wardlow Thompson, A.H. Leonard, & others. Slept a half hour at noon, at hotel. Aftn. at Fifth Ave. (Dr. Hall's Church) heard Sloan, McLaurin, Joseph Taylor, Fred. Galpin. In the Eve. Heard Pres. Angel James, Maurice Phillips & Bishop Ridley, of British Columbia.

Thursday, April 26 *Morn.* at Carnegie, heard papers on Comety, by H.M. King, Alex. Sutherland, and discussions. *In afternoon,* Mrs. J.P.E. Kumler presiding, Mrs. Smith Waterbury, Baird, Ida Fay Levering, Barnes, and Gordon spoke. *Eve:* Mrs. J.T. Gracey presiding Mrs. Joseph Cook read Mrs. Bishop's paper, & addresses were given by Mrs. McLearen, Miss Thoburn, Miss Lilivati Singh and Mrs. W.A. Montgomery

Friday, April 27 *Morn.* at Carnegie Hall, Self Support of Missionary Churches. Speakers: R.W. Lambuth & Underwood read by Speer. Discussion: wild-colored man, Ewing, and another. Went to hotel. Flickinger left at 1:00. At 2:30, at the "Church of the Strangers", heard George Scholl, Jas. M. Buckley & R.W. Thompson. Eve. Carnegie: heard Seth Lowe, S.B. Capen, D.G. Barklay, Ira D. Sandspring

Saturday, April 28 Young Men's Day. I. Ross Stevenson, Duncan, & C.B. Hall, spoke. Aftn, Whitman, Taylor & Eddy spoke. Eve., W.F. McDowell, Eugene Stock, and John R. Mott spoke. I (with Scribner, my constant companion) went to Astor Library, and at 5:00 to Central Park anc walked through the Park to Cleopatra's Needle.

Sunday, April 29 With J.W. Scribner, I attended Mad. Park Church and heard C.H. Parkhurst, 1 Cor. 6.19,

"Ye are not your own." Was at Carnegie Hall at 3:45, and went up to 4th Gallery. Missionairies spoke. In Eve, attended the Marble Collegiate Reformed Church, and heard the pastor, Rev. David James Burrell pr. on "Valley of Achor." Hosea 2.15. This is successor of 1st Dutch Ch.

Monday, April 30 Morn'g at Carn. H: heard Patten (read by Scudder) Battersby, F.H. Taylor, O.R. Avison. After Lunch went to Lenox library, 5th Ave. & 70th St. Staid till 6.00. Eve. at Carnegie, on Liquor Traffick, heard Battersby, Theo. Cuyler, and C.D. Hartranft & Chas. Williams.

Tuesday, May 1 At Carnegie, heard, in morn., A.J.F. Behrends, and egotist, wild; David H. Greer, an able speaker; & Rev. Geo. F. Pentecost, able & judicious. Staid to noon hour meeting. Spent afternoon in Lenox Library. Evening: Benj. Harrison presided. Addresses by Matthew D. Babcock, able and brilliant; W.T.A. Barber, good, but read lifelessly; Bishop W.C. Doane; Canon Edmonds; Owen; and B. Harrison. Closed conference.

Wednesday, May 2 Went with Prof. J.W. Scribner through Flatbush to the park; returned & looked at Brooklyn churches: Plymouth Church, Church of Pilgrims, etc. To Lenox Library an hour. Leave Grand Union Hotel at 12:30, leave Courtland St. Ferry at 2:00, pass on cars thru Jersey City, Newark, Brunswick, Phila., Harrisburg, reach Pittsburg[h] at 2:00 A.M.

Thursday, May 3 Leave Pittsburgh, at 2:20, reach Columbus at 6:00; Dayton at 9:30. Spend the day in writing, etc.

Friday, May 4 Rev. Wm. B. Stoddard came in the Afternoon. We went to H.J. Becker's; Floyd came. He and Stoddard sup with us. We attend Carson's meeting at Summit St. Floyd lodged with us.

Saturday, May 5 Spent forenoon in writing. In afternoon, Bp. H. Floyd & Dr. Becker came, and we went to Louding's, and thence to Depot. I returned. Called at Lorin's, met Bp. Barnaby at Station, supper at Dr. H.J. Becker's. Bps. Barnaby and Floyd, Radicals & Bps. Mills and Kephart, Liberals. I came home.

Sunday, May 6 Heard Bishop H.T. Barnaby pr. at Broadway M.E. Church at 10:30, Matt. 5.2. I dine with bishops at Rev. H.J. Becker's. Attend meeting that tells of the Ecumenical Conference for Foreign Missions. Barnaby & Floyd lunch with us. Floyd pr. at B'y M.E. Ch. at 7:30, Hebr. 12.2, "Looking to Jesus."

Monday, May 7 Bishop Floyd came. I went with him to Becker's and dined. Barnaby & Floyd came home with me, and an hour later went with Becker to see Bishop J. Weaver. They all, and Rev. T. Weyer, and wife sup with me. H. Floyd returned at 8:30, and staid with us.

Tuesday, May 8 I wrote out a joint pastoral address. Liberal and Conservative Boards of Bishops met in joint session in the U. Bib. Sem. at 11:00 and again at 1:00, and agreed on terms, as to property settlements, and adopted my joint pastoral address. Then Bishop H. Floyd went on the 3:28 tr. home and Bishop H.T. Barnaby came with me, and supped and lodged.

Wednesday, May 9 Went with Bishop H.T. Barnaby to Peter Loudings, and to Union Depot; and he leaves on 9:45 train; and I buy shoes $3.50, sandals 85 cts, etc. At home the rest of the day. Lorin and Milton call in the evening.

Thursday, May 10 Arose at 6:15. Wrote an article for the Conservator in the afternoon.

Friday, May 11 At home. Netta Wright and the children came in the afternoon, and Milton staid for supper.

Saturday, May 12 With Lorin's Milton, went to the bank and to the public Library. Mrs. Dr. Mitchell of Miamisburg and Agnes Osborne visited Katharine in the Afternoon. Had ice cream. Lorin called in the evening.

Sunday, May 13 In forenoon, heard Rev. H.P. McCormick, ex missionary to Mexico, and since Missionary to Porto Rico, who spoke of the island, its people, their longing for American teachers and deliverance from priesthood. Netta called in the afternoon. I heard Dr. M. Wilson at 7:30, II Chron. 22.15, on "character of Cromwell."

Monday, May 14 At home in the forenoon. Went to town at 3, went to Public Library and remained till after six o'clock.

Tuesday, May 15 At home till 9:30. Meet Frederick H. Short & wife at the depot and stay with them till they go back to Cincinnati on 11:55 train. In afternoon pay mine & Katharine's tax. Katharine went to Woman's League for supper & a business meeting.

Wednesday, May 16 Called at Jacob Swank's an hour before noon. Read over the reports of the New York Missionary Conference.

Thursday, May 17 At home. I was out but little all day. I called at Lorin's with Katharine in the evening. Wrote an article for the paper ("The Conference Personel") in the afternoon.

Friday, May 18 Katharine went to Columbus to-day with the debaters of Dayton High School. It rained in the afternoon. Katharine returned home about 2:00 in the morning.

Saturday, May 19 At home in forenoon and mostly in afternoon. Went to Oak Street Church & Rev. B.G. Huber's to see Bish. J.W. Hott, on the documents. It is somewhat rainy to day and considerably cooler than for two week's past.

Sunday, May 20 At 10:30, at Grace M.E. Church, heard Rev. C.W. Gullett pr. John 4:10, "Best wine at last feast," a wonderfully flowery discourse. Remained at home in the evening and read Albert Barne's on the XX chap. of Revelation, as I had read Henry Cowles in the afternoon. Each makes a clear case against Premillenarionism.

Monday, May 21 At home during the day. Wrote letters. Called at P. Louding's so as to send some world [word] about the Wilberforce's in my letter to Rev. R.A. Morrison. Wm. McKee called in the evening for me to acknowledge a sumons in case of Alexander and Rebecca Letz' will.

Tuesday, May 22 At home all day, except going over to Union Depot in the forenoon to mail some letters. Went to R.A. Morrison, and others.

Thursday, May 24 At home most of the day. I went to bank, Elder & Johnson's, and the postoffice just before noon. Guy Montgomery called just before supper. I went with Katharine to Lorin's in the evening Milton sings and marches.

Friday, May 25 Went to town in the forenoon, and bought small envelopes, Socks, thin coat.

Saturday, May 26 Got a letter from Wilberforce. Wrote letters. Called in the afternoon and read the Letter to Mrs. Wilberforce.

Sunday, May 27 Lorin and the children came about 10:00, & Milton staid till evening. I heard Rev. Stevenson pr. at 11:00, Judges 3:15, on Memorial Day, "God raises up Men." It rained in the afternoon and evening.

Tuesday, May 29 At home all day. Wrote my Annual Report for East District in the afternoon.

Wednesday, May 30 I went with Milton, jr., to decorate his grandmother Wright's grave. Spent the rest of the day in reading and writing, and getting ready to go away.

Thursday, May 31 Start at 7:00, via Arcanum and New Castle to May's, in Rush Co., Ind. I find at Arcanum no connecting train so I go on freight to Greenville and thence to Dunreith. Mr. Hudelston takes me to Thomas Wright's. Supper and lodging at Harvey Wright's.

Friday, June 1 Call at Eva Thomas's and John Wright's. Dine at Harvey's, and he takes me to Rushville, whence I go to Milroy, and thence with James F. Harris to his house, on my Grandfather Reeder's old farm. I have supper and lodging there.

Saturday, June 2 Go with Harris' buggy to Mt. Zion Church, 2 ms. s.w. of Andersonville, to the Ministerial Institute. I dined at Rev. Charles S. Miller's. Supper at J.F. Harris'. Rev. C.B. Small pr. at 8:00. I lodge at J.I. Lefforge's, a mile west of the Church.

Sunday, June 3 I preach at Mt. Zion at 10:30, Eph. 3.19. "All the fullness of God." I dined at Philander Lefforge's, in the old Peter Miller house at the corners. In afternoon, a Wesleyan pr. Mrs Sarah Ann Miller died about

4:00. I walk down to Graveyard at Hopewell. Sup at Rev. C.S. Miller's. Bp. H. Floyd pr. at 7:30. I lodge at James Frank Harris's.

Monday, June 4 Go in Harris' buggy to our old farm on County line, call at Mr. Worth's & Morgan Linville's, and went thence to Nicholas Frank Bowen's in Fayette Co., and dine there. We attend Allen Thomas Stone's funeral at Fayetteville & I made some remarks. Sup at Lucinda Moor's, and lodge at Chas. Stevens'.

Tuesday, June 5 Go early to Rev. Chas. S. Miller's & send rig home. Bp. Floyd and I conduct the funeral services at 2:00 at Miller's house. Burial at Hopewell. We sup and lodge at Miller's. I saw at the funeral Hulda & Emeline Simmonds, Emeline Gordon & others. Emeline Simonds is now Harrison Nichols' wife.

Wednesday, June 6 George Miller's son takes us to Milroy and we go thence to Bolivar, where Henry Walters meets us and takes us to Rev. Henry Akright's in Servia. The Missionary Board meets at 7:30, and Rev. Wm. Dillon pr. the annual sermon at 8:00. I lodge at Benj. Bashore's, 1 m. south. (Faye Ardery M. Charles Greenlee, this eve.)

Thursday, June 7 The Mission Board had sessions forenoon and afternoon. I board at Bashore's. Rev. D.K. Flickinger lectured on Africa at 8:00. (Miss Faye Ardery married to Chas. Greenlee last evening, in Hutchinson, Kansas.)

Friday, June 8 Board Sessions. I board at Benj. Bashore's. Bp. H.T. Barnaby pr. at 8:00.

Saturday, June 9 Board of Bishops met at 8:00 at H. Akright's. We dine there. We go on 12:07 tr. to Huntington and have a meeting to incorporate Mis. Society. I walked up to Bro. Brooks' in College Park & sup there. Heard Rev. C.L. Wood pr. at 8:00.

Sunday, June 10 I addressed the Sun. School ten min. Bishop H. Floyd pr. the bacalaureate sermon at 10:30, Rev. 3:20, "Be thou faithful." I dine at Prof. A.P. Barnaby's and sup at Rev. A.B. Lilly's. Call in afternoon at Mrs. Rufus A. Morrison's. Bp. Barnaby pr. at 8:00. I lodge at Pres. Kiracofe's.

Monday, June 11 Educational Board met at 8:30. Business was pursued forenoon and afternoon. I dine at Kiracofe's and sup at E. Clapp's. The glee club has an entertainment in the evening. I lodge at Kiracofe's.

Tuesday, June 12 The Board continued. I board at Kiracofe's. An entertainment by by [repeated in text] Literary Societies at 8:00, which I did not attend.

Wednesday, June 13 Publishing Board met at 8:00. Commencement at 10:00. Rev. Naftker's address. I dine at E. Clapp's. Educational Board at 2:00. Some other committees meet. Supper at Prof. J.H. McMurray's. Pub. Board met at 7:00, Growley session. I did not get to the musical entertainment.

Thursday, June 14 Went to Sayler's office and incorporated the Missionary Society. Went on 10:19 train via Wabash to Fairmount, & thence on 3:39 tr. to Fowlerton, Look over the place (farm) some and sup & lodge at R.W. White's. (Clarrissa Emeline Zeller was married to David Worth Dennis, to-day.)

Friday, June 15 Call at Millspaugh's Store, at Henry Simons, and go on 11:10 train to Fairmount & thence via Anderson and Richmond to Dayton. Arrive home at 7:00 and find all well.

Saturday, June 16 Was at home to-day. Writing some; resting some. Lorin & family called in the evening.

Sunday, June 17 Attended the United Presbyterian Church, Cor. High & McLain Sts. and heard Rev. C.E. McStravick pr. Isa. 59.1, on prevailing evils. At 7:30, heard J. Rosser Jones at Fourth Pres. Ch., Mark 9:27. He plays the anarchist. I was much disgusted.

Monday, June 18 Milton came for me to take him and Ivonette to the Ringling Animal show parade. Dr. H.J. Becker called in the afternoon. I went to Jac. Swank's after supper.

Tuesday, June 19 At home in forenoon. Katharine started to Oberlin at 9:40. In the afternoon, I called to see Rev. Mr. Eckert who is very low with consumption. He is on our street near Fifth.

Thursday, June 21 At home in the forenoon. Went to town about 3:00, and spent the hours in the Public Library. Lorin and family called in the evening. McKinley and Ro[o]sevelt were nominated unanimously at the Phil. Convention to-day, for president & vice president.

Friday, June 22 Nettie and family were with us, canning cherries.

Sunday, June 24 Was at home all day, except a walk a mile and back. Joseph Wilberforce called a half hour in the evening.

Monday, June 25 Wrote letters. D.K. Flickinger came at 6:40. We go to Phillips House & read letters from Africa and thence to Peter Louding's to see the Wilberforce's and thence home.

Tuesday, June 26 At home in forenoon, after going with D.K. Flickinger to Louding's and the train. At 2:00, attend Dennis Ensey's wife's funeral, Rev. J. Miller of Park Street Pres. Church officiating. Text: Mark 14:8, "She hath done what she could." Rev. Reichert was taken away from 39 Hawthorn[e] St. to ———[line appears in text] for burial.

Wednesday, June 27 Called at Lorin's, and Milton went home with me and staid till after dinner. Called again at Lorin's, in the evening, and saw Milton's "Cyclone" (wagon).

Thursday, June 28 At home. Wrote article for the *Conservator* & sent Appointments for conferences for publication. In the evening called at Lorin's and at Mrs. Richert's.

Friday, June 29 At home. Katharine did not come. Got word, by Mr. Rodgers, of the death of Rev. J.K Billheimer, who died this morning.

Saturday, June 30 Called to see Mrs. Bedell in Afternoon. Katharine came home from Oberlin on 2:55 train. Called at Lorin's in the evening.

Sunday, July 1 Went on 9:53 A.M. train to Westerville. Mrs. Billheimer and Mark on the train. Rev. J.K Billheimer's funeral at 2:00. Prof. Garst, Bp. Kephart and I spoke. Came on traction back to Columbus, and thence home arriving at Dayton at 8:00.

Monday, July 2 Was at home all day, except a little walk out. Milton was with us forenoon and afternoon. I did little except rest. Wrote Reuchlin a letter.

Saturday, July 7 Quar. Meet. Germantown. I did not go to the quarterly Sent Address of Board of Education to Dillon for publication. Called in forenoon at Bedell's neighbor's & learned that she had not returned after the funeral at Westerville.

Sunday, July 8 Went on 8:00 car to West Alexander, and thence to Germantown. Rev. R.G. Montgomery, P.E., preached John 6:28,29. I dine, sup and lodge at Lewis Wett's. Bro. E. Kiger and Joseph Thomas and wife there in afternoon. Rev. R.G. Montgomery came in the afternoon and staid till morning. Witts, Montg. & I talk much on Scriptures.

Monday, July 9 We call at Rev. T. Weyer's, Mrs. Long's, Mrs. Thomas's, and go on 10.07 train to Franklin, and thence to Dayton on the traction line. Bro. Montgomery dines with us, and goes on 2:55 tr. home.

Wednesday, July 11 Milton was with us nearly all day. In afternoon we took our ships to Wolf Creek & sailed them with feathers for sails. Dr. Becker came about 4 or 5 o'clock, and we talked an hour. Lorin & family called in the evening.

Thursday, July 12 Lorin's Milton & Leontine staid with us in forenoon & Lorin & wife dined with us. Revs. T. Weyer and J. Freeman & families called a half hour. Carrie Kaler was quite sick. Nettie and children are here.

Friday, July 13 At home forenoon. Went on 5:58 tr. to Union City. Called at John Judy's Restaurant. I lodged at the Branham House.

Saturday, July 14 Go on 6:40 tr. to Anderson and Fairmount, and Fowlerton. I dined at R.W. White's. Went about 4:20 to W.H.H. Reeder's & had supper there. I lodged at Oliver A. Glass's.

Sunday, July 15 I attended Sabbath School at Hopewell Ch., in Leach. I dined at W.H.H. Reeder's. Mrs. Greer & daughter, Mattie's aunt are visiting there. I remain till evening and at 8:00 pr. at Hopewell, Matt. 16:18, on God's revelation of truth, inwardly to all. I lodge at Oliver A. Glass's.

Monday, July 16 Marcus Glass takes me to Fowlerton & to White's. I go on 11:10 tr. to Fairmount. I dined at Ellis Wright's. In the afternoon, I, with Jas. F. Life, looked at real properties. I lodged at Ellis Wright's.

Tuesday, July 17 With Agent Brown, I look at Properties. Saw Wm. Lindsey in the forenoon and called to see him in the afternoon and then did not see him.

Wednesday, July 18 Went to Depot. Called at Lindsey's, but did not find him. He and Woods came to depot. I went to Wabash & Huntington. Dined at a restaurant. Called on Flickinger, Keiter, & Dillon at their offices. I went with Bishop H. Floyd to Pres. C.H. Kiracofe's & supped and lodged there. Attended prayer meeting at Col. Chap.

Thursday, July 19 Alvin K. takes me & Floyd to Mission Room. Ex. Com. meets forenoon & afternoon. We dine with Fiickinger at Bailey's. R.A. Morrison blue on Africa. After 4, I look at Properties, and lodge at R.A. Morrison's.

Friday, July 20 We go on 10:19 tr. to Wabash, and thence to Marion. I dine and sup at a restaurant. I look, with Worden, at properties. I go on 6:30 traction to Fairmount & lodge at Ellis Wright's.

Saturday, July 21 I made an agreement with Lindsey & went to Marion & dined at Restaurant. Lanfester showed me houses and lots. Went on 2:44 tr. to Union City and thence home to Dayton.

Sunday, July 22 At Pres. First Church, at 10:30, heard Rev. Tappan, Pres. of Miami University, on Gal. 6.2, "Bear Ye one anothers burdens", etc.

Friday, July 27 At home except an hour's trip to town. Called on Mrs. Wilberforce, looked at new Depot, failed to f ind Mr. Coleman, insurance agent. Lorin and Milton called in the evening.

Sunday, July 29 At First Presb. Church, heard Rev. A.A.E. Taylor, of Columbus, O., on Ps. 30.5, "Weeping may xx Joy cometh in the morning." [xx appears in original text] An essay! Lorin's Milton spent the day with us. In the eve. at Williams Street Baptist Church, heard Dr. Mullin, Louisville, Ky., on Josh. 1.1.

Wednesday, August 1 Wrote letters and investigated scriptures on eschatology. Found that Enoch, Abraham, Moses, David, Job, Solomon, Daniel, Paul, Peter, and John had intelligent conceptions of a future state unlike the hades of the heathen.

Thursday, August 2 Wrote letters and looked up scriptures. Milton spent the day with us.

Friday, August 3 Writing letters and studying on the scriptural, apocryphal and Ciceronian ideas of the future state.

Sunday, August 5 At Third St. Pres. Ch., heard Dr. W.O. Thompson pr 67th Psalm. At 3:30 heard him at Association Hall. In the evening heard Secretary Sinclair speak at open air meeting by Congregational Church at Boulevard, on Bartimeus.

Monday, August 6 Lorin's children with us to-day.

Sunday, August 12 At 3rd St. Pres. Church, at 10:30, heard Dr. W.O. Thompson on Rom. 14.16. A caution against being carried away by the political campaign. Heard Dr. Thompson again in the afternoon (3:30 at Assoc. Hall) on "If any man thirst." Called at Lorin's.

Monday, August 13 Went on 7:00 tr. via Union City to Fairmount. Lunch at Gas City. Sup at Ellis Wright's. Go with Wm. Dye and Tomlinson to R.W. White's, and lodge there. They had lost one of their twins lately.

Tuesday, August 14 I took Ellis's rig home and dined there. Afternoon, I contracted for a lot 66 X 165 ft., for $1,300.00 but deferred closing it till I could have abstract to date. So I go on 5:30 interurban line to Marion. Hear A. Rust pr. "If Ye abide in me," I find my home at Dallas Bilbe's, with H. Floyd. Bilbe's Chil: Mabel, Dwight, & Trula.

Wednesday, August 15 Conference opened in Horton Street Church, at 9:00. Bp. Floyd presiding. At noon, I went to Fairmount and got deed and paid $1,300.00 for lot. Return to Marion, leave deed for record & sup at Bilbe's. Dr. Kiracofe pr. at 8:00.

Thursday, August 16 I preside in forenoon. Dine at John Null's on the West Side of the River. I preach at 8:00, Rom. 2:7, on Immortality.

Friday, August 17 1 preside in the forenoon. Wolfard & C.B. Small were elected pres'g elders. Tharp pr. at 8:00.

Saturday, August 18 I preside in the forenoon. Z. McNew took an "open" transfer. Close at 5:00. Rufus A. Morrison lectured in tent at 8:00, on Africa. It was quite good.

Sunday, August 19 Bp. H. Floyd pr at 10:30, and we dined at Mrs. Susan Parlett's, H.W. Robbins pr. at 2:30. We sup at John Null's. J. Rees pr. at 8:00, "And he dwelt among us." We lodge as usual at Dallas Bilbe's.

Monday, August 20 I go to Fairmount and dine at Ellis Wright's. Ride out to my farm, 5 miles east, with Clark Leach. Andrew White takes me to Oliver A. Glass's, where I lodge.

Tuesday, August 21 Go to the farm, and thence to Wm. H.H. Reeder's. There I dine and sup, and then go to Oliver A. Glass's, birthday ice cream birth-day party. Lizzie Broyles and her daughter, Minnie Polhemus, with other relatives, and some others, were there. I lodged at Wm. H.H. Reeder's.

Wednesday, August 22 Oliver Glass took me to Fairmount. I went on 11:30 electric car to to [repeated in text] Marion. Get deed, pay tax, and go on to Bolivar, where I hire a rig to Laketon, Ind. I find my home at Howard John's. I pr. at 8:00, 1st Cor. 13:13.

Thursday, August 23 St. Joseph Conference opened at 9:00, and proceeded well. Rev. Mygrant pr. at 8:00.

Friday, August 24 Conference proceeded. Appeal, etc. Rufus A. Morrison lectured on Africa at 8:00. It was a good lecture.

Saturday, August 25 Conference continued. In afternoon, Rev. H. Akright was elected presiding elder. Ther report in J.H. Smith's case was voted down. Recess after 4:30 till evening service. Mr. John's 7-year old girl is Ruth.

Sunday, August 26 Bp. Barnaby pr. at 10:30, Rom. 15.29. Johnson took up a large collection for him. We dine as usual. At S.S. Anniversary at 3:00, Wright, Wright Smith, and Duart, a lay man, spoke. Bp. Barnaby pr. at 8:00, John 13.2, "Having loved his own," etc.

Monday, August 27 Went on 11:54 tr. to Huntington. Dine at a new restaurant at Jefferson St. Bridge. Meet the Mis. Exec. Com. at 2:00. We conclude to take the Wilberforce family to Huntington. Sup and lodge at E. Clapp's. Was at Official Church meeting at College Chapel at 8:00.

Tuesday, August 28 Go to Publishing Establishment & stay till noon. Go on Erie R'y to Markle. Hire conveyance ($1.00) to Zanesville. Board at Noah Walker's, 2 sq. n. of U.B. Church. Rev. C.S. Johnson pr. a good sermon & able, at 8:00, 1 John 3:2. "We know."etc His Walker's wife a Harvey, gr. daut. of Jeremiah Conway of Henry Co.

Wednesday, August 29 Conference opened at 2:00, and progressed well. Board as usual. Walker's son is Orval.

Thursday, August 30 In the morning, I visited the cemetery, a quarter mile south, & see statues of Wm. Hoverstock and former wife, in marble. Rev. R.A. Morrison lectured on Africa at 8:00, eve.

Friday, August 31 Conference continued. Willet Skinner's memorial service at 3:00. R.G. Montgomery and Wm. Miller are elected pres. elders. Sta. Com. met at Noah Walker's at 6:30. There was a bitter anti Morrison feeling, and I am treated shamefully. Alas for poor human nature! I was wakeful much of the night.

Saturday, September 1 Sta. Com. met at 8:00, A.M. at Walker's. Conference continued. In afternoon, I had a tilt with P.B. William and Dillon, who injected partyism into the discussion on Moral Reform. Conference closed at 3:30. Dillon pr. at 8:00, on "Christ hath once suf-

fered, for all," etc. 1 Pet. 3:18. I was wakeful from 12 till 3 o'clock.

Sunday, September 2 I preach in the tent (S.W.) at 10:30, Dan. 4.25, "He ruleth in the km. of men." Dine on the ground with Bowman's. Spoke in Aftn. in S.S. Anniversary. Supper at Wm. Hoverstock's. Lovefeast and communion in the evening. Lodge at N. Walker's as usual.

Monday, September 3 Went on 6:30 hack to Ft. Wayne. This is Labor Day Celebration. I went on 1:45 tr. to Toledo, and thence on 5:00 tr. to Cygnet, and walked back to Trombley, and went thence on electric car to Jerry City. Found Conference home at Wm. Deusler's, north of U.B. Church.

Tuesday, September 4 Wrote many letters to-day. Called at 4:30 at Isa. Miller's a half mile north of Densler's, and saw M.H. Tussing. Board at Deusler's. She is a second wife and Qr. Conf. preacher. He has 40 acres of land & oil wells. His income is $2400.00 a year.

Wednesday, September 5 I stay at Deusler's. Rufus A. Morrison came about 7:00, eve. Miss Eliz. Stevens pr. at 8:00, Luke 19:13, "Occupy till I come." Did pretty well.

Thursday, September 6 Conference opened at 9:00, and progressed well forenoon & afternoon. At 7:45, R.A. Morrison lectured on Africa to a very large congregation. He lodged at Deusler's.

Friday, September 7 Conference progressed well. In the afternoon, J.A. Ferguson was elected presiding elder. Stationing Com. met, 6:30, at Deusler's. Pres. C.H. Kiracofe came, at 7:00 p.m. S. Stevens pr. at 7:45, Rom 13.10, "Love is the fulfilling of the Law." Kiracofe and I stay at Deusler's. Stevens is quite able.

Saturday, September 8 Conference continued. Discussion on Moral Reform, and Edw. Day's party amendment. Close at 4:00. Pres. Kiracofe lectured at 7:45 on Education; text, Gal. 6:7, "What a man soweth."

Sunday, September 9 I pr. at 10:30, Gen. 15:16. I spoke just one hour. Dine at Dick Caskie's, and sup there. At 8:00, G.C. Lashley pr. Luke 17.31, "Remember Lot's wife." I stay at Duesler's as usual. Lashley was quite prosy.

Monday, September 10 I went with S. Stevens to Lonis Zimmerman's in Rising Sun, in buggy and dine there. We call at Horace Smith's. We go on to Burgoon, and sup & lodge at Rev. Silvarus Stevens. Their little son is affected with (fits) spells.

Tuesday, September 11 Go on 8:20 tr. to Mansfield and thence to Orrville. Stay at Mrs. John Lefever's.

Wednesday, September 12 Went on 7:35 a.m. train to Massilon, and thence on 9:50 tr. to Canal Dover . Albert Overholt takes me to Samuel Carnathan's, near the Crooked Run Church. I dine, sup and lodge there. E.R. Kile pr. at 7:30, Rom. 8:13, a "second work" sermon.

Thursday, September 13 I board at S. Carnathan's. East Ohio Conference opened at 9:00, and progressed well. Dr. H.J. Becker dined with me. Dr. D.K. Flickinger and Mrs. A.R. Kiracofe came. H.H. Young pr. at 7:45, 1 Cor. 15:10, "By the grace of God, I am what I am. "

Friday, September 14 Conference business progressed well. Discussion on Moral Reform. In afternoon, we had discussion on missions by Mrs. Kiracofe and Dr. Flickinger. H.J. Becker is elected pres. elder. The Stationing Com. met at 6:30, at Carnathan's . H.J. Becker pr. at 7:45, 1 Cor. 12.28, "First apostle, then prophets," etc.

Saturday, September 15 Conference progressed well and closed at 4:00. Educational discussion in forenoon, publishing in afternoon. Sup at Leonard Overholt's. Mission Meeting at 7:30; Flickinger and B.O. Hazard & wife spoke. Cash Coll. for Africa, $6.76.

Sunday, September 16 I preached at 10:30, Ps. 144.15, 147.20, "God hath not so dealt with any nation." We ordain Benjamin Otterbein Hazzard. I dine at Albert Overholt's. Flickinger pr. at 7:30, Ps. XV. Communion followed. It was good.

Monday, September 17 I go with others to Canal Dover, and thence to New Philadelphia. I dine sup & lodge at B. Frank Fisher's. We attended a Lutheran funeral in the afternoon, and walked through the Cemetery.

Tuesday, September 18 At 1:20 p.m., I left Fisher's and run on electric car to Urichville & thence to Dennison,

where at 2:45, I start to Pennsylvania, arriving at Pittsburgh at 7:00 (eastern time) and start on 8:30 train to Harrisburg. I put on heavy flannel, but caught some cold, it being a cool night in the mountains.

Wednesday, September 19 I arrived at Harrisburg about 4:30, and go on to Carlisle at 5:00, arriving about 6:00 A.M. I call at Rev. W.O. Weidler and find my home there, 1 1/2 sq n.e. of C. Valley Depot. Rev. S.J. Nicklas is moving to Carlisle & boarding at W.O. Weidler's, J.A. Mummart pr. at 8:00, 1 Pet. 1:3,4,5; preached quite well; is very promising.

Thursday, September 20 Pennsylvania Conference opened at 9 o'clock, and progressed well. Rev. M.F. Keiter preached at 8:00.

Friday, September 21 Conference continued. R.A. Morrison arrived in afternoon at 6:00. We held a missionary meeting at 8:00 eve. Not much subs[cr]iption.

Saturday, September 22 Conference continued. The com. on Hench's case reported. Report was adopted, requiring concessions. The memorial services of Rev. J.S. Wentz were held at 3:00. DM. Hench, proving obstinate, a prosecutor was appointed. Rev. R.A. Morrison lectured on Africa at 8:00. Collection was $5.77.

Sunday, September 23 I preach at U.B. Ch. at 10:30, Job 14:14, "If a man die, ...live again." Communion followed. Collection for Carlisle Church: $15.06. I was at Weidler's till eve. Pr. at 7:30, Rev. 11.15. Collect $5.00, for Carlisle Ch. Carrie Raffensberger is converted. Weidner's Children are: Estelle, Lovett (married), Flora, Sarah, Robert (about 18).

Monday, September 24 The brethren mostly leave for home. Morrison and I visited the Indian School, with G.S. Seiple & Harry Huber. Charley Speedrock, our Indian guide, b. in N.Y. City. Dine at Weidler's. Afternoon a company of us (Seiple, Harry H. & wife, Flora Weidler, Mises. Miller and McCaw included) visit Boiling Springs, on Trolley, and we visit Dickenson Col. Staid at Hershey House. I go on 6:05 train to Harrisb.

Tuesday, September 25 I go to Depot at 8:00 A.M. I wrote a letter to Flickinger and a card to Katharine and go on 3:35 train to Williamsport (Cup of Coffee & crackers there), and thence to Corry, Pa., arriving there at 2:45. I lodge at Rev. Samuel Evans'.

Wednesday, September 26 Remain at Evan's during the forenoon. Rev. R.W. Mercer came after dinner. We go at 3:00 to Conference (via Glynden) at Britton Run. I get supper at Melvin Pickard's, who is groggy. Rev. T.J. Butterfield pr. at 7:30, John 10,27, "My sheep hear my voice," etc., an excellent sermon. I board at Oliver H. Bloomfield's, a half-mile north.

Thursday, September 27 Erie Conference opened at U.B. Church, at 9:00 and progressed well, forenoon and afternoon. I dined at Pierce's, a 1/4 m. west, but board at Bloomfield's. R.W. Mercer preached at 7:30, Mark 11.13, "Nothing but leaves."

Friday, September 28 Conference proceded well. I dined at Mr. Pratt's, soninlaw of Mrs. Fraliche, who was there. Sup at E.S. Welman's in town. The stationing committee met there at at [repeated in text] 6:30. I pr. at 7:30, Titus 2.14. Lodge at Bloomfield's as usual. Rev. R.J. Pettit boarded there, and took me back and forth. He was pastor there.

Saturday, September 29 Conference continued. I joined issue on party resolutions. I dine at Bloomfield's. Supper at Elmer S. Welman's. Rev. W.H. Hodge pr. at 7:30. I lodge at O.H. Bloomfield's, Children: Milton, Hope, Ruth. Conference closed at 4:00.

Sunday, September 30 I preached at 11:00, Matt. 25.46, last clause, "life eternal." Coll. amounted to $30.75. I dine at Bloomfield's with S. Evans and T.J. Butterfield. I.I. Boorum pr. at 7:30. I lodge at Bloomfield's. She and oldest daughter seem quite pious; he is kind and smart, but not religious.

Monday, October 1 Bro. Welman, Elmer's father, takes me to Union City. I dine at Rev. N.R. Luce's. He is almost blind. I go to Peter K. Drury's to supper. I lodged at Luce's.

Tuesday, October 2 I go on 9:13 Erie train to Akron, Ohio, and thence on 3:13 C.A.C. train to Columbus,

arriving at 7:40. Go to Board of Trade Building and heard John G. Wolley and Prof. Samuel Dickey, of Michigan. With Dr. H.J. Becker, I stay at Dr. D.K. Flickinger['s], 201 S. Front St.

Wednesday, October 3 Go on 7:35 train to Lancaster; thence to C.L. & W Junction on C.M.V. R'y; thence on Col.& O.S. R'y to Laurelville. Wm. Poling takes Flickinger and me to Fielding Poling's and we dine there. Fielding Poling takes us near the Pleasant Ridge Church to Wm. Hutchinson's. J.O. Trovinger pr. at 7:30, James 1.27 & Dr. H.J. Becker exhorted.

Thursday, October 4 Conference opened promptly at 9:00, as my conferences usually do (mean time). Business proceeded rapidly. Flickinger elected Chairman. H.J. Becker preached at 7:15 Matt. 10.14, "Shake off the dust of". Warm day, and in eve., a warm crowded house. We board at Wm. Hutchinson's. Letty & son a year old, illigitimate, I learn.

Friday, October 5 Conference progressed well. J. Hoffhines and N. Allebaugh elected P. Elders. Stationing Com. met at Church & orchard, D.K. Flickinger pr. at 7:15 on missions, Eph. 3.8, "Preach among Gentiles, unsearchable riches of Christ." Warm house, indeed. I exhort 10 minutes.

Saturday, October 6 Stationing Com. met in Orchard at 7:30. Conference continued and closed at 5:00. Memorial of Rev. J. Everhart at 3:00; Rev. D. Folk, G.W. Tuttle and E. Blausser, spoke. Discussion of reports. Dr. Becker lectured on travels in Holy Land, at 7:00; Collection for him $11.25.

Sunday, October 7 I preach at 10:30, Acts 20.28. S.S. Anniversary at 2:30; Becker & I spoke 20 minutes each. Rain after forenoon meeting, hard. Owing to rain the evening meeting became a prayer meeting, though there was quite a congregation. Lodge as usual.

Monday, October 8 Go very early to South Perry for mail. Young Hutchinson takes Flickinger and me to Laurelville. We go on 8:13 tr. to C.L. & W. Junction; and H.J. Becker and I thence to Washington C.H., where we wait till 4:20; reach home (Dayton) at 6:10. Netta and the Children called. Went to bed at 9:00, and slept 9 hours.

Tuesday, October 9 I rest to-day. Went to Winter's Nat. Bank and to Post office in Afternoon. Went to bed early.

Wednesday, October 10 At home all day. Went to town at 2:00, and left measure for new coat & vest at Leibenburg's. Left umbrella at 9 W. 5th St. for a new cover. Finished recording in diary (from notes taken) from Aug. 13 to Oct. 8, 1900, at 10:30 eve.

Thursday, October 11 Registered at about 9:00. At home. Wrote several letters. Prof. J.T. Shaw, of Oberlin, called in the evening and "took tea" with us.

Friday, October 12 At home in the forenoon. Attended the Democratic meetlng at 12:30 and heard Charley Baker and W.J. Bryan. Both speeches were highly partisian. Write several letters.

Saturday, October 13 Go on 7:00 train to Union City & Fairmount. Arrive at F. about 2:00. Call at Ellis Wright's. At 3:00, I go with Rhoda W. to their farm (Wid. Helms) and from Frank Kirkwood's, walk to W.H.H. Reeder's. Sup & lodge there.

Sunday, October 14 I called at O.A. Glass's, and went with him to Hopewell Church, and pr. at 10:30, John 15.1, "Vine & branches." I return with Oliver and dine there. He takes mc to Salem M.P. Church to S.S. Rally, where I spoke awhile. I lodged at Levi Simons'.

Monday, October 15 I went to Robt. W. White's, on my farm, and thence to Fowlerton. Sold my corn to Chas. Leach, to be delivered in November, at 30 cts, bush. Dine at Charles Malone's. I sup at White's, and go on 6:10 tr. to Fairmount. Lodged at Ellis Wright's.

Tuesday, October 16 I looked after my Fairmount lot business, and dined at Ellis's, and went on 5:15 car to Alexandrla, and thence afoot and by caught up conveyance to Ed. Frazier's, 2 1/2 miles east, and lodged there.

Wednesday, October 17 I gave Grace (Ed. and Emma's only daughter) much of the genealogy of the family, which she wrote down in a book. She took me, after

dinner, to John W. Broyles' in Alexandria, where I found only their two girls, Laura and Lizzie, at home. I went on car to Fairmount and thence on 6:30 car to Gas City & heard ex Gov. W.S. Taylor, of Ky. Returned to Ellis's.

Thursday, October 18 In Fairmount till after dinner, when I went with Rhoda and children, to Cumberland, to Carl Simon's funeral, son of Adrich, pr. by Pres. T.C. Read, of Upland College, Ps. 23.4. Went back to Kirkwood's corner and walked to Joseph Cain's; supped & lodged there, in Fowlerton.

Friday, October 19 Went to R.W. White's, looked over east woods, dined at W's, and went to Robert B. Reeder's. Mrs. Douglas and Mrs. Mitchel, sisters of Robert Glass's, came and lodged there. Mrs. M. was army nurse at Louisville, and told of Army degredation and of its female attendants, as one who "Spake from authority."

Saturday, October 20 I went with Wm. and Robt. to Leach, and went on 11:10 tr. to Fairmount. I dined at Robt. Hastings with his three daughters & their cousin of Knox, Ind., Rariden Smith's daughter. I called at C. Brattain's, Mrs. Chas. Atkinson's, and Mrs. Mary Ann Bond's. I sup and lodge at Ellis W's.; Rev. Pell with them for supper.

Sunday, October 21 Rev. W.J. Oxley, pastor, pr. at U.B. Church at 10:30, Matt. 11.28 30, "Labor & heavy laden." Spoke 20 min. & I 10 or 15. I dine with Oxley at Roland Smith's. I sup & lodge at Ellis Wright's. I preach at M.E. Church at 7:45, Dan. 4.25, "He ruleth in km. of men", etc.

Monday, October 22 Went on 8:30 interurban car to Gas City and thence on 9:15 train to Union City, and on 1:05 tr. to Dayton, arri. at 2:33. Found all well. Melvin Pickard of Britton's Run, Pa. called, in the afternoon, to borrow $10.00, which I lent him, "expecting nothing." He was on a spree.

Tuesday, October 23 Went to town; got umbrella (newly covered $1.00) and note paper & "Day in Athens," Socrates. At home the rest of the day. Benj. Van Cleve Andrews born. I called at Lorin's in the evening.

Friday, October 26 At home all day, writing. The boys

(Wilbur and Orville) in the evening arrived at home from Kitty Hawk, N.C.

Saturday, October 27 At home forenoon, mostly reading. Went with Milton afternoon, saw Louding's monkey. Got my coat & pants at Joe Levenburger's—$22.00. Milton took supper with us. Read to-day Capt. Louis Lannette's project of an ice tunnel to the North Pole! He is an Arctic explorer & of the French navy.

Sunday, October 28 Heard (lst Presb.) M. Wilson pr. a good sermon, Jer. 22.16, "Judged cause of poor & needy." Lorin's dined with us. At home all the rest of the

Monday, October 29 At home writing most of the day. Called at Bedell's in forenoon and went to town. In the evening I attended Republican meeting at Lauding (in Library Park) and heard D.B. Henderson, Speaker of House, Corporal Tanner, and Gov. Nash. Tanner spoke well.

Friday, November 2 Katharine went on 7:00 tr. to Columbus to Teachers' Convention. I wrote up genealogical Notes of the Benham's for Hon. Eldridge H. Benham, of Neosho, Missouri.

Saturday, November 3 At home writing and culling the daily papers. Walked to the Public library and back home, in the evening.

Sunday, November 4 At the Central Catholic Church (corner of 4th & Wilki[n]son Sts.) at 7:30 Morning service, house full. At 10:30, with Milton jr., heard Howard L. Torbet at Grace Church, on Luke 14.16-23; a good speaker. Milton & Ivonette dined with us. Heard at 7:30, Zed Cop, at School Street, 1 Thes. 5.21. Telling how he would vote. Silly.

Tuesday, November 6 Voted early for McKinley and Roosevelt. At home the rest of the day. In the evening, to get the election dispatches, went to Journal bulletin board, and staid till 11:00, when Neurs (Dem.) sent up red lights to indicate Republican victory.

Wednesday, November 7 Read of the landslide in McKinley's favor, and rejoiced.

Thursday, November 8 At home all forenoon writing.

Took a book to Library, and then rode out to J. Swank's. There I encountered Miss or Mrs. Boyd, Dowieite worker, who came to convert the Swank's! Sharp controversy. Called at H.J. Becker's, who is having artificial gas put into his house.

Friday, November 9 Weather fair. I started on 9:45 train to Liberty Center, via Toledo. Reach Liberty at 6:02. Israel Poutins and his father Wm. Poutins met me & took me 4 1/2 miles N.W. to Poutins's. Israel's Children: Byron 12; Harry Milton 7. The old folks live with Israel.

Saturday, November 10 Remained at Poutins's during the forenoon. Afternoon went to the new Church and saw the trustees and arranged for the dedication. Sup & lodge at Poutins's. Rev. L.S. Wilmoth pr. at 7:30. Wilmoth is former pastor. Rev. C.L. Snyder is the present pastor.

Sunday, November 11 Weather snowy. I pr. at 11:00 at Victory Chapel, 1 K 8.11, raised $332.50— $82.50 more than called for—and dedicated the church, 2 ms n.w. of Liberty. Dined at S.W. Graffice's, son of Rev. J.T. Graffice of Sandusky Conference. I pr. at 7:30, Gen. 15.16. Porter & wife stay at Poutins's.

Monday, November 12 Israel Poutius takes me and Wilmoth to Liberty. Call to see Mother Eliz. Whitmore. Go on 7:20 tr. to Wabash, miss connection three min. and to wait six hours. Go on 5:15 tr. to Fairmount. Stay at Ellis Wright's.

Tuesday, November 13 I am about town in forenoon. Dine at Ellis W's. Wrote letters till 4:00. Went to Robert Hasting's. Called at Roland Smith's on my way. Sup and lodge at Hasting's. Robt. an enthusiastic Republican.

Wednesday, November 14 Return to town. I called at Bales' and at Ellis W's., got blue grass seed at Ulerey's, at $1.50 a bushel. Go on 9:39 train to Fowlerton, dine at R.W. White's on the place. Clear off brush in Afternoon. Sup & lodge at White's.

Thursday, November 15 I went on 11:10 (11:30) tr. to Fairmount, and dined at Ellis's. I looked up shingles and mended roof on my house. Lodge at Ellis W's.

Friday, November 16 Worked awhile on mending the roof on my Fairmount house. Intended to go on 8:30 car to Gas City, but it was 20 min. late. Went on 10:30 car to Alexandria, which was 20 m. late. Dined at J.W. Broyles's. Went on car (an hour late) to Anderson & on 4:25 tr. to Richmond. Call at D.K. Zeller's an hour. Go on 9:55 tr. (35 m. late) home, arr. about 11:00. None knew of my coming.

Saturday, November 17 I was at home all day. Slept some—read and wrote. Called at Lorin's in the evening. This is the seventy second anniversary of my birth.

Sunday, November 18 I heard Rev. W.P. Miller preach at Park, Presbyterian Church, 1 John 1:1, "Word of life." a good sermon. Milton, Jr. was at our house to-day. I called a half-hour at 4:00 at Jacob Swank's, a minute at Dr. Becker's, and a half hour at Mrs. Bartles. Staid at home in evening.

Monday, November 19 At home writing for E.H. Benham on genealogy.

Tuesday, November 20 At home writing as yesterday. Called at Milton's.

Wednesday, November 21 At home. Wrote letters. In afternoon, called at Joseph E. Gustin's 53 Reigel Street, a soninlaw fo Philemon Holt. Mrs. Hariet (Holt) Gustin gave me the genealogy of Philemon Holt's family.

Thursday, November 22 Wrote and read in the forenoon, and part of the afternoon. Go to town at 4:00, and get Crognenole board for Milton and toys for the girls.

Friday, November 23 At home writing. About 3:30, I go to J.E. Gustin's and get additional facts concerning the Holt family. It rained a little as I returned. Harriet gave some omissions, additions and corrections.

Saturday, November 24 This was quite a rainy day, greatly belying   as for some weeks, the predictions of the Weather Bureau. I read in America, Andrew's copy, of Benjamin Van Cleve's Memoranda, and at 3:00 went to Mrs. Fay Dover's, Van Buren St., and to Mrs. Anna

McKnight's 1600 Wayne Ave., who is a dau. of Thomas Dover dec. and has Benj. Van Cleve's notes. Sat up till abt. midnight.

Sunday, November 25 At 10:30, I heard Rev. Edgar W. Work preach at 3rd St. Pres. Ch., 2 Cor. 11:26,27 & Hebr. 11:38, of Heroisms of To-day, (i.e. of home & frontier Missionaries)   an excellent discourse. Called 5 minutes at Lorin's. At home the rest of the day and evening. Milton came after dinner and staid till 8:00.

Wednesday, November 28 Busy writing in the morning. Dr. D.K. Flickinger came at noon, dined with us, after which we called at Peter Loudings, and at the *Telescope* Office, to show the Missionary secretaries & treasurers etc. F's new African Mis. Map, to sell them 500 copies. Flickinger goes to Columbus on 3:55 train, and I buy ink, etc. and return home.

Thursday, November 29 At home all day writing. We ate our turkey alone. Lorin and family called in the evening an hour. Horace Stokes and his family (and Motherinlaw Ewing) are at Mrs. Corbett's, and Mrs. Ewing is with them. This is Thanksgiving Day, and personally, ecclesiastically, and nationally, we have much to thank God for. S.L. Herr d. at 7:30.

Friday, November 30 Writing most of the day. Called at Joseph E. Gustin's a moment and at Philip O. Gustin's, 512 W. Albany St., a half hour.

Saturday, December 1 Called again at both the Gustin's; saw Coleman about transfer of insurance policy; called at S.L. Herr's late residence, and saw the grandmother and Herr's children.

Sunday, December 2 I attended Grace M.E. Ch. at 10:30, and heard Dr. T.H. Pearne preach on "The name of Jesus," reading Matt. 1:21,22; 16:13 17; 17:1 5; Acts 3:2 5; 4:7 10,11, the best sermon I ever heard him preach—a very good sermon. At 3:30, at Assoc. Hall, heard Dr. Thos. O. Lowe deliver a very good discourse. Called a few minutes at Lorin's, on my way home. Lorin lived 117 Horace St.

Monday, December 3 Was at home forenoon writing letters. In the afternoon at 2:00, I went to S.L. Herr's funeral conducted in the house. Many, including myself, were outside. In the evening, I read most of the President's message.

Tuesday, December 4 I spent the day closely at home writing. Nothing remarkable occurred.

Wednesday, December 5 Go to Sidney, on 9:45 tr., and to Rev. S.L. Livingston's, on his farm. Saw Shuey Esq. and his daughter in law (nee Florence Shelby) and her 3 y. old son Webster. Livingston met me and proceded home 3 ms North, where I dine and remain till morning. I looked a little at the place.

Thursday, December 6 Livingston and I looked all over his farm, and at his farm. I saw his son Clifford and daughter Edith. Dined there. Go on 1:37 train home. Look at needed repairs on Livingston's house on Cyrus Street.

Friday, December 7 Called at Gustin's and got some additional dates. Went to Prudens and bought Christmas presents for my grandchildren. At home the rest of the day, reading and writing.

Sunday, December 9 Heard Dr. H.F. Colby at 10:40, Matt. 8.8, a good sermon. Lorin, Ivonette and Milton ate dinner with us. Heard Prof. Burroughs, of Oberlin, lecture at Asso. Hall at 3:30 on Righteousness. Lesson on Amos. At home the rest of the day.

Monday, December 10 At home most of the day and copied in the eve. Rev. John French's Memoirs for Rev. J.A. Ferguson. I called in the afternoon at U.B. Book Store, Cor. of 4th and Main Streets.

Tuesday, December 11 I wrote on the French Memoirs till 9:00, went to Mr. Curl's, 20 Cyrus Street, to look after repairs about the property, which is S.L. Livingston's. I got lumber, and had window light replaced and door lock mended. Had a talk with Becker at R'y station, and at my house.

Wednesday December 12 Wrote in forenoon. In the afternoon went to Curl's and laid foundation of well and cistern platform. Wrote in the evening, after Dr. H.J. Becker's visit of an hour.

Saturday, December 15 Went with dau. Katharine to town to shop. In the evening went (walked) to Public Library and back; got Thurlow Weed's Auto Biography, and read many pages.

Sunday, December 16 Heard Rev. Maurice Wilson preach, morning, Subject, "Minister Wu's Exploitation, of Confucianism," text 1 John 5:20, a fine sermon.

Monday, December 17 Went to Livingston's house, 20 Cyrus St., to see if carpenter had come, Mrs. Carl out of humor. Went to see Coleman on transfer of house insurance. Took Harry C. Andrews Van Cleve memoirs home in the evening. It was a dark day.

Wednesday, December 19 Went to Livingston's house, to see what had been done and to Mrs. H.M. Simpson's. She not at home. At home the rest of the day. My Clergy certificate was received.

Thursday, December 20 At home in forenoon. Went to Mrs. Simpson's in the afternoon, had a talk with her about the registry of her Grandfather Benjamin Van Cleve's family, and borrowed Benjamin Van Cleve's oldest Manuscript book of perhaps 140 pages.

Saturday, December 22 Writing in forenoon. Went in afternoon and took Mrs. Simpson's book home.

Sunday, December 23 At 10:30, heard Rev. Howard L. Torbet, pr. Gal. 4.4. Pretty fair effort, but rather sophomoric, at Grace M.E. Church, Dayton, Ohio. Called at Harry C. Andrews', at 4:00, and saw his mother, Mrs. Harrison of Monroeville, Ind. My son Reuchlin and family, from Kansas City, arrived on 5:50 (6:10) train; wife Lulu; children: Helen Margaret, 11; Herbert, n.8; Bertha,4.

Monday, December 24 At home. Reuchlin and family and some of Lorin's children are with us. In the evening, the Christmas-tree was set up, and things put on it and about it. Helen and Herbert staid at night at Lorin's.

Tuesday, December 25 Children and Lorin's came and had a time about the Christmas tree. Mr. Corbett and wife called a short time in the forenoon. Ed. Ellis called in the afternoon, a short time. Mrs. Bedell, her son Mr.

Hewitt & wife, and her sister Anna Ramsey called an hour. Lorin's left about 8:00. It is Bertha's birth-day anniversary; 4 years old. Helen is 11; Herbert nearly 8.

Wednesday, December 26 Reuchlin and family, except Helen, went to Bedell's for dinner. Milton was with us all day. Wm. Andrews called in the evening. I went to the library, got Herbert a drawing transparent slate.

Thursday, December 27 Reuchlin and his family and myself dined and supped at Lorin's. At night the club, called the "Ten Dayton Boys," met at our house in their annual feast. They remained till after midnight.

Friday, December 28 We were all rather sleepy; for I awoke early. Reuchlin's went in the evening to visit Rev. H.F. Shupe's.

Saturday, December 29 At home all day. Lorin's called in the evening; also Ed. Ellis called to see Reuchlin & family.

Sunday, December 30 Heard Rev. Maurice Wilson preach at 10:30, Ps. 135.6, on the Past Century, dwelling especially on the religious achievements. At home the rest of the day. Reuchlin & family attend Summit St. Church. Lorin & Milton with us to dinner & Nettie and her other children in the evening. Clare Andrews called a few minutes.

Monday, December 31 At home all day. Reuchlin's visited Ed. Ellis's in the evening. Milton was with us most of the day. This evening closes the Nineteenth Century (as men count) or the Year 1904, as it should have been. I have lived 72/100 of this century. I was awakened by the midnight clatter, but fell asleep in two minutes.

Notes at the end of the diary:

Mrs. Eliza B. Beall wrote me, Dec 7, 1899, as follows: "Mr. Milton Wright, Dear Sir: I am glad to know womething of my few surviving relatives, and hasten to answer your questions. My Father Jesse Reeder, died in St. Louis, in 1854. He was a member of the Presbyterian Church. I know not the year in which Uncle Johathan died. Yours, Eliza B. Beall."

Old Records
There is a transfer of personal property by Jesse Reeder, dated May 30, 1774, to Martin Baker, Who was he? There was a statement that Richard Reeder died at Parkersburg, Va., Feb. 15, 1878; aged 102 years. (From Mrs. Semele Short.)

The farm owned by George Reeder, son of Joseph and Anna, was to be sold at auction May 13, 1898. It had been in the hands of the Eversons. It is situated about six miles East of Cincinnati. There my mother was born, and probably all the children older than Mary Brown, of her Father's family. (Mary was probably born on the Sycamore Farm.)

Reeders and their Wives
George Reeder & Margaret Van Cleve. Jonathan Reeder & Sarah Morris. Reuben Reeder & Rebecca Kennedy. Jesse Reeder & Phibe Wheeler, 2nd Miss Kennedy; 3rd Miss McKnight. Ralph Reeder 1st Mary E. Timpson, Miss Travis, 2nd, Micaiah Reeder m. Jane Cowen.

Memoranda
Paul Lawrence Dunbar was born June 27, 1872, in Dayton, Ohio. His parents were Joshua and Matilda Dunbar, both of whom had been slaves. He graduated from Central High School.

The following have delivered the Annual Missionary Address: 1890, H.J. Becker, at Mt. Zion, Ind. 1891, H. Floyd, Elida, Ohio. 1892, C.L. Wood, Stryker, Ohio. 1893, D.B. Sherk, Waterloo, Ind. 1894, J.K. Alwood, Marion, Ind. 1895, C.H. Kiracofe, Van Orin, Ill. 1896, M. Wright, Charlotte, Mich. 1897, H.J. Barnaby, Messick, Ind. 1898, Wm. Miller. 1899, W.H. Clay, Otterbein Ch. Ohio. 1900, Wm. Dillon, Servia, Ind. 1901, D.K. Flickinger, Middleburg, Pa.

Joseph Reeder, of Loudoun Co., Va., who m. Susana Gano sold nine hundred (900) acres of land, nine miles from Leesburg, Va., to General Wolverton. On payment of a certain amount, which he failed to pay, his title-bond required that he was to have a deed. He never made payment, but without a title transferred the land. So the title still remains in the Reeders. As his executor, Joseph Reeder, who m. Anna Huff, did not press the claim in his lifetime, Sarah (Brand) his dau. destroyed the original deed. The above was so stated by Rev. Joseph Reeder, son of David Reeder, & grandson of Joseph of Va., Loudoun County.

Freeman's
1. John Porter Freeman, born in Lebanon, N.H. Jan. 9, 1772, d. in Rush Co., Ind., Sept. 28, 1854, aged 82 years., 8 mo., & 19 ds. 2. His son Kinion Freeman born in Brookfield, N.Y. Feb 28, 1807, d. Dec. 8, 1873, from an abscess. Died on the farm on which Hopewell Church stands. 3. Flavia (Tuttle) Freeman, wife of Kinion, d. suddenly at Clarksburg, Ind. April 7, 1888. She was born in N.Y. May 5, 1814. She was an intelligent pious woman. 4. John Porter Freeman, Jr., son of Kinion & Flavia, b. in N.Y. May 9, 1835, d. Aug. 3, 1876, killed by a timber at a barn-raising in Rush County, Ind. 5. Martha Delila Freeman, dau. of K. & F. Freeman b. in N.Y., March 30, 1833, d. of lung trouble at Clarksburg, Ind., July 17, 1888, unmarried. 6. Bertha Freeman, dau. of J.P. and E. Freeman, B. Dec. 25, 1871; d. Dec. 18, 1881.

Bishop Jonathan Weaver was born, March 23, 1824. Wm. John Shuey, b. Feb. 9, 1827. Josiah Davis b. Apr. 19, 1810. Clapp Memorial: David Clapp & Son, 291 Congress St. Boston. Price $5.00; letter, Dec. 22, 1899.

McClelland says: "Etymology is slippery ground." It is an art, to make scripture history and incidents vivid. Swear by His name: Ps. 63.16; 16:8; Deut. 8.18; 6.13; Acts 2.30; Isa. 45.23; 65.16; Jer. 4.2; 12.16; Deut. 10:20.

1 9 0 1

Tuesday, January 1 Having been spared for 72-100ths of the old century, I am permitted to enter upon the new. Praise the Lord for His merciful kindness. Reuchlin and family dined with us. Lorin and family came afternoon and staid till after 9:00. I called at Wm. Weidner's. My brotherinlaw, D.K. Zeller died this evening; I received telegram.

Wednesday, January 2 Reuchlin and family dined at Lorin's. Mrs. Lottie Andrews and Mrs. Olinger called in the afternoon. I was at home all day, except a call at Lorin's.

Thursday, January 3 Myself, Reuchlin, Lorin and Wilbur went to Richmond, Ind. to D.K. Zeller's funeral. We dined at John G. Zeller's. Solomon Jacob and Joseph Zeller and Zartman, Abe Kumler, and Mrs. Lizzie K. Miller were there & Mr. B.F. Crawford & others. Revs. Hughes officiated in the funeral. Text, Jas. 4.14. Burial at Earlham. We return on 5:00 train, to Dayton.

Friday, January 4 Reuchlin, Helen and I go to Woodland Cemetery and to the extreme eastern part of the city, in the forenoon. In the evening, Reuchlin's family called at Joseph Boyd's awhile. Lorin & family were at our house in the evening, and till quite late.

Saturday, January 5 Lulu & Bertha started at 9:50 for Columbus and other points to visit relatives and friends. Reuchlin left on traction car at 4:00 for Richmond, via Eaton, on his way home to Kansas City, Mo. Ed. Ellis went with him to Eaton.

Sunday, January 6 I took Herbert, my grandson, to Grace M.E. Church. It was communion day. Rev. D. Berger assisted the Assistant pastor, Rev. Howard L. Torbett, in the Communion service. In the eve. at 7:30, heard Rev. Howard [blank] at Conover St. Church on Matt. 16.26, "What shall it profit?" He is something of an actor, with the assurance of a showman.

Monday, January 7 Went with the children—Helen & Herbert—to the Soldier's Home, in the forenoon. In the Afternoon, I took Helen with me to Public Library, and Elder & Johnson's, Newsalt's, etc. Lorin and Netta called for Milton in the evening.

Tuesday, January 8 I took Helen and Herbert to their Aunt Jennie Bedell's in forenoon and met Mr. and Mrs. Fred. M. Short at Union Depot and spent over an hour with them, there. Called at Dr. Becker's before supper. Milton was with us after School.

Wednesday, January 9 I took the children to see the Holly Water works, in the forenoon. It was a dark, foggy and somewhat rainy day. Milton came after school, as usual.

Thursday, January 10 The forenoon was rainy, the afternoon free from it. I took Helen and Herbert to the Library Museum, and to Lorin's office. Children called at Bedell's, a few minutes. Milton and they had a great romp in the evening.

Friday, January 11 The day was a little rainy throughout. I went to town afternoon and purch[as]ed Schouler's History, U.S. and spent an hour in the Library, Lulu (Reuchlin's wife) came from Columbus at 6:40. Lorin came after Milton as usual.

Saturday, January 12 The weather is quite cold to-day. Lulu and children go to town, forenoon and afternoon. Katharine goes [to] the Helen Hunt celebration in forenoon. In afternoon, the little boys go with me to sail their boats, & lose both of them. Lorin & Netta called in the evening.

Sunday, January 13 Atterded Dr. Maurice Wilson's Church (lst Pres), who preached an excellent sermon from Josh. 1:4. Lulu, Herbert and Milton were with me. In the evening, heard Rev. H.H. Fout, P.E., pr[e]ach at 1st U.B. Church, a good sermon, Jas. 5:20, on Soul Saving. Lorin's called in the evening.

Monday, January 14 I was at home. Went to town in Afternoon. Lulu and the children are getting ready to return home, and I to go to Huntington. Lorin's called in the evening .

Tuesday, January 15 Lulu and children left at 9:30. I Left home at 7:00, went via Union City and Ridgeville to Briant, Jay Co., Ind. Visited Rev. A. Worth and Sarah E. Worth (my cousin). Their gr. dau. Ruby Read is 11 1/2 years old. Their son Andion called in the evening. At Ridgeville, I saw Wood, a music student at Huntington.

Wednesday, January 16 Go on 7:20 tr. to Ft. Wayne, and thence to Huntington. Rev. Wm. Dillon meets me & takes me to his house to dinner. Ex. Com. (Missionary) meets at 1:30. Bp. Floyd and I sup at Pres. C.H. Kiracofe's. Bro. Floyd pr. at 7:30, Ps. 1:1–6. I lodge at Rev. A. Morrison's.

Thursday, January 17 I called in morn. at Mrs. Wilberforce's. Bro. Brooks takes Bp. Floyd and me down town, and I go on 10:07 train via Wabash to Fairmount, and dine at my nephew Ellis Wright's. I go on 3:39 tr. to Leach. Sup at R.W. White's. I pr. at Hopewell at 7:00. (Protracted Meeting), Isa. 1.18. Stay at Ol. Buller's.

Friday, January 18 I attend meeting at 10:00. Dine at Samuel Hill's. Sow some grass seed in Afternoon. Rev. W. J. Oxley, pastor, pr at 7:00. Miss Delaney is converted. I stay at Oliver Buller's.

Saturday, January 19 I attend forenoon meeting, and dine at Joe Cain's. I sow blue grass seed in the morning and Andrew White sows for me in Afternoon. I pr. at 7:00, Matt. 12:30. I sup at White's. I lodge at Oliver Buller's. Mrs. Greeler (Delaney) joined Church.

Sunday, January 20 I pr. at 10:00, Hebr. 10:35, I dine with Oxley at Frank Kirkwood's. I pr. at 6:30, Luke 15.18. Mrs. Tomlinson came for prayers, almost before the invitation, and joined church, in the forenoon. I lodged at Oliver Andrew Glass's.

Monday, January 21 I go to White's and to the Church. I go on 11:42 train to Fairmount. Dine at restaurant. Called at Mrs. Little's. I sup and lodge at Ellis Wright's.

Tuesday, January 22 At Ellis's. Measure my lot. Go on Aftn train to White's. I pr. at 7. Eph. 2.16. I lodge at O.A. Glass's. Queen Victoria of England died at Cowes, Isle of Night, at 6:30 Afternoon. Hers has been a very long and successful reign.

Wednesday, January 23 I was at meeting at Hopewell, in Leach, in the forenoon. I sowed blue grass seed in the afternoon, and pr. at 7:00, Rom. 6.17, and much interest was manifested. I dined and supped at White's. Lodge at Oliver Buller's.

Thursday, January 24 I sow bluegrass seed in morn. Attended Church at 10:00, I dine at O.A. Glass's. The weather was cold afternoon and evening. Rev. W.J. Oxley pr. at 7:00, Mal. 3.7. I lodge at Buller's.

Friday, January 25 I finish sowing blue grass seed in my Woodland, and call at Church, and then go on 11:42 train to Fairmount. I dine & sup and lodge at Ellis Wright's. I called at Mrs. Mary Ann Bond's a few minutes.

Saturday, January 26 I staid mostly at Ellis's till 3:38, and then go to Leach, and sup at White's. Pr at 7:00, Ez. 73.11. Lodge at Charles Malone's at Fowlerton. Some snow fell in the night. Rev. John Fohl died in Chambersburg, Pa. this evening at 9:00.

Sunday, January 27 I teach Oliver Buller's class in Sabbath school at Hopewell. I preached at 11:00, Matt. 16.18. I dine and sup at O.A. Glass's. At 4:30, we called at Robert. B. Reeder's. I preached at Hopwell at 9:00,

Ps. 16.11. I lodged at Frank Kirkwood's, 1/2 m south of the church.

Monday, January 28 I went to R.W. White's and dine, sup and lodge there. Nothing of particular interest, except that White broke his mud-boat & tried to mend it. I engaged Andrew Wilt and Andrew White to cut logs for me to-morrow.

Tuesday, January 29 We cut cull logs all day in the west woods. Meals at Wnite's. I lodged at Oliver Buller's.

Wednesday, January 30 I help timbercutter's select timber till 11:00 and after 3:00. I dine at John Corn's, at Rebecca Jane's surprise birth-day anniversary. I sup at White's and go on 6:00 train to Fairmount. Stay at Ellis Wright's.

Thursday, January 31 I go on 7:30 traction car to Gas City; on 9:13 tr. to Union City, and on 1:05 tr. to Dayton. Found all well except Netta, who had grip. Leontine came with Carrie and was sweet as could be.

Friday, February 1 At home all day, only I called at Lorin's in the forenoon.. Wrote some letters and copied my diary notes.

Saturday, February 2 At home forenoon. Wrote some letters. In afternoon at 4:00, walked to Jacob Swank's and Sylvester Spidel's and back. Wrote out Samuel Spidel's obituary for the *Conservator*, and mailed it.

Sunday, February 3 Heard Rev. Maurice Wilson (lst Pres. Ch.) Hosea, 8.12, an excellent discourse. The day is rainy. I called at Lorin's a half hour in the afternoon. To day I read, in the revised version, thirty-seven (37) chapters of Genesis, mostly aloud. To-night, I slept 8 hours. I generally sleep 7 or 8 hours.

Monday, February 4 I read from the 38–50 chapters of Genesis. I cannot read the story of Joseph without weeping. I was at home all day.

Tuesday, February 5 I wrote some letters and read consecutively to the 13th chapter of Exodus. I was at home all day.

Wednesday, February 6 Bishop Jonathan Weaver died this morning near Oak Chapel in this city at 3:25, aged nearly 77 years. Peace to his soul. Lorin and Netta called in the evening. Milton had come after school and wrote Herbert a letter on the type-writer. As usual, he is never ready to go home, nor willing to stay all night.

Thursday, February 7 At home reading and writing. Mrs. E.S Lorens called in the afternoon to invite Katharine to supper Sat. evening.

Friday, February 8 Made some tops out of spools for Lorin's Children. Got ready to go to Bishop Weaver's funeral. Went at one o'clock. It was held at Oak Chapel, Huber, Funk, Bp. Kephart, Hot, Mills & Rev. Wm. McKee spoke. After returning, I went to the Public Library. We call at Lorin's, in Eve.

Saturday, February 9 Read much in the papers to-day. Wrote several letters. Katharine went to E.S. Lorenz's for supper in the evening.

Sunday, February 10 Heard at Summit St., Rev. W.J. Shuey's able address on Education at 10:30. Milton was with me. Lorin's were with us to dinner. At 7:30, heard Bishop J.S. Mills preach at First U.B. Ch., on Spiritual Enlightenment (text prob. 2 Cor. 3.18). It was a sermon of good ability.

Monday, February 11 I was at home all day, closely engaged in writing out a sketch of the Wright's, from John Wrighte, of Kelvedon, Essex Co., England, (1500) down to the family of my brothers, cousins, etc. It was a very large day's work.

Tuesday, February 12 I was at home all day taking copies of the Jerome Holt genealogy; that is Anna (Van Cleve) Holt.

Wednesday, February 13 Netta and the little girls called, and Ivonette dined with us. I called at "Aunt Mary" Englehart's in the afternoon.

Saturday, February 16 Engaged in reading and writing. Completed the reading of the Bible to Leviticus, revised version. Lorin and Netta called in the evening.

Sunday, February 17 Heard Rev. D. Burghalter pr. at his church, Memorial Reformed, on East 5th St., 2 Cor. 11:2,3, a good sermon. In the afternoon, at 3:30, heard F.S. Scoel at Assoc. Hall on "Conscience in Work," deliver an able address. He is Pres. of Wooster University. He is an able rather than popular speaker. A boy (Leonard) broke the ice & drowned to-day, above 5th St. Bri. Read six chapters in Leviticus and did much other reading.

Monday, February 18 (This is Tuesday's record, I think) Read and wrote all day. Wrote for R.R. rates on B & O and for Pa. R.R. Katharine went to the H.H. Club.

Wednesday, February 20 (This is Wednesday's record) I read over my Diary of 1886, retracing the fading parts. Completed the Consecutive reading of the Bible (revised v.) to the close of Leviticus. The house across the street from ours was moved away to-day.

Thursday, February 21 Wrote several letters in the forenoon. Read the "Independent." Wrote many letters in the afternoon about railroad rates to General Conference. Cal[l]ed to see Funk about their experience with the Passenger Associations on reduced rates. Ivonette and Milton came home with me for supper, and Lorin & Netta called in the evening, with Leontine.

Friday, February 22 Wrote many letters. Went to town to mail them in the afternoon. Called to see Albert Shearer a few minutes at his hardware store.

Saturday, February 23 Wrote Announcement of Committee on Revision for General Conference, went to Depot, and to the Library, in forenoon. Wrote letters and read in the afternoon, and revised manuscript.

Sunday, February 24 Heard Rev. F.M. McMillin (Pastor) preach at Memorial Presb. Ch. at 10:45, Rom. 8:9, a good sermon, though misinterpreting "the Spirit," and dismissing Carrie Nation with his dictum.

Monday, February 25 Arose before 5:00, and wrote and posted several letters.

Thursday, February 28 At home, most of the day reading. Went to the Library just before supper. Hon. Wm.

M. Evarts died at 9:10 this morning. He was considered one of the greatest lawyers of America.

Friday, March 1 At home all day. Wrote many letters. Katharine went to Cincinnati with her High School sch[o]lars to attend the debate against Walnut Hills High School. She dined with Mrs. Semele Short, 609 Mound St. They got home very late.

Saturday, March 2 Go to Miami City Station at 7:00, and had my "Clergy Certificate["] with me, but thought I had left it, so go back. Go on 8:10 interurban to West Alexander and thence to Rockford, Ohio and Allen W. Koeppel took me to his house for supper and lodging. I had boarded there at Mission Board meeting, last June a year.

Sunday, March 3 I preached for Rev. T.M. Harvey at 10:30, Matt. 5.12, "Great is etc." and at the close solemnized the marriage of Gay Montgomery and Lucy F. Bice. I dined at Bice's. Pre[a]ched at 7:30, Eph. 2.16. I lodge at Koeppel's.

Monday, March 4 Gay Montgomery takes me to Ohio City, and I go on 10:26 tr. to Warren. Dine with Wolfard at J.W. Gnards. Supper at Elijah Morrison's. I pr. at our Ch. at 7:30, Isa. 1:18. I lodged at Gnard's. Wolford took the night train to Kokomo. Mrs. Gnard was an Alexander.

Tuesday, March 5 Called at E. Morrison's, Capt. D.L. Elliott's and father Mygrant's. Dine at Rev. J.C. Valentine's three-fourths mile north. I went on 12:04 tr. to Marion, and thence on inter-urban car to Fairmount. Supper and lodging at Ellis Wright's.

Wednesday, March 6 I went on the C.I.E. R.R. to Fowlerton, and returned to Fairmount on noon train. Dined at Ellis's, and went to Marion, and supped and lodged at Mark Hillshammer's, on the west side of Washington Street, 6th house.

Thursday, March 7 Paid tax on my Fairmount property, and went on 9:02 train to Union City. The train for Dayton was two hours and a half late, so I got there after 5:00; found all well. Milton was visiting us.

Friday, March 8 At home all day except a walk to the Library and back.

Saturday, March 9 At home all day; mostly writing a sketch of the Reeders for cousin Robt. B. Reeder to be used in a chronological history of Grant County, Ind.

Sunday, March 10 Heard at Third Street Pres. Church, Pres. W.O. Thompson, of Ohio State University, on Acts 19:28, "Great is Diana," etc., an able and manly discourse. He read it, and read it well. Called at Lorin's. Walter Stokes' oldest daughter, Mrs. [blank] Hoppin, there.

Tuesday, March 12 At home. Went to town. Called at Lorin's.

Wednesday, March 13 At home. Called at the Library. Ex-Pres. Benjamin Harrison, one of our greatest and purest president's, died at 4:45, this afternoon.

Thursday, March 14 At home. Dr. H.J. Becker called an hour. Went to Library in the afternoon.

Friday, March 15 Read in the forenoon. Settled accounts in the family, on living, up to date.

Saturday, March 16 I was at home in the forenoon engaged mostly in reading. Read to-day to Deut. 16th Chap., in Rev. Ver. Went to Jacob Swank's in the afternoon; prayed with them.

Sunday, March 17 Arose at 6:00. This is the fortieth anniversary of my son Reuchlin's birth, and he was born on a clear, but quite cool Sunday forenoon. He has been a good and dutiful son. Heard at Grace M.E. Ch. Rev. T.M. McWhinney, of "Christian" Church Eulogy of Benj. Harrison: Sermon, Luke 10:42. Quite an orator, nearly 78 years of age. At 3:30, heard Judge Spencer.

Monday, March 18 At home in the forenoon, reading and writing. In the afternoon, at 4:00 I called an hour on H.J. Becker; has tonsilitis. Katharine went to the Helen Hunt Club in Dayton View.

Tuesday, March 19 In the forenoon, wrote a letter to Daniel Koerner, and finished the consecutive reading of

the revised version of the Bible through Joshua. I began in February. In the afternoon made out a program for Board Missionary meeting in May, and went to the office and mailed it.

Wednesday, March 20 At home in forenoon, especially reading. In the afterno[o]n I called on Dr. H.J. Becker a half hour. He is better of tonsilitis.

Thursday, March 21 At home all day. I am mostly reading. I finished reading Revised Version to 1 Samuel. Reached the 550 page of Vol. I of Blaine's Twenty Years in Congress.

Saturday, March 23 Engaged mostly in writing, but some in reading. Went to the Public Library after supper to return the first Volume of Blain's "Twenty Years in Congress" and get second Volume. Editor Arthur Edwards, of the "North Western Christian Advocate" was buried in Chicago to-day. Emilie Aguinaldo is captured to-day.

Sunday, March 24 Heard at First English Lutheran Church (Main St.) Rev. D. Frank Garland, pastor, pr. at 10:30, Matt. 7:2, "With what measure you mett." Fair & fairly read. In the evening, 7:30 heard Dr. August Pohlman, of Muhlenburg Mission, Mourovia, Liberia; an address on African Missions. Dramatic & amusing. Lorin Blodgett died in Phila. to-day. Lorin named for him.

Monday, March 25 At home. Went to the Post-Office and called at Haines at Penn. R.R. office.

Tuesday, March 26 At home. I read much and wrote many letters—wrote to coast delegates to General Conference, advising them of ways to get reduced fare east of Chicago.

Wednesday, March 27 At home all day reading and writing. In the evening I finished reading the Bible consecutively to 2nd Samuel.

Thursday, March 28 At home most of the day. Dr. H.J. Becker called at 3:00, afternoon, and staid some time, couseling over matters at Pleasant Valley, East Ohio Conference. I wrote letters and cards. Read till after midnight in Blain's Twenty Years in Congress, a very fascinating book.

Friday, March 29 At home most of the day. Took Blain's 2nd volume to the Library having read about 200 pages of it, and I called at Lorin's.

Saturday, March 30 Went on 8:46 train to Richmond, on my way to Fairmount. Called at Mrs. Caroline Zeller's, (my wife's sister's) ten minutes, reached Fairmount, Ind., at 1:33. Called at my nephew's, Ellis Wright's, (residence & store.) Went to Fowlerton, on 3:38 tr. and walked to Wm. H.H. Reeder's. Lodged there.

Sunday, March 31 I remained at Wm's till evening. Glasses and R.B. Reeder's were there; also Robt. B. Broyles and Chas. Milton Broyles. Rev. W.J. Oxley pr. at 8:00, Eph. 2:8 & I exhorted. I lodged at O.A. Glass's.

Monday, April 1 Oliver took me to R.W. White's, and we staked off for the ditches in the new field. I went on 11:43 tr. to Fairmount, and dined at Ellis Wright's. I called on Brown, the real estate Agent, at his & Wilson's request, and also in the evening. Lodged at Ellis's.

Tuesday, April 2 I paid Miller Driggs & Co. $142.28, the cost of my ware room back of their store. I went on Wabash railroad to Wabash, and thence to Ft. Wayne, and thence to Vicksburg, Port Huron and Stratford, Ontario, arriving at 5:00 A.M. There were some additional costs on my ware-room, amounting to about $150 in all.

Wednesday, April 3 I lunched at 8:00, at Stratford, mailed letters and cards, and went on 10:00 tr. to Palmerston, and on 12:30 mixed tr. to Port Elgin, arriving there at 6:30. I lodged at Wm. Nicholson's near the U.B. Church.

Thursday, April 4 I went at 8:00 with Father Nicholson to the Port, now filled with ice, far out on Lake Huron. I dine at Mrs. R.A. Clark's & Rev. J.G. Connor, her soninlaw. I sup and lodge at Mrs. Martin Eby's. Her daughters at home were Lizzie, Nellie, Amanda, 20, Katie, 18, and Edna, 13. Rev. A.R. Springer pr. at 8:00. Many came on late train.

Friday, April 5 Conference opened at 8:30 (9:00) and business proceeded forenoon & afternoon. Rev. J.B. Bowman dined with me at Mrs. Katie Eby's. I pr. at 8:00, Matt. 28:19,20. Go—& teach all nations. I had a prelude on the Crucifixion.

Saturday, April 6 Conference continued and closed at 5:00. Rev. A.F. Stoltz dined with me. D.B. Sherk was elected presiding elder. Rev. C.W. Bachus was much dissatisfied with his appointment to Niagera Mission. He talked sharply to D.B. Sherk. J. Howe pr. at 7:30.

Sunday, April 7 I preached at 10:30, Col. 4:17, "Take heed to the ministry," etc. Dine sup & lodge as usual. Howe supped with us. S. Swartz held a S.S. Anniversary at 3:00. I pr. at 7:00, Eph. 3:19. I had a prelude at 10:30, on the Resurrection. At 9:00 at the Town Hall, D.B. Sherk spoke on Temperance & I followed. Staid at Mrs. Katie Eby's.

Monday, April 8 Mrs. Eby got us an early breakfast, and we went to the 6:25 morning train. We reach Berlin at 11:00. I dine with D.B. Sherk's, slept two hours, supped at M. Eshelman's, pr. at 8:00, at U.B. Church and lodged at Rev. J.B. Bowman's.

Tuesday, April 9 I called at Father Rosenberger's. He is very well but of very infirm memory. Called at D.B. Sherk's and Father Detweiler's, and Mrs. I.L. Bowman's, and then go to 11:00 train. Reach Port Huron at 2:00, had lunched at Stratford, lunched again at Detroit, waited 3 hours at Toledo. Left at 12:00.

Wednesday, April 10 Reached Dayton at 4:45 A.M. Went to town at 11:20, ordered a suit & bought a hat. I wrote many letters Yesterday at Port Huroon and last night at Toledo. Slept part of the afternoon of to-day. Called at Lorin's in the evening. Ivonette and Leontine piled onto my knees. Milton's school report was good.

Thursday, April 11 At home in the forenoon writing. Mr. Beamer, agent of the Interstate Press Col. called, and I engaged "The World's History and Its Makers", $16.75; paid $1.75. I went to town and exchanged the hat I bought yesterday. Cost $5.00.

Friday, April 12 I made ready to go east, and went to Cincinnati on 11:35 train. Lunched in Public Library on Vine Street, sketched from Rev. John Gano's Memoirs items of genealogical interest, his sister Susana being (as supposed) a Reeder ancestress of our family. Spent the evening in the Library. Start at 9:10 on Ches. & Ohio R.R. for Staunton, Virginia.

Saturday, April 13 I had slept about five hours last night. Near Thurmond, a great stone had rolled onto our track and it hindered us an hour, before it was blasted and removed. I arrived at Staunton three hours late. J.E. Hott met me. We lunched and went to his house in Spring Hill. A very rainy night.

Sunday, April 14 A very rainy day, and no meeting. I remained at Bro. Hott's. Children: Guy, Mary 13, Blair 11, Alpha 10; Charley 9, Jon Kurt 5; Coya[h], 2. James Sheets called an hour in the afternoon. Bro. Hott lives in the parsonage of Augusta Circuit. Coyah is named for D.F. Wilberforee's ancestress.

Monday, April 15 The day was cloudy but there was not much rain in the forenoon. Hott & I took a walk up north. Called at the store. Preached at 8:00, at the U.B. Church, Ps. 25.14. I lodged at Hott's. Saw Burton and others at the meeting. Two joined Church.

Tuesday, April 16 I go with Rev. J.E. Hott to Olivet Church to the Ministerial Association, which met at 9:30. My boarding place is at George F. Perry's, 1/4 m north-west of Olivet. I supped at Bro. Markwood Knott's, W.J. Funkhouser pr. at 8:00, Isa. 65:7. I lodge at Perry's.

Wednesday, April 17 The Woman's Branch Mis. Association had a meeting at 9:30. I dined at Joshua F. Daggy's. In the Afternoon, a Virginia Branch W.M.A. was organized. H.W. Lindamood pr. at 8:00, Gal. 4.4, I supped and Lodged at Perry's. Their children: Anna, Bessie, Charley, Willie (girl).

Thursday, April 18 Virginia Annual Conference session opened at 9:00 a.m., and proceeded well. I went to J.M. Andrews, 2 miles S.E. for supper. Old folks are Dunkard's. The Young folks are bright. Rev. J.W. Chambers pr. at 8:00, John 4:38. I slept a full night—8 hours.

Friday, April 19 Conference progressed well. Rev. G.W. Allman dined with me at Perry's. Some rain fell to-day. The evening and night were quite rainy. I did not go to the evening meeting, but Rev. Joseph M. Crowell pr. at 8:00, with 11 persons present. Had full sleep.

Saturday, April 20 It is quite rainy and the creek was quite full. I supped at Markwood Knott's. The Conference business closed early. J.W. Chambers pr. at 8:00, Heb. 12.1. I dined, supped and lodged at George F. Perry's.

Sunday, April 21 I preached at 10:30, Titus 2.14. I dine at [blank] Douglas' & [blank] Kiracofe's 3/4 m. S.W., with J.E. Hott, J.W. Chambers, I preached at Olivet at 8:00, 1 Cor. 14.1, on Charity as better than other gifts. I stay at G.F. Perry's. It was a rainy evening, and the congregation was small.

Monday, April 22 Bro. G.F. Perry took me to Staunton. We dine at the Palmer House. I go to the C & O Depot. Write some. I go on the 7:39 train west, I slept a few hours. We find Ohio River very high. Reach Cincinnati at 9:20, late for connections. I go on 12:30 tr. to Dayton.

Tuesday, April 23 I reached Cincinnati over an hour late & miss all connections. Call at Public Library. Go on 12:30 Big 4 train to Dayton. Miss connection to Lima. A man finds my ticket and acts strangely. I am at home 3 hours. I went on 5:45 tr. to Union City, Anderson & Indianapolis. Stay at the Sherman House.

Wednesday, April 24 Breakfast & lodging $1.00. Go on 6:45 train via Anderson to Wabash and thence to Huntington. I dine at Rev. Wm. Dillon's with Miller, Wood, & Floyd. Publ Est. Board meets at 1:30, *Adjourned early. I go to Prof. A.P. Barnaby's, and sup there. I lodge at Pres. C.H. Kiracofe's. Bishop H. Floyd with me. * Mr. Crane (Expert) made report.

Thursday, April 25 I open the College devotions. The Board of Education meets at 8:15. We have report of the Financial Secretary Kiracofe, and of Treasurer Stemen. A sharp controversy ended in recognizing Edwards College at Albion, Washington, subject to the approval of Gen'l Conference Publ. Board at 2:00, another meeting Ed. Bd., 7:00.

Friday, April 26 I go from Pres. Kiracofe's to Wm. Dillon's and Publ. House. Talk with Keiter and Prudential Committee. I go on 10:19 train to Wabash and thence to Fairmount. Dine at restaurant. I go on 3:38 tr. to Fowlerton & to R.W. White's. He is setting out my appletrees. Go to Oliver A. Glass's, where I Sup and lodge.

Saturday, April 27 I call at W.H.H. Reeder's, and walk to White's. Andrew Wilt and I measure the clearing, which was six acres & three quarters, and the other ground included made the field seven acres and 135 rods. I go on 11:42 train to Fairmount & thence to Anderson & Richmond. Called at Mrs. M. Caroline Zeller's. Home at 6:00. All well.

Sunday, April 28 I walked to Miami Chapel. Looked at Otis and Ida's graves & Rev. Wm. Rhinehart's. Heard Rev. W.M. Van Sickle preach on Mark 12:41–44, Luke 21:14, a good sermon. The widow's Gift. I called at Lorin's an hour in the afternoon. False fire alarm in the evening.

Tuesday, April 30 At home all day, except a brief trip to town to get my new coat and pantaloons, which cost $22.00.

Wednesday, May 1 Went at 10:30 with Milton and Ivonette, to see the Wallace Show Parade. Waited at the Fairground till noon. I was writing in the afternoon.

Thursday, May 2 I was busy writing letters in the forenoon. In the afternoon, I called at Jacob Swank's. I saw Alta Becker a moment at their house. I met Pruner and had 15 minutes' talk.

Friday, May 3 Wrote in the forenoon. Went to town in the afternoon, left bankbook for posting. Bought a quarter ream of commercial note paper for 35 cts. It is nice paper. At 8:00, Katharine went to the High School Debate between the Columbus and Dayton Schools. Dayton's got the decision.

Saturday, May 4 At home most of the day considerable of which was spent in putting together the statistics of East District for the Conference Year preparatory to my annual report. Went to town in the forenoon. Katharine took an Oberlin girl on a ride to Carrollton. We called at Lorin's in the evening an hour.

Sunday, May 5 Lorin and the children called in the forenoon. I was not very well to-day, and did not go to church anywhere. Orville and Katharine went with Ed. Sines and his girl [blank] in a ride, with Milton along.

Monday, May 6 I prepare to go east. I early wrote to Albertson & Hobbs, Nurserymen, Bridgeport, Ind., Ellis Wright & W.H. Kindel. Make out tax list in afternoon. I go on 5:50 train to Columbus and Pittsburgh. Little Ivonette was with us to-day. I start at 5:50 for Chambersburg, Pa. Was on a through train. Bp. E.B. Kephart on the train to Harrisburg, Rev. Brubaker.

Tuesday, May 7 Arrive at Harrisburg at 9:10, A.M. Go on 12:00 tr. to Chambersburg, Pa., and stop off till evening train. Go on to Mason & Dixon, arriving after six o'clock. Find a home at Mrs. Caroline Stein's[.] Session of the Missionary Board at 7:30. Dr. D.K. Flickinger pr. An. Mis. sermon at 8:00.

Wednesday, May 8 Missionary Board in session. I, being president of the Board, presided. Alwood's questions on treasurer's report. Bishop Barkley's address in the evening. Mission Collection of about $50.00 The Bishop's Board met at Mrs. Strine's at 6:00.

Thursday, May 9 Bishops' Board at Leshers at 7:00. With others, I went on Morning train to Chambersburg & found my home at Fred. F. Seippel's, 482 N. Main Street. General Conference opened at 2:00, in King Street U.B. Ch., I presiding. D.B. Sherk pr. at 7:30, Rev. J. Howe, of Ontario was my regular fellow boarder.

Friday, May 10 Bishop H.T. Barnaby presided to-day. Most of general reports of officers were read. Adjourned afternoon for lack of business. Bro. Seippel's daughter at home is Maud. Sister Seippel's sons at home are John and Merle D'Anbigua. N.D. Wolfard pr. at 8:00.

Saturday, May 11 Bishop H. Floyd presided. D.F. Wilberforce, of Africa, had arrived and was introduced to Conference. Publishing Agent reported and the attempt was made to approve his reports. Wilberforce spoke at 8:00 on Africa.

Sunday, May 12 I heard Bishop Barnaby preach at 10:30 on "His son Jesus Christ." Rom. 1.3, a fine sermon. I preached at 1st Lutheran Church at 7:30, to a large congregation, Ps. 92.8. I had attended S. School in the morning, but staid at home in the afternoon & slept some.

Monday, May 13 Bishop H.L. Barkley presided to-day. The Publishing Board reported in the forenoon. In the aftn. at 2:00, the Agent's Report was considered. M.L. Keiter's defense, and a warm discussion. Report and Board's Report was referred to Com. of seven. Mrs. A.R. Kiracofe reported for W.M.A.

Tuesday, May 14 Wright presided to-day. The St. Joseph appeal was sustained in A.G. Johnson's case. J.K. Alwood made a lengthy and odd report on Moral Reform. I supped at R.P. Nicklas's. I was before Com. of seven. Heard last part of Becker's lecture.

Wednesday, May 15 Barnaby presided. Conference reconsidered the vote (i.e. took the paper from the table) relating to reply to Liberal Bishops' letter. Episode on the Bishop's pastoral letter. The action on Revision Com. report was completed.

Thursday, May 16 Went to Gettysburg Battle field. Viewed Seminary Ridge, Cemetery Ridge, Cemetery Hill. Dined at the Pitzer House. In afternoon viewed the Confederate battle line, "peach orchard["], Little Round Top, Round Top, High Water Mark. Saw Picket's Field. Returned to Chambersburg. Rev. J.K. Alwood pr. in the evening.

Friday, May 17 Bishop Floyd presided. Elections began at 10:30. Bp. Barkley was elected Coast Bishop by 36 votes, on 1st ballot. Bps. Wright, on 1st ballot for gen'l bishops, received 32 votes; Barnaby, 32; Floyd, 31. Becker elected editor on 3rd ballot by 25 votes; Clay is elected Publ. Agt. by 27 votes.

Saturday, May 18 Bp. Barkley presided[.] Becker chosen delegate to Methodist Ecum. Conf. I reported as Supt. of Litigation. New Dis. goes into effect Aug. 1st. *Bishops were stationed. Closing remarks by the bishops. J.N. Lemasters pr. at 8:00. *I was placed on S.W. Dist., Floyd on N.W. Dist, and Barnaby on East Dist.

Sunday, May 19 Dr. H.J. Becker pr. at 10:30, at King Street Church, on Rev. 21.21, "Each several gate was one pearl." Fanciful; but eloquent at close. Holiness

Meeting at 3:00. I led United Brethren Christian Endeavor at 6:30. Sup at Rev. J.S. Sollenberger's. Bp H. Floyd pr. at 7:30. I out with Seiple, Becker & Clay, over Clay's trouble.

Monday, May 20 We were on 9:45 train to Harrisburg and on 1:55 train to Pittsburgh. A number of delegates are aboard. Go on 9:15 tr. to Columbus and Dayton. At Pittsburgh, at the Depot, Bish. Barnaby said the general opinion was that the Board ought to meet, and refuse to let Clay take his office. He told C.L. Wood the same. This he three years denied.

Tuesday, May 21 I arrived at Dayton at 3:30 A.M. Go home and sleep some. At 10:00, meet Mr. F.H. Short & Semele Short at Union Depot. Mrs. Merrie with them. Call at High School. Drive over by my house. Wrote letter in Aftn. Slept some. Milton was with us Aftn & evening.

Thursday, May 23 Wrote letters. Went to the depot and mailed a letter. Nothing unusual occurred except Buffalo Bill's Wild West show, which I did not see.

Friday, May 24 Went to "town" in the forenoon. Nothing unusual occured to-day. Called at Lorin's, in the evening.

Saturday, May 25 Went to town in forenoon and to H.J. Becker's but he was not at home. I failed to get ready to start on the 11:20 D&U train to Grant County.

Sunday, May 26 Went to Evangelical Association Church on Commercial Street to hear Rev. S.R. Spreng, but found the service was in German. Then went to Central Christian Church & heard Rev. Cahill on Prov. 11:24, favoring another Com. congregation in the city. At home the rest of he day. Lorin and his little girls called in afternoon.

Monday, May 27 Go via Union City to Gas City, Fairmount and the farm. Saw Rev. Jas. Parker, of Oregon, on the train & John Kilbourn from Brookville. Reached Fairmount at 1:00 P.M. I dined at Ellis Wright's. I went on 3:38 tr. to Leach. Sup & lodge at Robt. W. White's. Paid A. Wilt remainder on clearing.

Tuesday, May 28 I go to W.H.H. Reeder's & dine there. R.B. Reeder called. I bought Wm's grey mare Princess at $125.00, and got $20.00 more on an old note. I lodged at Oliver A. Glass's.

Wednesday, May 29 Wm. Reeder takes me to R.W. White's, where I turn the mare in pasture. I settle with White for two years, paying him a balance of $3.75. After an early dinner, I went on 11:43 tr. to Fiarmount. Write at Ellis's. Call at Bond's. Lodge at Robt. Hastings.

Thursday, May 30 I dined at Ellis's and went on 3:38 tr. to my farm. I led the evening prayer meeting at Hopewell Church. I lodged at White's. In forenoon was out with Myrl and Ancil to cemetery to decoration. At 2:00 was at Congregational Church. Address of Verlin Davis.

Friday, May 31 I piled some tile in the forenoon & clear up some brush in the afternoon. I went to O.A. Glass's and lodged. There was a hard rain in the night. I rode over, on my Princess.

Saturday, June 1 I cut out a way through my woods, in the forenoon and burned brush and logs in the afternoon. I dined and lodged at White's. Emmett White helped me in the Afternoon.

Sunday, June 2 I preached at Hopewell at 10:30, Ps. 108.4. I dined and supped at O.A. Glass's. Joseph Broyles and Eliza and their son Wm. were there. I pr. at Hopewell at 8:00, 2 Pet. 3.9, "Not willing that any should perish," I lodged at Oliver Buller's.

Monday, June 3 I went to the farm and dug an open ditch in the newly cleared field, & after an early dinner went to Fairmount. I sup & lodge at Ellis's.

Tuesday, June 4 I feel stupid & sleep some. Concluded to not go home, but go hence to Huntington next Monday. I board at Ellis Wright's. I heard a sermon at the Baptist Church in the evening by Rev. Mr. Fry of Summitveille. There was a ministerial Association.

Thursday, June 6 I stay at Ellis's. I attended prayer meeting at the U.B. Church, which was led by Rev. Smith, the Wesleyan pastor.

Friday, June 7 I received looked-for forwarded letters and I answer them in the afternoon. I called at Mrs. Mary Ann Bond's at her request, in forenoon. Ellis bought Mrs. Bogue's barn for $100.00. I boarded at Ellis's.

Saturday, June 8 I called again at Mrs. Bond's. I wrote some, and in the afternoon went to Marion and lodged at Mark Hillshummer's, 6th house north of the bridge, on Washington Street.

Sunday, June 9 I preached at Horton Street United Brethren Church at 10:30, Ps. 108.4. I dine at Rev. Thornton Rector's where Rev. Cyrus Smith lives. I call at Dallas Bilbe's, and sup at Rev. W.C. Ketner's. I pr. at 8:00, Ps. 92.8. I lodged at Mark Hillshammer's.

Monday, June 10 I went on 9:22 tr. to Wabash, and thence to Huntington. I dined with D.K. Flickinger at Mr. Bailey's. I met the Miss. Ex. Com. at Mission Room at 1:00. I sup at a restaurant. I call at Brooks'. Hear half the concert. Lodge at Bailey's.

Tuesday, June 11 Attend Publ. Board meeting at 9:00. Dine with W.H. Clay at Midway Restaurant. I called at Rev. Wm. Dillon's. I attend the Educational Board meeting at 2:00. Sup at Prof. T.H. Gragg's. Col. Entertainment at 8:00. Lodge at Prof. T.H. Gragg's.

Wednesday, June 12 Breakfast at Prof. Gragg's. Call at Kiracofe's. Ed. Board met at 8:30. Had two ballots. Graduating exercises at 10:30. Alumni dinner at 12:00. I was toastmaster. Publ Board met at 2:00. I called at Bailey's, lunched at restaurant. Ed. Board met at 6:30. Musical Entertainment. Rain. I stay at Kiracofe's.

Thursday, June 13 Met Publ. Board at 8:00. Dine at Rev. E. Clapp's. Met Educa. Board at 2:00. Elected Ex. Committee, & committed election of Pres., faculty, etc. to Ex. Com. I lodged at C.H. Kiracofe's with Bp. Floyd.

Friday, June 14 Met Supervisory Com. at 7:30 at Rev. R.A. Morrison's. Go to Publ. House. Go on 10:19 tr. to Wabash & thence to Marion. Call to see Mrs. Millie J. Wiley 1208 S. Washington St. about sale of her lot in Fairmount. Sup & lodge at Ellis's in Fairm.

Saturday, June 15 Go on 7:15 tr. to Gas City & thence to Union City & home to Dayton, arriving at 3:00.

Sunday, June 16 I heard at Grace Church, Rev. Mr. H.D. Ketcham, M.E. pres. elder on Rom 1.17. Ivonette & Leontine came before I went to meeting. At home the rest of the day, except a call at Lorin's and a walk to [blank] Gustin's 53 Reigel Street, with Milton.

Monday, June 17 At home. Write some letters. Slept some. Mrs. Susan W. Flickinger, wife of Rev. D.K. Flickinger died in Columbus to-day at 11:30 A.M.

Tuesday, June 18 Little of interest occurred to-day. I was writing some letters and sleeping some. Lorin's little girls came and we took some walks—in the evening.

Wednesday, June 19 The day was spent about as yesterday. It rained near night.

Thursday, June 20 Katharine and Milton went on a picnic to Glen.Miller (near Richmond) Ind. They had a good time and returned about 8:00, eve. I Wrote to Mrs. Millie J. Wiley (Marion) about buying her lot in Fairmount.

Sunday, June 23 I heard at 10:30, Rev. D. Frank Garland preach at Main Street Lutheran Church, James 4:7,8, a good sermon. I was at home the rest of the day.

Monday, June 24 Spent the day in writing out any annual report on East District, and in writing an article on Music in the Cchurches, Which I walked over to the post-office to mail at 9:00 eve. Ivonette came to stay with us two days.

Tuesday, June 25 At home all day, mostly reading. I called at Jacob Swank's in the evening.

Wednesday, June 26 Made out my application for a clergy certificate on the Western Passenger Association District, mail it and a copy of the Conservator to Eben E. McLeod, 626 Monadnock Building, Chicago. Called a half hour at H. Sophia Simpson's 227 McPherson St. O. Chanute spent the evening with our boys.

Thursday, June 27 Mr. O. Chanute, spent most of the forenoon and till after 2:00 with us. He is an authority on aerial navigation. I write some letters.

Friday, June 28 In afternoon of to-day, I received a telegram from Mrs. Lizzie Riley Norton, announcing the death last night, of Pres. David Shuck, at Hartsville, Ind. He died the evening of the 27th. I went to Cincinnati, and lodged at Palace Hotel near cor. of 6th & Vine.

Saturday, June 29 Went on 7:15 train to Greensburg & Rugby and thence to Rev. John Riley's in Hartsville, where I staid till morning. Pres. David Shuck had been an invalid there for over a year, being much paralyzed.

Sunday, June 30 Riley took me to Rugby where I preached at 10:30, Eph. 3,19, I returned to Riley's to dinner. Funeral Services at the house at 3:00; burial at cemetery; then went to Church, where I preached, 2 Sam. 3:38. I afterward called at Rev. John Selig's. I lodged at Rev. A.H.K. Beam's. Very hot day.

Monday, July 1 Mrs. Norton & daughter took me to Rugby & I went thence to Cincinnati, and thence to Dayton arriving at 2:38. Rev. J. Selig & wife went to Cincinnati to attend a Knapp Holiness camp meeting. "Rev." Fogle is along. I call at Lorin's after 8:00. Turns cooler. It had been very hot.

Thursday, July 4 Milton came up and fired off his "day" fireworks. I went to the Cemetery, the twelfth anniversary of Susan's death. Milton in the evening enjoyed his Roman Candles, his sky rockets, his spinning wheels and other fireworks; & the little sisters & Lorin were with him.

Friday, July 5 Joseph Wilberforce called. I went to Peter Louding's. D.F. Wilberforce and Joseph and Christopher dined with us.

Saturday, July 6 At home in the forenoon. I aim to go on traction via Miamisburg to Germantown at 6:00. I miss the car and remain in Dayton.

Sunday, July 7 At Main Street Lutheran Church, at 10:45, heard J.G. Butler, of Memorial Church, Washington, D.C. James 4:12, "What is your life," etc. A good sermon, though the delivery was indistinct. Wilbur

& Orville started at 6:00 p.m. for Kitty Hawk, N.C. The day was cool & pleasant.

Tuesday, July 9 Milton and Leontine with us all day.

Wednesday, July 10 I was at home all day. Lorin's Milton and Leontine supped with us.

Thursday, July 11 At home. Went to town at 5:00 P.M. and bought shirts (4) and socks (4) and celluloid collars (2). The children (Lorin's) were with us to supprr. Lorin's second son was born this afternoon. They call him Horace Alfred.

Friday, July 12 Katharine started at 9:53 a.m. via Big 4 R'y to Geneva, O., to visit Mrs. Mella King & Miss Harriet Sillaman. Milton and Leontine sup with us.

Saturday, July 13 At home all day except two calls at Lorin's. Wrote considerably.

Sunday, July 14 Went on 9:00 Traction line to Crawford's, and walked to Olivet Ch. Heard half of W.H. Kindel's sermon on "Proclaim liberty land. I dine & sup with George Warvel's with Kindel's. I pr. at 8:00, 108 Ps. 4 v. Lodge at Aaron Wysong's who live in new house.

Monday, July 15 Walk to Traction & go on 7:00 car to Dayton. Call a few minutes at Lorin's in the evening.

Tuesday, July 16 At home all day, mostly studying sermons. Called at Lorin's a few minutes in the afternoon. It is a very warm day.

Wednesday, July 17 At home, reading and writing. Called at Lorin's in the evening, and we had a hard rain while I was there.

Thursday, July 18 At home all day, except that I dined at Lorin's and went to town and purchased blankbook, paper clip, buttons for cuffs, cheap white neckties, etc. It is a very warm day and sultry evening. Lorin came in the evening and made a draft for my new store room in Fairmount, Ind.

Friday, July 19 Spent the day closely, in writing diffi-cult letters, important ones. At sunset called ten minutes at Lorin's.

Saturday, July 20 I arose at 5:00. I called 5 minutes at Lorin's. I went on 9:00 train to Richmond and called at Mrs. C.E. Zeller's. I went on 11:00 train to Anderson, and on 12:40 train to Fairmount. I sup at Restaurant & lodge at Ellis Wright's. Rhoda away.

Sunday, July 21 I breakfast at Ellis Wright's. He takes me to Hopewell. Rev. W.G. Oxley pr. at 11:00, Rom. 5.1. Ellis & I dine & sup at 8:30, Eph. 5:14. Services all about 35 minutes long. I lodge at Oli. Buller's.

Monday, July 22 I went to R.W. White's . I hoe around my young appletrees. It is the hottest day of the year. About 103 degrees . White is having his oats cut . After supper I go to Oliver Glass's and lodge. Rode Princess.

Tuesday, July 23 I returned to White's and finish my hoeing. I lease him the place another year. After supper, I go on the train to Fairmount. I stay at Ellis Wright's.

Wednesday, July 24 I stay at Ellis's. Write some letters. The weather is still very warm. For about four weeks the Thermometer has run over 86 degrees, much of the time 95 degrees, 100 degrees. Slept well.

Thursday, July 25 Staid at Ellis's. Wrote many letters. The weather is about 100 degrees. Slept well.

Friday, July 26 I start via Gas City, at 7:20, for home. I get home at 2:30 P.M. via Union City. Get things ready for supper. I call in the eve at Lorin's 15 min. Slept well. Warm night.

Saturday, July 27 Wrote on a sermon. Got ice at 1:00.

Sunday, July 28 Ther. 100. It was a very hot day, and I did not go to Church. I dined at Lorin's.

Monday, July 29 Ther. 100. Another very warm day. Katharine returned from Geneva, O., at 6:25 p.m.

Tuesday, July 30 Ther. 100. At home. It rained at Cincinnati and turned some cooler, as dispatches state.

Wednesday, July 31 Got a forwarded letter from Wilbur, saying they had their machine nearly completed. He and Orville are at Kill Devil Hill, a few miles from Kitty Hawk, N. Carolina. It is comfortable, but quite warm to-day. Did much letter writing.

Friday, August 2 Ther. 70 degrees at 6:30 a.m. Kath. Got a letter from Orville saying that they had tried their new "flying" machine the Saturday before with some success.

Saturday, August 3 Ther. 87 degrees at 4:30 p.m. A pleasant day. I went to town in the forenoon, bought several articles, had my teeth scraped of lime and a tooth extracted.

Sunday, August 4 Ther. 73 degrees at 6:00 a.m. I was belated about getting to 1st Baptist Church & did not go. Worked on preparation of sermons. Milton came in Aft'noon & staid till 9:00.

Monday, August 5 Ther. 68 degrees at 6:30 a.m. At home all day. Prepared a sermon. Wrote considerably.

Tuesday, August 6 At home. Wrote many letters. Lorin and his little girls called in the evening.

Wednesday, August 7 Ther. 92 degrees. At home. It was a very busy day. I was largely preparing sermons, or especially revising recently prepared sketches of sermons.

Thursday, August 8 Wrote letters. Went to town in afternoon, loaned American Loan and Savings Association $1500.00. Got articles for self & Katharine. Supper at Lorin's. Lorin & Katharine start at 6:00 for the Jersey Coast on the car Aragh. I called a half hour at Peter Louding's.

Friday, August 9 Arise at 6:00. Get my breakfast and start at 8:00, via Hamilton to Glenwood, Ind. Clifford Long met me and took me to Mrs. Lucinda Moor's (my Bro. Wm's widow's) where I remained till morning. Before dark I visited my parents' graves on the old "home farm."

Saturday, August 10 I called on Chas. Stevens whose family are gone to Grant Co., after which Clifford and Bertha take me to Rushville. I go with Mr. Kolb to Harvey Wright's, my brother's, eight years older than I, who is taking a cancer out of his cheek.

Sunday, August 11 I attended the Baptist Association in my brother's woods. Rev. Mr. Radcliffe pr. at 10:00, Rom. 10.1. trying to make out that there are two salvations—that of the text in this life. Rev. Todd pr. at 11:00, Rom. 8:28, maintaining that the "all things" were only those of the context. I dined on the ground with McKee's & other Relatives. Rev. Robt. Thompson (grandson of Wilson's) pr. at 1:30 maintained that "God" loved all us a certain sense." Rev. Mr. Thomas closed.

Monday, August 12 I took Dr. George Wright, Harvey's second son, to to [repeated in text] Knightstown. Returning, I called at Jabez Rhoad's (she Harvey's second daughter) and at John Wright's. Dined at Harvey's. Afternoon at David Kirkpatrick's & sup there with other relatives. Stay at Harvey Wright's.

Tuesday, August 13 Thomas Wright takes me to Rushville, and we call at Dr. Dillon's, she being Thomas W's second daughter. I go on 10:46 tr. to Guynneville, Ind, & find my home at Rev. H.W. Robbin's, a few rods South of the Church. Rev. J.M. Habrich pr. at 7:30.

Wednesday, August 14 August 14th, White River Conference, in its fifty-fifth session, convened at 9:00, Bishop Milton Wright presiding. Read and commented on Rom. 12th Chap. Conference progressed well. Rev. R.A. Morrison pr. at 8:00.

Thursday, August 15 Conference continued and progressed well. I dined at Wm. Myers', brother of Mrs. Robbins. Rev. D.F. Wilberforce lectured at 8:00. Rev. W.H. Clay came in the evening.

Friday, August 16 Conference continued and progressed well. I dined at Riley Wagner's. Pres. C.H. Kiracofe pr. at 8:00.

Saturday, August 17 Conference progressed well. Rev. J.C. Valentine pr. at 8:00, Heb. 6.19. Hope an anchor.

Sunday, August 18 We abandoned the idea of holding meeting in the grove; for we had a little rain. I pr. at

10:30, Col. 3.1, and ordain O.M. Wilson, G.E. Swartz, and R.W. Harlow. I dined as usual at H.W. Robbins. Bishop H. Floyd pr. at 3:00, and the Sacrament followed. Rev. A. Rust pr. at 7:30, Isa. 11:10. I stay at Robbins.

Monday, August 19 I went to Indianapolis on 5:46 tr., and went to Austin Winchell's, 1200 E. Ohio St. In the Afternoon, I went to Rev. D. Stover's. Dr. George Wright's, and to [blank] Snyder's, and thence to A. Winchell's & lodged there. Daniel Stover was my Pres. Elder in 1847–8.

Tuesday, August 20 I called at Lulu Beeler's, (she being Dr. Geo. Wright's daughter) on E. Ohio St. went to Dr. George Wright's and dined. In the Afternoon, I went to Wm. Glossbrenner Reubush's 1315 Bell[e]fontaine St., and to Austin Winchell's, and lodged at the Spencer House, close to the Uni. Depot.

Wednesday, August 21 I went on 4:00 a.m. tr. to Louisville, Ky., & across on Locomotive cars to New Albany. Applied at Young Men's Ch. Asso. Rooms for help. Lacked just 53 cts to pay fare to Winslow. Commercial Bank charged me a fee to cash a draft I had got at Indianapolis! Went on 9:10 tr. to Winslow, where Cicero Henacher met me. Home at his house. I pr. at 8:00, John 13:1.

Thursday, August 22 Indiana Conference (Mission District) opened at 9:00. The sessions forenoon and afternoon were short. Rev. J.M. Johnson pr. pr. [repeated in text] at 7:30. I boarded at Cicero Hennacher's ten rods west of Friendship church, Pike Co., Ind.

Friday, August 23 Miss Phebe I. Clark, an educated blind girl, aged 27, was received into Conference. The sessions were short. Rev. J.M. Johnson pr. a sermon to the preachers at 2:00, which was good and instructive. I pr. at 7:30, Luke 10:27, on the Great Commandments. Board at Hennacher's.

Saturday, August 24 Conference proceded. It was mainly discussion on the reports. I pr. at 7:30. Rev. J.F. Miller is slow to accept the pres. Eldership.

Sunday, August 25 I pr. at 10:30 Isa. 53.12, and raise $41.00 on Missionary subscription. I dine & sup at Wm.

T. Roe's. He had gone off with the "Evening Lights." I preach at 7:30, 1 Cor. 12.16. After Meeting, Hennacher's soninlaw took me to Oakland City, and I go thence to Princeton & miss connection there. Stay at a boarding house, hotel being full.

Monday, August 26 I go on the train via Terre Haute to Hoopeston, Ill; and thence to Gibson City, where I visit J.F. Croddy, my cousin, raised in my father's family. Edward Milton & Bertha are at home. Franklin can barely walk about with canes. His wife's maiden name was Cynthia Mitchell.

Tuesday, August 27 I stay at Franklin's till 4:00, having called on Rev. Miss Niswonger. I went on train to East Lynn. Wm. Martin takes me to Mr. E.B. Weis's near Fountain Creek Church. Rev. W.H. Elliott pr. at 7:30. I stay at Weis's.

Wednesday, August 28 I attended the Ministerial Association at Fountain Creek Church. I delivered an address on Logic. I made my home at Weis's.

Thursday, August 29 The Annual Session of East Illinois Conference opened at 9:00 A.M., and business proceeded well. Rev. D.K. Flickinger was present. Rev. J.L. Neniger pr. at 8:00. Rev. G.M. Frees pr. at 2:00 to preachers.

Friday, August 30 Conference continued. Rev. D.K. Flickinger pr. or lectured at 7:30. I raise $105.00 missionary subscription. The Stationing Committee met at 7:00 at Weis'.

Saturday, August 31 I called at John Judy's, at 7:00, morn. Sta. Com. met at Weis's at 8:00. The Com. had contrary elements in it E.O. Clapp. Mrs. G. Waters pr. at 7:30.

Sunday, September 1 I pr. 10:30, Rom. 12.3, "More highly than ought to think." I ordain M.C. Snethen and G.W. Ogle. I dine in Claytonville, at Rev. D.D. Fetters', where I slept an hour. I pr. at 7:30, Col. 3.1-4 . Lodge at E.B. Weis's.

Monday, September 2 Was taken very early to Claytonville, & Wellington & Watseka. Oscar & Richard Braden met Dr. Flickinger & myself and took us to their house. Uncle John Braden of Greensburg is visiting there. Go to Robt. Braden's 5 ms. away in afternoon. We lodge at my cousin Braden's, in Watseka.

Tuesday, September 3 We dine at Cousin Lizzie Swinford's, with Braden relatives. We go on 2:00 tr. to Chicago. We lodge at the Wyoming House.

Wednesday, September 4 Go on 8:00 tr. to Kent, Illinios, on Chi, & Gr. Western. I board with J.L. Grimm at Mrs. Keeler's. Rev. A.X. Harrison pr. at 7:30, Gal. 6.14.

Thursday, September 5 Conference opened at 9:00, and business proceeded with dispatch. Grace L. Smith pr. at 7:30, Matt. 11.28,29.

Friday, September 6 Business proce[e]ded well. Dr. Flickinger left at 10:00, and Dr. C.H. Kiracofe came in the afternoon. Wm. Beers was elected presiding elder. The Stationing Committee met at 6:30, at Mrs. Eliz. Keeler's. Rev. J.H. Grimm pr. at 7:30, Ps. At 4:00, Pres. Wm. McKinley shot twice by Leon Czolgosz.

Saturday, September 7 The sessions were largely spent in discussions of general reports. I supped at Studebaker's, a half mile south. Dr. C.H. Kiracofe pr. at 7 30, Prov. 4.23, "Keep the heart."

Sunday, September 8 I preached at 10:30, Isa. 62.1, and ordained Elmer E. Plumley, Dr. Kiracofe dined & lodged with us. We visit Grandmother Keeler. We had a nice rain after meeting was over and the people at home.

Monday, September 9 Tne people mostly start home. I dine at Hockman's in town with E. Plumley and C. Bender. I start at 12:26 for Dubuque, where I got a bank draft, Rail-way guide & neck-ties. I went thence on 5:30 (6:00) train to Cedar Rapids. I lodge at the Grand.

Tuesday, September 10 I slept 6 1/2 hours. Got a lunch, and went on 6:45 (7:00) train to Ottumoa, on Chi. Mil. & St. P. Ry. Pres. McKinley is reported to be improving. I go on 1:40 tr. to Chariton. Wrote letters and cards. I attended the opening services of M.E. Des Moines An. Conf. Rev. Ream of Horton pr. a good sermon, Luke 11.13.

Wednesday, September 11 I slept 7 hours. Went on 4:35 tr. to Worth, Missouri & Rev. Lennuel Beauchamp takes Rev. A.D. Thomas & me to his house, 4 1/2 m. S.E., where we staid till morning. Their Children are: Wm. & Mary (twins), and 5 married children. The rainy weather clears off.

Thursday, September 12 Missouri Conference, at Prarie Chapel, opened at 9:00, and made good progress in business, tho few were present. I boarded at Rev. Abner Norman's, 1/4 m. south. Rev. A.D. Thomas pr. at 8:00, Acts 17.31.

Friday, September 13 The Conference continued. I dine at Rev. Ed. M. Beauchamp's, 1 m. West. Their children are Della, John, Ruth and Leah. It rains after supper & rains much, so that we have no meeting this evening. I board at Norman's. He is 70; his wife 17. They have a child 8 months old.

Saturday, September 14 I dine at Joseph Beauchamp's. He is a college mate of my wife's, and great admirer of her. Conference closes at 4:30. Rev. H.F. Cunningham pr. at 8:00, Rev. 3.20. Pres. Wm. McKinley expired this morning. His last words: "Goodbye, goodbye to all; it is God's way; His will be done." He repeated, "Nearer my God, to thee."

Sunday, September 15 Pres. T. Roosevelt took oath yesterday. I preached at 11:00, Rom. 8:2. I dined as usual at Norman's. I called an hour at Joseph Beauchamp's. I pr. at 8:00, 1 John 4.1. I lodged at Ed. M. Beauchamp's.

Monday, September 16 Rev. Ed. M. Beauchamp takes Thomas Garlock and me to Worth, & we take the tr. to St. Joseph & Forest City, arriving at the latter place at 1:20. Frank Petree meets me on hack and takes me to his house in Oregon. Estella, his wife, is my sister's dau. Rev. H. Crampton called.

Tuesday, September 17 I wrote letters in forenoon & called at Frank & Arthur Petree's law office. Petree's children: Lou Estella 9, Leo Webb, 8, Harris Earls, 6, Jay Ralph, 4. [Since born March 1, 1902, Charles Benjamin.] Mrs. Petree, Sen., called in the evening. I am hoarse from an influenza.

Wednesday, September 18 I went via St. Joseph to Bailieville, Nemaha Co., Kan. I dine at a hotel, free. Rev. F.W. Bertschinger takes me to his house for supper. Rev. T.P. Stewart pr. at the Church at 7:30. I make my home at Alexander Gillespie's, one mile north, across Clear Creek.

Thursday, September 19 The Church is Clear Creek. Conference opened at 9:00, and business moved well. Rev. E. Atkinson preached at 7:30. He boarded also at Gillespie's. I am growing hoarser every day. In the afternoon Rev. W.M. Scott & Bishop Wright delivered memorial addresses on Character of Pres. McKinley.

Friday, September 20 Conference proce[e]ded as usual. I dined at Amos Coffin's. His wife was a Gillespie. In the evening, Mrs. Brown, a Qr. Conf. preacher, pr. I am Still hoarser. (Mrs. Brown later married Rev. S.B. Mcgrew.)

Saturday, September 21 Conference proceeded as usual. We dine at Lee Davis's. Rev. H.M. Branham pr. at 7:30, Ps. 17.15 "Satisfied when I wake." I am very hoarse.

Sunday, September 22 The day is warm. I pr. at 11:00, 1 Thes. 2.1,2. I dine at Rev. F.W. Bertschinger's, 1 1/2 ms. south. Rev. W.M. Scott pr. at 7:30, Isa. 53.1. "Who hath believe. I lodge at A. Gillsepie's. I was quite hoarse from the influenza.

Monday, September 23 I went with Geo. Gillespie to Axtell. We dine at a restaurant. I met the Presbyterian preacher who is antisecrecy. I go on 12:27 tr. to Kansas City. Rev. Godman, M.E. P.E. is aboard he also antisecrecy. Rev. Scott, Adams & Lashley are aboard; also Rev. Clark, Baptist. Reuchlin met me and took me to his house, 3836 Euclid Ave.

Tuesday, September 24 I went down town with Reuchlin & bought presents for him & family. I spent the afternoon in talking with Reuchlin and Lulu. Lodged there.

Wednesday, September 25 I went down to the depot and started on 10:55 R.I. & Pac. tr. via Topeka, McFarland and Bellville to Ezbon, Jewell Co., Kansas. Reach Ezbon at 7:56 A.M. and Rev. R. Goldsworth took me to J.M.

Pixler's nine miles north. Their children are: Maud 15, Pearl 14, Harvey Merle 7 months old. J.H. Spall with us.

Thursday, September 26 West Kansas Mission dist. Conference informally met in R. Goldsworth's tent and adjourned till 2:00. There were very few present. Afternoon Session did business. Rev. J.H. Spall pr. at 8:00, in the large tent, Prov. 30.30-38. I board at Pixler's. Rev. Spall did well.

Friday, September 27 The session continued. Rev. G.W. Wilfong came at 10:00. He preached in the tent at 8:00, Gal. 6.7, a good sermon.

Saturday, September 28 Conference continued and closed. Rev. G.W. Wilfong pr. again at 8:00, Ex. 20.3-17, on the Decalogue, an able sermon.

Sunday, September 29 I preached at 11:00 in the tent, Isa. 62.1. I dine at R. Goldsworth's tent, near the large tent. Rev. J.F. Foster pr. at 3:00, I sup at J.M. Pixler's. Rev. R. Goldsworth pr. at 8:00, & I exhorted. We next had our farewell song. Stay at J.M. Pixler's.

Monday, September 30 Mr. Joseph M. Pixler takes me to Ezbon, and I went on 9:03 tr. to Mankato. I went to Rev. J.S. Rocks and staid there till morning. In the afternoon, I called at John Depo's. Rock's were full of conversation.

Tuesday, October 1 At 9:00, I start to Wichita via McFarland. The day was warm and clear. I reached Wichita at 7:00, and George M. Glenn met me and took me to his house, 428 Campbell St. Mrs. Fannie (Reeder) Glenn is my cousin. Children: Mabel 14, Georgie 12, Ruth 4; Helen 9 months. Lodged there.

Wednesday, October 2 I went to town with Mr. Glenn & to his office, Room 66 Winne Bldg., bought some presents & returned to Glenn's house. Chas. Greenle & Faye (Cousin Sina's daughter) dined with us. I went on 2:25 tr. (Mo. Pac. R'y) to Eldorado. Rev. C.B. Sherk took me to David Lucas's. Rev. H.D. Sill pr. at 8:00. Phil. 3.8, "I count all things—loss."

Thursday, October 3 I board at D. Lucas's. Arkansas

Valley conf. opened at our church in Eldorado, at 9:00 and business was transacted lively. Rev. A.W. Geeslin of Missouri joined on transfer. He pr. at 8:00, Ps. 40.1, an excellent sermon, and the after meeting was fine.

Friday, October 4 Conference progressed well. A.W. Geeslin pr. at 8:00, Luke 11:3, "Give us day by day our daily bread." Good speaking meeting followed. We had rain in the morning.

Saturday, October 5 Conference proceeded and closed at 5:00. Geeslin, Sherk & Tripps and I dined at Rev. S.F.C. Garrisons, two miles out in the country. Rev. C.B. Sherk preached at 8:00, Gal. 2.20, "Life I now live in the flesh." Board as usual. Wm. Wright, my sweet brother died 33 years ago, (1868).

Sunday, October 6 I pr. in U.B. Church in Eldorado, at 11:00, 2 Cor. 10.15. I dine with Rev. C.B. Sherk at Kelling's and Norton's, three miles in the country. Sadie Norton is one of H.D. Tatman's converts & Pres. C. End. Soci. Sup at Lucas. I pr. at 7:30, Ti. 2:14. Communion. Norton's & Kelling's join Church.

Monday, October 7 I dine at John B. Marcum's with Sherk, and we go to Rev. D. Herbert Sill's to supper & lodge at A.J. Sill's, near Kechi. I pr. at Kechi U.B. Church at 7:30, Eph. 3.19. Did not have much liberty in preaching.

Tuesday, October 8 Rev. C.B. Sherk, after an early breakfast, takes me to Wichita, and I go on Santa Fe tr. to Wellington, Kan., and Curtis, Woodward Co., Okla. Rev. R. Ward came aboard. John F. Solter met us and took us with a mule team to Elihn Maupin's, 20 miles on the way to Richmond, Okla., where we sup & lodge. Slept well.

Wednesday, October 9 I staid at Maupin's till afternoon, when we go to Richmond and put up at John W. White's (Merchant), where I found my conference home. Roy Ward pr. at 7:30. He evidently, while bright, does little in study.

Thursday, October 10 Oklahoma Mission Dist. Conference opened at 9:00, and progressed well. J.L. Ridgway preached at 8:00 an eloquent sermon on Matt. 7:24-27.

I boarded at White's.

Friday, October 11 Conference continued. The Case of the Williams, on Mrs. Williams' medical practice, came up, and was referred to a committee of trial. J.H. McNew pr. at 2:00 to the preachers. I pr. at 7:30, John 14.2.

Saturday, October 12 The report on the Williams' case was adverse to them and they asked their names stricken from the roll, which was granted. Conference closed at 5:00. I dined at Jas. Taylor's with F.M. Higgins. I pr at 7:30, Rom. 4.7,8. Rev. Degree, Adventist, was there.

Sunday, October 13 I pr. at Richmond Schoolhouse at 11:00, Rom. 8.2. I dine at Carmany's, he being a Liberal, a mile east of Sch. H. He is one of the Blue River, Ind., Carmany's. J.E. Rector & wife with me. I pr. at 7:30, 1 John 4.1. Lodge at J.W. White's.

Monday, October 14 I rise at 3:30, get breakfast at 4:30, and start with Revs. J.E. Rector and J.L. Ridgway to Woodward, at 5:00. Dark for some miles. We reach Woodward, 39 miles at 11:25 and start at 11:30 to Wellington & Winfield. Reach Cherry Vale at 1:55, and put up at Axtell house, a good hotel, $1.00. This was a fine day.

Tuesday, October 15 I wrote letters and a card at the Hotel. The train to Fredonia was 3 hours and 40 min. late, so I got there well in the afternoon. Rev. H.E. Smith met me & took me to his house where I supped & lodged. I pr. at new U.B. Ch. at 7:30, Acts 24.15, on Resurrection. Good congrega.

Wednesday, October 16 H.E. Smith's and I go on 10:50 tr. via Chanute to Welda. Dine at Rev. P.N. Lambert's. Afternoon, Rev. S.B. McGrew took me to Joseph M. Kauble's in the edge of town, where we board. At 7:30, Rev. E.M. Votah preached. The weather is very fine. Water scarce in this place & vicinity.

Thursday, October 17 Neasho conference opened at 9:00, and progressed well. There was a crowd in from the Washington Society friendly to Harrell's controversy. Rev. McGill introduced. Moral Reform was discussed in the Afternoon. Rev. A.L. Hope of Kan. Conf. pr. at 7:30, 2 Cor. 5:20, "Be ye reconciled God." Fine weather.

Friday, October 18 Annual conference progressed well. I dine at Rev. P.N. Lambert's again. At 2:00, S.B. McGrew pr. to the Conference. Rev. H.E. Smith pr. at 7:30.

Saturday, October 19 The report on Tatman & Harrell recom. that they be held till reconciled. Adopted L.G. Messenger transfer's to Oklahoma. Rev. *McGill pr. at 7:30. Stationing committee met at 7:00. *He was United Presbyterian.

Sunday, October 20 I preached at 11:00, Hebr. 8:10,11. I dine at J.M. Kauble's as usual. I pr. at 7:30, 1 Cor. 12.31. "The more excellent way." Lodge at Kauble's as usual.

Monday, October 21 Rev. P.N. Lambert, came after an early breakfast, and I start for Colony, at 5:00. I go thence on early train to Pleasanton, Mo. Lunch there & go on aftn tr. to Lamar. Rev. J.B. Crom meets me & takes me to his house, 3 1/2 miles away. We stay there till 1:00 at night. Has a son Floyd.

Tuesday, October 22 At 2:00, we leave Lamar on train to Springfield. We lunch for breakfast there. We leave at 11:00 for Chadwick 36 miles south. We hire a rig & go 14 miles south to Swan Postoffice. There we lodge with Milton Merrick, George Burger's soninlaw.

Wednesday, October 23 We walked two miles to George Burgers, senior, and remained there till morning. He is from Germany. He has seven very promising sons. The oldest (Charles) is at Central College. His son George is in the store at Swan. Oscar, Noah, etc. Rev. J.B. Crom pr. at Lone Star Ch. at 7:00, Song of Solomon, 5.3.

Thursday, October 24 South Missouri Mission Dist. Conference opened at 9:00, at Lone Star Chapel, 16 ms. South of Chadwick. I board at Neilse Christian Peterson's, a Dane, 3/4 of a mile west of the Church. Rev. D.S. Buck pr. at 7:00, John 15.4, a good sermon.

Friday, October 25 Conference continued. I dine at Lynn Dilks' 1 mile south. Mrs. Eva Dane (P.O. Swan) pr. at 2:30, Ps. 16.11. Rev. G.W. Masters pr. at 7:00, Acts 16.30, and S. Snell exhorted. I board at Peterson's. Daughters: Maud 19; Elsie, 13.

Saturday, October 26 Conference continued. I gave a lesson at 10:30, on 13th Chap. of John. I dined with Snell's at Wm. Leinler's, his soninlaw's. L.G. Cowdrey pr. at 7:00, 1 Cor. 1.8. There was a little Rain to-day.

Sunday, October 27 Sunday School Anniversary at 10:00, I made a short address. I pr. at 11:00, 2 Tim. 3.16. I dine at Adolphe Stolpe's and sup there. I pr. a communion sermon at 7:00, John 1.29. Communion followed. I went to George Burger's to lodge.

Monday, October 28 Noah Burger aged 19, takes us to Chadwick. We (Crom's & Buck) go on to Springfield on 3:00 train. We lunched out of basket at Chadwick, and at Restaurant at Springfield. Crom, Buck and I attend the Opening of the Baptist General Association at 1st Baptist Church, evening. I go on 11:10 tr to St. Louis. Rev. McHanway pr.

Tuesday, October 29 Arrive at St. Louis at 7:30, having slept 4 hours on chair car. Leave on 8:44 tr. on Vandalia Line, Arr. at Indianapolis at 2:55; reach Anderson at 8:45. Fairmount by electric line at 7:30. Lodge at Ellis Wright's. Leon Czolgosz was electrocuted at Auburn Prison; a sane man insane with anarchism.

Wednesday, October 30 I went on 9:31 tr. to Fowlerton. I dined at R.W. White's. I rode "Princess" over to Robert Reeder's. Lodge there. The Syrian pedler from Beyroute, supped at Robert's.

Thursday, October 31 I called at W.H.H. Reeder's and Ol. A. Glass's. Dined at R.W. White's. I went to Fairmount on 11+ tr. Ellis & Rhoda away. I sup & lodge at Ellis's. Tried to teach Myrl multiplication table. I slept eight hours.

Friday, November 1 Paid City Clerk the water rent & left with Ellis Wright a check for $5.00 for Wm. D. Dye, and went on 8:10 car to Gas City, and thence on 8:13 tr. to Union City and on 1:05 tr. home to Dayton. Found all well. Called at Lorin's. Lorin & Milton called an hour in the eve'g. Slept nine hours.

Saturday, November 2 Was very busy arranging things and writing. The day was warm. Retired before ten o'clock (eve) and slept 8 hours.

Sunday, November 3 I remained at home all day, my clothes not being cleaned up for church going. It rained afternoon and evening. I called at Lorin's a half hour. I slept 8 hours tonight.

Monday, November 4 I was at home all day. I wrote several letters and some cards. I[t] was a cool day, but very nice. I read up considerably in the September "Outlooks." Katharine went to the Helen Hunt Club in the evening.

Tuesday, November 5 This is election day. I voted in the forenoon; voted for every Republican, except Burnham. Wrote many letters and cards. I went to town at 9:00, and watched McKinley Club Bulletins from Grocery opposite. Seth Lowe elected Mayor of New York City. Evening cool.

Wednesday, November 6 The election news seem to indicate that the Republicans have carried most possible states, except Kentucky. The Republicans carried this county for every office. Write letters. At home all day.

Thursday, November 7 Li Hung Chang died to-day. At home all day except a call at Lorin's about 5:00 p.m. I was reading mainly; writing some. I read to a very late hour, "Ritchie King's Daughter" a not well composed religious temperance fiction. It is too abrupt in its improbabilities.

Friday, November 8 At home mainly reading. Went to town about 4:00 & got presents for Lorin's children, Milton being nine years old to-day. They are bright sweet children, Ivonette 5; Leontine 3, Alfred 4 mos. (Later we called him Horace.)

Saturday, November 9 At home all day, reading, writing. I read much. At 4:30, Dr. H.J. Becker came. He seems very Conservative, and very complimentary to me. I nearly read through Justin McCarthy's England in the XIX Century.

Sunday, November 10 Attended at 1st Presb. Church. Mr. Wilson's text was Cor. 3.3, "Your life is hid," a good sermon. Lorin's children came in the afternoon.

Monday, November 11 I was at home all day, mostly reading. Dr. H.J. Becker called at 4:00 p.m.

Tuesday, November 12 At home reading and writing letters. Lorin & Ivonette Jr. called in the evening.

Wednesday, November 13 At home. Wrote letters. I called at Jacob Swank's at 4:30 p.m. a half hour.

Thursday, November 14 At home all day reading and writing. Some snow fell in the afternoon melting, but left a white sheet at sunset, and the temperature fell considerably.

Friday, November 15 Very little snow fell about noon, and the ground became nearly bare.

Saturday, November 16 At home, except a trip to the bank & bt. ink. Wrote several full cards.

Sunday, November 17 At 11:00, heard Rev. H.F. Colby, Baptist, Col. 1:24, on the church, a good sermon. Lorin and family are with us to dinner & till night. At 3:30, Heard Rev. W.O. Thompson, D.D. at Association Hall, Luke 16.31. Sufficient Evidence. A fine address. At 7:30, I heard Rev. C.W. Gullette at Grace M.E. Church on healings, 1 Pet. 3:15.

Monday, November 18 At home all day, reading "World's History and it's Maker's," a better book than I thought at first. Wrote several letters in the evening. Katharine went to the Helen Hllnt Club, in the evening. This is Lorin's birthday, he being 39 years old.

Tuesday, November 19 At home in forenoon, except I went to the new (Fourth) Reform Church, Home & Summit Sts, to buy a ticket to Sam R. Jones lecture. Called at Albert Shearer's and at Lorin's.

Thursday, November 21 At home writing and reading. Wrote R. Morrison on By Laws for U.B.C.E. and some other letters. Went to hear Rev. Sam Jones at 4th Reformed Church at 8:00, evening. He is the finest humorist that I ever listened to.

Friday, November 22 At home. Get ready to go away. Called at Albert Sheraer's and at Lorin's, in the evening.

Saturday, November 23 Start at 7:00 for Fairmount, via Union City. Waited an hour after train was due at Union City, and on interurban 50 minutes at Jonesboro. Called at Ellis's store at Fairmount. I went on 3:39 tr. to Leach, and supped and lodged at R.W. White's on my farm. John Wright died to-day, Son of my brother Harvey.

Sunday, November 24 I preached at 10:30 at Hopewell Luke 11.13 (?) [Question mark is part of the text] Dine & sup at Oliver Buller's. I preach at 7:00, I John 4.1. Lodge at White's.

Monday, November 25 I dine at R.W. White's and go on noon train to Fairmount. I lodge at Ellis Wright's. *Expert Crane's Report:*Receipts $67274.70, Disbursements 64692.77, Balance 2581.93 A possible reduction 1111.19, Possible deficit 1470.74.

Tuesday, November 26 I go on 7:10 interurban car to Marion. I see Mrs. Millie Wiley on the sale or trading of lots. She is of low ambition about Fairmount property. Co on forenoon train to Huntington. I dine at Midway restaurant. At meeting of Publishing Board at 2:00, Mr. Geo. D. Crane of Ft. Wayne expert accountant, made complete report. M.F. Keiter appeared short $1,400—possibly $2,500. Sup at Foote's; Lodge at Kiracofe's.

Wednesday, November 27 Missionary Executive Committee met at 8:00. I dine at Foote's. Educational Exec. Committee met at 2:00. I was only advisory at each. I threw a shell into the camp of the Bible School projectors. I sup at W. Dillon's, and lodge at C.H. Kiracofe's at College Park.

Thursday, November 28 I call at Linker's and the Wilberforces rooms in the Stemen Addition. I go on the 10:19 train to Wabash, where I miss connection and wait till 5:01 train. So I go on to Fairmount and stay at Ellis Wrights. They and Hunt's & Heddrick's did not return from the Marion Soldier's Home till about 8:00. I wrote much at Wabash & at Ellis's. Lodge at Ellis's. Saw Mrs. Sarah Haines.

Friday, November 29 Dine at Ellis's. I went on 12:20 train to Louisville, Ky. I left my overcoat on the Indianapolis car. (The train waited an hour at Anderson) I went from Louisville to New Albany on the dummy car.

I staid at St. Charles Hotel: $1.00 for lodging and breakfast—unusually good cooks and waiters.

Saturday, November 30 I went on 9:10 train to Marengo. Rev. J.T. Miller met me and took me to Rev. J.M. Johnson's, one mile north of the depot, where I board till Monday. Miller preached at 6:45, Rev. 8.20.

Sunday, December 1 I preached at 10:30, Luke 11.13. Prof. Johnson's soninlaw & wife and son came. Rev. Daily and James Chester Weathers dine with us at Johnson's. I preached at 6:45 from 11Tim 3.16. I was at the S.S. in the afternoon. Wm. Goldman is the superintendent.

Monday, December 2 Miller & I dine at Wm. Goldman's, and we have supper at T.S. Heistand's. Meeting at 2:00. I preached to 100 people at 6:45, Rom. 4.8. We stay at Rial Key's. His wife is "Aunt Sibbe."

Tuesday, December 3 We dine with several others at Dr. J.E. Fetzer's. Had a good meeting at 2:00. We had supper at Abram Key's. His wife is "Aunt Rebecca." I preach at 6:45, Acts 26.28. We lodge at Theophilus Key's. He is cousin to Rial and Abram.

Wednesday, December 4 We dine at James Chester Weather's, who is a Disciple. We attended afternoon meeting. We eat supper at Mrs. Jane Weathers', a daughter of Dan Lopp's, brother of Jolen and Andrew. Miller pr. at 6:45, Isa. 1.16-21. We stay at Prof. Johnson's.

Thursday, December 5 We dine at Rev. Martin Goldman's, aged about 78; his wife Prof. Johnson's sister. Meeting at 2:00. We have supper at Alexander Peru's, born in Upper Canada, April 17, 1812; in his 89th year. I Pr. at 6:45, Luke 9.24.

Friday, December 6 Wm. Goldman takes my negative. We dine at Solomon Alderton's. Saw extracts from Pres. Theodore Ro[o]sevelt's Message. We sup and lodge at Prof. Johnson's. Miller pr. at 6:45, Rev. 22, on "Come."

Saturday, December 7 We arose at daylight. No 2:00 meeting. I stay at Johnson's. Miller pr at 6:45. We lodge at Rial Key's.

Sunday, December 8 I preached at 10:30, Matt. 16.18,

the latter part on the organic Church. We dine at Johnson's. I preached at 7:00, Gal. 1.4,5. We stay at Johnson's.

Monday, December 9 I dined at J.M. Johnson's. Meeting at 2:00. I pr. at 7:00, Matt. 19.27.

Tuesday, December 10 We dine at Theophilis Key's with Prof. Johnson & wife. Meeting at 2:00. Supped at Johnson's with Rev. Todd, Liberal, P.E. I Pr. at 7:00, 2 Cor. 8.9. Two converted. Lodge at Johnson's.

Wednesday, December 11 Nothing at 2:00, I dine and sup at Prof. Johnson's. I preached at 7:00, 1 Pet. 4.18. We lodge at Rial Key's.

Thursday, December 12 We dine at Alex Peru's. Meeting at 2:00. We ate supper at Mrs. Jane Weathers. Miller pr. at 7:00, Isa. 35.8, using blackboard. His proposition that unconverted indorse his sermon! We lodge at Rial Key's.

Friday, December 13 We go to Johnson's and thence to J. Wm. Goldman's, where we dine. I, at 2:00, expound the first Psalm, at the day meeting. We sup at George Destar's. a teacher & medical student. It rained. I pr. at 7:00, Matt. 13:44. We stay at Johnson's, he having got home.

Saturday, December 14 There are several inches of snow and the weather turns cold. I dine sup & lodge at Prof. J.M. Johnson's. No 2:00 meeting. Pr. at 7:00. Stay at Johnson's.

Sunday, December 15 The thermometer is below zero. I pr. at 11:00, 1 Cor 15.20. Was a little unwell. I dined at Theophilus Key's. I taught S.S. class at 2:00. Supper and lodging at Prof. Johnson's. I pr. at 7:00, Zech. 13.9.

Monday, December 16 I get ready, and Miller & Rial Key accompany me to depot. The train is over an hour late. Our Connection for the B&O S.W. at New AIbany is close. Antiquated restaurant keeper at depot delays me closely. Reach Cin. at 5:45, Dayton at 8:00. Wrote Article for *Cons*.

Tuesday, December 17 I was at home all day, reading and writing. I called at Lorin's in the evening. As usual,

Ivonette and Leontine were in a great glee about my coming.

Wednesday, December 18 I was at home all day.. Katharine went to Cincinnati. Milton wrote a letter, himself, to his Grandpa Corbett, enclosing a doller for himself and all the grandchildren. I wrote several letters in the afternoon. Day pretty cold.

Thursday, December 19 I was at home all day, except a trip to town, to bank and for purchases for Reuchlin's children. I wrote many letters. The mercury in the morning was below zero.

Friday, December 20 Probably this is the coldest morning of the season thus far. I wrote much; remained at home all day. Milton sups with us and helps the children pack a Christmas box for Reuchlin's folks.

Saturday, December 21 I was considerably unwell today, though not sick, and did little except read especially in the revised Bible American edition.

Sunday, December 22 Not being well, I remained at home all day. Lorin brought Alfred up, a real nice boy of five months. Netta and the rest came later. I studied and wrote on Mormon questions propounded by Mr. Moore of Richmond, Oklahoma.

Monday, December 23 At home all day. I wrote early and till midnight. The weather was warmer. My health was better. Milton supped with us. I wrote W.H. Clay criticising his mysterious letter & his criticism of other departments & their offices.

Tuesday, December 24 I spent the day at home. Lorin's Milton & sisters were with us part of the day. I wrote an article for our church paper on The Eminence of Joseph. I was up late at night.

Wednesday, December 25 I rewrote my article. We dined alone. I called at Lorin's in the evening. I expressed a package in the evening, mailed some letters at the post-office and called a half hour at Peter Louding's. He tells of their exper. with Wilber's.

Sunday, December 29 Was belated and did not get to

Church. Leontine & sister came up.

Monday, December 30 Katharine started at 9:00 for Chicago, to be at Margaret Goodwin's wedding to-morrow evening. Leontine came and staid till after dinner. I read & write. I was at home all day.

Tuesday, December 31 Wrote most of the day. Went no where. We had a nice time. Awoke at midnight to hear the bells and steam whistles, thought it day dawn, but soon fell asleep again. Margaret Goodwin mar[r]ied Cola Winn Meacham & moved into a flat; m'd at 8:00.

Notes for 1902, Jan. 1st.
Mary Osborn married Emmon's at 6:00, last evening. Flora Belle Greenwood married [blank] Smith.

Memoranda
Ralph Reeder's first wife was Mary E. Timpson, of English descent. He died in 1862. Reuchlin Wright 3836 Euclid Ave. K.C. Mo. Mrs. Eliza Wiley 457 N. 7th St., Terre Haute, Ind. Anna M. McKnight 1600 S. Wayne St., Dayton, O.

1902

Wednesday, January 1 Seventy-th[r]ee years of Divine blessings to me! Lorin's three older children dine with us; —turkey very best! Sweetest children! As always, I am busy reading and writing, am real well.

Thursday, January 2 I am at home. A deputy called to see if I represented Auglaize conference, on Levi Zehring's estate. Katharine got home from Margaret Goodwin's wedding at Chicago.

Friday, January 3 I called at Lorin's a half hour in forenoon. I made affidavit on date of William Wright's death, and so forth & sent it to Reuchlin, to Tonganoxie, Kansas. Write many letters.

Saturday, January 4 A letter came from Bishop H.T. Barnaby & I reply to it & write other letters. I sat up very late.

Sunday, January 5 I attended the African M.E. Church at 11:00, and heard Rev. Dickinson, P.E. preach, 1 Kings 8.36. He of Hamilton. Lorin called at 5:00. I pr. at 8:00, Zach. 13.9 at Af. M.E. Church, audience fair size. Pastor Rev. Collins.

Monday, January 6 I wrote about 15 letters & cards—seven of them to Conf. Secretaries for statistics—and did some reading. I had arisen at 4:00 Morn.

Tuesday, January 7 At home mostly, writing. Called at Lorin's a half hour. Went to Library at 4:30 & staid till 6:30, Looking up Smith genealogy.

Wednesday, January 8 Arose at about 4:30, & wrote two letters & one card before breakfast. Went to Public Library an hour and a half in forenoon, & an hour in the evening. Wrote a number of letters on McNew's pro. evang. tour!

Thursday, January 9 Wrote letters to Neosho men; also to Clay & Clapper. Spent some hours in Public Library.

Friday, January 10 Spent part of forenoon in reading and writing. Spent an hour in Public Library, and traced our Schenck ancestors to antiquity in Holland.

Saturday, January 11 I spent all day at home except a call at Lorin's. Wrote much; spent considerable time in arranging old papers. Wrote answers to the Mormon's questions.

Sunday, January 12 Somehow was belated about getting ready to go to Church. Milton and Leontine took supper with us.

Monday, January 13 Was at home reading early; washed three vests & two pair of pantaloons in forenoon. Attended Bishop Jas. Wm. Hott's funeral at 1:00, at Oak St. U.B. Church.

Tuesday, January 14 At home. In afternoon sent off application for "Clergy Reduced Rate Certificate," to W. Pas. Association. Was, which is uncommon, wakeful tonight.

Wednesday, January 15 Arose very early. Wrote many letters and cards. After breakfast answered Barnaby's & Flickinger's letters on Publ. Estab. matters. Went to town afternoon awhile, & then slept two hours. Slept long to-night.

Friday, January 17 Wrote out my reply to Mr. G.M. Moore's Mormon Questions, and mailed the reply type-written, with a copy to Mrs. Ada White, Richmond, Oklahoma. "Lottie" worked for us in the afternoon. Grant M. Moore.

Saturday, January 18 At home engaged as usual. Lorin called in the evening Mrs. Nora Jones came in the afternoon to do Katherine's housework.

Sunday, January 19 Heard at 10:30, Rev. Maurice Wilson preach on Esther 4:14, a Missionary discourse. At home the rest of the day. Lorin's two older children dined with us. Lorin & the babe came in aftn.

Tuesday, January 21 It is a snowy day partly melting as it falls. I write letters, many, as usual.

Wednesday, January 22 At home mostly. Took up Gamalie Bailey's history and character, and went to Public Library, and consulted with notes, the 17th volume of At. Month. Spent the evening on Wilson's Hist. Slave Power.

Thursday, January 23 Spend the forenoon in taking notes on Wilson's Rise & fall of Slave Power. Went in Aftn. and finished examination of Atlantic Monthly.

Friday, January 24 Wrote Clopper and Tharp. Went to town mail letter & buy underwear and socks. Get ready to start to Grant Co. Ind. in the morning. Write several letters.

Saturday, January 25 I start at 7:00 via Union City at Fairmount. I missed interurban car at Jonesboro, and waited another hour. Reach Fairmount at 2:00, see Mrs. Bond; go to Fowlerton on 3:35 tr. & go to Wm. H.H. Reeder's. Slept 6 hours.

Sunday, January 26 Wm. & Mattie take me to Hopewell Ch. I Pr. Zech 13.9. Dine at Ol. Buller's (Wm. Reeder & wife there.) Pr. at 7:00, Rev. 2.17, "Hidden [unreadable]. U.B.C.E. Meeting at 6:00. They adopt bylaws. Stay at Ol. Glass's. Slept well.

Monday, January 27 I dined at R.W. White's. Edith sick. I mark some trees in afternoon for the saw mill. Go on 6:15 tr. to Fairmount and walk to Union Ch. & pr. 2 Cor. 5:11. I supped at Henry Simon's. Talked of right of way. Stay at Wm. Keiver's. Slept 5 hours.

Tuesday, January 28 Call at Robt. Hastings with Rev. M.V.Bartlett. Go on to Ellis Wright's & dine. Receive Mrs. Bond's bequest note, cancel it at her request & retain it. I get other letters on it. Get my valise. Stay at Ellise's. Slept 3 hours.

Wednesday, January 29 It had snowed in the night, which was cold. Wrote letters and cards in the forenoon. In aftn. paid $149.49 on paving Washington St. Saw Mrs. Bond—got addi. pattern [?]. Supped at Hastings. Pr. at Union, Isa. 1.18. Walk to Ellis's. Lodged. Slept 4 hours.

Thursday, January 30 Go on 8:10 interurban car to Gas City & thence on 9:12 car to Union City & on 1:05 home. Mr. Oliver & family moving to Wayne, Tenn. McGee's going with them. They are on the cars from Union City. Slept 6 hours.

Friday, January 31 At home all day except a call at Lorin's. Milton is just getting over the measles. I read some & write some.

Saturday, February 1 At home all forenoon except a call at Lorin's about noon. I go in the afternoon to Germantown to Quarterly meeting. Sup & lodge at J.W. Fouts. Pr. at 7, Isa. 1:18, "Reason."

Sunday, February 2 Rev. Wm. Miller pr. at 10:30, Acts 13.38. I introduce communion. Dine with Miller at Lewis Wetts, 3/4 m. n.w. I pr. at 7, 2 Cor. 5.11. We lodge at Wesley Fouts. It was a very cold night.

Monday, February 3 Weather fair. Ther. low. We start at 7:00 for Dayton on Electric cars & reach home at about 8:30. At home the rest of the day. Got letter from W.H. Clay about bequest notes on file.

Tuesday, February 4 Weather clear. Ther. low. I arose at 5:00 & brushed the snow off the porch and cement walks. Called at Lorin's. Ivonette & Leontine have the measles.

Wednesday, February 5 The gas pressure was very light after the early morning. Ivonette is quite sick with measles. Read some, wrote some letters. Called at Lorin's in forenoon. To town.

Thursday, February 6 Weather, Clou. Ther. 35 degrees. I breakfast and go in the raise to Lorin's to see how the children are. They seem a little better. I went in Aftn. to town, bought a clock, left deed for W. Cemetery lot for record. Slept 8 hours.

Friday, February 7 At home all day. Did some necessary work preparatory to going to Huntington.

Saturday, February 8 I was at home all day except a call at Lorin's. The children are over the worst with the measles. I did little except read; and looked over documents relating to Publ. Board business.

Sunday, February 9 I heard at First Presbyterian Ch. Rev. Dr. E. Trumbull Lee, of Cin. pr. on Prov. 25.1, an able & eloquent sermon on "The Hiding of God." At home the rest of the day. Milton dined with us. I get ready to go to Hunting.

Monday, February 10 Start at 5:35, via Lima, to Huntington, Ind. Arrived on a belated train at 11:00, earlier than regular tr. Dine at R.A. Morrison's. Visit Publ. Estab. Sup & lodge at Bp. Kiracofe's.

Tuesday, February 11 Called at Wilberforce's. Dine at Restaurant. Publ. Board met at 2:00. Was promised liberty to ask questions. Sup at Prof. Gragg's. Lodge at Prof. Kiracofe's.

Wednesday, February 12 Keiter read his explanations. The Board in bad faith, refused to allow minority to ask questions. Dine at Restaurant. Sup & lodge at Foot's. He consulted Pros. Atty.

Thursday, February 13 The farcical investigation continued all day. The evening session was on other matters. I got in resolution Calling for reports on bequest notes. Dine & sup at Rest. I lodged at R.A. Morrison's.

Friday, February 14 "Investigation" continued. Keiter closed his arraignment! We are refused right to ask ques-

tions. Resolution of Floyd's is passed; 4 yeas, 3 nays. Minority file protest. Montgomery & I called by Justice. Sup & lodge at Kiracofe's.

Saturday, February 15 I call at Judge Watkins' office. I go to Wabash & Fairmount, Kiracofe, Floyd & Small being aboard. Kiracofe tells me of M.F. Keiter's arrest for forgery. Dine, Sup & lodge at Ellis Wright's. Surprise party to Rhoda.

Sunday, February 16 I preach, at 10:30, John 15.5, "Without me." Dine & sup at Wilbur Kester's. I preach at 7:00, 1 John 4.8. "God is love." Beginning of protracted meeting. I lodge at my nephew's. This is Rhoda Wright's 34th birth day anniversary.

Monday, February 17 I wrote to Judge Watkins & to Clay. I saw Mrs. Bond. Went via Gas City & Union City & got home at 3:00. Talk with boys. Wrote letters. Slept 7 hours. I have slept short hours for more than a week.

Tuesday, February 18 Arose very early. Wrote to W.H. Clay & to Bishop Barnaby. Passed the rest of the day as usual. Called at Lorin's at 12:00. Wrote some letters. Slept 7 1/2 hours. Dr. Newman Hall died to-day in England.

Wednesday, February 19 Arose very early & wrote some letters. Spent the day largely in reading. Wrote some letters. Went to bed at 9:30, and slept 8 hours.

Thursday, February 20 I was at home all day except a call at Lorin's. Spent much of the afternoon in filing old periodicals. Solemnized, at our home, the marriage of Ward E.H. Shock and Lillie M. Perdue at 7:30 in the evening. Slept 7 1/2 hours.

Friday, February 21 Went to Town & bought articles. Mr & Mrs. William Dillon called. He took dinner with us. Spent part of the afternoon in clearing out old periodicals.

Saturday, February 22 Was at home. Wrote some letters and mailed them at the post-office. Sent out 25 circulars.

Sunday, February 23 I was unwell, so I mostly lay abed

& slept much. Lorin & his two little girls called.

Monday, February 24 I was still not very well. Wrote and read some. This morning I recieved a copy of *Conservator* and a copy of *Herald* (Huntington). Got reply from Grant M. Moore, the Mormon.

Tuesday, February 25 Some better to-day. I took times deliberately. Sent to printer copy of Publ. Board action and Minority's Protest.

Wednesday, February 26 About as usual. I am doing less than usual on account of my health requiring abatement of effort.

Thursday, February 27–Saturday, March 1 At home. Engaged about as usual. Health improving.

Sunday, March 2 At Grace M.E. Church, I heard a very eloquent sermon by Rev. C.W. Gullette from 1 Tim. 4:16, "Take heed to thyself." Called at Lorin's in the afternoon.

Monday, March 3 I was at home all day except a call at the Post Office and at Lorin's. Carrie Kaler called & found Katharine gone to the Helen Hunt Club.

Tuesday, March 4 I was at home. About 11:30 had a telephone communication from W.H. Clay, Huntington, Ind. Getting ready to start to Huntington, Ind. Carrie Kaler called. Minnie Elsie Winchell m. Charles R. Heard to-day.

Wednesday, March 5 Leave home at 5:00 a.m. & go via Lima & Ohio City, arri. at Huntington at 12:00. Call at Publ. Estab. See Price & Rosebrough & Judge Watkins. Sup & lodge at Rev. H.C. Foote's.

Thursday, March 6 Board convened at 9:00. Our Demand was voted down. I dined a Lon. Bailey's. Session at 1:30, & at 7:30. Crazy majority. I sup at Foote's—lodge with Wood at W.H. Clay's.

Friday, March 7 Read copy of Crane's report by copy. I go on 10:19 tr. via Wabash to Fairmount. I call at Mrs. Bond's. Her strange talk. Dine Sup & lodge at Ellis Wright's in Fairmount.

Saturday, March 8 I go on 9:35 tr to Fowlerton. Dine at R.W. White's. Go at 4:00 to Ol. A. Glass's. They are at Matthews. Sup & lodge there. W.H.H. Reeder has removed to the Parks' place in Jefferson Township.

Sunday, March 9 I pr. at Hopewell at 10:30, John 4:34, "Worship in spirit." Dine with Rev. M.V. Bartlett & Bro. Nye at Oliver Buller's & I also sup & lodge there. Pr. at H. at 7:30, 1 Ki. 2:2, "Show thyself a man."

Monday, March 10 I go to White's & after early dinner to Fairmount. Called at Mrs. Bond's & Hollingsworth's. I supped & lodged at Ellis Wright's.

Tuesday, March 11 I go on 8:00 car to Gas City & thence to Dayton arri. at 4:00, hindered by a hot journal.

Thursday, March 13 Was at home. Called at Lorin's in the afternoon. Wrote the genealogies for J. Frank Heal, Sylvan, Wisconsin.

Friday, March 14 At home all day reading, writing & resting after those awful board meetings. Voted at the Republican primary. It inclines to rain.

Sunday, March 16 Heard M. Wilson at 1st Pres. Ch., John 14.22 at 11 o'clock. Called an hour at Lorin's. Heard Rev. John H. Thomas of Oxford, son of Prof. Thomas E. Thomas, at 1st Bapt. Ch., Gen. 45.7, on Providence.

Monday, March 17 Weather cold. At Home all day. Carrie Kaler came again to work for us, instead of Mrs. Jones. Wrote several letters. Wilbur concludes to go to Huntington, Ind., to-morrow.

Tuesday, March 18 Weather, cold. Wilbur left home at 5:00 A.M. for Huntington, Ind. to examine the Publishing House books and papers. Ivonette & Leontine are with us to-day & to-night.

Wednesday, March 19 Weather mild. Took a walk to town at noon. Lorin's took supper with us. Lorin's take supper with us. [Last sentence is crossed out of diary].

Thursday, March 20 Weather mild. At home all day. Lorin's moved to-day to their new house in *Riverdale.

Lottie Jones washed our bed clothes. *30 Plant St.

Friday, March 21 Weather mild. At home all day. Wilbur returned at 6:40 from Huntington. I spent the day largely in reading. Wilbur found Keiter's books and reports very crooked.

Sunday, March 23 At 10:30, hear Rev. W.P. Miller pr. at Park St. Pres. Ch. John 8:12, "I am the light of the world," etc. At home the rest of the day. Read much of II Chron & Jude.

Monday, March 24 Wilbur made out some statements of crookedness in Keiter's Books & reports which I forward a copy of to Rev. D.B. Sherk. Lorin sold his old property for $2675.00.

Tuesday, March 25 I was at home all day. Katharine visited Lorin's in the afternoon and evening. I wrote Bishop Barkley, giving him the time of the annual meeting of the Board of Bishops.

Wednesday, March 26 At home all day. I received a letter from W.H. Clay informing me that S.M. Sayler had made demand (for Clopper & others) the payment of the Bealor note.

Thursday, March 27 At home all day. I sent out to the trustees of Publ Estab. a plan to settle the present controversy. Looked over many old letters, destroying some.

Saturday, March 29 At home. Sent out copies to Kiracofe, Flickinger & Wood.

Sunday, March 30 Unpleasant on account of rain; so I remained at home, not caring to witness Easter display. Took Milton home in the evening to 30 Plant Street.

Monday, March 31 At home. Spent the day largely in reading the Bible & other books bearing on it. Got from Chi. Barnes Notes on Daniel. Answered Rev. Glegen Asbury Reeder, 373 Jennings Ave., Cleveland, Ohio.

Tuesday, April 1 At home mostly. I called at Wm. Weidner's in the afternoon. Lorin & Netta called in the evening. I had an influenza chill about 6:00 eve.

Wednesday, April 2 Was abed mostly. I took 16 grains of quinine and about five o'clock, piled on bed covers and took a sweat till 8:00. Mary (Osborn) Emmons called to see Katharine.

Friday, April 4 Seemed some better, only in the lower channels there seemed some difficulty. I tried Dr. Hall's treatment with more difficulty than usual.

Saturday, April 5 The difficulty mentioned above annoyed me & I applied hot irons with some alleviation. Got an answer from Bp. Floyd denying the issue of my propositions.

Sunday, April 6 My health did not admit of my going to Church, tho I am improving. Walked over a mile on our own pavement—over 1 1/7 m.—Milton came & staid two hours.

Monday, April 7 At home. I rec'd a letter from Tharp declining my proposition for referees in my circular letter to Publ. Board Trustees. I am better of my rectal difficulty. Spring Election.

Tuesday, April 8 Went to Kile's in the forenoon & bought 1 3/4 reams of commercial note paper. Wrote letters in the afternoon.

Wednesday, April 9 At home. The *Conservator* giving Becker's Article and Barnaby's characterization of some circular came in Afternoon. Read Apocryphal book Tobet, first time.

Thursday, April 10 Read book of Judith the first time. It is quite a Jewish fiction. We spent the day in preparing an expose of Keiter's defalcations. Lorin & wife called in the evening.

Friday, April 11 At home. Orville finished the typewriting of my proposed tract. Katharine brought over Lorin's little girls to lodge with us.

Saturday, April 12 At home. In the evening I took Lorin's girls home. D.K. Flickinger called in the afternoon. Dr. T.D. Wette Talmage died this evening.

Sunday, April 13 At home all the day. Carrie Kaler (our

domestic), was sick & Dr. L. Spitler came in forenoon. I slept considerable, and read considerably, all in commentaries etc. Walked 15 min. eve.

Monday, April 14 Engaged our tract printed. Wrote letters. Remained at home. Carrie was at work to day. Katharine was at the weekly meeting of the Helen Hunt Club.

Tuesday, April 15 I was at home all day, mostly reading, as I did not feel strong & energetic.

Wednesday, April 16 Felt better to-day. Read the proofs on my tract and prepared concluding copy. Miss Alice Hall and sister called in afternoon; also Chas. Parkhurst.

Saturday, April 19 Prepared envelopes for sending out tract, and mailed about 500 in the evening.

Sunday, April 20 I heard Rev. D. Frank Garland preach an able sermon at 10:30, First Lutheran Church, 1 Cor 4.7. At home the rest of the day.

Monday, April 21 Mailed some pamphlets. Gave out going to Grant Co. Ind. in the m.orning.

Tuesday, April 22 At home. Visited Lorin's after supper. Got approving letters on tract from Dillon & Clay.

Wednesday, April 23 At home. Got letters approving tract from Worman & from C.W. Blanchard of Elkhart & disapproving from Titus. Answered Titus letter.

Thursday, April 24 At home. I received letters from several approving my tract. Sent out a few more tracts. Read and wrote the rest of the day.

Friday, April 25 Got an advance page of *Conservator*, containing the four trustees' article, "Misrepresentations"—rightly named.

Saturday, April 26 Sent to Miller & Wood copies of our reply to "Misrepresentations." Lorin called in the evening to take Milton home.

Sunday, April 27 Called at Peter Loudings in the forenoon more than an hour. Lorin and his girls dined with us.

Monday, April 28 I go on 7:00 a.m. train to Gas City & on a belated interurban to Fairmount. Called at Mrs. Bond's. Dined & supped at Ellis Wright's & lodged there.

Tuesday, April 29 Went with Mrs. M A. Bond to Huntington, Ind. Dined & supped at Rev. H.C. Foote's. Met C.W. Watkins in the evening at his office. Lodged at Rev. W.H. Clay's.

Wednesday, April 30 The Keiter forgery trial began at 9:00. Examination of witnesses, all day. Dine at Restuurant. Supper at Foote's. Lodge at Clay's.

Thursday, May 1 Trial continued. Dined at Restaurant. The trial was on charge of the State that he had raised a bequest note of Mrs. M.A. Bond's from $1000 to $3000. The evidence largely was in letters he wrote to her.

Friday, May 2 Evidence continued in Keiter's case. Supper & lodging at Prof. H.T. Gragg's.

Saturday, May 3 Forgery case argued, C.W. Watkins makes a fine effort. Judge Branyan read a long charge to the jury. I went on 7 evening train to Lima. I dined at the restaurant.

Sunday, May 4 Reach home 4:55. Sleep a few hours. It is a warm day.

Monday, May 5 Slept two hours in afternoon. We prepared a tract for publication. I bought 200 envelopes to send out tract, and Katharine helped to address them in evening.

Tuesday, May 6 Got letter from Clay and pages of the *Conservator*. I mail pamphlet No. 2 in the evening. We finally sent out over 2000 copies of the tract.

Thursday May 8 I went on 11:15 tr. to Union City and North Grove. Sup and lodge at Daniel D. Weaver's just north of town. Their Children: Madge 16, Ray 14; Floyd 3 1/2. Rev. C. Bender pr. at 8:00.

Friday, May 9 Bishops' Board met at A.F. Rank's at 8:00, and all dine there. Missionary Board met at 2:00. Wolfard pr. at 8:00, the Annual sermon. I board at Weaver's.

Saturday, May 10 The Board meeting continued during the day. Rev. D.B. Sherk dined with me. C.B. Small on the way to the depot chode with me. D.B. Sherk is to pr. at 8:00. I go to Fairmount & stay at Ellis Wright's.

Sunday, May 11 Ellis with family takes me to Hopewell Church, in Leach. M.V. Bartlett pr. & I exhort. I dine at Oliver Glass's. I call at Oliver Buller's, sup at R.W. White's & return home with Ellis.

Monday, May 12 I called at Mrs. Bond's. I go on 8:58 tr. to Wabash & thence to Huntington, where I dine at Wabash Restaurant. Wilbur & I consult & prepare. I sup & lodge at Rev. H.C. Foote's.

Tuesday, May 13 I dine at Midway Restaurant. The Publ. Board met at 2:00. Agent's Report. I sup and lodge at Prof. H.T. Gragg's, in Stemen's Addition.

Wednesday, May 14 The Board continues and closes at at [repeated in text] 4:00. I got in peace proposition, which was voted down; also a resolution on right to be heard in *Conservator*. Dine at Midway. Sup & lodge at S.A. Stemen's.

Thursday, May 15 Wilbur had returned from Somers. We spend forenoon in Clay's office. Dine at Midway. We go on 12:45 tr. to Lima & thence to Dayton, arriving at 6:25.

Saturday, May 17 Took Lorin's children to the parade. There were nineteen elephants & eight camels. Milton came home with me to dinner. We walked. Heard Prof. G. Fred Wright on glaciers.

Sunday, May 18 Heard Rev. [blank] pr. at First Pres. Chu. Phil. 1:21, a good sermon. In Aft. 3:30, heard Prof. G.F. Wright lecture on Scenes in Asia. Lorin's Children (three) spent the day with us.

Monday, May 19 At home in forenoon. Katharine & I went on a drive in Afternoon to the Soldier's Home with Prof. G. Fred Wright. I heard him at 8:15 at Asso. Hall on Confirmation of Old Tes. History.

Tuesday, May 20 Met Fred H. Short & wife & Miss Donahue at 10:55 & spent till 12:00 with them. At home

the rest of the day.

Wednesday, May 21 At home. Wrote many letters, telling how leading men stand.

Friday, May 23 Wrote many letters, to find out where ministers & people stand on investigation of Keiter's books. After supper visited Lorin's, 30 Plant St.

Saturday, May 24 Went to town in forenoon, bought various articles. It rained in the afternoon.

Sunday, May 25 At Grace M.E. Church, heard Rev. H.C. Jennings, Publisher, Cin., on Prov. 29.18. He read the sermon. Milton visited us & staid till sunset. He is always a welcome guest to his uncles & aunt. He enjoyed the books & ice cream.

Tuesday, May 27 I went on the 11:15 tr. via Cin. & Greensburg to Rugby, Ind. arr. at 8:10. I heard Rev. A. Rust pr. at 8, John 14.13. I lodge at Mrs. [blank] Marlin's. Son's name is Lloyd. She was a Simmons. I call[e]d at John Braden's in Greensburg.

Wednesday, May 28 At 10:45, I taught a class in Theology at the Ministereal Institute. I dine at Wm. Galbreath's. His wife was a Smiley. I lectured at 4:45 on prayer. Sup at Marlin's. Go to Hartsville, to A.H.K. Bean's. Quite a cool night.

Thursday, May 29 Called at Mrs. Miller's, Tyner's, S. Rohrer's, Jno. Anderson's & J. Riley's. Returned on hack to Rugby. R.A. Morrison dined at Marlin's. Long talk with Morrison. Floyd pr. at 8, Heb. 12.1.

Friday, May 30 I start on 7:38 tr. for home. Reach home at 2:38. Feel loss of sleep and cares considerably. The Institute was turned into a Keiter Exhibit. I had some talk with Wolfard & Floyd at Rugby depot, on our controversy. (Slept seven hours.)

Saturday, May 31 Rainy this morning. I received and wrote many letters. Went to town and to Lorin's in the Afternoon.

Sunday, June 1 Lorin called in the forenoon. Milton with us in Afternoon. At 7:30, heard Maurice Wilson pr. on the "Recent General Assembly and the Revision of the Confession."

Monday, June 2 Wrote letters in the forenoon. Afternoon went to town & called at Sophia Simpson's a few minutes. Wrote letters in the evening.

Tuesday, June 3 At home. Wrote letters. Took a walk in the evening via Ross Wick's new Church and Germantown Street.

Wednesday, June 4 Began early but affected little to-day. Made some effort to shape a letter for somewhat general Circulation.

Thursday, June 5 At home, largely writing. I called in the afternoon to see "Aunt Mary" Englehart, who fell and hurt herself sometime ago, & since has had old rheumatism—80 years old.

Saturday, June 7 I went on 9:00 tr. to Richmond & dined at John G. Zeller's. Called to see Caroline Z. awhile. Went on to Ft. Wayne. Called at Geo. D. Crane's office, but he was out. Arrive at Huntington at 6:30. Lodge at Rev. H.C. Foote's.

Sunday, June 8 Rev. W.M. Clay came after me & I dine & sup with him. Lodge at S.A. Stemen's. Heard Pres. Kiracofe's baccalaureate at 10:30. I preached the annual sermon Heb. 6.1, "Let us go on to perfection," at 7:30.

Monday, June 9 I go down town & dine at Rev. Wm. Dillon's. Call at Publ. House & go with Clay for supper. Attend Glee Club Entertainment at Auditorium at 8:00. Lodge at S.A. Stemen's. His Mother, Mrs. Fogle is there.

Tuesday, June 10 I went down town. I dined at Fred A. Loew's. Attend Publ. Board meeting at Publ. House at 1:30. We authorized the purchase of a press. Sup at Dillon's. Attend the Inter-Society entertainment at 8:00. I lodge at Stemen's.

Wednesday, June 11 The Commencement Exercises at 10:00. Chas. E. Dubl, J. Henry Light, Fred E. Lowe, Jessie E. Geib, & Cora Tester graduated. Also Mrs. J.B. Metz in Music, & Miss Emma O. Warren in Elocution.

Dine at Hall. Sup at Morrison's. Board met. Lodge at W.H. Clay's. Slept 5 h.

Thursday, June 12 Board meeting at 8:00. Vote for President: J.H. McMurray 6; Kiracofe, 3; A.P. Barnaby l; Morrison l, blanks 2. Attack on Johnson aftn. Adjourn. I dine & sup at W.H. Clay's. I lodge at Rev. Wm. Dillon's. Slept 3 hours.

Friday, June 13 I go on 5:01 Wabash train, via Defiance & Deshler, home, arriving at Dayton at 8:00, a wreck at Kirkwood hindering an hour & thirty minutes. Slept 6 or 7 hrs. (We were not in the wreck.)

Saturday, June 14 At home all forenoon & till after supper. I called at Lorin's an hour after supper.

Sunday, June 15 I went on 8:00 traction to Germantown. I pr. at 10:30, Hebrews 6.1, "Let us go on to perfection." I dine at Lewis Wettz'. Sup at Chas. Coulthard's. Call at Long's. Lodge at J. Wesley Fouts.

Monday, June 16 I go home on the 5:45 car. Attend at 9:30 the funeral of Rev. C.W. Gullette, pastor of Grace M.E. Church.

Tuesday, June 17 Hear something of the Bealor note suit. At home all day.

Wednesday, June 18 At home. Wrote letters. Went to Brookville and Supped at Rev. A. Zehring's. Lizzie much Keiterized!

Thursday, June 19 To-day, Netta and the children, except Milton, spent with us; and Lorin was with us to supper also. The School Board increased Katharine's Salary to $100.00 a month.

Saturday, June 21 I went on 9:00 tr. via Richmond & Muncie to Fowlerton. Lunch on the cars. Look over my farm & sup at R.W. White's. Go via Jonesboro to Fairmount. Lodge at Ellis Wright's.

Sunday, June 22 I Go on Interurban car to Union Church. Pr. for Rev. Bartlett on baptism, Acts 2.88. I dine at Allen Underwood's with M.V. Bartlett's. Call at

R. Hasting's. I lead pr. Meeting at Fairmount. Lodge at Ellis Wright's.

Monday, June 23 I called at Mrs. Bond's. Her mother (Carter) there. Call at Mary. Hollingsworth's, dine at R. Hasting's, call at Lide Paine's. Went on 3:05 tr. to Fowlerton. Sup at R.W. White's. I lodge at Oliver Buller's.

Tuesday, June 24 I go on 7:19 tr. via Richmond home, arriving in Dayton 11:05 a.m. I saw Rev. Jas. Rector on the tr. between Benedum & Muncie & his sister Mrs. Johnson. News of postponement of King Edward's Coronation.

Wednesday, June 25 At home. Letter from C.W. Watkins informs me of Jas. M. Hatfield as attorney confessing judg[e]ment in the Bealor note suit.

Saturday, June 28 At home. I got a letter from Clay more fully explaining the action of the Prn. Com. on the Bealor note. Also a letter from Wood, I wrote to them. I called at Jacob Swank's. Swank's live with Minnie Seitters.

Sunday, June 29 At home resting. Lorin brought Ivonette. She behaves so nicely!

Monday, June 30 At home. Rev. Wm. Dillon called in the afternoon. Lorin and Netta called in the evening.

Tuesday, July 1 At home. I wrote some letters. Miss Wuichet called to see Katharine in the afternoon.

Thursday, July 3 At home. Received a letter from Wood & telegram from Clay. I answered both, by letters. Wilbur & I consulted Young in the evening, about Bealor note; to remedy confession of judg[e]ment

Friday, July 4 Start on 9:00 tr. to Fowlerton, via Richmond. Dine not. Supper at R.W. White's. Lodge at Oliver Buller's.

Saturday, July 5 Ther. 95 degrees. I go on early train to Fairmount. I dine at Mary Bond's. N.D. Wolfard arrests the passage of my character in Quar. Conf. on

Keiter's complaint. I sup at Hollingworth's. Lodge at Ellis Wright's.

Sunday, July 6 Ther. 95 degrees. Called at H.ollingworth's to talk to Bartlett & Kabrich. Ellis takes me to Oliver Glass's. Dine & sup there. I pr. at Hopewell at 8:00 Matt. 16.17. Lodge at O. Buller's.

Monday, July 7 Ther. 95 degrees. I went on 7:00 tr. to Richmond & Dayton, reaching home at 11:00. Called at Lorin's with Katharine in the evening.

Sunday, July 13 Heard Rev. Maurice Wilson preach, Matt. 16.13–28, a good sermon, at 10:30.

Monday, July 14 At home. I went to post office in the afternoon. Received a letter from Bartlett in answer to mine.

Tuesday, July 15 At home. I wrote to M.V. Bartlett in answer to his inviting me to write to him concerning Keiter's complaints. (This letter was written yesterday, not to-day.) This is for Monday.

Wednesday, July 16 At home. In the afternoon, I got a letter from N.D. Wolfard, notifying me that charges are brought against me and the time of trial at College Park is August 7th. This is for Tuesday.

Thursday, July 17 At home. Lorin called with Nettie in the evening.

Saturday, July 19 I to-day received the notice from N.D. Wolfard of time & place of trial. I wrote letters to Reuchlin, Huber, Lemasters, Ferguson, Wm. Miller, N. Alebaugh, Wm. Beers, A.L. Hope, A.W. Greslin, and D.B. Sherk.

Sunday, July 20 Remained at home. Lorin & his little girls called an hour in the forenoon. I studied afternoon and evening on Acts 3:21.

Monday, July 21 The boys resumed the preparation of my third pamphlet & completed it. I wrote to J.D. Snyder, R.V. Gilbert, S. Diller, & F.L. Haskins. We needed a little fire all day.

Tuesday, July 22 At home all day except a call at Lorin's in the evening. Wrote to S.A. Stemen and Louis R. Noble, of Mattoon, Ill. a descendant of Daniel Reeder, son of Joseph 3rd.

Wednesday, July 23 At home. Wrote some letters. Lorin called in the evening. Got the proofs on my third pamphlet—The Bealor Note Case.

Saturday, July 26 At home. We received in the afternoon part of the 2000 edition of my pamphlet, "The Bealor Note case," and mailed a few hundred of them. Lorin called in the evening.

Sunday, July 27 Katharine took care of Lorin's children, while he and Netta went to Franklin to the Chaut. Assembly. I went to bring her home in the evening.

Friday, August 1 I had a chill in the forenoon. Lorin and his little girls called about 8: 00 in the evening.

Saturday, August 2 (By mistake I turned two leaves.) I spent the day at home. I bought at Mose Cohen's a new suit of clothes & shoes at Haas ' for $12.40.

Sunday, August 3 At home. Lorin called in the afternoon.

Monday, August 4 I was at home. Lorin called in the evening. Wilbur is getting ready to go to Huntington, Ind.

Tuesday, August 5 At home. Write some letters. Wilbur started on 5:30 train to Huntington, Ind., to prepare evidence on my trial for the 7th. I get ready to go to-morrow.

Wednesday, August 6 Went to Huntington, Ind., on 5:40 morning train, via Lima. Supper & lodging at S.A. Stemen's. I had cholera—up often in the night.

Thursday, August 7 This day was set for my trial by Keiter, Barnaby presiding. After fruitless efforts to agree on the third committeeman, "the court" adjourned at 8:30, eve. I sup at Clay's. Lodge at S.A. Stemen's.

Friday, August 8 Came home. Sent out a few leters.

Rested mostly. My ailment continues.

Saturday, August 9 Wilbur came home at noon. At home all day. Dr. Jewett called in the afternoon and left me some medicine for my bowels, there being an epidemic of this.

Sunday, August 10 At home. Lorin and his little girls called in the afternoon. I am better in health to-day.

Monday, August 11 At home. My health is improving. The epidemic was very general and was called the cholera. It is said to have attacked about 2000 persons in the city.

Tuesday, August 12 I am making preparation to start to Indiana conference in the morning.

Wednesday, August 13 Left Dayton, on 6:30 a.m. train for Cincinnati, North Vernon, New Albany and Marengo. Wrote cards & letters. Spent three hours in the Park at New Albany. Find Home at Prof. J.M. Johnson's. J.C. Allen preached at 8:00.

Thursday, August 14 Conference opened at 9:00 at our church in Marengo. There were few present. J.C. Allen was elected secretary. J.T. Miller pr. at 8:00.

Friday, August 15 Conference continued. I dine at Abram Key's. Memorial service for A. Meyer & [blank] was held at 2:00. John Riley pr. at 8:00.

Saturday, August 16 Conference continued. J.W. Goldman was licensed to preach. B.F. Flenor pr. at 8:00. I got a letter from Katharine.

Sunday, August 17 I pr. at 10:30, Luke 1:32,33. I dined at Theophilus Key's. I supped at Johnson's. I pr. at 8:00, 2 Tim. 3:16. I lodged at Johnson's.

Monday, August 18 This was a very rainy day. I called at Abraham Key's. Rev. John Riley left in the afternoon for Milltown where his daughter Celia Gibbs lives. My health was quite feeble.

Tuesday, August 19 I called at Goldman's. I went on 11:35 tr. to Princeton and on 1:21 tr. to Terre Haute. I

Lorin Wright with his children: left to right, Milton, Leontine, Ivonette

put up at the "Northern" opposite to the Depot. I was quite weak, but rested well.

Wednesday, August 20 I went on the 9:45 tr. to Pana, Ill., and thence on 2:50 tr. to Mowequa. I called at D. Mull's. I went out to Obed with Bro. Klar. S.C. Allman pr. at 8:00. I board at O.E. Clapp's, in the Parsonage.

Thursday, August 21 East Illinois Conference opened at 9:00, and the session was pleasant. D. Fetters pr. at 8:00 and Mrs. G. Waters exhorted. Pres. J.H. McMurray came.

Friday, August 22 Conference progressed well. W.B. McMunn was elected pres. elder. The stationing Committee met at 5:00 at the Church. Mrs. G. Waters pr. at 8:00, but I did not attend.

Saturday, August 23 Conference progressed well, and closed before 4:00. Mrs. A.R. Kiracofe started home at 1:00. W.B. McMunn pr. at 8:00. I did not attend.

Sunday, August 24 I pr. at 11:00, Gen. 49:70. I dine at Bro. Weakley, 1 3/4 m. north. I pr. at 7:30, Eph. 2:4.

Monday, August 25 E.O. Clapp takes me to Mowegua, and I go to Elwin and lodge with Rev. W.W. Knipple. McMurray dined at Knipple's & went on to Mendota. (The boys [Wilbur and Orville] to-day started to N. Carolina.)

Tuesday, August 26 I go on 12:08 tr. to Forreston, and Samuel Breaw met me and took me to his house east of Adeline, where I lodged. His is a very pleasant family.

Wednesday, August 27 Bro. Breaw took me to Rev. Wm. Beers in Adeline. Bro. Beers read me his & Bp. Barnaby's correspondence. Go to Mt. Carroll. Sup at Bro. Christian's. C.Bender pr. at 8:00. I lodge at John Fulrath's.

Thursday, August 28 Rock River Conference opened at 9:00. Nice sessions. W. Dillon and Prof. McMurray came. J.L. Buckwalter pr. at 8:00, and a very precious testimony meeting followed.

Friday, August 29 Conference continued. Miss Grace Smith pr. at 8:00. I slept six hours, to-night. I board at John Fulrath's, an ex-member of the church, who is very kind to me.

Saturday, August 30 Conference continued & Closed at 4:20. Passed good resolutions on our church controversy. W. Dillon pr. at 8:00.

Sunday, August 31 I pr. at 10:30, 1 John 4:8. W. Dillon pr. at 7:30, "Grieve not the Holy Spirit," etc.

Monday, September 1 John Fulrath took me to Mt. Carroll to Rev. A.X. Harrison's. I wrote letters in the afternoon. Lodged at Harrison's.

Tuesday, September 2 I go on the 6:00 p.m. train to Cedar Rapids and staid at the hotel.

Wednesday, September 3 I went on to Hedrick and Fremont. Met A.D. Thomas and J.G. Garlock at Hedrick. Mrs. Yoeman & the son of [blank] took us out to Semus Yoeman's. L.H. Williams pr. at out Church, at 8:00.

Thursday, September 4 Arose at John D. Yeoman's. Conference opened at 9:00 at our church, 4 miles north of

Fremont. Rev. A.D. Thomas pr. at 8:00, a good sermon. I board at John D. Yeoman's.

Friday, September 5 Conference continued. It rained at night; so I did not preach.

Saturday, September 6 Conference closes at 4:00. A.D. Thomas pr. at 8:00. His sermons were very fine and produced a fine impression.

Sunday, September 7 I pr. at 11:00, and at 7:30.

Monday, September 8 John D. Yeoman takes me to 6:30 Central Illinois tr. at Fremont, and I go with Thomas and Garlock to Hedrick, & thence to Kansas City. Buy underclothing. Lodge there.

Tuesday, September 9 Go on 6:45 train to Tonganoxie & to Reuchlin Wright's. He is my son. I looked over his farm which is two miles east of Tonganoxie, Kan. We took a ride out north & west.

Wednesday, September 10 I went on the Missouri Pacific R'y to Clifton. Supper at Robert Burke's. Went out 8 miles north to Roscoe Church & found my home at the parsonage with Rev. John C. Hope's. No meeting at night.

Thursday, September 11 Kansas Conference opened at 9:00 & progressed well. A. Chrisian Endeavor meeting was held at 8:00 p.m.

Friday, September 12 Conference progressed well. Rev. A. Ritchie of Lecompton pr. at 2:00 and F.W. Bertschinger at at [repeated in text] 8:00. Got letters from Brantford. I dined at [rest is blank].

Saturday, September 13 Conference closed at 4:00. F.D. Heckard pr. at 2:00, and Mrs. Anna B. Reis at 8:00.

Sunday, September 14 I pr. at 11:00, 1 John 4:16, and at 7:30, 2 Tim 3:15.

Monday, September 15 Rev. J.C. Hope took me to Clifton, and I home at Robert Burk's. I wrote letters.

Tuesday, September 16 I remained at Burk's till evening train and went on Chi. R.I. & Pac. tr. to Smith Center.

John Truan, took me to the Bryan House and paid my bill. He is Bertschinger's fatherinlaw.

Wednesday, September 17 Rev. F.W. Bertschinger came and took me to his house a half mile north of Carvallis Church. Rev. Robt. Goldsworth pr. at 8:00.

Thursday, September 18 West Kansas Conference opened & progressed well. J.H. Spall pr. at 8:00. He did right well. He is perverse spirit and peculiar genius.

Friday, September 19 Conference continued. I supped at Bro. W.F. Hix's. J.D. Lamb pr. at 8:00. He is a nice young man, with a nice wife.

Saturday, September 20 Conference continued and closed at 4:00. W.L. Horton pr. at 2:00. Robt. Goldsworth pr. at 8:00. There was rain, so I did not attend.

Sunday, September 21 Some rain, but I pr. at 11:00, Ps. 92.8. The afternoon was very unfavorable. Very rainy afternoon and night. There was no evening meeting.

Monday, September 22 There were washouts on Rock Island Ry. I staid at Bertschinger's. Heavy rains at night. Creek very high, again.

Tuesday, September 23 Remained at Bertschinger's. Spall and Lamb came from Hix's. Lamb lodged with me.

Wednesday, September 24 We go to Smith Center & get the first through train to McFarland, and go thence to Hutchinson. Stay at Midland Hotel in Hutchinson.

Thursday, September 25 Go to Stafford and by livery to Zion Church. I dined at Central House. Conference in the afternoon. Home at A. McCune's. C.B. Sherk pr. at 8:00.

Friday, September 26 Ark Valley Conference Continued. Board at Bro. Abner McCune's a mile east of the church; Zion's Church is near Leesburg. Rev. H.D. Sill pr. at 8:00. I staid from church.

Saturday, September 27 Conference continued & closed early. Supper at Henry Garey's, McCune's fatherinlaw's. I dined at Thomas Deselm's. A.D. Thomas pr. ʒ 00. I did not attend.

Sunday, September 28 I pr. at Zion Church at 11:00, Rev. 21.7. I dine at G.F. Thomas's a half m. north of McCune's. D.H. Sill made the S.S. Anniversary address at 4:00. I pr. at 8:00, 1 John 3:2. I lodge at A. McCune's.

Monday, September 29 Staid till afternoon and went to Joseph Guire's and lodged. He lives 3 m. north west of the church. I named their oldest child Wilbur, when here nine years ago.

Tuesday, September 30 Missed the train twenty rods, and staid at the hotel in Stafford till evening train. Dr. Lorimer Ardery met me and took me to his house, 118 Ave. A. East. Mr. Charles Greenle and Faye came in the evening. He started to Washington City.

Wednesday, October 1 I went via Anthony to Cleo, Woods Co., Okla. J.E. Rector took me to New Home Sch. house. L.D. Thornburg pr. at 8:00. I home at Joseph Roberts 1 m. west.

Thursday, October 2 Conference opened at 9:00 & progressed well. There is drizzling rain. Rev. J.L. Ridgway pr. at 8:00. I did not attend.

Friday, October 3 Conference progressed well. Drizzling rain. J.H. McNew preached. Three were converted. I did not attend.

Saturday, October 4 I delivered an address to the ministers at 3:00. Conference closed at 4:00. The weather was more settled. The aftern. was clear.

Sunday, October 5 I pr. at 11:00, 1 Cor. 12.31. I dined at W.J. Nash's, 1 1/2 mile north-west. I pr. at 7:30, Isa. 55.1. Two joined church. I stay at Roberts'.

Monday, October 6 J.L. Ridgeway takes me to Ringwood & I go on to Enid & Wichita. I stay there with George W. Glenn's (my Cousin's). Children: Mabel, 16; Georgie, 14; Ruth, 5; Helen, 3.

Tuesday, October 7 I go on 3:00 aftern. train to Ft. Scott & stay at Lockwood Hotel.

Wednesday, October 8 I go on 7:00 tr. to Devon. I got many letters and wrote many cards in answer at the post office. Dine at boarding house. Went to J.F. Gearhart's saw Rev. J. Wilkison. Go on to Mrs. Eliz. Odell's. H.E. Smith pr.

Thursday, October 9 Conference began at 9:00. Rev. L.V. Harrell pr. at 8:00. I board at Mrs. Elizabeth Odell's.

Friday, October 10 Conf. Continued. Several went to see Rev. Jas. Wilkison in the afternoon. Rev. P.N. Lambert pr. at 8:00.

Saturday, October 11 Conference continued. H.E. Smith was elected pres. elder. Stu. Com. met at 6:00. S.B. McGrew pr. at 8:00. I received letters this evening from Katharine & from Wilbur.

Sunday, October 12 I addressed the M.E. Sunday School at 10:45. I pr. at 11:00 2 Cor. 5:11. I dined at Rev. John Clay's, 1 1/4 m. north of Berlin P.O. I preach at 7:00, Matt. 7:28. I lodge at Odell's. Her children Oscar, abt 25, Ozel, 21; Ethel, 19; Four joined ch.

Monday, October 13 I remained at Mrs. Elizabeth Odell's till 3:00 p.m. & go with Jas. Gearhart to Redfield and lodge at Eddy Stockmeyer's, a barber, soninlaw to Gearhart. They treated me nicely.

Tuesday, October 14 I went on 10:31 tr. to Ft. Scott. Mailed several letters & cards. Met S.B. McGrew on 2:35 tr. & go to Mansfield, Mo. Supped at Springfield. I put up at Ozark Hotel & slept.well. Fine weather.

Wednesday, October 15 Went on the hack to Ava. Dine & lodge at Harnden's, John's. They saw me at Fry Chapel, Iowa over twenty years ago. I pr. at M.E. Church at 7:30, Rom. 2:6,7. Harnden's a very nice family.

Thursday, October 16 I go thirteen miles to Star Schoolhouse by livery, and opened Conference at 10:00, read 1 Pet. 1.1-15. I dine at Geo. Siler's. I sup at D.B. Sager's one m. s.w. Home at Siler's. I saw Moon's eclipse.

Friday, October 17 Conference continued. Speaking meeting at 3:30. Sup & lodge at Siler's. Mrs. Eva G. Dane pr. at 7:00 on excuses of laborers. There were several seekers. A warm day.

Saturday, October 18 Conf. continued. I dined at Jerry Mendel's. I saw the "horny cow". Rev. S.B. McGrew pr. at 7:00 Eccl. 6.6. I got two letters. (The cow's hoofs were like horns, and the same way at several joints.)

Sunday, October 19 I pr at Star Schoolhouse at 11:00, Rom. 2.16, "My Gospel." I dine & sup at Jerry Mendel's. I pr. at 7:00, Ti. 2:14. There were six seekers & three bright conversions. I lodge at Siler's. Warm day.

Monday, October 20 Joseph Sager takes me to Ava. I dine at J.L.B. Harnden's. I go on the stage to Mansfield. Sup at Restaurant and go via Springfield to St. Louis. Slept 5 hours.

Tuesday, October 21 Arrive at St. Louis at 7:30. I lunch & go on 9:00 a.m. tr. to Wabash, Ind., arriving at 5:00 p.m. Sup & lodge at Rev. W.H. Clay's, in Huntington.

Wednesday, October 22 I attend College prayer services. Talk with Dillon at the College. Called at Morrison's and talked with him. Dined at Stemen's. Go with him to Publ. House. Talk with Flickinger on Mis. districts. Call at Dillon's. Lodge at Livingston's.

Thursday, October 23 Am pres. at Chapel Services by Morrison's. Call at J.C. Valentine's. Dine at Prof. T.H. Gragg's, & talk till 2:30. Went to Dillon's. Saw Spencer, and Watkins. Meeting at Dillon's. Sup & lodge there.

Friday, October 24 Went to Publ. House and on 10:19 tr. to Wabash & Fairmont & Fowlerton. Dine at Ellis Wright's & sup and lodge at R.W. White's.

Saturday, October 25 I walked to Oliver Glass's & dined. With family went to Robt. B. Reeder's & I remain till morning.

Sunday, October 26 Robt. Reeder takes me to Oliver Buller's and to Hopewell Church to S. School. I gave a Bible Reading at 10:30. I dine at Robert's & he takes me to Fairmount. Call at Mrs. Bond's, Atkinson's, & Hollingsworth's. Lodge at Ellis's.

Monday, October 27 I go home via Gas City & Union City. I arrive at 4:00 p.m. I am having a very bad cold. Katharine, Carrie Kaler & Harriet Silliman are are [re-peated in text] all at home. Lorin called, & Nelson Emmons.

Tuesday, October 28 Spent some time in recording in my diary. Rest some. Kath. and Hattie go to a sewing school in the evening, at the League.

Wednesday, October 29 At home all day and till 7:00 evening, when I went to Lorin's & spent an hour. Letter from Orville said they would not be home before to-morrow.

Thursday, October 30 I went and banked $300.85 in checks & currency; also to see the framework of the new Main Street Bridge. Telegram from Orville says (in French) they will not be home till Friday afternoon. Girls again go to writing school. Very slight spitting rain.

Friday, October 31 At home reading & writing. Met the boys at the train at 3:15 p.m. on their return from Kitty Hawk, N. Carolina.

Tuesday, November 4 At home. Voted a straight Republican ticket.

Wednesday, November 5 Letters of interest from McBride and Clay. Lorin came in the evening.

Thursday, November 6 Hariet Silliman went away this forenoon. Katharine started to Indianapolis at 6:00, eve., to Meeting of Central Ohio Teacher's Association.

Friday, November 7 Start at 9:50 for North Star, Michigan. Arrive at North Star at 8:19. Revs. C.L. Wood, E.D. Root and M.O. Root met me and took me to Wm. Fleckner's, my host of 11 years ago.

Saturday, November 8 I dined at E.D. Root's. Children: Floyd 6, Myrtle 3, & babe. Go with the Roots & Wood to East Washington Church, near Ashley. I sup & lodge with A.M. Mcdonald's, 3/4 m. west. C.L. Wood pr. at 7:30 Rom. 12.1. Children: Will, Maud 16, Ray 8.

Sunday, November 9 Love feast at 10:00. I pr. at 11:00, 1 Chron. 29:9,14 & raise $626.25, & dedicate the church. Dine at McDonald's with Wood, J.S. Beers, J.

Gnyn & others. I pr. at 7:00, Eph. 2.4, & lodge at McDonald's.

Monday, November 10 Rev. E.D. Root comes & takes Wood & me to the parsonage in North Star. Dine at Root's. Go to Alma & sup & lodge at C.L. Wood's. Children: Cora 20; Lester 17; Alyer 9. I pr. at U.B. Church at 7:30, Rom. 2.6. Audience abt. 35.

Tuesday, November 11 I go on 7:36 tr. to Toledo & Dayton. Ar[r]ive at 6:10. Slept some on the cars. A foggy day. Went the wrong end of St. Car line for Union Depot at Toledo.

Wednesday, November 12 At home all day. Receive copies of the call. Write some letters.

Thursday, November 13 Go to post office & get a supply of envelopes etc. Sent several letters; one to Noble, a descendant of the Reeders, of Daniel Reeder.

Friday, November 14 Friday I am at home. Write J.W. Chambers, C.L. Wood and S.A. Stemen, making suggestions to the latter on the programme for the convention.

Sunday, November 16 I remained at home all the day. Milton came in the afternoon.

Monday, November 17 This is my birth-day anniversary —the 74th. Letters came from Reuchlin & from his three children, referring to my birth day. The day was slightly rainy.

Tuesday, November 18 This is the 40th anniversary of my son Lorin's birth day. I was at home all the day. Lorin & Netta called in the evening.

Friday, November 21 I was at home all day. I sent on my Annual report of South West District for 1901, having been delayed by tardy statistics. Milton came at 4:00.

Saturday, November 22 At home except a call at the bank to deposit my gas check. Milton came in the afternoon & staid till after supper.

Sunday, November 23 I was at home all day. Miss

Wuichette, a high school teacher, called on Katharine. Milton came in the forenoon & staid till about 5:00. Lorin called at 4:00.

Monday, November 24 Started with Wilbur via Lima to Huntington, Ind. to a Convention. Start on 9:55 train. Saw Geo. D. Crane at Ft. Wayne. We lodge at S.A. Stemen's.

Tuesday, November 25 Rev. D.B. Sherk came & we talked till 10:00. Went to the publishing House. Dine at Wm. Dillon's. Convention opened in the afternoon. Sup at [blank] Evening session. Lodge at S.L. Livingston's.

Wednesday, November 26 Convention continued. Barnaby & Wright's discussion. R.A. Morrison remarks, & Wilbur's reply. Dine at Dillon's. Sup & lodge at A.J. Stemen's. Keiter sues nine of us for $11,000.00 damages.

Thursday, November 27 Go to Publ. H. & to Watkins office with others. Dine at Restaurant.. Go on Traction to Wabash. Go thence to Fairmount. Lodge at Ellis Wright's. Perhaps three inches of snow. Engaged Watkins to defend us.

Friday, November 28 Called at Mrs. Bond's. Went to Fowlerton. Saw Bartlett. Dine at R.W. White's. Went on 1:27 tr. to Richmond & home.

Sunday, November 30 At home all day. Milton came in the afternoon & Ewing Stokes. Rather a cloudy day. I called an hour at Lorin's. Saw Horace Stokes there.

Monday, December 1 At home all day. Wrote Clay and Watkins & Huber. Milton, and Ewing Stokes took supper with us.

Thursday, December 4 The weather is cool like, not very cold. I got coat & vest at DeWees's for $20.00. Wrote many letters. Milton supped with us.

Friday, December 5 I am at home all day. I receive and answer some letters. Reports of blizzard and storms in the eastern States. It is mild here to-day.

Saturday, December 6 At Home all day. Engaged as usual

in letter writing. Prof. G.F. Wright, Prof. H.A. Thompson, and Miss Steele of Oberlin, now Matron at Xenia Soldiers' Orphan's Home, called.

Sunday, December 7 Prof. G.F. Wright dined with us. I heard him at Association Hall at 2:00 address the boys, and at 3:30, the men, on the Uncertainties of Science & Certainties of Religion. A fine address.

Monday, December 8 Weather cold. I am at home all day. I am studying a parsonage dedication sermon John 21.29. I write many letters. Eleanor Wagoner called in the evening. Pressure of gas too low.

Tuesday, December 9 At home all day. I receive and answer letters. The pressure of natural gas was very low, hardly sufficient for our fires at all.

Thursday, December 11 I to-day wrote letters, and sent to C.L. Wood an Open Letter to sign. Is is addressed to the majority trustees, and is intended for publication in *Conservator*. Drizzling rain to-day.

Friday, December 12 I went on 5:40 morning train via Lima to Huntington. I was at Print. Estab. Office. I sup & lodge at S.A. Stemen's.

Saturday, December 13 I saw Watkins; also M.L. Spencer. I went on loco. car to Ft. Wayne & thence to Montgomery, Mich. I sup & lodge in the parsonage, O.G. Alwood, pastor. I pr. at 7:30, 1 Tim. 6:20, "Oppsi. of sei."

Sunday, December 14 I pr. at 11:00, John 19.27, "His own home." Raise $307.00 & dedicate the parsonage. Dine at Alwood's. Visit Rev. G.W. Hoag's. Pr. at 7:00, Eph. 3.19. "Love of Christ." Lodge at Rev. L.I.C. Young's.

Monday, December 15 I go on 9:+ [plus sign in text] tr. to Ft. Wayne & on trolley car to Huntington. I lodged at W.H. Clay's. Yesterday (day before yesterday) the British & German vessels fired on Puerto Cabello, and reduced it to ruins in 45 minutes.

Tuesday, December 16 I stay at the Office till 3:15. Go on trolley to Wabash & thence on Railway to Fairmount.

I staid at Ellis Wright's. Mrs. Catharine Northern was there.

Wednesday, December 17 I call[e]d at Mrs. Mary Bond's. I went on 9:01 tr. to Fowlerton. I was an hour at meeting at Hopewell Church. I dined at Oliver Buller's. Went on 6:10 tr. to Fairmount. Staid at Ellis Wright's.

Thursday, December 18 I went on 9:01 tr. to Wabash & thence to Huntington. Dine at Midway Restaurant. At the office. Lodge at S.A. Stemen's.

Friday, December 19 We began Keiter's Quiz at 9:00, and he had to give himself away. Adjourn at 4:00. Dine sup & lodge at Wm. Dillon's.

Saturday, December 20 M.F. Keiter's Quiz was resumed at 9:00, Yopst reporting. Badly worried. We dine at Restaurant. Come home on 2:35 Erie train arriving at 9:00.

Sunday, December 21 I heard Rev. H.C. Jameson pr. at 10:30, Isa. 9.6. I was at Home the rest of the day.

Monday, December 22 I sent application for Clergy Certificate on Central Pass. Association. I went on 9:00 tr. via Richmond & Anderson to Fairmount. Called at Mrs. M.A. Bond's & Mrs. Berg. Hollingsworth. Supper & lodge at Ellis W's.

Tuesday, December 23 Ex-judge Watkins came on 9:00 tr. After delay Lesh came & they took Mrs. M.A. Bond's deposition to Long's Office. I go at 2:00 to Gas City & thence to Piqua home, arr. at 9:20.

Wednesday, December 24 Patrick Alexander, a wealthy Englishman from Bath, near Easton, came to see Wilbur & Orville on Areonautics. I am busy mailing Pamphlets. Bought Christmas for grandchildren. Snow in eve. Lorin & Nettie called.

Thursday, December 25 I was at home all day. It is a quiet Christmas. Several visitors called in. Milton took supper with us. My presants were a diary from the children & a pocketbook from Lorin.

Friday, December 26 I went to Lorin's to take some presents from Reuchlin's to the children.

Saturday, December 27 At home all day except to go to the post-office, and call at Mrs. Bartel's in the evening, "Aunt" Mary Englehart having died there at 7:00 this morning.

Monday, December 29 In the afternoon, 2:00, I was at "Aunt" Mary Englehart's funeral at Mrs. Emma Bartle's. It was conducted by Prof. G.A. Funkhouser. J.P. Landis prayed. Mr and Mrs J. Gilbert sung.

Tuesday, December 30 I was at home writing letters. Wilbur went to Springfield, Ohio, and collected several notes for his Aunt Elmira Koerner.

[The following is at the end of the diary:]

Sarah (Wright) Harris's Children
1. Edward M. Harris
   Mary A. Heddrick
2. James F. Harris
   Zena Johnson
3. Laura Winchell
   Austin Winchell
4. Ella Rees
   Napoleon Bonaparte Rees
5. Charles W. Harris
6. Harvey B. Harris
   Hope E. Harsbarger
7. Orval Harris
   Emma
8. Estella Petree
   Frank Petree
9. Kate Van Fleet
   Marshal Van Fleet
10. Clara Gilbert

Conferences 1903
Indiana—Manfield S.H. & Leavenworth, Marengo. From Marengo 12 ms. Leavenworth a river station. East Illinois—Davis Chapel, Missal. Rock River & Eagan, Ill. Missouri—Gibbs, Mo. Kansas—Sabetha, Kan. West Kansas, Corvallis & Smith Center, Kan. Ark. Valley, Summer Ch & Mt. Hope, Kan. Oklahoma, Mt. Vernon Ch & West Point & Glencoe, Okla (Santa Fe) 9 m. Neosho—Otterbein Ch. & Parsons (F.D.R. 3) Dennis or Galesburg, Kan. 7 m. from Dennis, South Missouri— Lone Star Chap & Swan, & Chadwick, Mo. White River, & Messiok.

Salary Received—1902
Indiana 40.00, East Illinois 124.72, Rock River 207.45, Missouri 43.85, Kansas 94.00, West Kansas 42.20, Ark. Valley 43.08, Oklahoma 29.55, Neosho 33.71, White River 160.60. Total 819.16 South Misouri 28.00 total 847.16. *Traveling Expenses,* 1902 54.27

Bishop's Salary, 1902
Indiana 40.00, East Illinios 124.72, Rock River 207.45, Missouri 43.85, Kansas 94.00, Ark. Valley 43.08, West Kansas 42.20, Oklahoma 29.55, Neosho 33.71, South Missouri 28.00. Total 686.56. White River 160.60. Total 847.16. Traveling Expenses 54.27

Our contract with the C.I.&E. Railroad is said to be recorded in Book 63, in Marion, Ind. Price says: Keiter borrowed 1700.00 August 1898. Gave Sept 27, 1898 the first &700.00 note. Dec. 22, 1900, note received. See "Camisards" in "Universal Library," Am. Volumes, pp 403, Vol. II.

G.W. Barker, 155 Laselle St., Chi., Ill., second-hand Book-Store. J.F. Heal, Viola, Wis. Harvey Wright R.R. 3. O.A. Glass R.R. 2 Fairmount. D. Koerner R.R. 2. H.J. Barnaby R.R. 60, Ross. Prof. Z. Test, 209 14th St., Richmond, Ind.

Jacob Swank was 88 years old May 19, 1902. A.L. Hope 1115 N. Olive 15th St. Abilene, Kans. Wm. Miller Box 67, Uniopolis, S.J. Nicklas, 118 Pomfret St., Carlisle, Pa. S.A. Stemen Box 345 Huntington, Ind. H.E. Smith, Box 352, Fredonia, Kans. Bp. H.L. Barkley, 403 Prescott St., Portland, Oregon. Sina E. Ardery, 118 Ave A. East, Hutchinson, Kan. G.W. Barker, 155 Laselle St. Chi., Ill. Geo D. Crane, 24 E. W. St. Ft. Wayne, Otto B. Bowman, Dr. George Wright, 1077 W. McCarty St., Indianapolis, Lorin's Telephone Neighbor: Theo. Morris, Green 2481. Present at Fairmount Qr. Conf. July 5, 1902: M.F. Keiter, T.V. Rector, A. Rust, J.M. Kabrich, & O.M. Wilson. Leroy Sweedland's wife is the one M.F. Keiter is alleged to have flirted with across the street from his office, in 1901.

1903

Thursday, January 1 Another year comes in and finds us all in good health. Lorin, my son, and Netta, his wife, and their children: Milton, 10 years old, Ivonette, 6, Leontine, 4, and Horace, 18 months, dined with us. I write several letters. It was a pleasantly cool day.

Friday, January 2 This day has slight rain. I wrote many letters to-day, largely to ministers and people in White River Conference, to get up some communications with the layity there. My open letter came back; its publications refused by Kiracofe.

Saturday, January 3 Went at 10:00 on trolley to Germantown. I dined with Lewis Wetz. Rev. C.S. Johnson the Pres. Elder preached at 2:00. Quarterly Conference followed. I sup at Rev. W.H. Kindel's with Rev. D. Woggaman & wife. Bro. Johnson pr. again at 7:30. I lodge at J.W. Fout's. His sister and brotherinlaw, Peter Stout were there visiting.

Sunday, January 4 I called at Mother Long's and had considerable talk with her. She is quite an invalid from rheumatism. At the church, we had a good lovefeast meeting at 10:00. Rev. C.S. Johnson pr. on the seven sayings, on the cross, of Jesus. Communion; I officiated in. I dined at Lewis Wetz' with C.S. Johnson, Kiger & L. Long there. I pr. at 7 o'clock, Heb. 12.28-9. I lodge at J. Wesley Fout's with young Rev. Judy.

Monday, January 5 I return home on 7:00 car. Found I had exchanged overcoats on leaving Fout's. Spent the day mostly in writing. Several inches of snow fell. Lorin called an hour in the evening. The arbitration of the claims of Germany and England against Venezuela seems assured.

Tuesday, January 6 This is a pleasant, cold day. I spend the day in writing letters. I wrote to Revs. J.M. Johnson, D.O. Tussing & Wm. Stewart, and to Levi Meyer. Rev. L.A. Wickey, of Penn. died to-day. He was a man of great talent, but for some reason had fallen back into the quarterly conference relation only.

Wednesday, January 7 This is a cold day and somewhat snowy. I write some letters. Mr. Peter Staudt, of Union City, brings my overcoat, which I had exchanged at Germantown. To-day Keiter's quiz on oath was resumed and he refused to show his bankbooks, his check books, & certain notes, all of which he had promised, Dec. 20th.

Thursday, January 8 I was at home all day. I sent Netta, Lorin's wife, a wrist pocket book, and bought an analyne purple rib[b]on for my typewriter, I received word that Keiter is obstreporous about further "quizzing." In the afternoon his attorneys refused to appear further, or let him appear, saying that it was simply persecution.

Friday, January 9 I write several letters; and write out for Mrs. Nora Shirley the Van Cleve descendants to the same generation as my mother. Also the Covenhovens & the Schencks, beginning with Martin Schenck. Nora is a grand daughter of Jemima (Holt) White, and daughter of John White.

Saturday, January 10 I was at home all day, engaged as

usual. It was a tolerably cold day, but moderated toward evening, and there was considerable of snow in the night. I got a card from B.G. Huber saying that Rev. L.A. Wickey has died, that P.0. Wagnar has resigned his charge to go to M.E. Church, & that dear Rev. S.J. Nicklas is much afflicted.

Sunday, January 11 I was too unwell to attend church, and was at home all day. The trouble however was of the nature of disturbance of the bowels; not much unwell otherwise. Snowy in the morning, and several inches of snow on the ground. It thawed a little, but turned quite cold in the evening.

Monday, January 12 Arose early, as usual. Thermometer is below zero. Katharine dined at Hotel Atlas with Miss Wuichett. Wrote many letters. Sent J.F. Croddy five dollars. I had a long night's sleep. Sent J.F. Croddy the Record of Christian Work for 1903. Examined John 21, on the use of agapao and phileo in the dialogue of Jesus with Peter, for *love.*

Tuesday, January 13 The pressure of natural gas is lower than heretofore. I wrote letters, especially a long one to Bishop H.L. Barkley. The daily papers are full of news of distress over the scarcity and high price of coal. The treaty with Columbia for privileges and guarantys to U.S. in building the Panama Canal moves slowly.

Wednesday, January 14 I was at home. I wrote a few letters only. The day was warmer, and the gas pressure sufficient. I called at Lorin's an hour in the evening. I took Horace a bell wagon & horse. I got interesting letters from C.L. Wood and from J.A. Burkholder.

Thursday, January 15 The weather is warmer. I was at home all day. Was not in very good plight for work. To-day, the great Williams libel was argued by the prosecuting attorney and Col. Bob Evans, and by the Young's. Lorin called an hour in the evening.

Saturday, January 17 Weather thawing. L.M. Oler & wife, of Neosho County, Kansas, dined with us. He is a cousin of Wm. A. Oler's, is a son of James Oler. She was born in Dayton. Her people were by the name of Foland, and she is a neice of John Francisca's. I go to Germantown on the 2:30 traction. J. Slifer does not

meet me as promised. I call at Long's; Lodge at L. Wetz.

Sunday, January 18 Thermometer zero. Weather cold and very bright. I preached at 10:30, Ps. 25.14. I dined at Mother Long's, and lunched there in the evening. Bro. H. Long her son, was there. I preached in the evening at 7:00, Matt. 13.44, and had a speaking meeting following. I lodged at J. Wesley Fouts'. Ft. San Carlos was shelled to-day by the German Cruiser Panther. No notice and no provocation!

Monday, January 19 Weather fair and mild. I came to Dayton on the 7:00 car. I examined on a tax against the Germantown U.B. Church, on which it is advertised for sale tomorrow and wrote a card to Bro. Fouts, and later a letter. The Auditor promised not to put up the property for sale. I wrote many letters. I slept nearly eight hours.

Tuesday, January 20 I was at home all day. Nothing of much interest occurred. I got letters from Rev. J. Selig and Mrs. Alice H. Crull. I wrote cards to several. There was slight fall of soft snow in the evening.

Wednesday, January 21 Weather moderate. I was at home. Sent Mrs. M.A. Bond copies of the documents used in the forgery case. Wrote a reply to A.X. Harrison's letter, and a letter to Herbert. A little soft snow in the morning. To-day the bombardment of Ft. San Carlos was continued by the German Cruisers, Vinetta, Panther and Falke. Twelve Venezuelans killed, 15 badly wounded.

Thursday, January 22 Weather very fair. At home all day. I wrote a little. The weather was mild and very fair. News came of the continued shelling yesterday of Ft. San Carlos, at Lake Maricaibo, by German cruisers. It looks as if the German Emperor William wants to get into a great War. General Bello is the brave commander of the fort.

Friday, January 23 Weather is gloomy. I am at home all day. I spend most of the evening in revising sketches of sermons—some preached & some never preached. The weather is of quite a damp coldness in the evening. The Venezuelan trouble is gloomy.

Saturday, January 24 Weather snow, meduim. Snowing

this morning. Perhaps three inches of snow fell in the forenoon. I was at home. I slept considerably, having slept but five hours last night. The foreign situation does not improve, thought the British press seems to be antiGerman, and in the German Reichstag, Herr Bebel, criticises the Emperor's course.

Sunday, January 25 Weather moderate. On account of my cold I did not leave home to-day. I read some, but did little. Lorin and his little girls come in the afternoon and staid an hour. They were very nice. They wrote on my type-writer. Leontine was a can of good humor and Ivonette spent most of her time with me in her quiet way.

Monday, January 26 Weather Fair, mild. I am at home all day. I wrote a few letters. I am much better of my cold of a week past. Mrs. Mary Emmons called in the afternoon. The Venezuelan trouble is thought to be on the way to a peaceful solution. The English press largely condemns Germany's course at San Carlos.

Tuesday, January 27 Weather c[l]oudy but mild. At home. The day is very damp. I am confined to the house by the half rainy weather. I wrote several letters, D.P. Smith, Mrs. John Cranor, Wm. Heath, John Null, and Mrs. Chas. Hawley; friendly letters merely.

Wednesday, January 28 Weather Cloudy, damp. At home. I write Mrs. Mina Reeder of Burghill Ohio, and Rev. Glezen Asbury Reeder of Cleveland, on Reeder genealogy. I get little exercise on account of the damp weather.

Friday, Janaury 30 Weather Windy, but bright. I went to town, principally for a walk, but bought envelopes and a half dozen etcetaries. In the evening a [I] wrote out & mailed a circular letter to Barnaby, Floyd, Montgomery and Tharp on the settlement of our church controversy. Katharine went on the evening to the High School graduation exercises.

Saturday, January 31 I was at Home. I wrote several letters. I got a friendly one from Rev. G.W. Allman of Va. It seems as if nearly all sections of the Church are my confiding friends. More and more assurances come in every week.

Sunday, February 1 Almost raining. I heard, at Will-iams St. Baptist Church, Rev. Stevens talk and Rev. F. H. Croddy speak about 15 minutes from Matt. 16.17. Lorin called and left his little girls for dinner. They have a good day, staying till about four o'clock. A favorite exercise is writing on my type-writer, by them.

Monday, February 2 I was at home all day. I got many letters. I wrote several, besides letters soliciting funds for President Shuck's Monument. I answered Clay's peculiar letter.

Tuesday, February 3 Weather Rainy, warm. I was at home. Not a letter came to-day. Wrote a letter to Mrs. Lucretia P. Edwards, widow of Bishop D. Edwards. She now lives with her daughter Mary Flesher in Englewood, and it is a suburb of Chicago. I wrote few letters and read some.

Wednesday, February 4 Weather Windy, and cold. At home. Rev. Wm. Dillon visited us and dined with us. He had been at his daughter Minnie Fagan's, in Springfield. She has been very sick.

Thursday, February 5 Weather Fair & moderate. At home reading and writing. In the afternoon, I visited Father Jacob Swank on Western Ave., whom I found very low with old age, and who may die soon.

Friday, February 6 Weather Fair & moderate. In the forenoon called at Swank's again, and, in Afternoon at 5:00, telephoned them and found him each time as yesterday, very low.

Saturday, February 7 I went to Seitters in the forenoon to see Father Swank. About 1:00 we were telephoned that he died—died at 12:00. I went up in the afternoon, to Seiters again.

Sunday, February 8 Weather Half-way rainy. I feel very languid to-day and remain at home all day. It is a damp day. I read considerable. Miss Wuichet called in the afternoon.

Monday, February 9 Weather Pleasant. I was at home in the forenoon. Attended Jacob Swank's funeral at 1:00—text Ps. 112.6—burial in Woodland Cemetery. Five of his children were present, and six of his grandsons were the pallbearers. His age was 88 years, 8 months and 18 days.

Tuesday, February 10 I went in the forenoon to John J. Reeder's, 415 Haynes St. He has been sick 15 months. He is a grandson of Daniel Reeder whose graveyard is 1 1/2 miles east of Centerville, Ohio. It is thought that the above Daniel was a son of William Reeder, the half brother of my great grandfather Joseph Reeder. Not certain.

Friday, February 13 Weather mild. Wrote letters. Called at Seitters' to see Mrs. Agnes Swank in the forenoon. Mr. Larue died suddenly, this morning. I called there a few minutes. The boys broke their little gas motor in the afternoon. Mr. Geo. L. Larue was once Auditor of Hamilton Co. Ohio. Lived on Hawthorne St. Protocols between Venezuela and the allies were signed.

Saturday, February 14 The dispatches say, that last night, Minister Herbert W. Bowen and the representatives of the Allies (England, Germany, and Italy) signed the protocols concerning the Venezuelan blockade.

Sunday, February 15 Slight rain, sleet, & snow in evening. I spent the day in reading, mostly, much in my Greek English New Testament. I compared the relations of the Father and Son as set forth in the Scriptures, collecting the passages expressing the dependence of the Son before & after his habiliment in flesh, and also attribution of Divinity.

Monday, February 16 It is a snowy day, and grows colder. I spend the day mostly in writing letters. The Venezuelan blockade was raised to-day, which caused great rejoicing there and at Buracoa. Reports of extreme cold weather come in the day's dispatches.

Tuesday, February 17 Weather Cold. Snow on the ground, 8 or 10 in. The gas pressure was too low in the afternoon. I did not do much but read. Nothing of importance to record.

Wednesday, February 18 Weather Cold & fair. I read and wrote. Nothing very unusual occurred. I am in rather more vigorous health than usual. The boys increased the flow of gas by putting "a snorter" in the radiator in my room. Our gas radiators are of their invention and their making.

Thursday, February 19 Very cold morning, but moderated toward evening. I wrote a letter to G.W. Allman and to J.A. Burkholder & L.S. Coulson & to Clay and to Stemen. The gas pressure was very low but I kept comfortable. I read in Josephus considerably his imitation of Sallust in putting speeches in the mouths of Eliazur, Jacob, Laban etc.

Friday, February 20 Weather fair & moderate. I was at home all day. I wrote letters to Pa. & Va. and a long one to S.B. McGrew, he having enclosed one from Rev. W.H. Clay asking him to urge me to enter a lawsuit to have the judgement in the Bealor note set aside.

Saturday, February 21 Weather Fair & moderate. I received a letter from Wm. Morrow of Mercer, Ohio, telling of where Rev. C.S. Johnson & Rev. W.E. Strete stand and what they are doing. I write several letters. I call at Lorin's an hour in the evening. Lorin and Nettie each have the grip, but are not bedfast. Revs. Strete and Johnson are working for Keiter's cause.

Sunday, February 22 Weather fair & moderate. I spent the day mostly in reading on scriptural subjects treated in the Cyclopedias: as the Bible, the Pentateuch etc. In the Evening, I also read ten Psalms and compared the versions of them in the English revised and the American revised. Orville and Katharine visited Lorin in the eve.

Monday, February 23 Thermometer 24 degrees. Weather fair, but misty toward evening. I wrote a few Letters. Called at Mr. Gustin's, and went to Post-office & bank, but both were closed because yesterday was Washington's birth day. I received a card urging me to come to Huntington, to enter suit against the judgment on the Bealor note.

Tuesday, February 24 At home. Wrote Letters. Saw Mr. Geo. Young about 30 minutes at noon, on Bealor Note matter.

Wednesday, February 25 Weather moderate. I went on 9:45 tr to Lima, and on a 1:45 extra to Huntington. I called at C.W. Watkins' office, and found C.L. Wood there. We go to W.H. Clay's to supper. We met the attorneys at Watkins' office at 7:00. We lodge at Clay's.

Thursday, February 26 Weather Thawing. I called at Wilburforce's, Prof. T.H. Gragg's and at Rev. S.L. Livingston's & went with Wood to Watkins' Office and to the publ. office. We dine at the restuarant. We meet the attorneys at 2:00. I go on 3:29 electr. car to Wabash & thence to Fairmount. I sup & lodge at Ellis Wright's.

Friday, February 27 Very muddy and some rain. I called at Mrs. Bond's, and went on 9:35 train to Fowlerton. Dine at R.W. White's. I went on 1:15 tr. to Richmond, and thence to Dayton. The afternoon was somewhat rainy.

Saturday, February 28 The morning is gently rainy. I spent the day mostly in reading, but wrote a few letters. The rivers here are quite high. I read the argument of Alfred Russel Wallace, maintaining that the sun is the Center of the universe, and our planet the only habitable one. It is in the *Independent.* Both his propositions doubtful.

Sunday, March 1 Cool, but moderate. I remain at home. Lorin called in the forenoon. They have pretty well got over the grip.

Monday, March 2 I am at home. I got a letter from Hon. Frank Reeder, of Easton, Pa., giving important items concerning the Reeder family. Also a letter from W.H. Clay. I wrote a few letters.

Tuesday, March 3 Weather slightly rainy. I wrote several letters. I went to Public Library at 5:00 af'n., and copied the John Reader and Henry Feake genealogical items.

Wednesday, March 4 Cloudy & warm. I wrote several letters and read some. I got news that the Keiter faction dominated over the majority in Penn. session of Conference. G.S. Seiple was its leader.

Thursday, March 5 Weather Warm, cloudy, almost rain in the evening. I did not do much, being somewhat dull. Received a Letter from Penn. telling of the Conference. I read much in the Supplement to Encyclopedia Brittanica, on the Gospels, Judges, etc. Dr. Willis J. Beecher shows much ability in those articles. Josiah Muir,

of Morristown, N.J. inventor of paper car wheels d. today.

Friday, March 6 Weather Warm. I went to Post office & Library in the forenoon. I found "American Ancestors" in the library, and spent an hour in looking over its many volumes

Saturday, March 7 Early this morning, we had lightning and thunder, and a little rain. I wrote some letters. Lorin called in the evening. I was at home all day.

Sunday, March 8 Weather Damp and warm. I attended the Third Street Presbyterian Church at 10:30. It was communion occasion. President W.O. Thompson of the Ohio State University officiated. The order was: 1. The Reading of 1 Cor. 11:23 30. 2. Congregation read the "Apostles' Creed." 3. Sung a hymn. 4. Communion Prayer. 5. Deacons receive & distribute the elements. 6. Closing remarks. 7. Return thanks. 8. Sang, "Blessed be the tie." (used separate glasses)

Monday, March 9 Cloudy but a little cooler. Cloudy all day. I am at home all day. I spent the forenoon mostly in arranging letters from relatives, in families and according to date. I wrote several letters in the afternoon and evening. The news is that the rivers Ohio, Mississippi and Missouri, north and South are very high.

Tuesday, March 10 The rain falls hard at intervals, this morning, and it proves a rainy day. I wrote several letters. Lorin called in the evening. Bertha Croddy was married, at 7:00 this evening at John Mitchel's, in Pontiac, Ill. to Edward Glaze.

Wednesday, March 11 Weather is cloudy, but not rainy and is warm. The sun shone part of the afternoon. I called at Mrs. Bartles and at John H. Chapman's 921 N. Broadway. I did not do much work this afternoon.

Thursday, March 12 Cloudy, no rain. I wrote long letters to Revs. J.C. Hope and C.R. Paddack, whose letters came to-day. In the evening, I mailed copies of old carbon copies of letters to R.H. Clopper, to C.W. Watkins, Esq. Read the noble decree of the Czar of Russia giving religious freedom to his subjects, and instituting other reforms.

Friday, March 13 Weather mostly cloudy. At home. Read some. Went to the public Library in the afternoon.

Saturday, March 14 Weather, cloudy & warm. The grass is green and buds are springing. I was at home all day. Nothing of note occurred. Ida Graybeil called in the evening. Allen J. Kuhns called in the afternoon.

Sunday, March 15 Weather, Cloudy & mild. I hear Rev. Maurice Wilson pr. Zech. 4.1 6, a good sermon. His sermons seem to have behind them a desire to make his congregation better. His sermons are finely composed, but for oral delivery and he reads with power.

Monday, March 16 A rainy day. I was at home all day. Bishop H.L. Barkley came in the afternoon and remained till 11 o'clock at night.

Tuesday, March 17 Weather warm. I was at home all day. Slept some. Did not do much. To-day the treaty with Colombia for the Panama Canal Route was ratified by the Senate, there being but five votes in the negative; Morgan & Pettes, Teller, Martin & Daniel.

Wednesday , March 18 Weather, fair & warm. The grass is as green as May. I am at home all day. I wrote a letter to Hon. Frank Reeder, of Easton, Pa., in reply to one from him on the Reeder ancestors.

Thursday, March 19 The day is warm and the sky hazy, sunshine *part* of the time. It was quite warm to-day without fire. I did but little to-day. I called at Lorin's in the evening. The Cuban Reciprocity treaty was ratified by a vote of 44 to 22, to-day. Later: the vote seems to have been 50 to 16.

Friday, March 20 Weather warm. I failed to reach the depot in time to go to Liberty, Ind. John J. Reeder's son called and said his father wished to see me before removing to Ohmer Park, and I went to see him.

Saturday, March 21 Weather, Warm, fair. I went on 8:00 train via Hamilton to Liberty. Saw Rev. S.T. Mahan at Liberty. I Walked to Daniel Koerner's, except one mile I rode with Mr. Quick. Daniel is my deceased wife's brother—has been blind about a year. He is quite old.

Sunday, March 22 Weather, warm & fair. I walked to Bath Church, 2 ms S.West & preached for Rev. John Selig, who dined with me at Koerner's. Samuel and Daniel Harbine were very cordial with me. I pr. from Heb. 12:28. In the evening, I called at Fred. Brookbanks', who lives close by in Father Koerner's old house. He married Orpha Booth, a teacher in Dunlapsville, in October.

Monday, March 23 Pleasant in the morning, blustery in the afternoon & evening. Fred takes me to Liberty & I go on 9:00 tr. to Glenwood. Ralph Bowen met me and took me to N.F. Bowen's, where I dine & remain till morning. Mr. Bowen's wife, Sarah Catharine, is my deceased Brother William's daughter. Ralph, now 18, is their only son.

Tuesday, March 24 Weather, Damp & cold. Sarah Catharine took me to Mrs. Lucinda Moore's. Mrs. Moore was William's wife, whose second husband was Anson Moor. Her Soninlaw Clifford Long and her youngest daughter Bertha (Moor) live with her. Clifford is much afflicted with epilepsy. Catharine takes me in the afternoon to Charles Stevens', his wife Flora being my bro. William's daughter.

Wednesday, March 25 Cool but moderating. Stevens' only son is Ray, eight year's old. Charles takes me to Glenwood, and I go on 10:35 tr. to Rushville. There, at the depot, I saw William and Milton Churchell. My brother Harvey took me out to his house, 8 miles north, on Little Blue River. Drusilla McKee, his oldest daughter, called in the afternoon. I remained there. Milton Churchill is quite wealthy.

Thursday, March 26 Harvey & his wife Delila took me to John McKee's, but finding no one at home, they took me to his son Thomas's where we dined and called at Ed. Frazier's, three miles north, whose wife is Harvey's daughter, Emma. We returned to Harvey's. Charley Gray & Eva (Harvey's daughter) live with Harvey & Delila.

Friday, March 27 Weather, Pleasant. Harvey took me to Jabez Rhodes' where I dine, and go to Knightstown and take the 11:36 tr. to Fairmount. I call at Ellis Wright's, and at his Hardware store, at Haisley's office, at Mrs. Atkinson's and at Mrs. Bond's. I go on 6:11 tr.

to Fowlerton & stay at R.W. White's on my farm.

Saturday, March 28 Weather, Cloudy & mild. I go on 6:53 tr. to Richmond and thence home, arriving at 11:30. Milton & Ivonette had just come to make a visit for the rest of the day.

Sunday, March 29 Weather, Bright & mild. I missed the electric car and so gave out going to Olivet Qr. Meeting. I remained at home during the day. I read considerably.

Wednesday, April 1 Weather, Fair & mild. Spent the day in writing on the typewriter for D.B. Sherk. Quoted largely from Keiter's examination of Dec. 20, 1902. Katharine went to Dr. Quinsaulus's lecture at the High School building in the evening.

Thursday, April 2 Weather, Fair & no fire. I was at home very busy writing all day on my type-writer, mostly to Rev. D.B. Sherk. I called a half hour at Lorin's in the evening.

Friday, April 3 Weather, Rainy & warm. Finished up writing to D.B. Sherk, of Berlin, Ont. Word came of the death of James S. Corbett, step father of Ivonette, Lorin's wife. He died last night at Santa Barbary, California. He was in his 62nd year.

Saturday, April 4 Weather, Bright but cool. I was at home writing. Katharine went & brought the little girls (Lorin's) over to stay till tomorrow.

Sunday, April 5 Weather, Fair, comfortable. I heard Pres. W.O. Thompson pr. at Third St. Presby. Church, Phil. 2.6. The congregation was large. In the afternoon, I heard Rev. H.C. Jameson, of Grace M.E. Church, speak at Association Hall, at 3:30 on Thoughts & Character.

Monday, April 6 Weather, mild & bright. It clouded up toward evening. Lorin's little girls are still with us. To-day is the spring election. I voted the Republican ticket, except for councilman at large and constable. I have not done much to day.

Tuesday, April 7 Weather, some rain in the morning. The weather became clear before noon. It is warm enough without fire. In the afternoon, I went on Spring

Valley traction to White's Crossing & to Walter Weller's to Daniel H. Reeder's graveyard. His tombstone says: "Daniel H. Reeder died July 29, 1828, aged 60 years, 8 months & 17 days." Mrs. Sarah (McLain) Swanie died this morn at 5:30, aged 86 years, 4 months, 2 days.

Wednesday, April 8 I was at home all day. I did but little. This was little Ivonette's birth day and she enjoyed her presents, a new dress, silver thimble, finger ring & pocket book. Netta came in the evening and took the little girls home.

Thursday, April 9 At home in the forenoon. At Mrs. Sarah Jane Swaynie's funeral at 2:00. Called at Seitter's at 4:00 to see Mother Swank. Got my watch back from repairs, $1.00 cost.

Friday, April 10 Weather, mild & fair. Ontario Conference in Session. Mr. James Stewart Corbett's funeral occurred to-day. Services at the M.E. Broadway Church at 9:30. Revs. Haynes and Wones spoke well. I went with Lorin's to the burial at West Carrollton. Reached home at 1:30 Aft. Katharine started to Chicago.

Sunday, April 12 Weather, mild. I did not care to witness the Easter displays, so I staid at home. The spectacular taste seems to be growing on the Protestant churches.

Tuesday, April 14 Weather, Mild. I was at home. I got a letter from J. Howe, giving me copies of resolutions adopted by the conference. Ontario spoke out quite decidedly as to our controversy.

Wednesday, April 15 I was at home. I called at Public Library in the afternoon.

Thursday, April 16 Weather mild. I was at home. Wrote several letters. Nothing unusual occurred to-day. It was the thirty sixth anniversary of Wilbur's birth day. He has been a strong stay to me.

Saturday, April 18 Weather, sunshiney & mild. I went to the Public Library in the forenoon. I put a new ribbon on my typewriter in the afternoon. Wrote some letters. The maple trees are leafing out. The grass is high & green.

Sunday, April 19 Weather Ware & a ittle rain. At 10:30, I heard Pres. W.O. Thompson preach from Job. 1:9 11, "Doth Job fear God for nought," etc., a good sermon. He is a fluent (even rapid) speaker, has a solid mind, a very fine judgment. His manner is earnest, his tone rather monotonous, his voice rather flat. Evidently his aim is to elevate his congregation and do them good.

Monday, April 20 Weather, mild—hazy, with sunshine. Catharine arrived at home from Chicago about 7:00, a.m. Slightly hazy but sunshiny. The boys received their illuminum casting for their light weight engine, to-day.

Tuesday, April 21 Weather, Some sunshine with haze. Went over to town before noon, at home the rest of the day.

Wednesday, April 22 Weather, Moderately fair. I wrote many letters. I was at home all day. Lorin called in the evening.

Thursday, April 23 Weather, hazy sunshine. Wrote several letters in the early morning. Spent two hours of the forenoon in the Public Library. In the afternoon began the annual report of South West District. Spent the evening in sketching in Jas. Russel Lowell's Biography.

Friday, April 24 Weather, Cloudy & warm. Worked on the report of my District. Read in the evening from Prescott's Congress of Peru. Lorin called in the evening.

Monday, April 27 At home. Worked assiduously in arranging the facts evinced by the records, as to the Benham ancestry. Called at Lorin's in the evening.

Tuesday, April 28 At home. Writing and reading. Took a walk in the afternoon and looked at the new cement bridge on Main Street, on which they are now laying the tracks for the electric cars. I also looked at Van Cleve Park.

Wednesday, April 29 At home. In the afternoon, I sent a Check for seventy five dollars to Marion to pay my tax, and a dollar bill to Huntington to pay taxes there. Wrote letters to Alwood and to R.W. White.

Thursday, April 30 Nice day. At home mainly engaged in writing. Lorin dined with us.

Friday, May 1 Weather, rained some. At home. Lorin dined with us. The anticipatory opening of the Louisiana Purchase Exposition took place to-day. President Ro[o]sevelt and ex President Cleveland made great speeches on the occasion.

Saturday, May 2 At home. Beacham's finished painting the house. In aftn. I hear Rev. J. Campbell Morgan at Third Street Lutheran Church on The Religious Outlook. He is a pretty good orator, though not a graceful speaker. John Dodds, died this morning. Orville's eye is sore from a piece of emory that flew into it.

Sunday, May 3 I to-day read and studied the Song of Solomon. I am inclined to adopt Dr. Mason Good's Divisions of the Song as published in Adam Clarke's Commentary. Whether it was a spiritual type of Christ and the church seems to me very doubtful, it is a pure love song.

Monday, May 4 Orville discovers that his sore eye is caused by a piece of emery or something being imbedded in his eye just over the pupil. Charles Taylor takes it out; and later the doctor removes further fragments. John Dodd's funeral occured this afternoon at Oak Street U.B. Church conducted by Revs. Huber & McKee. I was not present.

Tuesday, May 5 I spent the day at home. Wrote some letters. Lorin dined with us. Orville's eye is much better.

Thursday, May 7 I read some and write letters. I bought a monoglass.

Friday, May 8 In the afternoon, Katharine went with me in a walk on Wolf Creek levy, where we saw various kinds of birds: Lapwing, jackdaw, etc.

Saturday, May 9 The girls (Katharine and Carrie) cleaned up my room to-day. I walked up to Mr. Seitters', but did not find the folks at home.

Sunday, May 10 Went on 8:00 tr. to Olivet. Rev. W.H. Kindel pr. at 10:00 Acts 16.25. Dine at Geo. Warvel's. Kindel & wife & Eubanks & wife werethere. At eve.

meeting, I pr. on 1 Pet. 1.1 4. I went home on 10:00 traction.

Tuesday, May 12 At home all day. Wrote a few letters. Preparation is being made to repaper the Dining Room.

Wednesday, May 13 At home. Received letters from Clay giving account of Quarterly Conference transactions at College Park and Etna,Ave. They were most illegal.

Sunday, May 17 At 10:30, I heard Rev. A.B. Leonard of New York City pr. Isa. 40:4,5, on the Progress of the 19th Century. 1. In exploration, 2. In travel, 3. In publication, 4. Christian cooperation, 5. Open door, 6. In evangelization. Very warm day.

Monday, May 18 At home all forenoon writing. Went out to John J. Reeder's in the afternoon, who lives on Creighton Ave., in Ohmer Park. I went on Spring Valley traction line.

Tuesday, May 19 Mr and Mrs F.H. Short came to Union Depot to the annual election of officers of the Cin. H. & D. R'y, and I met them there. Miss Carrie Donahue was with them. Katharine met them a few minutes. Miss Donahue is a daughter of Caroline Donahue, and granddaughter of Eden Boroughts Reeder. He was a descendant of Stephen Reeder.

Wednesday, May 20 At home. The house was all torn up & house cleaning going on.

Thursday, May 21 Rev. W.H. Kindel came and spent the forenoon and till 2 o'clock. Lorin moved to-day, to 1243 W. 2nd St.

Friday, May 22 Lorin's family breakfasted with us. Wrote some letters.

Saturday, May 23 At home. I called at Bedell's in the afternoon to see Mrs. A.L. Billheimer.

Sunday, May 24 Weather, Hot. morning—hot day. Heard Rev. Maurice Wilson pr. at 10:30, Luke 1.4, on "Some Certain Things." Looked up afternoon The testimony of the new Testament as to the Old Testament.

Called at Lorin's. Lorin's children came and remained to lunch.

Monday, May 25 Hot morning hot day. Nothing unusual.

Tuesday, May 26 Cooler in Morning. Hot evening and night. I voted at the Republican primaries in the evening.

Friday, May 29 Start on 9:00 tr. to Fowlerton, via Richmond, and Anderson to Fairmount, Ind. Arri. at 3:00. Called at Ellis' store and house. Went on 6:11 tr. to Fowlerton. I lodged at R.W. White's on the farm.

Saturday, May 30 Had a settlement of accounts with White. Went to Wm. Reeder's & dined. Sup at Robert Reeder's. I lodged at Oliver A. Glass's.

Sunday, May 31 We went to Joseph Broyles' and I remain till 4:00, when their son Charles took me to Summitville, and I went to Fairmount on the interurban car. I attended the Quaker Church and heard the Pastor Harvey preach.

Monday, June 1 I went on 9:01 train to Wabash & thence to Huntington. I dined at a restaurant and went to the Conservator Office. Went on 3:30 car to Ft. Wayne, and thence north on 5:00 train to Academy intending to stop at Carroll's Crossing. Walked three miles to Theodore Bowser's & lodge.

Tuesday, June 2 I staid at Bowser's till after dinner, and he took me to George Gloyd's, where Bishops Board met. Barnaby & Floyd wished to exclude me, but Barkley refused. Spent the afternoon talking over our differences. Bishop Barkley pr. at 8:00. I lodged at Bowser's.

Wednesday, June 3 The bishops met at George Gloyd's, 8:30 morning. Barbaby & Floyd protested in writing against my presiding & pocketed their dignity. We then had an harmonious session. I dine & sup at Gloyd's. I pr. at Union Chapel at 8:00. I lodge at Bowser's.

Thursday, June 4 I go to G. Gloyd's. The bishops talked but did no further business. Barkley and I filed a written reply to the other bishops protest. We dine at Gloyd's. I preside at Mission Board at 2:00. I sup at Bowser's.

Bishop Barnaby pr. Annual Sermon at 8:00. I lodge at Bowser's.

Friday, June 5 The Mission Board session continued. Committees met at 7:30. Reports on Finance, Home Missions, Foreign missions, and frontier missions, and completed business nearly. I dine sup & lodge at T. Bowser's. Wm. Dillon pr. at 8:00. Rev. D.B. Sherk lodged with me.

Saturday, June 6 I called at Bro. Heck's to see Dr. J.H. Alwood, a half hour. We had a session at 8:30. Topics were discussed. Alwood made a tilt on the African Mission. A.F. Stoltz spoke. Dillon dined with me at Bowser's. We go to Huntington. Sup & lodge at Clay's. N.E. Deune's pr. at 8:00. I lodge at Clay's.

Sunday, June 7 I called at Rev. S. L. Livingston's. I taught Pres. McMurray's Sab. School Class. Heard Bishop Bark pr. baccalaureate at 10:30. Dined at A.A. Powell's, with Wilberforce boys. Call at E. Clapp's. Sup at Powell's. Call at Gilbert's. C.B. Whitacre pr. at 8:00. I lodged at Livingston's.

Monday, June 8 Went to the Publish'g House. I dine at Prof. T.H. Gragg's; also supper. The Glee Club Concert at 8:00. I lodged at S.L. Livingston's.

Tuesday, June 9 The Educational Board met in the College at 9 o'clock. Johnson resigns and Livingston is elected on the Board. Clay elected Secretary of the Board. I dine at Pres. Jas. H. McMurray's. Publishing Board met at 2:00. Debate on Saler's employment by Ex. Com. & Hatfield. Debate on peace proposition. Sup at Clay's. Lodge at Stemen's.

Wednesday, June 10 I called at Livingston's. Ed. Board met at 8:00. General Secretary's report. Commencement at 10 o'clock. Dr. Bradshaw's address. Three graduates. Alumni dinner at College room. Floyd is toast master. My toast was "Truth never fails." Publ Board at 3:00. My reply. Peace voted down. Sup. Concert at 8:00. Lodge at Livingston's.

Thursday, June 11 Pub. Board meeting at 8:00 a.m. Finish up. I spoke on Peace. I went on 10:19 tr. via Wabash and Anderson home. Call at Mrs. Caroline

Zeller's. Saw Emma Dennis as I went there. Reach home at 6:30. Attended High School Commencement with Katharine. Slept 5 hours.

Friday, June 12 At home. Slept 2 hs. Called at Lorin's. Lorin looked over my legal expense books, etc. I made out my tax assessment.

Saturday, June 13 Weather Fair, pleasant. With Milton & Horace, I took a long walk along Wolf Creek. I went to town at 3:30. Called at Louding's & at Pub. Library. Called at Lorin's in the evening and left Ed. Smith's plan for my Grant County (Ind.) house. Wrote several letters. Slept 7 hours at least.

Sunday, June 14 Weather, Fair & mild. Heard Rev. S.D. Bennett pr. at 10:30, Boardway Christian Church, Heb. 6.12. Called at Lorin's, Kumler Huffman's, and John Nicholas'. Miss Wuichett called. Heard Rev. Henry C. Jameson pr., Grace Church, at 7:30, Luke 18.29.

Monday, June 15 Weather, Fair, mild. Nothing of special interest to-day. I took Horace on a walk in the forenoon. Wrote Barkley a letter.

Wednesday, June 17 Went to town in the forenoon. Wrote several letters. I found several letters written to me or to Wilbur last August. Among these were one from A. Worman, dated Aug. 14; from J.K. Alwood, Aug. 15; C.L. Wood, Aug. 11; M.F. Keiter, Aug. 8; N.D. Wolfard, Aug 14; M.V. Bartlett, Aug. 16; and A. Rust, Aug. 16th.

Friday, June 19 At home. Katharine started for Oberlin commencement.

Saturday, June 20 At home writing. Wrote to several leading men in the church about the protest of B. & F. & B. & my reply and gave copies, and of resolutions offered in the Publishing Board, etc. I have slept better at night than usual, this week—more hours.

Sunday, June 21 Orville does the cooking to-day. At First Lutheran Ch. (Main St.) I hear Rev. J. Frank Garland preach an able and eloquent sermon, 2 Tim. 4.7,8. I attended Episcopal prayer-meeting at 5:00, at Christ's Church on 1st St.

Tuesday, June 23 At home. Employed as usual. Wilbur went to Chicago to-night.

Wednesday, June 24 The day passed as usual. Wilbur delivered an oral address before the Society of Western Engineers in Chicago in the evening. Katharine is at Oberlin Commencement.

Thursday, June 25 Nothing unusual to-day. Wilbur got home at 6:00 afternoon.

Saturday, June 27 Went on 9:30 Electric to Miamisburg & Isaac Swartzel's—dined. Go with Isaac to Germantown; call at Mother Long's; Rev. C.S. Johnson pr. at 2:00, H.J. Becker objects to passing my character. Passed by 9 to 2. Went to Lewis Wetz. Johnson pr. at 7:30. I lodge at L. Wetz.

Sunday, June 28 Father Wetz is quite drowsy & in the day becomes helpless. Bro. Johnson pr at 10:30, Communion. I dine at Rev. W.H. Kindel's. Talk with C.S. Johnson. I go to L. Wetz. Call at Mother Long's. H.J. Becker pr. at 7:30. I lodge at J.W. Fouts'.

Monday, June 29 Call at Long's and at Kindel's. See J. Slifer at his new house. Come home on the 10:45 electric. At Home. Slept 2 hours. Call at Lorin's in the evening & take Horace on his usual walk.

Tuesday, June 30 At home. Nothing unusual. Lewis Wetz of Germantown died about 7:00 p.m.

Wednesday, July 1 Ivonette came to-day to visit us for days. Wrote letters to J. Gonser, W.H. Hodge, J. McBride, .G.M. Freese, B.G. Huber.

Thursday, July 2 Wrote many letters. Rev. Wm. Dillon & wife dined with us. They are to remodel their house in this city—on Third St.

Friday, July 3 I Went on the 8:30 electric car to Germantown. Called at Long's. Dined at Rev. W.H. Kindel's. Pr. Lewis Wetz' funeral at U.B. Ch. at 2:00. Supper at the house. Came home on 6:45 electric. Great racket over the eve of the Fourth.

Saturday, July 4 Went in the forenoon to the "Ten Day-ton Boys" picnic on the Salem Pike & spent the day there. It was quite a hot day, but pleasant in the shade. I returned to Lorin's & staid till the children had exhausted their fireworks, which were rather inferior.

Sunday, July 5 I spent the day at home. Slept considerably as I was wakeful last night. I called at Lorin's in the evening.

Monday, July 6 I was at home. I did not do much, lacking as I did in nervous force. I walked to Scitter's grocery and back in the evening.

Tuesday, July 7 At home as usual. Rested & slept a good deal. Prof. David Dennis & Emma (Zeller) came at 3:35 aftn.

Wednesday, July 8 Katharine and I took Prof. Dennis & wife to the Soldiers' Home, Cash Register, Dayton View etc. They left for home on 6:30 train.

Sunday, July 12 I was at home. I missed morning service by falling asleep. I went to an evening service, but found it an Endeavor meeting.

Monday, July 13 At home. In the afternoon I called at cousin H.S. Simpson's, at her request, to write out a notice of her Sister Mary Ann Drill's death who died the 7th of this month near Redkey, Ind. Our cousins Ed. E. McKnight called while I was there. They are Edward E. Mcknight and Anna Maria (Dover).

Thursday, July 16 At home. Pope Leo XIII died to-day.

Sunday, July 19 Heard Rev. D. Frank Garland, Main St. Lutheran Ch., John 8:12, "I am the light of the world," It was not one of his best discourses.

Monday, July 20 At home all day. Wrote letters.

Tuesday, July 21 Went on 8:38 tr. via Richmond to Fowlerton. Prof. D. Dennis & wife on the train from Richmond. I go to R.W. White's on the farm. I called in the evening at Ed. Smith's. I lodged at White's.

Wednesday, July 22 I go on 7:40 tr. to Fairmount. I called at Clinton Brattain's, also at Berge Hollinsworth's. I called at Mrs. Mary Ann Hilligoss's—Mrs. Bond's. I dine at Ellis Wright's. Went on 12:59 tr. via Anderson to Dayton. I saw Rev. S.W. Keister on the train.

Thursday, July 23–Thursday, July 30 At home. Nothing remarkable. Caught up somewhat on sleep. . . . [Wrote] letters and cards. Elmer Caylor a former neighbor boy, called in the forenoon. . . . [M]ostly reading. Walked to town in the afternoon.

Friday, July 31 At home writing letters. I got my new suit at DeWeese's.

Sunday, August 2 Bishop H.L. Barkley who had lodged at the Atlas Hotel, came in about 8:30 A.M. We called at Lorin's in the afternoon.

Monday, August 3 Spent the day in getting ready to go to Messick to-morrow, Bishop Barkley being here.

Tuesday, August 4 Started at 8:43 A.M. for Messick, with Bishop H.L. Barkley, to attend White River Conference. At Richmond, I called to see Caroline Zeller 10 min. Arr. at New Castle at noon. Called in Aftn. an hour to see Peter Keuther (89 years of age) at Mrs. Hinshaw's. I have known him 46 years—true as steel. Saw many preachers. Go to Messick on 7:40 tr. Swartz pr. at 8:00. I lodge at A. Messick's.

Wednesday, August 5 At 7:30, a com. gave me a paper. At 8:00, I give verbal ans. & ask till tomorrow to file written ans. At 9:45, C.B. Small calls a preliminary meeting. It resolves that I shall not preside, but Floyd. At nine o'clock both he and I call the house to order. Adjourn to 10:30. Sheriff at 9:30 serves an injunction on me. H. Floyd presides. I board at Messick's. Kiracofe pr. at 8:00. Tharp, Kabrich & Barkley board there.

Thursday, August 6 Conference continues. Wilbur came yesterday at 8:30. We and Bishop Barkley board at Albert Messick's. We prepared my written answer to com. yesterday and handed it in at 4:00. W.H. Clay, E.D. Root, Wm. Dillon, were present. Wilbur dines and sups with me, and lodges at Cornwell's.

Friday, August 7 Conference continued. My case is reported on by committee at 2:00 recommending expulsion. I speak an hour & 40 minutes in self defence. Oler spoke 30 or 40 min. against me. Postpone till tomorrow at 8:00. Morrison & Wolfard elected P.E.'s. Barnaby pr. Barkley and I take tr. to Lynne. We lodge at hotel at Lynne.

Saturday, August 8 I go on 6:36 tr. to Arcanum & thence by Electric R'y home. Arr. at 9:00. Rest & write some. Wilbur staid and heard Small, Barnaby, Floyd, Wolfard, etc. At 12:05, 22 elders voted to expel me, and two (Selig and Kinneman) for me. Wilbur staid and came home via New Castle & Richmond, at 6:00. Wilbur boarded at Messick's & Cornwell's each day.

Sunday, August 9 At home all day. Rev. S.J. Nicklas died to-night, in Pennsylvania, a bright and lovely man. M.F. Keiter, the embezzler, was the inspiration of the illegal prosecution against me, at White River Conference.

Tuesday, August 11 Went to Richmond on 8:43 tr. and thence to New Castle on 11:00 tr. Dine at Restaurant. Engage Wm. A. Brown as attorney. Call at H. Root's. Go on to Logans port. Lodge at Murdock Hotel, two squares north of the depot.

Wednesday, August 12 I go on the forenoon train to Bruce Lake. Home at Bruce's. Bp. Floyd came afternoon. Rev. J. Hatfield pr. at 8:00.

Thursday, August 13 Conference opened at 8:00. Bishop Barkley came in forenoon. Drs. Wm. Dillon and W.H. Clay came. Dr. W. Dillon pr. at 8:00 a good sermon.

Friday, August 14 Conference continued. M. Claypool was elected presiding elder. Stationing Com. met in the evening. Bp. Barkley pr. at 8:00 & raised $100.00 on Floyd's salary. I contributed $5.00 of it.

Saturday, August 15 Resolutions censuring White River Conference and declaring its action void were adopted and also a resolution censuring Bp. Floyd. Went with Bishop Barkley to Logansport on the evening train. Put up at the Murdock Hotel.

Sunday, August 16 Attended the Presbyterian Church at 11:00 and heard Rev. L.M. Clifford of Sidney, O., pr. on ["]Conversation, Grace, seasoned with salt." Went on 1:15 tr. to New Castle and put up at Bundy House. Bp. Barkley & I heard at 8:00, the Christian preacher (Campbellite) pr. a good sermon.

Monday, August 17 Saw Judge Morris and Wm. A. Brown in the forenoon & ordered a damage suit against the Conference for the injunction trick. I went on 3:10 tr. to Richmond and thence home arriving at 6:00.

Tuesday, August 18 At home all day, writing letters and otherwise getting ready to go to Indiana conference. Worked till late at night.

Wednesday, August 19 I went on the early train to Cincinnati and via North Vernon to New Albany. Wrote many letters at the post office at the latter place, and went on to Marengo reaching there at 7:15 in the evening. Lodge at Rev. J.M. Johnson's with Bishop Barkley who had arrived in Forenoon.

Thursday, August 20 We wait at the Hotel till the brothers Parkhill came after us, and then went on to Mansfield School House. Bp. Barkley and I dine at Stanley Parkhill's which was our Conference home. Conference opened at 2:00. I presided. I pr. at 8:00, 1 Cor. 1:30, "Wisdom righteous." Lodge at Parkhill's.

Friday, August 21 Conference proceded. Bp. B. & I dine at J. Edmond Parkhill's. Bp. Barkley pr. at 8:00. We sup & lodge at S. Parkhill's. Rev. Daniel Bavis pr at 2:00.

Saturday, August 22 Conference proceded. Barkley, Johnson & I dined at Mrs. Blackman's. J.M. Johnson was elected P.E. We sup at Oliver Bunch's. Bp. Barkley pr. at 8:00 on th Armor of Righteousness. We lodge at S. Parkhill's. Phebe A. Blackman is Mrs. Blackman's daughter, Pres. Township S.S.A.

Sunday, August 23 I pr. in the Sch. House yard, John 8.12, "Light of the world." J.T. Miller, J.M. Johnson, Bp. H.L. Barkley, and I dined at James Shafer's, 1 m. east. Have a fine watermelon. Sup there. Bp. Barkley pr. at 7:30, on Ezekiel 33:11. Read Sta. Com's report. We lodge at S. Parkhill's.

Monday, August 24 Stanley Parkhill takes Bp. B. and me to Marengo. We go on 10:36 tr. to New Albany. We

dine at a restaurant near Balt. & Ohio depot. We go on 2:12 tr. to N. Vernon & Cincinnati. B. goes via Richmond and Grand R. R'y. north. I go on 6:30 tr. home to Dayton.

Tuesday, August 25 Write many letters and get ready to go to Sagan City, Ill. Start at 8:55 Penn. tr. to Chicago. Lorin & Nettie called in the evening I read proofs on my new pamphlet on peace. I went on the night (Penn.) train to Chicago.

Wednesday, August 26 Arrived in Chicago at 7:20. Bishop H.L. Barkley met me at Union Depot. I lunched in Depot Restaurant. Dined at Hotel near. We went on Chi. M & St. P. R'y to Leaf River. Sup at Rev. J.L. Buckwalter's. He takes me & Dr. Clay to Egan. Prayer Meeting. I lodge at Noah Speaker's.

Thursday, August 27 Conference opened at 9:00. Margileth chairman, C.A. Gordon, Sec'y. I board at Noah Speaker's, an ex U.B. aged 83. Mrs. Sharp his housekeeper. Dr. W.H. Clay pr. at 8:00, and did well. Weather cloudy.

Friday, August 28 Strong resolutions were adopted against the White River action and recognizing me as a lawful bishop. Dr. Clay left in the evening. A.X. Harrison was elected presiding elder. Stationing Com. met at N. Speakers after supper. C.A. Gordon pr.

Saturday, August 29 Conference continued. Stationing Committee's Report read at 4:00. Harrison and Wm. T. Flakarty dined with me, but were not welcomed much by my host & hostess. Resolutions were reconsidered and St. Joseph resolutions substituted. A.X. Harrison preached at 8:00. I board as usual.

Sunday, August 30 I pr. at 11:00, 1 Cor. 9:16, "Woe is me if". Coll. nearly $60.00. I dine as usual. I called at 4:00 at David Kretzinger's, next north of the Church & lunched there. I pr. at 7:30 32 min. John 8:12. "The Light of the world." Lodge at Speaker's.

Monday, August 31 A young man takes me and Rev. Caskey & [blank] to Foreston and they go on to Mundota, & I on to LaSelle, where I lunch and write much at the postoffice, and go on to Streator on the

C.B. & G. R'y. I hire a rig for $1.00 and go out to Jac. Phillips, and lodge.

Tuesday, September 1 I go over to Missal with hired man, & dine at Mrs. G. Waters' with Revs. G.M. Freese & W.W. Knipple. I went afternoon with G.M. Freese to Widow A.B. Powell's. She is quite a Keiterite & talked quite sharply to me, Freese & Knipple. I board there. W.W. Knipple pr. at 8:00.

Wednesday, September 2 Bishop H.L. Barkley came at 2:00. He boarded at Mrs. G. Waters. He pr. at 7:30, from Isiah 11th Chap. a happy effort. About six came from the Ministerial Association at Waldron on 10:00 tr. & dined at Mrs. Powell's.

Thursday, September 3 Rev. W.B. McMunn assumed the Episcopate & tried to run the Conference. I held the ground and the dissenters retired. We did most of the business with five preachers besides the bishops & one lay-member. Adj till 4:00, finished & Barkley & I went to Streator & thence to Chicago.

Friday, September 4 I went on 2:45 Monon [?] tr. to Indianapolis and thence to Hamilton and on 1:30 tr. home. Found all well. I retired early & slept well. I called at Lorin's a minute in the afternoon. He has sold his Plant St. property for $3,500.00 cash. I slept about 8 hours. I slept 3 hours in the train.

Saturday, September 5 I record my diary. I spent the day at home and largely in writing letters. Wrot[e] to A.H. Roach, Ed. Beauchamp, D.O. Tussing, A.J. Ware, J.C. Coulson, A.L. Hope, J. Seelye Beers. We called at Lorin's in the evening, Katharine & I. I slept about 7 hours.

Sunday, September 6 I Spent the day at home mostly resting. I called at Lorin's in the evening and saw Harry Andrews and wife there.

Tuesday, September 8 Lorin Wrote letters for me; also Katharine. Lorin sent out tracts for me. Bishop Barkley came at 8:00 & lodged with us.

Wednesday, September 9 Went out to Crawford's with Bishop H.L. Barkley and put up at Eubank's. Augliaze conference began at 2:00. Motion to recognize me ruled

out by Bp. Barnaby, S.P. Overholtz pr. at 8:00, 23 min. Very sultry. Harvey is 83 years old. (Dr. George Wright, my nephew, died this morning, in Indianapolis, of typhoid fever, after five day's sickness.) (He was Harvey's Son.)

Thursday, September 10 Conference continued. Resolutions for signatures were circulated by Rev. A.J. Stemen. Bp. Barnaby pr. Matt. 22:11,12 at 8:00. Bp. Barkley left at 5:00. I dined at Aaron Wysong's.

Friday, September 11 Resolutions were presented in the forenoon. Bp. Barnaby ruled them out & refused to recognize any appeal from his decision. I dined at Rev. W.A. Hanshew's. I came home in the evening. Car broke axle ahead of us near the Soldier's home. I reached home about 8:00. Cora Tester preach. Quite warm.

Saturday, September 12 I went on 7:00 traction car to Crawford's & walked up to Olivet. At 3:00, Memorial services over Revs. Geo. Christopher Warvel and D.F. Thomas. I spoke of Warvel. Lizzie Warvel present. I dined at Mr. G. Warvel's & supped at Aaron Wysong's. Mrs. Harvey pr. in tent at 8:00. I lodge at Eubank's.

Sunday, September 13 Weather, Quite warm. Lovefeast at 9:30. Bp. Barnaby pr. at 10:30, 2 Cor. 5:1. I dine with George Warvel's on the ground. I address the S.S. Anniversary at 3:00 Young Mills takes me to the crossing and I go on the traction home, arriving at 6:00. I called at Lorin's a half hour. Bishop Barnaby told Chas. Weyer that he did not speak against me at White River Conference. He did.

Monday, September 14 Spent the day busily mostly writing letters. Lorin helped me on type writer forenoon and awhile afternoon. I slept well. Katharine resumed teaching in High School another year. Leontine started in the kindergarten to day.

Tuesday, September 15 Rose early. I was very busy getting ready to start to Missouri. Get my Answer to Kiracofe's editorials ready. I start on 11:40 tr. on Monon Route to Chicago, & on 10:00 tr. p.m., Santa Fe Route, to Hurdtland, Mo. Breakf & dine there (1 1/2 m. from Depot). Go on noon tr. to Gibbs, the 16th.

Wednesday, September 16 Reach Gibbs. Bp. Barkley & A.D. Thomas met me. Called at "Rev." J.L. Hall's. Sup at Mrs. Jane Garlock's near Prarie Bird Church, 2 1/2 m. N.W. of Gibbs, Mo. Rev. E. Beauchamp pr. at 7:30, John 3:3, a good sermon. My conference home at Mrs. Garlock's.

Thursday, September 17 Conference opened at 9:00 A.M. & Bishop Barkley & I presided, and it made good progress. Bishop Barkley & others home with me at Mrs. A.J. Garlock's. Bp. Barkley pr. at 7:30 a very striking sermon. After meeting, Garlock took him to Laplata, to go on early train to Kansas City & thence to Portland, Oregon. Bright day.

Friday, September 18 The day is bright & cool. Conference proceded well. I dine at Jacob Garlock's. Rev. D.W. Baker pr. at 2:00, about 12 min, Rev. J. Lisk pr. at 7:30, & quite a lively speaking meeting followed.

Saturday, September 19 Conference proceded and closed at 5:00. Each member gave me their hand to stand by me. Stationing Committee met at the Church after Conference adjourned. Rev. L.H. Williams pr. at 2:00. Rev. A. Norman at 7:30. Mrs. Crawford came as an earnest seeker—was converted before next evening.

Sunday, September 20 I pr. at 11:00, 2 Tim. 4:1, "Preach the word." Ordained E. Beauchamp. A. Norman took up Coll. for me, $56.45. I dine at the Church with Davidson's. I called at Jacob Garlock's and got a cup of coffee. S.S. Anniversary at 3:00. Rev. A.B. Thomas pr. at 7:30, Hab. 3.2. "Revive thy work." Few men could preach like him.

Monday, September 21 Rev. J.G. Garlock took me to Laplata (9 ms west) and I went on 10:19 tr. to Kansas City. I wrote letters there. I went on 4:20 tr. to Edminster & to Reuchlin's.

Tuesday, September 22 At Reuchlin's, I looked at the farm, crops, cattle, hogs, etc. Rode out with the family —called at Mr. McCaffrey's. Return to Reuchlin's. Wrote a little. In stocking feet, Herbert's height is 4 ft. 4 3/4 in.; Bertha's is 3 ft., 9 3/4 in.

Wednesday, September 23 I went from Tonganoxie to Senaca and thence to Hiawatha. Return on freight tr. to Sabetha & find conference home at Wm. C. Deaver's. Rev. A. Ritchie & Mrs. L.E. Hart also stay there. Rev. J.C. Hope conducted a U.B. C. Endeavor anniversary at 8:00, eve.

Thursday, September 24 Kansas Conference opened at 9:00. Every member, and all the people were my friends. Board as usual at Deaver's. Rev. E. Atkinson dined with us. It was a cool morning and a beautiful day. Rev. J.C. Hope pr. at 8:00, a good sermon, and a good testimony meeting followed.

Friday, September 25 Conference business proceded rapidly. A.L. Hope was elected pres. elder, in afternoon. Stationing committee met at the Church at 4:00. Mrs. L.E. Hart pr. at 8:00, Mark 16.3, "Who shall roll away the stone," a fine sermon. An excellent testimony meeting followed. I never heard a finer preacher (woman) than Sister L.E. Hart.

Saturday, September 26 Business proceded as usual, & closed at 5:00. Rev. A. Ritchie pr. at 8:00, a good sermon, Rev. 3.11, "Let us man take thy crown." Many spoke in the testimony meeting which followed.

Sunday, September 27 I pr at 11:00, in U.B. Sabetha Church, Acts 20.24. "The ministry-----received." At 3:00, there was a S.S. Anniversary, and Mrs. Anna B. Ries & Mrs. L.E. Hart & Mr. Squires (a Soldier) spoke & I also. I pr. at 7:30, 1 Cor. 12.31, "More Excellent Way." I slept six hours.

Monday, September 28 I go to both depots & saw Burk, also A. Ritchie and Mrs. L.E. Hart. I went on 12:35 tr. to Fairbury (Nebr.) and thence on 5:00 tr. to Mankato, Kan. I lodge at Rev. J.S. Rock's. Bro. Burk & wife and Misses Singular & Vincent were on the train to Hanover. All of them live at Cliffton.

Tuesday, September 29 I wrote to the Neosha preachers; also to Rev. D.H. Sill; full cards & to Bp. Barkley. I saw J.S. Rock's brother John and Rev. E.R. Baber, at Rock's. I went on 7:40 tr. to Smith Center & lodge at the Sherman House.

Wednesday, September 30 I wrote letters & cards. Rev.

F.W. Bertschinger came and took me to his house, 4 ms s.w., I dine, sup & lodge there. His children: Wright, 9; Hazel, 7; Ruth, 3; Esther, 5 mo. It is my conference home.

Thursday, October 1 Revs. J.D. Lamb, W.A. Perkins, & Tim. Wilfong came & Pixler & we began W. Kansas Conference at 2:00, & adjourned at 4:00. Rev. J.D. Lamb pr. a good sermon at 7:30, 1 Sam. 2:30, "Them that honor me," etc. I board as usual. Rev. J.N. Lemaster, a great preacher and good man of East Ohio, died to-day.

Friday, October 2 Conference business proceded as usual. Rev. George Wilfong and wife were present all day lunched on the ground, as their usual custom is. Rev. W.A. Perkins pr. at 7:30, Rev. 22.9, "Worship God." He is a lively but not impressive speaker. I board at Bertschinter's.

Saturday, October 3 The Conference passed reports on various subjects in the forenoon. I called at W.H. Hicks' after dinner. The treasurers reported in the afternoon. Conference adjourned at 4:00. Rev. J.D. Lamb pr. at 7:30, Rom. 8:31. I board at B's. The weather is fine.

Sunday, October 4 I pr. at 11:00, Rev. 19.6 & Ps. 93.1, "The Lord reigneth." J.M. Pixler dines with us. I pr. at 7:30, John 8:12, "Light of Life," Communion followed. The house was very full—crowded.

Monday, October 5 I arose at 5:30, and wrote in the forenoon. Bro. Bertschinger took me in the afternoon to Smith Center, and there I met Geo. Wilfong & talked with him a good while. I there wrote to J.C. Coulson and W.J. Funkhouser. I went on 6:46 "Buttermilk train" to Bellville and got the last room at Hotel Republic, a double room shared by a traveler.

Tuesday, October 6 I went on 8:35 train (Un. Pac.) to Junction City, & was hurried onto a belated train to Galesburg. I mailed documents to J. Selig, C.W. Rector & T.E. Kinneman. I also wrote a letter to Wilbur & Orville on the train. Peter Eisenbrant met me and took me to my Conference home at Luther Martin Oler's, near the Church.

Wednesday, October 7 I wrote in the forenoon and called at the Church in the afternoon. I visited with the family & others. Revs. Herbert Smith and E. Votaw, and Bro. Spencer & wife in afternoon & others at dark. Rev. Elbert Smith pr. at 7:30, Luke 17.33, "Whosoever shall lose his life," and E. Votaw exhorted.

Thursday, October 8 Neosho Conference was opened at 9:00. I commented on Job, 5th Ch. Business progressed well. Many dine & sup with us at Oler's. Rev. L.V. Harrell pr. at 7:30, and I exhorted.

Friday, October 9 Conference business proceded. Publishing interests report was reconsidered and referred to a Committee which reported in the afternoon & the report was adopted unanimously. I took supper at C.E. Boka's, 3/4 m. south. H.D. Tatman pr. at 7:30, Ps. 84.11, "A day in thy courts," I board at Oler's.

Saturday, October 10 The Conference proceded. I dined at Peter Eisenbrandt's, a m. west. Com. reported on the complaint of Eldorado Quar. Conf., against H.D. Tatman, for violation of contract & mischarges of coal etc. Correspondence ordered. Rev. P.N. Lambert pr. at 7:30, Luke 15.18, "I will arise & go to my father."

Sunday, October 11 Lovefeast at 10:00. I pr. at 11:00, 1 Thes. 2.20, "For ye are our glory & Joy." I dine at Luke Byrne's, 1 1/2 m. N.E. Children: Mamie, 26; Evalee, 16; Hazel, 8. I return to Oler's. Missionary meeting at 7:00. H.D. Tatman & N.C. Pierce spoke, and I raised $90.00, subscription. I lodged as usual.

Monday, October 12 Many are leaving. Wm. A. Oler takes me to Abraham Cary's in Parsons. I had much talk with him over the church controversy. Got a draft at Nat. bank. Supper at W.A. Crane's. I went on 6:28 train for Springfield, Missouri. Arrived at 12:30 and lodged at the Baldwin House, 7407 College St. Slept in a room with two corn husker boys.

Tuesday, October 13 I had a good breakfast. Bill was 50 cents. I went to the Depot and write and mailed letters and cards. At 9:45 our train starts to Chadwick. There Wm. Cook met me and takes me in a covered lumber wagon to his house, 1/2 m. s. of Lone Star U.B. Church, which is my conference home. Children: Ethel, 12; Linnie, 10; Clyde, 8; Virgie, 6; Martha, 6 mos. I lodge there. I dined at hotel at Chad.

Wednesday, October 14 I went to the Lone Star Church. Rev. Hiram Brown was in bed with kidney trouble. I gave him osteopathic treatment & he was up before night. I wrote J.E. & F.M. Higgins. I dined at Cook's, and supped at McGrew's in Church. Mrs. L.A. McGrew pr. at 7:30, and two lifted their hands for prayer. D.S. Buck, J.B. Crom & G.W. Masters came in the evening.

Thursday, October 15 Conference opened at 9:00. I commented on 2 Cor. 3rd Chap. Business proceded well. D.S. Buck dines with me at Cook's. He is much excited on Socialism, which he advocates. Hiram Brown & Rachel his wife were received into conference. D.S. Buck pr. at 7:30 and Rachel Brown exhorted. Daughtery and Miss Wyand knelt for prayers & D. professed conversion.

Friday, October 16 Conference proceeded in the forenoon. Masters & Walk dined with me. Resolutions in my favor adopted unanimously. Rev. S. Snell pr. at 7:30, Mark 1.15, "Repent & believe the Gospel." J.B. Crom exhorted. Miss Wyandt is converted.

Saturday, October 17 Conference closed at 4:30. Rev. J.B. Crom dined with me at Cook's. Rev. H. Brown pr. at 7:30, Mrs. Eva G. Dane followed, and D.S. Buck called for seekers, & Mr. Dane and about six others gave their hands for prayers.

Sunday, October 18 There was a S.S. Anniversary at 10:00, I being one of the speakers. I pr. at 11:00, Gal. 4:4,5, "When the fullness of time." Dined at Adolph A. Stolpe's. Call at Daugherty's & sup there. I pr. at 7:00, Acts 16.31. Thirteen at the altar & Dane and 7 others converted. Four join Church forenoon and five in the evening.

Monday, October 19 Wm. Cook takes McGrew & wife, Crom & myself to Chadwick. We had a lunch which we ate at a private house in town. We go on 1:35 tr. to Springfield, Mo., where Crom & I lunch at a restaurant. We wait & Rev. D.R. Sappenfield came & talked an hour. I sent a check for $75.00 on Citizen's Bank to Lee Hall to pay Grant Co. taxes. I go at 9:20 on Frisco Line to Wichita, Kan.

Tuesday, October 20 I arrive at Wichita at 8:00 a.m. I go to Mis. Pa. Depot. Write letters and full cards. Lunches 45 c. I could not find G.M. Glenn's. I go on 5:00 tr. to Haven, where C.B. Sherk met me & took me to Bro. Geo. R. Manning's, near Sumner church. Sup at M's & pr. at 7:30, Ps. 1.6. My Conf. home at Manning's.

Wednesday, October 21 I have a long task to arrange things in my valises. Several came in to conference. I write letters. I pr. at 7:45, 1 John 4.16, "God is love, and he that abideth in love," (1 Cor 13:1 13). J.H. Watson & C.B. Sherk board also at Manning's & I Rollins.

Thursday, October 22 Conference opened at 9:00 and proceeded well. Rev. A.W. Geeslin pr. a good sermon at 7:45.

Friday, October 23 Business continued. I pr. at 7:45 Acts 16.31. There were six seekers and two conversions. Rev. J.H. Watson joined the local society.

Saturday, October 24 We finish up conference business about 4:00. Rev. J.H. Watson pr. at 7:45. Sta. Com. met at G.R. Manning's, C.B. Sherk was elected P.E. in the Afternoon. He resigned later & I appointed A.W. Geeslin.

Sunday, October 25 There was a S.S. Anniversary at 10:00. I was one of the speakers. I pr. at 11:00, Rom. 7:13, "Exceeding sinful." Dined at Mrs. Clare Mitchell's, 2 m. n.w. I lunch at Manning's. I pr. at 7:00 Acts 16.31. I lodge at Manning's. Mrs. Hopkins in Mrs. Mitchell's mother.

Monday, October 26 I wrote some letters in the forenoon. Rollins and Watson start home. Bro. Manning takes me in the Afternoon to Mt. Hope. I wrote letters and cards at the depot. I went on 8:25 tr. to Witchita I lodged and breakfasted at the Keystone Hotel on Main St.

Tuesday, October 27 I went on 8:30 tr. via Guthrie to Glencoe, Okla. arriving at 5:00. Rev. W.H. Willoughby met me and took me to his house which was my good Conference home, 6 1/2 m. s.e. of Glencoe. I supped and lodged there. Children: Nathaniel Gerald, 17; Leo Adams, 17, Lester Adams, 11.

Wednesday, October 28 Arose at 6:30, and wrote letters in the forenoon. In afternoon Willoughby took me via Lamar's to Rev. J.L. Ridgway's, where I saw A. Rector, L.D. Thornburg & wife. Rev. J.E. Rector pr. at Mt. Vernon Church at 7:30, and a testimony meeting followed. I saw clear indications that my presiding was not intended.

Thursday, October 29 I opened prayer service about 9:15, and presided most of the forenoon. A paper presented, signed by J.E. Rector, L.D. Thornburg, J.L. Ridgway, J.E. & F.M. Higgins, & E. Maupin, asking for a chairman, I acceded to as to "a chairman" only. J.H. McNew was elected & after forenoon, he mostly presided, but I kept my place & rights. McNew pr. 7:30.

Friday, October 30 I kept the Bishop's Chair, advised, ruled on Discipline, and presided briefly. Mrs. Laura Holcomb Harnois, who came last evening preached at 7:30. There was very hard rain in the night. Rev. S. Kern was received on transfer from Iowa Conference.

Saturday, October 31 Amended minutes of day before yesterday were read & approved, also yesterday's minutes. Rev. L.G. Messenger of Neosho was received on transfer. Rev. S. Kern & wife, Rev. D.A. Robinson, and Rev. Carter & wife dined with us at W's. At my direction, J.E. Rector was elected P.E., and also appointed by me. I sat on Sta. Com. as chairman. Rev. J.W. Riley pr. at 7:30.

Sunday, November l I pr at 11:00, 2 Cor. 4.17, "Weight of Glory." I dine at Lemar's, 2 m s.w. Call aftern at J.L. Ridgway's. I pr. at 7:00, Rom. 4:16. Testimony meeting followed. Many specially came to me in the pulpit, after dismissal and bade me a hearty farewell. The hearts of the laity were with me. A vote of thanks was given me for my presiding.

Monday, November 2 I staid at Bro. Willoughby's till afternoon, when he took me to Glencoe, in some rain, and I supped & lodged at Whitted's hotel. I wrote letters there to Clay, my boys, and to Katharine. Rev. Joseph Wilson Riley who boarded at Willoughby's missed

conveyance to Blackwell, and came on later.

Tuesday, November 3 Went to the train without breakfast & ticketed to Lawrence, Kan. I lunched at Guthrie & at Arkansas City, at which last place a woman & boy removed my valises & overcoat "to jump" my seat. I wrote a letter to Wood & a full card to C.B. Sherk & Wm. Dillon and mailed on train. Lodged at Railr. House.

Wednesdsay, November 4 I went to Un. Pac. Depot. Missed train five minutes mailed many letters & full cards. Dined at a restaurant. Went on 3:55 tr. (4:55) to Longanoxie & walked out to Reuchlin's, my son's. Left my valises at the depot. The Panama Revolution occurred yesterday.

Thursday, November 5 I rested & took care of myself & wrote letters and cards. Reuchlin brought my valises in the forenoon.

Friday, November 6 I was at Reuchlin's all day. My cold was a little better. I wrote several letters & cards.

Saturday, November 7 I go on the 9:40 tr. via Meneger Junction to Leavenworth. Rev. M.S. Scott met me and took me to his house, where I dine with Revs. A.L. Hope & T.P. Stewart. Children: Wesley & Judson. Married daughter next door. We go to Mrs. Anna B. Reis, call at Church. Home at R. Lesher's, 1010 Kickapoo St. Rev. T.P. Stewart pr. at 7:30.

Sunday, November 8 Hope & I ride out with Lesher to the Fort & hear the band music. Saw buildings & grounds. At 11:00, Rev. E. Atkinson pr. a good sermon, Matt. 28.28, "Lo I am with you alway[s]." I dine at Lesher's. I pr. at 3:00 and raise $265.00, l Pet. 1:4, "Lo an inheritance incorruptable," was my text. At 7:30 A.L. Hope pr. "Strive to enter." We raise about $50.00 more and dedicate Rehoboth Church.

Monday, November 9 I arose at Lesher's & go on 7:30 traction to Kansas City, and on 10:10 tr. (Mo. Pac) to St. Louis and arrive on time, at 6:01 eve. Go on 8:15 Vandalia Lines for Dayton. Slept several hours on the way.

Tuesday, November 10 Arrive at Dayton at 7:00 a.m.

Breakfast. Arrange & read letters & rearrange papers, a large task. I went to the bank in the afternoon. I called at Lorin's in the forenoon. Slept considerably in the afternoon.

Wednesday, November 11 At home all day, except a call at Lorin's & the drug store, and a mile and a half walk. I Recorded in my diary, for the past two months.

Thursday, November 12 I Got a telephone message from Rev. D.D. Fetters, of Bruce Lake, Ind., who is a brother to the undertaker next to our boys' store. He called an hour at 10:00. I write letters & took a walk in the evening, and called at Mrs. Bartles' to see Mrs. Ramsey at Mrs. Billheimer's request. I Called at Lorin's.

Friday, November 13 Weather, Mild & warm. I spent the time at home writing to Flora Stevens, Mrs. Mosier, and Harvey Wright. I called at Lorin's in the afternoon. At 7:00 in the evening, Katharine and I with Lorin & Netta attended the exhibition of the Kindergarten— Leontine being one of the pupils—Miss Plummer the teacher.

Saturday, November 14 Weather, mild. At home all day. I slept an hour. Wrote letters. I went to town, looked at the new cement bridge on Main Street, paid Van Asdal, Conover, & Co. for carpets etc., bought a hat at London Hat House, 29 E. 3rd St., $5.00. Ida Grabil spent the evening with Katharine.

Sunday, November 15 Weather, Fair & mild. I heard Maurice Wilson preach at 10:30, Rev. 21.13, "There was on the North three gates," etc. It was a fanciful but good sermon, he attaching fanciful meaning to the many gates & the several sides. At home the rest of the day. Wrote to cousins Flora & Semele.

Monday, November 16 Weather, mild, cloudy, rain. At home all day only an hour's call at Lorin's in the afternoon. I wrote some letters.

Tuesday, November 17 Weather, Cloudy & cooler. I am seventy five years old. I was born in J.Q. Adams administration. It is now Theodore Ro[o]sevelt's administration. The former was the sixth president; the latter is the twenty sixth. No nation has ever had so many good,

and so few evil, chief rulers. Lorin & family took supper with us. He is 41 tomorrow.

Thursday, November 19 At home all day only called at furniture stores in Afternoon to look at sectional book cases. To-day, among other letters, I wrote a long one to L.S. Coulson.

Friday, November 20 I was at home in the forenoon writing letters to Bishop Barkley and to Rev. John B. Thomas. In afternoon went to Springfield, Ohio, to see Dr. Wm. Dillon. Went & returned on traction.

Saturday, November 21 In the forenoon, Katharine & I bought Milton a part of a sectional book case, $7.75. At home the rest of the day, mostly reading and writing.

Sunday, November 22 Went to town & back afoot; walked to Miami Chapel, and back. Heard Rev. W.H. Klinefelter pr. a thanksgiving sermon, Ex. 34:22, did well. I was at the grave of our twins, and that of Rev. W.R. Rhineheart. In the afternoon., Katharine & I went riding with Lorin & Milton, to Runneymede and Far Hills.

Monday, November 23 Received letters from Orville. Wrote the boys and registered the letter containing ten five dollar bills. Called at Katharine's room in High School Building, at 12:20. Called at Lorin's in the afternoon.

Wednesday, November 25 Received a letter from Orville dated the 19th. A postscript said the shaft had arrived for their motor. They are at Kitty Hawk, N.C.

Thursday, November 26 We had Charles Perry Parkhurst with us to dinner. I called at Lorin's in the evening. Mrs. Corbett and Horace Stokes were there.

Friday, November 27 At home writing. I attended Mrs. Potts' funeral at 2:00. Revs. Elliott and Gaddis officiated. She resided in the same house on Williams' St. when I moved to Dayton in 1869.

Saturday, November 28 At home. I cleaned out my radiator (stove) in the forenoon. Miss Wuichet visited Katharine in the afternoon. Nettie went to Delaware,

O. to visit Horace Stokes', her brother.

Sunday, November 29 Attended First Lutheran Church and heard Rev. D. Frank Garland preach an able sermon, Luke 23:27. Lorin, Milton and Horace dined with us, and also all the children supped with us.

Monday, November 30 I went on 9:00 tr. via Richmond to Fowlerton. Thence walked to O.A. Glass's & via Wm. Reeder's returned to Fowlerton & lodged at R.W. White's. I supped, talked over business affairs, etc. and lodged there.

Tuesday, December 1 I went on 8:40 tr. to Fairmount & finding Ellis Wright from home returned to Fowlerton & White's. Made settlement with him and went on 5:40 tr. back to Fairmount and staid at Ellis Wrights.

Wednesday, December 2 I with Ellis looked over the ground, and his company agreed that I should build for them to rent a 32 X 50 ft ware room, and Mr. Wiley & I made out the plan & bill of lumber. And I went to Fowlerton and examined as to timber for pillars & engaged Mr. White to cut them & haul them and some lumber I had. I returned to Ellis' on 5:40 train. Lodge there.

Thursday, December 3 I attended to a little business in forenoon & called at Hillegoss's. At 2:10, after consulting Attorney Chas. Parker, I went to Gas City on traction and went on via Union City to Dayton, arr. at 6:00. Found Orville at home after some machinery for the boy's flying maching. They had the second time broken the shaft to the propeller.

Friday, December 4 At home. In the afternoon I received a card from W.H. Clay saying that Judge Daily had yesterday dismissed Keiter's complaint against the nine. Keiter took exception to Appeal to the Supreme Court. I spent most of the day in copying (Canada), H.M. Bowman's manifold argument in favor of Keiter.

Saturday, December 5 Finished copying part of Bowman's "article," and sent the original back to Huntington, Ind.

Sunday, December 6 Heard H.C. Jameson, Pastor of Grace M.E. Church, pr. an able sermon, Eccl. 12:13,14.

He is eloquent after the style of A.J. Pierson. I was at home the rest of the day.

Monday, December 7 At home, mostly writing, and called in the evening to see Lorin about returning the check from "The Consumer's Gas Trust Co," Indianapolis. Mrs. Clare Andrews, Netta's sister, was there with her little boys, Corbett & Benjamin.

Tuesday, December 8 Weather, mild. I wrote a long letter to Rev. P.A. Black, of Oregon & in the evening read nearly all of Pres. Ro[o]sevelt's able message. The Cin. *Tribune's* second editorial to divert from Ro[o]sevelt's candidacy to Hannah's appears, this time suggesting Senator Hale or Frye of Maine. Orville gets ready to return to Kitty Hawk, N.C.

Wednesday, December 9 Orville started at nine o'clock, with his new propeller shaft, for Kitty Hawk, North Carolina. (This new (propeller or) shaft was made of spring steel and was some larger than the former ones.)

Thursday, December 10 At home all day. Wrote letters. I moved my book case upstairs.

Saturday, December 12 Weather, Warm. Rains a little. At home. Wrote some letters.

Sunday, December 13 Weather, Cold. 1/2 in. snow. I heard M. Wilson pr. Ps. 86.8, "None . . . works like . . . thy works," a good sermon.

Monday, December 14 I spend the day largely in getting type writer copies of the description of the Wright Flyer, and copies of a sketch of the inventors.

Tuesday, December 15 Katharine sick; misses School the first time in about four years. Dr. Spitler came. About 4:00 came the telegram "Misjudgment at start reduced flight (to) one hundred (and) twelve (feet)—power and control ample—rudder only injured—success assured keep quiet." Wilbur Wright. It was from Kittyhawk, North Carolina, and related to Wilbur & Orville's Flyer.

Thursday, December 17 In the afternoon about 5:30 we received the following telegrarm from Orvill[e], dated Kitty Hawk, N.C., Dec. 17. "Bishop M. Wright: "Suc-

DECEMBER, 1903.

cess four flights Thursday morning all against a twenty-one mile wind started from level with engine power alone average speed through the air thirty one miles—longest 57 seconds. XXX home Christmas. Orville Wright."

Friday, December 18 The *Enquirer* continued following headlines on the Wright's flying. Dayton *Journal* and Cin. *Tribune* contain nothing! though I furnished press reporter the news. At home. Looked a little after the news and a little about getting it out. Mr. Folkerth, reporter of the Cin. *Post* interviewed us. (The above is supplemental to last page on Friday)

Saturday, December 19 Got some papers containing notices of the Wrights and "Wright Flyer." At request of Indianapolis *Journal,* sent pictures of Wilbur & Orville and of last year's glider. Wrote Bishop Barkley and others.

Sunday, December 20 Attended First Pres. Ch. and heard Rev. Maurice E. Wilson pr. on "The Kingdom of Christ,"

Dan. 7:13,14. He said "Evolution has thrown a flood of Light on original Sin." "Bold as a lion, fierce as a tiger, proud as a peacock," etc. Otherwise, it was a good sermon. Call at Lorin's a half hour in the afternoon.

Monday, December 21 Saw Geo. R. Young a minute and met William A. Walley at the Phillips House at 9:00 to negotiate for supplemental gas leases on my farm. Met again at Young's office at 12:30 and agreed on terms, and drew up a tentative form of lease. Went at 4:00 with Katharine to buy Christmas presents. Christmas box to Reuchlin's. Go to bed early. Half rainy.

Tuesday, December 22 I Was at home all day. Reporters were calling and asking for pictures of the machine and of the boys. I wrote some letters.

Wednesday, December 23 I was at home. Wrote some. Bert Strang called in the interest of the *Commercial Gazette.* Katharine got a telegram from Orville, saying He and Wilbur would be at home to night. They came at 8:00. They had some interviewers on the way, but suppressed them.

Thursday, December 24 Weather, Mild, rainy. I was at home all day, except a call at Lorin's in the evening; and I went to the Christmas entertainment at Broadway M.E. Church. Ivonette and Leontine had parts in it.

Friday, December 25 Weather, Mild. I wrote a few letters forenoon & Afternoon. We as a family dine at Lorin's. Mrs. Corbett was there. Ivonette & Leontine spend the afternoon with us. Lorin had to go to his work in American Express Depot office, after dinner.

Saturday, December 26 Weather, colder. Wrote only a few letters. Miss Bertha Comstock's interview with W. & O. for Chi. *Trib.* in forenoon & J.D. Sider's for N.Y. *World* in evening. I made out and sent on an application for Clergy Certificate, to Centr. Pas. Asso'n. in the afternoon. I bought Horace a darkie doll.

Sunday, December 27 Weather, cold. Attended First Pres. Ch., Dr. Wilson. Text, 1 John 2.16 17, "The world passeth away, but he that doeth will of God abideth forever." Was introduced to Dr. Parmeter of Herkimer Co., N.Y. I call at Lorin's afternoon. Lorin and Netta and

Ivonette with Ivonette (so sweet) called an hour in the evening.

Monday, December 28 Weather, mild. Mailed several letters. I bought at Prugh's Game and book for Ivonette, table & dishes for Leontine and book & darkey doll for Horace. In the afternoon I sent out letters and documents to East Ohio ministers. Katharine visited Mrs. Mary Emmons, formerly Mary Osborn.

[The following is at the end of the diary:]

Gunckel's Eulogium

Rev. W. R. Funk, in an article on Mr. Lewis B. Gunckel said: "Mr. Gunckel was a discerner of men. He studied characteristics in client and opposition alike.xxx Of the opposition , he said, and his opinion is worthy of consideration in the light of present events: "I always thought Bishop Wright an honest meaning man, who struggled for what he thought was a principle; but the great majority of the other leaders of that side were simply position-seekers." Milton Wright.

Memoranda

The past year (1903) was full of stirring events. I was serene ana happy through it all, though grieved at the folly of many, and the wickedness of not a few. I believed that God would at last vindicate the right.

Paid Geo. Young $5.00 about Nov. 1902 for advice in the Bealor note Case, and $5.00 April 28, 1903 for advice in the same case.

(From the Arabic.)

None have I taught to bend the bow And set the swift shaft free, Who have not, at the last, for thanks. Their arrows aimed at me.

Exposure of Fraud

"The toleration of the wrong, not the exposure of the wrong, is the real offense."—Pres. Ro[o]sevelt, as quoted by the I*ndependent.*

Bishop H.T. Barnaby said at Auglaize Conference at Olivet, Sept. 13, 1903: "Knowledge is a settled conviction of a fact, without doubt."

Keiter's Over-charges

Crane found 1533. Keiter replied to 274 only. That is one to 5.54.

First powered flight, December 17, 1903. Kitty Hawk, North Carolina

1904

Friday, January 1 All at home to-day. I have lived 75 years past My wife Susan, lived 58 yrs. My father Dan. lived 71 yrs. My mother Catharine lived 66 yrs. Mr. Gr. F. Dan Wright lived 75 years. My Gr. M. Sarah Wright lived 86 years. My Gr. F. George Reeder lived 77 years. My. Gr. M. Margaret Reeder lived 80 years. My Grt. Gr. F. Benoni Bright lived 42 years. My Grt. Gr. M. Eliza (Smith) Wright lived 61 years. My Grt. Gr. F. John Van Cleve lived 41 years. My Grt. Gr. M. Catharine (Benham) Van Cleve lived 81 years. Snow in the night.

Saturday, January 2 It is a very snowy day. I go to Miamisburg but snow had closed the traction to Germantown. So I returned. Qr. Meeting at Germantown. I wrote letters. It snowed but little in the night.

Sunday, January 3 Thermometer 20 below zero. I attend Broadway Christian (New Light) Church. Rev. S.D. Bennet pr. Luke 13.24, "Strive—enter—straitgate." Joseph Boyd called an hour in the afternoon; and Agnes Osborn, a half hour at 5:00 aftn. Agnes starts to-night to Chicago to continue her course in the University.

Monday, January 4 At home all day except a call at Lorin's in the evening. As usual, I wrote some letters. Our mails came with new carrier, on new route after 10:00 & after 3:00!

Tuesday, January 5 I wrote Rev. F.E. Kinneman & Alice Crull, etc. Letter came from Flora Stevens & Ray. Bills came for cost of my new warehouse in Fairmount. Katharine spent afternoon ard eve. at Mary Emmons'.

Wednesday, January 6 At home. I wrote several letters suggested by old letters I had run across. Received a paper giving account of the sixtieth anniversary of Harvey & Delila Wright's wedding, Dec. 27, 1843. Wilbur and I meet Malone and Walley on the subject of oil lease, at Young's office.

Thursday, January 7 Met Malone and Walley at Young's Office. We fail to agree and they leave.

Friday, January 8 Lorin brings me as a nice present a six-shelves to my writing desk.

Saturday, January 9 Moderate weather. I made arrangement to get our mail at the station near cor. of Williams & Third Sts. I went to town in the Aftn and sent Ray Stevens a nice linen book, Cinderella, Jack the Giant Killer, etc.

Sunday, January 10 Mod. weather. I arose early. At 10:30 I heard Rev. Merle H. Anderson pr. at 3rd St. Pres. Church, Col. 1.19. He is quite young, has a splendid voice and good ability. May he be humble. I called a half-hour at Lorin's in the evening.

Monday, January 11 At home mostly as usual. I sent two drafts amounting to $303.62 to pay for bills on my warerooms. Sent them to Ellis Wright. I paid the last time to Winter's Bank for drafts!

Wednesday, January 13 At home as usual. I wrote to D. Koerner in answer to his dissatisfaction over all the lower rooms of the Publishing House not being rented.

Thursday, January 14 At home. Three volumes of Lyman

Attott's commentaries came by express. I sent for Wilson's Ear Drums. I wrote D. Koerner on Hypocrisy of the cry about my "going to law." Ida Grabil visited our young folks.

Sunday, January 17 Heard Rev. D. Frank Garland preach, an able and eloquent sermon, Ps. 48:12,13. At home the rest of the day. Milton and his sisters spent the afternoon with us. It is a moderate, cold day.

Monday, January 18 This is a moderate winter day with little or no thawing. I receive Wilson's eardrums which do not seem to benefit me. I wrote Driggs, Wright & Wiley, also Ellis. Lide (Harry) Hawk called in evening to learn Mrs. Dillon's address.

Tuesday, January 19 At home as usual. Efforts of the Fowlerton Window Glass Company to telephone to us. I spent some hours retracing in ink my diary of 1877, which I found fuller than I had supposed. Wrote letters to some of our old Liberal preachers.

Wednesday, January 20 At home. Mr. Brown and Leick of Fowlerton, came to see me about gas and oil leases on my land. I went to town, bought an eight-day clock, letter paper, etc. Clock $4.50. Thawing and some rain.

Friday, January 22 At home. Collected interest on Loans. Brought eight-day clock home for my study. Called at Lorin's. The water in the river is within ten or twelve feet of the top of the levy. Rain ceases about 11:00. Mr. O. Chanute supped with us.

Saturday, January 23 At home. There is a "skift" of snow. A moderate day with no thawing.

Sunday, January 24 I remained at home all day and slept a good deal having been short of sleep last night. Lorin's three children spent the afternoon and evening with us. A steady cold day. At 7:30, I heard Rev. D.L. Meyers at the Fourth Pres. Church, Heb. 11.27.

Monday, January 25 Weather mod. I went on 8:43 train via Arcanum, Shirley, and Anderson to Fairmount, arr. about 2:00. Called at Driggs' hardware store and then went to Ellis Wright's. Supped & lodged there. Snow fell early, late and all night.

Tuesday, January 26 The snow is about 12 inches deep. I mostly staid indoor, but went to the store a short time.

Wednesday, January 27 Cold Weather. I went to see Mrs. Holloway & Mrs. Frank Davis about the sale of their lot next to Bryan's. I dined at Ellis' and went on 3:05 train to Fowlerton. I called at Frank Kirkwood's a half hour, and Wm. Reeder came after me & took me to his house where I sup and lodge.

Thursday, January 28 Cold Weather. I dined at Robert B. Reeder's, and he took me to Oliver A. Glass', where I sup and lodge.

Friday, January 29 Cold Weather. Oliver took me to the farm (R.W. White's) where I dine. John Deitrich came in the forenoon and talked Long, representing the "Eastern Oil Co." F.J. LaDuron came afternoon and talked oil for Royal Window Glass Co. & took me to see Levi Simons' wells. Go to Fairmount & staid at Ellis'. Long's [last word is unreadable]

Saturday, January 30 Weather moderate. I went on 8:08 traction to Gas City and thence to Union City & home arr. at Dayton about 4:00. Read letters and wrote Clay. It thawed some to-day.

Sunday, January 31 I was at home all day. Lorin's three older children were with us in the afternoon and to supper. Lorin and Netta called an hour in the evening with Horace (baby brother).

Monday, February 1 Received a phone from R.W. White saying gas poachers were about to come on my land. I go on 6:00 tr. to Union City & Muncie. Lodge at the Southern Hotel, near the depot.

Tuesday, February 2 Went on 7:00 C.I. & E. tr. to Fowlerton, to White's & Levi Simons, and dine at Simons. Go on to Marion. Consult St. John & Charles. Lodge at Harfield House. Snow blockade at Deer Creek Hills.

Wednesday, February 3 Go on 7:00 to Fairmount. Get security on bond. Return & confer with Attorneys. Return to Fairmount. Dine at Ellis Wright's. Go at 3:05 to

Fowlerton. Supper and lodging at R.W. White's on my farm.

Thursday, February 4 The 6:43 tr. to Richmond was 1 hr and 10 min late, so I saw Wm. Millspaugh about price's on White's [unreadable] lot and Foster's. Reached Richmond about 10:40 and Dayton about 12:15. I wrote White & Dillon in the evening.

Sunday, February 7 I heard Rev. Garland pr. at 10:30, Gen. 20.1–3. Not a happy effort. Lorin and Netta went to her Uncle Walter Stokes' funeral in Lebanon, and all the children were with us all day. They called for them in the evening. The river full of floating ice, and water high. Great Baltimore fire began.

Monday, February 8 Weather mild. At home. News came to-day that the Japanese last night, with torpedoes, disabled three Russian ships at Port Arthur, about midnight.

Tuesday, February 9 Cooler Weather. The evening papers abound with the Story of the Japanese raid on the Russian ships at Port Arthur, disabling the battleships, Retvizian and Cesarevitch, and the cruiser Pallada.

Wednesday, February 10 Cold Weather. At home. Wrote J.S. Beers a long letter. War has been proclaimed between Russia and Japan.

Thursday, February 11 At home. The cablegrams seem to indicate that Japan is getting the better of Russia at sea, and is occupying Seoul. I wrote long letters to Wm. Dillon & to Wm. Beers. I received a letter from M.L. Spencer about the depositions he took at Hagerstown, Md. Katharine and Miss Wuichet walked out to Fairfield, for exercise.

Saturday, February 13 I was at home all day, except an afternoon trip to town for various small purchases. Prepared letters of Circulars for the Penn & Va. preachers.

Sunday, February 14 I called at Lorin's & dropped some valentines. At 10:30, I heard Rev. Garland pr. Ex. 20.7. Milton and the girls visited us.

Monday, February 15 I went on the 8:43 train to India-

napolis. I put up at my sister's daughter's Mrs. Laura Winchell's, 2214 N. Illinois Street. Her soninlaw & daughter live with them. Mr. Heard & Minnie & Harold (12 mo. old). Clarence & wife, visited there.

Tuesday, February 16 I remained at Austin Winchell till 11:00 & went to Lebanon, Ind. Went to Dr. John A. Morehous's. At 8:00 I married Otto B. Bowman & Mary Morehouse. Byron Bowman and Miss Geotz and Prof. R.A. Clark & Miss Purviance were there; also many relatives & Neighbors. Lodged at Davis's.

Wednesday, February 17 I went on traction road to Indianapolis, called at Fay Wright's office at 404 S. Meridian St. Went to Rushville. Called at Dr. G.P. Dillon's, & Thomas Wright takes me to Harvey's, my brother's, 8 miles north.

Thursday, February 18 John & Drusilla McKee, Jabez & Frances Rhoads, Emma and Grace Frazer, & Effie & David Kirkpatrick came in to see me, and spent several hours.

Friday, February 19 Charley Gray took me to May (6:40 tr.) and I went to New Castle, saw W.A. Brown a few minutes, and went via Richmond home, arr. about noon. Slept some—read some.

Sunday, February 21 Heard Rev. Garland preach on Sabbath observance, Ex. 20.8. Congregation very small, it being somewhat rainy. I called at Lorin's a half hour.

Monday, February 22 I went on 8:43 tr. via Richmond, Economy & Muncie to Fowlerton. Dined at a restaurant. Went to the farm (R.W. White's) and to Levi Simons'. Went on 5:40 tr. to Fairmount & sup and lodge at Ellis Wright's. F.D. Updike, of C.J. Oil Co. called and talked to me. He had been to Dayton to see me.

Tuesday, February 23 I went on 8:10 In. U. car to Marion. Saw Att. Charles and we had conference with Att. Brownlee, and later some telephone communications with him. I went on 5:00 car to Fairmount. Sup & lodge at E.W.'s. Ellis has been indoors nearly a week.

Wednesday, February 24 I remained at Ellis Wright's all day. We had some telephone messages from ny attorney at Marion. I did only a little writing. Ellis was at the store a few hours in the afternoon.

Thursday, February 25 I remained at Ellis Wright's. I found Ellis is an Oddfellow. Att'y Charles telephoned me to come to Marion early. Brown M.D. called & left Ellis medicine.

Friday, February 26 I went on 6:10 car to Marion. Mr. Charles wrote up a form of contract and Att. Brown had an interview with us, and Mr. Charles went to Wabash. Later we had an interview with Updike & Brown. After an hour's warfare on terms of expiration of lease, we agreed signed new lease, released old one, dismissed suit. I went home, saw Sam Stover and Fred. Landis.

Saturday, Febuuary 27 Wrote some letters, went to town, deposited a check & bought a monoglass, which proved too weak. Slept nearly two hours. Lorin and Milton called in the evening.

Sunday, February 28 The day was gloomy and it drizzled rain and I remained at home all day. Lorin and Netta and their girls went to Lebanon, and their boys staid with us. I slept several hours.

Monday, February 29 I went on 5:40 tr. via Lima to Huntington, Ind., arr. at 11:25. Dined at restau. & went to Att'ys Spencer's & Watkins' offices. Dr. Dillon & I sup and lodge at S.A. Stemen's. We called W.H. Clay over.

Tuesday, March 1 I go to the College exercises at 8:00, & lead devotions and make a short address on Uprightness. I called at S.L. Livingston's & at Publ. Office, & then go on 11:47 tr. to Wabash and Marion. Pay St. John & Charles for services $50.00. Go on to Fowlerton. Sup & lodge at White's & get written lease with him on farm. Co. are drilling for oil.

Wednesday, March 2 I go to Fairmount on 7:40 tr. & to Wabash & thence to Huntington on 9:01 tr. Dine at restau. I was at Pub. Office a few min. Sup at Clay's, lodge at Livingston's. J.L. Buckwalter pr. at college at 7:00, Eph. 2.5, "Mind be in you." Good sermon, but wrong construction of the text, as is usual.

Thursday, March 3 Blustery day. I remain at L's till 4:00. I write to J.C. Coulson (Pa.) and home. I call at the office, and sup and lodge at H.C. Foate's. Children Heiley & Evelyn Debora.

Friday, March 4 I went to Publ. Office at 8:30. Dine at restau. with O.B. Bowman. I sup & lodge at S.L. Livingston's. His sons away. Stanley, Clifford and Chester. Daughters at home, Nellie & Edith.

Saturday, March 5 I went to Office and W. Dillon went to Delphos. I dine at Prof. Gragg's & remain till 4:00. I sup and lodge at S.A. Stemen's. His daughter, Mrs. Johnson of Andrews and two children are there.

Sunday, March 6 I preached at College Chapel at 10:30, Ps. 119.30, "I have chosen the way of truth." I dined at Prof. T.H. Gragg's and remain till nearly night. Rev. Han Shu & wife there. I sup & lodge at Livingston's. We converse on facts & documents.

Monday, March 7 I have quite a talk with L. on theological subjects. I call at Geigers & at F.H. Cremean's. Talk on Flyer. They have a son Lorin. I dined at Market St. restaurant. I called at Publish. Office. I go on 2:35 tr. to Lima & reach home at 8:35. I gave Clay check of $70.00, on loan to Com.

Tuesday, March 8 I sent telegram & letter to Clay concerning Keiter's second year's books, and Wilbur & I wrote later in the day. At home.

Wednesday, March 9 I am at home all day. I wrote to Reuchlin. I slept much. Katharine rides out to Harrisburg with Miss Wuichet and they walk back, twelve miles, as they come by Polk Church.

Thursday, March 10 At home. In afternoon get letter from Clay on some figures not understood. Wilbur and I answered.

Saturday, March 12 At home. Get letters from Clay and Dillon on Smith's examination of K's books. I wrote several letters.

Tuesday, March 15 Wilbur went on the 5:50 morning train via Lima to Huntington. I slept several hours as I had lain awake last might to awaken Wilbur.

Wednesday, March 16 At home. Sent off Yearbooks and pictures to the relatives. Wilbur got home at 9:00, eve.

Thursday, March 17 At home. Rev. W.H. Kindel visited me in the afternoon.

Sunday, March 20 I attend the First Baptist Church. The pastor, Rev. Howard P. Whiden pr. Acts, 26.19. Obedience to the Heavenly Vision. He is a small, delicate man, and a fine orator.

Monday, March 21 Weather fair. I was at home all day. James Manning, an old neighbor, from whom I bought my house, called for a friendly visit. Milton, Jr., called in the evening.

Wednesday, March 23 This is a beautiful warm sunshiny day. I called on Prof. Blumenschein in the afternoon to see him about music lessons for J.G. Wilberforce. I called at Lorin's in the evening.

Sunday, March 27 Lay down for a nap & slept too long to get to church. Milton dined with us and Leontine came an hour in the afternoon.

Tuesday, March 29 At home. Catharine (Van Cleve) McFadden died at her home, eight miles north of Dayton, at 7 o'clock this morning. She was my Mother's Cousin, a daughter of William Van Cleve.

Wednesday, March 30 At home. Agnes Osbo[r]n dined with us.

Thursday, March 31 At home. Wrote to Rev. J.S. Rock & to Wm Miller.

Friday, April 1 Went to Tippecanoe on the traction but could not across the river to get to Mrs. C. McFadden's funeral. She is my mother's cousin, a daughter of William Van Cleve. Her age was about 87 years.

Saturday, April 2 Went on 11:00 train (traction) to Crawford's. Wm. Eubanks met me & took me to his house. Quarterly Conf. after W.S. Strete had preached at 2:00. I sup at at [repeated in text] Daniel Woggoman's.

I pr. at 7:30 (at Olivet) Prov. 25.2. Lodge at Wm. Eubanks.

Sunday, April 3 At Sab. School at 9:30. An excellent speaking meeting followed. W.E. Strete pr. at 11:00, John 14.19. I assisted by Strete's request in the communion. I dine with many others at Geo. W. Warvel's. Strete pr. at 7:30. I lodge at Aaron Wysong's.

Monday, April 4 I came home on traction arriving at 9:00. I spent much of the day sleeping & resting.

Friday, April 8 At home. Call[e]d in the afternoon at Swank's and John Nicholas's.

Saturday, April 9 At home. Wrote several letters. In the evening I saw Albert Shearer who had been at Catharine McFadden's funeral, April 1st.

Sunday, April 10 I attended Third Street Presbyterian Church and heard Rev. Merle Anderson pr., Acts 17.11.

Tuesday, April 12 I went on the 8:43 tr. to Richmond and thence to Fowlerton, Ind. and to R.W. White's. The first oil well, recently struck, was being divested of salt watter [sic] & oil pumping began at 7:00 eve. I lodged at Oliver Buller's.

Wednesday, April 13 I Went on 6:40 tr. to Fairmount & thence to Marion. Paid my taxes. Came back to Fairmount, dine at Ellis'. Go to Fowlerton & sup & lodge at White's. The oil well is a good one, at present running 50 barrels a day.

Thursday, April 14 I go on the 6:40 tr. to Richmond. Call at Caroline Zeller's. Go on traction 11:00 car home arrive at 1:00. Primary election at 4–6 o'clock. Lorin went to Cleveland to-night.

Friday, April 15 At home all day. Call at Lorin's in the evening. Lorin had returned home.

Saturday, April 16 Wrote an article for the *Conservator,* stating the facts of the Controversy.

Sunday, April 17 I attended Third St. Pres. Church and heard Maurice E. Wilson preach, Rev. 21:13, a rather fanciful sermon. I had heard it at his own Church. I called at Lorin's in the afternoon.

Monday, April 18 Revised and rewrote my article, "The Real Issue."

Tuesday, April 19 I went to New Castle, Ind., via Arcanum and at the Court-house compromised my suit for damages, the defendant paying me $175.00 and Costs. Mr. Ben Koons was with me & very friendly. He lives near Moreland. David W. Kinsey Cashier of the Citizen's State Bank is also a friend.

Wednesday, April 20 I was at home all day. Wilbur went out to Sim[m]s to work on his flyer.

Thursday, April 21 I was at home all day. Leontine and Horace were with us all day. Both behaved very nicely.

Friday, April 22 I was at home all day. Received a letter from C.H. Kiracofe concerning an article in reply to the manifesto of the "Big Four" in the paper. I wrote to W. Miller & C.L. Wood, and sent each a copy of the editor's letter.

Saturday, April 23 I was at home. I received Wm. Dillon's article to read that the editor had declined to publish.

Sunday, April 24 I was very dull to-day, not very well and I remained at home. Lorin's children visited us. Lorin called in the afternoon. It rained a little in the forenoon and considerably in the afternoon.

Tuesday, April 26 I was at home. I received a letter and card from C.L. Wood about the discussion started in the late Conservators. The day was rainy.

Thursday, April 28 I was at home. I did less work than yeaterday. It was another damp day. I called at Lorin's in the evening.

Friday, April 29 I was at home. The boys went to Sim[m]s to work on their machine.

Saturday, April 30 I was at home. The boys again went to Sim[m]s. This is the seventy-third anniversary of the birth of my wife, Susan Catharine Koerner. She lived to

be 58 years old. Her father, John G. Koerner, lived to 86; her mother, Catharine Fry, to be 92 years old.

Sunday, May 1 At Main Street Lutheran Church heard Dr. Garland on Hebr. 6.7–12, this being the 5th anniversary of his pastorate. I heard G. Campbell Morgan, at Third St. German Lutheran Ch. on "What is a Christian man?", 2. "What he will do?", at 3:00. Lorin & Netta called in the evening.

Monday, May 2 I went on the 8:43 tr. via Richmond to Fowlerton. I had supper & lodging at R.W. White's. The second oil well is well on the way in drilling. Another derrick is up. White's oats are up. I trimmed my orchard.

Tuesday, May 3 I sold my corn, 60 cts per 100 lbs, $107.64. Dine early at Whites & go on 11:42 train to Fairmount & out to see Ed. Smith at Thomas Dyson's. Return on 3:05 tr. to Fowlerton & White's. W.R. Br. of W.M.A. met at Hopewell Ch. I lodge at Oliver Buller's.

Wednesday, May 4 I called at Wilson Simons, at Dick Nottingham's Stable & John Leach's, & Chas. Malone's. I opened the services at W.M.A. meeting. Dined at O.A. Glass's. Supper at White's. At the meeting in the evening. I pronounced the benediction at the close. Lodged at Ol. Buller's.

Thursday, May 5 I called at the oil well (which was drilled to sand at midnight) and went on 6:45 train via Richmond home.

Saturday, May 7 I was at home. Looked over many letters and special documents. Sent to R.W. White two copies of contract for building the house on my farm & two copies of sepcifications, signed.

Sunday, May 8 I heard Mr. Anderson, pastor pr. at Third Street Presbyterian Ch., Ex. 15:23, "Waters of Marah." I saw John H. Weller, Mr. Fred. Shrot's friend, there. Lorin's children came up in the evening.

Monday, May 9 I went on 5:40 m. train via Lima to Wren, Ohio. I see Mr. Drear, a traction promotor, on the cars, and Rev. T. Weyer. I dine with Weyer at Wm. Bowen's. We call in afternoon at Mr. Frysinger's, whose wife lay a corpse. Bp. Barkley came in eve. We lodge at Bowen's.

Tuesday, May 10 Weyer pr. the funeral at 10:00. The bishops met at 2:00 at the church. Barnaby & Floyd absent. We transacted business. We dine and lodge at Bowen's.

Wednesday, May 11 Bishop Floyd came at 7:15, but absent all forenoon tho invited, but present in aftern, but we adj. at his suggestion. In aftn. I call with Floyd an hour at J.K. Wagers, at 3:00. We board at Bowen's, who have no children.

Thursday, May 12 Bp. Barnaby came at 7:15, but did not meet with us. Floyd came to Church to ask us to go to J.K. Wagers for a talk, and to notify Barkley of a board meeting there. We declined to go from the Church. Barnaby & Floyd came to Church, but soon left. Mission board met at 2:00. Becker read protest.

Friday, May 13 Board meeting forenoon & afternoon, following printed program. I presided. Spread their protest on journal. D.P. Sherk dined with us and lodged last night. Miss Lena Winkle, just from Africa, present. Floyd pr. at 8:00.

Saturday, May 14 The Board met at 8:30, completed the program and made final adjournment at 11:00. I ate an early dinner, and went with Barkley and Montgomery by livery to Ohio City. Reach home via Lima at 8:35. Slept 7 1/2 hours.

Sunday, May 15 I hear M.E. Wilson (lst Pres.) at 10:30, John 21.9, not one of his best. Ivonette and Leontine dine with us.

Monday, May 16 I was at home. I went to town collected interest on loans, bought presents for Lorin's children, etc. I wrote many letters about the Board meetings of last week.

Tuesday, May 17–Friday, May 20 [W]riting on a reply to the four Trustees. At night I had a chill. . . . I took quinine to day, not feeling well.

Saturday, May 21 I called at Albert Sheraer's & talked with Edith who was alone.

Sunday, May 22 Heard Rev. Holmes Whitmore (Episcopal) on Matt. 9:37,38, on Theological Education. A fair discourse. The cars are running over the temporary Third Street bridge. The old bridge is partly torn down. Composed a sermon on the ministry.

Monday, May 23 It rained early in the morning. Went out to Sim[m]'s Station to see the brothers attempt to fly. Too little wind. Went and came with Lorin's. Encountered rain on our return.

Wednesday, May 25 This is Wednesday's record. At 2:30, we were at Huffman's farm at Simm's station to see an aeronautical flight, but a rain came up & hindered. Many were disappointed. I went and came with Lorin.

Thursday, May 26 Went at 9:00 car to Huffman farm at 2:00 Orvill[e] flew about 25 ft. I came home on 3:30 car. It rained soon after.

Friday, May 27 I was at home. Went to town in the forenoon. Wilbur and Orville went to work on their Flyer.

Saturday, May 28 Went at 8:30 on traction to Isaac Swartzel's. Came home. At 7:00, I sent off the reply of the three trustees to the four: "The Facts and the Records." Called at Lorin's.

Sunday, May 29 I went on 12:30 traction to I. Swartzel's to pr. his wife's funeral, expecting to start at 6:25 via Arcanum to Deer Creek, Ill., to pr. Rev. G.M. Freese' funeral. Went on 6:25 train, to Illinois.

Monday, May 30 I reached Bloomington, Ill., at 5:47, and Deer Creek at 9:40. Levi J. Freese took me to John Stumbaugh's and after din[n]er to Rev. G. M. Freese's. Rev. W.W. Knipple was there. We remained. Stumbaugh is a son [in?]law of Freese.

Tuesday, May 31 Funeral at 2:00. Text Acts 7:24. Many vehicles in the procession. We remain till morning.

Wednesday, June 1 Levi took me to Deer Creek and I go

on 7:40 tr. to Gibson City. Visit J.F. Croddy. Call in eve. at Mitchel's.

Thursday, June 2 Nan Croddy, John's wife, came from Fisher. I go on 4:04 tr. to Alexander. Lodge at Kent House, in Alexandria, Ind.

Friday, June 3 I go on 5:35 car to Fairmount. Breakfast at Ellis Wright's. Engage George Coons to paint my house there. Go on 9:20 tr. to Fowlerton. Call at White's. Dine at restaurant. Go on 1:10 tr. via Richmond home. Arri. at 5:30.

Sunday, June 5 Heard at Grace M.E. Church H.C. Jameson pr. on Immortality as an Incentive, Job 14:7–14. Lorin and family called in the evening.

Monday, June 6 Made out my assessment. Looked at various fronts with reference to my new store building at Fairmount. (I did not build it this year.)

Friday, June 10 I went on the 5:40 train via Lima to Huntington, Ind. Wm. Miller with me from Lima. We dine at Midway Restaurant. Publ. Board met at 2:00. Wood & I sup at Clay's. Oratorical exercises at 7:30. I lodge with Miller at Livingston's. Anna Rowenhorst there, Stanley's intended.

Saturday, June 11 Board meeting at 9:00. Wm. Miller and I dine at Midway. I hear Rev. W.H. Kindel at 7:30. I lodged at S.A. Stemen's.

Sunday, June 12 Rev. O.G. Alwood pr. baccalaureate at 10:30. Did well. I dined at Isaac Stemen's. Called with C.L. Wood at S.A. Stemen's. Sup there. W.H. Clay pr. at 7:30, "Whatsoever is pure." I lodge at Prof. T.H. Gragg's. (Allen M. Harris died in Richmond to day and his family phoned me to pr. funeral.)

Monday, June 13 Publ. Board met at 2:00. Adjourned finally. I sup at Clay's. Glee Club exercises at 8:00. I lodged at Prof. Gragg's.

Tuesday, June 14 Educational Board met at 9:00. I dined at Rev. F.H. Cremean's. I sup at O.B. Bowman's & also supped there with Wm. Dillon. Dr. Johnson of Los Angeles fried the beafstake. Inter-college exercises at 8:00.

I lodge at O.B. Bowman's. Dr. Moorehous & wife there.

Wednesday, June 15 At 8:00, saw Mr. M.L. Spencer on the Bealor note suit. Commencement exercises at 10:00. The two Allen's, Miss Romig & Miss Davis graduated as B.S. & Phillips as A.B. At Allumnal dinner. Go on 3:29 traction to Wabash & to Fairmount. Lodge at Ellis Wright's.

Thursday, June 16 I go on 9:20 tr. to Fowlerton. Dine at R.W. White's. I go on 1:10 tr to Richmond & reach home in Dayton at 5:15.

Saturday, June 18 Went out in the forenoon to J.J. Reeder's in Ohmer Park. Went in afternoon to Simm's Station. Went going on 6:30 car to Germantown; only John C. Wright (cousin Samuel's son) came & I remained at home.

Sunday, June 19 I went on 8:30 tr. to Germantown. I was at Sabbath School. I preached at 10:15, Dan. 4.25, "The Most High ruleth in the kingdom of men" etc. Dined at Jac. Slifer's, in town. Called at 3:00 at Sarah Eiseley's—several there. Supper at Slifer's. I pr. at 7:30, John 7.17. I lodge at J.Wesley Fout's.

Monday, June 20 I fail to reach 5:45 car; so I go on 6:45 car to Dayton. Arrive at 8:00. The boys make some experiments with their flying machine. Mrs. Hall sews for Katharine. I read Root's great speech in the evening, at Convention in Chicago.

Tuesday, June 21 I wrote letters. I got Floyd's letter proposing an armistice. I walked to town & back. Called at Lorin's in the evening.

Friday, June 24 Katharine started to St. Louis, to the Exposition, to spend a few weeks with Mrs. Margaret Meachem, her college room-mate.

Saturday, June 25 At home. I went in the afternoon to John J. Reeder's in Ohmer Park & wrote a letter for him to Hon. R.M. Nevin.

Sunday, June 26 I heard Rev. Maurice Wilson pr. his last sermon, before Sept., from John 11.44, "Loose him and let him go." It is a fine day—cool in the afternoon.

Lorin and all his family came in the evening.

Thursday, June 30 At home. Sent out several hundred of the Smith Report on Keiter's books.

Friday, July 1 At home. Prepared the manuscript for press on my "Conservator as a Peace Agent" pamphlet, and took it to the printer.

Saturday, July 2 I went at 9:50 (10:15) on the train to Miamisburg. Waited at the bridge an hour for traction car to Germantown. Dine at Jac. Slifer's. P. Elder (Strete) pr. at 2:00. Qr. Conf. peaceful. I sup at Kindel's with A. Zehring & wife. I pr. at 7:45, Ex. 28.34. I lodge at Jacob Slifer's.

Sunday, July 3 I attned S.S. at 9:00. Lovefeast followed. W.E. Strete pr. at 10:45. I introduced sacrament. Dine at Edwin M. Scott's. He married Sarah Eiselly, Wednesday. Mrs. Hulsizer, his sister, and the Sisters Scott there. W.E. Strete pr. at 7:45. I lodge at W.H. Kindel's.

Monday, July 4 I went on 5:45 car home arrived 7:15. I went to Woodland Cemetery and cut the grass on Susan's grave. Wrote letters to several of the pres. elders of my district, giving time of their annual Conferences.

Tuesday, July 5–Friday, July 8 At Home. Wrote many letters. The proof on my new tract came in the afternoon.

Saturday, July 9 At home. Wrote some letters. Received part of the edition of "Conservator as a Peace Agent," and mailed some in the evening.

Sunday, July 10 I heard Howard P. Whidden on "Be ambitious to be quiet," 1 Thes. 4.11 in which tho he strained the real meaning of the text, he preached an able discourse. He is a good extempore preacher, and a fine workman.

Monday, July 11–Friday, July 15 At home writing letters and mailing . . . tracts. Lorin's helped.

Saturday, July 16 Go on 8:43 train to Richmond & Fowlerton. Dine and sup at R.W. White's. See Levi Simons, & Oliver Buller. Levi takes me to Wm. Reeder's. I sup at Levi's & lodge at Reeder's.

Sunday, July 17 Called at Robert Reeder's more than an hour & went with his children to Church at Hopewell, in Fowlerton. I stop an hour in McConkle's house. Bro. Cole came. Pastor Bartlett had me preach at 11:00, Isa. 11:1–12. Dine at White's, lodge at Buller's.

Monday, July 18 I go to my oilwells, and see about arranging windows in my new house and go on 8:20 u. to Marion. I saw Mr. Charles & go to Fairmount. Dine at Ellis Wright's. Go via Gas City home. Engine broke near Trotwood & delayed us. Home about 8:00.

Tuesday, July 19 Wrote; mailed some tracts, slept a little.

Wednesday, July 20 Sent notices of time of Conferences to Indiana ministers. Milton directed some pamphlets on typewriter. I paid Young and also Funk.

Sunday, July 24 At home. Called at Lorin's in the evening.

Monday, July 25 At home writing letters. Katharine returned home from St. Louis at 6:00 p.m.

Wednesday, July 27 At home writing letters. Afternoon, Katharine wrote 39 letters notifying my preachers of the time of conferences. Lorin and Netta called in the evening.

Thursday, July 28 I went on 9:50 tr. to Lima, O., to sell my oil. Got home on 3:00 train.

Saturday, July 30 At home. Mr. Walker, son of the Pres. of the Commonwealth Jewel Company called and we had a talk. I orally agreed for the company to drill another well, if done soon. Wilbur and Orville completed the reconstruction of their Flying machine.

Sunday, July 31 Heard Rev. E.E. Baker pr. at First Lutheran Church, John 5:17. He was pastor there eleven years, is now of Oakland, Calif. Lorin's children visited us in the afternoon.

Monday, August 1 Getting ready to go to my conferences. The boys went out to Simm's, but found the weather unfavorable to their experiments.

Tuesday, August 2 I started at noon for Marengo, Ind., and made all connections nicely. I attended prayer-meeting. I lodged at Rev. J.M. Johnson's.

Wednesday, August 3 We go on 9:20 tr. to Velpen. John Lee's son took us out to Philip Davis's. Quarterly Conference at 2:00. We lodge at Phil. Davis's.

Thursday, August 4 An. Conference opened at 2:00. Five ministers besides myself, and one lay delegate were present at some time during the session of three day's. Johnson & I board at Joseph Colgate's, 1 1/4 mile from the church. Rev. J.T. Miller pr. at 8:00, 1 Cor. 13.13.

Friday, August 5 Conference continued. We board at Colgate's.

Saturday, August 6 Conference continued. I dine at Rev. Daniel Davis's. We supped at Mack Robinson's. J.M. Johnson pr. at 8:00, Dan. 2.44. We lodge at Colgate's.

Sunday, August 7 I preached at Cup Creek Church, 122 Ps. 1 v. We dine at Phil. Davis's. Mr. Slunders takes us to Velpen. We stay at Velpen Hotel kept by Mr. Geddes.

Monday, August 8 We start on the 4:10 tr. I breakfast at New Albany and reach Dayton at 2:20. Found all well.

Friday, August 12 At home. Rev. W.H. Kindel and R.S. Kindel called an hour. He says C.S. Johnson and D.W. Wogoman have come out on my side of the church controversy.

Saturday, August 13 Warm day, I was at home engaged as usual. Wilbur made two flights of 800 and 1304 feet respectively, & Orville one of 640 ft. The speed was 35 and 40 miles to the hour. They were made in Huffman's field at Sim[m]s Station, in the afternoon.

Sunday, August 14 I attended Riverdale U.B. Church and heard Bishop E.B. Kephart pr. 2 Pet. 1.16, a good sermon. It was at the Liberal conference.

Monday, August 15 Wrote letters and copied some let-

ters. The boys worked on their machine at Sim[m]'s.

Tuesday, August 16 I was getting ready to go to Rock River Conference. I went on 9:00, eve. train via Richmond & Logansport to Chicago. I slept 4 hours on the way.

Wednesday, August 17 I arrived in Chicago at 7:15 A.M. I breakfasted at Oxford Hotel. I went and got a clergy certificate of Western Passenger Association and went on C.B. & Q. tr. to Buda, Ill. Lunch at a Restaurant, and walk a mile to North Western Depot, and thence with Revs. Flarkarty & Waters on 7:05 tr. to Manlins. Young Plumley takes me to Greenville Ch. Wm. Beers pr. Lodge at Nicholas'.

Thursday, August 18 Rock River Conference opened at 9:00. By special resolutions Barnaby and Floyd's Appt. of Becker to hold the conferences wes condemned and I was recognized as the lawful bishop. Conference progressed well. I board at James Nicholas's, a half mile south Daughter is Mary. Miss Lillian Lewis boards there. J.J. Margilleth pr. at 8:00 well.

Friday, August 19 Conf. continued. We had much rain. Mrs. Gianetta Waters pr. at 8 o'clock, and we had quite a lively meeting.

Saturday, August 20 Conference continued. Wm. Beers & wife & Theron 0. Lewis dined with us. The stationing committee met at Nicholas' at 6:00. W.W. Oberheim pr. at 8:00. Missionary Subs. followed about $88.00.

Sunday, August 21 We had a good lovefeast. I pr. at 11:00, 1 Pet. 1.25. Coll. at $37. I dine, sup & lodge at Rev. J.W. Cortwright's, in the parsonage. No meeting at night on account of hard rain which began at 5:00.

Monday, August 22 Many came in at Cortright's. I dined at Sidney Barber's one-fourth mile south of the Church. I go across to Nicholas's and he takes me to R.A. Lathrop's in New Bedford, and I sup & lodge there. He is sick with bowel trouble.

Tuesday, August 23 I remain at Lathrop's till evening. Miss Carrie Daggett, night telephone operator, boards there. Bro. Cortright took me to his house where I lodge.

Wednesday, August 24 Rev. J.W. Cortright takes me over to Sheffield, and I go thence to LaSelle and to Elwin via Decatur. I sup & lodge at Rev. W.W. Knipple's. He reads me his communications with Kiracofe, extinguishing the latter.

Thursday, August 25 Knipple and I go on the 7:05 morn. tr. to Decatur. We called on Bro. B.F. Price, who is paralyzed. I got a $200 draft on the Nat. Bank of Decatur on First Nat. Bk of New York and railway guide & went on noon tr. to Faylorsville. Dined at John Dapperts and remained till morn. I got many letters and papers here.

Friday, August 26 John Dappert took us to Mound Chapel, 6 1/2 miles south, and E. Illinois Conf. opened at 9:00. Kimpple, Hamilton, and Davis & Dappert present. Business proceeded well. Home at Elmer A. Brooken's, Dappert's soninlaw. Sup at Ollie Chesterman's. Rev. W.M. Davis pr. 8:00, Heb. 2:3. Rec. letters forwarded by Wilbur & ans'd Floyd & Morrison.

Saturday, August 27 Conference finished business in the forenoon. I mailed a letter to Floyd and card to Morrison. D.W. Hamilton dined with us, also a Mr. Jones from Taylorsville. Rev. Ressler pr. at 8:00, Prov. 18:24, "show himself friendly." He formerly lived in this neighborhood.

Sunday, August 28 I pr. at 11 o'clock, Hebr. 11:10. Dine at Louis Henney's. I pr. at 8:00, 2 Tim. 3.16. I lodge as usual.

Monday, August 29 We walked over to Mr. Kretzingers and Rev. Resler took Knipple and me to John Dappert's in Taylorville. In afternoon, we with them, visit some of their relatives in the country. Return to Dappert's. Knipple had missed train, but now went on 9:25 train home.

Tuesday, August 30 I went on 9:29 tr. to Bloomington & on Wab. 10:35 tr. to Hannibal, Mo., and there wrote Wilbur. Reached Keokuk in the night and staid at the Hotel.

Wednesday, August 31 I went on 8:20 tr. to Douds, and

thence to Rev. Wm. Heger's (Free Methodists) where I was sick (bowels) in the afternoon, but rested and slept well at night.

Thursday, September 1 I staid at Heger's till afternoon, and had my conf. home there. Missouri Conference opened at 2:00, and we had a pleasant session. I supped at Mr. Hewit's 1/4 m. n.e., E.M. Beauchamp pr. at 7:30, Ps. 34.8, a good sermon. A good testimony Meeting followed. Lodged at Heger's. He is a Free Meth. preacher.

Friday, September 2 Scott Adamson took me to church. Pleasant session. Dined at Chas. Dyer's west 1/4 m. M.E. Garlock pr. well at 7:30, John 10.9. Peterson exhorted. I lodged at Heger's. It rained in the night. Those entertaining conf. are nearly all Free Meth. of a good & modified sort.

Saturday, September 3 Bro. Heger takes us to church. Conf. proceded well and closed at 5:00. I dine and sup at Dyers. Stationing Committee met at 1:00 at the outdoor stand. Rev. A.L. Williamson pr. at 7:35. It was a fair pleasant day. I boarded at Heger's, a very pleasant family.

Sunday, September 4 I pr. at 11:00 in the grove, Dan. 6.23. I also pr at 3:00, Hebr. 11:16. Dine with Heger's on the ground, sup at Dyer's. A very pleasant day. E.M. Beauchamp pr. at 8:00. I lodge at Heger's. I liked him and wife & children very much. He is a man of fine judg[e]ment.

Monday, September 5 Bro. Heger took me to Selma to the noon train, and I go via Eldon to Kansas City and lodged at New Albany Hotel, near Depot. I lunch at Eldon & Cameron Junction. I reach City at 9:15.

Tuesday, September 6 I went on 7:15 tr. to Edminister. Herbert meets me and I go in the buggy to Reuchlin's. We went in the afternoon to Turner's after Bertha. I lodge at Reuchlin's.

Wednesday, September 7 I staid at Reuchlin's till 4:35, and went via Meneger Junction to Leavenworth. I walked up to the United Brethren Church. On the way I lunched and called at New's. There was a Christian Endeavor entertainment at 8:00. Scott brought me many letters. I lodge at H.W. Coldron's.

Thursday, September 8 Kansas conference opened at 9:00, and progressed well. I home at Coldron's. His sons: Byron, Bert, etc. Daughters: Anna (at home), Jessie Jack, of Deming, New Mexico, and Mrs. Shelly, living in town.

Friday, September 9 The conference goes in forenoon to visit State's Prison. We have a session in the afternoon. Rev. D. Miller, Liberal P.E. was present. J.C. Hope was elected P.E. Stationing Committee met at 4:30 at the Ch. Rev. E. Atkinson pr. at 8:00 a good sermon, Mart. 6:10, "Thy kingdon come," etc.

Saturday, September 10 I got my laundery, bought a telescope (valise), sent letters, etc. Conference continued, and closed at 4:00. F.V. Smith pr. at 8:00. I board as usual at Coldron's. I found this a good home, and the family were very pleasant.

Sunday, September 11 I pr. at 11:00, Dan. 7:23. Sacrament followed. I called in afternoon at Reis's. Sunday School at 3:00. A. Ritchie sups with us. J.C. Hope pr. at 8:00.

Monday, September 12 I went on 7:50 tr. to Edminister, & to Reuchlin's. It rained at night and next morning.

Tuesday, September 13 I remained at Reuchlin's. I wrote some and slept some. Mr. McHaffey was there in the forenoon. He was a little groggy as well as quite an actor.

Wednesday , September 14 This was Helen's 15th birthday anniversary. I mailed letters. I went on 11:05 tr. to Manhattan, Belleville and Mankato, arr. 9:00. Lodge at the Hotel.

Thursday, September 15 I visited J.S. Rock. I go on belated train to Ezbon. Rev. J.D. Lamb meets me and takes me to Rev. Wm. L. Horton's, at whose house West Kansas Conference opened at 3:00. Rev. W.A. Perkins pr. at 8:00, at Ash Creek Sch-house.

Friday, September 16 Conference continued at Horton's house. Rev. D.M. Harvey, of Liberal Church & wife there. R. Goldsworth pr. at 8:00 at Sch. H. I home at Horton's.

Saturday, September 17 Conference at Ash Creek School House. W.A. Perkins was elected P.E. I dined at J.M. Pixler's, where I boarded in 1901. Conference closed at 4:00. F.W. Bertchinger pr. at 8:00.

Sunday, September 18 Testimony Meeting at 10:00. I pr. at 11:00, Luke 17.23, "Greater born of women." I dine and sup at Rev. J.D. Lamb's. I pr. at 7:30, Rev. 5:9, "Sung a new song." I lodged at Horton's as usual.

Monday, September 19 I went with W.A. Perkins to Lebanon, 12 miles, by 8:00. All trains were behind to-day. I went via Belleville and McFarland to Wichita. I lodged at Cousin Fanny Glenn's (Geo. M. Glenn's) on Campbell St. Mabel, 18, Georgie, 16; Ruth, Helen are their children.

Tuesday, September 20 Wrote letters in the forenoon. I went on 1:30 Frisco tr. to Fredonia. I sup and lodge at Rev. H.E. Smith's. Rev. H.E. Smith's. Rev. H.D. Tatman called. Rev. L.V. Harrell lodged with me.

Wednesday, September 21 I dined at Rev. H.D. Tatman's. I got my overcoat, sent by express. I sent my peace proposal to the editor. I sup & lodge at Smith's. Rev. L.V. Harrell pr. at 8:00, Acts 1.8.

Thursday, September 22 Neosho Conference opened at 9:00. I commented on John 13th Ch. Business proceeded well. I dined and supped at Tatman's. Rev. N.C. Pierce pr. at 8:00, Gen. 5.24, "Enoch walked with God" A good speaking meeting followed. I lodged at Smith's, my Conf. home.

Friday, September 23 Conference proceeded. I dined and supped at at [repeated in text] Tatman'.s Rev. A.A. York pr. at 7:45. A good speaking meeting followed.

Saturday, September 24 Conference proceeded well and closed before 5:00. Dined with Pierce at Rev. Barnett's Cumb. Presbyterian. P.N. Lambert pr. at 7:45. A good testimony meeting followed.

Sunday, September 25 I made a Sunday School address at 10:40. I pr. at 11:00, Dan. 6.28. Dined with Pierce & York at Mr. Maybee's. I pr. at 7:30, Rev. 5.12. Sacrament follows.

Monday, September 26 Tatman made a great fuss against Smith. I dined at Tatman's. Tatman made very little showing at the informal meeting held at the Church at 2:00, I sup & lodge at Smith's. L.V. Harrell pr. at 7:45, Matt. 6.10. Maybee & wife joined church.

Tuesday, September 27 I go at 2:45 on the early Frisco tr. & we leave at 3:15 for Springfield, Mo. Slept 4 or 5 hours. Wrote letters on the train. Reached Springfield at 3:00 p.m. I went to Rev. S.B. McGrew's, 625 Division St. Go to the post-office. About 40 at meeting. Hiram Brown pr.

Wednesday, September 28 I remained at McGrew's all day, my conf. home. I preached at the church, just opposite, at 8:00, Luke 10:37. About 45 present.

Thursday, September 29 Rev. J.B. Crom came, conf. having been announced locally to begin at 9:00, J.B. Crom conducted devotions. Session proper opened at 2:00 and proceeded well. Mrs. Eva. G. Dane and Geo. Burger arr. at 6:00 p.m. G.W. Masters pr. well at 7:45, Heb. 2:1–3. About 50 present.

Friday, September 30 Conference progressed well. I received a letter from Katharine. Rev. G.W. Hughey visited Conf.. We had a talk about the M.E. Gen. Conf. which he attended at Indianapolis in 1856. He pr. us a fine sermon at 7:45, 1 Cor. 1:23,24, 1 1/2 hours in length! Dined with us. 309 Walnut St.

Saturday, October 1 I wrote to Katharine. Got a bank draft for $100.00. Conf. closed at 4:00. I called at Sister Stickney's to see Geo. Burger. Mrs. Eva J. Dane pr. at 7:35, John 6.35. Bro. McGrew's had temporary care of Harley Fink, an illegitimate boy born at the poor-house.

Sunday, October 2 I preached at 11:00, Rev. 5.13. I dined at Eliza Jane Stickney's. Mrs. Philinda Allen of 1316 Grant St., and Geo. Burger there. Mr. Howard's, Mrs. Stickney's soninlaw, there. I sup at John Gabriel's. I pr. at 7:30, Titus 2.13,14. I had addressed the S.S. at 3:00. Board at McGrew's. Some 8 asked for prayers.

Monday, October 3 I dined at Bro. Harris's. I went to bank and to the Depot. Called at Allen's 1316 Grant St., an hour. Sup & lodge at McGrew's. I pr. at 7:30,

Acts 1.11. Several asked for prayers.

Tuesday, October 4 This is a warm day. I went to Frisco Depot and took the early (5:05) tr. to Wichita, and thence took the 5:00 train to Hutchinson and lodged at Cousin Elsina E. Arderey's, (Dr. Lorimer Arderey) 118 A. Street East.

Wednesday, October 5 It is quite cool. I go on 9:30 tr. to Stafford. Rev. J.H. Watson meets me, and I dine with him at Mr. Johnson's, ex-Rev. Gallagher took me to Robt. J. Clinkscale's, 1 1/4 m. north of Zion Church, my Conf. home. Children: Mary, 20, Bourke, 12. DeSelm work's there.

Thursday, October 6 I called at the parsonage (D.R. Sappenfield). Conf opened at 2:00. C.B. Sherk pr. at 8:00, 2 Tim. 1:12. I dine, sup & lodge at Clinkscale's.

Friday, October 7 Conference continued. I dine at Sappenfield's. C.B. Sherk pr. at 8:00, 1 John. [rest is blank]

Saturday, October 8 Conf. continued and closed at 5:00. I. Rollins pr. at 8:00, Zech. 8:23. The session has been very pleasant and harmonious. I dined at T.B. Deselms', two miles east.

Sunday, October 9 I pr. at 11:00, 2 Ki. 2.9, "Double portion of thy spirit." I dine at Joe Guyer's, 4 miles northwest. Her brother, Bombgardner there. Children: Wilbur, Gladys, etc. The Parents were students at Lane University. I pr. at 8:00, Rev. 7:14. Communion. I lodge at C's with Sherk and Rollins.

Monday, October 10 I remain at C's till afternoon, and C. took me to Stafford & I go on 3:15 train (Mo. Pac.) via Conway Springs & Wichita to St. Louis via Kan. City.

Tuesday, October 11 I arrive at Kan. City at 8:15, and go on 10:10 tr. to St. Louis. Saw some of the awful wreck near Warrensburg. I arrive at St. Louis at 7:15. I go on 18th St. to Wash. Ave. and lodge at Mrs. Mary A. Sargent's, 3131. This was my lodging place while attending the Lou. Pur. Exposition.

Wednesday, October 12 Lodging 50 cts, breakfast 25 cts. I went on Olive St. cars (two blocks east) to the Exposition. I spent most of the forenoon in "Varied Industries" Building, and afternoon visited "Machinery" and "Transportation" buildings. Lunch (15), and I sup with Meachem at the Alps. Go via Olive St & Compton Ave. home.

Thursday, October 13 I spent the forenoon in "Manufactures," "Forestry, Fish & Game," "East Indies," "Philippines", "Aeronautics," etc. Reached Sargent's at 7:25. Last night I attended pr. meeting at Pres. Church. cor. Conway & Wash. Pastor's comments were fanciful.

Friday, October 14 I took my baggage and checked it at Union Depot. I then went to the Exposition and visited "Electricity," "Liberal Arts," "Fine Arts" "Education," "Agriculture" & went to "Machinery." Saw Rev. Mr. Meachem. Went to Union Depot & at 11:35 started, on the Vandalia Line, home.

Saturday, October 15 We reached Indianapolis about 7:35, and home (Dayton) at 11:00. All from home except Marie the house-maid. Found and read many letters. Slept some. Emptied my valises, etc, etc.

Sunday, October 16 I remained at home and rested. My nearest neighbor, Wm. Webbert Wagner died about 7:00 in the evening. I had known him 33 years or more.

Monday, October 17 Rev. Mr. Myer of Fourth Pres. Church called to see about my taking some part in Mr. Wagner's funeral. His nephew, "Will" Wagner, called in the evening to give me some dates about his uncle.

Tuesday, October 18 I wrote up a memorial paper. The funeral occurred at the house (next door) at 2:30. Burial in Woodland. I read the Memorial paper at the funeral and made a few remarks, and went to the burial in Woodland Cemetery.

Friday, October 21 Went to town in forenoon. At home reading and writing. I got a telegram in the evening from Rev. Aaron Worth, saying that Sarah E. Worth, my cousin, died at 4:00 p.m.

Saturday, October 22 I go on 11:00 tr. via Union City and Ridgeville to Briant, Ind. I sup & lodge at Worth's. His sister & her son & daughter. "Cousin" Arelia was there, and Agnes' daughter came in the night.

Sunday, October 23 I wrote out a memorial paper. Funeral by Rev. Seekins of Fairmount. Pastor is Rev. Carter. Dine at Worth's. I pr. at 7:30, Rev. 5.13. Lodge at Worth's. Sarah was buried just west of town. I read the memorial paper at the funeral.

Monday, October 24 I went on 8:00 tr. via Ridgeville and Jonesboro to Fowlerton arr. at 3:00. I went to White's, and supped and lodged there.

Tuesday, October 25 I made a settlement with White. I dined at Oliver Glass's. I called in the afternoon at R.B. Reeder's. I went on 5:40 tr. to Fairmount. Supper and lodging at Ellis Wrights.

Wednesday, October 26 I went to Marion and paid my tax and went on 9:43 tr. via Delphos to Monticello, Ohio, to Auglaize Ministerial Institute. Lunched at Delphos. I sup and lodge at at [repeated in text] Conrad Wash. Sites, Wm. Dillon pr. at 7:30, Eph. 4:30, "Grieve not H. Sp,"etc.

Thursday, October 27 The Institute continued in the forenoon. I dine at Sites'. I went on 1:54 train home, arr. at Dayton at 5:30. The Institute, without discussion, unanimously adopted Wm. Dillon's resolution denouncing the fraud of casting 49 and even over 50 ballots for Pres. Elder when only 47 members were present.

Sunday, October 30 I heard Rev. Howard P. Whidden pr. at 11:00, Isai. 26.15, on the Lou. Pur. Exposition, a fine sermon. I called an hour at Lorin's.

Tuesday, November 1 Went out to the aeronautical grounds at Sim[m]'s Station. The boy's fail[e]d to get the Flyer well into the air.

Wednesday, November 2 Went again to Sim[m]'s. Wilbur made one flight of 3/4 mile.

Thursday, November 3 Went out to Sim[m]'s. Wilbur flew 3/4 of a mile and landed breaking the machine some.

Friday, November 4 Sent out many letters to the preachers on the election of delegates.

Saturday, November 5 Wrote letters, etc. Mary Peffers closed her week of house
keeping for us.

Sunday, November 6 I heard Rev. D. Frank Garland pr. from Judges 5:23, "Curse ye Meroz."

Tuesday, November 8 I voted for Ro[o]sevelt and Fairbanks, and went out on 11:00 car to Sim[m]'s Station. The boys made no flight. Went to Main Street and got the election bulletins. Roosevelt is overwhelmingly elected. This is Milton's birth-day anniversary, the twelfth.

Wednesday, November 9 The news is still more favorable to Roosevelt, 325–343 electoral votes & unprecedented pluralities. I go on 11:00 car to Sim[m]s. At 2:00, Wilbur flew three (Lacking one-fourth) miles in 5 minutes and four seconds. The distance was only limited by failure of engine.

Saturday, November 12 Went in the forenoon to John J. Reeder's in Ohmer Park. At home the rest of the day.

Sunday, November 13 I heard Rev. Maurice E. Wilson pr. Matt. 6.10, on Social duty—not apposite! Ivonette & Leontine came & spent the day. They behave so nicely.

Tuesday, November 15 Wrote letters in the morning. Went on 11 traction to Sim[m]'s. Wilbur at 4:00 made a two-mile flight. Orville had flown 1/2, 1/3 and 1/8 mile earlier. Reached home at 5:00.

Thursday, November 17 At home. This is my seventy-sixth birth-day anniversary. Mine thus far has been a highly favored and happy life. Bless the Lord, for His mercy endureth forever. I get ready to start for Canada to-morrow.

Friday, November 18 I left home on the 5: 35 a.m. train to Toledo. Go thence on 2:17 tr. to Buffalo, N.Y., arriving at 10:25 (11:25 E.T.), where I lodge at Arlington Hotel, 75 cts. This is Lorin's forty-second birth-day an-

niversary. He was born at my father's home in Fayette Co., Ind.

Saturday, November 19 I go on the 5:47a.m. Mich. Central train to Stevensville. I breakfast at Rev. J. Howe's. D.B. Sherk & I dine at Mrs. Aramantha Baker's. I sup & lodge at Rev. J. Howe's. Counsel with three of the five trustees & Sherk, Howe and Hendershot at 9:30, even'g.

Sunday, November 20 I preach at 10:30, Judges 5.1,2. We raise $334 and dedicate the "First Church of Stevensville" 26 X 40 ', concrete-block. I dine at Bro. Edward Spear's, in the country. Father and Mother Plato (Sister Spear's parents) also there I preached at 7:30, Rev. 7.13, 14 . I lodged at Rev. J. Howe's, in "parsonage."

Monday, November 21 I remained at Howe's till after 3:00, and he took me to Wm. Spear's to supper, and I preach at Garrison Road Church at 7:30, Dan. 6.23. I included too much for effect. We lodged at Mrs. Jacob Shisler's, not far from the Church. Her sons bought Texas lands.

Tuesday, November 22 We dined at Bro. Nathan Day's. We supped at Br. Merner Shupe's. I preached at Sherkston Church at 8:00, Matt. 16.17, on Expeimental Religion. We lodged at Isaac Sherk's.

Wednesday, November 23 I go on 7:50 tr. via Brantford, Harrisburg and Galt to to [repeated in text] Berlin, arr. at 1:00, Go to Rev. D.B. Sherk's, but dine and sup at W.H. Becker's, where I see his mother & sister Divit. Call at Rev. J.B. Bowman's. Attend pr. meeting. Saw Snyder, Deitwiler, Miss Musselman, etc. Lodge at Sherk's. Slept 10 hours!

Thursday, November 24 After Shopping, I dined at Rev. A.R. Springer's, the pastor's. At 3:20, Rev. Springer took me to Rev. S. Swart's for Supper in the country, and at 8:00, I pr. at Manheim, 1 Cor. 1:30, "Wisdom, righteousness", etc. I lodged with Springer at Samuel S. Herner's, a teacher & Q. Conf. Preacher.

Friday, November 25 We return to Berlin. I studied my address for evening. I dined at W.H. Hilborn's. I sup at

Moses Eshelman's. I gave an address at 8:30, (Gen. 50.20), on "Divine Providence & Missions." I lodged at Sherk's.

Saturday, November 26 I got and read many forwarded letters. Rev. S.H. Swarts took me to his house, where I dined. In the afternoon, he took me to Amos Hilborn's, in New Dundee, where I sup & lodge. His bro. Aaron & wife sup & lodge there.

Sunday, November 27 I pr. at N. Dundee at 10:30, Matt. 11.11, on John Baptist. I dine at Gotleib Betschen's, 1 1/2 ms. North. He took me to Berlin to Rev. J.B. Bowman's. I sup there. I pr. in Berlin at 7:00, Rev. 7.2,3. About 3 inches of snow fell last night & lay all day.

Monday, November 28 I leave Berlin at 11:00 (11:40). Part of the way there were 6 or 7 inches of snow. I lunch on the train and reach Port Huron at 3:45 (2:45 Western time). I reach Durand at 6:20, and Alma at 8:45, and visited Wood [?] and Rev. E.D. Root till 2:00 morning. Slept three hours. I lodged at Rev. C.L. Woods.

Tuesday, November 29 I left Alma at 7:29, reached Toledo at 12:55, took C.H.& D tr. at 2:15 (2:47) and reached Dayton at 6:05 (7:00) and found family well.

Wednesday, November 30 I was at home all day. Wrote letters. Slept an hour in the Aftn. I called at Lorin's an hour in the evening.

Thursday, December 1 At home all day. Wrote some letters. At Lorin's a half hour in the evening. I went to the Torrence Huffman's farm on 12:00 Car, and saw Orville at 4:00, fly two and 3/4 miles.

Friday, December 2 At home forenoon. I go to aeronautical, but owing to cold wind there was no attempt to fly.

Saturday, December 3 I was at home all day. Wrote letters. Nothing unusual occurred, except that Ida Whitehead, after four weeks service, left this afternoon. Her fault was whineing about the work and her ill health. She left voluntarily. She did good work.

Sunday, December 4 I, at First Baptist Church, heard

Rev. Howard P. Whidden preach, 2 Cor. 1.12, "On the Simple Life." He is a fine thinker and orator.

Monday, December 5 Went to Huffman farm, but saw no flying.

Tuesday, December 6 Went to Aeronautical grounds in the afternoon, but there were no flights. I wrote letters in the forenoon. In the evening I read the President's Message through in full. It is an able & unique document. Wrong on Woman's exclusion from bread-winning and revival of whipping-posts.

Wednesday, December 7 Again I went to "Aeronauts." No flight. We are using the back stairway put in yesterday by the carpenters.

Thursday, December 8 I remained at home all day. The carpenters are still tearing up the house to put on two additional rooms. I get a letter from my farmer, saying that the oil company is pumping my third oil well.

Friday, December 9 I went at 1:00 to Sim[m]'s. It was a damp—windy day. The boys failed to get off in any flight. I got home on 6:00 car. It began to snow at nightfall. The Aeronautical ground is a very level field of eighty-seven acres, on Torrence Huffman's farm.

Saturday, December 10 I was at home all day. I got several letters bearing on the election of delegates, and one from Barkley. I write several answers. There were several inches of snow.

Sunday, December 11 I remained at home all day. Lorin, with Horace, called an hour in the afternoon. Horace is very stout, and promising every way. Milton came about 4:00 and remained till night. He is of good size, good-looking, and well-informed.

Monday, December 12 Mrs. Louise Murray came this morning to do our house-work. I wrote letters to-day. Lathers are busy on our house, and clutter up everything.

Tuesday, December 13 The plasterers are plastering our new upper rooms. I write letters. John Wright came in the evening. He lives in Pittsburgh, Pa. He copied a part of the Wright Genealogy, reaching back to John Wright of Kelvedon, in Essex County, Eng., as early as A.D. 1500.

Wednesday, December 14 I wrote letters and a number of full cards. Plasterers still at work. John Wright in the evening continued to copy the Wright genealogy, and completed it.

Saturday, December 17 I went to town at 9:15 & on the 10:00 car to Germantown arr. at 11:30. Dined at J. Wesley Fouts'. Rev. C.S. Johnson, P.E., pr. at 2:00, Mark 11:22, I sup at Kindel's with many others. Ja. pr. at 7:00, Eph. 5:14. I lodge at J.W. Fout's. It snowed this morning.

Sunday, December 18 At Sab. School at 9:00, & I taught the whole School. A precious testimony meeting followed. Elder Johnson pr. at 11:00, John 19:19. I introduced the sacrament. We dine at Isaac Swartzel's two ms. in country, with Johnson, Kindel's etc. I pr. at 7:00, Rev. 7.3. I lodge at Edwin M. Scott's, in Lizzie Long's house.

Monday, December 19 I go on 6:00 car to Dayton arri. at 7:20. Read letters, slept 2 hours, Mr. A.J. Root came at 4:30. He read his articles for his bee Journal. He went on 8:00 car to Springfield. Mr. Root seems to be a fine old gentleman. He lives in Medina, Ohio.

Tuesday, December 20 I was at home reading and writing. I went to town this afternoon and bought Helen a red mohair dress and Bertha an oil cloth blackboard.

Wednesday, December 21 I was at home all day. I received a letter from Bishop H.L. Barkley and sent him a long answer. I answered a letter from W.H. Willoughby. We sent a Christmas box to Reuchlin.

Thursday, December 22 I wrote a long letter to Lucinda (Wright). I sent for a clergy certificate to Cen. Pass. Association.

Friday, December 23 I wrote a long letter to Emma Zeller Dennis. It is a rainy day. I wrote cards to Wood and Barkley. I read considerable in the weeklies.

Saturday, December 24 At home. I wrote a letter to S. Kearn and one to W.H. Clay. A little rain to-day.

Sunday, December 25 At 10:30, heard at Grace M.E. Rev. H.C. Jameson pr, Luke 1.10,11, a sermon of extraordinary excellence. Lorin's family dined with us. The children were sweet as can be. A little rainy especially at night. I read much.

Monday, December 26 I wrote to A.F. Stoltz, W.W. Knipple and A.X. Harrison. It rained to-day to fill a great need. I read considerably in "The Strenuous Life," by Theo. Roosevelt.

Tuesday, December 27 This is a warm winter day. But it turned cold in the evening. I wrote letters and many cards. I got not a letter. This is the sixty-first anniversary of the marriage of my brother Harvey Wright, and Delila, (Stephens)—both alive and well, to their great age.

Wednesday, December 28 It is a cold raw day. I write some letters and many postals. I got a letter from Emma Z. Den[n]is, saying that Prof. had a set back on stomach trouble about two weeks ago.

Thursday, December 29 I had thought of going to Grant Co., Ind., to-day, but decided to post-pone. I received my Clergy Certificate on Cent. Pass. Asso. this morning, No. 5793. It proves a most beautiful and moderate day.

Friday, December 30 The weather is mild and delightful. I write some letters. Nothing of very special interest occurs.

Saturday, December 31 A delightful day. I wrote a letter to Mrs. Mary Wyatt, Philomath, Oregon, an old pupil of mine in 1858! I finished reading through Roosevelt's "Strenuous Life." The first two-thirds is not only able, but very interesting. The addresses in the last part have much repetition. I sat up till an hour of 1905 had come in. The year came in with bells, whistles and guns.

1905

Sunday, January 1 I sat up last night till 1:30, so I staid at home all day. I read and slept. Lorin and Netta were with us an hour in the evening. Port Arthur fell to-day.

Monday, January 2 Leontine with us all day, a package of amiability, and tact. Turkey dinner. Mrs. Murray, after quinsy for a week, resumes work. I retrace my diary of 1857, where such was needed.

Tuesday, January 3 I retraced, in part, my diary of 1859. Horace was with us 4 hours; ate turkey; much interested by Orville and Wilbur. Wilbur saw Hon. Robt. Nevin, in evening. Milton spent the evening with us.

Wednesday, January 4 News of Stoessel's surrender continues to come. Write Reuchlin much gossip & get his letter. Walked to town & bought Diary & slippers. Called on Albert Shearer, at his store. His father's cancer is cured.

Thursday, January 5 I went on 9:00 tr. to Richmond & thence on 11:10 train to Anderson. Buy Myrl Wright a nun veiling dress & Ancil performing clowns, "Humpty Dumpty." Reach Fairmount at 3:00 & sup & lodge at Ellis Wright's. Called in eve at Oliver Buller's, hour.

Friday, January 6 I went on 9:05 tr. to Fowlerton & farm. Look at oil wells, Hay, and power-house. See C.E. Wommer, the pumper. Dine, sup & lodge at White's. At Hopewell, W.L. Crom pr. at 7:00, Luke 10:42. Some seekers. Oliver Glass sought prayers to-day.

Saturday, January 7 Went on 7:00 tr. to Richmond & on traction parlor car to Dayton, arri. at 11:15. I read

letters and wrote some. I slept an hour. (Rev. D.W. Hamilton died to-day.)

Sunday, January 8 I remained at home all day except a call in the forenoon at Lorin's. Milton called in the afternoon and staid to supper.

Monday, January 9 At home all day. Get news of the election of Huber, Coulson & Seiple, in Pennsylvania. Write some letters. It snowed some in the night.

Tuesday, January 10 At home all day. Letter from J. Gouser says that A.H. Roach is elected delegate to Gen. Conf. by nearly double the vote that H.J. Becker received. Postal from Knipple says D.W. Hamilton died at 5:45, the 7th. Katharine Louise d. 1892.

Wednesday, January 11 Alas, that Hamilton should die! I remained at home. Wrote some letters and read considerably. The weather is thawing.

Thursday, January 12 It is thawing weather. I am at home all day. I mail letters to H.E. Drew, C.W. Watkins, Chas. M. Perry, etc. Orville has a chill—perhaps grip. (Lorin was married in 1892.)

Friday, January 13 I was at home all day. Orville is better. I called at Lorin's. Ivonette has been sick with tonsilitis. Horace shows me the pictures in Ivonette's book. I wrote to O.G. Alwood and others. Moderately cold, sleight snow.

Saturday, January 14 At home. Steady cold weather. Read some; wrote some letters. Letter from C.W.

Watkins indicating the putting off of the Bealor Note case till after Gen. Conference. Orville is about well; Wilbur, unwell.

Sunday, January 15 Called at Lorin's a half hour. Heard Dr. Garland preach at 10:30, 1 John 4:16, "God is love," a fine sermon. I slept in the afternoon, having risen very early in the morning. Quite a cold day.

Monday, January 16 It thaws a little. I make a general adjustment of my drawers, in desks. Wrote to cousin M.E. Johnson, Waveland, Ind. Wilbur and Orville are both better.

Tuesday, January 17 It thaws some to-day. Letter from Wm. Miller saying that he and Wm. Dillon & S.L. Livingston are certified as delegates to Gen. Conference. Wrote some letters and many postals.

Wednesday, January 18 Moderate weather. I received a copy of our Year Book and a card from D.B. Sherk, telling the result there on delegates. Wrote let[t]ers and many cards. Katharine is kept home by grip.

Thursday, January 19 It is thawing, foggy weather. I am at home. I learn from Clay that H.E. Smith is the delegate from Neosho. Write Clay. Write a half dozen full cards. Lorin & Netta call to see Katharine who is right sick with a cold or grip.

Friday, January 20 Damp weather with some thawing. Katharine is better of the grip. I did not do much to-day.

Saturday, January 21 It is cloudy and a little foggy. Mildly thawing in the evening, after very little snowfall. Looked over many letters. Sent 50 cts for *Tribune* for six months. Katharine still in bed. Dr. Spitler came, about 5:00.

Sunday, January 22 Owing to wakefulness last night, I did not attend church to-day. Katharine sat up most of the day. Lorin's little girls dined with us to-day. It is a steady cold day. I slept to make up for loss. (Semi-revolution in St. Petersburg.)

Monday, January 23 At Home. Went to town to bank & sent Money-order for "North Am. Review." News

comes of the St. Petersburg Masacre. Sent brief answer to Morrison's registered letter.

Tuesday, January 24 At home all day. Spent some hours looking over old papers. Arranged books and papers. Katharine about, but not in school. Horace has tonsilitis.

Wednesday, January 25 Ther. 9 degrees above zero at 7 a.m. Evening very cold. I wrote several letters. Leontine and Horace are better. Katharine went to her school.

Thursday, January 26 At 8:40, Ther. 9 degrees above. Lorin's children are better. Got a letter from Reuchlin and answered it; also from Mrs. J.L. Dane South Harwich, Mass. Lorin & Netta called in the evening.

Friday, January 27 Mild, fair day. I get a small valise ($5.00) & spend an hour in Library, before noon. The paper-hanger's are at work to-day, and the plumbers on the bath-room. Katharine in School.

Saturday, January 28 I was unwell to-day, remained indoor, did nothing; took 20 gr. of quinine last night and to-day. It is probably grip.

Sunday, January 29 I felt that I must confine myself to my room to-day. But I was up nearly all day. Leontine was with us to dinner.

Monday, January 30 I was at home all day. Spent considerable time in looking over my earlier diaries, and recording part of 1877, which I had in blank book leaves. Dr. Wm. Dillon dined with us to-day.

Tuesday, January 31 I was at home. While better, I am not entirely recovered from the mild attack of grip. Netta and Leontine called. I took 16 gr. of quinine. Sat up till 12:30. Slept six hours.

Sunday, February 5 Lorin's children all dined with us. It was a cold and somewhat snowy day.

Monday, February 6 At home. Rose at 4:00. Looked over my Diary of 1898. I read considerably, especially Lincoln Steffen's article in McClure, on "Rhode Island; a State for Sale." I sit up late, running over my Diary of 1887.

Tuesday, February 7 At home. John Job Reeder, of Omer Park suburb, died at 10:30, this morning, & they telephone me. I go there afternoon.

Wednesday, February 8 I was at home, and spent the forenoon in preparing a memorial of John Job Reeder. Sat up very late. Slept but 3 1/2 hours. New rooms were finished (about) to-day.

Thursday, February 9 Got ready for the funeral. At 1:00, I read a memorial paper & preached the funeral of John J. Reeder, in Ohmer Park, text, Ps. 116:15, "Precious—death—saints." Occupied 25 min in all. Burial at Mt. Zion Reform Church, 5 m. south-east. Supper at Reeder's. Rev. Shults assisted in funeral.

Friday, February 10 Went to town in forenoon. Had a new roller put on my type-writer in the afternoon, $1.50. Wrote letters to Bishops Barnaby, Floyd & Barkley, about Revision Committee.

Saturday, February 11 At home. Caught up with sleep. Wrote to A. Earl Wright, J.A. Ferguson, and Wm. Beers, besides postals to W.W. Knipple and others.

Sunday, February 12 Went on traction to Germantown. W.H. Kindel pr. at 10:00, John 4.6, "Jacob's well was there"— no text. I dined at J.W. Fout's, with Kindels & Flinchbach's. Sup & lodge at Jacob Slifer's. I pr. at 7, Ps. 2:12, "Blessed trust thee." Temperature, 6 below at 7:00.

Monday, February 13 I go on 7 1/2 car to Dayton. Several letters await me. I answer inquiries about our majority in General conference, from J. Freeman and J.C. Hope.

Tuesday, February 14 I remain at home. Wrote D.B. Sherk. Did not do much. Rec'd letter from H.C. Foote & $45.00 on the loan to Smith committee. Learn of Keiterman's plans somewhat. Warmer in evening.

Wednesday, February 15 Nothing of special interest. It is warmer than yesterday. I wrote but two letters. Orville and Wilbur's rooms are papered yesterday and to-day.

Thursday, February 16 Wilbur has stomache trouble to-day. Nothing unusual occurs. This is a moderate day.

Friday, February 17 Wilbur still unwell. At home as usual. It thaws considerably to-day, but still leaves the sidewalks icy.

Saturday, February 18 A fair, mild day like yesterday. Wrote many letters and cards. Miss Wuichette visited Katharine in the afternoon. Sat up till midnight, looking over diaries of 1880 & 1881.

Sunday, February 19 Thaws considerably. At First Christian (Campbellite) Church of West Side, I heard a soldier Perry on Job 14.14. Lorin's children were all with us afternoon, and he and Netta in the evening. They are so lovely.

Monday, February 20 At home. Luese away. I write for *Cynosure,* and add personal note; also wrote J.P. Stoddard, and Semele Short. Weather is thawing, taking off the ice of several weeks.

Tuesday, February 21 Spent the day in reading and restoring my diary of 1881. To me it was a busy and interesting year. I wrote C.A. Blanchard and some other letters and postals. The thaw continues.

Wednesday, February 22 Washington's Birth Day. Ro[o]sevelt's address in Phila. Franklin Masters, our neighbor, is buried to-day, age 81 years. Postal from C.L. Wood, and I wrote him at length. Still Thawing.

Thursday, February 23 The thaw proceeds slowly. I get news of the Condoner's councils in Huntington, and their plans. Write Wood, D.B. Sherk & Barkley.

Friday, February 24 Still Thawing slowly. Did little to-day. I wrote to Pres. McMurray, assuring him of my favor for college president, and saying that one should not be discarded for a single error.

Saturday, February 25 At home. Thawing, but turns cool toward night. Sent out many letters and cards.

Sunday, February 26 Called in at Grace M.E. Sunday Sch. Heard M. Wilson pr. at First Pres. Ch. at 11, John 20:19, Omnipresence of Christ. Construction of text fanciful & treatment like wise. Ivonette & Horace with us.

Monday, February 27 At home all day. Thaws again. I wrote many postals. To-day about two inches of snow that fell last night melted.

Tuesday, February 28 Thawing slowly. Fair day. Received Barnaby's letter from Chambersburg refusing any part with me in preparing for or organizing Gen. Conference. Wrote a few letters.

Wednesday, March 1 At home. Mild days continue. The plans of the condoners continue to reveal themselves. The condoner's of Keiter's embezzlement is referred to above.

Thursday, March 2 I am at home, except two hours in the afternoon at Mrs. Agnes Swank's and John Nicholson's. Informing letters continue to come in. The day was mild and fair.

Friday, March 3 At home. A mild day without rain. I wrote letters. I visited the marble works and looked at monuments for Pres. Shuck. Engaged a granite marker for Susan's grave, a head-stone.

Saturday, March 4 Started via Richmond to Fowlerton, Ind. on 8:40 tr. Arrive after 1:00. See my fifth oil well shot about 3:00. Sup & lodge at Robt. Wilson White's on the farm.

Sunday, March 5 Walk to Wm. H.H. Reeder's. Robert B. Reeder & family came and spent the day with us. I supped and lodged at Flora & Oliver Glass's.

Monday, March 6 I went to the farm. I sold my haystack for $20.00 cash to White. I went on 11:38 tr. to Fairmount. I spent the afternoon & night at Ellis Wright's.

Tuesday, March 7 I went on 8:00 traction car to Marion. I paid $95.94 tax on my farm. I consulted Mr. Charles (St. John & Charles). I then went to Anderson & dined at John Wilson Broyles', Lizzie my cousin. At 4:00, I went to Fairmount. I supped at E. Wright's; lodge 0. Buller's.

Wednesday, March 8 I went to Marion on 7:00 car. I got $80.00 from Columbia & Pittsb. Co. for right of way

on east line of farm. Paid $28.03 tax on town lot. Charles charged nothing. Dined at Ellis Wright's. Went to Fowlerton. Sup & lodge at White's. Oil well pumped to-day.

Thursday, March 9 I started on 7:00 train to Muncie. Called at the Kirby House. Saw G.W. Bartlett, receiver of C.I.& E. Ry.[?] Wrote several letters. Lunched at Restaurant. Went on to May's. Gusta (McKey) took me to Alma Fry's & to Harvey Wright's.

Friday, March 10 I called at Saml. Kirkpartick's, & M. Thomas's in the forenoon & at Sena Wright's & Thos. Wright's in the evening. Effie Kirkpatrick & her sisterinlaw & Gusta (Mc) dined with us & Frances Rhoads & Emma Frazier & Grace came afternoon.

Saturday, March 11 Quarterly Meeting at Olivet. I did not attend. Charles Gray took me to May's & I called 15 minutes at Clara Benner's. Went to Dunreith & on traction & thence to Richmond. Called 30 min. at C.E. Zeller's. Got home at 11:00 A.M. Saw Milton Wright Osborn of Mays on car.

Sunday, March 12 Went on 8:00 car to Crawford's. Walked thence to Olivet Church. Testimony at 10:00. Johnson preached at 11:00, Rom. 10.4, "Christ—end of the law," Dine at Isaac Martin's, a.m. n.-w. Call at Wm. Eubanks. C.S. Johnson pr. at 7:00, Heb. 2:1,2,3. I stay at Geo. W. Warvel's.

Monday, March 13 Went at 8:10 with Rev. W.H. Kindel to Crafford's & miss car. Wait at Johnsville an hour. Arrive at home at 10:00. Write to S.A. Stemen, A.K. Harrison, & B.G. Huber. It was a very fair day.

Tuesday, March 14 At home all day. Rev. Wm. Dillon dined with us. He is to have his left eye operated on to-morrow morning at 8:00, to remove a cataract.

Wednesday, March 15 Wrote some letters in the forenoon. Put some checks and money in the bank in afternoon. Wrote Wood and Clay in afternoon and evening in regard to Barnaby's article forthcoming. What mendacity he exhibits! Alas, the fine gold.

Thursday, March 16 Mrs. Dillon telephones of the op-

Milton Wright, ca. 1900

eration yeaterday on Dr. Wm. Dillon for a cataract in his left eye. Rev. W.H. Kindle dined with us. This is a beautiful spring day.

Friday, March 17 At home all day. Wrote some letters. I received another letter from R.A. Morrison. What cheek he has!

Sunday, March 19 Heard H.P. Whidden, at 10:40 Rev. 2.10, "Be thou faithful," a fine sermon. Ivonette with us. Lorin and Netta called aftn. Heard Rev. D.L. Myers at 7 1/2, Jer. 18.4, "Marred in hands— potter." A good discourse.

Monday, March 20 I was at home all day. I spent the evening in revising a circular letter to delegates on Barnaby's Article. A man began digging for our new cistern.

Tuesday, March 21 Wrote Wm. Miller and B.G. Huber early. Wrote copies of circular letter. Went at 2:00 to see Dr. William Dillon at Miami Valley Hospital. The weather has been mild since I last noted it.

Wednesday, March 22 I was at home. I wrote out circular letters. I learn of another article Bishop Barnaby is putting into the Conservator. Manning's old house is being removed.

Friday, March 24 It is a fair mild day. Our new cistern is finished. I sent out several circular letters to delegates.

Sunday, March 26 Heard Rev. D. Frank Garland pr., Ruth 2.12. After this, the ground for the new church was discussed by the Congregation. Referred to Committee of fifteen. Milton & Horace with us all the afternoon.

Tuesday, March 28 Writing. Went out to the cemetery in the afternoon. Woodland to see the headstone at Susan's grave. Cost $25.00. The weather is fair and warm. Kath. goes to Agnes Osborn's & lodges.

Wednesday, March 29 Wilbur & Orville go out to the Huffman farm. Katharine rides out with Miss Wuichet. It is a very fine day.

Thursday, March 30 This is another most beautiful day. Katharine rode out again with Miss Wuichet.

Saturday, April 1 This is another delightful day. I was employed as usual. The primary (nominating) election was in the afternoon. I wrote some letters.

Sunday, April 2 I heard Rev. H.C. Jameson pr. a very eloquent sermon, "All things are yours," 1 Cor. 3.21. Milton was with us to dinner.

Monday, April 3 There was a little rain this morning. Fire is hardly needed. The grass is green and growing, & the maple leaves are starting. I was at home all day.

Wednesday, April 5 This is another very beautiful day. I spend the day largely in anotations on Barnaby's article of March 22nd, I also wrote some what lengthily to Bishop Barkley. Rev. W.W. Knipple came at 7 p.m.

Thursday, April 6 Rode over to east side with Rev. Knipple in forenoon and to Soldier's Home in afternoon. Knipple leaves at 6:00. Parkhurst's visit.

Friday, April 7 To-day, early, has almost slight rain, and in afternoon a little snow, very little. I called at Lorin's an hour in the evening.

Sunday, April 9 The day was beautiful. Ther. about 75 degrees. I heard Waync B. Wheeler on the Anti-Saloon. I gave $6.00. The meeting was at the First Lutheran Ch. Ivonette dined with us .

Tuesday, April 11 It was mostly a cloudy day. Nothing unusual occurred. I got my type-writer paper at U.B. Establishment 1500 sheets at $2.25. Called at Lorin's in the evening .

Friday, April 14 At home. The boys and I had considerable discussion as to preparation for Gen. Conference. Received Oler's impudent letter to-day.

Saturday, April 15 It is a pleasant day. I received letters from S.A. Stemen, Bishop Barkley, and J.A. Burkholder. I wrote some letters.

Sunday, April 16 A very little snow fell in the night. At

8:00, the ther. stood 34 degrees. Mrs. Louise Murray went home, not notifying us that she did not intend to return.

Tuesday, April 18 I was at home. The weather was very nice. Mrs. L. Murray came after her clothes. She had telephoned that we should look for other house help.

Thursday, April 20 Went to bank. Bought two shirts. It is a fine day after rain in the morning.

Friday, April 21 It is a fine day. I am at home engaged in gathering up documents for General Conference.

Tuesday, April 25 At home looking over documents. The day was cloudy, but the temperature was such as to not need a fire. Get ready to go away.

Wednesday, April 26 Went on 5:35 tr. to Lima and on 11:35 tr to Huntington. Walk to S.A. Stemen's; sup & lodge there. Several come in at 8:00 for consultation.

Thursday, April 27 I go to Watkins office. Dine at H.C. Foote's with Barkley, Wood and Clay. Publ. Board meets at 2:00. Expert Swain's report. D.T. Sutton's note read. Hatfield brings in a surprise bill. Sup & lodge at Foote's.

Friday, April 28 Board met at 8:00. Worry over Hatfield's bill. Dine at H.C. Foote's. Sup & lodge at F.H. Gragg's. J.M. Hatfield brought in a bill for work done on the suit for a rehearing, which the majority of the board did not acknowledge.

Saturday, April 29 Fred. Clay takes me to 6:25 traction, and I go to Wabash and Marion, Union City, home. Paid tax on New Duling Ditch. Call at Lorin's at 7:30.

Sunday, April 30 Heard D. Frank Garland at 10:30, Matt. 22.39, "Love thy neighbor as self."

Monday, May 1 Wrote many letters to delegates to accompany Wilbur's new tract. It is nice weather.

Tuesday, May 2 Still wrote letters. Wilbur's tract came in the afternoon and I mailed letters with the tract to many delegates.

Wednesday, May 3 I was engaged in looking up papers that I might need at Gen. Conference. In the evening, Lorin looked up the figures on my Legal Fund book.

Thursday, May 4 Bishop H.L. Barkley came about 6:00 in the morning to consult on an agreement with the other two bishops. Went at 9. I made out my legal fund report.

Sunday, May 7 I hear Rev. H.J. Jameson at 10:30, on 2 Cor. 4:4, "Glorious gospel." Lorin's children visited us. I wrote the Bishop's Address in the afternoon and evening.

Monday, May 8 I am Getting ready to go to Caledonia, Michigan. I start at 2:30, via Lima and Ft. Wayne. I lodge at Rich. Hotel, 75 cts for lodging & breakfast.

Tuesday, May 9 I go on 8:50 train to Grand Rapids, Michigan. Arrive at Caledonia at 5:30. C.B. Sherk takes me to his bro. Amos's, and I lodge there. Mission Board meets at 7:30.

Wednesday, May 10 Mission Board meeting continued. It closed about 3:30, afternoon. Bp. H.L. Barkley, D.B. Sherk and I go to C.F. Parker's, 3/4 m. E. of Gaines Church.

Thursday, May 11 Peace convention at Church a fiasco. Consultation at Mrs. Hannah Bowman's (and C.F. Parker's) at 8:00. Gen. Conference was opened by Bishop Barkley at 2:00. I am recognized as a legal bishop. Dr. W.H. Clay pr. at 7:30.

Friday, May 12 Mis. Sec's report. Referred back to him. Bp. Barnaby presided. Publ. Board meeting at H.T. Barnaby's. He and Floyd scrap much. D.H. Shelly preached.

Saturday, May 13 Gen. Conference continues. Bishop Floyd presided. In afternoon, resolutions on White River were referred to a special committee. Quite a debate on them.

Sunday, May 14 Bishop H. Floyd pr. at 11:00, at Gaines. Rev. B.G. Huber pr. at 7:30, a fine sermon.

Monday, May 15 Morrison offers the McMurray peace plan. Tabled by 31 to 16, we offered our plan to Committee to go up on appeal, and not impeach White River. Becker failed to steal Roach's seat by 14 to 31. Barkley presided.

Tuesday, May 16 Bp. Barkley presided on Wednesday, C.L. Wood was elected bishop by 32 votes; Firman L. Hoskins by 29; O.G. Alwood by 28; H.L. Barkley was reelected Coast bishop by 47 votes; Foote, publisher, Clay, Editor, Howe, Mission Secretary.

Wednesday, May 17 The election of Gen. Officers began at 2:30. Bishops: Wood, 32; Hoskins, 29; Alwood, 28; Barkley (Coast), 47; Clay, Editor, 30; Foote, pub. Agt., 32. J. Howe, Mis. Sec., 28 to Morrison, 13; T.K. Gragg, Sec. Education, 31, to McMurray, 14.

Thursday, May 18 Bp. Floyd after the opening, declined to preside. Barkley presided. Bps. Barnaby and Floyd henceforth sulked. Wm. Beers moved to give McMuma the seat that was Knipple's.

Friday, May 19 My appeal for 1902 was sustained, against White River Conference. The trial occupied most of the day. In the evening at 7:00, the second Appeal (1903) was tried at at [repeated in text] Mrs. Hannah Bowman's. I was sustained next morning.

Saturday, May 20 Gen. Conference closed at 9:30. I go to 2:16 tr. at Ross and via Ft. Wayne to Lima. Sleep 3 1/2 hours at Huffman Hotel. Reach Dayton about 4:30 in the morning.

Sunday, May 21 Remained at home. I slept 2 hours in Afternoon. Called at Victor Grumbaugh's to see Carrie (Kaler). Spent the evening at Lorin's.

Monday, May 22 Eden S. Kemp died about 7:00, A.M. Assessor came. Wrote some letters.

Tuesday, May 23 Wrote letters in the forenoon. In the afternoon went to the bank and post-office. Called at Peter Louding's and at Cor. of Monument & Ludlow to see Chris Wilberforce. Chris came at 8 eve.

Wednesday, May 24 I was at home writing letters. I slept 11/2 hours. I corrected my tax (assessment) which I had given too high. Called to see Mr. Feight a half-hour..

Thursday, May 25 Spent forenoon in writing a letter to Jesse I. Leforge in reply to a kind one from them, and sleeping a half-hour. Dr. Tizzard capped my tooth— $5.00— afternoon. Letter from British war office, to Wright brothers.

Friday, May 26 I wrote letters and slept 1 1/4 hours. It was fair and warm after last night's rain. Mr. John G.

General Conference, 1905, in Caledonia, Michigan

Feight our nearest neighbor to the north is improving.

Saturday, May 27 I was at home. Wrote several letters. The boys (W & O) for several days have worked on their Flyer at the Lorrence Huffman farm.

Sunday, May 28 At 10:40, heard Rev. Jacob Speicher, of Kieh, Yang, China. He said 3,000 had been gathered as regular hearers in ten years. He is quite intelligent. Text Acts 14:27. Joseph G. Wilberforce called in the evening.

Monday, May 29 I wrote to D.B. Sherk and S.A. Stemen on the Wilberforce's. A warm day. Rain at night, and thunder. J.W. Carr of Anderson, Ind. was elected Super't. of Dayton Public Schools, by 7 to 5.

Tuesday, May 30 Orville, Katharine, Milton, Leontine and I decorated Susan's grave, in Woodland Cemetery. The headstone ($25.00) was put up in April. It was a rainy forenoon.

Wednesday, May 31 I start at 9:50 for Indiana, via Richmond to Dunreith & Mays. Dine at Grant House, Dunreith. Chas. Gray takes me to Harvey Wright's. Lodge at John McKee's. Saw Stella Rhoads at Mays.

Thursday, June 1 Call at David Kirkpatrick's, and again at Harvey's. J. McKee takes me to Rushville. Clifton Long takes me from Glenwood to Lucinda Moor's. I call in eve at N.F. Bower's, but lodge at Moor's.

Friday, June 2 Lucinda Moor, Kate Bowen and I dine & sup at Charles Steven's. Heavy rain at 4:00. Colvin Stevens there. I lodge at N.F. Bowens. He owns the old McPherson farm, 2 miles S.E. of Orange. C. Stevens lives on the old Wright farm.

Saturday, June 3 I dine with Bowen's at Moor's, and after an early dinner, Stevens takes me to Philander Lefforge's at Neff's Corners. Call at Sally Ann Cook's, Geo. Miller's, Ryan's, Sup & lodge at Jesse I. Lefforge's. Call at Sarah Miller's & Ellen Barber's.

Sunday, June 4 Somewhat rainy morning. I pr. at 10:30 at Mt. Zion, 2 1/4 m. south-west of Andersonville. Matt. 11:11. Dine at Phi. Lefforge's. Pr at 3:30, Acts 11:24. Lodge at Jas. Frank Harris's, my sister's son's.

Monday, June 5 I go with James to my native farm. Call at Mrs. Morgan Linville's. Go by Hopewell Church. Harris takes me to Rushville, & via Hamilton I reach home at 2:30. Call at Lorin's. Morgan Linville died a few months ago.

Tuesday, June 6 At home all day. I wrote a long letter to Reuchlin. Received a letter from Rev. B.G. Huber, telling of a plan of King Street Church to secede.

Wednesday, June 7 I wrote to Huber. Milton and Horace go in the afternoon to the pony-monkey show.

Friday, June 9 At home. Wrote letter to S. Kern, etc. Dentist took impression of my mouth for lower teeth at 2:00-3:00 afternoon. Lost my bank-book and some letters. Overhauled boxes in lumber room.

Saturday, June 10 Got ready and went to Huntington starting at 11:00 via Union City, Winchester & Ft. Wayne. Sup and lodge at S.L. Livingston's. Inter-society entertainment at 8:00. Fred L. Folker, Bertha Randolph, Chas. A. Clay, D.A. Powell, & Frank L. Clapp had parts.

Sunday, June 11 Sabbath School at 9:30. Bac. Sermon at 10:30, by C.B. Whitaker, 1 John 2:13, "Young Men." Dine at Clay's; Call at Prof. Gragg's, and sup at O.B.Bowman's & lodge there. H.C. Foote pr. at 7:30.

Monday, June 12 I called at Mrs. Brooks & Rev. F.C. Cremean's. Dined at W.A. Hanshu's. Supped at Prof. T.H. Gragg's and lodge at Livingston's. Glee-Club entertainment at 8:00.

Tuesday, June 13 Pub. Board met at 8:00. I dine with Bishop C.L. Wood at J.R Gilbert's. Educational Board met at 2:00. I Sup at Pres. McMurray's. Seniors' entertainment at 10:00; Oratory, 2:00.

Wednesday, June 14 Ed. Board etc. E.I. Bosworth, D.D. Oberlin, spoke on "The Appeal of the Future Life." At 10:30, Nellie B. Livingston, (A.B.) Mrs. A.D. Luke, Fred N. Clay, R.S. Kindel, Daniel Powell, E. Romig, V.L. Weaver (B.S.) graduated. Banquet. Ed. Board 2:30. Sup at F.C. Cremean's. Lodge at Livingston's.

Thursday, June 15 Ed. Board met at 7:00, Mis. Ex. Com.

at 9:40. Go on 10:18 train to Wabash & thence to Fairmount. Dine at Ellis Wright's. I go on 3:05 tr. to Fowlerton. Sup & lodge at R.W. White's. Children have scarlet fever. White paid me $46.37, on corn R.B. Reeder bought.

Friday, June 16 I go on 7:05 tr. to Richmond & thence to Dayton, arr. at 11:00. Call at Tizzard's to test "trial" plate to my lower jaw. Called at Lorin's in the evening. Saturday, June 17 Miss Wuichet visited us. In afternoon, I bought summer wear, at Elders & Johnson's and at Rike's.

Sunday, June 18 I heard, at First U.B. Church, Bishop J.S. Miller, 1 Cor. 12.27, an able sermon. Afternoon at 2:00 I attended the Corner-stone laying of "First U.B. Ch. S.E. cor. 4th & Perry Streets. A.B. Shauk, "conductor," W.J. Shuey, H.H. Fouts, and A.A. Maysillas [?] chief speakers. Bp. Mathews off'g.

Monday, June 19 Wrote letters to Huber and Clay in forenoon. Went to town in the afternoon, and wrote letters to Matthews and Hacker on Shuck monument fund.

Tuesday, June 20 Went to town and got my lower teeth at W.E. Lizzards; $5.50. Bought four shirts at Deweese' and four pr. of socks at Rike's. Afternoon, looked in vain for Livingston's tax, at Treasurer's office.

Wednesday, June 21 Went on 5:35 tr. via Lima to Huntington, Ind. Dine at Stemen's, sup at Clay's and lodge at Livingston's. Ed. Board met at 2:00. (Gragg's rec. room). Pres. McMurray accepted the presidency. Session at 7:30, elect profship. Adj. sine die. Somewhat warm day.

Thursday, June 22 Mis. Ex. Com. at J. Howe's at 8:00. I go on 10:18 tr. via Wabash to Fairmount & dine at Ellis Wright's. He gave me a $1.25 pen-knife. I go on 2:08 traction via Gas City home. Mr. A.I. Root there. Eve. mod. warm.

Saturday, June 24 I went on 9:00 car to Miamisburg and to I. Swartzel's & dined. Went with Swartzel to Germantown, called at Lizzie Long's and Sarah Thomas', and attended Qr. Conf. C.S. Johnson pr. at 2:00.

I sup at Jac. Slifer's. Pr. at 8:00, Heb. 4:10. Lodge at Slifer's.

Sunday, June 25 Doweyite at lovefeast! C.S. Johnson pr. 2 Cor 4:6-9 at 11:00. I intr. Sacrament. I dine at Rev. W.H. Kindel's with Woggoman's and Sophia Zehring. Lunch at Kindel's. I pr. at 7:30 Prov. 25:2. Lodge at Edwin M. Scott's, near the Church.

Monday, June 26 Scott takes my picture at his gallery, I call at Jacob Fout's. I went on 8:15 car to Miamisburg & home.

Tuesday, June 27 I wrote letters of condolence to J.C. Coulson and D.B. Sherk. I mailed them in town and saw Albert Shearer at his store. Katharine was at a picnic in the afternoon.

Wednesday, June 28 I wrote to Reuchlin a long letter on the victories of General Conference. At 7:00, eve., I called at Seiter's to see Mrs. Agnes Swank, but learned she is at W. Milton, near death from a cancer, cut out.

Thursday, June 29 I spent the forenoon mostly in classifying papers in my drawers, and in the afternoon went out to the field at Sim[m]s.

Friday, June 30 I went and paid S.L. Livingston's tax. I called at Seitter's (J.A.) and Minnie told me her mother was yet alive.

Saturday, July 1 I was at home all day. By telephone learned from J.A. Seitters that Mrs. Agnes Swank remained about the same. Called at Lorin's in the evening.

Sunday, July 2 At Pres. Ch. S.S. heard Daniels and Gillespie on Senacharib's defeat. Also heard Rev. M. Wilson pr. on "Civic Helpfulness," Isa. 41:6. Aftn, Wrote an article, "Great Preachers." Lorin and family called in the evening. I called at Henry Wagoners.

Monday, July 3 Nothing very unusual at home. Mrs. Agnes Swank died this morning at West Milton. The boys went at 1:00 to Huffman's field to work.

Tuesday, July 4 Went to Susan's grave and placed a boquet on it and adjusted the grass nicely. In afternoon, called an hour at J.A. Seitters'. the home of the deceased Agnes Swank. They call him Albert Seitters.

Wednesday, July 5 At home, forenoon. Attended Mrs. Agnes Swank's funeral at Home Street (Liberal) Church, at 2:00 aftn. I called at Lorin's in the evening.

Friday, July 7 I copied Floyd and Barnaby's letter of Sept. 1st, 1903 to E. Ill. and enclosed a copy to each of our bishops. I called at Lorin's in the evening.

Saturday, July 8 Katharine started to Geneva, Ohio to Sillaman's.

Sunday, July 9 Wrote a letter to Cousin Mary Virginia Johnson, Waveland, Indiana. At 10:30, attended First Eng. Lutheran Church and heard Pastor Garland preach a great sermon, Phil. 4:12, "I know how to abound."

Tuesday, July 11 I aimed to start at 2:50 to Fairmount, but was too late for the train. I bought Horace a toy automobile as a birth-day present.

Wednesday, July 12 I start to Fairmount on 8:10 D & U train. Lunch at Union City & go on via Gas City. Look at the Wheeler property. Sup at Ellis Wright's and lodge at Oliver Buller's.

Thursday, July 13 Dine & sup at Ellis's. In afternoon, called at C. Brattain's. Chas. Ellsworth Atkinson and William Simons, (lately hurt). Go to Fowlerton 6:10 tr. Call at Wm. Reeder's and lodge at C.A. Glass's.

Friday, July 14 Oliver takes me via Wm. Reeder's to R.H. White's, where I look at the farm. I went on 2:00 tr. to Benedum. Call at Rev. Jas. A. Rector's, Curtis Rector's and C.W. Rector's. Sup with Jas. Women. Go on 6:45 tr. Home, 10:45. Weather hot.

Saturday, July 15 Rested and slept considerably. Wrote to Wood and Clay, and to Reuchlin. Called at Lorin's. The weather was quite hot.

Sunday, July 16 I did not feel very well; so I remained at home all day. Milton, Ivonette & Leontine spent the afternoon with us, and Horace was with us an hour.

Wednesday, July 19 I drew, in a check on the Fourth National Bank, one thousand dollars and sent it to Prof. T.H. Gragg, Secretary of Education, as a donation from Mrs. Sarah Shisler's funds, for running expenses on Central College. Learned of the Modoc Meeting. A very hot day.

Thursday, July 20 I got letters from Katharine who is at Geneva, Ohio, visiting the Sillaman's; also a letter from W.H. Clay, telling of F.H. Cremean's information by Tharp of Morrison's plan to have Conference a week previous to the time. Wrote letters to White River.

Friday, July 21 Learned more of the Michigan Council. Wrote C.A. Allen, Sims, Heasley etc. It was much cooler to-day.

Saturday, July 22 There was nothing of special interest to-day, only of Michigan's apparent attitude. I wrote Bishops Wood, Barkley & a card to Hoskins. The temperature was nice.

Sunday, July 23 Heard Garland at 10:30, 2 Sam. 23:15; applied to longing for youthful days. I mailed a letter to Clay. Lorin's boys came in the afternoon.

Monday, July 24 At home all day. Read in the evening many old letters—mostly mine to William which I lately got at Lucinda's. Lucinda was his wife.

Wednesday, July 26 I received Bp. Wood's letter enclosing Morrison's and McMunn's. Morrison's plan to have gen'l. officers to agree to stay away from conferences! Wrote Wood, Foote, C.B. Sherk & Sims.

Thursday, July 27 Rec'd a letter from Huber. Answer, and also wrote Bp. Hoskins. Left teeth plates at Lizzard's for repair. Called a half hour at Lorin's in the evening.

Friday, July 28 I got letters from S. Wood and Chester Allen. I wrote to Bishop Hoskins, etc. I got my teethplates. $1.50. Wrote Bertha Wright and to C. Allen. Some rain.

Saturday, July 29 At home. Saw Crites' letter on Sunfield convention. Wrote Clay, Hoskins, and C.B. Sherk & Wood & Eva Gray. The air has been pleasant all the past week.

Sunday, July 30 Heard A. Clinton Watson, Assistant Pastor of the First Baptist Church on "Law, Grace and Truth," John 1.16,17. Joseph and Christopher Wilberforce supped with us. Albert Shearer called in the evening.

Tuesday, August 1 At home all day. I did nothing but read. No letters received. In the evening, I found my bank-book which I had thought lost June 9—found it in *old* desk!

Wednesday, August 2 At Home. I went to bank, dentists, and store in forenoon. Katharine came home at 6:55 from Cleveland or rather from Geneva, Ohio. I called to see Mrs. Rachel Wagner in the forenoon. Daniel Koerner died to-day.

Thursday, August 3 Learned by telephone at 7:30 of Daniel Koerner's death. I go on 11:55 tr via Hamilton to Liberty, Ind., where I hire a livery rig, $1.25. Stay at Elmira's. Saw Mrs. McMann, Long etc. Wrote on a Memorial paper.

Friday, August 4 Continued writing. Rev. J. Selig pr. Daniel Koerner's funeral at 10:00, I read Memorial. Burial at Old Franklin Church. Selig & Paddock dined at Elmira's, and others.

Saturday, August 5 Silvanus Koerner took me to Liberty. I hired a rig at Rushville and went to Harvey Wright's, $1.25.

Sunday, August 6 Luther Newhouse, Jabez Rhoades, John Whitton's, David Kirkpatrick, and families & others came in.

Monday, August 7 Called at Thomas Wright's, Sena Wright's, Mr. Thomas's, and dined at Harvey's. I went with David Kirkpatrick's to Knightstown and went home on traction cars, arr. at 8:00. See Tom. Huston at Knightstown. Emma & Grace Frazier came.

Tuesday, August 8 I go on 8:15 tr. to Fairmount, via Gas City. Saw O.R. Scott, Chas. Parker, etc. Rec'd deeds for Wheeler lot in the evening. Price $1400.00. Sup and lodge at Ellis Wright's on Sycamore St.

Wednesday, August 9 Look up business somewhat, dine at Ellis's, leave deeds at Marion for record and go on traction to Huntington. Sup and lodge at W.H. Clay's.

Thursday, August 10 I called at Prof. T.H. Gragg's, and J. Howe and S.A. Stemen and I consult there on frontier and foreign missions. I went on 10:18 tr. to Wabash and Fairmount. Dine & lodge at Ellis's.

Friday, August 11 I write to Wood, Barkley & Reuchlin. Arrange for sanitary sewer contract with Nick Winslow. I go on 3:05 tr. to Fowlerton. Sup and lodge at R.W. White's.

Saturday, August 12 I went on 7:03 tr. via Richmond to Dayton, arri. at 11:00. Saw the Loudings and Mary Harris about word on the report of Wilberforce's death, in the evening.

Sunday, August 13 Joseph Wilberforce called in the morning. I heard Rev. Stevens pr. at Wmstreet Baptist Church: Phil. 2.20. Lorin's children came in the afternoon.

Monday, August 14 No mail to-day, only a letter to Emma. Sent a copy each to Silvanus, Elmira, and Caroline (Zeller) of memorial paper rec'd at Daniel Koerner's funeral. Miss Wuichet dined with us.

Tuesday, August 15 Wrote letters to Bishop Wood and others. Called at Winter's Bank and at the post-office. Called at Mr. Feight's.

Wednesday, August 16 John G. Feight, aged 74 to-day, died this morning, a little before 7:00. He has been our nearest neighbor since the beginning of 1871. Friendship never marred.

Thursday, August 17 St. Joseph Conference begins to-day, 9:00. E. Tuttle Lewis, Episcopal assistant pastor, called withe John E. Feight. Joseph Wilberforce called at 5:00. Mrs. Carrie Gumbaugh called. Wrote on Mr. J.G. Feight's Memorial.

Friday, August 18 Finished up the memorial and read it at the funeral at 1:30. Rode out to burial with Rev. Lewis.

Saturday, August 19 At home. It is Orville's and Katharine's birth day anniversary. Called at Lorin's at 4:30, rain.

Sunday, August 20 Heard Rev. J.H. Jameson pr. on Job 3.23, a very fine sermon, at Grace M.E.

Monday, August 21 At home all day. I received a letter from Chief D.F. Hilberforce to-day, which shows that he is not dead as reported. I wrote Howe. I sat up till 11:00.

Tuesday, August 22 San. Sewer on Hawthorne St. was begun to-day. Miss Wuichet visits us in forenoon. Got Huber's letter afternoon. Wrote a few letters only. Katharine went to Osborn's & lodged.

Wednesday, August 23 Received a telegram from Bp. C.L. Wood, and go via Richmond & Jonesboro to Fairmount. Lodge at Oliver Buller's. Bishop Wood had adjourned the conference for lack of subordinate quorum.

Thursday, August 24 I looked after business in town. I boarded at Ellis's. I did not go to the conference, which the bishop again adjourned to 9:00 tomorrow.

Friday, August 25 I went with Bishop Wood and we at 9:00 adjourned Conference to meet at Fowlerton to-morrow. We go to Fowlerton and to White's on 3:00 train. Call at R.W. White's. Lodge at Glass's.

Saturday, August 26 Call at Lewis Hayden's & Chas. Malone's. Conference session at 9:00. Steele & Kinneman present. We go to Huntington. Lodge at Clay's.

Sunday, August 27 Bishop F.L. Haskins preached at the College, using no text. I dined at F.H. Cremean's, Casidy, Wechsler and wife, being there. Prayer Meeting there at 3:00. Chr. Endeavor at 7:00. Lodge at Livingston's.

Monday, August 28 Went to Pub. House at 8:00 and 3:00. Dine at I. Stemen's; sup at Hosoe's; Lodge at J.R. Gilbert's. Mis. Ex. Com. at Livingston's at 8:00, eve.

Tuesday, August 29 Start at 7:30 traction to Marion. Lost my pocket-book with $29.00 at Court-house.

Called at M. Hillshammer's. See Police. I go on 2:47 tr. via Piqua home. Arri. on Traction at 8:00.

Wednesday, August 30 Write many circular letters to White River Laymen. David Baker, of Portland, Ind. dined with us. He seemed considerably flighty. Wanted to find Benj. "Van Cleve's Notes." I did not tell him where they are.

Sunday, September 3 Called at Lorin's. Heard Whidden pr. a good sermon on 1 John 5.4, Victory of Life. He is the pastor of the First Baptist Church, on Main Street, north of Second Street.

Monday, September 4 Wrote out resolutions for White River sessions. This is "labor day," a legal Holiday. I sent out many circulars.

Tuesday, September 5 Went on 9:00 tr. via Richmond to Fowlerton, and thence on 5:40 tr. to Fairmount, and on traction via Wabash and Huntington. Staid at European Hotel. Bought 1000 mile book, to-day.

Wednesday, September 6 I went on 6:30 tr. to Markle with R.S. Kindel. Walk to Ross Athens', 3 miles. Dined. Conf. opened Macedonia Church. O.G. Alwood presiding. Bp. Wood there. Sup & lodge at Ellis Denny's. Beougher pr. at night.

Thursday, September 7 At 9:30, Denny takes us to Markle. We dine "Midway." at Huntington and go on traction via Wabash to Fairmount & Fowlerton. Wood and I lodge at R.W. White's.

Friday, September 8 White River Conference resumed at Hopewell Ch. at 9:00. (9:30). I dine at Oliver Glass's, & sup there. W.H. Clay pr. at 8:00. T.E. Kinneman, R. Steele, J. Jackson, Chas. R. Paddack & M. Wright answer roll call.

Saturday, September 9 Conference adopted lay delegation at 10:30. Dine, sup and lodge at Glass's. Closed at 4:00. W.L. Crom was excited, and spoke out. T.E. Kinneman pr. at 8:00. W.C. Galbraith (of Rugby) came at noon. I was elected editor of Conf. min.

Sunday, September 10 Testimony Meeting at 9:30.

Bishop C.L. Wood pr. at 10:30, Luke 1:53. Rainy day. Dine at R.W. White's. Go on 6:40 tr to Fairmount. Lodge at Ellis Wright's.

Monday, September 11 Look after business and start on 11:00 traction. Dine at J.W. Broyle's in Alexandria. Go via Anderson and Richmond home, arri. at 5:05. Called at Lorin's at 7:30.

Wednesday, September 13 Made out synopsis of White River Minutes and sent them to Clay. Prepared pamphlet minutes also. Wrote Wm. Meyer and Anna Lawrence, and some others.

Friday, September 15 Wrote many letters to Nebraska preachers to persuade them to meet Bishop Hoskins. Finished up pamphlet minutes.

Saturday, September 16 Arose at 4:00. Got ready to go to Fairmount. Started at 8:10 via Union and Gas Cities. Look after business and start 4:30, on traction, call at Recorders at Marion. Lodge at J. Howe's, Huntington.

Sunday, September 17 Call at C.B. Whitaker's. Hear pastor F. C. Cremean pr. at 10:30. Dine at Mat. Wechler's. Sup at Willis Cassady's, after pr. meeting. Lodge at J. Howe's. Was at Christian Endeavor meeting at 6:30.

Monday, September 18 Go to Publishing House. Prepare Wh. River Conf. Minutes for the printer. Dine at Restaurant with Otto Bowman's. Lodge at W.H. Clay's.

Tuesday, September 19 Went to Publishing House & spent forenoon—read proofs. Dine at restaurant. At 2:00 met Mis. Ex. Committee in Mission Room. Rev. Stoltz gave much statements. Lodged at J. Howe's.

Wednesday, September 20 College opening. I read Scripture & made 10 minutes address. Ex. Mis. Meeting at Howe's at 8:30 and at 10:30. Went on 2:30 traction to Fairmount & Fowlerton. At White's, I lodge.

Thursday, September 21 Went on 7:04 train to Richmond & home. (Went on 2:30 traction to Fairmount and Fowlerton. Staid at R.W. White's—Sept. 20.)

Friday, September 22 (I go on 7:04 train home via Richmond. Arrive at 11:00. I am busy writing letters, the rest of the day—Thursday.) At home writing.

Saturday, September 23 At home all day writing letters. Christopher Wilberforce came about 5:00, and staid an hour. We talk about his going to school and appointment to Africa, etc.

Sunday, September 24 Heard Pastor H.P. Whidden preach at 10:30, Eph. 7,15. "The Baptist Brotherhood." Pretty good. Lorin's boys spent the afternoon with us.

Tuesday, September 26 Wrote letters and postals till 1:45. Went to Torrence Huffman's field, and saw Wilbur at 4:15 fly in 18 minutes and 8 seconds eleven miles and nearly one sixth.

Wednesday, September 27 At home forenoon, working hard at writing. In afternoon, go to Huffman's & see Orville fly nearly two miles.

Thursday, September 28 At home all day, except to buy ribbon and carbon paper for type-writer. I wrote many letters. T. Bell's letter avows him on the loyal side.

Friday, September 29 At home all day. I did not see it, but Orville flew to day, in one flight, twelve miles.

Saturday, September 30 At home all day. Catharine went to the Springs beyond New Paris, Ohio. Orville made a flight of ten miles to-day, which I did not see.

Sunday, October 1 Heard Pastor Frank Garland pr. a noble sermon on Rev. 2.7, "Hear what Spir[it] saith to Chs." Lorin's children all came afternoon & staid to supper. I wrote an article, Zion's Faults and Glories.

Monday, October 2 At home all day. Wrote an article for the Christian Conservator, Zion's Faults & Glories. Dined at Lorin's. It was partly cloudy to-day. Revs. B.F. Harris and Dunkin called.

Tuesday, October 3 At home all day, writing letters. Orville flew over fifteen miles, in afternoon, in 25 minutes and some seconds, which I did not see.

Wednesday, October 4 Wrote letters in forenoon. At 2:00 I went to Sim[m]'s. At 4:32 Orville flew in 33 minutes and 20 seconds 21 miles, lacking one-tenth. The Webberts there. Kath. & I came home with Bilman's in automobile.

Thursday, October 5 In forenoon, at home writing. In the afternoon, I saw Wilbur fly twenty-four miles in thirty-eight minutes and four seconds, one flight.

Friday, October 6 Started at 8:10 for Fairmount, via Union C. & Gas City. Lunch tr., Cold supper at Ellis's & lodged there. Attend to business aftern. Insurance on Mill St. property.

Saturday, October 7 I look after business forenoon and attend Clarence Ketterman's funeral at 11:30, Friends Ch., Crom preached. Dine at Ellis Wright's with Myrtle Reeve. Buy wallpaper $7.85. Went on 2:00 car to Alexandria, sup at T. Bell's, Walk to Star crossing; Insurance, Scott. Lodged at Ellis's.

Sunday, October 8 Call at C.O. Ribble's. Hear T.E. Kinneman pr. at 11:00 at Union Chapel, II Cor. V.l, a good sermon. Go on 1:10 tr. to Fowlerton. Dine and sup at R.W. White's. Hear Kinneman pr. at 7:00, Lodge at Wm. Reeder's. Boys Ovid & Glenn.

Monday, October 9 Went to Fairmount on 7:40 tr.. Look after business all day. Dine at Restaurant. Sup at Ellis's. Go to Fowlerton. Lodge at O.A. Glass's. Mrs. Glass & daughters there from Tipton Co.

Tuesday, October 10 I Go on 7:03 tr. to Economy. See Henry Oler, Wm. Lamb, Henderson Oler, Francis Cain. Grant Mendenhall, & Rev. Arthur Rector. Grant takes me to John, Ulysses, and Edgar Manning's. Dine at Edgar's. John's wife takes me to see him. Talk at Depot. Reach home, 6:00.

Wednesday, October 11 At home all day writing letters. Nothing unusual occurs.

Thursday, October 12 At home. C.W. Linker & Joseph Wilberforce came in the afternoon & talk an hour. I go on 5:00 traction to Dublin. Arrive at 9:30. Stay at Tweedy's Hotel; lodging, 35 cents.

Friday, October 13 Breakfast at restaurant. Call at George Wilson's, Joseph Gray's, Eliz. Cranor's, J. Selig's, Lewis Cranor's. Champ's away (?). Went to Wm. L. Lawson's & sup. Dine at George Wilson's. Lodge at Solomon Crull's. Elsie is 13 years old, tho very small in 1897, when I boarded there.

Saturday, October 14 I go via Cambridge to Brookville. Call at G. Moulton's. Dine at Thomas Milbourn's. See him at Canning factory. Go by livery to Oakforest, $1.00. Oler's Conf. Personal coarseness. Sup David Lanning's. Oler pr 7:00. Lodge.

Sunday, October 15 Heard Oler pr. Dan. 12:3, Sacrament. Dine at Harvey White's. Dan. Harbine takes me to Brookville. Sup and lodge at Thom. Kilbourn's. Hear W.A. Oler pr. Ps. 50:23. Talk with A. Edrington. Harbine is silly.

Monday, October 16 Write and mail letters. I called at 10:00 at Alex. Edrington. Hire livery and Go to G.W.W. Stewart's and Wm. Strader Lacey's. I go on 5:17 tr. to Cambridge & to Danl. Lawson's.

Tuesday, October 17 Lawson takes me to Wiseman's, and to Wm. Hawley's. Dine. Josie Wiseman takes me to Widow Rebecca Haskett's and to Susan Riggle's & to Mr. Riggle's & to traction car. Go to Ogden, Lyon's, & Jabez Rhodes'. Sup at L's, lo. at Jabez's.

Wednesday, October 18 Jabez takes (after visit to Ed. Frazier's) to Harvey Wright's & to S. Blue River Church to Susan Newhouse's funeral, aged 90. Hall pr. it. Day very rainy. I dine, sup & lodge at Harvey's. Drusilla, Florence & Cora & Stella and Whitton & Gusta call.

Thursday, October 19 Write letters in forenoon. Charlie Gray takes me to Rushville. Jesse I. Lefforge takes me to his house. Supper. Meet Geo. Cox at Phi. Lefforge's. Lodge there, at Neff's corners.

Friday, October 20 Philander takes me to Milroy & I go to Greensburg & Rugby. Dine at Simmond's. Sup & lodge at Wm. C. Galbraith's. J. Selig came via St. Louis Crossing.

Saturday, October 21 Selig & I visited in Hartsville,

A.H.K. Beams, Wertz, John Bline's, G.C.Mensch, Wm. Smith, Sarah Rohrer, Carrie Rawlins, Dine at Beam's. Call at Galbraith, C. Barger's & Westley Mobley's. I pr. at Rugby, Rom. 4:13. Qr. Conf. Selig pr at 7:00, lodged at Galbr.

Sunday, October 22 A nice day. Lovefeast at 9:30. I pr. at 10:30, Rev. 1:5. Sacrament. Dine with Rev. S. Crom's, at Hartsville. Attend S.S. at 2:00. Call at Wesley Laurence's & at Nan. Lawrence's. Selig pr. at Rugby, Joel 2:18. I lodge at Galbraith's.

Monday, October 23 Go with Selig to St. Louis Crossing & via Cambridge & Richmond, get home at 2:00. Write some. Eleanor & Rachel Wagner call. It is nice weather.

Tuesday, October 24 I rise very early. The day is a little rainy. I get letters returned from Rugby. I wrote letters. Get my book from the bank. I call at Lorin's a half hour at 7:00. Horace gives me his picutre.

Wednesday, October 25 At home all day. I write letters to Rev. J.T. Holmes, Stuart & others. Rev. D.O. Fulton declares on the loyal side, in a letter to me. A slightly rainy day.

Thursday, October 26 I am Very busy getting ready to go away. I start on 2:45 tr. to Guynneville, Ind. Sup and lodge at William Myer's, 1/2 m. west. Adopted daughter: Hazel Ellen Myer.

Friday, October 27 Ben. Frank Nugent takes me to Alfred Arnold's, Wm. Riley Zike's, Peter Myer's, Geo. Beucher's, 1/2 m. S. Mt. Carmel, Phebe Engles, Uriah Coxe's, near Hargrove, & Jas. Arnold's. Dine at Beucher's, sup & lodge at Wm. Myer's.

Saturday, October 28 Visit Melisse Van Scyoc & Philip Six's. Dine at Wm. Myer's. Pr. at 2:00, 1 Pet. 1:1. Quar. Conf. Sup & lodge at Earnest Wagoner's. She a daughter of Pres. Davis. Her Sister Lucile (14) there. She is very intellectual. I never saw a smarter girl than Lucile.

Sunday, October 29 I pr. at Gwymmeville at 10:30, Matt. 16.17. Dine and sup at B.F. Nugent's. I pr. at 7:00, Acts 3.17, on final Restitution. Lodge at Wm. Myer's.

Monday, October 30 I went on traction car (8:30) to Rushville and on 11:04 tr. to Fairmount. Lunch at Anderson. Sup and lodge at Ellis Wright's.

Tuesday, October 31 Write letters. Lunch at Ellis's. I go to Marion and pay my tax. I sup and lodge at Ellis Wright's.

Wednesday, November 1 I write letters. I go on 9:05 tr. to Fowlerton. Dine at R.W. White's and return on 5:38 tr.. Pay C.O. Ribble $25.00 on settlement, on $60 deal. Lodge at Ellis's.

Thursday, November 2 I paid the pavement tax, $20.24 on the Wheeler lot. I went to Alexandria and dined at J.W. Broyles'. Went on to New Castle and out by livery to B.F. Williams', (cost $1.50) and on train to Cambridge. Walk out to Geo. Wilson and lodge. Rev. Joe Williamson.

Friday, November 3 In forenoon, I called at Selig's and Jas. Tweedy's, and dine at Rev. J. Selig's. Josie Wiseman came. I sup at James Tweedy's. Ruby Smith, his granddaughter, keeps his house. I lodge at Selig's.

Saturday, November 4 Geo. Wilson goes to Brookville. I find no place for Qr. M. so we have Qr. Conf. at Jacob Snyder's 1 m. n.w. where I dine & sup. I go on 5:30 traction to Dayton—home.

Sunday, November 5 It is quite a rainy day. Lorin's children come in the afternoon. George Feight called.

Monday, November 6 I took a hot bath this morning and covered up and sweat all forenoon. Wrote few letters.

Tuesday, November 7 This is election day. It is somewhat cloudy. I voted for Johm M.Pattison for governor.

Wednesday, November 8 At home. Martin Luther Oler of Kansas called in the evening. I held a conference near his home, a few years ago, some eight miles from Parsons, in Labette County.

Friday, November 10 Wrote busily till noon. Katharine went to Columbus to the High School Teachers' Association. I start to Cambridge, Ind., on the 4:00 traction car. See Josie Needham at Richmond. Call at Beecher Johnson's and Dublin. Lodge at John Selig's.

Saturday, November 11 Rev. Geo. Wilson & I go on tr. to Laurel. See Richard Kinion Freman, girl & boy Edmund. Jesse I. Lefforge takes us home, near Andersonville. Dine, sup & lodge there. Qr. Conf. at Mt. Zion at 2:00. I comment, John 12, 13 chapters.

Sunday, November 12 I teach S.S. Rev. Geo. Wilson pr at 10:30, 1 Jno. 1.7. Communion. I dine at Phi. Lefforge's. I call on Mrs. Jo. Mitchell, aged 90, Smith Scott & Ellen Barber. Roland Larue of Connersville called. I pr. at 7:00, Matt. 6.9. "Heaven." Jas and Zena Harris at meeting & Jo. Abercrombia. I lodge at Phi's in Anderson.

Monday, November 13 Jesse takes me in his automobile to Milroy, after a call on Sarah Miller's. I go on 10:49 tr. to Fairmount. Sup and lodge at Ellis Wright's.

Tuesday, November 14 I went at 9:16 tr. to Fowlerton. I dine at R.W. White's. Call at John Leach's. I walk to Oliver A. Glass's and lodge there.

Wednesday, November 15 I called at Wm. H.H. Reeder's. See Mr. Chas. Park there. Marcus Glass took me to C.H. & C. Depot. I return to Fairmount. The surveyors make out boundaries of my lots. Wiley protested. Lodge at Ellis's.

Thursday, November 16 I remain at Ellis' forenoon. Go to White's. Sup and lodge there. White found Hopewell Church could be unlocked. The seceders had put something into the keyhole.

Friday, November 17 Go on 7:04 tr to Economy. Dine at Calvin Wiles'. We go to Grant Mendenhall's, Wm. Elvin Oler's, & to Fremen Nelson's. I lodge at John M. Manning's.

Saturday, November 18 I walk to Economy. Call at Annual Edward's. Henry Oler's, Francis Cain's, and Pleasant Adamson's. Dined at John M. Manning's, Pr. in Economy at 2:00, on Lord's Prayer, John 6:7. Sup and lodge at J. Manning's.

Sunday, November 19 I pr. at 10:30, Matt. 16,17. Communion. Dine with many at Oliver Scantland's, four miles east. Sup and lodge at John M. Manning's. I pr. at 7:00, Prov. 25.2.

Monday, November 20 I called at Mrs. Susan Manning's to see the Manning Genealogy. Wnet on 8:30 tr. to Richmond. Called at Caroline Zeller's. Reached home at 1:00, by the traction. Fire at the corner, N.E. of us. Little damage.

Tuesday, November 21 At home. Went to town forenoon. Also went in afternoon and got medicine of Dr. L. Spitler for my persistane hoarseness (Laryngitis). It is a very pretty mild day. Birthday of Smith and Sarah Wright.

Thursday, November 23 I wrote in the forenoon. Horace and I took a walk in the afternoon. Wrote Clay on the origin of the Conservator. It is a very nice, mild day.

Thursday, November 30 Thanksgiving Day. Wrote a little: Starved on nothings. Horace with us in the forenoon. Milton Ivonette and Leontine with us to supper.

Sunday, December 3 Attend communion services at D. Frank Garland's Church (First Lutheran).

Monday, December 4 I went on 9:00 trac[tion] to Fairmount, via Union, Muncie, Anderson. Sup and lodge at Ellis Wright's.

Tuesday, December 5 *County surveyor completes survey of my lots. See Olivia* Buller at Hardware Store & talk with him over church matters. Board at Ellis Wright's.

Wednesday, December 6 Go on 9:00 tr. to Fairmount & to Wm. Millspaugh's and thence walk with John Franklin Heal to Robt. B. Reeder's & dine. Call at Wm. R's & O.A. Glass'. Sup & lodge at Wm. H.H. Reeder's. Boys: Ovid and Glenn.

Thursday, December 7 With Wm. Reeder, visit Myrtle Reeve's school. Dine sup and lodge at R.W. White's.

Friday, December 8 Get letters from Kinneman & others. Telegraph Clay. Get answer. I call at Owen

Nottingham's. I board at R.W. White's.

Saturday, December 9 I call at Levi Simons, Wilson Simons, Dick Nottingham's, Chas. Malone's, Lewis Hayden's, & Frank Kirkwood's. Rev. J. Howe came at 11:00. Pr. at 2:00, 1 Thes. 5:13-28. Howe pr. at 7:30, 1 Cor. 15:58. Board at White's.

Sunday, December 10 Rev. J. Howe pr. at 10:30, Rom. 12.1. Communion. Buller's, Howe and myself dine at O.A. Glass's. Sup there. Buggy broke down. J. Howe pr. 7:00, Zech. 4.6, to a larger congregation. Lodge at R.W. White's.

Monday, December 11 I go on 7:03 train via Muncie & Union City, Home. Arri. at 12:00.

Tuesday, December 12 At home. A Frenchman (Croquelle) and John F. Johnson visited Wilbur and Orville. The Frenchman was Croquelle a newspaper correspondent, who wrote up a most unconscionable story.

Wednesday, December 13 Attended Good Roads Convention, Association Hall. W. Bradburn, Prugh and Rice spoke.

Friday, December 15 At home. Rev. W.H. Chandler called a half hour in the afternoon. He lives in Wheaton, Illinois, but is laboring as a congregational evangelist in that state.

Tuesday, December 19 At home. Katharine came home from school sick. Dr. Spitler came and pronounced it an influenza.

Friday, December 22 At home. Katharine is out of bed to-day. Mrs. Stevens, teacher, call[e]d on Katharine.

Sunday, December 24 Heard Rev. H.C. Jameson pr. at Grace Ch. Isa. 9.6, a fine discourse. Remained at home the rest of the day.

Monday, December 25 Lorin and family were with us to dinner. Miss Alice Hunter called to see Katharine this afternoon. She is teacher of English in high school.

Tuesday, December 26 At home. Weather very mild. Netta W. and Gwendlyn Stokes called in the afternoon.

Thursday, December 28 The morning was beautiful, and a fire hardly needed. A Frenchman by the name of Arnold Fordyce came to investigate and drive a trade for a flying machine. They agreed on terms. A little rain.

Friday, December 29 Damp, but snowy. Cooler toward eve. The articles preparing with Mr. A. Fordyce. I wrote some letters. An Interview with Mr. Fordyce and his picture are published in evening News.

Saturday, December 30 It is a beautiful, mild day. I receive and answer letters. In the afternoon, Wilbur and Orville sign up the contract with Mr. Arnold Fordyce, of Paris, to furnish a flyer etc. for One Million Francs.

Sunday, December 31 Cloudy, and scattering, round snowdrops are flying. Afternoon sunshine. The weather the past year has been fine. The delegates election showed a two-thirds majority for the right, and they stood firm in Gen. Conference. With May 20th, my long service as a bishop ended. I was editor of the Telescope 1869-1877, bishop, 1877–1881, and 1885–1905; thirty-two years a general officer of the Church. Attended the M.E. Wesleyan colored church.

Memoranda
C.E. Wommer is oil pumper on my farm. Albert Dunning, Fairmount, Ind., is field boss. Hiram Fisher, Oil measurer, Matthews, Ind.

Bis pueri senes—Old men are twice boys.

Corn for 1905, at 35 cents a bushel came to $240.80. Henry Scott, delegate to the Auglaize Conference, in 1903, at Olivet, told me that Bishop Barnaby told him that he (B) did not make a speech against me at Messick, Indiana. He told Rev. Charles Weyer the same in the tent Sunday afternoon. He did speak against me one hour and 23 minutes! and I have a full, long-hand report of what he said.

PART FIVE

1906–1917

"My health the past year has been excellent for one so old. My brothers and sisters are not alive. Wilbur, a bright star among the Wright intellects, has been gone nearly four years. Street cars start past today."
Milton Wright, January 1, 1916

Milton Wright spent the last years of his life being the proud father of the Wright Brothers and the doting grandfather of many grandchildren. He continued to be involved in the lives of his grown children, encouraging them in their endeavors. He tutored his grandchildren, marched in a suffrage parade in Dayton, and wrote letters daily to family and friends. His house took on the modern conveniences of electricity and plumbing. He saw streetcars running on Dayton streets and would fly in an airplane built by his son. He met many early aviators who came to learn to fly at Huffman Prairie and fed many of them at his home. He took his grandchildren fishing and to the circus. The family suffered the loss of Wilbur to typhoid in 1912. The Bishop's diaries record the sadness and heartache the family felt. Orville purchased a car that same summer and took his father and other family members on frequent outings around the countryside. The Dayton flood of 1913 is recorded in detail. The Bishop moved with Orville and Katharine to Hawthorne Hill in Oakwood in 1914. His last entry is recorded on April 2, 1917. Milton Wright died on April 3, 1917, at the age of eighty-eight. He filled his days and his diaries with the things that mattered most to him and was thankful for a long and rich life.

Milton Wright, family, and friends on the porch at Hawthorne Hill, ca.. 1916

1906

Monday, January 1 Weather, fair. Temp., 33 degrees at 9:00. "Thy youth is renewed like the eagle." "As the heaven is high above the earth, So great is His mercy toward them that fear Him." I arose at 5:30. I get letters from Wood and Willoughby. Wilbur & Orville get letters from England, France and Austria. It was a beautiful day. I remained at home.

Wednesday, January 3 Weather, rainy. Therm., 48 degrees at 9:00. Remained at home except to buy some shirts at DeWees'. Read and wrote.

Friday, January 5 Weather, fair. Ther., 32 degrees at 7:00. At home. Wrote many letters. Orville and Katharine supped at Robt. Osbornes. The boys pictures in the News.

Saturday, January 6 Went on 11:55 tr. to Miamisburg with Rev. Wm. Miller and to Germantown. Miller pr. at 2:00, 46 Ps. 1 v. Cr. Conf. We sup at J. Slifer's. I pr. at 7:00, 103 Ps. We lodge at J.W. Fout's.

Sunday, January 7 At S.S. I teach the woman's class. Testimony meeting followed. Rev. Wm. Miller pr. at 11:00, Ps. 118:25, a good sermon. I hold the communion. We dine at Straight's. I call at Sarah Thomas', Lizzie Long's and at E.M. Scott's. Miller pr. 7:00, John 21.22. We lodge at E.M. Scott's. His father was a cousin of E.M. Stanton's.

Monday, January 8 A little snow fell yesterday and several inches fell in the night. The cars were belated. I reached home about 10:30.

Tuesday, January 9 I go on 9:45 tr. via Richmond and New Castle to Mays. I called on Berth Benner's and Fry's. Frances took me to Harvey Wright's. I gave books to Benner's boys and Lois Fry. I sup and lodge at Harvey's.

Wednesday, January 10 I remain at Harvey's. T. Wilhelm and Florence and Cora called; also Drusilla McKee and John Whiton and Augusta.

Thursday, January 11 I called at Ed. Frazier's and Jabez Rhoad's, on my way to Knightstown, I go on 11:00 tr. to Fairmount. There, I transacted business and went to Fowlerton & to R.W. White's. I leased my northeast deadning to Wm. L. Royal. Lodge at White's.

Friday, January 12 I contract with Andrew White to clear ten acres in southwest deadning for seventy dollars. I go to Fairmount & to Huntington via Wabash. Mission Executive Committee met at 2:30. I sup at Wm. Dillon's and lodge at J. Howe's. I called at Otto Bowman's.

Saturday, January 13 I was at College prayer & then conducted. I went to publishing house, and on 10:30 traction car to Ft. Wayne and to Lima and to Swanders. Sup & lodge at Christopher Shearer's. Martha, Mary, Clara and Effie are the sister's at home. Ed. & Warren were there that day, also Fannie ——— [blank]. Thawing & foggy.

Sunday, January 14 Slightly rainy. I remain at Shearer's all day. Harriet, my cousin, is partially paralyzed. She was seventy-six years old in October. Shearer's have six sons and six daughters. Albert, John, Ed., William,

Charles, Warren, the five daughters above & Minnie. The children all living.

Monday, January 15 I went on 9:40 traction to Dayton—on steam cars from Sidney. Wrote a letter or two.

Tuesday, January 16 Weather, colder. Joseph Wilberforce came at 9:00, and we went to Probate Judge to look after D.F. Wilberforce's Naturalization records. Copies had been sent to Sec. Root and to Freetown, as we learned from the Judge.

Wednesday, January 17 I was at home all day. I called at Lorin's in the evening. Ther. 29 degrees at 8:00.

Thursday, January 18 Weather, fair. Ther. 37 degrees at 7:30. I was at home all day. Carrie Gumbach called on a visit in the evening. I was dull and did not do much today, but I copied Hon. O.H. Smith's sketch, of Silas Wright and sent to Rodney P. Wright, Cambridge, (A.) Mass.

Saturday, January 20 Weather, little rain. Ther. 68 degrees at 12:00. At home. I gave my usual annual donation of five dollars to the Miami Hospital. Wrote a long letter to James M. Stewart of Brookville, Ind. and one to Kinneman. Agnes Osborn supped and lodged with Katharine.

Sunday, January 21 Weather, fair. 78 degrees at 1:00. Heard Maurice E. Wilson pr. a good sermon at 11:00, Eph. 6.1. "It is right." Saw Grandma Leitch on my way home, 85 years. Horace was with us to dinner. His physical health and energy, his decision, his amiability and his beauty and intelligence make him a favorite.

Monday, January 22 Weather, rainy. There was a high degree. At home. Read much in Schouler's History of the United States. He is a pretty good historian, only his style is artificial. Mrs. Smith of Fifth Street, came in the afternoon to do our house work. Poe's works came by express from "Lit. Digest."

Tuesday, January 23 Read much in Poe's 1st Volume. Wrote several letters. A pretty day. Bishop E.B. Kephart died to-day in Indianapolis, aged 72. Little Ivonette has tonsilitis.

Wednesday, January 24 Weather, fair. Therm. 26 degrees at 7:30. At home. Beautiful day. Ther. from 26 to 40 degrees. Wrote several letters. Clay informs me of our rehearing case being argued Monday at Wabash. I read much.

Thursday, January 25 Weather, clo. Ther. 32 degrees at 8:00. Went to bank & A. Shearer's store in the afternoon. Wrote many letters. Netta has tonsilitis, or quinsy, or mumps.

Friday, January 26 Weather, fair. Ther. 36 at 10:00, 50 at 11:00. I was at home as usual. I read much, and wrote letters. Netta is still quite sick and Lorin stays at home.

Sunday, January 28 Weather, cloudy. Ther., 35 degrees at 8:30. I Preached at 11:00 at Wesleyan Church (AMC) Ps. 126.3. Full house. Pastor Bastis protracting. Ivonette and Horace were with us most of the day. Rev. B.F. Farris called to see me. He talked with Orville about the Flying machine.

Monday, January 29 Weather, hazy. Ther. 34 degrees. I went to Cincinnati to F.H. & Semele Short's Golden Wedding. Saw their son Frank Bloom, Allen Reeder (aged 89), Miss Donahoo, a Mr. Reeder, Dr. Norton (aged 85), Lawyer Probasco, etc. Came home on 4:00 train, arr. at 6:00.

Tuesday, January 30 Weather, Fog. Ther., 57 degrees at 10:30. At home. Write out a sketch of the Reeder Family for Mrs. Mary A. Bellamy, of Knoxville, Iowa. Agnes Osborn visits us in the evening. Also Joseph G. Wilberforce and Miss Constance Henderson. *Amy French's grandaughter.

Wednesday, January 31 News of the death of Rev. Wm. Miller's wife, Lizzie. In the evening I am telephoned to assist in the funeral Friday.

Thursday, February 1 Ther. 33 degrees at 8:30. I received copies of Warren church and parsonage deeds, which shows a stolen church.

Friday, February 2 Ther. 12 degrees at 7:00. Went via Springfield to Uniopolis. Mrs. Lizzie Miller's funeral at 2:00 at the Church (M.E.). Rev. John Freeman pr. Jno.

1 9 0 6

14.2. I spoke (in all for both) 30 minutes. Burial cemetery three miles away. I supped at Miller's, went in cab to Wapakoneta and reached Dayton, 8:35. Shearer, Wilson & Jesse McKenzie, Mullenhour & his raltives were there—at the funeral.

Saturday, February 3 Ther. 14 degrees at 7:00. I am at home. The day is a pretty one. Wilbur and Orville get a cable message from Arnold Fordyce, Paris, saying that the French Government would deposit 25,000 francs, as per contract, by February 5th.

Sunday, February 4 At 10:30, heard Rev. George Walton King, at Park Presbyterian Church, preach, Phil. 3:13,14. Met Rev. J.F. Colby on my return home, who asks about the boys's flying. I called at Lorin's in afternoon. His horse "Joe"died this morning. A little snow in the evening.

Monday, February 5 Weather, fair. Ther. 3 degrees at 7:00. Much snow had fallen in the night, and it melted little in the day. Katharine's school room was not properly heated; so she dismissed at 10:00. Wilbur & Orville got telegrams that $4842.61 are deposited in Morgan's New York Bank by the French as forfeit money; or option money.

Tuesday, February 6 Weather, fair. Ther. at 7:00, 2 degrees below. Rev. B.G. Huber writes me of what I had known in the plan to hire Dr. H.J. Becker at Chambersburg! Still seeking whom he may devour! I am engaged as usual. The day is decided but not severe winter.

Wednesday, February 7 Weather, fair. Ther. 5 degrees at 7. At home engaged as usual. After midnight, I saw the eclipse of the moon.

Thursday, February 8 Weather, fair. Ther. 12 degrees. At home. Got word that Joseph G. Wilberforce was hurt and went to town to know. His finger was badly hurt. I did not see him. He had gone to the hospital, as I learned some weeks later.

Friday, February 9 Weather, fair. Ther. 12 degrees at 7:30. I visited the tri-conference of Congregationalists, United Brethren (Liberal), and Methodist Protestants

in the forenoon. Answered Rev. C.A. Mummart's request for advice on Chambersburg matters. Prof. Woerthner and wife visited us in the evening.

Saturday, February 10 Weather, fair. Ther. 20 degrees at 8:00. It was a nice day. I was reading and writing. Agnes Osborn visited us at supper. Paul Lawrence Dunbar died yesterday.

Sunday, February 11 I heard Rev. D. Frank Garland preach at 10:30, Acts 11.19–21, a good sermon on Work for Laymen. Leontine and Horace visited us to-day.

Monday, February 12 It was a warm day. Paul Lawrence Dunbar was buried to-day. The funeral was at Eaker Street M.E. (colored) Church. He was Orville's classmate in High School. (This record skipped a leaf!) Ther. 13 degrees, 7. At home. Wrote many letters.[Entry was placed on the wrong page]

Saturday, February 17 Weather, cloudy. Ther. 21 degrees at 7:00. Snow in the evening. I got a letter from Clay at 2:00 enclosing proof on an editorial. I telegraphed him to omit it. Wrote several letters. W.J. Hammer of New York, came in the evening to see the boys.

Sunday, February 18 Spent the day mostly in reading and studying the Scriptures. Lorin's children, except Milton, were with us. Mr. Hammer called again.

Monday, February 19 Ther. 28 degrees at 7:30. Telephone message of Mrs. Lee's death, New Point, Ind. It turns out a warm, sunny day, 56 degrees at 3:30.

Tuesday, February 20 Went on 12:10 (12:40) tr. via Cincinnati to Newpoint, Ind. Ivan Wilkison came and took me to his Mother's where I found Rev. C.R. Paddack & (her sister) wife. I supped and lodged there.

Wednesday, February 21 At 11:00, at Memorial Presbyterian Church, I preach, Rev. 21,4, Mrs. Lee's funeral. Rev. Mr. Taylor assisted. I saw Miss Cooms and the wives of David Morgan and Geo. Umphrey. I go from New Point to Rugby, where I attend prayer meeting. I lodge at W.C. Galbraith's.

Thursday, February 22 I went on 7:35 tr. to Greensburg

& called an hour on Uncle John Braden's and left on 10:25 tr. for Rushville, and thence on 12:00 traction to to [repeated in text] Gwynneville. Did not find any at home at B.F. Nugent's; so I walked to Wm. Myer's where I sup & lodge. Myrtle Kiser & Wilcoxen there.

Friday, February 23 I called an hour at Earnest Wagoner's, and went on traction to Rushville. Rode out to Harvey Wright's with Joey McBride. Dine, sup & lodge there. Drusilla was there, and Effie and Cora called at the gate. Harvey's cancer is very painful.

Saturday, February 24 Mr. Laser took me to Sexton to 6:20 tr., which I just reach, and I go on to Dunrieth and take the 8:41 tr. home arriving at 11:00. Alma & Lois Fry were on the train to Mays, and they move to Muncie, Monday. Thunder & rain, eve.

Sunday, February 25 Weather, fair. Ther., 45 degrees at 10:00. I heard Rev H.C. Jameson pr. a very able and eloquent sermon at 10:30, Job. 19:23–27, at Grace M.E. Church. Monsieur Fornier, an attache of the French embassy at Washington, came and dined with us. Left on 10:00 train. Gen. Thomas J. Wood, died in this city, early this morn.

Tuesday, February 27 Weather, fair. Ther., mild. At home as usual. Received a letter of inquiry concerning genealogy from Mrs. Mary Alice Bellamy, of Knoxville, Iowa, she being a grand daughter of Amey French, the daughter of Elizabeth (Reeder) Tingle.

Wednesday, February 28 Weather, fair, Ther. mild. Joseph G. Wilberforce called more than an hour in the forenoon. He broke his finger a few weeks ago. It is nearly well.

Sunday, March 4 I remained at home to day. Lorin's Milton and Horace were with us, and they lodged with us the first time in their lives.

Monday, March 5 Horace staid mostly in my room all forenoon. I wrote many letters, day and evening.

Tuesday, March 6 To-day, I see the statement in the Triweekly New York *Tribune,* that in the last quarter of a century, 10,000,000 acres of desert land in the United States, have been made productive by irrigation. For twenty years, and much more, I have believed and said that the arid land this side of the Rocky Mountians would be reclaimed!

Wednesday, March 7 Wrote out a sketch (8 large pages) of the Reader family; for Mrs. Mary Alice Bellamy, Knoxville, Iowa. She is the granddaughter of Amey (Tingle) French, and daughter of Jededia Tingle French. Mrs. French was my Mother's second cousin, Daughter of Elizabeth Reeder. Called at Lorin's.

Thursday, March 8 Finished and sent off the memorial sketch.

Friday, March 9 I went on 9:00 tr to Indianapolis. I called at 402 S. Meridian Street to see Fay and Harvey Wright, grand-nephews. Spent afternoon at Austin Winchell's, and had supper there. Laura W's father Chas. Harris (feeble) was there whom I had not seen for years. I go to Mohawk. Lodge at Dr. O.A. Collins.

Saturday, March 10 I dined at Dr. Collins. I pr. at 1:30, Ps. 16.11. Strange farce of Quarterly conference! T.B. Leary, James and Amos Deshond and their father! I sup at Clarence Brooks. I pr. at 7:30, Eccl. 12.11. I lodged at Amos Deshond's. Before supper, I called at Susan Nickum's to see Mrs. John Jackson.

Sunday, March 11 I called at Mrs. Wm. McConnell's. I preach at 11:00, Ex. 20.11. Dine at Mrs. Wm. McConnell's, John Kuhn's and wife there, also Mrs. John H. Cushman & boy. I go with Cushman's to their home 2 1/2 ms South-east of Fortville. Much snowfall. Sup & lodge there.

Monday, March 12 I ate early dinner, and she took me to Fortville. I went on 11:35 tr to Fairmount. Saw Oliver Buller in the bank & R.W. White at hardware store. I supped and lodged at Ellis Wright's.

Tuesday, March 13 I wrote letters & saw Joe Paril who paid me $35.00 on his ware-room on my lot, and Ellis Wright paid me $78.85 rent collected by him. I dine at Ellis Wright's and go on R'y via Anderson home. Mr. Grimes called; he is a writer. Wrote up flying by boys.

Wednesday, March 14 I was at home all day, and wrote Louis R. Noble, Mattoon, Ill. about the Reeder family. Lorin and Netta called an hour in the evening, with Horace, who wants his uncles to now make him a big flying machine so it will be ready when he is big!

Saturday, March 17 Ther. 14 degrees at 7:00. This St. Patrick's Day. He was not a papist, but one of the greatest of missionaries, and the Irish Church was for centuries one of the best in Europe. It is the 106th anniversary of my Mother's birth, and the 45th of my son Reuchlin's. I wrote him, and sent him five dollars, as a present.

Sunday, March 18 Ther. not cold. It is a snowy day, followed by a snowy night. I remained at home all day. A letter came from Reuchlin and one to Horace, enclosed. Horace thought that "Grandpapa made it," but Milton told him that Uncle wrote it.

Tuesday, March 20 Fair day; snow melted some. Commander Henri Bonel, Capt. Fornier, Arnold Fordyce, and Attorney Walter V.R. Berry came to negotiate some changes in the Flyer contract.

Wednesday, March 21 Ther. at 6:00, 26 degrees. Fair day and much melting of the snow. The French Commission came again, and terms were agreed upon. I was present.

Thursday, March 22 I was at home. Read over my Diaries of 1857, I wrote but little.

Friday, March 23 I read over my Diaries of 1859 and diaries of parts of 1869 and 1871. The three Frenchmen again visited Wilbur and Orville.

Saturday, March 24 To-day, I largely spent in classifying and fastening together my accumulated documents on our genealogy. Perhaps few have succeeded better in tracing ancestors in so many branches as fully and as far back as I have. Fordyce, Bonel and Berry supped with us & spent the evening.

Sunday, March 25 Heard Dr. Whidden pr at 10:40 on Young Men. Wrote an article on Spurious Christianity. The weather is thawing.

Monday, March 26 Went to Main Street and bought a few small articles. In the afternoon, I rewrote an article for the Conservator. Mrs. Stevens and Neice and Miss Wuichet visited Katharine. I attended Mrs. Stuckey's funeral at the Mitchell house on Third Street.

Tuesday, March 27 Letter from David H. Reeder, La Porte, Ind. I go to A.H. Reeder's, in 707 Superior Ave., to get Allen L. Reeder's address, which is Riverside, Cincinnati, Station G. Wrote to Allen, letter and Sketch of the Reeder family to the Children of Joseph III.

Thursday, March 29 At Home. This is Allen Lake Reeder's eighty-ninth birth-day.

Friday, March 30 I was at Boy's office when Arnold Fordyce came. In the afternoon at 2:30, Beri Bonell, Capt. Regnier, A. Fordyce and Walter V.R. Berry came. Negotiations closed. Bonnell will cable the war minister to see if he will yield certain points. Agreement doubtful.

Saturday, March 31 Was at home. Mr. Chas. Parkhurst and Agnes Osborn ate supper with us.

Monday, April 2 Mr. O. Chanute, Chi., came. His visit with the four Frenchmen in Wright brothers' office. He, W.W. Berry and Arnold Fordyce, sup with us. To-day John Alexander Dowie is deposed as a leader in Zion and W.G. Voliva succeeds him. His leaders, & even his wife Jane Dowie, repudiate him. Selah.

Tuesday, April 3 Wrote a long letter to Bishop F.L. Hoskins. Called on Sophia Simpson.

Wednesday, April 4 At home all day. Attended Joseph G. Wilberforce's & Constance M. Henderson's wedding at George Nook's, 217 Pontiac Ave., at 8:30, eve. Rev. O.B. Heavlow, Covington, Ky., officiated, of C.M.E. Church.

Thursday, April 5 I went on 5:30 A.M. tr to Lima and Huntington. Lunched at a restaurant. Mis. Ex. Com. met at 2:00. Joe Wilberforce forgiven. Determined not to send Stoltz back to Africa this year. Supper at H.C. Foote's and I lodge there.

Friday, April 6 I settle with Foote on Establishment legal expenses loaned by me from the Shisler fund. Ex. Com. met at 9:00. Determined to send Joseph G. Wilberforce and Constance to Africa in June. I went on 11:23 car to Fairmount. Sup & lodge at Ellis Wright's. Called an hour at 0. Buller's.

Saturday, April 7 Finished up business in Fairmount. Dined at Ellis's. Went to Fowlerton. Supper at R.W. White's. Walked to Wm. H.H. Reeder's. Lodged there.

Sunday, April 8 Rainy day. Oliver and Flora dined with us at Reeder's. I lodged at Reeder's.

Monday, April 9 William takes me to the 7:17 train, and via Richmond, I reach Dayton at 11:00. It was a pretty day. Mt. Vesuvius is still in a rage.

Tuesday, April 10 At home all day. Spent the time reading and writing. Alex. Dowie is in Chicago at a hotel.

Wednesday, April 11 At home. Nothing of note in my affairs. It is a delightful day. J.A. Dowey quiet.

Thursday, April 12 At home all day. It is a fine, warm day. Dowie talks of legal measures to regain Zion property. Joseph G. Wilberforce called at 1:00, and Rev. Wm. B. Stoddard at 2:30. He is of Washington, D.C.

Saturday, April 14 At home. Mrs. Katie Smith quit working for us. She has been an unusually nice woman in her ways, though not a very good house-keeper.

Sunday, April 15 I did not attend any of the Easter shows in the churches, which are becoming exclusive and intense.

Monday, April 16 At home. Wrote up and sent to Ruby Oliver a synopsis of the the [repeated in text] ancestry she is interested in.

Wednesday, April 18 At 2:00, Ther., 78 degrees. News comes of an earthquake at San Francisco, to day. Many lives lost and much property destroyed. Martial law is proclaimed. I forgot W.B. Stoddard's address at the German Lutheran Church.

Friday, April 20 At home. Mr. Partick Y. Alexander, an Englishman of wealth, sups with us. News from H.C. Foote of Judge Plummer's decision against us, at Wabash.

Saturday, April 21 I wrote letters to my nieces, Ela Rees, Lincoln, Kansas, and Stella Petree, Oregon Missiori and Kate Van Fleet, Alamosa, Colorado. The weather is warm.

Sunday, April 22 Called at Lorin's, and Ivonette and Horace came home with me. Heard the pastor, (F.G. Coffin) of Broadway Christian Church, preach Rev. 3.4. He is good in thought, language and delivery.

Monday, April 23 At home. Transcribed Gr. mother Reeder's accasional diary of 1852 to 1858.

Tuesday, April 24 At home. Wright Brothers received cablegram from Arnold Fordyce, Paris. Negotiation reconsidered. He is hopeful.

Wednesday, April 25 Got the Conservator containing Clay's note on the Bealor suit. Wrote him what I thought of its admissions.

Friday, April 27 Started at 10:50 for Fairmount via Richmond and Anderson. Arrived about 2:00. Looked after business. I supped and lodged at Ellis Wright's. Called at Hollingsworth's in the evening.

Saturday, April 28 Looked after business and then went on 9:17 tr. to Fowlerton. Dined at R.W. White's. Qr. Conference at 2:00. I pr Rev. 2:11. We measured cleared land 10 5/7, and I paid Andrew White $40.00 more for clearing = $75.00 in all. Supper at White's. J. Howe pr. at 8:00. We lodge at White's.

Sunday, April 29 I preach at Hopewell at 10:30, 1 Cor. 1:23,24, communion. Dine at Lewis Hayden's with J. Howe. J. How[e] pr. at 8:00—35 present; Malone's too. Lodge at R.W. White's.

Monday, April 30 I go on 7:17 tr via Richmond home. Arrive at 11:00. Bishop Matthews on train & Rev. W.F. Parker. Parker is Liberal pastor at Frankfort. He weighs very heavy. Matthews lives in Chicago. Grant Mendenhall was on the train from Economy to Richmond.

Wednesday, May 2 At home. Nothing unusual, except K's card from Mr. Meachem saying physicians give no encouragement for Margaret's recovery. Margaret was Katharine's room-mate four years in Oberlin.

Thursday, May 3 I wrote to C.W. Linker in Africa. A telegram to Katharine says that Margaret (Goodwin) Meachem died in Chicago, this morning. She was four years Katharine's room-mate at Oberlin College. Katharine started to Chicago at 9:30, eve.

Friday, May 4 At home. I wrote Bishop Barkley a long letter. I ordered my mail to be delivered at 1127 West Third Street.

Saturday, May 5 I wrote a program with notes for Bishops' Annual Meeting, for Bishop Barkley, in the forenoon. I went on 2:45 tr. to Glenwood & telephoned N.F. Bowen's to come for me and started on. Ed. Winchell & wife overtook me and brought me to Orange (formerly Fayetteville). Ralph took me to Bowen's where I lodged. It was first Danville.

Sunday, May 6 Went to Lucinda Moor's, and I dine and sup there. Heard A. Moody Shaw preach at 3:00 at Sains Creek Church. I lodged at Charles Stevens'. (Lucinda Moor's first husband was my brother William, who died in 1868. Boen and Stevens are her sonsinlaw. Lucinda's youngest daughter Bertha Long lives with her.)

Monday, May 7 I remained at Flora Stevens' till 2:00, and then went to Mrs. Bertha Long's. However I called in the forenoon at Colvin Stevens' an hour. Mr. Clifton Long has been in the epileptic assylum at Indianapolis about a year. Chas. Stevens' at 4:00 took me to Glenwood, and I went to Rushville and Charles I. Gray took me to my brother Harvey's.

Tuesday, May 8 I dined at my nephew's (Thomas Wright's) a half mile north. In the afternoon, Elder Tharp of Liberty and a Mr. Newhouse called at Harvey. I lodge at Harvey's, who has a very bad rose cancer across his left ear.

Wednesday, May 9 Charles Gray took me to 8:41 tr. at Dunrieth, and I get home at 11:00. Found several letters.

Thursday, May 10 I was at home. Wrote some letters. Went with Lorin's children to Ringling's parade in the forenoon. The Lower House of the Russian Parliament was opened to-day. Hail to the dawn of the liberty of "all the Russians," Autocracy will henceforth be ever decreasing till its sepulchal days.

Sunday, May 13 At Grace M.E. Church, I heard Bishop J.W. Hamilton of San Francisco, on Judges 3:20, "A message." It was not a great sermon, but he is a masterful speaker. Lorin's girls and Horace dined with us. I read the first Book of Maccabees through.

Monday, May 14 Wrote Bishop C.L. Wood on White River's time of conference.

Tuesday, May 15 At home. Ordered a coat and vest, of Perry Meredith.

Friday, May 18 Spent two hours in the Public Library in the forenoon. Put on a new type ribbon, and soon after broke the wire governing the letter t. I got letters from J. Howe and Clay telling of the suit entered at Marion about Fowlerton Church, by Seceders.

Saturday, May 19 At home. Got my typewriter repaired. Miss Jennie Steele of Oberlin called on Katharine in the evening.

Sunday, May 20 I heard Dr. A.H. Strong, Pres. of Rochester Theo. Seminary, N.Y. at 11:00, Matt. 17:20, "If faith as a grain of mustard seed" etc.; at First Pres. Church.

Wednesday, May 23 Started at 9:00, via Richmond to Fowlerton. Saw J.M. Manning, J.T. Vardaman & wife and Atkinson on the cars. Lunch at Restaurant in Fowlerton. Went to R.W. White's and Lewis Hayden's. Go to Fairmount. Sup & lodge at Ellis Wright's. O. Buller called at 7:30.

Thursday, May 24 Oliver Buller and I go on 8:00 car to Marion. Called at St. John & Charles' office. They are at Peru. We go back to Fairmount. Dine at Ellis's. Saw Buller, Parker etc. Bought Joseph Paril's warehouse for $200, he to have 16 2/3 months rent (use) for half that amount. Sup at Ellis's. Went to R.W. White's at farm.

Friday, May 25 I went on 7:17 tr. via Richmond, home. Arr. at 11:00. Wrote several letters and cards to mail at 3:00. Mr. Caldwell, of Toledo, called to see if Bishop Barkley was here.

Thursday, May 31 Went on 8:00 car with Oliver Buller to Marrion. Saw Attorney's St. John & Charles an hour. I went on 12:28 tr. to Knightstown. Went thence to Jabez Rhoads. Sup. He takes me to Harvey W's.

Friday, June 1 Afternoon, Thomas Wright takes me to Rushville and I go on to Milroy and thence with James F. Harris to his House. Sup and lodge there. They have spent the winter in Florida. Her father, Dr. Johnson, died in Clarksburg this spring.

Saturday, June 2 Started to Lefforge's, and Otis L. Miller met me, and I went to his house, 1 1/2 miles east and dined. The Quarterly meeting at Mt. Zion had been re-called because the Lefforge families had been called to Illinois by their brother's funeral. I went to Milroy & home via Knightstown & Richmond.

Sunday, June 3 Heard Rev. Henry C. Jameson pr. at 10:30, Gal. 6:14. He was a great preacher at the Grace M.E. Church.

Wednesday, June 6 I go on 8:14 tr. via Arcanum, Shirley, Anderson and Wabash to Huntington. Sup at J. Howe's. Lodge at Dr. Morehouse's, where my home is for a week. Dr. Dillon lectured at 7:30 on Religious Errors.

Thursday, June 7 Missionary Annual meeting begins at 10:00 in College Chapel. I sup at Otto B. Bowman's. Bishop F.L. Hoskins preached an able missionary discourse at 7:30, Rev. 6:1.

Friday, June 8 Board meeting continued. I supped at Morehouse's & dined also. Oratory entertainment at College.

Saturday, June 9 Closed Missionary meeting before noon.

Sunday, June 10 Attended Sunday School at 9:30, Clay's class. Rev. S.L. Livingston preached a fine baccalaureat sermon at 10:30. I dine at Otto B. Bowman's & sup there. I pr. annual sermon before the Board of Education at 7:30, Micah 6:8, "Do justly, love mercy."

Monday, June 11 Dined at S.L. Livingston's. Educational Board opened at 2:00.

Tuesday, June 12 Publishing Board met at 9:00. I was not present. I called at Chrispopher Wilberforce's, and W.H. Clay's, & dined at S.L. Livingston.

Wednesday, June 13 Called at L.M. Davis', F.H. Cremean's and at Willis Casidy's. Graduating exercises at 10:00. Five graduates, Miss Miller, and Rothfus, among them. Alumni dinner at 12:30. W.H. Clay toastmaster. Went on 4:20 traction to Wabash & thence to Ellis Wright's, Fairmount.

Thursday, June 14 Went to Marion with 0. Buller & R.W. White. Saw St. John & Charles. Went to Anderson on traction. Lunch. Go home on tr. arri. at 5:30. Had a long sleep at night. School Board advanced Katharine's wages from 120 to 140 dollars per month.

Friday, June 15 At home. Rearranged my book-case. Called at Lorin's in the evening.

Saturday, June 16 I went on 11:55 train to Miamisburg, and thence on traction to Germantown. Rev. William Miller pr. at 2:00. Quarterly conference followed. I sup at Jac. J. Fouts. W. Miller pr. at 8:00. We lodge at J. Wesley Fout's.

Sunday, June 17 At Sunday School at 9:00. Wm. Miller pr. at 10:30. I administer the sacrament. We dine at Rev. J. Cost's. Call over an hour at John Slifer's. I pr. at 7:30, John 1.4. I lodge at E.M. Scott's.

Monday, June 18 Start to Dayton on 7:15 traction. Wm. Miller goes to Wapakoneta on 9:50 train from Dayton. News came of the death of Gov. Patterson, who died at about 4:00 afternoon to-day.

Friday, June 22 Katharine started on a visit to Geneva, Ohio this forenoon. My brother Harvey Wright died about 3:00 this afternoon, and I received a telegram. His age was 85 years, 9 months and 13 days.

Saturday, June 23 I go on 9:00 tr to Knightstown and with Ed. Frazier to his house, and after dinner to Harvey Wright's, & returned to Frazier's and supped and lodged.

Sunday, June 24 Wrote a memorial paper. Went to Harvey's. Funeral at 2:00, at Center Church. Rev. Robert Thompson pr. at 2:30, 2d Tim. 4:7,8. I returned to Harvey's. Probably there were five or six hundred people at the funeral. (Some say 1,000).

Monday, June 25 I went on the 6:40 tr. to Mays, and home by 11:00.

Thursday, June 28 At home. It is a very warm day. Christopher Wilberforce called a half hour in the evening. It is a very warm day and night.

Friday, June 29 At home till 2:50; then go via Union City to Fortville, Ind., where Rev. T.E. Kinneman meets me and takes me to his house 4 miles away. Sup and lodge there. It was a very warm day and night.

Saturday, June 30 I went with Kinneman to James Selby's and to Mrs. Indiana Helms, where I dine. At 2:00, I comment on John 1.1–14, and we hold Quarterly conference. I go to Kinneman's where I sup & lodge.

Sunday, July 1 I preach at 10:30, after a testimony meeting, Rom. 6.22. I dine with Rev. John Jackson at Mrs. Lednum's, and go to Kenneman's. Sup and lodge there. I preach, again, at Plainview Church at 8:00, 2 Tim. 3.16.

Monday, July 2 Kinneman takes me to Fortville and I go on traction via Union City home to Dayton, arriving at 2:00. Katharine also returned in the afternoon from a visit to Silliman's and Mella King's at Geneva, Ohio.

Wednesday, July 4 It is seventeen years this forenoon since Susan died. I went this afternoon and spent an hour at her grave in Woodland Cemetery. Her's was a sweet spirit. Hers was a careful life, and one of implicit faith in God.

Thursday, July 5 At Home. Wrote a long letter to Rev. J. Howe. I called at Lorin's in the evening.

Friday, July 6 Called in the forenoon at Peter Louding's. Mrs. Lucy M. Louding, his wife, died early yester day morning.

Saturday, July 7 At 2:30 was at Lucy M. Louding's funeral at First U.B. (Liberal) Church, corner of Perry & Fourth. Rains about night fall. W.J. Shuey pr. the sermon.

Sunday, July 8 Heard D. Frank Garland, John 20.26, at 10:30. Lorin's three younger children came afternoon; and Lorin and Netta, a half hour.

Wednesday, July 11 This is Horace's fifth birthday anniversary, and I get him a "trombone", a firewagon and horses and 5 marbles. I called at Peter Louding's a few minutes in the evening.

Thursday, July 12 At home. Wrote a long letter to Reuchlin.

Friday, July 13 Went on 11:00 traction car to Richmond. Called at Caroline Zellers' a half-hour. Went on 2:10 Limited to Cambridge City. Wm. T. Lawson takes me to his house 1 1/2 m. n. of Dublin. I preached there at 4:00, Rom. 2:6, had a brief council followed by Quar. Conference. Sup and lodge at Lawson's.

Saturday, July 14 Went with Lawson's (who were marketing) to Cambridge City and went on 8:30 tr. to Laurel, and Jesse I. Leforge takes me in automobile to his home one-half mile west of Andersonville. Dinner. I preach at 3:00 & hold quarterly conference at Mt. Zion Ch. Sup & lodge at Phi. Lefforge's in Andersonv. Dr. Marshall & Sam. Barber and wife called in.

Sunday, July 15 I called at S. Barber's, Smith Scott's & Mrs. Prudence Moore's. The two last not in. I pr. at Mt. Zion, one m S. of Neff's corners, at 10:30, Ps. 84:11. Sacrament. Dine at Otis L. Miller's, 1 1/2 m. West. I pr. at 3:30, Lu. 16.9. N.F. Bowen & Chas. Stevens and wives present & I go with them. We called at Sally Ann Cook's. I sup at Charley Stevens' & lodge at Lucinda Moor's, near Orange.

Monday, July 16 Mrs. Bertha Long, takes me to Glenwood to 10:36 tr., but as train would not stop, I took the 11:58 train home and arrived about 3:00. Slept and rested some.

Tuesday, July 17 At home. It is time of quite a panic over the glanders in the city.

Wednesday, July 18 At home. Wilbur is testing his remodeled Flyer engine. Orville is completing his new flyer engine.

Thursday, July 19 At home. Katharine took Ivonette and Leontine to the Soldier's Home in the evening.

Friday, July 20 At Home. I did little except to read very much. Orville is beginning to try his new engine.

Saturday, July 21 At home. It was a dull day to me. Orville is still trying his engine.

Sunday, July 22 I heard at Williams' Street Baptist Church, E.R. Dow of Chicago, Ps. 62.11, "Power belageth unto God." He is a fluent, earnest, effective speaker. Netta and the children go to Delaware for a visit to Jessie Stokes, her sister in law.

Sunday, July 29 At Broadway Christian Church, I heard at 10:30, Rev. W.M. Dawson, who is a good speaker, from Yellow Springs, Phil. 4.13. I read in Kitto's History of the Bible, from the time of Malachi to the birth of Christ.

Monday, July 30 At home. Wrote to J. Howe, C.L. Wood, Lena Winkel & J. Jackson. Went to town. In the evening, the children take an automobile ride with Mr. S. Crane, Spencer Crane.

Tuesday, July 31 At home. In the evening, Netta and the Children return from Delaware. Joseph Wilberforce and Constance and Christopher called in the evening.

Saturday, August 4 Wrote Huber a statement about the Bealor Note decisions. Leontine took supper with us.

Sunday, August 5 Rev. Charles R. Watson pr. an able and eloquent sermon at First U.B. Liberal Church, at 10:30, Ps. 145.11. Lorin's children came, and Lorin and Netta in the evening.

Wednesday, August 8 Wrote out, for Fay Wright sketches of the Freeman and Porter families. Mr. Gleickey, an attache of the British Embassy at Washington called to see Wilbur and Orville.

Friday, August 10 Wrote to W.W. Knipple. I went in afternoon (2:25) via Lima to Huntington, Ind. Sup at W.H. Clay's. Lodge at Pres. T.H. Gragg's.

Saturday, August 11 I met the Mis. Executive Committee at 9:00. We remained in session till 1:00. I dine with Bishop Wood at a restaurant. Go out to S.A. Stemen's (2 m.) to Red Bridge, on traction line.

Sunday, August 12 We go to College Park, to testimony meeting. Rev. Wm. Miller, P.E., pr. at 10:30, Ps. 97.1 & Rom. 8.28. Preached excellently. I introduce the sacrament. I dine at S.L. Livingston's. Sup at J. Howe's. Call at O.B. Bowman's. Heard Bishop C.L. Wood pr. at 7:00, Hebr. 6.19. I lodged at Jacob Howe's.

Monday, August 13 I went on 6:00 tr. via Kingsland, to Montpelier, and walked six miles to Lorenzo W. Blount's. I dined, and got much information and assurance. Blount took me back & I go on via Heartford and Jonesboro to Fairmount. I lodged at Ellis Wright's.

Tuesday, August 14 I rode out five miles with Ellis. Next I saw C.T. Parker and settled with him. Dined at Ellis'. Settled with him. Went on 3:05 tr. to Fowlerton. Sup at R.W. White's, Mistake Sun. train. I go to O.A. Glass's.

Wednesday, August 15 I went on 7:17 tr., via Richmond, home arriving at 11:00, forenoon. I wrote letters.

Sunday, August 19 It is Orville and Katharine's birthday anniversary—he 35 and she 32 years old. I heard at 10:30, Rev. H.J. Jameson pr., Acts 11.26, What to be a Christian. He is the best preacher and pulpit orator, the M.E. Ch. ever had in Dayton. Horace supped with us and Leontine came after; and Lorin & Netta at dark.

Monday, August 20 I am at home. The boys are still adjusting and testing their new motors. Lou Lane came to work for Katharine.

Tuesday, August 21 Received telegram of Henry Walter's

death. Go on 2:50 train via Union City to Bolivar, Ind. Allisbaugh met me at Wabash and asked me to go no further! I went to Huntington and lodged at Huntington House.

Wednesday, August 22 Went to the Publishing House. Dined at Midway Restaurant. Walked to Park. Talked to Dillon. I supped at Livingston's. Lodged at J. Howe's.

Thursday, August 23 I went with Howe and others to Glenmore and to Greenbrier Church to Auglaize Conference, which opened at 9:00. I found home at D.N. Key's. I supped at George Alspaugh's, 1 m. S. He loves beer! J. Howe pr. at 8:00, quite well.

Friday, August 24 I dine at Middaugh's. He is blind. I sup at Hey's. Mis. Meeting at 7:30. I lodge at Hey's.

Saturday, August 25 I dine at Frank Dull's, a half mile west. Saw a Tussing, layman, brother of D.O.T. Memorial of Mahin & Lizzie Miller, at 2:30. Conf. adj. at 4:00. I sup at Key's. I pr. at 8:00, Rom. 2.6.

Sunday, August 26 Testimony meeting at 9:00. Bishop Olin G. Alwood pr. in the grove 1/2 m. west at 10:30, "Praise ye the Lord," Ps. 146, 147, 148, 149, 150, 1st verse. Coll. 50.00. I dine at Key's. S.S. Anniversary at the Church (at 3:00) on Account of rain. I sup at Wesley Walters, 3/4 m. west. Bp. Alwood pr. at 8:00, Matt. 22.42, "What think." Lodge at Key's.

Monday, August 27 Key took me to Wm. Walters', 1 1/2 m. n.w. where I dine. Walters took me to Ohio City, where I lunch (sup) at a restaurant, and go on 8:46 tr. to Van Wert where I lodge at Hotel Marsh.

Tuesday, August 28 Breakfast (restaurant) and go on 6:10 tr. to Alvordton & thence 9:50 to Kunkle, Ohio. Find conf. home at Jacob Daso's, first house east of the church. Many come to conference. Rev. Carpenter pr. at 8:00, John 13.4,5, "Wash the disciples' feet."

Wednesday, August 29 Bishop Firman L. Hoskins opened conference at 9:00 with much eloquence. Dennis Sect'y. Letter from Katharine and enclosed letters from Kinneman. Wrote K. & Wood. Sup at Mr. Smith's with Hoskin's. Wm. Dillon pr. at 8:00, John 7:46, "Never

man spake," Good, but tame. I slept well.

Thursday, August 30 Got letter & enclosed letters from Katharine. Called at Smith's. Saw many and received kind words. Rev. C.L. Snyder pr. a good sermon at 11:00. I pr. at 8:00, Rom. 8:2, "Law of spir of Life," to 500 people. It was a "halleluia" time. I slept well.

Friday, August 31 Conference continued. Memorial services in the afternoon, for two sisters Dunlap and [text has a line, no name] J. Howe pr. well at 8:00, on Christianity.

Saturday, September 1 Conference continued and closed at 10:00 at night. Wm. Clark pr. at 8:00, Matt. 5.16, "Let lights shine." He is an exhorter and revivalist.

Sunday, September 2 I called at Smith's. I led in the opening prayer at 10:30. Bishop F.L. Hoskins pr. a very able and eloquent sermon at 10:30, James 4.14, "Life a vapor." Coll. $76.00. S.S. Anniversary at 3:00. I spoke on "Duty of Parents to S. School." Wm. Dillon pr. at 8:00, moderate. Two seekers after much exhortation.

Monday, September 3 I go on 9:29 tr. to Mt. Peleer & thence to Ft. Wayne & via Richmond, home, arriving at 5:30. Expenses: 1.85 to Wabash, .35 to Huntington, .65 to Glenmore, .15 to Van Wert, .90 to Alvordton, .15 to Kunkle, .85 to Ft. Wayne, 1.40 to Richmond, .65 to home, 2.00 Hotel fare, 9.15 total. Collections 1.00,.50.

Thursday, September 6 At home. Wrote letters. Saw Baldwin's air-ship float out west. Wilbur went after it— got home at 10:30, at night.

Friday, September 7 Wrote several letters. Wilbur and Orville helped Baldwin bring his air-ship back to Fair Grounds. Emma Dennis and Mrs. Witt called in the afternoon.

Saturday, September 8 I spent most of the day looking up the use of seventh day in the Scriptures, and authorities on the use of sabbaton, taking texts in each case. In the evening, we had a time with Horace, who resented being sent up to our house. He said, "I want to go home!" I finally subdued him.

Sunday, September 9 I heard the farewell of Rev. H.C. Jameson at Grace M.E. Church, where he has been pastor four years. His text was 1 Cor. 15.58. Stability, Patience, Work, Success. He was able and eloquent. I called in the evening at Lorin's a half-hour.

Monday, September 10 Received a letter from Levi J. Freese, enclosing fifty dollars toward Pres. David Shuck's monument. Wrote letters to John M. Manning, Alpheus Huddleston, Wm. Lawson, G.W. Stewart, Wm. Myer, F.L. Hoskins & T.H. Gragg.

Tuesday, September 11 I wrote John Brooks, Wm. Oler, John Oler, Sylvester Wood, Wm. Smith and St. John & Charles. At 4:00, I attended the Republican State Convention, at Welfare Hall and heard Herrick and Foraker speak. A woman had a fight with the conductor on trolley car, as I came home.

Wednesday, September 12 Wrote Wm. Matthews, Cin. Was at the Republican Convention at Welfare Hall from 10:00 till 1:00. Saw Gov. Harris, Burton, Daughterty, Keifer, etc. Fight over Dick's chairmanship, over resolutions, etc. I did not care for the ratification meeting at night.

Thursday, September 13 At home. Called at Sines' to borrow the *Journal*. She was 75 years old, August 30th. Wrote to Marshall Hacker and Wm. A. Oler about Pres. Shuck's monument.

Friday, September 14 Wrote many postal cards. Learned, by Bishop Hoskins and Pres. Gragg's letters, of the defeat of the rebelious in Michigan conference session. In the afternoon about 3 o'clock, my neighbor, Thos. J. Sines was killed by the cars. He is past 74 years of age. Henry Wagner told me to-day that he was 79, last March. Mrs. Sines was 75, August 30.

Saturday, September 15 Went to U.B. Publishing Establishment and to D. Berger's, to see Autobiography of Lydia Sexton. Senseny found it in Historical Library, & gave me new edition of "Our Bishops." At 4:00, V.F. Brown conducted Mr. Sines' funeral & I read the Memorial.

Sunday, September 16 Called at Mrs. Sines, a half hour. Heard Maurice E. Wilson pr. at 11:00, Jer. 48.11, a fine

sermon. Leontine & Horace dine with us. Lorin & Netta called in the evening.

Monday, September 17 At home. Wrote letters in the forenoon. Wrote in the afternoon a sketch of Rev. Jeremiah Kenoyer & mailed it at the town post-office.

Tuesday, September 18 Wrote many letters, quite warm in the evening. Netta had a chill to-day. I called there in the evening. I slept eight or nine hours in the night.

Saturday, September 22 Wrote Pres. Elder's Report to conference.

Sunday, September 23 A little fire, morning, comfortable at noon without. Heard Dr. Whidden at 11:40, John 4.24, & Ps. 95.6, on Worship; as usual, a fine discourse.

Tuesday, September 25 Called at Lorin's. I found Netta's Bro. Horace's new "wife" was there. Netta talked straight to her—told her she did not want to see her, and could not harbor her. So the brazen woman left. I got harness man to mend my valise, 25 cents. I pack to start to conference and start at 7:40 via Richmond to Cambridge City. Lodge at Central Hotel.

Wednesday, September 26 Find no one at Alpheus Huddleston's. I go on the 8:30 train to Laurel. It is raining. Philander Lefforge takes me to his house in Andersonville, where I dine. I go on to Jesse Lefforge's, my conference home. Bishop Wood is there. It is rainy, and the evening meeting is recalled by telephone.

Thursday, September 27 The conference opened at 9:30. The bishop, Kinneman and Wright present, and some brethren & sisters. We dine at Philander's. J. Howe came in afternoon. I sup and lodge at Jesse I. Lefforge's. C.R. Paddack and wife came. T.E. Kinneman pr. at 7:00.

Friday, September 28 Conference continued. I dine and sup at Jesse's, and lodge there. Rev. J. Howe pr. at 7:00, Zech. 4.6, "Not by might," etc.

Saturday, September 29 Conference continued. T.E. Kinneman and John Freeman were elected Pres. Elders. We dined at Mr. Martin's, two miles northwest of the church. Kinneman left at 3:00. Afternoon session. Supper at Philander's. Bishop C.L. Wood pr. ably at 7:30, Acts 2.8, "Endurment with Power," Lodge at Jesse Lefforge's.

Sunday, September 30 C.R. Paddack led lovefeast. Bishop Corydon L. Wood pr 1 John 3:1,2. Raise $66.00 collection for the bishop. Wood and I dine at George Cos's, 1 m. south and $\frac{1}{2}$ m. east. She Morgan Linville's daut. Goldie, 17, Stella, 15, Leslie, Floyd. Wood pr at 7:00, Acts 4:12, "No other Name." Sermon able and impressive. Next conference at Economy. Adjourn. Lodge at Jesse's.

Monday, October 1 Jesse takes us to Milroy. Go to Wabash & Huntington. Exec. Mis. Com. met at 4:00. Sup & lodge at W.H. Clay's. I call at A.A. Powell's, M. Weckler's and Prof. Loew's. Lodge at Clay's.

Tuesday, October 2 After breakfast, call at Pres. T.H. Gragg's, & S.L. Livingston's. I see Chas. Clay, L.M. Davis & M. Wechler, Ex. Com. meeting at J. Howe's at 8:30. I go on to Wabash and reach Fairmount, at 12:45. Dine and lodge at Ellis Wright's. Call 1/2 hour at Oliver Buller's. Saw Mr. Charles at Marion, 20 minutes in afternoon.

Wednesday, October 3 Go with O. Buller to Wesley Hayden's and thence to White's, O.A. Glass's. Dine at Wm. Reeder's. Go on 2:08 train to Richmond and thence to Dayton, arriving at 6:00. Found all well.

Thursday, October 4 Called about 3:00 at 311 Chicago Avenue, and talked a half hour with Bessie Ramey, C.E. Wilberforce's affianced, an intelligent, modest colored girl, 19 years old last May 7th. She is well accomplished. Dr. Stewart & wife and Harry Ford & wife came to supper, with us.

Friday, October 5 I called at 10:00 at 14 Simpson Street to see the Wilberforces, but only saw Joseph J. Wheeler and wife, in whose house they live. They spoke well of the boys and of their women. Christopher E. Wilberforce called in the evening.

Saturday, October 6 At home writing. Mr. Spencer Crane supped with us. Joseph Wilberforce called a half hour

in the evening. They think of starting to Africa, sailing the 20th, as missionaries. One day, the past week, Rev. P.A. Black, of Assotin, Wash. call[e]d an hour.

Sunday, October 7 I wrote to J. Howe. I heard Dr. Whidden preach at 10:40, 1 John 4.11,"God's Love to us." He is a very fine thinker.

Monday, October 8 Went to the public library, wrote several letters. Brothers got a Grapone.

Tuesday, October 9 At home writing all day. Called at 7:30 p.m. at 14 Simpson Street to see the Wilberforces. Remained only a few minutes. Saw only Joseph and Constance.

Wednesday, October 10 I received a letter from Rev. J. Howe, directing that the Wilberforces come on to Huntington, Monday, the 15th. I had Orville telephone this over to Constance Wilberforce's aunt Nola Nooks, 1939 Main St. Wrote a note to the Wilberforce's. Went on 2:30 tr. to Lima and thence by train to Elida.

Thursday, October 11 Lodge at John Freeman's last night. Urania Cochran (his sister) came at 7:30, last evening & John H. [unreadable] & wife in the night. To-day, his brother Arile, and sisters Sarah Reece, Mary Kierns, and families, came also Revs. Chas. & Thomas Weyer & wives, and M.R. Ridenour, Mrs. Bet. Brenneman, Corbet Baker and many others, about 50 in all. Dinner in a tent. I spoke 56 minutes. I went home on 5:00 traction and 6:10 tr. Arri. at 9:00. Bell m. a dau. of Reece—a beauty.

Friday, October 12 At home writing. Wrote the Wilberforces. Wrote also a letter to D.F. Wilberforce in Africa.

Saturday, October 13 Christopher Wilberforce came and I lent him $15.00 to pay bills etc. Wrote letters, a notice of the Freeman reunion, etc. Joseph Wilberforce came in the evening, and his brotherinlaw, Heavlow, perhaps 12. Lent Joe $12.00, for purchases, mainly.

Sunday, October 14 Heard a discourse from Dr. M.B. Fuller, Pastor of Grace M.E. Church, at 10:30, Acts 13:22, "David son of Jesse to do all my will." Earnest, fluent, and of fair ability. Milton called in the evening looking up the history of Homer. I called at Lorin's an hour.

Monday, October 15 Christopher E. Wilberforce and Bessie Ramey were married at 12:30, at the home of the bride's mother and grandparents, 311 Chi. Ave. Wedding dinner. They and Joseph and wife Constance start to Huntington on 2:25 Lima train. I look after their freight and bargain for Pres. David Shuck's monument. Paid freight.

Tuesday, October 16 I spend the day in paying off bills Joseph had stated to me; Mrs. Burkle, Homestead Ave.; Niswonger, Albany St., Rose Nooks, Dakota St., Excelsior Laundry, Main St., and T & J.J. Wheeler, 14 Simpson St.

Thursday, October 18 At home writing. Katharine went to Alice Hunter's in Dayton View. Agnes Osborn came home with her, and lodged. Col. (Rev.) J.W.P. McMullin died to-day at Lafayette, Ind., aged 80. I heard him at Depot Church, Indianapolis, 1855.

Sunday, October 21 Heard Maurice E. Wilson pr. Luke 12.6,7. 1. Simple illustration. 2. God notices each sparrow. 3. Cares much more for us. 4. Poetry. It expresses great truths. 5. Family: (1) Father seen in Christ illus. Seen Paris, has seen France. parents sacrifice year by year. (2) Liberty of children so far as obedience & order admit. We are defended both for own sake and sake of the km.

Tuesday, October 23 At home engaged as usual. I received a copy of Conservator and a letter from J. Howe. Mrs. Albert called on Katharine in the evening.

Wednesday, October 24 Everything as usual. Got a copy of R.A. Morrison's bluff to Trustees of Hartford circuit.

Friday, October 26 At home as usual. I got several letters and a card from J. Howe saying a telegram from Africa tells that Minnie (Mull) Linker is dead!

Sunday, October 28 Cool and a strong breeze. I heard Rev. D. Frank Garland pr.at the new Lutheran Church, corner of First and Wilkison (not near finished), 1 Tim.

4.16, "Take heed to thyself," a fine sermon. Miss Winifred Snyder and our Leontine supped with us.

Monday, October 29 Went to bank and store in forenoon. Order a coat and vest of Perry Meredith. Bought a variety of paper for writing.

Thursday, November 1 Spent the day in clearing out my old files of papers, tracts, letters, boxes, etc.

Friday, November 2 I continue my work of yesterday, and find the National Era of 1847, 1848, 1849, 1850, 1851, 1852. I did not know I had so many. Katharine had a party of teachers to dinner: Misses Myers, Walter and Mrs. Stevens.

Saturday, November 3 Went to Winters' Bank and collected seventeen dollars of W.A. Oler, on which there were bank charges of 15 cents and my expenses for, letters and street car fare were 25 cents more, all from 01er's hatefulness.

Sunday, November 4 Lorin, Ivonette & Horace called in the forenoon. In the evening at 7:30, I heard Rev. Asa McDaniel on Rev. 2:8, "Open door," at Williams Street "Christian" Church. He is animated, but sophomoric.

Monday, November 5 I spent almost the whole day in arranging in order my old periodicals, to pack them away.

Tuesday, November 6 Voted a full Republican ticket; I generally scratch some. This is my protest against Hearstism and Campbellism—Jas. Campbell. I went about 8:30, and watched the stereoptican announcements at the corner of Third and Main Sts., of the results of the election, which were favorable to the Republicans at home and in other states, generally.

Wednesday, November 7 In afternoon, as yesterday, I spent more than an hour arranging periodicals, etc. This is nice weather—fire scarcely needed. Eva Gray writes me that Cora Wilhelm is married to Fred. Bullen. She is a pretty girl. They were married Oct. 17th, and live near Lewisville, Indiana.

Thursday, November 8 Wrote some, read some, and spent an hour in arranging files of periodicals. The weather is fine. This is the fourteenth anniversary of Milton's birthday. He was born in 1892, the day of Pres. Grover Cleveland's election.

Friday, November 9 I spent the forenoon in arranging periodicals. I went on 3:00 traction to Cambridge City, Ind., and lodged at Central Hotel, $1.00 for lodging & breakfast.

Saturday, November 10 I went on 9:30 tr. to Laurel. J.I. Lefforge met me and took me to his house, one-fourth mile W. from Andersonville, where I dine with Rev. T.E. Kinneman and A.A. Powell, and Sally Lewis. Kinneman pr. at 1:30, John 4.23. I sup at Philander Leforge's in Andersonville. I pr. at 7:30, Acts 11.26, "Christians." Lodged at Martin's, a mile W. Corners.

Sunday, November 11 Rev. T.E. Kinneman pr. at 10:30, Mt. Zion, near corner of my father's, first eighty of land, 1829. I administer the sacrament. I go home with my Nephew, Jas. F. Harris & Zena and remain till next day. They live on the old Reeder homestead. I called in the morning at Sally Ann Cook's. I boarded at her father's, John Cook's, when I taught school at Neff's Corners, in 1854–5. She is about 74.

Monday, November 12 James took me to Milroy, and I go on 10:59 train to Fairmount. I call at Ol. Buller's. I saw Chas. T. Parker and insured my farm house for $1,000.00. I sup and lodge at Ellis Wright's. They purpose wintering in Melbourne, in Florida, on Indian River; James Harris & Zena also purpose wintering at St. Petersburg, where their son Orlo is.

Tuesday, November 13 I called at Buller's again, and we went to Marion and saw Attorney Wm. H. Charles. I paid my tax. We returned and I dined at Buller's, and went on 3:05 train to Fowlerton. I supped and lodged at R.W. White's. Called at John Leach's and rented him the new field.

Wednesday, November 14 I go on 7:17 tr. to Richmond & home, arriving at Dayton at 12:00, noon. Mr. A.I. Root supped with us, on his way to St. Louis. He is from Medina County, Ohio, the bee culture man, very friendly to our boys.

Thursday, November 15 I was at home, reading and writing. I was inclined to be drowsy, and slept considerably.

Saturday, November 17 This is the seventy-eighth anniversary of my birth. I was born in a log cabin in Rush County, Indiana about 100 rods north of the south line and about one mile and a half (add 10 rods) west of the east line of the county. In 1840 (March lst) we removed ten miles north-east onto Sanes Creek, in Fayette County, three miles due south-east of Orange, once called Danville, later Fayetteville.

Sunday, November 18 Lorin called with Horace. I got ready too late to attend church.

Tuesday, November 20 I was at home. About this time one of the editor of the Scientific American called to see the Wright brothers.

Thursday, November 22 I was at home. The boys received a telegram that F.S. Lahm of Paris and Henry Weaver at Mansfield, Ohio would arrive at 6:00. They were an hour & 40 min. late. They supped with us. Lahm is an American 26 years in Paris, France, on business. He is also a balloonist. His son won the prize in a great balloon race. Weaver is Lahm's brotherinlaw.

Friday, November 23 Messrs. Lahm and Weaver spent most of the forenoon in Wright brothers' office and I was presnt most of the time. The boys dine with them. I dine alone. The New York Herald reporter also called again. Mr. Weaver & Lahm married women that were sisters to each other.

Sunday, November 25 I heard Dr. Howard P. Whidden preach, Deut. 8.2, & Phil. 3.13. It is a very beautiful mild day. Leontine & Horace dined with us, and were sweet as can be. Before the sermon Dr. Whidden gave a sermonette on "The Ten Links"—Ten Commandments, which he held to be still in force, as I do.

Monday, November 26 I was at home all day, and wrote many letters. It was five years ago this evennng, that the Publishing Board met and ordered Mrs. M.A. Bond's bequest note delivered to her. About what was said, several afterward swore falsely, either by wishes affecting their memory or otherwise.

Tuesday, November 27 I received a letter of inquiry from John M. Manning and answered it at considerable length.

Wednesday, November 28 Charles Shearer called in the forenoon at the brothers' office. He lives at Minneapolis, Minn. He is my cousin Harriet's son.

Thursday, November 29 Mr. Spencer Crane dined with us. I called an hour in the evening at Lorin's. This is a mild and very beautiful day for Thanksgiving.

Friday, November 30 This last day of November is very mild. There is much in the papers about the Wright brothers. They have fame, but not wealth, yet. Both these things aspired after by so many, are vain.

Saturday, December 1 The day is mild with very little rain in the morning. I was at home.

Sunday, December 2 I felt dull and staid at home all day. Lorin and Netta dined with us. Milton and Horace came after supper.

Wednesday, December 5 Patrick Alexander, of England, Dined and supped with us, and at 10:00 p.m. he and Wilbur and Orville started to New York. The weather is very mild.

Saturday, December 8 A little cooler. The *Enquirer*, the *News* and the N.Y. *Herald* give reports of the Wright Brothers being noticed at the aeronautical exhibit in New York, and dined last Evening at the Century Club by John Brisbane Walker, the *Herald* also noticing their engine on exhibition.

Sunday, December 9 A very mild day. Little rain. I heard Rev. John R. Mott at First Presbyterian Church on the Rapid advancement of belief and practice of faith in Christ and Christianity in America, Europe and Asia, especially among schools, colleges and universities. The *Enquirer* reports that the "brothers" went to Philadelphia Yester day afternoon. Ivonette and Leontine with us.

Tuesday, December 11 Slightly rainy. At home. Mrs. S. Crane called in the evening. He is the automobile man.

Wednesday, December 12 The Wright brothers arrived at home from Washington at 9:00 a.m. It is a damp day.

Friday, December 14 Cloudy in forenoon, and slight rain afternoon. Fire is scarcely needed. I did but little to-day.

Monday, December 17 There are fully two inches of snow. Winter! Orville started for New York at 3:15 to see Mr. Chas. Flint, a wealthy man, that telegraphed the "brothers" to come.

Wednesday, December 19 Orville returned from New York, his train several hours late, arri.g at 2:00. He reported a successful prospect of a deal with Charles Flint and Co.

Thursday, December 20 Things as usual. Messrs. Lahm & Weaver telegraphed that they were coming on the Erie evening train, which they however missed. Mrs. Carrie (Kaler) Gumbaugh ate supper with us.

Friday, December 21 Cloudy. There lies a 2 in. of snow. Ther. at 10:00 a.m., 34 degrees. F.S. Lahm, of Paris, France and Henry Weaver of Mansfield, Ohio visited the Wright brothers, and interviewed witnesses of their flights.

Sunday, December 23 At the Episcopal Church on First Street, 1st assistant rector Lewis pr. Gal. 5:1 on Liberty. Misconceived the text.

Tuesday, December 25 Christmas. Lorin's children called, and later Lorin and Netta. Mr. Spencer Crane supped with us. It was a pretty day.

Wednesday, December 26 Matters are as usual. At 6:00 p.m. Mr. (Flint Co.) Nolte of New York came. The Wright brothers see him at the Algonquin, this evening.

Thursday, December 27 To-day is a little icy and almost rainy. The brothers had an interview with Mr. Nolte in the forenoon. He waits a letter from his company.

Friday, December 28 Mr. Nolte received a letter, and the brothers spend the forenoon with him, and go again in the afternoon, after counseling between themselves.

Saturday, December 29 I was at home, only I paid my own and Candace Livingston's tax.

Sunday, December 30 I did not consider that health allowed me to go to Church. Wilbur & Orville rode on the train to Richmond with six aero club men, and called on Caroline Zeller and Prof. David Dennis's. Returned at 5:00. Lorin's three younger children were with us.

Monday, December 31 It was a mild day with no freezing at night, as it has been mostly or altogether since the 28th. Nothing of special interest occurs.

Soon after the presidential election of 1840, a poem was published in the Whig papers, one stanza of which ran thus: "When pumpkins shall now on top of a tall steple, And pancakes shall fall like rain; When Brownson and Bancroft can humbug the people, Van Buren may come back to power again." The Bancroft referred to became the great historian George Bancroft; and O.A. Brownson was the distinguished philosopher and theologian— first a Presbyterian, then a Universalist, and last a Roman Catholic.

Jennie May Gott, daughter of James Williams and Martha A. Hott (m. Ramey) died at our home, 7 Hawthorne Street, Dayton, Ohio, July 14, 1873, aged 1 year, 10 mo. & 11 days.

William R. Rhinehart died May 9, 1861, aged 60 years, 6 mo. & 11 days. His gravestone in Miami Chapel Cemetery, at Dayton, Ohio, is a sandstone (or limestone) slab 4 feet, 4 inches high, 22 inches wide and 1 1/2 inches thick.

Harvey Wright had his first cancer in the year 1900, taken out in September. He has had seven altogether. The first was on the left side of his face between the eye and ear. The last was a rose cancer on his left ear, reaching before and behind, about the size of a man's hand. He died June 22, 1906, aged 85 years, 9 months and 13 days, and was buried in Centre Cemetery, June 24th. Robert Thompson preached the funeral in Center Church, 2 Tim. 4.7,8. Probably 800 or 1000 people were at the funeral. His height was 5 ft. 10 in., and his usual weight about 150 pounds. His complexion was meduim, his hair dark, his features regular.

1907

Tuesday, January 1 Vivian Harris m. Earnest F. Smith. In 1807, Thos. Jefferson had been president six years, my father was a lad of sixteen, and my mother a girl of 7 years. Then the population of the United States was scarcely 7 million. To-day is cloudy and no freezing. Family ate turkey together.

Wednesday, January 2 It is a cloudy, damp day. Nothing of special interest presents itself. Vivian Harris, daughter of Harvey B. Harris' daughter, was married yesterday to Ernest F. Smith, Woodbine, Iowa.

Thursday, January 3 A little rain after a rainy night. Temperature 58 degrees at 9:00 a.m.

Friday, January 4 At home as usual. Dr. L. Spitler called before noon. I am considerably unwell.

Saturday, January 5 I called at Dr. Levi Spitler's at 9:00. My ailiment proved to be Diabetes Insipidus, not Diabetes Mellitus.

Sunday, January 6 On account of my ailment, I remained at home. All Lorin's children, except Milton spent the day with us .

Monday, January 7 I was at home. Reporter for McClure's Magazine tried an interview with the Wright brothers. Our hired girl, Hattie Williams, left.

Wednesday, January 9 I was at home, unwell, but able to walk down to the store. I received a letter from White, my farmer, giving me account of work on farm, prices of grain, etc.

Thursday, January 10 Perhaps my health is improving slowly. I do much of my sleeping in the daytime, my ailment interrupting it in the night.

Sunday, January 13 I was at home. Lorin's little girls came in the forenoon and staid till evening.

Monday, January 14 Nothing unusual occurs. My health gains, if at all, slowly. A card comes from Ellis Wright, who is in Melbourne, Florida, to spend the winter, and his family. I wrote again to Wm. C. Galbraith, Rugby, Indiana.

Wednesday, January 16 I received a letter from Wm. C. Galbraith reporting favorably of the David Shuck Monument, at Hartsville and sent the McKenzie Brothers, Delphos, Ohio, a check of $140.00 to pay for the same.

Thursday, January 17 Mr. [blank] Nolte of New York again returned to Dayton, to negociate for the Flyer, or agency for it, by Flint & Co. Lorin, Netta, and Ivonette called an hour in the evening.

Saturday, January 19 I went to see the doctor, in the forenoon.

Sunday, January 20 Not well enough to attend church. The boys started at 3:00 p.m. for New York.

Monday, January 21 Katharine got a card from Wilbur at Xenia, where they had to wait the cars several hours.

Tuesday, January 22 I wrote several letters. In the evening, Katharine had a supper for several of the teachers.

Saturday, January 26 Wilbur and Orville got home from N.Y. City about 6:00, in the evening.

Sunday, January 27 I read several of the minor prophets including Zecheriah and Malachi in the revised version. Leontine was with us in the forenoon, and Ivonette in the afternoon.

Tuesday, January 29 I am at home. Dennis Ensey died this evening, very aged, 95 (?). His mother, Sarah Ensey, was a half sister of my grandmother Margaret Reeder. He lives in Dayton.

Wednesday, January 30 Still at home. Agnes Osborn dined with our folks at 3:00.

Thursday, January 31 A rainy day. The sidewalks were slippery.

Sunday, February 3 I was at home all the day. Leontine with us in afternoon.

Monday, February 4 I saw Dr. Spitler at 9:00. Wilbur and Orville received a letter from Flint & Co., accepting their terms on Commission for sale of the Flyer.

Tuesday, February 5 Wilbur started at 10:00, evening to New York. Our neighbor Eby dropped dead this evening.

Thursday, February 7 As usual, Wilbur telegraphs of the proposition to Germany—50 machines for a half million.

Saturday, February 9 We got a letter and telegram from Wilbur, who is on his way home. Mr. Eby's funeral is this afternoon.

Sunday, February 10 At home. Slept a good deal. Milton and Horace came. Miss Winifred Ryder supped with us.

Wednesday, February 13 I took a long walk up North Broadway. It is a very mild and beautiful day. I wrote several letters.

Sunday, February 17 I was at home all day, mostly reading. Leontine and Horace were with us.

Tuesday, February 19 A very beautiful mild day. I got for J. Howe an etching of the Wilberforces, Joseph and Wilbur and their wives.

Thursday, February 21 The weather is cooler, but not very cold. I took the Wilberforce etching to U.B. Pr. Est. to have an electrotype made. It is a moderately cold day, and a cold night follows.

Friday, February 22 I went at two o'clock and got the electrotype and sent it to Rev. J. Howe by Adams Express.

Saturday, February 23 The *News* states that Bishop Dickson died this morning about 6:30, aged 84. He was 87.

Sunday, February 24 I attended Broadway Christian Church and heard the pastor Coffin preach, at 10:30. Leontine and Horace dined with us.

Monday, February 25 I went on 8:10 D.U. train via Gas City to Marion. I saw and talked with both St. John and Charles, Attorneys on our Hopewell suit. Went to Fairmount, called at Oliver Buller's and went on train to Fowlerton and to Wm. Reeder's. Lodged there. Fine, mild weather.

Tuesday, February 26 I called at Oliver A. Glass's, who is moving to Wabash Co. to-morrow. I next went to R.W. White's, on my farm. In afternoon, we planned the ditching of my new ground towards Fowlerton. Dined, supped and lodged at White's. It is fine weather.

Wednesday, February 27 I go on 7:40 train to Fairmount. Fix up my business with C.T. Parker and Driggs and Wiley. Went to Marion, saw attorneys. Saw Ex Rev. Fields of Gas City at Waiting Room in Marion. Dine, sup and lodge with O. Buller's. It is a fine day.

Thursday, February 28 I went via Gas city & Union City, arriving at home at 3:45. Mild but gloomy dark day. Rather chilly.

Friday, March 1 Rained at night. At home. Wrote to Howe and to Reuchlin.

Saturday , March 2 Went to the bank in the forenoon and deposited four checks - (Wise, $200.56, Oil, $21.03, C.T. Parker, $11. & Driggs $56.55.) Wrote Clay & Wm. Miller. Cool but nice day.

Wednesday, March 6 Went to Dr. Spitler's office. Wrote to Rodney P. Wright. It has been a very nice day.

Friday, March 8 As usual. Katharine went afternoon on a visit to Richmond to see her cousin Emma Dennis. It is a mild, beautiful day.

Saturday, March 9 Sent points to prove to St. John & Charles, Marion, Ind. Fine weather continues.

Sunday, March 10 At 10:30, heard Rev. A. Clint. Watson, pastor's assistant at First Baptist Church, pr. at Williams Street Baptist Church, 2 Tim. 1.10, a good sermon. Ivonette and Horace came in the afternoon.

Monday, March 11 At home. This evening, the *News* published as an advertisement a burlesque on the John H. Patterson meeting.

Tuesday, March 12 I was at home all day. I did not do much. As the "advertisement" of last evening made a great sensation, the *News* tried to make out that it was a boomerang! It rained hard in the afternoon.

Wednesday, March 13 Cloudy and slightly rainy. Rained at night. News "closes the incident," it says!

Thursday, March 14 Every thing about as usual. The day is cloudy in part. I wrote to St. John and Charles on matters of evidence.

Friday, March 15 It is one of the most beautiful days of the year and very mild. Wrote to Pres. Gragg & to J. Howe; also to G.W. Allman and J.H. Parlett, in Virginia. I walked to Washington Street Bridge. Report of unprecedented rise of waters at Pittsburg[h].

Sunday, March 17 I heard A. Clinton Watson preach (at 11:00) at Williams Street Baptist Church, 1 John 5.12. Horace was with us to dinner and supper, a bright well-behaved and lovely boy of 5 ys & 8 months. Milton was with us to supper.

Monday, March 18 Walked to the post-office and bank (2 1/4 miles) without the least fatigue. This is a green among lovely days. I study and write in the evening on the perpetuity of the decalogue.

Wednesday, March 20 The boys rigged up their floats and hydroplanes and tried them on the Miami. Katharine started on the evening 11:05 tr. to Chicago. The day was very beautiful, and no fire was needed.

Thursday, March 21 The brothers again spent the day in the Miami basin. They drove their craft with aerial screw propellers. The day was beautiful and a little cooler (not much) than yesterday. I got a letter from G.W. Allman.

Friday, March 22 In the early evening, the temperature was the highest since last fall. The temporary river dam at Washington Street gave way last night, some rods.

Saturday, March 23 The weather is still warm and beautiful. Walked out to Wm. Weidner's on Kilmer Street, at 4:00 Afternoon, and back.

Sunday, March 24 I heard Rev. D.L. Myers, on History of passion week, at Fourth Presbyterian Church, at 10:30. Lorin and Ivonette called in the evening, and Milton & Horace later. Wilbur started to New York at 10:00 eve.

Monday, March 25 Katharine arrived at Home from Chicago at 7:40. I wrote cards to G.W. Allman and C.B. Sherk, to R.W. White and to Walter S. Neal and to Mr. Wilson, of Marion, Ind., to straighten out tax list. Also wrote to Prof. Wood on use of my lot for garden.

Tuesday, March 26 At home. In the afternoon, I walked to the Germantown Street Bridge to see the washout in the east side of the temporary dam.

Wednesday, March 27 I wrote Ray, and T.E. Kinneman. It rained last night and some this forenoon.

Saturday, March 30 Nice Weather. Mailed an Article. Ten Command's Alive, to W.H. Clay.

Sunday, March 31 I remained at home and slept considerably, having had a short night's sleep. Lorin's girls dined with us, and the boys came soon after dinner. Lorin's & Netta called an hour in the evening. I read some in Neander, & Ency. Brittanica.

Monday, April 1 A nice day, a little cooler. Wrote my fourth article on the decalogue, Tuesday 2nd.

Wednesday, April 3 It was a fair day. Start to Fowlerton via Richmond on 9:00 a.m. train. Dine sup & lodge at R.W. White's on my farm. Looked over the farm a little and at the new tile ditches in the recently cleared field in the south-west corner of the farm. Settled with White for two years past.

Thursday, April 4 It was a nice day. Went on 7:40 tr. to Fairmount; called at Oliver Buller's and at Hollingsworth's. Called at C.T. Parker's office. Driggs and Wiley paid me $36.00 rent on ware to Apr. 1st. I go on to Marion & Wabash. See Neal on taxes. Ex. Com. Mission meet at J. Howe's. I lodge at Howe's.

Friday, April 5 I call at Stemen's, Livingston's, M. Wechler's, and Gragg's. I dine at Livingston's. S.A. Stemen's boy took me to Erie Depot at 3:00. I, via Lima, reach home at 8:45. The day was cloudy and the wind damp and chilly. I find a letter of congratulation from H.H. Hinman of Oberlin, antisecrecy worker, on Wright brothers success.

Saturday, April 6 I was at home. I slept much. Moses Taggart sent congraturations to me and the Wright brothers. He is the Grand Rapids attorney that won our case in the Michigan Supreme Court, some years ago.

Sunday, April 7 I was at home all day. It was a slightly rainy day. Lorin and Horace were with us an hour in the evening.

Tuesday, April 9 I received congratulations from C.N. Spencer and Mrs. Grace (Scribner) Spencer, who live in Washington, D.C. I largely spent the day in retracing parts of my diary of 1884, where recorded with an analine pencil. Only the best black ink should be used in recording.

Wednesday, April 10 I spent the day as usual. Katharine

had Mrs. Stevens, Miss F. Wuichet & one other teacher to dine with her.

Friday, April 12 At home. Milton Matthews and Miss Wuichet called in the evening. It was Frances Wuichet, Charles' daughter.

Sunday, April 14 I remained at home all day, except a call at Lorin's. Leontine came home with me.

Saturday, April 20 It is a pretty day, mildly cool. At 3:00, J.G. Feight's old home, next north of us, was sold at auction at $4175.00, the two houses, having seven and six rooms respectively.

Sunday, April 21 I attended Williams Street Baptist Church at 10:45. Rev. Stevens pr. on the Miracles of Pentecost, Acts. 2.9. I can hear him more easily than most speakers. Miss Winifred Ryder supped with us.

Monday, April 22 I was at home. I spent the day in Reading. I read considerably in Smiley on the Atonement.

Tuesday, April 23 At home. George Feight and Ida Grabill called in the evening, together. Letter from David V. Baker, Portland, Ind. His mind is wild. I did not answer it.

Thursday, April 25 Called at 5:00 p.m. at Peter Louding's. He has been quite sick four weeks. (The above should be for Friday the 26th.)

Friday, April 26 Agnes Osborne was with us at supper, and in the evening.

Saturday, April 27 Went to town at 2:00 and saw the fireman's record run for the moving pictures, I just happening there not knowing it was to be then.

Sunday, April 28 It is a beautiful day, warm enough without fire. I heard at Broadway Christian Church the pastor, F.G. Coffin pr. 10:30, Ps. 85.6. Miss Winifred Ryder was with us to supper and Lorin & wife and the children (except Ivonett[e]) an hour in the evening.

Monday, April 29 Yesterday at 2:30 were the services at

the laying of the corner-stone of the new Y.M.C.A. building at the corner of Third and Ludlow streets. Secretary of War W.H. Taft officiated, and delivered an address. I was present. At home to-day. Went to Pub. Library and walked back.

Tuesday, April 30 I got medicine at 8:00—of Dr. Spitler. I get ready to start at 2:25 to Berlin, Ontario. Went via Toledo, Detroit & Port Huron to Berlin, Ont.

Wednesday, May 1 Arrived at Berlin at 5:25 eastern time. Breakfast & dinner at Rev. A.R. Springer's on Alma Street. Slept three hours. Sup at Rev. J.B. Bowman's, after a call at M. Eshelman's. Bishop O.G. Alwood pr. at 8:00. I lodged at Eshelman's.

Thursday, May 2 I Board at Rev. J.B. Bowman's. Rev. Wm. Dillon dines & sups with us. The Annual Session of the Missionary Board begins at 9:00. My com. of Foreign Missions meets at 11:00 a.m. and 5:00 p.m. Wm. Dillon pr. An. sermon at 8:00. Mat. 6.2,3. I lodge at M. Eshelman's.

Friday, May 3 My Com. met at 8:00, a.m. In to-day's session of the Board, there was a lively discussion on the prospect of incurring a large debt by appropriating $1200.00, to the North-west mission. I discussed Education & missions. Supper in Basement. Start at 8:00, via Galt, to Wabash.

Saturday, May 4 I caught cold on *cold* car last night. At Detroit, and on the way to Wabash, our train was delayed about six hours. I reach Fairmount about 4:00 p.m. I sup & lodge at Ellis Wright's. They reached home from Florida, Monday, the 29th of April.

Sunday, May 5 I remained at Ellis' in the forenoon. In the afternoon, I was at the burial of Corporal Hugh Parker, who died at Vancouver, Washington, the burial being military, and the attendance large. Called an hour at Oliver Buller's. Lodged at Ellis'.

Monday, May 6 Went to Marion on 8:00 car. Paid St. John and Charles $100.00 for services in Hopewell Church suit. Return to Fairmount & dine at Ellis Wright's. I look after business somewhat. Go on 3:00 tr., to Fowlerton. Sup at R.W. White's. Rev. Harry

Malson and bride called an hour in evening.

Tuesday, May 7 Ernest White took me to 7:30 train and I go via C.C.& L train to Richmond and Dayton, arriving at 11:20 a.m. Slept some and posted my diary. I feel better, but my cold is not abated.

Wednesday, May 8 I felt the effects of my cold. I did nothing but read. Herbert N. Casson made an hour's call in the evening. He is the author of the article, "At last we can Fly," in the April American Monthly.

Saturday, May 11 I was at home. At 4:00, afternoon, I walked to Peter Louding's, but found him sleeping, and did not awaken him. His niece, Miss Harris of New Orleans, is taking care of him.

Sunday, May 12 Heard Dr. Maurice Nilson pr. at 10:45, at First Pres. Ch., Deut. 11.10–11. Called at 4:00 at Mrs. David Webbert's. I used to be at their house in Kearney, Nebraska in 1877–1880. Her husband died several years ago in Nebraska.

Monday, May 13 There was nothing of unusual interest to-day. Agnes Osborn was with us "at tea," and she and Katharine went to a musical entertainment at Association Hall, in the evening.

Tuesday, May 14 I spent the day largely examining the Bible on the subjects of dispensations, covenants, Testaments, etc.

Thursday, May 16 I was at home. Wilbur got a telegram from Flint, and at 10:00 p.m. started for New York to take ship for London. He goes to talk with agents, in London, Paris and Berlin.

Friday, May 17 I went to the Library in the afternoon, and walked home.

Saturday, May 18 I got ready to go away and started at 2:25 via Lima to Huntington, Ind., where I arrived at 8:00, the train being an hour and ten minutes late. Lodged at S.A. Stemen's. In forenoon, I met Rev. Samuel Scott who will be 88 in November. He lives on Germantown Street.

Sunday, May 19 I called early at J. Howe's, O.B. Bowman's etc. I attended Sunday School. R.S. Kindel pr. at 10:30, Ex. 4.2. I dined and supped at Prof. F.A. Loew's. I attended the Christian Endeavor meeting at 6:00 p.m. and I preached at 7:00, Rom. 5.11, on the oneness of all the dispensations. Lodge at Livingston's.

Monday, May 20 I call at Prof. T.C. Gragg's and at Dr. Morehouse's, and go to the Publishing House. Conferred with "Judge" C.W. Watkins. I dined at A..A. Powell's Restaurant, and supped and lodged at J. Howe's.

Tuesday, May 21 I go on 8:38 traction car to Marion. I saw St. John at his office and saw Mr. Charles at circuit court room. Reached Fairmount at 1:00. I called at Oliver Buller's, and supped and lodged at Ellis Wright's.

Wednesday, May 22 With Buller, I go on the 7:00 traction car to Marion. Conferred with William Charles, and he arranged to have the Hopewell Church trial postponed till June 14th. I go to Jonesboro on traction and on the 1:55 C.C. & L. train via Richmond to Dayton. Peter Louding, buried.

Saturday, May 25 I was at home. I copied Points to Prove in our church case at Marion, Ind., for C.W. Watkins.

Sunday, May 26 At Third Street Pres. Church, at 10:30, I heard Rev. Merle H. Anderson pr., Luke 18:15, on Children and their baptism.

Wednesday, May 29 Orville received a cablegram from Wilbur in Paris. Agnes Osburn supped with us.

Thursday, May 30 Decoration Day. I got medicine of Dr. L. Spitler in the afternoon.

Friday, May 31 I was at home. In the evening, Orville and Katharine attended the High School debate with the Shortridge High School of Indianapolis. Dayton won.

Sunday, June 2 At home all day. Lorin's girls dined with us and Leontine stays till bedtime. She is bright, full of application, helpful and sweet-disposed.

Monday, June 3 Katharine received a letter from Wilbur mailed at Queenstown, Ireland, dated May 24th. He had crossed the ocean in six days in the steamer in Campania. He reached London the 25th.

Tuesday, June 4 At home getting ready to go away tomorrow.

Wednesday, June 5 I went at 9:00 via Richmond (S. cars) to Fowlerton, Ind. Fare, 2.04. Wm. & Mattie Reeder on the train from Richmond. Dine at White's. Go on 5:30 tr. to Fairmount. Supper at Ellis Wright's, lodging at Oliver Buller's.

Thursday, June 6 I am at Buller's till 1:00 p.m. We go to Marion and see Mr. Will Charles & C.W. Watkins. I go on 5:00 tr. to Treaty and go out to O.A. Glass's, 2 ms. North and 2 East. Supper and lodging there. They removed the last of February from Fairmount township, Grant County.

Friday, June 7 It is somewhat rainy. Oliver, in the afternoon, takes me to Lagro, and I go on traction to Huntington. Call at Publishing house. Rev. S.L. Livingston takes me to his house, where I sup. and lodge, at S.A. Stemen's, Bp. O.G. Alwood pr. at 7:30, Acts 20.35, "More blessed to give than," to Chr. E. Society.

Saturday, June 8 Mis. Ex. Com. met at College Building at 9:00. I dine at S.A. Stemen's. I preside in a joint council of the Com. & Woman's Board at 4:30. Program of Department of oratory at 8:00. I sup & lodge at Stemen's.

Sunday, June 9 I taught S.A. Stemen's class (S.S.) Rev. Wm. Miller, 83 years old, pr. Bacalaureate sermon at 10:30, Ps. 104.34, "My meditation of Him—sweet." I dine at O.B. Bowman's. Talk with Rev. J. Freeman. Christian Endeavor meeting at 6. Bp. Wood pr. at 7:30, Rom. 8:37, on victory. Lodge at Livingston's.

Monday, June 10 The Educational Board met at 9:30. Reports of Pres. of College and Treasurer were read. I dine at W.H. Clay's. Sup at Wm. Dillon's. At 9:00 Program of Graduates of Music and oratory. Misses Mary M. Doub and Elsie Starbuck performed—Miss Daub in readings, very well. I lodge at Stemen's.

Tuesday, June 11 Board meeting's. I dine at Livingston's and sup at J. Howe's. Exercises of Graduating Class at 2:00, quite good. At 8:00, Inter-Society Program.

Wednesday, June 12 This is Commencement Day. Dr. S.D. Fess, Pres.of Antioch College, delivered a very good address, and five graduated in Clas. Course, six in Scientific and five in other departments. I was toast-master at the Alumni Dinner. Ed. Board & Com. meetings. Lodge at Stemen's.

Thursday, June 13 Ed. Board met at 9:00, after meeting of faculty. We have a meeting with the seceders at 2:00, and at 4:00 with Com.: Wood, Tharp, Morrison and myself. They seem anxious to re-unite, and say Keiter has lost his popularity. I miss car & sup at Foote's. Woods & I formulate memos andum of agreement. Lodge at Howe's.

Friday, June 14 Bp. Wood, Morrison and I spend several hours in formulating terms of agreement, and I went on 4:20 traction to Fairmount. Sup and lodge at Ellis Wright's. I had dined at Powel's Restaurant.

Saturday, June 15 I go on 7:00 traction to Anderson & thence by locomotive cars to Dayton, arriving at 11:00. Spent the rest of the day partly in sleeping. I had considerable loss of sleep the past three nights.

Monday, June 17 I was at home. Mrs. Stevens, and Misses Myers and Wuichet dined with Katharine. We got letters from Wilbur, in Paris.

Tuesday, June 18 I spent the day at home, mostly writing. It is the warmest day of the year, so far.

Wednesday, June 19 I was at home, writing letters and postal cards. Cablegram from Wilbur in Paris about rising 1000 feet on Flyer. Shall they agree to do so in demonstration?

Thursday, June 20 Nothing very unusual occurred. Mr. Baldwin (nephew of Rev. B. Baldwin) called.

Friday, June 21 Orville went in afternoon to Springfield to see Toulin on an additional patent—automatic control of the Flyer. Letter came from Wilbur, in Paris,

enclosing an interview published in a daily. It showed his noncommunicativeness.

Saturday, June 22 Lorin's family went out to Idlewild. Lorin dined with us. Orville received another letter from Wilbur detailing the original plan of a stock company for the Flyer.

Sunday, June 23 I spent the day in reading in John's Archaeology and other religious books.

Wednesday, June 26 At home. Orville went to Springfield again.

Thursday, June 27 At home. In afternoon, Hattie McFadden and Mrs. Herbert (Anna) Allen (and Ruth 7 years old) called an hour.

Sunday, June 30 At home, till 10:00. Went out in Lorin's surrey, and spent the day with them in Idlewild, where the family are summering.

Tuesday, July 2 At home. Wilbur sent cable dispatch that the French deal was off.

Wednesday, July 3 Dispatch that the French deal was on again.

Thursday, July 4 I went to Woodland Cemetary and put boquets on Susan's grave. She died eighteen years ago to-day.

Saturday, July 6 We had a cablegram from Wilbur saying write him in London—"letters to Paris total loss." (Several letters sent to Paris were afterward returned to us.)

Sunday, July 7 Heard a young preacher at Williams Street Baptist Church, on 1 Cor. 1:2. He did quite well for a young man. We received letters from Wilbur in Paris.

Thursday, July 11 Mr. J. Slifer and Mr. William K. Fouts called last evening to get me to preach the funeral of Jacob J. Fouts, in Germantown.

Friday, July 12 Went to Germantown on the 10:00 traction. Delayed—reached Germantown at 12:20. Preached Jacob J. Fouts funeral at 2:00, at his house, 1 Thes. 4.14.

He was buried at the cemetery west of town. I dined and supped at Fout's. I reached home at 6:30.

Saturday, July 13 News from Wilbur by *gram* said that Orville should come soon to Paris, France. He expects to contract with the French Government, probably.

Monday, July 15 Orville is packing Flying Machine and getting ready to start to Paris, France.

Tuesday, July 16 Orville is still busy preparing to go away.

Wednesday, July 17 Orville received a telegram from Charles Flint telling how to direct his material, and when the ship "Philadelphia" would sail.

Thursday, July 18 Orville was re-crating his aeroplane. He started at 10:00 p.m. for New York and Paris. Agnes Osborn lodged with Katharine.

Friday, July 19 Katharine dined with Miss Myer, the H. Sch. teacher.

Saturday, July 20 We had a telegram From Charles Flint saying Orville had to-day sailed on the the [repeated in text] Steamship Philadelphia for Europe. The Machine was to-day loaded on the car to start to-night to New York. We got a letter from Wilbur.

Sunday, July 21 Katharine and I went out with Milton in the surrey and spent the day at their cottage in "Idlewild." He brought us back, about six o'clock.

Monday, July 22 We had letters from Wilbur and Orville. Mr. and Mrs. Charles T. Parkhurst took supper with us.

Tuesday, July 23 Agnes Osborn and Miss Myer (teachers) dined with Katharine.

Saturday, July 27 I read all of John Fetterhoff's Autobiography, and the life of Paul Laurence Dunbar.

Tuesday, July 30 At home. Katharine cabled in the evening to Wilbur and Orville.

Wednesday, July 31 Lorin dined with us as usual; and Katharine had a separate dinner with some of the teachers. A little before 8:00, eve., Katharine received a telegram from Flint Co. for Charles Taylor to come to New York by Friday Morning. She phoned to him at Chautauqua grounds, Franklin.

Thursday, August 1 Charles Taylor starts on 11:00 train for New York and Paris. Lorin's and we ride out into Dayton View in the evening in his surrey.

Friday, August 2 Lorin and family took supper with us.

Sunday, August 4 I attended the Williams Street Baptist church and heard Rev. Mr. Stevens preach Jas. 4.14. Spent the afternoon and evening in reading commentaries on 4th & 5th chaps. of James.

Tuesday, August 6 I called at Smith Premier type-writer office.

Wednesday, August 7 I went on 9:00 a.m. train via Richmond, to Economy, Ind. I dined at John M. Manning's. John took me to Grant Mendenhall's and Calvin Wiles'. I sup at Manning's & go on evening train to Fowlerton & lodge at R.W. White's.

Thursday, August 8 I called at Lewis Hayden's and Robt. Reeder's, with R.W. White, and went to Fairmount on 11:30 tr.. Dine at Ellis's. Went to Summitville & supped at Peter Wright's. Oliver Buller came up with me on the interurban car. I lodge at Ellis Wright's.

Friday, August 9 Remained in Fairmount. Mrs. Reeve and Myrtle came. Mr. Wed. Helms dined there.

Saturday, August 10 I Went on 9:05 train to Fowlerton, and walked to Wm. H.H. Re[e]der's and dined. Wm. took me to Robt. B. Reeder's & to R.W. White's. I sup at Rev. Harry Malson's and lodge at White's. Harry's mother and his brother Lawrence (19) are visiting there. They are from Parkersburg, West Virginia.

Sunday, August 11 Bro. Malson borrowed Wesley Hayden's horse and we went from there to College Hill School-house, where he preached at 11:00, after Sunday-School, John 14.15, speaking 25 minutes and I followed on "The love of Christ." We went back to R.W. White's where I lodged.

Monday, August 12 White took me to Fairmount, and I went to Marion on traction, Saw St. John, and went to John Niell's, 3 ms. north-west and remained till morning. I knew them from youth up.

Tuesday, August 13 I went on the early train from Marion to Muncie, and thence by traction to Farmland & saw Revs. C.B. Small & Abr. Rust; went back to Muncie and thence to Mays, where I called at Bert Benner's & there saw Rhoads & Frances, & Stella took me to Delilah Wright's. Sup & lodge.

Wednesday, August 14 Drusilla McKee & Wilhelm called. Edward Frazier took me afternoon to 3:20 traction car at Knightstown & I go to Dayton, 0.; fare, $1.45 on limited. I saw Albert Huddleson on the cars at Cambridge City.

Thursday, August 15 Resting. Read & wrote some. Lorin's dined with us, and are moving back to town.

Friday, August 16 At home. Got a letter from Wood, enclosing Morrison's and finished a letter to Woods.

Sunday, August 18 I attended First Baptist Church and heard Rev. E.A. Hanley of Cleveland, pastor elect of F.B. Ch. Providence, R.I., 2 Tim. 1:9. Ivonette and Leontine dined with us. I wrote to Reuchlin. We got a letter from Orville this morning.

Monday, August 19 A letter from Wilbur at Berlin came to-day.

Wednesday, August 21 I walk to Washington Street bridge to see repairs of the east levy at washout, at the temporary dam of the river.

Thursday, August 22 We got another letter from Wilbur.

Friday, August 23 Katharine spent the day with Mrs. Frances (Wuichet) Matthews, who is sick.

Saturday, August 24 Katharine received a letter of the 15th from Wilbur at Berlin and one the 14th at Paris from Orville. Both are hopeful of a deal at either place. Fred. H. Short died in Cin. at 2:00 to-day.

Sunday, August 25 I attended the Fourth Presbyterian Church and heard Prof. G.A. Funkhouser on Eph. 5.25, an interesting discourse on every one becoming a missionary in some department of Christian work. Lorin and all the family called an hour in the evening.

Monday, August 26 I go on 8:10 train to Union City & Marion. Left my valise at Miami City Station. Connected for Huntington, and reached there at 2:20. Lunch with weed-mowers at the ravine. Ex. Com. Missions met at 7:00 in College Chapel. Some talk on Reuniting in White River Conference.

Tuesday, August 27 Regular proceedings of Ex. Com. at 9:00. In afternoon have a counsel with a few on the reuniting. I dine at Livingston's and sup at Howe's & lodge at Livingston's.

Wednesday, August 28 Bishop C.L. Wood and I dine at Rev. J.A. Mummart's. Confer with R.A. Morrison at 1:30 on the reuniting, and I go on the traction to Fairmount. Sup at Oliver Buller's and lodge at Ellis Wright's.

Thursday, August 29 I go on nine o'clock train to Fowlerton. Dine at R.W. White's. H. Malson calls a few minutes. I go on 2:07 tr. to Richmond and reach Dayton at 6:00.

Friday, August 30 I was at home. Miss Winnif. Rider returned from her vacation trip home in Massachusetts and supped with us. She and Katharine went to the High School roll call at 7:30, evening.

Saturday, August 31 At home. I wrote a second article on "White River Conference Sessions," and mailed the first.

Sunday, September 1 I attended the First United Brethren Church, corner of Fourth and Perry Sts., and heard the pastor, Rev. J.P. Miller pr. on Luke 6th and 48 & 49 verses. He is a good speaker. Miss Winifred Rider came back from Cleveland (Madison) on a belated train.

Monday, September 2 Katharine and Miss Rider attend the Superintendent's meeting. Miss Rider meals and lodges with Katharine.

Tuesday, September 3 High School and the district schools open. Horace begins his school experience. Miss Rider goes to Mrs. Greenwood's to stay till her rooms (in a flat) are ready for her.

Thursday, September 5 Write letters to Reuchlin and Wilbur from whom I received letters this morning. I go on the 2:25 tr to Sidney and after two hours wait, on traction car to Swanders and to Christopher Shearer's. Hariet is quite feeble.

Friday, September 6 I go on 6:48 train to Cridersville, where Harry Freeman meets me and takes me and S.A. Stemen & wife to Victory Church, to Augliaze Annual Conference. I dine at Rev. Uriah Miller's, 1/2 mile S., & sup & lodge at E.W. Sellers, 2 miles south. I pr. at 8:00, Rev. 16:13 & 19:19. Short sleep.

Saturday, September 7 I attended Conference. Dined at Bro. Shaw's, 3/4 m. southwest with Rev. John Freeman and families. I go to Cridersville after adjournment, and (after 2 hours' wait) home on the 6:44 train, arriving about 9:00. I slept well.

Sunday, September 8 At home. It was a rather dull forenoon. I answered Rev. W.C. South's letter which had been misplaced, and I had not seen it till afternoon to-day. I called at Lorin's in the evening, a half hour.

Monday, September 9 Received a letter from R.A. Morrison. I was dull and did little.

Tuesday, September 10 At 4:00, Edith Shearer was Married to Harry Newton Hall, at the First Reformed Church by W.A. Hale. I was present. Ring ceremony. It was a rainy morning.

Wednesday, September 11 All as usual. Miss Anna Feight supped with us and remained till 9:00.

Friday, September 13 At home. Spent the day in reading. Lorin and family called in the evening.

Sunday, September 15 I remained at home. I spent the day in rest and reading. I wrote a letter in the evening to Wilbur and Orville, on my type-writer.

Thursday, September 19 As usual to-day. Letter from Orville in Paris, dated Sept. 8, 9, 10. Wrote postals to 0. Buller and R.W. White. Wrote to Wilbur and Orville.

Friday, September 20 I was at home reading. M.L. Oler and wife spent the afternoon with us, and took supper with us. Wrote to William Charles, Esq., at Marion, Indiana.

Saturday, September 21 At home. Wrote a letter to Wilbur and Orville. Katharine went to Miss Myers to supper. I mailed postals to J. Freeman & M. Wecholer.

Sunday, September 22 I heard Rev. M.B. Fuller pr. at Grace M.E. Church, Ps. 82.6, "Ye are Gods," etc. Katharine took supper with Miss Winifred Ryder. I called a half-hour at Lorin's.

Monday, September 23 I am getting ready to go away to-morrow. Katharine received a letter from Wilbur, dated Paris, Sept. 13th. Lorin's called in the evening.

Tuesday, September 24 I started to Fowlerton at 9:00, Harry M. Malson & wife are on the train. I dined at R.W. White's. I went on 5:30 tr. to Fairmount, and supped and lodged at Ellis Wright's.

Wednesday, September 25 I went on 7:00 car to Marion, and on 8:00 car to Boehm's Crossing. At 11:00 we go on to Mt. Zion and find conference home at Mrs. Martha Gaiser's. The loyal W.R. Conference met at 5:00 and 7:00, C.E. Small pr. at 8:00, Phil. 1:23. Wood, Malson and White and I board at Gaiser's.

Thursday, September 26 White River Conference opened at 9:00. C.L. Wood presided; Tharp Chm., Elias Clapp, Secretary. The reunited Conference proceeded harmoniously. The characters of all examined passed without objection. W.A. Oler pr. at 8:00, Acts 3:19. We home at Gaiser's. This was the first lawful session participated in by most of these ministers since 1901.

Friday, September 27 I met the boundary Com. at 8:00. Conference continued through the day. Morrison & Floyd were elected pres. elders. I was elected on stationing Com. by 14 votes. The committee met at Mrs. Gaiser's at 5:30, and at 7:00. C.B. Small and Pliny H.

Wolfard were dismissed. H.C. Foote pr. at 8:00, Mr. Freeman of N. Grove here. Board as usual.

Saturday, September 28 Conference continued, forenoon and afternoon. Pres. T.H. Gragg came. He was sick at night. Abr. Rust pr. at 7:30, Eph. 3.17-19. Conference adjourned after the sermon. There was rain in the afternoon. Bro. Freeman of North Grove fairly groaned over the pastorate, there, of M.F. Kelter. Freeman a lay delegate.

Sunday, September 29 There was a testimony meeting at 9:30—good. Bishop Wood pr. at 10:30, John 4.24, a fine sermon. Tharp took a collection of over $78.00. I pr. at 3:00, 1 Tim. 3.16, to a full house. H. Floyd pr. at 7:00, Hab. 3.2, "Revive us." Wood followed. Board at Mrs. Gaiser's every day and every meal during conf.

Monday, September 30 Arose early. I go to Poneta and take the 7:30 tr. to Hartford City. I called at William L. Van Cleve's house. I go on the 9:55 tr. to Union City. There I write a letter to C.B. Sherk. I went on 1:55 tr. to Dayton arriving about 3:40.

Tuesday, October 1 I was at home & wrote seven letters and a card. Ed. Sines called in the evening, also Miss Rider.

Wednesday, October 2 I was at home all day. Nora Nooks called, in the afternoon, to learn how to send goods to Constance Wilberforce, in Africa.

Friday, October 4 I was reading and writing. Lorin's called in the evening. Katharine went to Miss Hunt's. Agnes Osborn came home with her.

Saturday, October 5 I wrote many letters. Katharine and Agnes, went to Lebanon and Fort Ancient, via Franklin. Rev. William McKee died this morning. I had known him since Thanksgiving, 1868, about 39 years.

Sunday, October 6 It is a pleasant beautiful day. I attended church at Grace M.E., in the morning. It was a communion service.

Monday, October 7 I wrote many letters—among them to Blue River members. We received a letter from Orville,

dated Paris. Ida Grabill lodged with Katharine, her mother being away in Dark[e] County.

Friday, October 11 We received several letters from Wilbur & Orville.

Saturday, October 12 I was at home. Katharine's new gas range came. Cost, 35.00. Wrote to G.W. Allman, Va. Leontine & Horace staid with us to-night.

Sunday, October 13 I heard George Walton King pr. at Park Pres. Church, Heb. 2.1. He is quite theatrical.

Monday, October 14 I spent the afternoon in writing up portions of the Van Cleve genealogy for William L. Van Cleve of Hartford City, Ind.

Tuesday, October 15 I was at home. Wrote to James W. Van Cleve of St. Louis. Studied the text and connection of Rev. 5.9,10.

Wednesday, October 16 I was at home, except a trip to the bank and to Rail Road offices. Getting ready to go to Scioto conference, via Columbus.

Thursday, October 17 Started at 7:30 for Scioto Conference, at Zion Ch., near Junction City. Rev. J.W. Chambers met us, and I took Mrs. Swearengen to Zion Ch. in a buggy, while Chambers & Howe walk. Conference in session. I sup & lodge at Joshua Folk's, a mile west. Rev. J. Howe pr. at 7:00, John 12.32. Speaking meeting.

Friday, October 18 Conference continues. I dine at Rev. W.S. Tuttle's, 1/2 m. east. I sup at George Moffit's, 1/2 m. northeast with A.H. Roach & others. Rev. H.C. Foote pr. at 7:00, Rom. 1.16. Rev. H.R. Smith (Amer. Wes.) of N.C. Ass. spoke following. I board at Folk's. I boarded at Joshua Folk's at the conference of years ago.

Saturday, October 19 Conference continued. I dine at David Middaugh's, 1 1/2 m. southwest. Conf. adj. at 4:00. Sup at J. Folk's. I pr at 7:00, Rev. 5.9,10, and lodge at Joshua Folk's. There were there: Mrs. Guiton and daughter, Mrs. Denizen, Miss M.L. Lemon, Mrs. J.W. Chambers.

Sunday, October 20 Testimony meeting at 9:00, led by

Roach. Bishop O.G. Alwood preached a good sermon at 10:30. Coll. nearly 55.00. I assisted in ordaining J.A. Storer. I dine in the church with Adcock's. It rains without. I spoke 15 minutes at S.S. Anniversary at 3:00. Sup at Milton Folk's, 1/4 m. west. Bp. Alwood pr at 7:00, Ps. 84.11. I introduced the sacrament. Lodge as usual.

Monday, October 21 I go at 7:00, to Junction City, and on 7:52 F.O.C. tr. to Columbus, Miss Harriet Neese of Dayton Widow's Home, with me. The Big Four tr. an hour late, arri. at Dayton at 1:20. Find letters awaiting me, at home.

Tuesday, October 22 Racing balloons were sighted to-day.

Wednesday, October 23 Things as usual. Williams Street is being torn up for its paving. I ordered a new suit of clothes, of Perry Meredith.

Thursday, October 24 Mr. Diensbaugh called with Captain Hildebrant. They are calling on witnesses of Wilbur and Orville's flying. (Capt. Hildebrant afterward contributed a long article, to the chief German paper, affirming the unquestionableness of the evidence of the flights and complimenting me as the "venerable priest.")

Friday, October 25 Wrote some letters. I received a card from Bishop C.L. Wood, saying his health is improved and that he expects to continue on his round of conferences.

Saturday, October 26 I wrote letters all day. There was a little rain in the afternoon. Sent a check to pay my Indiana taxes. Wrote to H.M. Malson, Reuchlin, Drusilla McKee and others.

Sunday, October 27 I remained at home. It was a dark day with a little rain. Leontine and Horace came and staid till afternoon.

Monday, October 28 Wrote the pastor of 1st Baptist Church of Providence for the address of some of Rev. Stephen Gano's descendants. Received a letter from Orville dated Berlin, Oct. 16, 1907, giving hopeful indications of sale of their flyer. Lorin, Milton and Netta called an hour in the evening.

Tuesday, October 29 Nothing unusual to day. Agnes Osborne and Katharine went to Thomas' Orchestry in the evening, and Agnes lodged here.

Wednesday, October 30 Paper from Des Moines giving som[e] account of Martin Tuttle & his father and brothers. I knew them at Orange (Fayetteville), Indiana. Perhaps, I now for forty years had not heard from them.

Thursday, October 31 At home as usual. Katharine went in the evening to a hal[l]o[w]een party at Miss Myer's sister's. I sat up till her return at midnight.

Saturday, November 2 I was at home. Agnes Osborne was with us in the evening.

Tuesday, November 5 This is election. Ed. E. Burkhardt is elected mayor. Kentucky goes Republican.

Wednesday, November 6 Election news comes in.

Thursday , November 7 I was at home. Katharine and Agnes have a supper in the evening for many teachers, who stay till a late hour.

Friday, November 8 Katharine starts at 7:00 a.m. for Columbus to attend the Central Ohio Teachers' Association. Ivonette and Leontion[ne] lodge at our house. Milton Jr. is fifteen years old to-day.

Saturday, November 9 I bought Webster's Unabridged Dictionary as a birthday present for Milton.

Sunday, November 10 Still unwell, I remain at home. Katharine and Winifred got back from Columbus after 6:00, eve.

Monday, November 11 I was at home. Letters from Wilbur.

Tuesday, November 12 At home. Perhaps a little better of my influenza.

Friday, November 15 Katharine staid at Milton Matthews'.

Saturday, November 16 I wrote a letter to the boys.

Frances Matthews died at 2:00 p.m. Katharine went and remained there.

Sunday, November 17 This is the seventy-ninth annivesary of my birth. The years have dealt gently. My brother Samuel Smith Wright, a brilliant flower, fell 65 years ago; my Father, 46; my Mother, 41; my brother William, (sweet spirit), 39; & sister Sarah, 39; Susan, 18; my brother Harvey, 2. Lorin & family dined with us to-day.

Monday, November 18 I am at home. I rewrote my letter of Saturday. Lorin's called in the evening.

Wednesday, November 20 Went on 9:00 (9:40) train via Richmond to Anderson, and thence by inter-urban to Fairmount. Call at several places, and sup & lodge at Ellis Wright's.

Thursday, November 21 I went on 9:18, Penn. tr. to Fowlerton. Call at R.W. White's on the farm, and go to Oliver Buller's and dine. Call at Wesley Hayden's. I go again to White's & have supper there. White gives me in cash $20.05 (besides 70 cts taken out for weighing) and a check of $22.65, hay money. Go to Fairmount, on 5:30 tr. Lodge at Ellis's.

Friday, November 22 I saw Chas. T. Parker & others. Went to Marion. Found the Fowlerton Church lawsuit dismissed. Return to Fairmount. Driggs & Wiley gave me a check for $48.00, on Ware Room rent. Engage Ribble to paint my ware-room. Lodge at Ellis Wright's.

Saturday, November 23 I went on 6:00 traction to Jonesboro, and on C.C. & L. R'y to Richmond & to home on Traction Limited, arr. at 12:30. Katharine in the evening went to Mrs. Negley's.

Sunday, November 24 Charles Taylor brought a letter from Wilbur, who is in New York. Letters of 12th and fifteenth came from Orville in Paris. Lorin and Netta called in the evening.

Monday, November 25 I was at home. Charles Taylor called in the afternoon.

Tuesday, November 26 Wilbur came home about noon,

from Eurpoe. Went May 16th. Lorin's called in the evening. Wilbur came home on the Steamship Baltic.

Wednesday, November 27 News reporter called about 12:00. I went to Stationery store at 5:00, and bought letter paper.

Thursday, November 28 Lorin and family and Winifred Ryder were with us to day. They remained till near 9:00, evening.

Friday, November 29 I went to bank and to store. Purchased underwear. Wilbur received a cablegram from Orville.

Sunday, December 1 I attended Williams St. Baptist Church and heard Rev. Mr. Stevens on Close Communion. I was at home the rest of the day. Letter from Orville, dated Nov. 19th, Paris.

Monday, December 2 At home, except a trip to town to exchang[e] underwear that was too small.

Tuesday, December 3 Wilbur started to Washington City at 2:45. I read the President's message in the evening, sitting up till very late. It is a very able document.

Friday, December 6 Wilbur got home from Washington at noon. Lorin's family, except Milton, called in the evening, an hour. Wilbur's ship was the Baltic.

Sunday, December 8 Was at communion at Dr. Wilson's church. Text 1 Cor. 11:25, "Do this," etc. King Oscar of Sweden died to-day.

Tuesday, December 10 Received a letter and enclosures from Rodney P. Wright, Cambridge, Mass. Wilbur received a letter from Orville, enclosing a copy of Capt. Hildebrant's report of his inquiries in Dayton about the aeroplane flights. Gen. Alexander Hamilton, grandson of the great statesman, died to-day, aged 92.

Wednesday, December 11 Horace came with his books for me to teach him.

Thursday, December 12 Horace came again and stayed

till afternoon. Wilbur had a Telegram from Orville at Jersey City.

Friday, December 13 Orville came home from Paris— at 7:00, morning. His ship was the "Oceanic".

Sunday, December 15 I attended Grace M.E. Church, at 10:30, and heard Dr. Fuller preach, Rom. 12:1. My hearing increases in dullness; so much I could only partly hear. I was at home the rest of the day.

Monday, December 16 At home. The children visited Ed. Sines and family who moved to 51 Bierce St, (Ave.) a few weeks ago, after being our neighbors over 36 years.

Tuesday, December 17 At home. Horace here. Misses Osborn and Ryder took supper with us.

Wednesday, December 18 Horace took the usual lessons in the afternoon. Lorin's children took supper with us.

Saturday, December 21 Went to Public Library in the forenoon; and bought and mailed a Bible (3.25) American, Pronouncing, Revised, to Ellis Wright. Finished a long letter to Rodney P. Wright, Cambridge, Mass.

Sunday , December 22 I went at 7:30 on traction car to Germantown, and preached at 10:30, 145 Psalm, 6 Verse. Called a half-hour at Mrs. Sarah Thomas's. Dined at J. Wesley Fout's. Reached home at 4:30.

Tuesday, December 24 I was at home. Rev. George Crum of Cincinnati formerly, now of Dayton, called on me. I subscribed for "The Circle", Magazine, for Reuchlin— $1.50. Over 35 years ago, I baptized some of his (Cr.) members by immersion—in 1871, I believe.

Wednesday, December 25 We all dined at Lorin's—a fine turkey—and remained till night.

Friday, December 27 I was at home. In the afternoon, Mrs. Stevens, Agnes Osborne and other lady teachers visited Katharine and Agnes supped with us.

Sunday, December 29 Heard Rev. Sherman F. Young, pastor of Broadway M.E. Ch., Ps. 85:6. He is a good speaker.

Tuesday, December 31 Funeral of Adam Hull at Broadway M.E. Church at 10:00. I led in the opening prayer. He was 86 yrs, 2 m. & [blank] days old. Wrote an article for the *Christian Cynosure* on "Secret Societies Ancient."

Notes for 1907-1909

The first day of January, Vivian Harris, Harvey's oldest daughter, m. Earnest F. Smith. In 1909, Jan. Ethel Harris m. to George W. Holland.

Grant County Farm
Crop of 1906
Corn 200.55, Hay 70.78, Pasture 20.00, Oats sold April 29.50, Oats sold August [blank]

(Spring of 1907)
Ditcher's work 32.97, Tile of Fowler 30.18, Tile on hand before [blank], Paper for rooms 4.00, Timothy seed 6.85.

Days of Birth
Milton Wright b. Monday. Susan C. Wright b. Saturday. Reuchlin Wright b. Sunday. Lorin Wright born Tuesday, Wilbur Wright b. Tuesday, Otis & Ida Wright b. Wednesday, Orville Wright b. Saturday, Katharine Wright b. Wednesday.

Feb. 1907. With shoes on, Milton Measures 5 ft. 2 inches, Leontine, 3 ft. 10 in., Ivonette 4 ft. 1 1/2 in. and Horace 3 ft. 3 inches. Herbert is reported to be 5 ft. 1 1/2 inches, in h[e]ight. Mashall H. Vanfleet, Kate H. Van Fleet, Alamosa, California. At Rushville, Ind., Dora Abercrombia, Sarah Ball, Dr. O.P. Dillon. (Now Dec) Eunice Moor [?]

1908

Wednesday, January 1 It is a mild beautiful day. I spent the day about as any other. We had a very fine Turkey for dinner. About four o'clock, I took a two-mile walk, and on the return called at Mrs. Kumler Huffmans, and at Lorin's. This is my 79th New Year.

Thursday, January 2 Another lovely day is this. Horace again came for me to teach. I took a walk, about 4:40, of about 1 1/2 miles.

Friday, January 3 It is fine weather, I took my hygenic walk. Horace took a short set of lessons.

Saturday, January 4 I was at home as usual. I took my walk. Called at Lorin's.

Sunday, January 5 I was bilious, making it unsafe to attend church. In the evening our young folks went to supper at Winifred Ryder's. I was reading and writing. The day was beautiful.

Monday, January 6 I was at home, except a walk to town on errands. Horace resumed his lessons to me. Governor Harris's message came, a concise and admirable document. I to-day began to write my autobiography. Another beautiful day.

Wednesday, January 8 The snow flies a little in the morning, and the day is a little colder than for several days before. Nothing very unusual occurs. I wrote several pages on my book.

Thursday, January 9 It is another nice day about the same temperature of yesterday. I am writing a summary of the Ancestral names in the several branches of the Wright Family. It almost makes one's head dizzy to think of so many! Netta has been sick two days.

Friday, January 10 A nice day. I called at 3:00, at Lorin's. Milton has had grippe two days. Netta is better, and up. Rev. S.B. McGrew died in Springfield, Missouri, to-day.

Saturday, January 11 I am at home as usual. It was a mild day. I wrote out especially a summary of our Schenck ancestry to several generations in Holland. Our ancestor Francis Gano came from France about 1686, tho' possibly our next Gano ancestor, Entiente Gano (Stephen Gano), may have come some years earlier. They were French Protestants, "Huguenots."

Sunday, January 12 I remained at home, the day being rainy, and my sleep being short last night. Leontine and Horace were with us in the afternoon, and all of Lorin's family except Milton in the evening. Milton is still unwell.

Monday, January 13 Horace came to his lessons, but does not seem very well. I largely spend the day in retracing with ink, the quotations I made, in the Lenox Library, New York, in 1900, from "Burke's Commoners", concerning the "Wright Family." The rule of the Library allowed extracts only in pencil writing. I have all branches of our family traced back to 1630–1686, in America, except those of the Huffs and Smiths, traced only to my great-grandmothers.

Tuesday, January 14 At home. It is a sunshine day, moderately cold. Nettie and children call about 4 o'clock.

Mrs. Davis closed her housework of some months to-day.

Wednesday, January 15 Another mild day tho clouded. Letters received from Reuchlin and from Flora M. Glass. Write several letters. Horace tries to teach me how to play dominoes! New housekeeper begins.

Thursday, January 16 It is a temperate beautiful day. Letters from Reuchlin, and Flora M. Glass; wrote to Reuchlin, Lefforge, etc. Wrote sketch of homeward trip from Riverside, Calif., via New Orleans, in 1887, from notes taken on the train. Milton & Horace came an hour in the evening.

Friday, January 17 This is another temperate, nice day. I wrote some letters, and a summary of ten ancestral families to enclose to Flora Glass, at Wabash, Ind. Horace progresses well with his lessons.

Saturday, January 18 This is a sunshiny, mild day. I wrote and mailed an article, "Pay for our college," to Conservator. Our young folks take supper at Mrs. Mary (Osborn) Emmons'.

Sunday, January 19 I was at home all day. Leontine, the nicest little lady, dined with us. I read and wrote, busily all day. It is beautiful mild weather.

Monday, January 20 Mailed letters to Mrs. L.H. Conover, and to Elmira Koerner. Orville went to Springfield in the afternoon. Lorin, Netta and Horace came in the evening. The day has been mild and sunshiny tho slightly hazy.

Tuesday, January 21 Went on 9:45 train to Troy, Ohio, to visit Alexander Heywo[o]d at the crossing of the Railroad at Franklin Street. Dined with them and came home on 5:25 train.

Wednesday, January 22 I slept much. Orville went on 3:00 train to (Mansfield) to Canton to see Lieut. Lahm's balloon ascension. I called at Lorin's at 4:00 and gave Horace lessons. The weather is delightful.

Thursday, January 23 A very little snow, but considerably colder. I did little to day. I wrote a few letters. Orville

did not return home to-day—till midnight.

Saturday, January 25 The weather was a little warmer than yesterday. Nothing unusual occurred except that Yoba Lakio, the High School student, called in the evening at 5:35.

Sunday, January 26 My sleep was short last night, and I remained at Home. It was somewhat rainy. Lorin's youngest three were with us to dinner and all with us in the evening, with the parents.

Monday, January 27 It was a pleasant cold day—the temperature abt. 25 degrees at 9:00. The boys are preparing to put in a bid to the United States Government on furnishing a Flyer. Horace recited as usual.

Tuesday, January 28 Temperature is about 30 degrees at 9:00. Wrote some. Lieut. F.H. Lahm made a balloon ascension, at Canton, and landed near Oil City, Pa.

Wednesday, January 29 The to-day's weather is pleasant, tho moderately cold. I write to Reuchlin and to Harvey B. Harris, & to L.V. Harrell.

Friday, January 31 Warmer. It rains some in the evening. Received and answered a letter from J. Howe. In the evening, I read the President's long special message. Roosevelt is a pic-nic!

Saturday, February 1 It is a blizzard like day. Nothing very remarkable occurs today. Katharine supped with Winifred Ryder. The king of Portugal and the crown prince were assassinated this evening. It was King Carlo.

Sunday, February 2 It is a cold day—8 degrees at 8:00, forenoon. Agnes Osborn and Winifred Ryder dine with us. Milton and Horace sup with us.

Tuesday, February 4 The temperature at 9:00 A.M. was about 20 degrees. Horace came after 1:00, and recited as usual.

Wednesday, February 5 After a little snow last night, the day was rainy. Things are as usual. Horace did not come for his lessons to-day.

Thursday, February 6 No rain to-day. Weather moderate. Horace recited well to-day.

Saturday, February 8 At home as usual. The *News* telephones the brothers, in the afternoon, that the War Department has accepted their bid in furnishing a flyer for $25,000.00. At 5:00, a telegram congratulates them, from Mr. Knabenshue, and one later from F.H. Lahm.

Sunday, February 9 I hear Bishop James.W. Thoburn pr. at Raper Church, Acts 1.8 "Ye shall be my witnesses," etc. It was an evangelical sermon. He is an admirable bishop. At 2:30, at Grace M.E. Church, Bishops Thoburn & Spellmyer and Mrs. ———, a missionary of China spoke.

Monday, February 10 This is a nice day. Horace's lesson in forenoon. The Wright brothers receive notice from Allen of the acceptance of their bid on a flyer for the War department. Munn Company applies for an article from them for the *Scientific American.*

Tuesday, February 11 Temperature, 44 degrees at 9:00. It is a beautiful day. Go to Main St. & buy a globe, rubber sandals, etc. It is primary election day.

Wednesday, February 12 I made it Lincoln Day for Horace. We had flags, new globe, map, pictures of Lincoln, etc. Yesterday's primaries show Taft victorious nearly everywhere in Ohio.

Thursday, February 13 Horace came in the forenoon. In the afternoon, I walked to Main Street & back. I got a map of Dayton.

Friday, February 14 I went on 12:30 traction to Germantown. Left my valise on the car. C.S. Johnson preached and held Quarterly Conference. Supper at Lizzie Long's. I preach at 7:00, 1 Cor. 12.31. I lodge at J.W. Fout's. (This is Sat. 15th's record.)

Sunday, February 16 Sunday School & speaking meeting, C.S. Johnson preached at 10:30, Matt. 24.30, & administered the sacrament of the Lord's supper. We dine at J. Slifer's on Cherry Street. I was sick in afternoon & night and sent for Dr. Brown. Took medicine all night, but slept a few hours.

Monday, February 17 I went on 8:30 traction car to Dayton. I gradually regained my appetite.

Tuesday, February 18 At home. Considerably unwell, but have no pain. I have food more suitable to-day. Lorin and Netta called an hour in the evening.

Wednesday, February 19 Ther., 37 degrees at 10:00. There is nothing unusual. I remain indoors. Earl Wright married Ethel Reeves to-day.

Friday, February 21 It was a beautiful, sunshine winter day. Twice I went to the brothers' shop to look after mail. Wrote to Reuchlin.

Saturday, February 22 The weather is nice. Wrote Reuchlin, and Rev. G.W. Keller.

Tuesday, February 25 Horace came again for his lessons. He is my six-year-old grandson. He is of short stature, strong build, energetic, active movement. His features are very regular and graceful, his eyes and countenance bright when excited, his complexion medium. He has self-assertion, but is meek and well-disposed.

Wednesday, February 26 I found my valise at the waiting room of the traction -Mr. Dailey having brought it from Hamilton. Horace reported to his mother that I had (my) "grip again" and she was alarmed, thinking it la *grippe!*

Thursday, February 27 Pretty cold to-day, but not severe. At 2:00, the funeral of Mrs. Elliot, Mrs. Sines' sister, on Oak St. I did not attend it.

Friday, February 28 Netta came with Horace to-day and heard him recite to me. I called at Henry Wagner's, as I do every week. He is near 81 years old and helpless, but suffers little. We have been neighbor's for 39 years. To-day was cloudy, but mild.

Saturday, February 29 This is the anniversary of the birth of my brother William, born in 1832. The day is cloudy, but mild. Miss Winnifred Ryder and her young friend Miss [blank] took supper with us.

Sunday, March 1 I attended Broadway M.E. Church. It

was a communion occasion. Lorin's girls came to supper and the rest, except Milton, came afterward. It rains at bedtime. On the whole, it has been a very mild winter, and, to those in the cities, a pleasant one.

Monday, March 2 The Miami River is pretty high. I went to the Library in the afternoon, at Third Street by the canal.

Tuesday, March 3 Horace came, saying "a 23rd cousin" kept him home yesterday. He counted nearly 100. I again went to the Library in the afternoon, affording me a 2 1/2 mile walk again.

Wednesday, March 4 I visited old neighbors, the Sines, 51 Bierce Ave. The mother is 77 or 78 years of age. Rev. Joseph Roy, former field secretary of Am. Mis. Association, and Antisecrecy man, died to-day, aged 80; also Senator Redfield Proctor, of Vt., aged 77.

Thursday, March 5 Ther. 45 degrees at 8:30. As usual to-day. In evening (8:00) heard Nature-fakir Long on habits etc. of animals, at Association Hall. He is evidently a sharp observer and perhaps a little whimsical. "Nature-fakir" is hardly an inappropriate name for him.

Friday, March 6 There is hardly any need of fire- heat to-day. In the afternoon, I took Horace to see Wolf Creek and the Miami River, the waters being the highest of the year.

Saturday, March 7 It is a beautiful day, and fire scarcely needed. The river has fallen perhaps eight feet. I saw Rev. Samuel Scott, who is 88 years old, walking the street as most men of 60 years. I have known him ever since I removed to Dayton, in 1869.

Monday, March 9 I took Horace to see the Chinamen in their laundry. Mrs. Davis is doing our housework again.

Wednesday, March 11 It is another beautiful day, and very mild. Orville & Katharine visit Miss W. Ryder in the evening.

Thursday, March 12 Mr. Roy Knabenshu, the aeronaut, visited Wilbur & Orville. It is a mild and beautiful day.

Friday, March 13 The day passed as usual. Katharine & others went in the evening to Richmond to to [repeated in text] hear the debate on ship Subsidy between Butler & Earlham Colleges. They return at 11:30, p.m.

Saturday, March 14 I walked in the afternoon to the Library and back.

Sunday, March 15 At Broadway Christian Church, I heard Rev. F.G. Coffin, on Eze. 13.1. He spoke much on the Cherebim of chapter 10. Lorin's children came in the afternoon. The day was hazy, the temperature very moderate. Wilbur started to New York.

Monday, March 16 A moderately warm day. I did not do much. Horace recited well. I slept better than usual. Mrs. Rebecca Hayden, of Fowlerton, was buried to-day, J.A. Rector preaching the funeral sermon.

Tuesday, March 17 It is a beautiful day. Horace is fast learning to read. I go over my papers, and put away a box of them. I slept none in the day. Orville got a letter from Wilbur about their French contract. Telegraphs assent to it with proposed changes.

Wednesday, March 18 A slightly rainy day. Horace does not come. News of Gen. Stoessel's sentence to ten year's imprisonment. Judge Wood sentenced Orchard to death, but recommends mercy. Orville injured his new engine badly, in continuing to test it.

Thursday, March 19 I gave Horace two lessons to day. The day was cooler and mostly cloudy in forenoon. Miss Winifred Ryder dined (supped) with us.

Friday, March 20 It is a mild pleasant day. Wilbur came home at noon. The young folks sup at Robt. B. Osborn's. Lorin, Netta & George Feight call in the evening. Bishop Charles H. Fowler, M.E., died to-day.

Saturday, March 21 Horace and Leontine dined with us. It is a beautiful, sunshiny day.

Sunday, March 22 I was at home all day. I did much reading in the Scriptures—especially on Daniel 9–27. I do not see how a Jew or unbeliever can get over its force. It seems to me that the seventy weeks (490 yrs) begin with 457 B.C. and end 33 A.D., or thereabouts.

Monday, March 23 Horace came at 1:00 and recited his "Tuesday's lesson." I get ready to go to Huntington in the morning, starting at 5:30. The Wright brothers get word that Weiler accepts their terms for French rights.

Tuesday, March 24 I go via Lima to Huntington, Ind., reaching there at 11:25. Dine at Restaurant near P.O. Mis. Exec. Meeting at 2:00. C.W. Linker reports orally. Linker's reception at 7:00 at College chapel. All Ex. Com. spoke & Mrs. Leow. Also Linker. I sup & lodge at S.A. Stemen's.

Wednesday, March 25 Ex. Com. met at 9:00, in College building. A.F. Stoltz is appointed to Africa. Linker to labor some here. I dine at Rev. J.W. Chambers', and sup at Pres. F.H. Gragg's. I lectured an hour on Church History prior to 1800. I lodged at Rev. S.L. Livingston's.

Thursday, March 26 Talk with Bishop Wood. I go to Publ. House with Livingston's, and on 10:10 car via Wabash to Fairmount. Dine in F. at a restaurant. See Chas. F. Parker, Esq., in his business office. I sup and lodge at Ellis Wright's.

Friday, March 27 I went on 9:25 tr. to Fowlerton. Dine and sup on the farm. Mrs. White sick. I walked to see the clearing (John Smith's) & the oil wells. Pipes are dug up. Went to Fairmount on 5:30 tr.. Settled with Driggs & Co. to Apr. 1st. Lodged at Ellis Wright's.

Saturday, March 28 Saw Squire Jones on renting him an office. I engaged Driggs to put a wire fence around my lot. At 11:00, I went to Marion and paid spring tax $63.44. Dine at restaurant. I went on 1:44 C.C. & L. tr. home via Richmond arri. at 6:00.

Sunday, March 29 At 3:00 (4:00) I was at the "Church of God" baptizing at Wolf Creek, near Western Avenue. Five women and one man were immersed after the usual forrmula. - I called at Lorin's on my way home. Yesterday, found a letter and book of poems from Rev. Th. Nield of Gleason, Tenn., an old correspondent of *Telescope.*

Monday, March 30 Horace recited much, and all better

than common, to-day. I wrote to R.W. White and Flora Glass in the evening.

Tuesday, March 31 A nice day. Nothing unusual occurs. I wrote to R.W. White and to J.F. Croddy. It may be said that there has been little cold weather, the past winter, and that the approach of spring is early, a fact grateful to the large number now unemployed.

Wednesday, April 1 Nothing unusual occurs. Horace makes a long recitation and stays till evening. It rains some to-day.

Saturday, April 4 It is a very mild and beautiful day. I called at Lorin's in the afternoon. The Brothers shipped their aeroplane for Kitty Hawk to-day. I slept 4 1/2 hours.

Sunday, April 5 I heard, at 1st U.B. Church, Pres. Lewis Bookwalter pr. Mat. 17.4 & Phil. 3.10 and Rom. 12.1. I could not hear much of what he said. Lorin's girls dined with us. They behave lovely. Lorin called an hour in the evening.

Monday, April 6 Wilbur started to Kitty Hawk, N.C., about 9:00 a.m. I spent the day largely in reading. I slept about six hours.

Tuesday, April 7 Horace read well to-day. After dinner, I opened up my box of old "Telescopes" stored in the cellar, and found them in better condition than I had expected. The body of Emanuel Swedenborg was exhumed to day, to be shipped to Sweden. I received a friendly letter from Lewis Bookwalter, to-day. I ordained him in 187[blank].

Wednesday, April 8 This is little Ivonette's 12th birthday anniversary. I got her a book on South America; and Leontine one on North America; and Horace one on animals and birds.

Thursday, April 9 Lorin's children got picture cards from Wilbur, mailed at Norfolk, Vir.

Friday, April 10 Orville shipped more matter to North Carolina. I received a picture card from Wilbur mailed the 8th from Wilbur, Elizabeth City, N.C., and Orville received a letter from him. Edwin Brown comes out as a candidate against Mr. Carr for Supt. of Public Schools.

Saturday, April 11 Orville received another letter from Wilbur, mailed at Elizabeth City. Rev. W.H. Chandler, Congregational, once a student of U.B. Seminary, dined with us. Is an organizer. Miss Ida Graybill called an hour in the evening.

Sunday, April 12 Ivonette dines with us. I remained at home. It is a very nice day.

Monday, April 13 I get my spectacle frames mended at Newsalts, and nose glasses improved.

Tuesday, April 14 Went to Newsalt's. Called at Leitch's an hour. The old lady was 89, Jan. 15th.

Wednesday, April 15 Orville received a letter from Wilbur, Kitty Hawk, dated April 10th. He found their old building pretty much wrecked. Orville is unwell—has some chill.

Friday, April 17 Rev. R.S. Kindel calls in the afternoon. I got Horace some toy gardening implements. I took a copy of Livingston's deed to Chadwick & sent to him.

Saturday, April 18 Katharine received a letter from Wilbur, at Kitty Hawk, dated the 14th. The day is cloudy, and very slightly rainy. Katharine takes supper at Winifred Rider's.

Sunday, April 19 I attended the Easter services at Emanuel Catholic Church, on Franklin Street, near Ludlow at 11:00. It is a beautiful day—no fire needed.

Monday, April 20 I went to the Court house and examined the plat of Farley Street and title, for S.L. Livingston. In afternoon, Mrs. M.L. Hearlow of Lexington, Ky. called, being in distress, for not getting letter from Constance Wilberforce, her dau., Bouthe, Africa. I tried to help her.

Tuesday, April 21 At 6:15 p.m., Orville started for Kitty Hawk, N.C. A perilous undertaking. The day is beautiful.

Wednesday, April 22 Nothing unusual at home. It is a delightful day. The daily paper tells of the death to-day of Henry Campbell-Bannerman, till lately the English premier. It also announces the death of Henry Ramey, Mrs. Bessie Wilberforce's grandfather, aged 91.

Thursday, April 23 At 2:00, I was at Henry Ramey's funeral at 311 Chicago Ave., DeSoto E. Bast officiating. Nearly 91 years old. This a beautiful day, but warm as June. Orville expected to reach Kitty Hawk, this evening. I reproduce my diary of 1857.

Friday, April 24 Received letters from Isaac Borum, & from White—check for corn. Small crop! One of Lorin's horses (Dick) died.

Saturday, April 25 Reports of dreadful storms and much loss of lives and property, in the southwest. I worked considerably on a revised copy of my diary of 1857.

Sunday, April 26 I went on the 8:30 traction car to Germantown. I was in Bro. Moses' S.S. class. Preached at 10:00, 2 Cor. 15.5. Dined at Jac. Slifer's. Called a half hour at Thomas's. Found no one awake at Lizzie Long's, and at E.M. Scott's. Sup at Slifer's. Preached at 7:30, Rev. 2.10. I lodge at Edwin M. Scott's. Their adopted child, Paul.

Monday, April 27 I go on 8:30 car to Dayton. Letter from Orville, the 23rd, from Elizabeth City, N.C. to Katharine. Automobile parade passes through West side about 4:30 p.m. I mailed Myrl Wright a nice hair-ribbon, for a birthday present.

Tuesday, April 28 Horace came with excuse for absence yesterday. I received letters from Emma Frazier and Bertha Long. Lorin is about to put in 31 bids on sprinkling.

Wednesday, April 29 This is Myrl Wright's sixteenth birthday anniversary; Ellis's daughter. I am at home, to-day, all day.

Thursday, April 30 This is the seventy-seventh anniversary of Susan's birth. I was at home to-day. There was a little snow, in the forenoon, melting as it fell.

Saturday, May 2 Telegram from Flint & Co. containing

Berg's request for accounts of flights. I wrote the Wright brothers enclosing Flint's Telegram and the *Herald's* yesterday's dispatch, abou[t] four mile flight across the Sound! What reports! The day was clear and cool. The clouds to-night kept off the frost.

Sunday, May 3 Heard at First U.B. Church at 10:30, Rev. Cyrus J. Kephart, Micah 6.8, "Do justly, love mercy," Ivonette and Leontine dine with us. Ida Graybill called in the evening.

Monday, May 4 I received a letter from Orville, dated April 28th. I wrote to them in the evening. They had made no flight with their aeroplane.

Tuesday, May 5 Wrote to White, my farmer, on straight rows of corn, both ways, and close plowing. Horace missed his attendance.

Wednesday, May 6 I went with Ivonette and Horace to the Wallace Show parade. We see it pass, 1st on Brown, 2nd on Maine [Main?] Street. Sunshine to-day. Katharine telegraphs to Nag Head for the Wright brothers, and writes them a letter. Weiller insistes on their coming to Paris by June 1st, as per contract with him.

Thursday, May 7 Letters from Reuchlin, and Elmira Koerner. It is rather a rainy day, but does not rain much. It has been so much of the time—for a week or two.

Friday, May 8 Pres. Henry Churchill King, Prof. J.W. Carr and Miss Rider dined with us. Lorin's children went to the Ringling Show. Pres. King lectured at Y.M.C.A. at 8:00. Agnes Osborn came home with Catharine, from the lecture, and lodged.

Saturday, May 9 Last evening's "Herald," to-day's "Journal," the "Cin. Commercial," the "Cin. Enquirer," and Dayton "News" had alleged dispatches concerning the Wright brothers' flights, the "Inquirer" reporting they had flown 3000 feet high, 30 miles long, and 8 miles out to sea! Kath. had a letter from Wilbur dated May 3rd. I wrote Reuchlin.

Sunday, May 10 I heard at 10:30, at Trinity Eng. Lutheran Ch., W.J. Gaby, Ps. 8.3,4. He is somewhat of an orator.

Monday, May 11 Letter from Orville dated May 7th, tells of a short flight, the 6th. I called at Sophia Simpson's. She has been sick. I received a letter from Jas. R.B. Van Cleve, Springfield, Ill., Pres. of Lincoln Bank. The above-mentioned was the first flight of this season, tho reporters have reported some marvelous ones!

Tuesday, May 12 Letter from Ray W. Stevens, my grand-nephew, Glenwood, Ind. Funeral of Wm. Harlow, across the street from us (a bartender) at 2:00. We had house cleaners at work. It is a warm day. We have been preserved from frosts by clouds, during the past cool spell.

Wednesday, May 13 The Dayton *Journal* has a highly commendable article, "The Wright Brothers." I received a letter from my niece, Mrs. Eva Gray, Greenfield, Ind. Also, letters from Clay and F.L. Hoskins, the latter asking me to meet the Board of Bishops, May 23rd and act in his stead!

Thursday, May 14 Katharine received this morning a special delivery letter from Wilbur and a letter by regular mail from Orville. I examined Mrs. Livingston's deed from Francis Loehr in the afternoon & copied. I called at Lorin's a half hour in the evening.

Friday, May 15 The "Journal" reports that the "Wright brothers wrecked their machine yesterday. Katharine went to a supper at the First Presbyterian Church, this evening. My room was quite warm yesterday and to-day, without fire. Uncle John H. Braden died to-day.

Saturday, May 16 Letter came from Flint saying that Weiller had consented to postponement of Wrights' coming to France. Warm day. Katharine attends a party at Miss Myers to High Sc[h]ool teachers going to Europe. In evening, she expresses Wilbur's trunk to New York. Telegram from Wilbur, at 10:00 p.m. Start's to France Wedn.

Sunday, May 17 Warm. At 10:45, I attended a prayer-meeting at Williams Street Baptist Church, conducted by the pastor, W.E. Stevens. Anna Feight and Winnifred Ryder visited us in the evening. I called at Lorin's a half hour.

Monday, May 18 Letter from Orville. I took Katharine's lunch basket to her at school.

Tuesday, May 19 Letter from Rodney P. Wright. Wrote Reuchlin and Barkley. The day is a little rainy.

Wednesday, May 20 I went to town and got my bank book. It is a pleasant day.

Thursday, May 21 Letters from Wilbur and one from [blank]. Wilbur is to sail for Paris to-day on the ship LaTouraine. I spent the day in righ[t]ing my lower part of the book-case. Agnes and Winifred supped with us. The weather is very warm.

Friday, May 22 Warm enough to sit in the open air. Katharine went to a party given to all teachers of high school. I spent the day arranging letters alphabetically.

Saturday, May 23 Orville arri. at home from Dare Co., N.C. at noon, after an absence of a month and two days. I took Horace' books home.

Sunday, May 24 Heard Rev. Asa McDaniel on Matt. 13.31,32.—The Mustard Seed. Beautiful day.

Monday, May 25 Train an hour late, so I miss connection at Richmond for Fowlerton, and go via Anderson, to Fairmount. I see C.J. Parker and Driggs, etc. Supper & lodging at Ellis Wright's. I hear a Prohibition Party speaker at Friends' Ch at 8:00, from Minnesota, a College man.

Tuesday, May 26 I went on 9:25 tr. to Fowlerton and the farm. Dine at White's. Return to Fairmount and stay at Ellis's. Was sick about day-light. The casing of three oil wells have been drawn, and the pumper's house removed, from my farm.

Wednesday, May 27 Sick in forenoon. Went in afternoon via Marion and Union City home, Arri. at 6:30.

Thursday, May 28 At home, feeling some the worse for yesterday's sickness. Ther. 93 degrees.

Friday, May 29 Not yet strong as before my brash. New York Herald & Collier's Weekly contain extensive articles on the Wrights and their Flyer. Ther. 93 degrees.

Tuesday, June 2 It is a beautiful day. I went to the main city in the afternoon. Katharine supped at Miss Myer's.

Thursday, June 4 At home. In afternoon, called at Alvin Weaver's and at William Weidner's. I called to see his sister who is a member of our Church. She was not at home.

Friday, June 5 Nothing unusual. I wrote to Wilbur, 32 Avenue Des Champs, Elysees, Paris, cp H.O. Berg. It is a beautiful pleasant day.

Saturday, June 6 Went to bank in the forenoon.

Sunday, June 7 Remained at home all day except a walk, and call of a few minutes at Albert Shearer's.

Monday, June 8 I left at 5:00, morn. for Huntington, Ind., via Lima, arri'g at 11:30. S.L. Livingston conveyed me to his house where I dine. Educational Board met at 2:00 in College Bldg. I sup at F.A. Loew's. I lodge at S.L. Livingston's. I only called in at the Inter-Society entertainment at Davis Hall.

Tuesday, June 9 Ed. Board met at 9:00. I dine at F.H. Cremean's. Afternoon session adjourns sine die at 5:00. I sup at Otto B. Bowman's. I lodge at Livingston's. I did not go to the oratorical department's entertainment. The Ex. Mis. Committee had a session at 5:00 p.m.

Wednesday, June 10 Ex. Mis. Com. met at 8:00 and completed business. Commencement exercises at 10:30. The address by Lawrence McTurnan, Asst. State Supt. of Public Instruction, was fine. I dined at J. Howe's, and went on 3:08 Interurban car via Wabash to Fairmount, and sup and lodge at Ellis Wright's.

Thursday, June 11 I saw C.T. Parker and went with Ellis to the farm. Dined at R.W. White's after looking over the farm. I went on 2:07 tr. to Richmond and home, arri. at 6:00.

Saturday, June 13 Orville busy with photopraph's with their Flyer. Caleb Powers is pardoned by Gov. Willson of Kentucky. Trial has been a farce for eight years, against an innocent and brilliant young man.

Sunday, June 14 Heard Rev. Mr. Sanderson pr. at 10:30, at 201 Champa. Ave., Phil. 2.7, 1st clause. A good sermon, to a few in a 13 X 16 ft. room. Duxon there.

Wednesday, June 17 The Republican National Convention is in Session in Chicago, "It is Taft." Mr. Herbert Balch, came and remained over night and till noon next day. His mother Harriet Maria (Sneider) Gallaher-Helm-Balch, was my second cousin, a very nice woman who died at Hood River, Ore.

Thursday, June 18 Herbert tells me that his Mother died in 1881, that his sister Gertrude Ingles lives near Hood River, that his niece Edna (Condon) Keisch lives in Chicago, that his brother—Helms is living, that his brother Frederick, died a distinguished author (about 1889). Herbert m'd a Guthrie & they have one child. He is 34. His uncle Jesse Snyder died a few years ago.

Friday, June 19 Wm. Howard Taft was nominated Yesterday afternoon at Chicago, by 702 votes, while Knox, the next highest received 68 votes, Hughes 65, Cannon, 61, Fairbanks, LaFollett, 25, Foraker, 16, Roosevelt 3, absent, 1. To-day James Schoolcraft Sherman, of New York, was nominated for vice president by over 800 votes. Katharine went to Oberlin. Lorin was run down by an automobile, at 5:30.

Saturday, June 20 Lorin is sore on his knees and head. The automobile driver is F.E. Walters, a saloon keeper of Eaton. A warm day. I did not do much. Lorin is feverish and his left leg pains him. The automobilist had been drinking. The accident was not *un*avoidable.

Sunday, June 21 I heard Rev. P.M. Camp at Summit Street on 1 Cor. 9.22,23. A medium preacher. Lorin is comfortable to-day. The forenoon is cool; the afternoon hot, very hot.

Monday, June 22 Lorin is doing well. The morning is cool. The afternoon and night are hot.

Tuesday, June 23 It is a hot day followed by a very warm night. I wrote to Rev. W.C. South and to Wilbur. Lorin's bandages were removed by the doctor, and he walked up to the brothers' shop, to-day.

Wednesday, June 24 At home as usual. It was a warm day. Grover Cleveland died to-day. He was a great man. Aged 71.

Thursday, June 25 Mrs. Barbary Hoffman (Kumler's widow) was buried to-day. Mrs. Bessie Dillon called in the forenoon. The morning was cool; the afternoon hot.

Friday, June 26 Lorin went to his office to-day. Katharine came home from Oberlin, this evening, Mrs. Harriet (Silliman) Robins with her. It was a comfortable day.

Saturday, June 27 Nothing special occurs with us to day. I call[e]d at Lorin's in the evening.

Sunday, June 28 Heard D.L. Myers at Fourth Presbyterian Ch., (Acts 16th Chapter) on the need of missionaries—Mexico, S. America, Africa, India. This forenoon, about one half the sun's disk was eclipsed. The eclipse came on about 9:00, and passed off at about 12:00.

Monday, June 29 Cooler toward evening. Selpt much to-day. Examined scriptures. The evening and night were cool.

Tuesday, June 30 Copied Grandmother Reeder's Notes -and sent copies to Cousins C.E. Wiley, Richard F. Braden & Flora M. Glass. Lorin, Netta & Ivonette called in the evening. The weather is pleasant.

Wednesday, July 1 At home. Katharine and Harriet visit Mrs. Dr. Stewart. Proofs on Orville's article for the Century come. I slept eight hours to-night.

Thursday, July 2 Katharine and Harriet visited Miss Mayer. Murat Halstead died to-day.

Saturday, July 4 I visited Susan's grave this forenoon. Wrote a letter to Wilbur, and cards to Elmira and Caroline.

Sunday, July 5 At Eaker St. Church, I heard Bishop H.M. Turner pr. Math. 11:12. "Kingdom—suffereth violence." Quite an original orator. I called at Lorin's at 5:00. Report in the *Journal* that Wilbur was scalded at LeMans Saturday, tho not severely.

Monday, July 6 The "dispatches" say H.O. Berg represents Wilbur's injuries as slight. The thermometer ran about 90 degrees in the afternoon.

Wednesday, July 8 Received a letter from Reuchlin. Wrote to him and to Wilbur. Kath, and H. went out to Soldier's home, at 5:00. LeMans dispatch says (Journal) Wilbur's physician orders him a week of complete rest.

Thursday, July 9 Received letters of the 28th Ult. from Wilbur at LeMans. Card and letter from Bishop Wood. The girls went to Robt. Osborn's to supper, and staid late.

Friday, July 10 I was at home. I called at Lorin's in the evening. The girls, (K & H) were at Dr. McLean's for supper. Wm. J. Bryan and John W. Kern were nominated at Denver Nat. Dem. Conven.

Saturday, July 11 Orville has a letter to-day from Wilbur dated July 3, at LeMans. I was busy writing to-day. This is the seventh anniversary of Horace's birth; I gave him a globe, a top and a soap bubble pipe.

Sunday, July 12 At 10:30, at Broadway M.E., heard pastor [blank] Young, Phil. 4.11, on Contentment. The day is quite warm.

Monday, July 13 Mrs. Harriet Robbins started home at 11:55, noon. Katharine had a letter of the 3rd Inst., from Wilbur. It was a very warm day.

Wednesday, July 15 K. Received a letter from Wilbur, dated LeMans, July 7th, saying his injuries were slight, and he had resumed work.

Thursday, July 16 Orville rec'd a letter from Wilbur, dated July 5th, telling how the accident occurred.

Saturday, July 18 Milton is sick with something like the fever.

Sunday, July 19 I remained at home to-day. Henry Wagner has a sort of bilious brash, but is better to-day. I received a letter from Wilbur telling more specifically about his 4th of July accident. Milton has less fever.

Monday, July 20 Milton has high fever to-day. Henry Wagner is better to-day.

Tuesday, July 21 Bishop H.C. Potter died this evening. Milton's fever is high to-day.

Wednesday, July 22 Milton's fever is still high.

Thursday, July 23 Dr. Spitler pronounced Milton's fever a mild case of typhoid.

Friday, July 24 Milton is quiet and notices things but little; sleeps considerably. A cable from Berg says that Wilbur is substantially well, and busy on his machine.

Saturday, July 25 Q.M. 2:30 Germantown. I did not notice it till evening—so was absent. Milton seems to be getting along well, tho his temperature at times runs up to 104 degrees.

Sunday, July 26 I went on the 8:30 traction to Germantown. The Quarterly meeting had been postponed three weeks. I pr. at 10:00, Rom. 2.16, "My Gospel." I dine at Jac. Shifer's & sup there. Call a few minutes at Lizzie Long's. Car belated. I get home after 9:00, by changing cars at Miamisburg. Hatt to stand.

Monday, July 27 Letters from Wilbur dated 14 & 15 July. Milton's fever is still strong and he for the first a little flighty. Ther. 90 degrees.

Tuesday, July 28 Milton more flighty. I paid my June tax, $8.44. Ther. 90 degrees.

Wednesday, July 29 Milton more flighty.

Thursday, July 30 Consultation of doctor's. Milton is quite sick.

Friday, July 31 At midnight last night, Milton's temperature went down to normal and continued so till morning, but it arose in the day, ran up, then lower. I wrote to Wilbur in the afternoon yesterday in answer to a letter of the 19th.

Saturday, August 1 Milton's fever is still pretty high.

Sunday, August 2 Near morning, Milton's pulses almost stopped beating, but he revived, and his fever ran high all day and all night. I called at Mrs. H.S. Simpson's and at Mrs. Ramey's. We received letters from Wilbur, I wrote to him.

Monday, August 3 Milton remains much the same. The nurse imagines that he looks better in the afternoon.

Tuesday, August 4 Milton seems better this morning, and later in the day, Dr. Spitler pronounced him decidedly better. It rained hard in the night.

Wednesday, August 5 Milton was restless and nervous last night. The doctor gave him codeine, and he slept five hours to-day. The day was a little cooler.

Thursday, August 6 Milton, on the whole, had a better day than usual.

Friday, August 7 Milton is still improving.

Saturday, August 8 The fever is rather high in the afternoon. But we think Milton is gaining. Wilbur is reported to have made a successful flight of two and 17/100 miles at LeMans, France, this afternoon at 3:00.

Sunday, August 9 Heard Rev. W.J. Gaby at Trinity Lutheran, Ex. 32.32. "Forgive—blot me."

Monday, August 10 Dr. Spitler went away and Dr. Conklin took charge of Milton's case.

Tuesday, August 11 Milton seems a little better to-day. Wilbur makes flights.

Wednesday, August 12 Milton has some congestion of the lungs, but gets no worse during the day. Wilbur makes a seven minutes flight at LeMans in the forenoon, and two short flights in the afternoon.

Thursday, August 13 Wilbur made a long flight (about six miles) and later broke a wing in landing. Milton is better all day to-day.

Friday, August 14 Milton continues to improve. In the evening, the Fair ground was opened as a park.

Saturday, August 15 Milton is still improving. To-day, the Quarterly meeting is at Germantown. I have for some weeks called at Lorin's two or three times in a day.

Sunday, August 16 Heard Rev. F.G. Coffin pr. at 10:30, John 11.35 & Rom. 12.15. (Most on laughing!) Called at Lorin's in afternoon. Albert Shearer called in the evening.

Monday, August 17 Milton is still improving and was moved down stairs and provided with a motor fan. Rev. R.S. Kindel dined with us.

Tuesday, August 18 Milton's temperament and pulses are about normal, in the evening. Orville is getting ready to go to Washington City.

Wednesday, August 19 Milton is about the same as last evening. Orville started to Washington City, this evening at 10:12, via Harrisburg, Pa. Both he and Wilbur peril their lives, perhaps Orville most by the unsuitableness of the grounds at Ft. Meyer.

Thursday, August 20 Mrs. Davis takes a vacation and Katharine runs the house.

Friday, August 21 Milton still improves. I am notified by Joseph Wheeler that memorial services for Mrs. Bessie Ramey will be held Sunday evening. (This notice was Tuesday or Wednesday and Mrs. S. Ramey called to see me about it.) I went to the bank in the afternoon. I paid Katharine $20.00 on my board.

Sunday, August 23 I was at home during the day, doing considerable reading especially on the Trinity. I examined scriptures on the subject, and read Luther Lee, who is very able on the subject. At 8:00, I attended the memorial of Mrs. Bessey Wilberforce at the Wesleyan Church, and was one of the speakers.

Tuesday, August 25 I saw Milton for the first time for several weeks.

Wednesday, August 26 The Chamber of Commerce held a meeting in the evening to consider the election of Edwin J. Brown as Superintendent of the Public Schools of Dayton. There was great indignation.

Thursday, August 27 I wrote to the editor of the Macon Republican (Mo.) concerning the Boones and Van Cleves; also to Mrs. L.H. Conover, Marlboro, N.J. inquiring of the parentage of Rachel Schenck. I also wrote to Wilbur.

Friday, August 28 I received a letter from Wilbur, dated the 15th, mentioning his flights, from 8th to wreck 13th, and telling of the French newspapers reports—of Bollee, Peltier et c. I wrote to Reuchlin and to Bertha Glaze.

Saturday, August 29 At home. Agnes Osborne lodged with Katharine.

Sunday, August 30 I preached, at 11:00, for Rev. [blank] Bast, at Wesleyan Methodist Church, on Wilki[n]son St., Matt. 20.27. Serve others.

Wednesday, September 2 Went to bank, bought slippers and typewriter paper 500 sheets for 70 cts.

Thursday, September 3 Katharine Wright went to Richmond on the 7:55 traction. I went to Courthouse at 10:00, for the argument on Ed. J. Brown's Superintendency. I also was there in the afternoon, Katharine returned in the evening.

Saturday, September 5 Heard Judge Alread's decision at 9:00. Mrs. Stevens came in the evening to supper. Miss Winifred Snyder called at 8:00. Received a telegram That Cousin J.F. Croddy died at 8:30, this evening.

Sunday, September 6 I pr at 10:30, at Broadway M.E. Church, 2 Cor. 13.5. I called at Lorin's to see Milton who begins to walk again.

^ The Public Schools are opened to-day. I wrote Semele Short and Effie W. Kirkpatrick. Orville is reported to have made two flights this evening at Ft. Myer—one of 11 minutes and 11 seconds, the other a little less than 8 minutes. This is fine progress.

Wednesday, September 9 We had a telegram from Orville about noon, saying: "Fifty-seven & 1/2 minutes, this morning; stop voluntary." In the afternoon he flew 62 minutes and 15 seconds; and then took Lieut. F.J. Lahm a flight of 6 min and 26 seconds. Secretaries Wright and

Straus, and Metcalf were present. Berringer came out at 11:00 p.m. to interview me. Asleep!

Thursday, September 10 In the evening, Orville, at Ft. Myer, flew 65 minutes and 52 seconds, and rose to the altitude (estimated by the reporter) of 200 feet.

Friday, September 11 Orville is reported to have made a flight of seventy minutes. Mayor E.E. Burkhart called at 3:00, in afternoon to consult about method of a public recognition of the Wright brothers on their return home. About 10:00 Miss Jessie M. Partlon, for "Newspaper Enterprise Association," Cleveland, came for an interview. Orville's flight to-day, 75 minutes, 26 sec.

Saturday, September 12 Orville is reported to have made two flights: one of 9 minutes with Maj. Geo. O. Squiers, and one of one hour and 15 minutes alone, rising 250 feet high. I[t] was toward evening.

Sunday, September 13 I heard W.E. Hammaker's first sermon at Raper Church, M.E., John 12.32, "If I be lifted up." He is quite theatrical. Lorin's brought Milton to our house, and he remained two hours, in the afternoon. It is his first visit—since his sickness—anywhere.

Monday, September 14 I dined at Lorin's. Orville made no flight to-day. I felt dull.

Tuesday, September 15 I called at Lorin's. I got ready and started to Conference, three miles north-west of Greensfork, Indiana, at Sugar Grove church at 12:00, by traction car. Spent two hours at Mrs. Caroline Zellers (sister-[in?]-law) Richmond. Went on 4:53 to Greensfork. Lodged at my old friend's, Wm. Hatfield's. Elias Clapp came. Wilbur flies 39 min. & 18 sec.

Wednesday, September 16 Levi Strickler's daughter took me to Oliver Wilson's. I dined there. Conference opened at Sugar Grove Church at 2:00, by Bishop C.L. Wood. Sup & lodge at Adam E. Howard's. Prof. Carl Wood's wife and sister there. Wm. Hatfield telephoned me of Wilbur's flight of 39 minutes. Rev. A. Rust pr. at 8:00, 1 Sam. 10:6.

Thursday, September 17 Conference adjourned at 10:30 for Committee work, and C.W. Rector preached, John

20:20, last clause. Dine at Howard's. Sup at Oliver Wilson's, with Bp. Wood and J. Howe. Bishop Wood pr. at 7:30, 1 Pet. 2:21, "In his steps." Mrs. Geo. Wilson, Maggie Stewart & Mr. H. Lamar take the place at Howard's of the Wood women. Orville injured. Orville's disaster at 5:00; Selfridge's death.

Friday, September 18 Wm. Hatfield telephoned me an account of Orville's Flyer accident as per Palladium (at 8:00) & later of Lorin's telegram. A.E. Howard takes me to Greensfork & I go home, arriving at 11:00. Dine & sup at Lorin's.

Saturday, September 19 We received a telegram from Katharine last evening saying that Orville's injuries were not dangerous, but painful. I wrote Katharine, sending her a draft for $50.00. I wrote Reuchlin. I wrote Wilbur in the evening. Leontine and Horace lodged with me. I board at Lorin's.

Sunday, September 20 Heard Rev. S.Y. Young pr. at 10:30, on Christian giving, without a text, at Broadway M.E. Church. In the evening, Lorin received a telegram from Katharine saying that Orville slept over two hours last night, and has little pain.

Monday, September 21 Slept none till bedtime. I wrote letters. Sent several enclosed letters to Catharine. A Dispatch from D'Auvours says that Wilbur flew 1 hour, 31 minutes and 25 seconds to-day, a great record.

Wednesday, September 23 We had a letter from Katharine of considerable length, dated Monday night, giving considerable concerning Orville's accident at Ft. Myer, last Thursday.

Thursday, September 24 In the afternoon I went to the National Theater and heard John J. Lentz, J.H. Newman, James M. Cox, Judson Harmon, Hanley and Wm. J. Bryan speak. Had boarded at Lorin's from noon the 18th all the time.

Friday, September 25 Dined at Lorin's. Supped at home.

Saturday, September 26 I breakfasted and supped at home. I dined at Lorin's. A telegram from Katharine says that everything is favorable in Orville's case.

Sunday, September 27 I heard Rev. M.B. Fuller pr. at 10:30, at Grace Church (M.E.) on the Christian Ideal, Luke 17.10. I came home by Albert Shearer's, and dined with them. Edith Hall, their daughter was there, from Joliet, Illinois. Lorin's called in the evening.

Monday, September 28 At home. Write some letters. Wrote to Orville.

Tuesday, September 29 Papers say Wilbur flew to-day three times: one flight 1 hour, 7 m., 11 sec.; second flight with aeroplanist Tissandier, 11 min, 3 2/5 sec, third with Count De Lambert, 6 min., 15 sec. We received a letter from Katharine dated 27th, 5:00 a.m., saying she had been with Orville by night and by day & his temperature had been high.

Wednesday, September 30 Called at Dr. Tizzard's at 2:00. Dentist out on Wednesday afternoons. Mrs. C. Davis came to see about work. I did not want her while I was alone.

Thursday, October 1 Dined at Lorin's. Wrote letters. Left my watch at Newsalt's to be cleaned. Mrs. Davis swept the house and righted up the rooms—75 cents.

Friday, October 2 Dined at Lorin's. I had the cap replaced on my tooth and my teeth cleared of lime, $2.00.

Saturday, October 3 I dined at Lorin's. I had a letter from Katharine saying that Orville's leg was doing well and that his ribs were practically well, and that it was safe to leave him at nights. I wrote to her and to Reuchlin.

Sunday, October 4 I heard Rev. W.E. Stevens pr., Williams St. Baptist Church, Col. 1:23. I dined at Lorin's. Wrote letters to Katharine & others.

Monday, October 5 I went to town, saw Prof. Loos, and paid water and gas bills. Dined at Lorin's.

Tuesday, October 6 I got a letter from Kath. dated Monday morning, saying that Orville's temperature again rose to 101 degrees, but he, with her care, slept more than usual.

Wednesday, October 7 I got a letter from K. saying that

Orville was better. I dined at Lorin's as usual. Wilbur took Mrs. Hart O. Berg in an aeroplane flight, the first woman that ever had a flight.

Thursday, October 8 In the afternoon, I went out the Jallappa road with Netta and her boys to get walnuts. We got about six! Wilbur, at D'Avours, takes Lieut. Gen. Baden-Powell, Count Serge Kaznakoff (a Russian), Mme. Bollee and Commander Bouttieaux, in flights, the last 75 feet high, and was congratulated by Dowager Queen Margharita, of Italy.

Friday, October 9 In the evening, I attended the Harding meeting, in Enterprise Hall. Heard J. Eugene Harding, Chas. H. Kumler and Geo. E. Hill, the last windy. Wilbur is reported to have made six short flights at Avours, with Lazare Weiller, M. Deutsch, DeLaMeurthe, etc.

Saturday, October 10 In afternoon, I went to town, but did not find my watch ready. I received at 8:00 a.m., yesterday's letter from Katharine. Orville's condition good, tho temperature 99 3/5 degrees. Wrote Katharine and Helen. Wilbur is reported to have flew, to-day 1 hour, 9 minutes, & 45 seconds. (Wrote the above on wrong page)

Sunday, October 11 Katharine writes Saturday morning, that Orville's temperature is normal, he suffers little severe pain, but is very uncomfortable. I attended communion at Trinity Lutheran Church. At 2:30, I heard Hon. Seaborn Wright speak on Temperance at Victoria Theater. Lorin's called in the evening.

Monday, October 12 At home. Went to Winter's Bank and left mine and Katharine's books to be posted. Sent Hellen six silver teaspoons as a wedding present.

Tuesday, October 13 A letter from Katharine dated yesterday says that Orville is doing splendidly. I write Katharine and Reuchlin. Prof. A.W. Drury called in the afternoon.

Wednesday, October 14 I went on 8:05, [a.]m. tr. to Marion (via Union City) called at John Null's, (saw Mr. & Mrs. Hoss) at 106 E. Street (north), paid my fall tax ($48.29), sup at Fairmount, at Ellis Wright's. Saw Chas.

T. Parker, my agent; setted with Driggs & Wiley—$72.00. Lodge at Ellis Wright's on Sycamore Street.

Thursday, October 15 I went to Fowlerton, looked over my farm, and dined at R.W. White's. He took me to William Reeder's. I telephone to Lorin's. Sup and lodge at Reeder's.

Friday, October 16 William takes me to White's. I dine there & settle accounts, Paying him $7.75. I then go to Robert B. Reeder's and sup & lodge. Wm & Mattie there, to supper.

Saturday, October 17 Robert takes me to the 7:30 tr, and I go via Richmond home, arr. at 11:00. Dine at Lorin's.

Sunday, October 18 At Broddway Christian Church, I heard Rev. M.D. Wolfe, of Haverhill, Mass., pr. 2 Cor. 5.17–19, at 10:30, "Rev." Ryder, of Lutheran paper, called to interview me. Dinner at Lorin's. Called at Henry Wagner's, talk with Rev. John Simons on Bank guarantee,

Saturday, October 24 At 4:00, Orville's overcoat came home from Stein's and, at 8:00, I sent it to him at Ft. Myer, by Adams Express.

Sunday, October 25 I heard Rev. William Greenough, D.D., Philadelphia, pr. at Fourth Presbyterian Ch., at 10:30, 2 Cor. 4.6, an able sermon, and sound. He is very aged. At 2:00, I attended the Old folks' meeting at Broadway M.E. Church at 2:30.

Monday, October 26 At 10:00, I was at Mrs. Lizzie (K. Kumler's) Miller's funeral, a[t] Summit Street Church, conducted by Pastor Peter Camp. W.J. Shuey, Prof. T.J. Sanders and Prof. Henry Garst each spoke about 15 minutes. At noon, I received a letter from Katharine saying that Lord Northcliff, General Miles had visited them Saturday.

Friday, October 30 Mrs. Lottie Jones spends the day in sweeping and cleaning the house, $1.25. The evening paper reports that Wilbur's motor exploded to-day, while his Flyer was in the air. Lorin & Netta called in the evening.

Saturday, October 31 It appears that injuries to Wilbur's motor were trivial. Carrie Gumbaugh came to look after our dinner to-morrow. I sent an article to the Tribune, New Castle, Ind. Lorin received a telegram from Katharine on her way home. Miss Carrie Breene sent me flowers—violets.

Sunday, November 1 Orville and Katharine came home from Ft. Myer, Va., arriving at 9:00 a.m. He is brought out from the depot on a wheeled chair. His mind is good as ever and his body promises to be in due time. Carrie Grumbaugh gets the dinner. Lorin met Orville at the depot & he and Netta dine with us. A few call. Flowers for Orville & Katharine came in.

Monday, November 2 Several came in to see Orville to-day, and flowers still came. He did not register for voting. Lorin came to stay with him at night.

Tuesday, November 3 I Voted for Taft, Harris and Harding, at 8:00. The day is a hazy sunshine. In the evening Lorin and I went over to town to see the telegram bulletins of the election. Taft appeared to be elected president, and Hughes governor of New York.

Wednesday, November 4 The morning papers make it clear that Taft has a large majority of the electoral votes, but that Watson, in Indiana, and Harris in Ohio are defeated for governors. Henry Wagner died at 5:20 p.m., aged 81 ys. We have been neighbors for 39 years; close neighbors 37 years.

Thursday, November 5 Attorney Toulman, of Springfield, called in the afternoon, and Rev. P.M. Camp, and Prof. A.W. Drury. I wrote several letters.

Friday, November 6 I called at Henry Wagner's. Orville received 50,000 francs on the French contract from Hart O. Berg -$9,687.92. I went in the evening and saw the Adams Express agent about Orville's overcoat and Katharine's furs, not delivered at Fort Meyer!

Saturday, November 7 I banked the check for the Wright brothers and paid gas bill for them, $1.20 and for us $1.80. At 1:30, I attended Henry Wagner's funeral, & spoke ten minutes.

Sunday, November 8 Called at Wagner's. At Williams St. Baptist Church, at 10:40, heard Rev. G.N. Bierce 2 Cor. 5.10, "We all must appear at judm. seat" etc. Prof. Werthner & wife and Mrs. Greenwood and others called. At 7:30, I heard Mr. Bierce again on The Young Men. In aftern, We rode out with Lorin's, beyond Miami Chapel, down the river.

Monday, November 9 I spent the day mostly in copying Mr. Pope's genealogical treatise on the Wright ancestry and writing to Rodney P. Wright.

Tuesday, November 10 I wrote some letters. Lottie Jones worked for Katharine and Mrs. Carrie Davis came back to keep house, in the afternoon.

Thursday, November 12 I went to town, Mrs. Heywood called, Mr. Morley and others. I wrote an answer to Ward S. Jacobs' questions, about the Wright brothers—Hartford, Conn.

Friday, November 13 Miss Hunter (Teacher) came. Chas. Taylor took Orville to the shop in a wheeled chair.

Saturday, November 14 Henry Webbert died at 1:30, morning. In the Evening, Editor Philippi took a picture of our dwelling, to use in an illustrated article in the "Telescope." This morning, we had our first considerable fall of snow flakes. My sleep was short to-night.

Sunday, November 15 I slept much to-day. Lorin, Netta and Horace called an hour in the evening. Prof. G.A. Funkhouser called a few minutes in the evening.

Monday, November 16 It is bright, but dry weather. I called at Henry Webbert's whose funeral occurred this forenoon, conducted by a Spiritualist. S.A. Stemen came to get me to go to Westfield, Illinois, to remove some misapprehensions of Mrs. Indiana Whitesell about her recent donations to the church.

Tuesday, November 17 Bright day. I arose early. This is the eightieth anniversary of my birth. "Thus far the Lord hath led me on, Thus far prolonged my days." I am older than either of my parents lived to be, and older than either of my grandfathers, and than three of my great-grandfathers. I have never felt much pain, nor seen many dark days. I am wonderfully preserved. Henry Webbert buried.

Wednesday, November 18 Nothing of special importance here occurred to-day. It is Lorin's birth day. He is forty-six years old. I received a letter from Reuchlin, enclosing one from Bertha. Orville went upstairs to-night to sleep, the first time since coming home.

Thursday, November 19 Went on to-day, on Dayton train toward Indiana and toward Terre Heaute, with a Mr. [blank] Wolsey on the way who got off at the Kingston for his home at Bloomington. I saw Prof. W.H. Wiley and wife at Terre Haute, and went on to Casey where I staid at St. Charles Hotel. Slept well.

Friday, November 20 Went on to Westfield, Called at [crossed out] and went on to Indiana Whitesell's and talked with her, and back to Fogler's, and dined. Went out in afternoon and called on Prof. R.A. Shuey's, call[e]d at Pres. Daugherty's, called at Rev. Daughterty's at depot, called at Prof. [unreadable] and at M.A. Fogler's, and teleph. Shrader.

Saturday, November 21 I got up at 5:00, and went to Ashmore with Shrader, and went on to Indianapolis, where I looked up and down Illinois Street, but found no Clarence Winchell. I walked back to depot, where I ticketed to Knightstown, where at Cambridge found myself awakened and got off and took car to Richmond. Went home on 10:00 train.

Thursday, November 26 Arose early. Read the paper. Lorin's came. I was at dinner from 1:30 to 2:30. I remained. Prof. Landis (Wilbur) came and staid an hour. I ate supper at 6:30, with Orville and Katharine.

Friday, November 27 I arose at six o'clock. I got paper and began to write. Was interrupted and wrote no more till after dinner.

Friday, December 4 (This should be for Dec. 10th) I spent to-day at home. Slept half the day. About 4:00 p.m. I went over to Anderton's and pruchased a 65 cents bottle of Higgins' ink. Lorin put up a lamp in my room. Henry Brook called to see Lorin and Geo. A. Feight. Horace was with Lorin.

Wednesday, December 9 Miss Myer, Agnes, and Ryder spent the afternoon with Katharine.

Thursday, December 10 I spent most of the day at home asleep, but about 4:00 went to Anderton's and purchased a 65 cent bottle of Higgin's Ink. Lorin came, with Horace, and put up a welchbagh burner in my upstairs room. Henry Brook called to see Orville, and Geo. A. Feight was with him.

Friday, December 11 Read in South's Sermon, 5th Volume. He is a most sublime orator.

Saturday, December 12 Between day-light and dark, I read much in the fifth Volume of the World's History & It's Makers; on Judith, Aphasia, Cleopatria, Joan of Arc, etc.

Sunday, December 13 I spent the day at home. Lorin's called in the evening. I received a letter from Mary H. Krout, of Honolula. She spends her whole time in literature. She went to Honolula for two months, and has remained two years.

Monday, December 14 I remained at home all day. Wrote letters to Rev. J.S. Rock & Wife, and to R.W. White.

Thursday, December 17 Winifred Rider, and Lorin, and his two boys, called in the evening.

Friday, December 18 Mr. Sidall, former student at Oberlin dined with us. I walked a mile South to Broadway Street. Lorin and wife & his two girls came in the evening.

Saturday, December 19 Mr. Sidall had a long talk with Orville and dined with us.

Sunday, December 20 Started to Grace Church, was too thinly dressed; staid at home. Miss Winif. Ryder dined with us. I spent afternoon in resting—not quite asleep. John Feight & wife came; Ed Ellis & Wife; Ed. Sines & A. Stoltz and Siddall, who remained till after supper. Lorin & all the children, except Leontine came.

Monday, December 21 We were all at home, but Wilbur. Alford, editor of the American Machinist called on

Orville in the forenoon. Katharine and Orville went to Springfield to see Toulin, the patent lawyer. Mr. Collins called to invite Orville to a dinner at 4th Pres. Church.

Tuesday, December 22 All at home. John Valter, a newspaper writer called at 4:00, in the evening, for an interview with Orville—peculiar in his facial motion.

Wednesday, December 23 It was a day of much buying, by Katharine.

Thursday, December 24 It was a day of general stir, getting ready for Christmas. Harrison and John A. Van Horne called to see me in the Afternoon. I knew the latter at Hartsville, 55 years ago, last April. Fred. Rike and Worman's called to leave Orville flowers. We had a supper in the evening, with Lorin's family.

Friday, December 25 We had breakfast at about 8:00. Like yesterday, the day was mild and bright. Went to Lorin's and ate dinner, somewhat elaborate, came home at 3:00. I walked up to the bridge and got back, as they arrived, Orville & Katharine took an additional walk.

Saturday, December 26 I arose about 7:00. Nothing new. I slept part of forenoon & part of afternoon. Prof. T. J. Sanders & Wife called to see us, in the afternoon. She was Rev. C.A. Slater's daughter, Burbank, Ohio. Their Son is a High School teacher, here.

Sunday, December 27 Received, a letter from Frazier, saying that she and Cora Dillon would come Monday. I remained at home all day. Albert H. Shearer and wife, Mrs. Sines, and others called. The company was unusually large.

Monday, December 28 In the afternoon, Mrs. Davis received a telegram from Cora Dillon & soon after, Miss [unreadable] and she came. All out except myself and them. Orville has a long conversation and shows his visitors pictures. Netta and Leontine came and the visitors go home with them & Lorin & stay.

Tuesday, December 29 I called at Lorin's at nine. The visitors go with Katharine to town, and get back to our house to dinner. They go on 1:00 Intururban to Indianapolis. I return home. Katharine out most of the after-

noon. The newspapers report a great earthquake in Italy, 50,000 lives lost in Messina.

Wednesday, December 30 At home, except a change of gold pen at Alderton's. I wrote letters to Eva Gray and to Reuchlin. At night Katharine took a sudden turn of mind, abandoning going abroad. I got a short night of sleep.

Thursday, December 31 Was in the room while my room was being got ready. A reporter from New York called to get a bid for a machine for a rich sport—$7,500, asked. Prof. Worthner and wife called an hour in the evening. I lodged in Orville's room. Thus closed another eventful year. Orville at Ft. Myer and Wilbur at LeMans, France, after Kitty Hawk.

Miscellaneous Notes from back of diary

Uncle J.F. Reeder's youngest daughter, Elmira, died of diptheria, Sept. 5, 1864.

In Sept. 1864, I bought a house and five acres in Henry County, paying $550.00 down and $150, christmas two years, without interest. Moved into it April [blank] 1865.

Harriet M. Snyder's second husband was J.B. Helms. Their son was born Oct. 16, 1857. Her Gallaher daughter was Almonia.

Martha A. Ellis, widow, daughter of Edmund F. and Anna Wright now lives on the old farm, in Miami Co., Ind.

For 1908

E[s]timates presented at Presbyterian Men's Society in Philadelphia, Feb. 13, 1908.
Jews 11,112,000, Greek Church 120,157,000, Roman Cath. 277,638,500, Protestants, 166,666,500, Mohammedans, 216,630,000, Heathen 838,278,000. Total 1630,482,000

Americans spend: for Church Work $250,000,000 Foreign Mis. 7,500,000 Chewing gum 11,000,000 Millinery 80,000,000 Confectionery 178,000,000 Jewelry 700,000,000 Liquors 1,243,000,000.

Uncle Porter Wright's son William Freeman Wright was born in the Gennesee Valley, New York, June 18, 1813; died in Centerville, Ohio, in 1816 or later.

Earl Wright married Ethel Reeves, Feb. 19, 1908.

Presidential Candidates, 1908
1. Wm. H. Taft & Jas. S. Sherman.
2. Wm J. Bryan & John W. Horn.
3. Thos. E. Watson & Saml. W. Williams.
4. Thos. L. Hisgen & John Temple Graves.
5. Eugene W. Chafin & Aaron S. Watkins.
6. Eugene V. Debs & Ben Hanford.
7. Martin R. Preston & Donald Munro.

1909

Friday, January 1 This is my eightieth New Year. "Thus far the Lord has led me on." Mr. Gordon call[e]d from the Home (Soldiers'). He is 79 years old. In the afternoon, J. Sprigg McMahon, Mayar Burkhart, Parmalee, and J.M. Coxe called on Orville. Prof. Funkhouser and Wife, Winifred Ryder and Lorin's called & Joe Boyd.

Saturday, January 2 I took a walk and returned at 3:00. Rev. R.S. Kindel and Ed. Sines were there. Earnest Mooney came in. And Alan Thresher and Heath came and spent an hour. I saw Kindel on the train. In the evening, Lorin & girls called, & Miss Valter, Hunter & Chas. Taylor. My room is repapered & new carpet.

Sunday, January 3 Heard Rev. [blank] at Wmst. Baptist, Ps. 8.4. Came home & slept an hour before dinner. Mrs. Wagner and Ed Ellis & Chas. Taylor call, and Misses Felker & Everhard, women physicians, called to see Katharine, later. Ellis's, and Mr. Emmond and Glenn Osborn, Misses Wagners, Drucilius, etc. Mr. Crane took us to Depot. Misses Valter, Hunter & Ryder there.

Monday, January 4 We ate breakfast at 7:00 dinner at 12:00, and supped at 6:00. Just before dinner, I put $600.00 in bank; bought two-inch augur at 90 cents. Afternoon I slept an hour. Got ready to go to Grant.

Tuesday, January 5 Start to Farm at 8:47, via Richmond. Go on to Fowlerton. Lunch on train. I sup at R.W. White's. I pr at Hopewell. Barrack Neal converted. A man and woman out for prayers. I lodge at Frank Kirkwood's. Have 4 boys. One in bank at Fairmount.

Wednesday, January 6 Walked to R.W. White's. At meet-ing. About 30 present. Dined with Jas. A. Rector. At last told Rector of Keiter's latest acts. All new to him! Went to stores to get sandals—found none—sup at White's. Pr at 8:00 Mat. 23.27. Stay at Kirkwood's with Rector.

Thursday, January 7 Go to White's. Go on 11:40 tr. to Fairmount. Call at Hasting's funeral. Dine at Ellis Wright's. Saw Chas. T. Parker. Call at Mr. Haisley's. Attend meeting at 7:00.

Friday, January 8 Dined at Ellis's. Went to Fowlerton. Sup at White's. I pr at 7:15, 1 Kings 18.17,18. I supped and stayed at Levi Simons'.

Saturday, January 9 Went to White's. Milspaugh came and we talked on sale of lot. I rejected it positively. At night, I pr at night. I stay at Wm. H.H. Reeder's.

Sunday, January 10 Went to Church and pr. 1 Pet. 1.2. Dine at Hugh Darien's. Whites all there. I sup at Frank Kirkwood's. Ten joined Church, including F. Kirkwood & wife.

Monday, January 11 Went to White's, and thence to Horace Reeves. He took me to Church. I pr. Ps. 92.8, to 27 persons. I went home with Wm. Reeder and lodg[e].

Tuesday, January 12 I went to Robert B. Reeders and dine. Wm & wife there. Wm. takes me to White's where I eat supper. Pr. at 7:30, 2 Cor. 5.10. I stay at Kirkwood's.

Wednesday, January 13 I arose at 6:00. Very cold. I went to Wm. Millspaugh's and they transfered the property to me. I went to town, and stayed at Ellis Wright's. I paid $325.00 for the property.

Thursday, January 14 I arose at Ellis's went down town. I went on the cars for Knightstown. Rode across in a "bus." Found Mr. Apple who took me to Jabez Rhodes where I lodged.

Friday, January 15 Rhoads all went to Delilah's, where we dine with Drusilla, Ed. Frazier's, Samuel Kirkpatrick & wife Hazel Wright, Earl Wright & wife came in the evening & staid till bed time.

Saturday, January 16 Went to Sena Wright's & back, to Sexton. Called on Frey's: Lois 8[?], Beatrice. Called at Howard Grubbs. I lodged at Frazier's. I went to Bert Brenner's at May's, banker. Saw Cora and Children.

Sunday, January 17 Dined at Thomas Wright's, with Jabez Rhoads & wife, Ed. Frazier & Emma & Aunt Delila, & Cora Dillon. I went with Cora Dillon and Russell Kirkpatrick to Rushville & lodge. P. Myers' folks located me after two days' search.

Monday, January 18 I go to Morristown on the 8:09 traction, to attend Peter Myers' funeral, having known him since 1857. Preached at 10:00 1 Cor. 15.56. Went to the Cemetery with the Protestant Methodist pastor, caught some cold. Returned with Mrs. Cora Dillon to Rushville.

Tuesday, January 19 I go on the traction car to Glenwood. Called at Lovicy Matney's and walked 3/4 of a mile till I met Sonnie Bowen who took me to his house where I dined, supped & lodged. He lately bought the Tom Stone House. I called at Moor's.

Wednesday, January 20 Rose at 7:00, washed. Went with Sarah Cath. to Chas. Stevens', and Lucy came over & dined with us. Ray is 5:3 in his stocking feet. I staid at Stevens.

Thursday, January 21 I go with Charles to John Meek's, on Garrison Creek. We then go to Aunt Lucinda's. Lovina is 13 years old & large. Israel is 10, Ewing 9, Milton 6.

Friday, Janaury 22 Sarah & Flora & Charles came & at 10:00, Sonnie took me to Glenwood, and I went on the 11:39 tr. via Hamilton home, arriving at 3:00. Found all well as common. It rained hard in the night.

Saturday, January 23 Arose at 5:30. Breakfast at 7:00. Went to boys' shop. In afternoon, went to Lorin's. Horace trying jumping high. I wrote to Wilbur and Reuchlin. I went to bed soon after nine. It was a cloudy warm day.

Sunday, January 24 Heard Bierce, at William Street Baptist, Gen. 5.22.

Thursday, January 28 Took coat & vest to to[repeated in text] cleaning establishment on Ludlow St. Lorin's called evening. Another party called.

Friday, Janaury 29 Called at Home. Carrie put the border on my paper. Wrote Mrs. Vanfleet at Alamosa, Cal. Wrote Wilbur at night. Snowed much. Carrie went with Miss [blank] to W. Chr. Asso.

Saturday, January 30 Much snow fell in the night. It is a rough day. I dine at Lorin's.

Sunday, January 31 Lorin called in forenoon.

Wednesday, February 3 Lorin's children at supper with us, and remained till nearly 9:00. Charley took them home. I paid half my year's tax here $4.15.

Thursday, February 4 I dine at Lorin's. Carrie visited a cousin near Ft. Ackinley.

Saturday, February 6 At home. Milton and Benjamin took supper with us.

Sunday, February 7 Attended Sherman Young's Church, and heard Him on the Black Man. He is a natural and sensible speaker.

Monday, February 8 Wrote on my Autobiography.

Tuesday, February 9 Dine at Lorin's. Wrote to Mary H. Krout, Honolula. Wilbur's letter in the News, asserting that he was innocent. This evening Ralph W. Bowen and Grace E. Smith were married.

Wednesday, February 10 Horace seems to have scarlet Fever. Send for Dr. Spitler. [last sentence crossed out in text]

Thursday, February 11 Dr. Spitler sees the coming out of the Fever. Milton and Ivonette & Leontine all come to our house, the next day.

Friday, February 12 Horace has broken out and is feeling better. Is much interested in Lincoln's pictures on the wall.

Saturday, February 13 Horace has broken out well and seems better to-day. He is full of laughter and talk. Ruby Oliver's husband died to-day at Blanchester, Ohio.

Sunday, February 14 I called at the window to see Horace, who is getting along well. I slept much to-day. Katharine took her first flight with Wilbur, at Pau, France, Apr. 15th.

Monday, February 15 Horace's fever had proved so far a light spell, and he sent for the funny pictures to-day, in the Sunday dailies.

Tuesday, February 16 Went on 5:30 tr. to Lima Crossing. Train came at 11:30. We are over four hours to Huntington. Committee still at Howe's room. Transact little business. I go in hack to Dr. W.H. Clay's house. I lodge there with Bishop Wood.

Wednesday, February 17 Call at College Chapel. Burton's remarks. Walk to Mission Room. Transact business by 12:00. Walk to Livingston's & dine. Go back. Pay tax— $1.18. Go at 4:00 to Wabash. At 5:40, leave there for Fairmount. Stay at Ellis's, who were away.

Thursday, February 18 Stay at Fairmount, till 3:05. Saw Parker and others. Dined at Ellis's. Sonnie & Kate came. I went to White's and to meeting at 7:00, at Hopewell. I led using, for a few minutes remarks: John 4.23. Closed the meeting soon after 9:00. Lodged at White's.

Friday, February 19 I slept well. Started at 7:35, arrive at depot. Start before 8:00 for Richmond. Get home at 11:00. Slept 1 h, 30 minutes. All well at home.

Saturday, February 20 Medicine used to-day, as Leontine is croupy.

Sunday, February 21 I arose after 6:00. I was sleepy in forenoon. Mrs. Sines called at 2:00. Lorin came at 5:30, & staid till 6:15.

Tuesday, February 23 Letter from Katharine. Boys go to Rome in March, early.

Wednesday, February 24 World is $53,700 behind. Wilbur's ride yesterday with Katharine, in Aeroplane. Children attend school.

Thursday, February 25 Orville and Katharine take a balloon ride in France. Wrote considerable in My autobiography.

Friday, February 26 Had to have cistern cleaned out. Wrote in my auto-biography.

Saturday, February 27 Wrote on my Autobiography. It was a nice day.

Monday, March 1 Nothing of special importance here. Wilbur is reported to have broken his rudder in France, at Pau. I wrote much on my autobiography. Word that Rev. L.G. Cowdry died to-day, comes in. A good man, full of the Holy Ghost & of faith!!

Tuesday, March 2 Leontine is thought to have tonsilitis. They have Dr. Spitler come. I wrote much of my autobiography.

Wednesday, March 3 Congress voted gold medals to the Wright brothers. I wrote much in my book. Leontine is taken home by Lorin.

Thursday, March 4 Pres. W.H. Taft was in[na]ugurated at noon. It was a very stormy day at Washington. It was nice here. Leontine seems better. Taft's cabinet: Knox, Hitchcock, Myer, Wilson, Neagle, McVeogh, Dickinson, Wickersham.

Friday, March 5 It is a mild, nice day. Leontine is getting along well.

Saturday, March 6 Leontine's fever left her. Doctor comes Monday to see if all is right.

Monday, March 8 A mild day. Rain seems probable. I write several letters—one to B. Blanch Baldwin, at New Cambria, Mo., and one to Aba. T. Cushing, in Boston. Each is a very remote cousin.

Tuesday, March 9 Wrote letters, and received one from Katharine, who was still at Pau, March 25th. We again got water in our cisterns.

Friday, March 12 Ivonette is quite well; over her rheumatism. King Edward is reported to have come to Paris.

Saturday, March 13 Paid Mrs. Grumbach ten dollars—in all thirty dollars—on board. The weather is mild.

Sunday, March 14 Nothing important to day. I saw the doctor at 3:00. Charley & Carrie go out to his Uncle's at Alexanderville.

Monday, March 15 Received a letter from Katharine dated March 4th. It gives account of Wilbur's bad accident in starting with Spanish Col. Vires. Went to Meredith Perry, ordered a suit.

Tuesday, March 16 I wrote considerable for my book. Charley & Carrie went to Frank B. Hale's for supper, a St. Patrick party.

Wednesday, March 17 Wrote considerable for my Autobiography. King Edward is reported to have visited Wilbur & Orville at their grounds at Pau, and witnessed Wilbur's two flights of seven and six minutes, the latter with Katharine.

Thursday, March 18 The papers say that Orville and Katharine have gone to Paris. I write much in the afternoon on my book.

Saturday, March 20 I went to Bank and drew 30$ and paid Carrie $10.00 paying to next Wednesday. I wrote much on my Autobiography.

Sunday, March 21 Received letters from Reuchlin, Bertha Glaize and Clara Gilbert. Answered Clara in the evening. Wrote Wilbur & Orville.

Monday, March 22 Wrote in Autobiography. George A. Feicht brought a likeness of the boy's golden Medals.

Tuesday, March 23 German paper came with likeness of the boys and their machine. *The Volk-Zeitung.*

Wednesday, March 24 I was slightly unwell to-day. I did not do much.

Monday, March 29 Writing on my life most of the day. My coat and vest came, Cost, $30.00.

Tuesday, March 30 At home. Lorin's are free on quarantine.

Wednesday, March 31 Leontine came to see me. They are just out of their quarentined home. She at her Grandmother's; Lorin's house being cleaned.

Thursday, April 1 I was sick last night, and to-day. I managed the case myself.

Friday, April 2 I wrote much on my Autobiography. Slept but two hours till 5:00 a.m., two more.

Saturday, April 3 Wrote much on my autobiography. Ivonette went home in the afternoon.

Sunday, April 4 Milton went home after breakfast, to stay. I went to Am. Wesleyan Connection Church and heard a most excellent discourse by Rev. Cyrus G. Baldwin, of Pamona, California. Text, 1 Cor. 13.13, Matt. 5.21–26. It was a sermon on Good Will. He is a son of Cyrus H. Baldwin—youngest ch. [entry ends here]

Monday, April 5 Called for my envelopes at the Post Office. They recognize and honor me as father of the Wright brothers with considerable ado. "Do they discard all use of tobacco," asked Withoft? "Yes, and all whiskey!" I replied

Wednesday, April 7 Wrote Wilbur a letter. Wrote on my autobiography, reached page 101.

Thursday, April 8 I slept most of the forenoon, being sluggish.

Friday, April 9 I was unwell, but not sick. Mr. P.M. Harmon died at 10:00 p.m., aged 84 years. Tariff Bill passes the House—3 over a Republican majority.

Saturday, April 10 I was at home. It is the time for which quarterly meeting at Germantown occurred. I did not go.

Sunday, April 11 I attended church at Williams Street Baptist Church. Heard Mr. Bearse on the Resurrection.

Wednesday, April 14 Caroline E. Zeller died this morning after one o'clock. John who came soon after telegraphed us. Wrote several pages of my book.

Thursday, April 15 Wrote several pages of my autobiography. Paid for my new suit $30.00.

Friday, April 16 Lorin, Netta and I go to attend Caroline's funeral at 8:47. Funeral at 2:00. Pastor and Hughes and his son seeak. We came home on 4:55 train. I wrote Wilbur a letter.

Saturday, April 17 Wrote several pages on autobiography.

Sunday, April 18 Went to hear Dr. M.B. Fuller at Grace M.E. Church. Text, Matt. 5.41, "If any man compel thee to go with thee a mile, go with him twain." Mailed a letter to Clara Wright.

Monday, April 19 At home. Wrote on my autobiography. Moving Picture of Wilbur's flights were shown at Theater.

Tuesday, April 20 Continued to write to page 120 of autobiography. I Dined at Lorin's.

Wednesday, April 21 We dined at Lorin's. And went there in the evening to look at the box of pictures.

Thursday, April 22 I had gastrology so I was inactive. Milton came after Irving's Life of Washington.

Friday, April 23 Stomach out of order.

Saturday, April 24 Lorin's family called. I was not well.

Sunday, April 25 Stomach out of order, I remained at home. Read considerably.

Monday, April 26 Stomach out of order. Spitler came in afternoon. Gave medicine and direction about dieting.

Tuesday, April 27 I am better. Went for mail forenoon, and to Lorin's afternoon.

Wednesday, April 28 I wrote sketch for W.H. Clay. Sent it on four o'clock delivery.

Thursday, April 29 Drew in cash sixty dollars at the bank. Get ready to leave home. Paid the Doctor $2.50.

Friday, April 30 I start at 8:00 to Marion, Ind. I pay first installment: sixty-three dollars & ninety-thre[e] cents. I went to Fairmount. Tell Bill Miller of Keiter's recent rescality. I see Charles T. Parker. I sup and lodge at Ellis Wright's.

Saturday, May 1 Windy raw day. I went on 9:24 train to Fowlerton & to R.W. White's. Dine. I went to Oliver Buller's supped and lodged. Oliver says getting hay to Cincinnati costs $2.00, per ton.

Sunday, May 2 Saw Heuston Dickinson and shaved with his rasor. Heard Jas. T. Rector preach Gen. 6.14. I dined at Frank Kirkwoods, and his second son takes me to Robert Reeder's where I see Joseph Broyles, Eliza, & Robert. I am sick at night. It is stomach trouble.

Monday, May 3 I am better, but really sick. I stay at Robert's till nearly night, when I go to William Reeder's. I lodge there.

Tuesday, May 4 I go on the 7.24 train to Richmond and to Dyyton, arri. at 11:15. I get good food. Slept well at night. Found letter from Katharine, Reuchlin, Capt. A. Hildebrant, Flora Glass, & Clay.

Wednesday, May 5 Wrote Reuchlin. Rested & dieted. Berkhart, J.S. McMahon called afternoon, to consult over Wright Brother's days, I wrote for the Invocation that day. The Children sailed for New York on the Kron

Prinzesion Cecile, due at New York next Tuesday.

Thursday, May 6 Lorin came and sewed his flying machine canvass. Lorin sold "Bill" for $200.00.

Friday, May 7 Went to Lorin's in the evening awhile. Artist called to see the picture on the wall, aeroplane.

Saturday, May 8 Bought some Fuchias at Ricter's. Rained hard, in the evening. Lorin sold his "Bob" to some Greeks. Called at Dr. Spitler's. Rev. Wm. B. Stoddard called, in my absence. Rev. R.S. Kindle called in afternoon. Paid him V.

Sunday, May 9 Attended Dr. Maurice Wilson's Church, and he spoke on the Anger of Deity. Rev. 6.17, Eph. 2:26. Dined at Lorin's and staid there till Grumbach's return from Cincinnati, after nine o'clock.

Monday, May 10 Wrote a report and forwarded it to the Publishing Board, of the trusteeship of the Shisler Estate. Nothing but expense reported.

Tuesday, May 11 Telegram from Katharine, telling of their safe arrival in New York, saying they will be home, Thursday. I wrote to Capt. A. Hildebrant, Berlin, Germany.

Wednesday, May 12 Telegram of yesterday delivered. Orville telegraphs that the children will come on noon train to-morrow. Ellington of Pau [?] calls. Herald sends a man with a snapshot. Lent him a picture. The city street is cleaned, and lights arranged for electric lights, to-morrow.

Thursday, May 13 Flags, Chinese lanterns and electric lights are being arranged. Eleven carriages met the Wright Brothers and Katharine at the Depot, and thousands, and a four horse carriage pulls them home, where thousands meet them around our house. Over 10,000 came at night.

Friday, May 14 I send papers to Reuchlin and Clay. Home as usual.

Saturday, May 15 Went on 11:00 train via Union City and Anderson to Wabash, arri. before 8:00, evening. Wait at Traction depot till after 9:00 for a car to Huntington, arri at about 10:00, and start to College Park. I overtake Mr. Brown, who takes me, living 9 miles in country. Sleep in Livingston's Third Story.

Sunday, May 16 Heard B. Baldwin preach a great sermon on the 45th Psalm, the Character of Christ. Board at S.L. Livingston's. At 3:00, I heard R.B. Mason, & attended testimony meeting in Chapel. A.J. Ware pr. at 7:30, I dined at O.B. Bowman's. I lodged at Livingston's. An excellent room alone, well supplicd. Food ample.

Monday, May 17 Was invited to a seat within the bar. Afternoon, picture of conference taken. Wood elected by 40 votes; Hoskins by 37, Barkley & Alwood by 30 votes, each. L.B. Baldwin elected editor on third ballot. Howe elected by 29 votes. Foote elected Pub. Agent. Cantata rendered by about 25.

Tuesday, May 18 I was elected on Miss. and educational boards. The day was spent on election of boards. I called at Cremean's in the morning. I dined at W.H. Kindle's. A woman (Whelock) interviewed me. Oratorical Exhibition at 8:00.

Wednesday, May 19 I called at Prof. T.H. Gragg's. Baldwin resigned and C.A. Mummart elected Ed. Conservator. Business proceeds. Session of Mis. Board & Ex. Com. Wood chairman of Ex. Com. I bought Scott on New Testament & Buck's The, Dic. paid 90 & 30 cents. I.R. Hughey pr. at 7:30. I was at Board meeting.

Thursday, May 20 I called at Matt. Wechler's. At 8:00, Ed. Board met. Elected Wood president. Had another meeting at O.M. Hypercriticisms of Dillon's proposed law on trials. That of 1901 substituted in its stead. I left at 12:45. Got home at 6:00. Found all well. I slept 8 hours. Margaret White is doing our work.

Friday, May 21 Katharine attended an entertainment at Cruiger's Eating House in her honor. I slept four hours. Cleared up my desk, Agnes Osborn came home with Katharine & staid.

Saturday, May 22 Got and planted tomatoes. I wrote Miss Breene and Mrs. O.P. McCabe acknowledging receipt of flowers.

Sunday, May 23 Heard the new pastor of Third Street Presbyterian Church, Rev. Chas. A. Campbell; preach an able and good sermon, Neh. 4.17,18. Called at Lorin's, afternoon.

Monday, May 24 Counte de La Valette sent in beauty roses.

Tuesday, May 25 I saw some reporters. Katharine supped with two women doctors; and several with her.

Wednesday, May 26 Katharine dined at Beckel House with Mr. & Mrs. Charles T. Parkhurst.

Thursday, May 27 Married Miss Eleanor L. Wagner to Forest Stoltz at 11:00, at our next door neighbor's, in the house where she was born. Katharine attended a club in the afternoon. It is nice weather.

Friday, May 28 Went to town in afternoon, returning certificate of marriage. It is a nice day.

Saturday, May 29 Wrote to Bishop Wood and to Sina Ardery, and several others. A very beautiful day.

Sunday, May 30 It rained, and I did not attend church. Lorin's dined with us. Company of doctors visited Wilbur. Albert Shearer called.

Monday, May 31 Decoration Day. It is warm enough in afternoon for a thin coat, which I put on. Judge Brown and wife called in the evening. Wilbur and Orville went on midnight train to Detroit to see Russell Alger, 5 Establishment.

Tuesday, June 1 Mrs. Weinrich called and Cyrus Kephart. Ben. Arnold interviewed me for an article on the boys.

Wednesday, June 2 The boys returned home before breakfast. It is a cloudy day. Left bank-book for adjusting at Winter's.

Thursday, June 3 Wrote letters to Reuchlin and to Mrs. T.M. White (Westfield, Ill.) and a card to Howe. Sent for Hartford Weekly Times.

Friday, June 4 Mr. Barrett, W.D.C., dined with us. Called to arrange for Washington medal. Slight showers.

Saturday, June 5 Got bank-book. Jew woman called Wilbur out to see her little girl. Mr & Mrs. Thresher called.

Sunday, June 6 Heard Rev. O.E. Hall, the new pastor of Williams Street Baptist Church, on "Why am I a Baptist?" Mrs. Sines dines with us.

White River Conference on May 17, 1909

Tuesday, June 8 Mr. J.F. Colby called. Ed. Ellis brought over some Pythian officers. Lorin and Ivonette called in the evening. I went to the clothiers but found no fitting suit.

Wednesday, June 9 I went on 8:40 train to Richmon[d] & Fowlerton. Went on 5:30 tr. to Fairmount. Staid at Ellis Wright's.

Thursday, June 10 Saw Parker afternoon and found renters in all my houses & the houses in good shape. I gave out adding to fences. Slept two hours, at Ellis's. Saw a report of the presentation of gold Medals to the Wright Brothers at Washington.

Friday, June 11 Called to see Mrs. Joan Holder in Fairmount. Went to Fowlerton, settled with hay-man, paid White all bills. Came home on 2:35 train. Found all well.

Saturday, June 12 Went after the copies of Mother's pictures—found them delayed.

Sunday, June 13 Went to Children's Day at First Presbyterian Church. Wilson spoke, Eph. V.l. Not a large "show." Corbett Andrews was one of the speakers.

Tuesday, June 15 Reuchlin came at 6:00 p.m.

Wednesday, June 16 Wm. Reeder and Mattie came, dined with us, and went to Mrs. Greenwood's. Mayor Burkhart came at 3:30 and took, in his automobile, me and Reuchlin and Katharine and Nettie all over the show ground, the Cash Register, Dayton View and the Soldiers' Home. Clara Wright came to Mrs. Greenwood's.

Thursday, June 17 Reception at 10:30. We came home and stayed till night. Jas. Whitcom Riley came afternoon & others. Effie Kirkpatrick. Went over at night, to fireworks.

Friday, June 18 It was a lovely day. Went at 10:30 to Fairground. Children sing. "Star Spangled Banner" made the invocation. Lieut. Allen spoke and presented the Congressional Medals. Gov. Harmon the Ohio Medal, Mayor Burkhart, presented the City medal. Return home. Attended the parade in afternoon. Also auto-mo-bile parade at night. Grand stand, 1st & Monument Ave.

Saturday, June 19 Wm. Reeder and Mattie start home, at 8:00. Boys pack their trunks and start at 10:00 p.m. for Ft. Myer. Wilbur and Orville pack clothes and start to Washington City on 10:00 train at night—via Harrisburg. Lorin's family came in evening.

Sunday, June 20 Went to hear C.J. Kephart preach, "To each man his work."

Monday, June 21 Ordered of Grimm brothers two new suits. Seventy-six dollars!

Tuesday, June 22 William Wright, of Chi. called, with Albert H. Shearer. I rode in the automobile to Herbert Allen's.

Thursday, June 24 Reuchlin and I went to Buck Island, and Loos shows the High School building. This week, I copied a Wright Memorial sent to me by Wm. Irving Wright, Fitchburg, Mass.

Friday, June 25 The work of Art from Larthe [?] was delivered. I bought two shirts and four collars of Kent, and a coat at Cohen's, $5.00. My two new suits came. The Work of Art, given by the people of Sarthe France was very nice.

Saturday, June 26 Took my coat over to improve. Got underwear, etc. Got some money. Left pictures of Mother (Wright) and Father Koerner, to have copied, at Horace Street. Lorin & family came up for ice cream. He and Reuchlin opened the art treasure from Sarthe. An angel of aviation pointing Wilbur & Orville to an eagle.

Sunday, June 27 Reuchlin & I hear Rev. Camp, at Summit Street United Brethren Church, Syrophenician Woman, Matt. 15.22,29. Saw some old Friends. We start at 5:58 p.m. for Washington City, Reuchlin & I.

Monday, June 28 We arrived in Washington at 1:00 p.m. Orville met us and took us to the Raleigh Hous[e], were we took rooms in the 8th story. The Senate adjourned & Congressmen came to Witness a flight. A rain went South. Wind strong.

Tuesday, June 29 We (Reuchlin & I) went to White House & to the Washington Monument Park. Heat was very oppressive. At 5:00 went to the Fort. Orville flew short distances only. He had an electric fan put in my room.

Wednesday, June 30 Reuchlin set the fan in motion—a great help. We went to the Smithsonian Institute. I saw all manner of birds, Ostrich, Emue, Condor, etc. In the evening at Ft. Myer, Orville flew better but broke a skid.

Thursday, July 1 We went to Smithsonian Institute. Saw animals & fish. Went to the Capitol. Saw statues. Looked in House of Representatives. Story below, heard Senator Root defend Corporation tax amendment. Went to Ft. Myer. Orville flew 5,8, and 9 minutes. We start home, Balt & Ohio, at 12:42.

Friday, July 2 Via Grafton, Parkersburg, Athens, Chillicothe, Blanchester, I reach Cincinnati at 5:30; home 8:40. Train an hour behind time. Orville made two nice flights, but his engine stopped over the machine shop & in descending he ripped the cloth on one wing. So he came home.

Saturday, July 3 Reuchlin left at 9:55, via Pennsylvania for Tonganoxie, Kansas. Tr. late starting. He went away much improved in health and looks.

Sunday, July 4 Orville came home to make covering for a wing. I hear Rev. Frank Garland in a patriotic Address. We called at Lorin's in the evening. Horace's chickens are doing finely. Twenty years ago this forenoon, Mrs. Wright died.

Monday, July 5 This is the day to celebrate the Fourth. There is considerable noise on the streets. Orville sews his cloth.

Tuesday, July 6 Orville leaves on the Pennsylvania train for Washington at 2:30. R.S. Kindel calls. I paid him out for the year. He takes a snap-shot of Orville. Dr. H. Russell, Pres. of the Anti-Saloon League called in the evening. Paper hangers distract Katharine.

Wednesday, July 7 Better paper hangers come. Times went better.

Thursday, July 8 Wrote an article for the Conservator, and sent it on. Paperers at work. Kitchen, Parlor and Katharine's room done.

Friday, July 9 Dr. Russell came and staid till 11:00.

Sunday, July 11 Called at Lorin's. Went to Seminary Park and heard Dr. Howard Russell speak at 7:30, on the Anti-Saloon League. He came home, and staid till 11:30. I gave Horace a dollar & Katharine geve him $2.00, for his birth day.

Thursday, July 15 We rode with Dr. Howard Russell, with Lorin's two girls. Went up Springfield Road; then came back through Dayton View.

Friday, July 16 We were at home. I dined at Carrie Grumbagh's. The boys did not fly at Ft. Myer, on account of rain. Lorin had a letter from Orville.

Saturday, July 17 To-day as usual at home. I called at Lorin's in the evening. His Charlotte will not go to roost without feeding. Horace's rooster sleeps in the shop. Orville flew about 12 miles, 90 feet high, 45 miles to the hour at Ft. Myer, at 6:00, p.m.

Sunday, July 18 I was sleepy, and slept most of the forenoon. I was awake, the afternoon. Dr. Howard Russell spent the evening with us. It rained in the morning.

Monday, July 19 Cool this morning. I encountered danger from the fire wagon. False alarm at the Malleable Works. Went to American Loan & Savings Association and collected $532.38, proceeds of $1500.00.note. Orville made two successful flights at Ft. Myer; 1st reported at 6:30 p.m, 41 miles an hour, 100 ft high, 25 minutes, 18 seconds, 25 1/2 circuits.

Tuesday, July 20 Orville's second flight is reported, yesterday 7:30 p.m., 150 ft high, 29 laps, 30 minutes time. Two flights 37 miles. Yesterday closed by darkness. Katharine went on 5:57 train to Washington. Lorin's came.

Wednesday, July 21 Yesterday, Orville flew at Ft. Myer, one hour twenty minutes and 41 seconds. Soared fast and 280 feet high. To-day he made two flights, one of

Dayton Homecoming Celebration, June 18, 1909

Fort Myer, Virginia, July 1909.
From left to right: Lt. Humphries, Orville Wright, Lt. Foulois, Reuchlin Wright, Milton Wright

them eleven minutes. Got telegram from Orville: two short flights speed 44 miles with one man.

Thursday, July 22 Yesterday Orville made two flights— one of them about 8 ms. long. Gladys Smith (little girl) here much of the day.

Friday, July 23 Yesterday hard rain in the afternoon. Milton shipped his model aeroplane to Anderson— $25.00 a week. Telegram from Washington: "No flights; weather unfavorable."

Saturday, July 24 Things as usual. No telegram: "No flights; weather unfavorable." but next morning paper reported an unusually successful flight by Orville, of over 20 minutes, 47 miles an hour, cutting all sorts of circles. Many Senators, Representatives, and army officers & diplomats present. Bleriot crosses English Channel.

Sunday, July 25 I call[e]d in at First U.B. Sabbath School, heard Holbrook, tell. Listened to H.F. Shupe, pr. John 12.21, "We would see Jesus." Wrote Katharine in the afternoon, at Washington.

Monday, July 26 We confidently expected a report of flight, at Ft. Myer, but a swift breeze hindered, and Orville rose without help of the derick, and flew about two miles, only. Mrs. Cobett and Mrs. Thompson a Lebanon old friend, called.

Tuesday, July 27 Day as usual. A little before 8:00, a telegram from Orville announced the good news, that with Lieut. Lahm, he had flown an hour & 12 minutes official flight. Joyful to us all. In morning, I received a letter from Perrila Maun, giving her father's photograph and dates of his family & his father's.

Wednesday, July 28 Things as usual. Telegram: "No flights. Weather unfavorable."

Thursday, July 29 Went to town in the afternoon. Left watch, left lower teeth at Tizzard's. Telegram: "No flights: weather unfavorable."

Friday, July 30 Bought sarge pants: $3.50. We had telegram from Katharine at 7:00, announcing that Orville had flew ten miles (officially) in 14 minutes and 42 sec-

onds. Home Sunday at 9:00. Lorin estimates that deducting the turn will give his average speed 43 miles: I 44 miles. Mrs. Wagner wonderfully rejoiced. It was a test flight.

Saturday, July 31 I went to town in the afternoon. Not a few congratulate me on Orville's success. I got my lower toothplate. Telegram from Wilbur saying Orville and Catharine will be home Sunday morning at 9:00.

Sunday, August 1 I start at 7:30 for Germantown, to fill an appointment at 10:30. Got there at 8:30. Called at Sarah Thomas', Went to Jacob Slifer's who died this morning. Preached at church at 10:15, Rom. 13.1. I went to Isaac Swartzel's for dinner. Went home by 3:00. Orville & Katharine came at 9:00.

Monday, August 2 At home in the forenoon. Get my watch at Newsalt's. Put in a 50$ order on my bankbook.

Tuesday, August 3 Letter from Perrilla Reeder Mann & great-grandfather Joseph Reeder's sword cane came. Expressage, 25 cts. Mr. Spurgeon of England and Mr. Corky, of Ireland, called to see the boys. Saw Wilbur. Albert Shearer called.

Wednesday, August 4 Wrote Perrilla Mann. Went to Germantown to assist in Jacob Thomas Slifer's funeral. Rev. W.H. Kindel pr Ps. 116.15. Forty minutes. He was a leader [?] there. Went home on 5:30 car. Clara Wright there.

Thursday, August 5 Clara started to Peru. Called at H.L. Simpson's and prayed with her. She gave me John Van Cleve's shirt & pants. Barnes called with petition. I sign it. Lorin and wife and two younger children called in the evening.

Sunday, August 8 I attended Broadway Christian Church and heard Rev. Mr. Bishop preach, Micah 6.8, Req. "to do justly." Mrs. Sines called before meeting. Orville and Katharine start to New York at 10:05, evening, to sail Tuesday for Berlin, Germany.

Monday, August 9 Wrote letters to Millspaugh at Amoritta, Okla., and Henry C. Nichols, New Palestine, Ind. He was a scholar of mine at Neff's Corner's when a very small boy.

Tuesday, August 10 Orville and Katharine sailed on the Crown princess Cecelie from N.Y. to germany. Letter from J.L. Lawrence, saying that Keiter's fraud in Tennessee had all been set aside by Judge Stout at Waverly, Tennessee, wholly deciding in Laundrum's (Abeh) favor. Keiter dare not appear.

Wednesday, August 11 Sent congratulations to Rev. J.M. Johnson, Marengo, Ind. over his monument to be unvailed the 27th, at the Crawford Co. Fair. Wrote Mrs. Mann, whose letter came back. Wrote Sina Ardery, told her of the will.

Friday, August 13 At home. H.C. Foote died at 3:40 morning. The body was taken to Adrian, Mich. for burial. Wood & Howe officiated at his home, the 15th at 4:00, at Huntington. Funeral at Adrian, also, by E.W. Mason.

Sunday, August 15 I went to Germantown. Preached at 10:00, Matt. 22.42. Dined at Shelby's. I called in the morning at Sarah Thomas's, talked and prayed with her. Called at Sleifer's. Went home at 4:00.

Monday, August 16 Went with grandson Milton to Fowlerton, arri. at 1:00. Valises at Stella Parkhurst's. Went to farm. Tired. Milton walking. R.B. Reeder came & took us to his house. We lodged there.

Tuesday, August 17 Dined at W.H.H. Reeder's. Ovid took us to train at Fowlerton and we went on to Marion, and took traction car to Van Buren, where af[t]er an hour, we went with G.W. Keltner to Dilman to G.W. Lee's, a merchant's. J.V. Rector pr. at chapel at 7:30. Eph. 5.14, a fair sermon, "Awake thou that sleepest." Lodge at Lee's.

Wednesday, August 18 Conference opened at 2:00, Bishop Alwood. Local preachers examined. Lee's daughter is 17, Myrtle Good, 16. Mrs. Lee sick. Rev. A.J. Stemen preached, Isa. 6. Well liked. Election of chairmen: Tharp 24, Oler 18 Floyd 6, Wright 1. [In text there are tick marks for each name, instead of numbers]

Thursday, August 19 Conference continued. Reports of pres. elders. O.G. Alwood lectured at 2:30, on the ministry. I preached at 7:30, Matt. 22.42, full house. I slept 6 or 6 1/2 hours.

Friday, August 20 I arose at 5:00 & dressed. Considerable conf. business. Small referred to Com. on Elders' orders. White of Hartsville is recommended. Reports read. We dine at Josiah Slushers. Met Branchla & wife, Henry Fry's dau. J. Howe pr. at 7:30. Oler, 25 & Rust, 16 elected. Wolfard, 7, Floyd, 7, Scattering, 2. P.E's, on 1st ballot. I examine C.E. Small.

Saturday, August 21 Milton & I go to Marion on Traction car, and thence to Fairmount. We stop at Ellis's. I was at band concert at night.

Sunday, August 22 I attended Mr. Gray's congregational church at 11:00 Went to Wesleyan Camp meeting in afternoon. Saw Pres. Baker, Seekings, Worth, Teters, etc. Heard Rev. Jennings. Two were ordained—woman & Negro man. Saw Mrs. Worth. I was at Congregational Church at night. Rev. Gray called at Ellis's, after meeting.

Monday, August 23 I went to Fowlerton. Dine at Robt. B. Reeder's. I got 180 ft. of lumber and had partition put between bedrooms. Paid Millspaugh, for their work, $10.00. Sup, lodge at White's. Unwell in the night.

Tuesday, August 24 I worked at House, and Milton went to Fairmount. I paid $3.90 tax at Marion. Milton came back with the wash, at 3:17. I dine at Parkhurst's. Went to White's for supper & lodging.

Wednesday, August 25 Went to Matthews; paid E.D. Clossoh $15.25 for lumber finish. We dined at Mrs. Parkhurst's. Went to White's & lodged.

Thursday, August 26 Went to Wm. Reeder's. Staid till night. They are fixing for next day. Went back to White's and lodged.

Friday, August 27 J.M. Johnson's monument to be unvailed at Marengo. I saw Van Antwerpt at the house Fairmount. Vergil took us to Reeder's, Reunion at W.H.H. Reeder's. Dine in his barn. Picture at table. Pictured at 3:00, Lizzie Broyles & family. All of Joe's, Eliza's,

Wm's, Flora's & Robert's there. Everts Slanker took us to Joe's.

Saturday, August 28 Staid at Joe's till 4:00. Robt. Broyles took us to John W. Broyles'. Had hard rain. Robert went home late. We lodged there. Kate Slanker has 3 boys: Evarts, Clarence & Lloyd. Davis have Adah. Alfred has Virgil & Clifford. Flora has Marcus, Smith, Floyd, Walter, Mabel, Lizzie.

Sunday, August 29 We went to Beech Grove to Sab. School. Lesson 13th First Cor. I was in Jas. M. Love's Class. I spoke 17 minutes. We called at Thos. Benton Markle's. Saw Melisse, Lorin, 18, Edith & John. Thurman (15) with his father. Dine at John's. Went to Chas Milton Broyles. Slanker's came. Went to Zion (M.E. Ch.) Barrett pastor there. Minton spoke on anti-saloon. Robert to White's.

Monday, August 30 Went to house in Fowlerton. Saw Amos Ailes and Van Antwerpt. Went to John Leach and telephoned to E.D. Slossen and engaged 8,000 shingles. Went to White's. Settled with him to date. Went to Fairmount & settled with Driggs & Wiley. Over $76 due me. Got my shirt of Chinaman.

Tuesday, August 31 Went with Milton afternoon to Wm. Reeder's. Went to Buller's at night.

Wednesday, September 1 Took Milton to White's and C.C.L. Depot. He went to Muncie, returned at 9:00 at night—was at Broyle's reunion. I went to Horace Reeve's. I went to White's & took horse to Buller's. I slept an hour there. Dinner. Went with Pearl to house in Fowlerton. Sup at Stella's. Staid at R.W. White's.

Thursday, September 2 Went to house. Settled wtih Amos Ailes for work, $15.55. Went on 11:43 train to Fairmount. Took the 12:26 train to Knightstown. Stella Rhoads met us and took us to Jabez Rhoads, where we sup & lodge.

Friday, September 3 Stella takes us to Delila Wright's where we remain. After dinner. Thomas's wife and Effie Kirkpatrick and Stella Wilhelm and Mabel Wright, & Drusilla McKee came. Milton and Stella Wilhelm and Mabel Wright, Fay's daughter, went to Sexton. We staid

at Delila's. She was 82, March 2nd.

Saturday, September 4 Mr. Frazier took us to Knightstown, and we got a train to Dayton, arriving at 11:00. Milton went with me home, and I staid. He went on to his home. I spent the afternoon & evening, straightening up and making my diary. Wilbur is at home.

Sunday, September 5 Awoke at 5:00. Got up at six. Called at Post-office & at Lorin's. Heard Rev. W.R. Funk pr. at Summit Street Church, John 17.3. Called about 4:00, at Lorin's. Slept pretty well till 4:00, morn.

Monday, September 6 Wrote letters to Mrs. Mann, Reuchlin, E.D. Clossen, etc. Called at Varsity Hall.

Tuesday, September 7 Wrote letters. Went to varsity Hall. Bought cuffs and collar (rubber). Voted for Kughns and Needham at Primaries. Wilbur got telegram from Russell Alger, and started to Detroit, at 11:25 at night.

Wednesday, September 8 Went and deposited money in Winters' Bank. Orville is reported to have flew alone 24 ms in 36 minutes, to-day, and 17 min. with Hildebrand, 200,000 reported. Ivonette & Horace staid here and to breakfast. Lorin and Milton are working on models of flying machine. Gen. H.C. Corbin died this morn.

Thursday, September 9 At home all day. Got a letter, morning from Katharine. Answered it afternoon & evening Wilbur got home about 6:00, eve. Orville is reported as flying 20 minutes "in a strong wind," and 15 minutes with Englehardt. Crown prince and princess saw the flights. Are at aero dinner to-night.

Friday, September 10 Bill from J.D. Van Antwerpt for $7.47. Sent that amount to Oliver Buller. Orville to dine at Royal Aero Club, Berlin, last night.

Saturday, September 11 Wilbur is preparing to ship his flying machine to New York to Fulton Hudson Exposition.

Sunday, September 12 It was a very warm day. Attended First Lutheran Church at 10:30, heard Rev. D. Frank Garland, Deut. 6.6,7. He preached an able discourse.

Lorin and his family dined with us. I read some in a story where great ado was made over trouble over Lydia was turned to joy over the marriage of the 16 year old girl, in English Society—from illicit cohabitation!

Monday, September 13 Some cooler this morning. Warm, at 11:00.

Tuesday, September 14 Cooler in the morning, but it was 91 degrees at 1:30. I read over Wilbur and Orville's letters. Wrote Wm. T. Lawson, sent copies of Landrum's and Lawrence's Letters.

Thursday, September 16 Letter from Perrilla Mann. Remail a letter to Orville. Cooler to-day. I received a telegram from W.H. Becker, Toronto, Ont., asking me to officiate at D.B. Sherk's funeral Monday, at noon. I telegraph that I will go.

Friday, September 17 I slept 7 hours, and arose early. I engaged a ticket to Buf[f]alo at 10:00 to-night. Wrote 8 pages of Sherk's funeral address. Started an hour late, at 9:00. I arrive at 7:00 (8:00 Eastern time) and start at 10:00 for Toronto, arri. at 2:00, at Mrs. Aldress. T.F. Best greatly helps me. He introduced me to Her.

Saturday, September 18 The foregoing was partly on Saturday. I lodged at W.H. Becker's, same Street West, 596 Brock Ave., being Mr. Aldred's address. Mr. T.F. Best was secretary of Y.M.C.A. at Hamilton.

Sunday, September 19 Went with W.H. Becker to M.E. Church. The pastor preached on Family Government, Dan. 49.4. Again, I dined at Aldred's and lodged at W.H. Becker's.

Monday, September 20 We start at 8:00 through the route to Berlin arri at Berlin at 15 minutes to 12:00. I dine at T.F. Swartz. Large audience. I occupied 25 minutes, Text, Acts 11.24. I read 8 pages of manuscript. At 1:00 p.m. C.W. Backus & Rev. Swartz spoke about 7 min. each. Saw Springer. Called at Bowman's and Eshelman's.

Tuesday, September 21 Bro. Swartz took me to starting place. Ticket via Galt, on traction to Detroit home, cost 9:00, sleeper 2.00. Staid at Detroit till 1/4 to 12:00, but entered sleeper at 9:00. Wrote obituary and mailed it in Detroit. Slept some on the way.

Wednesday, September 22 Arri. at home before six, in morning. Went to Lorin's to breakfast and dine, etc. Margaret (White) Allen is taking a week's vacation and Wilbur left for New York City, Saturday.

Thursday, September 23 I board at Lorin's. I do not much at home. Letter from C.L. Wood and from Reuchlin, this morning. Conservator comes.

Friday, September 24 I slept well last night. I get no letters before noon. I spend the morning, mostly reading. Milton's models came back from Eaton & Rock Island.

Saturday, September 25 Spent the day as usual. The Hudson-Fulton Exposition is opened in New York. The Clermont and Half Moon are attended by the navy of the world.

Sunday, September 26 Heard Rev. M.B. Fuller, Grace Church, Acts 17.22,23. What is religion? Very able and learned, but not satisfactory. I dined at Lorin's as usual.

Monday, September 27 Margaret Allen reported, and I staid at home. I wrote letters by day and at night to C.B. Sherk and J.F. Harris etc. Not suitable weather to fly in New York.

Tuesday, September 28 Wrote a card to J. Howe and to Wilbur defining, "What is religion?"

Wednesday, September 29 Wrote many letters. Wilbur is reported to have flown twice in New York; once from Governor's Island round the Statue of Liberty & back.

Thursday, September 30 There were no flights in New York, to-day. It was too variable in winds. Katharine wrote from Eisenach, Germany, that they spent yesterday morning at Weimar, went in afternoon to Eisenach, where they lodged last night, and about noon to-day, 3 oth start to Frankfort, then for a trip down the Rhine.

Friday, October 1 Again there were no flights, for the same reason. The children of Lorin came for dinner. I wrote Buller inclosing as check for $20.00. Milton shipped a model to St. Lonis. Netta and Lorin went to cousin Cowan's near Lebanon. Pearry's "Roosevelt" stop[p]ed below West Point!

Saturday, October 2 Went to town and exchanged 18 card pictures. Orville, at Potsdam is reported to have flown over 1600 feet high, 1637 ft. He took up the crown prince of Germany 60 ft. high, gets a present of a diamond and Ruby ring, Composing the letter "W" and a crown.

Sunday, October 3 Heard D.F. Garland on Christian Reflection, text, "Commanded the multitude to sit down." I slept in afternoon. Lorin and Netta came home, after supper. Curtis made a failure flight, at Governor's Island.

Monday, October 4 Wilbur flew from Governor's Island beyond Grant's Tomb & back in safety. He ha[d] a canoe attached. Dr. Dillon called an hour, on his way home.

Tuesday, October 5 Wilbur has gone to College Park, Maryland.

Friday, October 8 (This was yesterday) Man (Mr. Browncomb for Prof. A.W. Drury) brought manuscript of History of Wilbur and Orville to me to correct facts and had forms to sign of application for each agreeing to pay $278.00 each for their steele engravings! He was a rascal. I did not sign the applications.

Saturday, October 9 Got a letter from Wilbur. He sends for rasor-strap and envelopes.

Sunday, October 10 Heard Rev. [blank] Anderson preach at Third Street Presbyterian Church on cooper[a]tion. It rained as I went in and as I came home on the car. Walked with Ida Grabill under umbrella. Milton and Horace dined with me.

Monday, October 11 Mailed Brownscomb's manuscript to him.

Tuesday, October 12 Called at Brownscomb's as I did not want him to call at our house.

Thursday, October 14 Horace's "Pina" died and old "Blackie" Ran off. Called at Wagner's.

Friday, October 15 Lorin's learn nothing of Blackie.

Saturday, October 16 Orville is reported as flying at Potsdam, and he and Katharine having a talk with the Emperor. President Taft and President Diaz meet at El Paso. Margaret invited Lorin's family to dinner to-morrow.

Sunday, October 17 Went to Williams Street Baptist Church. Rally Day. Judge McCann speaks. He is well gifted. Lorin and family dined with us, except Horace who is sick & Netta, who is unwell.

Monday, October 18 Horace & Netta are better. Count de Lambert, with a Wright Flyer goes from Invissy field back and circles 300 feet above the Eifel tower. Alfonso quarrels with his premier over there being no chance to pardon Ferrer.

Tuesday, October 19 The Wrights are reported to have entered suit against Ralph Saulnier for restraining him from using a copy of Bleriots machine.

Wednesday, October 20 I write lists of Wrights from Helvedon, 1538, to the present time. To-night, there was a $700,000 fire in Dayton, in which the Computing Scale factory lost $200,000. It was on First St., and Monument Ave.

Thursday, October 21 Went to town, afternoon, left bank book for posting. Called at Sophia Simpson's and at Ramey's. Found Theo. Darwin Brown at out house and his brother Geroge R. After supper went with them to Street Cars. Sent Fay Wright, 538 Birch St., a copy of the generations of— Wrights and Freemans.

Friday, October 22 Wilbur is reported to fly 42 minutes by moonlight with Humphrey's, at College Park, Maryland.

Saturday, October 23 Slight rain to-day. Wilbur is reported to have flown four times from College Park. Orville is reported to-day, at Naples.

Sunday, October 24 Heard [blank] Myer preach at 4th Presbyterian Church, 1 John 1.7. "Cleanse from all sin."

I dined at Lorin's. David Dennis dined there. Supper at home.

Monday, October 25 I start to Gaston at 8:40. Reach Gaston, where Robert B. Broyles takes me to Joseph Broyles where I dine and Robert and I fix up our writings, after which he takes me to Oliver Bullers where I sup and lodge.

Tuesday, October 26 I go to Whites dine, and afternoon go with William Reeder and Robert B. Broyles (who came) over the farm. I sell the hay in the old house for $61.00 to Broyles. Robert takes me to the house in Fowlerton, and I go on train to Fairmount & stay at Ellis Wright's. Rev. Choate, of Kokomo, and [blank] Blunt of Ind is there.

Wednesday, October 27 I go to Marion and pay my taxes, & return. See Mr. Chas. T. Parker. Call in the convention and dine at the church. Go at 3:05 to Fowlerton and Wm. Reeder's. Sup and lodge there, Chas. Parks there.

Thursday, October 28 Ovid takes me to White's and I give notice to White to give possession March 1st. I go to Depot and to Richmond, and Dayton. Dine at home.

Saturday, October 30 Went on 12:50 car to Quarterly meeting at Germantown. Hired Wm. Dillon $475.00. Rev. W.H. Kindel preached, Rom. 12.11, "Not slothful in business" etc. Quarterly conference. Supped at Lizzie Long's. Came home on 5:30 car.

Sunday, October 31 Lorin and Horace called after breakfast. I did not attend church, was sleepy. Margaret cooked so good a dinner.

Monday , November 1 Stayed at home all day. Slept two hours. Wilbur has returned to Washington.

Tuesday, November 2 At home all day. Rained a little in the Morning. Election Day.

Wednesday, November 3 At home. Nothing of importance only Democratic victory in Dayton; Dem. Mayor in New York and *fusionists* prevail; Johnson beaten in Cleveland; Toledo & Cincinnati, Republican.

Thursday, November 4 Adriatic grounds at daylight in New York Harbor. Lands at 9 o'clock. Orville and Katharine are met by Wilbur.

Friday, November 5 A telegram from Katharine says they will be at home some time Sunday. I took up First Corrinthians.

Saturday, November 6 In afternoon, Lorin gets telegram that the children will be here at noon, Sunday. Study 1st Corrinthians.

Sunday, November 7 Lorin informed us of a telegram last evening, saying the Children are coming on Erie to be here at 5:30, this evening. The children get home at 6:+. All look to be in good health; Wilbur, Orville, Katharine.

Monday, November 8 Breakfast at 7:40. Wilbur and Orville go to Springfield to see Mr. Toulin. William Shank called. They came back about 2:+. Misses Rider & Osborn, and Mrs. Stevens called an hour, or more.

Tuesday, November 9 I began breakfast at 7:30. I sleep much of the forenoon. Orville starts to New York at 1:25 p.m. to clear the mists.

Wednesday, November 10 Lorin is finishing up cloth for lower half wing Govt machine, which Genl. Allen called for.

Thursday, November 11 Bathroom is being painted and the hallway. Orville returns from New York.

Friday, November 12 Painter finished job. Large fish for dinner.

Saturday, November 13 Orville went to Cincinnati. Leontine dined with us. Katharine and Leontine go in the evening to Miss Ryder's. Wilbur starts at 10:00, evening, to Washington, to get Lieut. Lahm's affidavit.

Sunday, November 14 Attended William Street Baptist Church. Heard Rev. Orthnells E. Hall on 2 Kings, 2.9, a good sermon.

Wednesday, November 17 Took coat and pants to cleaner.

Thursday, November 18 Rev. O.E. Hall called. He is pastor of Williams Street Baptist Church.

Friday, November 19 Suit came home from cleaners. Price $1.25.

Monday, November 22 Went on 5:25 cars to Lima and Huntington. Arrived at 11:00. Lunched at Depot. Called on J. Howe's Mission Room. Called at Publisher's. Rode to Howe's on cab. Remain over night. S.A. Stemen came in an hour. Called at Mummart's an hour.

Tuesday, November 23 Called at 7:45, prayers at College. Had an all day meeting at Mission Room. Dine at Howe's restaurant. Go to Howe's to night meeting of committee. We close at 11:00, & I lodge at Howe's. I suggested S.M. Crom as pastor to begin in the spring and Wm. Miller fill the vacancy. Wood opposed Miller's appointment.

Wednesday, November 24 Attended prayers at 7:45, and gave a short Thanksgiving address. Dined at S.L. Livingston's. A.B. Lilly takes me to the train. Go via Lima home, arri. at 6:00.

Thursday, November 25 Thanksgiving. Lorin's family with us. Remained till after 4:00. They have such nice children. I find that Wilbur & Orville have sold their United States Rights to August Belmont, Howard Gould, Cornelius Vanderbilt, Edward J. Berwind, Russell Alger, T.P. Shont's, Morton F. Plant, Andrew Freedman, Robt. J. Collier & Allen A. Ryan, $100,000.

Friday, November 26 *At Home. Katharine spends the evening at Mrs. Stevens'.*

Saturday, November 27 At home. Some women visit Katharine in the afternoon. Lottie Jones helps. Katharine goes to Ida Grabill's an hour in the evening.

Sunday, November 28 Spent the day at home. The boys arrived at home from New York at 6:00, evening.

Monday, November 29 Miss Kate Hierholzer called and engaged to work for Katharine.

Tuesday, November 30 Miss Katie Hierholzer called at 7:30, and began work for Katharine, this morning.

Wednesday, December 1 At home. Gas explosion reported at Argenbright's. Pole-discoverer Cook reported in an Asylum in Pennsylvania. Russell Alger and brother Frederick sup with us. They are fine appearing men.

Sunday, December 5 I was at Eaker St. M.E. Colored Church. Dr. Robins of Columbus spoke, Gal. 6.9, "Be not weary in Well doing." The pastor, J.C. Robinson, announced me as "the father of the Wright brothers."

Tuesday, December 7 Wilbur started for New York. In the evening, I read the President's Message, a business like document.

Wednesday, December 8 At home all day. Nothing of special interest occurs. Waterways convention is held. Taft speaks in favor of letting sale of bonds alone for the present.

Thursday, December 9 Katharine went to Miss Hunter's in the afternoon. I read Abbot's Introduction to the Epistle to Romans.

Friday, December 10 Rev. Gleason H. Reeder, of Mt. Vernon, Ohio, called an hour before noon. A large fish for dinner. He is a descendant of Benjamin Reeder of Pennsylvania, brother of Joseph Reeder of Va., born in 1716. Wilbur came back in afternoon from New York.

Sunday, December 12 I heard Dr. Ketman at Baptist Church, on the operations of the church in Missions, Sabbath Schools, colporteurs, and car work. Was introduced to him and Mr. Whidden by Dr. Colson. Wilbur went to New York to see a photograph of Curtis' machine contradicting his affidavit. Thus the lawyers abuse Curtis.

Monday, December 13 At home. Orville started at 8:00, eve. to Buffalo to trial before Judge Jno R. Hazel on Herring Company's infringement of patent.

Tuesday, December 14 At home all day. Wrote several letters. In afternoon Wright vs. Herring Curtis Co. came in U.S. Court, Judge John R. Hazel. H.C. Toulin their lawyer argued. Also Emerson K. Newell, N.Y., the lawyer for Herring, maintianed there was no infringement. Claimed their fame rested on their skill as aeroplane Chaffeurs."

Wednesday, December 15 The trial at Buffalo, N.Y. is before Judge John R. Hazel. Attorneys of Wright's: H.A. Toulin, Gen. Edward Wetmore, Local: C.W. Parker. Attorneys of Herring: Emerson K. Newell, Monroe W. Wheeler, [blank] Dunn. Parties: Wright Brothers vs. A.M. Herring & Glenn C.H. Curtis.

Thursday, December 16 Wright brothers at Detroit, Mich. to see an Aero Club organized. They go to Dayton in the night.

Friday, December 17 Boys came home for breakfast. Katharine went to Agnes Osborn's for supper. I found a sketch of the Nobles, and observe Caleb Leverich and Martha, children of Rev. Wm. Leverich.

Saturday, December 18 Dillon came just after noon. I copied some from Noble relatives. I fell asleep early, and slept disturbed in the night. Mrs. Deborah Cornell Wood, mother of Bishop C.L. Wood died to-day, in her 90th year.

Sunday, December 19 Was somewhat unwell. The children called Dr. L. Spitler, who said I had caught cold through me.

Monday, December 20 At home. Some better. Made out a table from Louis Reeder Noble's chart sent me several years ago, confirming our descent from the Leverich's.

Wednesday, December 22 Wrote letters to Mary H. Krout, Chicago. Wrote Reuchlin , etc. Report of Estrado's victory. Telegram to preach Rev. A.H. Roach's funeral. Could not go.

Thursday, December 23 At home. Katharine is specially preparing Christmas presents.

Friday, December 24 Mellville Brown's son (Brown) calls on Orville in behalf of Bradstreet to inquire of the boys company. Gets the names of directors, president, vice-

president, stock $1,000,000 ($800,000 pd in, $500,000 allowed for patents, "Wright Co., N.Y.).

Saturday, December 25 I arose before six o'clock. Lorin and family ate turkey with us. We had a very large fowl. Horace was much taken with his railroad track, and his wound up cars. The children had a fine Christmas.

Tuesday, December 28 Spent day in reading Murphy on Genesis. I am quite lame.

Wednesday, December 29 Dr. Spitler came by Katharine's invitation. I lie in bed all day, though slightly better.

Friday, December 31 The last day of the year. Wrote some letters. This has been a somewhat eventful year. In January, I attended Rev. James Rector's revival at Fowlerton and preached most of the time while there. The children come home from Europe and are much honored by thousands at the Depot and at their home. There is three days celebration in their honor. They go to Washington and fill (Orville) their contract with the U.S. Government and get $27,000. Reuchlin came and I went to Washington with him. Milton goes with me to Annual Conference and to the Reeder's first anniversary & to Wright's in Rush County. Our children, Orville & Katharine go to Germany, and see and converse with the Royal Family. They spend considerable time in Germany before coming home. The children all return home together, November 7th.

Cragum Farm
Dan Wright sold his claim north of Hopewell church, to a man by the name of Parker, probably in the latter part of 1822. He bought a house and forty-acre lot, as the deed shows, dated Feb. 27, 1823, of Elisha Cragum, paying for it One Hundred and fifty dollars. Signed by Elisha and mary Cragum. He bought west of it, 80 acres for $100.00. About 1836, he bought 40 acres of William Snelling.

Paulina Reeder b. in Hamilton Co. Ohio, m. Mr. Langworthy, in Dubuque, Iowa, died in Dubuque January 29, 1892

Frances Reeder b [blank] m. a Mr. Langworthy in Cincinnati

Phebe Harriet Reeder b. March 26, 1819, m. Scribe Harris, d. in Dubuque, Iowa, Jan 29, 1892.

Semele Reeder, b. Nov. 27, 1826, m. Bloomer married Frederick Short died Sept. 11, 1908, aged 82.
Joseph Reeder lived in Hampshire Co., Virginia, on the great Cacaphon River, died at Sarah Brand's, his oldest daughter's in Butler County, Ohio, Oct. 10, 1829, in his 87th year. His wife, Anna Huff, died in Hamilton Co., Oho, July 6, 1821. Her hair is said to have been red, and she died of cancer. She died in her 77th year. Ralph born Feb. 4, 1788 on Great Cacaphon River, in Hampshire Co., (now) West Virginia, died in Hamilton Co. Ohio July 8th, 1863. His daughter Paulina, b. Dec.

19, 1815, married Mr. Langowrthy d. Dubuque, Jan 29, 1892. Phebe Harriet, b. Mar. 26, 1819, d. Jan. 29, 1892, in Dubuque. Semele, b. Nov. 27, 1826, in Bloomer & Short, d. Sept. 11, 1908.

I taught School.
Matney's 3 in 1849, Gray's 6 on 1850–1, Hites 3 in 1851, Andersonville 3 in 1852 Fall, Hartsville 1 1/2 in 1853 Spring, Thomas's 6 in 1853–4, Neff's Corners 9 in 1854–4, Oregon 15 in 1857–9, New Salem 3 in 1860, Neff's Corners 3 in 1860, Hartsville 9 in 1868–9.

Judge John R. Hazel, Buffalo, N.Y.
Judge Hand, New York City
W.H. Becker 418 Borck Ave, Toronto, Ontario

1910

Saturday, January 1 I am in my 82nd year, in fair health, except lumbago. We dine at home together. Not much unusual.

Monday, January 3 News that the Wright Brothers were granted an injunction against Herring Company & Curtis.

Tuesday, January 4 Wrote to Clerk of Court at Waverly, Tennessee.

Wednesday, January 5 Nothing of very special interest occurred to-day. Notice of the death of [blank]. Also a fall for [blank]. Memorial Building dedicated. It is our largest auditorium. Wrote for Marion *Chronicle*. Katharine had Miss Myer, Mrs. Stevens and Agnes call and take a game with her.

Saturday, January 8 Wilbur had word of the suspension of Hazel's injunction, and the filing of $10,000 bond. They start to the meeting of the Ohio Society in New York, Monday, evening.

Tuesday, January 11 Miss Myer, Osborn and [blank] were here. Not far from this time Bertha Ried began to work for us; perhaps earlier.

Wednesday, January 12 In the afternoon, Mrs. Chas. Wuichet and her daughter inlaw, Mrs. Lane, and Agnes Osborn were here. Milton and Horace sup with us.

Thursday, Janaury 13 Katharine went to Young Men's association to the College Dinner, at 8:00 eve.

Friday, January 14 Wilbur arrived from New York at 3:00. Katharine at dinner at Mrs. Stevens in the evening. I read in Maccauly's sketches. Orville got home at noon from New York.(This is Saturday's)

Sunday, January 16 Moderate winter day. Horace spent the afternoon with us, and Lorin's, except Milton, the evening with us.

Monday, January 17 Katharine began to copy Class-letters.

Tuesday, January 18 I went to post-office and walked round two blocks. Wrote to J.F. Miller—advised him to try evangelism.

Wednesday, January 19 Things as usual. Katharine dines at Corner of Second and Main.

Sunday, January 23 I staid at home. I read in Wesley's works. Russell Alger and Frank H. Russell dine with us, on their way home.

Monday, January 24 I read in Volume III of Wesley's works. He went to Georgia an unconverted man.

Tuesday, January 25 I read considerably in Lawrence's Church History, the account of the rise of true Religion in the "dark ages."

Wednesday, January 26 Wrote several letters. Mrs. Eleanor Wagner had supper with us. I read in Lawrence's Church History.

Thursday, January 27 Slept most of forenoon, and also in afternoon. Seine very high; Paris, partly under water. A letter for Bertha Ried, came, mailed at Mechanicsburg (Champaign Co.) Ohio.

Sunday, January 30 Wilbur started to New York at 2:00, to attend the Paulhan trial, Tuesday.

Monday, January 31 Mr. Frank Russell, manager of the Wright Company dined with us.

Wednesday, February 2 Miss Myer, Miss Osborn and Mrs. Stephen supped at Katharine's.

Thursday, February 3 Wrote a letter to Dr. David H. Reeder, Laporte, Ind., giving him the Reeder parentage. He is a great-grandson of David, son of Joseph 3rd. His grandfather was David. Wilbur telegraphed to Orville to send him their picture of Paulhan's machine, which he did by "special delivery" mail.

Friday, February 4 Orville had a telegram from Wilbur expressing his surety of winning the suit. I paid $1.00 for cleaning coat and pants this week. Prof. David Van Horn and Rev. J.M. Coleman called to see me at 8:00 in the evening. J.M. Coleman is of Mercer, Pa., a Reformed Presbyterian.

Saturday, February 5 Was wearied beyond study. Walked most of a mile. Miss Vaulter (teacher) called in the evening.

Sunday, February 6 A bright, cool-like day. Lorin brought in letters and staid over an hour. Katharine dined at Winifred Ryder's.

Monday, February 7 Bright moderate day. I mailed a letter to Reuchlin. Enclosed a page of this morning's *Journal*. Wilbur came home from New York, at noon.

Tuesday, February 8 It is a pretty day, mild. Rev. C.I.B. Brane left me three copies of the *Telescope*. I got no mail to-day. I slept in the day—was dull. Agnes Osborn called in the afternoon. At 10:00 p.m. Wilbur and Orville start to Washington City, to receive, Friday, medals from the Smithsonian Institute.

Thursday, February 10 Katharine went afternoon to see Miss Greene Principal of the Normal School. A man, 104 Williams Street called to see me. This was his last. Lorin Netta, Leontine and Horace called. Story in the *Journal* about Wrights having purchased property in Dayton View.

Friday, February 11 I wrote Bishop Barkley. Orville got home at 9 a.m. Katharine took "dinner" at Robt. B. Osborne's, and came home through a heavy snowstorm. Chief Justice Fuller presented Wilbur and Orville, each, a gold medal, in behalf of the Smithsonian Institute. Taft, Senator Lodge and other dignataries were there. Lodge spoke.

Sunday, February 13 Lorin brought the letters and papers. In afternoon, Dentist Stewart and his wife called. I sent genealogies to Mary H. Krout, Chicago.

Tuesday, February 15 At home. Wrote to Stella Wilhelm and to Frank Petree, and to Aunt Delila. Agnes & three others call. Mr. F.H. Russell called in the evening.

Wednesday, February 16 Snow fell over a foot deep at night. Wrote to Reuchlin and to others.

Thursday, February 17 Schuffle off the snow from the walks. News from Pliny Williams that Judge Hand had decided the suit against Paulhan in favor of the Wright brothers. An injunction temporary granted. A telegram from Wilbur from Augusta, Georgia, says he finds a good place at Montgomery, Alabama.

Friday, February 18 It snowed very much. Snow was sixteen inches deep.

Saturday, February 19 There was considerable thawing. I broke the long icicles off the roof.

Sunday, February 20 Wilbur came home after midnight. It thawed gently to-day. Leontine, Horace and "Pekah" came afternoon. I read in my Greek Testament, 14th and 15th chapters of Matthew. I called in Forenoon at Lorin's. Milton came in the evening. Pekah is Clare Andrew's boy.

Portrait of Bishop Milton Wright by Jane Reece, 1910

Monday, February 21 Telegram from E.S. Lorenz, to know how deed should be made out to the boys—Wilbur & Orville. No trade yet. The snow is fully half melted off.

Tuesday, February 22 Only moderately cold. No thawing. Knabenshue is in town. He and Pliny Williamson dine with us.

Wednesday, February 23 The Chapman-Alexander revival is carried on in town.

Thursday, February 24 Katharine started at 10:30 a.m. for Pittsburg[h], to visit an old College chum Mrs. Cora Woodford, whom she had never visited before. Ed. Sines called in the evening.

Friday, February 25 Wilbur came home at 12:00 from N. York. Got out an injunction against Paulhan; security $25,000 for a month.

Saturday, February 26 Warmer weather, threatening rain; but no rain fell. There was considerable thawing.

Monday, February 28 Mr. Taylor & wife of Pen Yan, N.Y., called at noon. Meat pie for dinner. It does not rain to-day. Katharine came home at midnight.

Tuesday, March 1 The snow is passing away. Katharine is called by Mrs. Charles Kumler to visit the Miami Leaf Tobacco Company, to give them a talk.

Thursday, March 3 It was a mild bright day. Katharine went on 9:00 train to Richmond, to visit Emma Dennis, returned at 10:00 at night.

Friday, March 4 It was a mild, bright day. Katharine went to a piana performance, at night.

Saturday, March 5 Secretary Williams, of Oberlin College dined with us. It is a mild, but cloudy day. Rained afternoon. I have, in the past three days, written five pages on my Church History.

Sunday, March 6 Mild, somewhat cloudy day. Orville telephoned Horace to dine with us, and he came. Sunshiny at noon.

Monday, March 7 Wilbur left at 2:00 for the East to get affidavits to support those filled by himself and Orville in the retrial at Buffalo. In the afternoon, I reread my diary for 1906 & 1907 & 1908.

Tuesday, March 8 I was wrongly informed on time of train and failed to go to Fowlerton. I read my diary of 1908. Miss Lorenz called for a committee meeting. Left thinking it perhaps a mistake. Katharine sent word of its postponement, not given. It was a mild, nice day.

Wednesday, March 9 Weather, nice, mild. Left Dayton at 8:50, reached Fowlerton at 12:25. Went to John Leach's, and to Fout's. Engaged him to haul my corn. Went to Fairmount at 5:43. Visited Ellis Wright.

Thursday, March 10 Staid at Fairmount till 1:00. Go to Marion. I paid my tax. Saw Wm. Charles on my leases. Went to Elli's and lodged there. I saw C.T. Parker and found he had less than twenty-five dollars. My houses are rented at 5 & 4.00 a month; shop at 4, and warerooms at 8:00 & 4:00.

Friday, March 11 Nice weather in evening. Somewhat rain forenoon, pretty afternoon. Left Ellis Wright's at 8:30, call at Hollingsworth's. Go on 9:17 tr. to Fowlerton. Charley Milton Broyles takes me to Wm. Reeder's. I dine, rest a little, and William takes me to Robert Reeder's, and by the farm to Oliver Buller's where I lodged.

Saturday, March 12 Nice weather. Buller and I go in buggy up to determine fence posts (cement) on my farm. Decide Eastern fence-posts to be at proper place. I get out at Elevator & go to Depot to warm. Go to Farmhouse and stay till 2:00. Frout has all my corn at Elevator. I come home on 2:47 train. Detained an hour at Richmond to repair locomotive.

Sunday, March 13 I remained at home. Beautiful weather. I slept several hours. Horace dined with us, and visited Wm. Andrews, and called again on his way home. Albert Shearer called in the evening.

Tuesday, March 15 Fine weather. Roosevelt party reached Khartum. House of Representatives pass a bill to raise the Maine.

Thursday, March 17 Beautiful weather. In afternoon, Katharine had a meeting of the College Club. Entertainment etc. Speaker Cannon is overruled in a decision 163 to 111. The Democrats, 30 insurgents and about 12 other Republicans voting against him. (Yesterday this vote.)

Friday, March 18 No fire needed. Wrote letters afternoon to Eva Gray, Grace Frazer and Perrila Mann. Wilbur started to Buffalo at 8:00 evening. Speaker Joe Cannor upset in House of Representatives. Rev. Maxwell of Middletown called to tell of Constance Wilberforce.

Saturday, March 19 Katharine scours out her lumber house. Mrs. Nooks & Mrs. Maxwell call to see about Constance Wilberforce. She seems to consider herself deserted, and wants to come to America.

Sunday, March 20 Wilbur arrived home from Buffalo. The parties did not insist on a retrial, but they agreed to a future trial of the Appeal. F.H. Russell & family dined with us. Knaubenshue's called on us. The women went to look after houses. The men had Knabenshue's plans. Horace with us.

Monday, March 21 This morning, came a letter from S.A. Boroughs, and I answered it. It was from a descendent of Stephen Reeder, 963 Magnolia Ave., Los Angeles, Cal.

Tuesday, March 22 Wrote several letters: to Robert B. Broyles, to Con. Valley Association, Booth, to St. John & Charles, etc. Bertha Ried left us. She was exceeding smart colored girl. She was too smart and independent.

Wednesday, March 23 Horace has been sick since Monday evening. I called there, this morning. They are having their house papered. At 2:40, Orville starts to Montgomery, Alabama, to train men to fly. I examine the Encyclopedia, Britanica on the Gospels.

Thursday, March 24 Spring Weather. The weather has been fine and mild ever since March 3rd. It is an unusual March. I called at Lorin's. Horace is at play with Benjamin and "Pekah." A German girl, sent by Mrs.

Huffman called, and Katharine engaged her at $5.00, a week, to come on Monday a week.

Friday, March 25 Nice Weather. Katharine went shopping with Mrs. F.H. Russel. Dinner late. She employed Carrie Brumbach to get supper and went with Agnes Osborn on a walk. Agnes took supper with us. I read several able articles—one on "The Religion of the Present," by George A. Gordon, in the Atlantic Monthly.

Saturday, March 26 It was a fine day, forenoon and Afternoon. Cloudy at noon. I slept some. Reread Gordon's article.

Sunday, March 27 I was at the First Baptist Church. Heard an eloquent sermon on John 20.7,8. A number were baptized by immersion. I went home and to Frank H. Russell's to Dinner. He is a descendent of John Russell of Hadley, by his son Samuel. Russell lives on First Street.

Monday, March 28 Helen Lorenz' funeral, from New York, at E.S. Lorenz, City. Story of accident by Orville at Montgomery a fake, "Fall of 100 ft." Wilbur closes a deal with E.S. Lorenz for $10,500.00, at end of Fourth Street and Salem Ave., a lot.

Tuesday, March 29 At 10:00, I went on street car up Broadway, and to the lot on Broadway and Salem Avenue. I went thence to see Sophia Simpson. I walked home via River Bridge. H. Sophia is confined to her room, tho' able to walk and help herself somewhat.

Wednesday, March 30 Lorin's girls stay at our house at night.

Thursday, March 31 Lorin's girls again stay at night with us.

Friday, April 1 It is most beautiful weather, and has been such, since March 3rd. Lottie Jones helps clean the house. The girls Ivonette & Leontine stay with us at night.

Saturday, April 2 Beautiful Weather. Women are housecleaning. I sleep considerably. Wilbur went at night, to send a cylinder Orville had called for. Lorin's girls came again.

Sunday, April 3 Mild Weather. The day as usual. I slept for what I lost by Wilbur coming home late last night. Howard Russell called in the afternoon. We have had a month of unusually nice weather.

Monday, April 4 Lottie Jones and Celia———are cleaning our house. Got a letter from Reuchlin. I wrote a page of church History. Lorin's girls lodged with us. Mary Phillips began to keep house for Katharine.

Tuesday, April 5 Women are cleaning up my room. Wrote a letter to Reuchlin. I received a letter from Robert B. Broyles. He says he has 30 acres plowed for corn, and that his oats has come up nicely. Says the neighbors are saying that he has done more work than has been done in ten years past. Wilbur went at 2:40 to New York. Mrs. La Chappelle called. Mr. Krugg cleans our house paper.

Wednesday, April 6 Lottie still cleaning house. Mrs. LaShappelle dined with us & visited. Katharine went in the evening meeting at Y.M.CA.Building of the Street Cleaning Meeting. She is its treasurer.

Thursday, April 7 I received a letter from S.A. Burrowes, 963 Magnolia Ave., Los Angeles, and answered it. I sent him a corrected comparative Statement. I sent him in brief the Wright genealogy. Rev. J.M. Chandler called to see me. Is working as an organizer in Congregational Church. He is a Hurlessite still!

Friday, April 8 The carpet man finishes laying the carpets. A man attuned the pianaola.

Saturday, April 9 Orville came home in the forenoon. I received a letter from Preshia Roach giving May 8th as the time of Rev. A.H. Roach's funeral. I sent the Editor the announcement of the time and Roach's picture. LaChapelle called in the evening.

Sunday, April 10 Attended First Lutheran Church. Rev. Frank Garland preached Matt. 21.10, "Who is this?"'l. Not a deceiver, 2. A harmless enthusiast, 3. One of the best, but a man, 4. Son of God!' Horace & "Pekah" supped with us.

Tuesday, April 12 The weather has been fine from March

3rd till now. I arose early. I received a proposition in the Christian Science Monitor (Boston) to buy out the Wright's patents.

Thursday, April 14 I wrote to Mrs. Snooks and went to her house, 217 Pontiac Ave. I walked nearly four miles, returning by Miami Chapel graveyard. In afternoon, I cleared out the closet. Mrs. Sines called in the afternoon. I arrange to go to Fowlerton to-morrow.

Friday, April 15 Started to Fowlerton at 8:40, reached Fowlerton at 1:00, saw Robert B. Broyles, and staid with him. We looked over the farm and talked about fences & improvements.

Saturday, April 16 I talked with Broyles' about improvements and agreed to spend some $75.00 about the house and barn, of which he gave me a paper of costs, he agreeing to do the work at $1.00 a day. I went on the 11:40 tr. to Fairmount. I dined etc. at Ellis Wright's.

Sunday, April 17 I attended Church and heard Rev. Mueller in Sabbath School and preaching, morning and evening. In afternoon, I called at Dole Smith's. I learned that the United Brethren had no services in Fairmount.

Monday, April 18 I saw Mr. Parker and received the balance on our accounts, $31.90. Paid Wallace Jay, on pavement, $16.44.

Tuesday, April 19 I went to Marion and paid on Fowlerton house& lot, $2.67, tax. I then went on locomotive cars to Wabash and on traction car to Huntington, arri. at 11:00. I saw Mummart and Howe. I dined at a restaurant, with Howe. I walked with him to his house. I called at two or three places & supped at S.A. Stemen's. I lodged at Samuel L. Livingston's, my home. Rev. Charles G. Sterling's Scripture lecture.

Wednesday, April 20 The Board of Missions met at 9:00. We had a good session. I dined at Howe's one day. But to-day at W.H. Kindel's.

Thursday, April 21 Board Meeting Continued. The reports & Exec. Minutes. I dined at Howe's to-day. I supped at S.L. Livingston's. We in afternoon reported on Foreign Missions and appointed J.B. Woodard to

Africa as superintendent for three years. Mark Twain died. Board closed in the evening. He (Twain) was born in Florida, Mo., Nov. 30, 1835.

Friday, April 22 I supped at T.H. Gragg's. The Christian Endeavor gave us an entertainment.

Saturday, April 23 I was not present at the Quarterly Meeting, at Germantown. I forgot to go to Stemen's for dinner, and dined at Livingston's, my home.

Sunday, April 24 I heard H.L. Barkley, pr. at 10:30. I dined at F.H. Cremeans. Supped at Livingston's after meeting. I pr at 7:00, Matt. 16.15, "Whom do men say that I am," Occupied some 25 minutes. The compliments given at the close embarrassed me, being undeserved, I thought.

Monday, April 25 I dined at Bowman's, [unreadable]. I ate the other meals at Livingston's. Robert Kennedy Krout died in Crawfordsville at 12:55, this morning, aged 82 years, 1827, Sept. 8 was his birth-day. He married my cousin Caroline Brown.

Tuesday, April 26 Board meeting (Educational) at 9:00. Dined at Stemen's. Meeting at forenoon & afternoon, and evening. C.W. Blanchard is elected president. Gov. Hughes (Chas. E. Hughes) has accepted Taft's nomination as Justice of the Supreme Court of United States.

Wednesday, April 27 Went to 7:30 Board meeting. We had quite a scrap over changing the time of our board meeting to April. We elected the old members of the faculty at an advance of $100.00 each. Adjourned at 11:00. I went home on 12:35 train. Arri. at 6:00.

Thursday, April 28 Letter from Ray. W. Stevens. It stated Robert H. Krout's death. Also the Crawfordsville Journal came, giving a sketch of Robert H. Krout's life. Mrs. Stevens supped with us. Wilbur, at 4:00, started to New York.

Friday, April 29 Evening paper tells of Orville's flights at Montgomery, Alabama. Family goes to the High School Exposition & Horace comes to stay with me. A good play was reported, Milton acting a prominent part. Horace slept with me.

Saturday, April 30 Weather as warm as June. Letter from Grace Frazier, who was hurt the 16th by the fast train, at Dunreith, Ind. Horace dines with us.

Sunday, May 1 Bright Weather. Hear Rev. M.B. Fuller on Mark 2.10, "Miracles & faith." He spoke with much ability and earnestness, and lengthily. Horace came afternoon. Lorin & Netta called in the evening, and Milton. Talked of the Exhibition.

Monday, May 2 Day warm as June. [blank] painted the porch. I wrote letters, to Reuchlin and others. We went to bed before nine o'clock. Frank Henry Russell came and left his card. Letter from Caroline V. Krout, in answer to mine of Condolence for the death of her father. Senate confirms Gov. Chas. E. Hughes, as Justice Supr. Court.

Tuesday, May 3 Considerable cooler, after showers. Called at Mrs. Henry Wagner's. John Simons has bought lot in Peru, to build. Wilbur returned home about 2:00 p.m. from New York City. Had done little by going.

Wednesday, May 4 Mrs. LaChapelle called. Girls called in Afternoon to have a game. Prof. Gragg writes that C.W. Blanchard declines the Presidency of Central College.

Thursday, May 5 Went on 9:45 train to Lima, Ohio, and went to the widow Ave's. At 3:00 I united in marriage Wilbur F. Weyer and Emelia Ave. I ate a hearty supper. We had a lot of Chivirri boys that made quite a noise at 7:00. I went at 8:00 to the Lima house and lodged. At 85 cents for lodging and breakfast. Slept well.

Friday, May 6 Went on 7:05 train to Upper Sandusky, and thence to Columbus, arriving at 11:00 and leaving at 4:00, for Newcomerstown, at which place I stay at Snaveley's Globe Hotel, till morning, where I pay 85 cents for lodging and breakfast. I saw two of the Watson girls. (who played the violin at the wedding, the day before) three sisters. King Edward VII dies.

Saturday, May 7 I go south on 7:05 train to Whipple, arriving there at 9:35, where Perry Leroy Roach meets me and takes me over a rough road to his mother's, 12 miles (15 miles) out in Monroe County. His father Anson H. Roach, died Dec. 21, 1909, requesting, if possible, that I preach his funeral. His children were: Mary Emila, John Anson, Perrey Leroy, Louise Catharine, and Warren, Preshia's son. George V. (George Frederick) succeeds Edward.

Sunday, May 8 Rev. Mr. Robey took me to Hopewell M.E. Church, where I preached the funeral, 1 Thes. 4.14. The M.E. Pastor, P.H. Williams, and four other pastors, and a large congregation were present. I dined at Preshia Roach's. I sup at Leroy's & lodge at Mrs. Roach's. His son[-in-?]law, Harvey Lucas was there. Orville came home from Birmingham, Alabama.

Monday, May 9 It rained Sunday evening and Sunday night. I got to Town at 9:35 and dined at a restaurant and waited for 3:35 train to Newcomerstown, where I took the 11:55 train to Xenia, and on 7:35 train I reached home, at Dayton. I slept much of the day. Orville at Sim[m]s, made several flights. Wilbur is in New York.

Tuesday, May 10 Orville appeared at about 3:00, at Pennsylvania depot on his way to New York to attend in the Court of Appeals in defense of the decision in favor of their temporary injunction against Herring Company & Curtis. U.S. Marshall left notice for Orville & Wilbur to answer in Circuit Court of Cincin. Suit of Chas. H. Lampson.

Friday, May 13 Eight women came in to have a game with Katharine.

Saturday, May 14 Orville is flying. We went out to see him. He flew seven times.

Sunday, May 15 I remained at home. Nothing very unusual occurred. I read in Matthew. James W. Van Cleve died in St. Louis. He was formerly president of the Manufacturer's Association, and a leader in the fight against the boycott. He was 60 years of age.

Tuesday, May 17 Wrote on Matthew's Gospel. King Edward's body is borne on a gun carriage from Buckingham Palace to Westminster.

Wednesday, May 18 Orville flew in the forenoon 700 feet high. I saw him fly in the afternoon 1,520 feet. I was almost starved at supper at 8:00. Mr. Rule of Collier's

Weekly supped with us—a pretty modest man from such a journal. He and president of the St. Louis Aero Club flew with Orville.

Thursday, May 19 Orville made a number of flights at Sim[m]'s Station, one alone 1760 feet high. I wrote yesterday and to-day on Matthew. I wrote Oliver Buller a letter, authorizing him to sell the property in Fairmount, at $450.00. I afterward received a special delivery letter asking about renting it to Doc. McCormick of Fairmount. Katharine went to see Agnes.

Friday, May 20 It was rainy this morning. I wrote Reuchlin and Bertha. I also wrote to Oliver Buller.

Saturday, May 21 We went to Sim[m]s and saw Orville fly about 2,000 feet high. He prepared and tried a new machine once. He flew with A.L. Welsh, LaChapelle, and Lorin. The wind was pretty still. We came home in an automobile with Mr. Thresher.

Sunday, May 22 I went to First U.B. Church, heard E.S. Chapman, former pastor, preach Isai. 49.23. He preached politics. He called for me. I called at Lorin's in the afternoon. Miss Hunter called. Also Albert Shearer. Mailed a letter to Herbert.

Monday, May 23 Rev. William Dillon called in Afternoon. Told of Barkley's calling the Coast delegates together and nominating Baldwin—trying to pledge them to vote together. Mrs. Wm. H. Lanthurne called. Katharine went to visit Miss Winifred Ryder. No flying at Sim[m]s.

Tuesday, May 24 It rained this morning. Katharine was out in town most of the afternoon. Frank Russell and Roy Knabenshue called in the evening and left at 10 o'clock.

Wednesday, May 25 It is a nice day. Invitations come from Coin, Iowa, to attend June 2, the graduating exercises of High School (Mabel Harris), and from Basehor, Kan., Grammar School (Bertha Wright). Wrote letter to each. Mrs. LaShapelle called. We all went to Sim[m]s Station. Orville rose 1600 feet and 2600 feet in flights. Orville & Wilbur took a first flight together. Orville took me up 350 feet and 6.55 minutes.

The Bishop flying with Orville, May 25, 1910

Thursday, May 26 Katharine and Wilbur go to Sim[m]s Station in the afternoon. Orville makes some eight flights. In one he rose about 2100 feet high. In one he shut off the motor and descended some six hundred feet, safely. He flew in all directions and in very small circles. He spoke of cool trends of air, bending him down some 300 feet.

Friday, May 27 I went out to Sim[m]s at 3:30, on the car. Orville was flying with A.L. Welsh. He flew several times with Welsh & Chapelle. Welsh led many times. I came home on 5:30 car. Prof. Robert Koch, the bacterialist, died to day.

Saturday, May 28 I got up at 7:00, and breakfasted alone. Went to Sim[m]s. Orville and others took many flights. We went on a special 2:30 car. Returned on 7:30 car. Frank Russel and Roy Knabenshue and Mr. LaChappell and their wives, supped with us at 9:00.

Sunday, May 29 Attended First Baptist Church and heard Howard Whidden on Hebrews 13.2. Hospitality. Glen Curtis is reported to have flown from New York to Albany and back. An hour's rest on the way; 54 miles an hour.

Monday, May 30 This is Decoration Day. It is rather a windy day. Orville took no flights. I wrote some on Notes on Matthew.

Tuesday, May 31 To-day is extraordinarily cool for the last day of May. Albert Snyder and wife and Mother called. They live in Indianapolis. Mrs. La Chappelle dined with us.

Wednesday, June 1 The afternoon was windy. Very few flights at Sim[m]'s. I wrote some on Matthew.

Thursday, June 2 Orville Went early to Sim[m]s. It proved a cloudy forenoon. Katharine supped at Flora (Greenwood) Smith's, East End. I slept in my chair in the afternoon.

Friday, June 3 The boys flew nearly twenty times with both machines to-day. Brookins rose near 1000 feet, twice. Wilbur went to the grounds.

Saturday, June 4 It was not a good day for flying, but the boys flew some.

Sunday, June 5 I attended Grace M.E. Church and heard Dr. Fuller on John 17.21. Unity. Horace came afternoon. Wilbur started to New York. Katharine and Orville took a walk. Mr. Wald came to see Orville. Talked with me on Phillippines and tariff. Orville announced that applicants must be mechanics, expert, able to run a machine.

Monday, June 6 Not a good day for flying. I spend the day in looking over three years' volumes of the National Era. I find the Editor's article on Secrecy, and the account of the attempted mob in Washington. The former about March 9, 1848.

Tuesday, June 7 I went out late to Simm's. Orville glided downward 2000 feet and landed at the right place with ease and safety. Ed. Sines and wife were out with Mr. Clinger and wife, who brought me home in automobile.

Wednesday, June 8 Went to Sim's and had supper with Lorin's and Russell's, etc. Came home in the dark. Katharine suppers at Miss Stiver's. The "birds" flew much at Simm's, all low flights.

Thursday, June 9 It was a little rainy. Wilbur and Orville dine at Oscar Needham's; Katharine at Mrs. LaChapelle's. We all sup at home. Oscar Needham calls in at night. Tells of the working of the American Book Concern, in defeating Dr. W.O. Thompson.

Friday, June 10 Somewhat rainy to-day. Toulman's clerk dined with us. The aeroplanes are removed to Indianapolis. All of us ate dinner and supper together.

Saturday, June 11 Wilbur went to Indianapilis. I went with Orville and Kath. to see their new lot in the evening. We called at Lorin's.

Sunday, June 12 I went on 8:30 car to Germantown. Preached at 10:15, Matt. 7.24. Dined at Miss Lizzie Long's with Ed. M. Scott ' s . Preached at 7:30, Matt. 7.26, in Morn. three quarters of an hour. Evening, 25 min. Audience, morning, 14 , eve., 18 ! I lodged at E.M. Scott's at the old Wet's House.

Monday, June 13 Came home on 6:30 car. Bought box of typewriter paper, 85 cts. Mrs. LaChappele called after supper.

Tuesday, June 14 Katharine is unwell.

Thursday, June 16 Mr. Frank Russell called at noon. He was at Indianapolis yesterday. I received the news of the burning of Sublimity College building, in a letter from Jessie E. Glover near Sublimity, Oregon. I wrote to her, and to Prof. T.H. CIawford, at Corvallis. At High School commencement, Milton graduated. Dr. Thorn presided! Ed. Brown thc Superintendant. Pres. Herbert Welch, spoke.

Friday, June 17 Slept out my 8 hours, before noon. Warm last night and to-day. The International Aero club has an excursion to Indianapolis—about 300. Walter Brookins rises about 4,503 feet, gets lost, lights in a field, three miles from the Speedway, at Indianapolis.

Saturday, June 18 Arose late. Nothing unusual during the day. Miss [blank] Brett and Ryder supped with us in the evening. Toulmin's special letter to the boys came. I sat up till 11:00.

Sunday, June 19 Wilhur & Orville came home about 11:00 from Indianapolis. Wilbur started at 4:00 for New York. He went to apply for a modification of the decision of the Appelate U.S. Court, asking that Herring Co., and Paulhan be required to give bond.

Monday, June 20 I drew a Hampton Magazine, giving some proofs of Pearry, the Arctic Discoverer. I called at Lorin's and saw Horace, who is having mumps on both sidcs. He is playing with the children.

Tuesday, June 21 Orville and Katharine Start to Oberlin in afternoon. Ivonette and Leontine stay with me.

Wednesday, June 22 I start at 10:50 for Fowlerton, via Richmond. Sup with Robert Broyles; lodge at Oliver Buller's. Settled with Wilson Simon's. Gave a check for Edmund Dayley for $12.50 for ditching. I saw Joseph Broyles & Elizar and son Charles, on cars between Muncie & Gaston.

Thursday, June 23 Went to Fowlerton. Paid $15.90 for difference in tyle. Went on noon train to Fairmount. Dine at Restaurant. Staid at Ellis' till Friday afternoon. Saw Chas. T. Parker. Called at Mary Hollingworth's. Called at Mr. Holder's, Hiram Simons' son-inlaw's.

Friday, June 24 Saw Dr. Seal, health officer. Went in afternoon to Rushville. Called at Cora Dillon's and learned of Emma Frazier's death that morning of hemorrhag of the lungs. I staid at Mrs. Dillon's.

Saturday, June 25 Saw Russell's shop. His wireless telegraphy apparatus. In afternoon went to Delila Wright's, with the undertaker in automobile. I lodged at Thomas Wright's. I wrote Emma's obituary. Rev. Harry Frazier and daughter were there, and many others.

Sunday, June 26 Rev. John A. Thompson preached about 20 minutes. I read the obituary and prayed at the conclusion of his discourse. The Wrights of Indianapolis— Faye, Harvey, Walter's wife and little girl—Rhoda Williams, Luther Newhouse and wife, Rilla (Dan's widow) & husband, the friends all, were there. F.A. Bowen and Charles Stevens & wives there. Burial at Blue River.

Monday, June 27 I stayed at Delila's till afternoon. Went with Ed. Frazier (Wm. E. Frazier) to Rushville and on traction car to Griffin, where F.A. Bowen met me and took me to his house in Orange - formerly Danville and then Fayetteville. I lodgethere.

Tuesday, June 28 We go to Sonnie's farm. See Ralph, wife and little girl. Ralph's wife is Grace, his little girl is Mabel. We go on to Lucinda Moor's and Bertha Long's. I stay at Charles Steven's, whose Ray is 16, a fine boy.

Wednesday, June 29 I go to Lucinda's and lodge there.

Thursday, June 30 N.F. Bowen takes me in his automobile to Ellen Barber's in Sally Ann Cook's house at Neff's Corners, and by the two Rush County farms. Call at Mrs. Morgan Linville's (81 or 82 years old). Dine at James Harris's. Orlo doing the farming. I go to Jesse Lefforges's to supper. Phi. and wife and Otis Miller and family there. We got back to Orange at dusk.

Friday, July 1 I go to Glenwood at 8:00 and on traction car to Connersville. Wait 9:30 train to Hamilton and reach Dayton at noon. I find all the family at home, and all well.

Monday, July 4 All at home, and all well. Twenty-one years ago, this forenoon, Susan died. She was "the sweetest spirit earth ever knew." Heavy rain in the forenoon. The children go to [blank] Emmons' for supper. I called at Lorin's. Leontine is just getting over mumps. Horace has lately had them.

Saturday, July 9 At home. Have an electric fan and electric light put into my room. We had a nice shower in the afternoon. Orville's work.

Sunday, July 10 I was at home. Lorin's called in the evening.

Monday, July 11 Horace came early to get his (automobile) tricycle. Governor Harmon suspends Mayor of Newark a month.

Tuesday, July 12 It showers about daily. It rained this morning. My electric fan is put in and electric light. Katharine and I called an hour at Lorin's. Charles S. Rolls who twice crossed the Channel at Dover is killed. The "brothers" cabled condolence to his friends.

Wednesday, July 13 I wrote on Insurgents to Cyrus Smith, and a letter on Harvey's family to Reuchlin.

Sunday, July 17 Tolerably warm day. I was at home all day.

Monday, July 18 S.E. Kumler had a stroke of apoplexy.

Tuesday, July 19 I was at home. Mrs. Russell and her mother and Mrs. Guthrie and her mother visited Katharine afternoon. In the evening, Nettie and her three children came.

Wednesday, July 20 Milton is sick with appendicitis, a light attack.

Thursday, July 21 Milton still abed with appendicitis. The boys move a flying machine to Simms' Station, and make some experiments with wheels. They get home about 8:00, evening.

Friday, July 22 S.E. Kumler, stroke of apoplexy Monday, still alive. Milton is sitting up to-day. Samuel E. Kumler expired just after midnight, at his home on South Main Street.

Saturday, July 23 Mr. Griffith Brewer of England is expected to-morrow.

Sunday, July 24 Mr. Griffith Brewer arrived after 8:00 a.m. and continued with us.

Monday, July 25 Mr. Brewer continued with us. I attended S.E. Kumler's funeral at First U.B. Church, Kephart, Berger, Shuey, Funk had a part.

Tuesday, July 26 I went at noon to Miami Chautaqua Grounds. Heard at 2:00 Senator [blank] Doliver of Iowa speak on Abraham Lincoln. Came home with Mr. Aley, father of Mrs. Herbert Allen, cousin of W.J. Shuey.

Wednesday, July 27 Went to Simms Station. Orville flew three flights; about 15 minutes twice, about 20 minutes once; once 800 feet high, once 1200 feet. We were over an hour coming home. The cause, a fuse burnt out. Letter from Reuchlin says that Herbert has engaged to teach six months at fifty dollars per month—five miles south.

Thursday, July 28 I was at home all day. Knabenshue called in forenoon. Mr. Barnes dined with us. Katharine and Mrs. Knabenshue and Mr. Brewer and Mr. Plew of Chicago went to Simm's Station, in automobile. Several flights were made, in all two hours flight, by pupils. Barnes is a secretary and director of the Wright Company.

Friday, July 29 We went to Frank Russell's to supper. Mr. Barnes, Sec'y Wright Company, there. All our family were there. I heard scarcely anything that was said.

Saturday, July 30 I went to Simms with Wilbur, Katharine and Mr. Griffith Brewer. Orville & Mr. Brewer flew 23 minutes. Mr. Coffyn flew alone twice, the last time 13 minutes.

Sunday, July 31 Went to First Reform Church and heard Rev. [blank] Burkhalter on the Holy Spirit. Wilbur went to New York. Mr. Brewer had indigestion.

Tuesday, August 2 Mr. Brewer better.

Wednesday, August 3 Wilbur got home at noon. Had no business of importance at New York.

Thursday, August 4 I started at 9:45 for Blissfield, Michigan. Reached there by street fare 5 cents and Lake Shore R'y about 5:00. Called at a merchant's, Rothfuss's son not being at home. They look up camp, for me and I go to the church and his house. His married daughter gets me supper and his little daughter [blank] takes me to depot and I go at 7:40 to camp.

Friday, August 5 I arrived at 11:00 at Lake and lodged there and breakfasted. Slept six hours. Paid 75 cents. Paid $3.05 to Toledo; 55 to Blissfield and 87 cts to Toledo. Went with Rev. J.G. Connor to Campground, 40 rods away. Cure preached at 9:30. Bishop Alwood at 10:30, R.B. Mason raised about $70.00 at 2:00 and I pr at 3:00, John 17.17. I went to Mr.————, found all away. Staid at Kirshmiller's. Slept 7 hours.

Saturday, August 6 Went in automobile to Camp and heard John Freemen pr a good sermon on Imitating Christ. Mummart had Bible Reading on Holy Spirit. I affirmed many instances of the Greek neuter pneuma. It was a surprise to Mummart & Clay! Sup at tent. Rothfuss and wife and Mrs. [blank] and daughter stay also, at G.P. Hirshmiller's.

Sunday, August 7 Went to camp. Wood pr. well, after speaking meeting, from 1 John 3.1,2. Man baptized by sprinkling, before sermon. At the close Heighly Wood, E.C. Mason's son, and three others joined church. I pronounced the benediction on them. After sermon by Clarence A. Mummart, J.G. Connor baptized several at the Lake. I staid at G.P. Hirshmiller's.

Monday, August 8 R.B. Mason takes us to the cars. I go from Hillsdale to Fort Wayne, and thence to Wabash, and thence on traction to Jonesboro, and thence to Fowlerton. I go to Robt. Broyles' on the farm. I sup and lodge there. Levi Simons called to see one.

Tuesday, August 9 I look at the farm. I go to Richards' and see Oliver Buller, 5 minutes. Pay Robert B. Broyles on written account $46.66. Sup, lodge, breakfast and dinner at Robt. Broyles. Robt. takes me in buggy to C.C. & L. Depot. I connect at Richmond and get home a little after 6:00. Herbert Wright had come. Born Feb. 7, 1892, in Kans. City. He begins school, Sept. 1, 1910.

Saturday, August 13 I was up at night with dyssentary [*sic*]. The doctor (Spitler) called. Gave me tablets every two hours. I had no diarrhae; so took them accordingly. Lived on milk diet. Felt quite well. The disease he pronounced an epidemic.

Sunday, August 14 After (about 9:00) I had a little continued operation of the bowels. Was slightly sick. I used a piece of bread, cream of wheat, and coffee without sugar, unusual. I then resumed milk diet. I felt well, but slept half the time. At table, at 6:30. Slept half the time. Had a strange dream about conflict of conservation and Mormonism.

Friday, August 19 Edward M. Harris came in the afternoon. He is 64 years old in Sept. (28th) and last called in 1861. The boys flew at Simm's which Harris saw.

Saturday, August 20 Edward Harris went to Soldiers' Home. He left at 2:10 for Connersville. Wm. Andrews called in the evening.

Sunday, August 21 At home all day. Mr. Parmalee called to see the boys Monday afternoon. Alex. Ochilvie and Coffyn and Brookins called.

Monday, August 22 At home all day. Wilbur started to Chicago. Mr. P.O. Parmalee called.

Tuesday, August 23 This is the Day Prof. Dennis and family came, went after dinner to Simms', and our folks were brought home by automobiles of Cincinnati visitors, including Lorin's women and Horace. And we went to Centerville with Mr. Roy Knabenshue's and back by moonlight.

Wednesday, August 24 I wrote to Reuchlin and Mrs. Nora A. Shirley (Lincoln, Cass Co., Indiana), etc.

Thursday, August 25 I wrote some letters. Lorin's family came in the evening. A little rain; it turned much cooler. Wrote to Mary H. Krout.

Saturday, August 27 Went on 8:50 train to Richmond & thence to Gaston. Paid a dollar for a liveryman taking me to Joseph Broyles'. They were finishing their dinners. William A. Broyles and wife were away at Bloomington. Mrs. Boyd, and Mrs. Alfred Broyles were there and Otto Broyles. I staid at Joseph Broyles. Horace was with me.

Sunday, August 28 Robert B. Broyles drove us at Noon to Wm. H. Reeder's. I dined there. Supped at Robert's. Lodged at Will's.

Monday, August 29 Robert took us to the place. We looked at it. Nice corn. I dined at Kirkwood's. Went to Oliver Buller's. They took us to C.I. & E. depot, and I went to Ellis Wright's, where we staid.

Tuesday, August 30 Saw Wiley, and Chas. J. Parker. Corrected a mistake and paid Driggs & Wiley forty-two dollars & 25 cents, for settlement to Aug. 15th. Saw Parker and he paid me about $45.00. I went to Soldier's home returning at 9:30 at night.

Wednesday, August 31 Went with Horace to Wabash and by traction to Huntington. Dined at Restaurant. I went to Spencerville arriving about 3:00. Hired livery rig to Monticello. There put up at Mr. A.H. Clay's. Called to see Bish. Hoskins. Rev. Wm. Miller preached at 8:00, Isai. 66.1, a good discourse. We staid at Clay's.

Thursday, September 1 I attended fournoon session and joined Auglaize session, as a minister. I spoke at 11:00, Matt. 7.28 & 29 v. Dined at Clay's and went on 1:00 train via Ludlow Falls home. Arrived about 4:00.

Saturday, September 3 Mr. Alexander Ogilvie of England came to Dayton.

Tuesday, September 6 Miss Winifred Ryder supped and lodged with Katharine. I received a letter from Dr. G.W.H. Kemper and inclosing the Kemper Memorial.

Friday, September 9 I wrote letters, to Kate Van Fleet and Clara Gilbert. Mr. Russell and Ogilvie supped with us.

Saturday, September 10 It is pleasant weather. I wrote letters to Laura Winchell and Orval Harris. Katharine went to Simm's, to witness flights.

Sunday, September 11 Attended Broadway M.E. Church, and heard the pastor, Rev. T.J. Cocks pr. Josh. 1:1, "Joshua Son of Nun." 1. Obedience, 2. Courage, 3. Faith, It was a good sermon.

Monday, September 12 Wrote letters to J. Howe & Cyrus Smith. Got a knife at Albert Shearer's. Katharine went to Simms but there was no flying.

Wednesday, September 14 Ogilivie and Russell supped with Orville and Katharine.

Sunday, September 18 I remained at home. Alex. Ogilvie dined and supped with us. Mr. Coffyn and Brookins called in the afternoon.

Monday, September 19 Mr. P.O. Parmalee spent afternoon and evening with us. Wilbur started to Chicago, at 10:00 p.m.

Tuesday, September 20 Katharine started to Oberlin with Rachel Wagner, at 10:00 morning.

Wednesday, September 21 I am at home. Lorin's girls and Horace sup with me. Orville is at the Inter-Aero banquet, at 6:30 afternoon.

Thursday, September 22 Wilbur comes home from Chicago, before breakfast. Orville flew to Dayton, and back to Simms, 2,000 feet high coming, and 4,000 feet going. 100,000 people saw him fly. At 5:00, Orville comes on his flyer, about 2,000 feet high, turns at Williams Street, goes near our Home, flies along Third Street to the limits of the City, and rising to about 4,000 feet, goes up Mad River to their grounds. Came nine miles in ten minutes, returned slower. Many Thousands saw him. (This was Thursday, 22nd)

Saturday, September 24 I was at home. Katharine went to Simms and flew a thousand feet high with Orville, *last evening.* The papers estimate 100,000 witnesses, the 22nd, to Orville's flight.

Tuesday, September 27 This third day I made no record, except that Wilbur went to Chicago to-night.

Wednesday, September 28 Wrote to Elmira Koerner this week. Mailed a letter to Lucinda Moor, returning an old letter of Israel C. Evans to Daniel McNiel and Elizabeth McNiel. Wilbur Wright is at Chicago, to Witness Mr. Brookins preparation for a flight thence to Springfield, for $10,000 prize offered by the Chicago Record-Herald.

Thursday, September 29 Mrs. Sines (79 years old in August) called this morning. Mr. [blank]Osborn called to see Katharine. He is entirely deaf. To-day Walter Brookins flew from Chicago to Springfield, Ill. He stopped at Gilman, 75 miles at 11:30 and at Mt. Pulaski, 136 miles. It was 192 1/2 miles with two stops. He reached the state fair grounds at 4:27 p.m. Wilbur followed in a rail
way car.

Friday, September 30 Katharine went with Mrs. Sines to Simm's Aviation grounds. Wilbur came home from Springfield, Ill.

Saturday, October 1 Mr. Ogilvie dined with us. Katharine went in the evening to Woman's League, Mrs. Greene.

Sunday, October 2 I went to Summit Street Church and heard Rev. A.G. Clippinger pr. John 12.21. Attractiveness of Jesus. Mr. Ogilvie dined with us. I called at Lorin's in the evening. Wilbur goes at 10:00 p.m. to Washington, Penn., to inspect grounds of flight agreed upon by Khaubenshue.

Tuesday, October 4 Katharine went at 7:30 a.m. to Grace Church to the wedding of Miss Shaw & Wilbur Conover. Wilbur arrived at Home at noon, from Wash., Pa. Walter Brookins & Coffyn are at Washington, Pa.; Johnston at Richmond, Va., Hoxsey at Springfield, Ill. Turpin at Sedalia, Missouri, and Parmalee at Birmingham, Ala.

Friday, October 7 Mr. Ogilvie supped with us, and started to St. Louis.

Saturday, October 8 Mr. Hoxsey flies from Springfield, Ill. to St. Louis, Missouri. To-day, the Women's League edition of the Daily News was issued. Katharine reported the flying exploits and wrote an article for the paper.

Tuesday, October 11 Our cook, Mrs. Emma Ragan, was away.

Wednesday, October 12 John Feight took us out at 8:00 a.m. to Simms Station and we saw the new machine, 28 X 3 1/2 feet. Mary Noah, his Aunt from Omaha, was along. Also his son Howard, 5 years old. Misses Rider and Brett supped with us.

Thursday, October 13 Mr. Ogilvie called at 1:30, he being back from St. Louis. Katharine and Mrs. Russell & Wallace went at 4:00 to Wright Company's ground at Simms Station. Frank Russell's and Russell Alger called at 8:00.

Sunday, October 16 Katharine and I went to Summit Street and heard Rev. A.G. Clippinger discourse of "A basket of Summer Fruit." Amos 8.1. We dined at Joseph M. Phillips with Rev. A.G. Clippinger and his wife, Bishop Mill's daughter.

Thursday, October 20 News came of the rescue of Walter Welman and Company in their boats about 300 miles from land, east of Carolina. Lorin's & Mr & Mrs Russell supped with us. Agnes Osborn also. Wilbur started to New York.

Friday, October 21 Mr. Ogilvie dined with us. I went to town and bought several articles—among other things brought home an ear trumpet. It did me no good.

Saturday, October 22 Answered a letter from Ray Stevens. Orville tried his eight-cylinder engine and it worked well. Weighs 100 lbs more. We sup at Frank Russell's. 77 or 78 miles an hour. The machine is 22 feet long; 3 1/2 feet broad. His eight-cylinder engine weighs itself 100 pounds more than the four-cylinder one. It gives over 50 Horse Power.

Sunday, October 23 I dressed to go to Church but gave it up, and went to Lorin's. The *Journal* came late, owing to a ground-wire out of order. Mr. Alec. Oglivie dined with us. Lorin's came. Orville, Katharine and Mr. Ogilvie started at 4:00 for New York. I supped at Lorin's. Ivonette and Leontine came home with me and staid all night.

Monday, October 24 Lorin's girls breakfast with me. Bad day in New York. Moisant's and Graham-White's machines wrecked. Lorin's family ate supper with us, and the girls stay at night, and to breakfast.

Tuesday, October 25 Letter from Katharine came from New York. Lorin's girls breakfasted and whole family supped with me. The girls stay at our house. Johnston takes American record for h[e]ight in New York. Orville makes nearly seventy miles an hour with our racer.

Wednesday, October 26 Lorin's family as usual sups with me, and girls stay at night.

Thursday, October 27 Card from Katharine. Lorin's family come as usual, only Horace stays in Leontine's stead. Johnstone & Hoxsey were floated off by winds, to Middle Island and Brentwood, L.I. Johnson "55 Miles," Hoxsey, 25 miles.

Friday, October 28 Hoxsey and Johnstone returned. Drexel, Hamilton and Brookins are chosen for America's contestants. Latharn, Leblank & Aubrun for France; Graham-White, Radley and Ogilvie, for Great Britain. Milton closed his fifth week of school.

Saturday, October 29 Netta brought telegram to Lorin from F.H. Russell saying that Brookins' Racer fell with him, but that no bones are broken in the race. Lorin and family as usual, only Milton staid at night.

Sunday, October 30 Breakfast with Milton. I heard Rev. Frank Garland on Rom. 8.6, and thought he misunderstood "spiritually minded," mistaking it for miraculously helped, in Sampson's case. Lorin's dine with me. I sup there. The girls stay as usual.

Monday, October 31 Lorin's as usual. I look over old letters. Johnstone climbs at New York (Belmont) 9,714 feet; is higher than world's record. The girls—Ivonette and Leontine—come in with a party in masks. Emma Ragan went to a dance.

Horace Wright at nine years old

Tuesday, November 1 Lorin's as usual. Horace staid at night in place of Ivonette.

Wednesday, November 2 Lorin's come as usual. Lorin received a telegram from Orville, saying that he and Katharine will be at home at 9:00 tomorrow morning. Horace & Ivonette stay at our house with us. Lorin and Milton attend the International Aeroplane supper.

Thursday, November 3 Got letters from De Voe, Perrilla Mann and Elmira Koerner. Orville and Katharine came home at 9:00 a.m. They report eminent success. They got $20,000 for going besides $15,000 prizes. The Wright Company voted them $10,000 and declared a dividend of $80,000. The New York papers lauded them highly. Lorin's, except Milton came in the evening.

Friday, November 4 Mrs. (Leach) called afternoon. Mrs. Russell and her boys, Frank and Wallace, called.

Sunday, November 6 I was sleepy, and not very well. Wilbur came home from Baltimore at 4:00 p.m.

Monday, November 7 Orville and Katharine went to Simms to see Mr. Phil. O. Parmalee start to Columbus with several bolts of silk in an aeroplane. He flew there in 61 minutes, and delivered the goods.

Tuesday , November 8 Milton is eighteen years old, to-day. For six weeks, he has been teaching south of town in High School, at $65.00 a month. It is a pleasant morning for election day. I voted the Republican ticket, except for one man—Barnes. Wilbur started to New York at 4:00 afternoon. New carpet laid in two lower rooms. Election news unfavorable.

Wednesday, November 9 Harmon was elected governor of Ohio; Dix of New York; Woodrow Wilson of New Jersey; Judge Baldwin of Connecticut. Representatives in Congress indicate a Democratic majority. Several Republican Senators will not be reelected. Cannon & Payne (Repub.) were reelected to Congress.

Thursday, November 10 The elections show that many voters staid at home in New York, Ohio etc.

Saturday, November 12 Milton *walked* to Troy to-day. Lorin's supped with us.

Sunday, November 13 Orville started at 4:00, for Germany, Berlin, to instruct them how to build better machines.

Tuesday, November 15 Orville sailed on the Crown Princess Cecelia. Mrs. Russell and Mrs. Guthrie were here in the afternoon. Agnes Osborn supped with us.

Wednesday, November 16 At home. Wrote a letter to Rev. William Dillon. Sent him $5.00 more on salary. Katharine went to supper at Mr. Pierce's in Dayton View. She got home at 8:00. We got a letter from Wilbur, from New York City.

Thursday, November 17 This is the eighty-second anniversary of my birth-day. I am in good health. I am as spry as most men at half my age. Probably I do not appear older than most men at seventy. I got a picture card

from my nephew Edward M. Harris, Lincoln, Kans. I wrote a long letter to Rev. R. Beck, Grafton, California. Ralph Johnstone dashed to death in Denver.

Friday, November 18 With us at Lorin's was Mr. Frank Russell and wife, in the evening. Mr. F. Russell & Lorin met Wilbur at the train with Mrs. Ralph Johnstone, on the way to Kansas City, from New York City. I wrote cards in reply to birth-day cards from Grace Frazier, Stella Rhodes, Gusta Whitton & S.W. Wright; also to Flora Glass.

Saturday, November 19 Lorin went with Wilbur to Richmond, but came back as David and Emma Dennis had gone to Hamilton, to-day. Mrs. Russell, Mrs. Guthrie, and Mrs. Stevens came in for gambling with Katharine, and Mrs. Stevens staid for supper and went to Mrs. Hunter's to a party and returned and lodged.

Sunday, November 20 Heard at Broadway, Rev. T.J. Cocks, Esther 4.13,14. Horace visited us in the afternoon and I go home with him to supper. Katharine went to Miss Winifred Ryder's. Tolstoy died at 6:00 this morning, at Astapova, Russia. His home was at Yasnaya Poliana.

Monday, November 21 Wrote Harvey Harris and Sina E. Ardery. Katharine went to some kind of a gathering in the afternoon.

Tuesday, November 22 Wilbur came home at 6:00, evening, having visited Reuchlin yesterday. Lorin, Nettie and Horace came and staid till 8:00 evening.

Wednesday, November 23 Crippen was hung for killing his wife, in England. Chanute, Octave, died in Chicago, aged 79 years, nearly. We see that Orville arrived in Berlin, Germany, to-day. Octave Chanute was born in Paris, Feb. 18, 1832. His parents came to America in 1838. I do not believe that Crippen killed his wife.

Thursday, November 24 Wrote some. Went to the Lutheran Church, at the corner of Broadway and Germantown Streets and heard Rev. T.J. Cocks preach a thanksgiving sermon—very able. I went home, where Lorin's family and Winifred Rider dined with us. We, and Lorin's and Mr. Guthrie's went to Frank Russell's and staid till 8:00. Wilbur started at 9:00 for Chicago, to attend Octave Chanute's funeral.

Friday, November 25 Mr. Chanute's funeral (Episcopal) occurred in Chicago (Private-about 30 present), and he was taken to Peoria. Episcopal service at 4:00.

Saturday, November 26 Wilbur came home from Chicago in the morning.

Sunday, November 27 The day is somewhat rainy. Mr. Coffyn called in the afternoon.

Monday, November 28 Miss Ella Congdon called to see what periodicals Katharine wanted for next year. Mr. Remick or Remerick, a six foot Scotch-Irishman called to see me about buying stock in New York real estate. This last *belonged to Tuesday.*

Tuesday, November 29 A six-foot, 2 inch Scotch-Irishman called to see me about investing in New York real estate stock.

Wednesday, November 30 Women came in this afternoon to play cards. Wilbur started to New York about 4:00 afternoon. Mrs. Mella King came at 6:30, evening, some behind time. Carrie Grumbach helped about supper.

Thursday, December 1 I took my overcoat to the dry-cleaner. Bought a scull cap.

Friday, December 2 Katharine took Mrs. Mella King to Sim[m]s, where they see three short flights.

Saturday, December 3 Mrs. Russell brought some nice Roses while Katharine and Mella had gone out to see the Wright Company's shop. My overcoat came home cleaned, $1.50. Mr. Guthrie took the women out on a ride. Mrs. Stevens and Agnes Osborn supped with us, and Mrs. Stevens staid till 9:00. I finished my sketch of the Van Cleve family. Mrs. Eddy died to-day.

Sunday, December 4 I was too late to be ready for Church. Lorin brought the letters and papers as usual. At 5 00 Katharine and Mella go to Lorin's awhile. Miss Winifred Rider supped with us.

Monday, December 5 Mella King started home at 10:30. Katharine and I met, at Miss Reese's Photograph Gallery, for me to have my Photograph taken. A letter from Orville, written Thanksgiving Day (Nov. 24) came to-day. He writes from Berlin, Germany. He is well. Katharine attended a musical entertainment by a distinguished professor to-night.

Tuesday, December 6 Wrote J.F. Harris. Mrs. Guthrie called in the afternoon. Mrs. Wagner had supper with us.

Wednesday, December 7 Misses Mayer, Agnes Osborn and Mrs. Guthrie have cards with Katharine, and stay to a turkey supper with her.

Thursday, December 8 S.A. Steman came about noon and stayed to 4:35. Wilbur came home at 1:00 from New York. Wilbur has a letter from Orville, dated November 28th.

Friday, December 9 Katharine was away in the afternoon and at supper at Fourth Presbyterian Church till 8:45 evening. Wilbur was giving testimony in the suit against them at Cincinnati, and not at home for dinner.

Saturday, December 10 I wrote letters to Cyrus Smith, William Dillon, and Bertha Glaze. I sent a bank order for five dollars to Bertha, as a present. Re-wrote on my diary for 1857. Frank H. Russell and wife and her mother, Mrs. Ford, and Mr. Benj. Guthrie and wife supped with us. They staid till ten o'clock.

Sunday, December 11 Heard Rev. T.J. Cocks pr. at Broadway M.E. Church, 1 Cor. 13.13, a sound sermon. He has never made a failure that I have had.

Tuesday, December 13 Wrote several letters. Mr. P.O. Parmalee supped with us. Mr. Robt. Massa, an Oberlin student, called an hour.

Friday, December 16 Mrs. Evans, Mrs. Booth's mother, died. We saw no account of her burial.

Sunday, December 18 I went to Grace M.E. Church and heard Dr. [blank] Fuller pr. Luke 23.50,51. Spoke of His Looking for the Kingdom of God. 1. There were different ideas of the Km., 1. Abraham's, 2. David's, 3. Daniel's, etc. He said something I could not hear that seemed to smack of Darwinism. I slept most of the afternoon. Darwinsim is nonsense. Miss Winifred Rider supped with us.

Tuesday, December 20 Elmira Koerner, Daniel's widow, died, aged near 81.

Wednesday, December 21 Katharine got a sideview picture of me. Two young men from Benton County, Ind. called to see Wilbur. They wanted a job of flying! I had a telephone message of the death of Elmira Koerner. Rachel Wagner came home from Oberlin and she and her Mother supped with us.

Thursday, December 22 I wrote letters to-day. Katharine got dinner in town at restaurant. Katharine went to town after supper with Mr. & Mrs. Guthrie. She came home at 8:20. Mrs. Guthrie is going to see her folks at Elyria, Ohio.

Friday, December 23 Ivonette, my granddaughter, spent the day with us, helping dress Leontine's doll.

Saturday, December 24 Ivonette was with us part of the day, or afternoon.

Sunday, December 25 Lorin's dined with us. It was quite a day of Christmas gifts.

Tuesday, December 27 Miss Mayer, Miss Osborne and several others were in for a game of cards.

Thursday, December 29 Orville came home from Europe at 9:00 (10:00). Horace was with us much of the day. Milton was here part of the evening. The rest of Lorin's came in and staid till about 8:00.

Friday, December 30 Katharine has sorethroat to-day.

Saturday, December 31 I examined old letters and got facts for insertion in my 1857 Journal of Diary. See additional pages. John B. Moisant, the aviator was killed at New Orleans, this morning. Arch Hoxsey, fell to his death this afternoon, at Los Angeles, California. Katharine has the doctor (Conklin) this afternoon.

Notes on 1910
It seems hard to get the facts about the manner of Hoxsey and Johnstone's death. They are narrated by spectators so variable. It seems as if witnesses can not see when excited. It seems probable that Hoxie may have fainted from his high flight. I was at Auglaize Conference, in 1910. I arrived at Spencerville and hired conveyance Wednesday evening, Aug. 31, 1910. Conf. had adjourned. I called at Bishop Hoskins and talked with him. Wm. Miller preached a good, brief discourse. The speaking meeting was nice. I supped and lodged at A.H. Clay's. We were nicely treated. They have seven children. Horace, my grandson, was with me. Rev. Martin Bennett boarded there. We left Thursday afternoon. I joined the Conference. I was on transfer from White River, which I joined in 1853. I was a member of Oregon Conference from 1857 to 1859. I rejoined White River in 1861. I preached at Auglaize Sept. 1, 1910, at 11:00, Matt. 7.24,25. I thought I had little freedom, but the effort was praised. I taught that Jesus taught freedom from oaths in conversation; referred to commands to swear in Jehovah's name, and to oaths of Christ (adjured), and to oaths by the Apostle Paul. I interpreted Christ's instruction, "To resist not evil" as teaching martyrdom as the necessary position then. Paul claimed his rights as a Roman citizen. So we, in a Christian country, may claim ours. I spoke less than 30 minutes.

Pupils of the Wrights
Walter Brookins, Ralph Johnstone, Arch. Hoxie, P.O. Parmelee, Clifford Turpin, Frank Coffyn, A.L. Welch. Lieuts. Rogers of the Navy and Lieuts. Arnold and Milling of the Army. Gill, Brindsley, and Leonard W. Bonney, of Wellington, Ohio.

1 9 1 1

Sunday, January 1 Katharine was up to-day. I am in my eighty-third Year. My health is good. All my family are at home. My grandchildren in town called to-day. We had a turkey for dinner. I learned this morning of the death of Arch. Hoxsey yesterday afternoon, at Los Angeles. Moisant also lost his life at New Orleans yesterday. They ran too much risk.

Monday, January 2 I arose at 6:00. Got breakfasted about 8:00. Katharine was up to-day. Emma Reagan was not here to-day, nor yesterday.

Tuesday, January 3 We sat about the house—Wilbur and Orville. Arch Hoxsey was buried at Pasadena, Cal. to-day.

Wednesday, January 4 I was busy reading at home. I received letter from Pres. F.H. Gragg urging that I write Church History from Lawrence's time. Card afternoon from Rev. J. Howe, telling of death of 3 of Prof. Cremean's children. Wilbur and Orville went to New York to attend the Annual Meeting of Wright Company.

Thursday, January 5 Katharine went to Richmond to a luncheon of 12 persons, at her cousin Emma Zellar's. William's Agnes being one. She came home at 7:00, the car being an hour late. I dined at Lorin's. x Dennis.

Friday, January 6 I got a letter from Lizzie Long, saying that she had found the lost order on the bank for fifteen dollars. Katharine spent the afternoon in town. She came home for supper.

Saturday, January 7 A telegram from Orville says that he will be at home to-morrow at noon. Katharine spent the afternoon and evening till 7:00 at Miss Nutall's.

Sunday, January 8 Orville returned home from New York at 10:00. Wilbur is going to Washington. I remained at home all day.

Monday, January 9 I was rewriting my autobiography. Senator Beveridge reports unfavorably against Senator Lorimer.

Tuesday, January 10 I was writing, as yesterday. Pomerene was elected United States Senator to-day. Senator Crawford makes a careful speech, against Senator Lorimer.

Wednesday, January 11 Weather, warm. Nearly rainy. We have learned of McLean, of Connecticut, being chosen U.S. Senator above Bulkely, and of David Elkins being appointed to fill out his father's term, for West Virginia.

Thursday, January 12 I was busy rectifying last year's Diary. Mr. Wm. J. Hammer took supper with us. He is here to prepare an affidavit for one of Wilbur's lawsuits.

Friday, January 13 Mr. Hammer is about Orville's office. Katharine was at Mary Emmon's for supper.

Saturday, January 14 It is somewhat rainy. Katharine presided at the College Club, and was away till about 11:00 p.m.

Sunday, January 15 I was at home all day. In the evening,

Miss Ryder, Brete, Stevens, Osborne and Russell & wife [blank] and Miss Cones the Socialist, eat supper with us. Miss Cones is a beauty and an adept at behavior, very expert in answers, and conversation. Went away at 8:00.

Monday, January 16 I arose at seven. Wilbur came home at noon from Washington City. He went to Springfield to see Toulin. I got underwear at $2.00 and paper and envelopes, 30 cents.

Tuesday, January 17 I stay at home. Wilbur went to Springfield—came home at supper-time. Mr. Hammer is disposed to put in his whole history into a deposition!

Wednesday, January 18 Wilbur is again at Springfield, Mr Hammer's deposition. I went to the Wright Company's Shop out west. I called to see Mary Hatfield, 93 years old, at her daughter's Belle Weidner's. She thought I was W..J. Shuey! I wrote on my diary of 1859, very late.

Thursday, January 19 Katharine went to town and supped at Mrs. F.H. Russell's. I wrote in transcribing my diary of 1859.

Friday, January 20 I was at home. I transcribed much in my diary of 1859. Miss Osborn, Mrs. J.L. Stevens and xx were in for a game.

Saturday, January 21 I am recording my diary of 1859. Edwin Sines called in to see Orville. Katharine was out feasting.

Monday, January 23 My sample of pictures come from Miss Reece. Seven kinds. Two standing—one with hat on; two front views; three profile likenesses.

Tuesday, January 24 This afternoon, Netta Wright and her son Horace Went to Canton, Ohio, on a visit to her sister Clare Andrews and family. Lorin and Milton board with us while they are away. Ivonette and Leontine board at grandmother Corbett's.

Wednesday, January 25 I am recording a new diary of 1859, the old being small, disconnected and incomplete.

Thursday, January 26 Lorin and Milton eat meals with us. I finish my diary of 1859.

Friday, January 27 Lorin and Milton board with us. I write letters. And I revise my transcript of diary of 1859.

Saturday, January 28 I am critically examining my revised diaries of 1858 and 1859. Katharine and Mrs. Guthrie visit Mrs. L. Stevens. A man selling grape juice calls; and a manufacturer of engines. The one was silly; the other "smart."

Sunday, January 29 I staid at home. It was rainy, and warm. Ivonette and Leontine eat Supper with us, and visit in the evening. They are nice little girls. Ivonette is tall.

Monday, January 30 It is cooler and a sunshiny day. I wrote a long letter to Richard F. Braden, explaining about the Shorts' deaths, her half sisters; the relics, the Van Cleves in Dayton; the Van Cleves and Boones, and Mrs. Hatfield and Sophie Simpson's. Eleanor Stoltz called. Netta and Horace came home. I wrote also to Crystal Reeder.

Tuesday, January 31 Slight snow on the ground and cloudy. Katharine visits Mrs. F.H. Russell, this aftern. Katharine went out in an automobile with Mr. Guthrie's and others in evening.

Wednesday, February 1 Moderate weather. I got letters from Jesse Lefforge and Reuchlin. Mr. Meachem called in the evening. He dined and supped with us. Carrie Nation is sinking.

Thursday, February 2 Mr. [blank] Meachern dined with us. He was Margaret Goodwin's husband.

Sunday, February 5 I went to Germantown on the 8:30 car. I reached there about 10:00. Rev. John Freeman preached, Ps. 66.18, a good sermon. I dine at Fout's with Freeman and wife and Bro. Sunday. Sup there. Freeman pr at night, "Examine yourselves," 2 Cor. 13.5. I held a speaking meeting. Excellent. I left at 9:10. Got home at 11:00. Saw a Reform student on cars.

Tuesday, February 7 Letter from J. Howe, giving the

Orville and Wilbur Wright on the porch of the Hawthorne Street house in 1909

voice of Book Committee that I should be asked to write our Church History.

Wednesday, February 8 Katharine went to Mrs. Frank Russell's in the evening.

Thursday, February 9 Wilbur was home at noon from New York. I called at Lorin's at 5:30, Afternoon.

Friday, February 10 Katharine supped at Miss Meyer's.

Saturday, February 11 Miss Ryder supped with us— Winifred.

Sunday, February 12 Attended Communion service and assisted at Broadway M.E. Church, in Morning. Attended baptismal service in the evening. Two children of six years old, were baptized. Also about thirty grown or younger persons were baptized. The house was very full.

Tuesday, February 14 I was quite lame in my back. I slept two hours at least. This is valentine evening, and Orville surprised Horace as he stealthily brought valentines into the porch.

Wednesday, February 15 This is for the 14th. I was very lame in my back. I slept considerably. The children brought in Valentines. I wrote letters to Bishop Hoskins and others, on the 15th. Katharine got me a Church History at Telescope Office. She spends the afternoon at T.H. Russell's. Lorin and Netta called.

Thursday, February 16 Dr. Spitler came, at Katharine's call, and left me some medicine.

Friday, February 17 Winifred Rider supped with us, and Katharine went with her to High School, and lodged with her.

Saturday, February 18 Letter from J.T. Miller saying that Indiana Conf. is dissolved. I sent early letters to C.A. Mummart and Edwin H. Stow, our church poet.

Sunday, February 19 At Park Presbyterian Church, I heard William Gilbert preach John 12.21. He misconstrued the text to mean that they preferred his teaching to his redemption on the cross. Mrs. Wagner and [blank]

happened to be there to hear Huber. Horace came in the afternoon (and snowballed) and his mother & Sisters, later on.

Monday, February 20 Ema Ragan is not well and is absent. Katharine has the work to do. I somehow am wakeful to-night. I generally sleep well.

Tuesday, February 21 I write many letters to-day. Among them is one to C.A. Mummart showing that pneuma is chiefly used in N.J. for the Holy Spirit. It is a neuter noun. Emma still absent.

Wednesday, February 22 Emma again here. Mrs. J.L. Stevens came and she and Katharine visit Lottie Jones, who has been sick two weeks.

Friday, February 24 I wrote of William Otterbein.

Sunday, February 26 I heard Maurice E. Wilson preach at First Presbyterian Church, Matt. 11.28–30, a good sermon. I slept not more than four hours. Before going to bed, I looked up New Testament doctrine on Divine Evidence of the reality of Vital Religion.

Monday, February 27 I arose early and wrote my recollections of my first term as bishop, on the secrecy part. Visited C.J. Kephart and family.

Tuesday, February 28 Wrote an article on "Are the Scriptures Inspired?" and mailed it in the evening.

Wednesday, March 1 I wrote Sina Ardery of Uncle George taking me to a show in Clarksburg, in 1834.

Thursday, March 2 Revised my writing of Otterbein, etc. All Lorin's supped with us. Wrote to Reuchlin.

Saturday, March 4 Misses Mayer brought some coffee cake that her sister had made.

Tuesday, March 7 Katharine visited Miss Mayer. It rained to-day.

Wednesday, March 8 I wrote on United Brethren. Katharine was at Mrs. Russel's.

Thursday, March 9 I wrote on Lawrence's "United Brethren." Mrs. Ford, Mrs. Frank Russell, and Mrs. Henry, a sister of Russell's mother were at Katharine's in the afternoon. Lorin's, except Milton visited us an hour this evening.

Friday, March 10 Mr. W.S. Burgess from Boston, one of Wilbur's parties, dined with us. It is a nice day. I wrote my United Brethren History.

Saturday, March 11 I wrote on United Brethren History. Nice, fair day.

Sunday, March 12 My clock deceived me, and I did not get to Church. Frank H. Russell came before dinner. Milton and Horace came to bid Wilbur farewell. Wilbur started for New York and to Paris a quarter before four. Horace staid to supper.

Monday, March 13 Nothing of special interest to-day. I wrote to Robt. B. Broyles.

Tuesday, March 14 I look over papers, and find I have a deed for a lot in North Harvey, belonging to the Shisler estate, that I gave to some one, some years ago, and thought it had been disposed of! Mr. R.Bellville Osborn was knocked down by a street car and was hurt very badly.

Wednesday, March 15 Mr. Osborn is getting along well. It is Agnes' father.

Thursday, March 16 Writing on History of "United Brethren". John Gilbert died to-day. Mrs. J. L. Stevens sups with Katharine this evening. They go to hear Victor Murdock at Y.M.C.A.

Friday, March 17 We breakfast at 7:00, with Mrs. J.L. Stevens, here. I call at Gilbert's. Rev. Wm. Gilbert had bought his railroad ticket before his father's death.

Saturday, March 18 I attended John Gilbert's funeral at Summit Street Churct at 2:00. Rev. Clippinger, preached, text, 2 Cor. 4.6–8. [words missing?] Osborn, who is getting along well.

Sunday, March 19 Heard Rev. M.B. Fuller, of Grace Church, Phil. 1.21. It is a bright day. At Young Men's Chr. Associa heard a minister who was shallow. Horace and Leontine supped with us.

Monday, March 20 I spent the afternoon in writing for United Brethren book.

Tuesday, March 21 I worked to-day on a history of John Gotleib Koerner's family, which I rewrote. In the afternoon and for supper, Agnes Osborn, Mrs. (Lorenz) Stevens and Miss Mayer were with us.

Wednesday, March 22 I wrote up John G. Koerner and his family, to be preserved.

Thursday, March 23 Miss Winifred Ryder and Miss Kimball of Madison, Ohio, dined with us and spent the afternoon. Miss Ryder told of her father teaching here on West Side, boarding with Robert Norris, and hearing Henry Garst preach.

Friday, March 24 Orville and Katharine go to First Pres[b]yterian Church for supper.

Saturday, March 25 I do not much to-day. Write a little. Orville goes out to Simm's. Their machines not in good order.

Sunday, March 26 Heard Rev. Mr.[blank] Euland, at Grace M.E. Church, 2 Peter 2.9, a good sermon. Rev. Fuller is quite sick. The day is slightly rainy. Katharine went to Winifred Ryder's, awhile in the evening.

Monday, March 27 I wrote several letters to-day: to Samuel Hall, to Mrs. W.B. Baulware, to Rev. L.E. Cole, to Lizzie Brookbanks, C.R. Paddack.

Tuesday, March 28 Received a letter from Hon. Frank Reeder, who says that he knew Admiral Re[e]der for 40 years, who said the family tradition was that they were from England, and after a brief stay on Long Island, about the year 1700, settled in Maryland. He married Admiral Well's only daughter. The family lived on the same place six or seven generations.

Wednesday, March 29 Lieut. Rogers, Clif. Turpin and Ph. O. Parmalee sup with us.

Sunday, April 2 Heard [blank] at Broadway, on Acts 8.4. Lieut. Rodgers and his uncle Munsen called, afternoon. Mrs. Ford and Russells and Guthries call. Horace sups with us.

Monday, April 3 Somewhat snowy. Mrs. Ford starts home to Northern New York, to Mannville. She is Mrs. Russell's mother.

Tuesday, April 4 Rainy morning. The called session of Congress meets. Champ Clark is elected speaker of the House. Joe Cannon falls into the ranks. Gov. Hamon and Wm. Bryan are there, not members. Katharine attends the Christian League meeting.

Thursday, April 6 Katharine dined at Mrs. Guthrie's. Frank H. Russell dined with us.

Sunday, April 9 Went to Germantown. Heard Rev. J. Freeman, Gal. 6.9. I dine at E.M. Scott's, who is farming a mile north-west of the town. Freeman & wife, and Lizzie Long dine with us. I stay till 6:00, and come home on traction. I some way took a miserable cold, the first for years.

Tuesday, April 11 My cold and hoarseness is not much better. It is influenza.

Wednesday, April 12 Agnes Osborn sups with us, and She and Katharine attend the marriage of Lorenz daughter [blank] to Prof. [blank]Showers, the 11th. It was E.S. Lorenze's daughter.

Thursday, April 13 Lieut. Rodgers and Mr. Andre Roosevelt, both aviator students, sup with us.

Friday, April 14 Orville and Katharine supped at Russell's, with Lieut. Rodgers and Mr. Roosevelt of St. Louis, who buys a machine.

Saturday, April 15 At supper, we had Wood, [blank] McCormack (Reaper Man), McScutcheon, [blank]Ebberhart, F.H. Russell.

Monday, April 17 I wrote to Bro. J. Howe, that I would not be able to attend the board meeting. I had written

Bishop Wood to same effect at Junction City.

Wednesday, April 19 The Missionary Board was to meet at 2:00, at Zion Church, near Junction City, Ohio. It met and transacted its business. I did not attend.

Thursday, April 20 Mr. [blank] Roosevelt supped with us.

Friday, April 21 I slept much to-day. Lieut. Rodgers called in the evening. Marcus Glass graduated in Lincoln High School, this evening.

Sunday, April 23 I did not attend Church, not able. The Dr. (Spitler) came, and prescribed that I be kept in bed to avoid catching cold.

Monday, April 24 The Doctor left the same prescription. Left considerable medicine. Kept me in bed.

Thursday, April 27 The doctor did not come to-day. Katharine went to a College Club meeting. Lorin came at 4:30. Wrote to pay my taxes in Grant Co., Indiana.

Friday, April 28 Crystal Reeder graduated at Matthews High School, this evening. Also, Ovid Reeder, as president of the class.

Thursday, May 4 I walked to Third Street Bridge and back home.

Friday, May 5 I walked to Fourth Presbyterian Church and home again .

Sunday, May 7 Lieutenants Rodgers, of the navy, and Lieuts. H.H. Arnold and T.D. Milling of the army, supped with us. They are here to learn to fly.

Saturday, May 13 Summer weather. I wrote the "Three Dispensations," finishing to-morrow. Katharine went to Miami Hospital to see about her kid, Mr. Bonney.

Wednesday, May 17 Got my watch with new mainspring, $1.00.

Thursday, May 18 Katharine attended dinner at Miami Hospital to see that Mr. Bonney lived through it. He had gastric trouble and his doctor, Barker, and the Hospital doctor thought he had peritonitus, and favored an operation, and performed an operation, unnecessarily. Dr. Conklin advised against it. This was a former day.

Friday, May 19 Rev. Mr. Ford and Mr. F.H. Russell and his wife supped with us, and staid till bed-time. Mr. Ford was Russell's fatherinlaw, not living with wife.

Saturday, May 20 It has been very warm weather for over a week's time, the thermometer registering 94 degrees some day's. There was some change for the cooler this afternoon.

Tuesday, May 23 Mr. Bonney came to our house in the evening, to board. At the Hospital the diet was not adapted to him, and at Christian Association it was unsuitable.

Sunday, May 28 I remained at home all day. Lieut. Arnold called in afternoon & Lieut. Rodgers, and Mr. Frank Coffyn, who had been at Augusta, Georgia, and San Antonio, Texas, teaching Lieut. Folois. Corner Stone of Liberal U.B. Church laid at Corner of Third and Euclid Sts., at 3:00. I was present.

Monday, May 29 Mr. Leonard W. Bonney went to see Dr. Barker this morning.

Wednesday, May 31 Mrs.[blank] Roosevelt dined with us, and they went to Simm's Aviation grounds. Mrs. J.L. Stevens called. I went at 7:00 evening to Lorin's. Nettie and Leontine walked home with me.

Thursday, June 1 Katharine went to Simms with Anna Feight. She came home an hour earlier than the rest, to get supper, Emma Ragan staying home because a friend had convulsions on the death of her husband. Mr. and Mrs. Guthrie spent the evening with us.

Friday, June 2 Katharine gets breakfast. Ruth [blank] comes to do Katharine's work. Katharine goes to Simms, and Orville flies, to test some experiments. Supper at 7:00.

Sunday, June 4 I am at home. Horace comes as usual. Lieuts. H.H. Arnold and Milling sup with us. Orville cites at length his and Wilbur's experiments and trans-

actions. The Lieutenants leave at 11:00.

Saturday, June 10 Katharine went to Winifred Ryder's for supper and to spend the evening. To-day was very hot. The Government reports at some places were 98 degrees.

Sunday, June 11 It was a warm day. Russell's came in the afternoon and Katharine went with them in a carriage. Lieuts. Arnold called & Milling. Knabenshue & Russell came at nearly nine with Katharine, and I went with them to Milton's Schoolhouse in the automobile.

Monday, June 12 Katharine went to Agnes Osborn's for supper in the evening. A cable dispatch from London was delivered to Orville, and he could not read it. It proved not to be to his at all!

Tuesday, June 13 Katharine had Mrs. Russell, Mrs. Florence Guthrie and Mrs. Stevens in to see her in the afternoon. We had a little fire in the evening.

Wednesday, June 14 Mr. H. Beck, Winifred Ryder, Miss Brett, Agnes Osborn and Mrs. Stevens took supper with us. We had fire in the evening.

Thursday, June 15 The morning is cool. To-night is Commencement Evening at High School, and Katharine attended.

Friday, June 16 Somewhat cool to-day, and a little rainy. Orville and Katharine go to Frank Russell's, in the evening, after supper.

Saturday, June 24 Mr. Frank McClean of London, England, and Mr. Lockyer, son of a distinguished astronomer, dined with us. Mr. Lockyer himself is an astronomer. Mr. McClean is an aviator, and Kath. & Orv. knew them in London.

Sunday, June 25 Mr. McClean and Lockyer came and dined with us, and they rode in an Automobile to Dayton View, Cash Register, Oakwood and Centerville with Orville and Katharine. McClean is six feet high and well built. I called at Lorin's an hour.

Tuesday, June 27 Agnes Osborn and Mr. Howard Beck

were married at Fourth Presbyterian Church at 8:30. They went on 9:50 train north. Miss Mayer, Miss Hunter and Mrs. J. Steven called and went with Katharine to see the weddingers start on the train.

Friday, June 30 Mr. James "Ben" Guthrie and Mrs. Florence Guthrie are packing to remove to New York, and she tired out. Katharine had them dine and sup with us. And she and I rode in auto-mobile with them to Oakwood. We saw John F. Rodgers fly on his cousin Galbraith's machine, at J.M. Patterson's grounds. Orville and Katharine went with them to Russell's.

Sunday, July 2 Roy Knabenshue came and staid an hour. We went on a ride with him in an auto-mobile beyond Milton's School-house, and across to the Cincinnati pike & back home.

Monday, July 3 To-day was "the warmest in fifty years." I slept comfortably at night with the electric fan blowing on me.

Tuesday, July 4 It was hotter to-day than yesterday. Susan died twenty-two years ago. Lorin's went to Trotwood yester-day to a picknick.

Wednesday, July 5 I called at Lorin's in forenoon. Horace went to picnic yester-day and two of his little chickens died in the pen, of heat. We rode out to Oakwood and came up Cincinnati pike to Russell's, where we had ice cream. I got to bed at 10:00.

Thursday, July 6 I am at home. Mt. Zion Church, in Rush County, Ind., was struck, by lightning, to night, and burned down. The people got all out, except the stoves; all the windows, except two.

Friday, July 7 I staid at home. Jesse Lefforge wrote me of the loss of Mt. Zion Church.

Sunday, July 9 Rev. Wm. J. Gabey died at 7:30, morning at Miami Valley Hospital, from an operation for appendicitus. He was pastor of the Trinity Reformed Lutheran Church. I heard Rev. D. Frank Garland speak on his death at First Lutheran Church, at 10:30. I wrote Wilbur but failed to mail letter. Katharine went to [unreadable] Lieut. Rodgers called.

Tuesday, July 11 Horace's birth-day. I gave him a dollar. His Aunt Katharine gave him a dollar or two. Russell's gave him a book. Orville ordered him a tent. Lorin gave him a fishing pole. He dined with us. Gaby's funeral.

Wednesday, July 12 I went via Anderson to Fairmount. Ate at Richmond. I settled with Charles F. Parker. He had spent the rent in improvements. Went to Oliver Buller's. Ate Supper. Oliver came home. I lodged at Buller's.

Thursday, July 13 Settled with Mr. Welsh for Temporary warehouse to August 15th. Settled with Mr. Buller. He paid $15.01. I was at Friends Church at Homer Reeve's funeral. Stanton's Text, John 1.4. I ate at a restaurant. Rhoda Wright took me to Ellis Wright's. I lodged there.

Friday, July 14 Myrl Wright took me to the farm, on which Roy Millspaugh lives. I looked at the place and dined there, and talked with him on renting. I walked to Levi Simon's and talked with Mrs. Simons and Mrs. Korn and his daughter, the Hospital nurse. His son took me to Ellis's. Mrs. Haisley and some children there.

Saturday, July 15 I called to see Frank Kirkwood, and went to Wm. Reeder's and dined. I called at Robert B. Reeder's and went to 2:15 train. I reached Richmond at 4:20 and home at 6:00. Walter Harvey wanted to Rent the farm.

Sunday, July 16 Weather cool and pleasant. Walter Brookins came in the afternoon and sought the agency of California in the Flying business. Agnes (Osborn) Beck and Glenn Osborn came in the evening. Mr. Emmons and Mary (Osborn) called. Horace was here and staid till 10:00 at night.

Monday, July 17 At home. Katharine went to Fairview to a show by the College Club, with Mr. L.W. Bonney.

Tuesday, July 18 In afternoon, Miss Stevens, Mrs. Russell, and Mrs. Emmons came in for a game with Katharine. Mr. Guthrie came and took me on Broadway to Germantown pike to Soldier's Home & on 5th Str., back home. Katharine went with Mrs. Stevens to her niece's.

Wednesday, July 19 Orville went to Aeroplane Club for dinner and Katharine to Mrs. Russell's.

Sunday, July 23 We went (Orville, Katharine, myself and Mr. Brewer and his wife) with Mr. James "Ben" Guthrie, to Ft. Ancient, via Beavertown, Spring Grove, etc. Oregonia to Ft. Ancient, and returned by Lebanon and Centerville. Our fourth accident was the breaking of the off rear wheel of the auto-mobile.

Monday, July 24 Lieut. Frank H. Lahm & Mr. Brewer & wife were with us. They went to Simms. Lieut. Lahm lodged with us.

Tuesday, July 25 Lieut. Lahm lodged at Our house.

Wednesday, July 26 Orville and Lahm arrive at home late (9:30) from Simms, cars late.

Thursday, July 27–Saturday, July 29 The folks go to Simms Station.

Sunday, July 30 We, Orville, Katharine, Mr and Mrs. Brewer & Lieut. Lahm, went in an automobile to Milton's Schoolhouse and nearly Xenia, and back home. Mr. Brewer's go on the 7:40 train to Niagara Falls.

Tuesday, August 1 The folks attended the grounds at Simms.

Wednesday, August 2 Letter from Wilbur to Katharine from [blank] saying it is very hot in England. Orville started, to meet the Executive Committe[e] of Wright Company in New York, at 3:43 P.M. Mr. Andre Rosevelt & wife & Mr. Myer came, to have a play.

Thursday, August 3 I wrote to Jacob Howe, Katharine visited Miss Mayer.

Friday, August 4 Lorin's children all visited us, dinner and supper. Mr. Frank H. Russell supped with us and staid till 10:00. Arbitration treaties between the United States and England are signed by Secretary Knox and Ambassador Brice at 3:10 and with France a minute later.

Saturday, August 5 At home all day. The arbitration treaties are submitted to the Senate, and authorized by that body to be made public.

Sunday, August 6 The Morning *Journal* contains the treaty with England, full text. Milton, Leontine and Horace dined with us and supped with us. Ivonette was not very well.

Monday, August 7 Carrier delivered letters early. Mr. F. Russell supped with us and staid till 10:00. Lorin's got home from north Michigan.

Thursday, August 10 Wilbur and Orville arrived home from New York at 12:00 noon. Wilbur left home March 12th. Roy Knabenshue called after dinner. Lorin and Leontine called in the evening. Horace spent the evening with Wilbur and Orville. Ther., 87 degrees.

Friday, August 11 Wilbur and Orville are both at home. Orville starts at 9:40 p.m., to the meet at Chicago. It turns cooler about 8:00. It was 98 degrees in the porch, afternoon. Lorin and Netta called at 8:30.

Saturday, August 12 I "chilled" and slept some hours. Took a half-mile's walk just before noon and another in the evening. Wilbur and Katharine walked to their lot on Salem Avenue.

Sunday, August 13 As it is likely to be a warm day, I gave out going to Rev. John Freeman's last appointment at Germantown. After 3:00 p.m. we had a fine shower of rain. Horace came and staid till 8:00.

Monday, August 14 It was a warm day. Yesterday's report seemed to not have the Wright Company in it, at Chicago Meet. Atwood is reported on his aeroplane race from San Francisco to New York.

Tuesday, August 15 Some Aviators are reported to have fallen in the Lake at Chicago Meet. Atwell is reported to be near Chicago. He has a Burges-Wright machine. Wilbur and Katharine went to Oakwood, to see about the location.

Wednesday, August 16 Mrs. Bruff and a Mr. Aikman, pastor of the Christian Allowance (Cor. of Fifth and Walnut St.) called. They wished me to preach, the 24th at their meeting. Mary (Muller) Hinton is in the South.

Has two churches W. and K. again visited Oakwood nearly night.

Thursday, August 17 We all called at Lorin's in the evening.

Friday, August 18 Reuchlin and Bertha came from Kansas.

Saturday, August 19 We all took supper at Lorin's. It is Orville's and Katharine's 40th and 37th birth-day.

Sunday, August 20 Reuchlin and I attend the Park Presbyterian Church and hear J.G. Huber pr Phil. 4.8. It was a good sermon.

Wednesday, August 23 Katharine dines at Miss Mayer's. Reuchlin and Bertha go to Aunt Bedell's for supper. Bertha stays there.

Thursday, August 24 Katharine has Mr. Chas. F. Chandler for dinner. He is a nice behaved man. Lorin and Chandler go out to Simms. I wrote a card to Flora Glass, and sent a page of genealogical matter to Robert Reeder.

Friday, August 25 Reuchlin and I supped at Lorin's. Mr. Andre Roosevelt and wife spent an hour with us.

Saturday, August 26 Harry N. Atwood makes 20 flights, Averaging 63 1/4 miles. Captain Chandler comes home with Orville for supper, and stays till bed-time. Wilbur meets the Ten Dayton Boys at his office. Reuchlin takes supper at Mrs. Ramsey's. Harry N. Atwood completes, at 2:38, his flight from St. Louis to, New York City. Well done.

Sunday, August 27 Reuchlin and I attended Grace Lutheran Church and heard H.B. Burkholder pr, Mark 2.1–12. It is at the corner of May and Torrence St. The granddaughters, Ivonette, Leontine and Bertha dine with us. Reuchlin, Bertha, Ivonette, Leontine and our folks, take an auto ride to Milton's School-house and up Xenia Pike.

Monday, August 28 There are fine rains. Wilbur's complaint against motorman for failing to stop Oakwood st. car at corner is decided in his favor.

Tuesday, August 29 Lorin's and Reuchlin and Bertha and Orville and Katharine go out to Simms and the three girls fly with Orville. They all sup with us. Milton starts to Mackinac Island in forenoon. Mrs. Sines calls in the afternoon.

Wednesday, August 30 Reuchlin flew some ten minutes and about 400 feet high, with Orville, at Simms.

Thursday, August 31 H.N. Atwood's flights: 20 flights; Distance covered 1265 ms. Started St. Louis, Aug. 14, 8:05, Finished at Gov. Island 26, 2:38; Whole time: 28 hours, 31 minutes. The trip beats the world's record, 101 miles.

Friday, September 1 Reuchlin went to Simms and flew with Orville some half an hour. They rose about 1600 or 1800 feet high. They shut off the motor and sank some hundreds of feet.

Saturday, September 2 Prof. David Dennis and Cousin Emma came in an auto-mobile at 10:00. At three o'clock, they go home to Richmond, Ind., and take Bertha, Ivonette and Leontine with them. Ed. Sines came to see Reuchlin and talked an hour or so. Captain C.F. Chandler came home with Orville, late.

Sunday, September 3 Went to Grace M.E. Church. I am called on to speak. I was cheered as I arose. I sat on the rostrum and pronounced the benediction. Bishop [blank] Moore spoke. Text: 1 Tim. 1.15, "This is a faithful." Mr. Roosevelt was here. Joseph Boyd called in the evening. Bertha and Lorin's girls came from Richmond at 9:00. Horace wrote his grandmother.

Monday, September 4 Reuchlin and Bertha started to their home in Kansas, at 8:45. Lorin, Orville, Katharine, and Lorin's girls go to the depot with them. Our young folks go to Wright's Flying grounds and I to Lorin's to supper. They sup at Roosevelt's. Captain Charles de F. Chandler's name is on to-morrow's record.

Tuesday, September 5 I slept most of the forenoon. Captain Chandler dined with us. He is a modest, nice man. He starts to Washington to-night at 8:40. Orville sees him go.

Thursday, September 7 Wilbur started at 3:00 to New York to look after the lawsuit. I wrote Bertha Glaze, and enclosed my mortgage and notes on J.F. Croddy's lot. It was on $90.00, that I loaned him to pay off with. He never paid me anything. But I sent him from 10 to 30 $ each year.

Friday, September 8 Katharine visits at a party, at Mr. Andre Roosevelt's, Agnes (Osborne) and Howard Beck, being of the company.

Saturday, September 9 I was at home. Miss Winifred Ryder came for supper and staid till 9:00.

Sunday, September 10 I heard Rev. M.B. Fuller preach on The Transfiguration, Mat. 17.8. Horace came and staid till Lorin came after him at 8:00. Mr. [blank] DeLong, a former compositor (with Rigler) called on me.

Monday, September 11 Milton called in the evening and told of his trip to Mackinac Island, his fishing and so forth. I wrote letters to Lizzie Brookbanks, Flora Glass & others.

Tuesday, September 12 Katharine goes to Andre Roosevelt's (at F.H. Russel's) at 8:00, eve. Orville meets Charlie Taylor at O's office. A.L.Welsh calls. It rains hard at 11:00, eve. Katharine comes home at 12:00, as it rained very hard at 11:00.

Thursday, September 14 Rainy, I called at Lorin's. Bade Milton good by.

Friday, September 15 Milton went to Oxford, to College.

Sunday, September 17 Lorin's dine with us, and remain till 4:00. It is Leontines 13th anniversary of her birth.

Monday, September 18 Mr. Alex. Ogilvie came at 12:00 and dined with us. He and Orville go to Simms together.

Wednesday, September 20 I received a card from Lorin, written at Norfolk. Va., the 19th.

Thursday, September 21 Election in Canada. Winifred Laurier is badly defeated. Reciprocity is defeated.

Galbraith Rogers flies westward again.

Friday, September 22 Emma "went to Emancipation Day." I dined at Lorin's; he is at Kitty Hawk, N.C.

Saturday, September 23 Went to Grant Co. Ind. Went to Leroy Millspaugh's on my farm. Went to Ellis's. Lodged there.

Sunday, September 24 Ellis' hogs got into his corn. Myrl took me to Hopewell. Rev. Ralph Richardson preached Rev. 22.2. I dine at Frank Kirkwood's with Richardson. We attend a Methodist Protestant Sunday-School performance. I go to Ellis's in the evening. He staid at home and we talked all the evening.

Monday, September 25 I went to Millspaugh's and we fixed out our articles of Agreement. I went to Robert B. Re[e]der's for dinner. Went to William's for supper and lodging.

Tuesday, September 26 Millspaugh came and we signed up dulipcate articles; and I went to Fowlerton, and to Fairmount. I went on noon train to Knightstown. I found my way to Noah Rhoad's. Jabez came after me, and I had supper and lodging at his house.

Wednesday, September 27 Jabez took me to Delila's— Edward Frazer's. Delila after she told her troubles seemed well-content. I remained there till morning. Druzilla McKee staid there. Gusta Whitney and Alma Fry and her Lois [blank]were there and she went and brought Lois (11 years old) from school.

Thursday, September 28 Grace took me to Augusta Whitton's, and I went with her to Esta Grubb's at Rushville. Her boy is also a great-grandson of Harvey and Delila Wright. We found Nicholas Frank Bowen in Rushville, and I went to Orange with him. Dined. Supped with Ralph Bowen's on the farm. They took me to Lucinda Moor's.

Friday, September 29 I went, with Aunt Lucy and Bertha, to Chas. Steven's, where I staid till night. I went thence with Charlie to "Sonna" Bowen's. I lodged there.

Saturday, September 30 I went with Nicholas F. Bowen

to traction car (7:38) at Glenwood. I waited near two hours at Connersville and near two hours at Hamilton and got home at about 1:20. I slept some hours. The Austin Flood occurred in Penns. Italy declares war against Turkey.

Sunday, October 1 I slept well last night and late this morning. I was sleepy all forenoon. Wilbur came home from New York. Lorin is at home from Kitty Hawk, North Carolina. Leontine and Horace visited us in the afternoon.

Monday, October 2 P.M. General Hitchcock names Mr. Ovington as Aviator Mail Carrier from New York to Los Angeles, "Route 607,001." I wrote Reuchlin, of my trip to Indiana.

Wednesday, October 4 I find in the Conservator of to-day, that Rev. Mummart has resigned the editorhsip of the Conservator, and Dr. Dillon was elected, on the fortieth ballot, to succeed him.

Thursday, October 5 Wilbur and Orville and Katharine and Mr. Oglevie went with Mr. S. Crane in a Franklin auto-mobile to Fort Ancient and got back before supper-time. This is Registration day, and I registered; and Wilbur & Orville registered at night.

Friday, October 6 Milton came home from Oxford. There are about a hundred in his class there. This is for Friday.

Saturday, October 7 Lorin and Orville, with Horace and Mr. Ogilvie start at 6:00, eve for Kitty Hawk, N.C.

Sunday, October 8 I heard Rev. C.L. Work, a former pastor of the Fourth Presbyterian Church, at Park Street Presbyterian Church, Matt. 27.22, a fine discourse. Mr and Mrs Guthrie came in the evening. Katharine and I went via Mr. Russell's to Miss Mayer's. Father Mayer is nearly 87 year's old.

Monday, October 9 Katharine is out in town and Mrs. Guthrie dines with her. They spend the evening at Miss Mayer's and get home, a quarter before 12:00. Wilbur started to St. Louis at 11:30. Mr. Guthrie started to

Detroit, in afternoon, and Mrs. Guthrie stayed with Katharine.

Tuesday, October 10 It rained last night. I breakfasted at 7:20, and slept two hours. Mrs. Guthrie dined with us. She went to Elyria, Ohio, where her people live. Katharine attended the Young Women's League, where men tried to persuade them to unite with Young Women's Association. They unanimously dissented and expressed their views.

Wednesday, October 11 Wilbur came home in forenoon and started to New York in afternoon. I wrote Reuchlin. Wrote Milton a short letter. Mr. F.H. Russell came and lodged with us. Calvert Rogers has beaten the world's record in distance of flights.

Friday, October 13 Mr. Russell is with us. We went in Mr. Crane's auto-mobile to the depot with him and Katharine. And Crane took an extra ride with us (Nettie and her girls) in his Franklin automobile. Mr. Russell, a nice man left us with "put on" cheerfulness. He lacked capacity. Nettie and the girls lodge with us.

Saturday, October 14 It is slightly rainy in the morning. I am quite lame in my left knee, rheumatism. Wrote a letter to Treasurer of Grant County, Ind., about the amount of second payment of my tax.

Sunday, October 15 I remained at home on account of lameness in my left knee - rheumatism, which has troubled me several days. Wilbur came home from New York in the forenoon. Netta and the girls went home in the afternoon.

Wednesday, October 18 Went to Nook's on Pontiac Avenue. They sent the money to pay for Constance's return to America, but had it returned. Her letters say she is anxious to return, and others report her unwilling to come.

Thursday, October 19 Get letter from Orville and night telegram from Katharine from Geneva, Ohio. She says she goes to Oberlin Saturday at noon, and comes home Monday at 6:00.

Saturday, October 21 Katharine went from Geneva, to Oberlin.

Sunday, October 22 Wilbur and I dine at Lorin's. I am troubled with rheumatism in my left knee.

Monday, October 23 Telegram from Katharine saying Kate Leonard had arranged for some company in the afternoon, to-day, and that she would come at 6:00 to-morrow eve.

Tuesday, October 24 Telegram from Katharine that she would come home on 6:00 train eve. I went over in automobile with Spencer Crane to meet her. Her train was nearly a half hour late. Calvin Stevens died to-day, diabetus, uramic poisoning. Orville remained in the air nearly ten minutes without a motor.

Wednesday, October 25 Received a letter from Jesse Lefforge and answered it. News of Orville remaining in the air nearly ten minutes at Kill Devil Hill, in a fifty-mile wind, yesterday. Mrs. Sines called.

Monday, October 30 Orville and Ogilvie leave Manteo, and reach Elizabeth City.

Tuesday, October 31 Orville and Ogilvie and Horace get home a little after noon Halloween night.

Wednesday, November 1 Lorin gets home afternoon. I get a draft and send $82.47 cents to pay my tax in Indiana. Mr. Aleck Ogilvie starts home to London. Tailor came to fit two coats and one overcoat.

Saturday, November 4 The tailor brings me a new overcoat. The boys try a Curtiss machine, at Simms, and break it.

Monday, November 6 Receive my receipts for taxes in Grant County, Indiana, $82.47.

Tuesday, November 7 Election Day. Democrat's elect mayors in Ohio's principal cities, but the Republicans, in Dayton, by a plurality of nearly 500, elected Edward Phillips for mayor. Massachusetts gave Foss (Democrat) a sleight plurality. New York and Maryland and Nebraska voted Republicans in.

Wednesday, November 8 I wrote to J. Hoffhines. Orrville went, afternoon, to Simms Station to try a Curtis machine.

Thursday, November 9 Wilbur went out to try the Curtis machine. It is hard to fly with.

Friday, November 10 I wrote to Wm. Reeder. Richard Braden and Mary Krout about a monument to the Reeder graves; Grandfather and Grandmother's graves, and Aunt Sarah Croddy's.

Saturday, November 11 I called at Lorin's in the forenoon. Netta tells of roughness of the Sophomores to the Freshmen. Milton was laid up a few hours, and another at their house had his leg broken. Wrote John Croddy about his mother's monument. Suits of clothes brought home. Every day & Sunday.

Monday, November 13 Wilbur started to New York City, to see about Curtis's evidence.

Tuesday, November 14 Katharine dined at Mrs. Mary Emmons.

Friday, November 17 We had a birth-day supper at 7:00. I ate well of ice cream. Netta provided a birth-day cake, on which there were eighty-three lights — all blown out but one, and it burned clear out. Lorin's, except Milton, were here; and Wilbur is in New York City.

Saturday, November 18 This is Lorin's birth-day. He is forty-nine years old.

Sunday, November 19 Horace spent the afternoon and till after 8 o'clock with his uncle Orville. Mr. Raase Emmerson called in the forenoon. He is an expert in Railroad matters.

Wednesday, November 22 Katharine went to a supper at Y.W.L. Wilbur came home at noon. Mr. A.L. Welsh called.

Thursday, November 23 The day is somewhat rainy. Received a registered letter from John S. Collier a son of Simeon S. and cousin Margaret (Braden).

Friday, November 24 Katharine is busy with embossing a cushion slip costing much work.

Saturday, November 25 Found a June letter from John S. Collier, son of Simeon & Margaret (Braden), which had come, and I had not read, and answered it.

Sunday, November 26 The children went to look after a lot out south to build upon. Lorin & Netta and three children came and spent the evening with us.

Monday, November 27 To-day is somewhat cloudy and moderately warm.

Tuesday, November 28 Cloudy day. Turns somewhat cooler in the evening. Katharine brought my black eleven slippers.

Thursday, November 30 Lorin's folks and our folks and Winifred Ryder spent a very pleasant day together. It was a nice Thanksgiving Day. I was married 52 years ago the 24th of this month. The children had a play on guessing words.

Saturday, December 2 News of the taking of Nanking, China, by the revolutionists. The McNamara brothers confess their guilt at Los Angeles, $190,000 had been collected for their defense by the Unions!

Sunday, December 3 I sent an article to the *Conservator*. Wilbur started to New York at 4:47. I wrote to Reuchlin.

Tuesday, December 5 The McNamaras were sentenced at Los Angeles, the one for life, for killing 21 persons in the *Times* Bulding; the other for fifteen years for destroying another plant. President Taft sent a message on the trusts.

Wednesday, December 6 A.L. Welsh called at noon to tell of trouble he had with frozen ground.

Thursday, December 7 Miss Mayer brought a package for Katharine. I sent some manuscripts to E.C. Mason.

Friday, December 8 Some are aroused over Miss Weaver. Her father and mother died lately of typhoid fever, and she seems to be neglected. She has same disease.

Saturday , December 9 Miss Weaver was the object of attention by special friends, Miss Greene, and Katharine. Her uncle came to see her. Was not allowed to see her.

Sunday, December 10 I called at Lorin's in the afternoon and Horace came home with me. Lorin and Netta came at 6:30 and staid till 9:00.

Monday, December 11 I sent another article to Rev. E.C. Mason.

Tuesday, December 12 Wilbur came home at noon. The decision in the trial with Grayham-White resulted in his being enjoined, which stands good till reversed on appeal.

Thursday, December 14 It was a very gloomy day. Slightly rainy. Orville and Lorin attend Chamber of Commerce proceedings. Several Governors call in Dayton on their way to Cincinnati. Captain Roald Amundsen discovered the South Pole.

Friday, December 15 Russian Attache visits Orville, and he dines with him at the hotel. It is a cloudy day.

Sunday, December 17 At home all day. I read considerably. It has been cloudy for a week past. Captain Roald Amundsen, leaves the vicinity of the South Pole.

Tuesday, December 19 President Taft sent in his message, on Finance.

Wednesday, December 20 The bill abrogating the Russian treaty is passed by both houses and sent to the president.

Thursday, December 21 Weather is very mild. A little rainy in the morning. President Taft sends in a message to Congress on Finance. It is very able.

Friday, December 22 It was a little rainy all day. Katharine sends off an embroidered cushion to Mrs. F.H. Russell, Boston.

Saturday, December 23 I sent Sovenirs to Ed. M. Harris, Aunt Lucy, Myrl, Hazel Wood, Eva. Received and answered letters from J.L. Buckwater, Reuchlin, Harvey,

R. Bradan. Charles A. Phillips, councilman, dies.

Sunday, December 24 I was at home all day and the children were. At supper, we had our Christmas dinner, Lorin's family were with us. Many presents. I got the Imperial Atlas, lamp-electric, Year Diary, pulse-warmers—Calendar Cheer, calendar. Prof. A.B. Shauck dies.

Monday, December 25 I got up before 7:00. Newsboy delivered the Journal about 8:00. It is a cloudy day. Wu Ting Fang urges noninterference with Chinese Affairs.

Tuesday, December 26 Day much as usual. At night, I was much disturbed in my bowels.

Wednesday, December 27 I was somewhat unwell. I did little to-day. Emma came back looking quite unwell. She went home after she had done the dinner dishes.

Thursday, December 28 The first bright day for weeks. At 1:00 in sunshine Ther, 55 degrees. Lafollet comes out in his Ohio campaign for [unreadable] Ref. & *Recall*. Katharine dines at Mrs. Campbell's.

Friday, December 29 It is cloudy to-day and warmer. A republic is set up in China. Senator LaFollett speaks nearly three hours at Memorial Hall. Many Democrats there.

Saturday, December 30 A little rainy again. Report from Shanghai state that is agreed to leave the form of national government to a National Convention. Pres. [blank] King of Oberlin is given a dinner at Y.M.C.A. by the Oberlin graduates. Our children attend it.

Sunday, December 31 It is rainy this morning. Pres. King attends First Baptist Church. It is bright part of Afternoon. King speaks at Y.M.C.A. at 3:00. Wilbur attended with him. This year has been one of failing power. Pres. King went away at 12:00.

Ancestors, Wrights

Our first John Wright (?) [question mark is in text] m. Olive, was probably born about the birth of Henry VIII. He died, 1551. Purchased Helvedon Hall in 1538. Is said to have attained to baronetey. His son John was

born in Henry VIII reign. He lived through King Edward VI reign and through Queen Mary's into Queen Elizabeth's reign. He m. Avis Rook's. His son John was granted coat of arms, 1690. His son, John the 4th was clerk of parliament in Oliver Cromwell's days. His coat of arms was granted in Queen Elizabeth's reign.

1. *Our Ancestors Were,* perhaps John Wrighte and Olive. They lived in the reign of Henry VIII, Helvedon, Essex Eng.
2. John Wrighte & Avis Rooke Lived at Wrightsbridge, Essex, in the reign of Elizabeth.
3. John Wrighte and (Miss) Linsell had John & Samuel and a daughter, Mrs. Huartler, at Wrights
bridge. She dying and he married the widow Green, daughter of Lawrence Blisby, London; and they had Nathanial, Lawrence and Bennett, who married Edward Sarnes.
4. Samuel m (perhaps) and had Samuel. Little is known.
5. Samuel came to America probably in 1630, had a wife Margaret, and several children, Judah, born in Springfield, in 1641, and Helped, in 1644. There is a sister Hannah; and four of the children had families with a Hannah in them, and no Margaret.
6. His son James married Abigail Jess (or Joice) and he was in the "Falls Fight" with the Indians, May 19, 1775. He married Jess, or Joyce, and had a family of children, one,
7. Samuel, who married and had a large family of sons, the youngest
8. Benoni, who married Elizabeth Smith, who had five children, the third son Dan, and died at 41 years.
9. Dan m. Sarah Freeman at Lebanon, New Hampshire in 1785, Feb. 3. and had six children, two dying unmarried.
10. His son Dan, my father, born Sept. 3, 1790, married Catharine Reeder who was my mother.
11. I mar. Susan C. Koerner (Milton Wright) Nov. 24, 1859.

The Reeder Family

1. John Reeder settled at Springfield, Mass., in 1636. He went to Newtown, Long Island, about 1657.
2. Joseph Reeder, Newtown, 1657. Had two sons, Joseph and Jacob.
3. Joseph m. Eleanor Leverich, d. of Caleb, a prosper-

ous man and a presbyterian. They had sons Joseph and Jacob, the latter (Caleb was the son of Rev. Wm.) a useful man and a school

teacher in Newtown, d. in N.Y. 4. Joseph born in Newtown had a son William. This Joseph was born in Newtown, Apr. 24, 1716, and m. his second wife Susana Gano, b. May 23, 1722. They had many sons, the oldest Joseph, b. in New Jersey, May 6, 1743. He removed to Londoun Co., Virginia in 1763.

5. His grandson, George Reeder was born there, Sept. 24, 1767, lived on Great Cacapon River in Hampshire Co., and went with his parents to Columbia, east of Cincinnati, in 1790. He had an older sister Sarah, who married Jerry Brand, of Indian descent, a good and prosperous man. She died in Butler Co., Ohio aged nearly a hundred years. Her father died at her house. Her son Vincent, was a very good man. Reeder (George) was a wagon-master in carrying goods to the forts in Ohio. In June 2nd, 1796, he m. Margaret Van Cleve, in Cincinnati, her father, John Van Cleve, having been killed by an Indian, in an out-lot, of the city, he was clearing, June 1, 1791. He lived on a part of his Father's farm on Duck Creek, near Madisonville, in Hamilton County, till 1809–1811 at Sycamore, when re removed to Centerville, Ohio and became a dry-goods merch. He left Centerville, Ohio, in 1823, settling on 80 acres of woodland (James F. Harris' farm) in Rush County, Ind., where he died May 13, 1845. He had brothers, Jonathan, Jesse, Reuben and Ralph. Jesse and Ralph were great inventors. The farmer died in St. Louis in 1854. He was a fine looking man. His (George's) daughter Catharine was named for her grandmother Catharine Van Cleve, and she was named for her grandmother Catharine (Van Dyke) Benham. I named Catharine Wright for her mother and both her grandmothers. Catharine Reeder married Dan (not Daniel) Wright, Feb. 12, 1818, and I am their 5th child - a little brother George, dying at a few months old, before the birth of my sister Sarah. The family were: Samuel Smith Wright b. Nov. 21, 1818 Harvey Wright, Sept. 9, 1820 George Wright, date unknown Sarah Wright, Nov. 21, 1824 Milton Wright, Nov. 17, 1828 William Wright, Feb. 29, 1833. (Unnamed) Wright, died a well

developed child, at its birth. I named her Kate.

Milton Wright.

Freeman Ancestry

My grand-mother Wright was Sarah Freeman, the oldest daughter of Captain Edmund Freeman, one of the best of men.

The Freeman Family

1. Edmond Freeman, from England, brought his wife Elizabeth and children with him, in to Boston, in the ship Abigall or Abigail. He went to Lynn, and a little later to Sandwich, Mass. (being a short

time resident at Duxbury) 1637, where he settled in 1637, and died 1682, supposed to be ninety

two years of age. His second child was Edmond, his oldest son.

2. Edmond Freeman, b. in England, married 1st, Rebecca Prence, dau. of Gov. Prence, 2nd Margaret Perry, 3rd, [unreadable] Edmund, the 3rd child, and only son, was born Oct. 5, 1655, m. Sarah

4. Edmond Freeman, b. Aug. 30, 1683, m. [unreadable] Presbury) and had fourteen children, of which Edmund was the first that lived.

5. Edmond Freeman, the first son that lived, b. Sept. 30, 1711, graduated at Harvard College, 1733, m. Martha Otis, dau. of Nathanial Otis, granddau. of Judge John Otis, taught school for years went to Connecticut, where he died, aged 77 years.

6. Edmund Freeman, b in Yarmouth (N. Dennis) April 29, 1737, m. 1st. Sarah Porter, 2nd Theoda (Porter) Estabrook. He (His wives were cousins to each-other) had eight children, of which Sarah was the oldest. His second wife had six when he m. her. He was one of the best of men. He commanded a New Hampshire

Co. in the army against Burgoyne, and was present at the surrender of that general.

7. Sarah Freeman (Wright) born March 27, 1762, in Lebanon, N.H. m. Dan Wright of Hanover, N.H., Feb. 3, 1785, lived soon after, in Thetford, Vermont, went to Ohio, 1814, d. near Troy, O. April 1, 1848, aged 86 years. She had six children, of whom Dan Wright, Junior, was the third son, and child.

8. Dan. Wright, b. Sept. 3, 1890, m. Catharine Reeder, dau. of Geo. Feb. 12, 1818, had seven children of whom Milton was the 5th child and the 4th son.

1. John Van Cleve b. in Holland, in 1628, came to America about 1650 settled at [blank] He had a large family.

2. Isbrant Van Cleve b. [blank] lived on Staten Island, d. Middletown, N.J. was Captain. He m. Jane Vanderbilt in 1734.

Sarah Elizabeth Worth (Formerly Van-Cleve m. Heywood) died at 4:00 Oct. 21, 1904, in Briant, Indiana. She was my cousin, about five years older than myself. Her father, William Van Cleve, was my Mother's uncle, and her mother was my father's sister. Wm. Van Cleve was a very good-looking man— Capt. of militia.

Mary Virginia Brown is my cousin. She married 1st a Wiley, 2nd F.N. Johnson. She lives at Waveland (Now in Crawfordsville) Montgomery Co., Indiana. She is my cousin. She was the twin sister of Thomas Brown who died in the army. They were the youngest children of Aunt Mary.

Sarah Harris' Children
1. Infant died about a week old.
2. William Edgar d. at 18 mo.
3. Edward M. Harris b. [blank] m. Mary Amelia Heddrick
   James F. Harris m. Zena R. Johnson
   Laura H. Harris m. Austin Winchell
   Charles W. Harris m. May Waite
   Harvey B. Harris m. Hope E. Harshbarger
   Ella Harris m. Nap. Bonapart Rees
   Orval C. Harris m. Emma Harshbarger
   Catharine H. Harris m. Marshall H. Van Fleet
   Clara H. Harris m. Leonard Gilbert

All are living Jan. 1, 1912, except the two first.

Anti-secrecy Man
Several years ago, I came across a man at T.O.C. Depot, in Columbus, Ohio, by the name, Rev. J.E. Heifer, whose home was Charleston, W. Virginia. He belonged to the Ohio Synod of Lutheran preachers, which is antisecrecy in faith.

Pres. Z. Taylor's Dau.
Sarah Knox Taylor, Dau. of Pres. Zachary Taylor, was President Jefferson Davis's first wife.

My Grandmother
Sarah (Freeman) Wright born in Lebanon, New Hampshire, March 27, 1762, died at her granddaughter's Eliza Bates; five miles south of Troy, Ohio, April 1, 1848; momentarily, apoplexy, 86 years. Her funeral was preached by Rev. Lewis Pettijohn, of the American Wesleyan Connection. Funeral text was Ps. 39.9. "I was dumb, I opened not my mouth; because thou didst it." She was Buried at Bether grave-yard, near Asahel Wright's farm, ten miles north of Dayton.

Elizabeth Brookbanks, R.F.D. 5, Liberty, Ind.
Sina E Ardery, 413 Ave. A. East (correct) Hutchinson, Kansas.
Lulu D. Crandall, The Dalles, Oregon.
Flora M. Glass (correct) Rural 6, Wabash, Ind.
Ellis Wright, R.F.D. 22 Fairmount, Ind.
Wm. A. Broyles Dickey Co., Ellendale, North Dakota
Mary H. Krout, 310 Jamisen St., Crawfordsville, Ind.
Mr. A.E. Wallace, died,
Mrs. Sarah Jane Wallace, Peru, Ind., R.F.D. 11
Rev. Joh Riley, 3834 E. Wash. Indianapolis, Indiana
J.F. Harris, St. Petersburg, Pinellas Co., Florida
John S. Collier, Medicine Lake, Valley Co, Mont.
Eva Gray, wife of Charles I. Gray, R.F.D. 7, Greenfield, Ind. She was Harvey's daughter.
Curtis Wright, 304 West Macon St., Carthage, Missouri.

Flyers for 1911
Walter Brookins, got his hand swelled [?]
Philip O. Parmelee
Clifford Turpin
Frank Coffyn, not useful
A.L. Welch (killed) Honest
Gill
Brindsley
Lieuts. Rogers, odd, Milling, nice, and Arnold, nice behaved
Leonard W. Bonney, no account.
Alexander Ogilvie (nice) London, England
Simmons, Collier's man New York, a nice fellow.
I was born in John Quincy Adams' Administration. He was the sixth president. So I have lived through twenty-two administrations, March 4, 1913, including his.

1912

Monday, January 1 It is a bright, cool-like day. This is the eighty-fourth First Day of the Year I have seen. They have been years of toil, but little physical pain. Even rheumatism has been lameness rather than pain. Not a year has been devoid of much happiness. I spent about twenty-one years on the farm, ten years in teaching, and thirty-two in General offices of the Church, and fifteen in other itinerant work. I have enjoyed the Divine Goodness and meray all my life.

Wednesday, January 3 This is a bright day. It is cool, but not cold. Wrote to Reuchlin and to Rodney Wright, Mrs. Eudaly, etc. I was sleepy in the afternoon. Wrote cards in the evening to John Riley and to J.C. Young.

Saturday, January 6 All of us are at home, and we are all well. Wrote several letters. It is a very cold night. The thermometer goes below zero.

Sunday, January 7 I spent to-day at home. Horace ate supper with us and staid till 8:00. The morning was cold, but gradually the weather moderated.

Monday, January 8 I received a letter from W.H.H. Reeder enclosing 25 dollars toward Grandfather Reeder's monument, and answered it. I wrote a long letter to Jesse Lefforge and wife, urging some action at Mt. Zion.

Thursday, January 11 Wilbur went in the afternoon to New York City. I sent letters to Mrs. Lulu D. Crandall, the Dalles, Oregon, to Eva Gray, and to Richard Braden, I also mailed letters to W.C. Galraith, William T. Lawson, etc.

Friday, January 12 I wrote cards to eleven former acquaintances. Lorin's family supped with us and staid till bedtime.

Saturday, January 13 I was cleaning up my closet. Katharine went to Columbus, to visit the College Club. She reached home at midnight. I sat up till she came home. The mercury ran down to about zero.

Sunday, January 14 I forgot it was Sunday and worked at rearranging Conservators. I thought yesterday Friday. Horace came to see Orville in the afternoon, as he usually does. It was some warmer to-day.

Monday, January 15 It was a cold day. Katharine visited Mrs. Chas. Wuichet. I looked at and assorted papers. Prof. Sibert of Oberlin called in the evening.

Tuesday, January 16 Mrs. Eleanor Wagoner took dinner with us, to-day, or to-morrow.

Friday, January 19 I made a search of my papers relating to the history of Gamaliel Bailey. Found a paper giving considerable information, and Whittier's and George W. Julian's letters.

Saturday, January 20 I was in examination of Josiah Davis' letter, of Oswego, Kansas, Jan. 3, 1899, and John Riley's letter of Feb. 1899, and looking over accounts of Gamalid Bailey. Wrote of them into notices of the Indiana Conferences.

Sunday, January 21 I turned to themes appropriate for Sundays, and landed on an article showing that the washing of the disciples' feet was Wednesday night at Bethany. I wrote upon it in the afternoon. Horace came early and staid till 8:00. He was very good.

Monday, January 22 Orville brought Mr. Simmons home to dinner. I remodeled my article. Mr. Simmons was with us in the evening and till 10:00 at night. Wilbur came home about 8:00 at night. The Judge was "bought up" in the suit of 15,000 dollars in New York, and they reentered, suit.

Tuesday, January 23 Mr. Simmons dined with us today. I wrote to Mr. Harry Charles, and to Mr. L. Millspaugh. Lorin spent the evening with us.

Wednesday, January 24 I wrote to Ellis Wright, and to Oliver Buller, and to Eva Gray and (card) to Rev. J.S. Rock.

Thursday, January 25 I wrote and sent off to the *Conservator,* an article proving the washing of the disciples' feet on Wednesday night at Bethany. Katharine had Agnes Beck, Mrs. Stevens, and Winifred Ryder, for supper. It is moderate, fair weather.

Friday, January 26 Wilbur started to New York City in the afternoon. He went at Collier's (of the Weekly) urgent request to attend the Airclub's Annual dinner.

Saturday, January 27 I got my own breakfast. I wrote to Reuchlin, and to J. Hoffhines, Canal Winchester. Mrs. Stevens called in the evening and received the clock Katharine presented her, of which she was loud in praises.

Sunday, January 28 I got up at a quarter after 7:00, dressed and ate breakfast at 8:00. I slept most of forenoon. Orville argued that taxes raised the price of property, their equivalent, that the tariff abroad did not increase the price where produced; that the Civil War was over the tariff question! Leontine visited us. I wrote Wm. Knipple.

Monday, January 29 Wrote letters to J. Howe and others.

Tuesday, January 30 Lost my spectacles. I deposited $55.00 for grand-father's monument. Paid Dr. L. Spitler

his bill for $14.00. Got medicine. Katharine went to Chicago to see Harriet Robbins. I bruised my left elbow, and months afterward, a knot continued on my elbow.

Wednesday, January 31 I got my own breakfast. Wilbur came home at noon. I looked over my manuscript. Frank T. Coffyn at supper with us. Wilbur went in the night to Chicago, to see Lieut. Falois.

Thursday, February 1 I was at home with Orville. I began a revision of the history of Indiana Conference.

Friday, February 2 Wilbur came home about 8:00 from Chicago.

Saturday, February 3 Arose early. I wrote some History. Katharine's train was 4 hours late. She came home at 10:00, at night.

Sunday, February 4 Felt quite well, but had running off of the bowels. I wrote a letter to Ellis Wright. Horace came in the afternoon and Netta, Lorin and the girls after supper. All went home before 9:00.

Monday, February 5 Katharine was invited to Mrs. Talbot's to diner. She lives at Hon. George W. Houk's old property and is his daughter. She went. I was preparing for the Chruch History. Wrote letters to Rodney P. Wright; sent a card to Mrs. Hilleary, Mary Ann Rain's (Snyder's) daughter, at Oskaloosa, Iowa.

Thursday, February 8 I received a letter from William Little, a schoo[l]boy of 1850, from Marissa, Ill., and answered it. His wife (deceased) was Elizabeth Emeline Bell, another scholar, at Thomas's School-house.

Friday, February 9 Lieut. Fulois dined and supped with us. His account of his and Coffyn's exploits in Texas.

Saturday, February 10 Lieut. Benj. D. Fulois' testimony in the Glen Curtis case was taken to-day. He staid here.

Sunday, February 11 I got up early and got my own breakfast. Fulois is here. It turns some warmer. Fulois told how savagely our soldiers were killed in the Phillipines. Lieut. Foulois left, afternoon for Columbus.

Lieut. Thos. D. Milling came. He supped with us.

Monday, February 12 Lieut. Thomas Milling's deposition is taken to-day, in the Curtis infringement case. He sups with us. Katharine buys me gold-framed spectacles—$4.50. I paid her for them.

Tuesday, February 13 Lt. Thomas D. Milling remains in town and dines and sups with us. He is 24 years of age.

Wednesday, February 14 Wilbur began his examination on the testimony in the Curtiss' case. The amount of his intelectuality, in describing their invention, was marvelous. It must have greatly wearied him.

Thursday, February 15–Thursday, February 22 Wilbur's Testimony continued. . . . I am at home.

Friday, February 23 Katharine goes to Oberlin, to engage rooms for Mrs. E. Wagner, for her to stay with Rachel.

Sunday, February 25 Horace came and staid to supper. Night letter from Katharine saying Rachel did not need to come home, by telegraph to Orville.

Monday, February 26 Katharine came home from Oberlin, at 7:00, eve.

Tuesday, February 27 George Feight called as we closed our supper. I spent the day looking over the Wright records, and writing some new ones.

Wednesday, February 28 I was busy with Wright records. I had lengthy communication from Curtis Wright, about to-day.

Thursday, February 29 Spent the day on records of Wright family.

Friday, March 1 Wrote of the Wrights. Alpheus Barnes, Secretary of the Wright Company and Mr. Boyle, a New York lawyer supped with us.

Saturday, March 2 Examining the Wright records.

Sunday, March 3 Remained at home. Wrote to Ruby E.

Ebersole, at Bryant, Jay County, Ind. She is Sarah Worth's grand-daughter.

Monday, March 4 Wilbur started abt 4:00 to Washington and New York. He wishes to see General Allen at Washington. I wrote many letters, one to Rodney P. Wright argueing 1. That Samuel of Springfield was a son of Samuel son of John III. 2. That his wife was 1 Hannah 2 Margaret. Margaret was probably only wife.

Tuesday, March 5 I write the last of three replies to Curtis Wright, of Carthage, Missouri. I wrote to Harvey Harris. Wrote several other letters.

Thursday, March 7 Wrote Thomas M. Little of Connersville, Ind., who went to school at Gray's Schoolhouse to me in 1850–1, who tells me that Diantha (Rybolt), Agnes, Hugh & John Gray are yet alive; and Gibson and Miriam (Dailey) are also; that one of Gibosn's sons is Fayette County Circuit Judge, and another is the congressman; That Henry Pettus is still alive. Mr. Guthrie called in the evening.

Friday, March 8 Wrote to Helen Russel, at Knisely, Edgar Co., Kansas. Her husband is George N. Russel. Mr. French Cothior's solicitor, dined with us. And Mrs. Heathman, Mrs. Lucille Baldwin Van Slyke and Mr. French supped with us. Mrs. Van Slyke remained with us.

Saturday, March 9 Mrs. Van Slyke went with Katharine in an auto-mobile ride and dined with us. She and Katharine went to the College Club, at 4:00 where Mrs. Van Slyke was to speak.

Sunday, March 10 I could not attend Church. Miss Greene and Miss Campbell with Mrs. Van Slyke dined with us. Horace came as usual, and staid till his family came, and till 8:30. Mrs. Van Slyke and Katharine took supper at Mrs. Heathman's and remained till 11:00.

Monday, March 11 Mrs. Van Slyke went away about 9:00. The College Club regarded her as a fine lecturer. She is a great talker and actor. She outtalks Katharine!

Tuesday, March 12 Mrs. Eleanor Wagner breakfasted at our house and about 9:00 started to Oberlin, to keep house for Rachel, her daughter. I got letters from Curtis

Wright and from L. Grace Frazier.

Wednesday, March 13 I went to town at 4:00 and bought a "U.B." Year Book, and some Stafford ink and some Watterman's fountain-pen ink. I called at Shearer's Hardware Store, on Ludlow Street. His partner has retired from business.

Sunday, March 17 I was at home all day. Ivonette and Leontine came, and Lorin and Netta and Horace later in the evening.

Monday, March 18 I spent the day in writing. Among others wrote a letter to Curtis Wright, of Carthage, Missouri.

Friday, March 22 Received a letter from Mamie Hilleary of Oskaloosa, Iowa & answered it. Wrote a short letter to Edward Cowles. Mamie is [unreadable]. Ed. Sines called in the evening.

Saturday, March 23 A cloudy afternoon. It was fair in the forenoon. Got a letter from Curtis Wright. I received a letter from Hartford "Times" acknow[l]edging payment till in June. I called an hour in Afternoon at Lorin's. Teleagram from Wilbur says he is there to see Gill. He goes to Augusta. Milton is at home. Horace got 100 five times, plus.

Sunday, March 24 I arose very early. It is a very snowy, forenoon. In the afternoon Milton and Horace came. Milton staid two or three hours. Horace stayed till seven or eight. Much snow fell by the morning.

Monday, March 25 I wrote a letter to Curtis Wright and an argument maintaining that Samuel Wright's first wife was Hannah, our ancesstress, and not Margaret. Probably Margaret was our grandama's name. Her daughter Margaret was married in 165 and must be older than James.

Sunday, March 31 The children went out to see their lot in Oakwood. Horace came, and went home. Lorin, Netta & Horace came after supper and staid till 9:00.

Monday, April 1 To-day is a very nice day. I collect interest on $600.00 for five months, $10.00. Go to Miller's confectionary, and buy a record book, $.90, and stationery, amounting to $1.25. It is rainy in the afternoon.

Tuesday, April 2 Receive letters; one from Perilla Man giving me the address of Mary Jane Sparks (Brand) Elmwood. Place, Cincinnati. One from Rev. J.M. Johnson, enclosing D. Edwards' remarks on [blank] Heistand. Melting snow fell. I wrote of J.G. Koerner's family till bed-time. Slept 4 hours. Slept little more.

Wednesday, April 3 My stomach had little feeling. I only ate a little milk. Dr. Spitler came about noon. Left a little medicine. I lay in bed all day. I slept well in the night. Calbraith P. Rodgers dashed to his death on the Pacific Shore in California. Just how can not be told.

Thursday, April 4 I am much better. I ate cream of wheat porridge for breakfast; soup & crackers for dinner & rice. Wrote to Albert Koerner in forenoon and to Reuchlin in Aftn.

Friday, April 5 In after'n went to see about tombstone. Was offered one for $105.00. Expect to hear from Ola Harris soon.

Saturday, April 6 I count this day the last of the week. Letter received from J.M. Johnson. In afternoon, Wilbur and Katharine go out to Oakwood to the lot. Katharine and Orville go to Miss Myer's to a party, against my protest. I hold late hours an infringement of the Sabbath.

Sunday, April 7 Horace came before noon. He brought some easter eggs. He went out to the lot in Oakwood aft'd. with Wilbur and Orville. He went home at night.

Monday, April 8 Wrote on article of the Mormons. Wrote some of J.M. Johnson's characters. Went to town and bought shirts at Kent's. Ivonette birth-day supper—16 lights burning. I sat up till nearly nine o'clock.

Tuesday, April 9 Went to Mrs. Nooks and to Miami Chapel and looked over the cemetery. Mrs. Nooks showed me a picture from Africa of Constance Wilberforce, whom she thinks is all right. She is doubtless much mistaken!

Wednesday, April 10 Went to Mother's grave. Looked at Dr. Davis monument; Bishop D. Edwards' monument, Bishop J. Weaver's grave, and Celment L. Vallandingham's monument. I also Visited my Great-grandmother's Monument, Aunt Mary Swenney's; Benjamin Van Cleve's, and his wive's, and son John & daughter Sophie.

Thursday, April 11 I walked about a mile to-day. Gen. Frederick Dent Grant died to-day. He was the oldest son of Gen. U.S. Grant.

Friday, April 12 Went to Belle Famplin's (Sloop's, Weidner's), saw Mary Hatfield, 94 years old, who told me that Belle will marry Henry Gukes Saturday evening. Belle is moving to about 154 Kilner Street. Mary Hatfield is aunt Sally Ensy's daughter who is a half-cousin of my mother.

Saturday, April 13 Wrote letters at night to Ellis Wright, and to Leroy Millspaugh. I walked about a mile. Slept much of the afternoon.

Sunday, April 14 Attended Grace M.E. Church and heard the pastor, Rev. Daniel McGurk, pr. Matt. 24:12, on the Prevalence of Religion. I ate something at sup[p]er that did not agree with me, and I had some pain in my stomach. I slept pretty well, however.

Monday, April 15 I ate something at supper that disagreed with me. I was not well to-day. Ate a teacup of warm milk for dinner. In April 1865, at 22 minutes after seven oclock, Abraham Lincoln expired, he having the evening before been smitten by the pistol of John Wilkes Booth, the assassinator.

Tuesday, April 16 I was unwell. I ate too much and had pains in my stomach and bowels at night. Slept pretty well.

Wednesday, April 17 Dr. Spitler came about night. I did not need or call for him. I have mostly slept well at night.

Thursday, April 18 Agnes Beck, Winnifred Ryder and Miss Hunt "dined" with Katharine and spent the evening. I ate almost nothing, but was tolerably strong.

The number lost on the Titanic seems larger than before. Wilbur started to New York to make a contract with the Aero club.

Friday, April 19 I sent an article to the *Conservator,* "The Mormons further considered." I ate a little chicken and a little corn-starch, and felt better though not stronger. I ate about every four hours. Katharine went to Osborn's in the afternoon. It is now reported that 1595 perished by the Titanic. Over 800 were brought to New York by the Carpathia, K. reconciled to [unreadable]

Saturday, April 20 I ate some crackers to-day. I slept much of the day and night. Received a letter from Ola and Ora Harris. He does not remember well the exact location of the graves of our grandparents. His father will be here, the last of May.

Sunday, April 21 I attended First Presbyterian Church. Doctor Wilson's text was Luke 4:16, "As his custom was." Subject: worship. Afternoon, I looked up the Boyd lot and walked up to the Lorenze lot. Rode home on Street cars.

Tuesday, April 23 I partly got ready to go to Marion, Ind. Not well enough. Mrs. Sines called to see us. She looks well. Lorin prepares to go. Lieut. Kirtland "dined" at our house. He is an aviator in the army. I sat up till nearly 10:00.

Thursday, April 25 I was making four copies of William's article on Slavery, written about 1857.

Friday, April 26 Finished copying William Wright's article on Slavery. He showed fine feelings, and displayed much eloquence.

Saturday, April 27 Wrote letter to Flora Stephens enclosing her Father's article on Slavery. Wrote to Elizabeth Brookbank, inquiring after Father Koerner's "Wander Book."

Sunday, April 28 Breakfasted about 8:00. Lorin came, having settled with Robert B. Broyles, and got a bankable note. Lieut. Kirtlang came to dinner. I called at Lorin's an hour or more.

Tuesday, April 30 I heard at 3 o'clock, Rev. Newel Dwight Hillis lecture on New Germany. William 111; and German Lutheran policy everything, and France and England no where! He is an extremist. Wilbur and Orville arrived at home on Wright Company's automobile at 8:00 from Flying grounds. Lorin came with accounts. Rufus P. Hamilton d. Greenburg.

Wednesday, May 1 At 3 o'cl[o]ck heard Newel Dwight Hillis lecture to students of difficulties they would have to meet in the 20th Century. It was not very practical, but he evinced more faith in the genuineness and inspiration of the New Testament Scriptures than Lyman Abbot does.

Thursday, May 2 Wilbur began to have typhoid fever; first diagnosed, by Dr. D.B. Conklin, as probably mallarial fever, and later as a typhoidal fever.

Friday, May 3 Wilbur began to have high fever. Nothing else ailed him. He suffered nothing.

Saturday, May 4 Wilbur had Dr. Conklin called in. He still has high fever. There is no local disturbance any where. His tongue is much coated. The doctor thinks it may be malarial, or it may be typhoidal.

Sunday, May 5 I read in the evening John's Gospel, first and second chapters, in my Greek-English Testament. Orville and Katharine and Horace went out to the new lot, over south three miles. Wilbur is about the same as yesterday.

Monday, May 6 I got up early. I had slept well. I wrote John G. Zeller, 116 N. Arlington Ave., East Orange New Jersey, Emma Dennis, Main, and West 7th Streets, Richmond, Ind. and Cinthia Croddy. Wilbur is a little better to-day. Mr. Our Roosevelt called in the evening.

Tuesday, May 7 Wilbur is better. But still has considerable fever. Ed. Sines called in the evening.

Wednesday, May 8 Wilbur is some better. He has fever still. Mary Emmons called in the afternoon. Lorin's called in the evening. There seems to be a sort of typhoidal fever prevailing. It usually lasts about a week.

Thursday, May 9 It is a fair day. A little fire is comfortable; scarcely needed. Wilbur is about the same. I saw Mr. Merkle about a monument to grandparents' graves in Rush Co., Indiana, and purchased a nice one to be put on a stone at one hundred and five dollars, F.C. Merkle.

Friday, May 10 I took Lorin, and we agreed upon the lettering to be put on the monument, and how. We staid to see the Ringling parade which came in then. Many wagons and nice horses; several open carriages with bears, wild cats, hyena's, leopards, tigers, lions and lionesses. A dozen camels, twenty odd elephants, a steam whistle. Wilbur still has high fever.

Saturday, May 11 Wilbur is about the same at 8:00, this morning. No change in his condition. Mrs. Sullivan, a hospital nurse came last evening. The doctor comes twice a day.

Sunday, May 12 Wilbur continues the same. His fever rises in the afternoon. John H. Patterson & Mrs. Crane, his sister, called. The doctor called twice.

Monday, May 13 Wilbur continues to have strong fever.

Tuesday, May 14 Wilbur has high fever. William Andrews called in the evening. Lorin and Netta called. Mrs. Heywood brought snow-ball flowers. Miss Sheets came as a nurse.

Wednesday, May 15 Wilbur has not as high fever as some days. Roosevelt spoke in Dayton, to-night, and Orville went to hear him, but was crowded out, and heard a suffraget.

Thursday, May 16 Wilbur's fever is unchanged. Orville left for Washington City, at 9:00, to deliver a machine to the Government.

Friday, May 17 Letters from Reuchlin and Emma Dennis. Katharine mailed a letter to Reuchlin, informing him of Wilbur's sickness. He is about as he was yesterday.

Saturday, May 18 Wilbur is no better. He has an attack

mentally, for the worse. It was a bad spell. He is put under opiates. He is unconscious mostly.

Sunday, May 19 Wilbur ceases to take opiates, but is mostly quiet and unconscious. His sickness is very serious. He is mostly unconscious.

Monday, May 20 Drs. Spitler came afternoon and at night with Dr. D.B. Conklin. Wilbur's case very serious. He noticed little.

Tuesday, May 21 Orville's automobile came. The Doctors came at 7:30, thought Wilbur had held his own—Spitler thought a little better. I voted for Taft delegates to the Chicago Convention. Wilbur seems a little better at 8:00 in the evening. Prof. D.W. Denis and Emma & Silas came in the automobile after 2 o'clock. Staid not over an hour. Albert Shearer came. Also, Mrs. Corbett came.

Wednesday, May 22 Frank J. Southard picked the lock, got out his machine, early yesterday morning, and dashed to his death, at Simm's flying grounds. He was the first to lose his life there, contrary to advice! The doctors had Dr. Bushheimer of Cincinnati come in to consult in Wilbur's case. The doctor's think him better.

Thursday, May 23 The *Journal* represents Wilbur as changed for the worse—probably on Dr. Conklin's statement, tho' not to us. He seems about the same. This is 21st day.

Friday, May 24 Wilbur seems, in nearly every respect, better. The doctors have a long examination before noon. Spitler and then Conklin's father. Reuchlin came from Kansas, to-day.

Saturday, May 25 Wilbur seems a little better to day.

Sunday, May 26 Wilbur's symptoms are better to-day. Orville takes Ivonette to Miami City. Wilbur was worse in the night. Orville slept but little. Miss Votaw called. Katharine received a telegram from Lord Northcliffe. Many cards & telegrams. Northcliff [rest is blank]

Monday, May 27 Both Conklin and Spitler came at 7:00 morn. They think the case very bad. His fever was higher and he has difficulty with the bladder, and his digestion

is inadequate. Agnes Beck called. Reuchlin saw him in the afternoon. I slept with my clothes on. We thought him near death. He lived through till morning.

Tuesday, May 28 I slept some in the night. I awoke at 4:00. Wilbur is sinking. The doctors have no hope of his recovery. Mr. Toulman called, Col. Robt. Cowden, C.J. Kephart. At 6:30 eve. the doctor thought him dying. He revived in about an hour.

Wednesday, May 29 Wilbur seemed no worse, though he had a chill. The fever was down, but rose high. He remained the same till 3:15 in the morning, when, eating his allowance 15 minutes before his death, he expired, without a struggle. His life was one of toil. His brain ceased not its activity till two weeks of his last sickness had expired. Then it ceased.

Thursday, May 30 This morning at 3:15, Wilbur passed away, aged 45 years, 1 month, and 14 days. A short life, full of consequences. An unfailing intellect, imperturable temper, great selfreliance and as great modesty, seeing the right clearly, pursuing it steadily, he lived and died. Many called - many telegrams. (Probably over a thousand.)

Friday, May 31 Boyers are the undertakers. We get many letters and telegrams and cablegrams of sympathy from all people of every sort, and from all societies, and from dignities. Flowers come from individuals and societies, most beautiful. Maurice Wilson is at home at last! Arrange with the undertaker.

Saturday, June 1 I awakened before midnight and got up near two hours. I slept then till nearly 5:00. Arose and washed off and dressed till near seven. The undertakers put Wilbur in the burial casket. Took him to the church at nearly ten. Many relatives come; many friends. Wilbur's body lay in state at First Presbyterian Church from 10 till 1:00. Rev. Maurice Wilson assisted by J. Howe & conducted funeral services 3:00.

Sunday, June 2 The Reeder cousins (Wm and Robt.) went home, and Rev. J. Howe, Ellis Wright and Myrl went home at 6:00. I was at Lorin's several times. Orville & Katharine & Horace rode in the automobile to Middletown and back.

Facsimile of diary entries, handwritten:

Wea. Thur. May 30, 1912 Ther.

This morning at 3.15, Wilbur passed away, aged 45 years, 1 month and 14 days. A short life, full of consequences. An unfailing intellect, imperturbable temper, great selfreliance and as great modesty, seeing the right clearly, pursuing it steadily, he lived and died. Many called—many telegrams (probably over a thousand).

Wea. Friday 31 Ther.

Boyers are the undertakers. We get many letters and telegrams and cablegrams of sympathy from all people of every sort, and from all societies, and from dignities. Flowers come from individuals and societies, most beautiful. Maurice Wilson is at home at last! Arrange with the undertakers.

Wea. Sat. June 1, 1912 Ther.

I awaked before midnight and got up near two hours. I slept then till nearly 5.00 rose and washed off and dressed till near seven. The undertakers put Wilbur in the burial casket. Took him to the church at nearly ten. Many relatives come; many friends. Wilbur's body lay in state at First Presbyterian Church from 10 till 1.00. Rev. Maurice Wilson assisted by J. Prince & Confisted funeral service at 3.00.

Wea. Sunday 2 Ther.

The Reeder Cousins (Wm & Rob) went home, and Rev. J. Howe. Ellis Wright and Myrl went home at 6.00. I was at Lorin's several times. Orville & Katharine & Horace rode in the automobile to Middletown and back.

Monday, June 3 Wilbur is dead and buried! We are all stricken. It does not seem possible that he is gone. Probably Orville and Katharine felt his loss most. They say little. Many letters. Ezra Kuhn's comes, reads Wilbur's will, and leaves copies. I ride 20 ms. with Orville in auto.

Tuesday, June 4 We have our house fumigated by health officers in the forenoon. Orville and Katharine went to Howard Beck's near Lebanon, in the afternoon. Reuchlin was with me in afternoon. Miss Mayer called. Lorin's came in evening. Many letters morning and evening. Mr. Wilson called after supper, Miss Hunter called. Orville took Leontine & Horace a ride.

Wednesday, June 5 Reuchlin started home at 8:50 forenoon. Perhaps it is our last meeting on earth. In the evening Orville took me to Lorin's, and he and Katharine went to Springboro and back. Orville took me to Centerville, and to the Oakwood lot, after dinner.

Thursday, June 6 I felt Wilbur's absence as never before. Mrs. Sines called forenoon. Orville went to Troy, to get a new wind-break to his auto. Winifred Ryder called afternoon. Orville took me to Springboro and back. Prof. Loos & wife visited us.

Friday, June 7 Afternoon, I went with Orville to Simm's Station, where he gets gasoline and we come back by the Valley pike. Miss Heath came. After supper, I go to Lorin's, and Orv. & Kath. go to Eaton and back. As I come home, I learn of a fire-department horse being badly hurt by a street car. The horse was shot. The night was cool.

Saturday, June 8 Mrs. Oscar Needham called, and Winifred Ryder. Orville took me out through Liberty and up north. He took Kath. to Simms. Rev. Howard Whidden, pastor of First Baptist Ch. called.

Sunday, June 9 All at home in forenoon. After dinner, Orville took me down the road near the Pinnacles, and back by the Springboro pike. Horace along, and he went, and Katharine, to Trotwood and back by the Salem pike. He afterward went out to Oakwood. Lorin & Netta called.

Monday, June 10 Katharine slept little and is unwell. The doctor called. Ivonett came and got dinner. Carrie Grumbach got supper. I rode out with Orville northwest. I wrote letters to C.J. Kephart, Pastor B.L. Myers, and to Cinthia & Bertha.

Tuesday, June 11 Orville received word of A.L. Welch's death at Washington City, and with Lorin goes to the factory and sends Mr. Arthur Gaible to Washington, and comes home. Rev. Maurice Wilson called. (Probably Mr. Welch aimed at a dip and to rise again. But he miscalculated the distance to the ground.)

Wednesday, June 12 Orville and Katharine conclude to go to Washington D.C., and they start at 3:47. Carrie Brumbaugh & Nettie are here. I wrote letters to several before and slept an hour. I went to Lorin's for supper, and they came and stayed all night with me.

Thursday, June 13 Lorin's are with us.

Friday, June 14 I arose just before seven. I went to grammar School commencement, where Leontine graduates. Miss Crowell is principal. Kintergarten and little scholars sit on the floor. I by invitation offer the invocation. Forty-seven graduate. I slept an hour and did nothing in the afternoon. [blank]called in the evening.

Saturday, June 15 Lorin's lived with us. Milton came

home. He brought Forest Webster, an Oxford graduate, with him. He is a great debater, a democrat.

Sunday, June 16 Webster goes on home at 11:00. We all dine together and "Pekah" Andrews.

Monday, June 17 I answered many letters of sympathy.

Wednesday, June 19 Wrote many letters. Senator Root is chosen Chairman of the Chicago Republican National Convention by about 50 majority over McGovern of Wisconsin.

Thursday, June 20 Orville and I went down the Springborough pike and across by Centerville, up home. Miss Mayer called to see Katharine. The Republican Nat. Convention met and adjourned. Mrs. Wagner came home, and went to Eleanor Stoltz, her daughter's.

Friday, June 21 F.T. Coffin (flyer) dined with us. Mrs. Wagner and Rachel came home from Eleanor's. I bought a Railway Guide. Orville and I rode over town. I went to Lorin's. The Nat. Convention met at 11:00 and adjourned at 4:00. The votes on seating delegates were favorable to Taft. Rosevelt proposed a new party.

Saturday, June 22 The Taft men have their own way at Chicago and he is nominated in the evening. We go in the auto to Miamisburg and come home by Springboro pike. O. & K. go to Xenia and back.

Sunday, June 23 I am sleepy to-day. I walked a mile in the forenoon. I rode out with Orville about 12 west, after supper. Katharine & Orville go a long ride afterward. Orville and Horace and Alfred went to Yellow Springs & back.

Monday, June 24 Mrs.[blank] Grabill died. She had a sore on her arm, they thought developed into a cancer. She was a close neighbor. Mrs. Grabill was the name. Her daughter, Ida is a "Christian Scientist."

Wednesday, June 26 Orville and I go to W. Carrollton and to Springborough pike. We went circling over all kinds of roads before we came to W. Carrollton.

Thursday, June 27 Rode out in auto to Springboro pike

and home. I called to see Mrs. Grabill, Corpse, who was buried aft'n. Orville and Catharine go to Brookville and got on wrong end of Eaton pike. I Slept about six hours. Awoke finally at 7:15.

Friday, June 28 Orville and I go to Xenia and back. Katharine visits at Miss Myers, till we return.

Saturday, June 29 Orville takes Horace and A[l]fred (Pekah) fishing. They return in the afternoon. A man[blank] called at 9:00.

Sunday, June 30 In the afternoon, Orville and I go out to the assylum and are stopped an hour by the rain. We then go to Xenia and return. Horace and Alfred eat supper with us.

Tuesday, July 2 We went out west of Trotwood, and back home.

Wednesday, July 3 We go towards Centerville and across to Springboro pike, home. Wrote several letters. Mr. and Mrs. Chas. Wuichet call in the evening.

Thursday, July 4 Orville and I go to Centerville and return before supper. I slept considerably to day. Orville & Kath. go out riding, and I go to Lorin's in the evening. Clare Andrews there, and family.

Friday, July 5 We went beyond Dr. Winter's Church, then south and west to the Centerville pike and onto the lot, home.

Saturday, July 6 We rode to Miamisburg and across to the Springboro pike, home.

Sunday, July 7 Orville took Leontine and Horace to Xenia & back. I slept some to-day and was sleepy. Rode out west of town and got into a very hard rain some four miles out. Lorin, Netta and Horace called an hour, and Councilman Shank and wife also called.

Monday, July 8 I slept some in the fore'n Katharine and "baby sister" went to Leilah Roosevelt's birth-day party. I read the Dayton notices of Wilbur's death and burial. Orville and I went to Brookville and came back partly on the Jalapa Road.

Tuesday, July 9 I examined my comments on "Luke, the beloved physician." Orville and I go in auto down the river and across to Centerville pike to home. Sister Candace Livingston died at Huntington, Ind.

Wednesday, July 10 Mrs. Hariet (Sillaman) Robins, of Chicago, came in the evening.

Thursday, July 11 I slept mostly in the forenoon. This is Horace's eleventh birth-day anniversary. He is a good boy, much beloved in his family, and by his uncles and aunt. Orville and Horace and I go fishing below Waynesville on the little Miama. Waters muddy, no fish. Ate supper there. Came home via the Lebanon Pike.

Friday, July 12 I went on nine o'clock car to Germantown, to Candace Livingston's funeral, at 10:00, at the Liberal Church. J. Howe preached the sermon. I spoke 6 minutes. I dined at Oliver Gilbert's. I went an hour to Rev. John Freeman's. Came home on 4:10 car.

Saturday, July 13 Mr. S. Crane took us in his automobile beyond Miamisburg. We went to a view-point of the city, the river below and the Indian Mound. We went close to the mound, and on Southeast and back to Miamisburg, and up the west side of the River to Dayton. Lorimer is unseated in the United States Senate.

Sunday, July 14 We were rather dull. In afternoon, we went out to the Oakwood lot, and took supper there. Orville, Katharine, Harriet Robbins, Horace and myself went. Lorin's came when we got home. Orville took Leontine a ride in the auto. There were cloud bursts in Denver and locality, causing some deaths and much loss of propirty.

Monday, July 15 It rained hard in the forenoon. It rained in the afternoon, but not so hard. It had been very warm; after the last rain, it turned cooler.

Tuesday, July 16 Went to Simm's Station and over east and south to Trebine and on home.

Wednesday, July 17 Katharine and Harriet Robbins went on Morning train to Lebanon, and thence to Agnes Beck's, where they staid till next day. A silly colored man, Rev. [blank] called to see me.

Thursday, July 18 Orville took me on the Springboro pike to Centerville pike, home, in an hour and fifteen minutes. The girls had come home from Beck's. Mrs. Roosevelt called after Supper Leilah.

Friday, July 19 Mrs. Harriet Robbins went home to Chicago, on 9:00 morn. train. Orville & I went before supper to W. Carrollton and to Springboro pike home. This is Orville and Katharine's 41st and 38th birth-day anniversary.

Saturday, July 20 Received and answered a letter from Charles W. Harris of Coin, Iowa. Orville and Katharine went to Springboro and back, after supper.

Sunday, July 21 Orville and Katharine and Horace rode out in the auto before supper. I went with Orville to Xenia and back, after supper.

Monday, July 22 I slept much. I studied Ezekiel considerably. Mrs. Charles Kumler came. We had considerable talk about the climate and productions of California, which she had just visited on Mr. John H. Patterson's bounty. She was at a gathering at St. Barbary and Los Angeles. I went to the R.R. Station a mile east of Centerville & back, with Orville, in auto.

Tuesday, July 23 I wrote a long letter to Cinthia Croddy and to Bertha Glaze. After Supper, I went with Orville (in the auto) out the Jallapa Road nearly to Johnsville and came across to the Eaton Pike and home, 22 miles. The Miss Hunters called to see Katharine.

Wednesday, July 24 Ina C. Eberhardt and Chas. Will French and his wife called in the evening. I rode out the Springboro pike and to Centerville, where we had a shower, on home. Mrs. Wagner and Rachel were with Katharine.

Thursday, July 25 At 4:00 P.M., I married Isaac Wayne Swartzel and Mary Eliz. Long. Chas. William French called & showed his plan of building. After supper Orville and I went to nearly Xenia and back. Received, letter and wrote Reuchlin.

Friday, July 26 S.A. Steman and Wife called and staid two hours. Orville and Katharine went to Xenia and

Springfield— took their supper with them. They came back near 9:00. I went to Lorin's after supper. Mr. Olinger was there.

Saturday, July 27 Orville & Katharine went to Richmond via Jalapa road to near Eaton. They called at David W. Dennis', and look at places where we lived, and places where they attended School, and at Glenn Miller, and came back on National Road via Salem. Lorin's called in the even'g.

Sunday, July 28 I slept much of the day. Horace was with us to dinner, and till night. We went with Orville in auto to "Hills & Dales" and to Oakwood lot, when Orville went home and brought with him Ivonette and Leontine, and Kath. & Lorin's family followed, and we ate supper in the grove.

Monday, July 29 I slept much. Orv. & I went to Xenia & back. Katharine dined at Miss Myers'. She rode out with Mr. Crane and Lorin's family; came home at 9:00.

Tuesday, July 30 I went to Probate Court with the certificate of Swartzell's and Lizzy Long's marriage. Orville went to Victoria Theater to bring Katharine home from Suffragettes' meeting, to dine.

Wednesday, July 31 Read considerably. Went toward Centerville, with Orville and across by good private roads to Dayton.

Thursday, August 1 Orville and I go to Graveyard, 5 1/2 m. toward Centerville turn west on good roads, wind about, come into the Miamisburg & Centerville pike at iron bridge, and go to Centerville and home. Came to lot in Oakwood in 16 minutes from Centerville, home in 25 minutes.

Friday, August 2 I examined some of my oldest Diaries. After Supper, Orville took me up Springfield pike, across east of Dayton to Huffman Avenue, and home. Orville & Kath. went to hear Chinese Suffraget & interpreter. Enyart rode out with them before supper.

Saturday, August 3 Orville and I went down south, on the best roads, came out on the Centerville pike about a mile south of town and home, an hour and five minutes.

Sunday, August 4 Awoke about seven o'c[l]ock. Went with Orv. by and west of Soldier's Home, to Trotwood and home by Salem pike.

Monday, August 5 The men begin to level off Orville's lot for a new building in Oakwood.

Wednesday, August 7 Entart rode with Orv. and Kath. in Auto, to lot & beyond home.

Thursday, August 8 After supper, Orv. & I go by Springborough pike to Mi. & Centreville pike to Centreville, and them home.

Friday, August 9 I slept an hour in forenoon and in the afternoon. Enyart goes with Orville and Katharine again.

Saturday, August 10 I went to American Loan Association after 4 P.M.; am 10 minutes late. Take the Fifth Street cars to Soldier's Home. Saw Ryder and his wife. Saw deer in the park. Came home. Kath. at Miss Myers' to supper.

Sunday, August 11 Arose late. Went to bed after breakfast. Tried hot water bottle, with benefit. For about two weeks, we have had an unusually cool spell of summer weather. Orv. and I went out Germantown pike, west till we struck the road north to Trotwood and then home on Jallapa road.

Friday, August 16 We took an auto-ride, before dark.

Saturday, August 17 Wrote in answer to Mary H. Krout, giving her Reeder day, the 24th of August. Mr.[blank] Gill came. Also Lorin's except Milton, in the evening. The weather is very hot again.

Sunday, August 18 Heard Pres. Lincoln Hulley at First Baptist Church Prov. 16.32, "He that ruleth his spirit" is better "than he that taketh a city." An able discourse—perhaps an hour. Introduced at Close Orville took me to church, and met me near home with auto. It is a very hot day.

Thursday, August 22 Mrs. C.L. Stevens ate supper with us. Orville and Katharine and Lorin's two girls start after 6:00 afternoon, to Niagara Falls. Lorin & Netta and Horace stay at our house.

Friday, August 23 At home. Lorin's live with me. Milton sleeps at home.

Saturday, August 24 I am at home. Lorin's with me. Milton has his meals at our house.

Sunday, August 25 At home all day. Prof. A.W. Drury called over a half hour at noon, to invite me to come up and look at Euclid Avenue Church.

Monday, August 26 Emma Ragan came back again to work for us. A card from Niagara Falls, from Ivonette, says "the Falls are much more beautiful than I had expected."

Tuesday, August 27 I arose at 7:00. After breadfast, [breakfast] I took a half mile walk, out east.

Wednesday, August 28 Lorin's girls wrote that they were delighted with scenery in New York and with Pliny Williams and wife.

Thursday, August 29 They went to Washington, which they regarded the prettiest place of all.

Friday, August 30 Orville and Katharine and Lorin's girls came home from the outing.

Sunday, September 1 Orville started at 4:00 for a consultation of their lawyers at Boston.

Monday, September 2 Jas. F. Harris and Zena his wife, and their son Tyson, came in the afternoon. Chas. Taylor and his daughter called an hour in the evening.

Tuesday, September 3 We went with the Harris's to the factory, and to the site of the new house in Oakwood, and rode considerably over Dayton, after a trip over Hills and Dales. The Harris's started on 3:00 car via Hamilton, home. At the election, I voted for Woman Suffrage and against Initiative, Referendum & Recall.

Wednesday, September 4 Orville came home before six o'clock. Winifred Ryder ate supper with us.

Thursday, September 5 Orville started to Chicago on 9:30 forenoon train.

Friday, September 6 The Gov. thermometer reached 91 degrees, the second hottest day of the year.

Saturday, September 7 Orville returned from Chicago at 7:30. The man's son whom he went to see had died. For over a week, we have had the warmest weather. Yester[day] the government thermometer recorded 91 degrees. A day in July it was 93 degrees. It turned cooler this eve. The brick work of Orville's "Boyd" house is nearly completed.

Sunday, September 8 Orville and Katharine take a short Auto ride in the afternoon. I do the same. At 10:30 went to Friends' Meeting at Summit Street. Rev. Jas. Unthank read a portion of Matthew 6th, 19 v. to close—and commented well. Took as text Matt. 5.8, "Blessed the pure in heart, etc." Lively speaker. Lorin staid with me. Orv. & Kath. start to Chic[ago], 9:30.

Monday, September 9 Card that Harrises reached home safe the 5th. Crops good in the south; corn, cotton. Our Ther. at 98 degrees, at 1 & 2 o'clock. George Feight called in the evening and talked an hour. Lorin came at about 8:00 in the evening and staid till after breakfast next morning. George's story of Mr. Feight's talk to E.K. Caylor, over Alf's having whipped Elmer.

Tuesday, September 10 Orv. & Kath. came home at 8:00. It is a little cooler, 70 degrees at breakfast, 96 degrees at 11:00. At about 3 o'clock it was 100 degrees! Probable 93 degrees Gov Ther! It cools somewhat by evening. Orville and Kath. find Horace out skating.

Wednesday, September 11 At 2 o'clock, the Ther. said 84 degrees, 6 degrees less than yesterday. Kath. went to John H. Patterson's to dinner. John H. Patterson called at 7:00, evening, a short time.

Thursday, September 12 Father Fred. C. Mayer, the aged music Teacher, died in the afternoon. Mrs. Stevens ate supper with us, and Katharine, and she goes to Mayer's

and Orville goes after them, with auto.

Saturday, September 14 Katharine was at the funeral of Father Mayer at the family residence, and at the burial, in the afternoon, at Woodland Cemetery. Gill, the aviator, was killed by the collision of his aeroplane with that of Mestach's.

Sunday, September 15 Katharine was at Miss Green's to dinner. Sunday night Mr. A.A. Gaible went to Chicago to get the machine wrecked by Gill. It was injured.

Monday, September 16 We ate dinner at the little table in the sitting room. A man papered the dining room to-day.

Tuesday, September 17 Orville started to Washington City to meet Mr. Fish, a Lawyer from Boston. Fish he regards as a very accute lawyer.

Wednesday, September 18 Wrote an article on the The New Birth.

Thursday, September 19 I wrote the article, The New Birth, several times. Mrs. J.L. Stevens took supper with us. Orville went up to New York at night.

Friday, September 20 Orville saw Mr. Whetmore, their aged and effective lawyer in their Curtis suit. He started home on 4:00 train. I sent my article to the editor.

Saturday, September 21 Orville came home from New York before 8:00, morning. Miss Winifred Ryder and Mrs. J.L. Stevens, Rev. Lorenz's daughter, took supper with us. I walked down to Orville's new building, morning and evening, calling at Lorin's. Orville and Kath. ride out in auto to Centerville.

Sunday, September 22 I arose at 8:30. Slept much of the day. Studied the Acts of the Apostles, XIII and XV Chapters. Horace, my grandson, was with us to lunch, as usual. He is a great favorite with us all.

Tuesday, September 24 This afternoon Miss Cochran, of Cincinnait, came and was entertained by us over night. She with Katharine attend the meeting at 8:00 o'clock of Y.M. League. She is a great-granddaughter of Pres. Chas. Finney.

Wednesday, September 25 Miss Cochran (pron. Cockran) went away after breakfast. I went in Afternoon in auto to see Orville's lot, Mr. [blank] is well-along in excavating the cellar. I left Mrs. Sines visiting us. Miss Cochran (Francis) came near bedtime and lodged with us.

Thursday, September 26 Miss Cochran is offered for 10 months $65.00 a month as social secretary of the Dayton League. She went home. Her Father is a lawyer.

Friday, September 27 Miss Ryder, Mayer, Agnes Beck at supper. Mrs. J.L. Stevens visited us and translated Father Koerner's old copy of a church paper by pastor of Fothen, of Father Koerner's birth at midnight Feb. 16, 1791, his Father's name being John Thomas Koerner, a farmer of Fothen, and his mother being Eva Elizabeth (nee Polin) of Burkersdom.

Saturday, September 28 I rode out east to the Little Miami River, with Orville in the auto. In the evening, Orv. & Kath. rode out to Centerville. A telegram came and some telegraph communications. Orville noticed them. Some officers in Washington (at College Park) were killed in trying aeroplanes.

Sunday, September 29 I slept most of the forenoon. In the afternoon, the gas was shut off from 12:45 till 5:00. I read in Greek some chapters in the Acts, with unusual interest. Orv. & Kath. went out riding & Horace.

Monday, September 30 I have been lame in my back for a day or so. I went in the evening to Lorin's before supper. A horse was scared by fire-wagon, ran down street and fell about fifth. Not badly hurt. I slept none to-day, perhaps. Wrote to J. Excell and to White N.Y. publisher.

Tuesday, October 1 I am very lame to-day. I had intended going to the farm.

Wednesday, October 2 At home, except a look at Orville's Business House, in the afternoon, when Kath. & Agnes Beck were there. I am a little better of my lameness.

Thursday, October 3 I am not so lame in the morning, but lame as the day proceeds. Orville was going at 4 o'clock, to New York, to meet the Ex. Committee of the Wright Co., on royalty, but, not being very well, did not start.

Friday, October 4 Orville took me over Oakwood and near J.H. Patterson's and Houk's Runnymede (Talbot's). It is a pretty part of town.

Saturday, October 5 Prof. A.W. Drury called. He invited me to their communion, to-morrow. Would like to show me their Church, Euclid Ave. Orville took Katharine to Ida Grabill's, and took Leontine to Xenia and back. Lorin came in.

Sunday, October 6 Ate breakfast at 8:10. Orville took me by the lot to south of Milton's Sch. House, over east to Alpha and up Xenia pike home. It was a sunshiny day. I am at home in the afternoon, and mail a letter to Leroy Millspaugh.

Monday, October 7 I got up at 6:30, ate after 8:00. I remain at home all day. Read some in Commentaries. Lorin called in the evening.

Wednesday, October 9 Over 400 guests from over 40 nations visit Dayton and lunch at John H. Patterson's Cash Register Building. Orville is with Patterson and made a short speech. Katharine in the crowd of Dayton entertainers. They exhibit my picture. Rev. J. Howe came. We go to Orville's Third Street Building, and through Cash Register.

Thursday, October 10 Orville takes Howe in Auto to cars at 8:00, going to Scioto conference, at Greenfield. I was at home all day. Wrote to Gr. dau. Bertha, in answer to her letter.

Sunday, October 13 I rode in auto with Orville to Little Miami River, turned west, had good roads till we struck Springfield Pike south of Simon's Station. Lorin's visited us in the evening.

Monday, October 14 Write letters to Drusille and to Albert Koerner. Get ready to go to Grant County, Ind., to-morrow.

Tuesday, October 15 Lorin was kept at home by some

Orville and Katharine Wright and Harriet Silliman

court business. I did not find a way to go in the afternoon to Grant County, Indiana.

Wednesday, October 16 Lorin & I went via Richmond to Fowlerton. Hired a horse & buggy, and went to my farm (Millspaugh). Went to Ellis Wright's and found them setting a moved house. After supper, we went to Wm. Reeder's, where we lodged. Ovid is teaching school at "Leachburg" School-house.

Thursday, October 17 We went to Leroy Millspaugh's, and took the horse home to Fowlerton—$1.50. Hired conveyance to Fairmount $1.50. Saw Parker. He let renters get much behind—one $90.00 & another $45.00. Dined at Oliver Buller's. Went to Marion and paid taxes. Went on 2:45 tr. Union City, got home at 7:00.

Friday, October 18 Rained in forenoon & afternoon. I had a sore eye. I wrote letters to Reuchlin (card) and to Perilla Mann.

Saturday, October 19 Wrote a letter to Edward E. Cowles, Henrietta, Texas. Katharine visited Mattie (Hott) Huber in afternoon, and remained till after I went to bed.

Sunday, October 20 I slept part of the forenoon. Milton

came after dinner. His studies at Oxford are French, English, Economics, Chemistry, and English Speaking. Horace came as usual after dinner. Staid till after supper. Orville started at 4:00 for New York City.

Monday, October 21 Miss Hamil is a High School-teacher, and is a very bright woman.

Tuesday, October 22 Mrs. J.L. Stevens and Miss Hamil ate supper with us, and Mrs. Stevens translated Grandfather John G. Koerner's certificate from the Horseshoe, ax, Weapon and Wagon Society, in the principality of Reuss Hlanir, as master workman, 28th of Oct. 1809, he got certificate Oct. 4, 1817, from John Henry Degel, Obermeister. This was prob. about time of his coming to America.

Thursday, October 24 Orville returns home at 10:30 o'clock from Washington. Ralph Boen took sick with appendicitas.

Friday, October 25 Winifred Ryder dined with us. Barrett, of Pan American Union, Harry Garman of Davis Sewing Machine, Fred. Foucher, Sect'y of Chamber of Commerce and Wm. Frizzell, a lawyer, called in the afternoon.

Saturday, October 26 Rode with Orville after dinner to the lot—(filling cement by machine) and over Hills and Dales.

Sunday, October 27 Went at noon to near Xenia and back in auto. Horace came and staid till 8:20 at night. Emma Ragan did not show up, and Katharine did her own work.

Monday, October 28 Mrs. Williams appeared to get breakfast. I went before dark in auto to Orville's residence and on Centerville pike to the graveyard and out west and back to the pike and home. Lorin's girls called. Orville and Kath. took a ride in auto.

Wednesday, October 30 Rode into Xenia and back after dinner. Wrote to Rev. J.S. Rock. Went at 7:00 to hear Senator Beveridge speak. Hoover & candidate for Judge spoke. Beveridge began at 8:30, and spoke about two hours. He is a good orator. Vice-president Sherman died this evening. Ralph Boen was opperated on for appendicks.

Thursday, October 31 News of the complete defeat of the Turkish army 200,000 men, by the Bulgarian Gen.[blank] Brown, Republican candidate for governor, spoke in the evening at Dayton. Winifred Ryder dined with us. Brown had bad weather, making his autience small.

Friday, November 1 Miss Florence came and got breakfast. She is a nice "white" girl, of good manners. It was a cold like, damp day. Wrote J.F. Harris, a card.

Saturday, November 2 Wrote to Flora Stevens. The Allies are reported to have captured Andrianople.

Sunday, November 3 It is a nice day. I awoke early, but slept till 10:00, after breakfast. After dinner, rode down West side of the river to West Carrollton to Alexanderville, and out east to Davis' Church and Centerville pike and thence home.

Monday, November 4 Orville took me to see Taft, who came about 6:00 on the train to Cincinnati, where he votes to-morrow. Katharine went to Winnifred Ryder's for supper. Orville brought her home.

Tuesday, November 5 Election Day. I voted at 8:00 for William H. Taft. Little news came of the result of the election.

Wednesday, November 6 Woodrow Wilson is elected president of the United States. John H. Patterson and his daughter Dorathy called on a visit. She is a nice talker and nice-behaved girl.

Thursday, November 7 The news is that Taft is third in electoral votes. Orville took me to his lot and to Centerville. It is a nice cool day.

Friday, November 8 Orville took me after diner via the Asylum down the Bellbrook pike eight miles from home turned round, and off the pike, and came back west to the Centerville pike, and home. The wind was strong and cold. Wrote Grace, and to J. Howe. Cards to Drusilla and to ———.[blank after the lines]

Saturday, November 9 Katharine had no help all day. I was at home largely reading in Gerit Smith's Life. Orville and Kath. took a ride in the evening. Prof. G.F. Wright left his card, yesterday.

Sunday, November 10 Mattie [blank] came to do our house-work. I slept after breakfast. Orville took me after dinner, up north through Little York and back by Forest Ave. Street, home. Orville, Kath., Leontine, & Horace rode out to the lot. They remained till after 8:00, at our house.

Monday, November 11 At home as usual. Suffrage tea this afternoon. Went to Centerville and back home in auto.

Tuesday, November 12 Went down Springboro pike and across to Centerville pike home via lot.

Thursday, November 14 Mr. [blank] Donahue, of Cin. called in the evening half-drunk. I wrote a letter to Leroy Millspaugh.

Friday, November 15 Wrote to Isaac W. Swartzell. Rev. Maurice Wilson called in the evening. Katharine went walking with Mrs. [blank] Mr. Seibert and Edwin Shuey, Jr. came in to talk about college.

Saturday, November 16 Slept before dinner. Rode out with Orville to the lot and over hills & dales. Orville starts to Buffalo at 7:40, to Curtis' Trial. Flowers came in: Roses, Misses Louise Mayer & Justina Stevens; Chrisanthemums, by Lorin's girls. Card, Charles & Eva Gray; Letter from Estella Petree.

Sunday, November 17 I attended the First Lutheran Church. Text, "Go forward." He called for a subscription of $2,500.00. I came home. Carrie brought in a birth-day cake. Lorin's and Winifred dined with us. She is for Wilson. We went to see Lorin's new building, the north-east lower room being now occupied by [blank] a jeweler.

Monday, November 18 Winifred Ryder sent some large Chrisanthemums. Lorin went to Buffalo in the evening.

Tuesday, November 19 I arose at about 7:00. Slept part

of forenoon and part of afternoon. I wrote letters to the flowers girls; Winifred, Lorin's girls, Louise, and Justinia. Kath. renewed my library books. We had no help to-day.

Wednesday, November 20 Lorin went to Niagara Falls from Buffalo, which he had never visited before. Mrs. Justina Stevens and Kath. wnet out to the lot. Elizabeth came to work to-day. She had worked at Young's about six months.

Thursday, November 21 Lorin is at home. He said he heard Newel and Bull. He thought Fish set the case clear. Mrs. Wagner dined with us. Rev. F.A. Dental called. I gave him five dollars on salary. Katharine and Mrs. Wagner went out to the lot.

Friday, November 22 I bought slippers in the evening at the west-side store. Elizabeth scalded her feet, and went home.

Saturday, November 23 Elizabeth's scalds were not deep, and she came back and got breakfast. It is fine weather. The sky is slightly clouded. Orville and Mr. Brewer, of England came before noon. Mr. Brewer seems well. His name is Griffith Brewer.

Sunday, November 24 I slept part of the forenoon. In evening, Mr. Griffith Brewer showed some notes from Helvedon, England, one of the death of Ann Wright, wife of the Lord Manor, in 1617. It was inscribed on a stone. She died the 28th day of November, Ano Domini, 1617.

Monday, November 25 I slept some after breakfast and till dinner. We had excellent pudding. In the afternoon, Mrs. Weller, Mrs. Harry Snyder and Mrs. Jones, of literary committee, called to see Katharine. Orville and Mr. Griffith Brewer call in question Samuel Wright being connected with the Essex Wright family!

Tuesday, November 26 I slept part of the forenoon, and looked up some of my genealogical papers. Katharine went in the evening to a meeting of the gardeners. Dr. Conklin, Jr., called to see us.

Thursday, November 28 It is Thanksgiving Day. We are having good times, and our people as in 1892 are call-

ing for "a change." We had a turkey, which Winifred Ryder and Mr. Griffith Brewer helped us to eat. Orville's outing with children. Ryder called.

Friday, November 29 Mr. Brewer started for London, at 3+. Mr. Noel a reporter for the boys supped with us. Rev. William Dillon dined with us. Prof. Funkhouser and wife called.

Sunday, December 1 A beautiful, temperate day. I went with Orville in the auto to the house. Stone work commenced. Rode in the Dales. Dinner at 1:30. Milton came and went out with Orville & Kath. to the house and over Hills and Dales. Horace has gone to Canton, Ohio, with his mother, to visit the Andrews.

Monday, December 2 There was rain in the night and early in the morning. I slept, and awoke at 11:30. The skies cleared up and there was sunshine in the afternoon. Katharine attended Suffragett's meeting. Miss Frances Cochran had supper & staid till early bed-time. This is Cinthia E. Croddy's 65th birth-day anniversary.

Tuesday, December 3 It is cloudy in the morning. Julius Wohlirt called to see me. Is 54 in August, lives in Laporte, Ind. We called them "Woolard." Kath. went to a concert at 8:00.

Wednesday, December 4 It is a very mild, pleasant morning, like October weather. Received a letter from Reuchlin. He seems pleased with Baldwin. They approved of Helen's removal to Cottonwood Falls. I rode out to lot and in home.

Friday, December 6 It is a mild, pleasant October morning. It clouded up in the day. Katharine went to a playground association. Orville went to the country field, to try some experiments. It is gradually growing cooler.

Saturday, December 7 It was a rather pleasant day. I took some pains to arrange my genealogical documents. In the evening, I glanced some time over Berger's History of the U.B. Church.

Sunday, December 8 It is a cloudy day. I attended Summit Street (Friends) Church. Ira Johnson preached a fair discourse. He heard me at Hahn's Sch.h. when a little boy in Randolph Co., Ind. The discourse was brief. A few prayers before and words by many members afterward. Horace dines with us.

Monday, December 9 I was busy as usual. Katharine busy at a committee. Orville was trying his automatic flyer.

Tuesday, December 10 Katharine dined at Rike's and attended a committee meetings most of the day. In the afternoon and evening I wrote upon the type-writer the Koerner Family.

Wednesday, December 11 I thought well; I slept well. I wrote a Memorial of the Koerner Family on my typewriter. Practiced considerably on hand-writing. My brother Samuel Smith Wright's manuscript, left seventy-four years ago.

Thursday, December 12 Russell Alger, of Detroit visited us and ate supper with us. Mrs. Leontine Corbett, Lorin's Motherinlaw (perhaps aged 70) was married to Captain William H. Ainsworth, of Columbus, Ohio. I mailed the Conservator an article, "A Day of Joy."

Friday, December 13 From my home, I wrote to Cinthia Croddy. She is a poor, distressed cousin's widow. I sent her an order on the bank for ten dollars. This is John H. Patterson's 68th anniversary of his birth.

Saturday, December 14 It is a bright morning. Ther. 34 degrees at 9:00, foren. I write to C.L. Wood.

Sunday, December 15 I attended First United Presbyterian Church, on High Street, and heard President J. Knox Montgomery of Muskingum College pr. on the "Superiority of Effectual prayer," Isa. 62.6,7. He is a small man, but gave a great discourse. Miss Winifred Ryder and Miss Frances Cochran dined with us. Horace visited us, and Lorin called.

Monday, December 16 Frank S. Lahm, father of Dr. Frank C. Lahm, visited us, and dined with us. He is about to start a trip around the world. He has had a cataract taken out of each eye, and wears spectacles, of course. He is a very nice gentleman.

Tuesday, December 17 Robert Nevin, Sr., died to-day at 11:00. I knew him when he studied law on the West Side. He was a noted lawyer in criminal cases.

Wednesday, December 18 There was considerable snowfall in the afternoon. It lodged on the limbs of the trees.

Thursday, December 19 Finished up articles for the Conservator. Wrote a letter to S.C. Bowen. In the eve, Katharine went to see Winifred Ryder, who goes on a visit to Massachusetts to-morrow.

Friday, December 20 It is a cool sunshiny morning. The day was fair and the snow-skift melted before the sunshine. Kath & Lorin fixed up and sent off Christmas presents. I wrote to Estella, Citizens' Bank, and card to Rev. N. Allabaugh.

Saturday, December 21 It is the finest weather, the shortest day of the year. Orville took Charles Taylor's lots off his hands. I wrote to Bishop Wood.

Sunday, December 22 It is a pleasant morning. I heard Rev. Jas. B. Unthank pr Matt. 7.12. He applied it to politics and especially to business. Capitol, Employers and Labor must learn what is Just between them.

Tuesday, December 24 Lorin's except "Netta," are with us to supper. We had a nice Supper. Then many presents were distributed. Mine were "American Commonwealth" by Bryce, "The Beautiful Every Day," Miller, "Register of days of Week," "Handkerchief, Hellen. Calendar, 1913, "Buster."

Wednesday, December 25 After breakfast, we let Eliz. Snell go for the day. I read over Samuel Huber's Biography.

Friday, December 27 Katharine went to Miss Green's for dinner and to hear some women read. I got letters from Ella Rees and Jesse Lefforge, and answered Ella's.

Saturday, December 28 Katharine dined at Miss Mayer's. I wrote to Jesse Lefforge. Sent Check to Freeman $10.00 for Van Wert Church. Prof. [blank] Ferguson of Nevada University visited us. He is a very interesting man, is very natural in his conversation.

Sunday, December 29 I attended Summit Street Friend's Church. I was invited to take charge of the meeting, consented under the most self-imposed restrictions. Rev. James B. Unthank came, and continued from 1 Pet. 1.13. I read the 1st Chapter, and prayed not knowing the text. He spoke at considerable length. Horace was with us afternoon till bed-time.

Notes for 1912

Wilbur took sick with typhoid fever, May 2nd, or 3rd. He soon after made his will, Ezra Kuhn's officiating. The fever did not abate. He suffered little the first week. He was delirious the second week. About the end of the second week, he became unconscious, which mostly lasted to the close of his life, May 30th, about 3:15 in the morning. He had Dr. D.B. Conkling and Dr. L. Spitler during most of his sickness, and Mrs. Sullivan and Miss Sheets, two most faithful hospital nurses, the last weeks. He took nourishment about 15 minutes before he expired. For the last week or ten days, there was little hope of his recovery, but at any turn of his disease, we were encouraged. But at the last death came at an unexpected time. His brother Reuchlin and Lorin came from Lorin's home too late to see him die. His father came in when his pulses were stilled. He died without a struggle, without a moan. He died May 30, 1912, at 3:15 in the morning. In memory and intellect, there was none like him. He systemized every thing. His wit was quick and keen. He could say or write anything he wanted to. He was not very talkative. His temper could hardly be stirred. He wrote much. He could deliver a fine speech, but was modest.

Jont Franklin Reeder's Family
His wife was Nancy Furnish, not far from his age, July 19, 1827, who died in Grant Co., Ind. about 1847. His children were: Mary Jane, b. about the first of 1828, married Henry Richards, lost Effie in 1853, and died in 185[blank] leaving a son John, nearly two years old. She was a thoughtful child, and a good woman. His second daughter was Margaret Emila about 1831, who m. William Heal and died leaving an oldest son John Franklin, who lives in Viroqua, Wis., since moved to Marshfield, Wis.

George C. Reeder's Family
I. *John Reader,* from England, settled at Springfield, Mass., in 1636. He did not remain long, but lived in other places, and went to Newtown, Long Island, about 1657. Probably he was the father of John Reeder the ancestor of Andrew H. Reeder, Governor of Kansas in 1854, whose ancestors were at Newtown, in early times. He was *probably* the father of Joseph Reeder 1st. He seems to have been of a restless disposition.
II. *Joseph Reeder,* of London, about whom myths are told, as being a grandson of Wilhelm Leser, (William Reeder) who is represented as having gone from Hanover, Germany, to England, and one account says he was William III, of England. But William III was born in Nassau, Prussia, and in 1650, and was younger than his grandson, Joseph Reeder! So we dismiss the story as a myth. Joseph had two sons Jacob and Joseph. He is our first *certainly* known ancestor. His wife's name is unknown.
III. Joseph Reeder, son of the preceding Joseph, who married Eleanor Leverich, the daughter of Caleb, and granddaughter of Rev. William Leverich. Caleb "was a prosperous man and a Presbyterian." This Joseph had three sons, Joseph, Jacob & Benjamin.
IV. Joseph Reeder III mar. second wife Susana Gano & had (William (first wife's son) Elizabeth, (Lake) Joseph, Marg., Daniel. David, Susana, Eleanor, Elij.

The Brown Family.
Ryland T. Brown was born in Kentucky. He married Mary Reeder Nov. 25, 1829. She was born on Sycamore Creek, 25 ms from Cin. She died Oct. 19, 1865 in Indianapolis.

The Braden Children
John Braden b. in Ky. died in Watseka, Ill. He married Eliza Reeder Sept. 3, 1840. She was born in Centerville, Ohio, Apr. 15, 1821.

The Croddy Cousins
John Croddy was six years old, in 1842. In 1847, Uncle George sent for his father to take him and Mary away. And he was among strangers till he was of age. He became a very smart man. He married Nancy Lowe, and went to near Splitlog, Missouri. He lost a son. His sons living are Floyd, Bert & Reeder. His daughter is Lola Davis. He served in the Civil War. His address in 1912 & 1913 is Anderson, Mo. His sister was Mary born in

1831. She married Henry Evick. They lived in Niles, Mich. They had Gabriella, Adam and Cora Belle. Henry's first wife was Charlotte Williamson. His brother, Jont. Franklin Croddy, was born Nov. 21, 1841. His mother died August 18, 1842. His Aunt Katharine Wright took him to her home and raised him. In 1863, December 31, he married Cithia Mitchell. They had six children of whom Edward Milton and Bertha only lived. Bertha m. Ed. Glaze and had Van Cleve b. June 23, 1903 and Leslie.

(The Reeders Continued from four pages back)
Elijah (again), Cornelius, Jacob and Stephen. Joseph was born April 24, 1716; Sussana, his wife, May 23, 1722. In 1763, they removed to Loudon Co., Virginia (1763) after the birth of Stephen. They were m. in New Jersey [rest is unreadable]
V. Joseph Reeder, b. in N.J. m. in that state, Anna Huff, and in 1766, rem. to Loudoun Co., Virginia. In 1778, they moved to thegreat Cacapon River now in Hampshire Co., West Va. In 1789, they removed to Colombia, near Cincinnati, O. Their son, George, was born Sept 24, 1767 in Virginia.
VI. George Reeder, the third child, but oldest son of Joseph and Anna Reeder, was born in Loudoun Co., Va., Sept. 24, 1767. He m. Margaret Van Cleve, in Cincinnati, August 2, 1796. I have understood that George Reeder was born in Loudoun Co., Va. in 1869. They lived on the Duck Creek farm till 1809. When they removed to 100 acres of land on Sycamore Creek, Grandfather had very poor health. He would go to the woods, put on a load of logs (or a log) and the horse would haul it home, and grandmother would unload it and send the horse back. It was this year that their son John, who had been bitten by a supposed copperhead snake, but recovered, was killed by the falling of a dead tree, at school, which he was attending. I remember my mother often talked of the sycamore farm. Before John's death, she saw him go around the house apparently to scare her. She looked after him, and he was not there. She called to her Mother, and learned that John had been sitting near her all this while! He was killed soon after. She regarded his appearance at the house as an illusion in token of his death.

Rev. Aaron Farmer's Family.
Aaron Farman's first wife was Sarah Ann Branham. She bore him two sons and four daughters. One of the daughters, the youngest was Sarah Ann Smith whom I visited several times in Biggs, California, in 1887. She was an intelligent, pious lady. Her husband Lewis C. Smith, was a blacksmith, and they had three sons:[blank] She was then fifty-five years of age. She had lived in California, twenty years. Her brothers and sisters deceased, had lived pious lives. Gitty Miller, a widow, was his (Farmer's) second wife. She had six children by her first husband (Miller). By Mr. Farmer, she had one son and one daughter. Her daughter was Lucinda, Gale, then of Lamar, Missouri, to whom I wrote and had a satisfactory reply. I have since learned that all the Smith family except the youngest son, have died. She was converted at 16 years of age. At one session of White River Conference, a small appriation was made to her and her sister

William III of Eng. was born at the Hague Nov. 4, 1650. The Wilhelm Lesser tradition represents him as the grandfather of Joseph Reeder who lived about that time at Newport, L. Island.

Justus Wright's Genealogy
William I. Wright of Fitchburg, Mass, sent me the copy of a genealogy made out, by his aunt, deceased, of Justus Wright, a loyalist, in which Samuel of Springfield, is given without question, as the son of Samuel, the son of the third John Wright, of Wrightsbridge, Essex Co., Eng. I had reached the same conclusion before. Milton Wright.

John G. Koerner
John Gottlieb Koerner. Another old document, duly authenticated, says that he closed his service as apprentice of John Samuel Zeimer, after two years, and was declared master after two more years at the trade of wagoner, on October 28, 1809. The document is signed by John Henry Degel, the 4th day of October, 1817, at Schleiz, in Reussischen. The former obermeister is declared to have been John Gottlieb Barthold. The foregoing was made out about the time he emigrated to Baltimore.   Milton Wright

An old document was sent to me by Silvanus Koerner, giving date of John Gottlieb Koerner's birth as at midnight, February 16, 1791. It was signed by three witnesses. He was born in Forthen in Saxony. His father was John Thomas Koerner. His Mother was Eva Elizabeth Polion of Burkersdorn. The document was given in 1807, signed by the pastor of Forthen, Frederick Conrad Weisser, sealed with the Church seal. Milton Wright.

Esther L. Hamilton, Greensburg, Indiana, dau. of Freemara Kioyor [?] Etta Raines, granddaughter of Mary Ann Snyder, went to Texas, with Sally Eudaly and m. W.P. Rathford, lives at Ft. Stockton at Grand Falls. Mrs. Eudaly lives [blank] Sarah J. Wallace R.F.D. 11, Peru, Ind. Flora Glass, R.F.D. 6, Wabash, Ind. Etta (Rains) m. W.P. Rathford, lives at Fort Stockton, Texas.

John G. Zeller, 405 W. 15th St., N.Y. Emma Zeller Dennis, Main & 7th Street, Richmond, Ind. Mrs. Eva Gray R.7, Greenfield, Ind. Sally E. Eudaly, Grand Falls, Texas, Ward County. Mrs. Mamie E. Hilliary, 516 B. Ave. E. Oskaloosa, Iowa. Ellis Wright, F.R.D. 22 Fairom [?]

For my South eighty acres of land, in Grant Co., Indiana, I paid $250.00, to my Father Sept. 19, 1850, and One Hundred Dollars to my brother William, Sept. 24, 1855. I inherited an eighth of it. My father had bought Harvey Wrights and Sarah Harris's share before, paying them thirty dollars, each. For 53 2/3 acres north of it, I in July, 1860, paid 15 dollars an acre, and a little larger price for an extra acre and a third about the house, to give me fifty-five acres; I paid some more than fifteen dollars an acre for that acre and a third. I think I paid $30.00. In 1878, I traded my share in my father's estate for 320 acres of raw prairie land, in Adair County, Iowa, which was then valued at seven dollars an acre. In the yar 1900, I gave this land to my four sons. They sold $11,000.

Grandma O.E. Snooks, 217 Pontiac Ave., Dayton, Ohio. Leon Czolgoss the Assassin of President McKinley, was sentenced by Truman C. White, who died in Buffalo, New York (Feb. 7, 1912). Justice White, after an operation, retired from the bench in 1910, at the age limit. George N. Russel, D.V.S, is Hellen's husband. They are at Cottonwood Falls, 1912. Charles H. Lawson brought suit against the Wright brothers for infringing his invention on Lightening the wires of Kites! *Case was dismissed June 1912.*

[The following information was tucked away in a pocket in the diary:]

October 1855 Friday 19th Traveled through Bourbon, a small town in the timber. Before noon w[e] came to a [blank] her prarie. After noon we passed through a small grove or strit [?] of timber and out into the prairie where "the wide the unbounded prospect lay before us" Erican pike 3/4 of a mile from Monticello, Piatt Co.

Saturday 20th Passed through Monticello and Marian At the p.m. Got out into the raw prairie, met a man enquired the way to Litlesville. He told us we were on the wrong road. We struck across the prairie to hunt for it. About dark we found it & traveled 1 1/4 put up till Monday.

Monday, Oct. 22nd Arrived at Bloomington about noon. Chas. hunted up Mr. Leeaper step-Bro. of Dr. Laurence. I wrote a letter. Drove to the post-office, enquired for a letter & mailed mine. Drove out of town. Bought some hay. Turned around and wnet back to Mr. Leaper's & staid all night. We concluded to give up going through in the wagon.

Tuesday Oct. 23rd At 9 1/2 o clock, I embarked on the cars (Illinois Central R.R.) Run to Mendota there changed to the Chicago & Burlington R.R. Started for Burlington at 2 o'clock Landed in the City about 8 o cl.

Wednesday 24th The stages being full I started afoot. Mr. Wallace's 10 ms. W. of Indianaola. Went 3 ms beyond Mt. Plea[s]ant. 30 ms.

Thursday 25th Traveled about 18 ms beyond Fairfield. 38 ms.

Friday 26th Fairfield some 7 ms west of Oskaloosa. 37 ms.

Saturday 27th Traveled 11 ms. beyond Knoxville. 31 ms. Put up at a Mr. Smith's.

Elisha and Mary Cragun's deed to Dan Wright for forty (40) acres of land in Rush Co., Indiana, for One Hundred and Fifty Dollars, is dated Feb. 27, 1823. Harvey Wright has the deed. I have it now, in 1912.

1913

Wednesday, January 1 It is a pleasant, bright, still day. Orville took me in his automobile out on the Xenia pike nine miles and back. I received a letter from Ethel Saltus Ludington, wife of the publisher of the Ladies Home Journal. She a descendant of our Wright family. I answer it.

Thursday, January 2 I slept about seven hours last night but was sleepy to-day. I wrote a card to Hatty Kelly 500 [blank], Findlay, Ohio; to Helen Russel, and sent to Dr. W.H. Clay a request of Miss Shepherd for Ohio minutes.

Friday, January 3 This is a snowy day. Katharine went to Cincinnati, to see the Taft pictures. I wrote to W.H. Becker & wife to Shaskatoon, Schaskatchawan, in reply to theirs. Horace and "Pekah" came at night.

Saturday, January 4 Cloudy, slight snow, not much cold. I wrote some letters & cards. Orville fixed a sled for Horace and "Pekah," and took them out riding at night, behind his auto.

Sunday, January 5 Slight rain in the morning. There is snow on the ground and on the roofs of houses. Lieut. Arnold dined with us. He is an interesting man. Horace and Alfred Andrews (Pekah) visit us in the afternoon, and stay till bed-time. It rains off most of the snow, by morning.

Monday, January 6 It is a cloudy morning. The snow and ice are nearly all melted. I got a blue typewriter ribbon. I got a lot of typewriter paper.

Tuesday, January 7 I read considerably. Lieut. Henry Arnold dined with us. I sat up late. The weather is mild.

Thursday, January 9 Engaged in reading the discussion on Secret Societies in Gen. Conf. of 1869, at Lebanon, Pa. Lieut. Henry Arnold took supper with us.

Friday, January 10 A slightly rainy day. I did little. Wrote a little on Church History. Agnes, Miss Mayer and Mrs. Stevens are for a game with Katharine.

Saturday, January 11 Cloudy day, slight rain. I wrote to Flora Glass. In 1838 and 1839, Jeremiah Anderson taught our School. John Kemper and other boys made him treat to apples. They got them at my father's, who would not let them have them till Jeremiah came.

Sunday, January 12 There is a little frost, but it is dark and cloudy. It clears off in the afternoon, and is bright. Liut. Henry Arnold comes to dinner. Horace & "Pekah" (Alfred) come after dinner.

Monday, January 13 I was at home. Jeremy Anderson boarded with us. He pretended a great admiration for Margaret Bloomfield, who was reported to be the heir to ten thousand dollars. This was probably in the year 1848. He and S.S. Wright had an appointment to meet Jane Bowser there, but went a day too early.

Tuesday, January 14 Lieut. Henry Arnold dined with us.

Wednesday, January 15 It is a somewhat rainy day. I wrote on the Law. I sent S.A. Stemen a check for $10.00. I wrote a card to Mabel Harris at Coin, Iowa, Chas. Jr.'s daughter. Home Rule Bill passed the House of Commons 368 to 258. Ireland victorious!

Thursday, January 16 received a letter from Mrs. Frances Longworthy Gibbs, my second cousin, at Dubuque, Iowa, daughter of Paulina, uncle Ralph's daughter, whom I saw when she was sixteen years old. She her daughter, is now seventy-one. Received a letter from Lizzie Brookbank, Braidenstown, Florida. Arnold dined with us.

Friday, January 17 Mrs. Frances Langworthy Gibbs picture came; she is a second cousin. Good-looking. In afternoon, I went to Woodland, and to town - bought type-writer paper, collars & neck-ties. Lieut. Arnold visited us at supper, and starts to Washington, this evening. Mrs. Gibbs is four feet ten inches, in height. Raymond Poncaire, elected President of France.

Saturday, January 18 No rain. Wrote a letter to Mrs. F.L. Gibbs, Dubuque, Iowa. Received a letter from S.A. Stemen, and card from Jas. F. Harris. Pres. Taft speaks in New York against the early independence of the Phillipines.

Sunday, January 19 I heard James B. Unthank at Summit Street, on text. He favored the evolutional theory rather than the revolutionary, but admitted both. Horace and "Pekah" came. "Benna" came at supper. Rev. Phillipi called to see Orville.

Monday, January 20 The floods continue along the lower Ohio. Pres. Taft speaks against the early independence of the Phillipines. President Taft accepts a professorship in Yale Law School. I am at home.

Tuesday, January 21 Knete Nelson, Rep., is elected Senator, by Minnesota; Harry Lane, Dem., from Oregon; LaBaron B. Cott, Rep., from Rhode Island; F.M. Simmons, Dem., from N. Carolina. I am at home.

Wednesday, January 22 The Turkish Gov. decides to yield Andrinople to the Balkans. George W. Norris, Rep., from Nebraska; Thomas Sterling, Rep., from South Dakota, & W.S. Kenyon, from Iowa, are elected U.S. senators. I am at home.

Thursday, January 23 I am at home. The War party in Constantinople revolts, the cabinet resigns, and Namis Pasha, War minister, is assassinated. New York Senate passes a resolution to submit a woman's Suffrage Amendment to the Constitution to a vote. Woman Suffrage adop. in Montana. John H. Shields , Dem. elected in Tennessee.

Monday, January 27 Wrote to Reuchlin in answer to a letter from him. I wrote a number of cards about this time—one to Emma Dennis.

Tuesday, January 28 Milton calls to see us in the afternoon, while his class goes vacating. His health is not good. He is quite nervous.

Wednesday, January 29 Orville talks of going to Germany to attend the Patent trial there.

Thursday, January 30 Working on my comments on Matthew, which I found hid away on top of my desk, back by the door! Wrote a letter in answer to one received to-day from Mrs. Gibbs, Dubuque.

Friday, Janaury 31 Work on my comments. Mr. Rosevelt visits us at Supper. He has been in Paris. His wife and daughter are there. Leila. It is pretty cold again to night. It has been a warm month. Katharine brought some wild flowers, last evening, bloomed in Mrs. O. Needham's door yard.

Saturday, February 1 It is sunshiny, but the inch of snow, fallen last night, does not melt. I went at 2:30, to see the picutres of flower gardens, all over the world. Very nice. At Memorial Building.

Sunday, February 2 Cold morning. Bright and clear. Ground-hog Day. [blank]Campbell, the garden Sup. came for dinner. He is a very smart man. Ben. V. Cl. and "Peka" Andrews came with Horace, and they staid till eight o'cl. Yellow Stone has two sets of falls. It snows in the night.

Monday, February 3 Snows a little. Cloudy. I am sleepy. Income Amendment to the Constitution of U.S. becomes effective. Game: Mrs. Stevens, Beck, Mayer. Oscar Needham dined. Harlow E. Spring, Sec'y of Enterprise and Loan Association, commits suicide. The Allies close the armistice of two months.

Wednesday, February 5 Clear, cold weather. The Allies again bombard Andrinople. Katharine went to Agnes Beck's. I am writing on my type writer.

Thursday, February 6 Fair, clear cold day. I am making some type-written sketches of the Koerner Family. Joseph Boyd called. Looks better.

Saturday, February 8 I was at home. Weather moderates a little. Katharine gaded about all day. Gas was low. Rev. Clarence R. White borrowed $115 to pay off a couple of notes.

Sunday, February 9 Slept much. Wrote a letter to Ella Rees, enclosing a sketch of her mother and father. Miss [blank] Mayer, Joe Boyd, Carrie Grumb. called. Horace, Alfred & Benj. visited Uncle Orville. Not so cold. Lorin & family called an hour.

Monday, February 10 Mild weather. Revolution reported in Mexico. At 2:00, Orville and Katharine are finishing up ready to start to Germany, and Lorin and Netta are here. At 2:30, Lorin goes with them to the Depot.

Tuesday, February 11 Trouble in Mexican Capital. I am writing some report of the Reeder lineage.

Wednesday, February 12 They are about to take Edward Ellis's wife to the insane assylum. Revolution in Mexico City. Diaz rises against Pres. Madero.

Thursday, February 13 I received a letter from Katharine at New York, Tuesday evening, who said they arrived an hour late and consequenty had a dollar refunded on each of their fares. They would go aboard the Mauretania that night. Jury condemns John H. Patterson, at Cincin. Judge Holister.

Friday, February 14 Young Diaz seems to prevail in Mexico City. The British in London have a great meeting, on the death of Capt. Robert F. Scott and his company, in the antarctic region. He fixed the pole, a half-mile from where Amunden did.

Saturday, February 15 It is a bright, temperate day. There came a letter from Bishop Wood, one from Flora V.C., White, and the Dalles fr. Mrs. Randall. Copy of a paper given by my grandmother Reeder, Flora sent.

Sunday, February 16 Cloudy and dark in the morning. I remained at home. The girls have Company in the evening.

Mondy, February 17 I visited Orville's new business house. Judge Holister sentences John H. Patterson and his men, to terms of imprisonment. Ivaquin Miller died to-day, in California.

Tuesday, February 18 It was a very beautiful day. Mr. Ainsworth and his wife, (Mrs. Corbett) called in the evening.

Wednesday, February 19 It is a bright, mild and sunshiny day. Mrs. Dillon and Sibyl Sanderson Fagan called. Sibyl is a whistler.

Thursday, February 20 It is a mild pleasant day. I received letters from Reuchlin, Helen and S.A. Stemen. Wrote to Reuchlin. Netta went to "Caddo's."

Friday, February 21 Sent CatharineWiley, a letter stating the purport of grandmother Reeder's statements, and a copy of grandmother's register as given about 1850, and heading it with a statement of the first Van Cleve ancestors. It is a pleasant but rather dark day. The girls go to basket ball.

Saturday, February 22 I wrote of the Reeders on the type-writer. Wrote some in the day.

Sunday, February 23 I did not sleep fully, last night, but made it up to-day. Four of Aunt Caddoe's children came in the afternoon. I wrote a letter to Katharine in Berlin, Germany addressed to Orville, Berlin.

Monday, February 24 Lorin sold his property on Second St., to Norman Hash, at $5000.00 to-day. It is a nice day. I slept well at night.

Tuesday, February 25 A pleasant day. I wrote to Bishop Wood. I slept well.

Wednesday, February 26 Slight snow melts off. Lorin washed off my head, with an egg, after dinner. I slept well.

Thursday, February 27 Picture in Journal of Wilbur and the honor paid him at the Plains of Avours.

Friday, February 28 I was at home all day. Lorin was figuring on the purchase of the Pfout's property in Dayton View. Milton came home from Oxford, Ohio to stay till Monday.

Saturday, March 1 At home all day. This morning, Lorin purchased property on Grand Avenue and Grafton Streets at auction for $9100.00, it being the property of [blank] Pfouts, who died by his own hands.

Sunday, March 2 Went on 8:40 train to Knightstown, arrived 10:59. Lorin hired an Automobile to Delila Wright's. Found th. Drucilla Frances, Grace; Faye, Lula Bealor, Dan, and wives; Benner Clara & family; Kirkpatrick & Effie; Augusta, Alma & Esta & their families; Earl & wife; Ed. Frazier and Grace; Jabez Rhodes; Thomas & Florence & their daughter, Mrs. McDaniel, there, Rilla. Lorin and Ivonette and I stay at Delila's.

Monday, March 3 We went with Grace & Thomas to Effie's, who have fine house & dine. Thomas & Grace take us to traction at Knightstown. We go to Greenfield, where Charles Gray and Luther Newhous & their wives, come in to see us at Depot. Come to Dayton on 3:32 train arri. at 5:57.

Tuesday, March 4 I slept much last night and to-day. I wrote a letter to Paris, to Katharine. I received a letter from Reuchlin, and answered it. Woodrow Wilson is the president. Pres. Taft retired gracefully. Roosevelt's ambition helped to retire Taft.

Wednesday, March 5 A little snow, melting. Cloudy forenoon. Woodrow Wilson is president—the twenty-eighth president. Lottie Andrews and Ella Leitch called in the afternoon.

Saturday, March 8 I receive letter from Martha Wottering asking help to D.O. Tussing to lift a $600.00 mortgage! Wrote her. Also wrote letters to Sallie E. Eudaly, of Grandfalls, Texas, and got one from S.L. Livingston.

Answered them. Oliver Gilbert is dead. Cold seems no better.

Sunday, March 9 I am a little better of my cold. Lottie Andrews called and [blank], who married a Moonie. Ben & "Peca" called for supper. Lorin, at 10:00 a.m., received a Cablegram from Orville at Paris, saying, "Sail to-day, George Washington." Harry and Clare Andrews called. Ivonette was with them.

Monday, March 10 Netta goes to help her washerwoman. I am better of my cold. Unsettled day.

Tuesday, March 11 Ivonette staid out of School and helped her mother clean the old house on Second Street.

Thursday, March 13 Aunt Caddo was with us at Night. The newspapers gave the French decision in Orville's favor.

Friday, March 14 The girls went to the basket-ball game, at the Lakeside Rink. It was a nice day.

Saturday, March 15 It was a very pretty day. A little windful and cooler toward evening. I went to see the new house in Oakwood. The brickwork of the first story is done, and the east end partly on second story. Ivonette was unwell.

Sunday, March 16 There was snow in the night, melting, as it fell, on the sidewalks. A thin skiff on the ground. Benjamin was with us to Supper.

Monday, March 17 I had an explosion of the Dining Room stove in starting it. I filed soot all over my head and neck. It is a very nice day. Lorin's move to Pfout's house in the afternoon. I wrote to Ellis Wright.

Tuesday, March 18 It is a beautiful day. I got a night message from Orville, New York, saying they arrived the evening of the 17th, stay a day, arrive Wedns. noon, at home.

Wednesday, March 19 A nice, bright morning, and nice all day. Orville & Katharine return home from Europe at 12:15. Lorin and Netta & Horace dine with us. Mr.

Crane after dinner took's Katharine and me out to see the new house in Oakwood.

Thursday, March 20 It is a very nice day, but somewhat windy. I walked by Lorin's old house in forenoon, and around his first Residence in the afternoon. Horace dined with us. The Misses Mayers and Mrs. Stevens come in for a game.

Saturday, March 22 Fair, cold morning. Ther. 26 degrees above. Fair day warms up. I go to Oakwood. The second story of the new house is two-thirds up.

Sunday, March 23 It rains this forenoon. Horace came in afternoon; and they go to look at the new House. He writes a letter.

Monday, March 24 I apprehended a flood. Felt the danger of it.

Tuesday, March 25 Alarm about the waters rising. Russell Hartzell comes with a canoe after Mrs. Wagner, and takes in me. We glide down Hawthorne and on Williams Street to William Hartzell's & they receive us most Christianly. The waters rise six or eight feet by 9:00, night, begin to subside at 11:00.

Wednesday, March 26 The waters fall about a half inch, an hour and till next night. We have a neighbor next north who came in (by bridge). From others we are cut off entirely. Our children advertize for me. There was a Washburn girl about three years old drowned. She lodged. Snyder waded & brought her in from bushes; Catharine.

Thursday, March 27 Mr. Siler passed, saw me, and reported to Orville, who came after me and Forest Stoltz. He got an automobile which took us to E.S. Lorentz, opposite the Seminary, Where I saw Katharine. I dined there. Frank Hale and Charles Grumbagh took me to Lorin's, Corner of Grand & Grafton Avenue.

Friday, March 28 At Lorin's there are Father and Mother Ainsworth, Harry Andrews & his family, Chas. Grumbaugh, his sister and wife, a colored woman who took diphtheria & Milton Came by buggy from Oxford. There was much trouble about diphtheria, Clare & three children. Dr. Spitler came. Andrews visited Dr.[?] Patterson.

Saturday, March 29 Father Ainsworth and Lorin's go out. Yesterday, I went to the bridge and up river; and to Wright lot & back. To-day I walked to bridge and to First Street & back. After dinner, Health Officer quarentined the house! Mrs. Stevens called. Clare went to the children at Earl Andrews, near Osborn.

Sunday, March 30 Many did not come back, after quarentine. Only Harry, Corbett, & Mr. Tho. Costello, remained, and they worked at Harry's house, all day. Katharine came. I wrote to Reuchlin. Curfew came before I mailed my letter. It is a bright day. Harry's mother married Orange Harrison, who retired from M.E. itinerancy. Is practicing law. Has a cancer.

Monday, March 31 I went to School-house and mailed letter to Reuchlin; and, later, to Ellis Wright and Flora Glass. I slept an hour, afternoon. Saw Katharine. Andrews worked at his house. It is a bright day, windy.

Tuesday, April 1 It is a bright day. Mrs. Stevens called. Says Orville and Katharine staid at their house last night. They have stayed there two nights at least. I mailed cards to Richard F. Braden.

Wednesday, April 2 I wrote cards to Mary H. Krout, Sina E. Ardery and so forth. Mr. Gabel brought me letters in the afternoon from A.N. King, Robert & from William Reeder. Perilla Mann, Bertha Glaze, Mary Jane Follis. It was a fine day.

Thursday, April 3 The morning was cloudy, temperature mild. I wrote to many of the relatives, and mailed the cards. It was a drizzly day.

Friday, April 4 I wrote to Reuchlin and to Flora Stevens. The day is cloudy.

Saturday, April 5 I walked home after dinner. Found Orville drying his bonds, as Lorin had done in forenoon. In the morning, quarentine was lifted. Mrs. Stevens was at our house an hour. Mailed some letters. Got several letters. It was a nice day.

Sunday, April 6 It is a bright day. I slept nine hours. I slept two hours in the forenoon. Orville and Katharine came while I was sleeping. They came again later on.

Monday, April 7 Gas pipes did not work, and so Orville did not come for me. Lorin's pipes worked for supper. Clifford Andrews, Harry's brother, who was flooded, called an hour. Harry and Corbett staid at Lorin's. I received several letters.

Tuesday, April 8 I walked to Broadway St., before breakfast. It is a bright day, a little cool. Ivonette is 17 years old to-day. The family go to Miami City. I aimed to go on Oakwood cars to 412 E. Sixth St., to see about Mrs. Stine, B.W. Mason's daughter, but found no car. M.F. Keiter died, a Liberal preacher, at Bremen, Ind.

Thursday, April 10 It rains just a little. I went on Oakwood Car to 412 Sixth Street, to learn that the widow Cline, Rev. B.W. Mason's daughter, had escaped the flood. Wrote five cards. Katharine came an hour. Orville called a few minutes.

Saturday, April 12 Cloudy day. I go to the bank- leave book. I look at late effects of fires. I walk to our house. Dine there. Gift to relief fund, D.L. Dull, $5. Orville takes me to Lorin's. I got letters from M.H. Krout and others. A little rain in the night.

Tuesday, April 15 Some sunshine. I write to Ellis Wright. Milton came home about noon. Clare Andrews supper at somewhere else.

Wednesday, April 16 I go to New House at Oakwood. The brick-layers are at work. Get my bankbook. There $366.18 to my credit. I go on Third Street car home. A[f]ter dinner, Orville brings me to Lorin's. I slept nine hours. It was a bright day.

Thursday, April 17 The day is bright. I wrote Archie Reeder. Sent the "The Reeder Family." Went afternoon home, via Green line to get my *Conservator*, and writing paper. Slept nine hours.

Friday, April 18 It is a bright day. I sent "After the Dayton Flood," to the *Conservator*. Orville came after me, and took me home to stay. Man beat our carpet.

Saturday, April 19 It is a bright, pleasant day. Slight cooler than yesterday. I wrote a letter to Earl Wright. Orville washes off his automobile. Lottie Jones and some country boys work for Katharine. Geo. Feight called in the evening.

Sunday, April 20 It is a bright day. A little cooler. I ate at 7:00, breakfast. After noon Horace came, and Orville and Katharine took him to the lot in Oakwood, where they gathered wild flowers. After Supper, Orville took Horace home.

Monday, April 21 It is a fine, bright day. I wrote on "Recollections of Politics." I went with Orville to the new house in Oakwood. The brick-work is about up to the third floor. A large attic space is intended below the roof. The auto-mobile worked badly. News: that Agnes (Osborn) Beck has a boy.

Tuesday, April 22 It is a hazy, sunshiny forenoon, I wrote a letter to Eliz. Brookbank. Warm at noon. Dining room papered. I look after papers saved from the flood.

Wednesday, April 23 Morning like Yesterday morning. Thermeter high. It is a nice day out of doors. Miss Winifred Ryder called. I wrote on my typewriter on "My Acquaintance with Politics."

Thursday, April 24 I write on my political acquaintance. Receive a letter and write one to Reuchlin. The children went out to the Oakwood house. The brickwork is nearly done. Mrs. Stevens called.

Friday, April 25 A pleasant day. Orville took me out to the new house and on the Centerville pike, And across to Springboro road. We found that gravel had been washed over the fields, and the bridge over the Miami was gone. Went home by Cincinnati Pike.

Saturday, April 26 It is a little rainy this morning. Paper hanger still continues. Received a letter from Lizzie (Williams) M. Leffler, Scio., Oregon and ansd it. Lottie works for us.

Sunday, April 27 Before noon, it was hazy or cloudy, and a few drops of rain fell. Orville and Kath. went out to the new house. They later went to Lorin's.

Monday, April 28 It rained last night, and a little this morning. David, Emma and Silas came. Lorin & family also. Netta & the children remained nearly all the afternoon. The Richmond folks start home about 2:30. Man lays carpet in front-room.

Tuesday, April 29 It is a very nice day. The paper-hanger finishes his work. Our house is pretty much fixed up again. Lorin called in the afternoon. Mrs. Wagner took supper with us .

Wednesday, April 30 It is a fair day. I spent considerable time examining the titles of new books in the South book case. Devillo Gebhart called as an old time acquaintance to sell a piano. I fell out of bed, to avoid cakes of ice flying through the air.

Thursday, May 1 It is a nice summer day. Mrs. Daughtery came to work for Katharine. Girls came for a game. Orville went down the river to try his hydroplane.

Friday, May 2 It is a fine summer day. Orville went down the river again. Came home at 2:30 for a lunch. Mrs. Dillon called. Mrs. Daugherty sent a note, excusing herself on account of sore feet.

It is a fine day. Orville went down the river again to try the aeroplane. He spent the day there. Charley Taylor's daughter brought a telegram, asking Charley to send a cylinder somewhere.

Sunday, May 4 It is a nice spring morning. I breakfast at 7:00. After dinner, I went out in auto with Orville to Lebanon Pike, and across west & by the Oakwood House. Then Orville & Kath. took a ride.

Monday, May 5 It is a warm spring day. Gov. Cox suspends Martial law. Orville & I run around the Soldiers' Home. Orville & Kath. take a trip.

Tuesday, May 6 Martial Law ceased, morn. A pleasant, though somewhat cloudy day. Katharine presided at the Young Woman's League. The wagons came and hauled away the mud in the gutters of our street. Katharine is elected president of the League.

Wednesday, May 7 It is a fine day. I wrote Albert A. Koerner. I went with Orville in the Auto 7 miles on the Xenia Pike and back. I examined some of my old papers on the "Wright Family" and adapted them to our latest accounts.

Friday, May 9 It is somewhat cloudy in the forenoon. I received and answered Grace Frazier's letter. Lorin called, brought a Wistaria flower, Japanese. Kath. went at night to Mrs. Loos's to a party.

Saturday, May 10 Sunshiny morning, cooler. I wrote to Ray W. Stevens and to Harris Earls Petree. It is cooler in the evening.

Sunday, May 11 It is a sunshiny morning. We dismissed Journal carrier, and employed Eugene Heywood. Orv. & Kath. went after Horace. I slept in forenoon. Orville took Horace home after lunch in the evening.

Tuesday, May 13 May 13th, 1839, we had a killing frost in Rush Co., Ind. No apples that year. I spent some time in looking over old papers, relating to the Family. Rev. Unthank and his wife called. Told of Nicklas telling of a preacher whom I listened to, who often talked about flying. Drawing on imagination!

Friday, May 16 It is somewhat cloudy but pleasant. I spent the day in looking over old letters, destroying some. We went to Lorin's for supper. Home at 8:30.

Saturday, May 17 I am to-day 84 years and six months old. I am at home. Mary [blank] comes to work for us. Relief applicants come. Mary had headache and did not continue many days.

Sunday, May 18 I remain at home. Orville and Kath. take an automobile ride in forenoon. Horace and his cousins Ben. & Peka come and Orville takes them out to his new house in Oakwood. A nice day.

Tuesday, May 20 The election was to-day. News in the evening very favorable to the Commission Plan. I voted for it and 14 of the citizen's ticket.

Wednesday, May 21 The papers report the commission Plan adopted by a great majority, and the Citizen's Ticket elected by about 10,000 plurality. It rained in the afternoon and at night. The *Conservator* came giving us first news of Gen. Conf. W. Dillon reelected editor. Hoskins, Wood & Alwood Bish.

Thursday, May 22 I was working on old letters. I learn that Wood had 28 votes, Hoskins 35, Alwood was elected on 5th ballot. Dillon elected on 23 votes as editor. J. Howe was elected on 35 votes, as Sec. Mis. Soci. Clay got 12 votes for bishop, 14 for Pub. Agent. Oler 3 as bishop.

Friday, May 23 Wrote out, from J.M Johnson's notes, an article for the *Conservator*. I wrote to Rev. J. Howe. Otis Reeder died at his brother James at Waverly, Kansas.

Saturday, May 24 I sent two articles to *Conservator*; one "From J.M. Johnson", an other, the "Case of Andrew Ringer."

Sunday, May 25 Harace, Ben & Peka come in afternoon, and go out to Oakwood. At the Cash Register, there was an enthusiastic meeting over the Relief Fund. At about 8:50, at night, it was raised to $2,000,000, and increased to over that.

Tuesday, May 27 Rained a little. The Dr. came at noon. I wrote letters to Cinthia Croddy, and to Cousin Gibbs, at Dubuque. Mrs. Masters and Mrs. Kline call for relief, from the Red Cross, of which Kath. if the Committeeman.

Wednesday, May 28 The day is partly sunshiny. Katharine goes to Richmond, to see Emma Dennis. I sleep part of the forenoon.

Friday, May 30 I took supper at Lorin's. Orville and Katharine and Ivonette go to Oakwood and take supper outdoor there.

Saturday, May 31 Katharine anoints my back and rubs it. Orville goes out to Oakwood and have an out-door supper there. Orv. & Kath. are away at supper.

Sunday, June 1 It is partly cloudy. Threatening storm at 11:00. I slept from eight to ten oclock. Horace Ben and Peka come afternoon and stay till after lunch. Katharine anoints my back.

Monday, June 2 It is a nice day. I slept in forenoon. An Oregon, Missouri, paper comes with pictures of Lou Estella, Leo Webb, and Harris Earls Petree in it. They graduated in 1911, 1912, & 1913, and all stood at the head of their class. I rode after supper with Orville up Wolf Creek, down Salem pike, home. Called at Wm. Hartzell's, in a walk.

Tuesday, June 3 I am at home, as usual. Kath. anoints my back daily with mustard ointment.

Thursday, June 5 I lamed my back by an unpropitious turn. George Feight called in the evening, and he and Orville took a ride in the auto. Kath. is away at dinner, and at supper at Miss Mayers. Orv. flew up stream to Broadway. He carried three passengers besides himself.

Friday, June 6 Orville & Kath. went down the river to see about the hydroplane. Kath was away much of the day. It is a warm night.

Sunday, June 8 It was a cool morning and nice forenoon. I slept an hour. Horace came home with Orv. & Kath. from Oakwood and ate dinner with us. Ben. & Peka came and went out with Orv. to Oakwood. Prof. Woerthner was to meet them and tell the names of trees. They have 35 kinds of trees.

Monday, June 9 It was a nice cool day. Katharine away nearly all day. I remain at home. Horace ate dinner with us.

Wednesday, June 11 Horace ate dinner with us. In the evening, I got a telegram from Bert Benner, saying Aunt Delila died. I telegraphed that I could not attend the funeral, on account of lumbago.

Thursday, June 12 Katharine went to see Agnes Beck, was gone till in the night, near Lebanon.

Friday, June 13 In the evening, Dr. Edward F. Divine and three Red Cross women came and ate supper with us. Miss Bojsen is quite a talker. Miss Rankin is a tall thoughtful woman.

Saturday, June 14 Orville spent the day with the Hydroplane on the river, where Dr. E.F. Divine and his stenographer, Miss McHugh, and Miss Rankin and Miss Bojsen take a short ride with him. He also flies up to Main Street bridge and back, eight miles, round trip.

Sunday, June 15 I slept most of the day. Two women came inquiring for the old Wright house (Lorin's) and Norman Hash's. Orville is unwell to-day. It is the warmest day in the year, so far.

Monday, June 16 I got up at 6:30. Slept after breakfast. There was some thunder around in the forenoon. No rain. It is a very hot day. Dr. Spitler came to see Orville. Orville gets up my electric fan. Mrs. Rachael Wagner from Peru came. Orville took her out to Eleanor Stolt's.

Tuesday, June 17 It is a very warm day. Orville took me to Riverdale and to Lorin's. I sat up till after 10:00 at night.

Wednesday, June 18 It is a clear day. Breakfasted at 6:40. Slept a_ter breakfast. In the afternoon, I went to the Soldiers' Home. Came home at 6:00. Winnifred Ryder came to supper. It is a very warm day.

Thursday, June 19 Wrote to Reuchlin, and to Grace Frazer. It is a very hot day. Katharine and Mrs. Justina Stevens attended High School commencement at Steel's building.

Friday, June 20 This is the hottest day of all, so far. I answered Kitty Frazee's letter. Sioux City, Iowa, and Rev. John McBride's card from Kendallsville, Ind.

Saturday, June 21 It was a very hot day. In the afternoon a little before night, there was a sprinkle of rain, and the air turned down to 78 degrees. I rode with Orville out to the end of the Greenline road beyond Oscar Needham's late residence. Lorin's came. It rained in the night.

Tuesday, June 24 In the evening, I wrote on the attributes of Infinity and the qualities of the Finite Attributes of the Infinite: 1. Eternity 2. All Wisdom, 3. Unchangeable self-existence, 4. Space. 5. All true Love, 7. All power & Justice, 9. Spirituality.

Wednesday, June 25 Orville went out with me ten miles toward Xenia. His tire gave out and it took a half-hour

to put on a new one. Dr. Divine and his secretary Miss McHugh were at our house on our return.

Thursday, June 26 Flowers brought by John Patterson's direction to a few houses on the opposite of Hawthorn St.

Friday, June 27 Resodded on Hawthorn Street on Saturday. Some fences are torn away Saturday.

Saturday, June 28 Letters from J.F. Harris and Sallie Eudaly, answered. Orville looses auto-light by failure of battery connection. It is probably the hottest day of the year.

Sunday, June 29 It was a very hot day. Horace came in the afternoon and staid till after supper. Orville was threat[en]ed with arrest by a cop for rapid driving.

Monday, June 30 It was a roasting hot day. Milton came in the evening and staid an hour. Orville ran the hose over my roof and adjusted the fan, so I slept comfortable. He came near running over a 9 year old girl who stopped in the way of his auto.

Friday, July 4 In the afternoon, Orville took me to his lot in Oakwood Where Lorin and his family, Ben and Peka & William Andrews and wife, Willie Jenkins, and Wm. Shank's daugher, were where we ate supper, and went to the top of Orville's new house, and saw the fireworks at the fair grounds till 9 o'clock. Ella Leitch brought some cake.

Saturday, July 5 In the afternoon (Eve.) I rode with Orville past Lorin's up Salem Ave. and across to the end of the Green Line Cars and down home. We had a thunder storm.

Sunday, July 6 It is a cool, pleasant, day. Orville and Katharine take a ride in the auto. I sleep much at home.

Monday, July 7 I slept considerably. After supper, I rode with Orville to Lorin's and back. Harmon's Agt. called to see Katharine about furnishing the house in Oakwood.

Tuesday, July 8 I awoke at 5: 00 , and hungered till 7:00. I went to bed till nine, after breakfast. Orville went to meet the Wright Co., in New York.

Wednesday, July 9 It was a very hot day till a thunderstorm in the evening. Misses Mayers and Miss J. Stevens dine with us. The thunderstorm fired several barnes over south, and was attended in some places with hail.

Thursday, July 10 Orville's thin suit came from the cleaner's. The day is cool and pleasant. So also the night. Mrs. Rachel Wagner called in the evening.

Friday, July 11 Orville came home at 8:00, morning. Horace had a birth-day party, (his cousins) at home. My head swam on account of my back.

Saturday, July 12 I am better of my head swimming. In the evening my thin suit came.

Sunday, July 13 I went with Orville, in forenoon, to Aviation Grounds, and circle east to near Harshmanville, on home. Orville and Katharine, with Horace, Ben, and Peka, go to Oakwood and the kids supper with them, at our house.

Monday, July 14 Miss Florence Evans comes, and she and Katharine, explore the Young Women's League as a Committee on Appt. of committees. Mrs. [blank] is doing Katharine's work.

Tuesday, July 15 Mrs. [blank] doing Katharine's work. The weather flies back to warm—hot!

Wednesday, July 16 "Lide Hoffman" came in the evening, to consult on what for her to do. It is a warm night. I mail a six-page letter to Sina E. Ardery giving the present genealogy of the Reeders in America. Wrote card to Reuchlin in Sayner, Wis., and one to J.F. Harris at Washington, D.C.

Thursday, July 17 Lena Boley comes to do our work, at 10:00. Orville takes me to his lot, and puts up hammock to red-bud bushes, where spend afternoon.

Friday, July 18 We go again to Orville's lot on the north hill, and spend Afternoon. Read late in Encyclopedia Britanica, 11 edition.

Saturday, July 19 Orville and Katharine go out and spend afternoon. I read again in Encyclopedia Britanica.

Sunday, July 20 I read in Lawrence's Encyclopedia.["Encyclopedia" crossed out of text] Orville and Katharine visit Lorin's. She Mrs. Trofloupe writes as if for English aristocracy. The Established Church, and enemy of revivals.

Monday, July 21 I read Mrs. Trollope's accounts of her visit to America. Poor Stuff. She is however an engaging writer.

Tuesday, July 22 Called at Lorin's in the evening.

Thursday, July 24 It rained early in the morning. It is somewhat Cooler. At 10:00 Adam Howard of Sugar Grove, called upon me, and his nephew, called an hour. He knew of Keiter's being found a rogue.

Saturday, July 26 Isaac Swartzel and his wife Lizzie called to get their marriage certificate. I agreed to send one soon.

Sunday, July 27 Horace and "Peka" called afternoon, and Orville went with them to Oakwood. They lunched here. Miss Rankin and Boysen called in the evening. Red Cross visitors.

Monday, July 28 Kath. was called to town to see something about Young Woman's League business. Orville went for her but did not find her. She came home soon after.

Tuesday, July 29 We went to Orville's dooryard—supped there—and spent the evening on Orville's roof. It is 42 feet above the ground. He had a nice breeze there.

Wednesday, July 30 At 4 o'clock, we went to Orville's lot and ate supper on the roof of his house. Mr. Loeoning was with us. It was cool up there. We stayed till nearly 9:00. This is said to have been the hottest day of the very hot summer. In some places, it was 100 degrees, and others 106. Sent the Marriage Cert.

Thursday, July 31 This is a very warm forenoon, and also in the afternoon. We remain at home. Dr. E.F. Divine called in the evening to see Orville about some who said they knew him.

Saturday, August 2 I called at Lorin's in the evening.

Sunday, August 3 James F. Harris came about 2:00, from Washington City, on his way to Ola's, in Rush County, Ind.

Monday, August 4 James Harris went in the afternoon to visit Lorin's family. Mr. G.C. Loening and Katharine went to town to some evening show.

Tuesday, August 5 J.F. Harris, my sister Sarah's second son that lived, now 65 years old, went on the 8:00 train to Connersville, to visit his half-brother Albert Harris.

Friday, August 8 Orville and Katharine went, after supper, to Oakwood, and, next, to hear ex-Mayor [blank]and Dr. D. Frank Garland, speak on the new Charter. They regard Garland as a specially fine speaker. I go to Mrs. Wagoner's.

Saturday, August 9 Mr. Robbins, Harriet Silliman's husband, took dinner with us, and staid till 9:00 at night. A letter from J.F. Harris says he found all well at Connersville, at Ola's, and Aunt Lucy's.

Sunday, August 10 Horace and "Peka" came at 2:00 and staid till 5:00. Orville took me to Lorin's.

Tuesday, August 12 This is election day, on the adoption of the new city charter . I vote "Yes, " at 8: 00, morning.

Wednesday, August 13 The City Charter was adopted by more than two to one votes.

Saturday, August 16 In the evening, Orville takes me out to his house, which is mostly plastered, the columns set up, and the cornice on. We then went to Lorin's a few minutes on Grafton Avenue.

Sunday, August 17 Horace came to dine with us, and remained after lunch. Orville took him home and his cousin Peka,who had called in. The weather has been unusually warm for some weeks.

Friday, August 22 Agnes Beck dined supped and lodged with us. She and Katharine have been intimate friends since little girls together.

Saturday, August 23 Mrs. Agnes Beck took breakfast with us. She reports her grandmother as quite well. She is 91 years old. I wrote to Auglaize Conference. Also wrote to the Reeder Family who meet the 27th at Oliver Glass's in Wabash County.

Sunday, August 24 Orville and Katharine and Benney and Pekah go to the house at Oakwood. Mr. Loerning dined with us.

Tuesday, August 26 Katharine dines at Rike's. Some girls come in afternoon.

Wednesday, August 27 August 27, 1853, we had quite a frost. To-day the Reeder Reunion meets at Flora M. Glass's house, near Lincolnville, Indiana. I wrote Reuchlin to-day. It is a very hot night. My electric fan wards off the heat. I hear the Margaret Collier and her brother are at Glass's, Reeder Day.

Friday, August 29 Katharine went to the N.C. Register Club, to assist in a picknick of 1300 boy-gardners. In the evening, she attended the Suffragette entertainment in Dayton View. Orville and I spent an evening hour at Lorin's. Cooler to-day, again.

Saturday, August 30 Wrote Helen Russel and Bertha Glaze. It is cool to-day.

Monday, September 1 Winifred Rider took supper with us. It was very hot in the afternoon. She returned from a trip to Cape Cod and mostly at Andover, where her father is a professor. They live at Cambrige.

Thursday, September 4 Mr. Hardesty, of N.C.R., a grandson of Solomon Vonneida, comes in an Automobile, with a photographer, and has him take pictures of Bigger's house and of ours including me, etc. I sat on the porch all forenoon; it was pleasant. Hardesty acts in behalf of Welfare department, N.C.R.

Friday, September 5 Orville went out to Simm's to again try a new aeroplane.

Saturday, September 6 Mrs. S. Stevens dined with us and stayed most of the afternoon.

Sunday, September 7 Mr. G.C. Leoning dined with us.

Horace and "Pekah" stay all afternoon & till after lunch. Orville takes them home.

Monday, September 8 St. Petersburg, Penellas County, Florida. Mabel Shepherd, whose feet were frozen in the flood, called this evening.

Tuesday, September 9 Mabel Shepherd called again and Katharine went with her. I wrote to Ellis Wright about renting my farm. I also wrote to Reuchlin.

Wednesday, September 10 Orville and Katharine went to Xenia, to see about Mabel's entering School. I went to Lorin's to supper. Orville came and took me home.

Thursday, September 11 Miss Hunt called in the evening, to talk over association matters.

Friday, September 12 There was sleight rain, and clouds, in the forenoon. I wrote to Ray Stevens.

Saturday, September 13 Katharine went in afternoon to Young Women's Association Picnic out in Oakwood, and took her supper with her.

Sunday, September 14 I slept most of the forenoon. Horace and his cousins came in the afternoon.

Wednesday, September 17 This is Leontine's fifteenth birth-day anniversary. Prof.[blank] Rider came to see Winnifred. It was rather a rainy day and evening.

Thursday, September 18 Prof. [blank] Rider of Andover called a few minutes with Winifred, at 9:15.

Friday, September 19 Katharine in the evening attended a reception at the Y.W. League.

Saturday, September 20 Mr. Brewer and Mr. Oglevie, from England, came before 10:00. Horace, Ben. & Alfred came and stayed till after supper. Mr. James Jacobs called an hour.

Sunday, September 21 Mr. Griffith and Alexander Oglevie dine and sup with us.

Monday, September 22 I received a letter from Ray

Stevens. All well. Mr. Brewer and Oglevie dine and sup with us.

Tuesday, September 23 Mr. Brewer and Oglevie dine and sup with us. They went out with Orville & Kath. to the flying ground.

Wednesday, September 24 Received a letter from Reuchlin. I wrote one to Emma Zeller Dennis. She is a fine letter writer.

Thursday, September 25 Messrs. Brewer and Oglevie dine and sup with us. Orville and they spend the afternoon at aviation grounds.

Friday, September 26 Orville and Katharine go out to the aviation grounds in the afternoon, Mr. Brewer and Oglevie with them, who dine and sup with us.

Saturday, September 27 Katharine goes down to Howard Beck's, with some town girls, near Lebanon and spends the day. Orville and his visitors, go out to aviation grounds, to try an automatic machine.

Sunday, September 28 The weather is warmer. Orville and Katharine go to the new house at Oak-Wood. Messrs. Brewer and Oglevie dine and sup with us.

Monday, September 29 Mr. Brewer and Oglevie dine and sup with us.

Tuesday, September 30 Katharine and Orville and their visitors went to the aviation grounds, to try the automa[t]ic machine, with which Orville is much encouraged. After supper, Mr. Brewer started to Washington, on his way home. Lena Bolen left. She was one of the best girls we ever had.

Wednesday, October 1 Mr. Oglevie dines and sups with us. Horace is with us to Supper. I receive a letter of inquiry from Mrs. Edith Moore, Laclede, Missouri. She Sq[u]ire Boone's descendant. I wrote her.

Thursday, October 2 Mr. Oglevie started to New York to-night. He dined and supped with us.

Saturday, October 4 Orville and Katharine go to aviation field in the afternoon. They went to the Beckel House for supper with Mr. Lenning and his brother. I finish the article on Rev. John Fohl and forward it in the evening. Carrie got my supper for me.

Wednesday, October 8 Orville went to Cincinnati, to have a talk with Attor. Fish, his lawyer in the Curtis case, at 1:00. He came back at 8:00, Fish has a case tomorrow in the court at Cincinnati.

Saturday, October 11 Orville keeps the fire going in his new house. He spends the afternoon flying, or projecting with his automatic arrangement.

Saturday, October 18 Wrote a letter in answer to inquiries about how to trace the military record of her Ancestors, of Edith Baldwin Moore, giving my own experiences. She is at Laclede, Missouri. Those ancestors were the Masters. Mrs. Moore is a descen[d]ant of Squire Boone, who married Jane Van Cleve and went from the Yadkin to Kentucky with Daniel.

Sunday, October 19 The children make fire at the new house. Ben, Pekah, & Horace come. They stay most of the afternoon.

Tuesday, October 21 Katharine went to Geneva, Ohio.

Wednesday, October 22 Sent ten dollars to Cinthia Croddy. Rev. William Miller (aged ninety) and wife and his brother Charles, called an hour to see me. He is one of the best men I ever knew.

Thursday, October 23 It is slightly rainy. I get letters from Reuchlin and Ellis Wright.

Saturday, October 25 Katharine came home on 5:35 train which was three-quarters of an hour late.

Sunday, October 26 Orv. & Katharine took Horace to the new House, built fire and came home at 12:30. After dinner, Ben and Peka came.

Tuesday, October 28 Lorin dined with me. Ivonette and Leontine came to supper and stayed till toward bed-time.[This entry was crossed out of diary]

Thursday, October 30 Lorin Netta and Horace came to supper.[Entry crossed out of diary]

Sunday, November 2 Orville and Katharine returned home at 11:00 forenoon.[Entry crossed out of diary]

Monday, November 3 Orville and Katharine started afternoon to New York City. Clara (Carrie) and Charles staid with us.

Tuesday, November 4–Saturday, November 8 Ivonette and Leontine came to supper and staid till toward bed-time. . . . Lorin dined at our house. . . . Lorin took me to his house for dinner.

Sunday, November 9 Orville and Katharine came home from New York. Horace did not come as usual. Lorin and Netta came.

Sunday, November 16 Ben and Peka came after Horace who ate dinner with us.

Monday, November 17 Lorin's whole family, except Milton, ate supper with us. Mrs. Stevens called in the evening before supper.

Wednesday, November 19 I wrote Albert A. Koerner and Kate Van Fleet. I received a letter from Cory Dillon.

Thursday, November 20 Wrote to Cora, and to J.F. Harris.

Thursday, November 27 Winifred Ryder and G.C. Leining dined with us.

Saturday, November 29 Horace bought two Canary birds! Orville and Katharine went

Tuesday, December 2 Rev. M. Claypool and his son, pastor of Ev. Association at Philipsburg, Ohio dined with us.

Thursday, December 4 Katharine went to a concert at Victoria Theater.

Friday, December 5 Orville took me out to see the new house. Mr. Grumbach burns some leaves. It is too wet. Orville and Katharine went at 5:00 to Miss Dorathy Patterson's reception.

Thursday, December 11 "Pa Biggs" called in the evening to see Katharine. He is six feet 4 inches tall and his feet are twelve inches long.

Saturday, December 13 Orville is practising at Simm's Station and does not come home for dinner. Dr. Spitler called at six o'clock.

Sunday, December 14 Orville and Katharine and Horace went out to the new house. Horace went home to supper. Mr. Lenning came for supper.

Monday, December 15 Col.[blank] Reber dined and supped with us. Also Mr. Lenning supped with us. Reber is the son-in-law of Gen. Miles. He wants Orville to go to San Diego to teach aviators some of his theories. He is 6 ft 3 in. tall.

Tuesday, December 16 I got a letter from Reuchlin and card from James Harris. He tells of Carrie V. Harris, his Uncle James Harris's only child—who is at Woodville, Miss.

Wednesday, December 17 Mrs. J. Steven eats supper with Katharine. The supper at Aero Club is in New York this evening. Orville is there. It is the tenth anniversary of their first flight's at Kitty Hawk, N.C.

Thursday, December 18 Katharine dines at Rike's with Mrs. [blank] Orville attends another dinner in New York.

Friday, December 19 Mrs. J. Stevens sups and spends the evening with Katharine.

Sunday, December 21 Orville and Katharine phone to Horace & take him out to their house. Katharine went to a Y.W. League Supper; and Lorin & Netta came, and Horace goes with them. He was persistent in questions to Orville about pushing lots into the rivers at N.York. He fancied it on the Ocean.

Monday, December 22 Winifred Ryder ate supper with us. She goes to Boston in her vacation, starting soon.

Wednesday, December 24 Lorin's all ate supper with us. Milton is home in his vacation. He is in his third year in the State University at Oxford.

Thursday, December 25 Carrie Grumbach was excused. We ate dinner alone.

Friday, December 26 Edwin H. Sines, Orville's playmate, called awhile in the evening.

Sunday, December 28 Lorin, Netta and Ivonette went out to the new house with Orville and Katharine. Horace staid till 8:00 at night.

Monday, December 29 Orville went to Simm's Station. Mr. Loening called for supper and spent the evening at our house. His name is Grover Cleaveland Loening.

Notes at the end of the diary

Edward Milton Croddy, born March 29, 1875.

1913
Tues. 25, March, 1913
About 8:00 forenoon the waters burst onto our Street. I put on my overcoat, ready to go. A canoe came for Mrs. E. Wagner, and the boys said I could get in too. It glided across to Williams St. to William Hartzell's, next north of the Baptist Church. I walked in the door- saved my shoes. His wife is sick abed. She was Jemima Ellen Schell. Their sons were Russell, Layton, and Howard, 22 & 14. Their girls, Mary, 12, Mildred and Carrie, 6. A smart nice family. They belong at Lutheran Church. They treated us the kindest. Their house is a two story, plastered Atic above. Hartzell's (aged 42), parents died when he was young. Hers are living. He is intelligent, thoughtful, and Christian. The boys were out rescueing and Mrs. Pexton directed them to find Mrs. Wagner. Our children asked if they could take me. A young man carried me on his shoulders and set me in the canoe. We had no fire after Tuesday forenoon, only coal oil & alcohol. Our rations were limited, but sufficient. We had bread, eggs, etc. On Wednesday, we waited for the waters to go down, and Wednesday night. They discovered a child lodged in the next door yard north, and Daniel Snyder waded out & brought it to his house, where it lay till Wednesday morning, when I went in to see it. Just then its father came (Washburn) and took it away. While there, Mr. [blank] Siler, saw me and reported me to Orville. I slept a little Tuesday night, and more Wednesday night.

Mr. Hartzell slept three hours Wednesday night. A swift river flowed down Williams Street, and, toward Hawthorn Street, many sheds floated and were wrecked Tuesday. It carried off Hartzell's chicken house, and drowned his chickens, which had been moved to the barn. It seemed as if a widow and an old man had been Providentially provided for. We knew not what our near neighbors were doing, except Snyder's north of us. We had no word about our children till Thursday morning. Katharine had advertised for me Wednesday, on Hawthorn Street. Lorin a week before had moved from Second St. to 331 Grafton Avenue, Cor. Grand Avenue. I had counseled higher ground (that policy) for a year past. The flood was second to Noah's.

March 27, 1913
Orville and Mr. Stolts came after us and took us away in an auto-mobile, to E.S. Lorenz. I dined there and Charles Grumbaugh and Frank Hale took me, after dinner to Lorin's who moved a week before to Grand and Grafton. There I staid three weeks and one day, when we got gas, and I moved home again. We were quarantined at Lorin's a week because Drs. Smith and Patterson pronounced a colored woman serving at Lorin's as being a bad case of diphtheria. She had quinsy! At least two-thirds of the City was submerged. A considerable part, there was water in the second story of the buildings. The water came up 5 feet and five inches in our lower rooms. A few houses were washed away. Three or more fires broke out One burned just west of Orville's office, several buildings. Another burned several buildings, including the Park Presbyterian Church. Another burned several houses, south on Main Street, just north of the Fair Grounds, where there was quite a current of water flowed. The removal of the sediment and the cleaning of the dirt from the cellar, lower rooms, and door-yard took a hard month's work. The loss of books, furniture etc. amounted to a large part of a thousand dollars. Orville's automobile was submerged and injured several hundred dollars. In all he and the family lost one thousand dollars. Then his new building was injured nearly another thousand. Orville lost a pianola costing 500 dollars, and other furniture, amounting to three hundred. I lost a few books of value, and the family lost two or three hundred dollars worth. The dwellings, stores and shops of the city were injured many tens, if not hundreds, of millions. It has since been estimated at $200,000,000.

Rev. N. Allebaugh with me Aug. 21, 1912, that he had found a copy of the minutes of Scioto Conference of 1880, which says Rev. B. Gillespie died that year, he thinks in May. Johnathan Franklin Croddy died Sept. 5, 1908, at Gibson City, Ill.; he was buried Sept. 7th. Funeral by Rev. M.B. Leach at 11 o'clock, morn, at U.B. Church. I gave him $35.00 to pay on his Clay County home, and $90.00 to pay out on his Gibson City house and lot. I collected nothing, but gave him from ten to 30 dollars a year for many years of his life. Since, I have paid like sums to his widow.

J.F. Harris, 545 Cent. Avenue St. Petersburg, Pinellas Co., Florida.

The Man Who Threw the Bat that Struck Wilbur at the Soldiers' Home
Dr. Oliver Crook Haugh was electrocuted in Columbus, Ohio, November 4th 1906, just after midnight. He killed his father and mother and brother November 4th, 1905, and set fire to the house to conceal the crime. When asked if he had anything to say, he simply shook his head. It is said, however, that he never admitted his guilt. Attempts have been made to connect him with the murder of several women who were mysteriously strangulated. Also, he was said to have been involved in the murder of Mary Twobey, who died at Lorian, Ohio; and Anna Patterson at Chicago. He was divorced from his wife, who had two children.

My house in Grant Co., Ind. was reported finished Sept 3, 1902.

G.W. Bethers was Connor's neighbor, near Corvallis. Rev. Glezen Asbury Reeder, P.E. in M.E. Church at Cleveland Ohio, is a descendant of Benjamin Reeder of New Jersey, brother of Joseph, the 3rd. Squire Boone's descendants are: Mrs. Blanche Baldwin Bundun and Edith Moore, Laclede, Missouri.

Sallie E. Eudaly, Ward Co., Texas, Grand Falls. Her maiden name was Sally Snyder, born in 1840, her mother "Patsy" (Martha) Freeman Snyder. When the mother died she left Sally to my mother, but her father could not part with her.

I was born in Richland To., Rush Co., Ind., November

17, 1828. I remember being at Aunt Sarah Croddy's and Mary Brown's the summer before I was three years old. I went with Alexander Croddy for a pail of water; and Darwin scratched my eye, as we ran under the bed, in play. Just before a Camp-meeting at Hopewell, Dr. Brown & Aunt Mary came, and the doctor vaccinated me. I squalled like a good fellow. It left a perfect mark, the only time vacination ever affected me. I remember being at the Camp Meeting and my grandmother asking: "Do you hear those negroes singing in their tent."

The lawsuit of Landrumn was at Waverly, Tennessee. Judge Stout sat to hear case.

Flora V. White, 403 E. Main St. Portland, Ind. Clara Day, Richmond, Ind, 423 Kinsey St.; She has Uncle Benjamin's Bible. She is his granddaughter. Joseph Guernsey Cannon.

Sina E. Ardery 426 E. First St., Hutchinson, Ken. Mary H. Krout, 218 College Street Crawfordsville, Ind. Mrs. Eliz. M. Leffler, Scio, Linn Co., Oregon.

Emma Baldwin and her Husband Burton Baldwin were noted evangelists in the Radical United Brethren Church, their only son being Lorin B. Baldwin, a professor in Oregon.

Jonathan Franklin Croddy, born in Rush County, Ind., Nov. 21, 1841, died in Gibson City, Illinois, Saturday evening Sept. 5, 1908 at 8:20. His funeral was at the U.B. Church, the next Monday, Sept. 7, 1908, his funeral sermon being preached by Rev. M.B. Leach, and his burial in Gibson City. He came to my mother about Aug. 20, 1842, at nine months old, and lived there till he was married, which was December 31, 1863. I loaned him [rest is blank]

Distant Relatives.
Mrs. Ethel S. Ludington, Ardmore, Pa.
William C. Wright, 42 Mechanic St., Fitchburg, Mass. He furnished his Aunts, Justus Wright's Memorial It gave Samuel Wright's father (of Springfield) as Samuel, which is probably correct.

1914

Thursday, January 1 This, since November 17th has been my 86th year, and to-day is my 86th New Year Day. It is a hundred years since my father, at 24 years of age, came to Centerville, in this County. In Centerville, Feb. 12, 1818, my father and mother were united in marriage, by Rev. Dyer Burges, a Pres. Presbyterian minister .

Friday, January 2 It is fifty-three years since James Buchanan went out of office and Abraham Lincoln came in. What a fruitful half a century it has been! Slavery ended! and the colored people owning vast wealth, and making the most rapid advances in civilization! It seems slow, but it is so very fast!

Saturday, January 3 Mrs. E. Wagner and Rachel and Anna Feight dined with us. Rachel is her last year at Oberlin College, to which she goes back Monday. Anna Feight, is a sanitary cook, late in Colleges in New York. She, like Katharine, is in fine flesh. She kept house for her Uncle John till his death.

Sunday, January 4 Orville & Katharine, at 8:00 evening, took traction cars to Eaton, for locomotive on the Grand Rapids and Indiana, to Grand Rapids, Michigan. They go to select and buy furniture for their new house, in Oakwood.

Monday, January 5 The snow which began Sunday morning is still on the limbs of the trees. The temperature is very moderate. The day is cloudy. Lorin dined with me.

Wednesday, Janaury 7 Lorin dined with me. The day is cloudy. The temperature is moderate.

Thursday, Janaury 8 Orville and Katharine came home on 8:00 morning train. They purchased at Grand Rapids several thousand dollars of furniture, to be delivered the middle of March. I wrote full cards to several: Etta Ogden Hall, Drusilla, and Gusta; A letter to Oliver Buller.

Friday, January 9 Katharine was unwell—lay abed till evening. I wrote full cards to Clara, Estella, Kate Bowen, J.F. Heal, and Bertha Glaze. It was a warm, muddy day. I walked a half mile. I received a Briscoe automobile circular from James Guthrie.

Sunday, January 11 As usual, Orville and Katharine took Horace to the new house, and he staid in the afternoon.

Monday, January 12 Mr. Harry N. Atwood, a noted aviator—St. Louis to New York—supped with us. He learned to fly at Simm's Station.

Tuesday, January 13 Orville receives the decision of the U.S. Court of Appeals in the Curtiss case, in his favor, in a telegraph from Pliny Williams.

Wednesday, January 14 Katharine was away for dinner at the League. Further news on the Court decision is highly satisfactory.

Thursday, January 15 Katharine was away for supper. Orville went to meet Mr. Atwod who was over an hour late from Chicago. Telegram of congratlations from Glenn Curtiss at Nice, France!

Friday, January 16 Received a letter from Ellis Wright,

enclosing maps of the crops on my farm, 1913 and 1914. He says Ancil is just recovering from a spell of fever. He praises Myrl as being ingenious.

Saturday, January 17 I weighed at Hamburger's and at Hale's, 149 1/2 pounds. I wrote a letter to Herbert who had written me a nice birthday letter.

Sunday, January 18 Orville and Katharine took Horace out to the new house. Ben and Pekah Andrews came at 1:30 o'clock. They are smart boys.

Monday, January 19 Katharine went in the evening to a supper at the Y.W. League. Mr. Prentis called to consult Orville about a project to buy the house north of us on North side of Fourth Street.[Note in margin says "This is 20th"]

Wednesday, January 21 Secretary Barnes and G.C. Loenning supped with us. They remained till 9:40.

Friday, January 23 I get a letter from Ellis Wright, enclosing maps of the crops on farm for 1813 and 1814. He says Ancil is just getting up from a spell of sickness. He praises Myrl's ingenuity.

Saturday, January 24 I weighed 150 pounds at Hamburger's and at Hale's. I wrote to Herbert.

Sunday, January 25 Orville and Katharine go after Horace and take him out to the new house.

Monday, January 26 Orville and Katharine start to New York City, at [blank]

Wednesday, January 28 Lorin dined with me. Senator Shelby M. Cullom of Illinois died at 84 years.

Friday, January 30 William Little, a school boy of Fayette County, Gray's Schoolhouse, at 14, now 77 years old, called an hour in the afternoon. He married Emeline Bell, a school-girl at Thomas' Schoolhouse, later years, and they lived in Southern Illinois. Mrs. Wagner moved out to Eleanor Stoltz's perhaps temporarily.

Saturday, January 31 Orville and Katharine came home from New York, about 10:00.

Sunday, February 1 I went with Orville to the new house.

Monday, February 2 Katharine dined with Agnes Beck on Agnes 39th birth-day anniversary.

Tuesday, February 3 Katharine went to the Suffragette's supper.

Wednesday, February 4 Katharine was away for dinner. She went to the Musicale with Mr. Loenning.

Thursday, February 5 Rev. U. Miller, pastor at Germantown, called, took dinner. Also, Isaac Swartzel came with him. At night Orville attended supper in town and was recognized as having received the Collier prize for the greatest improvement in aeronautics within the year.

Friday, February 6 The paper published the receiving of the prize, the *Journal* and *News*. It is quite cold to-day.

Saturday, February 7 It is quite a cold day.[The following crossed out of diary] Horace goes to the new house with the children, and dines with us. I slept most of the day.

Sunday, February 8 Horace goes to the new house, with Orville & Katharine, dines with us.

Monday, February 9 Rev. W.J. Shuey was born in Miamisburg, Feb. 9, 1827. He is now 87 years old. This forenoon, I had a telegram from Charles I. Gray saying Eva is dead. She was a tall, good-looking, modest, smart woman. Her funeral is to be at Center Church at 1:30, Wednesday.

Tuesday, February 10 Orville and Katharine go to Cincinnati to see Mr. Jung, an Oberlin student. He is the author of the School law which was "amended'.

Wednesday, February 11 The papers publish of Orville's and Katharine's visit. Arangments are made for a company to go to Columbus tomorrow to see Governor Cox about extending the privilege to the legislature to Amend the school law.

Thursday, February 12 Seventeen men and women go

to Columbus and see the Governor, who refuses to interfere. Orville and Katharine are among them.

Saturday, February 14 We had an increase of snow to about 8 inches. It is not very cold to-day. Horace and cousin "Peka" come at night on a valentine excursion. Senator Augustus 0. Bacon of Georgia, died.

Sunday, February 15 Orville had word from Horace that he had a visitor (Cousin Ben) and could not come! He has come every Sunday, when Orville has been at home. He is a nice boy.

Monday, February 16 I wrote several letters, one to Flora Glass.

Tuesday, February 17 I mailed a letter to Gusta Whitton. I slept most of the day. Katharine goes to a League supper. Orville is called down to his office in the evening, by Jim Jacobs.

Friday, February 20 Mr. J.W. Conk, a Vetrenary Surgeon, 83 Years' old, 131 Fergueson Ave., calls to see me, and invites me to his birth-day dinner at Euclid Ave. He also leaves invitation for Orville, Katharine and Carrie Grumbach.

Sunday, February 22 Lorin, Netta and the two youngest children sup with us .

Monday, February 23 Orville and Mr. Grumbach went and worked on the finish of the doors of the new house. Lorin dined with us.

Tuesday, February 24 Orville and Charley spend all day at the new house staining the doors. Katharine goes to "Memorial" to hear Secretary Redfield speak. I wrote to Albert A. Koerner's wife.

Wednesday, February 25 Orville in the aftern. starts to New York City, to a business meeting. I send an Article to Conservator, "Of a Sound Mind."

Thursday, February 26 Mrs. J. Stevens' sups with us, and she and Katharine go to a concert. It is J.W. Couk's birth-day dinner at Euclid Avenue United Brethren Church.

Friday, February 27 Received a letter from W.A. Broyles, Park River, North Dakota.

Saturday, February 28 Katharine went to lunch somewhere, and Miss Green and Miss Ryder sup with her at our house. This is the birth-day of J.W. Couk—83 years old.

Sunday, March 1 It is snowy and blizzardlike in the forenoon; also part of the afternoon. Orville comes home at 9 o'clock morning. He and Katharine go for Horace for dinner. Horace stays till nearly supper. Dr. William G. Moorehead died in Zenia, this morning, at 6:00. He was a fine orator and anti-secrecy man.

Monday, March 2 Fair in the forenoon & afternoon. I went to Newsalt's and got glasses for my spectacles. I found them much better than the old ones.

Wednesday, March 4 Mrs. J. Stevens supped with us. She is aging very fast.

Friday, March 6 Mr. McPherson called an hour in the evening. He called some four years' ago. He is a railroad Expert.

Saturday, March 7 Katharine lunched at noon with Miss Alice Hunt at Rike's restaurant. Lorin and Netta came in the evening and staid an hour. They discussed the school situation.

Sunday, March 8 Snowy in the morning, Orville and Katharine got Horace. "Peka" (Alfred) Andrews came in after dinner.

Thursday, March 12 The Assessor called again for Orville's assessment. Mrs. Mary E. MacDowell spoke morning and evening in the City. She is from Chicago. Katharine went to hear her. Rev. C.A. Moore, the pastor of Broadway M.E. Church called to invite me to attend the reopening of his church, next Sunday.

Friday, March 13 The assessor called for Orville's assessment again this afternoon. It is a very pleasant day. Katharine is away. A man from N.Y. World came to consult Orville about a flight across the Atlantic.

Sunday, March 22 The children went after Horace. Mr.

G.C. Leoning called in the evening after supper.

Wednesday, March 25 Orville started to Washington City to-night on business, at 8:57. It is a nice March day.

Thursday, March 26 It is a rather pleasant day. Katharine went to town to hear Mrs. [blank] speak, who told of ropeing off certain Streets in Chicago, to make a place for children to play.

Friday, March 27 It is a moderate rainy day. I received a letter from Reuchlin to-day. Twenty-one from Baldwin City, including Herbert, started on a trip to California, the 23rd, to be gone about three weeks. Minnie Hanby, daughter of B.R. Hanby lives at Alhambra, a suburb of Los Angeles.

Saturday, March 28 Katharine lunches with Winifred Ryder at Keifaber's. It is a fair day. I wrote to J.A. Burkholder.

Sunday, March 29 Leontine and Horace dine with us, and they go with Katharine to the new house after dinner. It is a sleepy day to me. A telegram from Orville says that he visited Boston and New York and has a meeting of the Board of Directors of his company, before he returns home.

Tuesday, March 31 It is a pleasant day. Katharine and Lorin went to the new house. I wrote Mrs. J.S. Bellamy, Knoxville, Iowa, about Elizabeth Reeder, her great-grandmother. I received a letter from Flora Glass.

Wednesday, April 1 It is a rainy forenoon. Orville comes home in the forenoon, at 8:00, from Wash. He saw Col. Reber, had a talk with the Directors etc. of his company. They have not had a regular meeting since in December.

Friday, April 3 Dr. L. Spitler came at noon. He left a little medicine for me, and Orville a receipt.

Saturday, April 4 Pres. Henry C. King of Oberlin took lunch with us. The Oberlin Dinner occurred at 6:30, at Rike-Kumler's, at night.

Sunday, April 5 It is a bright, cool morning, and pleasant day. Horace dined with us, and Alfred (Pekah) came after dinner. They all went out to the new house.

Monday, April 6 Pleasant morning—cloudy afternoon. I gave Orville $978.46—a note on Leroy Millspaugh, and a note on Billman's Bank.

Tuesday, April 7 It is a somewhat rainy day. I wrote letters to Reuchlin and to Leroy Millspaugh. I got a letter from Mrs. J.S. Belamy, containing genealogy of the ancestral Leverich's, Reeder's, etc. She is of Knoxville, Iowa.

Wednesday, April 8 I spent the day looking over my genealogical sketches charts and letters.

Thursday, April 9 Reuchlin came before noon. He came at Orville's request to consult about their business.

Friday, April 10 I wrote to Cora Dillon, and to Rev. J.S. Rook. Mr. Moore called to see Orville & Katharine.

Saturday, April 11 Reuchlin supped at Lorin's. Katharine supped with Mrs. Hubard, at 1st & Main Club. Orville went Algonquin to see Aviator Atwood. It is a rainy day.

Sunday, April 12 Fair day. Enyart brought in an easter egg for three of us each. Reuchlin and children went over to the new house. Ben and "Pekah" Andrews came. Reuchlin went to see Lulu's Aunts at the Rose Davis house. George Feight called in. I mailed a letter to Flora Glass; found Reuchlin at home, when I came in. Lorin & Netta spent an hour.

Monday, April 13 Reuchlin started home about 9:00 A.M. I slept much of the day. Wrote Mrs. Hadley. Wrote J. Howe. It was a very fair day. Miss Mayer, Mrs. Stevens and Agnes Beck visited Katharine, in the afternoon.

Wednesday, April 15 Lieut. Milling visited Dayton, on his way to St. Louis. He did not call at our house, but sent his regards to me.

Thursday, April 16 Gen. Coxey's army at Alliance Ohio is small.

Friday, April 17 I am 85 years old, and 5 months. I am in good health.

1 9 1 4

Saturday, April 18 President Wilson had given till Sunday at 6 o'clock for Huerty to fire salutes.

Sunday, April 19 Horace and Leontine spend the day with us, and Pekah.

Monday, April 20 President Wilson reads a message to Congress, relating that Huerta has refused our demand that he salute the American flag, as a reparation for an insult to American Marines. The House of Representatives passes an authorizing resolution for enforced compulsion of Huerta.

Tuesday, April 21 It is a fine day.. The maple leaves begin to bud forth. Katharine receives gowns etc. from Rachel Wagoner, and the Oberlin students have a supper and a play. Vera Crux, in Mexico is taken by United States warship and marines.

Wednesday, April 22 The day is fine. The paper is full of war news. The honeysuckle begins to leave out.

Thursday, April 23 Orville and Katharine go to Tippecanoe to buy shrubbery. Horace went along and is presented with an English Hawthorn bush. It was afternoon. The bought about $300.00 worth.

Friday, April 24 There is an animal show in town to-day. There was no parade. Orville& Katharine went to the house, and the agent from Tippecanoe did not come till nearly dark. So they staid till half past seven.

Saturday, April 25 Mrs. Eleanor Wagner called to see me. Horace has an apricot to plant. In the afternoon, Orville and Katharine and myself went out to the house. Also Horace and Benjamin. Lorin and Netta came. We staid till after 5:00.

Sunday, April 26 Orville, Katharine and Carrie Grumbach go out to the new house.

Monday, April 27 Orville went at 2:00 on a business trip to New York. Katharine packed some books for moving.

Tuesday, April 28 We moved from 7 Hawthorn Street, Dayton, Ohio, to Hawthorn Hill, Harmon Ave., Oakwood, Ohio. I moved to 7 Hawthorn in 1871, some time in February. We moved to Iowa in [blank] 1878. We returned to Richmond in [blank] 1881, and came back to Dayton in 1884. We did with tallow candles, to-night. We arrived in a auto-taxicab at 3:45 afternoon.

Wednesday, April 29 I wrote cards to Ellis Wright, Flora Glass, Sarah C. Bowen, Drusilla McKey, Wm. Dillon, J. Howe. Red bud trees are in full bloom. Mrs. McCormick called to see us. A telegram from Orville says he will be at home to-morrow. We got connection with electric works to-day. We fitted up my room, the kitchen and dining rooms.

Thursday, April 30 We ate by 7:00. I walked over south through the woods. Orville came in the forenoon and went out to the factory—got home at noon. We got fire in the furnace in the afternoon. Lorin and Netta came in the evening and brought Ivonette and Leontine & Horace. We got the rug down in the upstairs hall. It is very pretty.

Friday, May 1 Mabel Creiger called with some eggs and flowers. I had quite a chat with her. Her father is town martial and constable of Van Buren Township. We set up furniture in the hall and put down the beautiful rug. We have had beautiful weather, this week.

Saturday, May 2 Mrs. Clare Andrews, and her two little girls called in the afternoon. Also Mr. Coffyn. Orville & Katharine went and brought Horace. Mrs. Agnes Beck called and staid till 8:00, and our folks took her "home." It was a very beautiful day.

Sunday, May 3 I arose at six o'clock. The blue-jays, Robins, and blackbirds were on the grounds and on the trees before the doors. A gray squirrel is a solitary visitor. The red bud has reached its best of bloom. Benjamin Van Cleve Andrews and Alfred came as we were eating dinner. There are some clouds but mostly sunshine. Miss Ryder & Lorin's all, come and staid till 8:00.

Monday, May 4 In the afternoon, another load of goods was hauled from the other house. They were largely of books.

Hawthorne Hill, Oakwood, 1914

Tuesday, May 5 I was busy much of the day putting my books in the bookcase. I became very tired. I wrote to Reuchlin, mailed to-day.

Wednesday, May 6 The hands dug up a red-bud tree at the left hand of the ring before the door, the left hand.

Thursday, May 7 I went to town to see the parade. Stopped at Harmon's furniture or carpet store. I went on to Lorin's and dined and staid there till 5:00. Orville took me home. The show was wrecked & there was no parade. Horace went to the show in the evening & got home at 11:30 o'clock!

Friday, May 8 It was rainy to-day. Mr. Polk (Poock) came and had evergreen shrubs put in front of the house. I wrote to Sina Ardery.

Saturday, May 9 Mr. Louis D. Poock sets out the schrubbery across the way. Mrs. S. Stevens dines with us and spends the afternoon. Carl Hotchkis, Horace's friend, calls to see us.

Sunday, May 10 It is a beautiful sunshiny day. We had no visitors, not even Horace. It is the time when the white bloom of our hawthorne appears.

Monday, May 11 Mrs. Clare Andrews and Mrs.[blank] Gordon, an Andrews cousin, called just before dinner, to invite us to the Van Cleve reunion. Mr. Grover C. Lenning called at 8:00.

Tuesday, May 12 I wrote a letter to Mary Krout. We had a little rain in the afternoon.

Wednesday, May 13 I walked out in the evening along Park Ave., met Orville and Katharine, and she got out and walked with me, and we came home to supper.

Thursday, May 14 The cement on the garage was finished. Carrie and I speculate on the strenght of the cement floor over the cellar. It is said that barges are now passing through the Panama Canal. Tampico is reported to be taken by the rebels in Mexico. [Down side of page is written "This for Wedns."]

Friday, May 15 Little of special interest occurs. The men finish setting out the shrubbery.

Saturday, May 16 I wrote to Eliz. Brookbacks, J.F. Harris and S.L. Livingston. I went to the old house and got some things and bought some rubber collars on my way home. Horace came before dinner and staid all night.

Sunday, May 17 I am 85 years and six months old today. Milton, Third year in Ohio State University, at Oxford, came and dined with us and staid till 6:00 train. Horace went home after supper on street car.

Monday, May 18 It was a beautiful day. I wrote to J.I. Lefforge and his wife. The workmen lay up the brick work on Orville's garage. I put many letters away in a box.

Tuesday, May 19 It is a clear day. Mr.[blank] Parrot and his daughter and her little girls called in just before supper. Orville left for Philadelphia, just a little after supper.

Wednesday, May 20 Orville delivered a written address before the Franklin Institute on his stablarizer, in Philadelphia.

Thursday, May 21 Mr. and Mrs. [blank] Chamberlain called at 8:00 in the evening. He is a former Representative of this county in the legislature, a littly blowy.

Friday, May 22 Orville came home about noon, and Captain Cowan was with him, quite an interesting man.

Saturday, May 23 H.J. Adams, a former mer U.B. Preacher of Kansas Conference, called to see Orville. He dined with us. Orville thought him crazy on an invention on electricity. He is very smart. He is from Portland, Oregon. He knew H.D. Latiman, at Salem, and told of his borrowing money of Charley Corby, and his beating an old gentleman from Cal. on a land trade.

Sunday, May 24 Fine forenoon. I slept most of it. Horace was here to day as on Saturday, as usual. "Peka" came after dinner. Lorin and Netta called in the evening .

Wednesday, May 27 It is a very dry, hot day. Plinny Williams called in the morning. Orville took him to the cars, and I ate dinner alone, Katharine and he arriving late. A sprinkle of rain occurred a little before supper. In the forenoon, a "professed inventor" from Fairfield,

Ohio, called to see Orville. It is cooler after the sprinkle.

Thursday, May 28 It is a month after the day we moved to this house—not yet settled. The rafters are completed on the garage. The tinners to-day about did half their work.

Friday, May 29 It is a warm, dry morning, and so all the day. The carpenters put on more than half the roof on the garage. Will Jenkins came after school with Horace. They ate supper with us, and remained with us all night. Will is a very nice boy, about 14.

Saturday, May 30 This is Decoration day. Katharine and Orville went to the florists to get flowers, engaged for decoration. It is just two years since Wilbur died. Oh, why did he go so soon? Orville is called to his office at 4:00 to see a young man from out West, and he stays till near 11 o'clock. Horace and Will Jenkins are called home to a garden party, and return at 8:00. They stay at night.

Sunday, May 31 A bright, cool day. The boys were up and out over the 17 acres. I wrote to Reuchlin. Orville took me in the automobile to Milton's Sch. house. Davit's Church, the Reformed Church, through Hills & Dales home. He took Horace and Will home. Mr. Atty. Loulman and his wife called in the evening.

Monday, June 1 There were small, brief showers in the morning. Carpenters put the rest of the roof on the garage.

Tuesday, June 2 Cool morning, & bright. Lorin dined with us. I took a walk south over to the creek. Katharine was to College pic nic and thence to the League.

Wednesday , June 3 Wrote to Barkley, Albert Koerner, etc. Sent Albert $10.00. Went to town evening and to Lorin's.

Thursday, June 4 We had nice little showers about 5 oclock, Eve. Katharine between them went to see Agnes Beck at Mary Emmon's. Wrote Cinthia Croddy & Bertha. Sent C. $10.00.

Friday, June 5 I finished an article, "Preachers in Indiana." United Brethren Preacher's.

Saturday, June 6 I wrote an article, "More Indiana Preachers." Horace came about noon. Orville and he caught a mole.

Sunday, June 7 Mr. Griffith Brewer came about nine o'clock in the morning. Ben and Alfred Andrews came after dinner.

Monday, June 8 I went to U.B. Publishing Estab. and got some writing tables in the afternoon.

Tuesday, June 9 John G. Feight & wife and Mr. Noe and his wife called in. Finished my article, "More Indiana Preachers."

Thursday, June 11 It is a fine day—rather hot. Orville did not come home at noon—went out to Simms and got home at 7:00. We received, from Rachael Wagner, the Oberlin commencement & invitation to attend. She wrote: "We are not going though," as she had said on announcing Katharine's invitation in 1898.

Friday, June 12 It is a nice day. I wrote to William Dillon, and to Arthur W. Wright giving him our probable genealogy to John Wrighte of Helvedon, Essex, England. I gave him, as Justus' Wright's genealogy that Samuel of Springfield was the son of Samuel of Essex, b. about 1570. His father died June 1606, aged 36 years.

Saturday, June 13 The day is nice and cool,—a most choice day. Adlai Stevenson died in Chicago Hospital, aged 80 years to-night.

Sunday, June 14 It is a nice cool day. I examined "Dispersion," 'Israel," etc. for the lost tribes. It was Rev. P. Beck's delusion. 2 Esdras 13.40, was Esdra's false theory. Not Saxons who were gross idolaters. William Jenkins comes to see Horace and stays at night.

Monday, June 15 It is a pleasant morning. Nothing very unusual occurs during the day. In the evening Mr. Smith and his wife, and Mr. Fernading and his wife called to see us. I sat up till they all left. At night, Mr. Brewer built up a nice fire and retired to his room.

Tuesday, June 16 Charles Grumbach made a nice fire in the east room. Mrs. Oscar Needham called to see Katharine.

Wednesday, June 17 I took sick while eating breakfast, and ate not another bite all day. Dr. Conklin came after nine in the evening, and said I looked better than when he had seen me before.

Thursday, June 18 We had a nice thunder shower early in the morning. Just before bedtime, I vomited bile and my stomach imediately regained its appetite.

Friday, June 19 At 9:00, I went to Lorin's. I ate every hour, one-fourth glass full of milk till about 7:00.

Saturday, June 20 I ate breakfast, Dinner and supper as usual. Orville and Katharine brought me some clean clothes. I walked down to Forest Avenue Presbyterian Church, with William Jenkins.

Monday, June 22 In the [blank] I went down to where Sophia Simpson lived formerly, on McPherson Avenue. I rode two squares north of Lorin's to Grafton Avenue. I staid at Lorin's.

Tuesday, June 23 A little before nine o'clock, I went to Orville's. Charles Grumbaugh met me at the cars, at the end of Brown Street. A woman & Dr.[blank] little girls called in the evening. Mr. G. Brewer called about noon. He flew till 8:00 in evening, at Simm's.

Thursday, June 25 Pliny Williams came and talked with Orville. He dined with us. There was a thunder shower about noon. Mr. Guthrie came in the after noon. He had often took me out in his automobile, when he lived in Dayton.

Saturday, June 27 My head swam considerably to-day. Some colored men brought a new bedstead for Mr. Brewer's room.

Sunday, June 28 My head is not swimming to day. The weather is delighly cool. Mr. Grover C. Loening dined with us to-day.

Monday, June 29 Mrs. Justina Lorenze Stevens dined with us. She recently had her tonsils cut out, and is weak.

She is to stay with Katharine a few days.

Tuesday, June 30 Mrs. Raymond and Gephart called a half hour in the evening. Col. Reber (U.S.A.) took dinner with us.

Thursday, July 2 It is a fair day, moderately cool. Mr. G. Brewer goes to the flying ground and stays all night.

Friday, July 3 It is a fair day. Orville came home at 2:00, and went to town again. Katharine & Mrs. Justina Stevens went down town.

Saturday, July 4 Susan died twenty-five years ago. Now, I am old and feeble. She was "the sweetest spirit earth ever knew." Ever since her death, a gloom has spread over Independence Day. It seems a day of mourning.

Sunday, July 5 It is a bright, cool day, though a little warm at noon, when I go in "auto" a little beyond Lorin's. I wrote an article, "The Great Revival." Mr. Dilks and his daughter called at 6:00. He is an Englishman, living on Oakwood Avenue.

Monday, July 6 It is a beautiful day. Mrs. Justina Stevens went home. She had much improved in health.

Tuesday, July 7 It is a pleasant, warm day. Lieut.[blank] Whiting and his wife dined with us. He is a very modest man.

Wednesday, July 8 It is a warm afternoon. I took my usual walk. Dr. Porter of whom we bought this land, and his wife, called, and staid to bedtime.

Thursday, July 9 It is a fair day. Pretty warm in the afternoon. I took my three-quarter mile walk. I slept rather scantily.

Friday, July 10 It is quite a hot day. I walked round the water-tower hill, and my three-quarter mile walk. The Constitutionalists took a large city in Mexico.

Saturday, July 11 Horace is thirteen years old to-day. They are up in Michigan. He wrote Orville that Milton and he caught forty fishes in three hours, and caught two messes of frogs! The day is very hot. It turns cooler

about sunset, but is warm in the night. Charles and Carrie go to Detroit to see Charlie's sister.

Sunday, July 12 It is a hot day. Orville goes down town, to see a man. Mrs. Lulu Williams gets dinner and supper for us. Lieut. Whiting and wife sup with us and remain till bedtime. Mr. G. Brewer goes out to Simms. To-day the therm. run to 103 degrees. We sat in the evening on the flat of the roof.

Tuesday, July 14 Charles and Carrie came back this morning. Orville went to New York City in the afternoon. It rained a little about 4:00. I slept comfortably, almost without cover.

Wednesday, July 15 It was a foggy morning, and somewhat cloudy day. Agnes Beck came. In the afternoon her girls came, Janet, 12 years old, and Elva, 10 years old. Agnes stays at night. Pres. Huerta, in Mexico, resigned. Francisco Carbajal, provisional president, succeeds him. The usurper's name is Victoriana Huerta.

Thursday, July 16 Fair morning. Weather warm. A show in town. No parade as usual this year. Orville came home at noon. Agnes went home in the afternoon.

Friday, July 17 To day is two-thirds of my 86th year. It is cloudy. There is a nice shower about noon.

Saturday, July 18 Fair forenoon. The birds are unusually active. Rev. U. Miller came. I gave him salary $10.00, mission money, $10.00, collections $5.00. Mr. G.C. Loening and Alpheus Barnes came. Dined with us. Barnes is secretary of the Wright Company.

Sunday, July 19 It is a clear, cool day. George A. Fight called to see us in the afternoon. Lieut. [blank] Whiting & wife called an hour, about 4:00.

Monday, July 20 We got rural delivery in our box on Oakwood Ave.

Wednesday, July 22 It is a warm day, 94 degrees. I received a letter from S.L. Livingston, and wrote a reply.

Thursday, July 23 The day is very warm. It was the warmest of the year, so far. Katharine went in the evening to visit Mrs. Dissinger. My electric fan helped me considerably.

Friday, July 24 It is a very warm day Katharine went down town with Orville. It turned cooler in the evening, but it was a pretty warm night.

Sunday, July 26 It is a hot day. Lieut. Whiting and wife dined with us, after one o'clock and remained till nearly bed time.

Monday, July 27 Katharine went to town with Orville. I give Carrie a check for $30.00, two weeks' pay. I received letters from Albert Koerner, Jesse D. Laforge and Edgar R. Harlan. It is a very hot day.

Tuesday, July 28 Katharine went to a picnick. It is much cooler to-day. The picnick was at the Cash Register Country Club Hills & Dales.

Wednesday, July 29 Mrs. Reeder and several other women called. Several women dined with Katharine. It is a cool day.

Thursday, July 30 Mrs.[blank] Elliot, wife of Katharine's class-mate, called in the afternoon. It is a very nice day. Lorin's returned from Three Rivers, Michigan.

Friday, July 31 The day is cool and nice. Katharine visited Mrs. neighb. McCormick. I am somewhat dizzy.

Saturday, August 1 We attended Lincoln Beechy and Oldfield's exhibition at the fair ground at 3:00. He made several flights, looping the loop and flying with the machine upside down in the last. He went so high as almost be lost sight of at times. He is the best aviator in America. Oldfield found it dusty and the circle too small. Horace came at night.

Sunday, August 2 It is a warm day. The thermometer on our north porch reached about 85 degrees. Alfred came to see Horace, and ate dessert with us. Lorin and Netta came in the evening, and staid an hour.

Monday, August 3 It is a fine morning. Alfred is with Horace to-day and to-night.

Tuesday, August 4 It is a clear, cool day. Alfred is still here. Katharine went to the Board meeting of the Young Woman's Christian League.

Wednesday, August 5 I walked to the Drug Store and back. I called at Koener's a half-hour. Katharine went to Simm's Station with Horace and Alfred. Alfred stayed at night with Horace.

Thursday, August 6 A letter from Reuchlin came. I had mailed one to him. Wrote one more. Some women came to see Katharine in the afternoon. It is a very hot day.

Friday, August 7 A very hot day. A barren thunder storm came up about 5:00 - not enough rain to fully to wet the surface of the ground. A similar storm there was last evening—less rain.

Tuesday, August 11 It was mostly cloudy to day. Several showers and light rains during the night. Pleasant temperature. Katharine went to a supper at Young Woman's League. She got home before nine o'clock. A preliminary election occurred to-day with a light vote.

Wednesday, August 12 Mrs. Fross & Miss Stiffen visited Carrie. Katharine went to the field and saw Orville fly. It appears that James M. Cox was nominated for Governor yesterday, and Timothy S. Hogan for U.S. Senator; Frank B. Willis by the Republicans, Warren G. Harding was nominated U.S. Senator. Garfield Prog. candidate for Senator.

Thursday, August 13 Katharine & Orville went down with Lieut. [blank] Whiting's and came home at 4:30, just ater John H. Patterson left. Patterson and Dorothy and Mr. Crane came about 8:00. We had quite a talk on the European War. Patterson spoke of William III of Germany's wisdom in developing Industrial pursuits in Germany.

Tuesday, August 18 Katharine ate dinner at Rike's with Whitings. She hired an automobile and took Mrs. Whiting and myself to Far Hills, Hills & Dales and to Dayton View. Miss McCormick came in with her and they and Mrs. Whiting staid the rest of the afternoon. Orville and Lieut. Whiting tried the airship on the River.

Wednesday, August 19 It is Orville and Katharine's birthday. He is 43 years old; she is 40. It was a very hot day.

Thursday, August 20 Charles drove the old automobile to meet Mrs. Agnes Beck, who came at 9:30. The day is very hot. Lorin and Horace go to the river, where the flyer took a dive. Agnes left a 7:00.

Friday, August 21 Horace went home, promising he would be back to-morrow. I rode in automobile out east. Corn looks finely.

Sunday, August 23 Sunday, I took a camp chair and went up the tank hill and viewed the buildings along the Centerville pike.

Monday, August 24 I was at home to-day, Horace visited us.

Tuesday, August 25 It was a cloudy, somewhat rainy day. [blank] Knabenshue dined and supped with us.

Wednesday, August 26 Mrs. Mella King and her daughter came at noon. Her daughter is Katharine Wright, aged 5 1/2 years. It is a very fine day.

Thursday, August 27 Germany seems victorious over Belgium and France.

Friday, August 28 Germany is repoted victorious in Belgium & in Lorain, but Russia is repoted victorious in eastern Prussia.

Saturday, August 29 Two Mrs. Packsons and another woman called to see the house. Mrs. King and Katharine dined down town. I grow hoarse from cold. It seems a little more favorable to the allies.

Sunday, August 30 Harvey Wright died aged as old as I am to-day, in 1906. He died of a cancer the 22nd of June 1906. Mella (Sillaman) King and her little daughter are here.

Tuesday, September 1 I cut down the bushes about the Sycamore tree south of the house.

Wednesday, September 2 I cut down some bushes about the wild rose patch beyond the sycamores. My hoarseness is mostly gone.

Friday, September 4 Mrs. King and her daugter Katharine Wright, started home about 10:00, to Geneva, Ohio. Ida Graybill dined with us.

Saturday, September 5 Orville and Katharine went down town. Bishop O.G. Alwood came. He is out on a $400.00 trip for the Chautaqua people. He remained till after dinner.

Sunday, September 6 Dr. [blank] Harris and his wife called in the evening an hour. Milton and Horace called. Horace stayed till morning.

Monday, September 7 Editor of "flying" took dinner with us. Winifred Ryder took supper with us. A letter from Reuchlin, the 4th, says that his motherinlaw Billheimer was that day seventy-nine years old. She is actively keeping house for Reuchlin while Lulu is visiting Herbert in Colorado.

Wednesday, September 9 Rev. J. Howe came at 6:00 and remained over night. Orville and Katharine took Ivonette home and went to the factory, got home about 10:30, at night.

Thursday, September 10 J. Howe spent the forenoon with Orville, and left at 2:45 tr. for Zion, Scioto conference.

Friday, September 11 Lieut. [blank] Whiting and his wife ate supper with us, his wife spent the afternoon with us. She has been sick.

Saturday, September 12 Lieut. [blank] Writing and wife started away at 1:15, and Orville and Katharine went to see them start.

Sunday, September 13 I rode afternoon up to Fairview Park and returned. Lawyer Thomas and Miss Thomas, his sister, and Mr. [blank] and wife were at our house on our return. Mr. Henry Woodhouse of New York dined with us.

Monday, September 14 John Wright came home with

Orville. He has some "inventions" to consult Orville about. Supper with us .

Tuesday, September 15 The hands completed their sodding along the road and their graveling.

Wednesday, September 16 I walked to the cars and back home.

Thursday, September 17 I walked east around by the Centerville pike to Park Avenue and home. Leontine is 16 years old to-day.

Friday, September 18 Ivonette and Leontine and Horace ate supper with us. I gave a dollar to each one of them.

Saturday, September 19 The children staid till after dinner, and Horace all night.

Sunday, September 20 Horace went home in the afternoon. I rode with Orville southeast of Beavertown on theWilmington pike, then west three miles north of Centerville to the Cincinnati pike home.

Monday, September 21 A war of millions is raging in Europe, in which the allies England, France and Russia seem to have the upper hand.

Tuesday, September 22 To-day is Emancipation Day. It is worthy of celebration by whites and colored people. "At midnight I will rise to give thanks to Thee, because of Thy righteous judgments." Ps. 119 ps., 62.

Thursday, September 24 Katharine went to the Woman's Suffragette supper and staid till after 10:00.

Friday, September 25 I went in the afternoon to Albert Shearer's - saw his grandson who is living there. I also called at Mrs. Eleanor Wagner's, where I saw Rachel, Eleanor Stoltz and her boy William. Mrs. Eleanor Wagoner and Mrs. Rachel (W.) called befoe I left. They had been out visiting.

Sunday, September 27 Lieut [blank] Maxfield dined with us, of the navy. Horace visited us, went home at 8:00 eve.

Tuesday, September 29 Gov. Cox and Willis are in a conflict of accusations. Willis accuses Cox of building up a machine. I went to drugstore and the grocery.

Wednesday, September 30 Mrs. Eleanor Wagner and Rachel and Eleanor Stolts and William (4 years old in December) and Mother Rachel Wagner (now 84 years old) visited us and dined with us. She lives with Etta Simons, at Peru, Indiana.

Thursday, October 1 The battle of Aisne in France, is now said to have lasted 19 days. To-day is a very nice day, as those of all the week have been. Katharine dined at the Notarial Club. Visited Mrs. McCormack in the afternoon.

Friday, October 2 It is a very fine day. I walked round Harmon Ave. to Lebanon Pike, to Far HIlls Ave. and up Harmon Ave. home. The women of Woman's League had a lawn party at our house. There were 175 or 180 of them.

Saturday, October 3 Katharine lunched down town.

Sunday, October 4 Lieut. Maxfield dined with us. Horace came and staid till bed time.

Monday, October 5 Katharine went to a Y.W.L. meeting at night.

Tuesday, October 6 Katharine went at night to the Library Convention.

Wednesday, October 7 I walked over a mile. Prof. Azariah Root, of Oberlin College, came & and staid all night. It was clear weather—about 175 degrees by the thermometer. There was some rain in the night.

Thursday, October 8 I wrote in the afternoon to Ellis Wright. Prof. A. Root again staid all night with us.

Friday, October 9 It is somewhat cloudy. The sycamore are all over a reddish brown; the ash & the pignut before the door, are yellow, the maples are reddish, yellow & mixed; the ash north, are yellow and mixed; So all around. Red oak brightly green, & some other trees. Lieut. Maxwell ate supper with us.

Saturday, October 10 It rained a shower before noon. Horace came in the evening.

Sunday, October 11 Lieut.[blank] Maxfield dined with us. I rode out to Beavertown with Orville. Horace goes home at bed-time.

Monday, October 12 It is a somewhat cloudy morning. We got a load of coal in the morning. At 10:00, Katharine went to a meeting of the Associted Charities. In the afernoon, she went to a League meetin and staid till late.

Tuesday, October 13 About 75 of the College Graduates came out in the evening (seven or 8 o'clock) and Manager Wait addressed them.

Wednesday, October 14 Orville and Katharine went to the Bryan meeting at Memorial Hall. Bryan, ex-governor Campbell, Probasco, & Guard spoke. Guard has a melodious voice, that is all!

Friday, October 16 Rainy in the morning, it fairs up before noon. Miss Kate Leonard and Mrs. Harriet (Sillaman) Robins came in the evening—Miss Leonard of Oberlin, and Miss Robins of Chicago. They were graduates of Oberlin in 1898, with Katharine.

Saturday, October 17 Some rain to-day. Mrs. Robins and Miss Leonard are with us.

Sunday, October 18 Lieut. [blank] Maxfield dined with us, and Miss Leonard and Mrs. Robins were also there.

Monday, October 19 Katharine and her visitors lunched at Rike's, and brought Mrs. E. Wagner and Rachel, and we went in automobile to Simm's Staition and through town by Lorin's and the lot on Salem Ave. out by J.G. Huber's to Mrs. Wagner's home. And we came out home, at 5:00.

Tuesday, October 20 The children went in the evening to hear J.R. Garfield, the Progressive Candidate for governor, speak. I received [blank]

Katharine Wright in 1914

Wednesday, October 21 The folks went to hear Mrs. Catt, Susan B. Anthony's successor speak. They pronounced it the best speach they had heard this fall. The folks lunched at Rike's with Agnes Beck.

Thursday, October 22 It is a very bright morning. I received a letter from Cora Wright [crossed out] Dillon. Mrs. Harriet Robins goes to Chicago in the forenoon, and Miss Kate Leonard to Oberlin in the afternoon.

Friday, October 23 Katharine dines down town where she is busy aiding in planning for the Women's Suffrage March.

Saturday, October 24 At 3:30, we were in the 1300 march in town. There was Mrs. Bolton and other aged women, perhaps no older men than, I in the march. There were 44 College women, in the procession. Orville marched by my side. The sidewalks were lined by many thousands of respectful spectators.

Sunday, October 25 Lorin's came to supper. Mr. Thresher and wife called in the evening. She is Dr. Colby's daughter.

Monday, October 26 I wrote a letter to William Miller.

Thursday, October 29 Mailed a letter to Ray Stevens, to Drusilla McKee and to Augusta Whiton.

Friday, October 30 Mrs. Justina Stevens came to Supper and went with Katharine to a musical exhibition. Staid with us all night.

Saturday, October 31 Mrs. Stevens continued at our house till after dinner.

Sunday, November 1 Horace visited Orville to-day.

Monday, November 2 Keneth Allen's moved into their new house south-east of our's to-day.

Tuesday, November 3 There was an animated—I might say excited—election throughout the States. Gov. J.M. Cox was beaten in Ohio, by Frank B. Willis; Geo. G. Harding was elected U.S. Senator by popular vote; most of the northern states went Republican; the Republicans almost overthrew the Democratic majority in Congress. The Rosevelt (progressive) party negligible.

Wednesday, November 4 Captain Bristol and Lieut. Maxfield dined with us. News show that Penrose is re-elected Senator by Pennsi. Nich. Longworth is Congressman from Ohio and J.G. Cannon from Illinois. Home Rule prevails in Ohio, and Female Suffrage goes down with prohibition. I wrote to Mrs. M.M. Harvey and sent ten dollars on salary.

Thursday, November 5 Katharine and Orville were down town most of the day. In the evening, She attended an out door picnic in the Hills and Dales, with McCormack's and parrots.

Friday, November 6 Kath. attended some meeting downtown in forenoon. And she and Orville went to Dr. [blank] for supper.

Saturday, November 7 Pliny Williamson and a Lawyer by the name of Morehouse dined with us. It is a beautiful day. Horace came in the evening.

Sunday, November 8 It is a rainy morning. It turned to snow before noon. At dinner time, there was a skift of snow which melted off in an hour or two.

Sunday, November 15 Horace came and staid till bed time.

Tuesday, November 17 I am 86 years old to-day. A set of carnation pinks were sent to me as a table boquet by Louise Mayer and her sister and Justina Stevens. It is a nice day. Lorin's family (Except Milton, Oxford) supped with us. There were eighty-six candles burning. Also I add 2, for seven dozen add 2, Lorin's 52 birthday is to-morrow; so it was a joint- supper.

Thursday, November 19 Orville had a visit from Horace to-night. Katharine had Agnes Beck and Mrs. Justina Stevens for supper and went to a musical concert with them.

Friday, November 20 Lieut. Maxfield called this evening.

Saturday, November 21 Lieut. Maxfield went away to-day. Katharine went to see a foot-ball game! Rev. W.H. Chandler called an hour. Says many menonites were excluded on account of being immersed, and have become Congregationalists. Mr. Folkerth's house had a slight fire. It was put out with chemicals. It is just west of ours. Horace came.

Sunday, November 22 Horace was with us all day, and till bed time.

Monday, November 23 Katharine went to the Associated Charaties, of which she is a member of the advisory Committee. At night, she and Orville went to John H. Patterson's.

Wednesday, November 25 Lorin's except Milton, including Corbett Andrews, and Winifred Ryder, dined with us, and staid till 4:00. A negro called inquiring for a dentist. We found later that the Camera, in a sack [?] was gone from the porch.

Thursday, November 26 Horace came in the evening and the children (Orville and Katharine had a weaner roast by the creek, in the woods.

Friday, November 27–Sunday, December 6 It is a nice day . . . a rainy day. Horace was with us at supper . . . Horace staid till bed-time . . .somewhat rainy . . . I am at home.

Monday, December 7 The day is a little rainy. There is a gale, 60 miles an hour, on the Atlantic Coast. Much destruction. Congress after six week's absence meets.

Friday, December 11 Orville and Katharine go to the supper at Rike-Kumler's, and to hear Star Jordan speak. The Laundryman's horse stumbled and fell down to-day in going down our gravel way. No damage apparent. Charley and I and Carrie help pull back the wagon off him.

Saturday, December 12 There is more snow to-day. Horace came to supper and staid till Sunday evening.

Sunday, December 13 Orville went to New York on 2:45 train. Lorin and Netty came before he started and remained till 8:00. Katharine went to a musicale on First St. at [blank] got home before seven.

Monday, December 14 A light snow on the ground. Katharine went down town dined there and returned home for supper. There is more than usual snow on the ground, and sun made no impression on it.

Wednesday, December 16 It was a cold bright day. Katharine lunched at the Y.W. League and was down town the rest of the day.

Friday, December 18 Orville saw Mr. Fish of Boston, to-day.

Saturday, December 19 Mrs. Justina (Lorenz) Stevens ate supper with us.

Sunday, December 20 Orville came home at 8:00 A.M. They went after Horace, who is becoming an interesting boy.

Monday, December 21 I got a letter from Rev. Horace D. Herr, of Humboldt, Iowa. His mother is at Winslow, Arizona at her daughter's, Florence Day's, Mrs. Lipp's.

Thursday, December 24 Lorin and Netta and their four children supped with us. Many Christmas presents. Among mine was "The greatest thing in the world," by Prof. Drummond.

Sunday, December 27 Horace went home about 8:30 in the evening. I read Mrs. Hariet Beecher Stowe's life by her son and grandson.

[The following is at the end of the diary in "address and telephone" section:]

When the Children Walked
Reuchlin began to walk at twelve months old. Lorin began at eleven months of age. Wilbur walked at 10 and a hallf months. Orville walked at a year old. Katharine walked at 10 months.

Milton Wright

My Years' Time

1. I was born Nov. 17, 1828.
2. Vaccinated, visited aunts Sarah and Mary, heard colored tent sing, 1831. Uncle Porter W. visit, promise book, 1831.
3. Attended Ross's School in 1834.
4. Show at Clarksburg in 1835. Went to Mrs. Bowler in 1836. Had the fever & whoop in 1835.
5. Went to Blackburn in 1834.
6. Went to Hogue in 1835.
7. Went to Jas. Johnson Walker, 1836.
9. Went to Jeremy Anderson 1832.
10. Remember the Whig ticket 1836 It had a marigmarole [?] on it.
11. Attended Wilson's sch. 1839.
[12 was omitted from his numbering]
13. Moved to Fayette Co. Mch 1, 1840.
14. Attended Jas. H. Rhoad's Sch, 1840.
15. Attended William Cotton's Sch. 1841.
16. Attend Jas. H. Rhoads Sch. 1842. Converted in June, 1843. Know John Rhoads the blackguard.
17. Attend James Kickan's Sch, 1844.
18. Knew George McAllum, sp. 1844. James Luttle's School, 1846.
[19 was omitted from his numbering]

20. Uncle George Reeder's Wed, 1848

21 Visited Alex. Haywood and Went Grant Co, in the year Spring 1849.

22. I joined Chruch in April 1847.

23. Taught Matney's Sch., Nov 1849

24. Spent summer in Grant, 1850.

25. Heard Hall pr. & I exhorted 1850.

26. Licensed to exhort in [blank] 1850.

27. Preached my first sermon, 1850.

28. Taught School at Gray's sch. House 1850.

29. Taught at Hite's School Sum. 1851.

30. Taught at Andersonville fall 1852.

31. Taught and attended Hartsn 1853.

32. Joined Annual Conf. in Aug. 1853.

33. Farmed in Grant Co (Farm'n) 1854.

34. Saw John Zahn at Farmington, 1854.

35. Taught at Neff's Corners [blank] 1854.

36. Taught at Neff's Corners Appoint to Indianapolis in 1855.

37. Rrevival at Indianapolis, fall 1855.

38. Revival at Indianapolis in 1856. Heard James H. Lane, Williard & co. & Joseph A. Wright speak. Attended M.E. Gen. Conference, saw Bishops, and great men. Heard debate on slavery. Ordained Aug. 1856 at Abbington, Ind. App. Andersonville Circuit 1856.

39. Went to Oregon in July, 1857. Taught at Sublimity in 1857–9. Traveled Marion Cir. 1858–9. Traveled Calipooca Mis, 1859.

40. Came home, was married, 1859.

41. Taught Sch. at N. Salem and Andersonville in 1860. Moved to Grant Co., Ind., fall of 1860. Traveled Marion Ct. Reuchlin b. 1861.

42. Elected P.E. & trav. Marion Dist 1861, 1862. Elected P.E. & Moved to New Cast, 1862. I did not live at New Castle. Lorin b. at my mother's, Nov. 18. 1862.

43. Moved to Dublin in Apr. 1863.

44. The Civil war began in April 1861, and closed in 1865. It resulted in the emancipation of all the slaves.

45. I traviled Dublin Dist. in 1862–3, and Indianapolis District in 1863–1864. I made no party speeches, but I, on Many occasions, condemned slavery and advocated the Union cause. In April, 1865, I was chosen to preach on the occasion of President Lincoln's death, which I did at the M.E. Church. I located in 1864, and three months after succeeded J.S. Wall on Dublin Curcuit. I had typhoid fever in 1865.

46. I was appointed while sick to Williamsburg Circuit, to which I went in October, 1865.

47. We had 220 accessions that year. In 1860, I was elected P.E. and put upon Marion Dist. I was reelected in 1867, put on Dublin Dist. I was elected to teach Theology, 1865. Wilbur was born April 16, 1867 in [unreadable text] by the two conferences & moved to Hart. I had a revival at Hartsville in 1869.

48. I was elected to Gen. Confer. 1869. This was the time of great debate on Secrecy. I was elected aditor of the *Rel. Telescope* and moved to Dayton June [blank] 1869. Lived at northwest corner of Third and [blank] streets till about November, moved into John Hemp's large brick on Second Street just east of Railroad, and lived there till 1871, when I moved into the house bought of James Manning, 7 Hawthorn St. (in April), 1871. There Orville was born aug. 18, 1871. I was reelected in 1873. Katharine was born August 18, 1874.

Harvey Harris's Ethel C.Harris married George M. Holland in 1909.

Mrs. Walton Brown Gephart. Stafford Avenue. Mrs Charles N. Raymond, 142 Second Street, West.

On Secret Societies.
Prov. 6.12–17, Rev.13.11–18, Rev. 14.9–11, 2 Cor. 6.14–18.

Visitors
J.W. Couk (83 y) called and invited me to his birth-day dinner at Euclid Avenue Church— Febr.20. McPherson called March 6. Rev. C.A. Mode invited me to Broadway Avenue Church, Mar.12. Pres King, Oberlin, lunched April 4. Mrs. J. S. Belamy wrote Apr. 7th. Reuchlin came— Apr. 9th. Pres. Wilson reads a message " 20 [meaning April] Vera Crux taken by U.S. Apr. 21. We move to Oakwood, Apr 28, 1914. Clara Andrews and Coffyn came May 2. Mr. Poock, shrubbery man came, May 8. Mrs. Gordon, an Andrews Cousin, May 11. Milton called May 17. Mr. Parrot & daughter called, May 19. Orville deliv. a written address at Philadelphia, 20. Mr. & Mrs. Chamberlain called 21. Capt. Cowan, signal Corpsc, May 21. H.J. Adams, Portland, Ore. May 23.

Renters

John McShay and Isadore McShay rented my Grant County farm in 1883–4.

A Fatal Accident

Miss Miriam Bloomer, daughter of James F. Bloomer, of Hotel Alms, Walnut Hills, Cincinnati, June 10, 1908, at her brother's, J. Ralph Bloomer's, at 40, East 26th Street New York, came suddenly to death by accidently drinking cyanide of potassium. She rushed suddenly into the room, to relieve the choking sensation caused by eating a cracker. She was 30 years of age, and is said to have been "queenly and regal." Her father was the son of Semele (Reeder, Bloomer) Short, a cousin of my mother. She is said to have been once the affianced of Nicholas Longworth.

Milton Wright.

Lallie Snyder, daughter of James and Patsy (Martha) Snyder, was born May 2, 1841. She married Mr. [blank] Sudaly, and has several children. Her present address (1914) is Grand Falls, Ward Co., Texas. Emmeline Zeller Dennis lives at the corner of Main & near 7th St., Richmond, Ind.

J.F. Heal, Marshfield, Wis. Sina E. Ardery, 426 East First Street, Hutchinson, Mass. Bishop Cyrus J. Kephart, 3936 Harrison Ave, Kans. City, Mo. Mrs. J.S. Bellamy, Knoxville, Iowa, 1402 Montgomery Ste. Mrs. Flora Glass, Route 6, Wabash, Ind. Rodney P. Wright 47 Granite Ste., Cambridge, Massachusetts. Curtis Wright, Carthage, Missouri. Mrs. Russell (Florence) Byrnim, 2315 St., Chicago, Illinois. Mary H. Krout, 218 College Street, Crawfordsville, Ind.

J. Franklin Croody and Cinthia E. Mitchel were married December 31, 1863.

Louise Russel was born July 16, 1809. She is my great-granddaughter.

1915

Friday, January 1 This is my eighty-Seventh New Year. Byron R. Newton, Asst. Secretary of the Treasury; R.B. Gebhart, banker, and Torrence Huffman dined with us; and Newton and John H. Patterson supped with us, Patterson remaining and talking an hour. Newton presented the new Post Office building and it was dedicated. I staid at home. It is a bright day.

Saturday, January 2 Interesting articles appear in the Dailies about the Dedication, and on the events and Deaths of 1914.

Sunday, January 3 Horace came and dined with us. The day is mostly cloudy. Horace remained till bed-time.

Friday, January 8 I walked out yesterday over a half mile, the first time I have been out in perhaps near three weeks. It is a clear, bright day to-day. I to-day walked a mile. Orville & Katharine took "dinner" at John H. Patterson's.

Saturday, January 9 It is a fine day. I walk over a half mile.

Sunday, January 10 Horace came in the afternoon and staid till bed time. His rat-trap caught a gray squirrel.

Monday, January 11 It is a rainy and snowy day. Orville has pain in his lame leg.

Wednesday, January 13 I sent an article, "The Eighth Psalm," to the *Conservator.* It was a pleasant day.

Saturday, January 16 I walked over a half mile.

Sunday, January 17 I am two months more than 86 years old. Horace came after dinner and staid till about 8:00. I walked over a half mile. John H. Braden died to-day, after a short spell of indigestion. April 23, he was born in 1862, at Adams, Indiana. He died at Kentland, Indiana. His wife was Lala Bell Fleming, and his children, Ruth, 14, Edward, 12, and John Jr., 6.

Monday, January 18 There was snow on the ground to-day. Orville does not come to table nor leave the house. Lorin dined with us and remained the afternoon.

Saturday, January 23 Lorin was with us some days this week.

Sunday, January 24 Horace was here, the afternoon.

Thursday, January 28 We moved to Oakwood nine months ago, to-day.

Friday, January 29 Lorin was with us three or four days this week for dinner.

Sunday, January 31 It was a rainy day and much of the 12 inches of snow went off. John H. Patterson came at six o'clock in the evening and staid an hour.

Monday, February 1 It was a foggy morning. Nearly half the ground is bare of snow.

Tuesday, February 2 The snow nearly goes off in the forenoon. Katharine goes down town in the afternoon, ends at Y.M.L. This is ground hog day. There is not a ray of sunshine.

Wednesday, February 3 There is almost no snowfall. I read a great deal to-day on Isaiah's Prophecies.

Thursday, February 4 It is a cloudy day, Sunshine in the afternoon. Katharine visited Miss Mayer. James Guthrie called in the evening.

Sunday, February 7 Horace visited us in the afternoon. Orville and Katharine took him home, about 8:00, eve.

Monday, February 8 It is a moderately fair day. I walked half a mile in the evening.

Tuesday, February 9 It is a fair day. I received a letter from Ruby E. Ebersole, "Reid it was," Cousin Sarah (VanCleve) Heywood's granddaughter, at Bryant, Indiana.

Sunday, February 14 Horace came in forenoon and staid till 8:00 at night. Orville took him Home. Lorin and Netta came in the afternoon. Thomas Wright died this morning at home. I received a telegram in the Evening from Cora W. Dillon. His wife died Feb. 27, 1911. He was born in Fayette County, Jan. 12, 1848. They were married in Rush County., Jan. 26, 1868.

Tuesday, February 16 Rev. C.W. Radcliff preached Thomas Wright's funeral at 2:00, at Center Christian Church in Rush County.

Wednesday, February 17 Dr. M. Wilson called an hour in the afternoon—and Mrs.[ ] and the teacher of French. Wilson is a pretty free-thinker for a Presbyterian. He thinks Dr. Riley a pretty good preacher, not very able. He worked a month with Sam Jones and regarded him as a great wit and sound man. Billy Sunday he regards as a great man.

Friday, February 19 Katharine was away at dinner time. I wrote a letter to Cousin Mary H. Krout and one to Elizabeth Brookbank. Netta and Ivonette called in the forenoon.

Saturday, February 20 Mrs. James Guthrie came from Elyria, Ohio, in the forenoon. She is a very handsome woman, and finely accomplished.

Sunday, February 21 Mrs. Guthrie took supper at Miss Mayer's with Katharine, and remained over night, to go home Monday,

Monday, February 22 Mr. Earl N. Findley, an editor of the New York Tribune, came in forenoon, and staid all night.

Tuesday, February 23 Mr. Findley remained all the forenoon, sleeping till 9:00. I received letters from Cora W. Dillon, a card from J.F. Harris and letter from Mrs. Frank F. Holt of Staunton, Virginia. She is descended from the Maryland Reeder's. J.F. Harris tells me of the death of Jesse Lafforge, the 14th of this month.

Wednesday, February 24 Mr. Glenn Martin, one the best aviators, dined with us (and Mr. Findley), to-day. Mr. Findley started back to New York about 8:00.

Thursday, February 25 The ground was covered with snow, this morning. It mostly melted off, by noon. The day is cloudy, and there is a little snow fall. Orville remained in the office at night to make bids on machines to be furnished to U.S. Navy.

Friday, February 26 It is a nice, sunshiny day. Orville and Katharine did not come home to dinner till half past 2:00.

Saturday, February 27 Mrs. E.S. Lorenz called to see Katharine. Horace called at noon and staid at night. I walked a half-mile.

Sunday, February 28 Mrs. O.H. Davison called at 4:00, to talk with Katharine on Suffrage. We have been here ten months to-day. It is a cold but fair day.

Wednesday, March 3 I walked 3/4 of a mile to-day. Wrote a letter to Myrl Wright.

Sunday, March 7 Orville started to Cleveland, to see Mr. Fish, at 11:00 at night. Horace spent the day with us. Bishop H.L. Barkley died in Portland, Oregon to-day, in the evening.

Monday, March 8 Katharine lunched with Mrs. Pierce at Young W. League.

Friday, March 12 Mr. Knabenshue came before breakfast, remained all day and the next night. Katharine took supper at John H. Patterson's and went to the League. It was a very bright day. I walked to the drug store and back.

Saturday, March 13 The court decision in John H. Patterson's case was announced. To have a new trial. Orville, Kath. & Knubenshue went to the depot to see Patterson come in. There was a large crowd—8:00 evening. Mr. Knabenshue went to Toledo at midnight.

Sunday, March 14 Horace came as usual. I rode by Lorin's, Orville's lot and the old home. We found that Mr. and Mrs. Dix had called to see us. Lincoln Beachy fell 7,000 ft to his death in San Francisco Bay, to-day, in his second flight, on a monoplane. Alas, that he must fly on Sunday! A monoplane cannot be as strong as a biplane.

Tuesday, March 16 It was a nice day. I walked a half mile to-day.

Wednesday, March 17 I wrote to Reuchlin on his his fifty-fourth birth-day anniversary. I walked a mile to-day.

Thursday, March 18 Received a letter from Otis L. Miller in reply to mine, in which he tells of the death of Prudence Moore (March lst) and Sally Ann Cook (Jan 23), and of the sickness of Theodore Walker, who recovered. His cousin Jesse Lefforge died Feb. 14th.

Sunday, March 21 Horace as usual. A somewhat cloudy day and cold wind. I rode out a few miles.

Wednesday, March 24 Mr. Knabenshue came before breakfast and continued here. The weather was mild. I walked 3/4 of a mile in the afternoon.

Thursday, March 25 Knabenshue still remained. It was mild weather. He went away at night.

Friday, March 26 Horace and Katharine were at the prize-giving to the gardener boys.

Saturday, March 27–Monday, March 29 The weather was mild. I walked 3/4 of a mile in the afternoon. . . . It was a thinly cloudy day . . . a thin sunshiny day. I walked 3/4 of a mile

Tuesday, March 30 Miss Winifred Ryder and Miss Kimball visited Katharine and supped with them. Edward W. Hanley was buried to-day. It is said to have been in attendance second only to that of C.L. Vallandingham. Hanley was a Catholic; his wife a Protestant.

Thursday, April 1 Iona Myrl Wright was married to Ovid L. Reeder to-day. I wrote Ellis Wright a letter wishing them much joy. It is a clear day.

Sunday, April 4 It is a clear, sunshiny day. George Nicholas Russel, Jr., was born to-day in Cottonwood Falls, Kansas, my first great grandson.

Tuesday, April 6 The day is fair. Mrs. Harriet E. (Copeland) Thompson, wife of Rev. H.A. Thompson, died at 1628 West First Street, this afternoon. She was an artist. She painted pictures of D.L. Rike, J.J. Glossbrenner, David Edwards, etc.

Thursday, April 8 This is a sunshiny morning. Ivonette dined with us to-day.

Friday, April 9 At 10:00 at night, the lightning struck our fuse, followed by quite an explosion, and we were without electricity till the next forenoon. Secretary C. Barnes and two Englishmen, Capt. Elder and [ ]dined with us on Saturday.

Saturday, April 10 Barncs, Elder and another man dined with us to-day. It rained about 3:30 afternoon. It was a hard shower.

Sunday, April 11 Horace came. Edw. Sines came in the afternoon.

Friday, April 16 Senator Nelson W. Aldrach of Rhode Island, died to day on Fifth Avenue, New York, aged 74 years. I walked a mile to-day.

Saturday, April 17 I am to-day 5 months over 86 years old, in good health for my age. It is fine April weather. There was probably a little frost to-night.

Sunday, April 18 It is a fine sunshiny day. Horace came at 9:00.

Monday, April 19 It is a nice April day. I walk over a mile.

Tuesday, April 20 Capt. Richardson of the navy stays with us at night. I walk about a mile.

Wednesday, April 21 It is somewhat cloudy and smoky today. Capt. Richardson dines with us.

Saturday, April 24 I sent for type-writer ribbon but Katharine was hurried home by threats of rain.

Sunday, April 25 A fair day. I rode out to Davie's Church and back. The road was good. Mrs. Justina Stevens came and remained till in the night.

Tuesday, April 27 Mrs. Agnes (Osborn) Beck came in the afternoon, and ate supper with us. It is a warm day.

Wednesday, April 28 It is just a year that we have lived in this house. The spring is probably a few days earlier than the last. Kenath Allen, our neighbor boy, came in. He is seven years old.

Saturday, May 1 Doctor Rev. Henry Francis Colby died at 7:00 evening. He was long pastor of the First Baptist Church. He was one of their best men. Aged 72. [This text was crossed through with "mistake" written over it]

Sunday, May 2 Report came of Rev. John Simons death at Peru, Ind.[This text was crossed through with "mistake" written over it]

Friday, May 7 The great steam passenger ship Lusitania, at 2:00, was torpedoed by submarines and lost in a few minutes with over twelve hundred, crew and passengers!

Saturday, May 8 Doctor Henry Francis Colby died at 7:00 this evening, aged 72 years. He was long pastor of the First Baptist Church in Dayton, and one of their best men. News of the destruction of the Lusitania fills the papers.

Sunday, May 9 News of the Lusitania disaster comes

teeming still in the papers. Horace comes in the afternoon and staid till his bed-time. He has failed to come only once or twice in the past months.

Monday, May 10 News of the death of Rev. John Simons, of Peru, Ind., comes in the paper.

Sunday, May 16 Horace came in the forenoon and staid till 8:00 at night. Mrs. Conover, the historian of Dayton, daughter of Dr. Reeves is 88 years of age, June 5th.

Monday, May 17 I am to-day 86 and 1/2 years old.

Friday, May 21 Agnes Beck dined and supped with us. Katharine and she went at night to Stivers' High School. Orville telegraphed that he would be home to-morrow afternoon.

Saturday, May 22 Orville telegraphed that would be at home to-morrow afternoon.

Sunday, May 23 Orville returned home from New York.

Wednesday, May 26 Mr. Nolty, a promoter, from New York, dined with us. He is a perfect gentleman in his manners.

Sunday, May 30 There was still rain. Horace came as usual. Lorin came and Netta, and staid till bed time.

Tuesday, June 1 I went to see the parade of Barnum & Bailies' show. There were several elephants. Two were quite large, with a man on each head. There were four lions, two tigers, and some bears. There was a nice lot of ponies. What an amount of expenditure—horses—vehicles—men and women employed! We had large rains in the evening! Agnes Beck dined with us.

Wednesday, June 2 The day was mosty fair. I walked about a half-mile.

Sunday, June 6 Horace was with us all day.

Monday, June 7 Upson of the Cash Register took supper with us.

Tuesday, June 8 Walter Brookens dined with us. Eckley

(cousin to Compositor) called. A student of Katharine's, now of New York called. Mrs. McCormack called and spent the afternoon in visiting Katharine.

Wednesday, June 9 Pliny Williamson and Mr. Morehouse dined with us. Mr. Morehouse was here last Nov 7th.

Saturday, June 12 It is a pleasant warm-like day. I read a good-deal in Encyclopedia Britanica, Vol. I & II.

Sunday, June 13 Horace as usual was with us.

Tuesday, June 15 Mr. Harry Clegg and his wife visited us in the evening. He wished to buy that part of Orville's land, lying between his south of us and his own recently bought.

Wednesday, June 16 The story was told in the *Herald* that Clara Wright was killed by a tornado. In the evening, a telegram corrected the report. She was only injured. "She rests easy", the telegram states.

Thursday, June 17 I am to-day 86 years and 7 months old.

Sunday, June 20 Lorin and Netta and Milton came in the afternoon and Horace went home with them. Some Oberlin women called in the evening.

Tuesday, June 22 Mr. Nolte was with us for dinner and supper, and till bed time.

Wednesday, June 23 Mr. F.R. Cordley and Nolte took dinner and Supper with us; went away at 7:00.

Thursday, June 24 Charles Williams of Oberlin, and Winnifred Rider took supper with us and staid till bed time.

Friday, June 25 Horace and William Jenkins came.

Saturday, June 26 Wm. Jenkins staid till bed time. Horace remained.

Sunday, June 27 Horace remained till bed time. I rode out before dinner with Orville in the automobile.

Tuesday, June 29 Mr. Knabenshue came and remained over night.

Wednesday, June 30 Mr. Knabenshue is with us still, remaining over night.

Thursday, July 1 Mr. Knabenshue talked of going on the train for Los Angeles, but not being well did not go.

Friday, July 2 Mr. Knabenshue did not go yesterday, but to-day to Toledo, at 10:00.

Sunday, July 4 Leontine and Horace came and she staid all day. She was as lovely as could be. She is as tall as her aunt Katharine.

Monday, July 5 Horace staid all day. Our folks attended a picnic in Orville's Woods, with William and Lottie Andrews, and Lorin & wife and boys, and Wm. and Jas. Jenkins.

Tuesday, July 6 Horace staid till bed time.

Sunday, July 11 Horace was with us all day. Leontine & Ivonette were with us the afternoon.

Monday, July 12 Orville started to New York in the afternoon.

Tuesday, July 13 The Miss Myers and Mrs. Stevens and Agnes supped with us.

Wednesday, July 14 Agnes remained with us till 8 or 9 o'clock. Her husband telegraphed that he was coming home on this morning train. I wrote to Ellis Wright.

Thursday, July 15 Mr. Earl N. Findley, of N.Y. Tribune and Mr. Jus. R. McMahon came home with Orville, on morning train. They dined with us.

Friday, July 16–Friday, July 23 All in good health.

Saturday, July 24 Earl Findley and John McMahon have been with us since the 15th.

Sunday, July 25 Horace came and staid till about 9:00 at night.

Monday, July 26 Orville went to New York. In the evening, Katharine and Mr. Findley and Mr. McMahon went to Lorin's, and came home at 9:25.

Tuesday, July 27 Mrs. Irvin and her sweet little girl; Mrs. Stoddard, and Mrs. Allen, and her boy, called an hour in the afternoon to see Katharine.

Wednesday, July 28 We are all well. We moved here fifteen months ago, to-day.

Thursday, July 29 Orville comes, from New York on 8:00 train. He suffered much pain from the agitation of the cars, on the way home. The afternoon is quite warm.

Saturday, July 31 Pliny Williamson dined with us, and remained till evening.

Sunday, August 1 We are all well, except Orville's lameness.

Wednesday, August 4 Mrs. Jas. E. Barlow called to see Katharine. It is cooler in the evening.

Friday, August 6 I wrote Reuchlin. We are all well. The day is cloudy and cool.

Sunday, August 8 We all remained at home. Horace came. Lorin and Netta came in the evening.

Monday, August 9 In usual health. Though Earl N. Findley has been somewhat sick.

Tuesday, August 10 Berger came out in an Automobile to see Orville, at supper time. I wrote Reuchlin at Ivins Hotel, 10th and Figueroa Sts., Los Angeles, Cal.

Wednesday, August 11 It is somewhat rainy. We are all well except Orville's lameness and Mr. Findley's stomach has hardly recovered. We had a hard shower in the afternoon.

Saturday, August 14 Mr. Fauver dined with us. He is rather a showy man.

Sunday, August 15 We are all well. Milton came in after,

Horace is here since his mother and Sisters went to Harry Andrews, Decatur, Illinois.

Wednesday, August 18 Pliny Williamson dined with us and remained over night.

Sunday, August 29 Horace was with us. Lorin and Netta came in the evening.

Tuesday, August 31 Lieut. Maxfield took supper with us. This was a very cool morning. I received a letter from Ray Stevens and from J.F. Harris.

Wednesday, September 1 It is warmer to-day. Orville and Katharine took lunch with Lieut. Maxwell, down town.

Tuesday, September 7 Mr. Knabenshue came and staid all day. Mr. Deeds called in the evening more than an hour.

Wednesday, September 8 Mr. Kabenshue continued till [than, which is crossed out]afternoon.

Thursday, September 9 All well but Orville, whose nerves are broken down.

Friday, September 10 Ancil Wright came about 10:00, and Ovid L. Reeder an hour later. They went out to the flying-ground in the afternoon and took supper at Y.C. League. The boys came to our house and staid at night.

Saturday, September 11 Ovid and Ancil went to Wright Company factory and spent forenoon. They dined with us. In afternoon, they went to Flying Ground and took supper at Lorin's.

Sunday, September 12 Ovid and Ancil go to Lorin's. Orville and Katharine go to see the boys start home. They did not go however as the traction had changed its arrangements. So they staid at Lorin's.

Monday, September 13 Orville has been worse for several days.

Tuesday, September 14 He is still quite helpless but he goes to town. Knabenshue returns this evening.

Family outing, ca. 1917

Wednesday, September 15 We went to Centerville and back in Knbenshue's automobile. Mr. Myer got a cigar at Centerville. They left before bed time.

Thursday, September 16 Mr. Knabenshue dined with us. In the evening, we went out to the flying ground at Sim's Station, in Knabenshue's automobile. He sups and lodges with us. I saw two flights at Sims. There are about 24 students of flying under Rhinehart's instruction.

Saturday, September 18 Leontine came, had a Latin lesson with Katharine. Roy took us a ride and we took Leontine home.

Sunday, September 19 I dined at Lorin's. Milton visiting at Oxford. I went Home with Orville and Kath. and

Knabenshue. After supper, we went down Lebanon pike across to Cincinnati Pike up to Dayton and out Salem Pike three miles, took Horace home and went home.

Monday, September 20 Mr. Roy Knabenshue continues with us.

Wednesday, September 22 My health is very good.

Thursday, September 23 Roy Knabenshue returned from Columbus *on tomorrow.*

Friday, September 24 Knabenshue came back from Columbus. My health continues good.

Saturday, September 25 Mr. Knabenshue is with us. Capt. Gustin is with us and Walter Brookens.

Sunday, September 26 Knabenshue went home to Toledo. Orville went down town, and Capt. Mustin and Walter Brookens came home with him and dined. Also, Horace was with us.

Wednesday, September 29 Orville and Katharine left at 2:30 for New York.

Sunday, October 3 Horace dined & supped with us.

Wednesday, October 6 Orville suffers much, and remains at home.

Thursday, October 7 Roy Knabenshue, Walter Brookens and Mr. Macey dined with us. Macey is a Witness at Buffalo in the Curtiss trial.

Friday, October 8 Knabenshue and Macey come in afternoon and stay two or three hours. Lorin came and took supper with us.

Saturday, October 9 Mr. Russell & Pliny Williams were here, preparing some writings. Mr. Howard came to help. Mr. Knabenshue dined with us. Lorin was also here.

Sunday, October 10 Dr. Hoppy, a specialist from Cincinnati, was here with Dr. L. Spitler. He pronounces Orville's ailment to be simply neuralgia. Knabenshue and Horace are with us.

Monday, October 11 Mr. Knabenshue left to-day.

Sunday, October 17 Horace was with us. Ivonette and Leontine were autoing and called. But I was asleep.

Wednesday, October 20 I am well. Mr. Knabenshue ate supper with us.

Friday, October 29 (This is for Decem,) of Cincinnati came as a hospital nurse. She has had some experience in neuralgia cases and is a smart woman.

Sunday, October 31 In the afternoon, I rode with Orville to Lorin's. Milton and Ivonette are at Oxford. Leontine is as sweet as can be.

Monday, November 1 Lorin went to Marion and saw

Albert Anderson Koerner who is not able to work. He is about house, He coughs very hard. He has tuberlocus. He gets 4 dollars a week from the Oddfellows. His wife is reputed to be a hardworking woman. She is reputed to be foolish over her son whom she will not allow to work at anything that soils his hands or clowthes. L. did not see her.

Tuesday, November 2 This is election day. Dayton votes for the issue of $40,000.00. Oakwould votes for the issue of bounds, to be issued to buy additional school play grounds.

Wednesday, November 3 Wm. Doup called to see me, a good-looking man of 44 years. He lives in Huntington, W. Va. He came up in Miami City. He studied law with Young He married a Miss McClure, He got into forgery, and was in the penitentiary for a time. He was evidently insane.

Sunday, November 7 Mrs. Justina Stevens took supper with us and Orville took her home and Horace.

Monday, November 8 We rode to Springfield to day and back home, 58 miles.

Tuesday, November 9 Mrs. McCormick and Agnes Beck dined with us.

Saturday, November 13 Orville and Katharine went to Cincinnati, to see a piannist and they took Leontine and Horace with them. They made 143 miles. Leontine they took home. Horace stays.

Sunday, November 14 We all and Lorin and Netta rode over twenty miles in the afternoon with us. ["with us" is crossed out in diary]

Monday, November 15 It is a very fair day, but somewhat cool. I have been quite well for a good while.

Tuesday, November 16 Clifford Andrews, a great-grandson of Benj. Van Cleve, called on some business of Mr. Harman. He is a brother of Harry Andrews.

Wednesday, November 17 Rode with Orville, Katharine Mrs. Justinia Stevens and Miss Myers north of Dayton through Vandalia. Had a supper joint with Lorin's, with 87 Candles burning. Ivonette wrote me and sent tuber-roses by express, from Oxford. Lorin's gave chrysanthiums and Miss Stevens carnations—all flowers very beautiful. It was a very bright fine day. My health was very good.

Thursday, November 18 Katharine was away at a suffrage meeting at noon, and at Y.W. League, at supper. It was [blank] years of Y.W. League. Notice of my birthday appeared in the Journal, and and the News. Letters of Congratulation from Alfred Fight, Winifred Rider and Young & Young.

Friday, November 26 Horace continued with us.

Saturday, November 27 We rode South in Orville's automobile. Mr. Robbins, came for Supper. He went to hotel to lodge.

Sunday, November 28 We went after Mr. Robbins Hariet Sillaman's husband and took a ride north through Vaandaily, home.

Tuesday, November 30 Men were at work at the door-yard, cutting away trees and grading.

Wednesday, December 1 Mrs. Elisabeth Brookbank, Daniel Koerner's youngest daughter, came at about 12 o'clock, from her home at Dunlapsville, Indiana. She visited Lorin's in the afternoon. Workers continue.

Thursday, December 2 Mrs. Brookbank is 62 years old. She has three sons: Charles, who has a store in Dunlapville; Frederick, who owns part of his grandfather Koerner's old place; and Roscoe who is married and lives at Washington, D.C. Lorin's (except Ivonette) took supper with us. Workers continue.

Friday, December 3 Mrs. Elizabeth Brookbank, went home just before noon. Workers continue on the door-yard.

Sunday, December 5 We rode up toward Vandalia. Winifred Ryder was along. Mr. John H. Patterson came in the evening and staid an hour. Horace was with us.

Tuesday, December 7 The workers continue to grade the door-yard. Roy Knabenshue took Dinner with us. Katharine attended the Young Woman's League, as she often does.

Saturday, December 11 Orville has great pain in his back, is unable to drive home. Katharine calls Charles Groombach to come and run his auto. He comes home about dark in the ambulenc. Lies easy on his bed. Dr. Conklin came. The roads are very icy. It is rather a gloomy day.

Sunday, December 12 It is a dark gloomy day. Dr. Spitler came at 10:00. Orville suffers much pain.

Monday, December 13 Orville is still troubled with great pain. Congress assembles.

Tuesday, December 14 Orville is thought to be better. The president reads his message, in favor of "Preparedness."

Wednesday, December 15 Orville's pain goes principally to his limb. He is deemed some better.

Thursday, December 16 Katharine and Leontine went to Oberlin. Orville is still uneasy, and requires close attention. The pain is shifted mostly to his limb. Lorin stays at night.

Friday, December 17 Orville, who has suffered much pain, seems to be improving. Lorin came in the evening.

Saturday, December 18 Orville has slept some six hours. Yet he is quite uneasy. Katharine's train which is due from Oberlin a little before six oclock, evening did not arrive till over an hour late. We ate supper about 8:00.

Friday, December 24 Lorin's family of children came, except Milton in the evening. Presents. Horace is given a bicycle.

Saturday, December 25 Dr. Hopin came from Cincinnati to consult in Orville's case with Dr. Spitler. They declare Orville's case purely Neuralgia. All Lorin's family came in except Lontine and staid an hour. Orville slept well during the night. Horace rode his new bycicle home. Lorin staid.

Sunday, December 26 I get up at 8:00. It is a sunshiny day. This is my 88th Christmas day.

Tuesday, December 28 To-night there was freezing of water that left icicles on the limbs of trees and bended them. I received photographs from Oregon of Henry J. Follis and his wife, the first I ever had.

Friday, December 31 Miss Omara Came from Cincinnati, as a hospital nurse. She is good-looking, smart and experienced in neuralgia.

[The following is at the end of the diary in the address and telephone section:]

Harvey moved to Rush County, in 1865. Thomas was born Jan. 12, 1848. He married Jan. 26, 1868, Miss Mary Elizabeth Vandall, who died in Feb. 27, 1911.His funeral was held at Center Christian Church, Febr. 16, 1915, at 2:00, Rev. C.W. Ratcliff preaching the sermon. Buried at Center. He died at his home, near May's Ind.

My first license to Exhort was dated Feb. 1, 1851. My permit to exhort was dated April 27, 1850. My quar. [?] Conf. license to preach was dated Jan. 17, 1852. My annual Conference license to preach was dated August 1853. I was ordained by Bishop D. Edwards, at Abington, Ind. August 1856.

Family Record
1. Dan Wright, born Oct. 3, 1790. died Oct. 6, 1861, aged 71 years.
2. Catherine (Reeder) Wright, b. March 17, 1800, d. Sept. 24, 1866. Their marriage occured Feb. 12, 1818, at Centerville.
3. Samuel Smith Wright Wright born at Centerville, O., Nov. 21, 1818, died in Fayette Co., Ind., July 18, 1842, age 23.
4. Harvey Wright, born Sept. 9, 1820, at Cent., died in Rush Co., Ind., Sept. 22, 1906, aged 85 past.

5. George Wright born about 1822, died at 8 months old.
6. Sarah Wright, born November 21, 1824, m. Charles Harris Aug. 184[blank] died Decem. 23, 1878, aged 44 years.
7. Milton Wright, born in Rush Co., Ind., November 17, 1728 marr'd Nov. 24, 1859, Susan Catharine Koerner,
8. Susan Catherine Koerner b. in Londoun County, Virginia, close to (3 1/2 mi) Hillsborough, Apr. 30, 1831, died in Dayton, Ohio, July 4, 1889, aged 58 years.
9. William Wright, born February 29, 1832, in Rush Co., Indiana, died October 5, 1868, aged 36 years.
1. Rev. Dyer Burge's, a presbyterian preacher, officiated in my parent's marriage.
2. Rev. John Wallace M.S. officiated in Chas. and Sarah Harris' marriage.
3. Rev. John Fohl M.B. officiated in my marriage.
4. Rev. Daniel Connor, I think, officiated at Harvey's wedding.

Grandfather and grandmother Reeder's graves are in the United Presbyterian Ground two miles east of Palmyra, immediately west of a nice granite monument of John McCorkle and James, and Sally McCorcle and Elizabeth Butler and A.P. Butler. Aunt Sally Croddy lies beside them. Uncle George Reeder was born May 15, 1818. He died 15 years ago, aged 82. Some of their children were buried near grandfather's grave.

Albert A. Koerner 250 Franconia Ave. Marion, Ohio

Sarah Jane Wallace, R.F.D. 11 Peru, Ind.

Flora M. Glass, Route 6, Wabash, Ind. Sina E. Ardery

Mary Jane Follis Box 147, Stayton, Oregon.

Alfred A. Thomas, 1110 U.B. Building Dayton

Grace Frazier left home Sept. 11, went to Chicago, and wrote home that she was going to some new country.

Lulu D. Crandall, The Dalles, Oregon.

1916

Saturday, January 1 Since November 17, I have been in my 88th year. To my great grand-father Joseph Reeder, I find no ancestor who lived so long as I have. He lived to be 86. My health the past year has been excellent, for one so old. My brothers and sisters are not alive. Wilbur, a bright star among the Wright intellects, has been gone nearly four years. St. cars start past, to-day.

Sunday, January 2 My ancestor, of France, is said to have lived to be 103 years old, Francis Jano. He was a fugitive Hugenot—a rich merchant. John H. Patterson called in the evening. I walked out with Carrie to see the streetcar track over east of us.

Thursday, January 6 Mrs. Weth, Hospital Nurse, came.

Sunday, January 9 Leontine and Horace dined with us. Mr. Deeds called to see Orville just before dinner. Katharine and Leontine do up the dishes, and let Carrie go to see her people. They did This nearly every Sunday of the Year.

Tuesday, January 11 Edwin J. Brown, Supt. of Dayton Schools, died, this morning, about 5 o'clock.

Thursday, January 13 Lorin came to see Orville.

Friday, January 14 Mrs. Frank McCormick called to see Katharine. Orville is a little better, sat up a little.

Saturday, January 15 Orville has been sick five weeks. He is still a little better to day.

Sunday, January 16 Mr. Deeds came again. He continued to come for some weeks on Sundays.

Friday, January 28 Miss Omara of Cincinnati came as an experienced nurse in neuralgia. Miss Weth was inexperienced, and not of much force. Miss Omara was a Roman Catholic.

Thursday, February 3 It is a sunshiny day, but the wind is cold. T.D. Brown, my Cousin, died at Crawfordsville, Ind., this afternoon. His wife died seventeen years ago. For several years, his reason was gone.

Thursday, February 10 Orville has two elm trees planted along the street. Cost: $35 or 40 dollars each. He altogether had six trees planted—two of them being maples.

Friday, February 11 Orville has another elm tree planted. Altogether he had four elms and two maples set out.

Monday, February 14 We received a telegram from Cora W. Dillon, saying that her father, Thomas Wright, died this morning. Thomas Wright was probably Harvey's son of the best judgment. George, next younger, had fine talent as a Baptist Preacher, but hardly so fine a judgment. George was a physician.

Sunday, February 27 Mrs. J.L. Stevens came. Horace came. Mr. Jacobs came. Orville and Kath. took them home after nine o'clock at night. Mr. Deeds and his little boy came. Miss [blank] and three Russian Boys and two McCarms came. She, probably a German Spy, though a High School teacher. Boy's pencil sketch of me, a picture.

Monday, February 28 Katharine went down town and was gone all the afternoon and till late bed-time. She has been at home closely during Orville's sickness of over two months.

Tuesday, February 29 This is Feb. 29th, leap year, and the 84th anniversary of my Brother Williams birth-day. What a sweet brother he was; and he was a great thinker and composer. He was almost perfect. But he was slow of utterance, and not very interesting. He talked very little.

Friday, March 3 Horace came before supper. He came almost every week.

Saturday, March 4 Horace staid all day.

Sunday, March 5 I walked a half mile, and more. I went in afternoon over ten miles, in town, in the automobile. We took Leontine home.

Tuesday, March 7 John H. Patterson visited us. He came about once a month.

Wednesday, March 8 We went in automobile three miles north of town.

Thursday, March 9 It is a sunshiny day. There is a skift of snow over the ground.

Saturday, March 11 We rode in the auto to Lorin's. "Peka" Andrews and Horace came home with us and staid till morning. They are moving back to Canton, from Illinois. Benj. Van Cleve and Peka are as tall and slender as bean-poles. The day is fair.

Sunday, March 12 We went in auto. to Lorin's. Benny rode out north-west with us, and on home. The day is fair.

Monday, March 13 We went in auto, over east part of town out as far as "David Winters" Reformed Church. Netta and Clare, and her little girls, came in the afternoon.

Wednesday, March 15 I had Larangitus. Dr. Levi Spitler came. He left me medicine for the rest of the day.

Thursday, March 16 I lay in bed closely, and take medicine.

Friday, March 17 I am today four months over 87 years old. Katharine went to a dinner at Sprig McMahon's. I still lie closely abed, and take medicine.

Saturday, March 18 It is a very pretty day. I got up and dressed myself.

Tuesday, March 21 Margaret (Braden) Collier died tomorrow, of dropsey, tomorrow, being 74 years old. She was born March 1st, 1842. Austin Winchel and Laura started home from St. Petersburg, F1y to day.

Wednesday, March 22 Margaret J. Collier died to-day. She was Aunt Eliza (Reeder) Braden's oldest daughter.

Tuesday, March 28 It is one year and eleven months since we moved to this place.

Sunday, April 2 Sally Ellen Eudaly died April 2nd, aged 73 years and 11 months. Her husband W.A. Eudaly died July, 1904. Her illness was short. Her son Milton F.; J. Ava S.; Violet May; William Goodman; and Pansy Ellen are yet alive, and fifteen grandchildren. She died at Fort Stockton, Tex. She was married August 10, 1859.

Thursday, April 6 It is a fair day. Pretty warm. We rode in auto north of Dayton.

Friday, April 7 It is a fair day. Pretty cool. Orville is having his driveway readjusted.

Tuesday, April 18 Miss Winifred Ryder was with us.

Wednesday, April 19 Winifred staid till after supper.

Sunday, April 23 Horace was with us. Winifred Ryder was with us. Mr and Mrs Deeds called an hour. She is a very fine-looking woman.

Tuesday, April 25 Orville and Katharine started for New York, at 2 t[his] afernoon.

Friday, April 28 It is two years to-day, since we moved into This house. The red-bud comes out some days later than it did then. We looked some for Orville and Katharine home from New York, but had no word from them. I walked before noon over a half mile circle.

Saturday, April 29 Orville and Katharine came on 9:45 train from New York, where the Wright Company held a meeting of its engineers.

Sunday, April 30 To day I am as old as William Otterbein was at his death. Rev. Wm. Dillon and his son Justin came on the 8:45 traction train from Springfield, on a visit. Minnie Fagan weighs 180 pounds. She must have some of her friends with her. Justin's have a daughter some eight years old. Dillon claims to be 74 years old.

Wednesday, May 3 The men are busy, tearing down the top of the hill north-west of the house; they fill the driveway with loads of gravel.

Thursday, May 4 Ivonette came in the afternoon, and had two Oxford student girls with her. I walk nearly a mile circle.

Friday, May 5 Three of the five girls came in the evening to see Ivonette at her home. They were Miss Elston, Mills, Miss Brochaur, Miss [ ]and Miss [ ] They were nice girls.

Saturday, May 6 We had a *Musicale* at our house about 4:00. Miss Eileen Mills and Ivonette Wright, pupils of Miss Clara Banford and Miss Bertha Elston pupil of Prof. Clem A. Fowner, Oxford, acting. About 30 invited guests were present. The six girls and Leontine and Lorine, Netta and Horace, and Winnifred Ryder, took supper with us.

Sunday, May 7 We rode out 7 miles north in the auto.

Sunday, May 14 Horace was with us. By Special delivery, a letter notified us of the purpose of Mary H. Krout, to visit us, Early to-morrow on her way home from Philadelphia.

Monday, May 15 Mary H. Krout, Cousin, Caroline's oldest daughter, of Crawfordsville, Indiana, visited us. We spent the day in conversation, and riding in the automobile. Manager Waite and his wife (six feet tall), and

his cousin and her mother dined with us. The mother was the motherinlaw of Kate Wiley. They live in Toledo.

Tuesday, May 16 Mary Krout went on 7 t [ ] train to Indianapolis, and in an hour on home to Crawfordsville.

Wednesday, May 17 I am half way in my 88th year, being 87 years and 6 months old.

Friday, May 19 We rode out to Cox's farm with Leontine, who ate supper with us. She then went home, and Horace came out with Orville.

Saturday, May 20 James Rice and wife and two little boys and a little girl, called to see us from Lorin's neighborhood. He formerly went to school to Katharine.

Tuesday, May 30 It is Decoration Day. We rode down town, with Mrs. Justinia Stevens, and on to Centerville.

Wednesday, May 31 I walked a mile in our porch. Katharine went to Richmond to comfort Emma Dennis.

Thursday, June 1 I walked a mile nearly every day, for several days.

Thursday, June 8 Mr. and Mrs. Frank McCormick took supper with us and staid till about 10:00. She is a very smart little woman, and a favorite of Katharine.

Friday, June 9 At the National Republican Convention, Charles Evans Hughes, was nominated on third ballot, practically unanimously, as the candidate for president of the United States. Accepted the nomination and resigned the Justiceship in the Supreme Court. Just a few minutes earlier, Theodore Rosevelt was nominated by the Progressive Convention. He deferred acceptance.

Saturday, June 10 Orville went on a trip to Boston, at 2:00, to attend a techniologist meeting next week.

Sunday, June 11 Miss Green, superintendent of the Normal School, dined with us. Katharine and I went with her to Park Presbyterian Church, and returned home at 2 o'clock.

Friday, June 16 Orville returned from Boston, in morning.

Saturday, June 17 I am 7 months over 87 years old.

Sunday, June 18 We rode south and west some 12 miles, in auto.

Monday, June 19 Mrs. Cora W. Dillon, on a visit to her mother's sister in Springfield, called a half-hour at Hawthorn Hill. We rode in town, in auto, some 8 miles, in afternoon.

Saturday, June 24 Mrs. A.M. Kittredge, and her daughters, Helen Louise, and Mrs. Thomas A. Watson called; 217 N. Ludlow Street, they live. T.R. Rosevelt wrote a letter declining the Progressive nomination, and urging the Progressive Party to support Charles Evans Hughes.

Sunday, June 25 Orville and Katharine visit Frank McCormick's. We rode on auto south-west.

Monday, June 26 At 3:00, I went to the show at the Fairgrounds. We saw seals, tigers, hyenas, lions, White bears, near a dozen elephants of various sizes, monkeys, camels, zebras, leopards, wolves, Gnu, lamas, river horse, Rocky-mountain sheep, etc. etc. We went into the Circus and paid for reserved seats. We saw many Clowns, a man posing at top of pole, woman on horseback, one on a gray-horse at the center rode on her feet trapese, four in show.

Tuesday, June 27 Katharine had a number of teachers to dine with her. Orville and I are not included. There were the Miss Mayers, Miss Hunters, etc. etc. in all to eleven. I did not get my dinner till 2:00.

Thursday, June 29 Esther Taylor called in the afternoon. She is thinking of attending Oberlin College. She is Charlie's daughter. She is a nice-looking and gifted girl.

Friday, June 30 Mrs. Wagner, and Rachel, and two girls, called in the evening.

Saturday, July 1 We went at 7:00 to Lorin's and took him and his two girls a ride in the automobile.

Sunday, July 2 Orville & Katharine started for Mr. Collier's in New Jersey, and to John Zeller's, on a visit.

Tuesday, July 4 Lorin, William Andrews, & Jenkin's children, had a picknick in Orville's woods. In the evening Jenkin's and his wife and his sister [blank]came. Fireworks in the evening.

Wednesday, July 5 Lorin took our silverware away.[to the Bank] [crossed out of original diary]

Friday, July 7 Mr. Buckwalter & wife came in the evening and Matilda Wirthing Mrs. Bookwalter's mother , & Andrew Kaler, Carrie's brother visited Carrie.

Sunday, July 9 Carrie is busy preparing to go away to Wawbec Island, Ontario. The post-office is: Wawbec Island, Penetanguishenc, Ontario, Canada. Lorin's came to supper and staid till bed-time. Orville and Katharine visited John Zeller. Mary Erickson, and her two boys were there. She is John's daughter. His son John is married; farming.

Monday, July 10 We are preparing to go to Wawbec Island, Ontario. Mrs. Creagor comes to see if we need help. We go on taxicab at 4:00; start on 4:23 train. Go on Big 4, to Springfield, London, Columbus, Delaware, Cleveland, on to Buffalo. I slept a little; jolted so I was not numb.

Tuesday, July 11 In the morning Orville came on cars from New York. We went from Buffalo west to Hamilton, and thence to Toronto, and North to Penetang, where we arrived at 2:00. There, in a half hour, we took a boat up Georgian Bay to Wawbec Island where we landed about 5:00, after a wearisome ride.

Wednesday, July 12 I slept till after eight o'clock. Arose and breakfasted. Went on a sail with Orville three miles on the Bay. I slept a nap; dined before 1:00 Slept an hour in afternoon. A skipper rowboat brought Miss Williams who brought us some milk.

Thursday, July 13 Mr. and Mrs. Werthner and her sister called. Orville& Kath. were away on the boat. This was in forenoon. Prof. Wm. B. Werthner and Mrs. Werthner and Miss Elizabeth Hippard, board at Mr. Frances Boarding House.

Friday, July 14 It is windy in the morning. It became exceedingly still, and we had a little rain.

Saturday, July 15 The steam [?] boat called about 6:00—later than usual.

Sunday, July 16 Mr. Clement called in afternoon. McKenzie's called while I was asleep.

Monday, July 17 Orville and Katharine went on the supply boat, I am 4 months less than 88 years old. McKenzie called in the afternoon. Orville had returned from Penetang. He went to send a telegram to Cincinnati. McKenzie had his son with him.

Tuesday, July 18 The Williams girls and Mrs. Hodgins came and brought their knitting. People knit for the hospitals up here.

Thursday, July 20 Thursday was a very hot day. Therm. 96 degrees.

Friday, July 21 It was cool to-day. Orv.& Kath. went to Prof. Werthner's hotel. Rev. Reinhold gave us some fish. No body came. Williams tarried long at the landing. Horace caught a pike 29 1/2 inches long.

Sunday, July 23 No visitors to-day. Charlie and Carrie, and we five, go out at dusk for a rowboat ride. I did little reading in the day.

Monday, July 24 The *Electric* made its first trip *before* 8:00.

Tuesday, July 25 We rode out north-west in boat with Prof. Werthner,wife and sisterinlaw. Went near Werthner's hotel. Got home late.

Wednesday, July 26 In the evening McKenzie's took Orville and Katharine a boat ride. I went to the dock to see the mail come in. I stayed late.

Thursday, July 27 Orville was away at supper time to McKenzie's. Charles & Carrie went to Penetang, in

morning boat; returned at 5:00. Hodgins and wife went away, to-day.

Friday, July 28 Orville received his long, delayed motor. It operates well. There is a strong southeast breeze, and it causes some waves on the bay.

Sunday, July 30 A shower in the evening, attended with wind. Williams hired boy Geo. Fisher, and William's are caught out in a boat. Orville looks after Them. Orville and Kath. eat supper at William's tent.

Monday, July 31 Katharine looks after a supply boat; finds it at last. Orville and the boys go hunting after minnows. We find them better than fishworms to catch Black bass. We dine at 1:30.

Tuesday, August 1 In the evening, Orv. & Kath. and Pekah & I went over to Lambert Island south of Ship Island, and over it. Come back by way of Wawbec Island,[?]. To-day is quite cool.

Wednesday, August 2 It is cool in the morning. It warms up in forenoon.

Thursday, August 3 Prof. W.B. Werthner and wife and her sister, Miss Hibbard sup with us.

Friday, August 4 I wrote an article, "James and his Epistle." Sent it by mail. We went round Portage Island, from North to North-west, and out toward Minnicog Hotel. Charles and Carrie are with us. Mr. Clement and family called, a half hour in the afternoon, Mrs. Prichard is along.

Monday, August 7 Orville and Kath. and Charles and Carrie, before supper, go and look at Lambert Island.

Tuesday , August 8 Prof. W.B. Werthner's start to Dayton, Ohio, and family.

Wednesday, August 9 Nothing unusual occurs. Pictures of ancient American places come to my address.

Thursday, August 10 Nothing special occurs. We have been here a month, 31 days.

Friday, August 11 We went on Motor boat past Campbell's, some 4 miles away. It is a fine ride. We came back the ride reversed round Wawbac Island. This was just before supper. The strait is only 100 ft. wide. Arthur Island was just before Bone Island. Arthur has, perhaps, 40 acres. Bone has [?] They are rich and evil spoken of.

Sunday, August 13 Mr. Johnson, William's partner, and Miss Williams came before supper.

Monday, August 14 Captain Punch's boat stuck over east, so we had no mail to-day. It went toward Penetang, in the evening.

Tuesday, August 15 Captain Punch did not make the forenoon call. Stewart McKenzie (14) dined with us. He is a smart, good-looking boy. We went to a bonfire by invitation to Mr. William's camp. We talked and had songs.

Wednesday, August 16 Mr. Wm. H. King, Mella and Katharine and Willie came about 4:00 afternoon. We went out boat-riding and our motor irrestistently struck, and Orville paddled home a mile and a half. We reached the boat-house before 9:00. Katharine Wright King is 8 years old, Willie is 10.

Thursday, August 17 I am to-day within 3 months of 88 years old. Mr. France's Caunch took us north-west to Home Bay, where there are scattered a number of Toronto University Professors. Saw many rocky islands, and many homes or part homes. Went two hours by sun. Got home at dark. We eleven and captain ate lunch on boat.

Friday, August 18 Nothing very unusual occurs. Captain Punch came about 6:00 Aft. in a lanch. Letter or card from Reuchlin's, who are moving from Baldwin City to 639 Freeman Ave., Kan. City, Kan. It is a warm day.

Saturday, August 19 This is Orville's and Katharine's birth-day—he 45, she 42 years old. She resembles her grandfather Koerner; he more like the Reeder's.

Sunday, August 20 Mr. France takes us 8 miles south to Honey Harbor. All but Horace and William Went.

Monday, August 21 Mr. William H. King went home to Geneva, Ohio. Captain Punch came twice. The thermometer ran about 80 degrees.

Tuesday, August 22 Nothing unusual, except that our steam boat comes *twice* a day; Captain Punch. It was a warm day. I wrote a careful description of Georgian Bay, to William H.H. Reeder.

Wednesday, August 23 Nothing unusual. The weather is temperate. Our children pile the brush for a bonfire. I wrote a letter to the Reeder Reunion; to Robert Braden, Reeder.

Thursday, August 24 Mr. S.J. Williams visits Orville. The boys add to the brush pile.

Friday, August 25 We had our bonfire. We had the prettiest flame, so far. I talked with Mrs. Williams and Mrs. McKenzie. People went away before 10:00.

Saturday, August 26 Nothing particular occured. Northern lights appeared in the evening.

Sunday, August 27 Our folks went out towards Campbell, in the boat. Miss Clement called to see Katharine. We had Pike fish for breakfast.

Monday, August 28 Mr. and Mrs. Williams called on their going away. He is a good
looking stout man.

Tuesday, August 29 Nella and Katharine went to Penetang, to get the times of the cars in going home.

Wednesday, August 30 We roast candy and they take me down to the fire, on the edge of the Bay.

Thursday, August 31 Orv. & Kath. and the children are invited to McKenzie's to tea, about 5:00.

Friday, September 1 Our folks go to Penetang to see about going home, fearing the threatened railroad strike.

Saturday, September 2 We start for home. We reach Buffalo, where our cars lie all night and till next afternoon.

Sunday, September 3 We lay at Buffalo, till about 3:00, when we go on to Delaware and Columbus and reach home about 3:00 afternoon.

Monday, September 4 This is "Labor Day" and it is expected the cars will be crowded. But as the people visiting were all alarmed as well as we about the strike, they over-thronged the cars on Saturday and Sunday, and we had to come on the third section of the cars. It was cool weather, however.

Tuesday, September 5 Today's cars will also be crowded. Probably with the previous efflux, there were fewer effected by Labor Day.

Saturday, September 9 Miss Justina Stevens came but as she had forgotten her spectacles, she could not examine great-grandfather John Phillip Freyer's fam. register.

Monday, September 11 Mrs. J. Stephens came and wrote a copy of John Philip Freyer's German Register (of his family register), and a translation of the same. John Philip Fry and Dorothy Boger were married the 6th (or 16th) of January, 1776. Her father's name was Joseph Boger(n) and her sister's name was Susana.

Tuesday, September 12 Silvanus Koerner and wife, and his sister, Lizzie, came at 11:00, and staid till 4:00. They came in an automobile. They went to visit some cousins of theirs at Camden, in the evening.

Wednesday, September 13 Our trunks from Penetang, Ontario, came. They had been dropped out at the Canada line.

Thursday. September 14 Carrie went to Irene Harding's wedding. She married Wert. We ate supper in the kitchen. Miss Harding was a clerk in Frank Hale's grocery where Charlie's worked and Carrie.

Friday, September 15 Orville got me a bright light for my room, in the evening, to read by. My central light is too high and the others too dim and to one side.

Saturday, September 16 Orville, Katharine and Winifred Rider went to Fort Ancient and back. Orville discovered where the mound Builders had stored up water.

Winifred took supper with us. They took Winifred home, after supper.

Sunday, September 17 I lack two months of being 88 years old. Mr. E.A. Deeds came while I was asleep in the afternoon, and Orville and Katharine went away with him. I have been inclined to sleep to-day. I am quite well to-day, and have been for three months, and more. Some times I have neglected to take note.

Tuesday, September 19 Orville went to the Aviator grounds, flying. He was using a machine intended to be used with his self-regulating invention.

Wednesday, September 20 Katharine went to the Hills and Dales Club. Mrs. Justina Stephens came home with her to supper. Orville spent the day out at the Aviator grounds, flying.

Thursday, September 21 Orville again spends the day at the aeronautical grounds. He and Catharine went in the evening to Lorin's.

Friday, September 22 Emeline (Zeller) Dennis came. While east, she visited grandfather Koerner's (grandmother) farm of 71 acres, three and a half miles from Hillsboro, Virginia. This farm, grandmother's inheritance, from her father's estate, they moved from to Indiana in 1832. Lorin and Netta and Horace ate supper with us. Emma went home.

Sunday, September 24 Horace Wright was with us as usual, and remained till bed time.

Monday, September 25 About 1:30 p.m. Orville and Katharine and I went to the Fair Ground. We saw the Political procession come in. There were squads from Cincinnati, and various counties. I scarcely saw the distinguished men. At memorial Hall at 8oclock, I heard Charles E. Hughes and [blank] and Ex-governor Herrick. Heard little.

Tuesday, September 26 The *Journal* gave [blank] and Hugh's speeches, and Herrick's. The *News* almost gave nothing.

Wednesday, September 27 Nothing very peculiar occurred

to-day. I wrote a letter to Reuchlin. Sent him a copy of John Philip Freyer's old register. They, John Philip Freyer and Dorothy Bogern, were married January 6th (or 16), 1776. Her father was Joseph Boger, and she had a sister Susana Boger. For her the oldest daughter of Phillip was named and probably my wife, Susan.

Thursday, September 28 Edwin Shuey, Jr. and Mr. Hatfield, Y.M.C.A. secretary called to ask a donation of Orville& Kath.

Saturday, September 30 I wrote a letter to Mrs. Loretta Sterrett giving the history of those children that I knew. In the evening I sent the Freyer Register by registered letter to Mrs. Starrett, Pataskala, Ohio. (I sent by Charles Broombach, and he failing to register the letter, returned it.)

Sunday, October 1 Mr. Edward A. Deeds called while we were at Dinner a moment, but returned with his family after 2:00 p.m., and the folks went riding with him. They went as far as Franklin & took supper at Mr. Deeds.

Monday, October 2 Orville dined down town. I sent the letter to Mrs. Loretta Sterrett, Pataskala.

Tuesday, October 3 Orville dined down town.

Wednesday, October 4 It is a deligtful day.

Saturday, October 7 The army engineer Bixby Brigadier General of Army, and Mr. and Mrs. Edward Deeds took supper with our folks.

Sunday, October 8 Albert Shearer, and William Hall, his grandson, called. John H. Patterson called. We took Albert to his Aunt's.

Monday, October 9 Cousin Samuel Wright's son John came in the afternoon. He was very full of talk, half of which I could not hear. Orville had started to New York, in the afternoon. I had not understood his going, though he had told me about it.

Tuesday, October 10 John staid till Katharine started to Oberlin. He was very full of talk.

Wednesda October 11 Mrs. Keneth Allen brought some nice flowers. They were zinia's or something like that.

Friday, October 13 Mrs. Creagor Brought some Cosmos flowers, Was afraid they might be frostbitten. Orville came home about 7:00 eve. Had been to Geneva and Oberlin.

Saturday, October 14 Orville went down town. John Wright came in the afternoon when I was writing to Henry C. Nichols New Palestine, Ind. I went down after a while; ate supper & came back to my room. John wanted to borrow money to buy his home in Pittsburgh. I finished the answer to Nichols.

Sunday, October 15 Orville had a visit from William Herbert Bixby, Brigadier General U.S. Army. Retired, 170 Lanier Place, N.W. Washington, D.C., in the evening.

Monday, October 16 Katharine came home from Oberlin about 7:00 eve.

Tuesday, October 17 I lack one month of being 88 years old. Orville meets Engineer Club, at night, and Katharine serves as Chairman of Reception Committee to receive one thousand members of Women's Clubs.

Thursday, October 19 Reuchlin and Lulu came about six o'clock. Katharine went to the Federation of women. She came home about 11:00. Reuchlin and Lulu appeared to be in *good* health.

Friday, October 20 The folks went out for a ride in the forenoon. I wrote a letter to William Hobson in the afternoon, and one to Milton. Our folks all went to the concert.

Saturday, October 21 Reuchlin's were at our house. Reuchlin went with Lorin to town. I had written a letter to William Hobson & wrote one to Milton Wright.

Sunday, October 22 Lorin's family, including Ivonette, dined with us. Reuchlin's also. They staid through the afternoon. John Wright came. Ivonette sung and Lulu played for her. We had many "Victor" songs. I ate supper and went to my room. I took up the Third Chapter of Romans (1–8v) which I have not been able to understand.

Monday, October 23 Reuchlin and Lulu went to see her Aunt Ramsey, at Mrs. Bartle's.

Tuesday, October 24 Reuchlin's went to Aunt Ann Ramsey's for supper & staid till bed-time. Orville and Katharine went to Miss Colby's wedding, came home by 9 o'clock.

Friday, October 27 Reuchlin's went out to Orville's flying grounds. I got a letter from Rev. Horace Lamar and one from Sarah Jane Wallace, R. II, Wabash, Ind.

Saturday, October 28 Lulu went to her Aunt Lizzie's, at Ravenna, Ohio. Ruchlin Went to Lorin's and remained over Sunday, till eve.

Sunday, October 29 Reuchlin came home at night.

Tuesday, October 31 Reuchlin went home this morning.

Saturday, November 4 Orville went to the flying ground.

Sunday, November 5 The papers are full of politics and predictions on the election. It is an unusual clash on an election. Colonel Harvey predicts the following states for Mr. Hughes: Cal. 13; Conn, 7; Idaho, 4; Ill. 29; Iowa, 13; Kan. 10; Maine, 6; Mass. 18; Mich. 15; Minn. 12; N. Hamp. 4; N.J. 14; N. Mex. 3; N.Y. 45; N.D. 5; Ore. 5, Penn. 38; R.I. 5; S. Dak. 5; Utah, 4; Vt. 4; Wash. 7; Wy. 3; Tenn. 12; Texas, 20. Believe Hughes will carry Del. 3; Oh. 24; Md. 13; Expect: Ind. 15, Wis. 13; Doubtful, Ari. 3.

Monday, November 6 Co. 6; Miss. 48; Montana, 4; Nebr. 8; Nev. 3,W.Va. 8–50. Yesterday or before McCormick said: Alabama 12; Ariz. 3, Ark. 9; Col. 6; Conn. 7; Dela. 8; Flor. 6; Geor. 14; Ill. 29; Ind. 15; Ken. 18; Lou. 10; Md. 8; Miss. 10; Mo. 18; Mont. 4; Nebr. 8, Nev. 3; N.J. 14; N.Y. 45; N.C. 12, Ohio 24; Okl. 10; S.Car. 9; Ten. 12; Tex. 20; Vir. 12; Wash. 7; W. Va. 8; Wisc. 13; -all 364 were for Wilson.

Tuesday, November 7 The election day was fair and warm.

I voted the Republican ticket. Orville the Democratic. I watched the "News" Signal Service on the election. It was much mixed and the results doubtful. Orville and Katharine doubtful, came home after midnight. I slept several hours.

Wednesday, November 8 The *Journal* claimed that Hughes had been elected. It is very doubtful. Chas. at 3:00, received telegrams from each party, that the election was very doubtful. The evening papers still left it doubtful, but the News had the best face. Orville had Com. meeting. I wrote Edith Livingston at Honolula, Hawaii.

Thursday, November 9 I got up late. The *Journal* nearly gives the election up. The East and North are for Charles Evans Hughes. The South and West are mostly for Woodrow Wilson. John Bear of Cedar Rapids died today.

Friday, November 10 The *Journal* concedes the reelection of Woodrow Wilson.

Saturday, November 11 Katharine went to Oberlin about 10:00, to preside in an Association next Monday. She takes with her a large basket for a spread for Leontine. The election is uncertain in its count.

Sunday, November 12 Horace as usual dined with us. Lorin, Netta, Lulu came. Also James Jenkins.

Monday, November 13 The Lawsuit against the Wright Company had been partly dismissed by the Judge, and the Jury disagreed on the rest. It was by Berger, a Jew, for damages. It will not be likely to be renewed. Orville was responsible only in the part dismissed by the Judge.

Tuesday, November 14 Katharine came home from Oberlin. Leontine and Esther have hard study, but are well.

Wednesday, November 15 Card saying John Bear of Cedar Rapids, was buried last Sunday. Services of great respect at U.B. Church, conducted by the Emerod's and N.R. Drury. He died the 9th. The card was from W.H. Meyers, 403 Second Ave.

Thursday, November 16 Received letters of congratulation from Reuchlin, Herbert and Bertha. Also from Jay R. Petrae. Emma Zeller Dennis, Lulu, Netta, Horace and Lorin came to dinner and most to supper.

Friday, November 17 88th Birth Day. Received many letters of congratulations: Richard Braden, Ed. M. Harris, Ella Rees, Sina E. Ardery, Cora Dillon, etc. My age is greater than that of any of my ancestors for several generations.

Saturday, November 18 Mr. Thresher, and wife, Dr. Colby's daughter, came in the evening, and their tall son. I received a card from Rev. O. Allebaugh.

Sunday, November 19 Mr. Deeds came in the evening. He comes quite often.

Tuesday, November 21 Katharine, Lulu and Netta go on a visit to Emma L. Dennis at Richmond, Ind.

Wednesday, November 22 Mrs. J.L. Stevens came, and ate supper with us. I learn from Lulu, that her brother Frederick had a little boy who died at a week old. Mark Wood's widow is married again to a nice man. She has a little Billheimer girl about 9 years old.

Thursday, November 23 The women went down town.

Friday, November 24 Lulu went to Netta's. Orville brought her home in the evening.

Saturday, November 25 Miss Winifred came to dinner and staid the afternoon. Orville staid down town.

Sunday, November 26 Lulu started for home this morning. Horace was here and James Jenkins came. McCormick and his wife came and spent an hour in the evening. Orville, as is his usual custom, and Katharine, takes Horace (and James) home.

Monday, November 27 It was a rainy day. I read in Britanica of the Pygmies, a real people. There are some 30,000 of them in the Phillippines. They are mostly over 3 1/2 feet in height, weigh perhaps 80 pounds, each.

Thursday, November 30 Lorin and Horace and Winifred Ryder dined with us. She remained with us.

Friday, December 1 Orville and Katharine and Winifred Ryder went to Cincinnati to get furniture for Orville's new building and came home before dark.

Sunday, December 3 Mr. E.A. Deeds came,and took out in auto. Orv., Kath. and Horace. Lorin stayed with me.

Monday, December 4 Congress Assembles. Pres. Wilson is paid quite an ovation. He is interrupted by the Female Suffragists, who when he came to that part of his message relating to increased suffrage for San Dominican threw out a banner asking "What he recommends for us," which a little page was lifted up to tear down.

Tuesday, December 5 I have a return to my old kind of bed springs. The new were uneasy.

Sunday, December 17 John H. Pattison came in the evening. Orville and Katharine, as usual, take Horace home.

Monday, December 18 It is a snow-bound day. Perhaps a couple inches of snow lies on the ground.

Thursday, December 21 There was a meeting of Oberlin students at 8:00, and their friends, about 50 in number; among them Rev. Bosworth, Prof. of Theology. It was a good time.

Sunday, December 24 Jay R. Petree came about dark. Lorin's all came. They had quite a time in music. Orville took them home in auto.

Monday, December 25 Many Christmas remembrances: Hattie Kelly, Ovid & Myrl, Louise E. Bauchamp, Estella Petree, James Guthrie & wife & dau. Pleasant day - about 2 inches of snow on the ground. Lorin's whole family, Bertha Elwyn, Wright, and Jay R. Petree dined with us and staid till 6:00, when they all went away.

Thursday, December 28 Mrs. Justina Stevens and Bertha Elwyn were with us to supper. Orville and Katharine took Mrs. Stevens home, and Elwyn to Lorin's. She is very fond of the ukalele, which Orville and Katharine give to her.

Friday, December 29 Elwyn came & dined with us.

Saturday, December 30 Bertha started home. She is a good looking, smart girl, 20 years old.

Sunday, December 31 Horace came. A magazine writer came in the afternoon and staid late at night.

[The following is written in the address section at the end of the diary:]

My father's mother was Sarah (Freeman) Wright. She died near Phoneton, and is buried there. (She died at the home of Mrs. Daniel Bates, about 5 miles below Troy, aged 86 years and a few days.) Her father was Edmund Freeman, our sixth ancestor of the name, Edmund, a long-lived and respected ancestry in New England who came in 1635. This my great-grandfather, commanded a company of New Hampshire troops in Gen. Gates army in the Saratoga campaign, and was present at Gen. Burgoyne's surrender. My grandfather, Dan Wright, was a young soldier 20 years old, from Lebanon, Connecticut. I have seen the honorable discharge of both. He was a young soldier in same army. My great-grandmother Freeman's father was Edmund Freeman whose first wife was Sarah Porter, daughter of John Porter a descendant of John and Rose Porter of Windsor, Conn. Gen. Ulyssus Grant and Grover Cleveland are also descended from this John Porter of Windsor. Edmond Freeman's second wife was a daughter of [ ]— a cousin of the first wife, the widow Estabrook, who had six children by her first husband, and three by her last. She was a smart woman to talk politics.

1917

Monday, January 1 This is my 89th New Year. Lorin's spent the evening with us; Lorin, Netta, Ivonette and Leontine.

Tuesday, January 2 Leontine goes to Oberlin College in the morning; Ivonett, to Oxford in the evening.

Wednesday, January 3 Orville goes to Washington, at 8:30 evening, to be consulted by the government, on reaching the Parks with Flying Machine.

Thursday, January 4 The weather is very warm for winter. Fair day. Much rain at night.

Saturday, January 6 Miss Green, teacher, and Miss Winifred Ryder and Mrs. Agnes Beck dined with us, and Miss Ryder and Green staid for supper.

Sunday, January 7 It is partly cloudy. It was a fair day withal. Most of the snow melted away. Horace came just before dinner.

Wednesday, January 10 Lorin, Netta and Horace came and staid till bed time.

Friday, January 12 Orville telegraphed that he would be at home tomorrow morning.

Saturday, January 13 Orville came home on the eight o'clock Penn. train which was behind time, on account of snow.

Sunday, January 14 About 5 inches snow fell. Lucian

Warner and wife came about 1:00, on a 4 hour's late train. They live at Bridgeport, Conn. They staid till bed—went on to Chi. She is a large, nice-looking woman.

Monday, January 15 Katharine is not well.

Friday, January 19 Orville and Katharine went down town in the evening. I looked over Drury's History of Dayton.

Saturday, January 20 The snow melted a good deal.

Sunday, January 21 Horace and Lorin and Netta were with us in the evening.

Tuesday, January 23 Katharine took dinner with Agnes Beck at Rike's.

Wednesday, January 24 Orville staid down town for dinner.

Saturday, January 27 Mrs. Justina Steven and Miss Winifred Ryder ate supper with us.

Sunday, January 28 Horace was with us to dinner and supper.

Saturday, February 3 Katharine had Dayton teachers at dinner today. There were about 18.

Sunday, February 4 Horace was with us all the day. He shows a good development of his intellect. Mr. Deeds called part of an hour.

Wednesday, February 7 Orville and Katharine start to New York about 8:00 in the evening.

Friday, February 9 This is W.J. Shuey's Birth-Day Anniversary - the ninetieth. Orville told me that I had an invitation to attend it. It is quite a cold day. There is a skiff of snow.

Saturday, February 10 Ema Zeller Dennis was in town on business and called a few minutes.

Sunday, February 11 I was most of the day alone. Lorin, Netta, Horace and Ivonette and Miss Bertha Eliton came and Miss Jenkins, at 4:30; went at 6:00.

Wednesday, February 14 Frank McCormic and wife took supper and staid till Prof. Fails dined with us and staid till bed-time. [Above text was crossed out of diary]

Sunday, February 18 Horace was with us.

Wednesday, February 21 It is a mild, warm day. I walked a mile. Frank McCormich and his wife were here for supper and Prof. Fails—or the day before.

Thursday, February 22 It is a nice day—a little cooler. Mr. Gardner, a publisher on aeronautics was with us to dinner and supper.

Bishop Wright on the porch at Hawthorne Hill, 1917

Friday, February 23 Orville and Katharine took supper down town.

Saturday, February 24 Lorin, Netta and Horace came for supper.

Sunday, February 25 Ivonette and Lorin and Netta came in the afternoon and staid till 9:00. A Danish consul and two other men called in the afternoon.

Monday, February 26 The ground is bare. It is rather a nice day.

Tuesday, February 27 Miss Steele came to read a French lesson in the forenoon. It is a colder day than yesterday. The ground is bare.

Wednesday, February 28 Prof. Woodworth of Iowa University, came after supper, and staid an hour.

Thursday, March 1 It was a cool like day, but fair.

Friday, March 9 Horace came.

Saturday, March 10 Scipio came. He weighs 16 pounds. He is a St. Bernard dog. He is a good-looking puppy.

Monday, March 12 Miss Steel called. Miss Wilson sung at Memorial Hall, in the evening. She is said to be very ordinary.

Tuesday, March 13 The trees are covered with sleet all forenoon.

Wednesday, March 14 Katharine went to Elyria to J.B. Guthrie's. She goes to-morrow to Oberlin to meet a committee on the meeting of her class on Alumni. This is a nice day.

Thursday, March 15 Katharine went from Elyria to Oberlin to meet a com. on meeting of the Alumni.

Monday, March 19 We expected Katharine on 6:00 train, but she did not come.

Tuesday, March 20 Katharine comes home from Oberlin.

Thursday, March 22 James B. Guthrie and wife took supper with us.

Saturday, March 24 Horace came

Sunday, March 25 Horace staid till after 8:00, eve.

Monday, March 26 It is a fine sunshiny day.

Tuesday, March 27 Katharine went and lunched with Miss Jeanneta Rankin and 30 (?) others at Mrs. Shoup's. Orville and Katharine went to Memorial Hall to hear Miss Rankin, the first woman elected to Congress, speak.

Wednesday, March 28 Orville and Kath went to Miss Stivers. Her sister was visiting her.

Friday, March 30 Mr. and Mrs. Louis Lord came at 9:00 & they dined with us. Horace also. Mr. Lord is Katharine's stopping place at Oberlin.(This is for to-morrow)

Saturday, March 31 Mr and Mrs Edward Seibert took supper with us. They are acquaintances of Lord's Mrs. White Mrs. Seibert mother.

Sunday, April 1 Horace is with us. So also Mr. and Mrs. Lord.

Monday, April 2 Mr. and Mrs. Lord's with us.

APPENDIX

Bishop Milton Wright Timeline

1828	Bishop Milton Wright born in Rush County, Indiana, November 17
1831	Susan Catherine Koerner born in Loudon County, Virginia, April 30
1840	Moved with family to Fayette County, Indiana
1843	converted on family farm
1847	joined United Brethren Church, Andersonville, Indiana
1849	began teaching in local schools to earn extra money
1850	preached his first sermon, November 17
1853	Bishop appointed supervisor of preparatory department at Hartsville College, a United Brethren institution; met Susan Koerner here admitted to White River Annual Conference
1855	first pastorate in Indianapolis
1856	ordained a minister of the faith at Abingdon, Indiana posted to Andersonville Circuit
1857	travels to and from Oregon: traveled by train to Philadelphia, steamboat to New York on North River; sailed aboard the *Illinois* on July 6 journeyed across Panama by rail boarded the *Golden Age* July 18, sailed for San Francisco sailed on *Commodore* from San Francisco to Portland took the *Hoosier* from Portland to Butterville preached first sermon August 23, 1857 sailed from Portland, October 7, 1859 at San Francisco, boarded *Sonora* for Panama City and on up the Atlantic Coast to New York and then home arrived Fayetteville, Nov. 14, 1859
1859	marriage to Susan Koerner, November 24 lived in Grant County, near Rushville taught school New Salem

1860   April, moved to Andersonville
        fall 1860 received regular church appointment, Marion Circuit, moved back to Grant
            County farm

1861   elected presiding elder, White River Conference
        Reuchlin born March 17

1862   Lorin born November 18

1864   moved around, then bought farm near Millville, New Castle, Indiana, for invest-
            ment; moved there 1865 not long after end of Civil War

1865   elected to first United Brethren General Conference

1867   Wilbur born April 16 on farm near Millville, Indiana

1868   returned to Hartsville College; Milton named first professor of theology in the his-
            tory of the UB Church
        attended first meeting of Nat. Christian Assoc Opposed to Secret Societies in Pitts-
            burgh

1868–69 attended National Temperance Convention, Christian Amendment Convention,
            which spoke out for women's rights

1869   rejection of Freemasonry—Milton was reformer, supporting abolition of slavery, tem-
            perance, and women's rights
        two factions emerged in church leadership: Radicals (Milton) and Liberals
        move to rented house in Dayton, spring
        editor of *Religious Telescope*

1871   move to Hawthorne St. house, April
        Orville born August 19

1872   delivered major address at National Anti-Secrecy Association in Cincinnati

1873   General Conference, Radicals win out
        re-elected to post of editor

1874   Katharine born August 19

1875   another address to Nat. Anti-Secrecy Association

1877   General Conference, elected Bishop in Church
       charged with responsibility for West Mississippi District
       much travel over next four years to Far West

1878   move to Cedar Rapids, Iowa
       Penaud Toy given to Wilbur and Orville
       address to State Anti-Secrecy Society of Illinois
       Reuchlin graduated from Coe's Collegiate Academy

1880   Milton built a new home in Adair, Iowa

1881   June, move to Richmond, Indiana, Henry County
       returned to Whitewater Circuit
       relinquished control of paper
       defeated in election for bishop
       Wilbur finished high school, but did not return to get diploma when family moved
       back to Dayton
       begins publication of *Richmond Star* and *Reform Leaflet*

1884   Wright Family returns to Dayton

1885   Bishop re-elected, assigned to Pacific Coast

1886   Orville and Ed Sines start *The Midget*
       Ten Dayton Boys Club organized at the home of Reuchlin Wright

1887   Orville enters Dayton Central High School

1889   Orville began publication of *West Side News* (1889–96)
       Susan Koerner Wright dies on July 4 at age 58
       United Brethren Church divides over secret society issue
       Milton re-elected bishop by Radical General Conference
       Secret Societies Controversy; Bishop assigned to supervise court litigation

1890   Orville and Wilbur convert West Side News into the *Evening Item* (April 30–August)
       Orville enters final year of high school at Central, leaves before graduating
       Paul Laurence Dunbar starts *Tattler,* Orville prints

1892   Orville purchases bicycle for $160.00

Wilbur purchases bicycle for $80.00
December 1892, first Bicycle Shop at 1005 W. Third St. (continued in business until 1907)

1893   Bicycle Shop moves to larger quarters at 1034 W. Third St.
        Wilbur and Orville attend World Columbian Exposition in Chicago

1894   Orville and Wilbur start weekly magazine *Snapshots*

1895   bicycle shop moves to 22 S. Williams St.

1896   Wrights manufacture own bicycles: Van Cleve and St. Clair
        experiment with gas engine
        make Wright Special bicycle
        Wrights members of League of American Wheelmen
        Orville has typhoid fever
        Otto Lilienthal dies

1897–98 continued in bicycle manufacturing and repair
        extensive reading about flight

1899   Wilbur writes to Smithsonian for information on flight
        kite constructed and tested
        letter to weather service

1901–5 Bishop involved in Publishing Establishment Controversy

1900   Wilbur writes to Octave Chanute
        September 6, Wilbur leaves Dayton for Kitty Hawk
        September 24, Orville leaves Dayton for Kitty Hawk
        October, active experiments
        return to Dayton late October

1901   Chanute visits Dayton
        July, return to Kitty Hawk
        Spratt, Huffaker visit
        Chanute visits
        August, return to Dayton
        October, air foil tests, mounted on bicycle
        wind tunnel balances testing October–December

1902   construction of 1902 glider

Wilbur goes to Huntington, Indiana, to defend his father in case involving laymen's misuse of church funds

return to Kitty Hawk; Sept.–Oct. gliding experiments

Lorin visits; Spratt, Chanute, and Herring visit

Langley's first letter to Wrights

October, Wrights leave for Dayton

December, propeller experiments and begin construction of 4-cylinder engine

1903   Wrights build second wind tunnel

test newly built motor

March 23, Wright brothers apply for patent, which was issued May 22, 1906

September 23, leave for Kitty Hawk; arrive Sept. 25

glider renovated and experiments conducted

October 9, commence assembly of 1903 machine

December 3, Orville returns to Dayton to replace broken propeller shaft

December 11, Orville returns to Kitty Hawk

December 14, first unsuccessful flight attempt

December 17, first successful powered flight, telegram to Bishop recorded in his diary

December 21 return to Dayton

Bishop is expelled from White River Conference

1904   Toulmin engaged as patent attorney

May, Wilbur once again occupied with U.B. Publishing House case involving his father; writes letters and travels to Huntington, Indiana

Wrights applying for French and German patents

construct new plane at Huffman Prairie

another trip to Huntington to defend Bishop

first use of catapult device for launching airplane

1905   January 1, *Gleanings in Bee Culture* article

May 2, Wilbur's tract dealing with misuse of funds of UB Publishing House is published and distributed to delegates of General Conference of the Church of the United Brethren in Christ

May 28, Wilbur was in Michigan to attend conference of his father's church

June, first flight with 1905 machine at Huffman Prairie

Aug. 30, Wilbur published editorial in *Christian Conservator*, "Will White River Conference Destroy Herself?"

Sept. 26, Bishop watches Wilbur fly

Milton retires as bishop

1906 press coverage of flying increases
May 22, patent issued, #821,393 flying machine
new engine; continuing tests

1906–7 negotiations trying to sell airplane

1907 hydroplane experiments Great Miami River
May 16, Wilbur to Europe hoping to sell plane; no deals
July, U.S. War Dept contract
Orville goes to Europe to join Wilbur
machine shipped to France, July 1907; stored until summer 1908
Charley Taylor joins Wilbur in August 1907
October 24, Milton is interviewed in Dayton about flights
November 11, Wilbur and Charley Taylor head home
December, Orville returns home

1908 February, formal contract signed with U.S. Signal Corps for airplane
Wilbur had done no flying since 1905
airplane shipped to Kitty Hawk, April 4
Wilbur arrives Kitty Hawk, April 9
Charley Furnas arrives in Kitty Hawk; Orville follows
May 17, Wilbur leaves for Paris
May 23, Orville returns to Dayton
August, Wilbur flies at Le Mans, Hunandieres Race Course, and Camp d'Auvours
September, Orville's first flight at Ft. Myer
September 17, crash kills Selfridge and injures Orville
September 18, Katharine takes leave from teaching and goes to care for Orville
November, Orville and Katharine return home to Dayton

1909 January at Pau
Orville and Katharine go to France to join Wilbur
February 15, Katharine passenger with Wilbur on flight
May 11, return to New York
June 2, return to Dayton
June 17–18, Homecoming Celebration in Dayton
June 18, Bishop delivers invocation
une 26, Ft. Myer flights success
June 27, Bishop and Reuchlin go to Ft. Myer to watch Orville fly
July 2, return home
July 20, Katharine goes to Ft. Myer to watch Orville fly
July 31, Orville and Katharine leave for Dayton, arriving home Aug. 1
August 2, Wilbur returns to Dayton

August 8, Orville and Katharine leave for Europe, Orville to fly there
August 16, Wilbur to New York to initiate patent suits against Curtiss
Orville and Katharine return to New York
Wilbur flying at Governor's Island, College Park
November 7, all return to Dayton
November 22, Wright Company incorporated

1910 Wilbur and Orville issued aviator licenses #4 and #5 by Aero Club of America
Wright School of Aviation established
Wright Exhibition Company formed
patent suit depositions
purchase of property for Hawthorne Hill
May 25, Orville takes Milton for flight at Huffman Prairie
Orville and Wilbur fly together
August 10, public appearance of first wheels on plane
September 23, Katharine flies with Orville at Huffman Prairie
November, Wright Factory in Dayton completed
exhibition flying continues

1911 patent suits, exhibition flying
October, Orville goes to Kitty Hawk

1912 patent testimony
May 2, Wilbur ill on visit to Boston
May 30, Wilbur dies at age 45

1913 January, Orville tests automatic stabilizer at Huffman Prairie
February, Orville and Katharine to Europe on business
March 17, return
March 25–27, Great Dayton Flood
Orville conducts hydroplane experiments on Miami River

1914 April 28, move to Hawthorne Hill

1915 Wright Company sold

1916 July 11–September 3, Katharine, Orville, and Milton vacation on Waubec Island in
Georgian Bay, Ontario, Canada.
September 19, Orville purchases Lambert Island

1917 Orville establishes Wright Aeronautical Laboratory
April 3, Bishop Milton Wright dies at age 88

INDEX

INDEX

INDEX

INDEX

INDEX

Woodbourne Library
Washington-Centerville Public Library
Centerville, Ohio